Political Developments in Contemporary China

Praise for Ian Jeffries' *China: A Guide to Economic and Political Developments* (2006):

> This book is highly useful not only to casual China watchers … but also to researchers and academics … an engrossing guide.
>
> (Marc Lanteigne, *International Affairs*)

China's role in global events today cannot be overestimated.

This book provides a comprehensive and detailed overview of contemporary political developments in China. Key topics covered include: China's international relations with its neighbours and with the international community more widely; demographic developments; Taiwan; Macao and Hong Kong, Tibet, Uighurs; human rights, health issues (including bird flu); food contamination and defective goods; and a chronology of political developments, congresses and Central Committee sessions since May 2006; the earthquake of 12 May 2008 and the 2008 Olympic Games.

The book continues – and adds to – the overview of developments up to May 2006 which were covered in the author's *China: A Guide to Economic and Political Developments* (2006), and is the companion volume to *Economic Developments in Contemporary China: A Guide* (2010) – both published by Routledge.

Ian Jeffries is Honorary Professor in the Department of Economics in the School of Business and Economics at Swansea University, UK. He is the author of numerous books in the series *Guides to Economic and Political Developments in Asia*, including volumes on North Korea, Vietnam, China and Mongolia.

Guides to economic and political developments in Asia

1 **North Korea**
A guide to economic and political developments
Ian Jeffries

2 **Vietnam**
A guide to economic and political developments
Ian Jeffries

3 **China**
A guide to economic and political developments
Ian Jeffries

4 **Mongolia**
A guide to economic and political developments
Ian Jeffries

5 **Contemporary North Korea**
A guide to economic and political developments
Ian Jeffries

6 **Political Developments in Contemporary China**
A guide
Ian Jeffries

7 **Economic Developments in Contemporary China**
A guide
Ian Jeffries

Political Developments in Contemporary China

A guide

Ian Jeffries

LONDON AND NEW YORK

First published 2011 by Routledge

711 Third Avenue, New York, NY 10017, USA
2 Park Square, Milton Park, Abingdon, Oxon OX14 4RN

Routledge is an imprint of the Taylor & Francis Group, an informa business

First issued in paperback 2016

Typeset in Times by Wearset Ltd, Boldon, Tyne and Wear

British Library Cataloguing in Publication Data
A catalogue record for this book is available from the British Library

Library of Congress Cataloging in Publication Data
Jeffries, Ian.
Political developments in contemporary China: a guide/Ian Jeffries.
p. cm. – (Guides to economic and political developments in Asia; 6)
Includes bibliographical references and index.

1. China–Politics and government–1976–2002. 2. China–Politics and government–1976–2002–Chronology. 3. China–Politics and government–2002– 4. China–Politics and government–2002–Chronology. I. Title.

DS779.26.J43 2012
320.951–dc22

2009049232

ISBN 978-0-415-58085-4 (hbk)
ISBN 978-1-138-97872-0 (pbk)

Contents

Acknowledgements vii

Introduction 1

1 **Demographic, historical and political background** 2
Population 2
Chinese civilization 5
The period 1911 to 1949 10
Communist China 11
Demography 29

2 **China and Taiwan** 47
A chronology of events since 4 May 2006 48

3 **The regaining of sovereignty over Hong Kong and Macao (and later developments)** 134
The regaining of sovereignty over Macao on 20 December 1999 134
The regaining of sovereignty over Hong Kong on 1 July 1997 137
A chronology of political events since 1 July 2006 138

4 **Tibet** 161
Historical background 161
Demographic, social and economic developments 167
A chronology of important events 171
A chronology of events since May 1995 171

5 Uighurs 326
A chronology of political events since 9 May 2006 329

6 Human rights 382
A chronology of developments in human rights since 16 May 2006 388
Religion: a chronology of developments since 3 May 2006 420
The use of the internet and mobile phones 432
Study abroad 470
Direct elections at the local level 471

7 Health issues 472
SARS and EV71 472
Bird flu 476
AIDS 516
Pig disease 523
Swine flu 525
Pneumonic plague 537
Food contamination and defective goods 538

8 Developments, congresses and Central Committee sessions since May 2006 634
The earthquake of 12 May 2008 758
The Olympic Games 821
General developments from 20 August 2008 onwards 866

Postscript 958

Bibliography 1016
Index 1027

Acknowledgements

I am much indebted to the following individuals (in alphabetical order):

At Swansea University: Robert Bidereux; Siân Brown; Dianne Darrell; Michele Davies; Chris Hunt; Nigel O'Leary; Mary Perman; Ann Preece; Paul Reynolds; Kathy Sivertsen; Fritz Summer, Chris West.

Professors: Nick Baigent, John Baylis; George Blazyca, Steve Brown, Mike Charlton, Steve Cook, Phillip Hanson, Paul Hare, Lester Hunt, Michael Kaser, Phil Murphy and Noel Thompson.

Russell Davies (Kays Newsagency).

At Routledge: Louise Collins, Emma Davis, Alan Jarvis, Eve Setch and Peter Sowden.

Copy-editor: Liz Jones.

At Wearset: Kelly Alderson, Matt Deacon, Claire Dunstan and Allie Waite.

Ian Jeffries
Honorary Professor
Department of Economics and Centre of Russian and East European Studies,
Swansea University

Introduction

> This book is highly useful not only to casual China watchers … but also to researchers and academics … Especially interesting was the middle section on political developments and the work of the various government congresses since the early 1990s, which provides an engrossing guide to the political priorities of the National People's Congress and other departments, including both domestic and international issues involving East Asia, the United States and elsewhere in the world. Also noteworthy was the section on China's emerging 'open door' policies which records Beijing's struggles with adapting to a globalized economy, with sections on liberalized trade, engagement with economic institutions, and currency policies, all areas of increasing interest to both analysts and policy communities. Additionally, those interested in the politics of healthcare in China will be especially impressed with the range of topics included … [including] the SARS crisis … AIDS and avian influenza … [Other topics covered include] the transfer of Hong Kong and Macao to Chinese sovereignty … the Taiwan question … township elections … market development, the reform of state enterprises … [and] agriculture.
>
> (*International Affairs*, 2007, vol. 83, no. 2, p. 409)

I was delighted with these generous comments about *China: A Guide to Economic and Political Developments* (Routledge 2006) by Marc Lanteigne. I can only hope that this companion volume on political developments finds equal favour.

Economic developments are covered in *Economic Developments in Contemporary China: A Guide.*

1 Demographic, historical and political background

(The background covers material up to November 2009. Please see the main text for more recent developments.)

Population

China is the largest country in the world in terms of population. On 6 January 2005 the figure was 1.3 billion. By the end of 2006 it was 1.314 billion.

The world population figure reached 6 billion in October 1999. India is the second largest country in the world by population, reaching 1 billion in August 1999. On 10 October 2006 the population of the United States was officially proclaimed to be 300 million.

China is the third largest country in the world in terms of land area, after Russia and Canada.

'The dominant Han today account for 93 per cent of the country's 1.3 billion people, according to official statistics' (*IHT*, 17 March 2007, p. 6).

China has to support about 22 per cent of the world's population on something like 7 per cent of the world's arable area. Thus it is no coincidence that agricultural reform was first in line after 1978.

'[There was] an increase in average life expectancy from thirty-five years in 1949 to sixty-eight years by 1978' (*IHT*, 20 August 2005, p. 2).

By 1986 life expectancy had risen to 66.9 for men and 70.9 for women (Jeffries 1993: 138).

'By 2005 life expectancy reached 72.4 years' (*FEER*, November 2007, p. 52). 'Despite a dramatic increase in prosperity and living standards in China since 1978 average life expectancy has increased by only 3.5 years, about half the gains in longevity in Japan, Singapore, Hong Kong and [South] Korea over the same period' (www.iht.com, 19 August 2005; *IHT*, 20 August 2005, p. 2).

Since roughly the mid-1950s the state has tried to control population growth, often in draconian fashion.

The present policy as regards population, formally introduced in 1979, is 'one child' per family with exceptions which have grown over time.

> At the time it was adopted in 1979, at the urging of Deng Xiaoping, the one-child policy … represented a huge change from the historical importance of

> large families in China and from a Maoist philosophy that encouraged parents to have more children because China would be strengthened by a big population ... According to 2000 census data, China had 117 boys born for every 100 girls.
>
> (*FEER*, 14 October 2004, p. 28)

> China hopes to achieve a normal balance of newborn boys and girls within six years [by 2010] by banning the use of abortions to select an infant's sex and by making welfare payments to couples without sons ... Government figures show that 117 boys are born in China to every 100 girls – a gap blamed largely on a policy limiting most couples to one child. In a society that values sons, many parents abort baby girls, hoping to try again for a boy ... The 'one child' limit allows rural families to have two children if the first is a girl, because Chinese peasants traditionally rely on sons to support them in old age.
>
> (www.iht.com, 15 July 2004)

[In 2003] 117 boys were born for every 100 girls, compared with a global average of 105 to 100' (*Guardian*, 16 July 2004, p. 19).

'In early January [2005] the government announced that the nationwide ratio had reached 119 boys to every hundred girls' (*IHT*, 31 January 2005, pp. 1, 7).

> The government has tinkered with ... the one-child policy ... It now allows husbands and wives who are themselves only children to have a second child, for example, and has eliminated a four-year waiting period between births for those eligible to have a second child.
>
> (*IHT*, 29 June 2006, p. 2)

> Zhang Weiqing, head of the National Population and Family Planning Commission ... defended the population plan – which he said had halted 400 million births in thirty years – and said it was wrong to call the programme a 'one-child' policy. The reality was more complicated, he said, with different provinces making their own adjustments as the situation demanded. Only just over a third of the population was limited to just one child. In nineteen provinces rural couples were allowed to have another baby if their first was a girl, the minister said. And in five provinces, including the southern island of Hainan and Yunnan in the south-west, all rural parents were allowed to have two children.
>
> (*Guardian*, 24 January 2007, p. 22)

> China's top family planning body has warned of a 'population rebound' as couples flout one-child policy rules. The widening wealth gap could lead to a rise in birth rates, Zhang Weiqing from the National Population and Family Planning Commission told state media. Newly rich couples can afford to pay fines to have more than one child, while rural couples are marrying earlier.
>
> (www.bbc.co.uk, 7 May 2007)

'Already the one-child family limits apply to only 35.9 per cent of the population' (*The Times*, 8 May 2007, p. 7).

'The government says it is drafting new laws to tackle the growing gender imbalance caused by the widespread abortion of female foetuses' (www.bbc.co.uk, 25 August 2007).

'China is planning to tighten punishments for sex-selective abortions … Although there are two laws banning doctors from telling pregnant women the sex of the foetus, the practice is common' (www.guardian.com, 26 August 2007).

> The authorities in China say they have found that most Chinese women would like to have more than one child. Family planning officials say their research indicates that 70 per cent of women want to have two babies or more … The research was conducted in 2006, but has only been released now … The *China Daily* reported the survey results, which showed parents would like a son and a daughter, at least. Jiang Fan (vice minister of the National Family Planning Commission): 'Our research shows that 70.7 per cent of women would like to have two or more babies' … Most women, or 83 per cent, want a son and a daughter, the survey said … Despite the survey results, the commission said China would achieve its goal to keep its population within 1.36 billion by the end of next year [2010]. Li Bin (minister of the commission): 'China's family planning policy underpins the country's economy and demographics.'
>
> (www.bbc.co.uk, 16 January 2009)

> A bias in favour of male offspring has left China with 32 million more boys under the age of twenty than girls, creating 'an imminent generation of excess men', a study released Friday [10 April 2009] said. For the next twenty years China will have increasingly more men than women of reproductive age, according to the paper published online by the *British Medical Journal* … [written] by two Chinese university professors and a London researcher … In 2005, they found, China had more than 1.1 million excess male births. There were 120 boys for every 100 girls … They blamed the imbalance almost entirely upon decisions by couples to abort female foetuses. The trend toward more male than female children intensified steadily after 1986, they said, as ultrasound and abortion became more readily available. The paper said: 'Sex-selective abortion accounts for almost all the excess males.' The researchers said the disparity was sharpest among one- to four-year-olds, a sign that the worst imbalances lie ahead. They also found greater distortion in provinces that allow couples a second child if the first is a girl or in cases of hardship. Those couples were determined to ensure they had at least one son, they noted. Among children born second there were 143 boys for 100 girls … They said enforcing the ban against sex-selective abortions could normalize the sex ratio in the future. The study was conducted by Wei Xingzhu (a Zhejiang Normal University professor), Li Lu (a Zhejiang University professor) and Therese Hesketh (a University College London lecturer).
>
> (www.iht.com, 10 April 2009)

'A baby boom in the 1950s and 1960s was halted by draconian population control that began in 1979, reducing the birth rate to 1.7 children per woman from more than six in the 1960s' (*IHT*, 22 April 2009, p. 2).

Chinese civilization

China is an ancient civilization. The question why China fell behind Europe after being ahead is an interesting one. Factors may include centralization which stifled initiative and enterprise, a sense of cultural superiority, a feeling that the regime was more secure with continuity rather than change and the preference of young men to become bureaucrats.

> For 500 years, from the fourteenth century until the 1830s, China accounted for a remarkable 30 per cent of world economic output. That is more than the US economy at the height of its global economic dominance after World War II – sustained for a half-millennium! But by 1979 ... China's share of global GDP was barely 1 per cent ... Today China accounts for about 5 per cent of world output.
>
> (Philip Auerswald, *IHT*, 12 August 2008, p. 8)

> In 1820 China accounted for about 30 per cent of the global economy ... The United States then weighed in with less than 2 per cent. But by the 1950s America was dominant and China ... accounted for only about 4 per cent of world economic activity.
>
> (Roger Cohen, *IHT*, 13 April 2005, p. 2)

> Up to the fifteenth century Chinese technological know-how was the most advanced in the world. China has the largest economy in the world for 1,800 of the past 2,000 years. As recently as 1820 it produced one-third of global output, and it remained the world's largest economy until 1885.
>
> (John Lee, *IHT*, 13 November 2008, p. 8)

> One of the basic questions asked by historians of Asia is why Japan responded quickly and effectively to the threat presented by the demonstrable superiority of the West, even as China responded slowly, reluctantly, unwillingly. The conventional answer has to do with Japan's tradition of cultural borrowing – mostly from China. It was a tradition of a country that always assumed it had something to learn, and learn it did, so that by 1905, in the Russo-Japanese War, Japan became the first Asian country to defeat a European power, decisively ... China, as is well known, possessed so deep and abiding a sense of cultural superiority, so strong a tradition of needing to learn nothing from the outside, that it was unable to adjust. It was so slow to see that it needed more than to learn a few material techniques to survive in the new globalized world that, in the end, its traditional system collapsed entirely.
>
> (Richard Bernstein, *IHT*, 21 April 2006, p. 2)

> In his book *The Levers of Riches* Joel Mokyr settles on a simple explanation for China's technological stagnation: the country's imperial state lost interest, Its purposes were better served by continuity than by progress, and there was no rival source of power and patronage to pick up the threads it dropped.
>
> (*The Economist*, 10 November 2007, p. 3)

> By the time Joseph Needham died in 1995 he had published seventeen volumes of his 'Science and Civilization in China' series, including several that he wrote entirely on his own. The Chinese began printing 600 years before Johannes Gutenberg introduced the technique in Germany. They built the first chain drive 700 years before the Europeans. And they made use of a magnetic compass at least a century before the first reference to it appeared elsewhere. So why, in the middle of the fifteenth century, did this advanced civilization cease its spectacular progress? So powerful has Needham's contribution been to the historiography of Chinese science that this conundrum is still known as 'The Needham Question'. Even the Chinese themselves use it … Among Needham's destinations … was Dujiangyan, a city badly hit by the recent [May 2008] earthquake in Sichuan province. There he was able to study a huge irrigation project that was created 2,300 years ago and which still stands today, though cracked by the earthquake. At that time only the Mesopotamians had made such strides in controlling their rivers … Needham never worked out why China's inventiveness dried up. Other academics have made their own suggestions: the stultifying pursuit of bureaucratic rank in the Middle Kingdom and the absence of a mercantile class to foster competition and self-improvement; the sheer size of China compared with the smaller state of Europe whose fierce rivalries fostered technological competition; its totalitarianism.
>
> (*The Economist*, 7 June 2008, p. 99)

'Sometime around the fifteenth century the creativity stopped – an issue known in the West as the "Needham question"' (*FT*, 2 July 2008, p. 15).

> China's claim to have invented paper was strengthened yesterday [9 August 2006] when archaeologists announced a discovery that suggests it was in use at 100 years earlier than thought … A scrap of paper made from linen fibre … measuring only 1.6 square inches … [and found] at the Yumen Pass, the gate between China and Asia, is believed to have been made in 8 BC, or 113 years earlier than the first known paper … Chinese history records that paper was invented in AD 105 by Cai Lun … [who] pounded together mulberry tree bark, cloth and fishing nets … However, the discovery of paper-like material made from silk in north-west China has fuelled debate in recent years that the invention could have been made two centuries before Cai Lun was at work … However … Fu Licheng, the curator of the Dunhuang Museum … said that the paper found at the Yumen Pass was

a more developed material than the disputed silk substance ... China exported its invention but kept its manufacture a secret. In AD 751 the Turks defeated China's armies in battle and captured Chinese papermakers who were taken to Samarkhand. The first Arab paper industry was founded in Baghdad in AD 793 and they, too, kept the process a secret. The invention did not reach Europe until about the 12th century ... China's other claims to fame are: golf, *chiuwan*, a precursor to golf recorded 500 years before it reached the West; pasta, a 4,000-year-old bowl of noodles being unearthed, proving they were eating them 2,000 years before the Italians; the wheelbarrow, China having descriptions of them 1,000 years before Europe; the compass, used on ships reaching Australia.

(*The Times*, 10 August 2006, p. 38)

Almost 2,000 years ago an astronomer named Chang Heng invented the world's first seismoscope ... Its centrepiece [was] a large bronze vessel surrounded by eight dragons, each holding a sphere in its mouth ... If an earthquake ever disturbed the vessel a ball would drop from a dragon's care into the mouth of a bronze frog. By observing which dragon had dropped a ball Chang Heng could ascertain the location of the quake ... The stirrup was invented by the Chinese. Printing, gunpowder, the use of the compass – the three inventions that Francis Bacon said defined the modern world – are all thought to have been made in China. So too, many think, were vaccination, toilet paper, segmental arch bridges, iron chains and perhaps chess – the list seems endless. And yet in the sixteenth century China's innovative energies inexplicably withered away and modern science became the virtual monopoly of the West ... Historians have long debated why the Chinese so signally failed to exploit their early promise. Lack of internal competition, some suggest. Others blame the long-held central ambition of every young Chinese man to become a Confucian mandarin, a bureaucrat, rather than an engineer or scientist.

(www.iht.com, 15 May 2008; *IHT*, 16 May 2008, p. 8)

The seismometer was invented by the Chinese in AD 132 as a way to detect tremors that might spell the end of a ruler's reign. Successive dynasties employed a master of omens who would record and interpret floods, famines and other disasters.

(www.iht.com, 16 May 2008)

The millennia-old Middle Kingdom can claim to have invented many things – fireworks, the umbrella, paper and the compass among them – but not the bicycle. According to Amir Moghaddass, a historian at the Technical Institute of Berlin, the Chinese first heard of bicycles from a customs officer named Binchun who visited Paris in 1866 and wrote of Parisians riding vehicles made of 'two wheels with a pipe in the middle'. Back then well-heeled Chinese generally got around in rickshaw or sedan chairs, both hauled by manpower. It was only after expatriate Americans and Europeans

> began cycling around Chinese cities that the fashion took off, Moghaddass wrote in his book *The Bicycle and the Chinese People.*
>
> (www.iht.com, 7 July 2008)

China is an ancient and continuous civilization ('The longest continuous civilization in the world': *The Times*, Supplement, 8 October 1999, p. 4). The Shang dynasty was founded in about 1550 BC. But the first centralized Chinese state occurred during the Qin dynasty (221–206 BC). The Han dynasty lasted from 206 BC to AD 220. Disunity followed until China was reunified under the Sui (581–618) and the Tang (618–907). The population of China reached 100 million by the end of the Song dynasty. The Song dynasty was in power from 960 to 1279. The Mongols under Genghis Khan invaded China in the thirteenth century and they established their capital at Beijing (meaning 'northern capital' and formerly called Peking in English). The Mongol Yuan dynasty ruled for nearly 100 years until the Mongols were expelled by the Ming in 1368. The Ming dynasty lasted until the Qing (Manchu) conquest of China in 1644. That dynasty ended in 1911 and a republic was proclaimed.

> The existence of the shadowy Xia dynasty – and with it Beijing's claims that China's civilization dates back 4,000 or even 5,000 years – has always been the subject of intense debate both in China and abroad. All this is supposed to end later this year [2000] when a government-appointed commission of 170 scholars is due to announce that after four years of research they have blown away the doubts about China's misty past … Critics say Beijing's attempts to promote nationalism have driven the project and that as a result the credibility of the findings has been compromised … Analysts worry that the study could provide new fuel to a growing fire of ethnocentric nationalism in China that could result in a more belligerent foreign policy stance on issues such as Taiwan and China's leadership role in Asia … Compared with the world's three other ancient civilizations – in present-day Egypt, India and Iraq – the origins of Chinese civilizations have always been controversial. That is because of the long transition period between the various primitive cultures that existed along the Yellow and Yangtze Rivers from roughly 8,000 to 3,000 BC and the beginnings of the country's written record during the Zhou dynasty in 841 BC … The existence of the Shang dynasty (roughly 1,500 to 1,000 BC) … as a 'civilization', with an organized state and a class system, is no longer in doubt … [The Shang dynasty lasted from the sixteenth to the twelfth century BC and the Zhou dynasty lasted from the twelfth to the third century BC] … The Xia, by contrast has remained the stuff of legend … Archaeologists working on the project say that the final report … will conclude that the Xia dynasty – and thus Chinese civilization – began around the year 2150 BC and continued for about 650 years until the Shang dynasty. The report is also likely to conclude that the reign of Emperor Yu, or the Great Yu – a mythical figure – marked the dynasty's founding. It will also trace the origins of the Xia back another 500 years by linking the Xia artefacts to those uncovered … in north-western

Henan. Some scholars believe the site was used by a mythological figure called the Yellow Emperor, the legendary ancestor of all Chinese people.

(Bruce Gilley, *FEER*, 20 July 2000, pp. 74–7)

In academic circles scepticism abounds over Huangdi ... the Yellow Emperor, regarded as the founder of the Middle Kingdom ... He is credited with the word 'emperor' and the imperial colour yellow, but Chinese legend also claims that he unified three major tribes in the Yellow and Yangtze River areas, invented the cart and the boat, and that his dialogues with the physician Qi Bo were the basis of China's first medical book, the Yellow Emperor's *Canon of Medicine*.

(*The Times*, 10 April 2002, p. 20)

[There have been] attempts in recent years to foster a cult of the Yellow Emperor, a mythical ancestor of the Han race, who supposedly lived 5,000 years ago. Senior leaders have taken part in ceremonies paying homage to him. Last October [2007] officials arranged for groups of ethnic minorities, including Tibetans, to join one such rite at a shrine in Shaanxi province where the Yellow Emperor is said to be buried ... The Olympic torch will be carried to the shrine in July [2008]. Yellow Emperor worship will enjoy a boost from the introduction of a new public holiday known as *Qingning*, Tomb Sweeping Day. This is a festival at which Chinese traditionally pay their respects to ancestors.

(*The Economist*, 5 April 2008, pp. 68–9)

Zheng He ... explored the Pacific and Indian Oceans with a mighty armada a century before [Christopher] Columbus discovered America ... At its [the armada's] peak [there were] as many as 300 ships and 30,000 sailors ... [compared with Columbus's three ships] ... Zheng He's first mission [was] in 1405 ... [and] his final voyage [was] in 1433 ... By the latter half of the fifteenth century the country had entered a prolonged period of self-imposed isolation that lasted into the twentieth century, leaving European powers to rule the seas.

(www.iht.com, 20 July 2005)

A prominent Chinese lawyer and collector ... Liu Gang ... unveiled an old map on Monday [16 January 2006] that he and some supporters say should topple one of the central tenets of Western civilization: that Europeans were the first to sail around the world and discover America. The Chinese map, which was drawn up in 1763 but claims to be a reproduction of an ancient map dated 1418, presents the world as a globe with all the major continents rendered with an exactitude that European maps did not have for another century and a half, after Columbus, Da Gama, Magellan, Dias and others had completed their renowned explorations. But the map got a cool reception from some scholars ... At issue are the seven voyages of Zheng He, whose ships sailed the Pacific and Indian oceans from 1405 to 1432. Historical records show he explored South-east Asia, India, the Gulf and the east coast of Africa, using navigation techniques and ships that were far ahead of

> their time … Gavin Menzies … a former British Navy submarine commander … [in] his 2002 book *1421: The Year China Discovered America* … claims that Zheng He visited America in 1421, seventy-one years before Columbus arrived there … [The book] laid out extensive but widely disputed evidence that Zheng He sailed to the east coast of today's United States and may have left settlements in South America. Menzies has welcomed Liu's map as evidence that his theory is correct.
>
> (*IHT*, 17 January 2006, p. 4)

> In June [2006] a medal was discovered in North Carolina [in the United States], complete with Ming dynasty inscriptions, that had been dug up kilometres inland from the coast. The six-Chinese-character inscription, 'Da Ming Xuan De Wei Ci', on the medal translates into 'Awarded by Xuan De of Great Ming'. It refers to the period between 1426 and 1435, the reign of Emperor Xuan Zong – long before Columbus's 1492 landing. Other researchers say that the high incidence of the genetic disorder Machado-Joseph disease among local Indians, which first appeared in Yunnan in China, could have been spread by the Chinese fleet in the 1430s.
>
> (*Independent*, 26 September 2006, p. 30)

> A replica sixteenth-century junk has sunk off Taiwan, one day short of completing an epic voyage to the United States and back. The Ming dynasty-style *Princess Taiping* was trying to prove that China's greatest admiral, Zheng He, could have reached North America 600 years ago … The junk [with a Taiwanese captain] broke in two after it was rammed by a freighter just off Taiwan's coast … Some historians argue that the Chinese discovered America, citing anchors and various other Chinese artefacts found scattered on the floor of the Pacific Ocean.
>
> (www.bbc.co.uk, 27 April 2009)

The period 1911 to 1949

As already mentioned, the Ming dynasty ended in 1911 and a republic was proclaimed. (China was defeated by Britain in the Opium War of 1841–2 and that was followed by de facto Western domination of China. This humiliating experience has influenced China's foreign policy to the present day.)

The Kuomintang Party (founded in 1924 by Sun Yat-sen) and the Communist Party of China (founded in 1921) co-operated in the drive to break the power of warlords, but in 1927, following the earlier death of Sun Yat-sen and under the new leader Chiang Kai-shek, the former party turned on the latter. The Kuomintang established a new government at Nanking. In 1936 the Communist Party were driven northwards from their rural bases in southern China (the so-called 'Long March'). Japan invaded Manchuria in 1931 and opened full-scale hostilities in 1937. Chiang and the Chinese communists under Mao Tse-tung then teamed up again against the Japanese invaders. But civil war again broke out after Japan's defeat by the Allies in 1945. The communists were the victors.

Taiwan was a Japanese colony between 1895 and 1945. Chiang Kai-shek's forces fled there on 10 December 1949 after losing the civil war. Beijing took over Taiwan's seat in the United Nations in 1971. President Richard Nixon visited China in 1972 and recognized the country and its 'One China' policy. The United States is against Taiwan ever seeking independence but helps Taiwan defend itself and expects any reunification to be achieved peacefully and voluntarily. China says that it will attack Taiwan if the island declares independence. Relations between China and Taiwan became particularly strained after the election of President Chen Shui-bian on 18 March 2000. The 'anti-secession' law was approved by the National People's Congress on 14 March 2005. This heightened tension, although China stressed that 'non-peaceful' means would be a last resort to prevent secession. Relations with China improved after the election of President Ma Ying-jeou on 22 March 2008. The United States has a policy of ambiguity as regards defending Taiwan, but it is generally assumed that it would come to Taiwan's rescue if Taiwan were attacked by China.

Communist China

The People's Republic ('communist' regime) was proclaimed on 1 October 1949 by Mao Tse-tung (Zedong), who died in September 1976. (The Communist Party was established in 1921.)

> New research suggests the Chinese nuclear tests from 1964 to 1996 claimed more lives than those of any other nation. Professor Jun Takada, a Japanese physicist, has calculated that up to 1.48 million people were exposed to fallout and 190,000 of them may have died from diseases linked to radiation ... No independent scientific study has even been published inside China ... Mao Tse-tung [Zedong] in 1955 [decided] to build the bomb ... The first test explosion [took place] on 16 October 1964 ... The scientists staged a total of forty-six tests around the Lop Nur site [in Xinjiang province in the Gobi Desert] ... 1,500 miles west of Beijing. Of these tests twenty-three were in the atmosphere, twenty-two underground and one failed. They included thermonuclear blasts, neutron bombs and an atomic bomb covertly tested for Pakistan on 26 May 1990 ... The last explosion in the air was in 1980, but the last underground test was not until 20 July 1996. Later that year China signed the Comprehensive Test Ban Treaty ... China had borrowed Soviet blueprints and spied on the West, according to *The Nuclear Express*, a book by Danny Stillman [director of technical intelligence at Los Alamos, New Mexico, home of America's nuclear weapons] and Thomas Reed, the former US air force secretary. It explains how China then exploited its human capital to win technological parity with the United States for just 4 per cent of the effort – forty-five successful test explosions against more than 1,000 American tests.
>
> (www.thetimes.co.uk, 19 April 2009)

The People's Republic of China became a member of the United Nations in 1971.

Although there were pockets of modern industry in the Treaty Ports and a commercial and monetary tradition, at the start of its socialist period China was, in other respects, a classically poor country. In 1949, 89 per cent of its population classified as rural. Average life expectancy was thirty-five years. The literacy rate was 20 per cent. The commodity structure of foreign trade characterized by mainly primary product exports and manufactured imports. In the period 1931–6 net investment was only about 3 per cent of net domestic product (Riskin 1987: 33). The new communist regime was also confronted with hyperinflation on taking control. In 1952, by which time the economy had largely recovered from decades of foreign and civil war, *per capita* GNP was only $50, while agriculture employed 84 per cent of the workforce and contributed 60 per cent to net material product (Riskin 1987: 269).

China is a one-party state, with the Communist Party determined to retain control. It was prepared to shoot protesting students in Tiananmen Square in June 1989. The stress is on 'unity and stability', and the regime is fearful of dissidents linking up with discontented workers and peasants and of mass movements such as Falun Gong.

> The new search for values from China's past is exploited by Falun Gong, a movement ordinarily seen in the West as a sect linked to rather mysterious traditional practices involving physical exercises as a source of well-being … Even though it is not a peasant movement, and frames its claims in intellectual terms, Falun Gong resembles popular movements that emerged during the final decades of the decadent Manchu empire … Falun Gong reproaches the [Communist] Party for having attacked China's 5,000-year-old traditional culture, attempting to destroy its three ancient religious traditions, Confucian, Buddhist and Taoist. It accuses the Communists of being the only regime in China's history to have attempted to eradicate all three ethical systems, in the past considered the source of legitimate government in China, providing 'the mandate of heaven'. This is a powerful and damaging attack on a Communist Party that presented itself as the vehicle of modernity in China.
>
> (William Pfaff, *IHT*, 25 August 2005, p. 6)

> The Communist leaders … came to power through mass movements and [the party] is likely to lose power only in the same way; it is therefore frightened of any group, even a non-political group like the Falun Gong, that has demonstrated its power to produce mass meetings and demonstrations, or of any publication, like that of *The Tiananmen Papers*, that threatens to embarrass the present Party leaders and undermine their personal position. But the Party is not frightened of purely academic discussions in which only general philosophical opinions and aspirations are mooted … The government cultivates uncertainty about what it will punish as a policy of deterrence …

> Political repression, though often savage and arbitrary, seems pragmatic. It is limited to what the government regards as genuine or potential threats to its position and is intended to discourage open political opposition; it is not an attempt at total mind-control … [In China reference is made to Russia, whose transition produced] what they [the Chinese] call 'chaos', crime, corruption, inefficiency and vulnerability to separatism and border terrorism.
>
> (Ronald Dworkin, *The New York Review of Books*, 2002, vol. XLIX, no. 14, pp. 66–7)

China is some 93 per cent Han. 'The country has fifty-five other groups' (*IHT*, 1 November 2004, p. 1). There has been unrest among ethnic minorities in peripheral areas, such as the Uighurs in Xinjiang (which borders Kazakhstan). The United States and China became closer after the 11 September 2001 terrorist attacks on targets in the United States. The United States has named one Uighur group as part of international terrorism, but critics stress the importance in general of not branding genuine independence movements as 'international terrorism' and thus not giving countries like China and Russia (in the case of Chechnya) an excuse for suppressing domestic rebels.

China regained control of Hong Kong from Britain on 1 July 1997 and of Macao from Portugal on 20 December 1999. Hong Kong is much more important than Macao in economic terms, e.g. in terms of foreign trade and foreign capital. But the people of Macao were much more enthusiastic at being under Chinese control than those of Hong Kong, the former hoping to get respite from criminal gangs. Their futures depend crucially on the reform path being maintained in China itself. The Hong Kong takeover was relatively smooth and China was praised by the West during the Asian financial crisis for not devaluing the Chinese yuan or the Hong Kong dollar. Hong Kong is subject to a 'one country, two systems' regime, with a supposedly high degree of autonomy (except for defence and foreign affairs) for fifty years as a Special Administrative Region of China. But this autonomy has been gradually eroded over time (albeit with increasing economic concessions (e.g. with regard to trade with mainland China) and mainland China has dragged its feet on further moves towards democracy for Hong Kong. Future democratization in China itself and overall success in Hong Kong and Macao are crucial to any prospects of a peaceful reunification with Taiwan. Taiwan remains a potential source of conflict between China and the United States. Both China and the United States are against Taiwan declaring independence, but in that unlikely event China has openly pledged to invade and the United States is, in effect, committed to defending the island.

China invaded Tibet in 1950. In 1959 there was an abortive uprising. The Dalai Lama fled to India and has still not been allowed to return, even though he accepts Chinese sovereignty and acknowledges economic improvements. The Dalai Lama is a believer in non-violence.

> The Dalai Lama said … the only solution is to allow genuine autonomy for the 6 million Tibetans … The regional authority would make policy on

> education, religious practice and the use of natural resources, while Beijing would retain the right to keep military forces in the region and oversee foreign affairs. An autonomous Tibetan government would not force out Han Chinese who had already settled in the vast Tibetan plateau … but would place limits on any future migration. The Dalai Lama said: 'Autonomous regions should be the native peoples' majority' … The Dalai Lama: 'Tibet is very, very backward. And every Tibetan wants to modernize Tibet. So, for that reason, remaining within the People's Republic of China is in our own interest as far as economic development is concerned, provided we have full guarantee to preserve our own culture, our own language, our own spirituality and full protection of environment.'
>
> (www.iht.com, 29 May 2009)

Critics of Chinese government policy see the influx of Han Chinese (further encouraged by the new railway connecting Tibet with the rest of China) as a threat to Tibetan culture. Violent protests erupted in Llasa on 14 March 2008.

China still considers the Dalai Lama to be a 'splittist'. An editorial in the Communist Party's *People's Daily* newspaper: 'The Dalai clique has always been proficient in playing with words. They put forward different kinds of concepts to dazzle people … [But] there is only one key word behind them – Tibetan independence' (www.iht.com, 27 April 2008).

> President Hu Jintao, forced to abandon the G-8 summit by the ethnic violence in Xinjiang, has said maintaining social stability in the energy-rich region is the 'most urgent task'. Mr Hu described the Sunday riots as a 'serious violent crime elaborately planned and organized by "three forces" at home and abroad'. 'Three forces' is a term China uses to refer to religious extremists, separatists and terrorists which, it says, menace Xinjiang.
>
> (*Independent*, 11 July 2009, p. 24)

A key policy of the party is 'unity and stability', keeping the country in one piece and avoiding what it sees as the anarchic conditions that prevailed in the Soviet Union just before it disintegrated in 1991, and in Russia in the 1990s. The party tolerates no threat to its monopoly on political power. That power enables it to conduct a policy of controlled economic reforms, allowing people's attention to be focused on improved living standards. (Economic reforms are discussed in the companion volume, which also deals with the global financial crisis.)

China stresses aspects such as the benefits of rapid economic development (including an impressive reduction in poverty) when discussing human rights. (See Table 1.) Ordinary people have generally benefited substantially in terms of rising living standards, although the growing urban–rural divide and rising unemployment, for example, are officially recognized areas of concern. People typically enjoy much greater freedom as regards work, movement and lifestyles. Many Chinese students now study in Western countries. ('More than 8 per cent of all students were party members in 2007, compared with less than 1 per cent in 1989': *IHT*, 23 May 2009, p. 4.)

Table 1 China: selected economic indicators

Economic indicator	*1990*	*1991*	*1992*	*1993*	*1994*	*1995*	*1996*	*1997*	*1998*	*1999*	*2000*	*2001*	*2002*	*2003*	*2004*	*2005*	*2006*	*2007*	*2008*	*2009*
Rate of growth of GDP (%)																				
Revised figures in brackets	3.8	9.2	14.2	13.5 (14.0)	12.6 (13.1)	10.5 (10.9)	9.6 (10.0)	8.8 (9.3)	7.8 (7.8)	7.1 (7.6)	8.0 (8.4)	7.3 (8.3)	8.0 (9.1)	9.5 (10.0)	9.5 (10.1)	10.2	11.1	11.9	9.6	8.7
Rate of growth of industrial output (%)	7.8	12.9	20.8	23.6	18.0	13.9	12.1	10.8	8.8		9.9		12.6	18.1						
Rate of growth of agricultural output (%)	7.6	3.0	3.7	4.0	3.5	5.0	5.1	3.5	3.5											
Grain output (million tonnes)	435.0	435.3	442.6	456.4	444.5				512.0	508.0		450.0		430.6	469.5	484.0				
Retail or consumer inflation rate (%)	2.1	2.7	5.4	13.0	21.7	14.8	6.1	1.5	–2.6	–2.9	–1.5		–0.8	1.2	3.9	1.8	1.5	4.8		
Population (billion)		1.158	1.170							1.259	1.265	1.272			1.300					
Balance of trade ($ billion)														25.50	31.90	117.0	177.47	262.2		
Foreign exchange reserves ($ billion)				21.2				139.9		154.67	165.6	212.2	286.4	403.25	609.9	819.9	1,066.0	1,500.0	1,946.0	

Source: Various issues of IMF, *World Economic Outlook*; United Nations, *World Economic and Social Survey*; United Nations Economic and Social Commission for Asia and the Pacific, *Economic and Social Survey of Asia and the Pacific*; *FEER*; OECD, *Economic Outlook*; FT; and *IHT*; Jeffries (1996a: 696).

But China has faced periodic censure votes in the United Nations Human Rights Commission since 1990 (Tiananmen being the year before), although all resolutions have failed to be carried to date. On 5 October 1998 China signed the International Covenant on Civil and Political Rights, although it has yet to ratify it.

Direct elections for village committees, which formally started in 1988, are not to be entirely dismissed despite being essentially under party control. The degree of democracy varies substantially, but they are seen centrally as a way of improving and controlling local government, combating corruption and venting local discontent. The first township election took place on 31 December 1998, and in 1999 experiments began with direct elections at the lowest level ('neighbourhood committees') in a number of cities, but progress has been disappointing.

China does not acknowledge that it has any political prisoners, claiming that over 2,000 people have been jailed for counter-revolutionary offences. The already weak dissident movement has been more or less decimated. Leading dissidents such as Wei Jingshen have ended up in the USA. Attempts to register the China Democratic Party in June 1998 (timed to coincide with the visit of US President Bill Clinton) led to jail sentences of up to thirteen years for allegedly attempting to 'overthrow state power'. There is an extensive labour camp network. (Former camp inmate Harry Wu estimated that there were 10 million inmates, while the Chinese government admitted to less than 1.5 million: *Guardian*, 19 May 1994, p. 27.)

On 22 July 1999 the Falun Gong movement was formally banned and in October 1999 it was officially described as an 'evil cult'. The regime sees the movement as a threat to the social stability deemed essential for economic reform and as a threat to the authority of the party at a time when ideology is declining and nationalism has not entirely filled the void. On 25 April 1999 more than 10,000 members had staged a peaceful demonstration around the leadership compound in Beijing, complaining about critical comments in the press and demanding legal status. Falun Gong means 'Way of the Law of the Wheel' and is an (slow-motion) exercise and meditation movement. It is influenced by Buddhist and Taoist principles expressed through breathing exercises.

Independent trade unions are not allowed.

China has exercised a degree of control over the internet far greater than originally forecast. The government is aware of its benefits but alert to the threat to party control over information and communication. US companies like Yahoo and Google have been attacked by critics at home for what is seen as assistance provided to the Chinese government in its control of dissidents.

Religious freedom has increased but is still restricted. For example, Catholics are allowed to practise under the auspices of the Official Chinese Catholic Association. The West estimates that many more practise underground (recognizing the authority of the Pope). China and the Vatican do not have diplomatic relations (although the latter has signalled its desire to establish them – at the expense of those with Taiwan – if agreement can be reached over issues such as the appointment of bishops). Attitudes to the unofficial churches have eased and vary somewhat across the country, but a close eye is kept on them.

China was criticized over the way it has handled AIDS and SARS in the country. China's record on bird flu is acknowledged to be better.

Deng Xiaoping

Deng Xiaoping was born on 22 August 1904 and died on 19 February 1997. He was the leading figure in the drive for economic reform, adopting a pragmatic approach (see quotations below).

'Deng Xiaoping opened the doors to economic reform ... Various economic experiments have been carried out at different levels of government, with the central government taking what works and implementing the reforms in the whole country' (Daniel Bell, *IHT*, 12 May 2009, p. 6).

Deng won the struggle within the Communist Party about how to maintain party control. ('In 1976 after Mao's death and the capture of the gang of four, Hua Guofeng, Mao's chosen successor, became top leader. But with little Beijing experience, Hua was no match for Deng, who step by step gained support to become top leader in 1978. At the Third Plenum in December 1978 Deng was anointed and launched his "reform and opening" ... He said he "crossed the river by groping for stones"': *FEER*, 25 November 1999, p. 43.) After relinquishing the titles of political office, Deng Xiaoping's only remaining formal title was 'Most Honorary President of the China Bridge Association'! But he remained the most powerful figure in reality.

Deng's argument (which is still generally accepted) is that concessions to the market and non-state ownership are essential for maintaining party control, while his opponents believed that the party's power is threatened by radical economic reforms (e.g. it leads to demands for political reform). (Deng's ideas on economic reform were influenced by people such as Zhao Ziyang.) Deng was aware of the extraordinary economic progress of the neighbouring 'Asian tigers' (and especially aware of the contrast between China and Taiwan). Deng strongly believed in political stability and considered this a prerequisite of economic progress. He was influenced and personally affected by the anarchy of the Cultural Revolution. He lost positions of power in 1966 and 1976, making political 'come backs' in 1973 and 1977. He did not become 'paramount leader' until his mid-seventies. He thought that calls for greater democracy and the student demonstrations of 1989 were a threat to stability and was ruthless in stamping them out.

> The goal [of the student protesters of Tiananmen] was to establish a bourgeois republic entirely dependent on the West. Of course we accept people's demands to combat corruption ... However, such slogans were just a front. The real aim was to overthrow the Communist Party and topple the socialist system.
>
> (June 1989)

'We put down a counter-revolutionary rebellion' (June 1989).

The following quotations illustrate, among other things, Deng's pragmatism.

'It does not matter whether a cat is black or white as long as it catches mice' (1961, in relation to agricultural reform). ('The phrase was revolutionary because it directly contradicted Mao Zedong's dictum "better red than expert"': H.D.S. Greenway, *IHT*, 7 November 2007, p. 5.)

'What do the people want from the Communist Party? First, to be liberated, and second to be made rich' (Third Plenum of the Eleventh Central Committee, December 1978).

'If today we still do not set about the task of improving the socialist system, people will ask why it cannot solve problems which its capitalist counterpart can' (August 1980).

'We should let some people get rich first, both in the countryside and in the urban areas. To get rich by hard work is glorious' (January 1983).

'Socialism must eliminate poverty. Poverty is not socialism' (June 1984).

'Development is the core truth.'

'Fish grow in muddy waters' (1985).

'Our experience in the twenty years from 1958 to 1978 teaches us that poverty is not socialism. You cannot eat socialism' (1985).

'If you want to bring the initiative of the peasants into play, you should give them the power to make money' (October 1985).

'A planned economy does not necessarily imply socialism … a market economy does not necessarily imply capitalism' (1992).

'We in China are faced with the task of transforming our backwardness and catching up promptly with the advanced countries of the world. We want to learn from you' (1979).

('In early 1979 Deng Xiaoping was barnstorming America to celebrate the historic agreement normalizing relations between the countries. At a stop in suburban Atlanta Deng toured a Ford factory that made more cars in a single month than China produced in a year. Aware of his country's economic inferiority, Deng … said he hoped to transform China into an industrial power by the distant year of 2000 … China manufactured 13,000 cars in 1979; last year [2004] the number exceeded 5 million': www.iht.com, 20 November 2005; *IHT*, 21 November 2005, p. 4. 'Chinese carmakers produced a record number of vehicles last year [2007], rolling out 8.88 million units, up 22 per cent': *IHT*, 14 January 2008, p. 13.)

The influence of Zhao Ziyang, Prisoner of State: The Secret Journal of Premier Zhao Ziyang *(Simon and Schuster, 2009)*

> Tapes [were] secretly recorded during his sixteen years under house arrest [by] Zhao Ziyang, the former premier and former General Secretary of the Communist Party … The tapes were smuggled out and will be published in English and Chinese this month [May 2009].
>
> (*Guardian*, 15 May 2009, p. 22)

> As Zhao Ziyang anticipated, he was immediately sidelined and soon vilified for 'splitting the party'. He was purged and placed under house arrest until his death in 2005. But in this long, enforced retirement ... Mr Zhao secretly recorded his own account, on thirty musical cassette tapes that were spirited out of the country by former aides and supporters.
>
> (*IHT*, 15 May 2009, p. 1)

> His last public appearance was on 19 May 1989 when he visited the young demonstrators in front of the Forbidden City and urged them to leave Tiananmen Square ... Standing beside him was his aide, Wen Jiabao ... the current premier.
>
> (*Independent*, 15 May 2009, p. 19)

> One striking claim in the memoir ... is that Zhao Ziyang presses the case that he pioneered the opening of China's economy to the world and the initial introduction of market forces in agriculture and industry – steps he says were fiercely opposed by hardliners and not always fully supported by Deng Xiaoping, the paramount leader, who is often credited with championing market-orientated policies. In the late 1970s, as the party chief in Sichuan province, Mr Zhao had started dismantling Maoist-style collective farms. Mr Deng, who had just consolidated power after Mao's death, brought him to Beijing in 1980 as prime minister with a mandate for change.
>
> (*IHT*, 15 May 2009, p. 4)

> While Deng Xiaoping is largely seen as China's architect of reforms, Zhao Ziyang's account gives the former party head more of a supportive role, making it clear that he himself was the first one to make breakthrough in economic thinking regarding the development of the Household Responsibility System ... and the rise of Special Economic Zones.
>
> (www.feer.com, 14 May 2009)

> [The book] casts light on Deng Xiaoping, the former paramount leader, suggesting it was Zhao Ziyang who was the real instigator of many of the country's economic reforms ... Mr Deng is credited with supporting reform but Mr Zhao writes that many of his ideas were his own. It was Mr Zhao who pushed for the break-up of farm communes in the early 1980s, he says. And it was he who persuaded Mr Deng to support the free-trade zones.
>
> (*FT*, 16 May 2009, p. 5)

'[In 1989 Deng Xiaoping's] only official title was Chairman of the Central Military Commission' (www.ft.com, 31 May 2009).

Selected quotes by Zhao Ziyang (*IHT*, 15 May 2009, pp. 1, 4; *Independent*, 15 May 2009, p. 19, *The Times*, 15 May 2009, p. 32; *Guardian*, 15 May 2009, p. 22; *FT*, 16 May 2009, p. 5):

> It is the Western parliamentary democratic system that has demonstrated the most vitality. This system is currently the best one available. It is able

> to manifest the spirit of democracy and meet the demands of a modern society … Of course the system is not perfect; it has its problems. Yet relatively speaking this system is best suited to a modern civilization … If a country wishes to modernize, not only should it implement a market economy but it must also adopt a parliamentary democracy as its political system. Otherwise this nation will not be able to have a market economy that is healthy and modern, nor can it become a modern society with a rule of law … It would be wrong if our Party never makes the transition from a state that was suitable in a time of war to a state more suitable to a democratic society … The ruling Party must achieve two breakthroughs. One is to allow other political parties and a free press to exist. The second … is the Party needs to adopt democratic procedures and use democratic means to reform itself … Different opinions must be allowed to exist, and different factions should be made legitimate … It is the Western parliamentary system that has demonstrated the most vitality. If we do not move towards this goal, it will be impossible to resolve the abnormal conditions in China's market economy.
>
> It was said that this event [Tiananmen] was aimed at overthrowing the People's Republic and the Communist Party. Where is the evidence? I had said at the time that most people were only asking us to correct our flaws, not attempting to overthrow our political system … I told myself that no matter what, I refused to become the General Secretary [of the Communist Party] who mobilized the military to crack down on students.
>
> For more than a week Bao Tong, a former senior Communist Party official now under strict surveillance, openly promoted an insider's account of Chinese political infighting … The book is the posthumous memoir by Mr Bao's boss, Zhao Ziyang … When the memoir became public last week Mr Bao, the most senior official imprisoned after the crackdown, quickly claimed responsibility. In a string of interviews with the foreign press that security officials did not initially seek to prevent, he said he had collaborated with other liberal party elders to slip cassette recordings out of the country for publication … Mr Bao said by telephone [22 May] that he had been informed he could no longer accept interviews.
>
> (www.iht.com, 23 May 2009)

China after Deng Xiaoping

There was something of a mild power struggle among Deng's successors, but there was essentially continuity of policy.

General Secretary Jiang Zemin (12 October 1992):

> We must hold high the great banner of socialism with Chinese characteristics … If we fail to develop our economy rapidly it will be very difficult for us to consolidate the socialist system and maintain long-term stability …

> The goal is to build a socialist democracy suited to Chinese conditions and absolutely not a Western, multi-party, parliamentary system ... [The development of a] socialist market economy [is the only way forward] ... We are convinced that a market economy established under the socialist system can and should operate better than one under the capitalist system ... [Macroeconomic levers should be the main means of control. The plan should, for example, set] strategic targets [include growth forecasts and deal with investment in the infrastructure. There should be an integrated national market with no regional protectionism].
>
> (Jeffries 1993: 497)

The leading personalities were the following:

1 Jiang Zemin, party leader and president (March 1993); he was described as the 'core' of the collective leadership (note the word 'collective') and he steadily consolidated his position (e.g. he was prominent during the October 1999 celebrations of the fiftieth anniversary of communist China);
2 Li Peng, prime minister until March 1998 when he was elected chairman of the National People's Congress; the least enthusiastic of the three as regards economic reform;
3 Zhu Rongji, senior vice-premier and the economics supremo until March 1998 when he was elected prime minister (while remaining economics supreme; the foremost economic reformer, he was once governor of the central bank, stepping down on 30 June 1995).

Among the economic problems facing them were inflation (though minor compared with that faced by many countries in Eastern Europe and the former Soviet Union in the early years of transition) and, starting in October 1997, deflation (a problem, for example, because large volumes of stocks depressed economic activity; the state has increased its spending to keep growth high enough to keep unemployment under control). (Modest inflation began to be recorded in 2003.) Persistent problems included heavy losses by many state enterprises, worker unrest (caused by factors such as unemployment, the non-payment of wages and benefits and corrupt management), a weak banking system (problems such as high ratios of non-performing loans), farmers' discontent, increasing economic disparities between coastal and inland provinces as well as between town and country, and corruption.

In November 2002 the party charter was revised to include Jiang Zemin's 'three represents'. 'The "three represents" said the party's mission was to represent "advanced production forces" (capitalists and technologists), "advanced cultural forces" (intellectuals) and "the broad masses of the people" (everybody else)' (David Ignatius, *IHT*, 21 September 2002, p. 4).

> The 'three represents': Jiang Zemin's controversial attempt to redefine the party's mission in order to guarantee the party's survival. He holds that the party should represent the needs of 'advanced forces of production' such as hi-tech industries and the private sector, advanced culture and the

> 'fundamental interests of the overwhelming majority of the Chinese people' – rather than the millions of blue-collar workers laid off by state-owned industries.
>
> (*FEER*, 7 November 2002, p. 29)

'[The term] "advanced productive forces" [is] communist jargon for capitalists' (*The Economist*, 9 November 2002, p. 15). In November 2002 private businessmen (private entrepreneurs) were formally allowed to join the party.

A so-called 'fourth generation' of leaders has appeared since the Sixteenth Communist Party Congress held in November 2002 and the Tenth National People's Congress held in March 2003. The positions mentioned were filled by the following:

1 Hu Jintao: the 59-year-old vice-president became General Secretary of the Communist Party on 15 November 2002, president in March 2003, chairman of the party's Central Military Commission on 19 September 2004 and chairman of the state's Central Military Commission in March 2005. Hu Jintao's mentor was Deng Xiaoping.
2 Wen Jiabao: prime minister. His mentor was Zhu Rongji.
3 Wu Bangguo: chairman of the National People's Congress. He was previously deputy prime minister dealing with reform of state enterprises and his mentor was Jiang Zemin.

Despite considerable prior speculation about exactly which positions Jiang Zemin would give up, the most orderly and peaceful transfer of power since 1949 has taken place. There was again essentially a continuity of policy, including that of collective leadership and attitudes towards economic reform. There were, however, some differences. For example, Hu seemed to have a more positive attitude towards greater transparency and democracy within the party (such as elections for lower-level party posts). But it was generally thought that his room to manoeuvre was limited. (Early on there was considerable speculation as to who would hold ultimate power, since Jiang Zemin remained chairman of the party Central Military Commission until 19 September 2004.)

Hu Jintao has not made any startling proposals to date, although he quickly identified himself with those people who and areas which have fared less well as a result of the economic reforms. He seemed to be concerned to place greater emphasis of the social costs of growth and less on growth as an end in itself. The term 'a harmonious society' became associated with him. But a communiqué issued on 11 October 2005 at the end of a Central Committee meeting showed that economic growth was not going to be sacrificed in the process. The communiqué stated:

> During the Eleventh Five Year Plan we must maintain fast and stable economic growth and support the building of a harmonious society. The meeting stressed that to push forward economic development and improve the lives of the people is China's major task … We need to put greater emphasis on social equity, enhance efforts in adjusting income distribution

> and strive to alleviate the tendency of the widening income gap between regions and parts of society.
>
> (www.iht.com, 12 October 2005; *FT*, 12 October 2005, p. 11)

(Likewise, although the (soon demoted) idea of 'green GDP' implies concern about China's severe pollution problems, it is clear that rapid economic growth is regarded as essential to maintain the rise in living standards and to keep unemployment at socially tolerable levels.) But the increasing income inequalities in China (especially between urban and rural areas) is causing increasing concern.

Overall, it seems that Hu Jintao has turned out to be more hard-line than expected. There is growing concern that unrest in the countryside (especially over such things as land seizures for urban and industrial development) and rising unemployment (aggravated by the global financial crisis) could threaten social stability.

> Three years after becoming China's top leader, Hu Jintao … president and Communist Party chief … has solidified his grip on power and intimidated critics inside and outside the Communist Party with the help of the man once seen as his most potent rival … Zeng Qinghong, vice president and the man in charge of the party's organizational affairs … They have clamped down on non-government organizations, tightened media controls and forced all of the 70 million members to submit self-criticisms as an act of ritualistic submission to their authority … In May Hu and Zeng convened top officials to warn that just as governments in Ukraine, Georgia and Kyrgyzstan had been toppled, the government in China could be, too. They argued that the United States had fostered social unrest in those places and had similar designs on China … They have since forced non-government organizations that focus on the environment, legal aid, health and education to find government sponsors or shut down. Many groups are also under pressure to stop accepting money from the United States and other foreign countries. The leadership has also fired editors at publications that defied orders from the party's propaganda department … They have also tightened rules on foreign investment in China's television industry.
>
> (Joseph Kahn, www.iht.com, 25 September 2005; *IHT*, 26 September 2005, p. 2)

> The Communist Party has chosen one of its oldest political tools – a Maoist-style ideological campaign, complete with required study groups. For fourteen months and counting, the party's 70 million rank and file members have been assigned readings that include speeches by Mao and Deng Xiaoping, as well as the numbing treatise of 17,000-plus words that is the party constitution. Mandatory meetings include sessions where cadres must offer self-criticisms and also criticize everyone else … The campaign [is] known as *bao xian* or 'preserving the progressiveness' … Hu Jintao, who is also general secretary of the party, has insisted that every member complete the programme … The third and final phase is now under way at village party

> branches and is to end in June [2006] … In recent years Hu's predecessor as the country's top leader, Jiang Zemin, ushered in study campaigns. More famously as many as 200 campaigns were introduced under Mao, from the angry purges of the Cultural Revolution era to mass mobilization efforts to exterminate rodents … In February [2006] the party's Central Discipline Inspection Commission announced that it had disciplined 115,000 party members for corruption in 2005 … One proposal debated in recent years by Chinese intellectuals calls for intra-party elections. But as yet such reforms have not materialized.
>
> (Jim Yardley, *IHT*, 10 March 2006, pp. 1, 8)

> Politically the government has intensified control. New restrictions are imposed on the media, non-government organizations and social activists. In part Chinese leaders acted in the belief that, at this stage of China's development, a firmer hand of the state is needed to maintain stability. They view the country's mounting social problems as the 'growing pains' of modernization that can be addressed with more fiscal spending.
>
> (Minxin Pei, *IHT*, 6 March 2007, p. 6)

Hu Jintao's speech given on 15 October 2007 at the Seventeenth Communist Party Congress included the following passages:

> [Economic development is of] decisive significance to build moderately prosperous society … and socialist modernization … Rapid development represents the most remarkable achievement [of the last five years].
>
> [One of the main goals is to build a] moderately prosperous society [by 2020]. [The aim is to quadruple *per capita* GDP by 2020.]
>
> [A] scientific outlook on development [is necessary] … Our economic growth is realized at an extremely high cost of resources and the environment … We must adopt an enlightened approach to development that results in expanded production, a better life and sound ecological and environmental conditions. We need to correctly handle the major relationships between urban and rural development, economic and social development and man and nature … There are still a considerable number of impoverished and low-income people in both urban and rural areas, and it has become more difficult to accommodate the interests of all sides … To realize social equity and justice is the Chinese Communists' consistent position … Balanced and sustainable [development is necessary].
>
> To stop or reverse [economic] reform and opening up would only lead up a blind alley.
>
> [Public ownership will remain] dominant … [but] all economic sectors [can] compete on an equal footing and reinforce each other.
>
> Hu Jintao succeeded in inserting his signature political theory, 'the scientific outlook on development' into the party constitution five years before he

> retires. Jiang Zemin managed only to write his equivalent 'three represents' into the party constitution when he was leaving the helm in 2002.
>
> (www.iht.com, 23 October 2007)

'President Hu Jintao praised the achievements made by his country during thirty years of reforms' (www.bbc.co.uk, 18 December 2008).

> President Hu Jintao … has vowed to continue the economic reforms … Speaking on the thirtieth anniversary of China's decision to open itself up to the outside world, President Hu Jintao told a crowd of 6,000 at Beijing's Great Hall of the People: 'Standing still and regressing will lead only to a dead end' … The first policies were approved on 18 December 1978. Hu said: 'Reform and opening up are the fundamental causes of all achievements and progress we have made … [Deng Xiaoping's vision three decades ago was] completely correct.'
>
> (www.cnn.com, 18 December 2008)

At the Seventeenth Communist Party Congress (held 15–21 October 2007) the likely future leaders were revealed: Xi Jinping (54 and likely future president) and Li Keqiang (52 and likely future prime minister).

Severe snow storms affected parts of China in early 2008. 'The worst winter weather in fifty years' (www.cnn.com, 31 January 2008).

> In the last week the government has worked as hard at public relations as at crisis management, with both of the country's top leaders travelling to some of the worst-affected areas. Prime minister Wen Jiabao, who has moved about China almost non-stop during this period, travelled early last week to the southern city of Guangzhou, where as many as 800,000 people had gathered at the train station at one point seeking to begin their annual leaves. President Hu Jintao travelled later in the week to a coal mine in northern Shaanxi province to encourage miners to redouble their efforts, including forgoing New Year celebrations, in order to spare the country's power grid from further brownouts. Hu, known for his circumspection in public, was quoted as saying he was unable to sleep because of the scale of the emergency.
>
> (www.iht.com, 3 February 2008)

'On Wednesday [6 February], which was New Year's Eve, top leaders visited some of the areas hardest hit by the severe weather' (www.bbc.co.uk, 7 February 2008).

> A powerful earthquake struck western China on Monday [12 May] … the country's worst natural disaster in three decades … The quake was China's biggest natural disaster since another earthquake levelled the city of Tangshan in 1976 … posing a problem to the Communist Party, which initially tried to cover up the catastrophe … The powerful initial quake struck at 2.28 p.m. near Wechuan county … The relatively vigorous flow of information and the fast response from top officials and rescue workers stood in stark contrast to the way China handled the Tangshan earthquake.
>
> (www.iht.com, 13 May 2008)

'The quake destroyed a massive swathe of Sichuan as well as the two neighbouring provinces' (www.iht.com, 21 July 2008). 'Prime minister Wen Jiabao flew to Sichuan hours after the earthquake struck' (www.iht.com, 13 May 2008). The regime's in many ways laudable response to the earthquake has been marred, for example by official resistance to the claim that shoddy construction of schools played a part in the death of so many children.

China hosted the 2008 Summer Olympic Games 8–24 August 2008 to great acclaim. But the international Olympic torch relay's early stages were bedevilled by anti-Chinese demonstrations (especially in London and Paris).

'The massive effort to clear the skies over Beijing for the Summer Olympics paid off, the city's environmental authority said Monday [1 September], with the capital seeing its cleanest air in a decade' (www.iht.com, 1 September 2008).

'The government set aside three "protest zones"' (www.iht.com, 17 August 2008).

> Authorities have received seventy-seven applications from people who want to hold protests … in three designated areas … during the Beijing Olympics, but all were withdrawn, suspended or rejected, state media said Monday [18 August] … Human rights groups and families of people who have applied to protest in the parks say some were taken away afterward by security agents, prompting critics to accuse officials of using the plan as a trap to draw potential protesters to their attention.
>
> (www.iht.com, 18 August 2008)

'The Foreign Correspondents' Club of China said at least fifty-nine reporters were harassed while trying to do their jobs' (www.bbc.co.uk, 28 August 2008).

'Mostly foreign activists staged a series of small illegal demonstrations near Olympic sites and at Beijing landmarks … A few journalists trying to cover the protests were roughed up by authorities then released' (www.iht.com, 25 August 2008).

> China concluded its debut as Olympic host Sunday [24 August] after sixteen days of nearly flawless logistics and superlative athletic achievement that co-existed awkwardly with the government's wariness of dissent and free speech … Its athletes topped the gold medal standings for the first time … Two athletes gave some of the greatest performances in Olympic history – Michael Phelps [of the United States] with his eight gold medals in swimming; Jamaica's Usain Bolt with three golds and three world records in the sprints [100 metres, 200 metres and 4 x 100 metres relay] … Led by Phelps and Bolt athletes broke forty-three world records and 132 Olympic records during the Games … Athletes shied away from making political statements and 'protest zones' established in Beijing went unused as the authorities refused to issue permits for them … China invested more than $40 billion in the Games … Olympic telecasts achieved record ratings in China and the United States, and the Games's presence online was by far the most extensive ever … Smog that enveloped the city early in the Games gave way to

> mostly clear skies, easing fears that some endurance events might be hazardous for the athletes.
>
> (www.iht.com, 24 August 2008)

> [China won 100 medals in total] ... [China] finished with fifty-one [gold medals], the highest figure for any nation at an Olympics in twenty years, and they won them across a wider range of sports than any team in Beijing ... The United States finished with 110 [medals in total] ... The Russians won thirty-six gold medals and eighty-eight overall in 2000; they won twenty-seven golds and ninety-two overall in Athens. This time the final tallies were twenty-three [coming third after China and the United States] and seventy-two.
>
> (www.iht.com, 24 August 2008)

The medal count for the top four countries was as follows (gold, silver, bronze, total): China (51, 21, 28, 100); United States (36, 38, 36, 110); Russia (23, 21, 28, 72); Britain (19, 13, 15, 47) (*IHT*, 25 August 2008, p. 18).

> [The] $43 billion price tag for the Games was almost completely absorbed by the state. China's fifty-one gold medals, easily the most of any nation, were the product of a state-controlled sports machine ... Critics say that the Olympics have underscored the deep resistance within the Communist Party to becoming more tolerant of dissent.
>
> (*IHT*, 25 August 2008, p. 15)

'Although the organization of the Games has been widely praised, rights groups have criticized the Beijing government throughout' (www.bbc.co.uk, 24 August 2008).

'What many outside China saw during the Olympics was a clampdown on dissent and a disdain even for the spontaneous street-party exuberance of previous Games ... Organizationally the Games went well' (*The Economist*, 30 August 2008, p. 63).

> President Hu Jintao has a favourite phrase these days: 'harmonious world', in which countries of different outlooks live together in peace. Mr Hu first unveiled this idea ... in a speech at the United Nations on 15 September [2005] ... Before 'harmonious world' came China's 'peaceful rise' – a term that fell by the wayside as officials bickered over whether it sounded a bit too menacing, or perhaps just the opposite as far as Taiwan was concerned.
>
> (*The Economist*, 19 November 2005, pp. 23–5)

President Hu Jintao (20 November 2005): 'China's commitment to a role of peaceful development is a choice that China must make ... China's development is peaceful, open and co-operative in nature' (www.iht.com, 20 November 2005).

China has gone out of its way to try to allay concern over its growing economic and military power. But many countries in Asia remain worried, not helped by China's territorial claims (over the Spratly Islands, for example).

China's rapid growth has become a factor of global economic significance. (See the companion volume, *Economic Developments in Contemporary China.*) This economic growth has been accompanied by increasing military might and a growing diplomatic stature. For example, China has hosted international, six-party talks about North Korea's nuclear weapons programme. On 9 October 2006, however, against China's wishes, North Korea tested a nuclear weapon. On 25 May 2009 North Korea conducted a second underground nuclear test.

China's relations with the United States loom large. The war against international terrorism since the 11 September 2001 attacks on the United States has brought the two countries closer together. China has used international terrorism to justify its tough policies on internal unrest among minorities. (See the section above on Taiwan as regards relations with the United States.) On 20 January 2009 Barack Obama replaced George W. Bush as president of the United States. The economy of the United States has been much weakened by the global financial crisis, but Presidents Hu and Obama have much in common in their response to it.

China has improved its relations with Russia since the collapse of the Soviet Union in 1991, both supporting the idea of a 'multi-polar' world (as opposed to a 'uni-polar' world dominated by the United States). Post-Soviet Russia was much weakened at first, but Vladimir Putin's Russia enjoyed an economic resurgence (albeit largely due to high energy and raw material prices) and has become a much more confident country on the international stage. China has much need of Russia's natural resources. By the autumn of 2008, however, Russia found that the global financial crisis was taking its toll on its economy. Both China and Russia have sought to use international terrorism to further crack down on internal unrest among minorities and resent what they see as other countries interfering in the internal affairs of others (given the sensitivity of Tibet and Chechnya, respectively). China and Russia have settled their own border disputes. But Russia's recognition of the independence of the Georgian breakaway regions of South Ossetia and Abkhazia on 26 August 2008 after Russia's brief war with Georgia (following Georgia's attempt to regain control of South Ossetia by force) did not see China follow suit.

China has also improved its relations with India, although it was disturbed by India and Pakistan conducting nuclear tests in May 1998. China itself announced a moratorium on further tests after it conducted its forty-fifth test on 29 July 1996. (The USA conducted 1,030 nuclear tests and the former Soviet Union 715: *IHT*, 12 December 1996, p. 7. There have been a total of 2,045 known nuclear tests since 1945: *IHT*, 12 September 1996, p. 17.)

China's search for raw materials such as oil has led to international criticism that it is mollycoddling gross violators of human rights such as Sudan and Myanmar.

Demography

China is the largest country in the world in terms of population. The population was 1.158 billion at the end of 1991 and 1.259 billion at the end of 1999. A figure of 1.265 billion was announced on 28 March 2001, the result of the fifth national census held on 1 November 2000. In 2001 the figure was 1.272 billion. On 6 January 2005 the figure was 1.3 billion. By the end of 2006 the figure was 1.314 billion.

The world population figure reached 6 billion in October 1999. India is the second largest country in the world by population, reaching 1 billion in August 1999 and 1.033 billion in 2001. (On 10 October 2006 the population of the United States was officially proclaimed to be 300 million.)

China is the third largest country in the world in terms of land area, after Russia and Canada.

'The dominant Han today account for 93 per cent of the country's 1.3 billion people, according to official statistics' (*IHT*, 17 March 2007, p. 6).

> By official estimates barely half the population can speak the official language [Mandarin] ... A government survey published last year [2004] said only 53 per cent of the population 'can communicate in Putonghua' [Mandarin]. In recognition of this broadcasters commonly include subtitles – the meaning of written Chinese characters is stable even as spoken dialects vary – on television to help people overcome comprehension problems ... China has fifty-five ethnic minorities ... China's Han [is] the ethnic group that makes up more than 90 per cent of the population ... The Han speak as many as 1,500 dialects, with the bulk of them concentrated in the southern half of the country ... Many of the Han dialects are almost entirely mutually incomprehensible.
>
> (www.iht.com, 10 July 2005)

> Although the Chinese share a common written language, linguists identify eight major spoken-language groups that are mutually unintelligible. The Communists, like the Nationalists before them, have gone to great lengths to impose a common spoken language, Putonghua, commonly known as Mandarin outside of China, as part of their drive to reinforce national unity. But regional language groups, which include Cantonese and Shanghainese, have been surprisingly resilient ... Cantonese is spoken by about 60 million people in Guangdong province and in Hong Kong and Macao, as well as among ethnic Chinese populations overseas.
>
> (www.iht.com, 15 January 2006; *IHT*, 16 January 2006, p. 9)

> Only about half of China's population can speak the national language, Mandarin, according to the state news agency Xinhua ... In a survey of 500,000 people around the country, the ministry of education found that only 53 per cent of people could 'effectively communicate' in Mandarin, Xinhua reported. In urban areas 66 per cent of residents spoke fluent Mandarin, while in rural areas only 45 per cent of those surveyed could

> 'effectively communicate orally' in the language, said Xinhua. Only 31 per cent of those aged between sixty and sixty-nine were able to speak it, compared to 70 per cent of people between fifteen and twenty-nine, the survey found.
>
> (www.bbc.co.uk, 7 March 2007)

China has to support about 22 per cent of the world's population on something like 7 per cent of the world's arable area. 'In 1979 only 11 per cent of the total land area of China was cultivated (50 per cent of India's land is cultivated), with just 0.12 ha *per capita* of the agricultural population (compared with India's 0.42)' (World Bank 1984: 35; cited in Jeffries 1993: 137). 'Only about half of China is habitable … [It] has 7 per cent of the world's cultivable land' (*FT*, 27 July 2004, p. 15). 'China is the world's largest agricultural producer, feeding some 22 per cent of the world's population with 10 per cent of its arable land' (*FEER*, 2 May 2002, p. 25). 'China attained food self-sufficiency in the mid-1990s, managing to nourish 20 per cent of the world's population from 7 per cent of its arable farmland' (*The Times*, 8 April 2005, p. 50). Thus it is no coincidence that agricultural reform was first in line after 1978.

'[There was] an increase in average life expectancy from thirty-five years in 1949 to sixty-eight years by 1978' (*IHT*, 20 August 2005, p. 2). By 1986 life expectancy had risen to 66.9 for men and 70.9 for women (Jeffries 1993: 138).

'By 2005 life expectancy reached 72.4 years; maternal, infant and under-five mortality rates declined to 47.7 per 100,000, and 19.0 and 22.5 per 1,000 respectively – levels comparable with middle-income countries' (*FEER*, November 2007, p. 52).

> Health experts agree that one of the major achievements of China's health system before 1978 was the provision of basic medical care for all urban and rural Chinese. These services, along with an emphasis on preventative medicine and national campaigns to eradicate endemic disease, contributed to an increase in average Chinese life expectancy from thirty-five years in 1949 to sixty-eight years by 1978. Despite a dramatic increase in prosperity and living standards in China since 1978 average life expectancy has increased by only 3.5 years, about half the gains in longevity in Japan, Singapore, Hong Kong and [South] Korea over the same period … Critics note that the government share of national health spending has plummeted from close to 100 per cent during the planned period to about 16 per cent today as the government has steadily withdrawn from providing health services. By comparison, public spending accounts for about 44 per cent of health outlays in the United States and an average of more than 70 per cent in other advanced industrial countries … The public's access to health care in China has been steadily declining for more than two decades … Critics … [talk of] exorbitant charges for medical services, wasteful over-servicing and widespread over-prescription of drugs … A hard-hitting report [was issued] earlier this month by the Development Research Centre, one of the government's top advisory bodies … The report was co-sponsored by the World

> Health Organization … [The report] noted 'to our shame' that the World Health Organization ranked the Chinese health system as one of the most unfair in the world. The report said: 'Most of the medical needs of society cannot be met because of economic reasons. Poor people cannot even enjoy the most basic health care' … In the absence of widespread medical insurance, many Chinese, particularly the 800 million living in rural areas, cannot afford treatment when they are ill … The return [has been witnessed] of deadly diseases including tuberculosis and schistosomiasis [a parasitic disease carried by water snails] that had largely been eradicated before 1978 … Health care outlays have now reached 6 per cent of GDP, a relatively high rate for a developing country. During the planned era outlays on health care were about half that proportion.
>
> (www.iht.com, 19 August 2005; *IHT*, 20 August 2005, p. 2)

'[The] government budget covers only 17 per cent of total health expenditure (compared to, for instance, 40 per cent in the United States)' (*FEER*, November 2005, p. 53).

> China has six people in the work force for every retiree, but that ratio could narrow to 2:1 between 2030 and 2050, according to a committee population survey, its first since 2000 … China is already home to more than half the old people in Asia and by 2050 its elderly are expected to exceed 400 million … Across the vast countryside more than half of the elderly did not have any medical insurance and fewer than 5 per cent received pensions.
>
> (www.iht.com, 18 December 2007)

Developments in demographic policy

Since roughly the mid-1950s the state has tried to control population growth, often in draconian fashion.

The 1953 census revealed a 1952 population of 575 million and shocked the party into a population control programme after 1956. Previously, exclusive blame for poverty was based on capitalism and imperialism, Mao opposing birth control as a 'bourgeois Malthusian doctrine' (Fang Lizhi, *Independent*, 18 January 1989, p. 19). It was not until the early 1970s, however, that the programme really took off, with the aim, set in 1980, of restricting population growth to 1.2 billion by the year 2000. A mixture of financial and non-pecuniary incentives and penalties were applied, especially to try to attain the goal of one child per family, formally adopted in 1979. This was relaxed somewhat in 1984–5 and tightened in 1987. After mid-1988 a surprising switch in policy took place, allowing families in rural areas to have a second child if the first was a girl, due to the difficulty of enforcing policy. 'But the policy was maintained for urban areas and tightened up generally for larger families' (Jeffries 1993: 174).

'The population of China will officially reach 1.3 billion [on 6 January 2005] … State media credited the government's population control policies over the past thirty years for delaying the date of arrival at the 1.3 billion figure by four years' (*The Times*, 4 January 2005, p. 32). '[China claims that its population] would today top 1.5 billion ... without government intervention' (*The Times*, 7 January 2005, p. 43).

The present policy as regards population, formally introduced in 1979, is 'one child' per family with exceptions which have grown over time.

> China's one-child policy was first implemented in 1979, but officially proclaimed only in the early 1980s ... According to Chinese estimates, only one in five youngsters is an only child. Faced with growing evidence that its population control measures are being ignored [e.g. false claims that children are twins], Beijing is aiming to switch to a two-child policy ... [although] there is no official policy change yet ... [China says that the one-child policy] has prevented 300 million births during the past decade and brought down China's birth rate from 33 per thousand to fifteen by the end of the 1990s.
>
> (*The Times*, 8 November 2004, p. 35)

> A little-known provision in China's family planning policy allows an only child married to another only child to have two children, providing the kids are spaced four years apart ... Now the first generation born under the one-child policy is starting to get married ... more and more couples will be eligible for exemption.
>
> (*FEER*, 23 November 2000, p. 98)

> China is starting to move away from its 'one-child' policy and compulsory birth quotas ... Targets and quotas have been abandoned in a trial project backed by the UN Population Fund in thirty-two rural counties. Beijing now plans to extend the voluntary approach to a further 800 counties ... The one-child rule has already been relaxed in most of rural China, where families are allowed two children if the first is a girl – and often if it is a boy. City dwellers are still limited to one child, unless both parents are single children themselves ... While birth quotas have been removed in the thirty-two pilot counties, families who exceed two children still have to pay a fine, known as the 'social compensation payment' ... Instead of paying the fine, couples can choose to have an abortion, especially if the pregnancy was unintended. Another important difference under the UN scheme is that families no longer have to apply to have their first child. In the past it might have been refused if the village 'quota' had been filled.
>
> (*Guardian*, 27 July 2002, p. 18)

> [On 22 July the USA] withheld $34 million in international family planning funds designated for the United Nations ... [because] any money to the agency ... [the United States claimed] helps the 'Chinese government to implement more effectively its programmes of coercive abortion'.
>
> (*IHT*, 3 August 2002, p. 6)

> China's one-child policy ... [was] launched in 1980 after the population topped 1 billion ... But implementation has always been spotty. Today only

about 20 per cent of children under fourteen are from single-child families ... The policy has been most effective in cities, where residents face heavy fines and can lose their jobs. But in the countryside, where parents depend on children to help them, especially sons, resistance has been widespread ... By the mid-1980s most rural communities allowed families with one daughter to have a second child after four years – in effect to try for a son ... In 1995 Beijing approved a pilot project in six rural counties where family planning workers would try to limit births by expanding health services for women, providing more information about contraception and allowing couples to make their own decisions. Then, in 1998, the UN population agency encouraged China to take the experiment a step further, providing funding and training to thirty-two rural counties ... that agreed to eliminate the birth permits, targets and quotas and stop promoting abortion as family planning ... [For example] under China's one-child policy, couples in this rural county [the county of Yushi] in Jiangxi province once needed a permit to have a baby. Women as a rule were fitted with IUDs after their first child, sterilized after their second. But times have changed. Yushi abolished the permits several years ago and let women make their own decisions about birth control. It stopped setting birth quotas and sterilization targets for family planning workers, too. The only punishment now for having an extra child is a fine, and even that is only occasionally collected in full ... Four years later ... [it is claimed that] population growth in Yushi has remained steady. In addition, infant mortality and other health indicators have improved ... as have relations between family planning workers and residents. Similar results have been reported in the other thirty-one counties ... [It has also been claimed] that officials across the country had been impressed by the results of the UN project, and that many were also abandoning birth permits and quotas ... [It is said] that cities and counties accounting for nearly a quarter of China's 1.3 billion people had eliminated birth permits and quotas over the last five years ... and about half the population now lives in jurisdictions that allow women to choose which type of contraception to use.

(*IHT*, 21 August 2002, pp. 1, 7)

China's first national family planning law came into effect more than two decades after its one-child-per-family policy was introduced. The legislation is aimed at preventing officials from arbitrarily fining and harshly punishing families which violate the policy. Couples who have more than one child will now pay a weighted form of compensation, while local governments must foot family planning budgets rather than relying on fines levied on parents.

(*FEER*, 12 September 2002, p. 12)

Beijing is considering the value of continuing the one-child policy ... At the time it was adopted in 1979, at the urging of Deng Xiaoping, the one-child policy ... represented a huge change from the historical importance of large

> families in China and from a Maoist philosophy that encouraged parents to have more children because China would be strengthened by a big population ... Some have said [there have been] cases of forced sterilization, abandonment of unwanted children and infanticide by parents who favoured sons over daughters. According to 2000 census data, China had 117 boys born for every 100 girls ... Fears of instability that could be caused by this imbalance is prompting officials to consider relaxing or scrapping the policy.
>
> (*FEER*, 14 October 2004, p. 28)

> China hopes to achieve a normal balance of newborn boys and girls within six years [by 2010] by banning the use of abortions to select an infant's sex and by making welfare payments to couples without sons ... Government figures show that 117 boys are born in China to every 100 girls – a gap blamed largely on a policy limiting most couples to one child. In a society that values sons, many parents abort baby girls, hoping to try again for a boy ... The 'one child' limit allows rural families to have two children if the first is a girl, because Chinese peasants traditionally rely on sons to support them in old age ... Researchers say China has millions fewer girls than it normally should, suggesting that many were aborted or killed after birth ... Another programme gives money to couples who have only one child or two daughters and no sons, or whose children are deceased or disabled ... Couples get 1,200 yuan, or $145, per couple a year after they turn sixty as compensation to families that practice family planning.
>
> (www.iht.com, 15 July 2004)

'Beijing said on 15 July that it would strictly ban selective abortion of female foetuses' (www.feer.com, 29 July 2004).

> [In 2003] 117 boys were born for every 100 girls, compared with a global average of 105 to 100 ... Officials said that they would offer welfare incentives to couples with two daughters and tighten the prohibition on sex-selective abortions ... Pilot programmes are already under way in China's poorest provinces. In some areas couples with two daughters and no sons have been promised an annual payment of 600 renminbi once they reach sixty years of age. The money, which is a significant sum in areas where the average income is [low] ... will also be given to families with only one child to discourage couples with a daughter from trying again for a boy ... In parts of Fujian province local governments have given housing grants ... to couples with two girls. The state will expand welfare programmes so poor couples rely less on producing a son to care for them in their old age. It will also push a 'caring for girls' propaganda campaign ... China's demographic distortions have clearly worsened since the introduction of the one-child policy. In 1982 the boy-to-girl ratio was similar to the global average ... Since 1980 family planning officials say the restrictions have prevented 300 million births that would otherwise [have occurred] ... Two laws have been

> passed banning gynaecologists from telling pregnant women the sex of their foetus once it is confirmed by ultrasound checks.
>
> (*Guardian*, 16 July 2004, p. 19)

> Despite some changes, China's one-child family planning programme remains a source of coercion, forced abortions, infanticide and perilously imbalanced boy–girl ratios, [US] State Department officials said [on 14 December 2004] … Couples who have unsanctioned children have been subject to heavy fines, job losses and forced sterilization … Testimony [in the United States]. .. focussed on a Shanghai woman who, since her second pregnancy in the late 1980s, has been assigned to psychiatric wards, coerced into having an abortion and removed from her job.
>
> (www.iht.com, 15 December 2004)

> One of the world's least controlled abortion regimes will be tightened … on 1 January 2005 … when the city of Guiyang … the provincial capital of Guizhou province … introduces a pilot programme aimed at halting the widespread termination of female foetuses. The new policy bans doctors from carrying out abortions on most women who are more than fourteen weeks into pregnancy. In many cases the parents delay making a decision until ultrasound checks can determine the sex of their child … China's laws do not set time limits for abortions … In 1982, shortly after the introduction of the one-child policy, the ratio was similar to the global average of 105 boys for every 100 girls … Because of the stiff financial penalties for second children, many couples have unregistered babies. There may be as many as 100 million of these 'illegal children'.
>
> (*Guardian*, 16 December 2004, p. 14)

'With over 40 million more men than women in the general population, China is seeking to strengthen laws on prohibiting the use of selective abortion of female foetuses' (*IHT*, 8 January 2005, p. 6). The National Population and Family Planning Commission: 'As a new measure, the commission will start drafting revisions to the criminal law in order to effectively ban foetus gender detection and selective abortion other than for legitimate medical purposes' (*IHT*, 8 January 2005, p. 6; *Guardian*, 8 January 2005, p. 18). 'Government figures show that 119 boys are born for every 100 girls, largely because parents abort girls to try again for a boy, under China's one-child policy' (*The Times*, 8 January 2005, p. 44). 'Beijing has set a goal of reversing the imbalance by 2010 … But demographers have said that in poor, rural areas girls are often not cared for as well as boys, resulting in higher infant death rates for girls' (*Guardian*, 8 January 2005, p. 18).

> In early January [2005] the government announced that the nationwide ratio had reached 119 boys to every hundred girls … China's imbalance has widened since population controls began in the late 1970s … [although the] preference [for boys] dates back centuries … Selective sex abortions … were already banned, but doctors often accepted bribes from parents who

wanted to guarantee a boy … [Experiments are being conducted to give] rural elderly people annual pensions … if they had only one child or if they had daughters … [and to give] female students from poor families free tuition as are students from families with two girls.

(*IHT*, 31 January 2005, pp. 1, 7)

The government has tinkered with … the one-child policy … It now allows husbands and wives who are themselves only children to have a second child, for example, and has eliminated a four-year waiting period between births for those eligible to have second child.

(*IHT*, 29 June 2006, p. 2)

Zhang Weiqing, head of the National Population and Family Planning Commission … said the government would make more effort to raise women's place in society and protect baby girls – with rewards, such as retirement pensions, for parents who have girls – as well as to crack down on illegal gender selection test and sex-selection abortions … China last year [2006] scrapped plans to make sex-selective abortion a crime … Mr Zhang defended the population plan – which he said had halted 400 million births in thirty years – and said it was wrong to call the programme a 'one-child' policy. The reality was more complicated, he said, with different provinces making their own adjustments as the situation demanded. Only just over a third of the population was limited to just one child. In nineteen provinces rural couples were allowed to have another baby if their first was a girl, the minister said. And in five provinces, including the southern island of Hainan and Yunnan in the south-west, all rural parents were allowed to have two children.

(*Guardian*, 24 January 2007, p. 22)

China's top family planning body has warned of a 'population rebound' as couples flout one-child policy rules. The widening wealth gap could lead to a rise in birth rates, Zhang Weiqing from the National Population and Family Planning Commission told state media. Newly rich couples can afford to pay fines to have more than one child, while rural couples are marrying earlier … [In April 2007] a survey by the National Population and Family Planning Commission found that the number of rich people and celebrities having more than one child was on a rapid increase, and nearly 10 per cent of people in this category had three children … In the countryside, too, the rules are being flouted. China's constitution says that men may marry at twenty-two and women at twenty, with late marriages and later childbearing encouraged. But according to Mr Zhang, 'early marriages are still prevailing in some parts of the country, especially in rural areas, which goes against the family planning policy'.

By the end of 2006 China's population stood at 1,314,480,000, according to the National Bureau of Statistics, with males accounting for 51.2 per cent of the population.

(www.bbc.co.uk, 7 May 2007)

> Most urban residents are restricted to one child, while those in rural areas are encouraged to have one but allowed more in some circumstances … 'The number of rich people and celebrities having more than one child is on a rapid increase and nearly 10 per cent of them even have three,' Xinhua cited a survey by the Family Planning Commission as saying. A Chinese health official has also said that rural women were risking maternal health by delivering babies in violation of the restrictions at home or in unregulated clinics.
>
> (www.iht.com, 7 May 2007)

'Zhang Weiqing, director of the National Population and Family Planning Commission … said China's wealthy were showing disdain for the [one-child] policy by paying to have as many children as they wanted' (*IHT*, 8 May 2007, p. 7).

'Already the one-child family limits apply to only 35.9 per cent of the population' (*The Times*, 8 May 2007, p. 7).

> The government says it is drafting new laws to tackle the growing gender imbalance caused by the widespread abortion of female foetuses. The practice is already banned, but new rules are expected to set out specific punishments for parents and doctors … Experts fear the phenomenon could have unpredictable social consequences. Some believe that with millions of men unable to find a wife, there could be risks of increasing anti-social and violent behaviour.
>
> (www.bbc.co.uk, 25 August 2007)

> China is planning to tighten punishments for sex-selective abortions … State demographers forecast that 37 million men will be unable to find wives by 2020. Already there are 18 million more men than women of marriageable age … Although there are two laws banning doctors from telling pregnant women the sex of the foetus, the practice is common … This summer [2007] the government said it will punish for the first time any medical institution that tells couples the sex of unborn babies … The government credits … a strict family planning policy that limits many couples to one child … for preventing 400 million births since the rules were introduced in 1979.
>
> (www.guardian.com, 26 August 2007)

> Hundreds of people in central China have been expelled from the Communist Party for violating the one-child policy … More than 90,000 people in Hubei province defied the policy in 2007 … These included 1,678 officials and party members, the agency said. Of these, 500 had been expelled from the party and 395 stripped of their posts … Urban couples are limited to one child, while rural couples may have two if the first is a girl. But as China has grown wealthier, couples who can afford to pay the fines are choosing to ignore the policy and have bigger families … A number of cases involving celebrities and officials were still being investigated.
>
> (www.bbc.co.uk, 7 January 2008)

> The authorities in Hubei said 93,084 people had breached the policy last year [2007], including 1,678 officials … Seven national and local lawmakers lost their political status … Yang Youwang (director of the family planning commission): 'More party members, celebrities and well-off people are violating the policies in recent years, which has undermined social equality' … In China's cities … the fine [is] a multiple of the main breadwinner's declared salary … Since the [one-child] policy was introduced … in 1980 … more than 400 million births have been prevented, officials believe. There is now an average birth rate of 1.8 children per couple in China, compared to six children when it was introduced … Enforcing the rules has been difficult, with families becoming increasingly mobile … Now the Hubei authorities have approved new rules barring offenders from government employment for three years, or holding elective office, or being political advisers.
>
> (*Independent*, 8 January 2008, p. 26)

> Celebrities' perks do not extend to having larger families, Beijing authorities have warned. Stars of sport and pop who violate the one-child policy will face harsher fines and tarnished credit records, according to a senior family planning official. The authorities believe the rich and famous are setting a bad example to ordinary Chinese couples, and barely notice the financial penalties because of their wealth … Deng Xingzhou (head of the municipal family planning commission): 'Celebrities and wealthy people would be more heavily fined for giving birth to more than one child. The commission is still deliberating on the amount' … The director of the state family planning commission has described famous offenders as a 'negative social influence', and officials in other parts of China have promised to tackle the issue by naming and shaming rich and influential offenders, or banning them from receiving awards and civic honours … Deng said the commission planned a threefold system of punishment based on tougher fines, the inclusion of family planning violations in personal files in the national credit system – affecting celebrities' ability to borrow – and the censure of party members … [Some analysts argue that] adding the credit record will make celebrities – especially businessmen – think more seriously … At present couples face up to ten times the local *per capita* income if they break the law. They are believed to average around 100,000 yuan (£7,000) in Beijing, where *per capita* income was 22,000 yuan last year [2007] … The government argues it must continue with its controversial rules … China's population is expected to continue growing over the next two decades, peaking at 1.5 billion … Officials argue that its introduction [the one-child policy] in the late seventies has reduced the population by an estimated 400 million people. They also say it is not a blanket rule, pointing to the rural couples who are allowed a second child because their first was a girl, or disabled.
>
> (www.guardian.co.uk, 21 January 2008)

'The exemption of multiple births from the one-child policy is thought to have encouraged some couples to turn to fertility drugs so they can enjoy a larger family without penalty' (*Guardian*, 22 January 2008, p. 15).

> China is studying how to move away from its controversial one-child policy, but any changes would come gradually and would not mean an elimination of family planning polices, a senior official said Thursday [28 February]. Zhao Baige, vice minister of the National Population and Family Planning Commission, said that government officials recognize that China must alter its current population policies ... Most urban couples are limited to a single child, while farmers can usually have two. Minorities are often allowed to have two or more children ... Chinese officials have argued that the policy has prevented roughly 400 million births ... The policy now allows urban couples to have two children if both spouses are themselves from one-child families.
>
> (www.iht.com, 28 February 2008; *IHT*, 29 February 2008, p. 2)

> [Zhao Baige said that China acknowledges] concerns about the effects ... of the one-child policy ... in creating an ageing society and gender gap ... Zhao Baige: 'We want to have a transition from control to a slowdown [relaxation], incrementally. The attitude is to do the studies, to consider it responsibly' ... Although the population has yet to peak – it is expected to rise from 1.3 billion now to 1.5 billion in 2033 – the birth rate has dropped below the replacement rate of 2.1. Rising prosperity in recent years has also helped to change attitudes. Zhao said 60 per cent of young women now say they want a maximum of two children ... Concessions already exist allowing people in their second marriage to have another baby if their spouse has none, and permitting couples without any siblings to have two children. But officials are nervous of announcing potential changes in the rules lest people pre-empt them. Discussions about relaxations of the law in 1983 are believed to have led to the birth of an extra 30 million babies that year.
>
> (www.guardian.co.uk, 28 February 2008)

'The one-child policy quickly cut the fertility rate ... to 1.8 – well below the replacement rate of 2.1' (*Guardian*, 29 February 2008, p. 25).

'Early action could help to slow an expected rapid ageing of the population, with 20 per cent of Chinese citizens expected to be over 60 by 2030 – more than double the current proportion' (*FT*, 29 February 2008, p. 8).

> The Chinese leadership has denied suggestions that it is about to alter its controversial one-child policy. Family planning chief Zhang Weiqing said there would be no change in the rule limiting families in cities to one child and those in rural areas to two. His comments come a week after another family planning official ... Zhao Baige, the vice minister at the National Population and Family Planning Commission ... said a policy change was under discussion.
>
> (www.bbc.co.uk, 6 March 2008)

> Zhang Weiqing declared that 'there can be no wavering, only stability' on the [one-child] policy … [Some] 30 per cent to 40 per cent of couples nationwide are permitted to have two or more children. In most cities parents who are themselves only children can have two offspring. In most rural areas parents can have a second child if the first is a girl.
>
> (*FT*, 7 March 2008, p. 12)

> China's top population official has ruled out changing the country's one-child family planning policy for at least another decade … Zhang Weiqing, minister of the State Population and Family Planning Commission, said China would not make any major changes to the overall family planning policy until an anticipated surge in births ends, roughly a decade from now … Zhang Weiqing: 'The current family planning policy, formed as a result of gradual changes in the past two decades, has proved compatible with national conditions. So it has to be kept unchanged at this time to ensure stable and balanced population growth' … Zhang said that 200 million people would enter childbearing age during the next decade and that prematurely abandoning the one-child policy could bring unwanted volatility in the birth rate … Zhang Weiqing: 'Given such a large population base, there would be major fluctuations in population growth if we abandoned the one-child rule now. It would cause serious problems and add pressure on social and economic development … After the new birth peak we may adjust the policy if there is a need' … Government officials often say the policy has prevented 400 million births, though some independent scholars and scientists cite a lower figure, around 250 million … Even with China's family planning restrictions, *The China Daily* reported that the population is growing by up to 17 million people a year and should peak at 1.5 billion by the mid-2030s.
>
> (www.iht.com, 10 March 2008)

'Some wealthy families … have more children and pay a $1,000 fine. In rural areas … families can petition for an additional child, but there's no guarantee the authorities will approve the request – they usually don't' (www.cnn.com, 15 May 2008).

> Infant mortality in China's countryside stands at 123 for every 1,000 live births compared with twenty-six in the richest countries, the experts wrote in a paper published in *The Lancet* medical journal. Of every 1,000 children sixty-four in the countryside will not live beyond their fifth birthday, compared with ten in the cities … While life expectancy in Shanghai is 78.1, that figure is 66.1 in Gansu, one of the poorest provinces … In 2000 infant mortality was 33.7 per 1,000 live births for girls compared with 23.9 per 1,000 for boys … Health care is taking up the bulk of household incomes, or a whopping 50 per cent in 2006 (more than eighteen times that in 1990) because of inadequate health insurance. This compares with 45 per cent in South Korea, 16 per cent in Sweden, 15 per cent in Japan and 11 per cent in

France ... Based on Chinese definitions, 22.8 per cent of Chinese were overweight in 2006. About 7.1 per cent in the population were obese in 2002.

(www.iht.com, 20 October 2008)

[According to] new research published in *The Lancet*, the medical journal, in richer rural areas infant mortality rates were twenty-six per 1,000 live births, similar to the rate in Mexico; in poor rural areas the level was 123, the rate in the Democratic Republic of Congo.

(*FT*, 23 October 2008, p. 15)

Old people's homes are a rarity in China, catering for only about 1 per cent of the over-sixty-fives, far less than in most Western countries. The vast majority of older Chinese live with their families. Care for the old within the family is not only a cultural expectation, based on the Confucian tradition of respect for age and experience; under a law passed in 1996 it is also a legal obligation ... There are far fewer young people around to take care of the elderly. This state of affairs is usually referred to by the nifty formula '4–2–1', meaning that the typical child today will have two parents and four grandparents to look after – a bit of an exaggeration, but not that far off ... The number of over-sixty-fives is expected to go up very rapidly, from about 166 million now to 342 million in only twenty years' time ... [There is] the prospect of 440 million pensioners by 2050 ... China is still a relatively young country, with a median age of about thirty. But, uniquely among developing countries, it is ageing extraordinarily fast, so by 2050 its median age will have risen to about forty-five. Over the next few decades the ratio of elderly dependants to people of working age will rise steeply, from 10 per cent now to 40 per cent by 2050. From about 2030 the country will have more elderly dependants than children, whereas in most other developing countries the opposite will remain true for the next few decades. China's pattern of ageing is very similar to that in Japan, Hong Kong, Singapore, South Korea and Taiwan. The difference is that in China this is happening at a time when the country is still relatively poor ... Average life expectancy at birth, at seventy-four, is now twenty-five years higher than it was fifty years ago ... There is no explicit population target, but the latest forecasts suggest that numbers will keep growing from about 1.3 billion now to a peak of around 1.46 billion by 2030 and then start declining gently.

(*The Economist*, Special Report on Ageing Populations, 25 June 2009, pp. 13–15)

The government in the city of Shanghai is to encourage some parents to have a second child ... Only parents who were themselves both only children would be eligible. The goal is to reduce the proportion of ageing people in the population and reduce future work force shortages ... China's family planning policy has been relaxed in recent years to allow second children, but what is different now is that Shanghai is actively encouraging the change.

(www.bbc.co.uk, 24 July 2009)

> Shanghai is urging eligible couples to have two children … Most newly married couples registered in Shanghai are both only children and so many may have two children … [China] allows urban parents to have two offspring if they are both only children. Rural couples are allowed a second child if their first is a girl … The US-based Center for Strategic and International Studies warned in April [2009] that by 2050 China would have more than 438 million people over sixty years of age, with more than 100 million aged eighty and above. The country will have just 1.6 working-age adults to support every person aged sixty and above, compared with 7.7 in 1975 … China aims to keep its overall population below 1.36 billion by the end of next year [2010].
>
> (www.iht.com, 24 July 2009)

> Shanghai is actively encouraging young couples to have a second child. City officials are planning to visit homes, slip leaflets under doors and offer emotional, counselling and financial incentives … In 2006 about 8 per cent of China's population was over the age of sixty-five. But the proportion is expected to triple to about 322 million people, or nearly a quarter of the country's population, by 2050, according to the United Nations.
>
> (www.iht.com, 25 July 2009)

> Shanghai [is] a city of nearly 20 million people … For more than a decade Shanghai has allowed couples to have two children if each parent is an only child, but few have done so … Some 21 per cent of Shanghai's registered population last year [2008] were aged sixty or older … twice the national average … Twelve categories of Shanghai couples are allowed to have two children, including those whose first child is disabled and those with a spouse who was a fisherman at sea for more than five years … In most rural areas couples have been allowed a second child if the first was not a healthy son. Ethnic minorities are also not limited to one child.
>
> (*FT*, 25 July 2009, p. 7)

> Shanghai's over-sixty population already exceeds 21.6 per cent of registered residents … [according to] the Shanghai Population and Family Planning Commission … By 2020 the population of elderly is expected to rise to 34 per cent of the city's population … The working age population [of China] is expected to start shrinking in about 2015. The overall population will peak in 2030, with China becoming the first country to grow old before it grows rich.
>
> (*The Times*, 25 July 2009, p. 37)

'Family planning officials [in Shanghai] will make home visits and offer financial advice to those wanting a second child … [China's population is] not expected to shrink until about 2033' (*Guardian*, 25 July 2009, p. 24).

> Shanghai has … the world's lowest fertility rate, with 0.7 births per woman of child-bearing age … Shanghai first announced an easing of the one-child

> policy in 2004, aiming to double the number of newborns by 2009. Those from one-child families or on second marriages were permitted to have more children and official enforcement of the policy relaxed. But the impact has been zero ... A recent UN report estimates that China's total population could peak as early as 2020. The median age was forecast to rise from thirty-four today to thirty-seven by 2020 and fifty by 2050 ... The Communist Party's brutal population policy reduced the national fertility rate from 4.8 in the 1950s to around 1.8 today.
>
> (www.iht.com, 7 August 2009; *IHT*, 8 August 2009, p. 7)

> More than 13 million abortions are performed each year in China, far more than any other country in the world, according to statistics disclosed by Chinese health officials. When unreported and medication-induced abortions are counted, the actual number is substantially higher, according to ... [a report in the] *China Daily* on Thursday [30 July] ... The rate of abortion in China – about 24 abortions for every 1,000 women between the ages of fifteen and forty-four – is far from the world's highest. Russia has by far the highest rate at 53.7 per 1,000, according to the United Nations ... Abortion has been legal in China since 1953, although sex-selective abortions were banned starting in 1994.
>
> (www.iht.com, 30 July 2009)

'China's population is probably 300 million to 400 million lower than it would have been without ... China's one-child policy ... Twenty million people enter the work force each year, instead of 40 million' (*The Economist*, 31 October 2009, pp. 37–8).

> India will become the world's most populous country in 2025, surpassing China, where the population will peak one year later because of declining fertility, according to the United States Census Bureau projections released Tuesday [15 December 2009]. The bureau suggests that the projected peak in China, 1.4 billion, will be lower than previously estimated and that it will occur sooner. With a fertility rate declining to fewer than 1.6 births per woman in this decade from 2.2 in 1990, China's overall population growth rate has slowed to 0.5 per cent annually ... China's labour force will peak at 831 million – 24 million more workers than today – in 2016. That is because the number of newcomers to the labour force in their early twenties is expected to start declining in 2011 after reaching 124 million ... China and India alone account for 37 per cent of the world's population of about 6.8 billion ... By the time the twenty-first century is a quarter over, the bureau estimates, the population of the United States will be more than 350 million.
>
> (www.iht.com, 16 December 2009)

> More than 24 million Chinese men of marrying age could find themselves without spouses by 2010, says the Chinese Academy of Social Sciences ... The gender imbalance among newborns is the most serious demographic problem for the country's population of 1.3 billion, says the academy ...

A reluctance among young urban Chinese to have a first or second child is exacerbating the problem.

(www.bbc.co.uk, 11 January 2010)

More than 24 million men of marriageable age in a decade may never find a bride because births of boys so far outnumber those of girls … The surplus of men, which will result in an army of bachelors – known as 'bare branches' – in China's poorest rural areas, has been described by senior officials as a grave problem that could lead to a surge in crime and stoke social instability – the greatest fear for the Communist Party … The latest report … by China's top think-tank … said: 'Sex-specific abortions remained extremely commonplace, especially in rural areas' … Officials have long acknowledged that the introduction of ultrasound scans for pregnant women in the late 1980s resulted in a surge of abortions of female foetuses as parents tried to ensure that their only child was a boy who could carry on the family line … The report said: 'The problem is more serious in rural areas due to the lack of a social security system. Ageing farmers have to rely on their offspring' … The normal sex ratio of birth of 103 to 107 boys for every 100 girls began to shift in the late 1980s. It rose from 108 boys in 1982 to 111 in 1990 to 116 a decade later … However, the report said that the trend of the gender imbalance had begun to slow since it soared to 119 males for every 100 females in 2005 … The National Population and Family Planning Commission says that abductions and trafficking of women and infants are rampant in areas where the ratio of boys to girls is particularly skewed. Abortion is legal and widely available. China bans tests to determine the gender of a foetus for non-medical reasons but these are still commonly carried out – mainly by underground private clinics in the countryside. Many countries ban abortion after twelve or sometimes twenty-four weeks of pregnancy unless the mother's life is at risk. China's laws do not expressly prohibit or even define late-term termination. Female infanticide is another problem – although this is rarely mentioned. Some families hide the births of daughters, never registering them with authorities, so they can legally try for a son but thus making it harder to measure the problem. It is men in poverty-stricken areas who will face the greatest difficulty in finding a wife, said … [a researcher at] the Chinese Academy of Social Sciences, which published this report.

(www.thetimes.co.uk, 11 January 2010; *The Times*, 12 January 2010, p. 29)

'China's population, which stands at about 1.3 billion, is growing at the rate of 0.6 per cent. It is expected to peak around 1.6 billion by 2050, the US State Department said' (www.cnn.com, 11 January 2010).

China's capital plans to relax some of its tough 'one couple, one child' family planning rules to allow more people to have a second baby … Currently only couples in which both husband and wife are only children are permitted to have a second child – and then only after a gap of at least four years between babies. That would now change with the gap to be eliminated – as has already been done in eleven other provinces and municipalities. Under the new policy, which has yet to be formally implemented, couples in which only one partner has no siblings would be granted the same privilege as two 'only child' parents to have a second baby. That would mark a first for China. The authorities appear to be anxious that urban couples are less willing to have a baby while their rural cousins take full advantage of policies allowing them a second if the first is a girl and after that they simply ignore the rules if they can get away with it ... In Beijing between 60,000 and 70,000 babies are born each year to recognized city residents – migrant or temporary workers who may account for at least 2 million or more of the city's 16.95 million residents are not included. That birth rate shows a negative growth trend, said Peng Yuhua, deputy head of the Beijing Population and Planning Commission. She said: 'According to the natural law of stable human replacement, every woman should bear at least 2.1 children. The number now in China has levelled at 1.8, while Beijing comes down to 1.0 right now.'

(www.thetimes.co.uk, 25 January 2010)

In January 2010 the Chinese Academy of Social Sciences (CASS) ... said that ... within ten years one in five young men would be unable to find a bride because of the dearth of young women – a figure unprecedented in a country at peace. The number is based on the sexual discrepancy among people aged nineteen and below ... Boys are slightly more likely to die in infancy than girls so there will be equal numbers of young men and women at puberty. In all societies that record births, between 103 and 106 boys are normally born for every 100 girls. The ratio has been so stable over time that it appears to be the natural order of things. That order has changed fundamentally in the past twenty-five years. In China the sex ratio for the generation born in 2000–4 was 124 (i.e. 124 boys were born in those years for every 100 girls). According to CASS the ratio today in 123 boys per 100 girls ... The use of sex-selective abortion was banned ... in China in 1995 ... In the countryside, where 55 per cent of China's population lives, there are three variants of the one-child policy. In the coastal provinces some 40 per cent of couples are permitted a second child if their first is a girl. In central and southern provinces everyone is permitted a second child either if the first is a girl or if the parents suffer 'hardship', a criterion determined by local officials. In the far west and Inner Mongolia the provinces do not really operate a one-child policy at all. Minorities are permitted second – and sometimes even third – children, whatever the sex of the first-born ... The crime rate has almost doubled in China during the past twenty years of rising sex ratios, with stories abounding of bridal abduction, the trafficking of women, rape and prostitution. A study into whether these things were connected concluded that they were, and that higher sex ratios accounted for about one-seventh of the rise in crime ... The skewed sex ratio ... has probably increased China's savings rate. This is because parents with a single son save to increase his chances of attracting a wife in China's ultra-competitive marriage market … [Another study] calculated that about half the increase in China's savings in the past twenty-five years can be attributed to the rise in the sex ratio … The census of 2000 and CASS study both showed the sex ratio stable at around 120. At the very least it seems to have stopped rising.

(*The Economist*, 6 March 2010, pp. 72–5)

The Chinese nation encompasses fifty-five fixed ethnic minorities and their territories … China's 1.3 billion people are officially 96 per cent Han; the rest range from Tibetans to Naxi to Manchus, categories fixed after the 1949 communist revolution.

(www.iht.com, 23 February 2010; *IHT*, 24 February 2010, p. 2)

2 China and Taiwan

> Taiwan was inhabited by non-Chinese peoples who spoke their own language and are ethnically and linguistically closer to modern Indonesians than to Chinese. Chinese fishermen and farmers began to settle along Taiwan's coastal areas, particularly in the sixteen and seventeenth centuries. Holland seized Taiwan in 1624.
>
> (*IHT*, 22 March 2000, p. 2)

'Large-scale settlement from the mainland only began in the seventeenth century and the original Malayo-Polynesian inhabitants remained a majority till the nineteenth century ... Today 40 per cent of the island's trade is with China' (*IHT*, 27 December 2003, p. 6).

> Except for a tiny aboriginal minority, well over 90 per cent of Taiwanese trace their ancestry to China. But only roughly 15 per cent of the population came to this island since 1949, the start of the communist era. In cultural terms this minority, many of them followers of the nationalist leader Chiang Kai-shek, known here [Taiwan] as 'mainlanders', still identifies closely with the motherland. To a large degree, today the rest of the population sees itself simply as Taiwanese.
>
> (*IHT*, 27 May 2005, p. 2)

'Aborigines make up less than 2 per cent of the population but have inhabited the island for thousands of years, longer than the majority Han Chinese ... [Taiwan] has thirteen officially recognized indigenous tribes' (www.iht.com, 3 July 2007).

> Without attempting to match the overwhelming US military might, experts say, the army has developed a strategy of 'area denial', where an array of precision weapons would be deployed in an attempt to keep US forces, particularly aircraft carriers, at a distance for long enough that China could overwhelm Taiwan's defences.
>
> (*IHT*, 11 June 2007, p. 1)

'The United States regards ... the Taiwan Strait ... as international waters, but China claims it as its own' (*IHT*, 8 December 2007, p. 2).

> Recently declassified government archives have revealed a previously unknown secretive plan by Taiwan's late President Chiang Kai-shek to take back mainland China … [As regards] the declassified information … photocopies went on public display in Taiwan for the first time in May [2009] … Details of this chapter in history were kept secret for forty-four years.
>
> (www.bbc.co.uk, 8 September 2009)

A chronology of events since 4 May 2006

4 May 2006.

> President Chen Shui-bian will not fly through the United States during his trip to Latin America during his trip to Latin America, the Taiwanese foreign ministry said Thursday [4 May] … The Taiwanese media reported that Chen had asked to make stops in New York and San Francisco, but the United States offered only to allow Chen to make a transit stop in Anchorage, Alaska.
>
> (www.iht.com, 4 May 2006)

9 May 2006.

> The Taiwanese foreign minister said Tuesday [9 May] that President Chen Shui-bian will forgo the offer of a US transit stop [in Alaska] on his return from Latin America … In five previous Latin American trips since taking office in 2000, Chen has stopped in major US cities, including New York, Los Angeles and Houston, all with the permission of the US authorities.
>
> (www.iht.com, 9 May 2006)

'China had by last year [2005] deployed 710 to 790 short-range ballistic missiles across from Taiwan, an increase from the estimated 650 to 730 missiles deployed a year before' (www.iht.com, 24 May 2006).

13 June 2006.

> Taiwanese lawmakers agreed Tuesday to hold hearings on a possible recall of President Chen Shui-bian, whose family members have been plagued by corruption allegations that have sparked calls for him to quit … The president has not been directly linked to corruption … This was the first time the Taiwanese have tried to formally recall their leader … Lawmakers will vote on 27 June on whether to hold a public referendum to recall the president.
>
> (www.iht.com, 13 June 2006)

> 'The president's aides and family members face allegations of impropriety, including his wife … Chen himself has not been accused of wrongdoing … Chen's son-in-law was arrested in May on suspicion of insider trading. The first lady, Wu Shu-chen, has been accused by the opposition of accepting favours from businesses … Supporters of a recall appear for now to be short of the required two-thirds majority … in the legislature.
>
> (www.iht.com, 14 June 2006; *IHT*, 15 June 2006, p. 4)

14 June 2006.

Taiwan and China said Wednesday [14 June] that they agreed to launch direct charter passenger flights between the two countries during major holidays … Negotiators have also reached a 'tentative consensus' on allowing Taiwanese companies to use special chartered cargo flights to fly goods and equipment between the two sides … Although they have allowed chartered passenger flights before, the service has been inconsistent and limited to the Lunar New Year – the biggest Chinese holiday. The new charter flights would serve four annual holidays: Lunar Chinese New Year, Tomb Sweeping Day, the Dragon Boat Festival and the Mid-Autumn Festival … [Taiwan] expects holiday flights will begin for the Mid-Autumn Festival, which falls on 6 October this year [2006] … Taiwan has banned regular direct flights between the two sides since they split in 1949 … The Taiwanese have said the direct flights pose a serious security threat, but improvements in radar technology have lessened the danger … An estimated 3 million Taiwanese travel to China each year for business or sightseeing … Taiwan began allowing charter flights to China during the Lunar New Year in 2003. But only Taiwanese carriers could provide the service and they had to stop in Hong Kong en route. A new round of squabbles blocked the flights in 2004. In 2005 and 2006 six Taiwanese and six Chinese carriers operated dozens of round-trip charter flights to take Taiwanese living in China home for the Lunar New Year. Although the flights were not required to stop en route, they were supposed to fly through Hong Kong airspace.

(www.iht.com, 14 June 2006)

Taiwan and the mainland agreed to allow up to 168 charter passenger flights each year during four annual holidays, including Chinese New Year. Chartered cargo and humanitarian flights will also be allowed for the first time and will be permitted throughout the year, although each will require individual approval … Only 173,000 mainlanders came to Taiwan last year [2005], while 4.1 million Taiwanese went to the mainland.

(www.iht.com, 14 June 2006)

Chinese and Taiwanese airlines would be allowed to operate 168 round-trip flights a year … starting from this year's Mid-Autumn Festival in October … From July Taiwanese companies can also apply for special cargo flights to move equipment to their factories in China. Charters for medical and disaster relief purposes will also be allowed on a specific basis. Aircraft will still have to fly via Hong Kong airspace, a condition laid down by Taipei.

(*FT*, 15 June 2006, p. 8)

27 June 2006.

President Chen Shui-bian offered to mend fences with China and the island's opposition Tuesday [27 June] after surviving an unprecedented parliamentary vote aimed at unseating him … Chen 'hopes to push for political consultations internally and cross-strait peace talks externally', the presidential office said in a statement … As expected, the main opposition Nationalist Party, or Kuomintang, and the splinter People's First Party lacked the necessary two-thirds majority to authorize a referendum on whether to remove Chen from office. Amid tight security 119 deputies voted to refer Chen's fate to the electorate, while fourteen cast null votes, meaning that the motion fell short of the 148 votes needed to pass … Lawmakers from Chen's governing Democratic Progressive Party boycotted the recall vote … Deputies from the Taiwan Solidarity Union Party, which usually sides with Chen, cast null votes … Chen's son-in-law was detained in May on suspicion of insider trading … Chen's wife has been accused of accepting millions of Taiwan dollars' worth of departmental store gift vouchers.

(www.iht.com, 27 June 2006)

Of the 221 legislators 119 supported the motion, well short of the 148 votes needed … [The Kuomintang] said the party would continue to collect signatures for a petition to recall the president, which 1.7 million people had signed by yesterday [27 June].

(*FT*, 28 June 2006, p. 13)

20 July 2006.

Patriot missiles streaked across the sky and F-16s bombarded ships Thursday [20 July] as Taiwan beat back a simulated Chinese invasion from the mainland in the island's largest ever military exercise. The 'Chinese Glory' manoeuvres were meant to test the Taiwanese army, navy, air force and marines against the forces of mainland China, just 160 kilometres, or 100 miles, across the Taiwan Strait … This is the first time Taiwan has shown the deployment of its Patriot-2 missiles … President Chen Shui-bian: 'China is acting against Taiwan to try to create the foundation of a future invasion' … [Taiwan] acknowledged that if China decided to move against Taiwan it could also opt for a so-called decapitation strategy – co-ordinated commando attacks and pinpoint bombing against the island's leaders and key institutions.

(www.iht.com, 20 July 2006)

1 August 2006.

Taiwan's government yesterday [1 August 2006] announced moves to liberalize cross-strait economic ties with China, lifting key restrictions on semiconductor technology investment [in China] and on business travel to the island by mainland nationals. The measures [are] to be implemented within a month … Restrictions governing business travel of Chinese citizens to Taiwan will be 'greatly relaxed', with multi-national companies allowed to bring Chinese employees to Taiwan for work or training … Currently Chinese nationals who intend to visit the island on business can only come in groups of fewer than thirty and the authorities take several months to approve visas ... [Taiwan] said Microsoft was considering holding a regional event in Taiwan and bringing up to 300 Chinese and that the government would relax the regulations to meet such requirements.

(*FT*, 2 August 2006, p. 7)

While the door has opened a crack to Chinese business visitors, they will still be admitted only if they stop off in a third country en route ... Taiwan's once total ban on mainland investment was replaced a decade ago by a rule prohibiting companies from investing more than 40 per cent of their net worth. Since then it has been lifted for a few selected products. Curbs on shipping have been eased and talks launched with Beijing on liberalizing cargo and passenger charter flights

(*FT*, 3 August 2006, p. 12)

6 August 2006.

Beijing has re-established diplomatic relations with Chad, one of Taiwan's few remaining allies ... Taiwan, in an effort to pre-empt the action, broke relations with Chad early Sunday [6 August]; Chad and China then established diplomatic relations at a ceremony in Beijing on Sunday night ... Foreign minister James Huang of Taiwan ... said that President Idriss Déby of Chad had told Taiwanese officials that China was arming rebels who are trying to overthrow him. The rebels have been blamed for some of the killings in eastern Chad and in the Darfur region of Sudan ... The switch in diplomatic relations raises the possibility that China may use its influence with Sudan militants and Chadian rebels, both of which it reportedly arms. Sudanese militias with government links and Chadian rebels have been linked to killings and rapes in eastern Chad and in the Darfur region of Sudan.

(*IHT*, 8 August 2006, p. 3)

8 August 2006.

China has executed a top official accused of spying for Taiwan and distributed a video of his trial around the country as a deterrent to other civil servants, according to reports on government websites. The official, Tong Daning, was a departmental head at China's $26 billion national pension fund, the National Council for Social Security Fund. Tong, who was executed in April, was the most senior Chinese official to be executed for espionage since the death sentence was carried out on Lieutenant General Liu Liangkun in 1999. Liu was also accused of supplying secrets to Taiwan ... There are regular reports of the exposure of Taiwanese spies in the state-controlled press ... Taiwanese companies and individuals have invested more than $100 billion in China and more than a million Taiwan citizens now live and work on the mainland ... There are signs of a thaw in the political relationship. The two sides have no official ties, but Beijing announced on 2 August that its top official responsible for Taiwan policy, Chen Yunlin, would visit the island in October to take part in an agricultural co-operation forum.

(*IHT*, 9 August 2006, p. 2)

5 September 2006.

> China's ambassador to Lusaka said Beijing might cut diplomatic relations with Zambia if voters [in an election on 28 September 2006] elected Michael Sata, an opposition candidate, as president, Zambia media reported yesterday [5 September] ... China is a leading investor in Zambian copper, the country's biggest export product by value. Mr Sata has been quoted calling Taiwan a 'sovereign state' ... and has also spoken out against Chinese labour practices in Zambia.
>
> (*FT*, 6 September 2006, p. 5)

> The Chinese ambassador to Zambia was quoted as saying that Chinese forms had suspended further investments in mining, construction and tourism because of threats posed by Michael Sata to China's relations with Zambia ... Sata, the leader of the Patriotic Front and President Levy Mwanawasa's strongest challenger, caused a diplomatic row between China and Zambia by indicating at a campaign meeting that he would expel Chinese investors and managers, who he claimed were exploiting Zambian workers.
>
> (www.iht.com, 5 September 2006)

14 September 2006. 'A Chinese airline will carry out the first emergency flight to Taiwan from China ... A seventy-year-old ... will fly to Taipei on Thursday [24 September]' (www.iht.com, 13 September 2006).

10 October 2006. 'Taiwan's National Day marks the establishment of China's first republic in 1911 following the overthrow of the Qing dynasty' (www.iht.com, 10 October 2006).

3–6 November 2006.

> Prosecutors in Taiwan said Friday [3 November] they have enough evidence to indict President Chen Shui-bian on corruption charges in connection with his handling of a secret diplomatic fund ... The prosecutors' move against Chen came after a month-long probe of how the presidential office handled the fund, which is used to sustain Taiwanese diplomatic efforts abroad. The fund is secret because of the sensitivity of Taiwanese attempts to maintain its fragile overseas foothold in the face of moves by rival China to undermine its position around the world. Chen's wife ... Wu Shu-chen ... two former aides and the president's accountant ... were indicted in connection with the handling of the fund on charges of embezzlement, forgery of documents and perjury, said Chang Wen-cheng of the Taiwan High Prosecutors' Office. He said that between 2002 and 2006 Wu took possession of $450,000 in fund expenses not covered by receipts ... [Wu was formally indicted] on charges of issuing fake receipts to extract about $450,000 from a fund that the president controls to support Taiwan's diplomatic initiatives overseas ... Chang told reporters that while Chen would not be indicted now, there was a strong possibility he would be after he leaves office ... [on suspicion] of graft and forgery ... Under Taiwanese law a sitting president cannot be indicted other

than on charges of sedition ... Chang said Chen had met with prosecutors twice to discuss the handling of the fund but that serious discrepancies have emerged in the testimony. Chen presented documents about six cases in which secret diplomatic funds were used, but investigation by prosecutors showed that only [the documents for] two cases were accurate, Chang said ... President Chen Shui-bian has characterized the corruption investigation as a politically motivated attack on his policies ... The latest charges are the most recent in a series of investigations into the affairs of Chen, his family and his inner circle. This summer [2006] prosecutors charged the president's son-in-law, Chao Chien-ming, with insider trading. Chao has denied wrongdoing. Prosecutors also investigated accusations that Wu might have obtained large numbers of gift certificates from a department store that was seeking government permission for a change of ownership. They subsequently said they did not have enough evidence to indict her ... At an extraordinary late night meeting [3 November] Chen's ruling Democratic Progressive Party demanded that the president explain his alleged role in the scandal to the Taiwanese people. 'We strongly demand that President Chen Shui-bian explain the unclear parts from the prosecutors' report,' said party chairman Yu Shyi-kun ... Late Friday [3 November] a small party allied with the president said it would support a recall motion against him [President Chen Shui-bian] if it comes up in the legislature. The Taiwan Solidarity Union has twelve seats in the 221-seat body ... [although] its support for a recall move would not be enough to push it over the required two-thirds threshold.

(www.iht.com, 3 November 2006; *IHT*, 4 November 2006, p. 3)

On Friday [3 November] public prosecutors indicted Wu Shu-chen on charges of issuing fake receipts to extract about $450,000 from a fund that the president controls to support Taiwan's diplomatic initiatives abroad ... [She] is accused of using the money for personal expenditures, including buying diamond rings and other luxury items for her children and grandchildren ... Two former aides ... and the president's accountant ... were also indicted on related perjury charges ... On Friday night party leaders urged the president to defend himself against the charges ... The country's next presidential election will be in 2008 ... Officials of the Kuomintang, or National Party, said Saturday [4 November] that they intended to introduce a motion Friday [10 November] to recall the president unless Mr Chen agrees to resign. That would be the party's third such effort this year [2006]. Political analysts said that the Kuomintang would need the votes of about a dozen members of Mr Chen's party to pass the recall motion, and that they did not seem to have the needed support ... Almost immediately after the indictment a small group allied with Mr Chen's party, the Taiwan Solidarity Union, asserted that it would support the opposition movement.

(www.iht.com, 5 November 2006)

President Chen Shui-bian ... on Sunday [5 November] refused to resign and denied prosecutors' allegations that he and his wife embezzled public money … Chen Shui-bian: 'The NT [New Taiwan] $14.8 million [$450,000], we absolutely did not put this in our own pockets … If my wife is convicted then, because the prosecutors believe my wife and I act together, I cannot escape. I am willing to resign before my term is up.'

(www.iht.com, 5 November 2006)

President Chen Shui-bian … acknowledged lying and other improprieties but asserted that this was necessary 'for the benefit of the country' … Chen acknowledged submitting false receipts to claim expenses from public funds and admitted that he had misled investigators. But he vigorously insisted that both steps were justified, invoking national security, Taiwan's international standing and the safety of intelligence operatives active in other countries … Chen made no effort to contradict the allegations. Instead, he offered a complex justification for the use of personal receipts to claim public funds and said he was constrained by national security considerations from telling prosecutors the truth about money spent in the interests of Taiwan's diplomatic efforts … Chen: 'I lied and I apologize. But they were white lies, and it was all for the benefit of the country' … Insisting that the judicial system must take its course, as he has many times in the past, the president also said he would step down if the lowest of three courts in Taiwan's legal system found him culpable … Chen: 'I am willing to stand trial and testify. I am also willing to give up my immunity as president to show my respect for the judicial system' … Chen's legal and political troubles, which have mounted for much of this year, now appear to be opening a deep rift among his supporters. He has already begun to lose crucial backing from legislative allies, including some from the Democratic Progressive Party … [This is] the most serious political crisis Taiwan has faced since it began a process of democratization in the late 1980s, political analysts say.

(www.iht.com, 5 November 2006; *IHT*, 6 November 2006, p. 4)

President Chen Shui-bian … asserted that the use of personal receipts along with his subsequent lies about having done so … were necessary in part because of problems in the government's accounting system and in part to provide cover for diplomatic missions that were matters of national security.

(www.iht.com, 7 November 2006)

Chen has admitted using false receipts to claim money from a fund set aside for affairs of national importance, but insisted it was used for 'secret diplomatic missions' which he could not disclose. Prosecutors, however, found that at least 1.5 million Taiwan dollars was spent on diamond rings and other luxury items for Wu Shu-chen. Chen said he would resign if his wife was found guilty.

(www.iht.com, 12 November 2006)

About fifty senior leaders and legislators from the governing Democratic Progressive Party, who convened a closed-door session at their party's headquarters, agreed to back the president as his opponents in the Legislative

> Yuan, or parliament, prepared to advance a motion to recall him. The agreement that emerged from the meeting ... threatened disciplinary action against any lawmaker who broke ranks to support the recall motion when it is put forward in a legislative session on Friday [10 November].
>
> (www.iht.com, 8 November 2006)

'The Democratic Progressive Party decision came after the Taiwan Solidarity Union, its smaller ally, on Monday [6 November] revoked its support for the recall' (*FT*, 9 November 2006, p. 14).

> The opposition leader in Taiwan, Ma Ying-jeou, will be questioned Tuesday [14 November] over the alleged misuse of 'special expenses' ... Ma, the mayor of Taipei and chairman of the opposition Kuomintang, or Nationalist Party, confirmed on Sunday [12 November] reports that he would be 'interviewed' by a prosecutor.
>
> (www.iht.com, 12 November 2006)

24 November 2006.

> Taiwanese lawmakers on Friday [24 November] failed to pass an opposition-backed motion that would have referred the recall of President Chen Shui-bian to the island's voters ... The motion fell twenty-eight votes short of the required two-thirds majority in Taiwan's 218-seat legislature. The main opposition Nationalist Party, its People First Party satellite and seven independents voted to support the motion, while lawmakers from Chen's Democratic Progressive Party did not participate in the poll. The twelve members of the Taiwan Solidarity Union – a DPP ally – deliberately spoiled their ballots.
>
> (www.iht.com, 24 November 2006)

9 December 2006.

> President Chen Shui-bian's democratic Progressive Party eked out the narrowest victory in the political history of Taiwan in mayoral elections in Kaohsiung, but the opposition Nationalist Party said it would seek a recount ... The central election commission announced that ... [the victor] had won by 1,120 votes, a victory margin of about an eighth of a per cent ... A Nationalist, or Kuomintang, candidate, Hau Lung-bin, won the mayoral election in Taipei by a wide margin.
>
> (*IHT*, 11 December 2006, p. 7)

> Taiwan's ruling Democratic Progressive Party has confounded expectations that corruption scandals would lead to a landslide drubbing by the opposition Kuomintang in mayoral elections ... The DPP lost in the capital's mayoral race, but by a far lower margin than forecast, and won in its traditional stronghold, Taiwan's second city, Kaohsiung ... The DPP's mayoral candidate in Taipei, Frank Hsieh, lost to Hau Lung-bin of the KMT, which already holds the mayorship. However, Mr Hsieh collected nearly 41 per cent of the vote, a much better showing than forecast.
>
> (*Independent*, 11 December 2006, p. 25)

'Surveys show that about 60 per cent of people [in Taiwan] favour maintaining the status quo in relations with China' (www.iht.com, 11 December 2006).

15 December 2006.

> The wheelchair-bound first lady of Taiwan passed out during the first session of her trial for embezzlement and forgery on Friday [15 December] … She was paralyzed from the waist down when a truck ran over her in 1985 … Wu's husband, President Chen Shui-bian … called the incident an assassination attempt and blamed the Nationalists for carrying it out, a charge that they deny.
>
> (www.iht.com, 15 December 2006)

'The son-in-law of President Chen Shui-bian has been sentenced to six years in jail for insider trading. Chao Chien-min was found guilty of using inside information to profit from buying shares in a property company' (www.bbc.co.uk, 27 December 2006).

29 December 2006.

> On 29 December Taiwan announced the easing of its restriction on technology used by Taiwanese semiconductor manufacturers operating in China. It is not a big gesture. The more advanced process permitted under the new rule is already being used by Chinese competitors, Taiwanese officials say.
>
> (*The Economist*, 6 January 2007, p. 46)

1–2 January 2007.

> In a speech on 1 January [2007] President Chen Shui-bian spoke of the 'myth' of one China and said only the people of Taiwan had the right to decide their future. But he did not set out any plans to rewrite the constitution accordingly. The following day [2 January] President Hu Jintao said China would 'not compromise on Taiwan independence'. He also said that it would never give up its efforts to reunify the country peacefully.
>
> (*The Economist*, 6 January 2007, p. 46)

8 January 2007.

> China criticized the United States on Monday [8 January 2007] for allowing the president of Taiwan to make a stopover on his way to Central America … A spokesman for the American Institute in Taiwan, the de facto US embassy on the island, said that Chen Shui-bian's stay in San Francisco would be 'private and unofficial' in keeping with US State Department guidelines for stops by senior Taiwanese leaders in the United States.
>
> (www.iht.com, 8 January 2007)

('Taiwanese scientists … [are] able to attend WHO [World Health Organization] meetings as technical experts, in accordance with a policy established in 2005': *IHT*, 6 January 2007, p. 2.)

('[Later in January] Taiwan ... announced that China had deployed some 900 missiles on the coast facing the island in recent years. Last August [2006] it had put the figure at 820': *The Economist*, 27 January 2007, p. 59.)

12 February 2007.

> President Chen Shui-bian renamed Taiwan's postal service 'Taiwan Post' yesterday [12 February] ... [It was formerly called] 'Chinese Post' ... Many state-run companies kept 'China' or 'Chinese' in their names after [1949] ... The Nationalist opposition ... said the name change would unnecessarily raise tension with China. Two more state companies will change their names later this month.
>
> (*Guardian*, 13 February 2007, p. 22)

'This month [February] Taiwan's central bank, post office and some state-owned companies have dropped from their names the word "China"' (*The Economist*, 17 February 2007, p. 63).

13 February 2007.

> The high court prosecutor's office in Taiwan said on Tuesday that it had filed corruption charges against Ma Ying-jeou, the leader of the island's main opposition party, whom many saw as a presidential candidate in 2008 ... Taiwan's top prosecutor's office announced that it had indicted Ma for misappropriating $339,000 in funds from an account he used while he was Taipei mayor. Ma acknowledged accounting for the funds improperly, but called it an inadvertent error rather than corruption. He said none of the funds were diverted for his personal use. He said he would step down as chairman of the Nationalist Party in accordance with the party's by-laws, but vowed to continue his bid for the presidency.
>
> (www.iht.com, 13 February 2007)

> Ma Ying-jeou ... is accused of forgery and of having embezzled $333,000 from a special allowance for public relations during his stint as Taipei's mayor from 1998 to 2006 ... [He] blames the weakness of the allowance's purpose. First he claimed he had interpreted it as 'public funds' and then shifted to argue that it was part of his salary ... Within hours the Kuomintang's Central Committee dropped the bar it had maintained on nominating indicted criminals as candidates, and decided to urge Mr Ma to stay on as chairman.
>
> (*The Economist*, 17 February 2007, pp. 62–3)

4 March 2007.

> President Chen Shui-bian yesterday [4 March] directly said for the first time since taking office that the island should pursue independence ... Chen Shui-bian: 'Taiwan wants independence, Taiwan wants name rectification, Taiwan wants a new constitution' ... In Chinese Mr Chen used a verb that could be understood as 'will', 'wants', 'must' or 'should'. Thus some of his

critics could interpret him as having pledged to declare independence, while his administration can claim that he only stated the obvious – the self-ruled island's wish to preserve the independence it enjoys … His party's official position … is that since Taiwan is independent already, there is no need for a declaration of independence … The president's remarks also appeared to further challenge the 'Five Noes', a set of pledges he made when taking office not to declare independence or take steps that could be understood as moving in that direction. He branded his new remarks as 'Five Wants', suggesting that he was replacing his former cautious position with a much more combative one … Mr Chen made the remarks in a speech to the Formosan Association for Public Affairs, the main non-governmental lobbying group for Taiwan independence.

(*FT*, 5 March 2007, p. 9)

President Chen Shui-bian … in a speech to a pro-independence group … said Taiwan should pursue independence, write a new constitution and change its official name from 'Republic of China' to Taiwan … Chen Shui-bian: 'Taiwan should be independent. Taiwan is a country whose sovereignty lies outside the People's Republic of China' … He spoke of a 'Four Wants' policy – namely independence, a new constitution, further developments and a change to the country's officially designated name … His latest comments are his strongest since taking office.

(www.bbc.co.uk, 5 March 2007)

The president, speaking in his native Taiwanese dialect, proposed what he called a 'Four Wants' policy: independence, a new constitution, development and new names for local companies that use the word China in their title. This is a shift from his previous 'Four Noes' pledge in 2000 not to move towards independence if China did not threaten the use of force … The word China was replaced by Taiwan on postage stamps on 28 February, an emotive date in Taiwan since it was the sixtieth anniversary of an uprising against Generalissimo Chiang's Nationalists that was suppressed and resulted in more than 10,000 deaths. Last week the Chinese Petroleum Corporation became CPC Corporation Taiwan, while China Shipbuilding Corporation is to change its name to CSBC Corporation, Taiwan.

(*The Times*, 6 March 2007, p. 33)

3 April 2007.

Taiwan opposition leader and presidential hopeful Ma Ying-jeou has gone on trial in a corruption case … he is accused of misappropriating $339,000 of funds while mayor of Taipei … He is facing four rivals from the ruling Democratic Progressive Party (DPP) who are seeking nomination from their party. The candidates are vice president Annette Lu, premier Su Tseng-chang, former premier Frank Hsieh and former chairman Yu Hsyi-kin.

(www.bbc.co.uk, 3 April 2007)

7 April 2007. 'The newly elected leader of Taiwan's main opposition party will visit China by the end of the month [April] ... Wu Poh-hsiung [was] elected Saturday [7 April] as chairman of the Nationalist Party' (*IHT*, 10 April 2007, p. 4).

26 April 2007.

> Taiwan's government rejected the route taking the Olympic torch to Beijing via Taipei that was announced by China on Thursday [26 April] ... [The] itinerary for the torch included a leg from Ho Chi Minh [Vietnam] to Taipei and then on to Hong Kong and Macao ... Taiwan said the torch should go on to another country rather than Chinese territory ... Taiwan will only agree to stage a leg of the Olympic torch relay if China respects the island's sovereignty, prime minister Su Tseng-chang said Friday [27 April].
>
> (www.iht.com, 27 April 2007)

'Officials in Taiwan ... do not want the torch to enter or leave via China' (www.bbc.co.uk, 27 April 2007). 'On Thursday [26 April] Taiwan's authorities rejected China's plans for the torch to pass through the island. Taipei said the plan was unacceptable and compromised the island's sovereignty' (www.bbc.co.uk, 28 April 2007).

28–29 April 2007.

> A China–Taiwan forum in Beijing [is held] ... More than thirty MPs from Taiwan's main opposition party, the Kuomintang (KMT), are taking part in the two-day event [28–29 April] ... A large group of Taiwan's business leaders are also taking part in the forum ... The gathering is the third of its kind since a visit to China by former KMT head Lien Chan in 2005. He was the first party chairman to return to the mainland since the KMT fled to Taiwan [in 1949].
>
> (www.bbc.co.uk, 28 April 2007)

1 May 2007. 'Taiwan has re-established formal diplomatic ties with the Caribbean island of St Lucia – taking the number of its diplomatic allies to twenty-five ... Beijing requires its diplomatic allies not to recognize [Taiwan]' (www.bbc.co.uk. 1 May 2007).

> [On 1 May 2007 the] tiny Caribbean island ... [of] St Lucia [population 168,000] ... signed an agreement ... [with Taiwan restoring] diplomatic relations ... St Lucia maintained diplomatic relations with Taiwan for thirteen years under prime minister John Compton. Compton's party lost national elections in 1997 and St Lucia recognized China. Compton's return to power in last December's elections [December 2006] marked the beginning of Taiwan's comeback, even though China pledged more money and technical assistance ... [The St Lucian] prime minister ... had indicated that any decision would be based on which suitor could offer a better deal to St Lucia ... St Lucia indicated last week that if it resumed relations with Taiwan it would still want to be friends with China. The Chinese embassy

> sent a rebuff on Friday [27 April] saying in a statement that China does not accept 'double recognition' … China called the move a 'brutal interference in China's internal affairs' … St Lucia's recognition of Taiwan is the first win for Taiwan in some time in its diplomatic rivalry with China. In 1969 Taiwan had full relations with sixty-seven countries, including the United States and much of Western Europe. Until Tuesday [1 May] that number had dwindled down to just twenty-four.
>
> (www.iht.com, 1 May 2007)

6–7 May 2007.

> Presidential candidates of Taiwan's ruling Democratic Progressive Party united Monday [7 May] around a moderate in relations with China to lead the independence-leaning party's ticket in the March 2008 elections. The decision by three DPP heavyweights to rally around former premier Frank Hsieh came a day after he easily defeated them in an internal party primary … In Sunday's DPP primary [6 May] Hsieh received 44.7 per cent of the votes, against 33.4 per cent for Su Tseng-chang, the incumbent premier. Su's poor showing convinced him [on 6 May] to drop out of the race, even before a second round on Wednesday [9 May] … Party chairman Yu Shyi-kun finished a distant third in Sunday's primary with 15.8 per cent, and immediately announced he was suspending all campaign activities. The fourth candidate, Vice President Annette Lu, garnered 6.2 per cent of the vote … Hsieh has tried to trim expectations that Taiwan can ever formalize its de facto independence … The selection of Hsieh as a candidate ended months of acrimony that threatened to undermine the DPP's chances in the presidential poll against former Taipei mayor Ma Ying-jeou of the main opposition Nationalist Party, which favours eventual unification with China … Hsieh, as mayor of the southern city of Kaohsiung from 1998 to 2005, pushed for exchanges with the nearby Chinese city of Xiamen and tried to promote better relations with Beijing under the slogan 'coexistence and reconciliation'. Sworn in as Taiwanese premier two-and-a-half years ago, he pledged to pursue 'peace through talks and negotiation', including an end to bans on direct air and maritime connections to the mainland.
>
> (www.iht.com, 7 May 2007)

'The opposition KMT's Ma Ying-jeou [is] widely seen as frontrunner in the 2008 vote' (*FT*, 7 May 2007, p. 8).

> Taiwan's ruling Democratic Progressive Party yesterday [7 May] chose Frank Hsieh – former premier with a record of pragmatism in dealing with the island's combative opposition and China – as its candidate for next year's presidential election … The DPP yesterday decided to skip a series of opinion polls intended as a second phase of its presidential primary process.
>
> (*FT*, 8 May 2007, p. 11)

'Frank Hsieh is a pragmatic politician who favours better ties with Beijing' (www.bbc.co.uk, 7 May 2007).

> Like President Chen Shui-bian, Frank Hsieh is a former lawyer who in the past defended dissidents under the authoritarian rule of the KMT … Mr Hsieh has called for 'coexistence and reconciliation', though he has also called for constitutional revisions aimed at making Taiwan a 'normal country' – a goal that has caused considerable anxiety in both Beijing and Washington … Ma Ying-jeou has pushed for better ties with China, particularly economic ones. He has not ruled out unification, though he says China must become a democracy first.
>
> (*The Economist*, 12 May 2007, p. 64)

12 May 2007.

> Taiwanese prime minister Su Tseng-chang has resigned … Mr Su is a former human rights lawyer and co-founder of the Democratic People's Party … The president has said he will announce Mr Su's successor later on Saturday [12 May] … The new prime minister will be the sixth to serve under President Chen Shui-bian during his seven-year term in office.
>
> (www.bbc.co.uk, 12 May 2007)

14 May 2007. 'President Chen Shui-bian has named Chang Chun-hsiung from his ruling Democratic Progressive Party as the island's new prime minister … Mr Chang is Taiwan's former top negotiator with mainland China' (www.bbc.co.uk, 14 May 2007).

> Chang Chun-hsiung chairs the Straits Exchange Foundation, a semi-official body originally set up to lead negotiations with China. However, since Beijing has refused to officially deal with Mr Chen's government, the SEF has lost this political function and been replaced by communication channels with even more tenuous links to the government.
>
> (www.ft.com, 14 May 2007)

7 June 2007.

> Taiwan said Thursday [7 June] that it was cutting all ties with Costa Rica after the Central American country established diplomatic ties with Beijing, endangering Taipei's alliances with countries in the region … [There may be] a chain reaction among at least a number of Taiwan's remaining seven Latin American allies … The agreement to switch ties was signed by foreign minister Yang Jiechi and his Costa Rican counterpart in being on 1 June … Costa Rica was the eighth country to break ties with Taiwan since President Chen Shui-bian took office in May 2000, after Macedonia, Liberia, Dominica, Vanuatu, Grenada, Senegal and Chad. In April the Caribbean island of St Lucia broke ties with China and recognized Taiwan … Only twenty-four countries now recognize Taipei and some of the most important ones are in Central America.
>
> (www.iht.com, 7 June 2007)

'By 1953 only twenty-three states had established diplomatic relations with Beijing … With the latest switch 170 nations now recognize [Beijing] … Taiwan has seen its support dwindle to twenty-four' (*Guardian*, 8 June 2007, p. 23).

[On 7 June] a former president of Taiwan, Lee Teng-hui, visited … [Japan's] Yasukuni Shrine … to pray for his brother … [The shrine] honours 2.5 million, including … tens of thousands of Koreans and Taiwanese drafted into the Japanese military during Japan's colonial rule … [Lee's] brother died fighting for the Japanese during World War II.

(www.iht.com, 7 June 2007)

Taiwan, which was a Japanese colony between 1895 and 1945, is a rare exception in Asia in that there is little anti-Japanese sentiment. While there have been protests against Japan from women forced into prostitution during the Second World War and from indigenous Taiwanese for atrocities committed by Japanese troops, those who harbour bitter feelings towards Japan are a small minority. For many of those Taiwanese who see the island as a separate nation to China, Japan's legacy helps their claim that Taiwan is not Chinese. Lee Teng-hui this week alluded to this argument, when he credited Taiwan's former colonial rulers with laying the foundation for Taiwan's modern democratic society.

(*FT*, 8 June 2007, p. 12)

15 June 2007.

Details have emerged from declassified US government documents regarding its success in halting Taiwan's budding nuclear projects in the 1970s. The recently declassified documents show that the administrations of Gerald Ford and Jimmy Carter applied heavy pressure on Taiwan to end its quest for sophisticated equipment that Washington feared would be used in the manufacture of a nuclear bomb … The leadership in Taiwan repeatedly denied that the island was trying to build a nuclear weapon, according to the documents, although they also show that from as early as November 1972 the US Central Intelligence Agency thought otherwise … The agency concluded: 'We believe Taipei's present intention is to develop the capacity to fabricate and test a nuclear device. This capacity could be attained by 1976' … The CIA said it was not sure why Taiwan began its alleged nuclear quest, but speculated that it was related to anxiety over the budding US relationship with Beijing … In February 1972 President Richard Nixon visited the mainland … The documents show that the Carter administration continued the US policy of leaning hard on Taiwan, making it clear that nuclear nonproliferation was a top priority for the new president … Washington switched diplomatic recognition from Taipei to Beijing in 1979, but continued to monitor Taiwan's nuclear programme.

(www.iht.com, 15 June 2007)

17 June 2007.

Taiwan's parliament has approved funds to buy weapons from the United States after more than six years of delays. The legislature passed $300 million in funds requested by the government as part of its 2007 defence budget. The three items are part of an estimated $18 billion package agreed with the US government to sell arms to Taiwan.

(*FT*, 18 June 2007, p. 8)

20 June 2007.

Officials in Taiwan vowed Wednesday [20 June] to proceed with a referendum on rejoining the United Nations under the name Taiwan, despite fierce objections from China as well as US warnings not to hold the vote … Taiwan lost the China seat in the United Nations to the communist government in Beijing in 1971 … A spokesman for the president of Taiwan said Wednesday that preparations for the referendum had already begun, including obtaining the 1 million signatures needed to get the issue on the ballot in one of the island's two coming elections … either legislative elections in January [2008] or the presidential poll two months later.

(www.iht.com, 20 June 2007)

19 July 2007.

Taiwan has submitted its first formal application to join the United Nations … This was the first time the country launched a bid for UN membership using its own name rather than the official title 'Republic of China' used in earlier attempts.

(www.bbc.co.uk, 20 July 2007)

'On 19 July the self-ruled island applied to join the UN as "Taiwan" – a departure from fourteen previous post-1971 applications as the "Republic of China", its formal name' (www.iht.com, 24 July 2007).

22 July 2007.

Taiwan plans to revise school textbooks to drop references that describe mainland Chinese historical figures, places and artefacts as 'national', the education ministry has announced … A ministry official said Sunday [22 July] that the authorities were considering dropping about 5,000 'inappropriate' references in Taiwanese textbooks to help 'clear up confusion' about the island's identity … [He] did not elaborate, but local news media said the revisions would include changing 'national opera' to 'Chinese opera', 'the Ming Dynasty' to 'China's Ming Dynasty' and 'this nation's historical figures' to 'China's historical figures'.

(www.iht.com, 23 July 2007)

23 July 2007.

The United Nations has rejected Taiwan's latest application to become a member of the world body, citing the organization's adherence to the 'One China' policy and its recognition of the Chinese government in Beijing … The United Nations rejected the application Monday [23 July], citing a 1971 resolution that stopped recognizing the government in Taipei as the representative of China, instead recognizing Beijing as China's sole representative to the world body ... The UN said: 'This resolution determined that the UN carries out a "One China" policy' ... Adherence to the 'One China' policy, as practised by the UN, means accepting that both Taiwan and China belong to the same national entity ... Taiwan was expelled from the UN in 1971 when its seat, which it held under the name Republic of China, was transferred to the Beijing-based government of the People's Republic of China.

(www.iht.com, 24 July 2007; *IHT*, 25 July 2007, p. 4)

The Republic of China has tried, without success, to reenter the United Nations since 1993. This year [2007] marks the first time that it has changed tactics by bidding to join the world body under the name Taiwan ... President Chiang Ching-kup proclaimed the end of martial law on 14 July 1987.

(*IHT*, 1 August 2007, p. 6)

A Taiwanese court acquitted opposition presidential candidate Ma Ying-jeou on corruption charges Tuesday [14 August] ... [He] was indicted earlier this year on charges he diverted $333,000 of public money into his private account while serving as mayor of Taipei between 1998 and 2006.

(www.iht.com, 14 August 2007)

23 August 2007.

Taiwan plans to increase defence spending by 16.4 per cent in 2008, to 341.1 billion Taiwanese dollars, the cabinet has announced ... The budget plan still requires approval from parliament ... Taiwan's military spending is still only a quarter of China's official military spending this year [2007] of $45 billion, a 17.8 per cent increase from 2008.

(www.iht.com, 23 August 2007)

6–7 September 2007.

With preparations for the 2008 Olympics gathering momentum, China and Taiwan appeared to be close to an agreement this month [September] on the island's role in the torch relay that will deliver the Olympic flame to Beijing. After a month of talks in which both sides made important concessions, Tsai Chen-wei, chairman of the Taiwanese Olympic committee, flew to Beijing on 6 September to sign an accord on the matter. But within twenty-four hours he returned to Taipei empty handed. At the last moment, Taiwanese officials say, Beijing had added a stipulation that only the Olympic flag of Chinese Taipei – the name under which the island competes in the Olympics – could be on display as the torch crossed the island ... Taiwanese officials say the Chen administration was prepared to agree that the Chinese Taipei Olympic flag would be the only one officially displayed. That flag, which bears the emblem of Taiwan's Olympic committee on a white background, has been used since the 1984 Games. But officials say they would be powerless to stop Taiwanese citizens from waving the flag of the Republic of

China, the island's official name – or any other flag, for that matter ... During the negotiations Taiwan had dropped its objection to the torch being passed from Taiwan to Hong Kong and then Macao – a link the Chen administration had complained would suggest that Taiwan was part of Chinese territory. And China had relented on characterizing the Taiwan leg in the official programme as part of its domestic route, in what appeared to be a significant concession from Beijing. Taipei was to be listed as one of the 'overseas' cities hosting the relay.

(www.iht.com, 17 September 2007)

15 September 2007.

At least 100,000 people have marched in Taiwan in support of a government plan to hold a referendum on joining the UN under the name Taiwan. The UN has rejected previous bids from the island to join the body under its official name, Republic of China ... The march, in the southern city of Kaohsiung, attracted hundreds of thousands of people according to organizers, while police said 100,000 took part. Kaohsiung is a power base for the ruling Democratic Progressive Party's (DPP) president candidate Frank Hsieh. The government intends to time the referendum with the presidential vote next March [2008] ... The opposition Kuomintang (KMT) also favours a referendum on joining the UN, but under the island's name Republic of China. The KMT held a separate rally in the central city of Taichung attended by its presidential candidate Ma Ying-jeou which attracted an estimated 50,000 people. The UN switched its recognition from Taiwan to mainland China in 1971.

(www.bbc.co.uk, 15 September 2007)

The opposition Kuomintang Party also mobilized tens of thousands Saturday [15 September] at its own rally in the central city of Taichung, calling for a referendum on UN admission under Taiwan's official name, Republic of China, or any other 'pragmatic' name ... Ma Ying-jeou has proposed the alternative vote on UN membership under the Republic of China name ... However, Beijing would almost certainly oppose a membership bid under any name ... Domestically, widespread support for UN membership [exists in Taiwan] ... Opinion polls indicate that more than 70 per cent of the island's 23 million people support a return to the United Nations for Taiwan, which in 1971 lost its seat, held in the name of the Republic of China, to the government in Beijing.

(www.iht.com, 16 September 2007)

The Olympic torch will not pass through Taiwan because negotiators could not resolve differences with the Beijing authorities, officials have confirmed. The two sides disagreed over the route the torch would take on its way to the Beijing Games in 2008. Taiwanese officials also objected to Chinese insistence that the use of Taiwan's flag and national anthem be limited at torch-related events.

(www.bbc.co.uk, 21 September 2007)

China welcomed on Thursday [20 September] the UN's rejection of Taiwan's bid to reenter the world body … A UN committee refused Wednesday [19 September] to place Taiwan's membership application on the General Assembly agenda, the fifteenth successive occasion it had been blocked … This time China waged a particularly hostile blocking campaign because the … government in Taipei submitted its membership application in the name of Taiwan instead of its official title, the Republic of China. It was a step the Communist Party in Beijing condemned as a move towards secession.

(www.iht.com, 20 September 2007)

21 September 2007.

The chairman of Taiwan's governing Democratic Progressive Party (DPP) has resigned after being indicted on charges of corruption and forgery. You Shyo-kun is one of three DPP members indicted by prosecutors on Friday [21 September]. He denies any wrongdoing … [The others indicted are] vice president Annette Lu and former foreign minister Mark Chen … Mr You maintained that funds he had received as part of a special allowance, given to about 6,000 high ranking public office holders, were all spent on public and not private affairs … Mr You has been charged with misusing $72,000 while he held several posts, including that of prime minister … Frank Hsieh and his running mate, Su Tseng-chang, were also investigated by prosecutors … [but] were cleared of all charges … There have been calls for an overhaul of the special allowance fund, which allows officials to treat guests or pay for gifts, and only requires them to submit invoices for half of the funds.

(www.bbc.co.uk, 22 September 2007)

The Pentagon estimates that China has deployed 900 missiles opposite Taiwan … The US and Taiwan militaries estimate that China adds up to 100 new missiles a year to its forces arrayed against the island … Faced with a threatening military build-up by China, an increasingly outgunned Taiwan is quietly pushing ahead with plans to develop missiles that could strike the mainland, defence and security experts say … Taiwan currently has no long-range missiles that could be used to attack distant targets in mainland China … There have also been unconfirmed news reports in Taiwan that the military is developing short-range ballistic missiles … The Bush administration has signalled that it opposes Taiwan developing offensive weapons, including missiles … There were reports in the Taiwanese media this month [September] that, under pressure from Washington, the Chen administration had dropped plans to deploy surface-to-surface missiles on Taiwan's outlying island of Matsu near the coast of China's Fujian province. Missiles deployed on Matsu would be able to strike targets on the mainland where China has concentrated air, missile and land forces opposite Taiwan … Defence analysts note that Taiwan publicly acknowledged for the first time this year that offensive missile strikes were now part of its planned response to an attack from the mainland ... Taiwan's ministry of defence denied that the missiles still under development were offensive weapons. It said that if a decision was made to deploy them, they would only be used if the island was attacked.

(www.iht.com, 28 September 2007; *IHT*, 29 September 2007, p. 6)

30 September 2007.

The governing Democratic Party passed a resolution ... 250 to seventy-three ... Sunday [30 September] asserting the separate identity of Taiwan from China and calling for a referendum on Taiwanese sovereignty. The resolution for a 'normal country', passed after a heated debate at a boisterous party congress, calls for the general use of 'Taiwan' as the island's name, without specifically abolishing the state's formal name, the Republic of China. It also called for the enactment of a new constitution ... The resolution said: 'We should rectify our name to Taiwan and enact a new constitution as soon as possible. A public referendum should be held at an appropriate time to underscore Taiwan as a sovereign state' ... President Chen Shui-bian decided to keep Taiwan's status ambiguous, fearing an outright call to change the island's official name to Taiwan could hurt Frank Hsieh at the [presidential] polls. The perceived softer stance has angered many pro-independence hardliners.

(www.iht.com, 30 September 2007)

10 October 2007.

Taiwan has marked its national day with a military parade for the first time in sixteen years ... National day military parades were discontinued in 1991 ... Two missiles developed in Taiwan – the Hsiung-feng III ship-to-ship missile and the Tien-kung III anti-tactical ballistic missile – were unveiled during the parade. But the Hsiung-feng 2E, a long-range cruise missile believed to be capable of targeting the Chinese mainland, did not appear.

(www.bbc.co.uk, 10 October 2007)

[Taiwan's national] day commemorates the 1911 overthrow of China's last imperial dynasty ... China holds its national day on 1 October, the date the ruling Communist Party proclaimed the People's Republic of China in 1949 ... Taiwan has developed a long-range, land-attack cruise missile with sufficient range to strike targets as far away as Shanghai. There had been speculation that this missile would be paraded alongside Taiwan's other advanced hardware, but officials in Taipei said early this week that the weapon was still under development and would not go on display.

(www.iht.com, 10 October 2007)

11 October 2007. 'President Chen Shui-bien ... has agreed to return as chairman of the ruling Democratic Progressive Party' (*FT*, 12 October 2007, p. 9).

17 October 2007.

> An opposition lawmaker blasted a move by the post office Wednesday [17 October] to stamp a slogan on outgoing mail in support of President Chen Shui-bian's contentious campaign to win a seat for Taiwan in the United Nations. The furore [was] created by the decision to place the slogan 'UN for Taiwan' on selected items of domestic and international mail ... While a clear majority of Taiwanese want the island in the United Nations, the Nationalist and Democratic Progressive Party are bitterly divided over what name it should use in pressing its application.
>
> (www.iht.com, 17 October 2007)

18 October 2007.

> President Chen Shui-bian on Thursday [18 October] denounced a peace overture from President Hu Jintao [see the 15 October 2007 speech given by Hu Jintao in the political chronology, Chapter 8], one that has received a cautious welcome here [in Taiwan] from both candidates in presidential elections to be held next March [2008] ... Chen Shui-bian: 'It is very clear that if we were to sign such a peace treaty under the framework of the One China principle then I think this would mean, for the 23 million people of Taiwan, a treaty of surrender ... Taiwan is an independent, sovereign country; Taiwan is not part of China, nor is Taiwan a local government of the People's Republic of China.'
>
> (*IHT*, 19 October 2007, p. 4)

24 October 2007.

> President Chen Shui-bian has launched a nationwide torch relay to highlight Taiwan's bid to join the United Nations ... [an] eleven-day, 1,200 kilometre (756 mile) journey around the island ... The president wants a national vote on whether the country should apply to join the UN under the name Taiwan ... Chen Shui-bian: 'Becoming a UN member under Taiwan's own name is the mainstream consensus. China and Taiwan are two separate states on either side of the Taiwan Strait' ... Taiwan is missing out on the Olympic torch relay because of differences with China over conditions ... [Also on 24 October] Ma Ying-jeou of the opposition Kuomintang ... also launched his own bicycle relay in support of UN membership – but under the official name, the Republic of China.
>
> (www.bbc.co.uk, 24 October 2007)

19 November 2007.

> The appointment of a Chinese judge to the highest court in the WTO has been blocked by Taiwan in a surprise decision. Taiwan lodged its objection citing fears of bias and the step forced a meeting [on 19 November] to be adjourned. China's Zhang Yuejiao was among four candidates nominated to the WTO's seven-member Appellate Body in June [2007]. She would have

been China's first judge on the body, which rules on trade disputes between the WTO member states.

(www.bbc.co.uk, 19 November 2007)

The WTO dispute settlement body had been due to approve the appointment of four new members of the WTO's Appellate Body, but Taiwan asked for that item to be removed from the agenda … 'because we have deep concerns on the question of impartiality and qualification of one of the recommended candidates to serve the Appellate Body'.

(*IHT*, 20 November 2007, p. 14)

27 November 2007. 'Taiwan dropped its objection Tuesday [27 November]' (*IHT*, 28 November 2007, p. 13).

('In a report to Congress in November, a commission examining America's relations with China gave warning that "the pace and success of China's military modernization continue to exceed US government estimates". China's principal aim, the report said, is to develop the wherewithal to delay or deter American military intervention in any war over Taiwan … On 11 January 2007 … a missile fired from a mobile launcher deep inside China … intercepted one of China's ageing weather satellites … The missile shot put America on notice that it can be challenged in space': *The Economist*, 19 January 2008, p. 24.)

('By November 2007 the Chinese military had deployed about 1,000 short-range missiles opposite Taiwan and was adding 200 missiles to this force each year, it [the Pentagon report] said': www.iht.com, 4 March 2008.)

21 December 2007. US Secretary of State Condoleezza Rice:

We think that Taiwan's referendum to apply to the United Nations under the name 'Taiwan' is a provocative policy. It unnecessarily raises tensions in the Taiwan Strait and it promises no real benefits for the people of Taiwan on the international stage.

(www.iht.com, 22 December 2007)

28 December 2007.

An appeal court has acquitted opposition leader Ma Ying-jeou of corruption charges. The ruling clears the way for him to represent the Kuomintang Party in the presidential election due to be held in March [2008]. Mr Ma had resigned as head of the Kuomintang Party following the indictment but denied any wrongdoing. Prosecutors have been seeking to overturn a lower court ruling which cleared him of embezzlement. Ma was accused of misappropriating $339,000 in funds while he was mayor of Taipei.

(www.bbc.co.uk, 28 December 2007)

A lower court originally exonerated Ma Ying-jeou in August [2007] on charges of diverting $333,000 of public money into his private account while serving as mayor of Taipei between 1998 and 2006. But prosecutors appealed that decision and added a new charge – breach of trust. Had the

> High Court upheld their appeal and sentenced Ma to at least ten years in prison – or had he been convicted on the breach of trust count – Ma would have been barred from the presidential race … In his defence Ma argued that Taiwan law recognized a special mayoral fund as an official subsidy of his salary. Ma always maintained that one of the main charges against him – using the fund without providing detailed accounting – had long been common practice among municipal leaders and other government officials. Rather than pocketing the fund, he said, he used it to make donations to charity … Early opinion polls give Ma a twenty-point lead in elections scheduled to take place on 22 March.
>
> (www.iht.com, 28 December 2007)

'Recent opinion polls are showing Ma ahead of his rival by 20 to 30 points. But publicly available polls in Taiwan have a credibility problem. Many are conducted by partisan media outlets and have proved unreliable' (www.iht.com, 10 January 2008).

> Both of the two major-party presidential candidates are moderates on cross-strait relations … [Although Frank Hsieh] would like Taiwan to be independent, he believes that China is too strong, US support too uncertain and Taiwan's economic interests are too tied to the mainland to make a bid for independence. He asserts that: '[Taiwan] cannot avoid mainland influence. We must understand their nationalism, must dialogue and communicate. We cannot realize our hopes while having very tense relations with the mainland' … Ma Ying-jeou would endorse Beijing's One China principle to get negotiations started, but only if Beijing and Taipei can each interpret this principle in its own way, the two sides agree not to use force, and final-status issues are shelved for thirty to fifty years. Ma hopes the mainland might eventually be willing to accept a Chinese confederation with the Republic of China as a member.
>
> (www.iht.com, 9 January 2008; *IHT*, 10 January 2008, p. 7)

1 January 2008.

> China plans to open a new commercial aviation route through the Taiwan Strait in a move that officials in Taipei said was a threat to regional peace and a danger to air safety. The new route between Hong Kong and Shanghai would track just inside the Chinese side of the unofficial dividing line through the middle of the Taiwan Strait, an area that both sides have mostly avoided since the 1950s, security and aviation specialists in Taiwan said. The United States has been drawn into the dispute and has held talks about the proposed route with Beijing and Taipei … In Beijing the State Council, or cabinet, and the Central Military Commission, or the top military decision-making body, approved the new air route off the south-east coast, according to a 5 December [2007] statement … [which] said that Chinese aviation officials were working on finalizing navigation arrangements, communications and co-ordination with Hong Kong and Taipei … In the final

New Year's address of his second and final term President Chen Shui-bian said that the new air route was part of China's efforts to expand the boundary of its airspace at the island's expense ... Chen said: 'In doing so China is once again challenging and attempting to unilaterally change the status quo in the Taiwan Strait' ... Security officials in Taiwan said the regular commercial aviation services along or near the dividing line would constrain the training and operations of the island's military, particularly its air force, which would be Taiwan's first line of defence in a conflict with the mainland ... Pressure from domestic and international carriers may have been a factor in Beijing's decision to approve the new route. Only 30 per cent of Chinese airspace is available for civil aviation, according to the International Air Transport Association, a trade group based in Montreal that represents more than 240 carriers. The group has been urging Beijing to expand its tightly controlled corridors. Increased congestion in the fastest growing major aviation market in the world, particularly in the so-called golden triangle routes connecting Beijing, Shanghai and Guangzhou, has led to costly delays at these major airports. Crowded skies over the Pearl River delta also cause up to twenty-five minutes' extra flying time for flights approaching Hong Kong from the north, with Chinese carriers most affected, according to the aviation authority ... Despite complaints from carriers, the Chinese military has been extremely reluctant to expand civil aviation corridors over the mainland ... Aviation officials in Taiwan said they learned from aviation officials in Hong Kong that China had applied to the International Civil Aviation Organization, the UN agency that co-ordinates the regulation of civil aviation, to register the route close to the mid-point of the Taiwan Strait ... Taiwan is not a member of the International Civil Aviation Organization ... As Beijing has accelerated its military build-up over the past decade, there has been a steady increase in the number of Chinese military aircraft, warships and research vessels crossing the dividing line, the defence ministry in Taipei has reported. Taiwan also operates regular military and civilian flights across the boundary to its outlying islands of Kinmen and Matsu near the mainland coast. Direct charter flights between the mainland and Taiwan during festival periods also cross this line. But security specialists said both sides had generally avoided using areas along the divide for civilian aviation or regular military activities. This constraint has served to minimize the danger of confrontation or miscalculation, they said.

(www.iht.com, 6 January 2008)

[On 1 January 2008] Taiwan reopened a giant monument in Taipei to ... Chiang Kai-shek as a memorial to human rights abuses under his rule. President Chen Shui-bian said the rededicated monument symbolized 'opening the door to democracy'. While a 10-metre-high (33 feet) bronze statue of Chiang remains in place, its guard of honour has been removed. Records of victims and milestones on the road to democracy now ring the statue, along with about 300 kites ... The monument was opened in 1980, five years after Chiang's death.

(www.bbc.co.uk, 2 January 2008)

12 January 2008. Parliamentary elections are held.

The first contest, on 12 January, is for Taiwan's legislature. The opposition Nationalist Party, the Kuomintang (KMT), is expected to retain its majority ... Turnout may be no more than 60 per cent, low by Taiwan's standards ... [There is to be] a new electoral system. Taiwan has adopted a 'single-seat, dual vote' system similar to those in Japan and Germany. Voters will choose one direct representative per constituency and a preferred party to provide 'at-large' members of parliament. There are 113 seats, of which seventy-three are directly elected and six reserved for aboriginal candidates. The KMT is expected to win sixty to sixty-five seats ... the ruling Democratic Progressive Party (DPP) ... thirty-five to forty-five ... The legislative-election campaign has been dominated by two issues. One is the DPP's drive to expunge from Taiwan symbols of Chiang Kai-shek, the KMT leader, who led its retreat from mainland China in 1949. This week the Chiang Kai-shek memorial hall in Taipei reopened as a 'democracy memorial', highlighting the human rights abuses of his regime. Second is a procedural dispute over two referendums to be held with the election. One, initiated by the DPP, relates to the KMT's 'stolen assets'. The other, introduced by the KMT, which this week nevertheless called a boycott of both referendums, covers alleged corruption by the DPP and President Chen Shui-bian ... Another referendum, to be held at the same time as the presidential election [on 22 March] ... will ask whether Taiwan should apply for membership of the United Nations using the name 'Taiwan' rather than its antiquated formal title, 'the Republic of China'. This appeals to the DPP's core supporters, who see themselves as Taiwanese, not Chinese.

(*The Economist*, 5 January 2008, pp. 51–2)

The number of seats will be reduced from 225 to 113 ... Legislators' terms will be extended from three years to four, and one-half of the thirty-four seats allotted to the parties based on their share of the political-party vote will be held by female legislators. Redistricting, based chiefly on population, has also changed the political landscape, and for the first time legislators will be elected from single-member districts (seventy-three seats, representing seventy-three districts). Voters will cast two votes, one for a district candidate and one for a political party – the latter determining the allocation of the thirty-four seats based on party performance. The remaining six seats will be allocated to aboriginal people ... Under the old system some constituencies elected as many as twelve legislators.

(www.economist.com, 8 January 2008)

The Democratic Progressive Party [DPP] has included a referendum in Saturday's election asking voters to support legislation that would allow the government to recover Kuomintang assets that were found to have been stolen from the public. The Kuomintang, once one of the world's richest political parties, governed Taiwan for fifty-one unbroken years before Chen Shui-bian's election in 2000. A second Kuomintang-backed referendum will also be held seeking backing for parliament to have powers to investigate senior government officials for corruption. But the Kuomintang has since decided to boycott the referendums ... The parliamentary elections will also test Taiwan's efforts to streamline its political system and improve the conduct of sometimes fiery and violent debate in the Legislative Yuan. Under a new system for this election, the number of parliamentary seats will be halved from 225 to 113. Of these, seventy-three will represent single-member electoral districts, six will be elected by indigenous people and thirty-four will be 'at-large' seats, drawn from a list of nominees based on their parties' share of the vote. Voters will cast a ballot for their local district or indigenous candidate and a second for their favoured political party. Government and opposition lawmakers say the new system should return more moderate legislators compared with the previous system, where candidates with more extreme views could win seats in multi-seat constituencies with only a small share of the vote ... Lawmakers hope a more efficient and civilized legislature will also improve public perceptions of politicians. 'People hate the Legislative Yuan,' said Joanna Lei, a Kuomintang lawmaker, noting that some opinion polls show that only gangsters are less popular than politicians in Taiwan.

(www.iht.com, 11 January 2008)

Some observers have said the new system may marginalize smaller parties in favour of the DPP and the KMT ... [One referendum] will ask voters to support legislation to force the KMT to return state assets the DPP says were illegally amassed during the 1950s ... [If the turnout is] less than 50 per cent ... neither of the referendums can be approved ... Kuomintang [KMT], which currently has a slim majority in parliament along with its allies, is hoping to win a two-thirds majority in Saturday's election. The two main parties are fighting for control of the newly scaled-down parliament, in which the number of seats has been cut from 225 to 113 in line with reforms adopted in 2005 in order to reduce corruption and improve efficiency ... [A turnout of] 59.2 per cent [was] achieved in the last legislative election in 2004.

(www.bbc.co.uk, 12 January 2008)

As Taiwan gears up for two elections, more than 200,000 residents are barred from voting, in part because of questions about their political loyalties. These are mainly Chinese-born spouses, mostly women, of Taiwan citizens ... Mainland-born spouses are not categorized as foreigners, eligible for naturalization. But at the same time they face daunting hurdles to full citizenship rights in their adopted homes. So tens of thousands of long-term residents ... are forbidden to work, open a checking account, take out a loan

> or register a business. Nor can they cast a ballot … Although foreign spouses, these days predominantly from South-east Asia, can gain citizenship and vote within four years of entering Taiwan, mainlanders must wait at least eight years to gain permanent residence status and a Taiwan identity card … that will allow them to vote. Foreigners can work within four months, but mainlanders cannot work within the first six years unless their family meets low-income requirements. Further limiting mainlanders' rights is the Taiwan government's ceiling on permanent residency permits. Only 6,000 are issued each year to mainland spouses. No such quotas apply to spouses from other countries. As a result, only 44,493, or about 18 per cent, of the approximately 250,000 mainlanders who have been allowed to immigrate here had voting rights as of late November [2007]. By contrast, around 44 per cent of foreign-born spouses have voting rights … The Taiwan authorities argue there are many reasons to treat mainlanders differently, from the decades of hostility between the two sides and the issue of where their real loyalties lie, to their sheer numbers. The increase in mainland spouses over the past decade is the largest wave of immigration the island of 22 million has seen since 1949.
>
> (www.iht.com, 8 January 2008)

The results were as follows:

> Taiwan's nationalist Kuomintang [KMT] has won a landslide victory in parliamentary elections. With all the votes counted, the KMT secured eighty-one seats … in the 113-seat chamber … [representing] 72 per cent [of seats] – up from 49 per cent it had in the previous legislature … The Democratic Progressive Party [DPP] got twenty-seven seats – or 24 per cent … Seventy-three seats were contested by a total of 296 individual candidates representing twelve parties … [The BBC analyst said] the two main parties' candidates for the presidential poll concentrated on local issues and shied away from discussing China in the run-up to the vote, a tactic the Chinese government has also adopted. Beijing has learned from its past misadventures during Taiwanese polls that verbal warnings and missile tests would backfire in favour of candidates from the DPP.
>
> (www.bbc.co.uk, 12 January 2008)

> President Chen Shui-bian resigned as chairman of the Democratic Progressive Party immediately after his party's defeat: 'I shoulder all responsibilities. I feel really apologetic and shamed' … Chen has been criticized for aggravating relations with Beijing by promoting policies to formalize Taiwan's de facto independence from China. Critics say that has allowed Taiwan's once vibrant economy to lose competitiveness and ratcheted up tension … If the nationalists go on to recapture the presidency, they will be in a strong position to end years of deadlock between Taiwan's legislative and executive branches and to stabilize the island's rocky relations with China … During Chen's two terms as president, the Nationalists used a

slender legislative majority to block many of his initiatives, including the purchase of a multi-billion-dollar package of US weapons. Also left stagnating have been negotiations to open direct air and shipping routes between Taiwan and China. Ma Ying-jeou took a high-profile role in the legislative campaign, pressing home his message that Chen's reluctance to engage China inflamed tensions with Beijing and hurt the island's economy ... Frank Hsieh has come out in favour of ditching Chen's across-the-board requirement that Taiwanese companies limit their investments in China to less than 40 per cent of their asset value. He has also indicated a willingness to expand direct charter flights across the Taiwan Strait ... Ma and the Nationalists go considerably further. They want to remove the asset requirement altogether and sanction scheduled flights between China and Taiwan.

(www.iht.com, 12 January 2008)

At the close of counting, the official central election commission said the Kuomintang had won eighty-one seats in the 113-seat legislative Yuan, the Democratic Progressive Party [DPP] won twenty-seven and the balance went to minor parties and independents. Almost 60 per cent of the 17 million eligible voters turned out in the first election under a new system in which the number of seats in the chamber was halved in an effort to streamline lawmaking and improve the quality of debate ... Chen Shui-bian: 'It is the worst defeat since the founding of the DPP. I feel very sorry and ashamed' ... Corruption scandals linked to his relatives had hurt the party's image, analysts said ... The DPP's candidate for president, Frank Hsieh, who kept a relatively low profile in campaigning for the legislature, faces an uphill battle in the race against the popular and charismatic Ma Ying-jeou. Ma, a Harvard-trained lawyer, has said Taiwan needs a strong military and close ties with the United States to counter the military threat from China. But he favours avoiding confrontation with Beijing while allowing closer economic ties.

(www.iht.com, 13 January 2008)

The Kuomintang, or Nationalists, had been expected to perform strongly, but the scale of the success surprised political analysts ... The Kuomintang once waged a fierce civil war against the communists on the mainland, but now advocates maintaining the status quo between the two sides without ruling out eventual reunification. In the meantime it supports closer economic and cultural ties with its neighbour ... The Kuomintang won 53.5 per cent of the vote compared with 38.2 per cent for the Democrats. Chen Shui-bian won office with 50.1 per cent of the vote in 2004. Some analysts interpreted the election outcome as a clear repudiation of Chen's policies aimed at shifting toward independence from China. Others said voters were also disillusioned with Chen's economic management and the parliamentary gridlock that has prevailed throughout his presidency.

(*IHT*, 14 January 2008, p. 2)

Ma Ying-jeou is of mainland descent … The DPP would likely benefit if turnout rises from 58 per cent in this election toward the near 80 per cent seen in the 2004 presidential election … It remains to be seen whether the KMT, which has strong links to protectionist forces, has the will to free up the domestic sector, which remains uncompetitive even as Taiwanese technology continues to lead the world.

(*IHT*, 15 January 2008, p. 7)

The Nationalists won eighty-five seats, including four for smaller aligned parties … There are 17 million Taiwanese registered to vote from a population of 23 million … A major election issue was the economy … Salaries have remained stagnant and unemployment is high in one of the world's top twenty economies, while the prices of consumer goods have soared … The Nationalists have promised to boost the economy by allowing Chinese tourists to visit the island and arranging direct flights between Taiwan and China.

(www.cnn.com, 12 January 2008)

The Nationalists and their allies had previously held 49 per cent of seats in the legislature while the DPP and its partners held 42 per cent … Many voters said that the trade restrictions had caused the island's once vibrant economy to lose steam … Many Taiwanese say that they prefer the status quo under which the island is nominally part of China but gets on with its own business … [But] Taiwanese politics are notoriously volatile and much could change in … the presidential election on 22 March.

(*The Times*, 14 January 2008, p. 33)

The KMT had been expected to retain its majority in parliament, but the size of the majority it has won is surprising. The nationalists will now control some 72 per cent of parliamentary seats compared to its earlier tally of around 52 per cent. Meanwhile, the DPP's share of seats has plunged to 24 per cent from the 42 per cent earlier held by the party and its 'pan-green' allies … But while disillusionment with the DPP is a big part of the reason for the KMT's victory, the full story is more complex. Many Taiwan analysts suspect that the DPP shot itself in the foot by agreeing to the new parliamentary system, which confers an advantage on the KMT because of its superior organization and resources. This effect was amplified by a low voter turnout, which especially hurt the DPP and the smaller pan-green parties, such as the Taiwan Solidarity Union (TSU). The TSU got less than 1 per cent of votes, compared to nearly 8 per cent in the previous election, suggesting that the party's supporters knew that voting for the TSU would mean very little but refused to vote for the DPP – possibly because of friction between the two parties in the run-up to the election. In the end Taiwan's smaller parties were largely shut out of power under the new system, winning only five seats. However, the election results were not all bad news for the DPP. Despite the

> KMT's landslide in terms of seats won, other indicators suggest the DPP retains significant support. The DPP actually won a slightly higher proportion of the popular vote than in the last legislative election (38 per cent versus 26 per cent). That the KMT's percentage of the popular vote was 51 per cent – about the proportion of seats it held in the previous parliament – also suggests that the Nationalists have not made major gains in terms of overall public support ... Under the new parliamentary system the DPP lost several districts where it had significant support but not enough to secure the seat ... Mr Ma has said that reunification would only be possible with a democratic China ... In 2008 China has largely kept silent throughout Taiwan's electoral season (although, bizarrely, several delegates, ostensibly from Taiwan, were appointed to the mainland's National People's Congress on the same day as Taiwan's election) ... It is a clear sign that Taiwan's voters are eager for the government to focus on economic policy-making ... Taiwan is increasingly economically dependent on the mainland: China is Taiwan's largest export market, Taiwanese firms have made investments worth tens of billions of US dollars on the mainland and an estimated 4 per cent of Taiwan's citizens live there. Moreover, this dependence is mutual: a significant proportion of China's exports, especially of electronic goods, are manufactured by Taiwanese firms operating on the mainland. The KMT can be expected to boost these reciprocal ties by accelerating the pace of cross-Strait economic integration. Ma Ying-jeou's proposed initiatives include allowing direct travel links with China and permitting Taiwanese firms to invest more than 40 per cent of their assets in China.
>
> (www.economist.com, 15 January 2008)

> The KMT's ideas for dealing with China ... [include lifting] a cap on investment in China by any Taiwanese company – 40 per cent of net worth – ... Direct Chinese investment in Taiwan would be allowed for the first time ... An agreement with China on direct scheduled flights and cross-strait shipping would be reached within a year. Ma Ying-jeou has said that as president he would not enter talks with China about reunification. But if China removed the hundreds of missiles it has pointed at Taiwan, he would discuss a peace agreement. Last October [2007] China's president, Hu Jintao, also called for a peace accord, but on 'the condition of the One China principle'. That is, Taiwan would have to accept it is in effect part of the People's Republic. Even the KMT balks at that.
>
> (*The Economist*, 19 January 2008, p. 54)

'Trade between China and Taiwan hit a record high last year [2007], rising to $102.3 billion' (www.iht.com, 12 March 2008).

'[Ma Ying-jeou has said that] he would ensure that the defence budget is equal to at least 3 per cent of Taiwan's GDP. He said: "[The military needs] to be strong enough to deter an initial attack from the mainland"' (www.iht.com, 12 March 2008).

14 January 2008.

> The Taiwan foreign ministry said Monday [14 January] that it had severed diplomatic ties with Malawi because the African country had established diplomatic relations with China … reducing the number of its allies to twenty-three. Most are small and impoverished nations in Latin America, Africa and South Pacific … China's diplomatic count now stands at more than 170 … [Taiwan] said that China had used underhanded means to steal Malawi away: 'We deeply regret that Malawi has decided to establish ties with China under Chinese threats and seduction' … [Taiwan] said China had offered Malawi $6 billion to get it to switch sides and criticized it for carrying out the move when President Chen Shui-bian was visiting Latin America … The foreign minister of Taiwan, James Huang, warned last week that China would try to embarrass Taipei around the time of Taiwan's legislative elections – they were held on Saturday [12 January] – and Chen's trip to Latin America. Huang had to drop a visit to Malawi this month [January 2008] – intended to shore up diplomatic support – because the African nation declined to receive him. Malawi is the third ally of Taiwan to defect to Beijing in the past eighteen months. Chad switched sides in August 2006 and Costa Rica did so in June 2007.
>
> (www.iht.com, 14 January 2008)

> [DPP presidential candidate] Frank Hsieh … took over the party's leadership yesterday [14 January] … One aide said Mr Hsieh wanted to suggest that China and Taiwan extend annual charter flights for Chinese New Year and, ahead of the election, beyond the holiday period.
>
> (*FT*, 15 January 2008, p. 11)

1 February 2008.

> Taiwan will hold two referendums on joining the United Nations, the island's election commission says … on 22 March, the same day as the forthcoming presidential election … Taiwan has no seat at the UN, having lost it to China in 1971. Its attempts to regain membership have been blocked … The Democratic Progressive Party-proposed referendum would ask whether voters 'agree that the government should seek to join the UN in the name of Taiwan to express Taiwanese people's will and enhance Taiwan's international status' … The referendum proposed by the opposition KMT [Kuomintang] will meanwhile ask whether the island should seek to 'return to the UN with a pragmatic and flexible approach'. The KMT referendum proposes joining the UN using either the official name, Republic of China, or any other suitable designation. The United States has already said it strongly opposes both parties' proposals.
>
> (www.bbc.co.uk, 1 February 2008)

13 March 2008.

> Outgoing President Chen Shui-bian: 'Some people may say the window of opportunity for Taiwan independence has already been closed. But I agree

even more with the view that the opportunity of Taiwan and the Chinese mainland merging, unifying, is becoming ever more remote' ... Mr Chen also challenged the claim that China's communist government inherited sovereignty over Taiwan when it won China's civil war against Kuomintang nationalist forces in 1949. This argument rests on the claim that sovereignty over the island, a Japanese colony from 1895 to 1945, was passed to the Republic of China in the 1943 Cairo Declaration by President Franklin Roosevelt of the United States, Winston Churchill, then the UK's prime minister, and Chiang Kai-shek ... Chen Shui-bian: 'Very clearly [the declaration] does not carry a date. And secondly the three leaders did not sign it. Moreover, afterwards they did not affirm it, let alone authorize its validity. Therefore, this is not a communiqué. It is merely a press release statement' ... Pro-independence campaigners in Taiwan have long argued that China never regained sovereignty over the island after Japan's defeat in the Second World War. However, this is the first time a Taiwanese president has embraced the argument ... According to opinion polls, more than 70 per cent of Taiwan's citizens see themselves as Taiwanese rather than Chinese, up from about 30 per cent before the Democratic Progressive Party took power ... While Ma Ying-jeou advocates forming a 'common market' with China and the Kuomintang still embraces the goal of eventually unification with the mainland, Ma has promised not to enter into talks with China on unification if elected. He has also opposed the 'one country, two systems' formula China sees as a solution for Taiwan and has declared that Taiwan independence as a future option cannot be excluded.

(*FT*, 14 March 2008, p. 7)

In the past two months the governing democratic Progressive Party has relaxed more and more restrictions on economic activity across the Taiwan Strait. It has allowed visits by Chinese tourists on international cruise ships, granted Chinese nationals married to Taiwanese citizens the right to work and is relaxing some restrictions on investment in China, including lifting a ban on indirect China-bound investment by local banks ... In February [2008] nearly 700 Chinese tourists arrived on a cruise ship. But after President Chen Shui-bian claimed that his efforts had paved the way for the new opening, the government in Beijing immediately said Chinese cruise passengers may not visit in future.

(*The Economist*, 15 March 2008, pp. 80–1)

16 March 2008.

Hundreds of thousands of people are expected to take part in rival political rallies across Taiwan. What is known as Super Sunday is the last chance for big weekend rallies before polls to elect a new president. The events, organized by the two main political parties, are also aimed at expressing public opposition to China's anti-secession law. Passed three years ago, it legalizes the use of force against Taiwan if the island formally declares independence.

(www.bbc.co.uk, 16 March 2008)

> In the final day of campaigning ahead of the island's presidential election Saturday [22 March] both major political parties condemned Beijing's suppression of protest in Tibet ... The ruling party of outgoing President Chen Shui-bian seized on the violence in Tibet ... as a warning of what could lie in store for the island if it was reunited with the mainland ... Ma Ying-jeou called for an end to the 'violence used by Beijing authorities'.
>
> (www.iht.com, 17 March 2008)

'Ma Ying-jeou said he would "not rule out" a boycott [of the Olympic Games] if the crackdown worsened' (www.bbc.co.uk, 18 March 2008).

18 March 2008.

> Prime minister Wen Jiabao yesterday [18 March] restated China's opposition to two referendums to be held alongside Saturday's election over whether Taiwan should seek its own UN membership, declaring that regional peace and security would be threatened were they to pass. Ma Ying-jeou responded that Mr Wen's remarks were 'barbarically unreasonable, arrogant, stupid and self-righteous'. He also threatened to boycott the Beijing Olympics over the recent violence in Tibet 'if the Chinese authorities continue to suppress the Tibetan people and the situation worsens'.
>
> (*FT*, 19 March 2008, p. 10)

20 March 2008.

> China's suppression of protests in Tibet and missteps by the opposition Nationalist Party have created a close race in Taiwan's presidential election on Saturday [22 March], as a seemingly insuperable lead for the Nationalist candidate, Ma Ying-jeou, has narrowed considerably, politicians and political analysts said ... The Democratic Progressive Party's candidate Frank Hsieh received an influential endorsement on Thursday [20 March]. Lee Teng-hui, a former Nationalist president of Taiwan, who now favours much greater political independence from the mainland, said that he would vote for Hsieh ... An unusual fracas last week has helped the Democratic Progressive Party warn voters against giving too much power to the Nationalists. Four Nationalist lawmakers roamed through Hsieh's campaign headquarters in an attempt to document whether the building lease complied with election laws. Hsieh's aides trapped the four in an elevator, accused them of trespassing and called the police ... Ma has apologized repeatedly since then ... Up through the middle of last week opinion polls had shown Ma with a lead of 20 percentage points. Taiwan election laws do not allow the release of polls during the final ten days before voting. But continuing surveys by both parties show that much of that lead has evaporated, with Ma now ahead by only a slender margin, politicians and political analysts said.
>
> (www.iht.com, 20 March 2008; *IHT*, 21 March 2008, p. 5)

'Ma Ying-jeou says it [the status quo] could go on like this for fifty years' (www.iht.com, 20 March 2008).

> In his state-of-the-union address to the Chinese parliament earlier this month, premier Wen Jiabao reiterated China's position: 'We will never allow anyone to separate Taiwan from the motherland in any guise or by any means. Reunification of the two sides is inevitable in the course of the great rejuvenation of the Chinese nation.'
>
> (www.bbc.co.uk, 22 March 2008)

> The military crackdown in Tibet and a warning from Wen Jiabao, the prime minister of China, that independence for either Tibet or Taiwan would be intolerable has helped the Democratic Progressive Party (DPP) candidate Frank Hsieh. He has narrowed a double-digit deficit in unpublished opinion polls and pulled within 5 percentage points of Ma Ying-jeou ... Mr Ma tried to shore up his flagging support by taking a tough stance against China's action. He threatened to boycott the Beijing Olympics should the bloodshed continue. Even that may have backfired, however. Rather against the odds Taiwan's baseball team this month [March] qualified for the Games – a triumph relished by the island's many baseball fans. Sabre-rattling by Beijing might be counter-productive in another way, too, improving the chances that two referendums to be held along with the presidential election, both of which China hopes will be roundly defeated, might actually be approved. One asks whether Taiwan should apply to join the United Nations using the name 'Taiwan'; the other asks if it should apply using 'the Republic of China' (its formal nomenclature) or something else. Parts of the Kuomintang [KMT] had been calling for a boycott of the referendums, which require a 50 per cent turnout for the result to be valid ... The KMT's ambitions for closer ties with China, including even a peace treaty and a 'Great China' common market, now look less like vote winners ... Mr Hsieh has taken every opportunity to label the 'Great China' market a 'One China' market, insisting the policy is tantamount to surrender to the communists. He has spread fears that under the plan Chinese workers and products would flood Taiwan, even though Mr Ma has repeatedly insisted that this would not be allowed to happen. The DPP has also attacked Mr Ma's planned peace treaty, claiming it would lead Taiwan to a destiny no different from that of Tibet, which signed an agreement with China in 1951 promising it great autonomy. In self-defence Mr Ma has reiterated his three 'noes' policy towards China – 'no independence, no unification and no military conflict'.
>
> (www.economist.com, 21 March 2008)

'Ma Ying-jeou has proposed a formal peace treaty with Beijing that would demilitarize the Taiwan Strait. But he has drawn the line at unification, promising it would not be discussed during his presidency' (www.guardian.co.uk, 22 March 2008).

21 March 2008.

> Ma Ying-jeou mooted an Olympic boycott, while Frank Hsieh warned that his rival could make Taiwan a 'second Tibet' ... Earlier this week Ma Ying-jeou talked of a possible Olympic boycott if the situation in Tibet deteriorated, but on Friday [21 March] he said he would not 'push the issue to the extreme' ... Before the protests in Tibet began, election campaigning had focussed primarily on economic issues.
>
> (www.bbc.co.uk, 21 March 2008)

> [During the campaign] Frank Hsieh, pointing to China's crackdown on Tibet, said the same thing could happen to Taiwan if it gets too close to Beijing. Ma Ying-jeou disagreed: 'Taiwan is not Tibet. Neither is it Hong Kong. We are a sovereign country and a democratic country.'
>
> (www.cnn.com, 22 March 2008)

> Ma Ying-jeou is not a charismatic figure. He calms rather than inspires. He is a soft spoken administrator who promises to govern by consultations. And he is just what many Taiwanese seem to want in a new president after eight years of tempestuous domestic politics and butting heads with China on the international front ... Independence is anathema to some leaders in the Nationalist Party who favour reunification with China. Ma has made it clear, though, that he is not willing to discuss eventual union with Beijing ... Ma has another weapon in his armoury – a Mr Clean reputation ... Ma, who has a doctorate in law from Harvard, is presenting himself as an exemplar of integrity with a track record of fighting corruption even in his own party.
>
> (www.iht.com, 23 March 2008)

22 March 2008.

> Ma Ying-Jeou won [the presidential election] by a convincing margin ... Ma prevailed 58.45 per cent to 41.55 per cent and Frank Hsieh quickly conceded defeat ... His inauguration [is] scheduled for 20 May ... [There was] a heavy voter turnout of 75.7 per cent ... Both parties' polls showed an increasingly close race in the final days of campaigning, in contrast with the last polls by media organizations nearly two weeks ago, which showed Ma ahead by 20 per cent. But in election day interviews voters echoed Ma's stance that close relations with the mainland and its fast-growing economy represent the island's best hope of returning to the rapid economic growth it enjoyed until the late 1990s.
>
> [Ma has attended] annual vigils for those killed during the Tiananmen Square killings in Beijing in 1989 and denounced the mainland's repression of the Falun Gong spiritual movement over the past decade. During the campaign he ruled out any discussion of political reunification while calling for the introduction of direct, regularly scheduled flights to Shanghai and Beijing and an end to Taiwan's extensive limits on its companies' ability to invest on the mainland ... His party and two tiny affiliated parties together

> took three-quarters of the legislature in January elections. Nationalists also serve as the magistrates, a position akin to mayor, in fifteen of Taiwan's twenty-five cities … Two controversial referendums, calling for Taiwan to apply for membership in the United Nations, fell well short of passage. Taiwan's referendum law requires a majority of eligible voters to vote on a referendum for it to be valid. Nationalists called for voters not to cast ballots for either initiative and slightly less than 36 per cent of eligible voters did so.
>
> (www.iht.com, 22 March 2008)

'The two plebiscites were approved by more than 80 per cent of votes cast but failed to pass because they did not meet the threshold of 50 per cent turnout' (*FT*, 24 March 2008, p. 4).

'Many Taiwanese waiting to cast their votes identified the faltering economy as their top priority' (www.bbc.co.uk, 22 March 2008).

> Ma Ying-jeou said he would like to work towards a peace treaty with Beijing, but would only do so if China removed missiles pointed at Taiwan … He ruled out an immediate visit to mainland China, but said he would focus on improving relations by 'substantive means', including direct flights. No incumbent president has visited the Chinese mainland since the Kuomintang was forced to retreat to Taiwan in 1949 … On Saturday [22 March] Mr Ma said economic normalization would take priority over concluding a peace treaty, which he said would be conditional on the removal of what Taiwan says are some 1,000 missiles aimed at the island.
>
> (www.bbc.co.uk, 23 March 2008)

23 March 2008.

> In Sunday's [23 March] further comments, Ma Ying-jeou acknowledged that the issue of sovereignty was the most difficult problem affecting bilateral relations, adding that mutual recognition was 'out of the question'. Instead, he proposed a middle road of 'mutual non-denial'. He said: 'We will not deny their existence but we cannot recognize their sovereignty [over Taiwan].'
>
> (www.bbc.co.uk, 23 March 2008)

> He will become the first non-native Taiwanese to become president. Ma Ying-jeou was born in Hong Kong to Chinese parents … The Kuomintang banned direct flights with China after they fled to Taiwan at the end of the Chinese civil war in 1949 … No incumbent president has visited the Chinese mainland since [1949].
>
> (www.bbc.co.uk, 24 March 2008)

> Ma Ying-jeou … said Sunday [23 March] he had no immediate plans to visit China and would work to fulfil his campaign pledge to improve relations with the communist neighbour, starting direct flights, allowing more tourists to visit and helping the island's financial industry to go to the

mainland … Ma Ying-jeou: 'I think the most urgent job for us to do is to solve many of the urgent problems in terms of our relations with mainland China. For instance, direct flights, to allow mainland tourists to come to Taiwan, to allow our financial services industry to go to the mainland' … Although thousands of Taiwanese have invested in China in recent years, the island still maintains a ban on direct shipping and air links across the 100-mile (160-kilometre-wide) Taiwan Strait. The government has also been cautious about relaxing restrictions on sensitive or strategic industries – like finance and technology – that want a bigger piece of China's booming market.

(www.cnn.com, 23 March 2008)

President-elect Ma Ying-jeou said Sunday [23 March] that he would pursue closer economic relations with mainland China, confidence-building measures to reduce the chance of an accidental war and eventually a peace agreement with Beijing … While Ma called repeatedly Sunday for closer relations with the mainland, he also showed again that, unlike some nationalist politicians, he is willing to criticize China in frank terms … He again denounced the Chinese crackdown in Tibet, saying Sunday that the Dalai Lama would be welcome in Taiwan and even describing him as a 'lovable Tibetan leader'. Ma said he supported the Dalai Lama's calls for autonomy within China. But while Ma repeated previous statements that he could not rule out a Taiwanese boycott of the Beijing Olympics if the crackdown continued and the situation in Tibet deteriorated further, he was also wary of tying the relationship with China to Tibet. He referred to Taiwan by its legal name, the Republic of China, and said it was a 'sovereign nation' with a completely different status from Tibet's … He said: 'I strongly condemn what they did in Tibet but I would never make a linkage between Tibet and Taiwan' … Ma repeated Sunday his earlier statements that he had no plans to visit the mainland and questioned the value of meetings between top leaders. 'Usually they are more ceremonial than substantive,' he said, adding that contacts between senior aides were often more productive.

(www.iht.com, 23 March 2008)

Ma Ying-Jeou, fifty-seven, offered on Sunday [23 March] a mechanism and a formula for achieving a peace agreement with the mainland. For starters he said that peace negotiations should be handled through two semi-official foundations set up with government backing in the early 1990s: the Straits Exchange Foundation, which Ma helped establish on the Taiwan side, and Beijing's Association for Relations Across the Taiwan Strait … The trickier task is to find a formula that balances Beijing's position that Taiwan is a breakaway province and Taiwan's position that it is a sovereign country as the legal continuation of the Republic of China, the government that replaced imperial rule in China. Ma said he accepted the so-called 1992 consensus, in which Taiwanese and mainland officials reached an informal document that there is one China but that the two sides interpret it differently.

> Ma offered another formulation Sunday, saying that sovereignty issues were too difficult to resolve but that the two sides would have to move beyond denying the legal existence of each other. He described the approach as 'mutual non-denial', while providing few details ... [He] continues to castigate Chinese leaders for human rights abuses and support the Dalai Lama's calls for Tibetan autonomy ... Ma may be at a disadvantage in reassuring Taiwan's people that he can strike a hard bargain with Beijing because he comes from a mainland family and was born in Hong Kong – although with a Taiwan connection, as he mentioned on Sunday ... He said: 'I was biologically conceived in Taiwan, although I was born in Hong Kong, so technically I was made in Taiwan' ... [He] obtained his doctorate [in law at Harvard] in 1981 ... [He has] two grown daughters, both of whom live in the United States ... The American Institute in Taiwan handles American diplomatic interests in the absence of full diplomatic relations ... Rebuilding Taiwan's relationship with the United States is part of a difficult balancing act that awaits Ma as he prepares for his inauguration on 20 May ... He needs to allay the suspicions of American conservatives who value Taiwan as a strategic counterweight to China and who remain distrustful of Ma's Nationalist Party because of its reluctance for years to approve the purchase of submarines and other military hardware first offered by President George W. Bush in 2001 ... Ma also has a long track record of infuriating Japan by arguing that it should hand over a cluster of small, contested islands to Taiwan – he even wrote his doctoral thesis at Harvard on the subject ... Ma said that Taiwan would be happy to accept Beijing's three-year-old offer of two pandas.
>
> (*IHT*, 24 March 2008, p. 4)

'Ma Ying-jeou is talking about confidence-building measures – a hot line between Taipei and Beijing is one idea – that would reduce the chance of an accidental military confrontation' (www.iht.com, 26 March 2008).

> Ma Ying-jeou said yesterday [23 March] that he expected to resume talks with Beijing through semi-official institutions, which had been interrupted since 1998. The institutions – Taiwan's Straits Exchange Foundation and Beijing's Association for Relations Across the Taiwan Strait – 'can become communication channels again', Mr Ma said ... The president-elect repeated that he would not discuss unification with China. He said: 'We are not negotiating Taiwan's future but how to end a state of hostility.'
>
> (*FT*, 24 March 2008, p. 4)

> The predictions were for a much narrower race. Yet Ma Ying-jeou won by a landslide ... Frank Hsieh began his political career as a lawyer defending opponents of the Kuomintang (KMT) regime. After admitting defeat this weekend he announced his retirement from politics ... The Kuomintang [is] a party historically dominated by mainlanders who had fought – and eventually lost – the civil war with the Chinese communists ... The Kuomintang

> Party … has traditionally advocated eventual reunification … Ma Ying-jeou promises to be 'a peacemaker not a troublemaker' after what he calls Chen Shui-bian's 'adventurism' … Mr Ma describes China as an economic opportunity but a security threat … Mr Ma wants to build mutual trust and advocates a peace treaty between the two sides, something President Hu Jintao has also endorsed. The starting point, says the president-elect, should be the '1992 consensus', in which both China and Taiwan agreed that there was but 'one China', while begging to differ on how to define it.
>
> (www.economist.com, 24 March 2008)

'Ma Ying-jeou … mentioned that he attends a memorial each year for the victims of the 1989 Tiananmen Square massacre' (www.economist.com, 26 March 2008).

> Of 1 million Taiwanese lining and working there [the mainland] some 200,000 came home to vote … Ma Ying-jeou, a Mandarin speaker, mugged up on the local Taiwanese language and showed that it was possible to campaign as if ethnic divisions had been healed – we are all Taiwanese now. That appealed especially to younger voters less haunted by the bitter past … Chen Shui-bian had come to office in 2000 as the champion of native-born Taiwanese resentful of the Kuomintang, a party dominated by those with roots in mainland China … 'Mutual non-denial' is Ma Ying-jeou's contribution to the arcane vocabulary of cross-strait theology. It is, in effect, a promise no longer to challenge the status quo, in which Taiwan is sovereign in fact though not in law … he is likely to press President George W. Bush for F-16 fighter jets, which Chen Shui-bian never got.
>
> (*The Economist*, 29 March 2008, p. 75)

> Already by May 2000 – the month President Chen Shui-bian first took office – polls indicated that a mere 23 per cent of Taiwan's citizens wanted unification with China either right away or the status quo now with unification later. By August 2007 the proportion favouring immediate or eventual unification had fallen to 14 per cent. Some 53 per cent preferred the status quo of de facto independence either indefinitely or with a decision to be made in the future, and 27 per cent wanted *de jure* independence either immediately or eventually. (In May 2000 around 17 per cent wanted immediate or eventual *de jure* independence.) Another poll indicated that in 2007 four out of five Taiwanese rejected the 'one country, two systems' formula the People's Republic of China proposes for solving the 'Taiwan problem'. Yet still other polls indicated that up to 80 per cent of Taiwan citizens rejected the claim the Republic of China is not a sovereign country or the notion that citizens of China should have a say in Taiwan's future. Some 75 per cent to 80 per cent wanted to enter the United Nations under one name or another … Ma Ying-jeou took a number of decisive steps to align his presidential campaign with Taiwan-centric consciousness … the widely shared consciousness that Taiwan is an autonomous entity with a distinctive history and a right to

> determine its own future free from interference by foreign countries … He began as early as the mid-1990s to learn to speak Taiwanese. Native speakers report that the results are mixed, but many express appreciation that Mr Ma made the efforts. Of more immediate political import, during the eight months preceding the election Mr Ma put some of his Taiwanese (and, to a lesser extent, Hakka … the Republic of China's various communal groups including Taiwanese, Mainlanders, Hakkas and Aboriginals) to use during a series of 'long-stay' visits to various parts of the island where Mainlanders are few and where suspicion that a Mainlander president might sell Taiwan out was common. Candidate Ma sought to engage average voters during his long-stay visits … His long-stay visits were widely reported and evidently helped convince many Taiwanese that voting for Mr Ma would be 'safe' … He has spent almost his entire life in Taiwan and has never even visited the people's Republic of China.
>
> (Daniel Lynch, www.feer.com, March 2008)

'With thirty-four female lawmakers now, or 30 per cent of the total, Taiwan was well above the international average of 17.8 per cent … [compared with] 20.6 per cent in China' (www.iht.com, 2 April 2008).

> Taiwanese investment on the mainland has dropped by nearly half during Chen Shui-bian's nearly eight years in office, to about $2 billion a year, as he enforced limits on how much capital could be invested by Taiwanese companies on the mainland – limits that [President-elect] Ma Ying-jeou said he would lift.
>
> (*IHT*, 25 March 2008, p. 12)

> China is already Taiwan's largest trading partner and investment destination. Taiwanese companies' cumulative investment FDI … in China … might be close to $300 billion, according to the [Taiwanese] government's latest estimates – which would make Taiwan China's largest source of FDI … [Critics say that] the ceiling [set by Taiwan] which limits companies' investments in China at 40 per cent of their net worth has failed to discourage them from mainland investments. It has just discouraged them from repatriating profits to Taiwan for fear of not being able to use the funds for further expansion on the mainland … The government [currently] bans the sale on the island of mutual funds that invest more than a tiny portion in China-linked equities … An estimated 2 million Taiwanese now live in Shanghai … Martial law was lifted in 1987 and democracy introduced in the early 1990s … In the early phase of his campaign Ma Ying-jeou said that his party's long-term goal remained eventual reunification. But he takes the position that, for now, Taiwan is a sovereign country.
>
> (*FT*, 26 March 2008, p. 13)

25 March 2008.

> The Defense Department announced Tuesday [25 March] that the United States had mistakenly shipped to Taiwan four electrical fuses designed for

use on intercontinental ballistic missiles but had since recovered them ... [The fuses] contained no nuclear material. They had been delivered to Taiwan in 2006 ... in or around August ... and were sent instead of helicopter batteries that had been ordered by Taiwan ... The error is particularly disturbing, [US] officials said, because of its indirect link to nuclear weaponry and because of the sensitivity of US arms sales to Taiwan, which China regularly denounces as provocative.

(*IHT*, 26 March 2008, p. 4)

The error is particularly sensitive because China vehemently opposes US arms sales to Taiwan ... Despite quarterly checks of the inventory, defence officials said they never knew the fuses were gone. Only after months of discussions with Taiwan about the missing batteries did the Pentagon finally realize, late last week, the gravity of what had happened ... Chinese leaders were informed of the mistake.

(www.iht.com, 26 March 2008)

26 March 2008.

A statement [issued by the Chinese foreign ministry on 26 March]: 'We ... demand the US side thoroughly investigate this matter and report to China in a timely manner the details of the situation and eliminate the negative effects and disastrous consequences created by this incident ... [China has brought a] serious representation [to Washington and China expresses] ... strong displeasure [over the error] ... [China demands an end to such weapons sales and military-to-military contacts between Washington and Taipei to] avoid damaging peace and stability in the Taiwan Strait and the healthy development of China–US relations.'

(www.cnn.com, 26 March 2008)

8 April 2008.

Ma Ying-jeou told the *Financial Times* that he would not personally engage in dialogue with Chinese leaders because this would be too controversial in Taiwan; he also said his government would take a gradual approach to deregulation of cross-Strait economic ties. Mr Ma hoped that Vincent Siew, Vice President-elect, could start building mutual trust through talks with members of the Chinese leadership at the Boao Forum for Asia in China at the weekend ... But he ruled out visiting China himself. He said: 'Once I go, you can imagine how many rumours would appear and how I would be discredited. Therefore, I believe that if I were to go, I would not necessarily be able to solve problems but it would cause me a lot of trouble' ... While he hopes to open non-stop charter flights to and from China every weekend and allow up to 3,000 Chinese to visit the island every year from July [2008], his government intends to move slowly on further cross-Strait economic deregulation.

(*FT*, 9 April 2008, p. 10)

'The incoming government [in Taiwan] has pledged to establish a weekly non-stop charter flight link with China by July [2008] ... Ma Ying-jeou has also promised voters that he will bring 3,000 Chinese tourists a day to Taiwan by July' (www.ft.com, 13 April 2008).

> From 11–13 April Taiwan's Vice President-elect, Vincent Siew, is to attend an economic forum on Hainan Island. China's president, Hu Jintao, will also be there and the two are expected to hold a meeting. Mr Siew, a former prime minister, will remain a private citizen until his inauguration on 20 May ... Ma Ying-jeou [has expressed] disapproval of proposed postage stamps marking his inauguration, which would use only the name 'Taiwan' ... In an interview with the *Financial Times* this week [published on 9 April] he said that it was natural for Mr Siew, a founding member of the Boao Forum, to visit China, but he himself would not go because this might generate negative 'rumours'. He apparently meant the concerns among DPP [Democratic Progressive Party] supporters that, in his haste for rapprochement, he might sell out Taiwan's interests.
>
> (*The Economist*, 12 April 2008, p. 66)

11–13 April 2008.

> Taiwan's Vice President-elect was to meet President Hu Jintao of China on Saturday [12 April] Siew would be the highest ranking elected Taiwanese figure to meet with China's president ... Beijing refuses to recognize the island's elected government and on Thursday [10 April] a Chinese foreign ministry spokeswoman referred to Siew only as chairman of the Cross-Strait Common Market Foundation, a private group that seeks to build economic co-operation between China and Taiwan.
>
> (www.iht.com, 11 April 2008)

'Vincent Siew was to meet Hu Jintao for twenty minutes on the sidelines of an economic forum in the southern resort of Boao' (www.iht.com, 12 April 2008).

> Taiwan's Vice President-elect Vincent Siew met with China's President Hu Jintao on Saturday [12 April] in the highest level political contact between the two governments in nearly sixty years. The meeting focussed on improving economic relations ... Hu Jintao: 'On this occasion I am happy to exchange opinions on the cross-Strait economy with Siew' ... [He was referring to the 160-kilometre-wide (100-mile-wide) strait between Taiwan and the mainland ... Siew, who was accompanied by a twelve-member Taiwanese delegation, said that closer economic relations between China and Taiwan would facilitate regional peace and improve the lives of ordinary Taiwanese and Chinese. He said: 'Reality proves that cross-Strait economic development is the common wish of people on both sides [of the Strait]' ... Taiwanese companies have already invested more than $100 billion on the mainland and in 2007 bilateral trade – heavily in Taiwan's favour – exceeded $80 billion.
>
> (www.cnn.com, 12 April 2008)

> China's President Hu Jintao held a historic meeting with Taiwan's Vice President-elect Vincent Siew. It was the highest level contact since their post-civil war split in 1949 … Before the meeting Vincent Siew said: 'I hope that through this meeting we can deepen the understanding between the two sides and also create a basis for common trust.'
>
> (www.bbc.co.uk, 12 April 2008)

13 April 2008.

> President Hun Jintao of China said he was thinking deeply about improving relations with Taiwan, state-run media reported Sunday [13 April], a day after an icebreaking meeting … Hu reportedly said the annual weekend conference in Boao, where businesspeople mix with world leaders, had 'inspired us to think deeply about Cross-Strait economic exchanges and co-operation under the new circumstances' … Hu endorsed two of Siew's key proposals: opening up Taiwan to more Chinese tourists and allowing weekend charter flights, Xinhua said. Direct air travel across the Taiwan Strait has been banned since the two sides split amid civil war in 1949 … [In the Xinhua report Hu Jintao said that] Taiwan had 'suffered twists and turns for reasons known to all' in recent years.
>
> (www.iht.com, 13 April 2008)

'The twenty-minute evening meeting was followed by more extensive talks Sunday [13 April]. This featured Siew, commerce minister Chen Deming of China and teams of industrialists and advisers on both sides' (*IHT*, 14 April 2008, p. 5).

'The Taiwan Strait is the most dangerous flashpoint in Asia … Much of China's increased defence spending is aimed at countering America's ability to keep Chinese forces from overrunning Taiwan' (editorial, *The Boston Globe*, *IHT*, 17 April 2008, p. 6).

> According to the Taiwanese government's latest count, Beijing has 1,400 tactical ballistic missiles pointed at Taiwan from the southern Chinese coast, as well as cruise missiles. That is up from just about 200 missiles when Chen Shui-bian took office in 2000.
>
> (www.feer.com, 19 April 2008)

14 April 2008.

> A landmark meeting over the weekend has 'started to thaw the ice' between Taiwan and China, according to Ma Ying-jeou … Mr Ma said he hoped negotiations across the Taiwan Strait could resume as soon as he takes office on 20 May … He said: 'Thanks to the … meeting, some of the barriers for the resumption of talks have been removed. The mainland authorities displayed goodwill at the forum' … [He said] Beijing had 'responded positively' to Taiwan's proposals of a further opening-up of the island to mainland tourists, including more direct flights.
>
> (www.bbc.co.uk, 14 April 2008)

Taiwan's central bank said yesterday [14 April] it would allow financial institutions to buy – but not yet sell – Chinese renminbi from individuals, in a step towards full convertibility between China's currency and the Taiwan dollar ... Ma Ying-jeou said this month [April] he aimed to allow convertibility on the main island of Taiwan this year [2008]. This would be vital to any opening of Taiwan to more mainland Chinese tourists, who would need to convert their renminbi to Taiwan dollars to make local purchases.

(*FT*, 15 April 2008, p. 8)

Chinese tourists were first officially admitted to Taiwan in 2002. But visits are capped at 1,000 a day and tourists must travel to the island via third locations because of restrictions on direct cross-strait flights ... President-elect Ma Ying-jeou has promised to reach agreement on more Chinese tourists and weekend cross-strait charter flights by early July [2008], expanding to weekday charters by the end of the year and regularly scheduled flights by summer 2009 ... Under the plan the cap would be tripled to 3,000 Chinese tourists a day, or more than 1 million per year. Last year [2007] 320,169 mainlanders visited Taiwan, only 81.900 of whom came as tourists, according to Taiwan's Mainland Affairs Council. The rest were listed as business travellers or 'others'. In a few years Ma hopes the cap could rise to 10,000 tourist visits per day.

(www.iht.com, 29 April 2008)

29 April 2008.

On Tuesday [29 April] Lien Chan, honorary chairman of the Kuomintang and a former Taiwan vice president, met the Chinese president ... Hu Jintao ... Taiwan's president-elect ... Ma Ying-jeou ... has stirred up controversy by announcing the appointment of Lai Shin-yuan as the next head of the Mainland Affairs Council (MAC). The MAC is the cabinet-level body responsible for Taiwan's relations with mainland China. Ms Lai's appointment is controversial because she is a former legislator of the Taiwan Solidarity Union, a political party that supports the island's independence from mainland China.

(www.economist.com, 30 April 2008)

Lai Shin-yuan ... has now said repeatedly she fully agrees with Ma Ying-jeou's cross-Strait stance ... She wrote in a February 2007 *Taipei Times* editorial: 'The blue-green struggle over the moot point of "unification versus independence" obscures the real problems concerning people's daily lives. Taiwan is a sovereign and independent nation. There is nothing to argue about. It is time to move on and leave this false debate behind.'

(www.feer.com, 9 May 2008)

5 May 2008.

Taiwan's deputy prime minister quit the governing [Democratic Progressive] Party Monday [5 May] to take responsibility for a diplomatic bungle

> that has cost the government millions of dollars. Chiou I-jen's announcement came three days after he acknowledged arranging for the foreign ministry to transfer $29.8 million to a Taiwanese man acting as an intermediary in a deal to try to get Papua New Guinea to officially recognize Taiwan. The man, Ching Chi-ju, and the money have disappeared … Chiou said … he did not take any bribes … Foreign minister James Huang said Friday [2 May] that the money was intended to be used as economic aid for Papua New Guinea, once it agreed to switch diplomatic relations from China to Taiwan. The effort was abandoned in late 2006 … China is recognized by 170 countries; Taiwan's diplomatic allies number twenty-three.
>
> (www.iht.com, 5 May 2008)

> Since 2000 Taiwan's foreign aid has become somewhat more transparent, with more aid distributed through the International Co-operation and Development Fund and third parties. The Taiwan foreign ministry says the island's total annual aid budget for its twenty-three allies is about $500 million.
>
> (www.iht.com, 8 May 2008)

> [On Friday 2 May] deputy prime minister Chiou I-jen … said two men hired to broker a deal with Papua New Guinea vanished in 2006 – along with the money – and were now being hunted … It [was] reported that Taiwan had begun legal proceedings to recover the assets, which were originally deposited in a Singapore bank account … held jointly by Wu Shih-Tsai, an ethnic Chinese in Singapore, and Taiwan-based Ching Chi-ju, who holds a US passport … The $30 million was intended as a deposit for negotiating a 'technical aid programme' with the South Pacific nation … The deal fell through, but the pair have not refunded the money. They are now being sought on charges of embezzlement.
>
> (www.bbc.co.uk, 5 May 2008)

'President-elect Ma Ying-jeou says he hopes Chinese students can be admitted to colleges on the island and inspire Taiwanese students to study harder' (www.iht.com, 5 May 2008).

6 May 2008.

> The foreign minister of Taiwan and two other top officials resigned Tuesday [6 May] over a botched attempt to win diplomatic recognition from Papua New Guinea, a scandal that has stirred public outrage against the outgoing government just two weeks before it is to step down … Foreign minister James Huang tendered his resignation over the case Tuesday. Vice premier Chiou I-jen also resigned from the cabinet, a day after he left the Democratic Progressive Party and said that he would retire from politics … He insisted Tuesday that he had not pocketed the money in the affair, amid [media] reports … that some of the $30 million may have been earmarked as kickbacks for Taiwan officials.

> Vice defence minister Ko Cheng-heng resigned later Tuesday ... In 2006 the government wired the $30 million to an account in Singapore that was controlled by two middlemen who had been enlisted by Taipei for the secret diplomatic gambit. After negotiations with Papua New Guinea foundered Taiwan requested the money back, but to no avail. Now one of the middlemen – Ching Chi-ju – is on the run ... Taiwan and China both refuse to establish official ties with countries that maintain ties with the other. All the major powers recognize Beijing, but the two sides have long competed for the allegiances of smaller countries, using promises of aid ... Now only twenty-three countries – mostly small, marginal ones – recognize Taiwan, compared with thirty when the ... [Democratic Progressive] Party took power in 2000.
>
> (www.iht.com, 6 May 2008; *IHT*, 7 May 2008, p. 4)

20 May 2008. 'Ma Ying-jeou was sworn in as president ... for a four-year term ... Vice President Vincent Siew was sworn in after Mr Ma' (www.bbc.co.uk, 20 May 2008).

> Ma Ying-jeou ... took office as Taiwan's president Tuesday [20 May] ... [saying]: 'We will adopt the principle of no independence, no unification and no use of force' ... In an interview last week ... he said it was highly unlikely that unification talks would be held 'within our lifetimes' ... In a break with his party's old guard, Ma has vowed not to negotiate with Beijing about unification during his term of office, which can stretch to 2016 if he is reelected to a second four-year term.
>
> (www.iht.com, 20 May 2008)

> Ma seemed to tie negotiations over Taiwan's political status to China's adopting the island's democratic system. He said: 'What matters is not sovereignty, but core values and way of life ... [I hope] that mainland China will continue to move toward freedom, democracy and prosperity for all the people.'
>
> (www.iht.com, 20 May 2008)

> President Ma Ying-jeou: 'Taiwan does not just want security and prosperity, it wants dignity. Only when Taiwan is no longer being isolated in the international arena can cross-Strait relations move forward with confidence ... In the light of our common Chinese heritage people on both sides should do their utmost to jointly contribute to the international community without engaging in vicious competition and the waste of resources.
>
> (*FT*, 21 May 2008, p. 12)

> Taiwanese prosecutors have announced they are mounting a corruption inquiry against ex-President Chen Shui-bian ... Prosecutors named Mr Chen as a suspect in a $450,000 embezzlement case. He denies wrongdoing. His wife, Wu Shu-chen, is already on trial in the same case, on charges of corruption and forgery.
>
> (www.bbc.co.uk, 20 May 2008)

'Chen Shui-bian's wife was indicted in December 2006 on charges of embezzling $484,000 from a special presidential fund' (www.iht.com, 20 May 2008).

23 May 2008. 'Taiwan and Beijing will resume direct talks next month, the chairwoman of the island's Mainland Affairs Council says. Lai Shin-yuan: "You will see very soon in June the beginning of institutional negotiations between the two sides"' (www.bbc.co.uk, 23 May 2008).

26 May 2008.

> The head of Taiwan's ruling party has departed for a six-day visit to China … Kuomintang (Nationalist Party) chairman Wu Poh-hsiung … is the first leader of a Taiwanese governing party to visit China since the two sides split in 1949 … Mr Wu will meet President Hu Jintao on Wednesday [28 May].
>
> (www.bbc.co.uk, 26 May 2008)

28 May 2008.

> The head of Taiwan's ruling party met with President Hu Jintao, the highest level encounter since the two sides split in 1949. Kuomintang (Nationalist Party) chairman Wu Poh-hsiung is in China for a six-day landmark visit … Hu Jintao: 'The love for compatriots shown by the whole Chinese people in time of disaster will become the power to drive co-operation between the compatriots across the strait and create the future together. We cannot guarantee there won't be any natural disasters … but through our mutual efforts we can ensure there is no war.'
>
> (www.bbc.co.uk, 28 May 2008)

President Hu Jintao:

> For half a month people from all circles in Taiwan have expressed their concern, love and generous support. The love for compatriots shown by the whole Chinese people in time of disaster will become the power to drive co-operation between the compatriots across the strait and create the future together. As long as both sides across the strait are concerned about each other and make exchanges with each other, a peaceful and stable development of relations across the strait can be expected.
>
> (www.iht.com, 28 May 2008)

> China and Taiwan agreed Thursday [28 May] to hold talks next month [June] on tourism and direct charter flights … An invitation sent by the Association for Relations Across the Taiwan Strait, the body set up to deal with relations with Taiwan, was accepted by Taiwan's Straits Exchange Foundation. Chiang Pin-kung (foundation chairman): 'We will organize a delegation. We have already reached general agreement on those issues and I hope our two associations can complete the talks under our good interaction' … The official Xinhua news agency said the Taiwan foundation was

> asked to send a delegation to Beijing from 11–14 June to discuss chartered flights across the Taiwan Strait and the issue of mainland tourists going to Taiwan. There are currently no regular scheduled flights between the mainland and Taiwan, with only a few chartered flights on holidays. Tourists from the mainland are also limited … Earlier this month (May) Chinese pressure thwarted Taiwan's bid for observer status in the World Health Assembly, a UN body.
>
> (www.iht.com, 29 May 2008)

'Bilateral talks had been suspended for a decade … China and Taiwan held regular consultations after a "consensus" was agreed in 1992. But the talks broke off acrimoniously as some Taiwanese politicians began to lean towards independence' (www.bbc.co.uk, 29 May 2008).

12 June 2008.

> For the first time in nine years representatives of China and Taiwan met formally [in Beijing] on Thursday [12 June] … China's official news agency Xinhua reported Thursday that the two official bodies – China's Association for Relations Across the Taiwan Straits and Taiwan's Straits Exchange Foundation – had agreed to set up offices in each other's capitals and exchange visits of high ranking officials … Negotiators from Taiwan and China opened their first formal talks in almost a decade … aiming to forge an agreement on expanded charter flights as a step towards restoring transport links severed fifty-nine years ago … The nineteen-member Taiwanese team is being led by Chiang Pin-kung, chairman of the … Straits Exchange Foundation, and includes two vice cabinet ministers – the highest ranking Taiwanese officials ever to participate in bilateral talks … Chen Yunlin [is the] head of Beijing's … Association for Relations Across the Taiwan Strait … The current [annual] level of … Chinese tourists to Taiwan … [is] about 80,000 … Charter flights are now limited to four holiday periods each year, for a total of 324 annual flights … They are packed with Taiwanese residents on the mainland returning home to visit family.
>
> (www.iht.com, 12 June 2008)

> Officials from China and Taiwan agreed Thursday [12 June] to set up permanent offices in each other's capitals to help co-ordinate future discussions on bringing the two sides closer together … The legislative body in Taiwan passed a bill amendment on Thursday to allow the renminbi to be exchanged in Taiwan … The Taiwanese government's financial supervisory commission and the central bank are now expected to work out details of the currency exchange. The bill amendment and the mechanism to be worked out by the financial institutions are intended only to allow mainland tourists to exchange renminbi for Taiwanese dollars. There are no provisions for allowing two-way convertibility between the currencies or for Taiwanese to buy renminbi.
>
> (www.iht.com, 12 June 2008; *IHT*, 13 June 2008, p. 2)

'The offices could reduce the chances of misunderstanding if tensions were to arise over issues like military manoeuvres' (www.iht.com, 13 June 2008).

'On their first day of talks the two sides agreed to set up representative offices to handle visas in each other's territories' (*The Economist*, 14 June 2008, p. 72).

'[The representative] offices will perform some consular functions' (*Guardian*, 13 June 2008, p. 27).

13 June 2008.

> Representatives of China and Taiwan agreed Friday [13 June] to start weekend charter flights next month [July] between the two sides ... President Ma Ying-jeou has said he would like to begin regular commercial service by 2009. The agreement reached Friday says the service would start on 4 July and begin with thirty-six flights per weekend between various cities ... That number could grow with demand. Chinese and Taiwanese airlines will each operate eighteen flights.
>
> (www.iht.com, 13 June 2008)

> China and Taiwan signed historic agreements to establish regular direct flights and allow more mainland tourists to visit the island. The deal means there will be more cross-strait flights every weekend, instead of just during holiday periods ... Early on Friday [13 June] they signed a deal to boost transport and tourism links ... The weekend passenger flights will begin on 4 July and there will be thirty-six flights each week, with China and Taiwan operating eighteen flights each. Previously direct flights were limited to four holiday periods each year. On other days cross-strait travellers had to fly via Hong Kong or Macao. From 18 July each side will also allow in 3,000 tourists per day – a move that triples the number of mainland Chinese who will be allowed into Taiwan.
>
> (www.bbc.co.uk, 13 June 2008)

> The Taiwanese delegation yesterday [12 June] said the two sides had agreed to have thirty-six non-stop charter flights every weekend from 4 July. The number of flights would be increased after the Beijing Olympic Games to ninety-six every weekend. Further talks on daily cargo flights and full regular scheduled direct flights would follow in three months.
>
> (*FT*, 13 June 2008, p. 8)

> Taiwan has quietly swallowed China's refusal to allow an early launch of charter cargo flights. China, it is thought, wants to protect its air cargo industry from Taiwanese competition ... Visitors to the Taiwan-controlled outlying islands of Kinmen and Matsu can already go directly.
>
> (*The Economist*, 14 June 2008, p. 72)

16 June 2008. 'Coastguard vessels from Taiwan entered Japanese waters near disputed islands to accompany a ship of protesters angry over the sinking nearby of a fishing boat from Taiwan, Tokyo said' (www.iht.com, 16 June 2008).

Nine Taiwanese coastguard vessels entered Japanese waters Monday [16 June] near disputed islands in the East China Sea to accompany a ship of protesters angry over the sinking nearby of a fishing boat from Taiwan, officials said. Japan immediately denounced the incident as a violation of its territorial waters, amid a spike in tensions over the islands, known as Diaoyutai in Chinese and Senkaku in Japanese. Officials in Taiwan called it a mission to uphold its sovereignty over the disputed territory. The vessels and the protest ship were in Japanese waters for about two-and-a-half hours near the islands, defying warnings from Japanese patrol boats, the Japanese coastguard said ... Japan contends that the captain of a Taiwanese leisure fishing boat is responsible for the collision last week with a Japanese coastguard vessel off the disputed islands. The Taiwanese captain contends that the Japanese vessel rammed his craft. No one was injured in the incident ... Japanese administers the islands, which are claimed by Taiwan as well as China. The value of the islands ... has grown in recent years following the discovery of potentially rich gas reserves in the area ... The small, uninhabited islands are in rich fishing waters between the Japanese island of Okinawa and Taiwan. The islands were seized by Japan in 1895 when it colonized Taiwan. They were administered by the United States after World War II until control was turned over to Japan in 1972. Both Taiwan and China maintain that the islands have been theirs for centuries.

(www.iht.com, 17 June 2008)

18 June 2008.

President Ma Ying-jeou of Taiwan called Wednesday [18 June] for a rapid expansion of economic relations between Taiwan and mainland over the next year or two that would go far beyond the weekend charter flights and expanded tourism announced last Friday [13 June]. Ma said he wanted broad access for Taiwan financial services businesses to the mainland market, an end to double taxation by government agencies in Taipei and Beijing, and the removal of investment restrictions. He also called for direct sea and air cargo links across the Taiwan Strait, regularly scheduled passenger flights, the drafting of common technical standards for the high-tech industry by both sides and the creation of a dispute-resolution system for commercial disagreements ... Ma said he wanted to open up cross-strait maritime shipping links that could get fresh fruit to the mainland in ten hours, in contrast to the four-day trip to Hong Kong ... Ma said he hoped China would agree to let Taiwan apply to international organizations if the island joined under a name other than Taiwan. One possibility, he said, would be to apply to join groups using the name of Chinese Taipei, which the Olympic committee here [in Taiwan] has been using since the late 1970s, and which the WTO now uses as well. He said: 'The name we are going to use in international organizations can vary. Without using Taiwan the mainland side should be slightly more agreeable than they were before ... [But] the mainland and the United States are opposed to our admission to any organization that requires statehood as a threshold. So we still have a long way to go' ... Only twenty-three countries, like Panama and Paraguay, still have diplomatic relations with Taiwan, while 171 recognize Beijing ... President Hu Jintao told a Taiwanese negotiator last Friday [13 June] that he was certain that a way could be found to address this competition, Ma said, warning that he did not want to see any more of Taiwan's allies lured away.

(www.iht.com, 18 June 2008; *IHT*, 19 June 2008, p. 4)

19 June 2008.

All Taiwan citizens can now travel to China on a money-saving ferry ride across the narrow Taiwan Strait, the cabinet announced Thursday [19 June] ... Starting Thursday anyone from Taiwan can fly to the strait islands of Kinmen or Matsu, a short domestic plane ride, then board ferries that run between those islands and Fujian province, in southern China, the cabinet decided. Previously only a few people could take the ferries ... Since the outlying island ferry routes opened in 2001, only residents of those sparsely populated islets and Taiwan businessmen based in China, plus a handful of others with special missions in China, have been allowed to use them ... The decision follows landmark talks last week between China and Taiwan. The two sides agreed to start direct weekend charter flights on 4 July. For security reasons these flights will detour through Hong Kong airspace and are likely to cost more than travel to Fujian via the outlying islands, local media say.

(www.iht.com, 19 June 2008)

30 June 2008.

Taiwan has lifted some restrictions on Chinese currency exchange ... For the first time Chinese bank notes will be officially available at authorized Taiwanese banks. They will also be available at foreign currency trading counters at tourist hotels, airports and gift stores ... From next month [July] up to 3,000 Chinese tourists will be allowed to visit Taiwan each day. The move will provide a legal channel for them to exchange their money for local currency to spend in Taiwan. The absence of a currency exchange service between Taiwan and China had led to rampant black market currency trading. Under the new regulations, anyone will be able to buy or sell Chinese yuan at authorized institutions, although the government has initially set a cap of 20,000 yuan – just under $3,000 – for each transaction. Yuan conversion by institutions and companies will still be barred ... Until now the conversion of Chinese currency could only take place on Taiwan's outlying islands of Matsu and Kinmen.

(www.bbc.co.uk, 30 June 2008)

4 July 2008.

Thirty-six round-trip routes will open between Taiwan and China ... eliminating wasteful Hong Kong or Macao stopovers ... Airports, airlines and travel agents [in Taiwan] are scrambling to prepare for Friday's [4 July] flights ... The flights run between Taiwan and the Chinese cities of Beijing, Guangzhou, Nanjing, Shanghai and Xiamen and back. Although the routes are dubbed weekend charters, they run Friday through Monday [7 July]. Only travel agents can sell tickets. President Ma Ying-jeou said he estimates 50 million Chinese would want to visit Taiwan.

(www.iht.com, 3 July 2008)

Six China-based airlines and five from Taiwan will operate thirty-six weekly round trips. Direct flights shave as much as six hours off the journey across the 161 kilometre, or 100 mile, Taiwan Strait ... Taiwan will admit as many as 3,000 mainland tourists a day starting 18 July. Spending by Chinese tourists overseas rose 11.8 per cent to $24.3 billion in 2006, the fastest growing of the top ten nations apart from South Korea, according to the World Tourism Organization.

(www.iht.com, 4 July 2008)

Beginning Friday [4 July] direct charter flights will shuttle as many as 12,000 mainland tourists to the island each weekend ... Now some in Taiwan are worried that Falun Gong could sour the mainland visitors' experience and hurt the tourist trade ... Falun Gong members ... say they will increase, not reduce, their presence at scenic sites ... Falun Gong ... has been banned on the mainland since 1999, but [members] can speak and gather freely in democratic Taiwan.

(www.iht.com, 3 July 2008; *IHT*, 4 July 2008, p. 5)

The opening [took place] on 4 July of regular direct charter flights between China and Taiwan ... These charters ... 'direct flights' ... must still take a lengthy detour through Hong Kong airspace. This is less cumbersome than the normal routine, which requires a landing and brief stopover in Hong Kong (or nearby Macao). But it still adds an hour and nearly 1,000 kilometres (625 miles) to the journey from Beijing to Taipei ... One sensitive site ... mainland tourists ... were not allowed to see was the memorial to Chiang Kai-shek ... The Chinese tourists were also prohibited from leaving their chaperoned groups.

(*The Economist*, 12 July 2008, p. 67)

About 4 million Taiwanese visit the mainland annually – travelling via Hong Kong and Macao, as do business people – and 1 million live there ... Members of Falun Gong, the spiritual group outlawed as an 'evil cult' in China, have said they will increase their presence at tourist sites ... But Taiwanese officials said they will intervene to stop anti-communist activists from making protests directed at visitors.

(www.guardian.co.uk, 3 July 2008)

'[Some] 4 million Taiwanese travelled to the mainland each year ... Few Chinese were allowed to travel to Taipei at all until the thaw in relations prompted by President Ma Ying-jeou's election this spring' (*Guardian*, 5 July 2008, p. 30).

The first regular, direct flight from mainland China for nearly sixty years has landed at Taipei's airport … At the same time … a Taiwan-based … flight with Taiwanese tourists was making its way to Shanghai … The new flights, which will take place from Friday to Monday only, will connect five major cities in China with eight airports in Taiwan.

(www.bbc.co.uk, 4 July 2008)

[There is] a political disagreement over the Chinese words for the name of the Olympic delegation from Taiwan, known in English as Chinese Taipei. The Chinese word for the first part of the name is officially Zhonghua. That comes from Zhonghua Minguo, or Republic of China, the name that the officially dominant political group, the Kuomintang, prefers for Taiwan. Mainland China signed an agreement with Taiwan in 1989 recognizing Zhonghua Taipei – Chinese Taipei – as the name for Taiwan's delegation. Years earlier Taiwan had promised the International Olympic Committee that it would make a gesture to the mainland by changing its delegation's original name and not using the official Taiwanese flag or the national anthem in the Olympics. But sports officials on the mainland often call the Taiwanese delegation Zhongguo Taipei. Zhongguo, which means Middle Kingdom, is the Chinese name for China. Referring to the Taiwanese delegation as Zhongguo Taipei implies that the athletes and the island they represent are part of China … In the 1950s the Chinese Communists lobbied the International Olympic Committee to banish Taiwan from the Games. But in the Cold War era Taiwan had strong backing from the United States, so in 1958 China withdrew from the committee in protest. That self-imposed exile did not end until 1979, after the United States recognized the Communist government. Mainland China and Taiwan did not take part in the Summer Olympics together until the 1984 Games in Los Angeles.

(www.iht.com, 6 July 2008)

Last month [July] Chinese officials announced they would refer to the Taiwan delegation by its official name, Zhongguo Taipei, rather than Zhongguo Taipei, the name favoured by people on the mainland. Zhongguo Taipei implies that Taiwan is part of the mainland, and Taiwanese officials are threatening to boycott the Games if China uses it.

(www.iht.com, 5 August 2008)

18 July 2008.

China has promised that from Friday [18 July] it would allow up to 3,000 of its citizens to visit Taiwan every day … Nearly 2,000 Chinese tourists will arrive in Taiwan this weekend, all travelling in mandatory tour groups … Up until now China has tightly regulated the number of people allowed to travel to Taiwan, with fewer than 300,000 visiting each year, compared to nearly 5 million trips made to China by Taiwanese visitors … The first group [consisted] of more than 700 visitors.

(www.bbc.co.uk, 18 July 2008)

24 August 2008.

> Taiwan is considering construction of a bridge linking Kinmen, one of its outlying islands, to Xiamen, a city in south-east China [in Fujian province] ... Kinmen was long known as Quemoy. In 1958, in a battle that lasted forty-four days, Chinese artillery troops hit the island with 500,000 shells ... President Ma Ying-jeou, who was in Kinmen for the fiftieth anniversary of the 1958 artillery battle between Taiwan and China, also said his administration planned to offer landing visas or multiple visas to mainland Chinese visiting Kinmen, to increase tourism exchanges.
>
> (www.iht.com, 25 August 2008)

3 October 2008.

> The Bush administration announced plans Friday [3 October] to sell $6 billion in arms to Taiwan ... [including] Apache helicopters ... Patriot III anti-missile ... Harpoon missiles, Javelin missiles, upgrades for Taiwan's E-2T aircraft and spare parts for the Taiwan Air Force ... The announcement of the package ... came in a notification to Congress.
>
> (www.iht.com, 3 October 2008)

> The announcement Friday came three months after Admiral Timothy Keating, the top military commander in the Pacific, announced a freeze on US arms sales to Taiwan. Analysts speculated the decision reflected US reluctance to anger China before President George W. Bush attended the Olympics in Beijing in August.
>
> (www.iht.com, 5 October 2008)

'The United States [said it] intends to sell $6.4 billion in arms to Taiwan ... [The] State Department deputy spokesman ... indicated the administration expects congressional approval' (www.cnn.com, 4 October 2008).

> Patriot Advanced Capability missiles [are] intended to intercept missiles fired from the coast of Fujian province, opposite Taiwan, where China has stationed some 1,400 ... The 1979 Taiwan Relations Act obliges American administrations to sell Taiwan arms for its own defence. In 2001 President George W. Bush offered it many of the items in this package, such as the Patriots. But Ma Ying-jeou's Nationalist Party, the Kuomintang, in opposition at the time, blocked the purchase, arguing it was too expensive ... Only two of Taiwan's weaponry requests were declined – plans to build diesel-electric submarines and for sixty Black Hawk utility helicopters.
>
> (www.economist.com, 9 October 2008)

4 October 2008.

> On Saturday [4 October] a spokesman for the president's office in Taiwan thanked the United States ... [He] welcomed a US decision to sell the island $6.5 billion in advanced weaponry ... China warned the move would damage relations between Beijing and Washington.
>
> (www.iht.com, 5 October 2008)

'The weapons package was proposed in 2001, the first year of the Bush administration, but had been delayed by budget squabbles in Taiwan and political concerns in Washington' (www.iht.com, 5 October 2008). 'From Taiwan a government spokesman expressed appreciation to the United States and stressed that the leadership in Taipei wanted to maintain a strong defence while striving to improve relations with China' (*IHT*, 6 October 2008, p. 8).

> The arms package … Washington's biggest for Taiwan in more than fifteen years … Taipei welcomed the arms package … [It was] originally agreed by the Bush administration in 2001, but had been stalled by feuding in the Taiwanese legislature and US displeasure at former Taiwan president Chen Shui-bian. Despite its scale, the years of delay and a removal of some items from the package … means its impact on the military balance across the Taiwan Strait has been reduced. Analysts say Taiwan must rethink its defence strategy as China's rapid military modernization sharply reduces the island's ability to achieve air superiority.
>
> (*FT*, 6 October 2008, p. 9).

6 October 2008.

> China has cancelled or postponed several military exchanges with the United States … A [US] Defence Department spokesman … said the [arms] sale does not violate the Taiwan Relations Act, which allows the United States to provide Taiwan with items for self-defence.
>
> (www.cnn.com, 7 October 2008)

> China has abruptly cancelled a series of military and diplomatic contacts with the United States … Beijing has notified the United States that it would not go forward with several senior level visits and other co-operative military-to-military plans … The Chinese action … [includes] the cancellation of an upcoming visit to the United States by a senior Chinese general, other similar trips, several port calls by naval vessels and the indefinite postponement of meetings on stopping the spread of weapons of mass destruction … A [US] Defence Ministry spokesman … said the [arms] sale did not represent a change in US policy and that Washington was only upholding the provisions of the Taiwan Relations Act under which the United States makes available items necessary for Taiwan to maintain a sufficient self-defence.
>
> (www.iht.com, 7 October 2008)

'A number of senior level visits and military-to-military exchanges due before November would not go ahead … China will also not participate in an exchange on humanitarian assistance and disaster relief' (www.bbc.co.uk, 7 October 2008).

21 October 2008.

> Pro-independence protesters in southern Taiwan pushed an envoy from China to the ground on Tuesday [21 October] while shouting that their

> island does not belong to Beijing. The attack on vice chairman Zhang Mingqing of the Association for Relations Across the Taiwan Strait was shown on television news broadcasts … Pictures from Taiwan television stations showed about a dozen protesters surrounding Zhang at a Tainan temple commemorating Confucius, then toppling him to the ground shouting anti-communist and pro-independence slogans … The attack on Zhang comes several weeks before a planned visit by Chen Yunlin, Zhang's boss.
>
> (www.iht.com, 21 October 2008)

'Zhang Mingqing was pushed to the ground in a scuffle and a protester jumped on the roof of his vehicle' (www.bbc.co.uk, 21 October 2008).

'Zhang Mingqing … was visiting Taiwan as part of an academic symposium … One protester jumped onto Mr Zhang's car when he tried to leave' (*FT*, 22 October 2008, p. 12).

('Wang Ting-yu, a local Democratic Progressive Party politician, and six associates have been charged': *The Economist*, 1 November 2008, p. 69.)

25 October 2008.

> Tens of thousands of pro-independence Taiwanese have demonstrated against China, accusing President Ma Ying-jeou of failing to stand up to Beijing. The opposition marchers in Taipei highlighted a recent scare over dairy products in China and accused Taiwan's government of playing down the issue … During Saturday's march [25 October], organized by the Democratic Progressive Party [DPP], protesters shouted such slogans as 'Opposing toxic products, defending sovereignty' … Former Taiwan President Chen Shui-bian, also of the DPP, joined the marchers and was cheered by the crowd.
>
> (www.bbc.co.uk, 25 October 2008)

> Tens of thousands of opposition supporters marched through Taipei Saturday [25 October] to protest an upcoming visit by a senior Chinese envoy, saying the trip was part of Chinese efforts to assert control over Taiwan … Saturday's march snaked for several miles through Taipei … The protesters, many wearing T-shirts bearing the slogan 'Defend Taiwan', also accused President Ma Ying-jeou of making too many concessions and moving too fast in relaxing restrictions on trade and investment with China … A second round of high level talks is to be held in early November by Chen Yunlin, chairman of China's … Association for Relations Across the Taiwan Strait … and his Taiwanese counterpart, Chiang Pin-kung … Taiwanese officials say the discussions with Chen will be limited to economic issues, including the introduction of direct cargo flights and an expansion of current weekend passenger flights to daily service … Ma Ying-jeou: 'We will safeguard Taiwan's interest and we will see to it that Taiwan's sovereignty or dignity will not be harmed.'
>
> (www.cnn.com, 26 October 2008)

> About 600,000 people took to the streets of Taipei at the weekend in the biggest display of disapproval of President Ma Ying-jeou's policies since his election earlier this year … [The] largely peaceful rally lasted most of Saturday … The protest was organized by the opposition Democratic Progressive Party, but was also attended by others unhappy over the flagging economy … China's top negotiator, Chen Yunlin, is due to arrive in Taipei for a new round of talks within the next few weeks. Mr Chen would be the highest ranking Chinese official to have visited the island.
>
> (www.ft.com, 26 October 2008; *FT*, 27 October 2008, p. 10)

> The demonstration [against President Ma Ying-jeou] in Taipei on 25 October was the biggest yet. The opposition Democratic Progressive Party (DPP), which organized it, claimed 600,000 took part … The protest was sparked by the planned visit to Taiwan of Chen Yunlin, Beijing's top negotiator for Taiwan, starting on 3 November, the first Taiwan–China negotiations ever held on Taiwanese soil. Mr Chen will be the highest level Chinese official to visit Taiwan since the end of the civil war in 1949 … At least one-third of Taiwan's 23 million population think that the self-ruled democratic island should be independent … the island has seen far fewer [Chinese] visitors than Mr Ma's target of 3,000 a day.
>
> (*The Economist*, 1 November 2008, p. 68)

3 November 2008.

> The most senior Chinese official to visit Taiwan in nearly sixty years arrived on the island Monday [3 November] for economic talks. Chen Yunlin, president of the Association of Relations Across the Taiwan Strait, leads a delegation of sixty for talks this week with his counterpart, Chiang Pin-king, chairman of the Straits Exchange Foundation … The talks will avoid volatile political issues and focus instead on economic co-operation, [Chinese] state media reported. Chen Yunlin: 'The mission is clear and well-defined. No political issues pertaining to cross-straits relations will be involved, nor will Taiwan's internal political affairs' … President Ma Ying-jeou noted the 1,300 missiles pointed at Taiwan and said China should ease its military threat … Chinese and Taiwanese officials agreed in June [2008] to set up permanent offices in each other's territories, in the first formal talks between the two sides in almost a decade … Cross-straits talks between the two delegations began in 1993 … A second meeting [took place] in 1998, but Beijing cancelled a 1999 meeting.
>
> (www.cnn.com, 3 November 2008)

'The highest ranking Chinese official to visit Taiwan since the two sides split in 1949 arrived Monday [3 November] for economic talks … [on a] five-day visit' (www.iht.com. 3 November 2008).

> Negotiators for China and Taiwan signed agreements Tuesday [4 November] tripling the amount of direct cross-strait charter flights to 108 per week, shortening air routes and opening dozens of seaports for direct cargo links

> ... The agreements mean there can be direct flights seven days a week, compared with four days in another landmark agreement signed earlier this year [2008]. They will let direct cargo shipments pass between eleven Taiwan seaports and sixty-three in China, tax free. They will allow sixty cargo flights per month and establish a mechanism for ensuring food safety.
>
> (www.iht.com, 4 November 2008)

> The [charter] flights are expected to run daily, with twenty-one cities on the mainland and eight in Taiwan receiving service. The planes will also fly a direct line between cities over a route north of Taiwan. Currently charter flights between China and Taiwan have to take a longer route through Hong Kong airspace because of security concerns ... The governments will open direct shipping channels for passengers and cargo. China will open a total of sixty-three ports (forty-eight seaports and fifteen riverports) and Taiwan will open a total of eleven ... Ships will not fly national flags. The two governments also agreed to expand free exchange of information regarding food safety issues. If any product is considered faulty or dangerous a government will recall it and halt any shipping ... China and Taiwan also agreed to start direct mail service ... Chen Yunlin also said Tuesday that the mainland would give Taiwan two pandas as gifts before the year's end. Chen will accept two rare animals from Taiwan, an endangered goat and a spotted deer.
>
> (www.iht.com, 4 November 2008)

'Chen Yunlin offered two pandas to Taiwan in exchange for a Formosa sika deer and a Formosa serow, a goat-like animal' (www.cnn.com, 6 November 2008).

'A Formosa serow [is] a goat-like animal native to Taiwan' (www.bbc.co.uk, 6 November 2008).

> [The] sweeping pact allows direct shipping links across the Taiwan Strait for the first time since the civil war. The deal also expanded the number of weekly passenger flights from thirty-six to 108. Cargo flights would be allowed for the first time, with sixty crossing the strait each month ... Taiwan and China ... agreed Tuesday [4 November] to hold high level talks every six months and focus on building closer financial ties in the next round of meetings ... [They] began relaxing restrictions on flights in July when their envoys met in Beijing. They signed a deal that would allow flights from five mainland cities. Tuesday's agreement allows planes to take off from a total of twenty-one cities.
>
> (www.cnn.com, 4 November 2008)

> Direct charter flights ... can operate daily rather than four days out of seven ... Private jet flights will be allowed ... Direct postal links will be expanded to improve delivery time, currently up to ten days ... Food safety alerts will be set up.
>
> (www.bbc.co.uk, 4 November 2008)

'The [South Korean] government estimates that … Taiwan's businesses … have invested over $150 billion in China. But the aubsence of direct links marginalizes Taiwan from global supply chains' (*The Economist*, 8 November 2008, p. 69).

> President Ma Ying-jeou met with Chen Yunlin in Taipei on Thursday [6 November] … The meeting lasted only five minutes … The two officials exchanged gifts: Chen presented Ma with a painting of a horse (Ma's surname means horse) and Ma gave Chen a piece of fine porcelain … Chen did not address Ma as *zongtong* – president. Doing so would have implied that the mainland recognizes the de facto independent status of Taiwan … The previous night Chen had been trapped by protesters in a hotel … while attending a banquet there … Chen is set to watch *Cape No. 7*, a made-in-Taiwan blockbuster movie that has become a source of pride for the island and which is expected to be shown in China, the first Taiwan film to be allowed a screening in years.
>
> (www.iht.com, 6 November 2008)

'Protesters … surrounded a hotel where the Chinese envoy was having dinner, preventing him from leaving until after midnight' (www.iht.com, 10 November 2008).

'[There have been] continuing protests by Taiwanese pro-independence groups … President Ma Ying-jeou: "I did not concede an inch of Taiwan's sovereignty so as president I have not made any mistakes. The Republic of China is a sovereign, independent country"' (www.bbc.co.uk, 6 November 2008).

> Chen Yunlin … left Taiwan today [Friday 7 November] after a turbulent visit that … sparked angry protests … Taiwan's main opposition Democratic Progressive Party … organized a rowdy street demonstration yesterday [6 November] as Ma Ying-jeou met Chen, who angered many by calling Ma 'you' instead of 'president' … At least 10,000 people filled the streets … Alex Chiang (National Cheng Chi University in Taipei): 'My estimate is that they represent at least a quarter of the population' … Through much of the night hundreds of riot police used batons and a water cannon to fend off groups of protesters who threw rocks and trash at them outside Chen's hotel … Opposition chairwoman Tsai Ing-wen … rejected any ties to the Thursday night clashes.
>
> (www.independent.co.uk, 7 November 2008)

10 November 2008. 'At least two groups of Chinese officials have cancelled plans to visit Taiwan because of violent protests against Chen Yunlin when he visited the island last week, a Taiwanese official said Monday [10 November]' (www.iht.com, 10 November 2008).

11 November 2008.

> Former President Chen Shui-bian was led away in handcuffs Tuesday [11 November] after six hours of questioning by prosecutors … Anti-corruption

prosecutors are investigating the ex-president over his alleged misuse of his discretionary 'state affairs fund' and a money laundering case involving the former first family ... Chen insists the charges are politically motivated.

(www.cnn.com, 11 November 2008)

Former President Chen Shui-bian is accused of money laundering and illegally using a special presidential fund during his eight years in office, which ended in May. He denies any wrongdoing and accuses the new administration of persecuting him to bow to the wishes of Beijing ... The former president is under investigation for allegedly embezzling 14.8 million Taiwanese dollars ($480,500) from the government.

(www.bbc.co.uk, 11 November 2008)

The former first family is suspected of sending at least a billion Taiwanese dollars to Japan, the United States, the Cayman Islands, Singapore and Switzerland and other places ... The former president and his wife, also a graft suspect in an ongoing trial, left the Democratic Progressive Party in August.

(www.iht.com, 11 November 2008)

Prosecutors sought his formal arrest on corruption and money laundering charges ... The detention was part of a widening corruption investigation that has already ensnared several of Chen Shui-bian's senior aides, as well as his wife, son, daughter and brother-in-law, each of who has been a defendant in the case. Chen's wife, Wu Shu-chen, is now on trial in Taipei for money laundering ... His wife was charged with corruption in 2006 and his son-in-law was arrested on insider trading charges ... Prosecutors are looking into whether Chen embezzled money while serving as president, and whether his family members and aides were involved in laundering millions of dollars worth of campaign funds.

(www.iht.com, 11 November 2008)

('The jailed former president of Taiwan, Chen Shui-bian, has been brought to hospital days after beginning a hunger strike in protest at his arrest ... Taiwanese media say there are plans to force-feed the ex-leader': www.bbc.co.uk, 16 November 2008. 'After five days on hunger strike, former President Chen Shui-bian was taken from his jail cell to a hospital Sunday [16 November] when a doctor found an irregular heartbeat, a prison official said ... A prison doctor recommended sending Chen to the hospital after examining him': *IHT*, 17 November 2008, p. 10. 'Former President Chen Shui-bian ... was hospitalized Monday [17 November] for complications from dehydration, the country's national news agency said. Doctors treated the fifty-seven-year-old former leader with injections of saline and glucose after he began experiencing 'an excessively fast heartbeat and tightness in chest', the Central News Agency said ... Nine other people have been arrested in the case, including Chen's former treasurer, and they have agreed to testify against him': www.cnn.com, 17 November 2008. 'Chen Shui-bian ... locked up on 12 November on suspicion of serious crimes ... at once started a hunger strike. He languished for five days in a cell isolated from other inmates, until his health failed. Dehydrated and his blood-sugar levels and blood pressure down to alarming levels, the fifty-seven-year-old former president was on 16 November taken to hospital and given intravenous glucose and saline drip. His health stabilized enough for him to be taken back to prison on 19 November … His lawyer said he would continue his fast': www.economist.com, 20 November 2008. 'Chen Shui-bian … ended a sixteen-day hunger strike Thursday [27 November]': *IHT*, 28 November 2008, p. 10.)

12 December 2008.

> Prosecutors in Taiwan have formally indicted ex-President Chen Shui-bian and his wife on corruption charges. The charges include forgery and money laundering … Mr Chen, his wife and twelve others were indicted on charges of corruption, money laundering, embezzlement and document forgery charges … The couple stand accused of embezzling millions of dollars in public funds and accepting a huge bribe in a land purchase deal.
>
> (www.bbc.co.uk, 12 December 2008)

> Former President Chen Shui-bian was indicted Friday [12 December] on several corruption charges, including embezzlement and accepting bribes. The former president is accused of embezzling $18 million. Prosecutors say he also took bribes, laundered money and illegally removed classified documents from the president's office … Thirteen others, including Chen's wife, son, daughter-in-law and wife's brother, have been indicted along with Chen. Prosecutors said Chen's son has a Swiss bank account with $22 million believed to be illegal proceeds.
>
> (www.cnn.com, 12 December 2008)

> Chen Shui-bian, who served eight years as president, was indicted Friday [12 December] on corruption charges, making him the first former president of the country to face criminal prosecution … Chen, who served from 2000 to May of this year [2008], faces charges that he and his family pocketed millions of dollars of campaign funds … Chen has denied the charges, saying his prosecution is a politically motivated attack by his successor, President Ma Ying-jeou. Ma and other leaders of the Kuomintang have rejected the suggestion that they are influencing prosecutors.
>
> (www.iht.com, 12 December 2008)

('Chen Shui-bian, accused of embezzling about 418 million, has remained free on bail after a nearly eight-hour hearing … Chen – the first former president to ever face prosecution – was freed last week after spending a month in jail … Chen is accused of embezzling about $18 million. Prosecutors allege he also took bribes, laundered money and illegally removed classified documents from the president's office': www.cnn.com, 19 December 2008.)

15 December 2008.

> Regularly scheduled commercial flights, shipping and mail between Taiwan and China resumed Monday [15 December] for the first time since 1949 …

> Current plans call for sixteen daily flights to or from Taiwan. Frequent charter flights began in July, but Monday marked the first formal service in nearly sixty years.
>
> (www.cnn.com, 15 December 2008)

> [Monday 15 December saw] the beginning of regular and direct flights ... Direct ship traffic and mail service also got under way ... Agreements [were signed] on 4 November to open up the direct links that began Monday ... As many as 108 direct passenger charters are due to operate each week across the strait ... as well as sixty direct cargo flights a month. The flights will come and go from twenty-one cities on the mainland and eight cities in Taiwan. Twenty cargo ships from both [China and Taiwan] ... were scheduled to set out across the strait on Monday. Sea voyages are now expected to take four days ... about half the time of previous indirect routes ... Passenger flights have been flying between China and Taiwan since July, but not daily and not regularly – only tourist group charters on weekends and holidays. The direct flights cut flying time in half.
>
> (www.iht.com, 15 December 2008)

> China and Taiwan are separated by a body of water just 160 kilometres (100 miles) wide. But flights and shipping routes have had to make detours through third countries or territories, usually Hong Kong or Japan ... Under the landmark agreements signed last month [November], the number of passenger flights will also increase to a maximum of 108 per week, starting this week, up from the previous thirty-six.
>
> (www.bbc.co.uk, 15 December 2008)

'When China offered thirty years ago to set up transport links with Taiwan, the island's government said no' (*The Economist*, 20 December 2008, p. 102).

19 December 2008.

> About 30 kg of the party drug ketamine on one of the first direct cargo flights between China and Taiwan ... a customs official [in Taiwan] said Friday [19 December] ... Airport Customs agents in Taipei found 66 lb of the powdered hallucinatory drug on Thursday [18 December] packed into eight boxes on a Chinese cargo plane ... [The] deputy Taipei customs office head: 'Our expectation was that direct cargo links could possibly lead to drug smuggling. I cannot say this was beyond our imagination.'
>
> (www.iht.com, 19 December 2008)

20 December 2008.

> A senior Chinese official has pledged that China will consider any request for assistance from Taiwan during the current global financial downturn ... The pledge to do more came at a meeting of politicians, academics and business leaders from the two sides of the Taiwan Strait called to discuss ways to co-operate in the financial and service industries. The Taiwanese

> responded warmly to the Chinese offer, and urged Beijing to start by making it easier for Chinese tourists to visit the island.
>
> (www.bbc.co.uk, 20 December 2008)

22 December 2008. 'China will provide $19 billion in financing over the next two to three years to Taiwan-based companies doing business in the mainland, the Taiwan Affairs Office of the State Council said Monday [22 December]' (www.cnn.com, 23 December 2008).

23 December 2008.

> A pair of giant pandas … 'Tuan Tuan' and 'Yuan Yuan' … arrived in Taiwan on Tuesday [23 December] as a gift from China … Taken together the pandas' names mean reunion … The offer to send Tuan Tuan and Yuan Yuan to Taiwan was first made in 2005 when Chen Shui-bian was still in charge. His government rejected it, but after Ma Ying-jeou's inauguration in May the way was clear to reverse that decision.
>
> (www.economist.com, 23 December 2008)

> [The pandas are] provocatively named the equivalent of 're' and 'union' by Beijing … Taiwanese identity has been strengthening. More than 95 per cent of its inhabitants are ethnic Chinese but there has been a sharp divide between those families who have been there for hundreds of years and those who fled to the island in 1949. Before Chen Shui-bian took power only 30 per cent of people thought of themselves as Taiwanese first. That has swollen to 70 per cent.
>
> (*FT*, 15 January 2009, p. 11)

'[As regards the proportion of] Taiwanese people in favour of unification with the mainland … Taiwanese opinion polls put the figure at less than 10 per cent' (*FT*, 23 December 2008, p. 6).

26 December 2008.

> Taiwan's government plans to ease restrictions imposed on spouses, mostly wives, from mainland China married to Taiwanese citizens. Current legislation prevents the mainlanders from working until at least two years after arriving. They have to wait eight years before they are entitled to apply for permanent residence. The rules for spouses of other nationalities are much more lenient … Under the proposed changes mainland Chinese spouses will be able to work within weeks of arriving, just like other foreign spouses. They will be able to qualify for permanent residency and voting rights in six years, instead of eight, they can also sponsor children from a previous marriage to come [to Taiwan] … [There are] more than 250,000 Chinese spouses in Taiwan … However … other foreign spouses only have to wait four years, not six, to gain permanent residence.
>
> (www.iht.com, 26 December 2008)

30 December 2008.

> Ex-President Chen Shui-bian has been returned to prison pending his trial on corruption charges, after a court reversed a bail order. The Taipei district court judges are reported to have said there was a risk he could collude with other suspects, destroy evidence and flee the island ... Mr Chen and his wife stand accused of embezzling millions of dollars in public funds and accepting a huge bribe in a land purchase deal.
>
> (www.bbc.co.uk, 30 December 2008)

> After twelve hours of deliberation, a panel of three district court judges approved the request ... [from prosecutors for] his return to state custody ... Judges [had] ordered Chen released after the indictment was formally presented, saying they did not believe he was a flight risk. However, Taiwan's high court was not satisfied with the decision and assigned a new judge to the case ... Chen's attorney: 'We question the work of the Taipei district court. Changing the judge is an interference with the justice system' ... Chen is accused of embezzling about $18 million ... prosecutors allege he also took bribes, laundered money and illegally removed classified documents from the president's office.
>
> (www.cnn.com, 30 December 2008)

20 January 2009.

> Former President Chen Shui-bian ... [has written] a lengthy prison diary ... In the 100,000-word declaration, the *Son of Taiwan* ... he says: 'I am a splittist and implementer of *de jure* independence for Taiwan' ... [The diary's] publication tomorrow [20 January] is eagerly awaited by the Taiwanese public ... He protested against his imprisonment by going on a sixteen-day hunger strike, though local media claim there are security camera pictures showing him secretly snacking on chocolate bars and crackers.
>
> (*FT*, 19 January 2009, p. 8)

21 January 2009.

> The son of former Taiwan president Chen Shui-bian yesterday [21 January] broke with his father and pleaded guilty in court to laundering millions in funds overseas for the family ... Chen Chih-chung and his wife, Huang Jui-ching, both promised full co-operation with prosecutors ... A day earlier [Chen Shui-bian] maintained his innocence at the opening of his trial [on 20 January].
>
> (*FT*, 22 January 2009, p. 8)

'The Central News Agency said: "Chen Chih-chung and his wife, Huang Jui-ching, acted as the proxy and a nominal holder of the former first family's controversial overseas ban account"' (*IHT*, 22 January 2009, p. 5).

10 February 2009.

> A former Taiwanese first lady pleaded guilty to money-laundering and forgery but denied embezzlement charges … Wu Shu-chen said she had accepted a $2.2 million political donation in connection with a land purchase deal – not a bribe as alleged by prosecutors. She admitted charges of forging documents in a separate case but denied using the money for personal gain. Mrs Wu is the wife of ex-President Chen Shui-bian, who was in office 2000–8 … Last month Chen Chih-chung, the Chens' son, pleaded guilty to money-laundering, as did Chen's daughter-in-law and Mrs Wu's brother.
>
> (www.bbc.co.uk, 10 February 2009)

> Wu Shu-chen said Tuesday [10 February] that she laundered $2.2. million and forged documents … She [said she] sent abroad the funds she received from a contractor in connection with a government construction project and that she forged documents related to a special presidential fund. Wu is also charged with looting a special presidential fund, taking bribes and laundering money.
>
> (*IHT*, 11 February 2009, p. 4)

'She did not admit to charges of embezzling money from the [presidential] fund or taking bribes in connection with the construction project. She has repeatedly suggested that the money was a political donation' (www.iht.com, 11 February 2009).

12 February 2009.

> President Ma Ying-jeou said on Thursday [12 February] that he was glad to have reduced tensions with mainland China and that he was not concerned that Taiwan was low on Secretary of State Hillary Rodham Clinton's list of priorities … America's new Secretary of State is preparing to visit Beijing with an agenda that barely mentions Taiwan … Ma also said he planned to push further this year [2009] for close relations with mainland China, even while acknowledging disappointment with the number of mainland tourists who have been allowed by Beijing to visit Taiwan. The Taiwanese government has set a limit of 3,000 a day, but actual arrivals have been closer to 500 or 600 a day.
>
> (www.iht.com, 14 February 2009)

> China, angered over a major US arms deal with Taiwan, broke off senior level military exchanges with Washington last October [2008] … The militaries of mainland China and Taiwan have had no contacts at all for many years … The Straits Exchange Foundation, the semi-official institution that handles Taiwan's negotiations … [has] a hotline to its mainland counterpart, the Association for Relations Across the Taiwan Straits.
>
> (www.iht.com, 18 February 2009)

14–16 February 2009.

> The director of the National Palace Museum in Taipei ... plans to travel to Beijing on Saturday [14 February] ... the first official visit by a director of the Taipei museum to China since [1949] ... A similar delegation of Chinese art officials comes to Taipei in March ... The artworks that the National Palace Museum seeks to borrow are obscure. They are mainly portraits and seals of Emperor Yongzheng of the Qing Dynasty, who ruled from 1723 to 1735 ... [The mainland has a] long history of insisting that the entire [imperial] collection belongs to Beijing. Taiwan makes no counter-claim against the mainland's holdings. The National Palace Museum in Taipei borrowed artworks from provincial museums in China for a large exhibition two years ago and promptly returned them.
>
> (*IHT*, 13 February 2009, p. 3)

> The Palace Museum in Beijing has agreed to lend works of art to the National Palace Museum in Taipei for an exhibition next autumn, temporarily bringing together a small part of China's imperial collection for the first time in sixty years, both museums said on Monday [16 February]. The art works – mainly paintings of Emperor Yongzheng, an eighteenth century ruler of China, and his concubines – are part of China's immense imperial art collection, long divided by strife. The Nationalists took nearly a quarter of the collection, including most of the best works, when they lost China's civil war to the Communists in 1949 and retreated to Taiwan ... The National Palace Museum plans to borrow the works for a three-month exhibition starting in October [2008] of art from the Qing dynasty reign of Emperor Yongzheng, who ruled from 1723 to 1735 ... The directors of the Beijing and Taipei museums also reached seven other agreements during meetings over the weekend in Beijing ... [including one which says that] the deputy directors of the two museums will meet annually ... But the two sides did not attempt to resolve the thorniest question of all: mainland China's legal claim to full ownership of the entire imperial collection, including the holdings of the National Palace Museum. The Taipei museum refuses to lend any works to the mainland for fear that they will not be returned, and has only rarely lent works from the imperial collection to other countries for fear of legal action.
>
> (www.iht.com, 16 February 2009; *IHT*, 17 February 2009, p. 2)

20 February 2009.

> Former Taiwan President Chen Shui-bian: 'My wife wired money abroad without my knowledge. That was certainly wrong. I did not manage my family well and for that I have to take moral and political responsibility' ... The former cashier in Mr Chen's presidential office this week pleaded guilt to graft ... On Friday [20 February] Mr Chen began a second hunger strike against what he claimed was misconduct by prosecutors in handling his case.
>
> (*FT*, 23 February 2009)

26 March 2009.

> The corruption trial of former President Chen Shui-bian began Thursday [26 March] … The trial is the first for a former head of state … Prosecutors say Chen embezzled $17.7 million, took bribes, laundered money and illegally removed classified documents from the president's office. Chen has countered that the bribe money was actually political donations. He has also said that a special presidential fund from which he is accused of embezzling does not clearly say what the money can and cannot be used for.
>
> (www.cnn.com, 26 March 2009)

> Prosecutors allege Chen Shui-bian and his wife, Wu Shu-chen, embezzled money from a special presidential fund and laundered it through Swiss banks during his eight years in office. They also accuse the couple of receiving bribes from a Taiwanese company to help it sell a piece of land to the government. Altogether the money involved in the case adds up to an estimated $15 million.
>
> (www.bbc.co.uk, 26 March 2009)

> On Wednesday [25 March] Chen Shui-bian issued a statement in which he charged: '[My conviction] was prepared in advance and the sentence was already determined. In order to win favours and protection from Beijing … [the Kuomintang] has launched a purge against me.'
>
> (www.iht.com, 26 March 2009)

26 April 2009.

> China and Taiwan have agreed to allow investment across the Taiwan Strait … In a joint statement they pledged to 'realize the normalization of cross-strait economic ties' … It was the third set of deals since Taiwan's new government came to power … In the past, while there has been a great deal of mainland investment from Taiwanese firms, Chinese companies have needed permission from the Taiwanese government to invest in Taiwan. In a joint statement the two sides said that they face a 'rare and historic opportunity' and that they would 'encourage and promote mainland businesses to … invest in Taiwan'.
>
> (www.bbc.co.uk, 26 April 2009)

'China and Taiwan signed a new set of agreements on Sunday [26 April], taking a big step towards opening up their financial services industries to each other and allowing direct investment in Taiwan from mainland China' (www.ft.com, 26 April 2009).

29 April 2009.

> President Ma Ying-jeou of Taiwan announced Wednesday [29 April] that Chinese officials had dropped their objections of Taiwan's participation as an observer at a UN body … China strongly hinted that it was prepared to let Taiwan participate in the World Health Assembly, the decision-making

body for the World Health Organization. But Beijing stopped short of explicitly saying that it had accepted a Taiwanese presence at a gathering of the assembly next month [May] ... China's health ministry said in a statement that the World Health Organization had invited Taiwan to participate next month, adding that 'the current arrangement reflects our overall concern and good will toward Taiwan compatriots, and this promotes the cross-straits relationship and the peaceful development of relations' ... Taiwan made its participation more palatable to the mainland by agreeing to use the name 'Chinese Taipei' instead of its legal name, the Republic of China, or the name by which it is best known, Taiwan. Mainland authorities blocked the WHO from providing direct assistance to Taiwan during an outbreak of SARS in the spring of 2003 ... Since being expelled from the United Nations in 1971 Taiwan has not been able to participate in its major component bodies because of Chinese pressure.

(www.iht.com, 29 April 2009)

[Taiwan] displayed an invitation letter from the WHO. China must approve any World Health Assembly role for Taiwan before the island can be formally invited ... [China] would only say that Beijing had a 'positive' attitude toward the issue ... Chinese officials said on Wednesday [29 April] they would work with Taiwan in controlling any spread of swine flu.

(www.ft.com, 29 April 2009)

After twelve failed attempts since 1997 to join the UN's World Health Organization as an observer, Taiwan has been invited to take part in the WHO's World Health Assembly in Geneva in May. This will be Taiwan's first participation in a UN event since it lost its seat to China thirty-eight years ago. It represents a big concession from China, which habitually bars Taiwan from any gathering that might suggest it has a claim to statehood. Taiwan will take part under the name 'Chinese Taipei', used in sporting events such as the Olympics and regional groups such as the Asia-Pacific Economic Co-operation Forum ... Taiwan has rejected any offer that describes it as part of the People's Republic of China and has insisted that the invitation came from the WHO, not Beijing ... During the deadly SARS crisis of 2003 Chinese objections delayed WHO experts wanting to assess the situation in Taiwan for several weeks. Taiwan's government was already permitted some contact with the WHO, but as an observer to the assembly it will have broader access to its data ... The latest [agreements], signed in Nanjing on 26 April, include one on financial co-operation, which will eventually allow Taiwanese financial institutions to start operating on the mainland. Others will allow a sharp expansion in direct cross-strait flights and improve co-operation in fighting crime and repatriating fugitives.

(*The Economist*, 2 May 2009, pp. 58–9)

[On 29 April China Mobile said that it would buy 12 per cent of FarEasTone Telecommunications, a big Taiwanese mobile operator ... The deal will need government approval … The number of [regular] flights increased from thirty-six a week to more than 100 a week in December [2008], and again to 270 from 26 April. Taiwan is pushing for the number to double again. Along with closer ties in aviation and telecoms, several other potential agreements have come from the thaw between Taipei and Beijing, starting with direct discussions between Chinese and Taiwanese financial regulators on greater co-operation. Taiwan will also open up to direct Chinese investment in services, manufacturing, property and rail projects. Taiwan has invested in China for decades, and by some reckoning more than 5 per cent of Taiwan's population now lives on the mainland in order to do business there. But Taiwan itself has long felt that it was too small, and China too threatening, to allow reciprocal ownership.

(*The Economist*, 9 May 2009, pp. 71–2)

Government initiatives to promote cross-strait business opportunities, such as tourism, have had little success so far. Beijing's concerns over allowing too many of its citizens to visit democratic Taiwan has meant there was just a trickle of tourists last year [2008], when Taiwan's public and its aggressive media were expecting a flood of wealthy Chinese spenders. Only last month [April 2009] did tourist numbers finally reach the daily quota of 3,000 visitors … The [Chinese] government-owned China Mobile proposed to take a 12 per cent stake in FarEasTone, a Taiwanese mobile operator, in the first mainland investment in a Taiwan-listed company.

(*FT*, 7 May 2009, p. 15)

7 May 2009.

Former Taiwan President Chen Shui-bian … has fired his lawyer and given up his legal defence to protest at what he claims to be an 'illegal trial'. In a statement Thursday [7 May] Mr Chen maintained his innocence but said he would not call any further witnesses and asked the judge to impose a sentence of life imprisonment upon him … The statement comes after Mr Chen's bail hearing on Thursday was cut short after the former president complained of feeling unwell, saying he had heart conditions and often broke out in a cold sweat at night. On Tuesday [5 May] prosecutors filed extra charges of receiving improper payments from senior banking executives against Mr Chen and his wife. A spokesman from Mr Chen's office said the former president would attend court hearings but would remain silent. He would not change his plea to guilty.

(www.ft.com, 8 May 2009)

9 May 2009. 'Former President Chen Shui-bian has been hospitalized after a three-day hunger strike' (www.iht.com, 9 May 2009).

June 2009.

President Ma Ying-jeou … told *The Economist* this week he believes China has even adopted the surprising policy of refusing requests from countries that recognize Taiwan to switch their diplomatic ties to China instead ... Ma Ying-jeou: 'We do see a measure of goodwill [from China]' ... [Presidential candidates in El Salvador and Panama said they wanted to establish formal ties with China, but] the mainland obviously declined their request for the sake of Taiwan ... Taiwan is now recognized by only twenty-three countries, mostly small ones. China has 171 diplomatic partners ... Taiwan has suffered a net loss of six supporters this decade ... Last year [2008] Mr Ma declared a 'diplomatic truce', meaning an end to the chequebook contest for recognition.

(*The Economist*, Special Report on Ageing Populations, 27 June 2009, p. 75)

16 July 2009.

Taiwan ... hosts the World Games at the port city of Kaohsiung this week ... The quadrennial games [is] an affiliate of the Olympics for sports [thirty-one of them] not included in the main event such as squash, canoe polo and fistball ... The games are the largest global event held in Taiwan in decades ... The games will be the biggest international sporting event ever held in Taiwan ... Thomas Tsai, president of the Chinese Taipei Olympic Committee, said both sides had been 'more willing to compromise' over previously contentious issues, such as whether the audience could wave the Taiwanese flag.

(www.ft.com, 14 July 2009)

China has boycotted the opening ceremony of the World Games in Taiwan ... China had not given an explanation but Chinese athletes would compete in the events ... Beijing's decision came after organizers allowed Taiwan's President Ma Ying-jeou to open the games. Beijing considers Taiwan a breakaway province and does not recognize Mr Ma as president ... The International World Games Association had made a last-minute decision to allow Mr Ma to open the games in recognition of the effort Taiwan had made as host nation ... Relations with China have improved significantly in the past year, since Mr Ma took office. This is the first sign of the lingering political tensions ... The thirty-one sports ... did not make it into the Olympics, such as water skiing, canoe polo and tug-of-war.

(www.bbc.co.uk, 16 July 2009)

China boycotted the opening of the 2009 World Games on Thursday night [16 July] ... Seventy-seven mainland Chinese athletes had completed the application process for competing in seven sports, including fin-swimming, boules and water-skiing. But none of them turned up for the opening ceremony ... The ceremony Thursday night was held in accordance with past practice at the Olympic Games and other international sporting events, under which Taiwan competes as 'Chinese Taipei' and cannot fly its national flag ... The World Games, held every four years, offer competition in non-Olympic sports.

(www.iht.com, 17 July 2009)

20 July 2009.

> Taiwan has restored the name of the island's former ruler, Chiang Kai-shek, to a memorial hall, less than two years after it was removed … The Democratic Progressive Party (DPP) took his name off the memorial hall in 2007 when they were in power. The hall was built as a tribute to Chiang after his death in 1975. The DPP removed his name from several landmarks and changed the name of the hall to the National Taiwan Democracy Memorial Hall. The DPP said Chiang was a dictator who was responsible for the deaths of thousands of people in Taiwan. But others remember him as laying the foundation for Taiwan's current economic prosperity. The ministry of education, responsible for the monument, said the DPP had changed the name of the hall in 2007 without parliamentary approval.
>
> (www.bbc.co.uk, 20 July 2009)

26–27 July 2009.

> The leaders of China and Taiwan have exchanged direct messages for the first time in more than sixty years. President Hu Jintao sent a congratulatory telegram to President Ma Ying-jeou after his Sunday [26 July] election to head of the ruling party … [the] Nationalist Party (KMT) … Neither man used their presidential titles in their messages … Mr Hu's message: 'I hope our two parties can continue to promote peaceful cross-Strait development, deepen mutual trust, bring good news to compatriots on both sides and create a revival of the great Chinese race' … Mr Ma said on Sunday that he had been expecting Mr Hu's telegram because he had received one from him when he was elected KMT chairman, in 2005. He held the post for two years.
>
> (www.bbc.co.uk, 27 July 2009)

> In his congratulatory telegram to Mr Ma, Mr Hu said: 'I hope our two parties can continue to promote peaceful development in cross-Strait relations, and help bolster mutual trust between the two sides in political affairs' … In response, on Monday [27 July], Mr Ma said: 'We should continue efforts to consolidate peace in the Taiwan Strait and rebuild regional stability.'
>
> (www.iht.com, 27 July 2009)

'Mr Ma's reply was addressed to Mr Hu as general secretary of the Communist Party … "We should continue efforts to consolidate peace in the Taiwan Strait and rebuild regional stability," Ma replied, adding that they should "put aside disputes"' (www.guardian.co.uk, 27 July 2009).

6 August 2009.

> A fortnight after Typhoon Morakot first struck Taiwan on 6 August the storm … the worst storm in fifty years … continued to wreak havoc on the island. Extensive flooding and landslides had claimed some 500 lives,

according to Ma Ying-jeou, the president, and caused at least $2 billion-worth of damage to property ... Morakot is also doing political damage. President Ma faces harsh criticism for his government's slow response to the disaster, and in particular for its surprising decision ... on 17 August ... to spurn foreign offers of aid in the early stages. Three senior officials have already offered their resignations. The reputation of Mr Ma himself has taken a knock ... This time the apologies he has made may not be enough to see him through. An opinion poll this week ... showed a dramatic drop in his approval rating: by 25 percentage points since June, to an all-time low of 16 per cent. Other polls give him higher ratings but show a similar decline ... He has promised a more efficient recovery effort and an investigation into the shortcomings of the government response ... In one striking proposal, Mr Ma said Taiwan's army would reorder its priorities towards handling big disasters. Now, he told a news conference, our enemy is not necessarily the people across the Taiwan Strait but nature. Taiwan would cancel orders for American military helicopters and buy disaster-relief helicopters instead ... China was quick to respond, not only expressing sympathy for the people it refers to as 'compatriots' but also providing $29 million in relief funds, prefabricated houses, sleeping bags and sanitation supplies ... On 16 August an American cargo plane arrived. It was the first American military aircraft to land in Taiwan in the thirty years since America severed its diplomatic ties with Taiwan in favour of China.

(www.economist.com, 20 August; *The Economist*, 22 August 2009, p. 47)

'Morakot means "emerald" in the Thai language' (www.iht.com, 12 August 2009).

'On Thursday [13 August] President Ma Ying-jeou publicly denied reports that his government had initially rejected help from other countries, a foreign ministry memo that proved otherwise was leaked to the local press on Friday [14 August]' (www.ft.com, 14 August 2009). 'The foreign ministry said the "poorly written" memo was written and sent without the president's awareness ... Typhoon Morakot did not carry strong winds but packed voluminous rainfall' (*FT*, 15 August 2009, p. 6).

The typhoon pummelled the island with three days of rain last weekend ... Some critics have chastised ... President Ma Ying-jeou ... for underestimating the devastation and for not immediately requesting international assistance ... On Thursday [13 August] the Taiwanese cabinet reversed an earlier decision and said it would accept foreign aid, including the heavy-lift helicopters needed to bring bulldozers deep into the mountains ... The foreign ministry asserted that the decision to turn down foreign help was actually a typographical error in documents it had sent abroad. Officials have strenuously defended their efforts, saying that the rainfall ... exceeded all predictions and that the remoteness of many villages had made recovery efforts especially complicated.

(www.iht.com, 14 August 2009; *IHT*, 15 August 2009, p. 1)

'President Ying-jeou: "We could have done better and we could have been faster" ... In China ... charities have raised more than $14.6 million in donations' (www.bbc.co.uk, 15 August 2009).

'President Ma Ying-jeou made remarks to a British television station in which he seemed to blame typhoon victims for their own misery. He said: "They were not fully prepared. If they had been, they should have been evacuated much earlier"' (www.iht.com, 15 August 2009).

'China has offered military aircraft, but Taiwan has declined the offer' (www.bbc.co.uk, 17 August 2009).

'[A] poll published Wednesday [19 August] ... put his [President Ma-Ying-jeou's] approval rating at 29 per cent, down from 52 per cent only three months earlier' (www.iht.com, 19 August 2009).

> Typhoon Morakot triggered landslides and severe flooding that trapped thousands of people in remote southern villages for days ... Chiu Yi, a politician with President Ma Ying-jeou's ruling Kuomintang Party, said that instead of waiting three days, the president should have declared a national emergency immediately to mobilize the military ... On Tuesday [18 August] Ma Ying-jeou said: '[The military's job is] to defend Taiwan, but now our enemy is not necessarily the people across the Taiwan Strait, but nature.'
>
> (*Guardian*, 20 August 2009, p. 22)

'President Ma Ying-jeou suggested that the main task of Taiwan's army should be prevention and rescue ... adding that an order for sixty American-made Blackhawk helicopters would be cut by fifteen, and the savings used to buy disaster relief' (www.iht.com, 24 August 2009).

'At least 500 people are still missing, thought killed by floods and mudslides ... So far the government has confirmed the deaths of 160 people in the typhoon' (www.bbc.co.uk, 22 August 2009).

> Flags are flying at half-mast during three days of national mourning to honour those killed by Typhoon Morakot two weeks ago. But anger, not sadness, remains the prevailing sentiment across Taiwan as President Ma Ying-jeou grapples with his worst political crisis since taking office last year [2008]. Despite repeated apologies for a slow response to the storm – which left at least 650 dead or missing after record rain caused huge landslides – Mr Ma has been kept busy warding off the sceptical news media and his political opponents, and calming furious survivors ... Mr Ma said Saturday [22 August]: 'The government is sorry. It failed to fulfil its responsibility to protect you' ... Mr Ma has said he will consider shuffling his cabinet; three senior aides, including his defence minister, have offered to resign ... In interviews last week even supporters described him as aloof, indecisive and inclined to technocratic language ... [The government failed] to apply last week for membership in the United Nations, a largely symbolic gesture that has occurred annually since 1993 ... [CNN published] an online survey last

week in which 82 per cent of respondents said Mr Ma should resign for his sluggish response to the storm ... though the poll did not claim to be scientific.

(www.iht.com, 24 August 2009)

The authorities in Taiwan will not try to recover the bodies of hundreds feared killed in an aboriginal village by a mudslide caused by Typhoon Morakot, and will instead turn the site into a memorial park, a township chief said Tuesday [24 August]. The park would sit above the landslide that buried the village. The typhoon's toll stands at 291 dead and 387 missing.

(*IHT*, 25 August 2009, p. 4)

As of 24 August the death count stood at 292, with 385 missing and presumed dead. Most were buried alive by mudslides or swept away by torrential rivers ... Displaced villagers credit Taiwan's robust civil society for filling the gap left by the government's poor job mobilizing resources. Buddhist relief organizations took the lead by rapidly opening shelters, feeding, and tending to the displaced. And thousands of volunteers – including many students on summer vacation – went to affected areas to help. Money and donations streamed in from private citizens all over Taiwan ... Preventative measures fell short. A government project is mapping out landslide-prone areas, and the emergency centre had the authority to force villagers to evacuate. That did not happen.

(www.feer.com, 25 August 2009)

Typhoon Morakot ... killed more people than previous estimates, the government announced [on 26 August] ... At least 376 people are now known to have died ... [and] at least 254 people are still missing ... Morakot dropped 102 inches of rain on Taiwan on 8 August before it roared on to mainland China the next day ... Initial reports in Taiwan said 123 people had been killed, but the death toll could top 300.

(www.cnn.com, 26 August 2009)

Premier Liu Chao-shiuan ... resigned Monday [7 September] amid strong criticism of the government's slow response to the most devastating storm to hit the island in fifty years ... [He] said he was leaving office because his cabinet had completed the initial rehabilitation work after Typhoon Morakot slammed into the island 8–9 August and left an estimated 670 people dead ... Liu's move sets the stage for the entire cabinet to resign. Liu said that would happen Thursday [10 September] ... President Ma Ying-jeou named Nationalist Party [Kuomintang] Secretary-General Wu Den-yih to replace Liu ... Typhoon Morakot, which dumped 3 feet (a metre) of rain in some locations, triggered massive flooding and mudslides in and around some forty villages in southern Taiwan. Critics blamed the heavy casualties on government inefficiency, saying authorities should have ordered residents in the area to evacuate their homes long before the storm hit. The government has also come under criticism for rejecting initial offers of foreign aid and for failing to immediately deploy troops to help with rescue operations. Opinion polls in Morakot's wake showed support for Ma and Liu plunging to below 20 per cent – a drop of 20 to 30 percentage points in only a matter of months. Even Mr Ma's Nationalist allies demanded a cabinet reshuffle … Liu said Monday that most of the 7,000 people who lost their homes in the storm have been resettled at military camps and other temporary shelters. The cabinet has earmarked $4 billion for reconstruction work.

(www.iht.com, 7 September 2009)

Prime minister Liu Chao-shiuan … resigned because of the government's widely criticized response to a deadly typhoon and said that his successor would replace the entire cabinet this week … the government had come under intense pressure for what many Taiwanese called its inept handling of Typhoon Morakot … [which] left at least 700 people dead or missing after three days of heavy rain set off huge mudslides. Mr Liu's resignation is the most serious political fallout yet from the typhoon … At the news conference on Monday Mr Liu said he first offered Mr Ma his resignation in mid-August. Mr Ma has asked him to stay, he said, but Mr Liu had 'firmly made up his mind' … Mr Liu said: 'I believe because so many people died, someone must take responsibility' … The prime minister appoints the entire cabinet, which has eight ministries established under the constitution and many newer commissions. The current cabinet will resign together on Thursday, Mr Liu said. Critics of the government say President Ma Ying-jeou and other leaders should have evacuated residents in vulnerable areas before the typhoon hit and accepted foreign aid earlier, among other things … President Ma Ying-jeou, who has the power to appoint the prime minister, chose Wu Den-yih as the replacement for Mr Liu … Mr Wu is a native Taiwanese and speaks the Taiwanese dialect fluently, which could give him an advantage over Mr Liu in trying to quell anger in the aftermath of the typhoon. Some of the worst hit areas were in southern Taiwan, dominated by native Taiwanese, who lived on the island well before the Chinese fleeing the civil war settled there.

(www.iht.com, 7 September 2009)

Premier Liu Chao-shiuan has resigned. He said: 'I am the top administrator and all of the political responsibility rests on my shoulders, so I offered my resignation to the president, and he has agreed' … Mr Liu told reporters that someone had to take responsibility for the fact that at least 600 people had died as a result of Typhoon Morakot … The government was heavily criticized for its slow response to last month's typhoon … Critics blame the heavy casualties on the government's failure to order evacuations before the storm hit. Other ministers are expected to offer their resignations on Thursday [10 September] … Mr Liu will be replaced by the ruling party's general secretary, Wu Den-yih.

(www.bbc.co.uk, 7 September 2009)

> Liu Chao-shiuan had announced his resignation at a news conference in mid-August to assume responsibility for the administration's handling of the typhoon ... But because the post-storm situation was grave, President Ma Ying-jeou asked Liu to remain and oversee relief work. Liu said Monday [7 September] that about 90 per cent of relief subsidies had been distributed to storm victims and about 92 per cent of displaced people had been temporarily resettled. He said he was resigning because he had completed his task ... The storm destroyed homes, farms and other buildings, and roads, causing about $3 billion in damage, President Ma Ying-jeou said ... At least 543 people are known to have died in the storm, according to Taiwan's Central Emergency Operation Centre. Hundreds are still feared missing.
>
> (www.cnn.com, 8 September 2009)

'[According to one poll] President Ma Ying-jeou's approval rating has slipped to 23 per cent from nearly 40 per cent in June' (www.ft.com, 7 September 2009).

27 August 2009. 'Taiwan said Thursday [27 August] that it will allow a visit by the Dalai Lama to pray for the victims of the typhoon-battered island. Taiwan President Ma Ying-jeou made the announcement Thursday [27 August]' (www.cnn.com, 27 August 2009).

> The president of Taiwan said Thursday [27 August] that he would allow the Dalai Lama to visit the island next week ... The Tibetan leader is expected to arrive Monday [31 August] for a six-day tour of southern Taiwan, which was ravaged by a typhoon three weeks ago that left at least 650 dead. The invitation was extended by several local government leaders in the south and was seen by analysts in Taiwan as a political manoeuvre aimed to embarrass President Ma Ying-jeou, whose approval ratings have plummeted over what is widely seen as a slow response to the devastating typhoon ... The Taiwanese officials who extended the invitation belong to the opposition Democratic Party, which has its traditional base of support in the south ... The Dalai Lama had been invited by the leaders of seven cities in southern Taiwan ... The president had rebuffed a possible visit by the Dalai Lama last November [2008], saying the timing was not right. The Dalai Lama has visited Taiwan three times in the past dozen years, most recently in 2001, when Chen Shui-bian, Mr Ma's predecessor was president.
>
> (www.iht.com, 27 August 2009)

'The Dalai Lama has visited Taiwan before, in 1997 and most recently in 2001' (*IHT*, 28 August 2009, p. 5).

> President Ma Ying-jeou has agreed to a request from the opposition to invite the Dalai Lama next week, to comfort the victims of deadly Typhoon Morakot ... After a five-hour meeting with security officials, he chose to allow the trip. President Ma Ying-jeou: 'We have ... decided to let the Dalai Lama visit as he is coming here to pray for the dead victims, as well as the

survivors' … Correspondents say China's criticism may be more muted than might otherwise have been expected because officials in Beijing are wary of playing into the hands of Taiwan's pro-independence opposition … President Ma came to power in 2008 … Last year [2008] he refused to grant permission for a visit by the Dalai Lama, saying the timing was not right as his government was working to improve relations with Beijing … [President Ma's] popularity has plunged to a record low of 20 per cent over his handling of the situation … Taiwan is home to a large exiled Tibetan community, and millions of Taiwanese are Buddhists … A spokesman for Taiwan's presidential office refused to say whether Beijing had yet been informed of the decision, but he said: 'Cross-Strait relations will not be negatively affected by allowing the Dalai Lama to visit.'

(www.bbc.co.uk, 27 August 2009)

President Ma Ying-jeou: 'We have decided to [agree to] the Dalai Lama's visit to pray for the souls of the deceased and seek blessings for the survivors of the typhoon' … A spokesman [for the president's office]: 'The visit is based on humanitarian and religious considerations which should not hurt cross-Strait ties.'

(www.thetimes.com, 27 August 2009)

A presidential spokesman: 'We welcome the Dalai Lama to come to Taiwan to take part in mass prayers … [The visit has been approved] for humanitarian and religious considerations … and we believe it will not harm cross-Strait relations' … Taiwan has a large exiled Tibetan community and the Dalai Lama has visited the island three times in the past twelve years, drawing crowds of thousands, although his last trip was eight years ago … Typhoon Morakot is believed to have killed around 670 people.

(www.guardian.co.uk, 27 August 2009)

A statement from Beijing's Taiwan Affairs Bureau:

'[The Dalai Lama is not a] pure religious figure … Under the pretext of religion he has all along been engaged in separatist activities. He raises the religious banner and continues to carry out attempting to split the country … Some of the people in the Democratic Progressive Party used the disaster rescue effort excuse to invite Dalai to Taiwan to sabotage the hard-earned positive situation of cross-Strait relations.

(www.bbc.co.uk, 27 August 2009)

The Chinese Taiwan Affairs Bureau said in a statement: 'No matter what form or identity Dalai uses to enter Taiwan, we resolutely oppose this. Some of the people in the Democratic Progressive Party are using the disaster excuse for an invitation to sabotage the hard-earned positive situation of cross-Strait relations' … According to official figures, published yesterday [27 August]. 543 people were killed and 117 were missing after Morakot caused the worst flooding in the island's history.

(*The Times*, 28 August 2009, p. 47)

'A spokesman for the Beijing government's Taiwan Affairs Office said it "resolutely opposed" the decision by Taiwan's president to allow the Dalai Lama to visit "in whatever form and capacity"' (*Independent*, 28 August 2009, p. 28).

'China said on Thursday [27 August] that it "resolutely opposes" a proposed visit of the Dalai Lama to Taiwan "in whatever form and capacity"' (www.ft.com, 27 August 2009).

'The final death toll is unknown, but could be as high as 650' (www.economist.com, 27 August 2009).

> The Dalai Lama will arrive in Taiwan on Sunday [30 August] for a trip that will include praying for victims of Typhoon Morakot ... While in Taiwan the Tibetan spiritual leader is also expected to give a public talk on compassion and religious harmony ... The Dalai Lama, who will return to India on 4 September, will also comfort and offer prayers for typhoon victims.
>
> (www.cnn.com, 28 August 2009)

> The Dalai Lama arrived in Taiwan [on Sunday 30 August] ... On Monday [31 August] the Dalai Lama will visit the worst hit village of Hsiaolin, where nearly 500 people were buried by a mudslide ... He will lead a mass prayer and address the island's Buddhist followers during his five-day visit. However, he has cancelled a press conference after criticism from pro-China groups about his decision to visit and a request from Taiwan to refrain from discussing politics ... At least 571 people were killed, with another 106 missing and feared dead in the typhoon ... President Ma Ying-jeou has announced he will not meet the Dalai Lama.
>
> (www.bbc.co.uk, 30 August 2009)

> The Dalai Lama ... headed straight for Hsiaolin, a village where at least 424 people died in Typhoon Morakot ... He said [Sunday 30 August]: 'I am a monk. I was asked to say prayers for peace. There is no politics. This is humanitarian in nature' ... Shortly after the Dalai Lama's arrival the Chinese government issued its second stern criticism of the trip. A spokesman for the cabinet-level Taiwan Affairs office: 'The Dalai Lama's visit to Taiwan is bound to have a negative influence on relations between the mainland and Taiwan.'
>
> (www.bbc.co.uk, 31 August 2009)

> The Dalai Lama: 'I have visited different parts of the world and I may have a political agenda there ... [But] my visit here is purely for humanitarian concerns' ... Wu Ph-hsiung, the chairman of Ma Ying-jeou's Nationalist Party, said Sunday [30 August] that his party had sought Beijing's understanding of the visit, but he did not give details or say whether China responded.
>
> (www.iht.com, 31 August 2009)

> The Dalai Lama: 'I am very, very strict, [the trip is of a] non-political nature. We are not seeking separation for Taiwan, but the fate of Taiwan

> depends on the more than 20 million people [here]. You are enjoying democracy and that you must preserve. I myself am totally dedicated to the promotion of democracy … [Taiwan should have] very close and unique links [with the mainland].
>
> (www.guardian.co.uk, 31 August 2009)

'The Dalai Lama on Monday [31 August] urged Taiwan to preserve its democracy even as closer cross-Strait economic ties mean it "should have a very close, unique link with China"' (www.ft.com, 31 August 2009).

> The Dalai Lama said Taiwan should have 'very close and unique links' with China but also enjoy democracy as he arrived at a devastated village Monday [31 August] to pray for victims of the worst storm to hit Taiwan in fifty years … He said: 'This is a humanitarian visit. On my side there is no political agenda. In any case Taiwan should have very close and unique links with mainland China, but at the same time Taiwan should also enjoy democracy and prosperity.'
>
> (*IHT*, 1 September 2009, p. 4)

'China … has cancelled upcoming trips to the island by top state officials … [but] not all cross-Strait events have been cancelled. Several new direct flights between the mainland and Taiwan started this week' (www.cnn.com, 1 September 2009).

'A spokeswoman for Taiwan's ruling Kuomintang Party told reporters that a senior Communist Party official had already cancelled a visit to Taipei, and a Chinese delegation would not take part in Saturday's opening of the Deaf Olympics' (www.bbc.co.uk, 1 September 2009).

> [China] stopped short of blaming President Ma Ying-jeou himself … China's retaliation has been desultory. A delegation led by Su Ning, China's deputy central bank governor, which was scheduled to arrive in Taiwan on 31 August, postponed its visit – but only by a week … President Ma Ying-jeou does not want to jeopardize trade negotiations that Taiwan hopes to launch with China in October. His government is keen to secure tariff cuts for industries that it believes will be put at a disadvantage when a free-trade pact between China and Asean takes effect next year [2010]. Mr Ma's goal is for Taiwan to secure a similar free-trade deal.
>
> (*The Economist*, 5 September 2009, pp. 66–7)

'The KMT confirmed it had sent a representative to Beijing to exchange views on the Dalai Lama's visit' (www.feer.com, 3 September 2009).

2 September 2009.

> Wu Shu-chen, the wife of former President Chen Shui-bian, was sentenced by a Taipei court on Tuesday [2 September] to a year in prison for abetting false testimony in the corruption case against her and her family. The couple's son, daughter and son-in-law were each sentenced to six months for perjury.
>
> (www.iht.com, 2 September 2009)

The wife of Taiwan's former president, Chen Shui-bian, has been sentenced to a year in jail for perjury. Wu Shu-chen was found guilty of asking her children to lie in court in an embezzlement case against her ... Mr Chen's son, daughter and son-in-law have each been jailed for six months ... [They] were also found guilty of perjury ... The verdict against Mr Chen himself is expected later this month ... The court also handed down an eighteen-month sentence to Diana Chen, the former chairwoman of Taipei 1001, one of the world's tallest buildings. Prosecutors accused her of bribing the former president and his wife for an executive position in a state-run securities firm.

(www.bbc.co.uk, 2 September 2009)

Wu Shu-chen ... [has been sentenced] to a year in prison for lying to prosecutors in her husband's corruption case ... [She] was convicted on charges that she helped her son, her daughter and her son-in-law provide false testimony in the wide-ranging trial of her husband, Chen Shui-bian.

(www.cnn.com, 2 September 2009)

10 September 2009. 'President Ma Ying-jeou swore in a new cabinet yesterday [Thursday 10 September]' (*FT*, 11 September 2009, p. 10).

11 September 2009.

Former President Chen Shui-bian and his wife, former first lady Wu Shu-chen, were convicted Friday [11 September] on corruption and money laundering charges and sentenced to life in prison ... Prosecutors said Chen embezzled $17.7 million, took bribes, laundered money and illegally removed classified documents from the president's office. The challenge for them was to prove Chen had handed out political favours in exchange for money. Chen has countered that the bribe money was actually political donations. He has also said that a special presidential fund from which he is accused of embezzling does not clearly say what the money can and cannot be used for.

(www.cnn.com, 11 September 2009)

Former President Chen Shui-bian was charged with embezzlement, taking bribes and money laundering, involving a total of $15 million while in office from 2000 to 2008 ... [He and his wife] were also fined $15 million ... Mr Chen has admitted accepting money but said it was campaign contributions ... Mr Chen and his wife were both sentenced to life for embezzling $3.15 million from a special presidential fund. They received lesser sentences on the charges related to accepting at least $9 million in bribes from a Taiwanese company to help it sell a piece of land to the government and of accepting nearly $3 million in kickbacks for helping a contractor gain a government project ... Their son and daughter-in-law received sentences ranging from twenty to thirty months for money laundering. Other relatives received suspended sentences. Two former advisers were given sentences of sixteen and twenty years in prison.

(www.bbc.co.uk, 11 September 2009)

Together they were fined a total of $15.2 million … Chen was charged with embezzling $3.15 million during his presidency from a special presidential fund, receiving bribes worth at least $9 million in connection with a government land deal, laundering some of the money through Swiss bank accounts, and forging documents. Wu Shu-chen was charged with money laundering and other graft offences … Chen's son and daughter-in-law were also convicted on money laundering charges. They were sentenced to two-and-a-half and one-year terms, respectively … Chen Shui-bian served two terms as president in 2000–2008 … Most Taiwanese were convinced he was guilty of at least some of the charges he faced, though some supporters believe his anti-China views played a role in his prosecution … Under Taiwanese law it is mandatory for the trial court to file and appeal in cases involving a life or death sentence … Mr Chen's most ardent supporters said the trial was a political witch-hunt.

(www.iht.com, 11 September 2009; *IHT*, 12 September 2009, p. 5)

Former President Chan Shui-bian … [was given] the maximum sentence and fined T$200 million ($6.1 million). Wu Shu-chen, his wife, was also convicted of corruption, given a life sentence and fined T$300 million, but will not have to go to prison because of her frail health … Mr Chen's daughter received a six-month sentence last week on lesser charges.

(*FT*, 12 September 2009, p. 5)

The young democracy is now divided between those who are celebrating the fact that even the most powerful are not immune from the legal process and those who see the prosecution, conviction and harsh sentencing of a former president as evidence that the courts are under the sway of politicians … It is generally believed by the Taiwanese public, analysts say, that Chen Shui-bian had been involved in some kind of wrongdoing, although there is also doubt that the former president has been fairly treated by the judiciary … The opposition Democratic Progressive Party produced a careful statement claiming that Taiwan's judicial system is flawed and supporting Mr Chen's appeal, but also saying that the ex-president should take responsibility for his actions, for example, by remitting large sums of money kept by his family overseas.

(www.economist.com, 12 September 2009)

Chen Shui-bian faces a new investigation. This time he is up for treason, a crime that can carry the death penalty. The bizarre charge springs from his own bizarre claim: that, during his tenure, he was an American agent. The thinking derives from a tiny band of fringe independence activists, now calling itself the Formosa National Legal Strategy Association. It argues that the San Francisco peace treaty, signed in 1951 to end the Second World War, did not award sovereignty over Taiwan to either Communist China or the Republic of China, over which the remnants of China's National Party, the Kuomintang (KMT), still claimed to rule. The association insists the

> treaty overrides all subsequent agreements, and Taiwan is still the territory of Japan's conqueror, the United States, its status comparable to that of Puerto Rico ... Mr Chen weighed in to back the association, claiming that, as president, he took orders from the Americans. After his sentencing in September he sued for his freedom in the United States Court of Appeal for the Armed Forces, proclaiming his innocence and arguing that America should intervene, as Taiwan was technically under its occupation. Mr Chen said he did this to clarify that Taiwan was separate from China ... The American appeals court declined the case in early October. The Supreme Court has also refused to consider the association's case.
>
> (*The Economist*, 24 October 2009, p. 72)

('One of the annual rituals performed at the United Nations General Assembly in New York is off the programme this year [2009]. For the first time since 1993 Taiwan is not to ask its little band of twenty-three diplomatic partners to propose it for UN membership ... This week officials made it clear that, besides shelving the bid for membership – already watered down last year [2008] to seeking merely "meaningful participation" in UN activities – Taiwan will not even try to join UN bodies that require members to be states. Instead it is only asking to join two specific UN agencies. It wants to become, like Palestine, an observer at the International Civil Aviation Organization. And it wants to join the United Nations Framework Convention on Climate Change. It is even prepared to be flexible over the contentious issue of the name the island uses ... Taiwan, the Republic of China, lost its UN seat to China in 1971' *The Economist*, 26 September 2009, p. 70.)

7 October 2009.

> Taiwan and China have opened the first joint exhibition by their two leading museums in six decades ... Taiwan and China hold their first joint exhibition of relics ... The exhibition – in Taipei's National Palace Museum – features items from the Qing Dynasty Emperor Yongzheng, including thirty-seven items of the royal collections from the Palace Museum in Beijing and 209 items owned by the Taiwan Museum ... The Taiwanese say there will not be any loans going in the opposite direction until an agreement is reached about Beijing's claims on treasures still in Taipei.
>
> (www.bbc.co.uk, 7 October 2009)

12 November 2009.

> New suspicions have been raised about the apparent attempted assassination of former President Chen Shui-bian in 2004 ... Investigators who re-examined the eve-of-election shooting found no blood or bullet holes in his underwear or trousers. At the time it was claimed Mr Chen had been shot and wounded in the lower part of his abdomen ... The investigator who compiled the new report concluded there were many suspicious aspects to the affair in addition to the lack of blood stains ... The new probe was

> ordered by the ruling Nationalist Party (KMT), which fielded the candidate who lost to Mr Chen.
>
> (www.bbc.co.uk, 12 November 2009)

5 December 2009

> A strong showing by the opposition party in local elections could serve as a warning to President Ma Ying-jeou … The Democratic Progressive Party [DPP] did well at the polls Saturday [5 December] … The DPP sharply closed the gap in several localities, winning 45.3 per cent of all votes against the Nationalists' 47.9 per cent.
>
> (*IHT*, 7 December 2009)

> President Ma Ying-jeou has ordered a thorough look at what went wrong on local weekend elections. These showed his ruling party … losing ground to the opposition … The elections for county magistrates and city mayors are being widely seen in Taiwan as a setback for President Ma and the Kuomintang. Although the party won a majority of the seats, the opposition Democratic Progressive Party gained nearly as big a percentage of votes, the largest percentage it has ever gained in local elections, narrowing the gap between the two parties … China has 1,500 missiles targeting Taiwan.
>
> (www.bbc.co.uk, 7 December 2009)

('Taiwanese companies have put more than $150 billion into 80,000 investment projects in China. There are now more than 270 direct flights between the island and the mainland every week': www.bbc.co.uk, 25 January 2010.)

> China on Thursday [7 January 2010] denounced the sale of advanced ai defence missiles by the United States to Taiwan, the first arms deal involving Taipei to be completed under President Barack Obama … [What is involved is] a $968 million contract for 253 Patriot Advanced Capability-3 missiles and related hardware. The deal also included the upgrading of Taiwan's existing Patriot missile defence system and the sale of spare parts.
>
> (www.ft.com, 7 January 2010)

'The sale … omits F-16 fighter jets and Black Hawk helicopters' (*IHT*, 14 January 2010, p. 4).

'The Americans did not agree to Taiwan's request for F-16 fighter jets and Black Hawk helicopters' (*The Economist*, 16 January 2010, p. 52).

'China says it has tested an advance missile interception system … Xinhua said: "[China has] tested a mid-course missile interception technology on domestic territory."' (*FT*, 13 January 2010, p. 5).

'China said Tuesday [12 January] that its successful test of anti-missile technology, coming amid rising tension over US weapon sales to Taiwan, was defensive in nature and part of military modernization' (*IHT*, 13 January 2010, p, 8). 'News accounts did not provide details about the test late Monday [11 January] and whether it destroyed its intended target' (*IHT*, 14 January 2010, p. 4). 'China announced that it had tested the country's first land-based missile defence system, a test that Chinese and Western analysts said was timed to convey Beijing's annoyance over the expected America arms sales to Taiwan' (www.iht.com, 30 January 2010).

'[China] did not specify whether a missile had been destroyed' (www.thetimes.co.uk, 13 January 2010).

> Xinhua on 11 January announced China's successful test of a land-based missile defence system ... The test apparently made China the only country after America to use a missile to destroy another in space. A Pentagon official confirmed that two missiles had been detected and that they had collided outside the earth's atmosphere. The Pentagon was not informed in advance ... China has been conducting on-and-off research into missile defence systems since the 1960s. But the technology it appears now to be mastering could just as well be used for attacking satellites.
>
> (*The Economist*, 16 January 2010, p. 52)

> The Obama administration has approved an arms sales package to Taiwan worth more than $6 billion ... The US Congress has thirty days to comment on the newest arms sales before the plan goes forward. Lawmakers have traditionally supported such sales ... The administration deferred a decision on selling F-16 fighter planes to Taiwan ... [but] added that they were not shutting the door to future F-16 sales ... [The Pentagon decided] not to include the fighters and a design plan for diesel submarines ... The last time the United States sold F-16s to Taiwan was in 1992 under President George H.W. Bush ... China has more than 1,000 ballistic missiles aimed at Taiwan ... The United States is Taiwan's most important ally and largest arms supplier, and it is bound by law to ensure the island is able to respond to Chinese threats ... The United States has been supplying Taiwan with arms under the Taiwan Relations Act, which Congress approved in 1979 and which mandates that the United States supply weapons that Taiwan could use to fend off an attack by mainland China forces.
>
> (www.iht.com, 30 January 2010)

'[The United States] left out the most controversial items: F-16 jets and diesel submarines' (www.iht.com, 11 February 2010).

'America is obliged under the Taiwan Relations Act of 1979 to provide the island with the arms it needs to defend itself' (www.economist.com, 2 February 2010). 'For six decades now Taiwan has been where the simmering distrust between China and America most risks boiling over. In 1986 Deng Xiaoping called it the "one obstacle in Sino-US relations"' (*The Economist*, 6 February 2010, p. 12).

'China has suspended military exchanges with the United States and threatened sanctions against American defence companies Saturday [30 January], just hours after Washington announced $6.4 billion in planned arms sales to Taiwan' (www.iht.com, 30 January 2010).

The Chinese government has announced a broad series of measures in retaliation … including the unusual step of imposing sanctions on American companies that supply the weapons systems … Xinhua said a planned visit by US Defence Secretary Robert Gates this year [2010] was being shelved … China is a major customer of companies like Boeing, whose McDonnell Douglas subsidiary builds the Harpoon missile being sent to Taiwan. Other companies that could be affected … include Sikorsky Aircraft (a unit of United Technologies), Lockheed Martin, and Raytheon.

(*IHT*, 1 February 2010, pp. 1, 4)

Beijing said it would suspend military exchanges with the United States, impose sanctions on companies selling arms, and review co-operation on major issues … China's latest views are what the United States would have expected, as the US view is that military exchanges are of limited use … Xinhua quoted the defence ministry as saying: 'Considering the severe harm and odious effect of US arms sales to Taiwan, the Chinese side has decided to suspend planned mutual military visits' … The foreign ministry said it would impose sanctions on US companies selling weapons to Taiwan, and that co-operation on major international issues would be affected. The United States, like the EU, has banned its companies selling arms to China since the 1989 Tiananmen Square massacre.

(www.bbc.co.uk, 30 January 2010)

Taiwan's Ministry of National Defence said yesterday [5 February] it had placed a rare order … [for] the Taiwan air force … for equipment from a European manufacturer … [The order involved] three helicopters from an EADS subsidiary … [worth] $111 million … The Chinese foreign ministry said: 'We understand these are rescue helicopters. We will continue to monitor the situation, especially the use of the planes' … [Taiwan said] the three EC225 helicopters were for search and rescue and had no military specifications … [that] 'the equipment is civilian'.

(*FT*, 6 February 2010, p. 6)

Taiwan's decision to relax some restrictions on investment in mainland China will help its flat panel manufacturers compete in the mainland's booming consumer electronics market, analysts and company officials said Thursday [11 February]. The top producer of liquid crystal display panels in Taiwan, AU Optronics, said it would apply to the Taiwanese government to build an advanced LCD panel facility in China as soon as possible. Until now Taiwanese companies have been allowed only panel modules – consisting of panels and frames – in China. The company expects China to become the world's number one market for flat screen televisions sometime next year [2011]. AU Optronics, which has 20 per cent of the market in China for the screens used in such televisions, said the new rules would help it compete against South Korean and Chinese rivals … The government in Taiwan, under pressure from its top technology companies and other businesses, has been relaxing limits on China-bound investment over the past decade. Taiwan said Wednesday [10 February] that it would let flat panel makers build screen-making factories in China, as long as their most advanced plants stayed in Taiwan and they keep equivalent investments on the island. The government also lifted some limits on investment in China by semiconductor companies, and will let them use more advanced manufacturing technology at their mainland plants. Also relaxed were China investment rules for Taiwan chip testers, packagers and companies involved in real estate, telecommunications, wind power and solar energy … The move by Taiwan on Wednesday followed the South Korean government's approval late last year of ambitious plans by those two companies for joint venture factories in China.

(www.iht.com, 11 February 2010; *IHT*, 12 February 2010, p. 18)

Taiwan's economy grew 9.2 per cent in the fourth quarter [of 2009], the government says, boosted by stimulus-fuelled demand from China … The economy contracted 1.9 per cent for all of 2009 … Economic growth of 4.7 per cent [is predicted] for 2010. Taiwan's export-orientated economy was badly hit by the global recession, but a wide-ranging stimulus programme in China – its biggest market – boosted high-tech and other sales in the second half of the year [2009].

(www.iht.com, 22 February 2010)

Taiwan's economy grew at an annualized rate of 18 per cent in the last three months of 2009, driven by demand for high-tech products from mainland China … Taiwan's economic growth is measured on an annualized basis – which shows what the annual rate would be if the latest change continued the whole year … Comparing the fourth quarter with the same period of 2008 its economy expanded 9.2 per cent.

(www.bbc.co.uk, 22 February 2010)

3 The regaining of sovereignty over Hong Kong and Macao (and later developments)

The regaining of sovereignty over Macao on 20 December 1999

> Current laws provided for popular election of only twelve of twenty-nine legislators. The chief executive is appointed by an electoral college of influential citizens, most of whom are seen as conservative allies of Beijing … The government of chief executive Edmund Ho has ruled for the eight years since China resumed sovereignty … The Sino-Portuguese Joint Declaration of 1987 and the Basic Law, Macao's mini constitution, make no mention of universal suffrage as the ultimate goal of political reform, as Hong Kong's Basic Law does … In what has traditionally been a placid political environment, the signs of public discontent are emerging. Several thousand people protested on 1 October [2007], China's National Day, for the first time. They marched on government house over a potpourri of grievances ranging from harsh new penalties for illegal parking of motorcycles, to corruption in government and the use of illegal labour. It followed a rowdy protest in May on similar issues. Another protest is expected in December to coincide with the anniversary of the handover to China … Macao's small democratic movement is also riding the wave of discontent to step up its campaign for direct elections for the chief executive and Legislative Assembly … Democrats say the [present] system stifles debate and encourages corruption and government secrecy … [On 3 October] democrats handed a proposal for reform to a representative of the chief executive's office, demanding a consultation with the government on increasing the number of directly elected legislators, in stages, and on the direct election of the chief executive … There is a common theme to recent anti-government sentiment, say legislators and political analysts. Living standards for the poor and middle class are being eroded, and the government of chief executive Edmund Ho … is out of touch. An annual report from the European Commission on conditions in Macao said in August that the gambling boom, instead of lifting the quality of life for the Macanese, had resulted in 'steep and widening inequality of incomes'. With imported workers – principally from mainland China but also South-east Asia – numbering about 70,000 or a quarter of the

> work force – the labour market has become more competitive and wages have not kept up with price rises and rents have risen by 200 per cent to 300 per cent … By most measures Macao has been a huge economic success. Last year [2006] the economy grew by 16.6 per cent, one of the fastest rates in the world. In the second quarter of this year [2007] growth was 31.9 per cent. Official unemployment in August was 3.1 per cent … The city's twenty-three casinos generated revenues of $6.87 billion in 2006, surpassing Las Vegas [in the United States] as the largest gaming market in the world … Political analysts say the popular frustration over widening income inequality is being exacerbated by a perception the government is corrupt and too close to the casinos and other business interests. Ho's government has been plagued by a succession of bribery scandals, the most damaging involving Ao Man-long, the secretary for transport and public works … Although Ao's arrest … last December [2006] on charges of accepting bribes and money laundering … helped Ho bolster his antigraft credentials, the case is viewed as the tip of a much deeper corruption problem and has provided momentum for public protest.
>
> (*IHT*, 8 October 2007, p. 2)

'Macao. A former Portuguese colony about 60 kilometres, or about 38 miles, west of Hong Kong, is the only place in China where casino gambling is legal' (www.iht.com, 5 November 2007).

> Macao's highest court sentenced a former minister to twenty-seven years in jail Wednesday [30 January 2008] for taking millions of dollars in kickbacks, in the Chinese gambling enclave's largest corruption case … [He was] arrested in December 2006.
>
> Ao Man-long, a former transport and public works minister, was found guilty on fifty-seven counts of taking bribes, laundering money and abusing his power to help property developers win lucrative construction tenders. In recent years Macao … has drawn several high profile Las Vegas operators who have invested billions of dollars in building upscale casino resorts to attract China's newly rich. Ao was accused of handling some of those construction contracts to companies in return for kickbacks.
>
> (www.iht.com, 30 January 2008)

> Edmund Ho, chief executive of the Macao Special Administrative Region, announced a new freeze on new gambling licences and land allocations for new casinos, saying Tuesday [22 April] that he was following directives from Beijing … Also among the new restrictions announced Tuesday was a moratorium on applications for new tables and slot machines at existing casinos.
>
> (www.iht.com, 23 April 2008)

> Macao [is] gloomy as more lay-offs hit [the] once booming casinos … The global economic downturn has not helped, of course, but Macao's hoteliers, casino operators and gaming experts say the real culprit is the visa controls being imposed by China. Two-thirds of Macao's gamblers come from

> mainland China – principally from neighbouring Guangdong province with a population, including migrants, of more than 110 million. The new regulations limit mainlanders to one visit every three months. Most experts see the regulations as Beijing putting the brakes on a white-hot economy that was stressing the territory's infrastructure, sending property prices soaring and causing social problems and labour unrest.
>
> (www.iht.com, 24 December 2008)

'The US-based Las Vegas Sands group has halted construction of five hotels, huge shopping centres and several new casinos. About 10,000 foreign workers and 2,000 workers from Macao have lost their jobs so far' (www.bbc.co.uk, 5 January 2009).

> The Communist Party, in trying to get control of an epidemic of gambling by public officials, announced a crackdown in 2005. That effort was flimsy and largely ineffective, but a drastic reduction in travel visas to Macao that began last summer [2008] has had more teeth. The new rules limit trips to Macao from the mainland to once every three months and for no more than seven days … To finance their gambling in Macao officials and managers have pillaged state funds, company accounts and municipal treasuries … Losses at tables bankrupted at least ten companies … The party's Central Committee for Discipline and Inspection recently issued a stern warning about corruption by party and government officials; the warning specifically mentioned gambling … Gambling … accounts for more than 78 per cent of its tax base, according to Macao's financial services bureau.
>
> (*IHT*, 15 January 2009, p. 2)

'China recently placed restrictions on its citizens visiting Macao, for fear of capital flight' (www.bbc.co.uk, 12 January 2009).

> A new state security law has taken effect in Macao to punish crimes of treason, secession or subversion against the Chinese government. It also punishes what it calls 'preparatory acts' of these crimes and the theft of state secrets. Rights watchdogs have criticized the ambiguous, catch-all language of the law. Democrat legislators have said the law in Macao is intended by China to set an example for less pliant Hong Kong. The Chinese government says the law is to fulfil Article 23 of the Basic Law governing the return of Macao and Hong Kong to Chinese sovereignty. It provides for sentences of up to thirty years for political crimes … In Hong Kong earlier Chinese government efforts to pass the law prompted huge protests in 2003 … Two members of Macao's twenty-nine-member Legislative Assembly voted against the bill last week.
>
> (www.bbc.co.uk, 3 March 2009)

'In the past year Macao has denied entry to several potentially bothersome visitors from Hong Kong, including a pro-Tibet student activist, a press photographer and members of its Legislative Council' (*The Economist*, 19 March 2009, p. 68).

Macao, now an autonomous special administrative region of China, is the only place in China where casinos are legal. Half of Macao's visitors come from the mainland. The figure is 82 per cent when neighbouring Hong Kong, also a special administrative region, is included.

(www.iht.com, 31 May 2009)

Only one candidate appears to be in the running to become Macao's new chief executive – former social and cultural affairs secretary Fernando Chui ... This means he will succeed Edmund Ho in December [2009] as the second chief executive since Macao's return to Chinese rule ... The vote is scheduled for 26 July, and Mr Chui only needs 151 votes in the election to become leader. Mr Chui is a member of one of the leading, richest families in Macao.

(www.bbc.co.uk, 17 June 2009)

Fernando Chui will automatically become the next chief executive of Macao ... having secured ... 286 nominations from the territory's 300-member ... pro-Beijing 'election committee' ... With fifty nominations required to enter the race no one else will be able to run against him ... Although it has a population of only 550,000 Macao is the world's largest gaming market, with casino revenues that exceed those of its two largest rivals – Las Vegas and Atlantic City – combined ... Beijing has ... limited visa access for Chinese tourists and gamblers. In the first quarter of this year [2009] casino revenues fell by 12.8 per cent against the same period last year [2008]. Macao is the only place in China where casinos are allowed to operate. Its gaming industry was liberalized in 2002.

(www.ft.com, 17 June 2009)

Legislative elections in Macao attracted a higher turnout than usual and strengthened the democratic minority, early results have shown.

[There was a] 60 per cent turnout ... [Macao] can choose only twelve out of twenty-nine seats ... Initial results published on Monday [21 September] showed Macao's pro-democracy camp winning three of the twelve directly elected seats – one more than in the previous poll ... The other seventeen seats are filled by appointees chosen by special interest groups or by Macao's incoming leader, Chief Executive Fernando Chui ... He will formally succeed Edmund Ho in December [2009], as the second chief executive since Macao's return to Chinese rule.

(www.bbc.co.uk, 21 September 2009)

The regaining of sovereignty over Hong Kong on 1 July 1997

The following are significant dates in Hong Kong's history:

1839–42. The Opium War between China and Britain.

26 January 1841. A British naval contingent raises the British flag on Hong Kong Island. (Hong Kong means 'fragrant harbour'.)

29 August 1842. Hong Kong Island is ceded to Britain in perpetuity in Treaty of Nanking.
October 1860. The Kowloon peninsula (3 square miles) is ceded to Britain.
9 June 1898. The New Territories (consisting of 235 islands and a mainland area adjoining Kowloon) is leased to Britain for ninety-nine years.
1941–5. Hong Kong is occupied by Japan.

A chronology of political events since 1 July 2006

1 July 2006.

The 1 July anniversary of the return of Hong Kong to Chinese sovereignty … [sees a] march for democracy … Under the Basic Law … it is theoretically possible for the city's voters to select all their political leaders, including the chief executive, in unrestricted elections after 2007. Changing the system to make this a reality would have required the approval of a two-thirds majority of Hong Kong's Legislative Council plus the backing of the chief executive and China's National People's Congress … Elections for Hong Kong's chief executive, the regional government leader, are due to be held in spring 2007 under the existing electoral system, which restricts voting to an electoral college of 800 prominent citizens, many of whom are handpicked. In 2008 Hong Kong will install a new legislature, but only half its members will be directly elected by the public.

(www.iht.com, 30 June 2006)

Organizers say 58,000 took part … [in] a rally calling for full democracy … Police put the figure at 28,000 … A pro-China rally held earlier in the day also attracted large numbers of people – police said 40,000 took part … The economy is doing well and new leader Donald Tsang is proving popular.

(www.bbc.co.uk, 1 July 2006)

More than 45,000 jubilant residents participated in a carnival parade in the morning organized by pro-Beijing groups celebrating the territory's reunification with the mainland, and roughly an equal number of eager protesters took to the streets in a pro-democracy march in the afternoon, demanding solutions to a number of issues, above all universal suffrage … Anson, who worked as chief secretary when Donald Tsang was financial secretary … [leaving] the government in 2001 … took part in the pro-democracy march … The pro-democracy march drew close to half a million in 2003 and 2004 … [In 2005] the number of participants [was] down to about 20,000 … [Anson Chan] first took to the streets in a march on 4 December [2005] calling for universal suffrage, in response to an electoral reform proposed by the government that was criticized by pro-democracy legislators as insufficient. The march drew 100,000 people and the proposal was voted down later that month. In spite of this political stumble the Tsang-led government has otherwise enjoyed relatively high popularity, with unemployment at its

> lowest point since 2003 and the government running a surplus for the first time since 1997. Tsang enjoys an average popularity rating of 60 per cent to 70 per cent, as compared with Tung Chee-hwa's 48 per cent when he resigned in March 2005 … A survey [was] released by the Public Opinion Programme at the University of Hong Kong last week showing that positive feeling about the mainland's policies toward Hong Kong has shot up by 20 percentage points to 56 per cent, its highest point since the poll was begun in 1999.
>
> (www.iht.com, 2 July 2006)

19 July 2006. 'Anson Chan announced Wednesday [19 July] that she was forming a political grouping to work for full democracy in the territory' (www.iht.com, 19 July 2006).

24 July 2006.

> On Monday [24 July] it [the Hong Kong government] released a discussion paper on how a chief executive might be chosen under a democratic system, although all the options require a committee to vet potential candidates first, which is a requirement of the Basic Law.
>
> (www.iht.com, 25 July 2006)

6 August 2006.

> Pro-Beijing lawmakers approved legislation Sunday [6 August] giving broad authority to the police to conduct surveillance, including wiretapping phones, bugging homes and offices and monitoring email. The bill was passed by the sixty-member Legislative Council in a vote of thirty-two to zero soon after pro-democracy lawmakers walked out of the chamber in protest … The Democratic Party and its allies had tried to introduce nearly 200 amendments through four days of marathon debates, but all were defeated or ruled out of order. Ambrose Lee, the Hong Kong secretary for security, welcomed the legislation, saying it was necessary to fight crime … But James To, the Democratic Party lawmaker who is chairman of the legislature's security committee, said the law gave too much discretion to the police and to the chief executive of Hong Kong. He contended that the law would make it too easy for the government to monitor political opponents … Since long before Hong Kong's handover by Britain to China in 1997 the police here have relied on a section of the city's telecommunications ordinance for their authority to conduct covert surveillance … Recent court cases have provided hints that the surveillance is extensive. Some experts said that establishing a clear legal framework for the surveillance represented an improvement.
>
> (*IHT*, 7 August 2006, p. 14)

24 September 2006.

> The most popular and influential democracy advocate has announced that she will not run for chief executive this winter … Anson Chan, who had

been Hong Kong's chief secretary and second highest official before and after the return to Chinese rule, criticized the highly restrictive rules that Beijing had chosen for the selection of chief executive … Election rules require a candidate to be nominated by at least 100 members of the election committee.

(www.iht.com, 24 September 2006)

11 December 2006.

Democracy supporters have won enough seats on an election committee to put a candidate on Hong Kong's leadership race ballot for the first time since the British colony returned to China rule nearly ten years ago, the democrats said Monday [11 December]. Pro-democracy lawmakers won more than 100 seats on the 800-member election panel, which will decide who can run in the March [2007] vote for the city's chief executive … Candidates for the chief executive need to be supported by at least 100 members of the committee to be included on the ballot. In the past two elections the pro-Beijing candidate coasted to victory unchallenged.

(*IHT*, 12 December 2006, p. 7)

('Only 204,000 registered voters can participate … Nearly half, or 373, of the 800 seats have already been determined because those races are uncontested or the electors are appointed': www.iht.com, 10 December 2006).

31 January 2007.

Hong Kong is poised to hold the first election in more than half a century that includes a democracy advocate seeking high office in territory controlled by Beijing. A pro-democracy politician, Alan Leong, announced on Wednesday [31 January] that he had obtained enough nominations to appear on the ballot to become the territory's next chief executive. But Leong acknowledged that he had no chance of beating the Beijing-backed incumbent, Donald Tsang, who is seeking reelection. The ballot on 25 March [2007] will be the first election for a chief executive since Britain returned Hong Kong to China in 1997.

(*IHT*, 1 February 2007, p. 8)

1 February 2007.

New rules have come into effect in Hong Kong designed to limit the number of pregnant women arriving from mainland China to give birth … The women are attracted by the chance to gain Hong Kong residency rights for their children, including health care and education. A Hong Kong birth also allows women to circumvent China's one-child policy and can give access to higher standards of medical care. Last year [2006] some 12,000 mainlanders arrived to give birth, leaving Hong Kong's medical facilities struggling to cope … As a further disincentive to cross-border births Chinese mothers will now have to pay double the hospital fees of their Hong Kong counterparts.

(www.bbc.co.uk, 31 January 2007)

25 March 2007.

Donald Tsang was reelected on Sunday [25 March] by a wide margin as Hong Kong's chief executive, following a campaign that drew unexpected interest as the first contested election for the territory's top job since Britain returned it to China in 1997. Tsang prevailed by a vote of 649 to 123 over Alan Leong, a former chairman of the Hong Kong Bar Association who was the first democracy advocate to obtain a place on the ballot here ... There were eleven bank ballots and five ballots [were] ruled invalid ... With strong backing from Beijing, Tsang's reelection was never in doubt. The electors are mainly wealthy business people and politicians with close ties to the mainland ... [The vote was held in] the nearly 800-member Election Committee ... Hong Kong held its first election debates, pitting Tsang against an opponent actively promoting democracy. Analysts said Leong, a trial lawyer, offered a compelling argument for democracy and was able to force Tsang to commit publicly to focus on universal suffrage during his next term, which expires in 2012 ... The elections represented the first time that a secret ballot has been used to choose the next leader of Hong Kong ... In an interview with five correspondents [on 23 March] Tsang said that he wanted to introduce a democracy plan in the next five years that would satisfy the 60 per cent of Hong Kong's people who consistently tell pollsters that they want a system of one person, one vote ... Leong said at a separate press conference after the vote that he planned to continue campaigning for universal suffrage to be introduced by 2012 ... The two most prominent figures in the pro-democracy movement here – Martin Lee, the founding chairman of the Democratic Party and Anson Chan, a former second-ranking official in the Hong Kong government – declined to run this spring.

(www.iht.com, 25 March 2007)

That Donald Tsang faced a serious and articulate challenger in the Civic Party legislator Alan Leong was itself a first for Hong Kong ... [which has a population of] 7 million ... Leong, a former chairman of the Hong Kong Bar Association, was the first democracy advocate to obtain a place on the ballot ... The government has failed to deal with increasingly dangerous air pollution, to act on promises to address rising income inequality and to spend money on social problems ... Tsang is in theory committed to pushing towards direct elections for all the legislature and the chief executive but only as far as 'consensus' and Beijing permit.

(www.iht.com, 27 March 2007)

Donald Tsang, Hong Kong's chief executive, easily won a second term after securing more than 80 per cent of votes ... He received 649 of 772 votes cast. Alan Leong picked up just 123 votes ... Alan Leong said his participation in what he called a 'rigged election' had nonetheless advanced Hong Kong's democratic movement and its demands for the introduction of full democracy by 2012, when the next chief executive election is held. Hong

Kong's 795-member Election Committee is dominated by business and community figures unwilling to challenge Beijing … During the campaign Mr Tsang pledged to produce 'a final arrangement' for the introduction of universal suffrage before the end of his second term. Yesterday [25 March], however, he refused to be drawn on whether he thought the next chief executive could be popularly elected.

(*FT*, 26 March 2007, p. 10)

Cardinal Joseph Zen said this weekend that the Vatican had turned down his offer to retire as bishop of Hong Kong and focus most of his energies on mainland China. Cardinal bishops traditionally offer their resignations when they turn seventy-five, as Zen did in January [2007] … Zen also explained the Hong Kong diocese's decision not to allow clergy to fill the church's seven positions as electors in the election on Sunday [25 March] to choose the next chief executive of Hong Kong, even though there is no specific Vatican policy against priests serving on the body. The diocese allowed parishioners to apply to fill the seven spots, but gave no indication on how to vote.

(www.iht.com, 25 March 2007)

4 June 2007.

[In Hong Kong] people gathered Monday [4 June] to commemorate the bloody [Tiananmen] crackdown … Thousands of people usually gather … At least thirteen little-known Chinese are still behind bars for their roles in the pro-democracy movement, a human rights group … the Chinese Human Rights Defenders … said Monday.

(www.iht.com, 4 June 2007)

1 July 2007. The tenth anniversary of the return of Hong Kong to China. Hong Kong was returned to China at midnight on 30 June 1997.

The largest part of Hong Kong's land area, the New Territories, had been Britain's under a ninety-nine-year lease granted in 1898. China never recognized that agreement, nor indeed the treaties ceding Hong Kong Island and Kowloon in perpetuity … China agreed to negotiations with Britain that led to the two countries' 'Joint Declaration', confirming Hong Kong's reversion to China at the end of the lease.

(*The Economist*, 30 June 2007, Survey on Hong Kong, p. 3)

Hong Kong's first decade under Chinese rule got off to a rough start. The Asian financial crisis erupted [on 2 January 1997] a day after the handover. Hong Kong was hammered and was finally recovering when it was hit by an outbreak of SARS … [which] killed nearly 300 people [299] in the city and ravaged its vital tourist industry.

(www.iht.com, 29 June 2007)

'President Hu Jintao arrived in Hong Kong [on 29 June] for special celebrations marking the tenth anniversary of Hong Kong's handover from Britain to

China ... This is Hu Jintao's first visit to Hong Kong since he became president' (www.bbc.co.uk, 29 June 2007).

'[On 1 July] Hong Kong's Chief Executive, Donald Tsang ... was sworn in for a second term in office by President Hu Jintao' (www.bbc.co.uk, 1 July 2007).

Donald Tsang:

> Democracy is growing in an orderly way ... [Political development should be] gradual and orderly ... We will develop a system that is more democratic ... A green paper will be published this year [2007] so that we can all work together to identify the most acceptable mode of universal suffrage to best serve the interest of Hong Kong ... The competition ahead is fierce. We are not only competing with neighbouring cities, but with cities around the world.
>
> (www.bbc.co.uk, 1 July 2007; www.cnn.com, 1 July 2007; www.iht.com, 1 July 2007; *IHT*, 2 July 2007, p. 3)

> Carrying small flags that bore the slogan 'One Person, One Vote', protesters marched through the heart of the city Sunday afternoon [1 July] in sweltering heat to demand greater democracy. The police put the march at 20,000, but organizers said that 68,000 had marched. By comparison a half million people marched the same route on 1 July 2003, when Donald Tsang's predecessor as chief executive, Tung Chee-hwa, was trying to impose stringent internal security legislation ... Media freedom has been a persistent issue here [in Hong Kong], with many media outlets owned by pro-Beijing proprietors. RTHK, a government department operating radio and television channels in competition with the private sector, was under tight British control in its early days but has evolved into a sophisticated news-gathering operation that frequently irritates pro-Beijing groups and the government with its aggressive reporting. A recent government commission suggested that a reorganization of RTHK include dispersing the staff to other government agencies and hiring a new, presumably more pliant, staff. Many of the demonstrators Sunday were carrying pennants from a group called SaveRTHK.org that read: 'One Person, One Vote'. The biggest surprise Sunday came when Cardinal Joseph Zen Ze-kiun, the Roman Catholic bishop of Hong Kong, chose for the first time to participate in such a march, and even helped carry a large protest flag in the front row of marchers ... He did not appear in his bishop's robes for the march, wearing instead a white short-sleeved shirt, black trousers and a white clerical collar ... Zen participated in prayer meetings before each of the four previous democracy marches on 1 July, and did so again on Sunday, but always refused to march before, saying that this would be disruptive.
>
> (www.iht.com, 1 July 2007; *IHT*, 2 July 2007, p. 3)

'The annual democracy rally attracted at least 6,000 people' (*Guardian*, 2 July 2007, p. 26).

Opinion polls [in Hong Kong] regularly rate the courts highly for their partiality and fairness ... The independence and integrity of the judiciary have also been paramount to the success of Hong Kong as a regional financial and business centre ... Democrats get a little uneasy at any suggestion that Beijing might seek to encroach upon the Basic Law's promise that the courts will exercise judicial power 'independently, free from any interference' and that the pre-1997 judicial system will be maintained ... At the end of British rule a new Court of Final Appeal took the place of the Privy Council in London as the region's highest court ... The Basic Law stipulates the right to appoint foreign judges. Hence, 18 per cent of judges are expatriates, as are fifteen of the sixteen judges on the Court of Final Appeal. On the Court of Final Appeal there is a system of rotating senior judges who have served on courts of the same rank in common-law countries like Britain, Australia and New Zealand ... The great fear of democrats is that the National People's Congress Standing Committee, which has the ultimate power to interpret the Basic Law, might try to curtail the freedom of the courts or issue a preemptive interpretation of the Basic Law if it fears it might lose on an important issue in the courts. On three occasions since 1997 the Standing Committee has issued such interpretations. Among the most controversial was in 1999, when it moved to limit the consequences of a ruling by the Court of Final Appeal on who had the right of abode in Hong Kong. The court had ruled that the children of parents who had the right of abode in Hong Kong also had that right. The ruling would have granted residency to hundreds of thousands of people in mainland China, although the exact number was hotly disputed. Fearing an influx of people, the Hong Kong government requested that the Standing Committee issue an interpretation of Basic Law provisions on residency rights. The Standing Committee's ruling had the effect of overturning the court's ruling for all future claimants, although the legal victory of the original group of Hong Kong Chinese litigants was allowed to stand.

(www.iht.com, 29 June 2007)

The Chinese government eased capital requirements for companies based in Hong Kong, giving them access to eleven new industries on the mainland ... The agreement, to take effect on 1 January 2008, cuts the amount of assets Hong Kong banks need to buy stakes in Chinese banks to $6 billion from $10 billion. Hong Kong tour operators, hospitals and other businesses will be given wider access to China's markets ... The mainland will introduce forty liberalization measures in twenty-eight services areas ... the agreement [is] the fourth supplementary accord to the Closer Economic Partnership Agreement (CEP) ... The first agreement was signed in June 2003 ... China will expand a zero-tariff programme for Hong Kong-manufactured goods including plastic flowers, chewing gum, black ink for printing, car engines and other items ... The zero tariffs will go into effect on 1 July [2007] ... Under CEP many Hong Kong goods already enjoy zero

> tariffs on entry to mainland China ... The CEPA framework came into effect in January 2004.
>
> (www.iht.com, 29 June 2007)

'Shanghai's port surpassed Hong Kong's this year [2007] as the world's second busiest behind Singapore. Another port in Shenzhen is expected to overtake Hong Kong next year [2008]' (www.cnn.com, 1 July 2007).

11 July 2007.

> The Hong Kong government embarked Wednesday [11 July] on a formal consultation with the city's people on the kind of democracy [that might be adopted] ... The government has promised to spend three months listening to the views of Hong Kong's 7 million people ... A consultation paper on constitutional development released by the government on Wednesday surveys several options ... Under an edict issued by Beijing the earliest the government can permit direct elections for the chief executive and entire sixty-member Legislative Council is in 2012. The paper, which largely dwells on the mechanics of electing the chief executive and legislature, sets out options for attaining universal suffrage by 2016 or beyond ... In the Basic Law, Hong Kong's mini constitution, universal suffrage is described as the 'ultimate aim' which is to be achieved by 'gradual and orderly progress' ... The Basic Law requires that even under a system of universal suffrage candidates for the chief executive must first have the support of a nominating committee. Among the issues discussed in the paper are how that nominating committee should be chosen, how many candidates should be allowed to run and procedures for the chief executive elections themselves.
>
> (www.iht.com, 11 July 2007)

> In mid-July the Hong Kong government opened a formal public consultation on the nature and timing of democratic reforms. Under current electoral arrangements the chief executive is elected once every five years by a largely pro-Beijing committee, comprising 800 representatives from the professions, social organizations and local and national legislatures. Only half of the sixty-seat Legislative Council is directly elected; the other half is chosen by professional groups called functional constituencies. Democrats have been pushing for the rapid implementation of a provision in the Basic Law, Hong Kong's mini-constitution, for 'gradual and orderly' progress towards the 'ultimate aim' of universal suffrage. The consultation paper released by the government in July sets out several options for reform and several target dates. It raised the possibility of direct, popular votes for either the chief executive or Legislative Council by 2012, 2016 or beyond. Government officials said they would propose a model for reform at the end of this year [2007] that would have wide community support ... Soon after the consultation began pro-Beijing figures signalled that China's communist rulers were opposed to the idea of direct elections being introduced in Hong Kong as early as 2012.
>
> (www.iht.com, 11 September 2007)

'Beijing must approve any changes' (*FT*, 12 July 2007, p. 10).

11 September 2007.

> Anson Chan ... a former Hong Kong chief secretary, the local government's second highest official ... announced Tuesday [11 September] that she would seek election to the local Legislature, giving a significant boost to a push for full democracy by 2012 ... Her candidacy in the 2 December [2007] by-election is a boost to the democratic camp, which is aiming to turn the contest for the seat into something of a referendum on public support for the introduction of full democracy by 2012 ... The seat [was] vacated by the recent death of Ma Lik, the former chairman of Hong Kong's largest pro-Beijing political party ... Opinion polls in various Hong Kong newspapers have shown strong public support for changes to be introduced in time for the next elections, in 2012.
>
> (www.iht.com, 11 September 2007)

'Although she will run as an independent, Anson Chan has been embraced by Hong Kong's two mainstream pro-democracy parties' (*FT*, 12 September 2007, p. 13).

7 October 2007. 'Up to 7,000 campaigners marched to government headquarters in a rally demanding full democracy by 2012' (*The Times*, 8 October 2007, p. 33).

'Anson Chan will help lead the march' (www.bbc.co.uk, 7 October 2007).

12 October 2007. Chief executive Donald Tsang:

> People can go to extremes like what we saw during the Cultural Revolution. For instance, in China, when people take everything into their own hands, then you cannot govern the place ... [It] was the people taking power into their own hands. Now that is what you mean by democracy if you take it to the full swing.
>
> (www.bbc.co.uk, 12 October 2007)

'Donald Tsang came under fire for citing the Cultural Revolution to argue that social stability should not be sacrificed for democratic development ... [He suggested] that China's Cultural Revolution was an extreme form of democracy' (www.bbc.co.uk, 12 October 2007).

13 October 2007. Donald Tsang: 'I am very sorry that I made an inappropriate remark concerning the Cultural Revolution during a radio interview yesterday, and I wish to retract that remark' (www.bbc.co.uk, 12 October 2007).

21–22 November 2007.

> China on Thursday [22 November] reversed a decision to block a US aircraft carrier strike group from visiting Hong Kong, but the change of heart by Beijing officials came too late to stop the US naval flotilla from returning to its base in Japan ... The 8,000-member crew was due in Hong Kong on

Wednesday [21 November] for a four-day visit to celebrate the US holiday of Thanksgiving. Some were planning to join family members who had flown from the United States, Japan and the Philippines. While the ships were nearby in the South China Sea, the Chinese foreign minister issued a 'last minute' refusal of the port call ... US Navy ships make frequent calls to ... Hong Kong.

(*IHT*, 23 November 2007, p. 2)

Two [US] minesweepers ... were sailing in international waters this month [November] when a serious Pacific Ocean storm threatened. The two vessels, relatively small, asked for permission to enter Hong Kong's harbour for fuel and safety. The request was denied ... About fifty US Navy ships visit Hong Kong each year.

(www.iht.com, 28 November 2007)

29 November 2007.

China blocked the visit of a US aircraft carrier battle group and other American warships to Hong Kong in retaliation for the Bush administration's upgrading of Taiwan's Patriot anti-missile batteries, the state media reported Thursday [29 November]. Beijing also denied that foreign minister Yang Jiechi had told President George W. Bush in a meeting Wednesday that the cancelled ship visits were a 'misunderstanding', as the White House had reported after the talks ... adding that China had 'grave concern' about US weapons sales to Taiwan ... [China] also asserted that Bush's meeting with the Dalai Lama in October had damaged ties ... The Pentagon lodged a formal protest Wednesday with the Chinese government after senior US naval commanders said they were particularly troubled by the unexplained decision to deny the minesweepers refuge ... Shortly after US Defence Secretary Robert Gates visited Beijing this month, the Pentagon announced that it would sell Taiwan upgrades to its Patriot missile system for about $940 million ... Patriot II missile systems and related equipment.

(www.iht.com, 29 November 2007)

The United States ... in apparent protest over the US aircraft carrier incident ... had the carrier sail through the Taiwan Strait on the way back to its base in Japan. That move prompted Beijing to express 'serious concern', implying that foreign vessels wishing to traverse the strait have to seek China's approval, even though the strait has always been regarded as international waters.

(www.iht.com, 20 December 2007)

('[On 21 December] US Defence Secretary Robert Gates dismissed as "specious" an explanation from China that it cancelled and refused port visits by American warships because Gates had not told officials in Beijing of planned sales to Taiwan ... [that] Gates had not informed them of arms sales to Taiwan that were announced in Washington shortly after the defence secretary's return from Asia ... Referring to his talks with the Chinese leadership in Beijing on

5–6 November Gates said: "In those conversations they raised at various levels our arms sales to Taiwan and I was very explicit that our arms sales were consistent with the Taiwan Relations Act and the joint statement … [I told the Chinese] that as long as they continued to build up their forces on their side of the Taiwan Strait we would continue to give Taiwan the resources to defend itself. So I think that to a certain extent I find that argument a little specious … [As regards the anti-satellite test] the foreign ministry did not seem to understand or know what had happened and there appeared to be some confusion … [Likewise the Chinese military in forbidding the port visits] may have made a decision that was not communicated to the political side of the government." ': www.iht.com, 22 December 2007.)

November 2007.

> In November the party closest to the Chinese Communist Party swept the polls in local elections … Nothing is simple in Hong Kong politics, where voters may support pro-Beijing parties perceived to be good at the practical business of running local councils, but favour the democrats when it comes to the big issues.
>
> (Stephen Vines, www.iht.com, 30 November 2007)

> The pro-democracy movement suffered a huge blow in last month's district elections [November] when Beijing-allied parties swept the board. Analysts put that loss down to voters' reluctance to rock the boat when the economy is on an upswing, due in part to Hong Kong's close relationship with mainland China.
>
> (www.iht.com, 2 December 2007)

'Democratic parties suffered one of their worst defeats at the hands of the pro-Beijing parties in local council elections' (www.iht.com, 3 December 2007).

'Last month [November] pro-democracy parties suffered heavy losses in district council elections, while Beijing-backed groups made huge gains. Analysts say the pro-Beijing parties benefited from a strong economy and good organization at district level' (www.bbc.co.uk, 2 December 2007).

2 December 2007.

> Anson Chan … is asking voters to support a model for direct elections of the chief executive and the legislature that is about as free and open as allowed under the Basic Law … [and] wants to have her model implemented by 2012, the earliest possible opportunity … Regina Ip also wants to see her model implemented in 2012, but is prepared to wait for several years longer to appease conservatives in Hong Kong and Beijing … Ip proposes that candidates for chief executive first win the approval of a minimum of 10 per cent of representatives of each of four main voting blocks in a 1,600-member nominating committee. The requirement for a nominating committee to vet candidates for their suitability is a requirement of the Basic Law. Chan says that would dramatically narrow the field of eligible chief execu-

> tive candidates. Some of the voting blocks – which are made up of representatives from business sectors like finance and manufacturing or the professions – are so pro-Beijing that not even 10 per cent of them would ever endorse a democratic candidate. Chan wants a pre-selection system that sets a much lower bar for potential candidates and so give the people a wider choice of leader.
>
> (www.iht.com, 1 December 2007)

'Anson Chan went into the election with a narrow lead in opinion polls … Regina Ip is supported by the city's powerful pro-Beijing establishment' (www.bbc.co.uk, 2 December 2007).

'According to a … poll on Friday [30 November], Regina Ip's popularity had risen to its highest, at 27.4 per cent, while Anson Chan had lost some of her support, down to 36 per cent' (www.iht.com, 2 December 2007).

'Anson Chan won a seat in Hong Kong's legislature after receiving … about 55 per cent of the vote, which saw a record turnout. Her closest rival Regina Ip received … about 43 per cent' (www.bbc.co.uk, 3 December 2007).

> In one of the most fiercely contested and symbolic elections since China assumed control of Hong Kong a decade ago, Anson Chan won a seat in the legislative Council by a decisive margin … Anson Chan won 54.6 per cent of the votes cast … Her main rival, Regina Ip, won 42.7 per cent of the vote … Although both candidates contested the election as independents, Chan was supported by a coalition of democratic parties. Ip was supported by pro-Beijing parties … Chan championed a liberal model for reform that would allow an open field for chief executive elections and a fully elected legislature by 2012.
>
> (www.iht.com, 3 December 2007p; *IHT*, 4 December 2007, p. 6)

> The Basic Law commits the central government to introducing democracy but offers only vague guidance on when and leaves unanswered many questions over the methods for implementing direct elections … In October the Hong Kong government concluded a three-month public consultation on democratic reform. Donald Tsang's report, submitted to the Standing Committee of China's National People's Congress, which is the ultimate constitutional authority on the Basic Law, summarized the consultation's findings. But he avoided committing himself on many controversial issues, like the workings of a committee to evaluate candidates for chief executive elections, which is a requirement of the Basic Law.
>
> (www.iht.com, 12 December 2007)

29 December 2007.

> The Standing Committee of the National People's Congress, China's parliament, issued a ruling on Saturday [29 December] saying it would consider allowing direct elections for the election of Hong Kong's leader in 2017 … The ruling: 'The session is of the view that … the election of the fifth chief executive of the Hong Kong Special Administrative Region in 2017 may be

implemented by the method of universal suffrage' ... The Standing Committee added that if the chief executive was elected directly, it would then consider introducing universal suffrage for the Legislative Council election in 2010. However, it ruled out full democracy at the chief executive election in 2012, saying only 'appropriate revisions' might be made to the selection method ... The move comes after Donald Tsang submitted a report requesting elections by 2012 ... Mr Tsang said in a report to the National People's Congress before the decision that a majority of Hong Kong wanted direct elections by 2012, although he said a delay until 2017 stood a 'better chance' of being accepted ... [The Basic Law] provides for the development of universal suffrage as the 'ultimate aim', but is vague about the date.

(www.bbc.co.uk, 30 December 2007)

[China's] announcement sparked protests by pro-democracy activists who sought an earlier date ... Hundreds of people marched through central Hong Kong in protest ... Qiao Xiaoyang, a senior member of China's parliament, flew to Hong Kong to explain the decision ... Changes would be made gradually, starting in 2012, the date of the next presidential race, he said, without saying what those changes may be ... Donald Tsang: 'A timetable for obtaining universal suffrage has been set. Hong Kong is entering a most important chapter of its constitutional history' ... Tsang urged all parties to put aside their differences and start thinking about how to implement direct elections for the chief executive in 2017. A task force will be set up to discuss how to amend electoral methods, with the first changes made in 2012, he said ... In 2017 a nomination committee is expected to select a 'certain number' of candidates that the Hong Kong electorate will then vote on, according to a copy of the decision announced Saturday that was released by China's parliament. The number of candidates and selection process was not revealed, but Hong Kong's leader had suggested between two and four candidates in a proposal he submitted this month [December] to Beijing, the document said ... Any changes to the electoral process still needs to win a two-thirds majority in the legislature, which is dominated by Beijing's allies, as well as further approval from China.

(www.iht.com, 29 December 2007)

The goal of full democracy for Hong Kong is far from guaranteed, despite a pledge by China to permit voters to elect their chief executive and legislative directly beginning in 2017, democratic politicians and analysts said Sunday [30 December]. A declaration by the Standing Committee of the National People's Congress on Saturday [29 December] explicitly recognized the desire of the people of Hong Kong to achieve democracy as quickly as possible ... Opinion polls [in Hong Kong] have consistently shown that a majority favour democracy at the earliest opportunity. After considering a report by Donald Tsang on the road to democracy, the Standing Committee decided that this meant the possibility of direct election of the chief executive in 2017 and the Legislative Council in 2020. But even that timetable could slip. The Standing Committee left crucial decisions over the electoral system to Hong Kong politicians, who are deeply divided over how best to implement the promise of democracy. Unless they can agree, direct elections would be further postponed. The decision of the Standing Committee states only that direct elections 'may be implemented' beginning 2017 … Tsang said he welcomed the decision because it had finally ensured that a 'timetable for attaining universal suffrage has been set'. He said on Saturday that: 'Hong Kong is entering a most important chapter in its constitutional history. We must treasure this hard-earned opportunity' … But democrats and conservatives loyal to Beijing face a long and difficult battle over models for the future electoral system, which could derail the timetable for direct elections. Politicians and analysts [in Hong Kong] expect a fierce struggle even over a modest package of interim reforms that the Standing Committee said could be introduced in time for the 2012 elections … Chinese officials tried to reassure the Hong Kong political elite in two separate briefings Saturday. Qiao Xiaoyang, a senior official of the Standing Committee, said in a statement explaining the decision-making on the proposed election timetable that the central government has made a 'solemn commitment' to grant universal suffrage. He said: 'By making clear the timetable for realizing this aim at an appropriate time, this is in line with the consistent position of the central government in supporting the democratic development of Hong Kong' … Still, changes to the electoral laws in Hong Kong are not easy to achieve. They require the support of two-thirds of a legislature in which neither democrats nor Beijing loyalists hold a commanding majority. They must also be supported by the chief executive and approved by the Standing Committee … Tsang said he would assign a task force to prepare proposals by late next year [2008] for how the electoral system could be reformed in 2012 … One of the most contentious issues is the operation of a nominating committee that will vet candidates for chief executive. Democrats insist that this not be used to ensure that only candidates satisfactory to Beijing are allowed to run.

(www.iht.com, 30 December 2007; *IHT*, 31 December 2007, p. 2)

Qiao Xiaoyang [is] deputy secretary of the National People's Congress … Half of Hong Kong's sixty-seat legislature is returned by largely conservative and pro-Beijing functional constituencies. While the National People's Congress said changes could be made to both the chief executive and legislative elections in 2012, it also ruled that the current fifty–fifty ratio between functional constituency and directly elected seats in the legislature could not be altered.

(*FT*, 31 December 2007, p. 4)

13 January 2008. 'Up to 20,00 people marched through Hong Kong yesterday [13 January] calling for the right to elect their government by 2012' (*The Independent*, 14 January 2008, p. 26).

28 January 2008. 'China on Monday [28 January] allowed a US warship to make a port call in Hong Kong two months after it turned away a US aircraft carrier battle group and set off a diplomatic dispute between the two countries' (*IHT*, 29 January 2008, p. 2).

16 February 2008. 'The prominent Asian banker David Li resigned from Hong Kong's cabinet [Executive Council] after settling civil charges of insider trading in the United States' (*IHT*, 18 February 2008, p. 10).

28 March 2008.

> One of the leading democrats in Hong Kong, Martin Lee, who has led the territory's long push for full democracy under Chinese rule, has decided he will not run again for legislative office, citing his age ... seventy in June ... and a desire to make way for new leaders ... Lee, who first joined the legislature in 1985, said he would step down as a lawmaker at the end of his current term in July but would remain a member of the Democratic Party ... He said: 'I'll still fight for democracy' ... [He was] a founder member of the Democratic Party.
>
> (www.iht.com, 28 March 2008)

May 2008.

> Gregory So Kamleung ... was a natural choice for one of the eight deputy ministerial jobs – a new tier of political nominees in the civil service – filled last month [May]. Yet Mr So's appointment as under-secretary of commerce has created a furore ... The storm broke when Mr So acknowledged that he held a foreign passport ... The Basic Law, Hong Kong's constitution, is explicit: foreigners can 'serve as public servants ... at all levels'. But Chinese language newspapers were outraged, demanding that all government officials disclose any second nationality ... China does not recognize dual nationality, but has winked at what is common practice in Hong Kong. It turns out that five out of the eight new appointees hold a second nationality. Mr So has begun the process of renouncing his Canadian citizenship. The other four have also announced that they are severing their foreign ties.
>
> (*The Economist*, 7 June 2008, p. 68)

6 June 2008.

> Education minister Michael Suen Ming-yeung lifted restrictions that forced four-fifths of the territory's more than 500 secondary schools to teach the 'mother tongue', i.e. Cantonese, the main language of its residents and of southern China. Schools may switch to English from next year [2009]. This reverses a decade-old policy adopted after Hong Kong's reversion to China in 1997 ... Twenty per cent of schools were permitted to continue teaching in English ... Ambitious parents ... know their offspring will need English to get ahead. Those who flee the public system for costly private schools or for the eight semi-private schools run on the British system did so. The rest

made extraordinary efforts to enter the minority of English language schools. They have huge waiting lists; Cantonese ones gaping holes … Private schools offering supplementary English tuition have mushroomed … A much debated but still undisclosed formula will allow an increasing number of subjects to be taught in English … Mandarin, or *putonghua*, [is] China's common language.

(*The Economist*, 14 June 2008, pp. 72–3)

9 August 2008.

Emily Lau (a member of the Legislative Council who is also the leader of Frontier, a small political group): 'We are protesting against the Chinese government's failure to live up to the undertakings it made seven years ago, when it made its bid to host the Olympics.'

(www.iht.com, 9 August 2008)

7 September 2008.

Hong Kong voters went to the polls Sunday [7 September] in legislative elections that threatened to set back the opposition camp … [The] issue of democratic reform has largely taken a back seat to concerns about wages, education and inflation … [Analysts have predicted the opposition camp, deprived of its signature issue, might lose as many as five of their twenty-six seats. Any more than that would cost them their veto power … About 3.4 million of the territory's 7 million people are registered to vote this year. A record 55 per cent of registered voters cast ballots in the election four years ago … Voters will directly pick thirty of Hong Kong's lawmakers, but the other thirty are chosen by a relatively small group of special interest voters, such as business leaders, doctors and accountants, who are expected to back pro-Beijing candidates.

(www.cnn.com, 7 September 2008)

Voters can vote directly for only half of the Legislative Council's seats, with the other half chosen by special limited constituencies … These 'functional constituencies' include groups of as few as 144 voters and are defined by professional allegiance, such as the financial sector, tourism and education. This year fourteen of the thirty functional constituency seats are uncontested, leaving a total of forty-six seats available … Voting turnout is expected to be moderate, comprising about half of the 3.3 million potential voters … [The elections in 2004 gave] democratic candidates … just twenty-five of the thirty seats available in the freely elected half of the Council … [This year] patriotic feelings towards China have surged after the tragedy of the Sichuan earthquake and the huge excitement and pride generated by the Beijing Olympics.

(www.bbc.co.uk, 7 September 2008)

Hong Kong residents voted Sunday [7 September] in legislative elections that threatened to set back the opposition camp and its push for greater democratic freedoms … Ordinary citizens were expected to cast fewer votes for pro-democracy candidates than in the last legislative race in 2004, when those politicians won new seats amid widespread anger over officials and policies backed by Beijing. This year the issue of democratic reform has largely taken a back seat to concerns about wages, education and inflation … Opinion polls suggested that high profile, pro-democracy figures like Emily Lau, who has been fighting for democracy in the Legislature for seventeen years, and the maverick activist Leung Kwok-hung might lose their seats. The conservative Regina Ip, a former Hong Kong security chief who caused an uproar in 2003 by promoting an anti-subversion bill, was expected to succeed in her bid.

(www.iht.com, 7 September 2008)

Hong Kong's pro-democracy camp has won more than a third of seats … and so retains a key veto over future major legislation. The pro-democracy opposition won twenty-three out of thirty elected seats in the Legislative Council … There had been predictions of heavy losses for the pro-democracy camp … Analysts had believed pro-government parties would make significant gains after the surge in pro-China patriotism sparked by the Beijing Olympics and the Sichuan earthquake. China had also promised the region some form of universal suffrage by 2017, blunting the democratic camp's campaign. Leading figures such as Emily Lau, Audrey Eu and Leung Kwok-hung, also known as Longhair, each fought off stiff competition to keep their seat. The pro-government party, the Democratic Alliance for the Betterment of Hong Kong, or DAB, has also done well, thanks to its strong organization. And the pro-China independent Regina Ip won her seat. But the pro-business leader Liberal Party leader, James Tien, lost his and has resigned.

(www.bbc.co.uk, 8 September 2008)

Hong Kong's pro-democracy politicians lost three legislative seats … but held onto their veto power over major legislation … Democratic parties claimed twenty-three of sixty legislative seats … down from their current twenty-six … Ordinary citizens vote for thirty of the seats, while the rest are chosen by special interest groups that tend to side with China's central government in Beijing. The result was better than expected for the opposition … Voter turnout dropped significantly this year … about 45 per cent of registered voters … the second lowest turnout rate since Hong Kong returned from British to Chinese rule in 1997. There was nearly 56 per cent turnout in 2004. The key threshold for pro-democracy parties was twenty-one. Fewer than that would have cost them their veto power … Thirty of the seats are chosen by more than 200,000 members of special interest groups like businesspeople, lawyers and accountants that tend to back Beijing. Fourteen of the interest group seats were uncontested. In the thirty directly elected seats … the Democratic Party and its allies actually increased their seats to nineteen, up one from 2004. The conservative camp, led by the

Democratic Alliance for the Betterment and Progress of Hong Kong, won eleven, down one ... [All of the democrats'] losses occurred in the special interest races.

(www.cnn.com, 8 September 2008)

The pro-business Liberal Party lost seats, while populists made gains with promises to introduce a minimum wage and reduce pollution. Most of the pro-democracy legislators kept their seats, despite a low turnout among the middle class and upper middle class voters who make up their main support ... Pro-democracy legislators ... need to hold at least twenty-one seats, one-third plus one, in the sixty-member Legislature to block such changes ... [as rewriting] the Basic Law ... Three leading figures in the pro-democracy movement – Martin Lee, Anson Chan and Sin Chung Kai – did not seek reelection. They dropped out to make room for younger politicians ... Pro-business lawmakers, a mix of independents and Liberal Party members, suffered heavy losses. The Liberal Party's chairman, James Tien, resigned as its leader shortly before it was announced that he had lost his seat. The Democratic Alliance for the Betterment and Progress of Hong Kong, or DAB, fared better. The most ardently pro-Beijing party, it also favours more government measures to help the poor and to combat pollution.

(www.iht.com, 8 September 2008)

Democracy advocates won twenty-four seats in the sixty-member legislature. They captured nineteen of the thirty seats selected by voting among the general public and five of the thirty chosen by business groups, the professions and labour unions ... But among both the pro-government political parties and the pro-democracy parties a sharp leftward shift occurred on economic policy. The Liberal Party, which is pro-Beijing and pro-business, lost three seats that it had been expected to win ... But the populist, pro-Beijing Democratic Alliance for the Betterment and Progress of Hong Kong, or DAB, showed unusual strength in fairly low income areas with a platform that combined Chinese nationalism with appeals for the government to help blue-collar workers and the poor cope with inflation ... On the opposition side the Democratic Party, which supports minimal government intervention in the economy, saw its support erode. Democracy-minded voters gravitated toward the Civic Party, Civic Act-Up and the League of Democrats, all of which favour a more active role on livelihood issues.

(www.iht.com, 8 September 2008)

The Liberal Party, the biggest pro-business party and hitherto the second biggest in Legco [the Legislative Council], won seven of the functional constituency seats. But its chairman, James Tien, and vice chairman, Selina Chow, both lost the directly elected seats they had won in 2004. Other Liberal Party candidates in directly elected seats were all defeated as well. Mr Tien and Mrs Chow quit their party posts, and Mrs Chow her seat in Hong Kong's cabinet, the Executive Council ... The Hong Kong Legislative

Council election results [60 seats], September 2008 (September 2004): Pro-democracy: Democratic Party 8 (9); Civic Party 5 (4); other 10 (12); Non-affiliated 7; Pro-Beijing: DAB 10 (12); Liberal Party 7 (10); Other 13 (13).

(*The Economist*, 13 September 2008, p. 73)

23–25 September 2008.

A run against one of Hong Kong's biggest and best-known banks stopped Thursday [25 September] as quickly as it had started … Bank of East Asia survived a run on Wednesday [24 September] and its stock rallied on Thursday thanks to swift co-operation among regulators, the bank and a tycoon nicknamed Superman by the local media: Li Ka-shing … The measures were the result of Hong Kong's unusually extensive experience with bank runs, which have not happened lately but were a chronic problem in this densely crowded city all the way up until the British returned it to Chinese rule in 1997 … Bank of Asia's problems this week started late Tuesday [23 September] with a flurry of mobile phone text messages suggesting that the bank was in difficulty.

(www.iht.com, 25 September 2008)

The Bank of East Asia [is] Hong Kong's largest locally owned lender … The ninety-year-old Bank of East Asia blamed 'malicious rumours' for the incident and said they were false … The Hong Kong authorities voiced their support for the bank and a tycoon bought shares. They rose on 25 September as normality returned.

(*The Economist*, 27 September 2008, p. 102)

Hong Kong police have arrested a man for allegedly spreading rumours on the internet about a bank run amid anxiety about the US financial crisis, the police said Sunday [28 September]. The man was arrested Saturday [27 September] for allegedly using a computer with criminal or dishonest intent but has not been charged.

(www.iht.com, 28 September 2008)

14 October 2008.

Hong Kong's financial regulators announced on Tuesday [14 October] that they would provide government backing for all of the territory's $773 billion in bank deposits through 2010 as government assistance for banks in Europe and the United States put pressure on Asian regulators to follow suit even though Asian banks tend to be better capitalized. The Hong Kong Monetary Authority also said it was prepared to provide capital to the territory's twenty-three locally incorporated banks if they needed it, following the example of the United States and Britain … Hong Kong banks are already among the most heavily capitalized in the world, and Joseph Yam, the chief executive of the Hong Kong Monetary Authority, said that he did not think either of the news measures announced on Tuesday would be needed … Hong Kong currently insures the first … $12,900 … in an account ... Yam said that he had discussed Tuesday's initiative with the People's Bank of China before announcing them, and said without elaborating that there was ample communication among Asian central banks.

(www.iht.com, 14 October 2008)

17 October 2008.

After weeks of wrangling with small investors, banks in Hong Kong agreed Friday [17 October] to buy back securities guaranteed by Lehman Brothers, which had soured after the collapse last month [September] of the US investment bank ... The Hong Kong Association of Banks announced Friday that it had agreed to a government plan to buy back at market prices the so-called 'minibonds' – complex structured products arranged by Lehman and sold to the public via Hong Kong banks. Investors have complained that they had been misled into believing the investments were safe. The bank association appointed Ernst & Young as an independent financial adviser to value the products.

(www.iht.com, 17 October 2008)

24 December 2008.

Cardinal Zen Ze-kiun, a sharp critic of China over democratic rights and religious freedoms, said Wednesday [24 December] that the Vatican has agreed to his request to step down next year [2009] as the head of the Roman Catholic diocese in Hong Kong ... He said he would spend more time monitoring Catholic churches in the mainland: 'I do not retire to rest. The mainland Chinese church is huge and complicated. Sometimes the Pope wants me to give him some advice, so I need more time to research it' ... Zen, who was born in Shanghai and fled to Hong Kong after the Chinese civil war, has led the diocese since 2002. Bishop John Tong Hon, sixty-nine, who was born in Hong Kong, has been designated as his likely successor. The Roman Catholic diocese of Hong Kong has an estimated 250,000 members. Macao has the only other Roman Catholic diocese in China.

(www.iht.com, 24 December 2008)

20 January 2009.

China's central bank has agreed a bilateral currency swap facility worth up to $29.4 billion with Hong Kong to try to ensure financial stability and support the autonomous region's depressed economy. As well as strengthening monetary co-operation between China and Hong Kong, the three-year swap could boost short-term liquidity for banking operations.

(*FT*, 21 January 2009, p. 10)

May 2009. '[Hong Kong] announced $2.2 billion in additional spending measures on Tuesday [26 May] ... Hong Kong's first quarter GDP fell 7.8 per cent over the same period last year, and 4.3 per cent quarter on quarter' (www.ft.com, 26 May 2009).

Last week saw a visit to Beijing by Chen Chu, the highest ranking elected official of the Democratic Progressive Party (DPP) … Ms Chen, the mayor of Kaohsiung, Taiwan's second largest city, stressed that she was visiting the mainland to promote her city, not to signal any political retreat from the party's independence stance. Trips to the mainland by DPP officials are nevertheless rare … Recently Taiwan increased the daily quota of visitors from China to 3,000, a ten-fold increase.

(www.iht.com, 26 May 2009)

1 July 2009.

Thousands of people joined a pro-democracy march on Wednesday [1 July], although the turnout fell short of a candlelight vigil held nearly four weeks ago to commemorate the twentieth anniversary of the Tiananmen Square crackdown in Beijing … The march on Wednesday [took place] on the twelfth anniversary of Hong Kong's return from British to Chinese rule … Many marchers said they were dissatisfied with government policies to deal with the economic downturn … But the largest single issue seemed to be the limits of democracy in Hong Kong … The police estimated that 26,000 people had assembled in Victoria Park on Hong Kong Island as the march began. The organizers said beforehand that they expected more to join the march along the way, and estimated late Wednesday evening that 76,000 people had participated. The police had estimated the crowd at the 4 June Tiananmen vigil, at the same location in Victoria Park, at 62,800, while the organizers put it at 150,000.

(www.iht.com, 1 July 2009)

'Numbers fell short of the 100,000 anticipated by the organizers' (www.bbc.co.uk, 2 July 2009).

14 August 2009.

The economy of Hong Kong has emerged from recession, posting growth of 3.3 per cent in the three months from April to June. The seasonally adjusted figures were better than had been expected and the government has raised its forecast of growth in the whole year … Hong Kong's growth was negative for four consecutive quarters, starting in the second quarter of 2008. The growth of 3.3 per cent compares with a revised contraction of 4.3 per cent for the first three months of 2009. The government was previously expecting the economy to contract by between 5.5 per cent and 6.5 per cent in the whole of 2009, and is now predicting a contraction of between 3.5 per cent and 4.5 per cent … Although there has been growth compared with the previous three months, the economy is still running below last year's levels, with a year-on-year contraction of 3.8 per cent.

(www.bbc.co.uk, 14 August 2009)

Hong Kong climbed out of recession in the second quarter [of 2009] … [Hong Kong is] heavily reliant on trade and banking … Data published

Friday [14 August] showed that Hong Kong's economy had grown 3.3 per cent in the second quarter from the first quarter, more than analysts had expected, adding evidence that the recovery was solidifying in much of Asia ... Although Hong Kong's economy grew in April to June from the first three months of 2009, it shrank 3.8 per cent compared with the [same] period last year [2008]. For the full year, the government now expects a contraction of 3.5 per cent to 4.5 per cent, rather than the 5.5 per cent to 6.5 per cent it had previously forecast.

(*IHT*, 15 August 2009, p. 11)

Hong Kong unexpectedly reported strong second-quarter growth after a year of contraction in a fresh sign that the global financial crisis could be coming to an end. The territory's GDP grew 3.3 per cent in the three months to June from the previous quarter on a seasonally adjusted basis, although it declined 3.8 per cent from a year before.

(www.ft.com, 16 August 2009)

18 November 2009.

A reform proposal unveiled by the government on 18 November aims to increase the level of democracy 'substantially' in 2012 when Donald Tsang's successor is chosen and a new legislature elected. Pro-democracy politicians are far from convinced ... Mr Tsang's proposal would add ten new seats to Legco in 2012. Five of them would be returned by direct elections and the other five by directly elected members of district councils, which are local consultative bodies. The election committee would be expanded from 800 to 1,200 members. But there has been no promise to abolish functional constituencies, either in 2012 or beyond.

(*The Economist*, 21 November 2009, p. 72)

As things stand, half of Legco's sixty seats are nominated through so-called 'functional constituencies', by just 211,000 people representing professional and business elites. Hong Kong's ordinary voters get to choose the other thirty ... The thirty democratically elected members cannot pass legislation without the say-so of their thirty unrepresentative brethren. The chief executive ... is selected by ... a 769-member 'election committee'. Donald Tsang's proposals would add ten new seats to Legco, half of which would be elected and half of which would be reserved for representatives of the lower-tier district councils. Meanwhile, the election committee to select the chief executive would be expanded to 1,200.

(*FT*, 3 December 2009, p. 17)

Thousands of Hong Kong residents marched to the Chinese government's liaison office today [1 January 2010], calling on Beijing to grant full democracy ... [They were] chanting 'one man, one vote to choose our leader' and carrying signs reading 'democracy now' ... The large turnout for the protest – police said 9,000 people took part – is a boost to Hong Kong's political

> opposition … Five pro-democracy legislators plan to resign later this month, hoping to turn the elections that the resignations would trigger into a referendum on democracy … In July 2003 500,000 marched to demonstrate against a national security bill.
>
> (www.guardian.co.uk, 1 January 2010)

> The complex case of the dissident, Zhou Yongjun, has raised questions about whether Hong Kong authorities handed him over to the Chinese police in violation of the 'One Country, Two Systems' form of governance … Mr Zhou was sentenced on 15 January to nine years in prison by a court in the city of Shehong … [he] was a prominent student protester in the days leading to the June 1989 massacre around Tiananmen Square … Mr Zhou fled to the United States in 1993 and became one of many stateless exiles … He is a permanent resident [in the United States] and is close to getting American citizenship. The Chinese government stripped Mr Zhou of full citizenship when he fled the mainland and has refused to reinstate it [according to a lawyer representing him] … In September 2008 he was apprehended by Hong Kong police and [later] handed over to the mainland when he tried to enter Hong Kong [via Macao] with a fake Malaysian passport under the name of Wang Xingxiang. Before handing him over, the Hong Kong police questioned Mr Zhou about a fraud investigation related to a Hong Kong bank account under the name of Wang Xingxiang … Hong Kong has no extradition agreement with mainland China … Mr Zhou's long-time girlfriend in Los Angeles … said that … Wang Xingxiang was another name used [by someone else] … [Thus] the overlap in names was an unfortunate coincidence … [Mr Zhou's lawyer] said the Hong Kong police had concluded that Mr Zhou was not the one who faked the signature on the funds transfer form given to Hang Seng Bank.
>
> (www.iht.com, 25 January 2010)

'Protesters, many of them young people proclaiming their interest in democracy, have opposed building an expensive high-speed rail link to Shenzhen and Guangzhou in mainland China' (www.iht.com, 28 January 2010).

> Five Hong Kong MPs resigned yesterday [4 February] to try to press Beijing into allowing direct elections in an attempt to revive the campaign for democracy … Opposition parties hope the resignations – one from each of the five electoral districts – will force a special election pitting pro-democracy candidates against pro-China ones in what the opposition says will be a de facto referendum on democracy.
>
> (*Guardian*, 5 February 2010, p. 29)

4 Tibet

Historical background

> Tibet's formation as a recognizable nation began as far back as the fourth century. In the early seventh century Tibetans, under Songtsen Gambo, converted to Buddhism and adopted a written language based on the Ranjana script – both imports from India ... Tibetans came to control much of their region, including parts of Nepal, Burma, India and present-day Xinjiang (China) and they did it the old-fashioned way, through warfare. They pointedly refused to defer to Tang Dynasty emperors and in the eighth century even briefly captured Changan, the Chinese capital, leading to the negotiation of borders between the two states. Effective Chinese control over Tibet did not come until the late eighteenth century and even then was mostly supervisory. Early in the last century even that began to fall apart, as did China's hold on other parts of its periphery. To enhance their position in India the British worked intermittently to reinforce the de facto Tibetan state.
>
> (Howard French, *IHT*, 27 October 2007, p. 2)

'China's communist troops entered Tibet in 1950 and the country claims to have owned the Himalayan regions for seven centuries. Many Tibetans say they were effectively an independent nation for most of that time' (www.cnn.com, 26 March 2008).

> The Tibetan view holds that Tibet was never subject to foreign rule after it emerged from the mid-seventh century as a dynamic power holding sway over an Inner Asian empire. These Tibetans say the appearance of subjugation to the Mongol rulers of the Yuan Dynasty in the thirteenth and fourteenth centuries, and to the Manchu rulers of China's Qing Dynasty from the eighteenth century until the twentieth century, is due to a modern, largely Western misunderstanding of the personal relations among the Yuan and Qing emperors and the pre-eminent lamas of Tibet. In this view the lamas simply served as spiritual mentors to the emperors, with no compromise of Tibet's independent status. In China's view the Western misunderstandings are about the nature of China: Western critics do not understand

that China has a history of thousands of years as a unified multinational state; all of its nationalities are Chinese. The Mongols, who entered China as conquerors, are claimed as Chinese and their subjugation of Tibet is claimed a Chinese subjugation. Here are the facts. The claim that Tibet entertained only personal relations with China at the leadership level is easily rebutted. Administrative records and dynastic histories outline the governing structures of Mongol and Manchu rule. These make it clear that Tibet was subject to rules, laws and decisions made by the Yuan and Qing rulers. Tibet was not independent during these two periods. One of the Tibetan cabinet ministers summoned to Beijing at the end of the eighteenth century describes himself unambiguously in his memoirs as a subject of the Manchu emperor. The idea that Tibet became part of China in the thirteenth century is a very recent construction. In the early part of the twentieth century Chinese writers generally date the annexation of Tibet to the eighteenth century. They described Tibet's status under the Qin with a term that designates a 'feudal dependency', not an integral part of the country. And that is because Tibet was ruled as such, within the empires of the Mongols and the Manchus. When the Qing Dynasty collapsed in 1911 Tibet became independent once more. From 1912 until the founding of the People's Republic in 1949 no Chinese government exercised control over what is today China's Tibet Autonomous Region. The Dalai Lama's government alone ruled the land until 1951. Marxist China adopted the linguistic sleight of hand that asserts it has always been a unitary multinational country, not the hub of empires. There is now firm insistence that 'Han', actually one of several ethnonyms for 'Chinese', refers to only one of the Chinese nationalities. This was a conscious decision of those who constructed twentieth century Chinese identity. (It stands in contrast to the Russian decision to use a political term, 'Soviet', for the peoples of the Union of Soviet Socialist Republics.) There is something less to the arguments of both sides, but the argument on the Chinese side is weaker. Tibet was not 'Chinese' until Mao Zedong's armies marched in and made it so.

(Elliot Sperling, *IHT*, 14 April 2008, p. 8)

Not far from National Stadium, Beijing's mammoth, just-finished Olympic arena, another construction project is still facing an Olympic deadline. The building will house Beijing's first museum exclusively dedicated to Tibet. Inside, curators will display antiquities, dynastic records and reproductions to demonstrate China's dominion over Tibet as far back as the thirteenth century. Many experts question China's historical claims, but few clouds of doubt are likely to darken the museum. Even the Dalai Lama is being edited out of the Chinese narrative. He will not appear after 1959 … A Tibetan scholar, Dolma Kyab, has been jailed since 2005 after writing an unapproved, multiple-volume history of Tibet … British troops invaded Tibet in 1903 and 1904 as the Qing Dynasty was nearing collapse. Today many Chinese recall the role of the CIA in Tibet during the 1950s and interpret

Western sympathy for the current protests as another foreign effort to destabilize and divide China ... Woeser, a Tibetan blogger, lost her editing job at a literary magazine based in Lhasa after writing a 2003 book, *Tibet Notes*, that included a friendly reference to the Dalai Lama ... At the heart of the historical dispute lies the Western concept of sovereignty. The Communist Party has prompted the concept of China as a diverse but unified nation of fifty-six ethnic groups. The majority Han constitute nearly 92 per cent of the population, but the remaining 8 per cent, including Mongols, Hui Moslems, Manchus, Uighur Moslems and Tibetans, are often said to be assimilated into the motherland over centuries of unbroken history. Many scholars say that narrative oversimplifies history to support contemporary political and territorial claims. Historians generally agree that the relationship between China and Tibet became fully intermingled during the Yuan Dynasty from the 1270s to 1368. The dispute is over the nature of the relationship. The Tibetan government-in-exile say Buddhist lamas established a 'priest–patron' relationship under which they became spiritual advisers to the Yuan rulers without sacrificing Tibetan self-rule or independence – an arrangement replicated in the last imperial dynasty, the Qing, which lasted from 1644 to 1912. Chinese scholars say this logic is disingenuous. They point to records detailing how Tibet was subject to certain laws of the Yuan and Qing rulers – a paper trail they say proves not just that Tibet is an inalienable part of China but also that Chinese emperors had the authority to select the Dalai Lama. Elliot Sperling, a leading Tibet specialist at Indiana University, said both sides massage their interpretations. He said Tibet cannot be regarded as truly independent during the Yuan and Qing dynasties given that records show Tibet as subservient to Chinese rulers and policies. But Sperling said China's claim to unbroken control of Tibet is also dubious. During the Ming Dynasty, from 1368 to 1644, Tibet had scant connection to Chinese rulers, he said. And describing the Yuan and Qing dynasties as 'Chinese' overlooks the fact that each took power after what was at the time viewed as a foreign invasion: Mongols established the Yuan; Manchus invaded and founded the Qing. Sperling: 'What China doesn't want to deal with is the fact that the Mongols had an empire. It wasn't a Chinese state. It was an empire' ... In this context, some scholars consider Tibet's past relationship with China more akin to that of a vassal state. China's government relinquished any remaining control over Tibet after the fall of the Qing in 1912. The current Dalai Lama and his predecessor ruled Tibet until 1951, when Mao invaded in what China maintains was a 'peaceful liberation' that freed Tibetans from a feudal theocracy ... Wang Lixiong, a dissident scholar in Beijing who has challenged some of the Communist Party's historical claims, said imperial China regarded itself as the centre of the world and had little concern about the political status of subservient neighbours like Tibet. But he said modern political needs have made this approach an inconvenient legacy. Wang, who is married to Woeser and is now banned from being published in China, said: 'Now we are in a Westernized political situation. We have this definition of sovereignty, so we fight over every inch of territory' ... Robert Barnett, a Tibetan specialist at Columbia University, said Tibet scholars inside China often do excellent work. But he said many scholars in China avoid specializing in Tibetan history after the thirteenth century because of the political overtones – and potential risks. He said one book was banned for including a sentence that questioned the official view that an eighth century Tibetan king was half Chinese.

(Jim Yardley, *IHT*, 17 April 2008, pp. 1, 8)

Mao's Cultural Revolution wrought havoc in the region and the Red Guards destroyed more than 6,000 monasteries and convents – just a handful survived ... In the aftermath of the late 1980s protest China's leaders thought a programme of rapid economic development in Tibet would stifle calls for political change ... But although they have poured billions into the region and increased the standard of living of many Tibetans, the sense of anger has not been defused. Some say that is because the measures were ill conceived. They benefited Han Chinese settlers more than Tibetans and focused on urban business development rather than rural and social programmes ... The high illiteracy rates in Tibet are a barrier for local people as they try to compete with Han Chinese migrants.

(www.bbc.co.uk, 27 March 2008)

The *Oxford English Dictionary* defines the term 'Dalai Lama' as follows: 'Tibetan [for] "Ocean Monk", because he is regarded as "the ocean of compassion"'.

In mid-May [2008] a serious young man of twenty-two who is revered as the 17th Karmapa – now the second most important figure in Tibetan Buddhism – will make his first visit to the United States. The trip comes eight years after his dramatic flight to India from a monastery near Lhasa at the end of 1999 when he was just fourteen years old ... The Karmapa, born Ogyen Trinley Dorje, arrived unannounced in Dharamsala, the Dalai Lama's base, in January 2000 ... The trip [to the United States] was planned before the protests in Tibet [which started in March 2008] ... This is the first time that a skittish India has allowed him permission to travel abroad. His flight from Tibet was a considerable embarrassment to China. The Karmapa Lama, spiritual head of the Kagyu order of Tibetan Buddhism, is now the only major Tibetan lama recognized as a reincarnation of his lineage by both the Dalai Lama and the Chinese government since it overran Tibet in the 1950s. The Panchen Lama, the third of a triumvirate and previously the second highest ranking among the three lamas, vanished into Chinese custody as a boy in 1995 and has been replaced by Beijing's own political appointee ... Because the Karmapa leads a different order of Tibetan Buddhism – the Dalai Lama is a Gelugpa monk – the young Karmapa cannot inherit his title.

(*IHT*, 8 April 2008, p. 8)

China's present control over Tibet dates from 1950 when the People's Liberation Army invaded Tibet and defeated the Tibetan army at Chamdo. China claims that Tibet was already part of China when it invaded, based on a claim to sovereignty over Tibet by the Qing dynasty dating from the eighteenth century. More recently China has claimed that its rule over Tibet can be traced to the rule of Tibet by the Mongols – known in China as the Yuan dynasty. There are at least three major historical difficulties with China's claim. Firstly, it is doubtful whether the relationship between the Qing and the Yuan on the one hand, and Tibetans on the other, was really one of sovereign and subjects. The Kangxi Emperor occupied Tibet in 1720. After his death in 1722 this occupation continued under his successor the Yongzheng Emperor until 1728, and there were further Chinese invasions in 1750 and 1792. However, after the end of the occupation in 1728, and after each of the later invasions, the Chinese armies withdrew and Tibet had virtually complete independence in practice. Secondly, neither dynasty made Tibet a part of metropolitan China. If it was a political relationship at all, it was one of dependency – what we call a colonial relationship. It is, therefore, a basis for concluding that Tibet is a colony and so is entitled to self-determination. Thirdly, and most importantly, there was no relationship – either similar to that between Tibet and the Qing Dynasty, or similar to the modern concept of sovereignty – between Tibet and the Chinese Republic, which succeeded the Qing Dynasty in 1911. In 1912 the 13th Dalai Lama made a formal declaration of Tibetan independence. Although the Chinese Republic responded by laying claim to Tibet, it never exercised control over it, save for certain far eastern regions where there had always been an ill-defined borderland. Tibet was entirely independent of foreign control between 1911 and 1950 ... Scholars agree that the pre-1950 Tibetan regime was backward. One aspect of its backwardness was its failure to appoint ambassadors to other countries or to apply to join the United Nations until invasion by China was imminent ... One month after China invaded Tibet on 7 October 1950 the Tibetan government appealed for help to the UN ... In 1951 China and representatives of the Dalai Lama signed the '17 point Agreement for the Peaceful Liberation of Tibet'. It provides that 'the Tibetan people have the right of exercising national regional autonomy under the unified leadership of the Central People's Government' (Article 3), that 'the Central People's Government will not alter the existing political system in Tibet' (Article 4), and 'will not alter the established status, functions and powers of the Dalai Lama' (Article 4).

These autonomy provisions were never observed ... The severity of Chinese repression in Tibet is well documented. There is severe repression of Tibetan Buddhism, which in 1997 was labelled as a 'foreign culture'. Virtually all classes in secondary and higher education are taught in Chinese, not Tibetan, resulting in a high drop-out rate among Tibetans. Urban development has generally benefited Chinese immigrants, large numbers of whom have moved to Tibet and now comprise about 12 per cent of the population … Tibetan culture is treated as inferior to Chinese culture, and most key posts in the government and the economy are held by Chinese. Those few Tibetans who are able to enter Chinese government service do so at the cost of alienation from their own people and culture … If Kosovo has the right of self-determination, the right of Tibet is infinitely stronger. The catalogue of gross oppression, the second class citizen status of Tibetans under Chinese rule, and the identity of Tibet as a country are much clearer than in Kosovo's case.

(Harris 2008: 18–20)

('Paul Harris is a Hong Kong barrister and founding chairman of the Hong Kong Human Rights Monitor. This article is adapted from an article originally commissioned and approved by the magazine of the Hong Kong Law Society, and then rejected as too sensistive after an extraordinary meeting of the society's editorial board': www.feer.com, 2 May 2008.) (Kosovo declared its independence, against the wishes of Serbia, on 17 February 2008.)

By the late 1990s the monasteries found themselves in crisis – on the one hand the [Communist] Party had begun to intrude into monastic space and on the other hand many senior lamas had begun to pass away because of old age. The most senior lamas, such as the Karmapa and Argya Rinpoche from Kumbum (Taer) Monastery, fled abroad, and the absence of senior lamas left a leadership vacuum in Tibet. In the past these senior lamas often acted as the moderate voice and as a calming influence on the monks and community, being used often by the [Communist] Party as mediators … No matter where a lama resides his monastery and the faithful continue to listen to him and look to him as their leader. Moreover, the Tibetan people in Tibet are scathing about Tibetan Communist Party officials. The people do not view the present Tibetan cadres as leaders, particularly in the Tibet Autonomous Region. They cannot offer a calming influence or serve as mediators between the people and the government. At best they are seen as opportunists and at worst collaborators … The flight of lamas into exile had unexpected consequences. The pro-independence demonstrations in Tibet in the 1980s and early 1990s did not spread much beyond Lhasa because most lamas were ambivalent and used their influence to calm their followers. This year [2008] almost all areas where protests occurred were in places where the senior lamas had left Tibet and gone to live in India … All the monasteries in Tibet look to the outside for leadership and as a source of religious teaching … This interchange of people and ideas is cultural rather than political.

(Shakya 2008: 15–16)

Before 1950 Tibet was no Shangri-la, but a country of harsh feudalism, poverty (life expectancy was barely thirty), corruption and civil wars. The last, between two monastic factions, was in 1948 when the Red Army was already knocking at the door.

(Slavoj Zizek, *IHT*, 31 May 2008, p. 8)

Nathan Hill: 'Tibet had a policy from 1792 to 1903 not to allow Westerners into the country' (www.bbc.co.uk, 18 February 2010).

Demographic, social and economic developments

'Tibet's native population is about 2.5 million' (*IHT*, 9 December 2004, p. 2). '[There are] approximately 160,000 Tibetans in exile in India. Tibet's exiled religious leader, the Dalai Lama, maintains headquarters in India' (www.iht.com, 1 April 2005).

'More than 5 million or so Tibetans recognize his [the Dalai Lama's] authority' (www.iht.com, 26 March 2008).

> Tibet has been expanding even faster [than China as a whole] … [Tibet's] economy grew by 14 per cent in 2007 … Tourism is also exploding, with the number of visitors last year [2007] approaching parity with the province's population of 2.8 million … Yet only around 15 per cent of Tibetans have completed secondary school where they would learn the [Chinese] language.
>
> (*FT*, 1 April 2008, p. 11)

> Only about 15 per cent of the Tibetan population has some form of secondary education and thus some degree of Chinese fluency, given that Chinese-medium education generally only starts in secondary school. As a result, the remaining 85 per cent are poorly positioned to integrate into the urban economic boom … The government recently ended its policy of guaranteeing employment for local high school and university graduates. As elsewhere in China, the old system has been replaced with competitive exams for the coveted posts of state-sector employment, although the exams, as elsewhere in China, are in the Chinese language. As a result, even well educated Tibetans are easily out-competed by Han Chinese migrants, even Han Chinese migrants from Chinese rural areas … In 2006 there was a large demonstration of Tibetan university graduates in Lhasa over the fact that out of 100 jobs that the government offered in open competition, only two were given to ethnic Tibetans … [There has been a] tightening of political control in response to rising tensions. This has especially been the case in the Tibetan areas of Sichuan, where increasing nationalistic agitation over the past several years has been a cause for alarm in both Chengdu, the capital of Sichuan, and Beijing. National and provincial governments across Tibet have responded by replacing existing leaders with more hard-line leaders and more repressive strategies of political control. In this context of reaction and counter-reaction what is utterly unprecedented in the demonstrations of last week was their duration. The fact that they turned violent on the fifth day in Lhasa appears to have been a popular reaction to the severity of repression carried out by the security forces during the previous four days of non-violent protests.
>
> (Andrew Fischer, www.feer.com, March 2008)

Rapid economic development in Tibet has bypassed the overwhelming majority of Tibetans who remain poor, disgruntled and suspicious of Beijing's largesse … Detailed statistics made available only up to 2005 reveal patterns of 'ethnically exclusionary growth', according to Andrew Martin Fischer … True, Tibet's economy doubled in size from 2000 to 2005. But this growth has been driven by the rapid expansion of the tertiary sector, which includes the government and party administration, and by a boom in construction of huge infrastructure works such as the Qinghai–Tibet railway and a new network of highways. The sheer cost of this state-sponsored development has been extraordinarily high. In 2001, for example, for every renminbi of Tibet's economic growth central government spending increased by 2 renminbi, according to Mr Fischer. In that year alone state spending increased by 75 per cent. By 2004 the situation had changed only slightly, with 0.65 renminbi of economic growth requiring only 1 renminbi of increased subsidies and state investment. Perversely, the disproportionally large government spending on the construction of big state projects, and on the expansion of the government and party administration, has widened social divisions within Tibetan society. A tiny share of the local population, including Tibetan cadres, administrators and other government workers, has become affluent at the expense of the overwhelming majority of Tibetans who remain poor, rural and illiterate. Unlike in other provinces where expenditures have been adjusted to boost education and reduce bureaucratic fat, security concerns have dictated the opposite in Tibet. Only 6 per cent of total government investment in Tibet in 2005 went towards education, Mr Fischer revealed. Meanwhile, 13 per cent was spent on government and party administration. As a result, 45 per cent of the Tibetan population were illiterate in 2005 and unable to benefit from the available economic opportunities, which inevitably require the knowledge of Mandarin Chinese … Huge amounts of China's natural resources are to be found in the autonomous region, including the country's largest chromium deposits and its third largest copper mine. Under the Great Western Development ('Go West') policy, launched by Jiang Zemin in 2000, the integration of Tibet into the rest of the Chinese economy was to be sped up with the construction of new infrastructure and the inflow of more economic migrants from other parts of China. But it was not until 2003, with the ascendance of the new leadership team of President Hu Jintao and Premier Wen Jiabao, that the central government made the development of China's hinterlands, including Tibet, an urgent policy priority … The autonomous region received more than 4 million tourists in 2007 – the first year that tourists outnumbered the local population of 2.8 million. At the same time economic migration into Lhasa has accelerated, with non-Tibetans numbering some 300,000 – twice as many as the ancient capital's Tibetan inhabitants. All this activity has little impact on Tibetans, most of whom remain in agriculture and animal husbandry. Profits from industry – much of which out-of-province migrants control – are more often than not sent back to the migrants' home provinces instead of being invested locally.

(www.economist.com, 10 April 2008)

State transfers to Tibetan areas in recent years have been astronomical in proportion to the size of the local economy. Before completing the world's highest railway in 2006, China announced 180 other major infrastructure projects for the Tibet Autonomous Region [TAR] worth 77.8 billion yuan (around $10.2 billion) to be constructed during 2006–10. The scale of these investments becomes apparent when measured against the TAR's GDP, which was 29.1 billion yuan in 2006. In fact, state subsidies account for around 75 per cent of the TAR's GDP ... GDP [has been] rising at an average of 12 per cent per annum [14 per cent in 2007] since the launch of the Western Development Scheme in 2000 ... [But] Tibetans have been among the big losers of China's economic miracle and within Tibetan areas the pace of modernization has polarized Tibet's economy, rewarding a minority of Tibetans with state jobs, but marginalizing the majority of Tibetans, who are poorly equipped to access new economic opportunities. Tibetans are mostly subsistence farmers and herders ... Most Tibetans have very limited access to off-farm employment ... Surplus low-skilled rural labour is not readily absorbed by secondary industry ... Tibetans must compete with migrants from other provinces who generally come with more education, skills and experience ... Unemployed rural Tibetan migrants are reported to have been behind some of the worst violence of the protests ... A central problem is the high rate of literacy among Tibetans – only 15 per cent of TAR residents have some degree of secondary education ... More than 40 per cent of Tibetans have no formal schooling at all, compared with China's national average of 8 per cent ... According to Chinese statistics, urban incomes in Tibet are five times higher than rural incomes.

(Hillman 2008: 8–11)

According to reports in internal news digests for senior Chinese Communist Party cadres, more than 30,000 Tibetans took part in nearly 100 'mass incidents' of varying size in Tibet and the provinces of Sichuan, Gansu, Qinghai and Yunnan ... The government spent 96.87 billion yuan ($13.8 billion) in the Tibet Autonomous Region [TAR] in the four decades from 1965 to 2005. Since 1993, 90 per cent of the revenues of the TAR administration have come from Beijing's largesse ... [Lhasa's] population has swollen to 300,000 with Han Chinese outnumbering Tibetans by two to one ... So far only a mid-ranked Tibet official, Danzheng Langjie, has been sacked for mishandling the March crisis.

(Lam 2008: 13–16)

Hu Jintao, who crushed protest in Tibet as party chief there in 1989, typifies the national consensus that China has delivered Tibetans from feudalism, ushering them toward modernity with infrastructure and investment. Tibet, in this view, should be grateful and the region's 'splittists' crushed.

(Roger Cohen, *IHT*, 7 April 2008, p. 6)

Should his people ever reclaim Tibet ... the Dalai Lama ... says an elected parliament and prime minister should rule; the Dalai Lama would occupy a religious station ... Typically, when the Dalai Lama dies, the royal court appoints a regent who rules until the next reincarnation comes of age.

(www.iht.com, 1 February 2009; *IHT*, 2 February 2009, p. 2)

Tawang, India ... [an] enclave in the Himalayas ... is perhaps the most militarized Buddhist enclave in the world ... Although little known to the outside world, Tawang is the biggest stumbling block in relations between the world's two largest rising superpowers. It is the focus of China's one remaining major land-border dispute, a conflict that is rooted in Chinese claims to sovereignty over all of historical Tibet ... China tried last spring [2009] to block a $2.9 billion loan to India from the Asian Development Bank on the grounds that part of the loan [$60 million] was slated for water [flood control] projects in Arunachal Pradesh, the state that includes Tawang. It was the first time China had sought to influence the territorial dispute through a multilateral institution ... The loan was approved in mid-June, infuriating Chinese leaders ... In June an Indian general announced that the Indian military was deploying extra divisions of troops and fighter jets here ... The roots of the conflict go back to China's territorial claims to Tibet ... China insists that this swathe of north-east India has historically been part of Tibet, and thus should be part of China ... The People's Liberation Army of China occupied Tawang briefly in 1962, during a war with India fought over this and other territories along the mountainous 4,030 kilometre border ... More than 3,100 Indian soldiers and 700 Chinese soldiers were killed ... in the border war ... Last year [2008] the Dalai Lama announced for the first time that Tawang was a part of India, bolstering the Indian government's territorial claims ... The Indian government recorded 270 border violations and nearly 2,300 instances of 'aggressive border patrolling' by Chinese soldiers last year [2008], the highest in recent memory ... Tawang became a part of modern India when Tibetan leaders from Lhasa signed a treaty with British officials in 1914 that established a border called the McMahon Line between Tibet and British-run India. Tawang fell south of the line. The treaty, the Simla Convention, is the basis for the Indian claim to Tawang but is not recognized by China, because to do so would mean acknowledging that the Tibetans had a measure of self-rule ... Since 2005 the two countries have gone through thirteen rounds of bilateral negotiations over the issue. A last round was held in August, with no result.

(Edward Wong, *IHT*, 4 September 2009, p. 2)

A chronology of important events

1720. 'China's Manchu Qing dynasty sends its army into Tibet to expel the Dzungar Mongols, bringing the area under Beijing's hegemony. The administration remains in Tibetan hands but the Qing later install their own representatives in Lhasa.'

1912. 'The Qing dynasty is overthrown. Tibet's government expels Chinese representatives.'

1913. 'The Thirteenth Dalai Lama proclaims Tibet independent.'

1918. 'The Tibetan army, led by British-trained officers, defeats the Chinese army. Tibet and China sign a peace treaty but China refuses to ratify it.'

1950. 'The Chinese communist People's Revolutionary Army invades eastern Tibet.'

1951. 'The Lhasa government accepts Chinese sovereignty over Tibet. Beijing promises to maintain the Dalai Lama's power and status and to respect local religious beliefs.'

1959. 'An abortive uprising in Tibet. The Fourteenth Dalai Lama flees into exile in India.'

Late 1970s–early 1980s. 'China softens policy on Tibet and makes contact with the Dalai Lama.'

1989. 'China declares martial law in Tibet after pro-independence riots.'

2002–4. 'The Dalai Lama's envoys hold talks with Beijing ... The Dalai Lama signals acceptance of China's sovereignty over Tibet but wants genuine autonomy for Tibetan areas.'

(The above chronology is taken from *FT*, 2 August 2004, p. 15)

A chronology of events since May 1995

May 1995. An Amnesty International report says that political and religious repression in Tibet increased in 1993 and 1994 (*IHT*, 30 May 1995, p. 4).

20 June 1996. The German Bundestag condemns what it calls 'China's continued policy of repression in Tibet'.

23 April 1997. President Clinton meets the Dalai Lama.

10 November 1998. The Dalai Lama meets President Clinton in the USA.

10 March 1999. Today is the fortieth anniversary of the uprising in Tibet (invaded by China in 1950) and the subsequent flight to India by the Dalai Lama.

5 January 2000. The third-ranking Tibetan Lama (the fourteen-year-old seventeenth Karmapa Lama, head of one of the four seats of Tibetan Buddhism) arrives in India (in Dharamsala, the seat in exile of the Dalai Lama, who fled Tibet in 1959; China took over Tibet in 1950). He arrived after a long trek from the Tsurphu monastery in Tibet, which he left on 28 December 1999. Both the Dalai Lama and China had recognized the boy's title in 1992. In contrast, the reincarnation of the eleventh Panchen Lama (the second-ranking Tibetan Lama) is in dispute. In May 1995 the Chinese authorities took away the seven-year-old boy recognized by the Dalai Lama and replaced him with another boy appointed by them.

8 February 2001. 'The Chinese government approved a plan to construct a railway from Golmud, in western China, to Lhasa, the capital of Tibet' (*The Economist*, 17 February 2001, p. 78).

23 May 2001. The Dalai Lama meets President George W. Bush at the White House.

'China marked the fiftieth anniversary of its rule over Tibet on Wednesday [23 May] with flag raising, praise for its policies in the region and condemnation of the Dalai Lama's meeting with President Bush in Washington' (*IHT*, 24 May 2001, p. 5).

'Mr Bush's meeting with the Dalai Lama was a step up in protocol from that extended by the previous administration. Bill Clinton used to drop by during a meeting between the Dalai Lama and top officials' (*FT*, 24 May 2001, p. 11).

4 April 2002.

> Tibet's longest serving dissident … the seventy-six-year-old Jigme Zangpo … has been released on 'health grounds' after two decades of stubborn refusal to renounce his pro-independence ideals … He is the second high-profile Tibetan prisoner to be freed this year. He had not been due for release until 2011. Earlier this year, in the run-up to the February summit between President George Bush and … President Jiang Zemin, the authorities ordered the early release of … Ngawang Choephel.
>
> (*Guardian*, 5 April 2002, p. 17)

(Tanag Jigme Zangpo, seventy-six … arrived in the United States yesterday [14 July] after winning release on medical grounds … He was first sentenced … in 1965 … [He] is the sixth Tibetan dissident to be freed this year [2002]': *The Times*, 15 July 2002, p. 13. 'He had been released in March and allowed home under a form of house arrest': *FT*, 15 July 2002, p. 6.)

10 September 2002.

> Two envoys from the Dalai Lama began meetings Tuesday with the Chinese government and will later travel to Tibet … [This] is the first time in more than a decade that Tibetan exile officials have publicly sent an envoy to China.
>
> (*IHT*, 11 September 2002, p. 1)

'[They are] the first officials from the exiled government to visit Tibet since 1985' (*Guardian*, 1 October 2002, p. 16).

27 May 2003.

> Secret negotiations between China and the Dalai Lama are due to resume after the arrival in Beijing last night [27 May] of two senior envoys of the Tibetan spiritual leader … Their visit to China last September [2002] was the first formal contact between the Chinese government and the Dalai Lama for ten years.
>
> (*Guardian*, 28 May 2003, p. 11)

(The visit lasted two weeks.)

9 November 2005. 'Last week President George W. Bush welcomed the Dalai Lama … in the Oval Office, but the White House was careful to give the meeting little publicity' (*The Times*, Thursday 17 November 2005, p. 47).

'President George W. Bush … met the Dalai Lama … at the White House on 9 November – but without press photographers' (*The Economist*, 19 November 2005, p. 25).

13 April 2006. 'The Dalai Lama abandoned his call for independence in 1988' (*Independent*, 4 April 2006, p. 24).

> [On 13 April 2006 there took place] China's first international religious meeting since the Communist Revolution in 1949 … The proceedings … of the First World Buddhist Forum … were dominated by the presence of Tibet's eleventh Panchen Lama, a controversial figure anointed by the Communists while still a child, and the absence of the … Dalai Lama … Gyaltsen Norbu … now sixteen … was named as Panchen Lama, the Himalayan region's second most important religious figure, in 1995. The Dalai Lama's nominee was whisked away and is thought to be held under house arrest … Gyaltsen Norbu shared the stage with Buddhist leaders from South Korea, Taiwan and Sri Lanka … About 1,000 Buddhist monks and theologians from thirty countries gathered in the eastern city of Hangzhou for the congress … Delegates emphasized the theme of the forum – 'a harmonious world begins in the mind' – which mirrors President Hu Jintao's campaign to build a 'harmonious society' … [There are] 27 million Tibetans … China has about 100 million Buddhists.
>
> (*Independent*, 14 April 2006, p. 25)

'The Dalai Lama's nominee – Gedhun Choekyi Nyima – is believed to have been under arrest since 1995, when he was six' (*The Times*, 14 April 2006, p. 47).

'China has accused the Dalai Lama of sabotage and provoking religious conflict after a group of Tibetan monks [in March] stormed a monastery near Lhasa and attacked statues of a deity denounced by the exiled leader' (*Independent*, 11 May 2006, p. 34). '[There are] approximately 110,000 Tibetans in Dharamsala [India]' (*Independent*, 3 July 2006, p. 20).

19 June 2006. See the 19 June 2006 entry in the political chronology, Chapter 8, for the opening of the Nathu-La Pass.

See the entry for 1 July 2006 in the political chronology, Chapter 8, for the opening of the Beijing–Lhasa railway. Beijing stresses the economic benefits, while critics stress the adverse effects on Tibetan culture and the environment.

> Beijing prepares a controversial plan to divert water from Tibet to the parched Yellow River in the country's west … with construction possibly starting as early as 2010 … Environmentalists and advocates of Tibetan autonomy have said the project threatens to tear the region's web of environmental and cultural interdependence.
>
> (www.iht.com, 1 August 2006)

21 August 2006.

> Mongolians are eagerly awaiting a visit this week by the Dalai Lama, although details of the revered Buddhist leader's travel plans remained secret amid concerns over likely protests from China. The Tibetan spiritual leader was to arrive Monday [21 August] in the Mongolian capital, Ulan Bator, almost four years after the last visit, which China condemned as part of an international campaign to promote political autonomy for Tibet. The Dalai Lama is being welcomed by the largest Mongolian monastery, Gandantegchinlen … Although his official schedule had yet to be announced, the Dalai Lama was expected to hold a series of lectures for the public and members of the Buddhist clergy and was to stay at a special government guesthouse outside the capital … Mongolians are overwhelmingly Buddhist … Although China has yet to issue any formal statement on the Dalai Lama's visit, news of which was officially announced late last week, Beijing has recently ratcheted up its rhetoric against the leader. 'His visits abroad are merely for the purposes of scraping together anti-Chinese elements and propagandizing and peddling his Tibetan independence thinking', a hardline communist leader in Tibet, Zhang Qingli, was quoted as saying on 8 August.
>
> (www.iht.com, 20 August 2006)

'The Dalai Lama arrived in Mongolia late Monday [21 August], defying likely protests from China … He was expected to hold several public lectures and meetings with Buddhist clergy … Organizers kept the schedule under wraps to avoid angering Beijing' (*IHT*, 22 August 2006, p. 6).

> Thousands flocked to Ulan Bator to welcome the Nobel Prize-winning leader-in-exile to Mongolia, where Buddhism has staged a revival since the country shrugged off Soviet control in 1991 … Mongolia's foreign ministry stressed the visit was sponsored by a monastery and not the government.
>
> (*FT*, 24 August 2006, p. 9)

('In 1989 the Dalai Lama was awarded the Nobel Peace Prize': *The Times*, 15 August 2006, p. 27.)

> China says it is to spend $1.3 billion on boosting infrastructure in Tibet. The world's highest airport and an extension to a controversial railway [from

> Lhasa to the second city Xigaze] are among 180 projects to be funded in the next three years, an official said … Improvements to drinking water and electricity as well as education and environmental conservation are also planned … The official said the aim was to improve the lives of Tibetans, particularly farmers and herdsmen. But critics fear Chinese development is threatening both the delicate Himalayan environment and Tibetan culture.
>
> (www.bbc.co.uk, 27 March 2007)

April 2007. 'In April the Chinese authorities arrested four pro-Tibetan independence protesters who had climbed to the Mount Everest base camp and hung a banner to protest plans to take the Olympic torch through the Tibetan Himalayas' (*IHT*, 14 August 2007, p. 2).

15 June 2007. 'Australian prime minister John Howard has met the Dalai Lama in Sydney … The seventy-one-year-old spiritual leader is on a eleven-day trip to Australia' (www.bbc.co.uk, 15 June 2007).

> China played down a visit this week by two emissaries for the Dalai Lama, but acknowledged Tuesday [3 July] that they had met with Chinese officials … A Chinese foreign ministry spokesman … [said] that they 'are not so-called envoys' … [They] arrived in China last week for a sixth round of direct talks with China … Direct contacts between the Dalai Lama's emissaries and China began in September 2002.
>
> (www.iht.com, 3 July 2007)

'Hundreds of prisoners of conscience, including Buddhist monks and nuns, remain in prison and reports persist of torture and deaths in custody' (*Amnesty*, July–August 2007, p. 16).

'In Tibet freedom of expression, religion and association are severely restricted. Hundreds of prisoners of conscience, including Buddhist monks and nuns, remain in prison and reports persist of torture and deaths in custody' (ibid.).

1 August 2007.

> Scores of people have been arrested in western China following a public protest for the return of … the Dalai Lama … A local resident … was detained after he climbed onto a stage … and asked the crowd if they wanted the Dalai Lama to return … Police and army reinforcements were sent to the traditionally Tibetan town of Lithang in western Sichuan province after the incident Wednesday [1 August] at an annual horse festival, said Radio Free Europe, which is financed by the US government, and the monitoring group International Campaign for Tibet … Radio Free Europe said about 200 Tibetans were taken into custody after the protest … China claims Tibet has been its territory for centuries, but Tibetans say they were self-ruled for most of that period … New regulations, which are to come into force on 1 September [2007], will 'regulate the management of the reincarnation if living Buddhas', the State Administration for Religious Affairs

said in a statement [on 3 August]. In 1995 the Dalai Lama and China's atheist communist authorities chose rival reincarnations of the tenth Panchen Lama, who died in 1989. The Panchen Lama is the second highest figure in Tibet's spiritual hierarchy. The six-year-old anointed by the Dalai Lama swiftly disappeared from public view.

(www.iht.com, 3 August 2007)

[A] local resident ... was arrested after asking festival-goers if they wanted the Dalai Lama back. People protesting at his arrest were also detained ... [One witness said that] twenty people were detained initially and another 200 following a protest at the jail ... [The local resident] called for the Dalai Lama to return and for the Chinese authorities to free the Panchen Lama, the second holiest figure in Tibetan Buddhism ... From 1 September all reincarnations of 'living Buddhas' would need government approval.

(www.bbc.co.uk, 3 August 2007)

Tibet's living Buddhas have been banned from reincarnation without permission from China's atheist leaders ... 'The so-called reincarnated living Buddha without government approval is illegal and invalid', according to the order, which comes into effect on 1 September ... Reincarnate lamas, known as *tulkus*, often lead religious communities and oversee the training of monks ... China already insists that only the government can approve the appointment of Tibet's two most important monks, the Dalai Lama and the Panchen Lama ... China has long insisted that it must have the final say over the appointment of the most senior lamas.

(*The Times*, 4 August 2007, p. 36)

China has introduced new rules that appear aimed at controlling the selection of the next Dalai Lama ... China will now have the final say over who can be selected as a reincarnated monk ... Although the new regulations do not mention the Dalai Lama by name, they effectively prevent his followers in exile from choosing his reincarnation. 'No outside organization or individual will influence or control the reincarnation of living Buddhas [eminent monks]', states one article of the new regulations. They also say that any reincarnation has to be approved by various levels of government. In the case of the most preeminent monks, who would include the Dalai Lama, China's cabinet has to give its seal of approval ... The current, fourteenth Dalai Lama, is now seventy-two. Since he fled Tibet in 1959 after a failed uprising against Chinese rule, he has travelled the world.

(www.bbc.co.uk, 1 September 2007)

The ceremonial wearing of animal fur has been raised to the status of a political question in western China, since the Dalai Lama issued a statement two years ago urging Tibetans to reject the long-time practice as inconsistent with Buddhism. Reportedly the Dalai Lama was responding to complaints from Indian conservationists that Tibetans' fondness for skins from tigers and other endangered species was hastening their disappearances.

> As word of the Dalai Lama's instructions spread across western China some Tibetan communities responded by publicly burning their furs, while others have simply dropped the use of fur in ceremonies. This perceived act of obedience to a man whom the Chinese government has long vilified as a 'splittist', meaning secessionist, appears to have angered the authorities.
>
> (*IHT*, 15 August 2007, p. 2)

23 September 2007.

> German Chancellor Angela Merkel is to meet the ... Dalai Lama on Sunday [23 September] in talks that have angered China ... Sunday's meeting will be the first time the Dalai Lama has been received at the chancellery ... Germany says the meeting ... is a private exchange.
>
> (www.bbc.co.uk, 23 September 2007)

('Beijing has already cancelled several high profile events, including a major business forum in Frankfurt and a meeting with the [German] finance minister ... in Beijing next month [December]': *IHT*, 20 November 2007, p. 3.)

16–17 October 2007.

> [On 16 October] President George W. Bush met privately with the Dalai Lama at the White House, as tensions escalated between the United States and China over Congress's awarding its highest civilian honour to the exiled leader ... The session was held upstairs in the Yellow Room of the White House residence, not the Oval Office, to send a message that Bush was receiving a spiritual leader, not a political one. Aides declined to disclose details, and the White House would not release a photograph of the two together, as it has during previous visits ... The Dalai Lama is in Washington for a week of festivities, including receiving the Congressional Gold Medal in a ceremony Wednesday [17 October] at the Capitol and delivering a speech on the Capitol lawn. Bush said he would participate in the award ceremony in his first public appearance with the Dalai Lama during this visit.
>
> (www.iht.com, 17 October 2007)

'President George W. Bush presented the Congressional Gold Medal to the Dalai Lama' (www.iht.com, 17 October 2007).

> [Earlier] an administration official said that the White House meeting would be at President Bush's residence, not in the Oval Office, 'which is appropriate and befits the Dalai Lama's role as a spiritual, not political leader' ... Beijing this week pulled out of a meeting at which world powers were to discuss the Iranian nuclear programme ... Beijing also cancelled its annual human rights dialogue with Germany to protest Chancellor Angela Merkel's meeting last month [September] with the Dalai Lama.
>
> (*IHT*, 17 October 2007, p. 8)

> George W. Bush will attend the ceremony in Washington, becoming the first sitting US president to appear in public with the exiled Tibetan leader ...

> Mr Bush met the Dalai Lama behind closed doors on Tuesday [16 October] in the White House residence, rather than the Oval Office, out of deference to China. It was their third private meeting in six years. But Wednesday's elaborate ceremony to honour the [1989] Nobel Peace prize winner on Capitol Hill will be a much more public affair.
>
> (www.bbc.co.uk, 17 October 2007)

'The Dalai Lama has met current or former US presidents on ten previous occasions but has never met a serving president in public' (*FT*, 17 October 2007, p. 12). 'The top US civilian award [is] a Congressional Gold Medal' (*Independent*, 17 October 2007, p. 29).

> According to reports from human rights groups and in the Hong Kong press, monks in Lhasa have clashed with the Chinese police over the past month ... The confrontation was sparked not by protests, but by some do-it-yourself work. Monks in the Drepung monastery were whitewashing and painting auspicious symbols on the walls of one of its buildings, assigned as a ceremonial residence for the Dalai Lama ... The painting celebrated his latest trophy: a Congressional Gold Medal from the United States – its highest civilian honour ... The reports tell of a similar showdown at another Lhasa monastery, Nechung, and of various other attempts by Tibetans to celebrate the congressional honour.
>
> (www.economist.com, 24 October 2007)

20 November 2007.

> The Dalai Lama says he is considering ... naming his own successor. Usually, following the death of a Dalai Lama, senior Tibetan Buddhist officials, guided by dreams and signs, identify a young child to succeed him. But the Dalai Lama said he feared China would try to influence the process. He said he was considering whether his successor should be picked by him, or elected by high ranking Buddhist monks [High Lamas] ... The Dalai Lama (on 20 November during a visit to Japan): 'If the Tibetan people want to keep the Dalai Lama system, one of the possibilities I have been considering with my aides is to select the next Dalai Lama while I am alive ... If China selected my successor after my death, the people of Tibet would not support him as there would be no Tibetan heart in him' ... Buddhists believe the current Dalai Lama is the reincarnation of his predecessors.
>
> (www.bbc.co.uk, 20 November 2007)

> The Dalai Lama said: 'Among the options being considered are a democratic selection by the high monks of Tibetan Buddhism, or the appointment of a successor by myself' ... The exiled leader accused the Chinese authorities of stepping up persecution of Tibetan monks and civilians, and called the region's relations with the Chinese government 'the most tense in recent years' ... The Dalai Lama arrived in Japan last week for a nine-day visit. He has been snubbed by Japanese officials, who want to improve relations with China.
>
> (*The Times*, 21 November 2007, p. 41)

22 November 2007.

A Chinese foreign ministry spokesman (22 November): 'The reincarnation of living Buddhas is a special inheritance of Tibetan Buddhism. The Dalai Lama's remarks clearly violate religious rituals and historical conventions [of Tibetan Buddhism]' ... Beijing bases its claim to final say over reincarnations on a precedent established by the Manchu-ruled 1644–1911 Qing Dynasty, which established loose suzerainty over the region.

(*FT*, 25 November 2007, p. 7)

[On 27 November] the Dalai Lama said: 'The Tibetan nation is 2,000 years old. The Dalai Lama institution is relatively recent – only a few centuries old. If I die it will be a setback for the Tibetan people for some time. But then the struggle will continue. If the Tibetan people decide that the Dalai Lama institution is no longer relevant, then it will automatically cease to exist' ... China's foreign ministry has issued a statement: 'The reincarnation of the living Buddha is a unique way of succession of Tibetan Buddhism and follows relatively complete religious rituals and historical conventions.'

(www.bbc.co.uk, 27 November 2007)

27 November 2007.

The exiled Tibetan Buddhist leader proposed yesterday [27 November] to hold a referendum among his 13 million to 14 million followers around the world – before his death – on whether he should be reincarnated or not. If the majority vote against it he said he would simply not be reborn, ending a lineage that tradition dictates dates back to the late fourteenth century when a young shepherd was appointed the first Dalai Lama ... The 1989 Nobel Peace Laureate ... the current Dalai Lama ... [is] the fourteenth ... He fled Tibet in 1959 after an abortive uprising against Chinese rule and has been living in India ever since, heading a 200,000-strong Tibetan exile community from the northern town of Dharamsala ... Yesterday the China foreign ministry condemned the Dalai Lama's proposals: 'The reincarnation of the living Buddha is a unique way of succession of Tibetan Buddhism and follows relatively complete religious rituals and historical conventions. The Dalai Lama's statement is in blatant violation of religious practice and historical procedure' ... The Dalai Lama said there was a historical precedent for a lama being reincarnated while still alive, giving the example of one of his teachers who died last year [2006]. He did not say how the referendum would be conducted, but said it should include all those in the Himalayan region, Mongolia and elsewhere who have traditionally followed Tibetan Buddhism. The 6 million Tibetans inside China would almost certainly be unable to participate, but another 7 million to 8 million follow Tibetan Buddhism in India, Bhutan, Nepal, Mongolia, Russia and the West ... The Dalai Lama: 'If my death comes while we are still as refugees, then my reincarnation logically will come outside of Tibet.

(*The Times*, 28 November 2007, p. 35)

> The Dalai Lama … has long said he may not be reincarnated at all, or, if Tibet is not free, that he may be reborn outside China … Recently the Dalai Lama has gone further, proposing that his successor be chosen while he is still alive, by himself or by senior monks. And this week he even suggested that Tibetans could hold a referendum to decide on the Dalai Lama's future.
>
> (*The Economist*, 1 December 2007, p. 71)

14 December 2007.

> Chinese authorities are taking an increasingly harsh stance on Tibet, pushing Tibetans to seek greater support abroad, the Dalai Lama said during a visit to Italy … addressing lawmakers in the lower house of parliament … He said that despite progress since 2001 Chinese officials in recent talks have 'intensified the accusation' of separatism and claimed 'there is no Tibetan issue'.
>
> (www.iht.com, 14 December 2007)

2 March 2008. 'China is to impose stricter rules on foreign rock and pop stars after singer Björk caused controversy by shouting "Tibet, Tibet" at a Shanghai concert. Her cry followed a powerful performance [on 2 March] of her song "Declare Independence"' (www.bbc.co.uk, 8 March 2008).

10 March 2008.

> More than 100 Tibetan exiles have begun a march from India to Tibet to protest against Chinese rule in the region. The marchers left Dharamsala on the forty-ninth anniversary of the Dalai Lama's escape from Tibet after a failed uprising against Chinese rule … The Dalai Lama said he approved of China hosting the Olympic Games because it provided the world with a chance to pressurize the Beijing government to uphold the Olympic ideals of freedom of speech and equality … The Dalai Lama said, 'China should prove herself a good host by providing these freedoms. Therefore, besides sending their athletes the international community should remind the Chinese government of these issues' … In Nepal Tibetan exiles have clashed with police in Kathmandu while trying to march to the Chinese embassy … Between 1,000 to 3,000 Tibetan exiles and their supporters gathered at a large Buddhist shrine, including many monks and nuns … The police barred the way when some protesters tried to march towards the Chinese embassy.
>
> (www.bbc.co.uk, 10 March 2008)

> The march will be one of several protests around the world before the 8–24 August [2008] Olympic Games, Tibetan exile groups said … Monday [10 March] marks the anniversary of a failed uprising against Chinese rule in Tibet … In the northern Indian city of Dharamsala on Monday the Dalai Lama denounced Chinese rule and said that: '[For nearly six decades Tibetans] have had to live in a state of constant fear, intimidation and suspicion under Chinese repression. In Tibet repression continues to increase with numerous, unimaginable and gross violations of human rights, denial of reli-

gious freedom and the politicization of religious issues' ... India shares a 2,485 mile border with Tibet 'so we could enter from anywhere'. Said Tenzin Tsundue, one of the main marchers and a leading Tibetan activist ... Every year some 3,000 Tibetans cross into Nepal, mainly through passes across the Himalayas on their way to Dharamsala.

(www.iht.com, 10 March 2008)

Indian police barred several hundred Tibetan exiles from marching to Tibet on Monday [10 March] to protest Beijing hosting this summer's Olympic Games ... Protesters also held demonstrations in New Delhi and Kathmandu, Nepal, where ten activists were detained after hundreds clashed with police. Meanwhile, the Dalai Lama, speaking at a separate event, accused China of 'unimaginable and gross violations of human rights' in the Himalayan region. The planned six-month march from India to Tibet began Monday to coincide with the anniversary of a failed uprising ... The local police chief [in Dharamsala] said the march contravened an agreement between New Delhi and the Tibetan government in exile ... Neither the Dalai Lama nor Tibet's government in exile have issued any official statement on the march ... In New Delhi more than 1,000 protesters marched and some wrapped themselves in bandages covered with fake blood and wore cutouts of the Olympic rings around their necks ... Jigme Yeshi (a member of the Tibetan Youth Congress): '[The bandages are meant to show] that the IOC [International Olympic Committee] has done a great injustice by giving permission ... to China to hold the Olympics' ... In Kathmandu police fired tear gas and beat up hundreds of Tibetans who threw bricks and stones at the police.

(www.iht.com, 10 March 2008)

The initial incident occurred Monday afternoon [10 March] when about 400 monks left Drepung Loseling monastery intending to march 5 miles (8 kilometres) to the city centre. Police officers stopped the march at the halfway point and arrested fifty to sixty monks ... The remaining monks held the equivalent of a sit-down strike and were joined by 100 more monks from Drepung ... The monks wanted the authorities to ease rules on 'patriotic education' in which monks are required to study government propaganda and write denunciations of the Dalai Lama.

(www.iht.com, 14 March 2008)

'The Dalai Lama said that: "[Tibetans' language, customs and traditions are] gradually fading away ... [as they become] an insignificant minority [in their homeland]" ' (*Guardian*, 11 March 2008, p. 29).

'As many as 3,000 Tibetan refugees arrive in India from China each year and India is home to an estimated 120,000 Tibetan refugees' (*FT*, 18 March 2008, p. 9).

'India is home to an estimated 130,000 Tibetan refugees' (www.iht.com, 17 March 2008). 'India is host to the largest Tibetan refugee population in the world, now about 100,000 people … India has never supported Tibetan independence' (www.iht.com, 19 March 2008).

> [There are] more than 150,000 [Tibetan] refugees and their supporters [in India] … India recognized Tibet as part of China in 1954 … The Dalai Lama [was] granted asylum … on condition the Tibetans would not engage in 'subversive activities' against friendly countries.
>
> (www.bbc.co.uk, 19 March 2008)

'In Greece protesters were barred from entering Olympia, which has hosted the games' torch-lighting ceremony since 1936. Instead, they lit a torch outside' (*Guardian*, 11 March 2008, p. 29).

'In Greece a dozen Tibetans lit a torch outside Olympia, site of the ancient Olympic Games, to launch a global torch relay they hope will cover more than twenty countries and end at the Tibetan border just as the Olympics start on 8 August' (*The Times*, 11 March 2008, p. 41).

11 March 2008.

> Leaders of Tibetan refugees in India say they are defying a ban preventing them from marching to Tibet in protest over China hosting the Olympics … In recent years India has not allowed large-scale public protests for fear of embarrassing Beijing … Meanwhile China on Tuesday [11 March] said that it had squashed a protest by Buddhist monks in Lhasa … China said [that on Monday 10 March] monks in Tibet's capital Lhasa staged a protest against Beijing's rule … Some reporters say that dozens were arrested.
>
> (www.bbc.co.uk, 11 March 2008)

'Some 100 Tibetan monks have been arrested' (www.iht.com, 12 March 2008).

12 March 2008.

> China has closed Mount Everest [Qomolangma] to climbers amid fears that activists could disrupt the Olympic torch ascent of the world's highest peak. The announcement that Chinese authorities had halted access to its side of the mountain that straddles the border between Tibet and Nepal came as paramilitary police were deployed against demonstrations by Tibetan monks in Lhasa … China has also declared the nearby Mount Cho-Oyu off limits … [There was] a second day of demonstrations by monks on a scale that has not been seen in nearly twenty years. Witnesses described soldiers firing teargas on Tuesday [11 March] to try to disperse more than 600 monks as they tried to march out of the Sera monastery on the edge of Lhasa. The monks were forced to a halt at the gates after police called in the military. The monks shouted 'Release our people', demanding the return of eleven of their number detained when they staged an anti-Chinese protest in protest of the Jokhang Temple, the holiest site in Tibetan Buddhism, in the heart of the city on Monday [10 March]. That protest coincided with demonstrations by

about 500 monks from the sprawling Drepung monastery outside Lhasa. The demonstrations ... are the largest since authorities imposed martial law after riots by anti-Chinese protesters in March 1989.

(*The Times*, 13 March 2008, p. 38)

'Police in India have detained more than 100 Tibetan refugees who were trying to march to the Chinese border ... The marchers ... [including] some foreigners ... were arrested 31 miles from Dharamsala' (www.bbc.co.uk, 13 March 2008).

Chinese officials have acknowledged that Buddhist monks were protesting in Lhasa this week ... Rights groups said the demonstrations were the biggest display of opposition to Chinese rule in Tibet since 1989 ... This week the Chinese leadership closed the north face of Mount Everest until after the Olympic Flame ascends in May for fear that activists might use it to stage photogenic Tibet-related protests.

(www.bbc.co.uk, 13 March 2008)

Police [in India] detained more than 100 Tibetan exiles as they marched to their homeland Thursday [13 March] ... The protesters began a hunger strike within hours of being arrested ... Indian officials fear the march could embarrass Beijing and banned the exiles from leaving the Kangra district that surrounds the northern Indian city of Dharamsala, the headquarters of the Tibetan government-in-exile. The march began Monday [10 March], the day Tibetans commemorated their 1959 uprising against China.

Nine foreigners who were marching with the Tibetans but were not arrested began a hunger strike of their own outside the building where the Tibetans were being held. The foreigners hail from the United States, Scotland, Germany, Poland and Australia ... Demonstrations also spilled over into traditionally Tibetan areas in the neighbouring province of Qinghai. Monks at two other monasteries – the Lutsang monastery and the Ditsa monastery – also held small protests but were not detained by police ... Demonstrations took place around the world [on 10 March], including a protest by 300 Buddhist monks in Lhasa, one of the boldest public challenges to China's rule in recent years ... Protests in Lhasa this week are believed to be the biggest in the city since Beijing crushed a wave of pro-independence demonstrations in 1989.

(www.iht.com, 13 March 2008)

Eight foreigners and three Indian citizens involved in the march were released later Thursday, but the police in Himachal Pradesh were still holding 101 others, who were all Tibetans. The Indian government says Tibetans are free to live and work in India as long as they refrain from political protests ... Soldiers and police have been deployed around two Buddhist monasteries [Drepung and Sera] in Lhasa where monks launched protests against Chinese rule earlier this week ... After two demonstrations Monday – one in which 300 or more monks from Drepung marched on the

> streets of the capital – the other in which a smaller group of monks from Sera protested – police arrested an unknown number of protesters … On Tuesday [11 March] police used tear gas to disperse an estimated 500 to 600 monks from the Sera monastery who were marching to demand the release of imprisoned fellow monks … Earlier Thursday [Chinese] foreign ministry spokesman Qin Gang confirmed that protests had taken place … Qin Gang: 'This is a political scheme by the Dalai group, attempting to separate China and try to make some unrest in the normal harmonious, peaceful life of Tibetan people.'
>
> (www.iht.com, 13 March 2008)

'Since Monday [10 March] there have been further demonstrations, including including Lhasa's third biggest monastery, Ganden' (*Guardian*, 14 March 2008, p. 19).

'Tibetans reported demonstrations by 400 in Lutsang monastery in Qinhai province, an area Tibetans call Amdo, as well as at the Myera monastery in Gansu' (*The Independent*, 14 March 2008, p. 29).

14 March 2008.

> Violent protests erupted Friday [14 March] in a busy market area of Lhasa, as Buddhist monks and other ethnic Tibetans clashed with Chinese security forces … Hundreds of people, including monks and civilians [were involved] … The protesters burned shops, cars, military vehicles and at least one tourist bus … Protesters set fire to other shops … Gunfire [was reported].
>
> (www.iht.com, 14 March 2008)

> Tibetan witnesses described Chinese police officers firing into crowds of protesters in the city's ancient Barkhor area … [Chinese reports say] two soldiers died … The apparent epicentre of protests Friday was the Tromsikhang Market, a massive, concrete structure built in the Barkhor area of Lhasa by the Chinese authorities in the early 1990s … The protest started Monday [10 March] when Buddhist monks began peaceful demonstrations against religious restrictions by the Chinese authorities … What actually sparked the violence [on Friday] is unclear, as accounts differed between Chinese and Tibetan residents. Monks from the Ramoche Temple, located a short walk from the market, reportedly began to march in the Barkhor area. The Ramoche monks intended to protest the rough treatment of monks who had marched earlier in the week, according to a Tibetan activist … When police began beating the monks ordinary Tibetans rioted in the Barkhor area … [It was reported that] Tibetan protesters were waving white scarves and shouting 'Free Tibet'.
>
> (*IHT*, 15 March 2008, p. 6)

> Clashes between protesters and security forces in Lhasa have left at least two people dead … Chinese properties – shops, restaurants, owned by ethnic

corpses had been counted, including twenty people killed on Saturday [16 March] next to the Drapchi prison in Lhasa … The Chinese official news agency Xinhua says ten people died on Friday [14 March], including business people it said were 'burnt to death'.

(www.bbc.co.uk, 16 March 2008)

Lhasa was reported quiet on Sunday [16 March], locked down by a heavy Chinese security presence. On Sunday businesses remained shut, the streets were empty and locals said a curfew was in force … The demonstrators, who on Friday [14 March] set fire to Chinese-owned shops and hurled rocks at local police, have been penned into an area of the old town by government forces … The Dalai Lama told the BBC he had received reports the death toll from the protests may be as high as 100, although he said the figure could not be verified … The Dalai Lama emphasized that he still supported Beijing's staging of the Olympic Games this summer … [He said] the Games were an opportunity for the Chinese to show their support for the principle of freedom … Chinese officials said the riots had been 'masterminded' by the Dalai Lama, an accusation he has denied … [On 15 March] pro-Tibet demonstrations were held in Nepal, New York, Australia and several European cities. A British journalist in Lhasa on Saturday [15 March] said police had used tear gas to disperse demonstrators defying a curfew. The authorities in Tibet have urged the protesters to hand themselves in by midnight on Monday [17 March], promising leniency to those who surrender … [There have been] demonstrations at one of Tibetan Buddhism's most important monasteries in the nearby province of Gansu … Riot police broke up a demonstration by monks from Labrang monastery on Saturday, for the second day … Chinese security forces fired tear gas to disperse a crowd of at least 1,500 monks as they marched through the streets chanting 'Free Tibet' … The situation is tense in Gansu's next-door province of Qinghai, which also has a large Tibetan population.

(www.bbc.co.uk, 16 March 2008)

Witnesses said police fired on about 1,000 monks protesting in Aba, Sichuan, on Sunday [16 March] … Reports put the death toll at seven … In Machu, Gansu province, hundreds of protesters marched on government buildings and set fire to Chinese businesses.

(www.bbc.co.uk, 17 March 2008)

The Dalai Lama (16 March):

It's a people's movement; I consider myself a people's servant; I cannot ask people not to do this, not to do that … Everyone knows my principle – knows [it is] completely non-violence … Violence is almost like suicide … I have no such power [to bring an end to the protests] … The Olympics should not be called off. The Chinese people … need to feel proud of it. China deserves to be a host of the Olympic Games.

(www.thetimes.co.uk, 16 March 2008)

'The Dalai Lama said he had been asked by activists inside Tibet not to ask them to curtail protests, but said he remained a firm believer in non-violence' (www.iht.com, 16 March 2008).

> The Dalai Lama endorsed the right of his people to press grievances peacefully against the Chinese authorities, and said he would not ask Tibetans to surrender to Chinese military police by midnight on Monday [17 March], as Beijing has demanded. He said he had no moral authority to do so and that Tibetans had beseeched him not to capitulate to that demand … The Dalai Lama: 'Whether the Chinese government admits it or not, a nation with an ancient cultural heritage is actually facing serious dangers. Whether intentionally or unintentionally, some kind of cultural genocide is taking place … They [the Chinese] have no experience of how to deal with problems through talk, only suppress … As far as material development is concerned, we get much benefit [from being part of China]' … Asked whether he endorsed the protest in Tibet … the Dalai Lama said Tibetans were entitled to air their grievances peacefully. 'Protest – peaceful way express their deep resentment – is a right,' he said … Asked if he could stop the protesters from defying the deadline, he replied 'I have no such power' … [There have been] six negotiating sessions between the Dalai Lama's representatives and Chinese authorities over the past six years.
>
> (www.iht.com, 17 March 2008)

'The Dalai Lama … argued that the Chinese treat Tibetans as second-class citizens in their own land. He said Tibetans need a full and genuine autonomy to protect their cultural heritage' (www.cnn.com, 18 March 2008).

> Thousands of Buddhist monks and other Tibetans clashed with the riot police in a second Chinese city on Saturday [15 March], while the authorities said they had regained control of Lhasa, a day after a rampaging mob ransacked shops and set fire to cars and storefronts in a deadly riot. Conflicting reports emerged about the violence in Lhasa on Friday [14 March]. The Chinese authorities denied that they had fired on protesters there, but Tibetan leaders in India told news agencies on Saturday that they had confirmed that thirty Tibetans had died and that they had unconfirmed reports that put the number at more than 100. Demonstrations erupted for the second consecutive day in the city of Xiahe in Gansu province, where an estimated 4,000 Tibetans gathered near the Labrang monastery. Local monks held a smaller protest on Friday, but the confrontation escalated Saturday afternoon … The demonstrations in Lhasa began Monday [10 March] and continued through Wednesday [12 March] as peaceful protests by Buddhist monks from three different monasteries. Some monks protested religious restrictions, while others demanded an end to Chinese rule and even waved the Tibetan flag … Chinese officials demanded the surrender of the 'lawbreakers' in Lhasa and offered leniency to people who turned themselves in to the authorities by midnight Monday [17 March]. Senior officials

described the unrest as 'sabotage' orchestrated by the Dalai Lama and credited the military force for rescuing 580 people from banks, schools and hospitals that were set alight by rioters. General Yang Deqing of the Chinese army said soldiers would not be employed and the protest were being handled by local police officers and the country's paramilitary force, the People's Armed Police ... Witnesses in Lhasa on Saturday reported seeing large numbers of military police, armoured vehicles and tanks ... It is still uncertain what set off Friday's unrest. Tibetan advocates say ordinary Tibetans began rioting after military police attacked monks trying to protest outside a monastery in the centre of the city.

(www.iht.com, 16 March 2008)

Rioting erupted Sunday [16 March] in a Chinese province that neighbours Tibet ... A police officer, speaking even as the main government building in Aba county, Sichuan province, came under siege, said that about 200 Tibetan protesters had hurled gasoline bombs and burned down a police station there. The Tibetan Centre for Human Rights and Democracy said that thousands of monks of the nearby Amdo Ngaba Kirti monastery in Sichuan had raised the banned Tibetan flag and shouted pro-independence slogans ... A woman in contact with a businessman in Lhasa said the streets were teeming with armed police officers in riot gear Sunday after word of renewed clashes overnight, when Hui Moslem Chinese attacked Tibetans in revenge for wrecked homes and property.

(www.iht.com, 16 March 2008)

There were unconfirmed reports that demonstrations by ethnic Tibetans had spread to the nearby provinces of Sichuan, Gansu and Qinghai ... Aides to the Dalai Lama said they had confirmed eighty killings on 13 and 14 March in Lhasa, including twenty-six victims killed just outside Drapchi prison. Tibetan exiles in Dharamsala said they had also received news that at least two Buddhist monks had set themselves on fire in protest ... For the second consecutive day protest appeared to have spread into Tibetan-populated regions beyond Tibet. Buddhist monks and the police reportedly clashed in Aba county in Sichuan province. A crowd of about 200 Tibetan protesters burned a local police station ... One witness said a police officer was killed in the confrontation.

(www.iht.com, 17 March 2008)

The regional government offered leniency to rioters if they gave themselves up by midnight on Monday [17 March] and provided information on lawbreakers. The Xinhua news agency said: 'Those who cover up or shelter the lawbreakers will be punished in accordance with the law' ... The Xiahe riots started as a show of support for the Lhasa demonstrations ... Xiahe is in the Chinese province of Gansu ... On Friday [14 March] hundreds of Labrang monks marched through Xiahe holding aloft Tibetan flags, which are banned in China. During the clashes on Saturday morning 1,000

> protesters marched to government offices and smashed windows in public buildings, including the local public security bureau headquarters.
>
> (www.independent.co.uk, 16 March 2008)

> At the Labrang monastery in neighbouring Gansu province monks said they had seen four people shot dead after riot police attacked the protesters … According to the Free Tibet Campaign, the riots have also spread to Kirti monastery in Aba county, in the province of Sichuan, where witnesses say they saw thirteen people shot by security forces … The Tibetan Autonomous Region only refers to part of Tibet but nearly 3 million Tibetans live in neighbouring provinces of China, such as Gansu and Sichuan.
>
> (*Independent*, 17 March 2008, p. 27)

('The population of Xiahe is roughly 45 per cent Tibetan, 45 per cent Han Chinese and 10 per cent Hui Moslem': www.guardian.co.uk, 16 March 2008.)

> Tibet Watch, a group based in Dharamsala, India, told CNN that thirty-four people have died in the Nwaga county area of Sichuan province in western China … Another protest took place in Machu county in north-western China … More than 200 people protested in Nyangden – near the Sera monastery north of Lhasa – Sunday [16 March]. Police used tear gas against demonstrators who took to the streets of Kama Kusang, east of Lhasa, on Sunday.
>
> (www.cnn.com, 16 March 2008)

'[During] the 1958–9 uprising, say Tibetans, up to 2 million were killed across the country and in other Chinese provinces' (www.guardian.co.uk, 16 March 2008).

17 March 2008.

> Tibet's governor … Champa Phuntsok … an ethnic Tibetan … said Monday [17 March] that thirteen people were killed … in violence that broke out in Lhasa last week, as Chinese troops fanned out to deal with protests that have spread to three neighbouring provinces … The death toll, which Champa Phuntsok said did not include three people who jumped out of buildings to avoid arrest, was a update over the government's previous figure of ten killed. He described the thirteen dead as 'innocent civilians' … Tibet's hardline Communist Party Secretary Zhang Qingli – the region's most powerful official – returned to Lhasa over the weekend … Zhang had been attending the national legislature's annual session in Beijing, which ends Tuesday [18 March] … In Sichuan province Monday government troops moved into a county in Aba prefecture where clashes between monks and police broke out Sunday [16 March] with reports of as many as seven killed.
>
> (www.iht.com, 17 March 2008)

> China raised the death toll from riots in Tibet last week to sixteen on Monday [17 March] but said security forces had avoided using lethal force,

> while scattered protests continued in ethnic Tibetan communities in neighbouring Chinese provinces. As police and paramilitary officers were deployed to quash demonstrations in Qinghai, Gansu and Sichuan provinces, a midnight deadline set by the Chinese authorities passed for those who took part in the demonstrations to give themselves up or face harsh penalties. Demonstrations also reached Beijing, with about eighty students at the central University staging a sitdown protest on the campus late Monday night ... Officials said the police and paramilitary police had been called in to deal with the protests, not the People's Liberation Army, which spearheaded the Tiananmen crackdown ... Liu Jianchao (foreign ministry spokesman): 'The PLA is not involved in the handling of the incidents. Their entering Tibet now is mainly to handle losses from the incidents ... The Chinese authorities have not used any lethal weapons in the whole process' ... Chinese officials said Lhasa was quiet Monday ... On Monday protests took place at the Chinese embassies in New Delhi and Paris, while another was being planned for London ... The senior Chinese political leader in Tibet, Champa Phuntsok [Qiangba Puncog, an ethnic Tibetan], said on Monday that security forces had used only water cannons and tear gas to disperse protesters in Lhasa. He said thirteen of those killed in the protest were 'innocent civilians' attacked by the mob. Another three Tibetans died when they jumped from the roof of a building after refusing to surrender to the police ... He said: 'This was organized, premeditated, masterminded and incited by the Dalai clique, and it was created under the collusion of Tibet independence separatist forces both inside and outside of China.'
>
> (*IHT*, 18 March 2008, p. 4)

'Champa Phuntsok: "There are thirteen common people who died in the beating, burning and smashing in the riots. They died of fire, asphyxiation and beating. Some of them were set on fire by rioters and died in the burning"' (www.cnn.com, 17 March 2008).

> Tibetan regional governor Qiangba Puncog [Champa Phuntsok]: '[Security forces] did not carry or use any lethal weapons. I can tell you as a responsible official that guns were absolutely not fired' ... Security forces in Lhasa are rounding up dissidents ... Tibetans in Nepal and India are continuing to protest ... Police in Nepal have dispersed a crowd of 100 Tibetan protesters and Buddhist monks ... Monday's protest by Tibetans was the first time in a series of demonstrations in Nepal that they have been confronted by police firing tear gas.
>
> (www.bbc.co.uk, 17 March 2008)

'Liu Jianchao (foreign ministry spokesman) said that: "[Law enforcement authorities] had shown maximum restraint [and the military had not been deployed] ... No bullets have been fired and no lethal weapons have been used"' (*FT*, 18 March 2008, p. 9).

> In November 2005 Zhang Qingli was appointed Communist Party Secretary of the Tibet Autonomous Region … Zhang had overseen a tough crackdown on many facets of Tibetan life. Tibetan government employees faced requirements to write denunciations of the Dalai Lama. Zhang reintroduced a policy that forbade Tibetan students and government workers to visit monasteries or participate in religious ceremonies. By 2006 Zhang had revived an 'anti-Dalai' campaign and intensified 'patriotic education' at Buddhist monasteries. Monks are now required to attend long sessions listening to recitations of China's interpretation of Tibetan history and to denounce the Dalai Lama.
>
> (*IHT*, 18 March 2008, p. 4)

> Zhang Qingli, who is Han, was appointed in 2005 after a spell crushing separatism in Xinjiang. When he took charge neglected rules banning students and the families of civil servants from taking part in religious activities began once more to be rigorously enforced … Mr Zhang urged more 'patriotic education' in monasteries, part of which involves denouncing the Dalai Lama. He banned displays of the portraits of the Karmapa Lama, who fled to India in 1999 … Some Tibetans believe Han Chinese now make up around half of the city's [Lhasa's] population … [Tibet's] GDP growth rate stayed above 12 per cent for the past seven years. In 2007 it was 14 per cent, more than two points higher than the national rate.
>
> (*The Economist*, 22 March 2008, p. 30)

'Lhasa now has twice as many Han Chinese as Tibetans' (www.iht.com, 18 March 2008).

18 March 2008. Prime minister Wen Jaibao:

> There is ample fact and we also have plenty of evidence proving that this incident was organized, premeditated, masterminded and incited by the Dalai Lama clique. This has all the more revealed the consistent claims by the Dalai clique that they pursue not independence, but peaceful dialogue, are nothing but lies … Their hypocritical lies cannot cover the ironclad facts … [The protesters] used extremely cruel means. This incident has seriously disrupted public order and life in Lhasa. This incident has inflicted heavy loss of life and the property of the people of Lhasa … [The protesters] wanted to incite the sabotage of the Olympic Games in order to achieve their unspeakable goal … Those claims that the Chinese government is engaged in so-called cultural genocide are lies … [China will continue] to protect the culture in Tibet … We will continue to help Tibet improve the livelihood of people of all ethnic groups. We will never waver in this position … We are fully capable of maintaining stability and normal public order in Tibet … [China] not only has the ability to maintain stability in Tibet and normal social order, but will also continue to support Tibet's economic and social development, to raise the living standards of all ethnic groups in Tibet, and to protect Tibetan culture, ecology and the environ-

> ment. This is an unwavering stand ... We appreciate the position and the steps taken by the Indian government in handling Tibetan independence activities masterminded by the Dalai clique.
>
> (www.cnn.com, 18 March 2008; www.bbc.co.uk, 18 March 2008; www.iht.com, 18 and 20 March 2008)

Dalai Lama:

> Violence is against human nature ... Violence is wrong. We should not develop anti-Chinese feelings. We must live together side by side ... If things get out of control then my only option is to completely resign ... Even [if] 1,000 Tibetans sacrificed their life, [this is] not much help. Please help stop violence from [the] Chinese side and also from [the] Tibetan side ... The Chinese prime minister accuses me of all these things I said. Absolutely not. Prime minister, come here and investigate thoroughly all our files, or record my speeches. Then the prime minister will know how much is distorted by local officials ... Investigate thoroughly [he said in response to Chinese claims that he instigated the violence]. If you want to start investigating from here you are most welcome. Check our various offices ... You investigate who is a liar ... I want to ask [Wen Jiabao], please show proof ... Independence is out of the question ... I received a call from Tibet – they said please don't ask us to stop.
>
> (www.bbc.co.uk; www.cnn.com, 18 March 2008; www.thetimes.com, 18 March 2008; *FT*, 19 March 2008, p. 10)

Tenzin Takhla (spokesman for the Dalai Lama): 'If the Tibetans were to choose the path of violence he would have to resign because he is completely committed to non-violence. He would resign as the political leader and head of state, but not as the Dalai Lama. He will always be the Dalai Lama' (www.cnn.com, 18 March 2008).

'About 100 Tibetan exiles and supporters ... held a demonstration in London' (www.bbc.co.uk, 18 March 2008).

'Exiled Tibetan groups claim there have been deadly clashes ... [in] Nwaga county in Sichuan province ... over the last couple of days with more than thirty protesters, including monks, women and children, killed by Chinese security forces' (www.cnn.com, 18 March 2008).

> Reports of further violence and protest continued. Tibetan sympathizers said confrontations had occurred in two locations in Sichuan province, with four Tibetans killed in one clash ... On Tuesday [18 March] a spokesman for Tibet's government in exile said it had confirmed ninety-nine deaths, including eighty in Lhasa, in confrontations with Chinese security officers. Pro-democracy groups also issued photographs of naked, bloody bodies that they asserted were of Tibetans slain by Chinese security officers in Aba county, also known as Ngawa, a Tibetan region of Sichuan province.
>
> (www.iht.com, 19 March 2008)

According to the Tibet regional government, 105 people involved in the protests had handed themselves over to police by 23.00 (15.00 GMT) on Tuesday [18 March] … Tibetan exiles say at least ninety-nine protesters have died in clashes with the authorities – in Lhasa and beyond … On Tuesday Tibetan activists released images they say support their claim of heavy casualties and Chinese brutality. They say the pictures depict protesters killed by Chinese security forces at Kirti monastery in Sichuan province on Sunday [16 March] … The Tibetan exile government said it had also heard reports of nineteen deaths in neighbouring Gansu province … Tenzin Takhla (senior aide to the Dalai Lama): 'Maybe China's grand strategy is to flood Tibet with an influx of ethnic Han Chinese. In Lhasa two-thirds of the 300,000 population is already Chinese. Rumour has it that after the Olympics China will settle 1 million Han Chinese into Tibet.'

(www.bbc.co.uk, 19 March 2008)

Qin Gang (a foreign ministry spokesman): 'What the international community should concern itself with, and should ask about, is precisely what role and function he [the Dalai Lama] played in this serious incident of criminal violence involving fighting, smashing, looting and arson. The one who should be tried and investigated is the Dalai Lama himself' … Qin later said he meant the Dalai Lama should be tried on moral grounds … The Dalai Lama complimented Beijing for having met three out of four conditions to be a 'superpower'. He acknowledged that China had the world's largest population, military prowess and a rapidly developing economy. 'Fourth, moral authority, that's lacking,' he said, and then for the second time in two days he accused Chinese officials of a 'rule of terror' in Tibet. But the Dalai Lama also sought to make conciliatory gestures. He condemned the burning of Chinese flags and attacks on Chinese property by Tibetan protesters. He also said he planned to meet Wednesday [19 March] in India with a group of Tibetan advocates who have vowed to march 1,400 kilometres, or about 900 miles, from Dharamsala to Lhasa. He said he would convey his 'reservations' about their effort. The first batch of marchers that set off from Dharamsala last week was arrested by the Indian police. The second batch was allowed to continue but remains well inside India … The Indian police arrested one group of marchers but have allowed a second to continue, to about 90 miles from Dharamsala … Some of the younger exile groups have advocated independence for Tibet, openly deviating from the Dalai Lama's 'middle way' of greater autonomy but not secession from China. On Tuesday [18 March] some of them burned the Chinese flag.

(www.iht.com, 19 March 2008)

19 March 2008.

Gordon Brown (UK prime minister): 'The premier [Wen Jiabao] told me in a phone call on Wednesday [19 March] that, subject to two things that the Dalai Lama has already said – that he does not support the total independence of Tibet and that he renounces violence – that he would be prepared to enter into dialogue' … Mr Brown also said he would meet the Dalai Lama during a visit to London in May … Also on Wednesday the Dalai Lama asked Tibetan activists not to undertake a controversial march from India to Lhasa … [Chinese] officials said on Wednesday that the Olympic torch – which will be carried across China ahead of the Games – will still go through Tibet despite the current troubles. It is due to be carried to the top of Mount Everest in May and to pass through Lhasa in June … The India-based Tibetan Centre for Human Rights said three people had been killed by security forces in Kardze, Sichuan province … Serious unrest was reported in provinces close to Tibet with large ethnic Tibetan populations. Video has emerged from nearby Gansu province showing Tibetans tearing down a Chinese flag and replacing it with a Tibetan flag. Hundreds of protesters can be seen on foot and horseback in Tuesday's incident at a school near Hezuo.

(www.bbc.co.uk, 19 March 2008)

On Wednesday [19 March] the Communist Party chief of Tibet, Zhang Qingli said: '[The Dalai Lama is] a jackal [wolf] in Buddhist monk's clothes, an evil spirit with a human face and the heart of a beast … We are engaged in a fierce battle of blood and fire with the Dalai clique.'

(*IHT*, 20 March 2008, p. 2; www.iht.com, 26 March 2008)

('The Tibet Party Secretary declared: "The Communist Party is like a parent to the Tibetan people and is always considerate about what the children need … [The party is the] real Buddha [for Tibetans]"': www.iht.com, 8 April 2008.)

'[The Chinese] authorities … claimed 156 offenders had surrendered themselves to police' (*Guardian*, 20 March 2008, p. 28).

20 March 2008.

Chinese police opened fire and wounded four protesters 'in self-defence' last Sunday [16 March] in a Tibetan area of Sichuan province, the Xinhua news agency says. The report is the first time Chinese authorities have admitted hurting anyone since protests against Chinese rule in Tibet began last week … China has admitted for the first time that anti-Beijing protests have spread outside the Tibetan Autonomous Region … Xinhua news agency reported huge damage to government buildings and shops after riots in Sichuan province on Sunday … The agency referred to protesters in Aba county, Sichuan, as 'mobsters', saying they had caused 'great damage' to shops and government offices … Officials said twenty-four people had been arrested after demonstrations in Lhasa and 170 protesters had surrendered to authorities … State media reported that 170 people had now handed themselves in – up from the 105 people they said had surrendered to police in Lhasa … It was not clear whether the twenty-four were among the 170 reported to have surrendered.

(www.bbc.co.uk, 20 March 2008)

> On Thursday [20 March] Chinese authorities admitted that members of the security forces had fired on Tibetan protesters. Police wounded four protesters in 'self-defence' last Sunday in Aba county, Xinhua news agency said. An earlier Xinhua report said police had shot the four dead, but it was quickly changed. Xinhua did not provide further details of the incident, but Tibetan activists say at least eight people were killed at a demonstration against Chinese rule near the Kirti monastery in Aba on Sunday.
>
> (www.bbc.co.uk, 21 March 2008)

'The official Xinhua news agency said protesters had attacked "shops and government offices" Sunday [16 March] in Aba [Sichuan] but made no mention of allegations by pro-Tibet groups abroad that troops had fired on protesters, killing several' (www.iht.com, 20 March 2008). 'The official Xinhua news agency said Thursday [20 March] that the police shot and wounded four rioters "in self-defence" during violent protests on Sunday [16 March] in Aba prefecture in Sichuan' (www.iht.com, 21 March 2008).

'China acknowledged for the first time that anti-government riots that rocked Lhasa last week have spread to other provinces … The official Xinhua news agency said there were "riots in Tibetan-inhabited areas in the provinces of Sichuan and Gansu"' (www.cnn.com, 20 March 2008).

'For the first time the [Xinhua news] agency said Chinese forces had opened fire in "self-defence" in Sichuan last week, wounding four protesters' (www.guardian.co.uk, 20 March 2008).

> In India the Dalai Lama said he was 'always ready to meet' with Chinese leaders, in particular President Hu Jintao, though he said he would not travel to Beijing to do so … The [Chinese] foreign ministry said it was 'seriously concerned' about a planned meeting between prime minister Gordon Brown of Britain and the Dalai Lama.
>
> (www.iht.com, 20 March 2008)

> The Dalai Lama Thursday [20 March] said he was powerless to stop anti-Chinese violence … The Dalai Lama: 'I have no authority. I have no power to tell the movement to shut up' … The Dalai Lama met Wednesday [19 March] with leaders of several Tibetan activist groups. Younger activists demand Tibetan independence and hope to derail the 2008 Beijing Olympics. The Dalai Lama, who calls for 'meaningful autonomy' and supports the Olympics, said Thursday [20 March] that he will suffer the consequences of the protesters' actions. He also said he is ready to meet with Chinese leaders, regarding Tibet, if there is something concrete to be accomplished.
>
> (www.cnn.com, 20 March 2008)

'The Dalai Lama was quoted as saying: "I [am] always ready to meet our Chinese leaders, particularly Hu Jintao"' (www.guardian.co.uk, 20 March 2008).

The Dalai Lama: 'As I mentioned earlier, to go to Beijing and meet leaders … That would be big news. Many Tibetans … may develop some unrealistic expectations. I have to think very carefully' … He said he would be willing to travel to Beijing in a matter of weeks if there was a 'concrete indication' that the Chinese were prepared to negotiate and if the protests in Tibet had concluded. His spokesman later confirmed that while he did not wish to simply provide the Chinese with a photo-opportunity that could be used against him, he was ready to discuss a 'mutually agreeable solution' to the issue of Tibet … [The Dalai Lama's] cautious 'middle way' has been criticized by some Tibetans, including the Tibetan Youth Congress which seeks full independence from China … Dharamsala is home to more than 1,000 monks … India is home to an estimated 100,000 Tibetans in total … The government-in-exile [is] properly known as the Central Tibetan Administration (CAT) … While the CAT is not formally recognized by any government, it does receive funding from a number of countries and international organizations.

(*IHT*, 21 March 2008, p.2)

A handful of radical Tibetan groups have said angrily that the 'middle way' has achieved nothing in nearly thirty years. They have called for an Olympic Games boycott, burned Chinese flags and refused to call off a march from Dharamsala to Lhasa … The Dalai Lama: 'I have no authority, no power to say "Shut up." I'm always telling them: "You are fighting for our rights. But today we are almost a nation dying. This moment important is survival. Practical solution is necessary"' … The Dalai Lama has flatly said that to call for independence would be to lose the support of world leaders, including that of his hosts in India … Samdhong Rinpoche (the prime minister of the Tibetan government-in-exile): '[I recognize the] energy and fire [of the younger, more radical exiles] … [But] they have all lived in a world of dreams. And they are driven by emotions.'

(www.iht.com, 21 March 2008)

The Dalai Lama said … [on 20 March] that he feared villagers in remote parts of Tibet were 'facing death' from Chinese troops in remote parts of Tibet from Chinese troops intent on seeking retribution for the protests, but emphasized that he was prepared to meet Chinese leaders to resolve the crisis … The Dalai Lama: 'I am really worried that a lot of casualties may happen. Then [there are] no medical facilities. So I am appealing to the international community, please think about these helpless unarmed innocent people who simply love Tibetan culture and are not willing to accept others' bullying. These are now facing death' … The Dalai Lama said that columns of army trucks were being sent across the Tibetan plateau and there were Chinese troops deployed in many villages.

(www.guardian.co.uk, 21 March 2008)

The Dalai Lama dropped his calls for independence in 1979 after Deng Xiaoping offered talks in return … No country recognizes his [the Dalai

> Lama's] 'government-in-exile' … The government's revenue, generated from donations and a small levy on Tibetans in India, is thought to be about $20 million. The New York Tibet Fund disburses another $3 million a year, which the Chinese consider a front for the US government because part of the funding comes from the State Department.
>
> (www.iht.com, 23 March 2008)

21 March 2008.

> Nancy Pelosi, [Democrat] Speaker of the US House of Representatives, spoke out while holding talks in northern India with the Dalai Lama … Nancy Pelosi: 'We call upon the international community to have an independent outside investigation on accusations made by the Chinese government that His Holiness [the Dalai Lama] was the instigator of violence in Tibet. The situation in Tibet is a challenge to the conscience of the world. If freedom-loving people throughout the world do not speak out against China and the Chinese in Tibet, we have lost all moral authority to speak out on human rights' … Nancy Pelosi said she was not seeking a boycott of the Beijing Olympics, but warned that the 'world is watching' events in China … [She] is one of the sharpest critics of Beijing's human rights record in the US Congress. Her visit at the head of a congressional delegation was planned before the protests began.
>
> (www.bbc.co.uk, 21 March 2008)

'Nancy Pelosi … rejected Chinese claims that the Dalai Lama incited the violence, saying the accusation "doesn't even make sense"' (*FT*, 22 March 2008, p. 8).

> John McCain, the presumptive Republican presidential nominee, said China's crackdown 'is not correct' and expressed hope Beijing would seek a peaceful resolution … McCain: 'The people there are being subjected to mistreatment that is not acceptable with the conduct of a world power, which China is.'
>
> (www.cnn.com, 22 March 2008)

'The authorities say 160 rioters have turned themselves in to the police and twenty-four people have been charged with "grave crimes"' (www.economist.com, 21 March 2008).

> The violence in Lhasa … has incited sympathy demonstrations in neighbouring provinces, prompting Beijing to blanket a huge area with troops and warn tourist and foreign journalists to stay away … Demonstrations have flared across Sichuan, Gansu and Qinghai provinces in support of protests that were started in Lhasa … Tibetan exile groups say ninety-nine people were killed – eight in Lhasa and nineteen in Gansu – while Beijing maintains that sixteen died.
>
> (www.iht.com, 21 March 2008)

> Outside of Lhasa Beijing has deployed troops across a wide swathe of western China where more than half of China's 5.4 million Tibetans live. Moving from town to town police set up blockades and checkpoints to keep Tibetans in and journalists out.
>
> (www.cnn.com, 22 March 2008)

'Chinese authorities have issued a list of twenty-one people wanted for their alleged role in anti-China riots in Lhasa last week ... The official Xinhua news agency said that two of the twenty-one suspects had already been arrested and a third turned himself in' (www.bbc.co.uk, 22 March 2008).

> The twenty-one people are accused of endangering national security and cited for beating, smashing, looting and arson ... Xinhua said two of the twenty-one suspects were arrested and a third turned himself in ... Police have arrested twenty-four people and another 183 turned themselves in, Xinhua said.
>
> (www.cnn.com, 22 March 2008)

22 March 2008. 'China [now] says eighteen civilians and a policeman were killed' (www.bbc.co.uk, 22 March 2008). 'China has said that nineteen people were killed in the Lhasa riots ... Hundreds of people have been marching through London ... the marchers, including many exiled Tibetans, also sang the Tibetan national anthem at the Chinese embassy' (www.bbc.co.uk, 23 March 2008).

'Beijing's official death toll from last week's rioting in Lhasa rose to twenty-two, with the Xinhua news agency reporting that five more civilians and a police officer died' (www.cnn.com, 22 March 2008). 'China raised its death toll by six, to twenty-two, with the official Xinhua news agency reporting that the charred remains of an eight-month-old boy and four adults were pulled from a garage burned down in Lhasa last Sunday' (www.cnn.com, 23 March 2008).

> Ethnic Han Chinese were the real victims of the Tibetan riots, the Beijing authorities said, and its security forces will respond severely ... Footage of ethnic Han Chinese being attacked by Tibetans in Lhasa has dominated state media in China ... 'Evidence shows that the violent incidents were created by the "Tibet independence" forces and masterminded by the Dalai Lama clique with the vicious intention of undermining the upcoming Olympics and splitting Tibet from the motherland,' thundered an editorial in the *People's Daily*, yesterday [22 March] China's official Xinhua news agency said eighteen civilians and a policeman died in Lhasa.
>
> (www.independent.co.uk, 23 March 2008)

> In Lhasa yesterday [23 March] local television issued the number seven list of those most wanted in connection with the riots on 10 March ... The latest list included six women and one monk and brought to forty-five the number of people the security forces were seeking ... The *People's Daily* ... accused Tibet's spiritual leader of planning attacks with the aid of violent Uighur

> separatist groups seeking an independent East Turkestan for their largely Moslem people in the north-western Xinjiang region of China. It said: 'The Dalai clique has also strengthened collusion with East Turkestan terror organizations and planned terror activities in Tibet.'
>
> (*The Times*, 24 March 2008, p. 32)

'Five young women burned to death in a Chinese clothing store during rioting in Tibet on 14 March ... Four of the women were Han Chinese. The fifth was a twenty-one-year-old ethnic Tibetan' (www.iht.com, 28 March 2008).

> On Sunday [23 March] ... the *People's Daily* said: 'The Beijing Olympics are eagerly awaited by the people of the whole world, but the Dalai Clique is scheming to take the Beijing Olympics hostage to force the Chinese government to make concessions to Tibet independence' ... Beijing has released tallies of statements of support from foreign governments – 100 of them, it said, from North Korea to Sudan to Tonga.
>
> (www.cnn.com, 23 March 2008)

> One of Thailand's six torchbearers said in an open letter that she had decided against taking part in the relay ... The official lighting of the Olympic flame is set for Monday [24 March] in Greece and some fear the arrival of the Olympic torch – scheduled to travel through twenty countries before the Beijing Olympics open on 8 August – could spark violent protest against China.
>
> (www.iht.com, 23 March 2008)

> A group of Chinese intellectuals has circulated a petition to stop what they call a 'one-sided' propaganda campaign against the Dalai Lama and to open direct dialogue with Tibet's spiritual leader. The petition was signed by more than two dozen writers, journalists and scholars.
>
> (www.iht.com, 23 March 2008; *IHT*, 24 March 2008, p. 1)

> A group of twenty-nine Chinese dissidents released an open letter yesterday [23 March] calling for talks with the Dalai Lama. The letter criticized the 'one-sided propaganda of the official Chinese media' and 'Cultural Revolution-like language' of many government statements and called for a United Nations investigation of the events in Tibet.
>
> (*FT*, 24 March 2008, p. 4)

'[There has been] a massive migration of over 7 million Han Chinese into Tibet ... In 1951 there were virtually no Han Chinese in the province, but now they are the majority' (Malcolm Rifkind, *IHT*, 24 March 2008, p. 6).

> Last October [2007], when the Congressional Gold medal was awarded to the Dalai Lama, monks in Tibet watched over the internet and celebrated by setting off fireworks and throwing barley flour. They were quickly arrested. It was for the release of these monks that demonstrators initially turned out this month.
>
> (Patrick French, *IHT*, 24 March 2008, p. 6)

24 March 2008.

> The Olympic torch has been lit at a ceremony in Greece that was briefly disrupted by protesters. Two pro-Tibet activists broke through the cordon of 1,000 police officers in Olympia and attempted to display a flag as China's envoy spoke … As Liu Qi, head of the Beijing Olympic Organizing Committee, spoke ahead of the torch lighting, two men ran up behind him attempting to display a black flag depicting the Olympic rings made from handcuffs. They were quickly bundled away by police and Mr Liu continued his speech uninterrupted … Before the ceremony a Tibetan activist confronted Jacques Rogge … head of the International Olympic Committee (IOC) … in a hotel lobby and said there should be free access for all media inside China, including Tibet, during the Games … The Olympic torch is being carried in a 136,000 kilometre (85,000 miles) around-the-world relay that will see it pass through twenty countries before arriving in Beijing for the start of the Games on 8 August … The Tibetan government-in-exile says at least 130 people have died in a crackdown by Chinese troops.
>
> (www.bbc.co.uk, 24 March 2008)

'During the ceremony campaigners broke through police lines and unfurled a Tibetan flag before being dragged away' (www.bbc.co.uk, 25 March 2008). 'The Tibetan goventment-in-exile says it can now confirm that 130 people died during the recent clashes … [It] had previously announced a death toll of ninety-nine' (www.bbc.co.uk, 24 March 2008). ('[The Tibetan activist confronting Jacques Rogge] demanded that Tibet be removed from the Olympic torch relay and that dignatories boycott the Games' opening ceremony on 8 August': *IHT*, 25 March 2008, p. 4.)

> One of the protesters, who were from the Paris-based media group Reporters Without Borders, which was demonstrating against media restrictions in China, was able to get behind a senior Chinese official who was giving a speech and unfurl a banner before being dragged away by police … The Associated Press reported last week that Chinese authorities had decided to prohibit live television broadcasts from Tiananmen Square, the site of 1989 pro-democracy demonstrations, for fear that the square could attract more protests … Beijing said yesterday [24 March] that it would allow a group of foreign reporters to visit Lhasa this week.
>
> (*FT*, 25 March 2008, p. 8)

> Beijing told several journalists Monday [24] that a group of about twelve journalists would be able to travel to Lhasa for a special government-guided tour of the city this week. Whether they will be allowed to interview people independently is unclear.
>
> (www.iht.com, 25 March 2008)

> The Chinese government has arranged for a trip for foreign media organizations to Tibet … The spokesman said that about a dozen foreign journalists

would be allowed into Tibet on Wednesday [26 March]. The group, which does not include the BBC, would be allowed to interview 'victims of criminal acts', he said.

(www.bbc.co.uk, 25 March 2008)

The Beijing torch relay was disrupted by pro-Tibetan and press freedom activists. Seven people were detained … Three members of the Paris-based group Reporters Without Borders were detained after running onto the stadium field while Beijing organizing chief Liu Qi was speaking. The ceremony went ahead and the flame was lit by the sun's rays. At the ceremony a Tibetan woman covered in red paint – symbolizing blood – lay in the road in front of a runner carrying the Olympic torch, while others unfurled flags and chanted 'Free Tibet' and 'Shame on China'. Two Tibetans were detained in that incident, while another Tibetan campaigner and a Greek photographer with him were held at another site, Tibetan activists said.

(www.iht.com, 24 March 2008)

'Reporters Without Borders made headlines again Monday [24 March] when three high ranking members were arrested at the Olympic flame-lighting ceremony after unfurling a black banner showing the Olympic rings as handcuffs' (www.iht.com, 25 March 2008).

'Demonstrations continued today in countries neighbouring Tibet. In north-east India police stopped nearly 500 Tibetan exiles from marching to the Chinese border to demand a halt to China's crackdown on protesters in Tibet' (www.guardian.co.uk, 24 March 2008).

Hundreds of monks, nuns and local Tibetans who tried to march on a local government office in western China to demand the return of the Dalai Lama have been turned back by paramilitary police who opened fire to disperse the crowd. Local residents of Luhuo said two people – a monk and a farmer – appeared to have been dead and about a dozen were wounded in the latest violence to rock Tibetan areas of China … About 200 nuns from Woge nunnery and a similar number of monks from Jueri monastery marched out of their hillside sanctuaries and walked towards the Luhuo third district government in the nearby town. They were swiftly joined by an estimated several hundred farmers and nomads, witnesses said. Shouting 'Long live the Dalai Lama' and 'Tibet belongs to Tibetans' they approached the district government office. However, paramilitary People's Armed Police swiftly appeared and ordered the crowd to turn back. Town residents reported that … shots were fired and two people appeared to have died … The authorities in Lhasa issued their number eight list of those most wanted in connection with the violence. The new list … of eight people brought to a total of fifty-three the number of those who are wanted … the Dalai Lama's government-in-exile in India said today [24 March] that the death toll in the clashes had risen to 130.

(www.thetimes.co.uk, 24 March 2008)

25 March 2008.

> A deadly clash erupted between protesters and the police in a Tibetan area in China's west, state media and a rights group said Tuesday [25 March], as the country's top police official called for stepped-up 'patriotic campaigns' in monasteries to boost support for Beijing. The demonstration in Garze, a prefecture in Sichuan province, started Monday [24 March] as a peaceful march by monks and nuns grew violent when armed police officers tried to suppress the crowd, which ballooned to about 200 after residents joined in, said the Tibetan Centre for Human Rights and Democracy in Dharamsala, India. China's official Xinhua news agency said the protesters attacked the police with knives and stones, killing one police officer. The Tibetan Centre for Human Rights said one [eighteen-year-old] monk died and another was critically wounded after security agents fired live rounds into the gathering … Meng Jianzhu, the minister of public security … said 'patriotic education' campaigns would be strengthened in monasteries … Meng was the first high level central government official to visit since protests began in the Tibetan capital on 10 March … Also on the trip was Zhang Qingli, Tibet's hard-line Communist Party leader … Zhang is known for his inflammatory statements. Speaking last year [2007] in Beijing, Zhang proclaimed that 'the Central Party Committee is the real Buddha for Tibetans' … The *Tibet Daily* said that thirteen people were formally arrested in Lhasa on Monday in a 10 March protest outside the Jokhang temple, Tibet's most sacred shrine. The thirteen chanted 'reactionary slogans' and carried a 'reactionary flag', indicating the snow-lion flag of independent Tibet. In Aba, another Sichuan province, Xinhua said 381 people involved in protests had surrendered to the police as of Monday.
>
> (www.iht.com, 25 March 2008)

'Tibet's government-in-exile said on Tuesday [25 March] that it could confirm 140 people had died in the recent violence – an increase of ten from Monday [24 March]' (www.bbc.co.uk, 25 March 2008).

> Police armed with bamboo sticks stopped a protest by Tibetan refugees and monks in front of the Chinese embassy in Nepal on Tuesday [25 March] and arrested about 100 participants. Chanting 'Free Tibet' and 'Chinese thieves leave our country', the protesters approached the visa office of the Chinese embassy in Kathmandu … Tibetans have been protesting near refugee camps or near the United Nations office in Kathmandu since 10 March, but this was the first anti-Chinese rally near the Chinese embassy … Nepal's border with China in the Himalayas is a key route for Tibetans fleeing Chinese rule in the region. Thousands of Tibetan refugees live with relatives in Nepal or in camps funded by aid groups. Most of the refugees eventually move to India.
>
> (www.iht.com, 25 March 2008)

'Tibetan exiles and monks protested for a second day outside of China's embassy visa office in Kathmandu (Nepal) on Tuesday [25 March], resulting in seventy-three protesters arrested, Nepalese police said' (www.cnn.com, 25 March 2008).

26 March 2008.

> A group of foreign reporters has been allowed into Lhasa for the first time since the violence began. The group, which does not include the BBC, would be able to interview 'victims of criminal acts' [a] foreign ministry spokesman said on Tuesday [25 March] ... More than 660 people have turned themselves in to police following recent violent protests in and around Tibet ... Xinhua news agency reported 280 people in Lhasa had handed themselves in by late Tuesday and earlier reports said 381 people in Sichuan had surrendered ... Authorities in Lhasa have also issued twenty-nine warrants and published a list of fifty-three people wanted in connection with the violence, Xinhua said.
>
> (www.bbc.co.uk, 26 March 2008)

> China said Wednesday [26 March] that 660 people had surrendered to the authorities in western China, following two weeks of anti-government protests and deadly riots in and around Tibet ... Beijing allowed a group of twenty-six hand-picked foreign journalists to travel to Lhasa on Wednesday morning to witness the damage in the city and interview victims of the riots ... Very few journalists have been able to report from inside Tibet. Shortly after the 14 March riots the government began forcing foreign journalists out of the city. Government blockades have also prevented foreign journalists from reaching Tibetan areas in neighbouring provinces. The foreign journalists invited to Lhasa on Wednesday are on a three-day, government-supervised trip. The Associated Press was among the organizations allowed to travel there. *The New York Times* was not offered entry. Whether the foreign media would be able to report freely, without government minders, was unclear. For more than a week, however, more than twenty journalists from China's state-controlled media have been allowed into Tibet and areas with large Tibetan populations to report on the unrest and efforts to restore order. The Chinese media have been driving home Beijing's message: that Tibetan separatists acted as terrorists, while the government responded with restraint in quelling the riots.
>
> (www.iht.com, 26 March 2008)

> State-run media announced on Wednesday [26 March] that more than 600 people had turned themselves in to police in Lhasa and in Sichuan province, where unrest also broke out. Police also published a list of fifty-three people wanted in connection with the riots, the official Xinhua news agency reported. At least twenty-nine people have been formally arrested, but it was not clear if they were among the fifty-three on the wanted list.
>
> (www.cnn.com, 26 March 2008)

> More than 600 people involved in violent protests in Tibet have surrendered to the authorities, China said yesterday [26 March] ... 280 people in Lhasa

and 381 in Sichuan province … The Tibetan parliament-in-exile … [says] at least 135 people are dead.

(*The Times*, 27 March 2008, p. 45)

In a telephone conversation with President George W. Bush, President Hu Jintao said China was willing to 'continue contacts' with the Dalai Lama. But he repeated the usual precondition, that he forgoes demands for independence (he has, in fact) and added another, that he stops 'activities to fan and mastermind violent activities' and efforts to 'sabotage' the Olympics. The Dalai Lama has denied any involvement. The last round of informal contacts between his representative and China was held last July [2007].

(www.economist.com, 27 March 2008)

27 March 2008.

Charles Hutzler (Beijing bureau chief for the Associated Press, was among a group of journalists who were taken on a government-arranged trip to Lhasa): 'A group of monks disrupted a government-managed tour by foreign reporters to Tibet's capital on Thursday [27 March], screaming there was no religious freedom and that the Dalai Lama was not to blame for recent violence there. The … fifteen-minute … outburst by about thirty monks came as the journalists, including an Associated Press reporter, were being shown around the sacred Jokhang Temple by government handlers in Lhasa … "Tibet is not free" yelled one young Buddhist monk … Government handlers shouted for the journalists to leave and tried to pull them away during the protest … The monks had rushed over to stop the reporters from being taken into an inner sanctum of the temple, saying they were upset that a government administrator was telling the reporters that Tibet had been part of China for centuries. They said that troops who had been guarding the temple since 14 March were removed the night before the visit by the reporters. One monk said they were upset that some people brought to the temple for the visit by the journalists "are not true believers but are Communist Party members" … The official programme [was] put on for the roughly two dozen American, European, Middle Eastern and Asian reporters from *The Wall Street Journal*, *USA Today*, Japan's Kyodo News Agency, KBS of South Korea, and Arab broadcaster Al-Jazeera … [An official video] showed how Tibetan protesters targeted many of the symbols of Chinese rule. They torched police stations, fire trucks and a Bank of China. The video showed a charred signboard from a Communist Party office … The Chinese government says twenty-two people died, while Tibetan exiles say the violence plus the harsh crackdown afterward have left nearly 140 people dead.'

(www.iht.com, 27 March 2008; *IHT*, 28 March 2008, p. 4)

Tibetan monks shouting pro-independence slogans caught Chinese officials by surprise Thursday [27 March] during a highly scripted tour for Western journalists in Lhasa's central Buddhist temple … Government handlers

> shouted for the journalists to leave and tried to pull them away during the fifteen-minute protest by about thirty monks at the Jokhang monastery in central Lhasa … The monks involved in the protest … rushed over to stop the reporters from being taken into an inner part of the temple, saying they were upset that a government administrator was telling the reporters that Tibet had been part of China for centuries, the Associated Press said … Tibet neighbouring provinces with large Tibetan populations are now under tight military control, with roadblocks and house-to-house searches for suspects. But there have been daily reports of protests and sporadic violence in some regions, people in those areas say.
>
> (www.iht.com, 27 March 2008)

'Many of the surviving properties had white silk scarves tied to the locks – an apparent signal to rioters that the owner was Tibetan and that their building should be spared' (*FT*, 27 March 2008, p. 1).

> The monks complained that they had been locked in the temple since the 14 March riot … The monks claimed that the heavy security presence around the temple had been withdrawn only for the media visit and said many of the people inside the inner sanctum of the temple were not genuine worshippers but had been brought in to the temple by officials to make it seem as if normal religious life had returned to the capital … Baima Chilin, vice chairman of the Tibetan government, denied that the authorities had artificially created the impression that the temple was busy and said the monks would not be arrested for their actions. However, he revealed that of 414 people arrested in Lhasa since the riot, some were monks … of the 414 people arrested for taking part in the four days of disturbances, he said, the vast majority were Tibetans.
>
> (*FT*, 28 March 2008, p. 5)

'The reporters described Lhasa as a divided city – with Chinese areas resuming normal business, but the old city, mainly populatd by Tibetans, still under police presence. The BBC's request to take part in the media trip was turned down' (www.bbc.co.uk, 29 March 2008).

> Poland's prime minister has said he does not intend to go to the opening of the Olympics in August in the wake of China's crackdown in Tibet … Czech President Vaclav Klaus has announced he will not be going to the opening ceremony although he said his motivation was 'not a threat to China'.
>
> (www.bbc.co.uk, 27 March 2008)

> Donald Tusk, Poland's prime minister, became the first EU head of government to announce a boycott on Thursday [27 March] … Tusk: 'The presence of politicians at the inauguration of the Olympics seems inappropriate. I do not intend to take part' … He was promptly joined by President Vaclav Klaus of the Czech Republic, who had previously promised to travel to Beijing.
>
> (*Guardian*, 29 March 2008, p. 21)

28 March 2008.

> The German Chancellor, Angela Merkel, yesterday [28 March] became the first world leader to decide not to attend the Olympics in Beijing … Germany is to stay away from the Games' opening ceremony in August … Frank-Walter Steinmeier, Germany's foreign minister, confirmed that Merkel was staying away … While announcing that German leaders were staying away from Beijing, Steinmeier denied they were boycotting or staging a political protest against the Chinese military and police campaign in Tibet and surrounding areas … British and US diplomats were among a group of outside officials allowed to travel yesterday to Lhasa for the first time since the crisis erupted a fortnight ago.
>
> (*Guardian*, 29 March 2008, p. 21)

'China will take a handful of foreign diplomats to Tibet … The UK, France and the United States are among the countries invited on a two-day trip to Lhasa' (www.bbc.co.uk, 28 March 2008).

> The government invited a small group of reporters, including the *Financial Times* to visit Lhasa on a two-day trip that ended yesterday [28 March]. A group of foreign diplomats arrived yesterday for a government organized trip … Baima Chilin, deputy governor of Tibet, said three Tibetans had been among the eighteen civilians killed in the riot.
>
> (*FT*, 29 March 2008, p. 9)

'Ethnic Chinese people reportedly make up a third of the population of some Tibetan cities' (p. 11).

> About twenty Tibetan high school children scaled a brick wall surrounding the United Nations compound in Kathmandu [Nepal] on Friday [28 March], carrying a small home-made sign that read 'Free Tibet' and asking the United Nations to help their cause … [It was reported] that police had arrested sixty demonstrators outside the compound.
>
> (www.iht.com, 28 March 2008)

> A UN spokesman … [said] the twenty-one students apologized to senior officials and guards for entering the UN compound … in Nepal's capital, Kathmandu … As the students climbed into the UN [compound], the police attention appears to have been diverted by a bigger demonstration nearby, from which they arrested eighty-nine people, say Tibetan activists.
>
> (www.bbc.co.uk, 28 March 2008)

> On Friday [28 March] the Dalai Lama made his most extended comments on the Tibetan violence, accusing the Chinese state-run media of trying to 'sow the seeds of racial tension' there but calling for 'meaningful dialogue' with Beijing about how to reduce tensions … In 1995 Beijing arrested the Panchen Lama, the number two in Tibetan Buddhism, a six-year-old at the time. He has never been seen since. China then anointed another youth as a

replacement Panchen Lama and has tightly controlled his education and public duties ever since. Under Tibetan Buddhism traditionally the Panchen Lama names a new Dalai Lama, theoretically giving Beijing control over the present Dalai Lama's succession ... The Dalai Lama has repeatedly promised that he has no desire to see Tibet break free of Chinese sovereignty. He has, though, pressed for what he calls 'genuine autonomy' under Chinese rule for Tibet, which is defined by the Chinese as an autonomous region, though smaller than historical Tibet. He refers to the Chinese constitution, which invokes the right of autonomy and self-government 'in areas where people of minority nationalities live in compact communities'.

(Howard French, www.iht.com, 29 March 2008)

29 March 2008.

EU foreign ministers meeting in Slovenia have rejected a proposed boycott of the opening ceremony of the Olympic Games in Beijing ... German foreign minister Frank-Walter Steinmeier said the German Chancellor had not planned to go to Beijing. So there was nothing to cancel and no link to Tibet.

(www.bbc.co.uk, 29 March 2008)

Foreign diplomats are in Tibet on a fact-finding visit approved by China ... The UK and the United States are among the fifteen nations invited on the one-day trip to Lhasa ... A group of seventeen diplomats from countries including Japan and Australia arrived in Tibet from Beijing on Saturday [29 March]. They are expected to return to the Chinese capital on Saturday.

(www.bbc.co.uk, 20 March 2008)

30 March 2008.

The Olympic torch has been handed over to Chinese officials at a ceremony in Athens amid scuffles between police and pro-Tibet demonstrations. A small group of protesters tried to break through a police cordon to enter the stadium ... The protesters tried to unfurl a banner which said 'Stop genocide in Tibet', but failed to enter the stadium or disrupt the solemn ceremony. At least six people were arrested. Police had warned they would confiscate all banners, signs or objects that might be thrown ... The handover came as pro-Tibet protesters tried to storm the Chinese embassy in Nepal's capital, Kathmandu ... Police baton-charged Tibetan exiles and Buddhist monks who were trying to storm an office of the Chinese embassy and arrested at least 100 people ... In India's capital Delhi exiled Tibetans launched an 'independence torch' to tour the world in an anti-China protest.

(www.bbc.co.uk, 30 March 2008)

Sunday's formal handover [30 March] was held in the Panathinaiko Stadium in Athens, where the first modern Olympics took place in 1896 ... Shouting 'Stop the killing' the protesters [in Kathmandu] attempted to open the [visa] office's metal gate before they were repulsed by a police baton charge.

> Police sources told the BBC that 113 people were arrested outside the embassy ... A Tibetan activist said more than eighty of those held were Buddhist monks or nuns, although he said many were wearing ordinary clothing to try to avoid being targeted by police ... Earlier the UN Office of the High Commissioner for Human Rights in Nepal said the constant mass arrests violated internationally recognized rights to peaceful assembly and to freedom of expression – rights to which Nepal is a signatory.
>
> (www.bbc.co.uk, 31 March 2008)

'[In Athens] the protesters, from all over Europe, were bundled into a police van after unfurling a banner that proclaimed "Stop the genocide in Tibet"' (*Guardian*, 31 March 2008, p. 18).

> The torch was handed over Sunday [30 March] in Athens to the organizers of the 2008 Summer Games. Outside the site of the ceremonies in Athens the police scuffled with pro-Tibet demonstrators and prevented others from unfurling protest banners. Twenty-one demonstrators were detained – seven Indians, one Nepalese and thirteen Greeks ... The protesters challenged a police cordon but failed to disrupt the final leg of Greece's torch relay – from the Acropolis to the stadium ... [The] flame travels to Shannan Diqu and Lhasa (in Tibet, 19–21 June); north to Qinghai province (22–24 June); Xinjiang (25–27 June); and Gansu (June 28–30) before heading inland.
>
> (www.iht.com, 30 March 2008)

> Shouting 'Free Tibet' and flashing red banners reading 'Stop Genocide in Tibet' demonstrators charged a police cordon on Sunday, trying to block the Olympic flame from making its final 100 yard run into a sprawling marble arena in Athens ... Even before the handover began, three supporters of Falun Gong were detained outside Panathinaiko Stadium for distributing leaflets on the spiritual movement outlawed in China.
>
> (www.iht.com, 31 March 2008)

> A group of 200 Tibetan exiles and Buddhist monks tried to storm the Chinese embassy visa office in Nepal's capital on Sunday [30 March] but police beat them back with bamboo batons. At least 130 protesters were arrested and some of the demonstrators and policemen were injured in the scuffle ... Tibetans have protested in front of the Chinese embassy visa office in Kathmandu in the past, but it was the first time they had reached the gate and tried to push through.
>
> (www.iht.com, 30 March 2008)

> Radio broadcasters and Tibetan activists have reported that fresh protests broke out in Lhasa as foreign diplomats wrapped up a tightly controlled visit organized by Beijing ... The Washington-based International Campaign for Tibet said a demonstration began Saturday [29 March] at the Ramoche monastery and grew to involve 'many people' ... The situation calmed down after a few hours. The SU-funded broadcaster Radio Free Asia reported

> several hundred people took part in the protests. Ramoche was the original; site of monk-led demonstrations that began peacefully on 10 March ... The reports of new protests came as a fifteen-member group of diplomats from the United States, Japan and Europe returned to Beijing after a two-day visit to Lhasa ... During their Lhasa tour diplomats met people selected by Chinese authorities, who accompanied them at all times, the American embassy said.
>
> (www.cnn.com, 30 March 2008)

> The Chinese media accused the Dalai Lama on Sunday [30 March] of closing the door to talks over Tibet's future ... Xinhua said: 'It was the Dalai Lama clique that closed the door of dialogue' ... Prime minister Wen Jiabao said Sunday that Lhasa was 'basically stable' and that 'social order has returned to normal' ... Xinhua said in another report Sunday that a suspect in the riots had confessed that the security department of the Tibetan government-in-exile has asked him to distribute leaflets about the 'Tibetan people's uprising movement' to monasteries and lay people in Tibet that encouraged the 14 March riots ... Xinhua said Saturday [29 March] that the police had found guns and explosives at a monastery in Aba county in western Sichuan province where state media first acknowledged the police had fired at protesters on 16 March, wounding four. The police found thirty guns, hundreds of bullets, explosives and knives at the Geerdeng monastery on Friday [28 March] Xinhua said ... While Beijing has imposed a military clampdown, a new protest was reported to have broken out Saturday in Lhasa as diplomats wrapped up a visit by Beijing ... According to the International Campaign for Tibet, the demonstration at Ramoche monastery lasted several hours.
>
> (www.iht.com, 30 March 2008)

> After two weeks in which China contended that Tibet's government-in-exile had instigated the riots earlier this month to tarnish the coming Summer Olympics in Beijing, the Chinese government on Sunday [30 March] issued for the first time what it said was evidence of the plot. The state-run media said the Chinese police had a confession written by an unidentified monk who said they received orders from supporters of the Dalai Lama ... In what an article described as the confession, the monk said: 'For the sake of protecting myself, [the Dalai Lama clique] asked me not to participate in the demonstrations in person, just in charge of stirring people up' ... On Saturday [29 March] China said it had seized a cache of guns, ammunition, explosives and sophisticated communications equipment at a Buddhist monastery in Sichuan province ... The Chinese government said it had arrested twenty-six people suspected of rioting in Aba county, Sichuan province.
>
> (www.iht.com, 31 March 2008)

'A senior Chinese official has urged India to "understand and support" China's policy towards Tibet ... India is home to more than 150,000 Tibetan exiles' (www.bbc.co.uk, 31 March 2008).

31 March 2008.

> The Olympic torch has been relit at a lavish ceremony in Beijing after arriving aboard a flight from Athens. President Hu Jintao took part in the event at Tiananmen Square ... [where] tight security was put in place ... On Tuesday [1 April] the torch goes to Almaty in Kazakhstan, its next stop on a tour of twenty countries.
>
> (www.bbc.co.uk, 31 March 2008)

> The audience [in Tiananmen Square] was limited to 5,000 invited guests, performers and journalists ... The Olympic flame is actually being split into two torches. One will be flown on Tuesday [1 April] to Almaty, Kazakhstan, to begin an international relay that will cover five continents. The other torch will be flown to Lhasa and then taken to a base camp below Mount Everest. There the flame is expected to be stored in a special lantern until May, when a team of climbers – escorted by two specially trained cameramen for Chinese state television – will attempt to carry the burning torch to the summit of the world's highest mountain and then back down. By then the international relay should be completed and the two torches will be reunited in Lhasa to begin a tour through the Chinese mainland that concludes in Beijing at the opening of the Games on 8 August.
>
> (www.iht.com, 31 March 2008)

> China stepped up attacks against the Dalai Lama on Monday [31 March] as authorities apprehended suspects in four arson and murder cases stemming from anti-government riots that engulfed Lhasa more than two weeks ago ... Jiang Zaiping, the vice chief of the Public Security Bureau in Lhasa, said investigators have arrested the suspects responsible for arson attacks on three shops – including the clothing outlet where five young women were burned to death – and one in nearby Dagze county ... A total of 414 suspects have been arrested in connection with the riots, Jiang was quoted as saying. Another 298 people have turned themselves in, he said.
>
> (www.iht.com, 31 March 2008)

'The ascent of Mount Everest and the tour through Tibet had infuriated pro-Tibet advocates even before violent protests erupted in Lhasa on 14 March and subsequently spread in western China' (*IHT*, 1 April 2008, p. 2).

> Tibetan exile groups continued their anti-Chinese demonstrations ... in India ... but the most radical among them have quietly called off a controversial march into Tibet, apparently heeding requests from their spiritual leader, the Dalai Lama ... Last week, without fanfare, they decided not to try to go to Lhasa now, but to advance to New Delhi ... One of India's senior ministers cancelled a trip to China, while the Indian Vice President earlier cancelled a meeting with the Dalai Lama ... In Nepal [it was reported] ... that hundreds of demonstrators split into small groups and

> tried to storm a Chinese consular office from different directions in Kathmandu. Police officers beat them with sticks and detained more than 280 people.
>
> (www.iht.com, 1 April 2008)

1 April 2008. 'India's football captain ... a Buddhist ... has refused to carry the Olympic torch during its journey through the Indian capital Delhi later this month [April] ... in protest against China's crackdown on Tibetan demonstrators' (www.bbc.co.uk, 1 April 2008).

'The Indian Olympic Association, which is organizing the flame's run in New Delhi on 17 April, invited several top Indian athletes to carry the torch, including India's soccer captain' (www.iht.com, 1 April 2008).

> China said Tuesday [1 April] that 'Tibet independence forces' were planning to use suicide squads to carry out bloody attacks, in the latest of a string of accusations that have taken aim at supporters of the Dalai Lama ... Wu Heping (a spokesman for the Chinese Public Security Bureau): 'To our knowledge, the next plan of the Tibetan independence forces is to organize suicide squads to launch violent attacks. They claimed that they fear neither bloodshed nor sacrifice' ... [Wu Heping] offered no firm evidence to support the claims ... Chinese state media have focused overwhelmingly on the victims of violence in Tibet, releasing the names of fourteen of the eighteen civilians and one police officer it says were killed in the Lhasa riots.
>
> (www.iht.com, 1 April 2008)

'Prime minister Samdhong Rinpoche (of the Tibetan government-in-exile): "Tibetan exiles are 100 per cent committed to non-violence. But we fear that Chinese might masquerade as Tibetans and plan such attacks to give bad publicity to Tibetans"' (*IHT*, 2 April 2008, p. 7). 'A previous Tibetan uprising in March 1989 saw martial law and troops firing on demonstrators ... [There are] the present-day Tibet autonomous regions as well as those Tibetan areas now under Qinghai, Gansu, Sichuan and Yunnan provinces' (www.iht.com, 3 April 2008).

> Public security ministry spokesman Wu Heping ... did not produce any evidence to back up the claims, but said China would release proof later. The prime minister of the Tibetan government-in-exile, Samdhong Rinpoche, denied China's allegations. Mr Wu claimed the wave of protests that erupted across Tibetan areas recently was part of a 'Tibetan People's Uprising Movement' ahead of the Olympic Games. He said police had recently discovered guns, ammunition, knives and explosives in the dormitories of Tibetan monks ... He went on to say that the recent anti-Chinese demonstrations were part of a well-thought-out plan to split Tibet and China ... Wu Heping: 'Back in 2007 the Tibetan independence forces in the United States plotted this very concept. They believe it will be their last chance to realize Tibetan independence' ... Chinese police claim the Dalai Lama set up an intelligence network in Tibet to collect and disseminate information. Secret activists used code to talk about

sensitive topics, according to Mr Wu, with the Dalai Lama apparently referred to as 'uncle'. Mr Wu said police have arrested a 'key member' of this network who confessed to being involved in separatist activities. They have also confiscated 176 guns, 13,000 rounds of ammunition and more than 3,500 kg of explosives, he added. China says eighteen civilians and two police officers died in the unrest in Tibetan and neighbouring provinces inhabited by Tibetans that began on 14 March.

(www.bbc.co.uk, 1 April 2008)

'India's foreign minister Pranab Mukherjee: "India will continue to offer him [the Dalai Lama] all hospitality, but during his stay in India they should not do any political activity, any action that can adversely affect relations between India and China"' (www.bbc.co.uk, 1 April 2008).

('At Beijing's request, the authorities have fortified security around the Chinese embassy in New Delhi, though it was not enough to stop Tibetan protesters from scaling a wall last week and unfurling banners inside the compound': www.iht.com, 4 April 2008.)

('Tibetan protesters forced their way into the Chinese embassy compound in New Delhi on 21 March ... India is home to more than 100,000 Tibetan exiles': www.feer.com, 6 April 2008.)

2 April 2008.

China's human rights record is getting worse, not better, because of the Olympics, a rights group says. According to Amnesty International, China is clamping down on dissent in a bid to portray a stable and harmonious image ahead of the Games in August. It urged the International Olympic Committee (IOC) and world leaders to speak out against abuses, including China's handling of protests in Tibet ... In a report entitled *China: The Olympics Countdown* the London-based group says the Olympics had failed to act as a catalyst for reform in China ... The report: 'Unless the Chinese authorities take steps to redress the situation urgently, a positive human rights legacy for the Beijing Olympics looks increasingly beyond reach. It is increasingly clear that much of the current wave of repression is occurring not in spite of the Olympics but actually because of the Olympics' ... Activists and dissidents had been targeted as part of an apparent pre-Olympic clean-up, it said, with many under some form of detention. The group also called on world leaders to speak out on the situation on Tibet, calling a failure to address the issue 'tacit endorsement' of human rights abuse. It accused Chinese troops of using lethal force on Tibetan protesters and urged China to release information about those who had been detained, saying it feared for their safety.

(www.bbc.co.uk, 2 April 2008)

3 April 2008.

More than 1,000 people have been arrested or turned themselves in to the police in connection with deadly rioting last month [March] in Lhasa, one of

> the city's top officials said. Trials will begin before 1 May, the deputy Communist Party secretary of Lhasa, Wang Xiangming, was quoted as saying Thursday [3 April]. Wang said 800 people had been arrested over the violence in Lhasa, while another 280 had surrendered to take advantage of a police offer of leniency. The government said twenty-two people died in the unrest. The publication of Wang's remarks came as Reuters, citing the World Uighur Congress, an exile group, reported that the police in Kashgar, in the Xinjiang region, had arrested seventy people, fearing trouble when the Olympic torch passes through the city in June ... The Tibetan tourism authority announced Thursday that the region would reopen to foreign tourist groups on 1 May, in time for a national three-day holiday.
>
> (www.iht.com, 3 April 2008)

'The police detained at least six Uighur Moslems on Thursday [3 April] at an anti-China protest during the Olympic torch relay [in Turkey]' (*IHT*, 4 April 2008).

> China has urged the Nepalese authorities to take stronger measures to prevent protests against Beijing's policies in Tibet. The call came in a statement issued by China's embassy in Kathmandu, where the police arrest dozens of Tibetan demonstrators almost every day ... Kathmandu is home to thousands of Tibetan exiles ... many Tibetans started arriving in Nepal in 1959, after the Dalai Lama went into exile in India following a failed uprising against China's rule of Tibet.
>
> (www.bbc.co.uk, 3 April 2008)

> Xinhua news agency said a riot erupted on Thursday [3 April] near government offices in Garze, Sichuan province ... A government official was 'attacked and seriously wounded' ... The agency reported last week that one Chinese policeman was killed and several others were injured during clashes in Garze.
>
> (www.bbc.co.uk, 4 April 2008)

> Fresh violence has erupted in a Tibetan region of south-western China, with disputed reports of at least eight people shot dead by police, even as the Chinese government on Friday [4 April] vowed swift and severe punishment of Tibetans accused of rioting and participation in last month's anti-government protests. Police officers fired on a crowd of protesters on Thursday [3 April] outside government offices in the Garze Tibetan autonomous prefecture in Sichuan province along the border with Tibet. A Tibet activist group ... the London-based Free Tibet Campaign ... said the shooting left at least eight protesters dead.
>
> (www.iht.com, 5 April 2008)

> As many as eight Tibetans may have been killed when paramilitary police opened fire during protests in Sichuan province, according to Tibetan support groups. They say the protesters were gunned down in the Garze

> Tibetan autonomous prefecture when police used automatic weapons on the crowds on Thursday [3 April]. China's state media acknowledged a confrontation had taken place ... but reported that police fired only warning shots to protect officials ... Xinhua said a member of the local People's Congress Standing Committee was 'attacked and seriously wounded' ... Xinhua: 'Police were forced to fire warning shots to put down the violence, since local officials and people were in great danger' ... According to the Free Tibet Campaign, the unrest was sparked when a government delegation tried to force monks at the Tonkhor monastery to denounce the Dalai Lama as part of a 'patriotic reeducation campaign' on 2 April ... That afternoon 3,000 riot police reportedly raided the monastery and arrested two monks ... who were found in possession of pictures of the Dalai Lama, an offence under Chinese rule. Next day 370 monks and 400 lay people marched to the civil authority buildings, demanding the release of monks and chanting 'We do not have freedom' and 'Dalai Lama'. They were confronted by hundreds of armed police who fired machine guns into the crowd, killing at least eight ... More than ten monks are still missing.
>
> (*Guardian*, 5 April 2008, p. 1)

4 April 2008.

> Tibetan refugees in Nepal have suspended their demonstrations against China because of next week's elections in the country. According to activists, the Nepalese government had warned that protesters would be arrested to prevent unrest during the election period ... The 10 April polls [will be] the first in Nepal since 1999 ... On Wednesday [2 April] China asked Nepal to ban further protests.
>
> (www.bbc.co.uk, 5 April 2008)

5–6 April 2008. The Olympic flame arrived in London on 5 April and moved on to Paris on 6 April after the London torch relay on that day.

> Before the Olympic flame even reached London four Free Tibet protesters were arrested, after abseilers unfurled a banner reading 'One World, One Dream, Free Tibet 2008' from Westminster Bridge yesterday morning [5 April] ... Up to 1,000 anti-Chinese protesters, including members of the Free Tibet Campaign, the religious movement Falun Gong and the Burma Campaign, have already indicated they intend to stage rallies along the route.
>
> (www.guardian.co.uk, 6 April 2008)

> Today [6 April] eight [British] athletes, celebrities and dignitaries are due to carry the Olympic torch in relay through London ... At least five people have refused to carry the torch, including the comedian Francesca Martinez. The relay route through central London is expected to be met by around 500 demonstrators.
>
> (www.independent.co.uk, 6 April 2008)

> Police officers were guarding the thirty-one-mile route and flanking torchbearers in a effort to prevent pro-Tibet campaigners from further disrupting the event. Crowds were lining the route across the city, with many waving Tibetan flags and 'Free Tibet' banners. Others carried signs reading 'Stop the Killing in Tibet', 'No Olympic torch in Tibet' and 'China talk to Dalai Lama' [and 'Torch of shame'] … Police officers grabbed a man in west London as he tried to snatch the torch from [a torchbearer] … Moments afterwards a second man released a cloud of foam from a fire extinguisher as he tried to douse the flame … Three demonstrators were also arrested as they attempted to board a bus following the flame as … the relay [got] under way at Wembley Stadium [ending up at Greenwich, the construction site of London's future Olympic stadium] … [A] human rights campaigner … jumped into the road carrying a sign calling for the release of Chinese activist Hu Jia, who was jailed on Thursday [3 April] … China's ambassador to the UK … carried the torch through China Town, following a different route to originally planned, before handing it over without incident.
>
> (www.cnn.com, 6 April 2008)

'The Beijing Organizing Committee noted thousands had come out "to welcome the torch"' (www.cnn.com, 7 April 2008).

> There had been contradictory reports whether [China's ambassador to the UK] … had pulled out of the relay, with the Chinese embassy refusing to confirm her place until the last moment … London's Metropolitan Police said it was aware of six organizations, including the Free Tibet Campaign, the spiritual group Falun Gong and a group calling for democracy in Myanmar, planning to protest. The force deployed 2,000 officers along the route … Several [torchbearers] dropped out to protest China's human rights record … [One] said he would not participate because China was not doing enough to stop violence in the Sudanese region of Darfur … The torch's global tour is the longest in Olympic history.
>
> (www.iht.com, 6 April 2008)

> The torch was protected by an inner guard of Chinese security men in blue and white Olympic tracksuits and an outer cordon of yellow-jacketed British police officers … The security cordon around the torch was so dense that the flame and those carrying it were often barely visible to crowds.
>
> (www.iht.com, 7 April 2008)

('Protest and controversy have surrounded the Beijing Olympic flame … and so has a phalanx of large and physically fit Chinese men in blue and white track suits … Employed by the Beijing Organizing Committee, the "flame protection squad" formed in August 2007 to safeguard the fire twenty-four hours a day on its … 130-day relay … Its members were picked from the ranks of the People's Armed Police, the security force spun off from the army that is responsible for riot control and "domestic stability"': www.iht.com, 8 April 2008.)

> What had been billed by the organizers as an occasion to celebrate Olympic sporting ideals turned instead into a daylong contest between China's supporters – many of them Chinese students and people of Chinese origin living in Britain – and groups and individuals who gathered to protest China's recent crackdown in Tibet and its wider human rights record, including its constellation of labour camps … The warmest reception for the torch came as it passed through the China Town area of central London. There and elsewhere where knots of Chinese supporters gathered there were cries of 'One World, One Dream', the slogan adopted for the Beijing Games.
>
> (*IHT*, 7 April 2008, p. 3)

('China's blue-clad flame assistants, whose aggressive methods of safeguarding the Olympic torch have provoked international outcry, are paramilitary police … The aggression with which the guards have been pursuing their brief has provoked anger, not least in London where they were seen wrestling protesters to the ground and were described as "thugs" by Lord [Sebastian] Coe … the Olympic medallist and organizer of the 2012 [London] Games … Kevin Rudd, the Australian prime minister, warned Beijing yesterday [8 April] that he would not allow Chinese officials to provide their own security for the Olympic torch when it is carried through Canberra': *The Times*, 9 April 2008, p. 29. 'Sebastian Coe … was heard telling an assistant that they tried to "push me out of the way three times. They are horrible." He said organizers in other countries should "get rid of those guys"': www.guardian.co.uk, 12 April 2008. 'The seventy young officers were sworn in as the Olympic Flame Guardians in August 2007, thirty to take responsibility during the torch relays overseas and forty to follow the torch inside China … London's Metropolitan Police said the guardians had no official role and often got in the way of officers trying to restore calm … Former Olympic champion Lord [Sebastian] Coe, who is now the head of the organizing committee for the 2012 London games, said: "They tried to push me out of the way three times. They did not speak English. They were thugs"': www.bbc.co.uk, 9 April 2009.)

> The idea of carrying a lit torch from the temple of Hera in Greece was invented by Hitler in 1936 to suggest a link between the German people and fellow Aryans in southern Europe. It was revived as a political act by Sydney in 2000 with a regional tour symbolizing Australia's links with the Pacific rim of Asia. Athens staged a world tour in 2004 in honour of the Games returning to their original home.
>
> (Simon Jenkins, www.thetimes.co.uk, 6 April 2008)

> Zhang Qingli (Communist Party chief of Tibet, speaking on 6 April): 'The social order in Lhasa and other parts of Tibet [has returned to] normal … [But] grave challenges remain ahead, as the Dalai clique is plotting for new sabotage activities … [The authorities have] to spare no efforts in preparing for the torch relay to ward off any possible mishap.'
>
> (www.iht.com, 6 April 2008)

> [On 6 April] the Dalai Lama said the recent demonstrations in Tibet were 'outbursts of long pent-up physical and mental anguish' that proved most Tibetans wanted freedom from Chinese rule. He said the protests had 'shattered the propaganda that except for a few reactionaries the majority of Tibetans enjoy a prosperous and contented life'.
>
> (www.iht.com, 7 April 2008)

7 April 2008.

> Protests against the torch relay ahead of the Beijing Olympics have spread to France's capital, Paris … The French protest came after thirty-seven people were arrested during the pro-Tibet protests which disrupted Sunday's relay in London … Officials [in Paris] twice extinguished the torch and put in on a bus for safety reasons … Security in Paris was extremely tight, with some 3,000 police on duty … A member of the French Green Party was restrained after attempting to grab the torch from the first of Paris's eighty torchbearers.
>
> (www.bbc.co.uk, 7 April 2008)

'The torch was [first] placed on board a bus shortly after setting off from the Eiffel Tower … "Boycott Chinese goods" and "Save Tibet" read some of the banners held by the demonstrators' (www.iht.com, 7 April 2008).

> Demonstrations in the French capital began only hours after the relay's procession through London had degenerated into a series of skirmishes between protesters and the police … Protesters began targeting the flame before it had even left the Eiffel Tower for the planned seventeen-mile journey to the Charléty stadium on the edge of Paris … Live television footage showed the extinguished torch being put into the vehicle alongside tracksuit-wearing Chinese security staff. The torch is lit from permanent flames enclosed within special lanterns carried with it. Designed to be carried on buses and planes, they are used to keep the flame intact overnight … The organizers of the Beijing Olympics have seen the planned celebratory passage of the torch on an 85,000-mile journey from Olympia, in Greece, become a focal point for human rights protests … At least five activists were arrested during today's [7 April] demonstrations. The flame was more heavily guarded than it had been in London and was barely visible inside a 200-metre cordon shielding it from protests as it left the Eiffel Tower. Police encircled the bearers with dozens of cars and motorbikes, 200 riot police and another 100 tracking the convoy on inline skates … Along the route some cheered and waved Chinese flags but many others chanted pro-Tibet slogans. Around 500 protesters congregated at Trocadero Square.
>
> (www.guardian.co.uk, 7 April 2008)

> Police decided not to go ahead with the final section of the relay … Despite the huge security presence, at least two activists got within little more than an arm's length of the torch before being stopped. One protester threw water

> at it, but failed to extinguish the flame ... Police grappled many other demonstrators to the ground, using tear gas to disperse those blocking the relay's route. They said twenty-eight were arrested ... Along the route some cheered and waved Chinese flags, but many others chanted pro-Tibet slogans.
>
> (www.guardian.co.uk, 7 April 2008)

'Militants from rights group Reporters Without Borders chained themselves to the Eiffel Tower and deployed a black flag with handcuffs replacing the Olympic rings' (www.independent.co.uk, 7 April 2008).

> French security officials have been forced to cut short the Paris leg of the Olympic torch relay following anti-Chinese protests along the route. The torch was extinguished three times due to the protests before being taken on a bus to the relay's end point.
>
> (www.bbc.co.uk, 7 April 2008)

> The last part of the Olympic torch relay has been cancelled ... after a day of chaos in which anti-China protesters forced the authorities to extinguish the flame at least five times, take to a bus and skip some scheduled stops, including City Hall ... Police have taken numerous protesters away, some with fire extinguishers ... at other times using tear gas to remove demonstrators who lay in the road and tried to block the route. The chaos comes one day after human rights activist demonstrators made the journey through London more like running the gauntlet than a journey of celebration ... While it was hard to gauge numbers it looked like thousands of demonstrators had taken to the streets – although some were Chinese backing the Olympics ... At least six groups had permits to protest the route, but only for demonstrations well away from the flame's path. The Paris mayor had ordered a banner to be hung from City Hall that reads 'Paris, City of Human Rights'.
>
> (www.cnn.com, 7 April 2008)

'Thousands of protesters forced an abrupt halt to the flame's passage through Paris after just 10 miles of the 17 mile planned route' (www.iht.com, 8 April).

'Thousands of people from around Europe, many with Tibetan flags, massed to protest the passage of the flames' (www.iht.com, 7 April 2008).

> Organizers were forced to cancel the last third of the Paris route Monday [7 April] after demonstrators threw water at the flame and tried to take the torch from its bearers. The security forces protecting the torch had to extinguish it several times and retreat to the safety of a bus, although the Olympic flame continually burns in a lantern brought along the route.
>
> (www.iht.com, 8 April 2008)

> The international tour has proven jarring for Beijing. What organizers had considered an occasion to celebrate the Olympics' sporting ideals of peace and harmony has turned into a day-long contest between China's supporters

> and demonstrators protesting China's crackdown in Tibet and its wider human rights record … Chinese officials had originally hoped that the torch relay would serve to highlight China's triumphal emergence as a global power. But it has turned into a high profile venue for protesters angry over the Chinese crackdown in Tibet, intolerance for political dissent, environmental degradation and other issues.
>
> (www.iht.com, 8 April 2008)

> Many of the eighty torchbearers wore badges intended to register the concern of French Olympic athletes … The Socialist mayor of Paris cancelled a ceremony to receive the torch because Chinese officials objected to a rights banner hung from the City Hall. It was outside the Parliament that the beleaguered Chinese organizers gave up and put the torch on to a bus for its final leg to the Charléty stadium in southern Paris … Protesters on the Trocadero Esplanade on the Seine [gathered] with banners reading 'Tiananmen 1989 – Lhasa 2008' and 'For a bloody world welcome to the Olympics made in China' … Reporters Without Borders draped big banners with its black 'Olympic handcuffs' from strategic points, including the Eiffel Tower, a building on the Champs Elysées and the front of Notre Dame Cathedral … Hundreds of Chinese students and members of the Paris Chinese community attempted to stage counter-demonstrations but were far outnumbered and shouted down by protesters.
>
> (www.thetimes.co.uk, 7 April 2008)

'The mayor of Paris infuriated China by making the Dalai Lama … an honorary citizen' (www.economist.com, 25 September 2008; *The Economist*, 27 September 2008, p. 86).

'The route of the Olympic torch relay through the Australian capital [Canberra] on 24 April has been changed due to security concerns, a government official said Monday [7 April]' (www.iht.com, 7 April 2008).

> Seven pro-Tibet demonstrators were arrested in San Francisco after tying anti-Chinese banners to the cables of the Golden Gate Bridge. The flame is due to arrive in the city on Tuesday [8 April] … The three climbers among them faced additional charges of trespassing. They had scaled the bridge to perch 150 feet (46 metres) above traffic, attaching 'Free Tibet' banners and a Tibetan flag.
>
> (www.bbc.co.uk, 8 April 2008)

'Extra police will line the torch's route as it travels 6 miles (10 kilometres) through San Francisco on Wednesday [9 April] … One runner who planned to carry the flame has already dropped out because of safety concerns' (www.bbc.co.uk, 8 April 2008). ('A fourteen-year-old girl dropped out Monday [7 April] out of security concerns … [leaving] seventy-nine runners': www.iht.com, 9 April 2008.)

'Three people scaled the Golden Gate in San Francisco on Monday [7 April] and tied the Tibetan flag and two banners to its cables. The banners read "One

World One Dream. Free Tibet" and "Free Tibet 08"' (www.iht.com, 8 April 2008). 'The torch's San Francisco stop is the sixth stop of a global itinerary [after Kazakhstan, Russia, Turkey, the UK and France]' (www.iht.com, 8 April 2008).

> Those who climbed the cables from which the bridge's deck is suspended were members of the Students for a Free Tibet ... The climbers – who were on the bridge for three hours – came down voluntarily and were arrested, after workers ... began cutting down their banner.
>
> (www.cnn.com, 8 April 2008)

'Sun Weide (a spokesman for the Beijing organizing committee): "No force can stop the torch relay of the Olympic Games"' (www.iht.com, 8 April 2008).

> The Chinese authorities have stopped issuing multiple-entry visas to foreigners and slowed visa processing in Hong Kong, a major gateway for travel to the mainland, in restrictions that will remain in place until after the Beijing Olympics ... A travel agent said Chinese authorities were now only issuing single or double-entry business visas to foreigners in Hong Kong.
>
> (www.iht.com, 8 April 2008)

8 April 2008.

> Hundreds of pro-Tibet protesters have marched in San Francisco as the Olympic torch arrived for the US leg of its international relay. Demonstrators carrying Tibetan flags marched to denounce Beijing's policy on Tibet ... On Tuesday [8 April] activists gathered near City Hall for their march to the Chinese mission and a late-night vigil.
>
> (www.bbc.co.uk, 9 April 2008)

> Groups were already rallying in the city on Tuesday [8 April], with Tibetan supporters carrying flags in the shadow of City Hall and a large crowd protesting in front of the Chinese consulate ... San Francisco was chosen as the torch's only America stop last year [2007] – shortly after a failed bid for the 2016 Games – in part because of its large Chinese population ... Chinese-American leaders here are particularly vexed at the actions of the city's Board of Supervisors, which voted on 1 April to condemn China's human rights record.
>
> (www.iht.com, 9 April 2008)

9 April 2008.

> A group of monks have for the second time interrupted an escorted media visit to the Tibetan plateau. About fifteen monks rushed to meet foreign and Chinese journalists at the Labrang monastery in Xiahe, Gansu province, where hundreds of monks rallied on 14 March ... The monks [were] quoted as saying 'The Dalai Lama has to come back to Tibet' ... [and] 'We are not asking for Tibetan independence, we are just asking for human rights,

we have no human rights now' … Almost 1,000 people had been detained over the protests, a Chinese official announced on Wednesday [9 April].

(www.bbc.co.uk, 9 April 2008)

More than a dozen monks staged an emotional protest Wednesday [9 April] in front of visiting journalists at a monastery in western China, calling for human rights and the return of the Dalai Lama … The monks, whose numbers grew to about two dozen during the ten minute incident, began shouting slogans … at the Labrang monastery in Xiahe in western Gansu province bordering Tibet. The group waved the Tibetan flag and shouted: 'We are not against the Olympics. We need human rights' … [and] 'We want human rights, we want the Dalai Lama back, we want to preserve our religion and culture' … Chinese foreign ministry officials on the journalists' trip observed the protest but did not attempt to block the monks … [A monk] said the monks have heard that about 2,000 people – monks, students and ordinary Tibetans – were detained in Gansu following last month's anti-government protests. In Labrang, he said, as many as twenty monks were taken away and only three or four have been released so far … Champa Phuntsok, the Chinese-appointed [ethnic Tibetan] head of the Tibetan Autonomous Region [chairman of the Tibet Autonomous Region government] … on Wednesday [9 April] said Tibetan police have detained 953 people suspected of participating in the 14 March riots. Of those 403 were formally arrested, he said. Another 362 people turned themselves in and 328 of those were released after confessing to minor crimes, he said. Police have ninety-three suspects on their most-wanted list and have already arrested thirteen of them.

(www.iht.com, 9 April 2008)

Champa Phuntsok … said 362 people had handed themselves in to police in response to a government ultimatum, but 328 were released on the grounds that their crimes were light and they had a 'good attitude' in confessing them. It was unclear if the remaining thirty-four were included in the tally [953] of detainees.

(www.guardian.co.uk, 9 April 2008)

[Chinese] officials arranged for a small group [of reporters] to Xiahe, Gansu province today [9 April] … But the visit took an unexpected turn as between fifteen and thirty lamas, carrying a banned Tibetan flag, burst out of a building at Labrang monastery and rushed across to the group of Chinese and foreign journalists.

(www.guardian.co.uk, 9 April 2008)

Officials in San Francisco shortened and changed the torch's planned route Wednesday [9 April] to bypass thousands of demonstrators, including those supporting and opposing China. They also cancelled a waterfront closing ceremony scheduled for Wednesday night … The route of the Olympic torch relay in Hong Kong on 2 May will be cut short to avoid the possibility of violent protest, a source was quoted as saying in the *South China Morning Post*. The source said in the paper's report: 'Hong Kong is the first stop on Chinese soil for the relay so the government will hope to avoid the embarrassing scenes' … Likewise, Indonesian authorities announced Thursday [10 April] that the torch relay in the capital of Jakarta … scheduled for 22 April … would be significantly shortened.

(www.cnn.com, 10 April 2008)

The nation's only chance to see the Olympic flame up close became an elaborate game of hide-and-seek here [in San Francisco] on Wednesday [9 April] as city officials rerouted the planned torch relay, swarmed its runners with blankets of security and then whisked the torch to the airport in a heavily guarded motorcade. The closing ceremony to mark the flame's only North American stop was also effectively cancelled in the face of thousands of protesters and supporters, who waited for hours in vain along the flame's announced route. Instead, officials decided that the flame would leapfrog protesters and travel on a central avenue about two miles away. There, surrounded by uniformed officers and police on motorcycles, it was run in stop-and-start fashion toward the Golden Gate Bridge, chased by a throng of surprised residents and members of the news media … About four miles into the route the torch was placed on a bus and taken to San Francisco's airport, where it will fly to Buenos Aires … Mayor Gavin Newsom said the decision to change the route was made shortly after the torch was lit outside AT&T Park, when it was briefly held aloft by Chinese Olympic officials and then promptly taken into a waterfront warehouse … As the start of the relay approached, thousands were lining the [original] route and several scuffles broke out between pro- and anti-China forces.

(www.iht.com, 10 April 2008)

The US stage of the torch relay passed off amid confusion and tight security in San Francisco on Wednesday [9 April] … The route was totally changed at the last minute amid anti-Chinese protests. Torchbearers were immersed in a cocoon of security, surrounded by dozens of police officers and Chinese guards in tracksuits. The Olympic flame was lit in Greece on 24 March and is being relayed through twenty countries before being carried into the opening ceremony in Beijing on 8 August. Demonstrators sought to disrupt the torch relay in Athens, Istanbul, Paris and London, while it passed successfully through Almaty (in Kazakhstan) and St Petersburg (in Russia). It is due to arrive in the Argentine capital, Buenos Aires, later this week … Thousands of spectators had been waiting hours to see the torch pass through San Francisco and demonstrators were out in force along the waterfront relay route. But immediately after the torch was lit the torchbearers turned into a warehouse building, disappearing for an hour. They reappeared at a new starting point across the city where it was handed to two runners, away from the protesters. The planned waterfront closing ceremony in Justin Herman Plaza was moved to a motorway flyover … In the end there was no riot. There was no real trouble, just some skirmishes as pro-China supporters engaged in verbal sparring with pro-Tibet backers. The shout-off came in short angry bursts.

(www.bbc.co.uk, 10 April 2008)

'Some protesters following proceedings on television managed to find the parade and flash the occasional pro-Tibet sign, but were otherwise frustrated' (www.independent.co.uk, 10 April 2008).

> [British] prime minister Gordon Brown will not attend the opening ceremony of the Beijing Olympics, Downing Street says. However, he will be at the closing ceremony, when the Olympic baton will be passed to London. A spokeswoman said Mr Brown had never planned to attend the opening ceremony and was not boycotting the Games … The Olympics minister Tessa Jowell will represent the UK at the opening in Beijing in August … Mr Brown has never specifically said he will attend the opening ceremony … On 27 March, at a press conference during France's President [Nicolas] Sarkozy's visit, he said: 'We will not be boycotting the Olympic Games; Britain will be attending the Olympic Games ceremonies' … On 1 April Mr Brown said: 'I think President Sarkozy said himself that he expected Britain, because we are to host the next Olympics, to be present at the Olympic ceremonies and I will certainly be there' … Mr Brown attracted controversy for receiving the Olympic torch outside 10 Downing Street, although he did not hold it.
>
> (www.bbc.co.uk, 10 April 2008)

'On Wednesday [9 April] prime minister Kevin Rudd of Australia used a speech at Peking University in Beijing to raise human rights concerns about Tibet' (*IHT*, 10 April 2008, p. 2).

> Kevin Rudd, a friend of China and fluent Mandarin speaker on his first trip to the country since taking office, used a speech to students at Peking University to talk of 'significant human rights problems' in the region. He called, too, for dialogue between China's government and the Dalai Lama.
>
> (www.economist.com, 10 April 2008)

10 April 2008.

> The Dalai Lama said he supports China's hosting of the Summer Olympics, but insisted Thursday [10 April] nobody had the right to tell protesters demanding freedom for Tibet 'to shut up' … He told reporters outside Tokyo on a stopover on a trip to Seattle: 'We are not anti-Chinese. Right from the beginning we supported the Olympic Games. I really feel very sad the government demonizes me. I am just a human, I am not a demon' … The Dalai Lama said the demonstrators had the right to their opinions, though he called for non-violence: 'The expression of their feelings is up to them. Nobody has the right to tell them to shut up. One of the problems in Tibet is that there is no freedom of speech … Autonomy [in Tibet] is just a

name; it is not sincerely implemented. The crisis is the expression of their [Tibetans'] deep regret' … He faulted Beijing for suppressing anti-government unrest in Tibet last month [March], saying its use of violence was 'an outdated method' that did not solve the underlying problems … Japan's government has been relatively quiet about the violence in Tibet and, out of deference to Beijing, does not deal officially with the Dalai Lama. Tokyo does, however, grant visas to the exiled Buddhist leader, who has visited Japan fairly frequently. Buddhism is one of Japan's main religions, along with the indigenous Shinto faith. No meetings were planned between the Dalai Lama and government officials although the wife of former prime minister Shinzo Abe greeted him on his stopover en route from India. He is to spend two weeks in the United States … The Dalai Lama said he is not behind the unrest and called Chinese claims that he is the mastermind 'a serious allegation'. 'Some in the leadership consider Tibetan Buddhism is a source of separatism,' he said, adding that Beijing has reacted to the protests with 'violent suppression'. But he added that if the situation improves he would even be willing to attend the Olympics' opening ceremony. He said: 'If things improve and the Chinese government starts to see things realistically, I personally want to enjoy the big ceremony' … In a separate statement Thursday the Tibetan government-in-exile said it did not support the disruption of the Olympic torch relay.

(www.iht.com, 10 April 2008)

The president of the International Olympic Committee [IOC], Jacques Rogge, offered a rare rebuke to the Chinese government on Thursday [10 April], calling on authorities to respect its 'moral engagement' to improve human rights and provide the media with greater access to the country ahead of the Olympic Games … The Chinese government immediately rejected Rogge's remarks, saying they amounted to an unwelcome meddling in the country's domestic affairs … Jiang Yu (a foreign ministry spokeswoman): 'I believe IOC officials support the Beijing Olympics and adherence to the Olympic charter of not bringing in any irrelevant political factors.'

(www.iht.com, 10 April 2008)

Jacques Rogge … said Chinese officials had said that awarding the Games to Beijing would help advance social change in China, including human rights. Mr Rogge said he considered that 'a moral engagement … and we definitely ask China to respect this moral engagement'.

(www.bbc.co.uk, 10 April 2008)

'Jacques Rogge, IOC president, said that when China was awarded the 2008 games, government officials promised it would "advance the social agenda of China, including human rights". He said: "We definitely ask China to respect this moral engagement"' (*FT*, 11 April 2008, p. 8).

'On Thursday [10 April] a spokeswoman for UN Secretary-General Ban Ki Moon said he has told the Chinese authorities that he "may not" be in a position to attend the opening ceremonies of the games due to scheduling issues' (www.cnn.com, 11 April 2008).

> UN Secretary-General Ban Ki Moon will not attend the opening ceremony of the Beijing Olympics, an aide has said. The decision was due to 'schedule issues' and had been made months ago, said [a] UN spokeswoman … [She] said: [Ban Ki Moon] had conveyed to the [Chinese] government some months ago that he may not be in a position to accept the invitation to attend this important event due to schedule issues.
>
> (www.bbc.co.uk, 11 April 2008)

'Indonesia said it would significantly shorten its leg of the Olympic torch relay. Hong Kong said that it might make slight changes in its torch route and would deploy 3,000 police for security' (*IHT*, 11 April 2008, p. 1).

'Indonesian officials said yesterday [11 April] they had cancelled a 22 April Olympic torch relay around Jakarta. Acting on a request from Beijing, they have changed the route to confine the torch to the vicinity of the main stadium' (*FT*, 11 April 2008, p. 8).

'Kenyan Nobel Peace Prize laureate Wangari Maathai has withdrawn from the torch relay's Tanzanian leg, due to concerns over human rights in China' (www.bbc.co.uk, 11 April 2008).

'The unrest in Tibet has helped to rally support for the leadership among ordinary Chinese' (*The Economist*, 12 April 2008, p. 67).

> Aggressive street demonstrations in London, Paris and the United States, and mounting calls for President George W. Bush and other world leaders to skip the opening ceremony of the Olympic Games in August as a show of protest against China's internal policies, have produced a nationalist backlash in China. There both the leadership and ordinary people resent what many see as a plot to disrupt the Games and damage China's image as a rising power, which the Olympics once seemed likely to burnish.
>
> (Steven Erlanger, www.iht.com, 13 April 2008)

> Most young ethnic Chinese strongly support their government's suppression of the recent Tibetan uprising … The 'Dalai clique' [is] a pejorative reference to the circle of advisers around … the Dalai Lama … Educated young Chinese are the biggest beneficiaries of policies that have brought China more peace and prosperity than at any time in the past thousand years. They can't imagine why Tibetans would turn their noses up at rising incomes and the promise of a more prosperous future. The loss of a homeland just doesn't compute as a valid concern. Of the twenty-nine ethnic Chinese intellectuals who last month [March] signed a widely publicized petition urging the government to show constraint in the crackdown, not one was under thirty.
>
> (Matthew Forney, *IHT*, 16 April 2008, p. 8)

> While there were protests in London, it was the aggressive effort to disrupt the procession of the flame in Paris that seems to have most upset the

Chinese, coupled with a huge banner on the Paris City Hall, put there by the city's socialist mayor, which read: 'Paris defends human rights everywhere in the world'. There was also a widely distributed photograph of a protester, in a cap with Tibetan colours, trying to grab the torch from a Chinese woman in a wheelchair, who was praised in Beijing for protecting the flame.

(*IHT*, 12 April 2008, p. 4)

The official website of the Beijing Games lauded her valour and posted a blow-by-blow account of the 7 April episode … A one-legged fencer from Shanghai endured a gauntlet of anti-Chinese demonstrators … Each time a protester broke through the barricades and lunged for the torch Jin Jing shielded it with her body.

(www.iht.com, 18 April 2008)

The Dalai Lama arrived … in Seattle … on Thursday [10 April] … his first visit to the United States since the onset of international protests over the crackdown in Tibet. But the trip was planned long before the recent troubles.

(www.iht.com, 11 April 2008)

11 April 2008.

Friday's tour [11 April] through Buenos Aires is the only stop the torch is making in South America … Japan said it will ban the torch's Chinese security detail [in Nagano on 26 April] … Australia, and now Japan, have said they will provide their own security when the torch arrives on their soil … The head of the IOC, Jacques Rogge … said the IOC had no right to tell China how to deal with sovereign issues like Tibet and human rights. On Thursday [10 April] Beijing had rebuked him for urging China to respect its 'moral engagement' to improve human rights.

(www.bbc.co.uk, 11 April 2008)

Argentine athletes carried the Olympic torch through the streets of Buenos Aires … A major security operation was mounted to try to avoid the scenes that marred the relay in the UK, France and the United States. Both anti-China protesters and supporters of the Beijing Games turned out, but only minor scuffles were reported and the torch was not impeded … Anti-China activists had promised some 'entertaining surprises', but nothing serious emerged, and the only apparent attempt to derail the relay were a few water balloons thrown at the torch, easily deflected by guards … Activist Jorge Carcavallo unfurled a giant banner on the torch route reading 'Free Tibet'. And members of the Falun Gong spiritual movement, which is banned in China, lit their own 'human rights torch' and marched along the route the flame was to take. Police separated the few dozen pro-Tibet demonstrators from a similar-sized group of Chinese residents … But most spectators appeared to be intent on supporting the torch as it passed.

(www.bbc.co.uk, 12 April 2008)

Argentines offered Olympic organizers a respite Friday [11 April] as the Olympic torch passed through their capital amid festive spirits and in an orderly manner. Protests were minimal and non-violent … Small groups of fenced-off demonstrators protesting China's human rights record exchanged jeers with hundreds of pro-China demonstrators … Three water balloons thrown at a torchbearer as he passed the presidential palace were easily batted away by guards … Organizers adhered to the original, pre-announced eight mile route without deviation. Police presence was heavy. Eighty people carried the torch. Most were Argentines but other Latin Americans also took part. Earlier in the day Argentina's branches of Free Tibet and the Falun Gong held a peaceful protest at the central Obelisk monument … About twenty-five Falun Gong supporters lit a 'human rights torch' and marched along the route to protest China's ban on the spiritual movement. Some traded insults with China supporters, but no violence was reported … Several Argentines carried a long 'Free Tibet' banner … Protesters were outnumbered by onlookers and journalists … About 500 China supporters … waved banners … The streets were not even closed to traffic. After speeches condemning China's human rights record the protesters marched to Plaza de Mayo … but they did not interfere with the torch … Pro-Tibet demonstrators tossed lotus flowers onto the route.

(www.iht.com, 12 April 2008)

China expressed indignation Friday [11 April] over a US Congressional resolution calling on Beijing to stop cracking down on Tibetan dissent and to talk to the Dalai Lama. State media [in China], meanwhile, labelled a group linked to the Dalai Lama's India-based government-in-exile a 'terrorist organization' … The group, the Tibetan Youth Congress, said China's communist leadership had long sought to destroy its effectiveness by smearing its reputation … [by] trying to brand it as a terrorist organization without any basis … The official Xinhua news agency accused the Tibetan Youth Congress of planning deadly rioting on 14 March, saying this 'exposed the terrorist nature' of the group The resolution passed by the House of Representatives Wednesday [9 April] … sponsored by speaker Nancy Pelosi … called on Beijing to 'end its crackdown on non-violent Tibetan protesters' along with cultural, religious, economic and linguistic 'repression'. While noting reports of deadly rioting in Lhasa and other Tibetan areas, the resolution called China's response 'disproportionate and extreme'. It said hundreds of Tibetans had been killed and thousands detained … The resolution also called on China to begin 'an unconditional results-based dialogue' with the Dalai Lama to address Tibetan concerns and work toward a long-term solution to the dispute.

(*IHT*, 12 April 2008, p. 4)

12 April 2008.

President Hu Jintao told visiting Australian prime minister Kevin Rudd: 'Our conflict with the Dalai clique is not an ethnic problem, not a religious problem. It is a problem either to safeguard national unification or to split

> the motherland' ... Mr Hu repeated China's position that it was ready to meet the Dalai Lama, but only if he met certain preconditions, such as desisting from trying to 'split the motherland'. 'incite violence' and 'ruin the Beijing Olympics' ... Speaking on US television during a visit to Seattle, the Dalai Lama reiterated his opposition to a boycott of the Olympics, but said China's record on human rights and freedom was 'poor'.
>
> (www.bbc.co.uk, 12 April 2008)

> On Saturday [12 April] President Hu Jintao made his first public remarks about the Tibetan unrest, blaming the Dalai Lama and defending Beijing's crackdown as a necessary response to protect national sovereignty. Hu said: 'No responsible government will sit idle for such crimes, which gravely encroach human rights, gravely disrupt social order and gravely jeopardize the life and property security of the masses.'
>
> (www.iht.com, 13 April 2008)

> In Seattle more than 50,000 people packed a stadium Saturday [12 April] to hear the Dalai Lama call for non-violence. He said: 'Twentieth century become like century of bloodshed. I think it is our own responsibility to make this century be century of dialogue.'
>
> (www.iht.com, 13 April 2008)

13 April 2008. 'Although few protests are expected [in Dar es Salaam], the planned 25 kilometre (15 mile) torch relay on Sunday [13 April] has been reduced to 5 kilometres ... Tanzania is the torch's only African stop' (www.bbc.co.uk, 13 April 2008). 'The relay run passed off without incident' (www.bbc.co.uk, 14 April 2008).

> China has arrested nine Tibetan Buddhist monks who have been accused of a bomb attack, according to the official Xinhua news agency. Chinese officials said the monks' homemade bomb exploded in a government building in eastern Tibet on 23 March ... Xinhua said the monks confessed to planting the explosive in Gyanbe township ... The alleged bombing is the first to be reported in Tibet since the anti-China protests began on 10 March in Lhasa.
>
> (www.bbc.co.uk, 13 April 2008)

> Xinhua denounced the Dalai Lama and his supporters as 'anti-human rights' Sunday [13 April], stepping up a campaign against the exiled Tibetan spiritual leader the day after Beijing announced the arrest of nine monks for allegedly bombing a government building in Tibet last month [March]. Xinhua reported late Saturday [12 April] that the monks, from the Tongxia monastery in eastern Tibet, had fled after a homemade bomb exploded at the building in Gyanbe township on 23 March. The report said the monks later confessed to planting the bomb. A local official confirmed the monks had been detained ... No other bombing has been reported in Tibet since the anti-government protests began on 10 March in Lhasa, turning violent four

days later ... [The] Xinhua commentary said Sunday: 'It is indeed the anti-human rights nature of the Dalai clique that impels the "pro-Tibet independence" separatists to undermine China's stability and unity, disgrace China worldwide, and even sabotage the Olympic torch relay by all sorts of violent means' ... The commentary cited an attempt last week by protesters in Paris to wrench the Olympic torch from a wheelchair-bound athlete as a violation of human rights and said the Dalai Lama dreamed of bringing back the feudal system of serf ownership. Another Xinhua editorial, on Saturday, criticized Nancy Pelosi, the speaker of the US House of Representatives, who recently met with the Dalai Lama and backed a resolution urging an end to repression in Tibet. It accused Pelosi of cynical double standards.

(www.iht.com, 13 April 2008)

Chinese media denounced the Dalai Lama and his supporters on Sunday [13 April] and called Nancy Pelosi 'the least popular person in China' for her stance on Tibet ... A Tibetan source with strong contacts in Lhasa said the city was swirling with reports of fresh clashes between monks and security forces at the Drepung monastery.

(*IHT*, 14 April 2008, p. 5)

14 April 2008.

The Olympic torch reached Oman, its only stop in the Middle East. The torch arrived in the capital, Muscat, on Monday morning [14 April] from Tanzania ... the parade in Oman is not expected to feature the human rights protests that have caused chaos in London, Paris and San Francisco. Oman has strong economic ties with China, [which is] a major importer of its oil.

(www.bbc.co.uk, 14 April 2008)

The Dalai Lama [in Seattle] said that 'some efforts' at diplomacy were under way between his representatives and those of the Chinese government ... he said: 'Just a few days these are going on' ... He said he had not been directly involved in the conversations ... Chinese forces found firearms hidden throughout a Tibetan temple in an ethnic Tibetan area of south-western China that has been the scene of anti-Chinese riots in recent weeks, according to state television ... The police, responding to what they said was a tip, found thirty firearms in the monastery in Aba prefecture in Sichuan province last month [March] ... The Chinese police also detained five air passengers, possibly Tibetans, whose 'suspicious remarks' prompted the return of their flight half an hour after takeoff from the southern city of Shenzhen, a newspaper reported.

(www.iht.com, 14 April 2008)

Lhasa plans to focus on luring Chinese tourists this summer [2008] ... Xinhua took an optimistic look at the collapse of tourism, a key industry in Tibet, saying that those who do make it to the so-called 'roof of the world' will find it refreshingly free of tour groups ... Xinhua reported from the city:

'Tourists visiting the city these days will find they need not stand in line for the usually hard-to-get tickets for popular attractions' ... Four million tourists went last year [2007] to see historic temples, experience Tibetan culture and enjoy breathtaking natural scenery. Visits had risen sharply since the opening of the first rail link to Lhasa, a holy city for Buddhists, in July 2006. Travel officials have frozen ticket prices for the summer season, when they can be twice winter levels, to attract more Chinese travellers ... The region will reopen to foreign tourists on 1 May, Chinese media reported, although government officials have not confirmed this.

(www.iht.com, 14 April 2008)

15 April 2008.

Yesterday [15 April] an event planned to mark the torch's visit to Nagano, Japan, was cancelled, even though officials said there would be no changes to the route of the torch relay itself... The torch arrives in Nagano on 26 April.

(*FT*, 16 April 2008, p. 9)

The Chinese foreign ministry demanded Tuesday [15 April] that CNN's Jack Cafferty apologize for remarks he made last week ... Cafferty (9 April): 'We continue to import their junk with the lead paint on them and the poisoned pet food ... They're basically the same bunch of goons and thugs they've been for the last fifty years' ... CNN issued a statement Tuesday: 'We are aware of concerns abut Jack Cafferty's comments related to China ... CNN would like to clarify that it was not Mr Cafferty's, nor NCC's, intent to cause offence to the Chinese people, and [CNN] would apologize to anyone who has interpreted the comments in this way ... Jack was offering his strongly held opinion of the Chinese government, not the Chinese people – a point he subsequently clarified ... on 14 April.'

(www.cnn.com, 19 April 2008)

('China on Thursday [17 April] snubbed an apology from CNN ... A Chinese foreign ministry spokeswoman: "Their statement did not make sincere apology for his remarks but turned its attack on the Chinese government to try to sow division between the Chinese government and the people. So for this point we cannot accept it at all"': www.iht.com, 19 April 2008.)

16 April 2008.

Thousands of Pakistani troops have been deployed to protect the Olympic torch which has touched down in Islamabad ... Security fears mean the torch will be paraded along a much shorter route than originally intended when it is taken to the city's main sports stadium later ... Around sixty Pakistani athletes are expected to carry the flame around the grounds of Jinnah stadium before a musical ceremony attended by President Pervez Musharraf ... Stop-overs in Argentina, Tanzania and Oman have been largely trouble-free.

(www.bbc.co.uk, 16 April 2008)

> Pakistan and India have changed plans for their Olympic torch runs because of worries about security and anti-China protests … The torch arrived in Islamabad on Wednesday on the first leg of its relay in Asia … Officials in Pakistan, a close ally of China, said they did not expect anti-China protests but that they had changed the venue for the torch run for security reasons … Pakistan has been hit by a wave of suicide bomb attacks by militants linked to al-Qaeda and the Taliban since an army assault on a radical mosque in Islamabad last July [2007] in which more than 100 people were killed. The Olympic Association had hoped to hold a torch run along Islamabad's main boulevard in front of parliament, but the event will now be held inside a nearby sports stadium. India has also shortened the route of its torch relay on Thursday [17 April], fearing that Tibetan protesters might try to disrupt the procession. The final route is still to be announced, but media reported the torch will travel less than a third of the original 9 kilometre (5 mile) distance in a heavily guarded New Delhi neighbourhood.
>
> (www.iht.com, 16 April 2008)

> Pakistan [is] a loyal ally of China … An interior ministry official said the government was concerned about the possibility of suicide attacks. Groups thought to be linked to Moslem Uighur militants opposed to China's rule in Xinjiang, the only Chinese province with a Moslem majority, have in the past targeted Chinese nationals in Pakistan … Pro-Tibet protests have never taken place in Pakistan.
>
> (*FT*, 16 April 2008, p. 9)

> Ceremonies to mark the arrival of the Olympic torch in Pakistan have taken place amid tight security … President Pervez Musharraf has just returned from a visit to China, with which Pakistan shares historic defence and economic links … In India, where the torch arrives on Thursday [17 April], there have been protests with at least fifty Tibetans being detained. The demonstration, which was in front of the Chinese embassy in Delhi, was quickly broken up by police.
>
> (www.bbc.co.uk, 16 April 2008)

'In Pakistan runners carried the Olympic flame around the outside of the Jinnah stadium in the capital of Islamabad on Wednesday [16 April] – an invitation-only event in front of a sparse crowd with heavy security' (www.cnn.com, 17 April 2008).

> Dozens of Tibetans wearing yellow 'Free Tibet' headbands were arrested in New Delhi on Wednesday [16 April] after they stormed through barricades and ran with banners towards the Chinese embassy, taking heavy security in the diplomatic heart of the city by surprise. The police intervened swiftly, arresting forty-seven of the protesters against Chinese rule in Tibet. But it was the second embarrassing breach of the tight security measures imposed by the police in New Delhi as the Indian capital prepared to play host to the Olympic torch relay on Thursday [17 April] … On Tuesday [15 April]

another twenty-seven demonstrators were arrested in New Delhi after breaking through police ranks to mount an alternative 'protest torch relay' along the central avenue along which the official torch will be carried. The New Delhi portion of the relay is widely expected to be one of the more sensitive, potentially volatile chapters in the Olympic torch's troubled worldwide tour ... Amid growing anxiety about the event, a number of sports stars and celebrities [in India] have announced that they will not be participating in the relay ... The Tibetan Solidarity Committee were making banners to carry in a 'peace run' that they hope to hold a few hours before the Olympic torch run ... Members of the Tibetan Youth Congress, which led the protests at the embassy on Wednesday and along the torch route Tuesday, said they were planning demonstrations for Thursday ... Lawmakers [in Australia] have already cut back the relay route. Pro-Tibet demonstrators expect at least 1,000 people to travel to the capital [Canberra] in a bid to interrupt the event.

(www.iht.com, 16 April 2008)

Weapons and explosives have been found in eleven Buddhist monasteries in the Tibetan-populated province of Gansu, according to China's state media. The items were discovered in the past two days in monasteries in the Gannan prefecture, Xinhua news agency said. According to Xinhua, ninety-four people were injured during assaults, looting, arson and vandalism in Gannan in mid-March ... More than 2,200 people are reported to have surrendered to the police in connection with the Gannan riots. Most have now been released, but about 100 monks are reportedly still being held ... Exiled Tibetan leaders say more than 150 people were killed by the Chinese security forces during the violence last month.

(www.bbc.co.uk, 17 April 2008)

'On Wednesday [16 April] the police said they had discovered dynamite, weapons and satellite dishes at eleven Buddhist monasteries in Gansu, in north-western China' (www.iht.com, 18 April 2008).

Chinese security forces have detained a well known Tibetan singer ... [Her husband] said Jamyang Kyi, who has performed extensively abroad, was detained in Xining in Qinghai province on 1 April and has not been seen since 7 April. Kyi is also a producer in the Tibetan language section of state-run Qinghai television.

(*Guardian*, 17 April 2008, p. 18)

The Chinese authorities have detained a prominent Tibetan television reporter and intellectual who is also a popular singer ... Jamyang Kyi, an announcer at the state-run television station in Qinghai, was escorted from her office on 1 April by plainclothes police officers in the city of Xining, according to colleagues and friends. The authorities also confiscated her computer and a list of contracts, they said. Her husband, Lamao Jia, who is also a journalist and writer, said he had received no word from his wife for more than a week and did not know where she was being held … A researcher at the Tibetan Centre for Human Rights and Democracy in Dharamsala, India, said he knew of nothing in her music or writings that might have provoked the authorities.

(www.iht.com, 18 April 2008)

'The Chinese press reported that nearly 4,000 "rioters" had been detained in Lhasa and other Tibetan areas since anti-Chinese riots last month [March]. More than half were said to have been released: 400 face formal criminal charges' (*The Economist*, 19 April 2008, p. 7).

17 April 2008.

Chinese cheer leaders and Tibetan protesters greeted the Olympic flame Thursday [17 April] amid a massive security clampdown for the latest leg of the international torch relay in India, home to the world's largest Tibetan exile community … Even the flame's late night arrival at New Delhi's airport was marred by small protests. Some two dozen Tibetan exiles chanted anti-China slogans and protested along a busy highway as the torch made its way into the city … Tibetan exiles number more than 100,000 in India … In recent weeks Tibetan exiles have stormed the Chinese embassy, which is now surrounded by barricades and barbed wire, gone on hunger strike and shaved their heads to protest China's crackdown on protests in Tibet … Thousands of Tibetans were also taking part in their own torch run … The alternative run began Thursday morning [17 April] … Several dozens of prominent Indians, including former defence minister George Fernandez, joined the Tibetans who were planning to march around the city with their alternative torch … Activists disrupted torch relays in Paris, London and San Francisco. However, stops in Kazakhstan, Russia, Argentina, Tanzania, Oman and Pakistan were trouble-free. But in India public sympathy lies with the Tibetans.

(www.iht.com, 17 April 2008)

'Public sympathy in India lies with the Tibetans … While India needs to bow to popular sentiment and allow some Tibetan protests, it must ensure it does not jeopardize its important relations with China, analysts say' (www.cnn.com, 17 April 2008).

The Olympic torch made a strange and lonely procession through central New Delhi on Thursday [17 April], with the event so comprehensively overshadowed by fears of the anti-Chinese protests that had marred its appearance in other cities that no members of the public were allowed close enough to witness it. The seventy-odd Indian athletes and celebrities who carried the torch down New Delhi's widest avenue were outnumbered by thousands of watchful members of India's security forces, who managed to stamp out any pomp and excitement, transforming the occasion instead into a tense security operation rather than a celebration … [It was] some of the tightest security ever seen in the Indian capital … Only elected guests and a

> few schoolchildren were permitted to attend … The relay itself was not disturbed by demonstrations but there were numerous small attempts to breach the heavy security in the streets around the route … On Thursday morning hundreds of Tibetan protesters marched through central New Delhi shouting 'Die for Freedom'. Demonstrators lit their own torch at the spot where the ashes of the Indian pacifist Mahatma Gandhi are buried and mounted a parallel, peaceful torch relay through central New Delhi … Police had granted permission for the march, but warned they would extinguish any flame carried by protesters … Police confiscated the torch, but marchers had six reserve torches and swiftly substituted another one … Several Indian celebrities and sports stars, including Sachin Tendulkar [citing a groin strain], the country's most popular cricketer, had withdrawn from the event, and two more invited athletes decided not to join the team of seventy torchbearers.
>
> (www.iht.com, 17 April 2008)

'Left watching the torchbearers were flag-waving Chinese officials and a few dozen school children' (www.guardian.co.uk, 17 April 2008).

> The Olympic torch completed the latest leg of its world tour in India's capital. New Delhi, amid heavy security to protect it from protests … Dozens of Tibetan activists were detained nearby, but the event passed off without the sort of anti-China demonstrations witnessed elsewhere. Earlier Tibetan exile groups organized a peaceful alternative torch relay involving politicians and celebrities … Apart from about 500 dignitaries and a group of school children invited to watch, the public was kept well away from the flame as it was carried 3 kilometres (1.9 miles) … a third of its original 9 kilometre (5 mile) distance.
>
> (www.bbc.co.uk, 17 April 2008)

'The Indian leg of the relay took place under tight security. At least 100 pro-Tibet activists were arrested' (www.bbc.co.uk, 18 April 2008).

> Thousands of protesters descended on the Indian capital from across the country, but extraordinary security measures kept demonstrators mostly at bay … The Indian capital was transformed into a fortress … Indian authorities did not disclose the relay route or the start time until twenty-four hours before the event … Tsewang Rigzin, president of the Tibetan Youth Congress, told CNN that at least 200 members of the pro-independence group and their supporters were arrested in various places in the capital. The congress boasts 300,000 worldwide members, it says … In another part of the city hundreds of Tibetan monks and supporters took part in a symbolic torch relay … More than 500 protesters were arrested Thursday [17 April] in Kathmandu, Nepal, in front of the Chinese embassy.
>
> (www.cnn.com, 17 April 2008)

> Nepalese police detained more than 500 Tibetan exiles near the Chinese embassy on Thursday [17 April] … monks and nuns and other Tibetans …

It was so far the largest number of Tibetans detained in Kathmandu since the exiles began almost daily protests last month [March].

(www.iht.com, 17 April 2008)

As many as 100 Tibetans were arrested in north-west China on Thursday [17 April] after they took part in a demonstration to protest the earlier detention of monks from a nearby monastery, according to witnesses and a Tibetan human rights group. Local residents said that the police beat and then arrested people at an open-air market in Tongren, a town in Qinghai province, after they refused to obey orders to leave. They said the town had been the scene of several disturbances in recent months, including an unauthorized gathering in February involving 300 monks who were dispersed by tear gas as they tried to make their way to a government building. On 16 March the monks in Tongren set off fireworks and burned incense on a hill above the monastery under the gaze of the riot police. A police official in Tongren confirmed that there had been detentions following 'unrest' but said that half of those detained had since been released. The disturbances on Thursday were the latest sign that the continuing unrest in Tibetan regions of China had yet to be quelled by the authorities. Since the 14 March riots in Lhasa 2,200 people in areas with heavily Tibetan populations, most of them in Qinghai and Gansu provinces, have been taken into custody, according to Xinhua. The authorities said that most of those who were arrested or had surrendered to the police had since been released … According to Xinhua, 2,200 people, 519 of them monks, have been taken into custody since the riots began in mid-March. The news agency said 1,870 of those had been released after questioning, but officials are still seeking scores of people who took part in the disturbances that the government contends killed nineteen people, nearly all of them Chinese. Tibetan exile groups place the figure at 140 and say most of the dead were Tibetan.

(www.iht.com, 18 April 2008)

18 April 2008.

A Buddhist temple has withdrawn from plans to host Japan's opening stage of the Olympic torch relay … Zenkoji Temple, in the city of Nagano, had been due to serve as the starting point for the parade on 26 April … The city has already cancelled one event planned around the relay because of security concerns. There is also a row brewing with China about whether or not its security officials will be allowed to run alongside … Japan says its own security measures will be sufficient, but China asked Japan to accept that its people should be in place to deter any demonstrators … Meanwhile the torch arrived in Thailand in preparation for a parade through the capital city, Bangkok.

(www.bbc.co.uk, 18 April 2008)

'Officials at the temple withdrew from the plan Friday [18 April], citing security concerns and sympathy for Tibetan protesters' (www.iht.com, 20 April 2008).

> The Olympic torch arrived in Thailand early Friday morning [18 April] under tight security for the latest leg of its round-the-world relay, on Saturday [19 April] through the capital, Bangkok … The torch is scheduled to leave Thailand for Malaysia on Saturday night.
>
> (www.iht.com, 18 April 2008)

'The head of Thailand's Olympic Committee said he expected the relay to pass off without major disruption … Thailand has strong links to China and the relay stage has been publicly endorsed by the revered royal family' (www.bbc.co.uk, 19 April 2008).

> The official Chinese news media have sought to temper nationalist calls to boycott foreign businesses accused of backing Tibetan independence, urging angry citizens to focus on economic development. Chinese internet sites have been awash with calls to stop buying French goods and stop shopping at the French retailer Carrefour after pro-Tibet protesters in Paris upset the Beijing Olympics torch relay. After prominent local news reports, Chinese officials and citizens have also vented outrage at a commentator on CNN television who spoke of Chinese 'goons' and 'junk' products. But in a sign that Beijing may be moving to cool public anger, Xinhua called for 'patriotic zeal to concentrate on development' … The commentary said: 'Patriotic zeal must enter into a rational track and must be transformed into concrete actions to do one's own work well. Thirty years of reform and opening up have created a China miracle. But we must be crystal clear that for China that has endured so much the future road will not be all smooth-going' … The Xinhua commentary echoes official handling of earlier surges of popular nationalism when officials sought to rein in volatile anger that could turn against the central government. In 1999, after Nato mistakenly bombed the Chinese embassy in Belgrade during the war against Serbia and killed three Chinese citizens, students and citizens surrounded and stoned the US embassy in Beijing and attacked US consulates … This time French companies are the main target, with campaigners calling for a boycott of Carrefour, accusing it of helping fund the Dalai Lama … But past nationalist boycott campaigns against US and Japanese companies have fizzled with little effect on sales.
>
> (www.iht.com, 18 April 2008; *IHT*, 19 April 2008, p. 13)

> In the past the government has encouraged nationalistic outbursts and then quashed them when passions grew too inflamed or when the protests had achieved the political purpose officials envisioned. In 1999 the authorities gave free rein to a brief spasm of anti-America protest after the accidental bombing of the Chinese embassy in Belgrade … In 2005 they allowed even larger anti-Japanese demonstrations which were fuelled by anger over textbooks glossing over Japan's wartime atrocities in China.
>
> (www.iht.com, 20 April 2008)

> Bloggers and commentators on web forums have reacted strongly against perceived bias in the Western media … China has made similar efforts to

rein in outbursts of public anger in the past. In April 2005 it called for calm after destructive anti-Japan protests triggered by the publication of a controversial history textbook.

(www.bbc.co.uk, 18 April 2008)

Beijing has called on its citizens to channel their 'patriotic zeal' into the economy in a sign the government wants to cool the nationalistic backlash against the West … Xinhua said in an editorial that patriotism should be 'cherished hundred-fold' but harnessed 'rationally' in the pursuit of the most important priority – 'sound and fast development' … Xinhua offered some support for a boycott of French goods in retaliation for protests in Paris against the torch, calling it the 'unadorned expression of patriotic zeal and a true representation of public opinion'. Carrefour, the supermarket bearing the brunt of the anti-French campaign, has introduced a generous offer [in the form of coupons] for customers as from 1 May, the start of the proposed boycott.

(*FT*, 19 April 2008, p. 8)

A South African trade union has refused to unload arms from a Chinese ship destined for Zimbabwe … President Robert Mugabe of Zimbabwe is locked in an election stalemate with the opposition over the delay from a 29 March election that has raised fears of violence. The 300,000-strong South African Transport and Allied Workers' Union said it would not unload the weapons in the port of Durban because Mugabe's government might use them to crack down on opponents.

(www.iht.com, 19 April 2008)

The arms shipment was ordered from China before the elections, but its arrival amid Zimbabwe's political crisis … brought new scrutiny on China at a time when its human rights record is already under scrutiny for suppressing protesters in Tibet and supplying arms to the government of Sudan … The Chinese ship is packed with ammunition, rockets and mortar bombs … The shipment weighed 77 tonnes and was valued at $1.245 million. The invoice was dated 21 January [2008] and the goods apparently left China on 15 March … China [has] long [been] an ally of Mugabe … On Friday [18 April] the Chinese ship pulled up anchor and moved off … [heading towards] Maputo, the capital of Mozambique.

(www.iht.com, 19 April 2008)

19 April 2008.

Thousands of people watched the Olympic torch pass through Bangkok during the Thai leg of a worldwide relay held amid tight security … Hundreds of anti-Chinese protesters were faced by Beijing supporters, but there was no major disruption … There was a brief scuffle within seconds of the start of the relay as a Thai and a foreign pro-Tibet activist tried to unfurl a banner. The sign was quickly ripped from their hands by a group of Chinese men who surrounded the protesters.

(www.bbc.co.uk, 19 April 2008)

'[In] Bangkok the relay was greeted by a few small protests' (www.iht.com, 20 April 2008).

> Protesters in several Chinese cities gathered to demand a boycott of French products and denounce campaigns for Tibetan independence. Hundreds of people demonstrated in cities including Beijing, Wuhan, Hefei, Kunming and Qingdao – often outside stores of the French chain Carrefour. Passions ran high, but the protests were closely patrolled by police.
>
> (www.bbc.co.uk, 19 April 2008)

> On Friday [18 April] and Saturday [19 April] protesters gathered in front of a half-dozen outlets of the French retailer Carrefour, including a demonstration in the central city of Wuhan that reportedly drew several thousand people ... On Saturday about fifty demonstrators carrying banners held a brief rally at the French embassy in Beijing before the police shooed them away. For the moment, however, most of the outrage is confined to the internet. More than 20 million people have signed online petitions saying they plan to stop shopping at the Carrefour chain, Louis Vuitton and other stores linked to France because of what they see as the country's failure to protect the torch during its visit to Paris two weeks ago. In a survey released Friday ... Xinhua said 66 per cent of those who responded said they would stay away from Carrefour during a month-long boycott planned for May. Public indignation has also been directed at Western news outlets, which are blamed for one-sided coverage of the torch relay and for anti-Chinese bias in their reporting on the disturbances in Tibet. In recent days foreign news outlets have been swamped by angry phone calls; two music videos circulating on the internet blast CNN ... Although Communist Party officials have the ability to block text messages and internet traffic they find objectionable, the censors have until now allowed more leeway for boycott organizers. In many ways they have been feeding the outrage by publicizing the threat by the French president, Nicolas Sarkozy, to skip the opening ceremonies [of the Olympics] and by repeatedly calling on CNN to apologize for remarks made by Jack Cafferty ... But in a sign that the government may now be worried about the intensity of popular passion, Xinhua said on Friday that it was time to curb nationalist zeal. While it applauded the boycott crusade, it advised people not to complicate the government's aim of encouraging foreign investment in China ... On Saturday it issued a stronger warning, highlighting government concern that anti-Western sentiment could affect public attitudes during the Olympics, when 1.5 million people are expected to arrive. It said in an editorial: 'Every son and daughter of China has the responsibility to show to the world in real action that China welcomes friends from all countries with open arms and will deliver an outstanding Olympics' ... Mindful of how a public grief after the death of a party official morphed into the pro-democracy protests in Tiananmen Square, the Chinese government recognizes that vitriolic campaigns against outsiders could easily pivot toward the Communist Party ... If the protests on

> Saturday are any indication, official tolerance for unsanctioned demonstrations is wearing thin. According to witnesses and news reports, most of the Carrefour protests were quickly dispersed by the police. In Beijing a rally that drew about fifty people to the French embassy and a nearby French school lasted an hour before riot police forced them to leave. By 3 p.m. dozens of uniformed officers had sealed off access to the streets surrounding the embassy … In a country where the press is tightly controlled, the growing popularity of high-tech communications has made such protests possible. Some 229 million people have internet access in the country and usage in China is growing by 30 per cent a year … Cellphone text messaging is ubiquitous, with more than 98 per cent of the country's 400 million cellphone owners regularly using text messages. Another 300 million people are registered on instant messaging networks like MSN and QQ … Many of the messages accuse Carrefour executives of providing financial support to pro-Tibetan advocates, a charge the company denies. Others say American fast-food chains should be boycotted as a punishment for the recent meeting by the Speaker of the House, Nancy Pelosi, with the Dalai Lama. In the past boycott campaigns in China have largely come to naught.
>
> (www.iht.com, 20 April 2008)

'Carrefour has 112 hypermarkets and over 2 million customers in China' (www.iht.com, 21 April 2008).

> Chinese censors have quietly warned cyber-police and internet businesses to delete all information related to protests against Western policies, nations or companies that have proliferated in the wake of the global Olympic torch relay and high level calls to boycott the opening ceremony of the summer games in Beijing. A notice issued last week by China's Internet Inspection Sector instructs recipients to reset the keywords used to block access to certain websites, relay the instructions through all internet distribution channels and then delete the notice in a timely manner … A planned event to give away patriotic T-shirts near Beijing's Qinghua University reportedly was halted by the police … Several Western reporters have had death threats since their phone numbers and other details were posted online. Chinese internet users called for a boycott of Carrefour, the French supermarket chain that has more than ninety stores in China … CNN has been singled out for using a photograph in March on its website that cropped out Tibetan rioters attacking Chinese targets, focusing instead on a Chinese military vehicle.
>
> (www.guardian.co.uk, 20 April 2008)

> Hundreds of Chinese students gathered in Manchester and London to protest at the Western media's portrayal of the Free Tibet movement. More than 1,000 people … gathered outside BBC Manchester and about 300 were outside the Houses of Parliament in London.
>
> (www.bbc.co.uk, 19 April 2008)

'Expatriate Chinese on Saturday [19 April] rallied in Paris as well as outside CNN's offices in California and the BBC in Manchester – which are accused of alleged media bias over Tibet' (*Guardian*, 21 April 2008, p. 18).

'Demonstrations in support of the Beijing Olympics and against the Free Tibet movement were staged over the weekend in Paris, London and Manchester' (*Independent*, 21 April 2008, p. 28).

'At the weekend thousands of Chinese joined demonstrations in London, Paris and Berlin' (*FT*, 22 April 2008, p. 9).

('Scenes ranging from civil to aggressive have played out at colleges across the United States over the past month as Chinese students have been forced to confront an image of their homeland that they neither recognize nor appreciate ... Traditionally silent on political issues [they] have begun to lash out at what they perceive as a pervasive anti-Chinese bias. Last year [2007] there were more than 42,000 students from mainland China studying in the United States, an increase from fewer than 20,000 in 2003 ... At Duke University in North Carolina pro-China students surrounded and drowned out a pro-Tibet vigil; a Chinese [female] freshman who tried to mediate received death threats and her family living in China were forced into hiding': www.iht.com, 29 April 2008; *IHT*, 30 April 2008, p. 4.)

20 April 2008.

> China has urged its citizens to be calm amid further anti-Western protests in the country, focused on French supermarket chain Carrefour. The official Communist Party newspaper, the *People's Daily*, said patriotism should be expressed rationally ... Xinhua said more than 1,000 people carrying banners had gathered in front of a Carrefour store in the city of Xian and there were also protests in Harbin and Jinan. Xinhua added that police were monitoring the demonstrations in three cities, which remained peaceful. The protests came after Saturday [19 April] saw hundreds of people demonstrating in cities including Beijing, Wuhan, Hefei, Kinming and Qingdao – often outside Carrefour stores ... The front-page Sunday [20 April] editorial in the *People's Daily* called on Chinese people to cherish patriotism 'while expressing it in a rational way'. It said: 'As citizens we have the responsibility to express our patriotic enthusiasm calmly and rationally and express patriotic aspiration in an orderly and legal manner. The more complicated the international situation is, the more calmness, wisdom and unity need to be shown by the Chinese people.'
>
> (www.bbc.co.uk, 20 April 2008)

> Nepal said it is prepared to use force – including gunfire – to prevent anti-Beijing protests during the Olympic torch relay up Mount Everest. The torch is scheduled to be brought up the peak from the northern, Chinese Tibetan side in early May ... Nepal does not want to alienate China, one of its two neighbours and a country it depends on for foreign aid and diplomatic support.
>
> (www.bbc.co.uk, 20 April 2008)

> In Nepal soldiers and police officers guarding the slopes of Mount Everest have been given authorization to use 'whatever means' required in the event of protests during the Olympic torch's run to the summit of the mountain in early May. The police and soldiers 'have been given orders to stop any protest on the mountain using whatever means necessary, including use of weapons', said ... a spokesman for the Nepalese Home Ministry. He added that such force was to be used as a last resort and that officers would first try to persuade protesters to leave and would arrest those who refused to do so.
>
> (www.iht.com, 20 April 2008)

> The Olympic torch arrived in Malaysia on Sunday [20 April] ahead of a relay that is expected to take place [on Monday 21 April] under heavy security, while other countries in the region tried to minimize the potential for conflict when the torch is scheduled to arrive in their respective countries.
>
> (www.iht.com, 20 April 2008)

'The torch is currently in a secret location in Malaysia, ahead of its relay through Kuala Lumpur on Monday [21 April]' (www.bbc.co.uk, 20 April 2008).

21 April 2008.

> Hundreds of flag-waving Chinese students gathered at the starting and ending points of the Olympic torch relay in Kuala Lumpur, far outnumbering the handful of people who carried pro-Tibet signs ... About 500 Chinese students attended the relay, carrying pro-China signs and heckling the few people taking a pro-Tibet stand ... An Olympics organizer said the Chinese embassy arranged for the students to be there. Several of the students told CNN that the Chinese government provided their transportation to the event and gave them the flags and shirts ... About 1,500 people attended the relay's start ... Few of them appeared to be local residents – a member of the Malaysian Olympics council explained it was a work day ... The flame will arrive in Jakarta, Indonesia, late Monday [21 April] for a torch relay there on Tuesday [22 April].
>
> (www.cnn.com, 21 April 2008)

> Police have already detained a Japanese family of three who unfurled a pro-Tibet banner at the starting point ... About 300 Chinese students studying in Malaysia greeted the torch at the airport ... Hundreds of anti-China protesters were faced by Beijing supporters, but there was no major disruption.
>
> (www.bbc.co.uk, 21 April 2008)

> A crowd of Chinese onlookers heckled and hit a Japanese family with inflated plastic batons on Monday [21 April] after the three unfurled a Tibetan flag before the start of the Malaysian leg of the Olympic torch relay. The family, comprising two adults and a boy, was detained by police, who also took a Buddhist monk and a British woman wearing a 'Free Tibet' T-shirt into custody. All five were later released ... The torch's next sched-

uled stop is Indonesia, where organizers said Monday the country will stage a shortened, invitation-only relay under heavy security to hinder anti-China protests … [The Malaysian] organizing committee … said the steps were taken for Tuesday's [22 April] relay after pressure from the Chinese embassy.

(www.iht.com, 21 April 2008)

France's president expressed sympathy for a disabled Chinese athlete who was jostled by a pro-Tibet activist as she held the Olympic torch in Paris. In a letter to the twenty-seven-year-old Paralympian fencer Jin Jing, Nicolas Sarkozy told her she had shown 'outstanding courage' in the face of the assault … A protester in Paris tried to snatch the torch from Ms Jin, who was carrying it in her wheelchair on its Paris leg. She was hailed as a hero in China's state-run media … Mr Sarkozy's letter stated: 'I would like to express to you my deep feeling about the way you were jostled in Paris on 7 April when you were holding the Olympic flame. I want to assure you that the incidents staged by a few people on this sad day do not reflect the feelings of my countrymen for the Chinese people' … Ms Jin was invited to visit France as a personal guest of the president … Meanwhile, Paris city council said it will honour the Dalai Lama … Bertrand Delanoë, the Socialist mayor of Paris, announced he would make the Tibetan spiritual leader an honorary citizen.

(www.bbc.co.uk, 21 April 2008)

After a wave of anti-French protests in China, President Nicolas Sarkozy of France is ending three top officials [the president of the French Senate, a former prime minister and Sarkozy's chief diplomatic adviser, and a former ambassador to the United States and the UN] there this week in a diplomatic charm offensive aimed at limiting the political and economic fallout from the controversy surrounding the preparation of the Olympic Games.

(www.iht.com, 21 April 2008)

State-run media reported on Monday [21 April] that officials are launching a two-month 'patriotic education' [campaign] in Tibet where Communist Party officials and local people will gather to denounce the spiritual leader … [China] says [the campaign] is designed to undermine support for the Dalai Lama and any separatist sentiment. The *Tibet Daily* newspaper said the campaign was to 'unify the thinking … of officials and the masses' … China's Communist Party has long used what it calls 'patriotic education campaigns' to impose discipline and reinforce its authority … The *Tibet Daily* said the latest drive would include television programmes and a series of sessions in which the Dalai Lama would be denounced by Communist Party members, other officials and local people. Campaigns requiring monks in Tibetan monasteries to denounce the Dalai Lama and declare their loyalty to Beijing have also been stepped up.

(www.bbc.co.uk, 21 April 2008)

> The Communist Party has started a political education drive in Lhasa, vowing a long campaign to attack pro-independence sentiment and support for the Dalai Lama … In a bid to reinforce control in Lhasa, party officials have begun an education drive focused on officials and party members, the official *Tibet Daily* reported Monday [21 April]. The paper said: '[The campaign to] fight separatism, protect stability and promote development … [will focus on] unifying the thinking and cohesive strength of officials and the masses, deepening the struggle against separatism and counter-attacking the separatist plots of the Dalai clique' … Party members would be assessed on their 'performance' in the two-month drive, which will include television programmes and organized denunciation sessions.
>
> (www.iht.com, 21 April 2008)

22 April 2008.

> The Olympic torch is to be paraded around a stadium in Jakarta [Indonesia]. For security reasons the original 20 kilometre (15 mile) route has been cut to a few laps around the capital's main stadium. It will be watched by 5,000 people, who had to apply for special entry cards … Police broke up a small protest by pro-Tibetan demonstrations near the stadium and detained several people. A banner reading 'No human rights, no Olympics' was unfurled, before police moved in … Human rights campaigners complained their activists had been detained despite having permission for their protest.
>
> (www.bbc.co.uk, 22 April 2008)

> The Olympic torch was paraded through a heavily guarded stadium in Jakarta after the police stopped about 100 anti-Beijing protesters from disrupting the latest leg of the [torch relay] … Earlier in the day there had been a thirty minute standoff between the police and protesters … There have been several small demonstrations outside the Chinese embassy in Jakarta over Tibet.
>
> (www.iht.com, 22 April 2008)

> China denounced a decision by the Paris City Council to bestow honorary citizenship on the Dalai Lama, saying Tuesday [22 April] that the move was 'another insult' that would harm diplomatic relations … even as French officials tried to smooth over relations with Beijing, the Paris City Council, led by Mayor Bertrand Delanoë's Socialists and the Green Party, voted Monday [21 April] to bestow the title of 'honorary citizen' on the Dalai Lama. Conservatives, led by President Nicolas Sarkozy, opposed the measure … The Chinese foreign ministry spokeswoman, Jiang Yu, said Tuesday: '[The move] wantonly interferes in China's internal affairs, seriously harms relations between China and France' … Jiang's statement did not mention Hu Jia, a Chinese human rights activist who will also be recognized as an honorary citizen of Paris. Hu was recently convicted of subversion charges and sentenced to three-and-a-half years in prison. Jiang also criticized a meeting [on Monday 21 April] between a US official … an Undersecretary of State … and the Dalai Lama.
>
> (www.iht.com, 22 April 2008)

A Chinese ship that was blocked from unloading its cargo in South Africa may return to China because of difficulties at African ports, Chinese foreign ministry spokeswoman Jiang Yu said Tuesday [22 April]. The ship, which is suspected to be carrying weapons destined for Zimbabwe, left South African waters Friday [18 April] after that country's High Court ruled that the cargo could not be transported over South African roadways to landlocked Zimbabwe – where violence continues in a dispute over election results. It was last believed to be headed toward Angola [to the port of Luanda], South African officials said. The United States has asked that other southern African countries not allow the ship to dock … [A US official said] the ship also tried to dock in Mozambique but was refused permission.

(www.cnn.com, 22 April 2008)

South Africa's High Court Friday [18 April] barred transport of the ammunition, rockets and mortar bombs across South Africa from the port of Durban to landlocked Zimbabwe after an Anglican archbishop argued they were likely to be used to crush the Zimbabwean opposition following the disputed 29 March election … South African officials said last week that they could not interfere with the shipment because there was no trade embargo against Zimbabwe … [On Monday 21 April] Levy Mwanawasa, who is president of Zambia and heads a bloc of fourteen African nations … the Southern African Development Community … called on other countries in the region not to let the ship dock in their ports. A spokesman for the Zambian government said Tuesday [22 April]: 'He [the president] said it would be good for China to play a more useful role in the Zimbabwe crisis than supplying arms. We do not want a situation which will escalate the situation in Zimbabwe more than what it is.'

(www.iht.com, 22 April 2008)

Zambia's president has called on other African countries not to let the ship … carrying weapons to Zimbabwe … enter their waters, in case the arms escalate post-election tensions … The Chinese vessel was said to be bound for Angola but the United States is reported to be pressurizing port authorities there and in Namibia not to allow them to dock … Despite reports the ship was heading for Angola, an ally of Zimbabwe's government, the director of the Institute of Angolan ports said the vessel had not asked for permission to dock in Angola.

(www.bbc.co.uk, 23 April 2008)

Britain and the United States put concerted pressure on southern African states and China to stop a Chinese ship carrying weapons for the Zimbabwean government docking in the region … Namibia and Angola, both allies of Zimbabwe, denied having been asked to allow the boat to dock.

(*Guardian*, 23 April 2008, p. 14)

23 April 2008.

> The Olympic torch arrived in the Australian capital, Canberra, amid tight security on the latest leg ... A metre-high wire fence has been erected along the route of the procession, which has been shortened because of concerns about security ... The torch will be relayed through Canberra on Thursday [24 April]. Australian prime minister Kevin Rudd: 'If any protester irrespective of their political point of view, engages in unruly, disruptive, violent, unlawful behaviour then the police will come down on them like a ton of bricks' ... There has been confusion about the role of Chinese guards who are travelling with the torch. The Australian government has insisted they will have no security role in Canberra, while the Chinese ambassador has said they may have to intervene if the flame is attacked.
>
> (www.bbc.co.uk, 23 April 2008)

> The Olympic flame reached Australia on Wednesday [23 April] ... There were small protests. In Sydney activists unfurled a huge banner over a prominent billboard for Coca-Cola – an Olympic sponsor – that urged China to open talks with the Dalai Lama. The police said they detained four people for questioning. Earlier in the city the police stopped two people from unfurling a banner on the landmark Sydney Harbour Bridge that demanded freedom for Tibet from Chinese rule. In Canberra about 150 supporters of Tibet attended a vigil on Wednesday evening outside the Chinese embassy and spelled out 'Free Tibet' with candles ... The police in Canberra sought to end lingering confusion about the role of Chinese security agents in the relay, with the police chief saying three Chinese 'flame attendants' will always be near the torch but will have no official security role ... After Australia the flame will head to Nagano, Japan.
>
> (www.iht.com, 23 April 2008)

24 April 2008.

> Thousands of pro-Chinese supporters swamped the route of the Olympic torch as it passed through the Australian capital Canberra on Thursday [24 April] ... The Australian police reported only seven arrests from a crowd estimated at 20,000. The Chinese authorities had mobilized their biggest weapon: the huge expatriate community, who came out in their thousands to dwarf a small but vocal band of pro-Tibet protesters. But there were some ugly incidents when groups of Chinese students surrounded and intimidated isolated pro-Tibet protesters ... The Australian police had warned pro-Tibet groups to stick together because they could not guarantee their safety if they struck out alone ... The 16 kilometre (10 mile) route was fenced off with waist-high barriers. Only two people tried to cross them, but they failed to get close to the torch and were quickly subdued.
>
> (www.iht.com, 24 April 2008)

> Canberra's Olympic torch relay took place relatively smoothly, despite fears of clashes between pro-Tibet and Chinese supporters ... There were pockets

of pro-Tibet protesters, but they were heavily outnumbered by thousands of Chinese ... many of them students studying in Australia ... who turned out to 'protect the flame' ... In the early stages of the relay there were scuffles between the pro-Tibet protesters and China supporters, leading to the arrest of five people. Police also arrested three protesters who ran out in front of the torch – though the relay was not disrupted ... There was also wrangling between the jogging Australian police officers surrounding the flame and the Chinese security guards accompanying the torch ... The Australian officers repeatedly pulled the three Chinese guards trying to run with the torch away from their positions alongside the torchbearers ... Pro-Tibetan campaigners held a candle-lit vigil outside the Chinese embassy ahead of the relay.

(www.bbc.co.uk, 24 April 2008)

A Chinese ship carrying armaments made by a Chinese state-owned company and bound for Zimbabwe has headed back to China without unloading its cargo of bullets and mortar bombs ... China's decision will be welcomed as a victory by the dock workers, trade unionists, religious leaders, Western diplomats and human rights workers who have been campaigning since last week to block delivery of the weaponry to Zimbabwe.

(www.iht.com, 24 April 2008)

25 April 2008. Xinhua (quoting an official): 'In view of the requests repeatedly made by the Dalai side for resuming talks, the relevant department of the central government will have contact and consultation with Dalai's private representative in the coming days' (www.cnn.com, 25 April 2008; www.iht.com, 25 April 2008).

'The last round ... of talks with the Dalai Lama's representatives ... was held in June and July last year [2007]' (www.bbc.co.uk, 25 April 2008).

The Dalai Lama was returning from the United States on Friday [25 April] ... [China's] dialogue with his envoys began in 2002, but then broke off last summer [2007] after six rounds of talks. Those talks – focused on the future status of Tibet and whether the Dalai Lama will be allowed to return to China – never made significant progress, and their failure is one reason cited by some analysts for the recent unrest ... Tenzin Takhla, the Tibetan spokesman ... noted that the Dalai Lama had ... not sought independence until 1974 ... The Dalai Lama has talked about 'genuine autonomy' within the Chinese state for what he describes as 'greater Tibet' – a region that includes the current Tibet Autonomous Region as well as Tibetan areas of neighbouring Chinese provinces ... [It has been noted that China describes the talks with the Dalai Lama's envoys as] meetings, never negotiations.

(www.iht.com, 25 April 2008)

'Earlier this month ... the Dalai Lama ... hinted in Seattle that a back-channel discussion was already under way' (www.iht.com, 26 April 2008).

'Lodi Gyari, the Dalai Lama's chief negotiator, had said that back-channel communications were continuing despite the unrest but were not encouraging' (*Guardian*, 26 April 2008, p. 21).

Riot police officers, protesters and Chinese well-wishers converged on Nagano in the mountains of central Japan on Friday [25 April] as the torch of the Beijing Olympics arrived … Dozens of protesters surrounded by hundreds of riot police marched through the city, which hosted the 1998 Winter Olympics, carrying Tibetan flags and banners saying 'Stop the Torch' as the flame arrived … In a last-minute change the 18.7 kilometre (11.6 mile) torch relay was to begin in a parking lot Saturday [26 April] instead of an ancient [Buddhist] temple … Five tracksuit-clad riot police officers will run alongside the torchbearers, who will also be followed by two Chinese officials … Groups including Amnesty International and Reporters Without Borders have announced plans to protest … Besides the protests in Nagano, a handful of young people raised the flag of Tibet's exiled government Friday at a highway rest stop when the caravan carrying the torch pulled over. There were no confrontations. After Nagano the torch heads to Seoul on Sunday [27 April] and then to Pyongyang, North Korea, on Monday [28 April]. Human Rights Watch, based in New York, urged South Korea on Friday to use the torch relay to highlight the plight of North Korean refugees in China … The torch next travels to Vietnam, which [on Thursday 24 April] expelled an American citizen of Vietnamese origin who planned to disrupt the relay there, state media reported Friday [25 April] … From Vietnam the torch heads to Hong Kong.

(www.iht.com, 25 April 2008)

The head of Interpol said Friday [25 April] that there was a 'real possibility' that the Beijing Olympic Games would be targeted by terrorists or that anti-China groups could attack athletes … Ronald Noble (speaking at the opening of the International Conference on Security Co-operation in Beijing): 'An attempted act of terrorism is a real possibility and a real concern that all Olympic host countries have shared in recent years. Recent Tibet-related protests have introduced significant additional complications to the normal security considerations for a major international event like these Olympics. In the light of recent events all countries whose athletes will participate and whose citizens will attend the Beijing Olympics must be prepared for the possibility that the groups and individuals responsible for the violence during the global torch relay could carry out their protests at the actual Games. These activities could range from disruptive behaviour, like blocking major transportation routes or infrastructure or interfering with competitions, to more violent acts like assaulting Olympic officials or athletes or destroying property. Worse yet, we must be prepared for the possibility that al-Qaeda or some other terrorist group will attempt to launch a deadly terrorist attack at these Olympics. The threat is compounded by the very nature of the 2008 Summer Olympics. China will open its doors to hundreds of thousands of foreign visitors and journalists and an audience of billions watching on television' … China has accused Uighur militants in the far western, Moslem-majority region of Xinjiang of plotting attacks –

> with al-Qaeda's support – to help achieve their goal of establishing an independent country called East Turkestan. Earlier this month [April] the Chinese authorities said they had detained forty-five East Turkestan 'terrorist' suspects and foiled plots to carry out suicide bomb attacks and kidnap athletes at the Games. China has also accused Uighur separatists of trying to bring down a civilian airliner … An Interpol support team will arrive in Beijing before the Games to train Chinese officers in crisis management and major event operations.
>
> (www.iht.com, 27 April 2008)

26 April 2008.

> The Olympic torch met with more protests and scuffles in Nagano. With security tight along the route, two demonstrators tried to seize the torch and a third threw eggs at the flame. All were arrested. But the relay passed off without serious disruption. The streets were lined with thousands of Chinese supporters, as well as dozens of protesters.
>
> (www.bbc.co.uk, 26 April 2008)

'Japanese nationalists and pro-Tibet activists clashed with pro-Chinese groups … Five men [were] arrested in scuffles' (www.bbc.co.uk, 27 April 2008).

> Tight security accompanied the Olympic torch … as thousands of police officers helped quickly end the few and sporadic protests in Nagano … A few sideliners waved Tibetan flags, but those were outnumbered by those holding large Chinese flags … The relay was running smoothly until a protester holding a Tibetan flag threw himself at a torchbearer, briefly holding up the latest leg. Police officers quickly tackled the man, dragging him away before arresting him. Uniformed and plain-clothes police also had to quell a scuffle involving pro- and anti-China spectators … Earlier a group of anti-Chinese protesters threw objects at the relay, prompting police to push back the crowd … Students for Free Tibet Japan has announced plans to demonstrate at the Nagano leg of the relay with banners and speeches, but no loudspeakers … The torch now heads to South Korea, where the next leg of the global relay will be held in Seoul on Saturday [26 April].
>
> (www.cnn.com, 26 April 2008)

'[In Nagano] a few sideliners waved Tibetan flags, but those were outnumbered by those holding large Chinese flags. Despite some scuffles, the relay went off uninterrupted' (www.cnn.com, 27 April 2008).

> The eggs and tomatoes flew, the Chinese flags waved and a determined police force got the Olympic torch through yet another city … Making its sixteenth international stop, the torch was greeted Saturday [26 April] by a sea of Chinese well-wishers and pro-Tibet protesters as it passed through Nagano in the central Japan Alps that played host to the Winter Olympics a decade ago. At least three protesters rushed the torchbearers during the four-hour, 18.7 kilometre (11.6 mile) relay … Five men – four Japanese and a

pro-Tibetan resident of Taiwan – were arrested … More than 5,000 Chinese – most of them students bussed in from Tokyo – descended on Nagano for the relay – blanketing the city in red flags. They far outnumbered the pro-Tibet crowd … Nagano residents were conspicuously absent from the crowds.

(www.iht.com, 27 April 2008)

Dozens of human rights activists took part in a demonstration near the Olympic Park [in Seoul] on Saturday [26 April] ahead of the torch's arrival. In addition to protests against the Chinese occupation of Tibet, the relay is also seen as an opportunity to raise the issue of China's policy of repatriating North Korean defectors. Vowing to stop the march, human rights lawyer Kim Sang Chul … [said] China had repatriated 75,000 North Koreas over the past fifteen years … Over the following few days the torch will stop in North Korea and Vietnam.

(www.bbc.co.uk, 27 April 2008)

The Dalai Lama yesterday [26 April] welcomed Beijing's offer to meet his envoy, but said that he wants serious dialogue to reduce resentment about Chinese rule that triggered riots in Lhasa last month [March] … The Dalai Lama: 'We have to explore the causes of the problems and seek a solution through talks … [But] merely meeting some of my men in order to show the world they are having dialogue [would be meaningless].'

(www.guardian.co.uk, 27 April 2008)

27 April 2008.

The Olympic flame began the seventeenth leg of its … global relay in Seoul, South Korea, Sunday [27 April] – with Chinese students vastly outnumbering demonstrators. A North Korean defector tried to set himself on fire but was stopped by police. Sporadic scuffles broke out along the route between demonstrators and Chinese students as police tried to keep the two groups apart … The 15 mile (24 kilometre) route started at Olympic Park, built when Seoul hosted the Summer Games in 1988 … After Seoul was granted the 1988 Games massive pro-democracy demonstrations broke out, prompting the then-military government to enact sweeping reforms. Among them was the decision to hold direct presidential elections … An hour before the start of the relay thousands of Chinese students thronged the park plaza … About 30,000 Chinese students study in South Korea. In other recent Asian legs of the relay a large number of Chinese students have attended. In Bangkok, Thailand, students told CNN the Chinese embassy there provided their transportation and gave them shirts to wear … [In Seoul] demonstrators protesting China's policy toward Tibet turned out at the rally. They were joined by other demonstrators critical of how China forcefully deports North Korean refugees back to their country when they escape into China. Under the North Korean penal code, leaving the country without state permission can be considered an act of treason, punishable by heavy penalties including imprisonment and forced labour, said Kay Seok of Seoul's Human Rights Watch. She said: 'They will invariably be interrogated about what they did in China, why they went to China and who they met there. And depending on the result of the interrogation, they will be sent to labour camps for a few months or to prison for a few years' ... From Seoul the torch heads to Pyongyang, North Korea. On Wednesday [30 April] it travels to Hong Kong. Three human rights activists who planned on protesting the torch relay there said Sunday [27 April] that they were barred from entering [Hong Kong] ... [One of the activists was] Danish sculptor Jens Galschiot [who] sculpted *The Pillar of Shame*, which depicts fifty torn and twisted bodies to symbolize those who died in a Chinese crackdown on Tiananmen Square in 1989 ... The torch relay ends its round-the-world jaunt of twenty-one cities in five continents in Beijing in August.

(www.cnn.com, 27 April 2008)

Pro- and anti-China demonstrators clashed in Seoul ... Rights protesters were targeted by Chinese students, who outnumbered their rivals ... The protests had been against China's forced repatriation of North Korean refugees and its crackdown in Tibet ... Police struggled to contain thousands of flag-waving China supporters who chanted slogans and threw rocks at demonstrators denouncing the torch relay. Meanwhile, police managed to restrain one North Korean defector who tried to set himself on fire to halt the procession.

(www.bbc.co.uk, 27 April 2008)

A North Korean defector tried to set himself on fire to halt the Olympic torch relay Sunday [27 April] in Seoul, where thousands of police guarded the flame from protesters blasting China's treatment of North Korean refugees. Hundreds of China supporters wearing red and waving the Chinese flag greeted the torch and threw rocks at demonstrators denouncing the torch run ... On other stops along the torch's globe-trotting journey it was China's crackdown on violent protests against Chinese rule in Tibet that triggered the run celebrating the August games. But in South Korea critics have focused on Beijing's treatment of defectors who try to escape their lives of hardship in the North ... Many defectors live in hiding in China, but if caught there they are deported and likely face imprisonment in life-threatening conditions. The man who tried to immolate himself, forty-five-year-old Son Jong Hoon, had led an unsuccessful public campaign to save his brother from execution in the North, where he was accused of spying after the two met secretly in China. About an hour into the relay Son poured gasoline on himself and tried to set himself on fire, but police stopped him. At the start of the relay a protester rushed toward the Olympic flame and tried to unfurl a banner calling for China to respect the rights of North Korean refugees. Dozens of police surrounding the torch quickly whisked him away. Later, as it approached the city centre, another North Korean defector tried to impede the run and was arrested. Police said a total of five people, including a Chinese student, were arrested. There were no further attempts to stop the torch on its four-and-a-half-hour trip through Seoul to City Hall, where it was met by some 5,000 supporters … Scuffles broke out near the relay's start between a group of 500 Chinese supporters and about fifty demonstrators criticizing Beijing's policies. The students threw stones and water bottles at the others as some 2,500 police tried to keep the two sides apart … Before the relay two South Koreans who had been chosen to run said they would boycott it to protest China's recent crackdown on violent protests against Chinese rule in Tibet … After Seoul the torch was scheduled to fly to North Korea for its first-ever run in the communist state Monday [28 April].

(www.iht.com, 27 April 2008)

Thousands of young Chinese assembled to defend their country's Olympic torch relay pushed through police lines on Sunday [27 April], some of them hurling rocks, bottled water and plastic and steel pipes at protesters demanding better treatment for North Korean refugees in China. Two North Korean defectors living in South Korea poured paint thinner on themselves and tried to set themselves on fire in an attempt to protest what they condemned as Beijing's inhumane crackdown on North Korean refugees, but the police stopped them … The South Korean police and Chinese students also overpowered at least two other protesters who tried to impede the run … The route was kept secret until the last minute and guarded by more than 8,300 police officers … When lone protesters demanded that China stop repatriating North Korean refugees, they were quickly surrounded by jeering Chinese. Near the park Chinese students surrounded and beat a small group of protesters … In another scuffle, at the city centre where the five-hour torch run ended, Chinese surrounded several Tibetans and South Korean supporters who unfurled pro-Tibet banners, and kicked and punched them … The largest scuffle erupted after the first torchbearer left the Olympic Park … Many of the Chinese gathered at the park surged toward about 150 protesters, mostly old South Koreans and North Korean defectors, who were shouting 'No human rights, No Olympics' from across a boulevard. Armed with plastic shields the police scuffled with the Chinese as they tried to separate the two groups who were hurling objects at one another. At least one Chinese student was hauled away … The torch run stirred little interest among South Koreans in general.

(www.iht.com, 27 April 2008)

China heaped more criticism on the Dalai Lama and his followers on Sunday [27 April], accusing them of using empty words and concepts as a facade for their goal of independence … An editorial in the Communist Party's *People's Daily* newspaper: 'The Dalai clique has always been proficient in playing with words. They put forward different kinds of concepts to dazzle people … [But] there is only one key word behind them – Tibetan independence' … On Sunday China continued attacking the … Dalai Lama

> … and encouraged protesters against Tibetan self-rule as patriotic heroes … In Kathmandu, the Nepalese capital, the police detained 150 Tibetans who held a protest Sunday near the Chinese embassy visa office. The protesters, who were mostly Buddhist monks and nuns, were demanding the end of Chinese rule in Tibet.
>
> (www.iht.com, 27 April 2008)

> The Chinese Communist Party's official mouthpiece has poured fresh scorn on the Dalai Lama, only two days after the government's abrupt announcement that it would meet his aides within days. Tibetan exiles had greeted the announcement warily and the Dalai Lama's nephew, Khedroob Thondup, a member of the Tibetan parliament-in-exile, yesterday [27 April] attacked it as a 'ruse' designed 'to deflect pressure and give false assurance to Western leaders' … The *People's Daily* commentary: 'The Dalai clique have always been masters at games with words and the ideas that they have tossed about truly make the head spin … Those who split the nation are criminals to history' … The renewed attack came as a leading Tibetan official launched an extraordinarily frank condemnation of the handling of recent protests in Tibet. Bai Ma, Chairman of the Chinese People's Political Consultative Conference Committee in Qinghai province, said: 'It is regrettable that authorities in Lhasa failed to take firm action to control the situation during the first few hours of the 14 March riots … They did not have enough police. They had guns, but they could not open fire without permission from above' … He told the *South China Morning Post* that the situation at the Drepung and Sera monasteries in Lhasa remained tense because of the patriotic education programme targeting monks. He said: 'The heavy-handed and arbitrary tactics [of the government] only create more animosity' … Hong Kong this weekend barred a Danish artist, Jens Galschiot, and his two sons, who had planned to protest over human rights violations when the torch arrives this week.
>
> (*Guardian*, 28 April 2008, p. 16)

'A second Olympic flame arrived at Mount Everest base camp in Tibet' (www.bbc.co.uk, 27 April 2008).

28 April 2008.

> The Olympic torch held its first-ever run Monday in authoritarian North Korea, where the flame was assured of a trip free of the anti-Chinese protest that marked other legs of the relay … The torch arrived earlier Monday [28 April] in North Korea by plane from South Korea … An attentive and peaceful crowd of thousands watched the start of the relay in Pyongyang, some waving Chinese flags … The event was presided over by the head of the country's rubber-stamp parliament who often acts as a ceremonial state leader, Kim Yong Nam … Kim Jong Il was not seen at the event, but was 'paying great interest to the success of the Olympic torch relay', said Pak Hak Son, chairman of the North's Olympic committee … The North has been critical of disruptions to the torch relay elsewhere and has supported

> Beijing in its crackdown against violent protests in Tibet. North Korea is one of the world's most tightly controlled countries, where citizens are not allowed to travel freely and civil rights are highly restricted … The relay began from beneath the large sculpted flame that tops the obelisk of the Juche Tower, which commemorates the national ideology of 'self-reliance' created by Kim Il Sung … Kim Yong Nam passed the torch to the first runner, Pak Du Ik, who played in North Korea's 1966 World Cup soccer team that made a historic run to the quarterfinals. As he began the 20 kilometre (12 mile) route through Pyongyang, thousands more cheering people lined the city streets waving pink paper flowers and small flags with the Olympic logo and chanting 'Welcome! Welcome!' … Some people along the streets held banners reading 'North Korea–China Friendship' … Other torch bearers were also seen running through a Pyongyang street, escorted by several people in training suits and some vehicles, but there was notably lighter security than seen on other torch relay stops … The relay finished after about five hours at Kim Il Sung Stadium … [which] was filled with tens of thousands … The UN children's agency UNICEF had been asked to participate in the North Korean leg of the relay but withdrew in March, saying it was not sure the event would help its mission of raising awareness of conditions for children. North Korea's children are often the most at risk of starvation in the regular food shortages that plague the country.
>
> (www.iht.com, 28 April 2008; *IHT*, 29 April 2008, p. 4)

> Tens of thousands of flag-waving North Koreans lined the streets of Pyongyang … This is the first time the Olympic torch has come to North Korea … Kim Jong Il was not seen at the event, with the head of parliament, Kim Yong Nam, officiating at the starting ceremony. The first runner was Pak Du Ik, who played in North Korea's football team when it claimed a legendary victory against Italy in the 1966 World Cup … A peaceful crowd, some waving Chinese flags, watched the start of the relay and thousands more people, waving pink paper flowers and chanting 'Welcome' lined the torch's route.
>
> (www.bbc.co.uk, 28 April 2008)

'North Korea on Monday [28 April] played host for the first time to the Olympic torch, as large crowds in Pyonyang waved red and white flags and cheered the runners' (www.cnn.com, 28 April 2008).

> South Korea's deputy foreign minister Lee Yong Joon expressed strong regret over the clashes in a meeting Monday [28 April] with China's ambassador to Seoul, Ning Fukui. Ning also said he regretted the 'extreme behaviour' by some young Chinese and expressed his condolences to police and a journalist who was injured.
>
> (www.iht.com, 28 April 2008)

'On Monday [28 April] the [South Korean] government expressed "strong regret" to the Chinese ambassador over the incidents. On Tuesday [29 April] prime minister Han Seung Soo said they had "hurt national pride considerably"' (www.bbc.co.uk, 29 April 2008).

> The government of Nepal expelled the BBC from the base camp on the Nepalese side of Mount Everest. The Nepalese authorities have imposed a complete communication ban on journalists from the base camp onwards ... The flame is not coming anywhere near the Nepal base camp but an American man with a pro-Tibet flag was sent down from the camp last week and China is worried ... The upper parts of the mountain are closed until the torch has been and gone.
>
> (www.bbc.co.uk, 28 April 2008)

> The Hong Kong government denied entry Saturday evening [26 April] to three Danish human rights activists who had hoped to protest at the torch relay, detaining them for six hours and putting them against their will on a flight back to London. At least one Tibetan monk has reportedly been stopped on arrival and forced to fly elsewhere ... The Hong Kong Alliance in Support of Patriotic Democratic Movements in China, a group that commemorates the Tiananmen killings in 1989 and seeks human rights improvements in Hong Kong, held a small demonstration Monday [28 April] to protest the government's decision to block entry of the Danish activists ... The International Olympic Committee has moved all six Olympian equestrian events from Beijing to Hong Kong after Beijing was unable to satisfy international veterinary groups that horses brought into mainland China could be kept free of equine diseases ... Hong Kong's business elite – which was generally pro-Japanese during World War II, pro-British before and after the war, and now pro-Beijing – is trying to organize large rallies in favour of the Beijing Olympics.
>
> (www.iht.com, 28 April 2008; *IHT*, 29 April 2008, p. 4)

29 April 2008.

> A court in Tibet jailed seventeen people for taking part in riots in Lhasa ... The prison terms are reported to range from three years to life ... Tibet and the surrounding provinces where the riots took place have been closed to foreigners since the unrest.
>
> (www.bbc.co.uk, 29 April 2008)

'Nepal has deported an American mountaineer who was found on Mount Everest with a "Free Tibet" banner and has banned him from all climbing in the country for two years' (www.iht.com, 29 April 2008).

> Chinese state media said seventeen people have been sentenced to terms from three years to life for their roles in riots in Lhasa last month [March] ... Xinhua said Tuesday [29 April] that authorities reopened a Buddhist monastery in Lhasa to tourists. Tibet and the surrounding provinces where protests broke out have been closed to foreigners since the unrest.
>
> (www.iht.com, 29 April 2008)

'One of the men given a life term was a … driver for a local real estate company' (www.iht.com, 29 April 2008).

> The sentences were the first punishments meted out to those accused of taking part in the looting, vandalism and violence in Lhasa … The other man receiving a life sentence, a monk … was blamed for leading a group of ten people who attacked the police and destroyed shops and a government office. The others, including five monks, were sentenced to fifteen or twenty years. According to the government, the violence claimed nineteen lives and destroyed seven schools, five hospitals and 120 homes. Tibetan exile groups say more than 1,490 people, most of them Tibetans, have been killed in the government crackdown that followed. They also reject the government's contention that fewer than 100 people are awaiting trial … The Tibetan Centre for Human Rights and Democracy said … that 5,000 people had been detained in recent weeks.
>
> (www.iht.com, 29 April 2008)

> A Chinese court sentenced seventeen people, including six monks, to jail sentences ranging from three years to life imprisonment for their roles in riots in Lhasa last month [March] … Xinhua said Tuesday [29 April] that a monk led ten people – including five monks.
>
> (www.cnn.com, 29 April 2008)

> Thirty people, including six monks, have been jailed … Sentenced to life were … a driver with a Lhasa real estate company and a monk … from Doilungdegen county in the Lhasa region … Xinhua said … [the monk] led ten people – including five monks … of the five two were sentenced to twenty years and the other three to fifteen years.
>
> (www.guardian.co.uk, 29 April 2008)

> Six Buddhist monks are among the first to be jailed … receiving sentences ranging from life to fifteen years … The three people sentenced to life were a monk … a driver for a property company … and a businessman from a county outside Lhasa … The five monks [led by the monk] all received jail sentences. Two monks were sentenced to twenty years and three to fifteen … Seven people were sentenced to about fifteen years in prison and the other two received sentences of three to fourteen years.
>
> (*The Times*, 30 April 2008, p. 35)

> China's ambassador to Seoul, Ning Fukui, said [on 28 April] he regretted the 'extreme behaviour' of the Chinese protesters and offered sympathy to wounded South Koreans … The Chinese foreign ministry, however, refused Tuesday [29 April] to condemn the students' actions. It said pro-Tibet groups were to blame. A foreign ministry spokeswoman: 'As to the disruptions and sabotage by the separatist forces, some students upholding justice came out to safeguard the dignity of the torch – I believe that is natural' … Dozens of South Korean activists protested Tuesday near the Chinese

> embassy in Seoul, chanting angry slogans and holding placards that read: 'We condemn the Chinese government for promoting the violent protests' ... The South Korean foreign ministry said the Chinese embassy had asserted it was not behind the clashes.
>
> (www.iht.com, 29 April 2008)

> South Korea said Tuesday that it would deport Chinese citizens who assaulted demonstrators protesting Beijing's policies during the Olympic torch relay in Seoul ... The violence surrounding the relay on Sunday [27 April] triggered a flood of strong anti-China commentary by South Korean internet users.
>
> (www.iht.com, 29 April 2008)

> Hong Kong officials on Tuesday detained two pro-Tibet activists at the airport before the local leg of the Olympic torch relay. A spokeswoman for Students for Free Tibet, Lhadon Tethong, said that two fellow activists, Kate Woznow and Matt Whitticase, were detained ... Woznow said she was put on a return flight to New York.
>
> (www.iht.com, 29 April 2008)

> The Olympic torch arrived in Ho Chi Minh City in Vietnam for the final international stop ... The parade is expected to pass off fairly smoothly ... But a group of activists have promised demonstrations linked to a territorial dispute with Beijing ... Some activists say they will rally against China's claim to the disputed Spratly Islands ... After Vietnam the torch goes to Hong Kong to begin the domestic leg of the relay. International protests have turned the torch's celebratory tour of twenty countries into what analysts describe as a public-relations disaster for Beijing.
>
> (www.bbc.co.uk, 29 April 2008)

30 April 2008. '[It is announced that] two Tibetans – a policeman and a suspected protest leader – have been killed in a rare gunfight in north-western China after a raid to arrest the wanted man ... in a remote county in north-western Qinghai province' (*The Times*, 1 May 2008, p. 40).

> A policeman ... an ethnic Tibetan ... shot dead in a rare gun battle in a Chinese village was killed by outraged Tibetans after he opened fire on a young monk, local sources said. The story emerging from the remote village in north-western Qinghai contradicts the official report issued by state media, which claimed that the police officer had died in a hail of bullets as he tried to arrest an insurgent leader. The police officer arrived at the village ... and shot him ... After the monk was killed angry villagers turned on the police officer, the sources said. They fetched guns, commonly used in the area for hunting and also in provincial border disputes among Tibetans vying to collect caterpillar fungus for traditional herbal medicines, and shot the police officer ... [According to Xinhua, the police officer] was leading a raid to capture a ringleader of the 21 March demonstration when he was

shot dead. Other police then killed his assailant … Such gunfights are extremely rare in China, where very few people own guns and where violence against the police is unusual.

(*The Times*, 2 May 2008, p. 37)

A gun battle in a rural area of north-west China earlier this week left a policeman and Tibetan insurgent dead, according to state-run media. It was China's first official admission that any Tibetans have died in the anti-government unrest that began in mid-March. The incident occurred in Qinghai province after the police tried to arrest a man who they say led a group of herders seeking to incite a riot a week after the 14 March disturbances that shook Lhasa … Tibetan groups say that more than 200 people, most of them Tibetan, have died in the crackdowns … According to Xinhua, the bloodshed on Monday [28 April] began after members of the Qinghai public security bureau tried to detain men who officials described as 'insurgents seeking Tibetan independence'. It said the men … resisted arrest and in the ensuing gunfire a policeman was killed. The account did not indicate who shot the officer or whether the men being sought had weapons. Private gun ownership is extremely rare in China … In a report Wednesday [30 April] a Tibetan advocacy group based in the United States said that the government crackdown included sweeps of Tibetan monasteries, the arrests of 160 monks and a massive 'patriotic education' efforts to stamp out sympathy for the Dalai Lama and pro-independence sentiment. The group, the International Campaign for Tibet, said several distraught monks had committed suicide in recent weeks and that the authorities had destroyed or defaced religious imagery and photographs of the Dalai Lama, which are banned by the Chinese government.

(www.iht.com, 1 May 2008)

A milestone of sorts was reached on Wednesday [30 April] with the reporting in China's carefully controlled media of the death of a Tibetan in a clash with security forces … This was the very first such report of a Tibetan death since the outbreak in March of demonstrations by Tibetans in their 'autonomous region' and in the surrounding provinces where Tibetans live in large numbers.

(www.iht.com, 2 May 2008)

Protests erupted Thursday [30 April] outside Carrefour stores in Beijing and three other cities … Changsha in central China, Fuzhou in the south-east and Shenyang in the north-east … with hundreds of people waving banners and shouting slogans … No violence was reported … In Beijing police detained five men and two women … In Shanghai three university students stood outside a Carrefour handing out stickers … Carrefour outlets in a dozen Chinese cities were the target of earlier protests.

(www.iht.com, 1 May 2008)

On the first day of a planned boycott of the French department store Carrefour there were a few low-key protests around the country. But most outlets

> did brisk business … On Thursday [1 May], the start of a three-day national holiday, there were reports of small rallies at nearly a dozen Carrefour outlets around China, but the absence of any mammoth groundswell of protest, coupled with the throngs of unapologetic shoppers, suggested that the nationalistic fury may be petering out … The government has been working hard to dampen the anti-French zealotry. In recent days government ministers have gone on television reminding people that the 40,000 employees at the nation's 112 Carrefour stores are Chinese. Newspaper editorials have … [been] urging citizens to heartily embrace foreign friends, about 1.5 million of whom will be arriving in Beijing in August for the Summer Games … Text messages championing the boycott have been blocked [by state censors] and typing 'Carrefour' into search engines returned blank pages explaining that such results 'do not conform to relevant law and policy'. Still, a few protests drew hundreds of people to Carrefour stores in Xian, Chingqing, Shenyang and Changsha, although police made sure the rallies were brief. A demonstration in Fuzhou reportedly drew 1,000 people … In Beijing, which has nine Carrefour stores, store clerks said the crowds were noticeably thinner, especially for a holiday. The only reported protest in the capital was at a Carrefour that serves the city's university district … Carrefour cancelled advertising for a May Day holiday sale in an apparent effort to lower its public profile amid calls for a boycott and protests.
>
> (www.iht.com, 1 May 2008)

'[In] Carrefour shops in Beijing staff said business was slightly slower than could be expected for a holiday but was nonetheless busier than normal' (*FT*, 2 May 2008, p. 6).

'Hundreds of people have staged protests in four Chinese cities against the French supermarket chain Carrefour … A handful of people have been detained outside one store in the capital' (www.bbc.co.uk, 1 May 2008).

> The Olympic torch returned to Chinese soil Wednesday [30 April] after a twenty-nation tour, landing in Hong Kong, where officials deported at least seven protesters before the flame's arrival … protesters who were considered a threat to the relay … The deported activists included three pro-Tibet protesters who were kicked out of the territory as they arrived at the airport Tuesday [29 April]. A fourth activist – an activist for an independent Chinese writers' group – was also turned away on Tuesday. Three Danish activists were deported over the weekend.
>
> (www.iht.com, 30 April 2008)

> On Saturday [26 April] the Hong Kong government denied entry to three Danish human rights advocates who had hoped to protest at the torch relay, detaining them for six hours and then putting them against their will on a flight to London. A Tibetan monk was stopped on arrival at the airport over the weekend and forced to fly elsewhere … Three pro-Tibet activists were

> deported after they arrived at the airport in Hong Kong on Tuesday [29 April] … The Hong Kong Alliance in Support of Patriotic Democratic Movements of China, which commemorates the Tiananmen Square killings in 1989 and seeks human rights improvements in Hong Kong, held a small demonstration Monday [28 April] to protest the government's decision to block the entry of the Danish advocates … Official Chinese news media have exhorted citizens in recent days to 'defend the torch' in each city of the relay route.
>
> (www.iht.com, 30 April 2008)

> The Hollywood actress Mia Farrow was briefly questioned at Hong Kong's airport Thursday [1 May] before officials allowed her to enter … to give a speech criticizing China's relations with Sudan … Officials were concerned that she might cause problems during the event … Mia Farrow: 'They wanted some reassurance that we were not here to disrupt the torch relay, which, of course, we are not' … Mia Farrow speaks about Darfur on Friday [2 May].
>
> (www.iht.com, 1 May 2008)

'The local Law Society journal has declined to publish an article setting out a legal case for Tibetan independence' (www.iht.com, 1 May 2008). ('Paul Harris is a Hong Kong barrister and founding chairman of the Hong Kong Human Rights Monitor. This article [published in the *FEER* in May 2008] is adapted from an article originally commissioned and approved by the magazine of the Hong Kong Law Society, and then rejected as too sensitive after an extraordinary meeting of the society's editorial board': www.feer.com, 2 May 2008.)

2 May 2008.

> Thousands of people turned out in Hong Kong to watch the Olympic torch parade [lasting eight hours] through the streets. Many people waved Chinese flags and cheered, significantly outnumbering small groups of protesters holding pro-Tibet or pro-democracy placards … There were some reports of confrontations and scuffles between pro-China supporters and protesters, but the early stages of the relay appeared to have passed off smoothly. After Hong Kong the torch will go to Macao.
>
> (www.bbc.co.uk, 2 May 2008)

> Runners carried the Olympic flame through Hong Kong on Friday [2 May] as large groups of flag-waving supporters shouted insults at pro-Tibet and human rights protesters, forcing them to seek refuge in police vans … A small group carried protest signs that said 'Olympic flame for democracy' and 'Build a democratic China'. Another group of seven activists were overwhelmed by torch supporters … Many torchbearers were apparently from mainland China because they chanted slogans and hurled insults in Mandarin, not the local Cantonese dialect … In the past week authorities used a blacklist to stop seven pro-Tibet and human rights activists at the airport.

They were questioned and deported, in a tactic authorities typically use ahead of events involving high ranking Chinese leaders.

(www.iht.com, 2 May 2008)

Thousands of mainland Chinese and Hong Kong residents cheered the Olympic torch through the streets of Hong Kong on Friday [2 May] during the largely peaceful first leg of its three-month trip through China. A small crowd jeered, threw a few eggs and physically blocked a march by about twenty demonstrators who tried to follow the torch relay while calling for human rights and democracy in China. The police shielded the protesters as they walked to a nearby park and later finished their march by a different route … A Hong Kong university student who tried to wrap herself in a Tibetan flag … ended up in an argument with a defender of China and both were bundled away for safety reasons by the police, who did not file charges … A separate Olympic torch event, organized by Dream for Darfur … also came to Hong Kong on Friday, the first time that the official and unofficial torch relays have come to the same city. Mia Farrow, the Hollywood actress who is chairwoman of Dream for Darfur's advisory board, lighted a torch in front of the Hong Kong government's headquarters and demanded that the Chinese government put more pressure on its allies in Sudan to stop widespread killings and other human rights abuses in the Darfur region of Sudan … Mia Farrow acknowledged that Beijing officials had started to put some pressure on Sudan's government at the United Nations and through direct diplomatic pressure … Mia Farrow called for world leaders to boycott the opening ceremonies in Beijing but not the athletic events.

(www.iht.com, 2 May 2008)

'The Chinese … could have followed some International Olympic Committee chieftain's advice and not organized an international torch relay' (www.iht.com, 8 May 2008).

Two Tibetan envoys are to arrive in Beijing on Saturday [3 May] for talks on ending the crisis in Tibetan areas of China … A statement from the Dalai Lama's office in Dharamsala: '[The envoys] will convey His Holiness the Dalai Lama's deep concerns about the Chinese authorities' handling of the situation and also provide suggestions to bring peace to the region.'

(www.bbc.co.uk, 2 May 2008)

'The two envoys will arrive in China on Saturday [3 May] for "informal talks with representatives of the Chinese leadership", said a statement from the Dalai Lama's office' (www.iht.com, 2 May 2008).

The Tibetan government-in-exile in India announced Friday [2 May] that the two envoys were on their way to an undisclosed location in China for 'informal' discussions. But in a signal of low expectations the announcement predicted that the visit would be 'brief'. The envoys, based in Switzerland and the United States, were scheduled to reach China on Saturday

[3 May] … The Tibetan statement said: 'During this brief visit they will convey His Holiness the Dalai Lama's deep concerns about the Chinese authorities' handling of the situation and also provide suggestions to bring peace to the region' … Alongside the statement on the envoys' visit to China the Tibetan administration in India sent out a list of Tibetans it said had been killed or beaten and arrested in China in recent weeks. In the same statement it condemned what it called the 'arbitrary sentences' China handed down on Tuesday [29 April] for thirty Tibetans, with terms ranging from three years to life in prison for convictions on charges that include attacking the police, burning vehicles and looting stores. The Tibetan statement said the defendants were given no more than a 'pretence of a fair trial'. Last week the government-in-exile greeted China's offer of dialogue by saying the crackdown inside Tibet would have to stop if talks were to be meaningful. On Friday [2 May] a spokesman for the Dalai Lama, Tenzin Takhla, went further by saying he hoped 'the Chinese recognize a majority of Tibetan people have deep resentments against Chinese policies'. From the Chinese side vitriol continued throughout the week as editorials in the press again painted the Dalai Lama as an instigator of violence inside Tibet. An opinion article in the *China Daily* said he and his followers were 'seeking to revive theocracy, the darkest and the cruellest system in Tibetan history'. On Tuesday a foreign ministry referred to him as 'the Dalai'.

(www.iht.com, 3 May 2008)

The secretary to the Dalai Lama said: 'During this brief visit the envoys will take up the urgent issue of the current crisis in the Tibetan areas' … Special envoy Lodi Gyaltsen Gyari and envoy Kelsang Gyaltsen will represent the Dalai Lama at the talks.

(www.cnn.com, 3 May 2008)

Thubten Samphel [the Dalai Lama's spokesman]: 'They [the envoys] will convey deep concerns over how the Chinese authorities are dealing with the current crisis and we will provide suggestions about how peace could be restored in the region' … However, he said that the future of Tibet would not be part of the discussions. Saying that the six rounds of talks over the issue had ended in the summer of 2006 because of 'a feeling that the Chinese were taking too hard-line, too inflexible a stance', Samphal said that the 'larger issues could perhaps be resolved in later talks' … The Tibetan government-in-exile has sent its two main envoys, both of whom have had past meetings with the Chinese government: Lodi Gyaltsen Gyari, based in Washington DC, and Kelsang Gyaltsen, the representative of the Dalai Lama based in Switzerland.

(www.guardian.co.uk, 3 May 2008)

3 May 2008.

Chinese state media renewed its criticism of the Dalai Lama as two of his envoys prepared to meet Chinese officials … Sunday's talks [4 May] will be the first such contact since the protests ... The meeting would take place in the southern city of Shenzhen.

(www.bbc.co.uk, 3 May 2008)

The 2008 Olympic torch relay wrapped up in the Chinese territory of Macao with a glittering show on Saturday [3 May], even as officials said weather conditions may force a delay of a torch run up Mount Everest, the world's highest peak ... Everest is located in Nepal and the Chinese region of Tibet ... It would be the first time the Olympic flame has scaled the mountain ... The torch run in Macao came to a spectacular finish amid casino lights and a fireworks show on Saturday. The former Portuguese colony, which came under Chinese rule in 1999, is the last stop for the torch before reaching mainland China. It was expected there Saturday night. The run was completed in Macao without incident. Security was tight, however.

(www.cnn.com, 4 May 2008)

4 May 2008. 'The Olympic torch has started its tour of mainland China ... [in] the resort of Sanya, on Hainan Island ... The torch is scheduled to visit every province in China before arriving in Beijing several days before the Olympics begin' (www.bbc.co.uk, 4 May 2008).

Envoys for the Dalai Lama began a series of meetings Sunday [4 May] with Chinese leaders ... Later in the week the two sides will carry out further meetings. President Hu Jintao told Japanese reporters Sunday that: 'I am confident that through joint efforts by both sides this visit will be able to achieve the expected results.'

(www.cnn.com, 4 May 2008)

'The official Chinese media has continued its attacks on what it calls the "Dalai clique" ... By contrast, Japanese media quoted President Hu Jintao as saying he hoped the talks would achieve "positive results"' (www.bbc.co.uk, 4 May 2008).

President Hu Jintao said he was hoping for 'positive results' from talks with envoys of the Dalai Lama that opened Sunday [4 May] ... Hu Jintao: 'When determining a person's position we must not only listen to what he says but also watch his deeds. The door to dialogue has always been open. We sincerely hope the Dalai side can show through action that they have genuinely stopped separatist activities, stopped plots to incite violence [and stopped trying to] sabotage [the Olympics] ... [These steps will] create conditions for the next rounds of dialogue' ... Hu added that he had hope 'contacts this time will yield positive results' ... Tenzin Takhla (a senior aide to the Dalai Lama): 'The meeting took place this morning [4 May]. It will continue tomorrow [Monday] and possibly the day after' ... Xinhua identified the Chinese negotiators as Zhu Weiqun and Sitar, both vice ministers of the Communist Party's United Front Work Department and responsible for winning over religious leaders and ethnic minorities ... China says the rioting in Lhasa in March had killed eighteen 'innocent civilians' and a

> police officer. It has not specified how many, if any, protesters have died, but the government said that troops used maximum restraint and avoided using lethal weapons … The [Tibetan] government-in-exile estimated last week that 203 Tibetans might have died in the unrest since 10 March.
>
> (www.iht.com, 4 May 2008; *IHT*, 5 May 2008, p. 4)

5 May 2008. 'Chinese officials and representatives of the Dalai Lama ended day-long talks without a breakthrough but agreed to more talks, Chinese state media said. The two sides would hold further dialogue at "an appropriate time", Xinhua news agency reported' (www.bbc.co.uk, 5 May 2008).

> The Dalai Lama says he is not so concerned about redrawing Tibet's political boundaries to include all ethnic Tibetan areas adjoining it (an idea he once backed strongly, to China's horror). The priority, he says, is to protect the culture and environment of Tibetans. But China will want a stronger retraction than this. It believes the Dalai Lama is still intent on carving out a single Tibetan territory covering a quarter of China's land area.
>
> (*The Economist*, 10 May 2008, p. 79)

6 May 2008. See the entry in the political chronology, Chapter 8, starting on 6 May for the five-day visit to Japan by President Hu Jintao.

8 May 2008.

> The Olympic flame has reached the top of the world … the top of Mount Everest … The Olympic flame had been carried up to the tallest peak in a special metal canister. As the flame neared the summit, they used a wand to pass the flame from the canister to the torch, which had been designed to withstand the frigid, windy, oxygen-thin air … The climbing team reached the summit exactly three months before the 8 August [the eighth month] ceremony [eight being a lucky number in China] … China persuaded Nepal, a long-time recipient of Chinese aid, to keep climbers off its side of Everest for the first half of May.
>
> The nineteen-member final assault team was comprised of both ethnic Han Chinese and Tibetan members … The team captain and the final torch-bearer were both Tibetans … The Everest flame is separate from the main Olympic torch … The main flame will cross every region and province of China, returning to Beijing on 6 August, two days ahead of the opening ceremony … [There had been] days of weather-related delays at Everest base camp … The summit attempt had been repeatedly delayed because of bad weather … On Thursday [8 May] the Free Tibet Campaign, an overseas group advocating Tibetan independence, said on its website that the torch relay up Everest was a 'callous attempt' by China to 'legitimize its baseless claims to sovereignty over Tibet'.
>
> (www.iht.com, 8 May 2008)

'The first and last of the [Everest] torchbearers were Tibetan women' (www.bbc.co.uk, 8 May 2008).

'Five climbers, two of them women, staged the relay ... The team was composed of twenty-two Tibetans, eight ethnic Han Chinese and a man from the Tuijia minority' (*Independent*, 9 May 2008, p. 26).

'Twenty-two of the thirty-one-strong [Everest] team were Tibetans' (www.guardian.co.uk, 8 May 2008).

> Nepal has reopened the summit of Mount Everest to climbers on its side ... [but] 'liaison officers' will continue to carry out security checks on climbers' baggage ... On Thursday [8 May] there were more angry scenes outside the Chinese embassy in Kathmandu as demonstrators tried to break through a security cordon. A number were detained.
>
> (www.bbc.co.uk, 8 May 2008)

> Lodi Gyari (a spokesman for the Dalai Lama, commenting on the talks in China): 'We have called for the release of prisoners, to allow those injured to be given proper medical treatment and give unfettered access to visitors, including the media. We have also called for an end to the "patriotic reeducation campaign" ... We disagreed more than we agreed. Our counterparts made baseless allegations against the Dalai Lama for derailing and sabotaging the Beijing Olympics. But we made it very clear that the Dalai Lama supported the Olympics from day one.'
>
> (www.iht.com, 8 May 2008)

'Officials in Dharamsala ... deny the Shenzhen meeting was a continuation of confidence-building discussions held between 2002 and July 2007

> Rather [said Lodi Gyari] it was an 'emergency conversation' about the present crisis. Mr Gyari said only the next round of talks would count as the resumption of a formal dialogue. The Tibetans had several demands: an end to the clampdown in Tibet, including the withdrawal of security forces from monasteries; no more 'patriotic education' requiring monks to denounce the Dalai Lama; an investigation by an international body into the causes of the unrest; the release of political detainees, and fair trials for those accused of rioting.
>
> (*The Economist*, 10 May 2008, p. 79)

11 May 2008.

> Police detained more than 600 female Tibetan protesters, including many Buddhist nuns, on Sunday [11 May] after breaking up several demonstrations against China's recent crackdown. It was the largest number of protesters detained on a single day since Tibetan exiles began almost daily protests in March against Chinese policies in Tibet and the first time that only women demonstrated. The protesters held three separate rallies in Kathmandu but were quickly stopped by police. More than 600 protesters were being held in detention centres in Kathmandu ... Nepal's police have broken up almost all anti-China protests by Tibetan exiles during the past several weeks and detained participants ... The Tibetan exiles have mainly

been protesting in front of the United Nations offices and the Chinese embassy in Kathmandu.

(www.iht.com, 11 May 2008)

12 May 2008.

The Dalai Lama said Monday [12 May] that formal talks between his envoys and their Chinese counterparts were expected to take place next month [June], even as Chinese officials kept up their public denunciations of the exiled Tibetan spiritual leader … The talks, for which exact dates have not yet been fixed, would represent the seventh round of talks since 2002 between the two sides. They follow what the Dalai Lama's aides described as emergency consultations in Shenzhen … Samdhong Lobsang Tenzin Rinpoche, the elected head of the government-in-exile, said later Monday that the delegation this time would have five or six Tibetan representatives and that they would try to propose an agenda for substantial negotiations for Tibet … The Dalai Lama said he had offered, in a letter to President Hu Jintao last March, to help pacify the protests inside Tibet, but had not received a response. The Dalai Lama said: 'My letter to Hu Jintao mentioned that. We are ready to send some people there and cool down the situation.'

(www.iht.com, 12 May 2008)

The president and foreign minister of Germany are refusing to meet the Dalai Lama, who arrives Friday [16 May] as part of a tour of European capitals that will include London, where he is to see prime minister Gordon Brown … Chancellor Angela Merkel, who broke ranks with previous German leaders by meeting the Dalai Lama last September [2007], is leaving Tuesday [13 May] on a week-long visit to Latin America. Merkel said last week she would be prepared to meet him again but did not specify a date.

(*IHT*, 13 May 2008, p. 3)

15 May 2008.

The Dalai Lama today [Thursday 15 May] expressed sadness at the deaths … in an earthquake [which struck on 12 May] and announced a prayer meeting for the victims. He arrived in Frankfurt to begin a five-day tour of Germany … A political row has erupted in Germany over the visit as senior figures, including foreign minister Frank-Walter Steinmeier and President Horst Köhler have declined to meet the Dalai Lama … Chancellor Angela Merkel will not meet the Dalai Lama as she is travelling to Latin America. However, the government announced that cabinet minister Heidemarie Wieczorek-Zeul, responsible for development issues, will meet him on Monday [19 May].

(www.independent.co.uk, 15 May 2008)

In March Tibetans burned 1,000 Chinese-owned shops (with a few people inside) and savagely attacked or stoned ordinary Chinese citizens, even a child

> of about ten … Last Month [April] the Chinese authorities ushered a group of journalists on a tightly scripted tour to show that Labrang [monastery in Xiahe] was calm – and then fifteen monks rushed up to the group. One was crying and all said that their human rights were systematically violated. After the reporters left those who joined that peaceful protest were imprisoned, beaten and in some cases subjected to electric shock torture, the monks say.
>
> (www.iht.com, 15 May 2008)

(For the effects of the 12 May earthquake on the torch relay, see the entry in the political chronology, Chapter 8.)

16 May 2008.

> The twenty-two-year-old living Buddha … arrived in New York … He had begun an eighteen-day visit to the United States … The Seventeenth Gyalwang Karmapa, Ogyen Trinley Dorje, [is] one of the most important leaders in Tibetan Buddhism … He made headlines across the world at age fourteen with his daring escape from China to India across the Himalayas in [December] 1999 … The [Indian] government officially accepted him as a refugee in 2001 … His followers regard him not only as the reincarnation of his predecessor, the Sixteenth Karmapa, Rangjung Rigpe Dorje, who died in 1981, but also as the seventeenth incarnation of the first Karmapa in the twelfth century, in an unbroken lineage going back 900 years. They revere him as leader of the Kagyu sect – called the black hat or black crown sect – one of the four major schools of Tibetan Buddhism. The Karmapa has been traditionally recognized as the third most important figure in Tibetan Buddhism after the Dalai Lama and the Panchen Lama … Ogyen Trinley Dorje is but one of two claimants to the title of Karmapa in the Kagyu tradition. A rival, Trinley Thaye Dorje, made a tour of Europe several years ago … The US followers of Ogyen Trinley Dorje point to his recognition by both the Chinese government and the Dalai Lama … The Chinese have not excoriated him as they have the Dalai Lama.
>
> (www.iht.com, 16 May 2008)

('Since March no Politburo member has publicly visited Tibet': *The Economist*, 17 May 2008, p. 71.)

18 May 2008.

> The Dalai … [said] in Nuremberg [Germany] that religious tolerance is imperative and … [that] it was tragic that religious differences often lead to bloodshed … He said: 'We need all the different religions to serve the people, because the people are different and have different goals' … Before the Dalai Lama spoke, Wolfgang Grader, leader of the Tibet Initiative Deutschland, called for more support for Tibetans. Grader said that Tibetans face more persecution now than in decades. He said some 5,000 Tibetans are in prison, most of them unjustly.
>
> (www.iht.com, 18 May 2008)

'On Sunday [18 May] more than 7,000 people turned up at a rally in Nuremberg where the Dalai Lama gave a rousing speech calling for greater religious tolerance' (www.bbc.co.uk, 19 May 2008).

19 May 2008. '[In Berlin] the Dalai Lama … met the country's economic and development minister, Heidemarie Wieczorek-Zeul … His trip [to Germany] has exposed sharp divisions with Chancellor Angela Merkel's government' (www.bbc.co.uk, 19 May 2008).

> The original venue was to have been the ministry but that was changed, apparently to play down the official nature of the occasion. Nevertheless, Heidemarie Wieczorek-Zeul said she was not going to talk to the Dalai Lama as a private citizen. She said: 'I am a member of the federal government.'
>
> (www.iht.com, 19 May 2008)

'Heidemarie Wieczorek-Zeul [is] a member of [foreign minister] Frank-Walter Steinmeier's Social Democratic Party' (*IHT*, 21 May 2008, p. 4).

'The Dalai Lama was received only by the lowly development minister and in a hotel rather than in her office' (*The Independent*, 20 May 2008, p. 26).

'[Some] 25,000 turned out at the Brandenburg Gate in Berlin to hear the Dalai Lama express his condolences to China over the earthquake' (*IHT*, 1 May 2008, p. 4).

> The British government has … [arranged for prime minister] Gordon Brown to meet the Dalai Lama [on Friday 23 May] at Lambeth Palace and not at Downing Street. By holding the meeting at the home of the Archbishop of Canterbury, the government is underscoring that it sees the Dalai Lama as a spiritual leader.
>
> (*FT*, 20 May 2008, p. 12)

20 May 2008.

> The Dalai Lama is due to arrive in London at the start of a ten-day visit … [He] will address parliament and give evidence on human rights to a parliamentary committee during his trip. Prime minister Gordon Brown will not receive him at 10 Downing Street but is due to meet him with the Archbishop of Canterbury at Lambeth Palace on Friday [23 May].
>
> (www.bbc.co.uk, 20 May 2008)

> During an eleven-day visit … the Dalai Lama … will meet [prime minister] Gordon Brown only at a scheduled encounter with the Archbishop of Canterbury, Rowan Williams, at what the prime minister's office has called 'an inter-faith dialogue with several other religious leaders'. But, breaking with a tradition established by two former British prime ministers – John Major and Tony Blair – Brown will not receive the Dalai Lama at 10 Downing Street, his official residence … The Dalai Lama is on a three-month tour of five countries, including the United States … [and] Germany.
>
> (www.iht.com, 20 May 2008)

21 May 2008.

The Chinese government is refusing to issue visas to Hindus trying to make the traditional summer pilgrimage to what they hold to be the home of Lord Shiva in Tibet, forcing thousands to delay or cancel the trip. Starting in June Hindus from Nepal and India embark on a multi-week journey … The trip [is] a once-in-a-lifetime event for most who make it … This year [2008] the Chinese government is refusing to grant any visas for travel to the Tibetan sites from Nepal, tour operators in Nepal say. The Indian foreign ministry said Tuesday [20 May] that the Chinese government cited unspecified 'domestic reasons' for the cancellation … The Olympic torch is scheduled to go through Lhasa on 20 June.

(www.iht.com, 21 May 2008)

The Dalai Lama (in London): 'I appeal particularly to inside Tibet to not disturb … the torch when they visit. I made clear right from the beginning we fully support Olympic Games. The Olympic torch is part of that. We must respect, we must protect that' … The Dalai Lama is expected to make a speech at the Albert Hall on Thursday [22 May]. Buddhist protesters are expected to target this, as well as his meeting with [prime minister] Gordon Brown. The protests will be staged by the Western Shugden Society, which is calling for freedom to worship seventeenth-century monk Dorje Shugden. The Dalai Lama has rejected worship of Dorje Shugden, saying it is an evil force.

(www.bbc.co.uk, 21 May 2008)

The Dalai Lama today [21 May] called for Tibetans to end protests against the Beijing Olympics, also telling MPs in London he would happily accept an invitation to attend the event if relations with China improved … His government-in-exile called for a temporary halt to all protests against Chinese rule over the territory while Beijing deals with the aftermath of the Sichuan earthquake … The government, based in the northern Indian town of Dharamsala, urged Tibetans not to demonstrate for at least a month … The statement said: 'In order to express our solidarity with the great natural disaster that befell on China, Tibetans across the world should shun demonstrations in front of the Chinese embassies in the respective host countries they live in' … Citing advice from the Dalai Lama, the statement encouraged Tibetans to 'explore the possibilities of establishing Sino-Tibetan friendship associations' … The Dalai Lama (in London): 'I appeal particularly to Tibetans. They should not disrupt the torch. I have made clear from the beginning we fully support the Olympic Games. The Olympic torch is part of that. We must protect it … I have no indication about an invitation to the Olympic Games. Some Chinese want me to go there. If the situation in Tibet were to improve and there was a long-term solution, then I am ready to go to the Olympic Games … The president himself [Hu Jintao] acknowledged that meeting [of 4 May] and he expressed seriousness about that meeting. That never happened in the past. After the next meeting and also after the Olympics I think we can see whether the Chinese government's desire to meet our people was only for the Olympics or more serious.'

(www.guardian.co.uk, 21 May 2008)

The Dalai Lama went out of his way to praise the response of the Chinese authorities to the Sichuan earthquake ... He said: 'I appeal, particularly inside Tibet, [people] should not disrupt the Olympic torch when they visit. We must respect, we must protect that.'

(www.independent.co.uk, 21 May 2008)

Last night [21 May] it emerged that the Dalai Lama had sent his personal representatives to the Chinese embassy in London where they paid their condolences to the victims of the recent Chinese earthquake. Beijing's decision to allow representatives of the spiritual leader to be received at one of its overseas embassies in this way is very unusual.

(*FT*, 22 May 2008, p. 9)

22 May 2008. 'The Dalai Lama told the foreign affairs committee [of the British parliament] ... his people were facing a form of "cultural genocide" at the hands of China' (www.bbc.co.uk, 25 May 2008).

23 May 2008.

The Dalai Lama said he had been informed by Tibetan residents that large areas of empty land had been marked out, as if for construction, in the past two years. The Dalai Lama: 'Then last year [2007] we received information – after the Olympics 1 million Chinese are going to settle in the autonomous region of Tibet. There is every danger Tibet becomes a truly Han Chinese land and Tibetans become an insignificant minority. Then the very basis of the idea of autonomy becomes meaningless' ... There has been an increasing influx of Chinese settlers into Tibet in recent years as transport has improved, but the exact figures are a matter of dispute. According to an official census in 2000, there were 2.4 million Tibetans in the region and 159,000 Han Chinese. The government-in-exile says there are more Chinese if migrant workers and soldiers are counted. The Dalai Lama says there is a Han majority in Lhasa ... Rivers flowing out of the Tibetan highlands include the Yangtze, the Yellow River, the Indus, the Mekong and the Ganges. The Dalai Lama: 'Due to carelessness these waters have been polluted and also reduced and I think billions of people's lives depend on these rivers ... [There has been] mining without proper care, deforestation ... irrigation without proper planning. In some valleys new diseases have developed which some specialists believe is the result of water pollution' ... The next talks between representatives of the Dalai Lama and China are scheduled for Beijing on 11 June.

(*Guardian*, 24 May 2008, p. 22)

The Dalai Lama:

> My efforts have failed to bring concrete results so criticism is becoming stronger and stronger ... If the violence grows out of control my only choice is to resign ... [In recent times many Tibetans have been showing] clear signs of frustration [with the lack of progress in talks with the Chinese] ... There are many Tibetans who have the view that our non-violent approach is not having an effect ... Is this [the Chinese talking Tibetan representatives] only being done for the Olympics or to deal with the real situation of Tibet? I do not know ... [What I want is just] realistic autonomy ... [for the current] Tibet Autonomous Region [not for historic Tibet] ... What we are seeking is genuine implementation of the rights of the [Tibetan] minorities. They are facing elimination of their culture and language. We are acting on behalf of all of them.'
>
> (*FT*, 26 May 2008, pp. 1, 5)

30 May 2008.

> Beijing's official tourism body is urging tour operators to stop selling holidays to France, the French foreign ministry has said ... However, Beijing said that it had 'simply reminded Chinese tourists to be careful about their security'. Estimates suggest that about 700,000 tourists from mainland China visited France last year [2007].
>
> (www.bbc.co.uk, 1 June 1008)

3 June 2008.

> Two prominent human rights lawyers have lost their licences after volunteering to defend Tibetans charged in the violent anti-China protests that erupted in March ... The two lawyers, Teng Biao and Jiang Tianyong, are known for taking on politically contentious cases, including those alleging official abuses of human rights ... The action against the two lawyers came after human rights groups say authorities initially considered denying licence renewals for numerous lawyers, only to relent in the cases other than those of Teng and Jiang ... In April [2008] eighteen lawyers signed a public letter volunteering free legal services to Tibetans arrested during an official crackdown against protests in western China. State media reported that thirty Tibetans, represented by government-appointed lawyers, were given sentences from three years to life during trials in April. Teng said Beijing judicial authorities were not pleased with the offer of free legal counsel and later warned the lawyers not to get involved in the Tibetan situation. By May Teng said his law firm applied for its standard annual renewal of licences. But the firm's licences were suspended. Teng said: 'They just informed my boss that I was the reason the whole firm was in trouble' ... But on 29 May authorities lifted the suspension and granted renewals for the other sixty or so lawyers in the firm.
>
> (www.iht.com, 3 June 2008; *IHT*, 4 June 2008, p. 8)

> Thubten Samphel, spokesman for the Tibetan government-in-exile said … Beijing officials had stopped ordinary Tibetans from leaving China for Nepal and India. He added that occasional protests by monks and nuns were continuing – even if they were quickly stopped by Chinese security forces. The Free Tibet Campaign said fifty-four nuns were arrested a few weeks ago after staging a protest in Garze county in Sichuan province. It said the nuns were angry because they were being forced to denounce the Dalai Lama … The Tibetan government-in-exile said about 250 died, most of whom were Tibetans killed in the ensuing crackdown.
>
> (www.bbc.co.uk, 4 June 2008)

5 June 2008.

> The police in Tibet have arrested sixteen Buddhist monks and accused them of involvement in three bombings. A police spokesman in north-eastern Tibet said Thursday [5 June]. All three bombings involved the use of home-made explosives and did property damage without killing or wounding anyone … Xinhua reported Thursday that the Tibet Department of Public Security had arrested the sixteen monks on 12 and 13 May in connection with bombings on 5, 8 and 15 April in villages near Qamdo. All the detainees have since admitted their guilt, according to Xinhua.
>
> (www.iht.com, 5 June 2008)

11 June 2008.

> The Dalai Lama arrived in Australia for a five-day visit … The Dalai Lama will deliver a series of lectures and meet immigration minister Chris Evans, acting head of government while leader Kevin Rudd is in Japan … Some human rights groups have criticized Mr Rudd for failing to meet the Dalai Lama. He will instead meet Mr Evans in Sydney on Friday [13 June] … Early in May [2008] … Chinese officials held talks with two envoys of the Dalai Lama. But a second round of talks set for this week was postponed following the devastating earthquake in Sichuan province … Chinese foreign minister Yang Jiechi (Tuesday 10 June): 'We maintain that the Dalai Lama's side must halt the separatist activity, ending violent acts of destruction against China, halt its activity to ruin the Olympics, [thereby] creating the conditions for further meetings.'
>
> (www.bbc.co.uk, 11 June 2008)

13 June 2008.

> Germany's foreign minister urged China on Friday [13 June] to hold further talks with envoys of the Dalai Lama. Frank-Walter Steinmeier and his Chinese counterpart, Yang Jiechi, also said they agreed to restart regular meetings on issues including climate change and human rights … Steinmeier earlier publicly rebuked German Chancellor Angela Merkel for meeting with the Dalai Lama and has criticized aspects of her foreign policy, particularly her blunt approach to issues in relations with Russia and China.
>
> (www.iht.com, 13 June 2008)

'Steinmeier said that he hoped more talks would resume soon between China and the Dalai Lama's representatives, and that "this will also lead to progress on advancing and protecting Tibetans' culture and religion"' (www.iht.com, 14 June 2008).

16 June 2008.

> The authorities in ... Xinjiang are telling people who want to watch the Olympic torch as it passes through the area to stay at home and tune in to the television instead. Spectators ... were also banned from climbing trees or gathering on bridges under which the flame will pass, state media said Monday [16 June] ... A three-day tour of Tibet was supposed to precede this leg, but the schedule was altered after a three-day suspension due to the earthquake in Sichuan. A curtailed trip to the Himalayan region will now follow after the torch leaves Xinjiang.
>
> (www.iht.com, 16 June 2008)

17 June 2008.

> Security was tight as the Olympic torch began passing through China's mainly Moslem Xinjiang region ... Police were out in force as the flame left People's Square in the capital, Urumqi, on its run around the city. The torch will spend three days in the region, which is home to around 8 million Moslem Uighur people ... Uighurs are the largest ethnic group, making up 8 million of the region's population of 20 million ... The relay has been moved forward by a week, in an apparent attempt to avoid unrest. The torch's visit to ... Lhasa has also been moved up ... The Chinese authorities announced extra security measures ahead of the torch relay in Urumqi, including random vehicle checks and a ban on firecrackers ... Many local people were asked to stay away ... Spectators were told not to watch the relay over footbridges or shout slogans that would 'harm the nation or the relay cities' in Xinjiang ... The majority of the crowd that gathered in the square [in Urumqi] were Han Chinese.
>
> (www.bbc.co.uk, 17 June 2008)

18 June 2008.

> China's torch relay moved on to the ancient Silk Road city of Kashgar on the second day of its journey through the mainly Xinjiang region. Hundreds of police lined the streets ... Officials fear separatists may target the relay but its run in Xinjiang's capital Urumqi on Tuesday [17 June] was calm. The relay was moved forward by one week in an apparent attempt to avoid unrest. In Beijing Olympic organizers confirmed that the torch will reach Tibet on Saturday [21 June]. A planned three-day stay there has been cut to one day ... The relay will run through Lhasa ... Kashgar is seen as one of the main Islamic centres in the region – more so than Urumqi, where Tuesday's relay passed off peacefully ... There was a huge security presence, with police searching people thoroughly ... As in Urumqi some residents

> told the BBC they had been told to stay at home and watch the relay on television … After the torch's run through the Silk Road oasis city of Kasgar, it moves on to the cities of Shihezi and Changjii on Thursday [19 June].
>
> (www.bbc.co.uk, 18 June 2008)

> More than 1,000 Tibetans detained during protests against the Chinese government remain unaccounted for, Amnesty International says. In a report the human rights group said there were reports that detainees had been beaten and deprived of food … The Dalai Lama has appealed for Tibetans not to protest during the Olympic torch visit to the region … [He] recently said he was fully supportive of the Games … and therefore the torch.
>
> (www.bbc.co.uk, 19 June 2008)

19 June 2008. 'Kevin Rudd, Australia's prime minister, said yesterday [19 June] he would attend the Beijing Olympics' (*FT*, 21 June 2008, p. 6).

20 June 2008.

> China has released more than 1,000 people involved in unrest in Tibet earlier this year [2008], Chinese media say … Those freed had been held for minor offences connected with the unrest in March. The announcement came one day before the Olympic torch reaches Lhasa … The announcement on the detainees came a day after rights group Amnesty International called for Beijing to account for those who were still in jail after the unrest … It was not clear the figure … [of] 1,157 … referred to the total of detainees freed since March [2008] or a newly released group of prisoners … [It was] also said twelve people had been sentenced for crimes related to the unrest, but did not specify the offences or the punishments … A total of forty-two people had now been punished over the March protests … Chinese security forces have been patrolling in the main square of Lhasa in the run-up to the torch's arrival.
>
> (www.bbc.co.uk, 20 June 2008)

'Xinhua quoted a senior official as saying 116 people remained in custody awaiting trial over the unrest' (www.bbc.co.uk, 21 June 2008).

> On Friday [20 June] Palma Trily … the vice governor of Tibet's Chinese-appointed administration … said that twelve more people had been sentenced for taking part in a 14 March riot in Lhasa … He gave no details about their offences or the punishments meted out. Palma Trily said another 1,157 people had been released from detention over minor offences related to the violent anti-government protests.
>
> (www.cnn.com, 21 June 2008)

> Lhasa was under tight security on Friday [20 June] … As a group of foreign journalists arrived to observe the relay the police stood on guard every 200 metres, or about 600 feet. Trucks full of troops and riot police could also be seen … Tenzin Takhla (a senior aide to the Dalai Lama): 'Since this is a

> proud moment for the people of China, the Dalai Lama has appealed to Tibetans not to protest.'
>
> (www.iht.com, 21 June 2008)

21 June 2008.

> The Olympic torch has been carried through Lhasa amid heavy security. The 11 kilometre (7 mile) parade passed off smoothly, with the flame carried past apparently hand-picked spectators … There was a staggering security presence in the city … Reporters representing about thirty international news organizations were allowed into the city in a closely monitored group to cover the torch relay … Each member of the crowd had a badge, suggesting that spectators were specially chosen or vetted for the ceremony … A planned three-day stay in Tibet was cut to one day because of scheduled adjustments linked to last month's Sichuan earthquake.
>
> (www.bbc.co.uk, 21 June 2008)

'The Olympic torch made its way without trouble Saturday [21 June] through Lhasa … During the Lhasa leg the Olympic flame was united with the one that was carried to the summit of Everest last month [May]' (www.cnn.com, 21 June 2008).

'The main Olympic torch was reunited with a separate [Everest] flame … [in a] cauldron' (*The Times*, 23 June 2008, p. 32).

> Hundreds of police and paramilitary troops stood watch and hand-picked onlookers cheered as the Olympic torch passed through Lhasa on Saturday [21 June] … No disruptions were reported, although the mood was far more subdued than at the torch's earlier stops in cities in China proper … The relay saw the main torch reunited with a separate one carried to the top of Mount Everest, with just under half of the 156 runners ethnic Tibetan … The torch has so far had a smooth run in China … The torch next travels to neighbouring Qinghai province, also hit this spring by protests in Tibetan-dominated areas, before gradually winding its way across northern China toward Beijing on 8 August. The Tibetan leg was cut from three days to one, ostensibly to make way for a 3–5 August visit to Sichuan province, the centre of a 12 May earthquake that killed nearly 70,000 people. Lhasa, which has been under a security lockdown since the March riots, all but closed down for the relay, with streets deserted and shops closed … Officers lined the route at intervals of as little as 10 feet, while badge-wearing onlookers, who had been carefully screened and individually approved beforehand, waved flags and chanted 'Go China'. A few dozen foreign reporters given special permission to cover the Lhasa leg were required to travel in a closely guarded convoy. They were only allowed to cover the opening and closing portions, isolating them from contact with ordinary residents. Almost all foreign visitors have been banned from the region since the protests, hamstringing the local tourism industry … Beijing organizers allowed only groups of selected journalists to attend the relays in Xinjiang

> and Tibet … Thubten Samphel (the official spokesperson of the exiled Tibetan government) said on Saturday (21 June): 'The Dalai Lama has been supportive of the Beijing Olympics and believes that China deserves to host the Olympics. Since the torch relay is part of the Olympics he has asked the people in Tibet to respect the event' … In a report that could not be confirmed, a Hong Kong-based monitoring group said 7,000 troops had been dispatched to stand guard along the two-year-old railway line to Lhasa, on alert for sabotage during the Saturday relay. The Information Centre for Human Rights and Democracy said the line has been attacked more than eighty times since it opened. Incidents have included the placing of obstacles on the tracks and gunshots fired at the windows of passing trains, it said.
>
> (www.iht.com, 21 June 2008)

> The visit of the Olympic torch to Lhasa came and went in about two hours on Saturday … Zhang Qingli, the Communist Party secretary of Tibet, stood beneath the Potala Palace, the historic seat of the Dalai Lama: 'Tibet's sky will never change and the red flag with five stars will forever flutter high above it. We will certainly be able to totally smash the splittist schemes of the Dalai Lama clique.'
>
> (www.iht.com, 23 June 2008)

> Chinese officials used the visit of the Olympic torch to the Tibetan capital on Saturday [21 June] to launch an attack on the Dalai Lama … Zhang Qingli (Communist Party secretary in Tibet): 'We will certainly be able to totally smash the splittist schemes of the Dalai Lama clique.'
>
> (*FT*, 23 June 2008, p. 8)

'A protest [took place] outside the Chinese embassy in Kathmandu Nepal, staged to coincide with the Olympic torch parade in Lhasa' (*Independent*, 23 June 2008, p. 19).

> Tibet has reopened to foreign tourists, Chinese state media says … The decision to allow them back in comes days after the Olympic torch's short, tightly controlled visit to the region passed off smoothly … Domestic tour groups have been allowed in since late April, Xinhua said … Access to the region for foreign journalists remains extremely limited.
>
> (www.bbc.co.uk, 25 June 2008)

'The government reopened Tibet to domestic tourists on 23 April and to tourists from Hong Kong, Macao and Taiwan on 1 May' (*The Times*, 26 June 2008, p. 37).

> China on Thursday [26 June] denied injecting politics into the Olympic Games, despite a rare rebuke from the International Olympic Committee [ILO] over remarks by a Chinese official about Tibet and the Dalai Lama. The IOC said it sent a letter this week to Beijing organizers expressing regret over a speech Saturday [21 June] by Tibet's Communist Party boss

> Zhang Qingli at a ceremony marking the Olympic torch's passage through Lhasa. The two-sentence IOC statement said: 'The IOC regrets that political statements were made during the closing ceremony of the Torch Relay in Tibet. We have written to BOCOG [Beijing Organizing Committee of the Olympic Games] to remind them of the need to separate sport and politics and to ask for their support in making sure that such situations do not arise again.'
>
> (www.cnn.com, 26 June 2008)

> China has cancelled the international leg of the Paralympic torch relay, which was due to pass through London ... Organizers of the Beijing Olympics said that the decision was because of the earthquake in the south-western province of Sichuan on 12 May ... The Paralympics will be held from 6 to 17 September and the first international part of the torch relay was scheduled to begin at around the same time as the start of the Olympics on 8 August. It was due to pass through the host cities of the next three winter and summer Olympics – Vancouver, London and the Russian Black Sea resort of Sochi – as well as Hong Kong ... Olympic organizers have also left Chengdu, Chonqing, Tainjin and Urumqi out of the sixteen-stop domestic torch relay ... The International Paralympic Committee said that the decision had been made to allow 'the Chinese government to focus on the rescue and relief work and show support for the people affected by the earthquake, especially persons with a disability'.
>
> (*The Times*, 27 June 2008, p. 45)

30 June 2008. 'Senior envoys of the Dalai lama are due in Beijing for formal talks with China's government ... The 1–2 July meetings follow informal talks held on 4 May' (www.bbc.co.uk, 30 June 2008).

'Two senior envoys from the Tibetan government-in-exile, Lodi Gyari and Kelsang Gyaltsen, travelled to the Chinese capital for the closed-door meeting' (www.bbc.co.uk, 3 July 2008).

'The rescheduling of the talks was announced during a visit to China by [US] Secretary of State Condoleezza Rice' (www.iht.com, 30 June 2008).

1–2 July 2008.

> Chinese officials and senior envoys of the Dalai Lama opened their latest round of negotiations over Tibet on Tuesday [1 July] ... The [1–2 July] discussions [are being] held at an undisclosed location in Beijing ... A day earlier [on 30 June] the French President, Nicolas Sarkozy, said he would decide whether to attend the Olympic opening ceremony after assessing the merits of the talks ... Foreign journalists are still forbidden from visiting many Tibetan regions of western China. Pro-Tibet advocacy groups have reported continuing violent confrontations between Tibetans and security officers ... But ... on 4 June the Dalai Lama led a prayer vigil on behalf of the victims of the Sichuan earthquake that was attended by officials in the Tibetan government-in-exile in Dharamsala, India. The Dalai Lama has also

> sought to tamp down more confrontational factions in the exile Tibetan community. China, meanwhile, has reopened Tibet to foreign tourists and says foreign journalists, if approved, can also visit. Chinese state media also reported that the authorities had released more than 1,000 Tibetans detained after the demonstrations.
>
> (www.iht.com, 1 July 2008)

('The Dalai Lama … hoped that the Chinese might agree to slow down Han immigration into Tibet … The Dalai Lama said that "direct contact" began in 1978 when his older brother met Deng Xiaoping and Party General Secretary Hu Yaobang on several occasions … The Dalai Lama: "We think Tibet is part of China. History is history, the past is the past. We concentrate on the present and future. I have said one thousand times we do not seek independence. China should manage defence and foreign policy. Inside Tibet Tibetans should be responsible for education, religion and the environment. We want the preservation of Tibetan culture inside the People's Republic of China … Buddhism … got to China some centuries before Tibet. So in that respect they are our elder brothers. Also Tibet, a landlocked place, needed modernization in many fields and Tibetans welcome it. No Tibetans want to return to the old system. We were spiritually advanced but materially backward. But what we also need is the preservation of our culture, our values and our religion … In the early 1980s I was hopeful. In 1983 I said I would go to China and Tibet. In 1984 my delegation visited Tibet. But in 1985 and 1986, when the Democracy Movement began in China, and with the departure of Hu Yaobang, their policies hardened and after Tiananmen in 1989 things were even more difficult"': *The New York Review of Books*, 17 July 1998, p. 4.)

> China's Communist party chief in Tibet delivered a new attack on the Dalai Lama on Wednesday [2 June], even as envoys of the exiled leader met for a second day with Chinese officials … Zhang Qingli: 'The 14 March incident was a seriously violent criminal incident by the Dalai clique. The organized and orchestrated incident was created by Tibetan separatists after long-term preparation, with the support and instigation of Western hostile forces. At a sensitive moment they harboured the evil intention of turning the incident into a bloodbath, of disrupting the Beijing Olympics and destroying Tibet's stability and political harmony.'
>
> (www.iht.com, 2 July 2008)

4 July 2008.

> An envoy for the Dalai Lama said that two days of talks with Chinese officials in Beijing this past week had been 'one of the most difficult sessions' held so far, but that he will return for more discussions in a few months … Lodi Gyari: '[I told my] Chinese counterparts very candidly that if there is not seriousness on their part it is almost pointless [to waste time with more talks].'
>
> (www.iht.com, 4 July 2008)

Lodi Gyari and Kelsang Gyaltsen (special envoys of the Dalai Lama): 'The Chinese side even failed to agree to our proposal of issuing a joint statement with the aim of committing both parties to the dialogue process. We were compelled to candidly convey to our counterparts that in the absence of serious and sincere commitment on their part, the continuation process would serve no purpose' ... The Tibetan envoys agreed to attend a further round of talks in October, after the Beijing Olympics.

(*FT*, 7 July 2008, p. 8)

Amnesty International reports that more than 1,000 Tibetans have disappeared and more than 200 deaths have been reported by the Tibetan Solidarity Committee ... Every month hundreds make the hazardous trek across the Himalayan Mountains [to India] ... [The] Tibetan diaspora [is] spread over twenty-nine countries.

(www.iht.com, 6 July 2008; *IHT*, 7 July 2008, p. 6)

Few monks remain in the province's three most important monasteries ... Dozens, possibly several hundred, have been arrested or are detained and under investigation for their roles in the anti-Chinese demonstrations and riots ... This, however, does not account for the empty halls in the three great monasteries, Drepung [the largest of Tibetan monasteries, whose name means 'rice heap'], Sera ['enclosure of roses'] and Ganden ['continent of completely victorious happiness'], that lie near the city [Lhasa] ... Tibetan sources have revealed that most of the monks, more than 1,000 in total, have been transferred to many prisons and detention centres in and around the city of Golmud in neighbouring Qinghai province. The detained monks are all young ethnic Tibetans from surrounding regions who had made their way to Lhasa ... The detention is part of a policy to rid the monasteries of any monks not registered as formal residents of the administrative region, known as the Tibetan Autonomous Region. Family members say that the monks have been told that they will be incarcerated in Golmud only until the end of the Olympic Games in Beijing ... They will [then] be ordered to return to their home villages ... Authorities have ordered all Tibetans without a Lhasa residence permit to leave the city and to return to their homes.

(*The Times*, 7 July 2008, p. 29)

9 July 2008.

French President Nicolas Sarkozy will attend the opening of the Beijing Olympics next month [8 August], his office said Wednesday [9 July] ... Sarkozy informed Chinese President Hu Jintao of his decision during talks on the sidelines of the G8 summit in Japan, his office said ... The Dalai Lama is expected to visit France in August. The French president has said in the past it is 'possible' he might meet with the visiting Tibetan leader ... Wednesday's statement ... said Sarkozy consulted his EU partners about his decision to attend the ceremony and he will represent both France and the twenty-seven-nation EU there. France currently holds the rotating EU presidency … British prime minister Gordon Brown has said he would skip the opener but attend the closer. Neither German Chancellor Angela Merkel nor Canadian prime minister Stephen Harper plan to attend the opening event.

(www.cnn.com, 9 July 2008)

President Nicolas Sarkozy of France, whose office announced Wednesday [9 July] that he would, after all, attend the opening ceremonies of Beijing's Olympic Games, was warned by China on Tuesday [8 July] not to meet with the Dalai Lama in France next month [August]. Kong Quan (China's ambassador to France): '[There will be] serious consequences [for Chinese–French relations if President Sarkozy meets the Dalai Lama] … [It] would be contrary to the principle of non-interference in internal affairs' … The Dalai Lama's visit to France, for a conference on Buddhism, comes after the opening of the Olympics.

(www.iht.com, 9 July 2008)

It is still not known whether the security forces shot anyone at all during the unrest of 14 and 15 March in Lhasa. Figures used by Tibetans abroad have fudged the issue. The Dalai Lama himself says more than 200 people have been killed by Chinese security forces since March. But he and his aides have provided scant detail. There is little doubt that several were shot in other parts of the plateau, most notably in Sichuan, where several dozen may have been killed. In the case of Lhasa the Tibetan government-in-exile has published a list of only twenty-three killed on 14 and 15 March. But it is unable to provide a consistent account of these incidents … Sporadic discussions between Chinese officials and the Dalai Lama's advisers over nearly three decades have achieved nothing. China has not allowed the Dalai Lama's delegates to visit Tibet itself since 1980, following three trips there during which Chinese officials were embarrassed by emotional displays of public support for the Dalai Lama's team. The last trip they made to any part of the Tibetan plateau was a visit to Qinghai in 1985. Deng Xiaoping met a representative of the Dalai Lama in 1979.

(*The Economist*, 12 July 2008, pp. 71–2)

12 July 2008.

Two monks at a monastery in western China were killed in a clash with paramilitary police … three Tibetan sources have told *The Times*. The monks, at a monastery in western Sichuan province, which borders Tibet, were killed in a clash on 12 July … It is the first report of the lethal use of gunfire against Tibetan protesters … since the fatal shootings on 2 April at the Tongkor monastery … Tibetan sources said that the trouble erupted when monks at the Gonchen monastery, one of the most prominent in the region and renowned as a centre for printing Buddhist sutras, or scriptures, attempted to mark a festival that fell on the tenth day of the sixth month of the Tibetan calendar. The festival pays homage to the birthday of Padmasambhava, or

> Guru Rinpoche, the founder of Tibetan Buddhism … The Nyingma sect, also known as the Red Hat sect, is the oldest sect of Tibetan Buddhism. Its name, meaning 'ancient' or 'old' in the Tibetan language, stems from its practice of Buddhism deeply rooted in the Tubo Kingdom of the eight century. Nyingma monks wear red hats, while the [monks of the] Gelug sect, formed in the fourteenth century, wear yellow ones. The Dalai Lama is the figurehead of the dominant Yellow Hat sect. The Red Hat sect claims as its founder Padmasambhava, the man credited with building Tibet's first monastery, Samye, in the late eighteenth century … Its monks can marry.
>
> (*The Times*, 18 July 2008, p. 35)

23 July 2008.

> Kathleen McLaughlin has been a journalist in China for more than seven years … She is one of the first foreign journalists to visit Tibet since March 2008 allowed to travel independently to Tibet, although regulations still require hiring a government-approved guide. During her five-day trip she is sending dispatches from Lhasa for the *Review* … Kathleen McLaughlin: 'When the Chinese government announced on 25 June that Tibet would reopen to foreigners, it seemed a natural step to apply for a permit … I asked my assistant to make sure the Tibetan foreign affairs office was clear that we are two journalists who will write about our experiences. I knew of no other foreign journalist approved for independent travel in Tibet since March … During our five days we … my Spanish colleague and I … will be accompanied by a minder and required to use a government-supplied car and driver … Our requests to visit the Drepung monastery – once the biggest monk-training school in Tibet – were rejected.'
>
> (www.feer.com, 25 July 2008)

'Kathleen McLaughlin: "A handful of foreign journalists (perhaps three small groups, including ours) has been allowed into Tibet to work independently since the riots"' (www.feer.com, 27 July 2008). 'Kathleen McLaughlin: "Government officers we met … point to figures showing that Tibet's economy doubled in size from 2000 to 2005, mainly due to Chinese central government investment"' (www.feer.com, 30 July 2008).

3 August 2008.

> [The Dalai Lama] approves of the Olympic Games being held in Beijing and he is not trying to seek full independence from China, just what he calls cultural autonomy … [The Dalai Lama was asked why he would] not overtly support the young generation of Tibetans who want a more proactive policy of confronting China … He said he would not condemn them as he believed in democracy and free speech. But nor would he support their tactics or their goals. He just kept asking (rhetorically) a simple question: with what are we going to fight them?; are we 6 million Tibetans going to confront the army of 1.2 billion people?; how?
>
> (www.cnn.com, 3 August 2008)

> Indian police detained fifty-six Tibetan exiles, including several monks and nuns, attempting to cross the border into China and protest the Beijing Olympics. Police said Tuesday [5 August]. The arrests were made late Sunday night [3 August] … about fifteen miles from India's border with China … In recent months Tibetan exiles have been staging protests and trying to march to Tibet to show their support for the uprising that erupted in Lhasa in March and to protest China being allowed to stage the Games, which begin Friday [8 August].
>
> (www.iht.com, 5 August 2008)

12 August 2008.

> The Dalai Lama sent a message of good will for the Olympics … at the start of his twelve-day visit to France on Tuesday [12 August]. The Tibetan spiritual leader is spending most of the duration of the Beijing Olympics in France, with only one political event of his schedule – closed-door talks with French lawmakers on Wednesday [13 August]. His trip is focused mainly on Buddhist teachings and reaching out to his flock of hundreds of thousands in France … The Dalai Lama: 'I fully support the Olympics in China … the People's Republic of China deserves to play host to the Games.'
>
> (www.iht.com, 13 August 2008)

('The Dalai Lama … [met] Carla Sarkozy, [France's] first lady, on Friday [22 August] before dedicating a Buddhist temple … He accused China of imposing a new, long-term "plan of brutal repression" against the Tibetans': *IHT*, 23 August 2008, p. 3. 'During his trip the Dalai Lama accused Chinese troops of firing at a crowd of Tibetans in China last week and said people may have been killed during the incident … He accused Beijing of imposing a new, long-term "plan of brutal repression" and building new military camps in Tibetan areas': www.iht.com, Friday 29 August 2008.)

14 August 2008.

> Nepalese police clashed with Tibetan protesters and detained more than 500 of them Thursday [14 August] while breaking up a demonstration in front of the Chinese diplomatic mission in Kathmandu. More than 1,000 Tibetan exiles had gathered outside the Chinese embassy visa office in Kathmandu shouting slogans against China and the Olympics … The area around the visa office in the heart of Kathmandu is declared a no-protest zone and demonstrations and gatherings are prohibited … Tibetans exiles in both Nepal and India have been staging frequent protests to show their support.
>
> (www.iht.com, 14 August 2008)

> The Chinese leadership and the Tibetan government-in-exile have delicately discussed a possible visit by the Dalai Lama to China, nominally to commemorate the victims of the earthquake in Sichuan province in May. That would be the first meeting between the Dalai Lama and Chinese leaders in

more than fifty years … The opportunity arises in part because the Dalai Lama publicly acknowledged last week for the first time that he could accept Communist Party rule for Tibet. Previously, the Dalai Lama had seemed to demand something like the 'one country, two systems' model of Hong Kong.

(Nicholas Kristof, www.iht.com, 14 August 2008)

About 2,000 Tibetan exiles, including children, monks and nuns, joined a protest rally in Kathmandu on Sunday [24 August], hours before the closing ceremony of the Olympics in Beijing … Participants walked silently for 8 kilometres (5 miles) to the outskirts of the Nepali capital … More than 20,000 Tibetans live in Nepal, the second largest home for them outside Tibet after India, having fled there after a failed uprising against Chinese rule in 1959 … About 10,000 refugees have been arrested in the past five months, but later freed … Also Sunday in Dharamsala in northern India … hundreds of Tibetan youths marched, vowing to keep alive their 'Free Tibet' campaign even after the Olympics.

(www.iht.com, 24 August 2008)

27 August 2008. 'The Dalai Lama … is suffering from exhaustion and has cancelled his international trips for the next three weeks … Planned trips to Mexico and the Dominican Republic were now shelved' (www.cnn.com, 27 August 2008).

28 August 2008. 'The Dalai Lama was admitted to a hospital in the western Indian city … of Mumbai … Thursday [28 August] to undergo tests for abdominal discomfort … His spokesman said: "There is no cause for concern"' (www.iht.com, 28 August 2008).

('The Dalai Lama's spokesman says the Tibetan spiritual leader has been discharged from the hospital [in Mumbai] where he has been undergoing tests for abdominal discomfort … The Dalai Lama was discharged Monday morning [1 September], but will remain in Mumbai for several days … He is in good condition but doctors have advised him to rest as much as possible. The Dalai Lama was admitted [to hospital] … with what his advisers called exhaustion … The Dalai Lama spends several months a year travelling the globe to highlight the struggle of Tibetans for greater freedom in China and to teach Buddhism': www.cnn.com, 1 September 2008.)

29 August 2008.

A major Buddhist monastery in Tibet reopened this week five months after being shut by the authorities … a staff member said Friday [28 August] … The Drepung Monastery, on the outskirts of Lhasa, reopened earlier this week … The fifteenth-century monastery had been closed to the public since 14 March … China has said that twenty-two people died in the violence, but Tibetan supporters have said that many times that number were killed in the protests and the subsequent military crackdown.

(www.iht.com, 29 August 2008)

12 September 2008.

> Nepal will start deporting Tibetan exiles living illegally in the country, a government official has said … Those found without proper documents will face deportation to where they came from … More than 200,000 Tibetan refugees live in Nepal … The Nepalese government spokesman said the verification of papers was being done with the help of officials from the United Nations refugees agency (UNHCR) in Nepal … A UNHCR official told the BBC that if the detained Tibetans did not have valid certificates they would be 'helped to proceed to a third country' … Until 1990 Tibetan refugees arriving in Nepal were allowed to stay and they now form the core of the exile community in the country. But since then, under Chinese pressure, the government in Kathmandu has not let newly arriving Tibetans remain, instead referring them to the UNHCR, which helps them move onto India.
>
> (www.bbc.co.uk, 13 September 2008)

7 October 2008. 'The Dalai Lama has been cleared to resume international travel after a medical check-up showed he has recovered from a recent abdominal ailment … he will be starting his international travels at the end of this month [October]' (www.cnn.com, 7 October 2008).

9 October 2008. 'The Dalai Lama was hospitalized Thursday night [9 October] in New Delhi … He is to undergo surgery to remove a gall stone' (www.cnn.com, 10 October 2008).

('The Dalai Lama has recovered from surgery to remove gallstones and will resume his travel schedule by the end of the month [October], a senior aide said Wednesday [15 October]. The Dalai Lama underwent surgery Friday [10 October]': *IHT*, 16 October 2008, p. 4.)

14 October 2008.

> Eight Buddhist monks convicted of bombing a government building in Tibet during an anti-government uprising in March have been sentenced to prison, two of them for life, a judge said … The others received sentences ranging from five to fifteen years.
>
> The monks had been found guilty of setting off a bomb in Gyanbe township … about 1,400 kilometres, or 850 miles, east of Lhasa … Chinese state media have reported that eight monks from the Tongxia monastery in eastern Tibet confessed to planting a bomb at the government building in Gyanbe on 23 March. No casualties or damage were reported … [The judge] said the monks did not appeal their sentences … The Free Tibet Campaign in London said the monks were sentenced on 23 September, but it was not made public … Beijing has said twenty-two people were killed in the riots … The Dalai Lama's government-in-exile in Dharamsala, India, has said at least 140 people died. More than 1,000 people were arrested, though human rights groups assert the number could be higher.
>
> (www.iht.com, 14 October 2008)

26 October 2008.

> This weekend the Dalai Lama told his followers he had lost hope of reaching agreement with China about the future of his homeland ... The announcement he is giving up attempts to persuade China to grant greater autonomy to Tibet will come as shock to many ... [There is to be] a special meeting of Tibetan exiles, now scheduled for November.
>
> (www.bbc.co.uk, Monday 27 October 2008)

29 October 2008.

> Chinese authorities are to arrange fresh talks with envoys of the Dalai Lama 'in the near future', Xinhua has said ... Xinhua quoted a government official as saying that Chinese authorities would 'arrange another round of contacts and negotiation with the private representatives of the Dalai Lama in the near future at the request of the Dalai Lama side' ... On Tuesday [28 October] Tibetan officials in exile in India called a special meeting to discuss foundering discussions with China.
>
> (www.bbc.co.uk, 29 October 2008)

> In a little-publicized parliamentary statement on 29 October UK Foreign Secretary David Miliband gave his strong backing to the talks and also backed the Dalai Lama's calls for autonomy as a basis for agreement. Mr Miliband also referred to a historic agreement dating back to the early twentieth century, which acknowledged China's 'special position' in Tibet, but asserted that Tibet had never been fully part of the country. Describing the policy as an 'anachronism', he asserted: 'Like every other EU member state, and the United States, we regard Tibet as part of the People's Republic of China' ... Many observers think ... the British decision might be linked with prime minister Gordon Brown's efforts to bring China into a new world economic order.
>
> (www.bbc.co.uk, 15 November 2008)

> Until that day [29 October] the British had described Tibet as autonomous, with China having a 'special position' there. This formula did not endorse the Tibetan claim to independence. But it meant that in the British view China's control over Tibet was limited to a condition once known as suzerainty, somewhat similar to administering a protectorate. Britain, alone among major powers, had exchanged official agreements with the Tibetan government before the Chinese takeover in 1951.
>
> (www.iht.com, 25 November 2008)

'UK prime minister Gordon Brown has taken the lead in urging China and other countries with big cash stockpiles to finance the IMF so that it can make more emergency loans' (www.bbc.co.uk, 15 November 2008).

> On 29 October, a day before Tibetan envoys arrived in China for the eighth round of talks, the British government announced that it was dropping its

formal recognition of a suzerainty relationship between Tibet and China. This recognition of a 'special position' for Tibet dated back ninety-four years, from a time when the British Empire used Tibet as a buffer region to shield India, then a British colony, from Russia. Britain was the only remaining nation to accord Tibet such a status, and its renunciation led to widespread criticism of the British government by opponents of Beijing.

(www.iht.com, 16 November 2008)

30 October 2008.

Chinese officials and envoys of the Dalai Lama are expected to resume talks on Friday [31 October] … A spokesman for the Tibetan government-in-exile in Dharamsala, India, confirmed that two senior envoys left New Delhi on Thursday [30 October] for a five-day trip to Beijing … The latest negotiations are the eighth round of talks since 2002 … In a statement released on Tuesday [28 October] the Dalai Lama expressed concerns about the negotiating process. He stated: 'I have faith and trust in the Chinese people; however, my faith and trust in the Chinese government is diminishing' … The precise agenda for this week's meeting is uncertain, though Chinese authorities have said they are only willing to discuss the future of the Dalai Lama himself and possible terms for his return to China. Tibetan envoys believe the talks should be framed around the future of Tibet, greater religious tolerance and other issues … Lodi Gyaltsen Gyari (one of the senior Tibetan envoys in the talks during a speech made earlier in October in the United States): 'The task at hand is to develop a system that would grant the kind of autonomy required for the Tibetans to be able to survive as a distinct and prosperous people within the People's Republic of China' … Officials have continued to block foreign journalists from visiting areas of western Sichuan province that saw especially violent confrontations between Tibetans and paramilitary forces.

(www.iht.com, 30 October 2008)

The Dalai Lama … says he will ask Tibetan exiles meeting next month [November] to decide if a new strategy is needed … He said: 'My faith, my trust in Chinese government, now becomes thinner, thinner. Unfortunately, they always say something, doing something different … Now I hand over direct responsibility to the people, concerned people.'

(www.bbc.co.uk, 30 October 2008)

5 November 2008. 'The Chinese government announced a total of fifty-five people have been sentenced in connection with the unrest in Lhasa in March' (www.bbc.co.uk, 5 November 2008).

China has sentenced fifty-five people for their involvement in anti-government protests that broke out in Tibet in March, state media reported Wednesday [5 November]. Following the riots in Lhasa Chinese police detained about 1,300 people, Xinhua said. About 1,100 of them were later released. The rest were put on trial ... Xinhua did not say what the fifty-five ... were charged with or what sentences they received. It also did not say whether the group included thirty people convicted in April of arson, robbery and attacking government offices in connection with the riots. Those people received sentences ranging from three years to life ... The subsequent crackdown left eighteen civilians and one police officer dead, according to the Chinese government. Tibet's self-proclaimed government-in-exile put the death toll from the protests at 140.

(www.cnn.com, 5 November 2008)

[China] said fifty-five people had so far been sentenced for the relay rioting that shook Lhasa on 14 March ... Following the violence police detained 1,317 people, of whom 1,115 were subsequently released. The rest stood trial ... The report did not detail the crimes or sentences of those convicted. Nor did it say what had happened to the 147 people apparently tried but not sentenced ... In late April China announced it had jailed thirty people for terms ranging from three years to life for their roles in the Lhasa riots that left eighteen residents and a police officer dead ... Since April groups abroad advocating Tibetan self-determination have reported additional sentences, but these have not been confirmed by China.

(www.iht.com, 5 November 2008)

6 November 2008.

Senior envoys of the Dalai Lama said Thursday [6 November] that they had presented Chinese officials in Beijing with a memorandum on 'genuine autonomy' for Tibetans living under Chinese rule. The envoys, Kasur Lodi Gyari and Kelsang Gyaltsen, left Beijing on Wednesday [5 November] after arriving on 30 October for an eighth round of talks.

(*IHT*, 7 November 2008, p. 10)

A senior official who met representatives of the Dalai Lama has struck a hard line, ruling out the kind of autonomy that Beijing has granted Hong Kong. The remarks by Du Qinglin, head of a government department in charge of the talks, were the first public comment by China since the two days of discussions ended on Wednesday [5 November] ... Du Qinglin: 'It is impossible for Tibet to become independent, semi-independent, or independent in a disguised form.'

(*Independent*, 8 November 2008, p. 38)

10 November 2008.

The Dalai Lama's calls for 'high level autonomy' for Tibet will never be accepted by Beijing, Zhu Weiqun, a vice minister of the Chinese Communist Party's United Front Work Department [which oversees dealings with religious organizations] ... said Monday [10 November] ... [He] said that envoys of the Dalai Lama had pressed his longstanding demand for 'genuine

> autonomy' for Tibet during talks last week [31 October to 5 November] … Zhu Weiqun: '[China will] never allow ethnic splitting in the name of genuine autonomy. In fact, this is seeking a legal basis for so-called Tibetan independence, or semi-independence or covert independence … If one day he [the Dalai Lama] really seizes power he will without any compunction or sympathy carry out ethnic discrimination, apartheid and ethnic cleansing' … [There are to be] talks by exiled Tibetans about the future of their cause … [The Dalai Lama] is not attending the 17 to 22 November exiles' meeting.
>
> (www.iht.com, 10 November 2008)

> Zhu Weiqun: 'Our contacts and talks failed to make progress and [the Tibetans] should assume full responsibility for it … They aimed at revising the constitution so that this separatist group could actually possess the power of an independent state … [China will not accept] independence, half-independence or covert independence' … The memorandum presented by the Tibetans … also contained other proposals that were unacceptable, such as a plan to withdraw Chinese troops from Tibetan areas, Mr Zhu said.
>
> (www.bbc.co.uk, 10 November 2008)

'Zhu Weiqun … [said that] ethnic cleansing would follow [independence] … The huge numbers of Chinese settlers who have gone to Tibet to live would be attacked, he said' (www.bbc.co.uk, 15 November 2008).

'Zhu Weiqun said there was no progress in last week's talks and blamed the Tibetan side. The current system was "perfect", he said, and in no need of revision. He added: "There is no other way" ' (www.guardian.co.uk, 10 November 2008).

17 November 2008.

> A critical six-day summit meeting of Tibetan exiles begins Monday [17 November] in India, the first since 1991. The Dalai Lama has called for hundreds of prominent Tibetans to gather in Dharamsala, the seat of the Tibetan government-in-exile, to help decide on a new strategy to deal with the current impasse … In the eighth and last round of talks, from 30 October to 5 November, the Tibetan envoys presented the Chinese government with a memorandum detailing the Dalai Lama's call for genuine autonomy, outlining eleven broad areas over which the Tibetans should practise self-governance … The Dalai Lama, seventy-three, issued a statement Friday [14 November] expressing his disappointment. He said: 'Despite this approach receiving widespread appreciation from the international community, as well as the support of many Chinese intellectuals, there have been no positive signs or changes in Tibet … [The special meeting will allow Tibetans to discuss] in a spirit of equality, co-operation and collective responsibility the best possible future course of action to advance the Tibetan cause.'
>
> (www.iht.com, 16 November 2008)

> The week-long meeting of 581 exile leaders … represents the first major reevaluation of the Tibetan strategy since the Dalai Lama outlined the policy, which rejects calls for outright independence, in 1988 … The closed-door discussions in India end Saturday [22 November] and their recommendations will be taken to parliament. The Dalai Lama, who is not participating in the discussions, will meet the exiled leaders on Sunday [23 November].
>
> (www.iht.com, 9 November 2008)

'The Dalai Lama has called hundreds of representatives from the world's 150,000 Tibetan exiles' (www.iht.com, 22 November 2008). 'The Dalai Lama is considered the reincarnation of Chenrezig, the bodhisattva, or god, of compassion' (www.iht.com, 23 November 2008).

> Tibetan exile leaders gathered in northern India on Monday [17 November] after the Dalai Lama acknowledged he has failed in his efforts to convince China to restore the territory's autonomy. The Dalai Lama will not be at the week-long conference in the northern hill town of Dharamsala, where he lives in exile. The meeting, he said, was intended to offer the exiles an opportunity to discuss 'the best possible future course of action' … He said in a statement posted on his website: 'Until now we have followed the Middle-Way Approach, and eight rounds of talks have taken place since contact with the PRC (People's Republic of China) was restored in 2002. Despite this approach receiving widespread appreciation from the international community, as well as the support of many Chinese intellectuals, there have been no positive signs or changes in Tibet … [The special meeting this week is being convened] with the express purpose of providing a forum to understand the real options and views of the Tibetan people through free and frank discussions. All the participants, as Tibetan citizens should discuss in a spirit of equality, co-operation and collective responsibility the best possible future course of action to advance the Tibetan cause.'
>
> (www.cnn.com, 17 November 2008)

> China on Tuesday [18 November] reaffirmed its hard-line stance … as more than 500 Tibetan exile leaders in India held closed-door discussions as part of a six-day meeting, the first major reevaluation of their strategy since the Dalai Lama in 1988 outlined his 'Middle Way', which advocates autonomy but not outright independence … A Chinese foreign ministry spokesman [18 November]: 'Any attempt to separate Tibet from Chinese territory will be doomed. The so-called Tibet government-in-exile is not recognized by any government in the world.'
>
> (www.iht.com, 18 November 2008)

'Young Tibetan leaders at a summit meeting of exiles are pushing … to declare independence from China, while the older guard continues to support a more conciliatory approach towards Beijing, participants said' (www.iht.com, 19 November 2008). 'Posters around town [Dharamsala] advertise the word *rangzen* – Tibetan for "independence". Not in years has it been heard so much in the streets here, falling from the lips of members of the Tibetan diaspora' (www.iht.com, 22 November 2008).

'The speaker of the parliament-in-exile said that of 17,000 messages from Tibetans inside Tibet, roughly 8,000 endorsed the Dalai Lama's position and 5,000 advocated demanding independence' (www.economist.com, 20 November 2008).

> After an intense debate on whether to begin a formal independence movement, the majority of delegates attending a conference of Tibetan exiles in northern India recommended Saturday [22 November] to continue to adopt the Dalai Lama's conciliatory approach to China, a Tibetan spokesman said … But most delegates also advised the Tibetan government to end the dialogue until China shows real willingness to negotiate … [The spokesman said] the Tibetan parliament will likely discuss the recommendations at its next session in March [2009].
>
> (www.iht.com, 23 November 2008)

> Tibetan exiles meeting in India have agreed to back the Dalai Lama's policy of seeking autonomy, rather than full independence … But the decision to support the Tibetan spiritual leader's approach to continue talks with Beijing was viewed as conditional on progress being made … The policy was given renewed backing by majority vote … The meeting concluded that if China makes no effort to meet the Dalai Lama's demands then other options, including calls for independence and self-determination, would be put forward. Delegates also suggested that the Dalai Lama's envoy should not return to China unless attitudes change in Beijing. The recommendations are non-binding.
>
> (www.bbc.co.uk, 22 November 2008)

> The Dalai Lama has called on Tibetan exiles to improve their contacts with ordinary Chinese people as they press for autonomy … He welcomed a decision by exiles meeting in India to back his policy of seeking autonomy rather than independence … Total independence was 'not practical' he told a meeting in Dharamsala … [and] also sought to end rumours he was planning to retire … The Dalai Lama: '[The] majority of views have come up supporting the Middle Way path to the Tibetan issue … There is no point or question of retirement … My faith in the Chinese people has never been shaken … [But my faith in the Chinese government is] getting thinner … [It uses] fear and ruthless suppression [to control Tibet].'
>
> (www.bbc.co.uk, 23 November 2008)

> The Dalai Lama: 'It is my moral responsibility until my death to work for the Tibetan cause' … The majority view during the meetings was that efforts to negotiate with China on greater autonomy – the Middle Way Approach – should continue. But for the first time other, more radical options have been given a formal hearing. Tenzin Tsundue (a prominent

Tibetan activist): 'This time what has changed is that we have adopted independence as the alternative. We are going to give a short period of time for China to respond appropriately.'

(www.bbc.co.uk, 23 November 2008)

The Dalai Lama warned Tibetan exile leaders on Sunday [23 November] to be prudent in their plans or risk failure, after they said at a conference that they might push for independence for their homeland if China refuses to grant it autonomy soon ... The Dalai Lama: 'The next twenty years, if we are not careful, if we are not prudent in our plans, there is a great danger of failure' ... [He said] that the meeting should not be viewed as final and that at least one more meeting of Tibetan leaders was likely in the next few weeks. He suggested that the meeting may be held abroad ... He also reiterated that he would remain the Tibetan people's spiritual leader: 'Till my death I committed. No idea of retirement' ... he has been saying since the early 1990s that he would only consider stepping away from his role as spiritual leader when Tibet has more freedom. He said: 'With certain degree of freedom when we return, then I will hand over all my legitimate authority' ... But he reiterated that he is semi-retired as a political leader, as he has done several times before ... The Dalai Lama told the delegates Sunday: 'My trust in Chinese officials is becoming thinner, but my trust in the Chinese people is still alive and strong ... [There is need for a] dialogue with the Chinese people' ... He suggested the possibility of bypassing the Chinese government and talking directly to the Chinese people.

(www.iht.com, 23 November 2008)

The Dalai Lama said a final decision on how to engage with China would only be taken 'in a month's time' after international supporters of the Tibetan cause had been consulted ... [He said] he supported 'democracy in China' and the failure of authoritarian states in the twentieth century was a lesson of history Beijing should learn.

(www.guardian.co.uk, 23 November 2008)

'The Dalai Lama ... [said] the Tibetan nation was close to a "death sentence"' (*Independent*, 24 November 2008, p. 28).

The Dalai Lama is considering appointing a regent to lead the Tibetan movement after his death until his reincarnation is old enough to take over. The idea was discussed this week at an unprecedented meeting of 600 Tibetan exiles ... The Tibetan exiles are keen to prevent China from hijacking his reincarnation ... The most likely candidate for the regency is the twenty-three-year-old Karmapa Lama, the third highest in the Tibetan Buddhist hierarchy ... He cannot become the next Dalai Lama as he leads a different sect of Tibetan Buddhism ... the Kagyu (Black Hat) sect ... The Dalai Lama, leader of Gelugpa (Yellow Hat) sect ... The Dalai Lama has proposed several alternatives, including holding a referendum among the world's 13 million to 14 million Tibetan Buddhists on whether he should be reincarnated at all. He told a news conference today [23 November]: 'If the majority feels this institution has become irrelevant, then it will automatically cease' … If the majority wanted to continue the tradition, he said he would be reincarnated as a young boy, or girl. He said: 'Girls show more compassion.'

(www.thetimes.co.uk, 23 November 2008)

26 November 2008.

China has postponed an annual summit with the EU originally scheduled for next Monday [1 December], the Europeans said in a statement on Wednesday [26 November]. The Chinese were angered by a new visit to several European countries by the Dalai Lama … According to the Europeans, the Chinese 'said their decision was due to the fact that the Dalai Lama will at the same time undertake a new visit in several countries of the union and will meet on this occasion heads of state and government'. One of those leaders is President Nicolas Sarkozy of France, who intends to meet the Dalai Lama in Poland in December [on 6 December] at a ceremony honouring Lech Walesa, the anti-communist leader of Solidarity and later Polish president. France holds the presidency of the EU until the end of the year.

(www.iht.com, 26 November 2008)

'Prime minister Wen Jiabao was set to attend the summit in Lyons next Monday [1 December]' (www.bbc.co.uk, 26 November 2008).

4 December 2008.

Addressing the European Parliament in Brussels [on Thursday 4 December], the Dalai Lama said he was 'seeking a genuine autonomy within China' … [and that] his movement was not 'a separatist' [one] … [He stressed] his commitments to 'strictly non-violent methods' to achieve his goals … Earlier the Dalai Lama urged the EU to stand up to China on human rights. He told the BBC on Wednesday [3 December]: 'Our friends should take a firm stand. That I think for the long run is an immense help to the Chinese people. [The] Chinese people also want freedom of expression, free media and rule of law. If you adopt an attitude of appeasement. In the long run [it is] in no-one's interest.'

(www.bbc.co.uk, 4 December 2008)

6 December 2008.

French President Nicolas Sarkozy held his long-awaited meeting with the Dalai Lama on Saturday [6 December] despite warnings from China that it could have a negative impact on ties between the two countries. The French president and the Tibetan spiritual leader sat down for a thirty-minute talk behind closed doors in Gdansk during celebrations marking the twenty-fifth anniversary of former Polish President Lech Walesa's Nobel Peace Prize … Sarkozy did not meet with the Dalai Lama when he was in France for a twelve-day visit in August ... The president's wife, former model Carla Bruni-Sarkozy, attended a much-photographed temple ceremony with the spiritual leader in France ... [France] currently holds the rotating EU presidency.

(www.cnn.com, 7 December 2008)

The French president, who did not meet the Buddhist leader when he visited France in August, would be the only European head of state to meet the Dalai Lama while holding the EU's six-month rotating presidency ... The exiled Tibetan leader is on a tour of European countries that has included meetings with the Belgian and Czech prime ministers as well as fellow Nobel Peace Prize laureate Lech Walesa, the former Polish president.

(www.bbc.co.uk, 6 December 2008)

Several times over the last week China demanded President Nicolas Sarkozy cancel the meeting ... China protested strongly to France on Sunday [7 December] ... He Yafei: 'This wrong act by France is a rude intervention in Chinese internal affairs and has hurt the feelings of Chinese people gravely. Sarkozy gave no consideration to numerous Chinese citizens' intense opposition ... [The Dalai Lama is a separatist and] political hooligan' ... The Dalai Lama won the Nobel Peace Prize in 1989.

(www.iht.com, 7 December 2008)

The police have detained fifty-nine people in Tibet on charges that they sought to foment unrest by spreading ethnic hatred and by downloading and selling banned songs from the internet, Chinese state media reported Thursday [25 December]. The detainees are accused of acting at the behest of the Dalai Lama ... Since 4 December public security officials have been sweeping the markets of Lhasa for compact discs that contain 'reactionary songs', according to the China News Service ... Rioting last March left at least twenty-one people dead ... According to the government, 1,317 people were detained, and 1,115 of those were subsequently released. Exile groups, however, say that hundreds are still in custody and that more than 200 Tibetans were killed during the ensuing crackdown.

(www.iht.com, 25 December 2008)

January 2009.

Tibet is to celebrate a new holiday: Serfs' Emancipation Day ... The new commemoration is meant to remind the world of the feudal system that had persisted for centuries in Tibet – the Dalai Lama has said that he would not want to see a return to that era. The date chosen by the regional government for Tibet's new celebration will be 28 March, with the first commemoration held this year [2009] ... In September 1949 China claimed Tibet. A military campaign to conquer the territory began in 1950. In September 1951 thousands of Chinese troops marched on Lhasa. In March 1959 after a widespread rebellion the Dalai Lama left Tibet to claim asylum in India ...

> The 1959 rebellion was finally suppressed with the deaths of nearly 100,000, according to official Chinese figures.
>
> (*The Times*, 17 January 2009, p. 43)

'This year [2009] … marks fifty years since the Dalai Lama fled Tibet. Members of the Tibetan People's Congress, the regional legislature, have proposed the occasion be known as "Serfs' Emancipation Day"' (www.ft.com, 18 January 2009).

> The government … has come up with a name to mark the date the Communists declared rule over Tibet after forcing the Dalai Lama to flee: 'Serfs' Emancipation Day'. On 28 March 1959 the Chinese Communist Party announced the creation of the Tibet Autonomous Region and dissolved the old Tibetan government. Legislators passed a bill on Monday [19 January] mandating an annual celebration of that event by designating a special title for the date. The bill will be reviewed by the ninth regional People's Congress … Xinhua reported: '[Serfs' Emancipation Day will] mark the date on which about 1 million serfs in the region were freed fifty years ago' … [Xinhua contends] that 90 per cent of the Tibetan population in the 1950s were serfs or slaves. The article added that the creation of the Tibet Autonomous Region 'came after the central government foiled an armed rebellion staged by the Dalai Lama and his supporters, most of whom were slave owners attempting to maintain serfdom'. Xinhua added: 'That meant the end of freedom and the abolition of the hierarchic social system characterized by theocracy, with the Dalai Lama as the core of the leadership' … The bill creating 'Serfs' Emancipation Day' was approved by all 382 legislators in attendance at the session … The move to mark the date comes just months before the fiftieth anniversary of the Dalai Lama's flight to India. The Dalai Lama left Lhasa on 17 March 1959, with an entourage of twenty men, six of them cabinet ministers.
>
> (www.iht.com, 19 January 2009)

18 January 2009.

> Chinese authorities have launched a security operation in Lhasa, running checks on almost 6,000 people [5,766] and detaining eighty-one … The *Tibetan Daily* said the 'strike hard' campaign was targeting criminals. However, campaigners for Tibetan autonomy said its timing – just two months before the fiftieth anniversary of the failed uprising against Chinese rule that resulted in the Dalai Lama's flight into exile – suggested it was meant to intimidate residents … The public security bureau in Lhasa began its campaign on 18 January … China first introduced 'strike hard' campaigns against crime and corruption in 1983, concerned that offences were soaring in the wake of economic reforms.
>
> (www.guardian.co.uk, 28 January 2009)

20 January 2009.

> Premier Wen Jiabao is due to travel to Europe next week, the foreign ministry announced – but his trip will pointedly exclude France. Mr Wen will

> visit Germany, Spain and Britain, as well as the EU in Brussels and the World Economic Forum in Davos. Correspondents say Beijing continues to snub Paris because of a meeting between President Nicolas Sarkozy and the Dalai Lama late last year [2008].
>
> (www.bbc.co.uk, 20 January 2009)

> Prime minister Wen Jiabao is to travel to Switzerland, Germany, Spain, Britain and the EU headquarters in Brussels on the 27 January–2 February trip ... Wen's itinerary does not include France, which prompted questions about whether Paris was excluded due to Chinese anger over French President Nicolas Sarkozy's meeting with the Dalai Lama last month [December 2008] in Poland ... [A Chinese spokesman] blamed Wen's tight schedule but said only France can resolve 'difficulties' in their relations.
>
> (www.iht.com, 22 January 2009)

28 January 2009. 'Several dozen pro-Tibetan demonstrators gathered peacefully in Davos [Switzerland] about a kilometre from the conference venue to protest over [Chinese prime minister] Wen Jiabao's presence at the annual meeting [of the World Economic Forum]' (www.cnn.com, 28 January 2009).

31 January 2009. Prime minister Wen Jiabao arrives in the UK for a three-day visit.

'Wen Jiabao is on a three-day visit to Britain focusing on building economic ties and fighting the global downturn' (www.iht.com, 1 February 2009).

> [On 1 February] five protesters were arrested after trying to approach premier Wen Jiabao during a Free Tibet Group demonstration. Several people vaulted barriers as he arrived outside the Chinese embassy in London amid a noisy demonstration ... A group of around 100 were chanting pro-Tibetan slogans and brandishing placards from behind barriers ... A dozen or so protesters vaulted over the barriers and made their way across the road ... Supporters of Mr Wen were also outside the [Chinese embassy].
>
> (www.bbc.co.uk, 1 February 2009)

> Five of the pro-Tibetan demonstrators were arrested when they tried to take the Free Tibet flag to the doors of the embassy ... One protester had concealed himself with the pro-Chinese group of about 100 people, who were gathered opposite a bigger crowd of people, many of whom were from the Free Tibet organization ... The police presence quickly quelled the rebellion and the majority of the protest passed off peacefully without violence.
>
> (www.thetimes.co.uk, 1 February 2009)

'A spokesman for the group of about 200 demonstrators said a small number of them were trying to take the Free Tibet flag to the doors of the building ... The protests passed off largely peacefully' (www.guardian.co.uk, 1 February 2009).

'Police detained several pro-Tibetan protesters ... Police soon confined the rest of the 200 or so protesters' (www.iht.com, 1 February 2009).

'Approximately 150 Chinese counter-demonstrators were also at the demonstration chanting pro-Chinese slogans' (www.cnn.com, 1 February 2009).

> As prime minister Wen Jiabao arrived at the university he was met by both pro-China supporters and people demonstrating against China's human rights record in its own country and in Tibet ... A twenty-seven-year old man has been charged after a shoe was thrown at the prime minister during a visit to Cambridge University ... The shoe was thrown at Mr Wen and he was called a 'dictator' as he gave a speech on the global economy on Monday [2 February]. The premier, on a three-day UK visit, described the incident as 'despicable'. The protest was similar to an event in December [2008] when US President George W. Bush was forced to duck to avoid [two] shoes thrown at him by an Iraqi journalist in Baghdad ... Throwing shoes is an insult in the Middle East.
>
> (www.bbc.co.uk, 3 February 2009)

> Witnesses said the protester shouted: 'How can the university prostitute itself with this dictator? How can you listen to the lies he is telling?' ... Prime minister Wen Jiabao continued with his speech after the incident, telling the audience: 'We come in peace. This is not going to obstruct China–UK relationships. History shows harmony will not be obstructed by any force, so would you let me continue.'
>
> (www.guardian.co.uk, 3 February 2009)

'The shoe missed prime minister Wen Jiabao and landed about a metre away from him ... He said: "This despicable behaviour cannot stand in the way of friendship between China and the UK"' (*IHT*, 3 February 2009, p. 1).

11 February 2009.

> The government has sentenced seventy-six people for taking part in the deadly riots in Tibet last March [2008] ... Details about the length of the sentences or the crimes committed [were not provided] ... [but it was] suggested that the government had shown leniency toward the 950 people who had been detained since the 14 March riots ... In a previous announcement last November [2008] the authorities said that fifty-five people had been sentenced to terms ranging from three years to life for crimes that included robbery, arson and disturbing public order.
>
> (www.iht.com, 11 February 2009; *IHT*, 12 February 2009, p. 5)

15 February 2009.

> Chinese police have detained several people after pro-Tibet protest in south-west China, campaign groups say. The protests flared at the weekend in Lithang county in Sichuan province. A number of Tibetans were beaten and twenty-one detained ... China does not allow foreign journalists unrestricted access to Tibet or restive areas surrounding it ... The protest began when a Tibetan monk shouted pro-Tibet slogans in a market place on Sunday [15 February]. Police beat those who joined him and arrested him ... Another

protest on Monday [16 February] drew more people, prompting further detentions and violence ... A total of twenty-one people were detained.

(www.bbc.co.uk, 18 February 2009)

Chinese officials have significantly increased security forces across Tibet in the face of a grass-roots movement to boycott festivities during the coming Tibetan New Year ... The movement aims to use the holiday period to mourn Tibetans who were killed during the government crackdown last March and express concern for those arrested or tortured ... Lithang, a town in Sichuan province, has been locked down this week. The problems in Lithang stemmed from a single person's protest on Sunday [15 February] ... A monk shouted slogans from a street corner supporting the Dalai Lama and calling for a New Year's boycott ... The next day hundreds of Tibetans took to the streets to demand the monk's release; riot police officers broke up the protest and arrested about twenty people ... The campaign for the boycott of Losar, the Tibetan New Year, has spread via text and email messages and fliers ... The call for a boycott ... has been endorsed by overseas Tibetans, including the government in exile in Dharamsala, India ... Foreign reporters are not allowed to visit Lhasa and central Tibet unless invited by the Chinese government.

(www.iht.com, 19 February 2009; *IHT*, 20 February 2009, p. 4)

Foreign tourists planning to visit Tibet have been told by travel agencies that the region has been closed to outsiders until the end of March ... China does not allow foreign journalists unrestricted access to Tibet or restive areas surrounding it.

(www.bbc.co.uk, 24 February 2009)

The Chinese government has quietly barred foreign tourists from entering Tibet before the fiftieth anniversary of a rebellion against Chinese rule, according to news reports ... Travel agencies have been told not to organize tours for foreigners into Tibet until after 1 April ... The government says that Tibet remains open and that foreigners can apply as usual for permits to travel there, but it has not said when they would be processed.

(www.iht.com, 25 February 2009)

China has introduced a heavy police presence into Tibetan regions of the country ahead of the start of Tibetan New Year celebrations on Wednesday [25 February], the first in a number of potential flashpoints over the next month. The fifteen-day festival, called Losar, is usually one of the most festive times of the year for Tibetans, but this year there has been an underground campaign to boycott the celebrations to mourn those killed during the wave of protests in the region last year [2008]. Chinese officials have been worried about the potential for unrest around other sensitive dates, including the fiftieth anniversary of the failed Tibetan uprising against the Beijing government that led the Dalai Lama to flee into exile on 10 March. The government has named 28 March as 'Serf Emancipation Day', a new

> holiday to celebrate the fiftieth anniversary of the official dissolution of the Tibetan government that was led by the Dalai Lama … The Chinese authorities say they are responding to the increased risk of crime in the region … In a statement on Tuesday evening the Dalai Lama said Tibetans should not respond to the 'provocation' of the security build-up. The campaign to boycott the traditional New Year, which Tibetan activists have described as an act of civil disobedience, has been building for several months … Diplomats and reporters who have recently visited Tibetan areas say there is some support for the boycott, although there is also plenty of opposition, including from shops and other service businesses for whom the holiday season is peak business … According to the Tibetan Centre for Human Rights and Democracy, a Dharamsala-based group, there was a two-day protest starting 14 February in Lithang county after a monk began chanting 'No Losar'.
>
> (www.ft.com, 25 February 2009)

26 February 2009.

> The State Department issued a report sharply critical of Beijing's human rights record … The 2008 Country Reports of Human Rights Practices: 'The government of China's human rights record remained poor and worsened in some areas … [Chinese authorities] committed extra-judicial killings and torture, coerced confessions of prisoners and used forced labour … [There has been] severe cultural and religious repression [of minorities in Tibet and other regions]' … [There has been] increasing harassment and detention of dissidents and activists who signed a petition calling for respect of human rights.
>
> (www.cnn.com, 26 February 2009)

'China's human rights record worsened in some areas in 2008, including the repression of dissidents and of minorities in Tibet, the report said' (www.bbc.co.uk, 26 February 2009).

> The State Department document … an annual US State Department report on global human rights … singled out China, Russia, Zimbabwe, Egypt and a handful of other countries as states where human rights conditions had deteriorated during 2008 … The section on China particularly criticized the government's treatment of its Tibetan and Uighur minorities and what it termed 'increased detention and harassment of dissidents and petitioners' The document stated that as many as 218 Tibetans died in the violence, far more than the twenty-one civilian deaths claimed by the Chinese authorities, and it cited 'numerous reports that the government or its agents committed unlawful or arbitrary killings' during the protests. It also referred to reports that as many as 1,100 Tibetans had disappeared after the violence, their whereabouts still unknown, including one 'highly revered' Tibetan Buddhist leader, Phurbu Tsering Rinpoche of Kardze.
>
> (www.iht.com, 26 February 2009)

27 February 2009.

Chinese police today [Friday 27 February] shot a burning Tibetan monk before they put him out, the Free Tibet campaign said. The monk had set himself on fire in a protest over Tibetan New Year rituals in Aba county, Sichuan province … The area saw some of the worst unrest during Tibetan protests last March … Tabe … a monk aged in his twenties … was immediately put in a van and taken to an undisclosed location. His present condition is unknown … Free Tibet said up to 800 monks had reportedly gone to Tabe's home village of Trinkin to say prayers, believing him to be dead … The group said Tabe's protest followed an attempt by almost 1,000 monks at Kirte to use a prayer hall to observe the Monman festival – part of the Tibetan New Year – despite being told not to do so … More than 100 monks from the Lutsang monastery in Qinghai province held a candlelit vigil and protest march on Wednesday, the US-funded Radio Free Asia reported today.

(www.guardian.co.uk, 27 February 2009; *Guardian*, 28 February 2009, p. 23)

1 March 2009.

Tibetan monks … took to the streets after they were banned from holding a traditional New Year's prayer ceremony Sunday [1 March], activists said. About fifty monks demonstrated outside the Sey Monastery in an ethnic Tibetan part of Sichuan province that was the scene of protests last year [2008] and where a monk set himself on fire on Friday [27 February], a group called Students for a Free Tibet said. The monastery has been sealed off by police officers.

(*IHT*, 2 March 2009, p. 6)

10 March 2009.

On 10 March 1959 Tibetans rose up in rebellion against the Chinese government. That rebellion failed and the Dalai Lama fled … A total of 80,000 Tibetans followed … The [Tibetan] government-in-exile says: 'Over 1,2 million Tibetans, one-fifth of a population of 6 million, have died as the direct result of China's invasion of Tibet' … [On 10 March 2009] the fiftieth anniversary of a failed uprising against Chinese troops which led to his exile … the Dalai Lama launched a fierce attack on Chinese rule in his Tibetan homeland … [China says the 1950 uprising] was a plot by Tibet's upper classes who wanted to maintain their feudal hold over their enslaved people … The government-in-exile says China's 'ruthless' clampdown following the protests [a year ago] left 210 peaceful protesters dead. It says about 5,600 people are under arrest or in detention, with 1,000 missing. China says eighteen civilians and policemen died in what it terms a riot. To prevent a repeat of those protests this year, there is a heavy security presence in Tibetan areas, including those outside the Tibetan Autonomous

> Region ... Thousands of Chinese troops and paramilitary police are said to have been deployed in Tibetan-populated regions amid fresh fears of violence on the sensitive anniversary. Campaign groups have already reported some unrest in areas around Tibet ... People who have visited Tibetan areas say there is heavy security and the situation is tense.
>
> (www.bbc.co.uk, 10 March 2009)

'[In 1959] the Dalai Lama fled to India with 83,000 followers' (*The Times*, 11 March 2009, p. 34).

'Four-fifths of Tibetans do not speak good Chinese ... In 1958 there were 114,000 monks and 2,700 monasteries in Tibet. By 1976 there were a little over 800 monks in just eight monasteries' (*FT*, 11 March 2009, p. 12). 'The Dalai Lama dropped the demand for independence in favour of "meaningful autonomy" in 1988' (*FT*, 14 March 2009, p. 11).

> Tension was high ahead of the fiftieth anniversary ... There are reports that extra security troops were deployed to the region to avert a repeat of last year's unrest ... Tibetan exiles say more than 200 people died when Chinese security forces clamped down, but Beijing denies this, saying twenty-two people, mostly Chinese civilians, died during riots.
>
> (www.cnn.com, 10 March 2009)

'The authorities say twenty-two people died, mostly because of rioters, while Tibetan exiles alleged that more than 200 Tibetans died in the crackdown' (www.guardian.co.uk, 10 March 2009).

'To forestall protest during the anniversary season, the Chinese government has deployed a massive security presence both in the autonomous region and in the neighbouring provinces of Sichuan and Qinghai' (www.economist.com, 10 March 2009).

> In the rugged Tibetan regions of China ... no reports emerged Tuesday [10 March] of any large-scale protests. The Chinese government, fearing civil unrest among 6 million Tibetans, has locked down the vast area, which measures up to a quarter of China, by sending in thousands of troops in the last few weeks and cutting off cellphone and internet services in some locations ... At least nineteen people were killed in Lhasa [in the 2008 riots], most of them Han Chinese civilians, according to the Chinese government. In the violent suppression that followed, 220 Tibetans were killed, nearly 1,300 were injured and nearly 7,000 were detained or imprisoned, according to the Tibetan government-in-exile. More than 1,000 Tibetans are still missing ... Officials from Lhasa said last week that 953 had been detained after the riots and that seventy-six of them were sentenced on charges of robbery, arson and attacking government institutions. The others have all been released, the officials said.
>
> (www.iht.com, 10 March 2009)

'There were few reports of unrest in the Tibetan regions on the [fiftieth] anniversary' (*FT*, 11 March 2009, p. 8).

'[The Dalai Lama spoke in Dharamsala] before some 10,000 Tibetans from around the world' (www.independent.co.uk, 10 March 2009).

The Dalai Lama (10 March 2009):

> [The Chinese government carried out] a series of repressive and violent campaigns [throughout the decades] ... These thrust Tibetans into such depths of suffering and hardship that they literally experienced hell on earth ... The immediate result of these campaigns was the deaths of hundreds of thousands of Tibetans ... These fifty years have brought untold suffering and destruction to the land and people of Tibet. Today the religion, culture, language and identity, which successive generations of Tibetans have considered more precious than their lives, are nearing extinction. In short, the Tibetan people are regarded like criminals deserving to be put to death ... Even today Tibetans in Tibet live in constant fear and the Chinese authorities remain constantly suspicious of them ... Hundreds of thousands of my people [have been killed and thousands of places of worship destroyed] ... Many infrastructural developments ... which seem to have brought progress to Tibetan areas were really done with the political objective of Sinicizing Tibet ... [They were done to move Han Chinese migrants into Tibet] at the huge cost of devastating the Tibetan environment and way of life ... There has been a brutal crackdown on the Tibetan protests that have shaken the whole of Tibet since last March ... We Tibetans are looking for legitimate and meaningful autonomy, an arrangement that would enable Tibetans to live within the framework of the People's Republic of China. I have no doubt that the justice of Tibet's cause will prevail, if we continue to tread the path of truth and non-violence ... [The two sides should] look to the future and work for our mutual benefit. Fulfilling the aspirations of the Tibetan people will enable China to achieve stability and unity.'
>
> (www.ccn.com, 10 March 2009; www.bbc.co.uk, 10 March 2009; www.guardian.co.uk, 10 March 2009; www.independent.co.uk, 10 March 2009; www.iht.com, 10 March 2009; www.thetimes.com, 10 March 2009)

'Pro-Tibet supporters have marched in London and other cities to mark the [fiftieth] anniversary' (www.cnn.com, 10 March 2009).

'Tibetans outside of China and their supporters held rallies around the world Tuesday [10 March] to mark the fiftieth anniversary of a failed Tibetan uprising against Chinese rule ... After the Dalai Lama's speech thousands of Tibetans marched through Dharamsala' (www.iht.com, 10 March 2009).

12 March 2009.

> The Chinese government lodged a formal complaint to the Obama administration on Thursday [12 March] over a resolution passed by the US House of Representatives that calls on China to 'cease its repression of the Tibetan people ... [and] respond to the Dalai Lama's initiatives to find a lasting solution to the Tibetan issue' ... Representatives voted 422 to one on Wednesday [11 March] to pass the non-binding resolution, which was

intended to mark the fiftieth anniversary of a failed Tibetan uprising against Chinese rule.

(www.iht.com, 12 March 2009; *IHT*, 13 March 2009, p. 2)

13 March 2009. Prime minister Wen Jiabao (13 March):

> Several days ago the Dalai Lama tried to rebut Chinese statements and said he has never asked the government to withdraw troops or remove Han ethnic groups. These are sheer lies. These are all written words on paper. Of course, the Dalai Lama can change his quotes. But he can never deny what he has already said [referring to a peace proposal the Dalai Lama made in 1988].
>
> (www.cnn.com, 13 March 2009)

16 March 2009.

> A bomb was hurled into a government building in a predominantly Tibetan area of western China amid growing concern over a period of unrest in the region. China's state-controlled media said Tuesday [17 March] that no one was injured in what it called a 'terrorist' attack. The blast occurred Monday [16 March] during a sensitive period for Tibet … A public security officer in the Tibetan Ganzi prefecture of Sichuan province said the blast had damaged a new police station. Last week a police car and fire engine in another Tibetan region were struck by a homemade bomb.
>
> (www.iht.com, 17 March 2009)

21 March 2009.

> Some ninety-three monks have been held by Chinese police after a riot in an ethnically Tibetan town, state-run media report. The monks were held after a crowd of at least 100 attacked a police station in Gyala township in Qinghai province on Saturday [21 March], Xinhua news agency said. The agency quoted officials as saying policemen and government staff had been assaulted and 'slightly injured'. The protest was apparently sparked after a monk detained for advocating Tibetan independence escaped from jail. Chinese authorities said the monk fled on Saturday and was still missing. But a Tibetan website said the monk had killed himself by jumping into a river.
>
> (www.bbc.co.uk, 22 March 2009)

> Nearly 100 Tibetan monks were arrested or turned themselves in Sunday [22 March] after hundreds of protesters attacked a police station in north-west China, state media reported. The protest appeared to be in retaliation for the disappearance of a Tibetan from police custody in Qinghai province, reported Xinhua, the official news agency. Six people were arrested over alleged involvement in the riot and another eighty-nine people surrendered to the police. All but two were monks, Xinhua said. On Saturday [21 March] several hundred people, including nearly 100 monks from the Lagyab monastery, attacked the police station of Lagyab and assaulted officers and

police, Xinhua said … The violence began after a man accused of supporting Tibetan independence escaped from police custody, Xinhua said. A Tibetan exile website says the man committed suicide after fleeing.

(www.iht.com, 22 March 2009; *IHT*, 23 March 2009, p. 7)

'A source … [said the man] had unfurled a Tibetan flag on 10 March' (*FT*, 23 March 2009, p. 8).

'The Tibetan-government-in-exile … said 4,000 people clashed with police in Tibet over the suicide of a Tibetan monk' (*Independent*, 23 March 2009, p. 24).

'Tibetan exiles … put the crowd numbers at variously 1,000 and 2,000' (*Guardian*, 23 March 2009, p. 16).

24 March 2009.

Google, the internet company, said Tuesday [24] that its YouTube video-sharing website was being blocked in China. The company said it did not know why the YouTube site was being blocked, but on Tuesday a report in China's official Xinhua news agency accused supporters of the Dalai Lama of fabricating a video that appears to show Chinese police brutally beating Tibetans following riots last month in Lhasa … The agency did not identify the video, but, based on its description, it appears to match a video, available on YouTube, that was released by the Tibetan government-in-exile recently. It purports to show police storming a monastery after riots in Lhasa last March, kicking and beating protesters.

(www.iht.com, 25 March 2009)

China said video footage that purportedly shows Chinese security personnel violently beating Tibetans last year is 'a lie' … A Chinese government official said many of the images and voices in the video had been pieced together from different sources.

(www.bbc.co.uk, 25 March 2009)

'The video itself makes clear that it contains three sets of pictures [from 1988 and 2008]' (*The Times*, 26 March 2009).

('The Chinese government has lifted its block of YouTube, the popular video-sharing website run by Google. On Friday [27 March] people in Beijing accessed the site without using special software to enter it through a proxy server, a common way of getting around internet walls put up by the government': www.iht.com, 30 March 2009. 'YouTube was blocked in China for most of last week and again on Monday [30 January]': *IHT*, 31 March 2009, p. 9.)

27 March 2009.

South Africa has denied the Dalai Lama a visa to attend a peace conference [to be held on 27 March] linked to the 2010 Football World Cup which the country is hosting … A government spokesman has denied suggestions that the ban was a result of Chinese pressure. He said he did not want anything

> to distract from South Africa's hosting of the World Cup. The Johannesburg conference is intended to discuss football's role in fighting racism and xenophobia … Archbishop Desmond Tutu has pulled out of the meeting in protest … Archbishop Tutu: 'We are shamelessly succumbing to Chinese pressure. I feel deeply distressed and ashamed' … South Africa is China's largest trading partner in Africa, with 2008 trade standing at $10 billion … The Dalai Lama has visited the country on two previous occasions, in 1999 and 2004.
>
> (www.bbc.co.uk, 23 March 2009)

'[A government spokesman said] the decision was made last month … [He] said the Dalai Lama has been welcomed twice previously in South Africa and would be welcome again in the future' (www.independent.co.uk, 23 March 2009).

> South Africa has barred the Dalai Lama from a peace conference in Johannesburg … The peace conference Friday [27 March] was organized by South African soccer officials to highlight the first World Cup to be held in Africa, which South Africa is to host in 2010. But because the Dalai Lama is not being allowed to attend, the gathering is being boycotted by fellow Nobel Peace laureates the Reverend Desmond Tutu, retired Anglican Archbishop of Cape Town, and former president F.W. de Klerk. Members of the Nobel Committee have also declined to attend … South Africa decided last month [February] to refuse to issue an official invitation, without which … the Dalai Lama cannot visit.
>
> (*IHT*, 24 March 2009, p. 2)

'The peace conference was billed as an opportunity to showcase South Africa's role as a human rights champion ahead of its hosting of soccer's World Cup next year [2010]' (www.cnn.com, 23 March 2009).

> A peace conference for Nobel laureates in South Africa has been postponed indefinitely after Pretoria refused the Dalai Lama a visit … [The] government spokesman confirmed that no visa would be issued 'between now and the World Cup' … The conference, scheduled for Friday [27 March], was intended to discuss football's role in fighting racism and xenophobia. But the chairman of the South Africa 2010 Organizing Committee said the conference was being postponed indefinitely.
>
> (www.bbc.co.uk, 24 March 2009)

28 March 2009.

> Officials in Tibet have designated Saturday 28 March as Serf Liberation Day … Chinese officials say 90 per cent of more than 1 million people living in Tibet were 'serfs' until China dissolved the pro-Dalai Lama Tibetan government on 28 March 1959, and began handing out aristocratic and monastic land to farmers and nomads … Instruments [were] supposedly used to torture serfs before the uprising was crushed.
>
> (www.economist.com, 25 March 2009)

> China marked fifty years of direct control over Tibet on Saturday [28 March] ... a new holiday ... [called 'Serfs' Emancipation Day'] ... In China's official version of events, Tibet in mid-century was a remote mediaeval backwater where most people lived in servitude to the Buddhist theocracy and nobility ... Hundreds of Tibetans in Dharamsala and in the Nepalese capital of Kathmandu held street protests against Beijing's rule.
>
> (www.iht.com, 28 March 2009)

> A ceremony in the regional capital and a lavish international Buddhist conference featured a rare appearance by the government's hand-picked religious leader ... The second World Buddhist Forum, in the eastern city of Wuxi, was addressed by the Beijing-backed Panchen Lama, the second highest figure in Tibetan Buddhism. The nineteen-year-old ... Gyaltsen Norbu ... [made a] rare appearance ... The forum attracted more than 1,000 monks, nuns and adherents from around the world ... Gyaltsen Norbu is not widely accepted by Tibetans as the Panchen Lama. Another boy, Gendun Choekyi Nyima, was named as the incarnation of the Panchen Lama by the Dalai Lama in 1995. The boy and his family disappeared soon after and have not been heard from since ... Buddhism arrived in China 2,000 years ago and has endured alternating periods of flowering and government-sponsored purges. Following the founding of the communist state in 1949, monks and nuns were forced from their monasteries, temples were converted to factories, and the religion mocked as backward vestiges of feudal China. Tibetan Buddhism and different types of Chinese Buddhism are practised differently, though there are close ties historically.
>
> (www.iht.com, 29 March 2009)

'Since 1959 ... life expectancy ... has increased ... to sixty-seven years from thirty-five-and-a-half' (*The Times*, 28 March, p. 49).

29 March 2009.

> An electronic network, based mainly in China, has infiltrated computers from government offices around the world, Canadian researchers say. They said the network had infiltrated 1,295 computers in 103 countries. They included computers belonging to foreign ministries and embassies and those linked with the Dalai Lama ... Researchers say they have no conclusive evidence China's government was behind [the network]. Beijing has denied involvement. The report comes after a ten-month investigation by the Information Warfare Monitor (IWM), which comprises researchers from Ottawa-based think-tank SecDev Group and the University of Toronto's Munk Centre for International Studies. They were acting on a request from the Tibetan spiritual leader's office to check whether the computers of his Tibetan exile network had been infiltrated ... Investigator Greg Walton: 'We uncovered real-time evidence of malware [malicious software] that had penetrated Tibetan computer systems, extracting sensitive documents from the private office of the Dalai Lama' ... [The researchers] say they believe

the system, which they called GhostNet, was focused on governments in Asia … According to *The New York Times*, the spying operation is the largest to have been uncovered in terms of the number of countries affected.

(www.bbc.co.uk, 29 March 2009)

A mystery electronic network apparently based in China has infiltrated hundreds of computers around the world and stolen files and documents, Canadian researchers have revealed. The network, dubbed GhostNet, appears to target embassies, media groups, NGOs, international organizations, government foreign ministries and the offices of the Dalai Lama … After ten months of study the researchers concluded that GhostNet had invaded 1,295 computers in 103 countries, but it appeared to be most focused on countries in south Asia and South-east Asia, as well as the Dalai Lama's offices in India … The researchers were clear that they had not been able to identify who was behind the network, and said it could be run by private citizens in China or a different country altogether. A Chinese government spokesman has denied any official involvement … The Chinese government regularly attacks the Tibetan exile movement as encouraging separatism and terrorism within China. The researchers found that the computers had succumbed to cyber-attack and that numerous files, including letters and emails, had been stolen. The intruders had also gained control of the electronic mail server of the Dalai Lama's computers … The news comes as researchers at Cambridge University prepare to release a report today [29 March] called Snooping Dragon, which looks at suspected Chinese cyber-monitoring of Tibetan exile groups.

(www.guardian.co.uk, 29 March 2009)

While one of the reports remains mute on the identity of the perpetrators, the other has no such qualms, warning that the Chinese government ran a series of cyber attacks on Tibetan exile groups. The Cambridge authors of 'The Snooping Dragon: Social Malware Surveillance of the Tibetan Movement': 'What Chinese spooks did in 2008, Russian crooks will do in 2010 and even low-budget criminals will follow in due course.' But the authors of 'Tracking Ghost-Net' argue that things may not be as they seem in the world of electronic espionage.

(*Guardian*, 30 March 2009, p. 16)

The Toronto team said they could not prove the Chinese government was behind the hacking but in a separate report those who researched spying on the Tibetan exile movement did not hesitate to point the finger … Ross Anderson (Cambridge University) and Shishir Nagaraja (University of Illinois): 'Agents of the Chinese government compromised the computing infrastructure of the office of His Holiness the Dalai Lama … and then downloaded sensitive data. People in Tibet may have died as a result.'

(*Independent*, 30 March 2009, p. 24)

The researchers said that the system was being controlled from computers based almost exclusively in China, but that they could not say conclusively that the Chinese government was involved ... In less than two years ... [the operation] has infiltrated at least 1,295 computers in 103 countries, including many belonging to embassies, foreign ministries and other government offices, as well as the Dalai Lama's exile centre in India, Brussels, London and New York ... Intelligence analysts say many governments, including those of China, Russia and the United States, and other parties use sophisticated computer programmes to covertly gather information ... The newly reported spying operation is by far the largest to come to light in terms of countries affected ... The researchers said ... they had found no evidence that US government offices had been infiltrated, although a Nato computer was monitored by the spies for half a day and computers of the Indian embassy in Washington were infiltrated ... The electronic spy game has had at least some real-world impact, they said. For example, they said, after an email invitation was sent by the Dalai Lama's office to a foreign diplomat, the Chinese government made a call to the diplomat discouraging a visit. And a woman for a group making internet contacts between Tibetan exiles and Chinese citizens was stopped by Chinese intelligence officers in her way back to Tibet, shown transcripts of her online conversations and warned to stop her political activities ... Although the Canadian researchers said that most of the computers behind the spying were in China, they cautioned against concluding that China's government was involved. The spying could be a non-state, for-profit operation, for example, or one run by private Chinese citizens known as 'patriotic hackers' ... Ronald Deibert (a member of the research group): 'This could well be the CIA or the Russians' ... At the same time two computer researchers at Cambridge University in Britain who worked on the part of the investigation related to the Tibetans, are releasing an independent report. They do not fault China, and they warned that other hackers could adopt the tactics used in the malware operation.

(www.iht.com, 29 March 2009)

The spying operation is by far the largest to come to light in terms of the number of countries affected ... The operation, [which] is still going strong, continues to invade and monitor more than a dozen new computers a week, the researchers said in their report 'Tracking Ghost-Net: Investigating a Cyber Espionage Network'.

(*IHT*, 30 March 2009, p. 1)

University of Toronto experts found 1,295 infected computers around the world and observed the operation stealing documents and watching and listening to users through webcams and microphones ... The report said circumstantial evidence suggested that the Chinese state had exploited this set of high profile targets for 'military and strategic-intelligence purposes'. It said many attacks appeared to come from Hainan Island, home of the Chinese military's Lingshui signals intelligence facility ... In 2007 Chinese military hackers penetrated the Pentagon computer network serving Robert

> Gates, the US Defence Secretary. Hackers originally from China last year [2008] broke into the White House computer system.
>
> (*FT*, 30 March 2009, p. 10)

> The Canadian report said: 'Chinese cyber espionage is a major global concern … [but] attributing all Chinese malware to deliberate or targeted intelligence gathering operations by the Chinese state is wrong and misleading' … But the report also points out that China is among a handful of countries, also including the United States, Israel and the United Kingdom, which are 'assumed' to have considerable cyber-espionage capabilities.
>
> (www.cnn.com, 30 March 2009)

('[In the UK] intelligence chiefs have warned that China may have gained the capability to shut down Britain by crippling its telecoms and utilities. They have told ministers of their fears that equipment installed by Huawei, the Chinese telecoms giant, in BT's new communications network could be used to halt critical services such as power, food and water supplies. The warnings coincide with growing cyber-warfare attacks on Britain by foreign governments, particularly Russia and China … Whitehall departments were reportedly targeted by the Chinese in 2007 … Computers at the Foreign Office and other Whitehall departments were attacked from China in 2007. In the same year … [MI5] warned 300 British businesses that they were under Chinese cyber-attack … Two years ago Chinese Trojan horse spyware was found in the offices of Angela Merkel, the German chancellor … An attempt by Huawei to merge with the US company 3Com, which provides computer security systems for the Pentagon, was blocked last year [2008] … [Huawei was set up] in 1988 after an edict from Deng Xiaoping that the country's defence industry turn itself into profitable companies able to acquire modern technology. A Pentagon report last week cited Huawei as a key part of the cyber-threat from China, noting that it retained "close ties" with the People's Liberation Army (PLA). Huawei denies any continuing links to the PLA': www.thetimes.com, 29 March 2009. 'Huawei's boss, Ren Zhengfei, is a former Chinese army officer': www.economist.com, 2 April 2009.)

30 March 2009.

> China says it is reopening Tibet to foreign tourists in early April … Even at the best of times foreigners needed special permission to visit Tibet … Visitor numbers [were] down by nearly half in the first nine months of last year [2008], according to Xinhua.
>
> (www.bbc.co.uk, 30 March 2009)

> The Chinese government will reopen Tibet to foreign tourists on 5 April after a nearly six-week ban, according to Xinhua. Foreign tourists were barred from visiting Tibet in late February before the fiftieth anniversary of a failed rebellion against Chinese rule … The anniversary passed on Saturday [28 March] without serious unrest … Chinese officials said 13,000 people in Lhasa celebrated Saturday.
>
> (www.iht.com, 30 March 2009)

'In the first two months of the year [2009] 120,000 domestic and foreign tourists visited Tibet, a jump of about 5 per cent over the same period last year [2008], according to the regional tourism bureau' (*IHT*, 31 March 2009).

> Tibetan discontent at Chinese rule has taken a new twist, with farmers refusing to till their fields ... Officials have sent for troops from the People's Liberation Army to work with farmers – or in their place if need be – to carry out spring planting in mountainous regions able to support only one crop a year. Local sources say that many farmers in areas of Sichuan province with large ethnic Tibetan populations have decided to down tools and leave their barley fields fallow this year ... The government has even ordered officials and party members to get on with the spring planting. The extent of the protest was impossible to gauge since foreign reporters are barred from Tibet and have been prevented from entering Tibetan populated regions. However, it appears to be serious enough to have prompted a statement this week from the Dalai Lama's base in India saying: 'The Tibetan government-in-exile of the Dalai Lama appeals to Tibetans not to make this sacrifice and to stop their refusal to till the fields' ... A Tibetan monk was killed and eight people wounded when Tibetan farmers and paramilitary police clashed in Luhuo county late last month [March]. The farmers had refused to commit to plant a certain amount of their land with crops. The dead monk had been organizing the farmers to refuse to plant crops, local residents said.
>
> (*The Times*, 11 April 2009, p. 40)

1 April 2009.

> China and France have agreed to restore high level contacts, ending a rift that began after French President Nicolas Sarkozy met the Dalai Lama last year ... The Chinese foreign ministry said: 'France refuses to support any form of Tibet independence.'
>
> (www.bbc.co.uk, 1 April 2009)

> President Nicolas Sarkozy of France and President Hu Jintao met Wednesday [1 April] in London before the G-2 summit meeting after months of friction [over Tibet] ... An unusual joint statement issued Wednesday by the foreign ministries of both countries: 'France fully recognizes the importance and sensitivity of the Tibet issue ... [and reaffirms] the position that Tibet is an integral part of the Chinese territory ... [France refuses to support any claim of Tibetan independence and both countries adhere] to the principle of non-interference in each other's affairs ... [The leaders have] decided to conduct high level contacts and new sessions in their strategic dialogue at an opportune time' ... France went to some lengths to emphasize that its position on Tibet in particular was not a shift from its long-held policy. In the joint statement the two sides noted that what was called the 'one China policy' and the French view of Tibet's status had first been formulated by Charles de Gaulle in the late 1950s and 1960s. It said the French attitude 'has not changed and will not change.'
>
> (www.iht.com, 2 April 2009; *IHT*, 2 April 2009, p. 4)

8 April 2009.

> Two Tibetans have been sentenced to death for their role in riots in Lhasa last year, Xinhua said on Wednesday [8 April]. They were found guilty of 'starting fatal fires' during the riot … Two others got suspended death sentences and another life imprisonment.
>
> (www.iht.com, 8 April 2009)

'The report did not say what charges they [the other three] had faced or when the rulings were made' (*IHT*, 9 April 2009, p. 8).

> These are the first definitive death sentences relating to the riots in Lhasa last March … The two men sentenced to death played a part in starting fires which resulted in seven deaths and the destruction of five shops in Lhasa, Chinese state media report … Two were given suspended death sentences – which are usually commuted to life imprisonment – and another was sentenced to life.
>
> (www.bbc.co.uk, 8 April 2009)

21 April 2009.

> A respected Tibetan lama went on trial on weapons charges on Tuesday [21 April] and three people were sentenced to long prison terms for deadly arson attacks during last year's rioting in Lhasa. The lama, Phurbu Tsering Rinpoche, the first senior Buddhist monk to face a serious charge linked to last year's demonstrations, is accused of illegally possessing weapons … The monk led a convent in Ganzi, a predominantly Tibetan area of Sichuan province.
>
> (www.iht.com, 22 April 2009)

> The abbot of two convents … is expected to be sentenced next Tuesday [29 April] on charges of weapons possession and embezzlement … The abbot … a living Buddha … is believed to be the most senior figure put on trial following waves of detentions aimed at suppressing a widespread Tibetan uprising last year … [He] was detained by security forces on 18 May, four days after a protest by more than eighty nuns from his convents … On Tuesday a court sentenced three Tibetans convicted of setting or helping set a deadly fire during the rioting in Lhasa. One Tibetan was given a death sentence with a two-year reprieve, a second was given life in prison and a third was given ten years in prison.
>
> (www.iht.com, 24 April 2009)

('A Chinese court has indefinitely postponed delivering a verdict in the case of a Tibetan abbot charged with illegal possession of weapons and embezzlement, a lawyer for the abbot said Monday [28 April]. The abbot, Phurbu Tsering Rinpoche … was originally scheduled to receive a verdict on Tuesday [28 April]': www.iht.com, 28 April 2009.)

24 April 2009. 'The Dalai Lama arrived [in the United States] on Friday [24 April] for a two-week tour' (www.iht.com, 26 April 2009).

Last week the Dalai Lama and more than 100 scholars from China [met in the United States] … He described the three- and four-hour audiences he had with Chairman Mao Zedong in Beijing more than a half century ago. He said he had once been attracted to the moral principles of socialism and had even asked to join the Chinese Communist Party.

(*IHT*, 7 May 2009, p. 6)

May 2009.

The Dalai Lama said … the only solution is to allow genuine autonomy for the 6 million Tibetans … The regional authority would make policy on education, religious practice and the use of natural resources, while Beijing would retain the right to keep military forces in the region and oversee foreign affairs. An autonomous Tibetan government would not force out Han Chinese who had already settled in the vast Tibetan plateau … but would place limits on any future migration. The Dalai Lama said: 'Autonomous regions should be the native peoples' majority' … The Dalai Lama said that autonomy was enshrined in the Chinese constitution, which guarantees the right of regional self-rule for ethnic minorities. Based on that, he said, the large area of western China that is predominantly Tibetan – including Tibet, but also parts of the provinces of Qinhai, Sichuan, Gansu and Yunnan – should be united under a single Tibetan authority … [China says this] would mean turning over one-quarter of China to Tibetan governance … The Dalai Lama: 'Tibet is very, very backward. And every Tibetan wants to modernize Tibet. So, for that reason, remaining within the People's Republic of China is in our own interest as far as economic development is concerned, provided we have full guarantee to preserve our own culture, our own language, our own spirituality and full protection of environment.'

(www.iht.com, 29 May 2009)

'The Dalai Lama said: "Whether intentionally or unintentionally, some kind of cultural genocide is taking place"' (www.iht.com, 6 June 2009). 'The Dalai Lama said … that all options for choosing his reincarnation were open, including ones that break from tradition' (www.iht.com, 7 June 2008).

A group of prominent Chinese lawyers and legal scholars have released a research report arguing that the Tibetan riots and protests of March 2008 were rooted in legitimate grievances brought about by failed government policies … The lengthy paper is the result of interviews conducted over a month in two Tibetan regions. It represents the first independent investigation into the causes of the widespread protest … The research paper was quietly posted last month [May] on Chinese websites, and an English translation was released this week by the International Campaign for Tibet, an advocacy group based in Washington. The authors of the report are members of a Chinese group called *Gongmen*, or Open Constitution Initiative, which seeks to promote legal reform in China.

Lawyers in the group also tried to file lawsuits on behalf of families whose babies suffered in the tainted milk scandal last year [2008], and two members have defended Tibetans in court this year. The authors of the report concluded that Chinese government policies had promoted a form of economic modernization in Tibet that left many Tibetans feeling increasingly disenfranchised over the decades. The researchers found that Tibetans had enormous difficulty finding work in their homeland, while ethnic Han Chinese migrants have a monopoly on jobs in restaurants, hotels and stores … The report said: 'An important perspective for interpreting the 14 March incident is that it was a reaction made under stress by a society and people to the various changes that have been taking place in their lives over the past few decades. The notion that appears impossible to understand is the implication that reasonable demands were being vented, and this is precisely what we need to understand and reflect upon … When the land you are accustomed to living in, and the land of the culture you identify with, when the lifestyle and religiosity is suddenly changed into a "modern city" that you no longer recognize; when you can no longer find work in your own land, and feel the unfairness of lack of opportunity, and when you realize that your core value systems are under attack, then the Tibetan people's panic and sense of crisis is not difficult to understand' … The report also cast blame on the governing structure in Tibetan regions, saying that there had been problems adapting Tibetan culture and society to the 'ruling state's systems'. It also criticized the central government for putting into power incompetent Tibetan local officials who, the researchers say, play up the threat of separatist movements to acquire more power and money from Beijing. The report quoted Phuntsok Wangyal, one of the founders of the Communist Party in Tibet as saying: 'They are unable to admit their mistakes and instead pull all of their effort into shifting accountability onto "hostile foreign forces"' … [*Gongmeng* said] the report had been submitted to the government, but that there had been no response.

(www.iht.com, 6 June 2009)

7 June 2009.

The Dalai Lama has been made an honorary citizen of Paris. The mayor, Bertrand Delanoë, made the award in what French President Nicolas Sarkozy described as a municipal matter, not an act of state … The Dalai Lama said on Sunday [7 June] that the rioting that erupted in Tibet in March last year [2008] had been fomented by agents of the Chinese state in order to justify a subsequent crackdown and smear local activists as rioters. The Dalai Lama said: 'Despite a heavy security presence throughout Lhasa from 10 March onwards, it remains unclear why the Chinese force of order remained inactive for so long in the centre of the city. On 14 March Tibetans unknown to anyone in Lhasa started to burn shops and throw stones at the Chinese without police interference, while film crews already in place filmed the scene and broadcast it throughout the world. Only then did the security forces crack down on the disturbances. It is not hard to suspect a deliberate staging of riots.'

(www.bbc.co.uk, 8 June 2009)

11 August 2009.

The Dalai Lama: 'The Chinese government considers our problem a domestic one. And we also ... We are simply waiting [for Beijing to send signals]' ... Between 2002 and 2008 nine rounds of negotiations were conducted between Chinese officials and his representatives.

(www.bbc.co.uk, 11 August 2009)

30 August–4 September 2009. For the Dalai Lama's visit to Taiwan, see Chapter 2.

14 September 2009.

A senior adviser to President Barack Obama met the Dalai Lama on Monday [14 September] in Dharamsala, in northern India, and discussed the exiled spiritual leader's views on how to preserve Tibetan identity ... Valerie Jarrett was the highest ranking Washington official to visit the Dalai Lama in Dharamsala, where he lives, since House Speaker Nancy Pelosi travelled there in March 2008. The Dalai Lama visited the United States in May [2009] and plans to return next month [October 2009] ... Ms Jarrett was accompanied by Maria Otero, under secretary of state for global affairs, who will be the administration's official in charge of the Tibet issue ... The Dalai Lama's office said in a statement ... that the Dalai Lama hopes to meet Mr Obama after the president visits China in November [2009].

(www.iht.com, 15 September 2009)

22 September 2009.

China has banned foreign tourists from travelling to Tibet ahead of a parade in the capital to mark sixty years of communist rule, an official said Tuesday [22 September], amid stepped up security across the country to ensure nothing mars the celebrations ... Foreign tourists would be banned from Tuesday onwards, but those who have already arrived would be allowed to stay ... The ban will be in effect until 8 October ... China requires foreigners to obtain special permission to visit Tibet ... The region has been periodically off-limits since riots in March 2008.

(www.iht.com, 22 September 2009)

The Dalai Lama was welcomed to Memphis ... [by] interim Memphis mayor Myron Lowery on Tuesday [22 September] ... The Dalai Lama is in Memphis to receive the International Freedom Award from the National Civil Rights Museum on Wednesday [23 September].

(www.iht.com, 23 September 2009)

6 October 2009.

> The Dalai Lama accepted a human rights prize from a US foundation Tuesday [6 October] … The inaugural Lantos Human Rights Prize, presented by House Speaker Nancy Pelosi, honours his commitment to ending global injustice … The award [was] from the Lantos Foundation for Human Rights and Justice … The foundation describes … the late Tom Lantos as a champion of human rights during his twenty-seven years in Congress … The Dalai Lama won't meet with President Barack Obama, who instead plans to visit with him after a presidential trip next month [November] to China … The Dalai Lama … whose name is Tenzin Gyatso … is slated to return to India before travelling to Japan, Australia and New Zealand.
>
> (www.cnn.com, 6 October 2009)

20 October 2009.

> A Tibetan exile group in India says that the Chinese authorities have executed four people for the roles in the riots that convulsed Tibet last year [2008]. According to the Tibetan Centre for Human Rights and Democracy, the four were put to death on Tuesday [20 October]. More than six months after they were tried and convicted of starting fires in Lhasa that killed seven people … Since March 2008 at least eighty-four people have been convicted during trials that rights groups say are opaque, cursory and unfair … Although they claim that Tibetans are sometimes secretly killed in detention, exile groups say the executions this week were the first in Tibet since 2002. They identified three of those killed … [two] man and a woman … According to the Congressional-Executive Commission on China, which released a report on Thursday [22 October] that documents the crackdown, at least 670 Tibetans have been jailed in 2009 for activities that include peaceful protest or leaking information to the outside world. The report detailed a widespread 'patriotic education' campaign that requires monks and nuns to pass examinations on political texts, agree that Tibet is historically a part of China and denounce the Dalai Lama.
>
> (www.iht.com, 24 October 2009)

> Two Tibetans have been executed for their involvement in riots in Tibet last year, the Chinese government has confirmed … The two men were sentenced to death in April for starting fires in riots that gripped Lhasa in March 2008 … There are reports that two more Tibetans have been executed, but that has not been confirmed … Security is still reported to be tight in Tibetan areas.
>
> (www.bbc.co.uk, 27 October 2009)

'Tibetan rights groups have said the executions were carried out on 20 October' (*IHT*, 28 October 2009, p. 7).

22 October 2009.

> Despite protest by the Chinese government, the Dalai Lama is going ahead with plans to visit a heavily militarized Tibetan Buddhist area in north-east

India that is the focus of an intense territorial dispute between China and India, a Tibetan official in India said Thursday [22 October]. The Dalai Lama is expected to visit the state of Arunachal Pradesh from 8 November to 15 November ... The Dalai Lama was scheduled to visit Arunachal Pradesh last year [2008] but cancelled his trip. Some people say in the area he was denied permission by the Indian government, possibly due to pressure from China. Tenzin Takhla, a spokesman for the Dalai Lama, said the Dalai Lama postponed his visit so as not to disrupt elections taking place in India around that time. The status of Arunachal Pradesh is one of the most intractable diplomatic issues between China and India. The dispute centres on the mountainous, mist-cloaked region of Tawang, a thickly forested area bordering Bhutan and Chinese-ruled Tibet that is dominated by the ethnic Monpa people, who practise Tibetan Buddhism and speak a language very similar to Tibetan. The Chinese government says Tawang was once part of Tibet, and so belongs to China. The Indian government says a self-governing Tibet signed a treaty with British-ruled India in 1914 that ceded Tawang to India on the condition that London recognize Tibetan autonomy. The British agreed at the time to acknowledge what they called the suzerainty of Tibet. But last year [2008] the British Foreign Secretary, David Miliband, retracted that recognition, saying it was a holdover from a colonial era ... Last year [2008] he [the Dalai Lama] announced for the first time that Arunachal Pradesh belonged to India. Tenzin Takhla said the Tibetan government recognizes the borders designated by the 1914 treaty, called the Simla Convention. China has been increasingly vocal this year [2009] over its claims to Tawang and possibly other parts of Arunachal Pradesh. On 13 October a foreign ministry spokesman denounced a visit to the state in early October by Manmohan Singh, the Indian prime minister. In the spring China tried unsuccessfully to block a $2.9 billion loan that India had requested from the Asian Development Bank ... [with] $60 million of the loan slated for flood control projects in Arunachal Pradesh ... India's most important Tibetan Buddhist monastery is in Tawang and the Dalai Lama appoints the abbot there.

(www.iht.com, 22 October 2009)

'Beijing claims about 90,000 square kilometres (35,000 square miles) of Arunachal Pradesh as its own territory' (*IHT*, 23 October 2009, p. 3).

The Dalai Lama passed through Taiwan ... when he fled into exile in India in 1959. The Dalai Lama appoints the abbot of the monastery in Tawang, one of the most important Tibetan Buddhist monasteries in India. He last visited the area in 2003 ... His spokesman said the Dalai Lama will visit Tawang for a week starting next Sunday [8 November] because his Buddhist followers have asked to see him.

(www.iht.com, 1 November 2009; *IHT*, 2 November 2009, p. 6)

Since 1949 China has resolved seventeen of twenty-three border disputes, offering concessions in fifteen of those instances and, overall, receiving less

> than half of the contested territory, said M. Taylor Fravel … The compromises have generally come at times of regime instability, when the Communist Party has felt threatened by external or internal forces, he added … Mr Fravel said: 'When it has compromised in the past, mostly in disputes on its land border, it was a relatively weak state. The question now becomes: how will a stronger China behave in its remaining territorial disputes over maritime sovereignty and with India?'
>
> (www.iht.com, 14 November 2009)

30 October 2009.

> A self-taught film-maker who spent five months interviewing ordinary Tibetans about their hopes and frustrations living under Chinese rule is facing charges of state subversion after the footage was smuggled abroad and broadcast on the internet and at film festivals around the world. Dhondup Wangchen, who has been detained since March 2008, just weeks after deadly rioting broke out in Tibet, managed to sneak out a letter from jail last month [September] saying that his trial had begun.
>
> (www.iht.com, 30 October 2009; *IHT*, 31 October 2009, p. 5)

5 November 2009. 'The Indian government refused Thursday [5 November] permission to all foreign journalists to cover the Dalai Lama's visit … to Arunachal Pradesh … Foreigners require special government permission to visit the mountainous state' (www.iht.com, 5 November 2009).

8–15 November 2009. 'Thousands of people have turned out to welcome the Dalai Lama … [He] is in Tawang in India's state of Arunachal Pradesh … This is only his fifth visit in fifty years' (www.bbc.co.uk, 8 November 2009).

'Thousands of people turned up at Tawang … On Sunday [8 November] the Dalai Lama led prayers at a monastery in Tawang after his arrival. The visit is due to last until 15 November' (www.cnn.com, 8 November 2009).

> The local administration, which expected 25,000 people, erected a small tent city for pilgrims, while other visitors sought shelter in local monasteries and guesthouses. India and China have been embroiled in a border dispute over the north-eastern state of Arunachal Pradesh since 1962 … The sixth Dalai Lama came from the region in the seventeenth century, and China fears the current Dalai Lama will say his successor could also come from the region, removing China's role in choosing Tibet's next spiritual leader.
>
> (www.iht.com, 8 November 2009)

> Tens of thousands of ethnic Tibetans began pouring into the town of Tawang in the early hours of Monday morning [9 November] to hear an address by the Dalai Lama … Its 300-year-old monastery is one of the most influential outside of Tibet … China and India fought a brief border war in 1962 – partly over Arunachal Pradesh – and the frontier has yet to be settled despite several rounds of talks … Several border disputes – including over Kashmir and Sikkim – have never been resolved … Mistrust between Delhi

> and Beijing has recently gained momentum with reports in the Indian media of Chinese incursions along the border ... When the two countries enjoyed better relations, especially in the late 1990s, Delhi did not allow the Dalai Lama to visit Arunachal Pradesh or any area contested by China.
>
> (www.bbc.co.uk, 9 November 2009)

'As many as 30,000 people ... heard [the Dalai Lama]' (*The Times*, 10 November 2009, p. 38).

> Indian officials clamped down Monday [9 November] on journalists covering the Dalai Lama's trip ... India refused to allow foreign journalists to travel to Tawang to cover the trip and tried to keep local reporters away from the Dalai Lama on Sunday [8 November] . As the Dalai Lama inaugurated a hospital wing in Tawang on Monday ... a media official with the state government told waiting reporters they were 'requested' not to ask any questions ... On Monday he [the Dalai Lama] was surrounded by a tight security cordon that made asking questions impossible.
>
> (www.iht.com, 9 November 2009)

12 November 2009.

> The Chinese government had a special message for President Barack Obama on Thursday [12 November]: he is black, he admires Abraham Lincoln, so he, of all people, should sympathize with Beijing's efforts to prevent Tibet from seceding and sliding back into what it was before its liberation by Chinese troops: a feudalistic, slaveholding society headed by the Dalai Lama. Qin Gang (a foreign ministry spokesman): 'He is a black president, and he understands the slavery abolition movement and Lincoln's major significance for that movement.'
>
> (www.iht.com, 14 November 2009)

> Qin Gang (a foreign ministry spokesman): 'He is a black president, and he understands the slavery abolition movement and Lincoln's major significance for that movement. Lincoln played an incomparable role in protecting the national unity and integrity of the United States.'
>
> (*Independent*, 16 November 2009, p. 21)

> China has sentenced a revered Tibetan living Buddha ... Phurbu Tsering Rinpoche ... to eight-and-a-half years in jail on charges of illegally occupying government land and possession of weapons ... [The trial] marked the first time a Tibetan arrested following last year's riots had been allowed to select his own defence lawyers. He had face a maximum fifteen years in prison on the two charges ... The court sentenced him to seven years in prison on the charge of illegally occupying government land and to an additional year for possession of bullets ... The monk was arrested on 28 March last year [2008], four days after nuns from two religious houses over which he presides took to the streets in demonstrations shortly after deadly rioting erupted in Lhasa. A police search of the home of the living Buddha, who

> presides over several religious houses and runs an old people's home, turned up an imitation pistol and 100 rounds of ammunition.
>
> (www.thetimes.com, 30 December 2009)

'Phurbu Tsering is a 'living Buddha' from Ganzi, a part of south-west China's Sichuan province dominated by ethnic Tibetans' (www.bbc.co.uk, 1 January 2010).

> A Chinese court has sentenced a Tibetan filmmaker to six years in prison after he made a documentary in which ordinary Tibetans praised the Dalai Lama and complained about how their culture had been trampled upon … The filmmaker, Dhondup Wangchen, and his friend, Golog Jigme, a monk, were detained shortly after finishing the film, *Leaving Fear Behind*, but managed to smuggle tapes out of the country.
>
> (*IHT*, 8 January 2010)

> China formally told the … the Palm Springs International Film Festival [in the United States] … this week that two Chinese films were being withdrawn from its programme in protest of the scheduled screening of a documentary about Tibet and the Dalai Lama. While Chinese officials told the festival's director that the filmmakers themselves had decided to withdraw their state-financed works, many China experts believe that this is the state sending a message, rather than the individuals … *The Sun Behind the Clouds: Tibet's Struggle for Freedom* … a documentary by Ritu Sarin and Tensing Sonam … follows the Dalai Lama over a year through protests over the status of Tibet that were timed to coincide with preparations for the Beijing Olympics.
>
> (www.iht.com, 9 January 2010)

> China is to build the world's highest airport, at an altitude of 4,436 metres (14,500 feet), in Tibet. The construction, at Nagqu, is likely to be a daunting task given the altitude and climate, with average temperatures staying below zero throughout the year. The airport will be just 764 metres lower than the Mount Everest base camp on the Chinese side, which is located 5,200 metres above sea level. Nagqu is in the centre of the Qinghai–Tibet plateau, about 186 miles from Lhasa, with a population of 400,000. The airport will be the sixth in Tibet … The airport is planned for 2011 with a construction period of three years … The new airport will beat the current altitude record holder – Bamba airport … which is also in Tibet … sits at an elevation of 4,334 metres. That airport overtook the one at Lhasa, which has been built at a mere 3,600 metres … China announced in 2008 that it would build ninety-seven new airports by 2010, so that four-fifths of the population would be within a ninety-minute drive of an airport … With the airport, Nagqu, which is also on the Qinghai–Tibet railway line, is expected to become the centre of an economic hub in the plateau region … An extraordinary railway line connecting Tibet to the rest of China opened four years ago, and the government is constructing six new rail lines in and around the

vast region, which is rich in natural resources ... Opponents claim that the developments are eroding the Tibetan way of life and damaging a fragile environment ... There is particular concern about Han migration, made possible by the Qinghai–Tibet railway ... At its highest point, the Qinghai–Tibet line hits 5,072 metres – a height that is above the peak of any European mountain.

(www.guardian.co.uk, 12 January 2010; *Guardian*, 13 January 2010, p. 22)

President Hu Jintao and other leaders ... at a Tibet planning conference which ran from Monday to Wednesday [18 to 20 January] ... decided that 'more efforts must be made to greatly improve living standards of the people in Tibet, as well as ethnic unity and stability' ... The Chinese government has invested $45.6 billion in Tibet since 2001, according to Xinhua. Tibet's GDP, estimated to be $6.4 billion last year [2009], has increased 170 per cent since 2000, the news agency said. Xinhua reported that the average income of Tibetan farmers and herders was expected to match the national level by 2020 ... At the conference ... senior leaders not only laid out policy for central Tibet, the area China designates as the Tibet Autonomous Region, but also drew up plans to develop ethnic Tibetan areas in the provinces of Sichuan, Yunnan, Gansu and Qinghai.

(www.iht.com, 24 January 2010)

Twice this month [January] senior Chinese leaders met to discuss Tibet policy. At the last conclave, which finished on 20 January, President Hun Jintao called for more efforts to improve the living standards of Tibetans. The *per capita* incomes of Tibet's rural population should be raised to the national average by 2010, he said.

(www.economist.com, 25 January 2010)

Last week state media reported that China planned 'leapfrog' development of ... [Tibet] and of Tibetan areas in neighbouring provinces ... Xinhua said China had invested 310 billion yuan in Tibet since 2001 and the economy was expected to reach 43.7 billion yuan in 2009, representing an annual growth of 12.3 per cent over the past nine years. The plan aims to raise the annual income of farmers and herders, who make up four-fifths of the population, to the national average of 8,582 yuan by 2020. At present they earn just 3,410 yuan.

(www.guardian.co.uk, 25 January 2010)

'The meeting established China's goal of bringing about "leap-forward development" and long-term security in the region' (www.bbc.co.uk, 2 February 2010).

The Dalai Lama's envoys will arrive in Beijing tomorrow [26 January] for their first discussions with the Chinese authorities in fifteen months ... The meetings will be the ninth round of the on–off talks ... Lodi Gyaltsen Gyari and Kelsang Gyaltsen will be accompanied by three other officials.

(www.guardian.co.uk, 25 January 2010)

'This will be the ninth round of discussions between China and the Tibetan government-in-exile since 2002 … The five-person group will return to India at the beginning of February' (www.bbc.co.uk, 26 January 2010).

> Last fall [2009] President Barack Obama declined to meet with the Dalai Lama while the Dalai Lama was visiting the United States. The move was widely seen as an attempt by Mr Obama to improve United States–China relations, but Chinese leaders continued to press the president on Tibet during his first state visit to China in November. State Department officials quickly abandoned a new phrase that had been coined to describe the conciliatory approach – 'strategic reassurance' – and which had been criticized by some Americans as being tantamount to appeasement.
>
> (www.iht.com, 26 January 2010)

> Chinese officials have rejected demands by the Dalai Lama that Tibetan areas of China receive greater autonomy and be governed as a single region, Xinhua reported Monday [1 February]. Du Qinglin is head of the United Front Work Department, the arm of the Communist Party that officially manages ethnic policy … During the talks Du Qinglin told the envoys that the concept of a 'Greater Tibet' and 'high level autonomy' violated China's constitution … Mr Du insisted that talks would progress 'only if the Dalai Lama completely abandoned such claims' … The Tibetan envoys … arrived back in India early Monday … The Dalai Lama has said he does not seek independence for Tibet but rather wants genuine autonomy for Tibetan areas – the Tibetans should be able to make their own policy regarding religious practice, education and immigration to the areas, he says. Furthermore, the areas that are mostly ethnic Tibetan should all be put under one administrative region, the Dalai Lama says. This would include central Tibet – what China calls the Tibet Autonomous Region – and parts of the Chinese provinces of Qinghai, Sichuan, Gansu and Yunnan.
>
> (www.iht.com, 1 February 2010)

'Zhu Weiqun (of the Chinese Communist Party's United Front Work Department): "The positions of the two sides are sharply divided" … Mr Zhu said there was no possibility of the "slightest compromise" on the issue of the sovereignty of Tibet' (www.bbc.co.uk, 2 February 2010).

> Zhu Weiqun … is the executive deputy minister … executive vice director … of the United Front Work Department, the arm of the Communist Party that officially manages ethnic policy … Mr Zhu said Tuesday [2 February] that the Dalai Lama was not a legal representative of the 6 million Tibetans in China, and that China would only discuss with the envoys the status of the Dalai Lama, not the future of Tibet.
>
> (www.iht.com, 2 February 2010)

> Last week a Nepalese government delegation visited Beijing … As Nepal's home minister, Bhim Rawal, met with China's top security officials, Chinese state media reported that the two countries had agreed to co-operate

on border security, while Nepal restated its commitment to preventing any 'anti-China' events on its side of the border. Details of the meetings were not yet known, but the two countries were expected to finalize a programme under which China would provide money, training and logistical support to help Nepal expand police checkpoints in isolated regions of its northern border. The reason for the deal is simple: Tibet … Nepal is now moving to close the Himalayan passages through which Tibetans have long made secret trips in and out of China, often on pilgrimages to visit the Dalai Lama in his exile in India … China is now exerting itself more broadly toward its small Himalayan neighbour, analysts say – partly because of its concern that Nepal could become a locus of Tibetan agitation, partly as another South Asian stage in its growing soft power fencing match in the region with India … From China's perspective, Nepal's geopolitical significance elevated after Tibetan protests erupted in March 2008, five months after Beijing played host to the Olympic Games. Those protests began inside China, in Lhasa and other Tibetan regions, but also spread across the border to Kathmandu, where an estimated 12,000 Tibetans live. Even as Chinese officials were able to block international coverage of the crackdown under way in Tibet, the protests in Nepal attracted global attention as photographs circulated of the Nepalese police subduing Tibetan protesters … Last fall [2009] Mr Rawal announced that Nepal, for the first time, would station armed police officers in isolated regions like Mustang and Manang on the border with Tibet. Meanwhile, Tibetan advocates say the tightening border security has already sharply slowed movement. Until 2008 roughly 2,500 to 3,000 Tibetans annually slipped across the border, according to the office of the Dalai Lama. By last year [2009] the number dropped to about 600, a change that Tibetan advocates attribute to closer ties between China and Nepal … Trade with China has quadrupled since 2003, according to government statistics, and Nepalese business leaders want to increase economic ties. When Nepal's foreign minister visited Beijing last September [2009], she asked Chinese officials for $1 billion in loans for infrastructure projects. In recent years Chinese airlines have opened routes into Nepal as the number of Chinese tourists has risen steadily. Nepalese government officials have already asked that China extend rail service into the Himalayas to the Nepal border. If that happens, Nepal would become a link on the same high altitude line that connects Tibet to Beijing.

(www.iht.com, 17 February 2010; *IHT*, 18 February 2010, p. 1, 4)

The Chinese government allowed a US navy strike group to sail into its territorial waters yesterday [17 February] despite rising tensions between the two countries over Tibet and Taiwan. But senior Chinese military officials declined an invitation to attend a reception aboard the USS *Nimitz*, which arrived in Hong Kong for a port visit. There had been speculation that China might deny the USS *Nimitz* and four other warships permission to enter Hong Kong.

(*FT*, 18 February 2010, p. 7)

> President Barack Obama is to go ahead with talks with the Dalai Lama at the White House today [Thursday 18 February] … The meeting is to be held neither in the Oval Office nor Obama's personal quarters but instead in the less grand Map Room.
>
> (*Guardian*, 18 February 2010, p. 18)

> Thursday's meeting will take place in the White House Map Room, not the symbolic surroundings of the Oval Office, where President Barack Obama normally meets foreign leaders and VIP guests. The Dalai Lama will also meet Secretary of State Hillary Clinton at the State Department.
>
> (www.bbc.co.uk, 18 February 2010)

> The meeting came near the start of a ten-day visit by … the Dalai Lama … to the United States … The Dalai Lama was ushered into the building out of view of the press, and the White House only released a still photo of the session … Secretary of State Hillary Clinton added a meeting with the Dalai Lama to her schedule on Thursday [18 February]; as late as Wednesday the State Department could not confirm the encounter.
>
> (*IHT*, 19 February 2010, p. 4)

'President Barack Obama spent more than an hour with the Dalai Lama' (www.guardian.co.uk, 19 February 2010).

A White House statement: 'The president stated his strong support for the preservation of Tibet's unique religious, cultural and linguistic identity and the protection of human rights for Tibetans in the People's Republic of China' (*The Times*, 19 February 2010, p. 41).

> According to a White House statement … the president praised the Dalai Lama's 'commitment to non-violence and his pursuit of dialogue with the Chinese government' … He also stressed the importance of having both sides 'engage in direct dialogue to resolve differences, and was pleased to hear about the recent resumption of talks'.
>
> (www.cnn.com, 19 February 2010)

> A State Department spokesman said: 'The Dalai Lama is a Nobel Peace Prize laureate, internationally revered religious and cultural leader and the Secretary [of State] will meet him in this capacity as recent Secretaries of State have done' … White House officials had said they would keep the visit low key, releasing a photo after the meeting between the Dalai Lama and President Barack Obama. But there was no joint public appearance.
>
> (www.iht.com, 18 February 2010)

> A small trade war with Denmark and China started in May last year [2009] after a meeting with the Dalai Lama. It ended in December, only after Denmark promised to act with 'caution' in future contacts with the Dalai Lama and declared it is 'fully aware of the importance and sensitivity of Tibet-related issues'.
>
> (*Guardian*, 18 February 2010, p. 18)

'In May [2009] China suspended diplomatic relations with Denmark after prime minister Lars Loekke Rasmussen met with the Dalai Lama, then resumed them only after Copenhagen promised to notify Beijing before inviting him again' (*IHT*, 19 February 2010, p. 4).

> In his first interview since his recent controversial meeting with President Barack Obama … the Dalai Lama … told CNN's *Larry King Live* that China claims Tibetans are 'very happy … much, much, much better than previous Tibet'. However, he noted that his Tibetan government-in-exile has received information indicating 'suppression … or restrictions' culturally and religiously of the Tibetan people … The Dalai Lama: '[Tibetans] are not seeking independence. That's why we are called middle way. We complain [about] the presence of policy in Tibet. It is actually very much damaging … But [on the] other hand we also do not want separation from China because … Tibet [is a] landlocked country, materially backward. Every Tibetan want modernized Tibet. So for that reason [we] remain within the People's Republic of China' … He sought to deflect attention away from his exile … He said: 'This is not our concern. Our concern is 6 million Tibetan people's basic rights and culture. These are our main issues.'
>
> (www.cnn.com, 23 February 2010)

> China has appointed its choice of the Panchen Lama, traditionally the second most important man in Tibetan Buddhism, to a top advisory body … The Chinese government chose Gyaincain Norbu to be the Panchen Lama in 1995. But he is not widely accepted by Tibetan Buddhists as the true incarnation of the Panchen Lama. The Tibetan boy selected by the Dalai Lama in the same year, Gendun Choekyi Nyima, disappeared soon afterwards – he and his family have not been seen since … Gyaincain Norbu was one of thirteen people to become members of the national committee of the Chinese People's Political Consultative Conference (CPPCC) on Sunday [28 February] … The committee [is] made up of private entrepreneurs as well as religious and cultural figures … The CPPCC begins its annual meeting this week, coinciding with that of the National People's Congress. Gyaincain Norbu lived in seclusion for his early life, but in 2009, aged nineteen, made a series of public appearances praising China's rule in Tibet.
>
> (www.bbc.co.uk, 1 March 2010)

> Gendun Choekyi Nyima … and his family vanished [in 1995]. The government has said they are in 'protective custody' … According to Xinhua, the reigning Panchen Lama … Gyaincain Norbu … who is just shy of his twentieth birthday, is the youngest person ever appointed to the consultative conference … The Chinese People's Political Consultative Conference (CPPCC) … is made up of wealthy businessmen, sports celebrities and prominent members of China's ethnic minorities … Last month [February] the state media liberally featured his elevation as vice president of the government-run Buddhist Association of China. In an address he swore to

> uphold the leadership of the Communist Party and promised to 'adhere to socialism, safeguard national unification and strengthen ethnic unity'.
>
> (*IHT*, 2 March 2010, p. 2)

'The CPPCC [is] a 2,252-member body' (www.iht.com, 3 March 2010).

> The son of a Tibetan herder, Gendun Choekyi Nyima was five years old when he was named as the Panchen Lama. Police travelled to the village north of Lhasa and, pro-Tibet exiles say, removed the child and his parents. Tibet's new governor, Padma Choling, revealed yesterday [7 March] that the young man, now twenty, is still living in Tibet.
>
> (*The Times*, 8 March 2010, p. 29)

> Padma Choling, an ethnic Tibetan, was appointed governor and chairman of the Tibet Autonomous Region in January [2010], but he reports to Zhang Qingli, an ethnic Han who is the regional secretary of the Communist Party … The new governor of Tibet said Sunday [7 March] that the Dalai Lama did not have a right to choose his successor however he wanted, but instead must abide by the 'requirements' of Tibetan Buddhist tradition … The government has already ruled that the next Dalai Lama must be approved by the government … The Dalai Lama has said the process could break with tradition, including having the next Dali Lama, the fifteenth one, identified and trained while he is still alive. He has also said his successor could be female or found outside Tibet.
>
> (www.iht.com, 8 March 2010)

> Hundreds of Tibetans are being rounded up in Lhasa and armed paramilitaries are patrolling the streets in advance of the anniversary of the fatal riots in 2008 … March 10 is regarded by Tibetans as the anniversary of the start of an abortive uprising against Chinese rule in 1959 that resulted in the Dalai Lama's flight into exile in India … The armed police patrols that have become routine in the Tibetan heart of Lhasa since 2008 were expanded to include cavalcades of trucks packed with paramilitary units … Lhasa residents told *The Times* that as many as 400 to 500 people had been detained in the latest crackdown … Tibet was closed to foreign visitors from Tuesday [9 March], with a moratorium on issuing the travel permits required by all non-Chinese wanting to visit the restive Himalayan region.
>
> (*The Times*, 11 March 2010, p. 27)

> For a second straight year, the Chinese government has increased security across parts of the vast Tibetan plateau to dissuade any Tibetans from holding protests this week to mark the anniversaries of ethnic uprisings … A few foreign journalists who were invited by the government last week to Lhasa reported seeing Chinese security forces with automatic rifles patrolling the streets … In Nepal the police on Wednesday [10 March] arrested thirty protesters who had been demonstrating in Kathmandu in support of the Tibetan cause.
>
> (www.iht.com, 11 March 2010; *IHT*, 12 March 2010, p. 4)

'The Dalai Lama lashed out yesterday [10 March], accusing them of trying to "annihilate Buddhism" in Tibet as he commemorated a failed uprising against China's rule ... He accused Chinese authorities of working to "deliberately annihilate Buddhism"' (*Guardian*, 11 March 2010, p. 21).

> On Wednesday [10 March] the Dalai Lama gave a speech in India on the fifty-first anniversary of his flight from Lhasa. He urged Tibetans everywhere to make contact with Chinese people and said a shift in attitude among ordinary Chinese might one day sway Chinese government policy toward Tibet.
>
> (www.iht.com, 11 March 2010)

> The Dalai Lama voiced his support on Wednesday [10 March] for Uighurs ... In an address in Dharamsala observing fifty-one years since he fled Tibet after a failed uprising against Chinese rule, the Dalai Lama referred to Xinjiang as East Turkestan, the name given to it by pro-independence exiles.
>
> (www.iht.com, 11 March 2010)

'Referring to Xinjiang as "East Turkestan", the name given to it by pro-independence exiles, the Dalai Lama said: "I would like to express my solidarity and stand firmly with them"' (*The Times*, 11 March 2010, p. 27).

5 Uighurs

> Although many Uighurs claim to be the indigenous people of the region, foreign historians say the Uighurs did not migrate from the Mongolian steppes to what is now Xinjiang until the tenth century. They eventually built tribal societies, mostly around oasis towns along the southern edge of the large desert depression called the Tarim Basin. Archaeological finds, especially recent excavations of amazingly well-preserved mummies, show that the first people to live in the region were probably West Eurasians, some of whom seem to have worshipped cows. The oldest of those mummies date back some 3,800 years ... The Chinese empire did not exercise political control over the territory in its current shape until the Qing Dynasty, ruled by ethnic Manchus, annexed the region in 1760 and later gave it the name Xinjiang ... [which] translates as 'New Frontier' or 'New Dominion' ... Ethnic Han began arriving in large numbers only after the Communist takeover in 1949.
>
> (*IHT*, 13 July 2009, p. 7)

'Xinjiang [was] settled by Uighurs in the tenth century after their migration from the Mongolian steppes' (www.iht.com, 13 July 2009).

'The Uighurs began adopting Sunni Islam in the tenth century' (www.iht.com, 19 October 2008).

'Xinjiang ... its name means "New Border" ... [was] originally conquered by the Qing Dynasty armies in the mid eighteenth century' (*Independent*, 9 July 2009, p. 21).

'The Uighurs ... converted to Islam in the fifteenth century. During the Qing Dynasty (1644–1912) China's Manchu rulers managed to subjugate the Uighurs and other local tribes but had to fight off periodic revolts' (www.feer.com, 10 August 2009).

'The Uighurs briefly established the self-governing First East Turkestan Republic in 1933 ... The region was formally incorporated into China in the mid-eighteenth century' (*FT*, 10 July 2009, p. 11).

'In the 1930s and 1940s a Republic of East Turkestan twice enjoyed a brief independence in parts of Xinjiang' (www.economist.com, 4 September 2008).

'People's Liberation Army soldiers … put down the short-lived independent East Turkestan Republic (1944–49)' (www.iht.com, 9 July 2009). 'China's army occupied the region in 1949' (www.iht.com, 11 July 2009).

'The region was brought under the complete control of communist China in 1949' (www.bbc.co.uk, 5 August 2008).

> The Xinjiang production and Construction Corps [is] a uniquely Chinese conglomerate of farms and factories created by decommissioned Red Army soldiers at the end of the civil war … Many Chinese consider the *bingtuan*, or soldiers corps, a major success. In one fell swoop Mao deployed 200,000 idle soldiers to develop and occupy a resource-rich, politically strategic region bordering India … The settlements run by *bingtuan* include five cities, 180 farming communities and 1,000 companies. They also report directly to Beijing and run their own courts, colleges and newspapers … In the early years the ranks of the *bingtuan* were fortified by petty criminals, former prisoners of war, prostitutes and intellectuals, all sent west for 'reeducation' … In 1949, when the Communists declared the establishment of the People's Republic of China, there were just 300,000 Chinese in Xinjiang. Today the Han population has grown to 7.5 million, just over 40 per cent of the region's population. The percentage of Uighurs has fallen to just over 40 per cent, or about 8.3 million.
>
> (*IHT*, 7 August 2009, p. 2)

'Together, Xinjiang and Tibet constitute about one third of China's land mass' (*FT*, 11 July 2009, p. 9).

'Xinjiang occupies one-sixth of China's landmass, with Tibet the second largest province' (www.bc.co.uk, 9 July 2009).

> The proportion of Han Chinese inhabitants rose from 6 per cent in 1949 to 40 per cent by around 2000 and migrants had begun to spread from cities into rural areas, where they found themselves in competition with Uighur communities for water and land.
>
> (www.guardian.co.uk, 5 August 2008)

'The percentage of Han in the population … of Xinjiang … was 40 per cent in 2000, up from 6 per cent in 1949' (www.iht.com, 9 July 2009).

> The proportion of Uighurs in Xinjiang shrank from about 75 per cent in 1949 to 45 per cent now … Xinjiang [has] … more than 8 million Uighurs (about 45 per cent of the population according to official figures, which tend to undercount Han Chinese migrants elsewhere in the country).
>
> (www.economist.com, 9 July 2009)

'In Xinjiang … Uighurs are the largest ethnic group, accounting for 45 per cent of the population' (*FT*, 14 July 2009, p. 6).

'Xinjiang's main ethnic division: 45 per cent Uighur; 40 per cent Han Chinese' (www.bbc.co.uk, 14 July 2009).

'Moslem Uighurs make up almost half the 21 million population of Xinjiang' (www.guardian.co.uk, 14 July 2009).

'The Xinjiang Uighur Autonomous Region is home to about 20 million people and thirteen major ethnic groups – of which the Uighur is the largest' (www.cnn.com, 19 July 2009).

'[There are] 9 million ethnically Turkish Uighurs in Xinjiang and a 2 million-strong diaspora' (www.feer.com, 10 August 2009).

> Amnesty International said recently that the Uighurs' identity and well-being are being 'systematically eroded' by government policies that limit the use of the Uighur language, restrict religious practices and foster job discrimination. It accused Beijing of arresting thousands of Uighurs on bogus terrorism charges.
>
> (*IHT*, 9 July 2009, p. 8)

> Three years ago, in its annual report on international religious freedom, the [US] State Department singled out Xinjiang for criticism in a section on China: 'Officials in the Xinjiang Uighur Autonomous Region tightly controlled religious activity, while elsewhere in the country, Moslems enjoyed greater religious freedom' … The government is phasing out the use of Uighur language in schools … A 2009 Amnesty International report on threats to Uighur identity charts the recent history of the Uighur language in education, beginning with a policy in the 1990s that eliminated Uighur as a language of education at the university level. Today, at Xinjiang University in Urumqi, only Uighur poetry classes are taught in Uighur, the report says. In 2006 the government began carrying out policies that make Chinese the main language of preschool instruction.
>
> (www.iht.com, 8 July 2009)

> A 2008 report by the United States congressional commission noted that government job websites in Xinjiang set aside most teaching and civil services positions for non-Uighurs … Nearly 1.5 million Xinjiang residents [are] already employed outside the region.
>
> (www.iht.com, 15 July 2009)

> Following Xinjiang Party Secretary Wang Lequan's declaration in 2002 that the Uighur language is 'out of step with the twenty-first century', the government started to shift the entire education system to Mandarin, replacing Uighur teachers with newly arrived Han Chinese. The authorities also organized public burnings of Uighur books. Control over religion was extended last year [2008] to prohibit traditional customs such as religious weddings, burials or pilgrimages to the tombs of local saints.
>
> (www.iht.com, 9 July 2009)

> Part of the reason why Han Chinese are so successful in Xinjiang is that Uighurs are blocked from competing. My Xinjiang work originally focused on cross-border trade with Central Asia. Uighurs have a hard time getting

visas and licences, and generally working in a system controlled by a Han-dominated government, so Hans from outside Xinjiang have been able to move in and occupy this niche.

(Calla Wiemer, www.feer.com, 10 July 2009)

A chronology of political events since 9 May 2006

9 May 2006.

China angrily demanded Tuesday [9 May] that Albania hand over five Chinese Uighur Moslems who are being resettled there after being released last week from the US prison at Guantanamo Bay, Cuba ... The five were released from the prison in Cuba on Friday [5 May] after it was determined that they were 'no longer enemy combatants', the US Defense Department said. The US authorities had asked nearly two dozen nations to provide asylum for the Uighur detainees because they did not want to anger the Chinese ... [China] said that Albania was mistaken in believing that the Uighurs were refugees, maintaining they were members of an East Turkestan grouping that the United Nations has listed as a terrorist organization ... The Albanian authorities have said they will 'seriously investigate the activities' of the former Guantanamo detainees, who have asked for political asylum. The five are believed to be among a group of about twenty Uighur Moslems cleared for release from Guantanamo Bay, where the Pentagon says 480 detainees still remain.

(www.iht.com, 9 May 2006)

US officials, citing concerns that the five could face persecution if they returned to China, said it took eighteen months to find a country that would take them ... China, Albania's sole ally during the communist regime of Enver Hoxha, still maintains good relations.

(*IHT*, 10 May 2006, p. 3)

('Most recently the country [Albania] has quietly taken several former Guantanamo Bay detainees off the Bush administration's hands when sending them to their home was out of the question. There are nine in the country so far and President Alfred Moisiu said he is open to accepting more': www.iht.com, 9 June 2007; *IHT*, 10 June 2007, pp. 1, 3). '[Albania has accepted as Guantanamo Bay detainees] five Uighurs ... an Egyptian, and Algerian and an Uzbek ... [i.e.] eight people [in total] ... At least fifteen of the seventeen Uihgurs who remain at Guantanamo Bay have also been cleared for release, but not even Albania will accept them – and neither will the United States. Instead, American diplomats say they have asked nearly 100 countries to provide asylum to the detainees, only to find that Chinese officials have warned some of the same countries not to accept them ... Beijing's ambassador to Albania has met at least three times with Sali Berisha, the prime minister, to demand the Uighurs' repatriation, Albanian officials said. Albania has since told Washington it cannot accept any more of the Uighur detainees ... Twenty-two Uighurs who ended up at Guantanamo were part of a group of about three dozen Uighur men who were staying at a hamlet in the White Mountains of eastern Afghanistan': www.iht.com, 10 June 2007; *IHT*, 11 June 2007, p. 3.)

> Oil and natural gas – lots of it – have been discovered ... in Xinjiang ... [There is] an energy boom in the region's Tarim Basin and Taklimakan Desert ... China is building a 4,200 kilometre, or 2,600 mile, pipeline from here ... directly to Shanghai and possibly Beijing. But the manner and terms under which the government is extracting resources from Xinjiang angers many of the region's 7.5 million ethnic Uighur Moslems ... In the 1930s the Uighurs and other Turkic tribes in the region, who until then had been on the fringes of various Chinese empires, formed an independent state called East Turkestan. In 1949 China annexed East Turkestan and turned it into an autonomous region dubbed Xinjiang, or new frontier. Beijing flooded the area with ethnic Han migrants.
>
> (www.iht.com, 7 November 2006)

November 2006.

> Xinjiang [is] an overwhelmingly Moslem region close to the rich poppy fields of Afghanistan and near the border with Kyrgyzstan and Tajikistan. With a population of about 20 million and an officially estimated 60,000 infections, Xinjiang has one-tenth of China's AIDS cases and the highest HIV infection rate in the country. The Chinese authorities estimate that Kashgar prefecture, with a population of about 3 million, has 780 cases, but public health experts here say the real figure is probably four times that and rising fast.
>
> Since 2005 the authorities in Xinjiang have been trying everything from needle exchanges and drug substitution programmes – approaches that first became popular in the West in the 1960s – to community programmes, often involving imams and mullahs.
>
> (www.iht.com, 12 November 2006)

> To dissuade Uighur youths from inheriting their traditional Islamic culture, the government has banned children from entering mosques, studying Islam or celebrating Islamic holidays ... Though Uighurs have traditionally followed a moderate blend of Sunni Islam and Sufi mysticism strongly influenced by local folklore and rural traditions, a rising Islamic mood is palpable in Xinjiang.
>
> (www.iht.com, 21 November 2006)

January 2007.

> [Albania] has become the new destination for a special category of prisoner – men whom the United States feels it is right to release but too risky to repatriate. Asylum has already been arranged for eight former Guantanamo Bay detainees who the United States says would face torture if sent back

home ... Among them ... are Uzbeks, Algerians, Tunisians, Egyptians and Libyans ... [There are] five former Guantanamo detainees from China's Xinjiang province ... [who are] ethnic Uighurs ... So far Albania has been the only place willing to take them in ... Some 100 countries rejected US requests to provide asylum to freed terror suspects before Albania stepped forward.

(www.bbc.co.uk, 11 January 2007)

February 2007.

China has executed an ethnic Moslem from the country's restive far western region for alleged separatist activities, a US broadcaster ... Radio Free Asia ... said Friday [9 February]. China did not confirm the execution of Ismail Semed, which his supporters condemned because they said the prosecution's case against him lacked evidence and that his confession might have been coerced. Semed, a member of the Uighur Moslem minority in Xinjian, was shot and killed Thursday morning [8 February] ... He was convicted in October 2005 of trying to 'split the motherland' and possessing firearms and explosives ... [According to Semed's widow] her husband said during his trial that his confession had been forced.

(www.iht.com, 9 February 2007; *IHT*, 10 February 2007, p. 5)

19 April 2007.

A Canadian human rights campaigner jailed in China after allegations that he was linked to terrorism was sentenced to life in prison Thursday [19 April] ... Huseyincan Celil was sentenced for 'taking part in terrorist activities and plotting to split the country' ... the official Xinhua press agency said ... The Xinhua report said he was a 'prominent member of the East Turkestan terrorist organization' ... Celil, a member of the Uighur minority group from the western Xinjiang region, was born and raised in China and drew the attention of authorities by campaigning for the rights of his people. He was arrested in China and tortured, but escaped from prison in 2000 and fled to Uzbekistan and Turkey before reaching Canada, where he was given citizenship. He was arrested in Uzbekistan in March 2006 while visiting his wife's relatives, and he was extradited to China in June.

(www.iht.com, 19 April 2007; *IHT*, 20 April 2007, p. 8)

'The Chinese authorities have used the "war on terror" to justify harsh repression of the largely Uighur people in Xinjiang province, closing mosques, restricting use of the local language and banning certain books' (*Amnesty*, July–August 2007, p. 16).

27 January 2008.

Suspected militants arrested in western China earlier this year were planning attacks on the Beijing Olympics [which starts on 8 August], a Chinese official says. Two people were reported to have been killed and fifteen arrested in a raid on 27 January [2008]) in Urumqi, Xinjiang province. Officials now say their aim was to attack the August Olympics. The alleged plot was disclosed as officials also revealed that a plane crew prevented an apparent attempt to crash a jet on an internal flight. The incident occurred on Friday [7 March 2008]. The flight also originated in Urumqi and was bound for Beijing.

(www.bbc.co.uk, 9 March 2008)

'Some argue that China is deliberately exaggerating the terrorist threat to the Olympics to crack down on groups within the country' (www.bbc.co.uk, 12 March 2008).

Chinese police broke up a terror plot targeting the Beijing Olympics and a flight crew foiled an apparent attempt to crash a Chinese jetliner in a separate case, officials said Sunday [9 March]. Wang Lequan, the top Communist Party official in the far western region of Xinjiang, said materials seized in a 27 January [2008] raid in the regional capital, Urumqi, showed the plotters planned 'specifically to sabotage the staging of the Olympic Games' … Earlier reports of the January raid in Urumqi said police found guns, homemade bombs, training materials and 'extremist religious ideological materials'. Two members of the gang were killed and fifteen arrested … Wang said the group had been trained by and was following the orders of a Uighur separatist group based in Pakistan and Afghanistan called the East Turkestan Islamic Movement, or ETIM. The group has been labelled a terrorist organization by the United Nations and the United States. East Turkestan is another name for Xinjian. China says its main terror threat comes from ETIM. Although the group is believed to have no more than a few dozen members, terrorism experts say it has become influential among extremist groups using the internet to raise funds and find recruits. Chinese forces reported raiding an ETIM training camp last year [2007] and killing eighteen militants allegedly linked to al-Qaeda and the Taliban … Wang cited no other evidence or sources of the information and earlier reports on the [27 January] raid had made no mention of Olympic targets … Speaking at the same meeting, Xinjiang's governor said a flight crew prevented an apparent attempt to crash a China Southern flight from Urumqi to Beijing on Friday [7 March]. Nur Bekri did not specifically label the incident a terrorist attack, saying it remained under investigation … China has largely suppressed the violence [in Xinjiang] … and no major bombing or shooting incidents have been reported in almost a decade.

(www.iht.com, 9 March 2008)

9 March 2008.

[On 9 March] Chinese officials … [said] they had successfully thwarted two terrorist attacks, including one targeting the Olympic Games. Officials blamed both attacks on separatists operating out of an autonomous region in north-west China … home to about 19 million people, most of whom are

> Moslems and other minorities. Many of them oppose Beijing's rule ... The flight had taken off from Urumqi, the capital of the Xinjiang Uighur Autonomous Region.
>
> (www.cnn.com, 9 March 2008)

'According to Chinese state media, a nineteen-year-old woman from China's Moslem Uighur minority tried to start a fire on a domestic flight' (*Guardian*, 14 March 2008, p. 40).

'Xinjiang is home to 8 million Moslem Uighurs ... many of whom resent the growing presence of Han Chinese' (*FT*, 10 March 2008, p. 7).

> [A spokeswoman for] Amnesty International said the government had not provided evidence to back up its claims of terrorism activity: 'What has been going on has been a much broader crackdown. They have become so fearful of any expression of Uighur identity that they see it as automatically equating to separatism, and that is equated to terrorism' ... Turkic-speaking Uighurs account for 8 million of the 19 million-strong population in oil-rich Xinjiang.
>
> (*Guardian*, 10 March 2008, p. 19)

> The obscure group ... the East Turkestan Islamic Movement ... is believed to have no more than a few dozen members and has carried out very few attacks ... The last known Uighur attack was in 1997 in Urumqi when bombs placed in buses killed nine.
>
> (*The Times*, 10 March 2008, p. 36)

> Xinjiang means 'new territory' in Chinese. It saw brief independence as East Turkestan, or Uighurstan, in 1933 and part of it was under Soviet tutelage from 1945 to 1949. Its population is still roughly 55 per cent non-Han – Uighurs and Kazakhs whose Turkic-speaking cousins stretch all the way to the Black Sea, Moreover, it also has an ethnic Korean minority in the north-east.
>
> (*IHT*, 18 March 2008, p. 8)

23 March 2008.

> China admitted [on 2 April] that protest took place in a restive western region, days after unrest in Tibet. Protesters 'caused a disturbance' in the market town of Hotan [also spelt Khotan] in China's Xinjiang Uighur Autonomous Region, according to the local government. But there are conflicting reports about what caused the incident and the number of people involved. Officials say protesters wanted independence for Xinjian, but other reports blamed local disputes ... According to Hotan local government, the incident took place on 23 March in the town's bazaar. A press release said: 'A small number of the "three forces" ... attempted to incite the masses and provoke an incident' ... No one was injured. The 'three forces' is a term used by the Chinese government for separatists, terrorists and extremists ... A spokesman for the Hotan local government told the

BBC that several dozen protesters had distributed leaflets calling for demonstrations. The protesters were calling on Uighurs, the main ethnic group in Xinjiang, to follow the lead of the Tibetans, he said … [He] said most of the protesters had been arrested and some of them had already been sent for 'reeducation' … But a report from Radio Free Asia (RFA), a US-funded broadcaster, said two local issues had led to the protests in Hotan. It said witnesses told the radio station that the death of a prominent local businessman and philanthropist while in custody had sparked anger. Protesters were also demanding the authorities scrap a proposed headscarf ban in Hotan, an oasis town … They also want China to stop using torture to suppress Uighur demands for greater autonomy, it added. RFA also claims there were two protests in two locations in Hotan involving hundreds of people.

(www.bbc.co.uk, 2 April 2008)

One Uighur demonstration, which appears to have been quickly suppressed, took place in the town of Hotan on 23 March … Officials said the protest had been staged by Islamic separatist groups seeking to foment a broader uprising in Xinjiang … A statement by the Hotan government: 'A small number of elements tried to incite splittism, create disturbances in the market place and even trick the masses into an uprising' … But Han residents said that as many as 500 Uighurs protested in the centre of the city. Some reports have said that the Uighurs were objecting to restrictions on wearing Islamic headscarves and head coverings. Some interviewees, however, said the protesters were seeking independence. The demonstrators were quickly arrested by security forces who took control of the area.

(*IHT*, 3 April 2008, p. 5)

About 500 Uighurs gathered in the city of Khotan on 23 March, reportedly hoisting banners and shouting pro-independence slogans before the police moved in and arrested many demonstrators … On 18 March a rumour spread quickly through the streets of Urumqi that a Uighur woman had detonated a bomb on a city bus, escaping before its explosion. Officials denied the incident.

(www.iht.com, 4 April 2008)

'Protesters wanted the right for Uighur women to wear headscarves and the release of political prisoners … Turkic-speaking Uighurs account for 8 million of the 19 million people in [Xinjiang]' (*Guardian*, 3 April 2008).

27 March 2008.

A nineteen-year-old woman has confessed to attempting to hijack and crash a Chinese passenger plane that had to be diverted earlier this month after suspicious liquid was found on board, Xinhua, the government news agency, said Thursday [27 March] the woman confessed to a 'terrorist' attempt on the 7 March flight from Urumqi … The flight was diverted to Lanzhou, in the western province of Gansu, after one or more passengers were found

> with suspicious liquids. The woman is from China's Turkic Moslem Uighur minority, Xinhua said ... A male suspect previously confessed to masterminding the plot to crash the China Southern flight, but no further details have been released.
>
> (www.iht.com, 27 March 2008)

> Passengers on domestic flights are now banned from bringing liquids on board. Unlike similar bans in the West, the new order applies to baby formula and medicines, as well as drinks. Passengers with infants will have to ask the airline itself to provide formula; those with liquid medicines will need to have them carried by flight attendants. The change follows the government's claim that terrorists sought to bring liquid explosives on board a flight between Urumqi and Beijing on 7 March ... Previously the restriction only applied to flights between China and countries with bans of their own.
>
> (www.economist.com, 27 March 2008)

3 April 2008.

> Reuters, citing the World Uighur Congress, an exile group, reported that the police in Kashgar, in the Xinjiang region, had arrested seventy people, fearing trouble when the Olympic torch passes through the city in June ... The Tibetan tourism authority announced Thursday that the region would reopen to foreign tourist groups on 1 May, in time for a national three-day holiday.
>
> (www.iht.com, 3 April 2008)

'The police detained at least six Uighur Moslems on Thursday [3 April] at an anti-China protest during the Olympic torch relay [in Turkey]' (*IHT*, 4 April 2008).

4 April 2008.

> Residents of hamlets near Gulja, a city in north-western Xinjiang, said that about twenty-five Uighurs were arrested Friday [4 April] on a tip that people in the area were making bombs. Residents said the police turned up three bombs in a cowshed, but the authorities were still looking for more devices ... In Xinjiang the government bans students and party members from practising Islam and tightly controls and polices the Moslem clergy. Many Uighurs also complain of discrimination, saying that they are rarely given jobs in the modern economy or allowed to study abroad with the same ease as the Han. During a previous wave of protests in Gulja in 1997, Uighur human rights activists say that dozens of demonstrators were killed on the spot by paramilitary forces and many others executed later ... In the western Xinjiang city of Kashgar, a traditionally important centre of Islam in the region ... the police have arrested seventy Uighurs in recent days in a sweep aimed at securing the city before the arrival of the Olympic torch, which is to pass through Kashgar in June.
>
> (*IHT*, 5 April 2008, p. 7)

10 April 2008.

> China said Thursday [10 April] that it had uncovered a criminal ring planning to kidnap athletes and others at the Beijing Olympic Games. The 'violent terrorist gang' was based in the restive western Xinjiang region and headed by a man identified as Abdulrahman Tuersun, public security spokesman Wu Heping said. He also gave more details on a second alleged ring that had been uncovered in January [2008]. Wu said thirty-five people, including Tuersun and another man, Kuerban Mutalifu, were arrested between 26 March and 6 April for plotting to kidnap athletes, foreign journalists and other visitors to the August Olympics … Wu: 'They wanted to make a global impact to sabotage the Beijing Olympics. We face a real terrorist threat' … The men's names appear to indicate they are members of Xinjiang's Moslem Turkic Uighur ethnic group … Since the 11 September 2001 terror hijackings China has tried to portray the simmering insurgency in Xinjiang as linked to terrorist organizations in central Asia and the Middle East … Wu said police confiscated almost 10 kg (22 lb) of AN-TNT explosive material, eight sticks of dynamite, two detonators and 'jihadist' literature in raids in Urumqi … He said the gang hatched the Olympic plot in November [2007] and travelled through Xinjiang last month seeking recruits, including those skilled in weapons and explosives production. They also sought jihadist fanatics to carry out suicide bomb attacks in Urumqi and other Chinese cities, Wu said … Wu also provided details about those arrested in January, saying they had been manufacturing explosives and were plotting to attack hotels, government offices and military targets in Shanghai, Beijing and other cities. Wu said ten men, led by a man named Aji Maimaiti, had been arrested and confessed to acting on orders from a radical Islamic independence group, the East Turkestan Islamic Movement, to prepare attacks targeting the Beijing Olympics. Those included remote control bombings, poisoning and poison gas attacks, Wu said, adding that thirteen practice bombings had already been carried out. He said the group sent members abroad for training and had a variety of funding sources. Plans called for poison and bomb attacks to commence next month [May] in Shanghai, Beijing and other cities, Wu said … Wu said: 'The goal was to disrupt the Beijing Olympics' … In raids on four locations in January police seized eighteen detonators and a variety of equipment to make bombs and poison, along with cash, three vehicles, two computers, a CD burner and 'jihadist' training materials, he said … While the United States has labelled the East Turkestan Islamic Movement a terrorist organization, the State Department also alleges widespread abuses of the legal and educational systems by the communist authorities to suppress Uighur culture and religion.
>
> (www.iht.com, 10 April 2008)

Some observers question if China is inflating a terror threat to justify a clampdown on dissent ahead of the Olympics. China brands the Xinjiang separatists as terrorists and has claimed more than 260 terror acts have been committed in the province [Xinjiang] over the past two decades.

(www.bbc.co.uk, 10 April 2008)

Human Rights Watch recently stated: 'China continues to use the "war on terror" to justify policies to eradicate the "three evil forces" – terrorism, separatism and religious extremism – allegedly among Uighurs. Uighurs who express "separatist" tendencies are routinely sentenced to quick, secret and summary trials, sometimes accompanied by mass sentencing rallies. The death penalty is common.'

(www.cnn.com, 10 April 2008)

4 June 2008.

Two [US] lawmakers chastised the Bush administration for allowing the Chinese government to interrogate Chinese Moslem detainees at the US military prison at Guantanamo Bay and demanded that they be freed in the United States ... Representatives Bill Delahunt, a Massachusetts Democrat, and Dana Rohrabacher, a California Republican, said Wednesday [4 June] that the Uighurs who were interrogated should be compensated and apologized to for any abuse they may have suffered while they were held in the detention centre at the US naval base in Cuba ... FBI officials reported that before the Chinese interrogators arrived US military personnel had awakened the Uighurs every fifteen minutes in a sleep-deprivation interrogation tactic ... A federal judge has called their imprisonment unlawful, but the Bush administration opposes releasing them unless they can go to a country other than the United States ... Under US law the Uighur men cannot be sent back to China because they are likely to face persecution and torture. The administration has been seeking refuge for them in other nations; five were sent to Albania in 2006. As of two months ago, seventeen Uighurs remained at Guantanamo, awaiting countries to take them.

(www.iht.com, 5 June 2008)

A [US] Department of Justice report this month [May] suggests that American troops softened up Uighur prisoners in Guantanamo Bay on behalf of visiting Chinese interrogators. The American troops starved the Uighurs and prevented them from sleeping, just before inviting in the Chinese interrogators.

(www.iht.com, 29 May 2008; *IHT*, 30 May 2008, p. 7)

Huzaifa Parhat has been detained for six years, despite his insistence that he was an innocent swept up in the chaos of Afghanistan ... A federal appeals court [in the United States] has ruled, in the first decision of its kind, that Parhat was improperly labelled as an 'enemy combatant' ... Parhat is one of seventeen Uighur Moslems being held at the US Navy base in Guantanamo. Their supporters maintain that they were captured by mistake and had no hostile intentions toward the United States.

(www.iht.com, 25 June 2008)

'More than twenty Uighurs were captured by the US military after its invasion of Afghanistan. Though imprisoned at Guantanamo Bay for six years, they have yet to be charged with any offence' (www.bbc.co.uk, 5 August 2008).

9 July 2008.

> Chinese police have shot dead five alleged Moslem militants in the north-western region of Xinjiang, reports state news agency Xinhua. It said police had raided an apartment in the regional capital, Urumqi. Officers opened fire when some of the group of fifteen Uighur Moslems inside – armed with knives – tried to escape … A police spokesman said that when officers surrounded the apartment they found themselves facing fifteen knife-wielding Uighurs shouting 'sacrifice for Allah', Xinhua said. The five women and ten men threatened to 'perish together' with the police when they found themselves cornered … The agency cited an unnamed police spokesman as saying the suspects had confessed that they had been trained to prosecute a 'holy war' against Chinese Han people and wanted to establish their own Uighur state.
>
> (www.bbc.co.uk, 9 July 2008)

> Police in western China shot and killed five members of a group planning a 'holy war' against Han Chinese … police told Xinhua Wednesday [9 July]. The five were among fifteen who were cornered in a police raid in Xinjiang province, the agency said. The fifteen were Uighurs, a Sunni Moslem ethnic minority who live in an autonomous region in Xinjiang … Police had been searching for three men in the group after they were suspected to have stabbed a Han woman and seriously wounded her at a beauty salon in May [2008] … When police surrounded the men's apartment Tuesday [8 July] they found fifteen men and women wielding knives and shouting 'sacrifice for Allah', a police spokesman told Xinhua … Police found more than thirty knives in the apartment … The suspects confessed they had all received training in launching a 'holy war' against Han people, whom they believe to be heretics, police told Xinhua.
>
> (www.ccn.com, 9 July 2008)

10 July 2008.

> Authorities say eighty-two suspected terrorists have been arrested for plotting to sabotage the Olympic Games in Beijing. They say they have broken up five terrorist groups in Xinjiang … China has suggested the threat it faces comes mainly from a group called the East Turkestan Islamic movement. China says this movement has links to al-Qaeda but international security experts have questioned the threat that China says it faces.
>
> (www.bbc.co.uk, 10 July 2008)

> China says it has destroyed five terrorist groups in a mainly Moslem autonomous region on suspicion of plotting to attack the Olympic Games … Authorities have arrested eighty-two suspected terrorists in the Xinjiang Uighur Autonomous Region in the past six months, according to state-run

> media ... The police also banned gatherings at forty-one places where illegal preaching or 'Holy War' training was taking place in the western Xinjiang province, the Xinhua report said Thursday [10 July]. In addition police also cracked down on followers of the Falun Gong spiritual movements, arresting twenty-five 'criminal suspects' ... Earlier this year [2008] China announced dozens of arrests in Xinjiang that it said were part of a plot by Islamic terrorists to attack cities – including Beijing and Shanghai – ahead of the summer Olympic Games, which begin on 8 August. China said the plots were linked to the East Turkestan Islamic Organization, a terrorist group based outside China which sent its leader Aji Mai Mai Ti to China last year [2007] 'to accelerate the preparation on terrorism activities' targeting the Beijing Games. The terrorist leader planned to target hotels in Beijing and Shanghai that were frequented by foreigners, as well as government buildings and military bases, according to a statement from the ministry of public security. The terrorist cell inside China, led by Aji Mai Mai Ti, carried out tests on poisonous meat, poisonous gas and remote explosive devices as part of their plans, the ministry said. The group also planned to kidnap foreign journalists, tourists and Olympic athletes 'to make influences on international communities to undermine the Beijing Olympics', the ministry said. The Xinjiang autonomous region is home to about 19 million people, most of whom are Moslems and other minorities ... Human Rights Watch said in a report earlier this year: 'China continues to use the "war of terrorism" to justify policies to eradicate the "three evil forces" – terrorism, separatism and religious extremism – allegedly prevalent among Uighurs. Uighurs who express "separatist" tendencies are routinely sentenced to quick, secret and summary trials, sometimes accompanied by mass sentencing rallies. The death penalty is common.'
>
> (www.cnn.com, 10 July 2008)

> The police chief of Urumqi ... was quoted as saying his forces had also detained 'sixty-six gang members' of the 'three evil forces' of terrorism, separatism and extremism, and destroyed forty-one training bases of 'holy war' from January to June [2008].
>
> (www.guardian.co.uk, 10 July 2008)

'On 9 July two terrorists were reportedly executed ... in the western province of Xinjiang' (www.economist.com, 17 July 2008).

27 August 2008.

> A confrontation in western China has killed two police officers and led authorities to detain at least twenty members of the Uighur ethnic group, according to an international organization that represents Uighur interests. Two officers were killed, more were severely injured and others suffered slight injuries on Wednesday [27 August] between Uighurs and police, said a spokesman for the World Uighur Congress, which is based in Germany. A Chinese police spokesman, however, said she was unaware of any police

deaths or of any incident in the region in question. The clash happened in Jiashi County, about 62 miles (100 kilometres) from the city of Kashgar … in China's Xinjiang Uighur Autonomous Region.

(www.cnn.com, 28 August 2008)

29 August 2008.

Chinese police officers investigating a spate of attacks last month in the far western region of Sichuan shot and killed six suspected rebels … An exile group … the World Uighur Congress … accused the police of gunning down the suspects – members of the Xinjiang region's Moslem Uighur ethnic minority – after they had surrendered … Xinhua, the state-run news agency, reported that police officers had encountered nine suspects in a corn field near the far western city of Kashgar on Friday night [29 August] … The police told Xinhua that its initial investigations had linked the suspects to attacks on 12 August and 27 August … On Wednesday [27 August] it was reported that two police officers had died … after a clash in a village in Jiashi County, a Uighur town.

(www.iht.com, 31 August 2008)

Two police officers who were killed … in an ambush in western China on 27 August were ethnic Uighurs … The attackers were also Uighurs … Two days after the attack police officers shot and killed six suspects and arrested three near Kasgar, according to a report Saturday [30 August] by Xinhua. The nine suspects were linked both to the 27 August attack and to one on 12 August, Xinhua reported … Some reports have said the victims of the earlier attack were also Uighurs … There are signs women are playing a prominent role in the violence unfolding in Xinjiang.

(www.iht.com, 2 September 2008)

7 October 2008.

A US court yesterday [7 October] ordered the immediate release of seventeen Chinese Uighurs imprisoned at Guantanamo Bay in Cuba since 2001 … In the first ruling to order the release of prisoners from Guantanamo, Judge Richard Urbina said there was no evidence the Uighurs were 'enemy combatants' or posed a security risk to the United States. Pakistan handed the Uighurs to the United States in 2001 after they fled from a camp in Afghanistan following the US invasion … The United States cleared the Uighurs for release in 2004, but had resisted sending them to China out of concern they might be tortured. The Bush administration has been unable to find another country to accept them. Judge Urbina rejected arguments that the United States could hold the Uighurs until another country offered to take them, saying the US constitution did not permit such indefinite detention … With the exception of Albania, which took five Uighurs in 2006, the United States has failed to persuade European countries … to help.

(*FT*, 8 October 2008, p. 13)

> A federal appeals court Wednesday [8 October] blocked the planned release of seventeen Chinese Moslems from the US military facility at Guantanamo Bay, Cuba ... A three-judge panel of the US Court of Appeals granted the Bush administration's motion for an emergency stay ... The Justice Department said only the executive branch – not the courts – may decide whether to admit an alien into the United States ... The United States said the seventeen had engaged in weapons training at an Afghan military training camp.
>
> (www.cnn.com, 9 October 2008)

> The government restrictions are posted inside mosques and elsewhere across Xinjiang. In particular, officials take great pains to publicize the law prohibiting Moslems from arranging their own trips for the hajj. Signs painted on mud-brick walls in the winding alleyways of old Kashgar warn against making illegal pilgrimages. A red banner hanging on a large mosque in the Uighur area of Urumqi, the regional capital, says: 'Implement the policy of organized and planned pilgrimage; individual pilgrimage is forbidden' ... Critics say the government is trying to restrict the movements of Uighurs and prevent them from coming into contact with other Moslems, fearing that such exchanges could build a pan-Islamic identity in Xinjiang. About two years ago the government confiscating the passports of Uighurs across the region ... Now virtually no Uighurs have passports, though they can apply for them for short trips. The new restriction has made life especially difficult for businessmen who travel to neighbouring countries. To get a passport to go on an official hajj tour or a business trip, applicants must leave a deposit of nearly $6,000 ... All official imams are paid by the government.
>
> (www.iht.com, 19 October 2008)

21 October 2008.

> China released on Tuesday [21 October] a wanted list of what it called eight terrorists who it said had threatened the Beijing Olympics and were bent on achieving independence for Xinjiang. The eight, all members of the mainly minority Uighur group, belonged to the East Turkestan Islamic Movement, or ETIM, which the United Nations listed in 2002 as a terrorist organization with links to al-Qaeda ... Two of the suspects ... had tried to bomb a 'large market place where many Chinese business people gather' before the opening ceremony of the Games, the [public security ministry] statement said ... A third had planned to attack a big oil refinery ... The statement named Memetiming Memeti, thirty-seven, as the head of the ETIM ... The ETIM head [is] also named as Memetiming Aximu among other aliases.
>
> (www.iht.com, 21 October 2008)

17 December 2008.

> A court in Xinjiang has sentenced two men ... ethnic Uighurs ... to death for an attack in August that killed seventeen paramilitary officers, the official Xinhua news agency reported on Wednesday [17 December].

The assault was the deadliest against security forces in China since at least the 1990s. The court determined that the men, who carried out the attack on the morning of 4 August in the remote oasis town of Kashgar, were trying to 'sabotage the Beijing Olympic Games that began on 8 August', Xinhua reported … The day after the attack Chinese officials said the men … rammed a truck into a group of about seventy officers from the People's Armed Police who were out for morning exercises and then attacked the officers with machetes and homemade explosives … The attack was the first and deadliest of four assaults in Xinjiang in August that officials blamed on Uighur separatists. The violence killed at least twenty-three security officers and one civilian, according to official tallies … The Xinhua report did not mention the East Turkestan Islamic Movement, a shadowy organization Chinese officials have long cited as the main separatist threat in Xinjiang. The day after the attack Kashgar's Communist Party secretary said the two men appeared to be members of that organization.

(www.iht.com, 17 December 2008)

China said Tuesday [23 December] that it wanted seventeen terrorism suspects who are Moslem Chinese returned if the US military prison at Guantanamo Bay in Cuba is closed … Although the US military no longer considers the seventeen Uighurs 'enemy combatants' they have remained at Guantanamo because the United States has been unable to find a country willing to take them. It has resisted sending them to China on the ground that they might face persecution there. A Chinese foreign ministry spokesman said the seventeen were members of the East Turkestan Islamic Movement.

(*IHT*, 24 December 2008, p. 6)

A federal court appeals court panel ruled Wednesday [18 February] that seventeen native Chinese Moslems in military custody at Guantanamo Bay, Cuba, cannot be released into the United States … While there is no evidence that the Uighurs plotted against the United States, the Pentagon says the Uighur detainees have ties to a militant group demanding separation from or an autonomous homeland in China.

(www.cnn.com, 19 February 2009)

4 January 2009.

The authorities in the western desert region of Xinjiang approved the arrests of nearly 1,300 people in the first eleven months of last year [2008] on suspicion of 'endangering state security', according to a report published Sunday [4 January 2009] in an official newspaper. The number of arrests on that particular charge represents an extraordinary leap over the number in 2007 … The prosecutors' departments in Xinjiang approved 1,295 arrests of individuals and indicted 1,154 of those people … In 2007 the number of people arrested across all of China on suspicion of endangering state security was 742, according to government statistics. Prosecutors indicted 619 of

> them. Of those 2007 numbers about half were from Xinjiang ... Since 2001, when the [George W.] Bush administration began its war on terrorism, the Chinese authorities have said that they are battling the 'three forces' in Xinjiang: separatism, terrorism and religious extremism ... The charge of endangering state security includes inciting separatism, inciting subversion, stealing state secrets and giving state secrets to foreigners. It can carry the death penalty. Government statistics show that of all the regions and provinces in China, Xinjiang has had by far the most number of cases of endangering state security.
>
> (www.iht.com, 5 January 2009)

2 April 2009. 'A man has died after detonating a bomb in an office building in ... Urumqi ... the capital of the Xinjiang region' (www.bbc.co.uk, 2 April 2009).

9 April 2009. 'Two [Uighur] men were executed Thursday [9 April] for an attack that killed seventeen in [Xinjiang] ... [on] 4 August 2008 ... [They] were sentenced to death on 17 December [2008]' (www.cnn.com, 9 April 2009).

10–11 June 2009.

> The United States has won agreement to transfer up to seventeen Chinese Moslems from the prison camp in Guantanamo Bay, Cuba, to Palau, a sparsely populated archipelago in the North Pacific ... Palau, which was a United States trust territory until its independence in 1994, maintains diplomatic relations with Taiwan rather than China ... [Palau said it] had 'agreed to accommodate the United States of America's request to "temporarily resettle" the detainees, members of the Uighur ethnic group, "subject to periodic review"' ... the agreement opens the door to the largest single transfer of Guantanamo prisoners ... The United States has not been able to persuade any country to take them, despite contacting about 100 governments ... [Palau has] barely 20,000 people.
>
> (www.iht.com, 10 June 2009)

'A senior US official said the United States was engaged in aid discussions with Palau, but denied reports the aid was tied to taking the detainees' (*FT*, 11 June 2009, p. 8).

> On Thursday [11 June] the president of Palau ... [said it was] not because of a reported offer of $200 million in aid and other assistance from the United States ... [that] that the island had agreed to take the Uighurs.
>
> (www.bbc.co.uk, 12 June 2009)

> The United States announced [on 11 June] that it had sent four Chinese Moslems [Uighurs] who had been detained at Guantanamo to the island of Bermuda ... [where they were] granted short-term asylum ... premier Ewart Brown: '[The detainees] will have the opportunity to become naturalized citizens and thereafter afforded the right to travel and leave Bermuda,

> potentially settling anywhere … As a British overseas territory with significant autonomy' … Because of its colonial status, Mr Brown said that it is 'important for everyone to understand that this process is not complete'.
>
> (www.iht.com, 11 June 2009)

'Britain has told Bermuda, a UK overseas territory, it should have consulted London before accepting them' (www.bbc.co.uk, 11 June 2009). 'The four who were sent to Bermuda were part of a group of seventeen Uighurs still at Guantanamo' (www.bbc.co.uk, 12 June 2009).

> Palau's decision to allow thirteen Chinese Moslems from the Guantanamo Bay prison camp to resettle there has sparked anger among islanders who fear for the safety of the tranquil tourist haven … Public opinion has appeared overwhelmingly negative … Palau President Johnson Toribong explained his decision as traditional hospitality … Toribong said: 'Palau's people are always on the side of the US government' … He said Palau would send a delegation to Guantanamo to assess the Uighur detainees … Four other Uighurs left Guantanamo Bay for a new home in Bermuda on Thursday [11 June]. Some residents of the North Atlantic island were also unhappy … The British Foreign Office complained that Bermuda's leaders failed to consult 'whether this falls within their competence or is a security issue for which the Bermuda government do not have delegated responsibility'.
>
> (www.independent.com, 12 June 2009)

> Five Chinese Uighurs cleared of suspected involvement in terrorism … [were] granted asylum by Albania in 2006, after other countries refused to take them … Far from lining in obscurity the four [remaining] Uighurs – one has since joined a sister who was granted asylum in Sweden – became celebrities in Tirana, appearing on television chat shows and giving interviews … The Tirana government provided … [them] with free apartments, lessons in Albanian and a monthly allowance … Albanian citizenship … [is possible] after five years' residence … The United States, which is committed to closing Guantanamo, has faced difficulty in finding countries to accept another seventeen Uighurs. Four Uighurs went to Bermuda last month [June]. The other thirteen were offered resettlement in the South Pacific Islands of Palau, but most are reluctant to go because they would not be given Palau passports.
>
> (*FT*, 11 July 2009, p. 6)

The violent demonstrations of July 2009

> Chinese police have detained a man who they say sparked a deadly ethnic clash at a toy factory in southern China … Xinhua said the man had posted a message on a local website claiming six Xinjiang boys 'raped two innocent girls'. Police say the false claim sparked a vicious brawl between Han

> and Uighur groups at the Guangdong factory. Officials have encouraged the hiring of Uighurs from Xinjiang, in an effort to reduce regional income gaps in China ... The fight took place in Shaoguan city, Guangdong province, and saw both sides wielding iron bars, leaving two Uighurs dead and 118 people injured.
>
> (www.bbc.co.uk, 30 June 2009)

> [There were] reports of ethnic clashes between Han Chinese and Uighur workers at a toy factory in the southern Guangdong province in which two Uighurs were killed and 188 wounded ... A group of Han Chinese fought with Uighurs who had been recruited to the factory recently ... Police have now arrested a Han Chinese for rumour-mongering after he was found to have made up the rape report in a fit of anger after losing his job at the plant.
>
> (*The Times*, 6 July 2009, p. 31)

> Uighurs say the riots that started Sunday – put down by volleys of tear gas and a massive show of force – were triggered by the 25 June deaths of Uighur factory workers during a brawl in the southern city of Shaoguan. State media have said that two workers died, but many Uighurs believe more were killed.
>
> (www.independent.co.uk, 8 July 2009)

> The rioting started Sunday as a peaceful protest calling for a full government inquiry into an earlier brawl between Uighurs and Han Chinese at a factory in the south in late June ... The internet appeared to have unified Uighur anger over the way Chinese officials handled the brawl in June. There Han workers rampaged through a Uighur dormitory, killing at least two Uighurs ... Photographs that appeared online after the battle showed people standing around a pile of bodies, leading many Uighurs to believe that the government was playing down the number of dead Uighurs.
>
> (*IHT*, 8 July 2009, p 5)

'Chinese officials say that two Uighur workers were killed by a small group of Han Chinese, who had been detained ... Rebiya Kadeer says ... there is evidence that a mob killed up to sixty Uighurs' (www.iht.co, 9 July 2009).

'Word of the Han assault [in Guangdong] reached Uighurs in their Xinjiang homeland, and rumours spread that hundreds of their kind had died' (*The Times*, 11 July 2009, p. 43).

> An anonymous internet posting claimed that a group of six Uighur men had raped two Han women ... In the government's version of events, the factory clash was the simple product of false rumours, posted on the internet by a disgruntled former worker who has since been arrested. A few days later they added another wrinkle to the story, saying the fight was prompted by a 'misunderstanding' after a nineteen-year-old female worker accidentally stumbled into a dormitory room of Uighur men.
>
> (www.iht.com, 15 July 2009)

Xinjiang experienced the biggest display of ethnic unrest in recent memory today [5 July] as thousands of Uighurs took to the streets in protest. The protesters smashed up buses, threw stones through shop windows and assaulted Han Chinese passers-by, according to a witness, who said the spark was the recent killing of Uighur migrant workers in Guangdong, southern China … The protests were said to have started when several thousand people rallied in the Grand Bazaar to protest the death of two Uighur migrants, and injuries suffered by hundreds of others, during an ethnic conflict between workers in a factory in Guangdong last month [June] … Xinhua reported that vehicles were set on fire and traffic guard rails overturned … Armed riot police moved in to restore order with tear gas, armoured vehicles and road blocks, according to a foreign student in Xinjiang. A large section of Urumqi was shut off to vehicles tonight, with police manning roadblocks at the perimeter, and witnesses reported large numbers of armed officers inside the cordon.

(www.guardian.co.uk, 5 July 2009)

The city of Urumqi in China's restive Xinjiang region has been hit by violence with cars burned and traffic blocked … An unspecified number of people also attacked passers-by and damaged property, Xinhua news agency said … The Xinhua report did not say how many people were involved, or suggest a motive. But an eyewitness … [said] that the rioters were Uighurs, numbering in their thousands.

(www.bbc.co.uk, 5 July 2009)

At least three people were killed in a rare outburst of violence in Urumqi … Witnesses said that up to 3,000 rioters went on the rampage, smashing buses and overturning police barricades during several hours of violence … About 3,000 Uighur and 1,000 police [were involved] … Riots are rare in Urumqi, where ethnic Han already outnumber the local Uighur population … [There is a] large presence of security forces.

(*The Times*, 6 July 2009)

At least 140 people were dead and more than 800 others injured … A witness in Urumqi told CNN that soon after the protest started … hundreds of protesters 'grew into easily over 1,000' … Police arrived quickly and tried to control the swelling crowd by erecting barriers in the street, but 'people pushed them over', the witness said … The witness said: 'They were throwing rocks at passing cars and buses' … Hundreds of People's Liberation Army soldiers [were] in the streets.

(www.cnn.com, 6 July 2009)

Violence in … Xinjiang has left at least 140 people dead and more than 800 injured, state media say … Uighur exiles said police fired indiscriminately on a peaceful protest in Urumqi. The Xinjiang government blamed Uighurs abroad for orchestrating attacks on ethnic Han Chinese … The Xinjiang government has blamed the latest unrest on businesswoman Rebiya Kadeer, the Uighurs' leader, who is living in exile in the United States. The government said in a statement (published in Xinhua): 'An initial investigation showed the violence was masterminded by Rebiya Kadeer' ... Eyewitnesses said the violence started on Sunday [5 July] with a few hundred people and grew to more than 1,000.

(www.bbc.co.uk, 6 July 2009)

The clashes on Sunday [5 July] began when the police confronted a protest march held by Uighurs to demand a full government investigation of a brawl between Uighur and Han workers that erupted in Guangdong province overnight on 25 and 26 June [Xinhua] reported Monday [6 July] that at least 140 people were killed and 816 injured ... At least 1,000 rioters took to the streets ... The riot was the largest ethnic clash in China since the Tibetan uprising of March 2008 and perhaps the biggest protest in Xinjiang in years ... Chinese officials said the latest riots were started by Rebiya Kadeer, a Uighur human rights advocate who had been imprisoned in China and now lives in Washington ... She denies the charges ... There was also a rumour circulating on Sunday that a Han man had killed an Uighur in the city earlier in the day ... Uighurs are the largest ethnic group in Xinjiang but are a minority in Urumqi, where Han Chinese make up more than 70 per cent of 2 million or so ... Urumqi is a deeply segregated city, with Han Chinese there rarely venturing into the Uighur quarter.

(www.iht.com, 6 July 2009)

The regional government said the violence was 'masterminded' by the World Uighur Congress, said Xinhua ... The Congress, a group based in Munich that advocates for the rights of Uighurs in China, said security forces had staged a 'brutal crackdown of a peaceful protest' and said it had no part in the protest. Protests spread to a second city, Kashgar, as 200 to 300 people chanting 'God is great' and 'Release the people' confronted the riot police in front of the city's main mosque, said an eyewitness ... China's central government moved swiftly to take command of the public depiction of the Urumqi protests and to cripple protesters' ability to communicate ... [For example] local internet service was largely disabled ... Xinhua said the toll so far was 140 dead and 828 wounded.

(www.iht.com, 6 July 2009)

Rebiya Kadeer, sixty-two, first gained fame as an astute businesswoman and then a favoured example of China's claim of multi-ethnic harmony. She built an empire of trading companies and a department store and was even appointed to China's national legislative body ... She was arrested in 1999 and sentenced to eight years for betraying state secrets ... She was released to exile in March 2005. She was soon elected president of two exile groups, the Uighur American Association, which represents the 1,000 or so Uighurs in the United States, and the World Uighur Congress, an umbrella group for forty-seven groups worldwide, with headquarters in Munich ...

The organizations say they reject ties to violence or Islamic extremism. They call for democracy and 'self-determination' for the Uighurs ... The World Uighur Congress had sponsored demonstrations outside Chinese embassies in several European cities last week to protest the killings of Uighur workers in Guangdong province in late June ... Beijing officials singled out the group along with Ms Kadeer as a culprit ... She said that while the groups she leads condemn the Chinese government's excessive used of force, 'We also condemn in no uncertain terms the violent actions of some of the Uighur demonstrators.'

(www.iht.com, 7 July 2009)

[This was] the single worst day of violence since troops crushed student demonstrations centred on Tiananmen Square in June 1989 ... Police said the number of dead was expected to rise. State television said at least one member of the paramilitary People's Armed Police had been killed.

(www.thetimes.com, 6 July 2009)

The *China Daily* put the number of protesters at 300 to 500 while the exiled Uighur American Association had it as high as 3,000. An unnamed Chinese official said the 'unrest was masterminded by the World Uighur Congress led by Rebiya Kadeer'.

(www.independent.co.uk, 6 July 2009)

Chinese police detained at least 1,434 people by Tuesday morning [7 July] ... Xinhua reported ... as protests spread to more cities ... Police halted people who had gathered in nearby Yili Kazak Prefecture and Aksu City and dispersed more than 200 people who had tried to gather in nearby Kashgar at the Id Kah Mosque, the largest mosque in China, the news agency said ... The regional public security department put the toll from riots at 156 deaths and more than 800 injuries, according to Xinhua ... With a massive presence of soldiers and anti-riot squads, the government said Tuesday, the unrest in this capital of China's far west Xinjiang region had been brought under control.

(www.cnn.com, 7 July 2009)

Officials say 156 people – mostly ethnic Han Chinese – died in Sunday's violence and more than 1,000 were injured. Uighur groups say many more have died, claiming 90 per cent were Uighurs ... New protests have flared in Urumqi two days after more than 150 people died in clashes between police and demonstrators. About 200 ethnic Uighurs faced off against police to protest over the arrest of 1,434 people over Sunday's unrest ... At least 200 people – mostly elderly women or women with children – have taken to the streets, complaining that their relatives have been arbitrarily arrested. Foreign journalists witnessed the protest during a tour led by government officials.

(www.bbc.co.uk, 7 July 2009)

> The Chinese government locked down this regional capital [Urumqi] of 2.3 million people and other cities across its western desert region on Monday [6 July] and early Tuesday [7 July], imposing curfews, cutting off cellphone and internet services and sending armed police officers into neighbourhoods … China's central government crippled internet service, blocked Twitter's micro-blogs, purged search engines of unapproved references to the violence, and saturated the Chinese media with the state-sanctioned media … But hundreds of Uighur protesters defied the police again on Tuesday morning, crashing a state-run tour of the riot scene for foreign and Chinese journalists. A wailing crowd of women, joined later by scores of Uighur men, marched down a wide avenue with raised fists and tearfully demanded that the police release Uighur men who they said had been seized from their homes after the violence … The confrontation later ebbed to a tense stand-off between about 100 protesters, mostly women, some carrying infants, and riot police.
>
> (www.iht.com, 7 July 2009)

> Several hundred people staged a new protest in Urumqi on Tuesday [7 July], demanding the release of relatives detained in connection with weekend demonstrations by ethnic Uighur residents … The crowd of 200 to 300 – mostly women and elderly – quickly formed as local authorities were taking members of the media on a tour.
>
> (www.cnn.com, 7 July 2009)

'About 300 Uighurs confronted riot police to demand the release of family members they said had been arbitrarily arrested in the crackdown' (www.thetimes.co.uk, 7 July 2009).

'Officials said 156 people had been killed in rioting in the worst ethnic unrest and provincial violence in the country since the Cultural Revolution' (*FT*, 7 July 2009, p. 7).

'One official described Sunday's unrest as the "deadliest riot since New China was founded in 1949"' (www.bbc.co.uk, 7 July 2009).

'It began as a protest about a brawl at the other end of the country; it became China's bloodiest incident of civil unrest since the massacre that ended the Tiananmen Square protests twenty years ago' (www.economist.com, 9 July 2009).

> The authorities swiftly imposed a curfew on … Urumqi … in an attempt to quell what the government has already described as the worst riots since the foundation of the People's Republic sixty years ago … Witnesses described vicious and apparently indiscriminate attacks on Han Chinese people, although numbers of Uighurs and other ethnic minorities were also injured.
>
> (www.guardian.co.uk, 7 July 2009)

'Thousands of Han Chinese roamed the streets of Urumqi today [7 July] looking for vengeance … Most of the victims appear to have been Han Chinese cut down by Uighurs armed with knives' (www.thetimes.co.uk, 7 July 2009).

'Thousands of furious Han Chinese with makeshift weapons marched from a central square … toward the main Uighur neighbourhood, where the riots began Sunday' (*IHT*, 8 July 2009, p. 5).

'Police fired tear gas on Tuesday [7 July] at Han Chinese protesters armed with clubs, lead pipes, shovels and hoes, news reports said' (www.iht.com, 7 July 2009).

> President Hu Jintao changed plans to attend a summit of major economic powers in Italy, instead returning home to address ethnic violence raking north-western China, state media reported Wednesday [8 July] … Taking Hu's place at the G-8 economic summit this week in Italy will be Dai Bingguo, China's state councillor … There is speculation that Sunday's protest, which took place in the predominantly Uighur-populated bazaar district, may have been a reaction to ethnic violence … at a toy factory in Guangdong province … Police have detained fifteen suspects in connection with that incident … The unrest in Urumqi was brought under control with a massive presence of soldiers and anti-riot squads, the government said Tuesday [7 July] … Curfews were in force in major districts of the capital. Several small protests erupted despite the heavy police presence and were quickly defused. More than 1,400 suspects had been detained by Tuesday morning, the Xinhua news agency said.
>
> (www.cnn.com, 8 July 2009)

'Thousands of security forces have been deployed in Urumqi … There are thousands of paramilitary police in the city … Fresh scuffles were reported as police tried to arrest protesters' (www.bbc.co.uk, 8 July 2009).

'Thousands more armed riot police poured into Urumqi's city centre … Many Urumqi residents believe the new arrivals, though kitted out as members of China's paramilitary police force, include regular army troops' (www.economist.com, 9 July 2009).

> Thousands of Chinese troops poured into Urumqi early today [8 July] in a massive show of force, as President Hu Jintao cut short a visit to Italy for the G-8 summit to deal with the outbreak of ethnic violence … Xinhua said China would be represented at the meeting … by State Councillor Dai Bingguo … Mr Hu's decision to return home came after another day of strife in Urumqi on Tuesday [7 July] as thousands of Han Chinese roamed the streets looking for vengeance after Sunday's riots, which left 156 dead and more than 800 injured. He left Italy early today 'due to the situation in north-west China's Xinjiang Uighur Autonomous Region', Xinhua reported … Although China is not a member of the G-8, talks at the summit were to include emerging powers including China and India.
>
> (www.thetimes.co.uk, 8 July)

> President Hu Jintao cut short a trip to Italy on Wednesday [8 July] to fly home after the deadly ethnic clashes in the north-western Xinjiang region, abandoning plans to attend the G-8 summit meeting as news reports spoke of continued unrest … Mr Hu arrived in Italy on Sunday [5 July] and was

also scheduled to visit Portugal … The Chinese foreign ministry said that Mr Hu was returning 'given the current situation in Xinjiang' where state media say at least 156 people have died in China's worst ethnic clashes in decades between Moslem Uighurs and Han Chinese. News reports from Urumqi, the regional capital, said up to 1,000 Han Chinese protesters gathered in Urumqi on Wednesday as squads of anti-riot police tried to break up the crowd. Reuters said scuffles broke out as police and security forces seized apparent ringleaders, prompting cries of 'release them, release them.'

(www.iht.com, 8 July 2009)

The situation in Urumqi is now under control after the deployment of thousands of troops, local communist officials have said … The city's Communist Party boss, Li Zhi, told a press conference that the government would execute all those found guilty of killings during the riots … [He said] that many people accused of murder had already been arrested and that most of them were students … Despite the security presence and calls for calm, there were reports of fresh violence on Wednesday [8 July] … A crowd of about 1,000 Han Chinese had faced off with security forces, with some angry that police were arresting young Han men … Officials say 156 people – mostly Han Chinese – died in Sunday's violence. Uighur groups say many more have died, claiming 90 per cent of the dead were Uighurs.

(www.bbc.co.uk, 8 July 2009)

[Urumqi] Communist Party chief Li Zhi … [said] many people had been arrested, including students. He said: 'To those who committed crimes with cruel means, we will execute them' … Li would not say how many of the 156 dead were Han … and how many were Uighurs … even though more than 100 of them have been identified and handed over to their families. He said both groups were responsible for the violence. He said: 'The small groups of the violent people have already been caught by the police. The situation is now under control.'

(www.independent.co.uk, 8 July 2009)

As north-west China's Xinjiang Uighur Autonomous Region settled into tense stillness on Wednesday [8 July] after three days of deadly ethnic violence … Li Zhi, the party boss in Urumqi … said that many suspected instigators of the riots had been arrested and that most were students … [He made a] promise to seek the death sentence for those responsible … Mr Li said that nine of the 156 known dead remained unidentified, their bodies too badly burned for families to recognize them. He did not specify the ethnicity of those who died, but one Han family member who reviewed photos of the dead, seeking to identify a relative, said in an interview that the great majority of the photographs were of Han victims.

(www.iht.com, 8 July 2009)

Advocates for the city's Uighur population angrily challenged both the official death toll and the suggestion that most victims were Han. Uighurs who

> witnessed the rioting in Urumqi estimate that between 400 and 1,000 Uighurs died in the violence, many shot on sight by the paramilitary police, according to a statement by a former president of the Uighur American Association, Turdi Huji … Rebiya Kadeer [said] that at least 500 people had died in the rioting.
>
> (*IHT*, 9 July 2009, p. 7)

'One official has said that thirty-three Uighurs were among the dead' (*The Times*, 10 July 2009, p. 41).

> There were no weapons visible today, but residents showed reporters' mobile phone and video camera footage of the earlier chaos … Police have generally allowed foreign media to cover the tensions. The Chinese media have covered the violence but have not made it a priority.
>
> (www.guardian.co.uk, 8 July 2009)

> China's top leadership has vowed to administer 'severe punishment' to those involved in the deadly rioting … The pledge was the first public comment by top leaders … President Hu Jintao met other leaders at a Politburo meeting on Wednesday night [8 July] … A statement issued Thursday [9 July] said that stability in Xinjiang was the 'most important and pressing task'. It said: 'The planners of the incident, the organizers, key members and the serious criminals must be severely punished according to law.'
>
> (www.bbc.co.uk, 9 July 2009)

'The old alleyways of Kashgar [are] now being rapidly torn down as part of an urban-renewal programme … [This] is fuelling yet more resentment among local Uighurs' (www.economist.com, 9 July 2009).

> Kashgar [is] a city of 3.4 million that is 90 per cent Uighur … It is rapidly being bulldozed in the name of modernization … [People have been detained] after publicly criticizing plans to tear down the old mud-and-straw homes that, until recently, flanked Kashgar's historic mosques.
>
> (www.iht.com, 23 July 2009)

> China has ordered mosques in Urumqi not to open for Friday prayers … Many mosques have been closed since the fighting broke out on Sunday. An unnamed government official … [said] that the order not to open for prayers on Friday, the holiest day of the week in Islam, was given on public safety grounds … A Uighur man said: 'The government is afraid that people will use religion to support the three forces' … The 'three forces' is a term used by the Chinese government for separatists, terrorists and extremists … On Thursday [9 July] China said it had 'a great deal of evidence' that some of those involved in the violence had 'Training from foreign terrorist groups including al-Qaeda'. Foreign ministry official Qin Gang did not say what the evidence was, but said the groups were 'inextricably linked with three vicious forces from abroad'.
>
> (www.bbc.co.uk, 10 July 2009)

> President Hu Jintao, forced to abandon the G-8 summit by the ethnic violence in Xinjiang, has said maintaining social stability in the energy-rich region is the 'most urgent task'. Mr Hu described the Sunday riots as a 'serious violent crime elaborately planned and organized by "three forces" at home and abroad'. 'Three forces' is a term China uses to refer to religious extremists, separatists and terrorists which, it says, menace Xinjiang.
>
> (*Independent*, 11 July 2009, p. 24)

> Chinese authorities banned prayer meetings at mosques … in Urumqi … on Friday [10 July] … In Kashgar foreign journalists and other visitors were instructed to leave … The *People's Daily* editorial echoed the remarks of President Hu Jintao, who cut short a visit to the G-8 summit meeting in Italy. In a statement issued along with the Communist Party's senior leaders, Mr Hu called on the authorities to 'isolate and deal a blow to the small group' who had a hand in the bloodshed. Mr Hu said: 'Preserving and maintaining the overall stability of Xinjiang is currently the most urgent task' … Urumqi appeared to be settling into an uneasy calm … As many as 20,000 troops from nearby regions had poured into Urumqi after the rioting began … On Wednesday [8 July] the government for the first time shifted some of the blame to the United States, which it accused of financing Rebiya Kadeer's organization, the World Uighur Congress, and other groups that advocate human rights and democracy for ethnic Uighurs in China. The accusation appeared in an article in the *People's Daily*.
>
> (www.iht.com, 10 July 2009)

> A night-time curfew has been reimposed in Urumqi, officials have announced. The curfew had been suspended for the last two days after officials said they had the city under control. Mosques in the city were ordered to remain closed on Friday [10 July] – but at least two opened at the request of crowds of Moslem Uighurs that gathered outside … Thousands of people – both Han Chinese and Uighurs – are reportedly trying to leave the city.
>
> (www.bbc.co.uk, 10 July 2009)

'Police say that more than 2,000 people have been arrested' (www.thetimes.com, 10 July 2009).

> China yesterday [10 July] revealed the ethnicity of those killed in rioting in Urumqi last week, and increased the official number of dead to 183. State media said that 137 Han Chinese and forty-six Uighurs were killed … Police sweeps of the city have so far taken in more than 2,000 suspects … Nicholas Becquelin of Human Rights Watch said that the riots appeared to pit the poorest of the Uighur poor against similarly poor Han incomers from other provinces … Relations between the better-off were less strained … Some Uighurs are also furious at the razing of swathes of their ancient neighbourhoods in Kashgar. Nervous that tension could spread there, foreign journalists were ordered to leave yesterday "for their own safety".'
>
> (*The Times*, 11 July 2009, p. 43)

'In both cases … the deadly riots in Xinjiang and those in Tibet early last year [2008] … young indigenous males appear to have set upon Han Chinese' (*FT*, 11 July 2009, p. 9).

> The government today raised the death toll to 184 and offered the first ethnic breakdown of the dead: 137 Han Chinese and forty-six Uighurs … One Hui Moslem also died. More than 1,000 were injured … [Urumqi] appears to be settling into an uneasy calm, policed by a security force of about 20,000 paramilitary, riot and regular officers.
>
> (www.guardian.co.uk, 11 July 2009)

('[In China as a whole] Hui Moslems [number] 10 million': www.iht.com, 13 July 2009.)

'Rioting … [has killed] at least 184 … More than 1,000 [have been injured]' (www.iht.com, 11 July 2009).

> Of the 184 people known to have died, 137 were Han Chinese, forty-six were from the indigenous Uighur community and one was an ethnic Hui … a male … local officials said … Some Uighurs believe their own death toll was higher … Uighurs living in exile outside China have also disputed the Chinese figures. Rebiya Kadeer said she believed about 500 people had died … According to the Chinese death toll released by state media, twenty-six of the 137 Han Chinese were female, while all but one of the forty-five Uighurs killed were male.
>
> (www.bbc.co.uk, 12 July 2009)

> Chinese riot police broke up a small demonstration by Uighurs leaving Friday prayers in a Moslem neighbourhood of Urumqi, arresting several … A crowd of several hundred gathered near the White Mosque along with riot police … Hundreds of Uighurs crowded into the mosque after authorities relented on a decision to close mosques.
>
> (*Independent*, 11 July 2009, p. 24)

> A notice by the public security bureau of Urumqi: 'Assemblies, marches and demonstrations on public roads and at public places in the open air are not allowed without permission by police' … The Urumqi security measures on public assembly came on the eve of a sensitive day of mourning … It is traditional for ethnic Han to mourn their loss on the seventh day after a death … Uighur religious leaders have condemned the violence, saying it is against the spirit of the Moslem faith and Uighur tradition.
>
> (www.cnn.com, 12 July 2009)

'The official toll of the wounded rose to 1,680' (*IHT*, 13 July 2009, p. 7).

'Many Uighurs assert that hundreds of Uighurs were shot dead by Chinese security forces and massacred by Han mobs' (www.iht.com, 13 July 2009).

'Two ethnic Uighurs have been shot dead by police in Urumqi' (www.bbc.co.uk, 13 July 2009).

> Chinese police shot dead two men and injured a third as the trio attacked a fellow Uighur in Urumqi today [13 July], officials have announced. The violence follows last week's inter-ethnic clashes between Uighurs and Han Chinese in Urumqi, in which the government says that 184 people were killed and 1,680 wounded. It has warned that the death toll could rise.
>
> (www.guardian.co.uk, 13 July 2009)

> Chinese police today [13 July] shot dead two Uighur men and wounded a third in the first official report of the use of firearms … Officials said that officers opened fire after they were attacked as they tried to prevent three men from assaulting another with knives and rods.
>
> (www.thetimes.co.uk, 13 July 2009)

> Police officers shot dead two armed ethnic Uighur men and wounded a third on Monday [13 July] after the three resisted officers during a violent dispute … The three Uighurs were brandishing sticks and knives and chasing after another Uighur, according to the Xinhua account, and the three turned on the police when confronted … The ethnic strife between Uighurs and the Hans … led to a spasm of violence that by government statistics left at least 184 people dead and 1,680 injured. Many Uighurs here dispute those figures, saying that hundreds of Uighurs have died at the hands of security forces and Han vigilantes … On 5 July more than 1,000 Uighur protesters held a march … Riot police tried to suppress the march, battles broke out, and mobs of young Uighur men rampaged through the centre of the city, killing many Han civilians. For at least three days afterwards Han vigilantes attacked Uighurs with sticks and knives.
>
> (www.iht.com, 13 July 2009)

> Yesterday's [13 July] announcement … [by] the city government … followed reports of the shooting by several foreign media organizations. The Associated Press reported that, according to a witness, the officers involved were paramilitary rather than regular police, and that the Uighur men had attacked the security officials rather than chased another Uighur. Xinhua said the incident was being investigated.
>
> (*FT*, 14 July 2009, p. 6)

'A Han man told the Associated Press that he saw three Uighurs with knives coming out of a mosque and attack paramilitary police' (www.guardian.co.uk, 14 July 2009).

'On 13 July the Beijing Bureau for Legal Affairs instructed lawyers considering the representation of Uighurs involved in the recent Xinjiang protests to "positively accept monitoring and guidance from legal authorities and lawyers' associations". Both associations are government controlled' (www.iht.com, 28 July 2009).

> More than 100 Chinese writers and intellectuals have signed a letter calling for the release of Ilham Tohti, an outspoken Uighur economist. Mr Tohti disappeared from his Beijing home last week and has apparently been

> detained … It was posted online on Monday [13 July] and demands information about his case … It also said that Mr Tohti's website … was an important site for dialogue between Han Chinese and Uighurs. In a televised speech on 6 July Xinjiang governor Nur Bekri accused the site of helping 'to orchestrate the incitement and spread propaganda'.
>
> (www.bbc.co.uk, 14 July 2009)

> Prominent Chinese intellectuals and writers have signed a petition calling for the release of a well-known ethnic Uighur economist in Beijing who was apparently detained last week … The economist, who had written critically about government policies toward the Uighurs, is the best known person to be detained so far in relation to the ethnic strife … [He] vanished from his Beijing home sometime last week and made a call to a friend to say he would be detained. Mr Tohti ran a website … that had become a popular forum for discussion of issues important to Uighurs … On 6 July Nur Bekri, the governor of Xinjiang, said in a speech that … [the] website had helped instigate the rioting by spreading rumours … Mr Tohti had been increasingly critical of the lack of jobs for Uighurs in Xinjiang and policies that had encouraged the influx of Han settlers … The petition to free Mr Tohti was started by Wang Lixiong, one of China's leading experts on ethnic minority issues and the husband of Woeser, a well known Tibetan blogger. The petition had 158 signatures as of Monday night [13 July]. The signers are mostly ethnic Han and from over China.
>
> (www.iht.com, 14 July 2009)

> The letter was posted online yesterday [13 July]: 'Professor Ilham Tohti is a Uighur intellectual who devoted himself to friendship between ethnic groups and eradicating conflicts between them. He should not be taken as a criminal' … Xinjiang's governor accused Tohti's website of helping 'to orchestrate the incitement' of last week's riot, but the letter's authors said it was an important site for dialogue between Han Chinese and Uighurs.
>
> (www.guardian.co.uk, 14 July 2009)

'Indonesia saw anti-Chinese protests yesterday [13 July]' (www.guardian.co.uk, 14 July 2009).

> China has demanded that Turkish prime minister Recep Tayyip Erdogan retract his accusation that Beijing practised genocide against ethnic Uighurs … Mr Erdogan made the controversial comments last Friday [10 July]: 'The incidents in China are, simply put, a genocide. There is no point in interpreting this otherwise' … He called on Chinese authorities to intervene to prevent more deaths. Turkey is secular but the population is predominantly Moslem and it shares linguistic and religious links with the Uighurs.
>
> (www.bbc.co.uk, 14 July 2009)

'Turkish prime minister Recep Tayyip Erdogan [said] that Chinese policy in Xinjiang was "like a genocide" and that China should "abandon its policy of assimilation"' (www.iht.com, 14 July 2009).

> Turkey has long been a haven for disaffected Uighurs, including Isa Yusuf Alptekin, the pre-eminent leader of Uighur nationalism until his death in 1995 ... Both countries [Kyrgyzstan and Kazakhstan] have sizeable Uighur populations – 50,000 in Kyrgyzstan; 300,000 in Kazakhstan (including prime minister Karim Massimov). There are also an estimated 1 million ethnic Kazakhs in Xinjiang, who complain they face the same sort of pressure on their culture and traditions as the Uighur ... The 'stans' have taken a dim view of Uighur nationalism. Kazakhstan, for example, has sent a few separatists wanted by China back to Xinjiang.
>
> (*The Economist*, 18 July 2009, p. 58)

> Al-Qaeda-linked militants in Algeria have called for reprisals against Chinese workers ... Events in Xinjiang triggered a call for an Algerian-based al-Qaeda affiliate for reprisals against Chinese workers ... Al-Qaeda in the Islamic Maghreb (AQM) promised to target Chinese workers in Algeria and north-west Africa ... AQM appeared to be the first al-Qaeda affiliate to officially state that it would target Chinese interests.
>
> (www.bbc.co.uk, 14 July 2009)

> The Associated Press reported that two extremist Islamic websites affiliated to al-Qaeda had called for the killing of Han in the Middle East, noting large communities of ethnic Chinese labourers in Algeria and Saudi Arabia ... Western experts see scant signs that terrorist groups operate in Xinjiang, where Uighurs are Sunni and follow a moderate form of Islam.
>
> (*The Times*, 15 July 2009, p. 31)

'Organizers of Melbourne's International Film Festival have defied calls from China not to show a documentary about ... Rebiya Kadeer' (www.bbc.co.uk, 15 July 2009).

('Chinese hackers have attacked the website of Australia's biggest film festival over a documentary about Rebiya Kadeer. Content of the Melbourne International Film Festival was briefly replaced with the Chinese flag and anti-Kadeer slogans on Saturday [25 July] ... In an earlier protest on Friday [24 July] Beijing withdrew four Chinese films ... Attacks on the festival's website began about ten days ago ... Police were investigating the website attacks, which appear to come from a Chinese internet address': www.bbc.co.uk, 26 July 2009.)

'In the end 192 people died and more than 1,000 were wounded, according to the government' (www.iht.com, 15 July 2009; *IHT*, 16 July 2009, p. 2). 'In Urumqi at least 192 people were killed and 1,721 injured' (*IHT*, 18 July 2009, p. 3).

> The Chinese authorities today [18 July] acknowledged shooting dead twelve Uighur rioters in Xinjiang ... Inter-ethnic violence over several days left 197 dead and more than 1,700 wounded ... Most victims had been bludgeoned to death with bricks and iron rods ... said ... Nuer Baikeli, governor of the region ... It was not clear whether the total of twelve rioters included two Uighur men shot dead by police earlier this week ... At least 1,400,

mostly Uighurs, have been detained. The region's chief prosecutor said on Thursday [16 July] that the initial investigation had concluded and he would soon issue arrest warrants.

(www.guardian.co.uk, 18 July 2009)

Nuer Baikeli, Xinjiang's regional governor, admitted in a public statement that Chinese police shot dead twelve Uighur rioters … Yesterday [19 July] thousands of ethnic Uighurs rallied in Almaty, the largest city in Kazakhstan, to protest against the crackdown on Uighurs in China.

(*FT*, 20 July 2009, p. 8)

China acknowledged Sunday [19 July] that security forces shot dead twelve people during ethnic riots in the north-west earlier this month … Nur Bekri, chairman of the Xinjiang regional government … did not say whether … [they] were Uighurs or Han … Officials also said that the death toll from the violence in the Xinjiang region had risen to 197 … The leader of the Turkistan Islamic Party, in a video that appeared on Islamic websites, blames the Chinese for 'genocide' against people in East Turkestan – what some Uighurs call the region of Xinjiang province … The remarks were delivered by Seyfullah, commander of the Turkestan Islamic Party and dated 8 July … The speaker urged his people to 'kill the Chinese Communists where you find them and besiege them and ambush them wherever you can' … The US State Department said the group has taken credit for violent incidents in the past.

(www.cnn.com, 19 July 2009)

Twelve of the nearly 200 people killed during an ethnic riot in the city of Urumqi on 5 July were shot by Chinese security forces, the state news agency report … Nur Bekri, the governor of Xinjiang, said policemen 'resolutely shot twelve mobsters after firing guns into the air had no effects on these extremely vicious thugs', Xinhua reported Sunday [19 July]. Mr Bekri did not reveal the ethnicity of the shooting victims … At least 197 people were killed and 1,721 injured during several hours of ethnic bloodletting in Urumqi, officials say … The government has given no estimate for the number of people killed or wounded in the revenge attacks.

(www.iht.com, 20 July 2009; *IHT*, 21 July 2009, p. 2)

The Bureau for Legal Affairs in Beijing has warned lawyers to stay away from cases in Xinjiang … Last year [2008], in the months leading up to the Beijing Olympics, the authorities arrested and tried more than 1,100 people in Xinjiang during a campaign against what they called 'religious extremists and separatists'.

(www.iht.com, 20 July 2009)

China on Tuesday [21 July] defended its policies on ethnic minorities, saying the violence that killed nearly 200 people this month in Xinjiang was provoked by separatists and not by its treatment of Uighurs … Wu Shimin, vice minister of the State Ethnic Affairs Commission, blamed an underground separatist movement of Uighurs and said China would never tolerate secession in Xinjiang.

(*IHT*, 22 July 2009, p. 8)

Wu Shimin, vice minister of the States Ethnic Affairs Commission, said the government's ethnic minority policies were 'effective' ... [He said] on Tuesday [21 July] that government policies 'had nothing to do with the violent crimes' that unfolded in Urumqi ... The statements were the most vocal defence by a government official since 5 July of the nation's ethnic minority policies ... Mr Wu said that although the overall ethnic minority policies are working, 'improvements might be made when necessary' ... He added that local governments might need to do a better job carrying out the policies. He said: 'The current policies include guiding principles set by the central government and regulations of local governments, but a deeper understanding is needed when it comes to making policies at the local level' ... Many Hans say the government gives Uighurs, Tibetans and China's other fifty-three ethnic minorities too many benefits. For example, they say, the government allows Uighurs to have two or three children without being fined, as Han are if they have more than one child. It also gives Uighur students extra points on standardized tests for university entrance. Other ethnic minorities are governed by similar policies, but the specific details vary with each minority ... About 10 per cent of the 1.3 billion people in China are ethnic minorities, according to government statistics.

(www.iht.com, 22 July 2009)

China's ambassador to Japan has reacted angrily to a planned visit to Tokyo by Rebiya Kadeer ... Mrs Kadeer is to meet members of Japan's ruling Liberal Democratic Party and give a news conference during her five-day visit, beginning on Tuesday [28 July].

(www.bbc.co.uk, 27 July 2009)

Normal internet access in China's troubled north-western region of Xinjiang may not be resumed for months, it has emerged, as officials begin to allow users to visit a small number of sites. The internet was blocked across the region three weeks ago ... Authorities also shut down text message services. Mobile phone users are now receiving texts again – but only in the form of a daily update from the authorities and weather reports. The first, on Sunday [26 July], told them the security situation had improved and urged them not to believe rumours. A block on calls to overseas numbers – from any phone – also remains in place.

(www.guardian.co.uk, 28 July 2009)

Limited telephone text messaging and internet access are now available in Xinjiang ... officials said Tuesday [28 July] ... [It was stated that] the government was now sending text messages to citizens, though they still could not send messages to one another ... Internet access to a few government

> and business-related websites is also available … The authorities in Xinjiang had also restored access for specialized operations like internet banking services and online stock exchange and university enrolment services.
>
> (*IHT*, 29 July 2009, p. 4)

> China has complained to Australia about the forthcoming visit of Rebiya Kadeer … Mrs Kadeer is to attend a film festival in Melbourne next week and will give a televised speech. Meanwhile, China summoned Japan's ambassador in Beijing to protest about Mrs Kadeer's visit to Tokyo, where she has met members of the governing party … A spokesman [for Japan] said she was invited by civil society organizations rather than the government … Mrs Kadeer is to attend the Melbourne International Film Festival, which is screening … on 8 August … a documentary about her life … At a news conference she said that 'nearly 10,000 people' disappeared in one night in Urumqi … Other sources put the number of those detained in Urumqi at 1,400.
>
> (www.bbc.co.uk, 29 July 2009)

> The Melbourne Film Festival's organizers ignored pressure from Chinese officials to cancel the screening. Instead, the moved it to a larger venue after publicity over the row sparked big demand to see it. China reportedly threatened Melbourne's mayor with ending a sister-city relationship with Tianjin.
>
> (www.economist.com, 19 August 2009)

> On Wednesday [29 July] … Rebiya Kadeer claimed that 'nearly 10,000' Uighurs had disappeared 'overnight' in Urumqi … Government numbers place the numbers of those arrested at 1,200 … The Japanese government said that Ms Kadeer was visiting as a private citizen … Ms Kadeer heads the World Uighur Congress, which advocates for Uighur self-determination … [China has] described her as 'a terrorist' and 'a criminal' who caused the death of 197 people, most of them Han Chinese. As proof, they cite a phone call she made to her brother in Urumqi shortly before the strife began, warning him to stay off the streets. Ms Kadeer does not deny making the call but says she was just looking out for his safety … Ms Kadeer says that most of the dead were Uighur, not Han, and that as many as 1,000 people were killed, many of them peaceful demonstrators shot dead by security officials.
>
> (www.iht.com, 30 July 2009)

'Security forces in Urumqi have detained at least 253 more people suspected of taking part in the ethnic rioting on 5 July, according to a report Thursday [30 July] in *China Daily*' (www.iht.com, 31 July 2009).

'Xinhua said yesterday [29 July] that authorities in western China had arrested 253 more people suspected of being involved in the violence in Urumqi, in addition to the 1,434 detained earlier over suspected involvement in the 5 July riot' (www.guardian.co.uk, 30 July 2009).

> China will begin trials in the next few weeks for suspects it accuses of playing a role in the deadly riots that shook the capital of Xinjiang region in early July, state media reported on Friday [31 July]. The *China Daily* said officials were organizing special tribunals to weigh the fate of 'a small number' of the 1,400 people who have been detained … On Thursday [30 July] the authorities published the photos of another fifteen people, all but one of them Uighur, who say they had a hand in the unrest. Those who provide information leading to an arrest can collect as much as $7,350 in reward money.
>
> (www.iht.com, 31 July 2009)

'In the past week the authorities have arrested 253 more suspects, many through tips from residents of Urumqi' (*IHT*, 1 August 2009, p. 4).

> Suspects detained over ethnic riots in Urumqi that left 197 dead and 1,700 injured will go to trial within a couple of weeks, *China Daily* said. Police say they have detained 1,653 suspects, but it is not known how many were later released. The newspaper's source said only 'a small number' will stand trial.
>
> (*Guardian*, 1 August 2009, p. 24)

> Chinese police detained 319 people suspected of involvement in deadly ethnic rioting in north-western Xinjiang region last month [July], after a 'wanted list' of [fifteen] suspects … made public on 30 July … spurred tip-offs, Xinhua said today [2 August] … The report did not give an overall total for the number of people now being held in connection with the riots. Officials have previously said over 1,500 had been detained.
>
> (www.independent.co.uk, 2 August 2009)

> Xinhua reported Sunday [2 August] … [that] police in Urumqi said they had detained 319 people in connection with the 5 July riots … The detentions came in addition to the 253 detentions announced on 29 July … Before that 1,000 suspects had been detained, Xinhua said. It was unclear, however, how many of the detainees had been released … The latest 319 people were detained after information was received from the public or obtained through the police investigation … Xinhua reported.
>
> (www.cnn.com, 3 August 2009)

'Security officials have detained an additional 319 people suspected of taking part in the unrest in Xinjiang, Xinhua reported Sunday [2 August] … The arrest, according to Xinhua, came days after another 253 people were taken into custody' (*IHT*, 3 August 2009, p. 4).

> Chinese police have recently arrested 319 people … This brings the total number of people detained over the riots to more than 1,500, although it is unclear how many people have since been released … The 319 people who have been detained recently are in addition to 253 detentions last week and more than 1,000 before that, according to Xinhua.
>
> (www.bbc.co.uk, 3 August 2009)

'Chinese authorities said Tuesday [4 August] that they had taken 718 people into custody in connection with last month's ethnic riots in Xinjiang, but an official with an ethnic Uighur group said the true number was far higher … The head of Urumqi's Public Security Bureau said that 718 'criminals who disturbed the peace' had been detained … The new report, released by Xinhua, left it unclear whether the 718 detainees represented the total of suspects captured since the 4 July unrest, or were in addition to previous arrests and detentions. The government had previously said that more than 1,500 people had been detained after the riots. Nor was it clear how many of the suspects have been charged with crimes. State radio … reported on Tuesday that eighty-three suspects had been accused of crimes ranging from murder and arson to assault and disturbing the peace … Omar Kanat, the vice president of the World Uighur Congress, said that … the new report of 718 detentions could only add to previously reported totals. He said: 'Many people are calling us every day, and they say the number of arrests exceeds five, six thousand. We cannot confirm that. But we know that the number of arrests are much more than the Chinese figures' … Most of the detained people are of Uighur descent, he said, adding that Uighurs in Xinjiang have told the organization in recent days about a new wave of detentions in Urumqi and surrounding areas.

(www.iht.com, 4 August 2009)

'Chinese police say they will charge eighty-three people … Xinhua also said 718 people had been detained … Urumqi's chief prosecutor: "Those arrested will face charges of murder, intentional injury, arson and robbery"' (www.bbc.co.uk, 4 August 2009).

Rebiya Kadeer: 'I did not tell them to come out on that day or that particular time to protest. It was the six-decade-long repression that has driven them to protest' … She does not rule out Xinjiang remaining part of the Chinese state – so long as Uighurs have self-rule within a democratic polity.

(www.feer.com, 10 August 2009)

An aircraft bound for Urumqi … has been threatened with a bomb attack, Xinhua reports. Officials told the airport not to allow the plane to land … Later reports said the plane had landed in Afghanistan. Xinhua earlier reported the incident as a hijacking. It did not specify whether the threat to the plane came from on board in its latest report.

(www.bbc.co.uk, 9 August 2009)

The Xinhua news agency says there has been a bomb threat to a plane from Afghanistan scheduled to land in Xinjiang … Xinhua earlier said the incident was a hijacking. It did not specify the airline, but said Urumqi airport has been told not to allow the plane to land.

(www.guardian.co.uk, 9 August 2009)

A flight to Urumqi was forced to return to Afghanistan last night [9 August] after a bomb threat … On Tuesday [4 August] officials said that security

> forces had prevented five organized terrorist attacks in Xinjiang. According to Xinhua, police forces and state security crushed five organized plots in Urumqi, Kashgar, Aksu and Ili ... Last March senior officials from Xinjiang reported that flight attendants had foiled an attempted attack on a Chinese passenger jet flying from Urumqi. A nineteen-year-old woman was later blamed for the attempt.
>
> (*Guardian*, 10 August 2009, p. 16)

> A plane scheduled to land in Xinjiang ... was diverted to southern Afghanistan by a bomb threat, state media said Sunday [9 August]. Xinhua news agency did not identify the airline or the type of plane, but said the airport in Urumqi had been told not to allow the plane to land ... Xinhua had earlier reported that the plane had been hijacked, but then said it had landed in Kandahar, Afghanistan, after a bomb threat. However, a press officer for Nato forces in Afghanistan, which control the Kandahar airport, said the alliance had received no report of a plane forced to land there ... In early August an internet message purportedly from the leader of an Islamist group fighting Chinese rule in a western province urged Moslems worldwide to attack Chinese interests in retaliation for what it called the oppression of minority Uighurs.
>
> (www.iht.com, 9 August 2009)

> An Afghan plane bound for Xinjiang was sent back to Afghanistan after a bomb threat was made ... The airline, Kam Air, said the plane left Kabul, Afghanistan's capital, and was crossing Kyrgyzstan on its way to Urumqi, when it was told to turn back Sunday [9 August]. Xinhua said that there had been a bomb threat and that Urumqi airport authorities had been told not to let the plane land. [However] the deputy chief of Kam Air ... said there had been no bomb threat. He said the plane had been inspected by Afghan officers and a foreign security company prior to departure in what he characterized as an unusually thorough security check. He said that Kyrgyz authorities told the crew that China would not allow the plane into its airspace, and that the plane, with 160 passengers aboard, was diverted to Kandahar.
>
> (www.iht.com, 10 August 2009; *IHT*, 11 August 2009, p. 4)

> The police in Kyrgyzstan detained two Uighur community leaders after they accused China of 'state terrorism' at a rally Monday [10 August] and called for an independent investigation of clashes last month in Xinjiang. About 500 Uighurs gathered at a building on the outskirts of the Kyrgyz capital, Bishkek, with photographs posted to the walls showing what they said was abuse of their kinfolk in China.
>
> (*IHT*, 11 August 2009, p. 4)

'The Chinese government has tried to pressure Australia's National Press Club in Canberra to cancel an address by Rebiya Kadeer. But the event, to be carried live on national television, will go ahead as planned' (www.bbc.co.uk, 11 August 2009).

> It has emerged that China cancelled a ministerial visit to Australia in protest against a recent visit by Rebiya Kadeer … The Chinese vice foreign minister was supposed to attend a summit earlier in the month [August] of Pacific nation leaders. The Australian foreign affairs department has confirmed that it was informed via diplomatic channels that the minister would be unable to attend the summit and that the Chinese delegation would be led instead by a junior envoy.
>
> (www.bbc.co.uk, 18 August 2009)

'The Dalai Lama called the recent riots in Xinjiang "very sad", saying he totally disagreed with violence and that "that kind of riot is no help to solving the problem"' (www.bbc.co.uk, 11 August 2009).

> The first wave of workers to make the annual migration to Xinjiang this year [2009] to pick cotton has arrived in the area … The workers are mostly ethnic Han and are the first large batch of migrant workers to make the journey to Xinjiang since deadly rioting broke out this summer … The Xinhua report on Friday [21 August] said most of the cotton pickers were women … About 1,600 workers from Henan arrived at their work sites from late Wednesday to early Thursday … In all 100 trains full of workers will arrive in Xinjiang through mid-September. Xinjiang makes up one-sixth of China … [and] is the largest cotton producing region in the country. The Xinjiang Production and Construction Corps, the state enterprise that runs the *bingtuan*, the vast farms set up in the 1950s and afterwards by the People's Liberation Army to help populate the frontier region … A *bingtuan* official told Xinhua: 'In half a month after the violence there was a huge shortage of tomato pickers. Many migrant workers did not dare to come here' … An official with the enterprise's labour and social security department said the farms run by the company plan to employ a total of 500,000 people to pick cotton this year [2009]. Sixty per cent are from outside Xinjiang, he added. That is a 17 per cent drop from last year [2008], but the decrease is because of lower acreage for cotton this year and more use of cotton picking machinery, not because of the violence in July, he said.
>
> (www.iht.com, 21 August 2009)

> Authorities unexpectedly released three political activists from detention on Sunday [23 August] … [Among the three was] Ilham Tohti, an economist, internet activist and ethnic Uighur who has been detained after deadly riots reputed in Xinjiang in early July … Mr Tohti ran a website called Uighur Online, a popular forum for ethnic Uighurs … to discuss issues important to them. After the July rioting Xinjiang's governor, Nur Bekri, charged that the site had helped foment the violence by spreading rumours.
>
> (www.iht.com, 23 August 2009)

'Ilham Tohti … who was detained shortly after the 5 July riots in Urumqi … returned home' (*FT*, 24 August 2009, p. 4).

Trials may begin this week for more than 200 people charged with crimes after riots last month … the state-run newspaper *China Daily* reported on Monday [24 August] … The charges include vandalizing public property, inciting crowds to cause bodily harm, murder, arson and robbery … *China Daily* said more than 290 lawyers, about twenty of them of Uighur descent, had been assigned to the trials, which will largely be open to the public … State media outlets stated earlier that 718 people had been detained and eighty-three charged in connection with the violence.

(www.iht.com, 24 August 2009)

Charges include vandalizing public property and transport, organizing crowds to cause bodily harm to others, robbery, murder and arson … The *China Daily* did not give a breakdown on how many Uighurs and how many Han would go on trial, but said more than 170 Uighurs and twenty Han lawyers had been assigned to the suspects … The trials are taking place at a sensitive time for China's leaders, in the run-up to celebrations for the sixtieth anniversary of the founding of the People's Republic of China on 1 October.

(www.bbc.co.uk, 24 August 2009)

There is confusion about how many people China plans to put on trial … and when this might happen … An official has now said the number is closer to eighty, and no date has been set … On Tuesday [25 August] an official at the Xinjiang government media office questioned the accuracy of the report: 'At present there is no scheduled date for the trial. I do not know how *China Daily* got that information, but it is not true. We will announce it to the media when there is a trial. We have not received any official notice on a change in the number of the suspects. So currently the number of suspects is still eighty-three.'

(www.bbc.co.uk, 25 August 2009)

An official with the news media office of the local Communist Party headquarters [in Urumqi] said Tuesday [25 August] that he had no information that any such trials would take place this week … He said he had no information on exactly when the trials would start … Xinhua has yet to report on any fixed trial date as of late Tuesday [25 August].

(www.iht.com, 25 August 2009)

President Hu Jintao has been visiting … Xinjiang for four days, state media reported Tuesday [26 August], in his first trip to the region since deadly rioting in July … He said: 'The key to our work in Xinjiang is to properly handle the relation between development and stability in the region' … In the violence in Urumqi at least 197 people were killed and 1,721 injured.

(www.iht.com, 26 August 2009)

President Hu Jintao called Tuesday [26 August] for a 'prosperous and harmonious' Xinjiang province during his first visit to the region since last month's deadly riots. President Hu said: 'The key to our work in Xinjiang is to properly handle development and stability' … He said the central government 'attaches great importance to the well-being of ethnic groups' and called the riots 'a serious criminal act masterminded by separatist forces at home and abroad'.

(www.cnn.com, 26 August 2009)

There have been fresh protests in Xinjiang … A witness told the BBC that as many as 2,000 ethnic Han Chinese have been demonstrating in Urumqi. The protesters are said to be angry at the deteriorating security situation in the wake of the July riots. A trigger for the protests appears to have been a spate of unexplained stabbings using hypodermic needles … People have been protesting in the streets since yesterday [2 September] … Xinhua said the stabbing victims came from nine ethnic groups, including Uighurs and Han. Protesters have accused the provincial government of being 'useless', and some even asked for the dismissal of regional Communist Party boss Wang Lequan, who is thought to be an ally of President Hun Jintao.

(www.bbc.co.uk, 3 September 2009)

Thousands of ethnic Han protesters swarmed around government buildings in … Urumqi … on Thursday [3 September] to demand that local leaders clamp down on ethnic Uighurs, whom they blame for a spree of recent alleged needle stabbings … Many protesters yelled 'Wang Lequan, step down', referring to the powerful regional secretary of the Communist Party who has run Xinjiang for fifteen years … In recent days rumours had spread quickly throughout Urumqi of Uighurs attacking Han with needles infected with HIV … The rumours appeared murky … A small protest ignited by rumours of widespread stabbings was held on Wednesday [2 September], witnesses said … The latest protests took place in the middle of a five-day trade fair in Urumqi that is aimed at attracting overseas investment to Xinjiang … Rumours of deadly needle stabbings have circulated in China for years … One well known case took place in Tianjin in 2002, when officials tried to quiet rumours of widespread infected-needle attacks.

(www.iht.com, 3 September 2009)

In recent days rumours had spread quickly throughout Urumqi of Uighurs attacking Han with needles infected with HIV … A report Thursday [3 September] on state-run Xinjiang Television said that 476 people, the vast majority of them ethnic Han, had sought treatment since 20 August for needle stab wounds … The same article quoted a health official as saying no one had been infected or poisoned from being stabbed so far.

(*IHT*, 4 September 2009, p. 5)

A resident said he had seen a group of Han Chinese protesters beating up an ethnic Uighur suspected of carrying out attacks with syringes, but he was rescued by police and taken to hospital … Rumours of AIDS patients attacking pedestrians with hypodermic needles have previously swept China, but were later shown to be unfounded … Nobody had been infected with anything or poisoned by the stabbings in Urumqi, the *China Daily* said … A visitor to Urumqi … said … many ethnic Han Chinese blamed the stabbings on Uighurs.

(www.independent.co.uk, 3 September 2009)

Over the past month more than 400 Han Chinese have been stabbed with tainted syringes by Uighurs, according to local news reports … A local woman told CNN that the stabbings were ethnically motivated and that government text messages to citizens have warned that the syringes contained an unknown disease.

(www.cnn.com, 3 September 2009)

More than 1,000 residents of Urumqi took to the streets yesterday [3 September] demanding the resignation of the region's Communist Party chief [Wang Lequan], in a rare open challenge to one of China's top strongmen … [Eye witness estimates varied considerably but] Xinhua said more than 1,000 took to the streets … Some observers cautioned that the syringe attacks could be just rumours.

(*FT*, 4 September 2009, p. 8)

At least five people have been killed … during days of protests by ethnic Han demanding a government clampdown on Uighurs in [Urumqi] … according to [Xinhua] … The casualty toll [was given] late Friday [4 September] … Xinhua did not report the ethnicities of the victims … Urumqi remained paralysed Friday as Han protesters continued to rally to call for greater security measures against alleged Uighur attacks, forcing the government to close schools, offices and shops to keep people off the streets and to block traffic from the city centre … Helicopters were seen swooping overhead in the morning in Urumqi, one day after tens of thousands of Han took to the streets to criticize the government for failing to prevent alleged needle-stabbing attacks by Uighurs … Some of the Han said the needles were infected with HIV. Groups of protesters continued to gather in front of the offices of the regional government Friday to demand the resignation of Wang Lequan … Mr Wang, a proponent of hard-line ethnic minority policies who has ruled Xinjiang for fifteen years, is a member of the Communist Party's ruling Politburo, and the outcry is a rare attack against a member of the country's governing elite. The rioting on 5 July was the deadliest outbreak of ethnic violence in decades, leaving at least 197 people dead and 1,721 wounded, according to government statistics.

(www.iht.com, 4 September 2009)

Five people have been killed … this week, officials say. It was unclear how the deaths happened, but thousands of Han Chinese have been protesting over a unexplained spate of stabbings with syringes. Many of the protesters blame ethnic Uighur Moslems for the stabbings. Riot police used tear gas to disperse angry crowds earlier, and China's top security official … Meng

> Jianzhu ... has arrived in Urumqi to try to restore order ... Authorities have announced a ban on 'all gatherings, marches or protests on roads or other public venues', Xinhua said. Large numbers of police were deployed overnight in the city after tens of thousands of Han Chinese protested in central areas on Thursday [3 September] ... Chinese media said that nearly 500 people, almost all Han, have sought treatment for stabbings in the past few weeks. Reports said eighty-nine people had 'clear syringes marks' but that no one had been infected or poisoned.
>
> (www.bbc.co.uk, 4 September 2009)

> The government in Xinjiang struggled to contain escalating unrest on Friday [4 September] as thousands of people confronted police in Urumqi ... accusing the government of incompetence in maintaining public safety. The protests increased in numbers and intensity for a third consecutive day ... Xinhua reported from Urumqi that more than 1,000 demonstrators confronted police near the Communist Party headquarters and that security forces had dispersed the crowds with tear gas ... Some witness accounts put the number of demonstrators much higher than the official count ... 'There are 100,000 people protesting in various places all over the city today,' said an official at the Xinjiang education department ... The government tried to calm the crowds with an announcement of arrests of suspects linked to the bloody race riots that killed 197 people in early July; 825 had been detained and 196 of them formally charged, state media said.
>
> (www.ft.com, 4 September 2009)

'Xinjiang is different from other Chinese provinces where the leaders rotate every few years. Wang Lequan has held senior positions there since 1991 and headed the regional party committee for fifteen years' (*FT*, 5 September 2009, p. 7).

> The latest unrest has left five people dead ... in Urumqi ... a deputy mayor said Friday [4 September] ... 'Authorities have issued arrest warrants to 196 suspects and prosecuted fifty-one' in a 5 July riot, Xinhua reported ... In recent weeks hundreds of people from several ethnic groups have sought treatment for syringe stabbings by Uighurs, Xinhua reported: 'Hospitals in Urumqi are treating 531 victims of hypodermic needle attacks. Statistics from the city's twenty-four hospitals say 106 of the 531 were showing obvious signs of needle attacks. The victims include members of ethnic groups such as Han, Uighur and Kazakhstan' ... There have been no reports of deaths from the stabbings. Authorities have detained twenty-one suspects, of whom six are in custody and four have been arrested for criminal prosecution ... The syringe attacks, which residents said began in early August, sparked the unrest ... [One] woman said the stabbings were ethnically motivated and that government text messages to citizens have warned that the syringes contained an unknown disease. Fears were likely heightened by the fact that Xinjiang has the highest rates of HIV infection in China, attrib-

uted to intravenous drug use. Rumours have abounded there of people trying to spread AIDS … Xinjiang serves as a convenient drug trafficking route, lying between the opium-growing regions of Afghanistan and South-east Asia and the heroin markets in Central Asia, Russia and Europe. It is estimated that more than 60,000 people in Xinjiang are HIV-positive … The Uighur America Association issued a statement late Thursday [3 September] urging the government to improve public safety. Rebiya Kadeer: 'I call on Chinese officials to guarantee the security of all people living in East Turkestan (Xinjiang), including Uighurs and Han Chinese.'

(www.cnn.com, 4 September 2009)

The public security minister, Meng Jianzhu, arrived in Urumqi to direct the police action … He said: 'The needle stabbing incident is a continuation of the 5 July incident, and it is plotted by unlawful elements and instigated by ethnic separatist forces. Their purpose is to damage ethnic unity.'

(*Independent*, 5 September 2009, p. 30)

China sacked the top official of Urumqi on Saturday [5 September] as the city crept back to an uneasy normality … A large deployment of military police appeared to have brought a measure of peace to the city … The city has been under heavy security after three days of fresh unrest this week … The city's Communist Party secretary, Li Zhi, was dismissed and replaced by Zhu Hailun, the head of Xinjiang region's law and order committee … Li Zhi became the most senior person removed since ethnic tensions erupted there [Urumqi] in severe rioting in early July … The *China Daily* said in an editorial: 'Saboteurs may be planning more unnerving disruptions to create a sense of insecurity as the nation counts down to its major celebration of the sixtieth anniversary [on 1 October]' … The minister for police, Meng Jianzhu, flew to Urumqi to oversee security … Beijing officials sent this week a special medical inspection unit from the People's Liberation Army to Urumqi to investigate a series of incidents in which people have allegedly been stabbed with needles. It is somewhat unusual for China's leaders to replace a senior local official so quickly after protests – in this case while large deployments of armed police are still blocking intersections in Urumqi and most shops are still closed … The latest protests were notable for including large crowds of people who specifically called on Friday [4 September for the removal of Mr Li's boss, Wang Lequan, the powerful party secretary of Xinjiang region … The crowds in Urumqi this week have been accusing Mr Wang and his aides of not being tough enough … Han have been moving in large numbers to Xinjiang since the 1960s, occupying many of the best jobs.

(www.iht.com, 5 September 2009)

A Communist Party leader and police chief in Xinjian have been sacked … Xinhua first announced that Urumqi Communist Party chief Li Zhi was to be replaced by Zhu Hailun, the head of Xinjiang region's law and order committee. A later statement added that Liu Yaohua, director of the Xinjiang Autonomous Regional Public Security Department, has also been dismissed.

(www.bbc.co.uk, 5 September 2009)

[A] Xinhua report, citing a notice from the municipal court, said penalties for those who stabbed others with syringes containing poisonous or harmful substances would range from three years in jail to the death sentence ... Twenty-five people have reportedly been held over the attacks in Urumqi ... Chinese officials have blamed Uighur Moslem separatists for the incidents ... Correspondents said Urumqi was calmer on Sunday [6 September], although the security presence was still heavy.

(www.bbc.co.uk, 6 September 2009)

A newspaper vendor said: 'Things are getting worse – they are pouring sulphuric acid in people's faces now' ... Although there is no evidence for such attacks, the persistence of such rumours shows how the city [Urumqi] is gripped by panic and mistrust.

(*FT*, 7 September 2009, p. 8)

Three of the four people prosecuted in an investigation into syringe attacks in Urumqi that authorities blame on Uighur separatists are drug users, state media have reported ... Xinhua said two people attempted to rob a taxi driver by threatening him with a hypodermic needle, and another stabbed police trying to arrest him. It also said some reported incidents were caused by mosquito bites or 'other psychogenic reasons'. But there is little detail of the cases against twenty-one more suspects detained in connection with the assaults ... Officials said Uighurs were among the victims.

(*Guardian*, 7 September 2009, p. 24)

Some 7,000 Communist Party members are to be deployed in Urumqi, state media say. The move is an attempt to reassure residents and ease ethnic tensions in the city, Xinhua reports. The officials will have face-to-face meetings with residents to explain government policies ... Regional party secretary Wang Lequan told a meeting on Sunday [6 September]: 'It is ethnic separatists who are creating an atmosphere of terror, undermining national unity, and are disturbing social order' ... Xinhua (attributing the remarks to Mr Wang): '[The 7,000-strong taskforce] will make it clear that the party and government are capable of punishing criminals ... They will enhance people's sense of security, to help the public stay cool headed, so as to not be easily swayed by people with ulterior motives.'

(www.bbc.co.uk, 7 September 2009)

China is sending 7,000 officials to Urumqi ... The officials, known as 'harmony makers', are meant to ease tensions ... Wang Lequan: 'The officials will go door to door to explain policies and solve disputes' ... The syringe attacks started 17 August ... Police received an additional seventy-seven reports of attacks between Sunday and Monday evenings [6–7 September]. But the report by Xinhua did not specify whether they were new attacks or ones that had just been brought to the attention of officials. Authorities said they had detained forty-five suspects in connection with the attacks, twelve of whom were taken into custody.

(www.cnn.com, 8 September 2009)

Both the government and Han residents accuse Uighurs of carrying out widespread stabbings since mid-August, using syringes, safety pins, needles and other sharp objects … China's press has taken to calling these 'syringe attacks', but the Urumqi authorities use the more general term 'needle-like objects'. They say that fewer than one-fifth of reported stabbings have left any obvious mark … Xinhua quoted exports who said that some prickings were mosquito bites or merely imagined.

(*The Economist*, 12 September 2009, p. 69)

'Three people were sentenced Saturday [12 September] to up to thirteen years in prison over a series of syringe stabbings' (www.cnn.com, 12 September 2009).

A court in Xinjiang sentenced three people to up to fifteen years in the first trials over a recent series of syringe attacks. The court did not give the defendants' ethnicity but their names suggest they are from the Moslem Uighur minority …[A] nineteen-year-old [male] was jailed for fifteen years for stabbing a woman in the buttock at a fruit stall … [A] thirty-four-year-old [male] and a twenty-two-year-old woman were given sentences of ten and seven years respectively. They were convicted of threatening a taxi driver with a syringe and stealing 710 yuan ($103) from him.

(www.bbc.co.uk, 12 September 2009)

'[The nineteen-year-old] was sentenced to fifteen years' jail, accused of using a pin to jab a woman while she bought fruit' (www.iht.com, 12 September 2009). 'The harshest sentence … was brought against [him] … for "spreading false dangerous substances" when he inserted a needle into a woman's buttocks on 28 August, Xinhua reported' (*IHT*, 14 September 2009, p. 4).

Nine suspects have been arrested for the recent syringe attacks in Xinjiang … The beating of Hong Kong journalists covering recent events in Xinjiang has also sparked conflict with the former British colony … Officials in Hong Kong have said they cannot do much to protect Hong Kong people in China, but politicians and press freedom watchdogs plan a Sunday march to defend against Chinese state controls. The latest arrests follow reports earlier in the week that the authorities had identified forty-five suspects behind the attacks – it is unclear how many of these are actually in detention or face formal charges.

(www.bbc.co.uk, 11 September 2009)

'Three Moslem Uighurs have been jailed for between seven and fifteen years for their role in a series of mysterious attacks using hypodermic needles' (*Independent*, 14 September 2009, p. 20).

'On Saturday [12 September] … [a] court in Urumqi sentenced three people, all ethnic Uighurs, to up to fifteen years in prison in the first trials over the attacks' (www.iht.com, 16 September 2009).

> Journalists have led a march in Hong Kong protesting against alleged police beatings of three reporters covering unrest … There three television journalists say that they were punched, kicked and tied up before being detained for three hours. The alleged assaults took place during a protest in Urumqi on 4 September … A senior Xinjiang official expressed regret for the journalists' treatment, but blamed them for stirring unrest. She also accused the reporters … of working without permits … Sunday's protest [13 September] was called by the Hong Kong Journalists' Association and was backed by several news outlets in the city.
>
> (www.bbc.co.uk, 13 September 2009)

> Sunday's protest was called by the Hong Kong Journalists Association and the Foreign Correspondents' Club and was backed by several news outlets in the city … About 700 protesters, including journalists, politicians and residents, marched on the Hong Kong office of the Chinese government carrying placards saying 'reporting the news is not a crime' … A senior pro-China figure in Hong Kong has said he will convey concerns about alleged police brutality against Hong Kong journalists to Beijing. Convenor of the Executive Council Leung Chun-ying's promise echoed the concerns of several pro-China figures last week … Last week several political figures known for defending China's policies expressed concern, and the pro-China *Ta Kung Pao* newspaper carried an editorial decrying what it described as an attack on press freedom.
>
> (www.bbc.co.uk, 14 September 2009)

'In Hong Kong hundreds of journalists, parliamentarians and residents marched to protest against the alleged police beatings of three reporters covering the Xinjiang unrest and demanded a government investigation' (*Independent*, 14 September 2009, p. 20).

> No dangerous chemicals have been found in blood samples from the victims of recent needle attacks in Xinjiang, state media have said. Rumours have been rife that the needles contained radioactive substances, poison or even HIV … A total of 531 people reported being attacked with hypodermic needles, with 171 showing 'obvious syringe marks', according to Xinjiang officials.
>
> (www.bbc.co.uk, 14 September 2009)

> Schools have reopened in Urumqi after being closed for ten days in the wake of a spate of syringe attacks which cause panic in the streets. Local authorities closed the schools and imposed traffic controls in the city on 4 September after mass demonstrations by tens of thousands of Han Chinese against what they said was a government that could not guarantee their

> safety against the attacks. All primary and middle school classes resumed yesterday [14 September].
>
> (www.independent.co.uk, 15 September 2009)

'The Xinjiang public security ministry ... on Tuesday [15 September] ... said the transport of weapons, ammunition, explosives and radioactive goods into or within Xinjiang would be suspended from 25 September to 8 October' (www.iht.com, 16 September 2009).

> China announced the break-up of a bomb-making plot in Xinjiang on Wednesday [16 September] ... The announcement said the authorities had arrested six people who had established three bomb-making workshops and assembled about twenty explosive devices in a town 430 miles outside Urumqi. The public security ministry said the suspects had planned to plant the explosives on cars, motorcycles and people ... The police did not identify the ethnicity of the suspects. But the names suggested they were Uighurs ... The Wednesday announcement was the first indication that antagonists with scores to settle were making bombs ... On Tuesday [15 September] the police announced they had detained a total of seventy-five suspects accused of needle-stabbing attacks ... A public security official said two of those detained confessed they stabbed a resident in a supermarket 'to create panic in society'. Others admitted that they had organized needle attacks to inflame ethnic hatred, according to Xinhua.
>
> (www.iht.com, 16 September 2009)

> Four more people have been found guilty of carrying out attacks with syringes in Xinjiang ... The four received sentences ranging between eight and fifteen years in jail ... the names of the latest four to be convicted indicate they are Uighurs.
>
> (www.bbc.co.uk, 17 September 2009)

> Lawyers say three Chinese Moslems held for eight years at Guantanamo Bay have accepted an offer to relocate to the Pacific island nation of Palau. The deals are the first among thirteen Uighur detainees who have been offered a new life on the island.
>
> (*FT*, 11 September 2009, p. 10)

> A documentary about Rebiya Kadeer ... *The Ten Conditions of Love* ... is to be shown in Taiwan's city ... But officials in Kaohsiung said the film would be shown this week, not during a festival next month [October] as originally planned ... The film was shown at the Melbourne Film Festival.
>
> (www.iht.com, 20 September 2009)

('[There was] denial of entry to Rebiya Kadeer. This was done in the name of "national interest", apparently linked to the finalization, expected soon, of a memorandum of understanding on cross-strait financial links': www.iht.com, 6 October 2009.)

> A high ranking al-Qaeda leader has called on China's minority Uighurs to prepare for a holy war against the Chinese government. Abu Yahia Al-Libi said Wednesday [8 October]: 'There is no way for salvation and to lift this oppression and tyranny unless you … seriously prepare for jihad in the name of God and carry your weapons against the ruthless brutal invader thugs.'
>
> (www.cnn.com, 8 October 2009)

> A court has sentenced a Han Chinese man to death for his role in a factory brawl … at a Hong Kong-owned toy factory in Guangdong province … that sparked the Xinjiang riots … Another man was given a life sentence … Nine others were given prison sentences of five to eight years.
>
> (www.bbc.co.uk, 10 October 2009)

'The fight [was] at the Early Light Toy Factory in Shaogang City … The clashes raged at a factory dormitory through the early hours of 26 June' (*IHT*, 12 October 2009, p. 6).

> A court has sentenced six men to death and a seventh man to life in prison on Monday [12 October] for their roles in the deadly ethnic rioting in Urumqi in July … The seven men had names that suggested they were Uighurs … All were convicted of murder, and some were also found guilty of arson and robbery … The sentences were the first to be handed down by a court in response to the rioting of 5 July.
>
> (www.iht.com, 12 October 2009)

'As well as murder, state media reported they were convicted of other crimes ranging from arson, leading mobs and causing "economic loss" … Fourteen people are still waiting to be tried' (www.bbc.co.uk, 12 October 2009).

> A court sentenced a further six people to death over ethnic unrest in Xinjiang … The six were part of a group of fourteen people who went on trial on Wednesday [14 October], charged with crimes including murder, robbery and arson … Activists have condemned the trials as sham, saying they have lacked transparency and fairness … According to a government white paper on Xinjiang, released last month [September], the July riots were caused by Uighur separatists promoting an independent 'East Turkestan'.
>
> (www.bbc.co.uk, 15 October 2009)

> Three new defendants were sentenced to death … and three others were sentenced to death with a two-year reprieve – a penalty usually commuted to life in prison. One of the condemned men appeared to be Han Chinese based on his name … the others had Uighur names, except for one defendant sentenced to death with a two-year reprieve whose name was not included in the report … Three other defendants were given life sentences and five were given prison terms of different lengths … All those given jail terms appeared to be Uighur except for a Han Chinese, who was sentenced to ten years in jail … The government has blamed the rioting on overseas-based

> groups agitating for more Uighur rights in Xinjiang ... Rebiya Kadeer condemned the sentences, saying the accused had been denied legal process.
>
> (*IHT*, 15 October 2009)

'The exiled World Uighur Congress said all the Uighurs who had stood trial so far had been denied a fair hearing, including the right freely to choose their defence lawyers' (*FT*, 16 October 2009).

> Rebiya Kadeer stepped off a plane in Tokyo on Tuesday [20 October] and immediately began accusing the Chinese government of secretly executing members of the Uighur minority and illegally detaining hundreds of others ... Last week she barnstormed New Zealand for a few days and then flew to Germany, where she spoke at the Frankfurt Book Fair, infuriating China, which was the guest of honour.
>
> (www.iht.com, 21 October 2009)

> At least forty-three ethnic Uighur men from far western China have disappeared, an advocacy group said in a report released Wednesday [21 October]. The report, by Human Rights Watch, asserted that the number of vanished Uighurs was likely higher, although the group could conclusively document only forty-three cases during weeks of secret investigations in Xinjiang.
>
> (www.iht.com, 21 October 2009)

> Human Rights Watch said the forty-three men and teenaged boys were taken in police sweeps of Uighur districts of Urumqi, and had since vanished without trace ... The youngest are reported to have been between twelve and fourteen ... Brad Adams (Asia director at Human Rights Watch): 'The cases we documented are likely just the tip of the iceberg.'
>
> (www.bbc.co.uk, 21 October 2009)

> Six Uighur Chinese detainees were flown from the US military detention centre at Guantanamo Bay, Cuba, the US Justice Department said on Saturday [31 October]. The transfer leaves seven of the Chinese Uighur detainees still confined at the naval base, along with 208 other men ... The transfer [of the six thus] leaves 215 detainees at the detention camp that President Barack Obama has pledged to close by 22 January [2010] ... Palau is one of only twenty-three countries that recognize Taiwan over Beijing ... The Centre for Constitutional Rights which represents three of the [six transferred] men said: 'Palau is courageous to offer our Uighur clients a temporary home. We are hopeful that other countries like Australia and Germany will resettle them permanently' ... Palau has agreed to take up to twelve Uighurs ... Four of the Uighurs were moved in June to Bermuda.
>
> (www.iht.com, 1 November 2009)

> Four other Uighur detainees were resettled in Bermuda earlier this year [2009] and another five went to Albania in 2006 ... The president of Palau told the BBC that the Uighurs would be given a temporary home for as long

> as two years … In addition to the six Uighurs who arrived on Sunday [1 November] the island has offered to take six of the seven others. One did not receive an invitation because of concerns about his mental health … Palau [is] a former US trust territory … The tiny nation has retained close ties to Washington since independence in 1994.
>
> (www.bbc.co.uk, 1 November 2009)

'[The president of Palau said] what he called a "temporary" resettlement could mean "a few months or a few years"' (www.guardian.co.uk, 1 November 2009).

> Security officials have launched a fresh dragnet [in Xinjiang] to track down accused rioters and other so-called terrorist elements … The 'strike hard and punish' campaign would focus on 'cases and clues related to violent acts of terrorism'. Security officials have launched similar campaigns in the past, largely aimed at Uighurs … The news report stated, however, that the police would also target other offences, including organized crime and trafficking in women and children. The campaign began Sunday [1 November] and will last through the end of the year [2009].
>
> (www.iht.com, 3 November 2009)

> The Xinjiang authorities … said the 'strike hard and rectify' campaign would run until the end of the year to 'further consolidate the fruits of maintaining and eliminate security dangers'. They said they would 'root out places where criminals breed, and change the face of the public security situation in these areas' … Local police would continue to hunt down suspects in the riots and 'keep a close eye on clues and cases involving terrorism and explosions'.
>
> (www.bbc.co.uk, 3 November 2009)

> Nine people have been executed for taking part in ethnic rioting in Urumqi in July … The report by the China News Service [on 9 November] did not give further details of the executions, except to say that the cases had all been reviewed by the Supreme People's Court, a legally mandated step in death penalty cases in China. The court did not say when the executions had occurred.
>
> (*IHT*, 10 November 2009, p. 7)

'They had been convicted of murder and other crimes committed in Urumqi' (www.iht.com, 9 November 2009).

> Chinese authorities have executed nine people in connection with the ethnic riots in Xinjiang … The nine men were convicted of crimes including murder and arson. The reports do not say whether those executed were Uighurs or Han. But if the executions were in line with previous statements by the Xinjiang government, the group consisted of eight Uighurs and one Han.
>
> (www.bbc.co.uk, 9 November 2009)

> A court sentenced five more people to death Thursday [3 December] for killing a police officer with a brick, kicking bystanders to death and other crimes committed during ethnic riots in Xinjiang in July. The Intermediate People's Court of Urumqi also sentenced two others to life in prison … The five identified in the official Xinhua news agency report had names indicating they were Uighurs, and it said the cases were heard in the Uighur language.
>
> (www.iht.com, 3 December 2009; *IHT*, 4 December 2009, p. 6)

'Five people [were sentenced] to death for murder and other crimes … Two other people were sentenced to life imprisonment … Eight other people received jail terms, including the two sentenced to life in prison' (www.bbc.co.uk, 3 December 2009).

'Three more people were sentenced to death … bringing the total to seventeen' (*The Times*, 5 December 2009, p. 48).

'China has handed down at least seventeen death sentences over the rioting' (www.iht.com, 19 December 2009).

> China's foreign ministry said a group of twenty-two Uighurs said to have sought asylum with UN officials in Cambodia were suspected criminals. Two of the group are reported to have said they saw security forces killing and beating Uighur demonstrators during rioting in Urumqi in July.
>
> (*FT*, 16 December 2009, p 8)

> The Chinese foreign ministry has hinted that it is seeking or will seek the return of twenty-two Uighurs who fled to Cambodia after the eruption of deadly ethnic riots in July in western China … The twenty-two Uighurs in Cambodia entered the country about a month ago with the aid of Christian missionaries in China that usually help North Koreans reach nations where they can seek refugee status. The Uighurs made their way to the Cambodian capital, Phnom Penh, where they applied for refugee status at a UN refugee office … The Chinese embassy sent a note to the Cambodian government in early December about the Uighurs … Three of the Uighurs who made it to Cambodia are children. Two Uighurs were detained in Vietnam en route to Cambodia, and five others who fled China have disappeared … The United States has declined to send Uighurs detained in Guantanamo Bay back to China and has also refused to grant them refugee status. Some of them have ended up in Albania, Palau and Bermuda.
>
> (www.iht.com, 18 December 2009)

> A group of twenty Uighurs … will be expelled, a Cambodian official says. He said they had to be expelled because they had entered Cambodia illegally … A Cambodian foreign ministry spokesman: 'I cannot say where they will be sent but I assume their final destination will be China, the place where they came from.'
>
> (www.bbc.co.uk, 19 December 2009)

> Twenty Uighurs ... will be deported, most likely back home, government spokesmen said Saturday [19 December] ... A foreign ministry spokesman said two other Uighurs have gone missing ... The United States and United Nations urged Cambodia to stop the deportation. A spokeswoman for the UN refugees agency said it had not finished evaluating the Uighurs, including two children, for refugee status ... [She said that] an evaluation of the Uighurs for possible refugee status had not yet been completed ... The Uighurs had been in joint custody of the UN refugee agency and Cambodian authorities ... A [Cambodian] foreign ministry spokesman said they were now under the 'sole protection' of the Cambodian government ... The expulsion comes as Chinese vice president Xi Jinping visits Cambodia on Sunday [20 December] as part of a four-country tour ... China says it is the top foreign investor in Cambodia.
>
> (www.iht.com, 19 December 2009)

> The Cambodian government on Saturday [19 December] deported [to China] twenty members of the Uighur minority ... [They were] put on a special plane sent from China that left Phnom Penh on Saturday night ... The expulsion came one day before Vice President Xi Jinping was due to visit Cambodia. China, which is Cambodia's biggest investor, had branded the Uighurs criminals and demanded their return.
>
> (www.iht.com, 20 December 2009)

> China has signed a substantial development package with Cambodia, just days after the Cambodian authorities repatriated twenty ethnic Uighur asylum seekers to China. The deals are worth some $1.2 billion ... The Chinese authorities said the Uighurs were suspected criminals facing investigation.
>
> (*FT*, 22 December 2009, p. 8)

> China signed fourteen deals on Monday [21 December] worth approximately $1 billion, two days after Cambodia deported twenty ethnic Uighur asylum seekers under strong pressure from Beijing ... The exact value of the agreement was not announced, but the chief [Cambodian] government spokesman ... said they were worth $1.2 billion ... In October [2009] prime minister Wen Jiabao of China met with Cambodia's prime minister, Hun Sen, in China, and concluded a deal worth $853 million.
>
> (www.iht.com, 22 December 2009)

'Several of the fugitive Uighurs told the United Nations in written statements that they had been involved in the unrest and feared lengthy jail terms or even the death penalty if they were returned to China' (www.iht.com, 22 December 2009). 'It was not the first time Cambodia has bent to Chinese demands for the return of its citizens. In 2002 the government handed over two practitioners of Falun Gong' (*IHT*, 23 December 2009, p. 5).

> A court in Xinjiang has sentenced a further five people to death for their role in July's deadly ethnic riots ... Reports suggest that the five sentenced to

death were Uighurs … The sentences bring the number of people condemned to die over the riots to a total of twenty-two. Five more were sentenced to death with a two-year reprieve, a sentence often commuted to life in prison. Nine people were executed last month [November] over the riots.

(www.bbc.co.uk, 24 December 2009)

The five sentenced to death were among twenty-two defendants that went on trial this week … Along with the five people to be executed, another five were sentenced to death but the execution will be postponed for two years … The others received sentences ranging from ten years in prison to life in prison.

(www.cnn.com, 24 December 2009)

The sentences, after a series of trials this week, bring to twenty-two the number of people given the death sentence since the trials began in September. The court in Urumqi gave five other people suspended death sentences, which are often equivalent to life in prison. Nine of those sentenced have already been executed … Those convicted in trials on Tuesday and Wednesday [22 and 23 December], according to the statement, were guilty of 'extremely serious crimes'. It described several defendants, all with Uighur names, who attacked Han residents as they drove or bicycled through the city, bludgeoning and stoning them … In recent weeks the authorities have detained ninety-four additional people whom they describe as fugitives. Not included in that number are the twenty Uighurs repatriated to China last week after seeking political asylum in Cambodia. Those Uighurs, including three children, told the office of the United Nations High Commissioner for Refugees that they feared long prison terms or the death penalty if they returned … The state-run English language … newspaper *China Daily* … described seven of the Uighurs as fugitives.

(www.iht.com, 25 December 2009; *IHT*, 26 December 2009, p. 5)

Chinese authorities gingerly began to lift an internet blackout on Tuesday [29 December], allowing partial access to a pair of official news sites … People in Xinjiang can visit the sites of Xinhua, and the Communist Party's main newspaper *People's Daily* … Even on those reliably policed sites, the region's web users were still barred from engaging in email, blogging or forums … In Xinjiang local authorities, banks and phone services have been able to send text messages, but private citizens still cannot. People can read news on a number of local government-run media sites that were restored in August, yet most of those sites are blocked to viewers outside the region … State firms and some large companies have been able to hook up to the web outside Xinjiang, but smaller businesses generally cannot. Even at popular online trading posts that have been switched back on, web users in Xinjiang can deal only with others in Xinjiang. Some have driven hundreds of miles away to Gansu province to conduct business.

(www.iht.com, 30 December 2009)

The region's internet users, who have had limited access to regional government, banking, entertainment and gaming websites since August, can now visit xinhuanet.com, a state-run news service, and people.co.cn, the online newspaper of the Communist Party ... Though Xinjiang residents can browse stories on the sites, they cannot post forum comments or use email ... Yang Maofa (director of the regional telecommunications administration): 'To prevent further unrest, the government blocked access to the web and suspended international calls and short message services in the region twenty-four hours after the 5 July riot because they were vital tools used by ringleaders to instigate the riots in Urumqi.'

(www.cnn.com, 30 December 2009)

The Chinese government continued to ease a six-month-old blackout on communications in Xinjiang by restoring some text-messaging services on Sunday [17 January] ... In recent weeks the authorities have restored limited internet service, allowing the region's 20 million residents to view pages from the Communist Party's main newspaper, *People's Daily*, the official Xinhua news service and two popular web portals.

(www.iht.com, 18 January 2010)

Authorities in Xinjiang have punished residents for spreading rumours and 'splittist' content via text messages, within days of turning services back on, according to local media ... The restoration of text messaging [took place] two weeks ago ... Human Rights Watch yesterday [28 January] urged China to disclose the whereabouts and status of twenty Uighurs – including two children – who were forcibly repatriated by Cambodia last month [December 2009], having sought refuge there.

(www.guardian.co.uk, 29 January 2010)

China must account for the whereabouts of [twenty] ethnic Uighurs forcibly repatriated [in December 2009] from Cambodia, a US-based rights group has said ... Human Rights Watch: 'There is no information about their whereabouts, no notification of any legal charges against them, and there is no guarantee they are safe from torture and ill-treatment' ... Human Rights Watch said a number of the group had given detailed accounts of past torture and persecution in China and that threats had been made against their families. The organization said China has a history of executing or imposing harsh sentences on Uighurs sent back from abroad and that there were unconfirmed reports some members of a group previously returned had been sentenced to death in western Xinjiang province ... The Uighurs fled Xinjiang after July's violent ethnic clashes in Urumqi which left at least ninety-seven people dead ... At least twenty-five people have been sentenced to death after the riots.

(www.bbc.co.uk, 29 January 2010)

China has criticized a Swiss offer of asylum for two ethnic Uighur inmates at the US military prison at Guantanamo Bay ... Switzerland had agreed on

> Wednesday [3 February] to take two Uighurs from Guantanamo Bay for humanitarian reasons ... They were captured in Afghanistan with twenty other Uighurs but not later classified as 'enemy combatants' ... The United States has found homes in Albania, Bermuda and the Pacific island nation of Palau for most of the group. Once the two are sent to Switzerland, which is expected to happen in the next month, five of the Uighurs will be left in Guantanamo ... US President Barack Obama has been trying to close the prison, but there are still about 200 detainees there. Switzerland has taken one other Guantanamo inmate, an Uzbek man.
>
> (www.bbc.co.uk, 4 February 2010).

> The [US] Supreme Court said on Monday [1 March] that it would not decide a case involving seven Chinese Moslems detained for eight years at Guantanamo Bay that had been set for argument in April. The seven, captured in Afghanistan in 2001, have been determined to pose no threat to the United States, but the government and the courts have not determined whether the men could be released into the United States, as they had requested. The court on Monday sent the case back to the lower courts ... The government has continued its efforts to relocate the men, and it had a breakthrough last month [February] when Switzerland agree to take two of the prisoners who had proved most difficult to place. But five Uighurs remain at Guantanamo, having rejected resettlement offers from Palau and an unidentified second country.
>
> (www.iht.com, 1 March 2010)

(See Chapter 8, leading up to and during the Olympic Games, for further information.)

(For the new law on the People's Armed Police and its role in Xinjiang, see the entry for 27 August 2009 in the political chronology, Chapter 8.)

6 Human rights

'Under a 1998 law state secrets are defined as "all other matters classified as state secrets by the national State Secrets Bureau", a catch-all phrase' (*The Independent*, 12 June 2007, p. 23).

'An estimated 300,000 Chinese citizens have been sent to "re-education through labour" camps across the country, often for political activities' (Wang Dan, *IHT*, 4 June 2008, p. 6).

> China's highest court will regain the power to decide on all death sentences under legal changes approved Tuesday [31 October] ... The move to recentralize control over executions in the hands of the supreme court beginning 1 January [2007] comes as the authorities face mounting criticism from human rights groups and Chinese legal scholars for what they say is the widespread and arbitrary use of the death penalty. Chinese courts have been embarrassed in recent years after a number of widely reported miscarriages of justice in which evidence later emerged that innocent people had been executed ... The National People's Congress approved the amendment to the law, which 'is believed to be the most important reform of capital punishment in China in more than two decades', the official Xinhua news agency said in a short dispatch. In an attempt to deter a wave of crime and corruption in the early years of China's economic boom, the authorities in 1983 delegated the power to lower courts to impose the death penalty for a wide range of offences ... Legal experts say that as living standards rise and China becomes an important international power, the country's senior leadership is uncomfortable that the death penalty is so readily applied. China does not disclose the number of executions it carries out under a criminal code where almost seventy offences carry the death penalty ... Amnesty International estimates, based on publicly available reports, that at least 1,770 people were executed in 2005 and 3,900 were sentenced to death. Some Chinese legal experts estimate that as many as 8,000 people are executed each year. In a 21 September report Amnesty said shortcomings in the legal system for people sentenced to death included the lack of prompt access to lawyers, the absence of the presumption of innocence, political interference in the courts and the use of evidence by torture.
>
> (www.iht.com, 31 October 2006)

> China enacted a legal change Tuesday that requires its highest court to approve all executions ... The official Xinhua news agency said: '[The legal change] deprives the provincial people's courts of the final say on issuing death sentences. Death penalties handed out by provincial courts must be reviewed and ratified by the Supreme People's Court ... China is believed to lead the world in executions.'
>
> (*IHT*, 1 November 2006, p. 4)

> From January [2007] all death penalty cases will be reviewed by the supreme court in a move some legal scholars believe could reduce hangings, shootings and lethal injections by up to a third. China is the world's leading executioner ... The number of executions ... is a state secret. Even by the most conservative estimates it accounts for more than half of the world total. According to Chinese domestic media, there are sixty-eight capital offences, only twenty-four of which are crimes of violence ... Amnesty International says many innocent defendants are tortured into signing confessions.
>
> (*Guardian*, 1 November 2006, p. 19)

'China executes an estimated 5,000 to 12,000 people a year – more than any other country' (*FT*, 1 November 2006, p. 9).

> The total number ... of people it executes ... is a carefully guarded secret but Amnesty International counted at least 1,770 executions in 2006 and the real amount could be as high as 8,000 ... China executes far more people than the rest of the world combined.
>
> (www.economist.com, 30 May 2007)

> Human rights experts have estimated that China executes 10,000 to 15,000 inmates a year. Beijing does not release official figures, which are designated state secrets ... China has more than sixty offences eligible for a death sentence, ranging from murder to public corruption and a range of economic crimes ... Amnesty International says China executed at least 1,770 people in 2005 – about 80 per cent of the world's total. The true number is thought to be many times higher. Amnesty International has cited a senior member of China's national legislature as saying some 10,000 people are executed each year ... Less than 1 per cent of all criminal defendants are acquitted.
>
> (www.iht.com, 8 and 9 June 2007)

> In 2005 an estimated 1,770 executions were carried out and nearly 4,000 people were sentenced to death, human rights group Amnesty International says ... Non-violent crimes such as tax fraud and embezzlement carry the death penalty. Other crimes include rape, robbery and drug offences. China does not publish official figures on executions.
>
> (www.bbc.co.uk, 8 June 2007)

> Amnesty International knows of at least 1,010 executions in China in 2006, but a Chinese legal scholar estimates that about 8,000 people are executed each year ... There are sixty-eight crimes punishable by death in China,

two-thirds of them non-violent crimes … Critics of the government, members of banned religions and anyone else deemed to be in need of 're-education' can be sent to a 're-education through labour' camp for up to four years without charge or trial … Evidence in court may be based on torture and political interference in trials is common … Torture is widespread in the criminal justice system … Allegations of torture are rarely investigated, despite a large number of deaths in custody … Nearly twenty years after the crackdown on demonstrators in Tiananmen Square, dozens of them remain in prison … People who stand up for human rights are harassed and arrested, and often sentenced on vague charges related to 'state secrets' … Websites are blocked or banned, searches are filtered and internet users are imprisoned after unfair trials. Sentences range from two to twelve years … Tens of thousands of Falun Gong practitioners are detained … The Chinese authorities have used the 'war on terror' to justify harsh repression of the largely Uighur people in Xinjiang province, closing mosques, restricting use of the local language and banning certain books. In Tibet freedom of expression, religion and association are severely restricted. Hundreds of prisoners of conscience, including Buddhist monks and nuns, remain in prison and reports persist of torture and deaths in custody.

(*Amnesty*, July–August 2007, p. 16)

Based on available public reports, Amnesty International estimated that in 2006 China executed at least 1,010 people – around 60 per cent of all executions across the world. However, the group said that credible sources had put the figure at much higher – between 7,500 and 8,000. During the same period there were fifty-three executions in the United States.

(www.cnn.com, 3 January 2007)

China leaves the world trailing [in] use of the death penalty. Indeed, the number of Chinese criminal executions remains a state secret. Foreign human rights groups make valiant efforts to scour local press reports and tally the sums, but reckon they hear about only a fraction of the cases. In 2006 Amnesty International counted 2,790 people sentenced to death in China and 1,010 executed. Other groups put annual executions at 7,500 or more. Even per head, using low estimates, China probably outstrips every country but Singapore. It also has a greater number of capital offences than anywhere else: more than sixty.

(*The Economist*, 12 January 2008, p. 48)

China's supreme court rejected 15 per cent of all death sentences handed down by lower courts in 2007 … Amnesty International says China carried out two-thirds of the world's executions in 2006. Official figures are a state secret in China. But China says the number has fallen since an amendment came into force in January 2007 requiring the Supreme People's Court to approve all death sentences.

(www.bbc.co.uk, 8 March 2008)

'Sixty-eight crimes still carry the death penalty' (*Guardian*, 11 March 2008, p. 29).

> The authorities put to death at least 470 people last year [2007], but may have killed up to 8,000, human rights group Amnesty International has said ... In China figures are secret ... More than sixty crimes can carry the death penalty in China, including tax fraud, stealing VAT receipts, damaging electric power facilities, selling counterfeit medicine, embezzlement, accepting bribes and drug offences, Amnesty said. Those sentenced to death are usually shot, but some provinces are introducing lethal injections ... At least 1,252 people are known to have been executed in twenty-four countries in 2007, a slight drop on the previous year. Just five countries – China, Iran, Saudi Arabia, Pakistan and the United States – were responsible for 88 per cent of known executions in the world.
>
> (www.bbc.co.uk, 15, April 2008)

> China executed more people than any other country in the world last year [2007] by putting at least 470 people to death ... [falling] from 1,010 in 2006 ... Amnesty International said ... Research by the US-based Dui Hua Foundation, which campaigns on behalf of political prisoners and researches conditions in Chinese prisons, indicates about 6,000 people were executed in 2007. The group's data are based on figures obtained from local officials.
>
> (www.iht.com, 15 April 2008)

'Death penalty statistics in China are difficult to assess, Amnesty International said [in its annual report], but, based on public reports, the group estimated that at least 470 people were executed in 2007' (www.iht.com, 28 May 2008).

> Chinese criminal law professor Liu Renwen estimated that 8,000 executions took place during 2006 in China ... The US-based Dui Hua Foundation estimated that 7,500 to 8,000 executions took place in the same year ... There were 1,250 people executed worldwide last year [2007], down from 1,591 over the previous twelve months.
>
> (www.guardian.co.uk, 15 April 2008)

> Amnesty International reported Tuesday [24 March 2009] ... [that] at least 2,390 people were executed worldwide in 2008, compared with its 2007 figure of at least 1,252. With at least 1,718 executions China was responsible for 72 per cent of all such penalties in 2008, the report stated ... The Chinese authorities also handed down at least 7,003 new death sentences last year [2008], although the report said the true totals of both executions and death sentences 'remain shrouded in secrecy'. Some countries, including China and North Korea, do not disclose the number of executions they carry out. In China's case 'real figures are undoubtedly higher', the report stated.
>
> (www.iht.com, 24 March 2009; *IHT*, 25 March 2009, p. 5)

(See also www.feer.com, 10 July 2009.)

> China is to reduce the number of people it executes to 'an extremely small number' ... Zhang Jun, vice president of the Supreme People's Court (SPC), said the court would in future impose more suspended death sentences. Two years ago China gave the SPC power to review death sentences handed down by lower courts. That has already led to fewer executions ... In September 2007, after the SPC was given its power to review cases, Chinese state media reported that executions were at a 'ten-year low'. Amnesty International said China executed 1,718 people in 2008 – 72 per cent of the world's total. The death sentence still applies to sixty offences in China, including non-violent crimes such as tax fraud and embezzlement ... [Zhang Jun said] that the SPC had been working to ensure that the death sentence was imposed only on those who had committed extremely serious or heinous crimes that led to grave social consequences.
>
> (www.bbc.co.uk, 29 July 2009)

> More than sixty crimes can draw the death penalty in China, including tax evasion, embezzlement and drug trafficking, but the government does not release figures on the number of executions, many of which take place immediately after a defendant's conviction ... Human rights groups like Amnesty International estimate that more than 1,700 people were put to death in China in 2008, a sharp drop from previous years in which as many as 15,000 executions took place. The United States, by contrast, put to death thirty-seven people last year [2008]. The number of executions in China began dropping in 2001 – not long after Beijing was chosen as the site of the 2008 Summer Olympics – but they have fallen more sharply since 2007, when the country's high court was given the power to review all capital punishment cases. Last year, according to *China Daily*, the court overturned 10 per cent of all death sentences meted out by lower courts ... Mr Zhang suggested that the number of eligible crimes would be scaled back through legislation and that provincial courts would be encouraged to mete out a sentence known as 'death penalty with reprieve'.
>
> (www.iht.com, 29 July 2009)

> The vice president of the Supreme People's Court said ... that the penalty should be reserved for a small number of serious crimes, particularly those that threaten social stability ... Zhang Jun: 'Judicial departments should use the least number of death sentences as possible.'
>
> (*IHT*, 30 July 2009, p. 4)

'Amnesty International ... believes that at least 1,718 people were executed in 2008' (*The Times*, 30 July 2009, p. 35).

'Human rights groups estimate 1,700 to 5,000 people were executed in China last year [2008]' (www.cnn.com, 30 July 2009).

> 'Death penalty with reprieve' sentences are becoming more common and are usually commuted to life in prison. That can later be reduced to twenty years or less with good behaviour ... *China Daily* said the Supreme People's

Court overturned 15 per cent of death sentences handed down in 2007 and 10 per cent in 2008. Independent analysts suggested the policy had caused a drop in executions of as much as 30 per cent year-on-year.

(*Guardian*, 30 July 2009, p. 20)

China is trying to move away from the use of executed prisoners as the major source of organs for transplants. According to the *China Daily*, executed prisoners currently provide two-thirds of all transport organs. The government is now launching a voluntary donation scheme, which it hopes will also curb the illegal trafficking in organs. But analysts say cultural bias against removing organs after death will make a voluntary scheme hard to implement. About 1.5 million people in China need transplants, but only about 10,000 operations are performed annually, according to the health ministry. The scarcity of available organs has led to a thriving black market in trafficking organs, and in an effort to stop this the government passed a law in 2007 banning trafficking as well as the donation of organs to unrelated recipients ... *China Daily* said on Wednesday [26 August] that more than 65 per cent of organ donations come from death row prisoners. China executes more people than any other country. Amnesty International said at least 1,718 people were given the death penalty in 2008 ... The system will be piloted in ten provinces and cities, and a fund will be started to provide financial aid to donors' families.

(www.bbc.co.uk, 26 August 2009)

China inaugurated its voluntary organ donor programme on Tuesday [26 August], hoping to overhaul a system that now harvests the vast majority of its organs from black market sellers and executed prisoners and leaves millions of ailing people without hope of getting a transplant. The new programme [is to be] run by the national Red Cross Society with help from China's health minister ... Chian does not publicly report execution figures ... Although prisoners must give written consent for their organs to be used, inmates 'are definitely not a proper source for organ transplants', said Huang Jiefu ... the vice minister of health ... It is almost unheard of for ordinary Chinese citizens to volunteer to donate their organs after death. Only about 130 people have pledged to donate their organs since 2003 ... The new organ donation system will start as an experimental programme in ten cities, including Shanghai, and later rolled out nationwide.

(www.iht.com, 26 August 2009)

Two years ago China ruled that organs from executed prisoners would be given only to family members, and that living donors could give body parts only to relatives or those with an 'emotional connection' ... A World Medical Association agreement, among others by China, requests countries not to use organs from death-row prisoners because of concerns about whether those people have truly given informed consent ... Huang Jiefu (vice minister for health): 'Transplants should not be a privilege for the rich

> … The [new transplant] system is in the public interest and will benefit patients regardless of social status and wealth in terms of fairness in organ allocation and better procurement.'
>
> (*Guardian*, 27 August 2009, p. 25)

> Donating organs is not a widespread practice in China. Officials said last year [2008] only thirty-six people donated organs … The nationwide number of donations fell last year to thirty-six, from forty-one the previous year [2007], and only about ten cases so far this year [2009] … Only 130 organ transplants have ever been performed in China using donors who consented to have their organs used after their death.
>
> (www.cnn.com, 26 August 2009)

'There has been a surge in living donors. About 40 per cent of transplants are carried out with organs from living donors, up from 15 per cent in 2006' (www.thetimes.co.uk, 26 August 2009).

A chronology of developments in human rights since 16 May 2006

'Prosecutors have reintroduced an indictment against a researcher for *The New York Times* … Zhao Yan … on accusations of fraud and disclosing state secrets, the same case that the authorities dropped only two months ago' (www.iht.com, 16 May 2006).

> Chinese officials stepped up a crackdown on defence lawyers on Friday [18 August 2006] in the latest sign that Communist Party leaders are determined to stamp out legal challenges to their authority. The Beijing police detained Gao Zhisheng, one of the country's most outspoken lawyers and dissidents, on suspicion of criminal activity … Separately, court officials in Shandong province held a closed criminal trial of Chen Guangcheng, a blind legal expert … Three of Chen's legal advisers [were detained] on Thursday [17 August] … Chen attracted attention when he tried to organize a class-action lawsuit on behalf of residents of the city of Linyi who had been forced to undergo abortions or sterilization in a campaign to meet population control quotas.
>
> (*IHT*, 19 August 2006, p. 3)

> A court sentenced a blind advocate of peasants' rights to more than four years in prison Thursday [24 August] … Chen Guangcheng was convicted of destroying property and organizing a mob to block traffic. He had earned the enmity of local Communist Party leaders in Shandong province, eastern China, when he sought to organize a class-action lawsuit against forced abortions and sterilizations there … A two-hour trial of Chen last week and the sentence announced Thursday appear to reflect a concerted effort by the authorities to punish lawyers and rights advocates who have represented people aggrieved about land seizures, environmental abuses, religious per-

> secution and population controls … The thirty-four-year-old peasant, blind since a childhood illness, taught himself the law. He became a minor celebrity in China after he helped handicapped people win cases against government agencies that did not grant them the full protections and benefits they are entitled to under Chinese law. But Shandong government officials turned bitterly against him in early 2005. It was then that he sought to represent thousands of local residents forced to abort foetuses or submit to sterilization operations so that Linyi City, Shandong, could meet its population-control quotas … Though central government investigators later concluded that abuses had occurred in enforcing population policies there, the local authorities put Chen under arrest for months and then charged him with destroying property and blocking traffic.
>
> (*IHT*, 25 August 2006, p. 2)

'Chen Guangcheng was sentenced … to four years and three months … for "wilfully damaging property and organizing a mob to disturb traffic"' (*FT*, 25 August 2006, p. 6).

('The Linyi City intermediate court, where Chen Guangcheng filed his appeal, overturned the sentence on Monday 30 October 2006 and sent it back to the lower court in Yinan county [for a retrial] … [The] appeals court [is] in Linyi, which is the same urban area where local officials ordered the crackdown on Chen … [This was] a rare victory in a case his supporters had called one of the most blatant abuses in China's legal system in recent years … While such practices … [as forcing] villagers to have late-term abortions and sterilizations … are illegal, local officials often resort to drastic measures for fear of being punished for exceeding birth quotas … Last month more than fifty leading scholars and rights campaigners from the United States, Europe and Australia mentioned Chen in a letter to President Hu Jintao. The cases of Chen, along with lawyer Gao Zhisheng, AIDS activist Hu Jia and *New York Times* researcher Zhao Yan were particularly troubling because China appeared to be using "state secrets laws to prevent defendants in politically sensitive cases from exercising their rights to fair and impartial hearings", the letter said': www.iht.com, 1 November 2006.)

> A Beijing court Friday [25 August] unexpectedly dismissed a state secrets charge against a researcher for *The New York Times*, but sentenced him to three years in prison on a lesser, unrelated charge of fraud. The verdict against Zhao Yan spared him a prison sentence of ten years or longer … Agents began detaining Zhao almost two years ago and accused him of leaking state secrets to *The Times*. He has consistently stated that he is innocent of both charges … Zhao, formerly a muckraking journalist for different Chinese publications, has been imprisoned since September 2004. Under Chinese law the time he has already served will count against his prison term … The court ruling stated that his release was scheduled for 15 September 2007. Zhao joined *The Times*'s bureau in Beijing as a researcher in April 2004. *The Times* has consistently rejected the charge that he leaked

> any state secrets to the newspaper … Investigators added the fraud charge several months after Zhao was arrested on 17 September 2004, on the state secrets charge … [The charge] accused him of leaking state secrets for a *Times* article about the transition among the top leaders. The article, published ten days before Zhao was detained, revealed that a former president, Jiang Zemin, had unexpectedly offered to resign from his final leadership position as military chief. The investigation did not accuse Zhao of being one of the anonymous sources cited for Jiang's resignation offer. Instead, security agents accused him of providing information about jockeying between Jiang and Hu Jintao over positions in the military's high command. A reference to this jockeying was included as context at the end of the article. As evidence, the investigation report cited a photocopy of a note in which Zhao had scribbled down a few sentences of political gossip about the jockeying. The note was left in *The Times*'s bureau in Beijing.
>
> (www.iht.com, 25 August 2006)

'[The court] found Zhao Yan guilty of fraud after allegations that he took … [a sum of money] from a villager in north-east China to help him avoid "labour reeducation" – a form of imprisonment' (*The Times*, 26 August 2006, p. 42).

> A Hong Kong journalist … Ching Cheong … has been sentenced to five years in prison after a Beijing court convicted him on charges of spying for Taiwan, state media reported Thursday [31 August] … The two cases [Ching Cheong and Zhao Yan] … have been interpreted as warning signals to journalists against prying into the inner workings of the highest levels of the Communist Party.
>
> (www.iht.com, 31 August 2006)

> An appeals court Friday [1 December] upheld a fraud conviction against a Chinese researcher for *The New York Times*, while a trial court convicted for a second time a blind legal expert who had exposed abuses in the country's population control policies … Zhao Yan will likely remain in prison until his three-year sentence ends next September [2007] … The blind legal expert, Chen Guangcheng, was convicted Friday morning on charges that he destroyed property and disrupted traffic. He was sentenced to four years and three months in prison.
>
> (www.iht.com, 1 December 2006; *IHT*, 2 December 2006, p. 5)

> China has at least thirty-one journalists behind bars, making it the world's leading jailer of reporters for the eighth year in a row, according to … the New York-based Committee to Protect Journalists [CPJ] … About three-quarters were convicted under vague charges of subversion or revealing state secrets, and more than half were internet journalists … The total number of journalists jailed worldwide rose to 134 as of 1 December [2006] – nine more than a year earlier. The number of jailed journalists in China has fallen by one from last year [2005] … Reporters Without Borders maintains its own tally of Chinese reporters and cyber-dissidents behind bars,

> with a count of thirty-two as of January this year [2006]. The Paris-based group list nineteen people, including five Tibetan monks who were arrested last year for allegedly starting an underground newsletter, who are not named on the CPJ's list. The two combined lists total fifty journalists.
>
> (www.iht.com, 8 December 2006)

'Human rights conditions in China deteriorated last year [2006] ... Human Rights Watch ... the New York-based group ... said in a report' (www.iht.com, 12 January 2007).

> More than 200 people [217], including twenty-nine children, have been rescued after working as 'slaves' in brick kilns in central China, state media reports. Tens of thousands of police moved in on kilns in Henan province, arresting 120 people ... They acted after media recently reported that children were being forced to work in kilns in neighbouring Shanxi province ... Xinhua said the victims had been 'enticed or sent by human traffickers to the kilns', where they were 'beaten, starved and forced to work long hours without payment' ... On Wednesday [13 June] 400 men from Henan made an online appeal for help in their bid to rescue children from brickworks hidden deep in the mountains of Shanxi. They said they had 'risked their lives' to rescue about forty, but believed at least 1,000 children had been kidnapped for sale to traffickers ... Last week [8 June] thirty-one disorientated workers were rescued from a brickwork factory in Shanxi . They were reported to have been duped into working at the factory, and faced a harsh regime in which they worked unpaid for twenty hours a day with only bread and water in return ... Eight were reported to be so traumatized by their experiences that they were only able to remember their names.
>
> (www.bbc.co.uk, Thursday 14 June 2007)

> The Chinese authorities say they have freed another 200 people who had been trafficked to work as slaves at brickworks in northern China. More than 460 people have been rescued in recent weeks from brick kilns in the central provinces of Henan and Shanxi ... The story attracted widespread media coverage after parents of some of the children set up an online campaign to free them ... Hundreds of people, some of them children thought to be as young as eight years old, were kidnapped, held captive and forced to work long hours for no pay. Many were beaten and starved. The online campaign claims that about 1,000 children have been forced into slavery – many of whom are still in captivity. Now President Hu Jintao and other senior politicians have called for an investigation into the scandal ... Forced labour and human trafficking are common in rural parts.
>
> (www.bbc.co.uk, 15 June 2007)

> Hundreds [of stories] ... have swept China in recent days in an unfolding labour abuse scandal that involves the kidnapping in central China of hundreds of children, and perhaps more, some reportedly as young as eight, who have been forced to work under brutal conditions – scantily clothed,

unpaid and often fed little more than water and steamed buns – in the brick kilns of Shanxi province. There have been reports of adults being forced to work under similar circumstances … A manhunt was announced mid-week for … the foremen of one of the kilns where thirty-one of the workers were recently rescued … Local authorities have sometimes turned parents away from the factories in collusion with the kilns. Other reports have said that local authorities, including labour inspectors, have taken children from freshly closed kilns and resold them to other factories.

(www.iht.com, 15 June 2007; *IHT*, 16 June 2007, pp. 1, 3)

According to the official Xinhua news agency, around 35,000 police rescued 468 people after checking 7,500 kilns. They made up to 120 arrests … The main official newspaper, the *People's Daily*, put at least part of the blame on corrupt local officials … Thirty-one people were freed [earlier] by police from slave labour at a brick kiln in Hongtong, a county in [Shanxi].

(*Independent*, 16 June 2007, p. 38)

According to the state media, they [the victims] were beaten by guards and kept from escaping by dogs. At least thirteen died from overwork and abuse, including a labourer who was allegedly battered to death with a shovel … Their plight was revealed by one of the biggest known police operations in the country's history. In the past week 35,000 police have inspected 7,500 kilns in the countryside of Shanxi and Henan provinces … They have arrested 120 suspects and freed 468 slaves, including 109 juveniles … The first case was revealed on 8 June … The huge police investigation was prompted by 400 parents of missing youths, who posted a petition on the internet last week, accusing local officials of ignoring their suspicions … President Hu Jintao and prime minister Wen Jiabao ordered an investigation.

(*Guardian*, 16 June 2007, p. 21)

'Local officials … said the number of children forced to work in the kilns … in Henan and Shanxi provinces … could rise to more than 1,000' (*The Times*, 16 June 2007, p. 53).

'Some 550 people have been liberated in recent weeks and families believe up to 1,000 children were enslaved … Many labourers were reportedly abducted off the streets of regional towns and sold on' (www.bbc.co.uk, 16 June 2007).

By Saturday [16 June] the police in Shanxi had detained twenty-five people suspected of involvement in what amounts to a slave trade, Xinhua said … Police have captured a man accused of holding workers in virtual slavery, state media reported Sunday [17 June] amid a national uproar over teenagers and men forced to work in brutal, furnace-like brick kilns … [The man] is accused of holding workers in a kiln [that he leased] in Hongtong county in the northern province of Shanxi. One worker died and the police rescued thirty-one others, thin and scarred. The police caught [him] … last Saturday [16 June] after a nationwide manhunt … [He] had coerced or lured workers to the site since March 2006, forcing them to work sixteen-hour days and subsist mainly on steamed bread ... A sweeping police crackdown in Shanxi and Henan has so far freed 568 people from kilns and other work sites, including twenty-two under the age of eighteen in Shanxi ... The owner of the kiln ... was detained in late May ... This is not the first time brutality in Shanxi's brick industry has stirred their concern. In 2003 Wen called for tough punishment after a teenage boy was forced into working in a kiln in Shanxi.

(www.iht.com, 17 June 2007)

Police in northern China say they have now arrested more than 160 people accused of involvement in slave labour in illegal mines and brick factories. Among them is the foreman of a brickworks in the northern province of Shanxi, who had been the subject of a nationwide manhunt. Almost 570 people trafficked as slaves – fifty of them children – have been freed in Shanxi and neighbouring Henan ... There has been unusually strong criticism in the state-run media with one paper calling the situation a shocking disgrace, but the reality is that forced labour is common in rural parts, our [BBC] correspondent adds.

(www.bbc.co.uk, 17 June 2007)

China has arrested two labour bureau officials over their alleged links to slave labour in brick kilns, amid reports Friday [22 June] that kiln bosses were hiding children and charging ransoms for their release. The pair are the first officials arrested in connection with the [enslavement] ... The two arrested officials are the head of the labour inspection team in the Yongji district of Shanxi province, who was charged with dereliction of duty, and one of his officers, charged with abuse of power ... Since the scandal broke last month more than 8,000 kilns and small coal mines in Shanxi and Henan provinces have been raided, with 591 workers freed, including fifty-one children, according to state media. The Shanxi police said another 359 people had been freed in the province, twelve of whom were underage, while ages of nine others were being checked, according to Xinhua. About 160 suspected kiln bosses have been detained in the two provinces, and at least one Communist Party secretary from the village level was expelled from the party after his son was found to be operating a kiln where thirty-one slaves were found.

(www.iht.com, 22 June 2007)

Child labour is a daily fact of life and one to which the government typically turns a blind eye ... Hu Jindou (Professor of Economics at Beijing University of Technology): 'Everything is about the economy now, just like everything was about politics in the Mao era, and forced labour or child labour is far from an isolated phenomenon. It is deeply rooted in today's reality, a combination of capitalism, socialism, feudalism and slavery.'

(Howard French, *IHT*, 19 June 2007, p. 2)

'Nearly 1,000 workers have been released following police raids in recent months, prompted in part by accusations posted on the internet that authorities were ignoring such practices' (www.iht.com, 29 June 2007).

> A doctor who exposed the cover-up of the SARS outbreak in 2003 has been barred from travelling to the United States to collect a human rights award … The doctor, Jiang Yanyong, a retired surgeon in the People's Liberation Army, was awarded the Heinz R. Pagels Human Rights of Scientists Award by the New York Academy of Sciences … Jiang rose to prominence in 2003, when he disclosed in a letter circulated to international news organizations that at least 100 people were being treated in Beijing hospitals for SARS. At the time the Chinese medical authorities were acknowledging only a small number of cases on the mainland and maintaining that the disease was under control there … SARS eventually killed more than 800 people worldwide … Jiang was initially hailed as a hero in Chinese and foreign news media. He used his new prestige in 2004 to press the ruling Politburo Standing Committee to say that the leadership had erred in ordering the military to shoot unarmed civilians staging pro-democracy demonstrations in Tiananmen Square in June 2989. Jiang, who treated Beijing residents wounded in the 1989 assault, contended that the official line that the crackdown had been necessary to suppress a rebellion was false.
>
> (www.iht.com, 13 July 2007)

> Dozens of local government officials have been punished by the Communist Party for their roles in a brick kiln slave labour scandal, but higher level officials were found to be innocent of any wrongdoing, a party discipline committee said Monday [16 July] … Ninety-five officials at the county level or lower were disciplined by the Communist Party for misconduct, with punishments including warnings, demotions and black marks on their records, said Yang Senlin, vice secretary of the Shanxi provincial party discipline inspection committee. Three were expelled from the party and thirty-three were fired from their jobs. Eight officials will be criminally prosecuted, including two who were already disciplined by the party … However, officials at the municipal level, which in China is higher than the county level, and above were found to be innocent of any wrongdoing … Yang Senlin: 'No corruption has been found among officials in Shanxi after a careful month-long investigation.'
>
> (www.iht.com, 16 July 2007)

> Chinese officials announced Monday [16 July] that an embarrassing labour scandal involving slave-like conditions affecting hundreds of workers at brick kilns in Shanxi province would result in just a handful of prosecutions, provoking anger among people who worked at the factories and widespread criticism among the general public. Shanxi province officials announced the punishment of dozens of officials in the scandal, but they said criminal prosecutions would only be opened against six officials, all low-level figures in

the Communist Party or in local government. The punishments for the others ranged from firings and demotions to expulsion from the party or administrative warnings ... Yang Senlin (vice secretary of the Shanxi provincial party discipline inspection committee): 'Other than the direct responsibility of the owners, the "black brick kilns" incident happened mainly because of lax supervision and dereliction of duty of grassroots party and government officials' ... Contradicting the accounts of many who were freed from the kilns ... Yang said there was no evidence of collusion or corruption on the part of local officials.

(www.iht.com, 16 July 2007)

One man has been sentenced to death and twenty-eight others jailed for their roles in a slave labour scandal at brick factories in northern China. The foreman of a kiln where more than thirty people were held captive was jailed for life, and an employee received the death penalty for killing a worker. Others were jailed on charges of illegal detention and forced labour. Since the scandal broke in June, more than 570 people forced into slavery in Shanxi and Henan have been freed ... The kiln where the accused foremen ... and his employee ... worked was owned by ... the son of a local Communist Party official ... [The son] was jailed for nine years ... On Monday [16 July] ninety-five officials in Shanxi province were punished for dereliction of duty in supervising the brick kilns ... Thirty-three were sacked from their posts and another sixty-two were given disciplinary warnings ... There are expected to be more trials connected with the scandal. Police in northern China have arrested almost 160 people suspected of involvement in the case.

(www.bbc.co.uk, 17 July 2007)

[The] kiln boss ... was sentenced to nine years in jail for unlawful detention ... [His] father was a village-level Communist Party secretary and he was expelled from the party after the scandal broke ... A total of twenty-nine people were convicted Tuesday [17 July] in seven different courts in Shanxi for their roles in the slavery scandal ... Another twelve are still standing trial.

(www.iht.com, 17 July 2007)

At least 20,000 police surveillance cameras are being installed ... in Shenzhen ... and will soon be guided by sophisticated computer software from a US-financed company to recognize automatically the faces of crime suspects and detect unusual activity. Starting this month [August] in a port neighbourhood and then spreading across Shenzhen, a city of 12.4 million, residency cards fitted with powerful computer chips programmed by the same company will be issued to most citizens ... Security experts describe China's plans as the world's largest effort to meld cutting edge computer technology with police work to track the activities of the population and fight crime, but they say the technology can be used to violate civil rights.

> The government has ordered all large cities across the country to apply technology to police work and to issue high-tech residency cards to 150 million people who have moved to a city but not yet acquired permanent residency. Both steps are officially aimed at fighting crime and developing better controls on an increasingly mobile population, including the nearly 10 million peasants who move to big cities each year. But they could also help the Communist Party retain power by maintaining tight controls on an increasingly prosperous population at a time when street protests are becoming more common … Shenzhen … next to Hong Kong … is the first Chinese city to introduce the new residency cards. It is also taking the lead in China in the large-scale use of law enforcement surveillance cameras.
>
> (*IHT*, 13 August 2007, pp. 1, 7)

> China Public Security, based in Shenzhen, [is] incorporated in Florida [in the United States] … China Security and Surveillance Technology [is] a fast growing company that installs and sometimes operates surveillance systems for Chinese police agencies, jails and banks, among other customers. The company … [also] based in Shenzhen … has just been approved for a listing on the New York Stock Exchange. The company's listing … [is] just the latest sign of ever closer ties between Wall Street, surveillance companies and the Chinese government's security apparatus … China Public Security Technology, like China Security and Surveillance, incorporated itself in the United States to make it easier to sell shares to Western investors … Human rights advocates contend that surveillance in China poses different issues from surveillance in the West … Critics say the surveillance is aimed at catching … [those] the Communist Party regards as threatening.
>
> (*IHT*, 10 September 2007, p. 10)

> China's supreme court has ordered judges to be more sparing in the imposition of the death penalty. An order on its website said execution should be reserved for 'an extremely small number of serious offenders'. It said the death penalty should be withheld in certain cases of crimes of passion or economic crimes. Amnesty International says China carried out two-thirds of the world's executions last year [2006], but China says it expects a ten-year low this year. The supreme court said murders triggered by family disputes should not always result in the death penalty. Crimes of passion should take into account the offender's payment of compensation, it said. Similarly, those convicted of economic crimes should be treated more leniently if they help recoup the money that was defrauded. The court suggested greater use of two-year suspensions on death penalties – allowing them to be converted to imprisonment … In 2005 an estimated 1,770 executions were carried out and nearly 4,000 people were sentenced to death, Amnesty International says.
>
> (www.bbc.co.uk, 14 September 2007)

'Zhao Yan, a Chinese research assistant for *The New York Times*, was expected to be freed Saturday morning [15 September] after serving three years in prison on a fraud conviction ... Zhao, forty-five, completed his full sentence' (www.iht.com, 14 September 2007; *IHT*, 15 September 2007, p. 5).

> Zhao walked out of prison at 8 a.m. ... The more serious state secrets charge was dismissed ... remarkable in a system where anyone charged with a state secrets violation is almost automatically convicted ... But the court convicted him on the fraud charge.
>
> (www.iht.com, 16 September 2007)

('China is already a world leader in this last category [of imprisoned journalists], according to Human Rights Watch, which counts "some thirty known cases of journalists imprisoned for their reporting activities"': www.iht.com, 17 November 2007.)

> In preparation for the Beijing Olympics and a host of other international events, some American companies are helping the Chinese government to design and install one of the most comprehensive high-tech public surveillance systems in the world ... Critics of China's human rights record said the work violated the spirit of a sanctions law [the US] Congress passed after the Tiananmen Square killings.
>
> (*IHT*, 28 December 2007, p. 11)

> China is to expand the use of lethal injections to replace execution by shooting ... Jiang Xingchang, vice president of the Supreme People's Court, said that the move was because lethal injections were considered more humane ... Beijing is gradually reforming its use of the death penalty. Last year [2007] the Supreme Court ordered judges to be more sparing in its imposition. Half of China's 404 Intermediate People's Courts – which carry out most of the country's executions – now use lethal injections, Jiang Xingchang [said] ... [he] said that the method would eventually be used in all Intermediate People's Courts, but he gave no timetable for the shift ... Chief justice Xiao Yang ... [said] that China was 'working towards' more limited use of the death penalty, but ruled out ending the practice.
>
> (www.bbc.co.uk, 3 January 2008)

> Based on available public reports, Amnesty International estimated that in 2006 China executed at least 1,010 people – around 60 per cent of all executions across the world. However, the group said that credible sources had put the figure at much higher – between 7,500 and 8,000. During the same period there were fifty-three executions in the United States ... Lethal injections were first introduced as a method of execution in China in 1997 ... China has attempted to reform its capital punishment system following reports in 2005 of executions of wrongly convicted people and criticism that lower courts arbitrarily impose the death sentence. An amendment to China's capital punishment law, enacted in November 2005, restored to the Supreme People's Court the sole right to approve all death sentences, ending a twenty-three-year-old practice of allowing provincial courts alone to sign off on executions.

Chief justice Xiao Yang said the authorities were keen to limit the use of capital punishment in the future. It should be applied only to 'an extremely small number' of serious offenders.

(www.cnn.com, 3 January 2007)

This month [January 2008] the chief justice, Xiao Yang, said China might one day like to abolish capital punishment altogether, But that day would not dawn soon, because Chinese people believe strongly in the notion of an 'eye for an eye and a life for a life'.

(*The Economist*, 12 January 2008, p. 49)

A prominent Chinese activist has been formally arrested more than a month after being taken into custody [on 27 December 2007]. Hu Jia, who publicizes human rights abuses across China, has been accused of inciting subversion of state power … His wife Zeng Jinyan, also a prominent activist, has been put under house arrest with the couple's two-month-old baby … Rights groups say Beijing is cracking down on dissent ahead of the Olympics in August [2008].

(www.bbc.co.uk, 1 February 2008)

Hu Jia gained international prominence for his advocacy on behalf of AIDS patients, farmers and the environment. He and his wife, Zeng Jinyan, are well-known bloggers who have faced official scrutiny for years for their writings on human rights in China … More recently, Hu was outspoken in saying that China had not fulfilled its promises to improve human rights conditions before the Olympic Games.

(www.iht.com, 1 February 2008)

Hu and his wife, Zeng Jinyan, are human rights activists who spent much of 2006 restricted to their apartment. She used the power of the internet to blog about life under detention while he wrote online about peasant protests and human rights cases. Hu's recent testimony to the European parliament about Olympics-related rights violations may have been the last straw.

(www.iht.com, 4 February 2008)

A Hong Kong journalist who was jailed on spying charges has been released after serving less than half a five-year sentence. Ching Cheong was detained in [April] 2005 … in the southern Chinese city of Guangzhou … and sentenced to five years in jail in a case that angered human rights groups. Chinese officials accused him of buying information and passing it to Taiwan – charges his family and his employer, Singapore's *Straits Times*, rejected … He is now returning to Hong Kong … Ching's supporters have always insisted he is innocent and human rights groups have waged a concerted campaign for his freedom … Supporters said he was arrested after travelling to China to collect documents linked to Zhao Ziyang … According to human rights group Reporters Without Borders, more than thirty journalists are currently in custody, along with fifty internet campaigners.

(www.bbc.co.uk, 5 February 2008)

The veteran journalist ... Ching Cheong ... was sentenced to five years in jail in August 2006 on charges of spying for Taiwan. He was detained during a visit to Guangzhou in April 2005 ... However, a Chinese court sentenced democracy activist Lu Gengsong ... who wrote about corruption ... on Tuesday [5 February] to four years in prison for 'inciting subversion of state power', a vague charge frequently used to silence whistle-blowers and critics of the Communist Party. The New York-based Committee to Protect Journalists [CPJ] welcomed Ching's release, but said China continues to jail more than any other country ... Bob Dietz (CPJ programme co-ordinator): 'We hope that in this coming year when China will host the Olympic Games, that the government will grant the same freedom to Lu and the twenty-eight other journalists who still remain behind bars.'

(www.iht.com, 5 February 2008)

The editor of a Chinese newspaper known for its aggressive reporting has been released early from prison after serving four years on corruption charges ... Yu Huafeng left prison on Friday [8 February] ... Yu was the third prominent journalist detained in China to gain release this month [February], following Li Changqing, the former editor of *Fuzhou Daily*, and Ching Cheong, a Hong Kong-based correspondent for Singapore's *The Straits Times*, newspaper ... Yu was arrested in 2004 after his newspaper reported the beating to death of a man in detention that prompted the government to limit some police powers. The newspaper also broke the news of a case of SARS before Beijing reported it to the WTO. While Yu and a colleague, Li Minying, were sentenced for embezzlement and graft, many believed the charges were trumped up by vengeful officials who had been embarrassed by the reports ... Yu was originally given a twelve-year sentence, but that was twice reduced. Li Minying was released last year [2007] ... Earlier this month [February] democracy activist and anti-corruption campaigner Lu Gengsong was sentenced to four years in prison on subversion charges, and well-known dissident Hu Jia formally arrested on a charge of inciting subversion.

(www.iht.com, 9 February 2008)

Yang Chunlin, a human rights advocate, will stand trial for subversion after he called for human rights instead of the Beijing Olympic Games ... Yang ... an unemployed factory worker ... in past years wrote petitions, denounced government corruption and urged democratic reform of the one-party state. Last year [2007] he helped organize villagers to sign a petition demanding return of disputed land. Yang declared: 'We do not want the Olympics, we want human rights.'

(www.iht.com, 13 February 2008)

A Chinese human rights lawyer ... Teng Biao ... who has defended dissidents and urged stronger citizens' rights ahead of the 2008 Summer Olympics, is missing, family and colleagues said on Friday [7 March], fearful that he may have been secretly detained by the police.

(www.iht.com, 7 March 2008)

[On 8 March] Beijing security agents released … Teng Biao … after detaining him two days earlier without notice and forcing him to endure intensive questioning at an unknown location, the [human rights] lawyer said … His whereabouts had been a mystery since he called his wife Thursday night [6 March] to say he would be home within twenty minutes. Instead, he never arrived … In December [2007] a friend of Teng's named Hu Jia was detained and later charged with subversion … Last year [2007] Teng and Hu co-wrote a public letter criticizing the Communist Party as having failed to meet its Olympic promises to improve human rights … In the essay Teng and Hu said: 'The Olympic Games will be held in a country where there are no elections, no freedom of religion, no independent courts, no independent trade unions; where demonstrations and strikes are prohibited' … Teng has also written other essays critical of the party.

(www.iht.com, 9 March 2008)

The [US] State Department no longer considers China one of the world's worst human rights violators … Its annual human rights report [was] released Tuesday [12 March] … on more than 190 countries … The report dropped China from a list of ten countries that it deemed the worst offenders: North Korea, Myanmar, Iran, Syria, Zimbabwe, Cuba, Belarus, Uzbekistan, Eritrea and Sudan.

(www.iht.com, 12 March 2008)

A Chinese activist who circulated an open letter titled 'We want human rights, not the Olympics' was sentenced Monday [24 March] to five years in prison … Court security shocked Yang Chunlin repeatedly with electric batons after the twenty-minute hearing when he tried to speak with family members, the China-based Civil Rights and Livelihood Watch said in a statement … Yang had been convicted of subverting the power of the state, a charge that authorities commonly use to clamp down on opposition activists … Yang had gathered more than 10,000 signatures, mostly from farmers, for the petition that pushed for greater protections for human rights ahead of the Olympics that begin on 8 August.

(www.iht.com, 24 March 2008)

Yang Chunlin … an activist who had petitioned for land rights … was shocked with electric batons when the police scuffled with his family, his lawyer said. Yang had gathered more than 10,000 signatures for an open letter titled 'We want human rights, not the Olympics'. Most of the signatures came from farmers demanding redress for land taken from them by officials for development … Last month [February] a court sentenced a democracy activist, Lu Gengsong, to four years in prison for 'inciting to subvert state power'. Another dissident, Hu Jia, was tried on the same charge last week but has not been sentenced.

(www.iht.com, 24 March 2008)

> On Wednesday [2 April] UK-based rights group Amnesty International accused Beijing of carrying out a 'wave of repression' ahead of the Olympic Games. The authorities were targeting those who criticized the government in a bid to present a stable and harmonious image when the Games began in August, the group said.
>
> (www.bbc.co.uk, 3 April 2008)

'Hu Jia was convicted of "inciting subversion of state power and the socialist system" ... and jailed for three-and-a-half years. He has long campaigned for the environment, religious freedom and for the rights of people with HIV and AIDS' (www.bbc.co.uk, 3 April 2008).

> A court on Thursday [3 April] sentenced ... Hu Jia ... to three-and-a-half years in prison [the maximum being a five-year term] after ruling that his critical essays and comments about Communist Party rule amounted to inciting subversion, his lawyer said ... Xinhua, the government news agency, reported that: 'Hu spread malicious rumours and committed libel in an attempt to subvert the state's political power and socialist system' ... China's subversion laws, like those over state secrets, are deliberately vague and grant prosecutors considerable leeway in determining 'subversive' speech – even though freedom of speech is included in the Chinese constitution.
>
> (www.iht.com, 3 April 2008)

'Hu was convicted of charges of "inciting subversion of state power", based on internet articles he had written and interviews he gave to foreign media, said his lawyer' (www.iht.com, 3 April 2008).

> China's highest court overturned 15 per cent of all death sentences in the first half of this year [2008], an official newspaper said yesterday [27 June], although the number of executions remains a state secret ... The court took back the right of final review from lower courts last year [2007]. Most were overturned for lack of evidence or because they were 'inappropriate', the *China Daily* quoted [the judge as saying].
>
> (*FT*, 28 June 2008, p. 6)

> The police in Beijing blocked dissident lawyers from attending a meeting with a pair of visiting US congressmen, the lawmakers and a human rights group said Tuesday [1 July]. Chris Smith of New Jersey and Frank Wolf of Virginia had planned to dine with the group on Sunday [29 June], but the police either detained the lawyers beforehand or placed them under house arrest, they said ... Smith and Wolf also said they presented a list of 734 political prisoners to Li Zhaoxing, chairman of the national legislature's foreign affairs committee and a former foreign minister. Smith said they asked Li to work for the release of the prisoners. Wolf, who like Smith has long been active on Chinese human rights issues, called the list the 'most extensive and complete' of its kind ever compiled.
>
> (www.iht.com, 1 July 2008)

The military trainers who came to Guantanamo Bay in December 2002 based an entire interrogation class on a chart showing the effects of 'coercive management techniques' for possible use on prisoners, including 'sleep deprivation'. 'prolonged constraint' and 'exposure'. What the trainers did not say, and may not have known, was that their chart had been copied verbatim from a 1957 Air Force study of Chinese communist techniques used during the Korean War to obtain confessions, many of them false, from American prisoners.

(www.iht.com, 2 July 2008)

One of China's longest-held political prisoners was released Tuesday [26 August] after serving sixteen years of a twenty-year sentence for setting up a political party in defiance of a ban by the communist authorities … Hu Shigen, fifty-three, a former lecturer at the Beijing Languages Institute, helped found the China Freedom and Democracy Party in 1991 … Hu was arrested in 1992 for planning to commemorate victims of the military crackdown on pro-democracy demonstrators in Tiananmen Square on 4 June 1989. He was convicted of counter-revolution, or subversion, in 1994 for setting up the political party and an independent labour union; he was sentenced along with more than ten co-defendants. Hu was given the heaviest sentence of the group. Kang Yuchun, a doctor, received seventeen years and Liu Jingsheng, a former chemical worker, was given fifteen years. Both Kang and Liu have been freed. Hu may not be interviewed by reporters because he is deprived of political rights for four more years.

(www.iht.com, 26 August 2008)

Hu Jia won the EU's top human rights prize Thursday [23 October] despite a warning from Beijing that his selection would seriously harm relations … Hu was selected by members of the European parliament from a shortlist of three that also included candidates from Belarus and Congo for the Sakharov Prize.

(www.cnn.com, 23 October 2008)

Hu Jia was chosen by the European Parliament as this year's recipient of the Sakharov Prize for Freedom of Thought, despite warnings from Beijing that his selection would harm relations with the EU. Last year [2007] Hu testified via video link before a hearing of the European Parliament about the human rights situation in China. Weeks later Hu was jailed and later sentenced to three-and-a-half years in prison on a conviction for subversion based on his critical writings about Communist Party rule … His selection comes after he had been considered a front-runner for the Nobel Peace Prize, which was awarded to the former president of Finland, Martti Ahtisaari … Song Zhe, the Chinese ambassador to the EU, wrote a critical letter to the president of the European Parliament on 16 October: 'If the European Parliament should award this prize to Hu Jia, that would inevitably hurt the Chinese people once again and bring serious damage to China–EU relations.'

(www.iht.com, 23 October 2008)

> A foreign ministry spokesman: 'We express strong dissatisfaction at the decision by the European Parliament to issue such an award to a jailed criminal in China, in disregard of our repeated representations' ... Song Zhe (China's ambassador to the EU): 'Not recognizing China's progress on human rights and insisting on confrontation will only deepen the misunderstanding between the two sides and is not conducive to the promotion of the cause of world human rights.'
>
> (www.bbc.co.uk, 23 October 2008)

'[According to Human Rights Watch] at least twenty-six Chinese journalists are in prison due to their work, many on ambiguous charges including "revealing state secrets" and "inciting subversion"' (www.feer.com, 31 October 2008).

> China reacted angrily Monday [24 November] to a United Nations report that says the government tortures political and criminal prisoners, calling its authors biased and driven by a political agenda. The report, issued Friday [21 November] by the UN Committee Against Torture, documents widespread abuse in the Chinese legal system, one that often gains convictions through forced confessions. The report recounts Chinese use of 'secret prisons' and the widespread harassment of lawyers who take on human rights cases. It also criticizes the government's extralegal system of punishment, known as reeducation through labour, that metes out prison terms to dissidents without judicial review ... The report was written by a ten-member committee of independent experts ... Last week the government reacted angrily to a report from the US Congress that criticized China for failing to fulfil its pledge to improve human rights and lift media restrictions leading up to and during the Olympics ... The report says: 'Illegal detentions and harassment of dissidents and petitioners followed the Chinese government and Communist Party's instructions to officials to ensure a "harmonious" and dissent-free Olympics. Individuals detained for circulating a "We Want Human Rights, Not Olympics" petition are now serving sentences in prison and "reeducation through labour" centres' ... On 13 November Guo Quan, an associate professor at Nanjing Normal University, was detained on suspicion of 'inciting subversion of state power' after he established an independent political party, according to human rights advocates. A day earlier Liu Xueli, an activist from Henan province who sought a protest permit during the Olympics, was sentenced to reeducation through labour. On Friday [21 November] a court in Chengdu handed down a three-year sentence to Chen Daojun, a journalist and political activist who was convicted of 'inciting to subvert state power'. Chen was sentenced in May after he published a series of articles on the Tibetan quest for greater autonomy and a spate of anti-Western demonstrations that erupted across the country after the Olympic torch relay was disrupted in Paris, London and San Francisco. Although prosecutors accused Chen of slandering the Communist Party, his lawyer suggested that the authorities were particularly

irked by Chen's participation in a demonstration this year [2008] opposing the construction of a petrochemical plant near Chengdu.

(www.iht.com, 24 November 2008; *IHT*, 25 November 2008, p. 6)

Local officials in Shandong province have apparently found a cost-effective way to deal with gadflies, whistle blowers and all manner of muckraking citizens who dare to challenge the authorities: dispatch them to the local psychiatric hospital. According to an investigative report published Monday [8 December] by a state-owned newspaper [*The Beijing News*], security officials in Xintai city have been institutionalizing residents who persist in their personal campaigns to expose corruption or the seizure of property. ... Although China is not known for the kind of systematic psychiatric abuse that occurred in the Soviet Union, human rights monitors say forced institutionalizations are not uncommon in smaller cities ... In recent years practitioners of Falun Gong, the banned spiritual movement, have complained of coerced hospitalization and one of China's best known dissidents, Wang Wanxing, spent thirteen years in a police-run psychiatric facility under conditions he described as abusive.

(*IHT*, 9 December 2008, p. 2)

Hundreds of Chinese activists issued a new public call for greater democratic freedoms on Tuesday [9 December], one day before the sixtieth anniversary of the UN Convention on Human Rights, but the police detained two of the signatories before it was even issued ... The on-line statement – called Charter '08 and signed by a diverse group of more than 300 [303] lawyers, writers, scholars and artists – represents an unusual open declaration calling for change ... The statement proposed nineteen measures to improve human rights in China, including promoting an independent legal system, calling for freedom of association and ending the monopoly of one-party rule.

(www.iht.com, 9 December 2008)

Charter '08 [is] a political manifesto that calls for an end to one-party rule, free elections, the rehabilitation of dissidents, religious freedom and an end to Communist Party interference in the courts. The manifesto [was] signed by 303 academics, economists, writers, lawyers and journalists ... Charter '08 comes at a time of growing economic uncertainty ... Already seventy-seven signatories of the charter – who now number 7,000 – have been questioned by the authorities.

(www.iht.com, 6 January 2009)

A number of observers inside and outside China see the Charter '08 initiative as the boldest challenge to the rule of the Communist Party since the 1989 Tiananmen Square protest. Among others, the signatories of Charter '08 are urging Chinese leaders to adopt a republican constitution with the separation of legislative, executive and judicial powers, to hold direct elections at all levels of government, and to guarantee citizens' freedom of expression, assembly and religion … The document links the 'massacre of pro-democracy student protesters' with China's failure to live up to the ideals of the Universal Declaration of Human Rights … Increasingly worried about a sickly economy sowing social unrest, the government is tightening state control over the media. Its main aim appears to be to smother dissemination of politically sensitive discussions and information on the internet.

(www.economist.com, 8 January 2009)

The document, signed by more than 2,000 Chinese citizens, was conceived and written in conscious admiration of the founding of Charter '77 in Czechoslovakia, where, in January 1977, more than 200 Czech and Slovak intellectuals formed a 'loose, informal and open association of people … united by the will to strive individually and collectively for respect for human and civil rights in our country and throughout the world'. The Chinese document calls not for ameliorative reform of the current political system but for an end to some of its essential features, including one-party rule, and their replacement with a system based on human rights and democracy. The prominent citizens who have signed the document are both from outside and inside the government, and include not only well known dissidents and intellectuals, but also middle-level officials and rural leaders … They want Charter '08 to serve as a blueprint for fundamental political change in China in the years to come.

(*The New York Review*, 15 January–11 February 2009, p. 54)

(The full text of Charter '08 can be found on pp. 54–6.)

Police detained dozens of human rights protesters who had gathered outside the ministry of foreign affairs in Beijing. China is planning to publish its first assessment of human rights in the coming months. However, about forty people gathered outside the ministry protested that ordinary Chinese citizens would not be allowed to contribute to it. The event came on the sixtieth anniversary of the UN Declaration of Human Rights.

(www.bbc.co.uk, 10 December 2008)

China marked International Human Rights Day on Wednesday [10 December] with newspaper editorials and television commentaries hailing the country's 'unremitting efforts' and 'non-stop progress' in promoting free speech and individual rights. It was also a busy day for public security officials, who were dispatched to quell a protest of about forty people who rallied outside the gated headquarters of the foreign ministry in Beijing. After calling for free elections and demanding a crackdown on corruption for about thirty minutes, the demonstrators were herded on to buses and taken away. For Liu Xiaobo, one of the most high profile dissidents in China, Wednesday also marked the third day of detention for what friends and relatives say was his role in drafting a bold public letter that demands political, legal and constitutional reform. The document, published on the internet and signed by 303 Chinese academics, artists, farmers and lawyers, was released to coincide with the sixtieth anniversary of the Universal Declaration of Human Rights, a product of the United Nations and a foundation for human rights laws around the world. In recent days the Chinese police have also detained several other signers, including Zhang Zuhua, a rights activist … The state-run *China Daily* marked Human Rights Day with a sprawling opinion piece by Wang Chen, minister of the State Council Information Office. The full-page article documents China's long pursuit of human rights, noting that the country has 229 laws and 600 administrative decrees that protect individual human rights. In 2004, Wang wrote, China added 'respecting and protecting human rights' into the constitution. He wrote: 'I firmly believe that so long as we unswervingly implement the constitutional principle of respecting and protecting human rights, constantly improve democracy and the rule of law, our society will become more harmonious and people will live a still better life.'

(www.iht.com, 10 December 2008)

More than 160 prominent writers, scholars and human rights advocates outside mainland China have signed an open letter to President Hu Jintao asking him to release a well known intellectual … Liu Xiaobo … who was detained earlier this month. The letter was posted on the internet on Tuesday [23 December] … Among the writers signing the letter are three Nobel laureates in literature … as well as other scribes who regularly champion freedom of expression … Just as notable is the fact that an array of foreign China scholars have signed the petition … Some of the scholars who signed the petition are already on the Chinese government's blacklist, while others still have regular access to the country … Well known scholars in Hong Kong … also signed the letter … Liu, a fifty-three-year-old critic and dissident, was taken by security officers from his home on the night of 8 December and has not been heard from since … He was one of the driving forces behind Charter '08, a bold manifesto demanding democratic reforms and accountability from the Communist Party that was signed by more than 300 Chinese from various backgrounds and recently posted on the internet. Other people who signed the manifesto have also been detained and questioned by the authorities. All except Liu have been released … His wife and family members have received no word of his whereabouts or condition … The letter notes although Liu was twice detained for several years, he has never been convicted of any crime.

(www.iht.com, 23 December 2008; *IHT*, 24 December 2008, p. 7)

'Human Rights Watch, which released the letter, said Liu Xiaobo's detention was the most significant Chinese dissident case in a decade' (www.bbc.co.uk, 23 December 2008).

Liu Xiaobo is under 'residential surveillance' … house arrest … at a secret location in Beijing, human rights groups say. The measure generally precedes a trial ... Until now nothing had been heard of the former professor since his detention by police on 8 December.

(www.bbc.co.uk, 2 January 2008)

The government is moving to crush a group of prominent dissidents and intellectuals that has released a rallying call for democracy, human rights and rule of law. The group of about 300 writers, peasant farmers, students, professors, journalists, economists, and political activists from across the country all signed a document, known as Charter '08, that provides a detailed and wide-ranging blueprint for peaceful political, legal and economic reform in China. Since then nearly 7,000 Chinese and foreign intellectuals inside and outside the country have signed Charter '08, which warns of 'the possibility of a violent conflict of disastrous proportions' if Beijing does not move quickly to reform the one-party authoritarian state. Chinese intellectuals and dissidents are calling the document the most significant of its kind for at least a decade and possibly since the 1989 Tiananmen Square protests. Its name is a reference to Charter '77, the 1977 call for human rights issued by dissidents in former Czechoslovakia ... Since it has begun circulating one of the organizers has been detained without charge and friends and relatives had no word of his whereabouts until yesterday [2 January] ... Liu Xiaobo's wife was allowed to meet him on the outskirts of Beijing yesterday [2 January] and was told he was being held under house arrest at an undisclosed location, according to rights groups ... At least seventy of the charter's 303 original signatories have been summoned or interrogated by police, and China's powerful Central Propaganda Department has warned all domestic media not to interview or carry articles by anyone who signs the charter. The interrogations gathered momentum this week and all those called in have been ordered to retract their support for the charter ... Signatories include mid-level government officials and Communist Party academics. The charter was made public through the internet on 10 December to mark the sixtieth anniversary of the Universal Declaration of Human Rights ... Senior officials have shown increasing concern over the potential for unrest as a result of lay-offs and crumbling growth. The charter could serve as a rallying call for up to 1.5 million unemployed recent graduates.

(*FT*, 3 January 2009, p. 1)

Charter '08 calls for all Chinese citizens inside and outside the government to embrace the 'rapid establishment of a free, democratic and constitutional country' and the end of one-party authoritarian rule by the Communist Party. Many of the signatories are not known for their radical views or political activism ... Charter '08: 'As these conflicts and crises grow ever more intense ... the decline of the current system has reached the point where change is no longer optional' ... All mention of the charter in Chinese is blocked from websites, search engines and even emails. Propaganda officials have banned domestic media from interviewing any signatories or

> publishing any of their work. According to Amnesty International, the authorities now consider the charter a 'counter-revolutionary platform' … Xu Youyu, Professor of Philosophy at the Chinese Academy of Social Sciences, a government think-tank, was asked by a senior academy official for details of the charter, and then told the document was illegal and ordered to retract his signature… Professor Xu Youyu: 'I absolutely refuse to retract my support for this document' … Beijing moved yesterday [2 January] to silence parents of victims of the poisoned milk scandal, underscoring the determination to quell unauthorized action in response to social and economic problems … Parents of children killed when their schools collapsed in the 12 May Sichuan earthquake … [said] this week they had been warned that continuing to pursue compensation and talking to foreign journalists were illegal activities that would land them in jail. China has no such laws, according to rights groups and lawyers.
>
> (*FT*, 3 January 2009, p. 5)

'Chinese law states that foreign reporters need only the consent of their interviewees, not the police' (www.bbc.co.uk, 5 January 2009).

> Charter '08 called for democracy and the rule of law in China … It condemned recent economic modernization efforts as having 'stripped people of their rights', and called for political reform and a new, liberal, democratic constitution … The writer Wen Kejian has been detained … Police have also ransacked the Beijing home of Zhang Zuhua, one of the main authors of the charter, confiscating his passport as well as his computers, books and notebooks. Professor Xu Youyu, a leading philosopher at the Chinese Academy of Sciences, has been told by police to retract his signature … [China has also] cracked down on citizens who have campaigned against other abuses … [such as] parents of children affected by the recent tainted milk scandal … Parents of children who died in collapsed schools during the Sichuan earthquake have been told to stop talking to foreign journalists.
>
> (www.guardian.co.uk, 4 January 2009)

('[According to] Zhang Zuhua, a political theorist who helped … draft Charter '08 … considerably more than 8,000 Chinese citizens have joined the original 303 signers': www.iht.com, 1 May 2009.)

'[Although] Bao Tong … seventy-six … one of the highest officials imprisoned after the Tiananmen Square protests … still lives under house arrest … [he has] been able to publish a series of essays calling for political change' (*IHT*, 7 January 2009, p. 6).

> A high profile Chinese lawyer demanded Wednesday [7 January] that the government open its books to the public, in an unusually direct display of the legal activism that the Communist Party sees as a growing threat to its rule. Yan Yiming, an attorney who has made his reputation taking on companies that misled investors, presented an application to the finance ministry headquarters demanding that it publish details of its 2008 expenditures and

2009 budget. China's Communist Party discloses only the barest outline of its spending plans to a submissive parliament every year. Yan wants the government to live up to its pledges of transparency and accountability, especially with so much of the nation's faltering economic fortunes now resting on state spending plans ... In a second application Yan requested that the National Development and Reform Commission, China's top economic planning body, open to public scrutiny its management of the 4 trillion yuan ($585.5 billion) economic stimulus package recently unveiled by Beijing. His challenges will test landmark access-to-information rules that came into effect last year [2008]. The regulations, the first of their kind in China, require that governments disclose information about issues affecting the public interest in a bid to combat rampant corruption and discourage cover-ups enabled by often secretive decision-making ... If his application fails he said he may file a lawsuit against the ministry, something that no one has ever attempted ... Yan first caused a stir in 1998 when he tried to sue a state-owned television maker in Sichuan. As the legal environment evolved to give more protection to shareholders, he won a string of cases against firms that had falsified financial information ... His law firm earned more than 10 million yuan in 2007, placing him in the elite rank of independent lawyers in China.

(www.iht.com, 7 January 2009)

In December [2008] more than 300 of the country's most prominent activists issued a wide-ranging appeal for democratic reform. On 12 January a group of them were at it again ... with a demand for a boycott of national state-owned television ... Charter '08 ... issued online in early December ... was initially signed by 303 intellectuals ... Organizers say that thousands more have added their names (by sending their details to an email address), although the identities of many are difficult to verify ... Chinese internet service providers [have] removed postings about the document. A blog-hosting service, Bullog, home to several personal sites supportive of the Charter, was shut down ... Among the twenty-two people who signed the petition [on 12 January] are seven, including its drafter, Ling Cangzhou, from Charter '08's first group of signatories. The petition accuses state broadcaster CCTV of playing down reports about protests and other negative news.

(*The Economist*, 17 January 2009, p. 52)

A veteran democracy activist has been sentenced to six years in jail for helping set up an opposition party ... A court in Hangzhou sentenced Wang Rongqing on charges of 'subversion of state power' ... Wang had helped to set up a political group called the China Democracy Party in the late 1990s.

(www.bbc.co.uk, 8 January 2009)

In China ... British medical journal *The Lancet* claimed 90 per cent of the organs for its 11,000 annual transplants come from executed prisoners.

> The government claimed in 2007 that it had curbed the practice, anticipating criticisms in the 2008 Beijing Olympics.
>
> (www.feer.com, 7 January 2009)

> [There is an] increasing assertiveness of advocacy groups in pushing China's government to follow its own rules and account to the public for its actions … [China is seeking] to expand its co-operation with non-governmental organizations in alleviating poverty, stemming the spread of AIDS and halting environmental degradation … The *China Statistical Yearbook* counted 386,916 non-governmental organizations at the end of 2007 without defining what the category encompasses.
>
> (www.iht.com, 13 January 2009; *IHT*, 14 January 2009, p. 2)

> 'Black jails' [are] detention centres holding protesters without official procedures or right to appeal … [They are] against the law. But local officials call them study classes … Tens of thousands of citizens every year travel to Beijing to complain at government 'petitions and appeals' offices that promise to help settle citizens' grievances.
>
> (www.iht.com, 9 February 2009)

> The government plans to hand out $6.6 billion to Xinhua, the official state news agency, and China Central Television (CCTV) to expand abroad [it was reported in January]. CCTV will start Russian and Arabic channels this year [2009] to supplement English, Spanish and French programming. Xinhua will add to its more than 100 foreign bureaus and China will get its second official English language daily [it was reported on 14 January].
>
> (www.iht.com, 17 February 2009; *IHT*, 18 February 2009, p. 2)

> China has submitted its first report on its human rights record for review by the UN Human Rights Council … The report will be reviewed by a three-country panel [Nigeria, India and Canada], which will then make recommendations by Wednesday [11 February] … All UN member states are expected to report at regular intervals on their human rights record under the newly launched UPR process.
>
> (www.bbc.co.uk, 9 February 2009)

'Under the new system … the Universal Periodic Review (UPR) mechanism … all UN member states are to be reviewed once every four years' (www.feer.com, 22 February 2009).

> The State Department issued a report sharply critical of Beijing's human rights record … The 2008 Country Reports of Human Rights Practices: 'The government of China's human rights record remained poor and worsened in some areas … [Chinese authorities] committed extra-judicial killings and torture, coerced confessions of prisoners and used forced labour … [There has been] severe cultural and religious repression [of minorities in Tibet and

other regions]' ... [There has been] increasing harassment and detention of dissidents and activists who signed a petition calling for respect of human rights.

(www.cnn.com, 26 February 2009)

'China's human rights record worsened in some areas in 2008, including the repression of dissidents and of minorities in Tibet, the report said' (www.bbc.co.uk, 26 February 2009).

> The State Department document ... an annual US State Department report on global human rights ... singled out China, Russia, Zimbabwe, Egypt and a handful of other countries as states where human rights conditions had deteriorated during 2008 ... The section on China particularly criticized the government's treatment of its Tibetan and Uighur minorities and what it termed 'increased detention and harassment of dissidents and petitioners' The document stated that as many as 218 Tibetans died in the violence, far more than the twenty-one civilian deaths claimed by the Chinese authorities, and it cited 'numerous reports that the government or its agents committed unlawful or arbitrary killings' during the protests. It also referred to reports that as many as 1,100 Tibetans had disappeared after the violence, their whereabouts still unknown, including one 'highly revered' Tibetan Buddhist leader, Phurbu Tsering Rinpoche of Kardze ... The report also charged that China had stepped up the repression of dissidents and petitioners, especially near the time of the Olympics, and that it muzzled both the state-controlled press and potential critics to silence any negative portrayal of the government during the Games ... But it also offered scattered instances of approval of Chinese human rights policies. The number of non-governmental; organizations in China rose more than 9 per cent in 2007, the last year for which records are available, despite harsh restrictions on the groups, the department stated. China also 'experimented with various forms of public oversight of government' from phone hotlines to public hearings on proposed legislation, in an effort to give citizens some say in policies.
>
> (www.iht.com, 26 February 2009)

> The family of one of China's most prominent dissidents surfaced in America after being spirited out of China. Geng He, wife of Gao Zhisheng, a lawyer whose causes included disgruntled investors and the outlawed Falun Gong, made the trip in January [2009]. She paid human traffickers to smuggle her and her two children across south-east Asia by motorbike.
>
> (*Guardian*, 14 March 2009, p. 18)

> The government insists there are fewer than 2,500 cases of human trafficking each year, a figure that includes both women and children. But advocates for abducted children say there are hundreds of thousands ... Although some are sold to buyers in Singapore, Malaysia and Vietnam, most of the boys are purchased domestically by families desperate for a male heir, parents of abducted children and some law enforcement officials who have

investigated the matter say. The demand is especially strong in rural areas of south China, where a tradition of favouring boys over girls and the country's strict family planning policies have turned the sale of children into a thriving business … Peng Gaofeng, who started an ad hoc group for parents of stolen children, said some of the girls were sold to orphanages. They are the lucky ones who often end up in the United States or Europe after adoptive parents pay fees to orphanages that average $5,000. The unlucky ones, especially older children, who are not in demand by families, can end up as prostitutes or indentured labourers. Some of the children begging or hawking flowers in major Chinese cities are in the employ of criminal gangs that abducted them … The reluctance of police to investigate such cases has a variety of explanations. Kidnappers often single out the children of migrant workers because they are transients who may fear the local police and whose grievances are not treated as high priorities. Moreover, the police in China's authoritarian bureaucracy are rarely rewarded for responding to crimes affecting people who do not have much political clout. Mr Peng said the police prefer not to even open a missing persons inquiry because unsolved cases make them appear inefficient.

(www.iht.com, 5 April 2009; *IHT*, 6 April 2009, pp. 1, 8)

China's cabinet released on Monday [13 April] what it called the country's first national human rights action plan, a lengthy document promising a wide range of civil liberties that are often neglected and sometimes systematically violated in China. The rights China promised to protect under the two-year plan include the right to a fair trial, the right to participate in government decisions and the right to learn about and question government policies. It calls for measures to discourage torture, such as requiring interrogation rooms to have designs that physically separate interrogators from the accused. There are also specific protections for children, women, senior citizens, ethnic minorities and people with disabilities … The document does not phase out China's extensive and controversial system of administrative detention, which gives broad powers to local law enforcement officials, including the ability to send people to prison camps for 'reeducation through labour' without a trial. And while the document guarantees a wide range of rights to detainees and petitioners, there is no promise to close unregistered jails that municipal and provincial governments have set up in Beijing and elsewhere to detain petitioners who want to present their grievances to higher levels of government. The 'National Human Rights Action Plan 2009–2010' emphasizes economic and social rights instead, such as a 'right of urban and rural residents to a basic standard of living' … There is a promise that unemployment will remain below 5 per cent in 2009 and 2010 for urban residents who remain in the communities in which they are registered to live and do not try to migrate in search of better jobs. The plan does call for China to go considerably further in areas where it has already begun making changes, such as releasing more information about

> government decision-making, and to extend to the countryside policies that so far have mainly benefited cities.
>
> (www.iht.com, 13 April 2009)

'A court on Thursday [16 April] ordered the release of a lawyer … Liu Yao … on parole after reducing his prison sentence from two years to eighteen months' (www.ft.com, 16 April 2009).

> China says it is to tighten control of its prisons after cases of suspicious deaths in detention came to light. About fifteen people have died in police detention this year, according to widespread media reports … The authorities were reporting just five deaths a few weeks ago … Senior judges and prosecutors will now inspect some of China's nearly 3,000 detention centres, where criminal suspects are held. The aim of the campaign is to prevent what officials call 'unnatural deaths' in the country's jails. It comes in addition to a campaign to improve the work of prison officers that was announced earlier this month.
>
> (www.bbc.co.uk, 19 April 2009)

> In the decade since the government began repressing Falun Gong, a crusade that human rights groups say has led to the imprisonment of tens of thousands of practitioners and claimed at least 2,000 lives, the world's attention has shifted elsewhere … But ten years on the war on Falun Gong remains unfinished. In the past year as many as 8,000 practitioners have been detained, according to experts on human rights, and at least 100 have died in custody … In recent months scores of practitioners have been given long prison terms … The group at its peak claimed millions of followers around China … The decision to ban the group entirely was made after 10,000 Falun Gong adherents staged a silent protest outside the gates of Zhongnanhai, the Communist Party's leadership compound in Beijing, to complain about reports in the state-run media that the group said were defamatory. Security forces apparently had no knowledge of the demonstration, which took place on 25 April 2009, and they began treating the group as a treat to national security.
>
> (www.iht.com, 28 April 2009; *IHT*, 29 April 2009, p. 5)

> Falun Gong practitioners in the United States estimate at least 100,000 adherents have been locked up in prison, psychiatric hospitals or 'reeducation through labour' camps in China's notorious gulag system since a vicious campaign to stamp it out began in July 1999. They say about 3,200 followers have been tortured to death while in custody, including more than 100 last year [2008].
>
> (*FT*, 10 June 2009, p. 10)

'Falun Gong has been treated most harshly. Supporters outside China claim 2,000 have died in custody since 1999, and the UN alleges that the group's members feature disproportionately among those who have suffered torture and abuse' (www.guardian.co.uk, 18 July 2009).

> The Falun Gong information centre, based in New York, says the Chinese government has carried out a violent campaign against practitioners over the last ten years. It claims more than 3,000 people have been killed and tens of thousands tortured in China's crackdown on the movement ... Although the group is banned in mainland China, it is legal in Hong Kong ... There have been demonstrations against China's crackdown on the movement in Hong Kong, Taiwan and the United States over recent days ... There are still people in the mainland who ignore their government's ban and continue to practise in secret.
>
> (www.bbc.co.uk, 22 July 2009)

> China is setting up a DNA database to help trace missing children ... Thousands of children in China are stolen or sold each year ... The children of migrant workers are usually targeted ... In a society that favours male heirs, it is often boys who are taken.
>
> (www.bbc.co.uk, 1 May 2009)

> After six months in detention ... Liu Xiaobo ... has been formally arrested and charged with subversion ... Xinhua: '[Liu Xiaobo has been arrested for] agitation activities, such as spreading of rumours and defaming of the government, aimed at subversion of the state and overthrowing the socialist system in recent years' ... Xinhua said Mr Liu had confessed during a preliminary police investigation ... Mr Liu was detained in December [2008] after signing Charter '08 ... Charter '08 initially had 303 signatories and now has more than 8,000.
>
> (www.iht.com, 24 June 2009)

> Dozens of prominent Chinese academics have signed a petition calling for the release of Liu Xiaobo ... In the petition the fifty-two signatories of the petition said his comments had been rational and constructive, and showed a sense of social responsibility.
>
> (www.bbc.co.uk, 26 June 2009)

> Government officials on Friday [17 July] shut down the office of a prominent lawyers' group known for taking on cases involving civil rights and corruption ... The group of voluntary lawyers, called *Gongmeng*, or Open Constitution Initiative, represented parents suing Sanlu Group, a large dairy company, over tainted milk that led to the deaths and illnesses of children across China in 2008. In May [2009] it released a report that said economic policies by the government had resulted in the marginalization of Tibetans over the decades ... In a separate government action, the licences of fifty-three lawyers in Beijing were cancelled.
>
> (www.iht.com, 18 July 2009)

'On Wednesday [29 July] the funder of *Gongmeng*, Xu Zhiyong, was taken into police custody' (www.iht.com, 30 July 2009).

> China's nascent legal rights movement ... has been shaken by the detention of a widely respected rights defender who has been incommunicado since

> the police led him away from his apartment twelve days ago … Xu Zhiyong … who has made a name representing migrant workers, death row inmates and the parents of babies poisoned by tainted milk … is accused of tax evasion … Teng Biao … a colleague … helped Mr Xu establish the Open Constitution Initiative, a six-year-old non-profit legal centre that the authorities closed last month [July] … Last week China's justice minister gave a speech saying lawyers should above all obey the Communist Party and help foster a harmonious society. To improve discipline, the minister said, all law firms in China would be sent party liaisons to 'guide their work'.
>
> (www.iht.com, 10 August 2009; *IHT*, 11 August 2009, pp. 1, 4)

'Xu Zhiyong has been formally arrested for tax evasion … He was seized from his home on 29 July' (www.ft.com, 18 August 2009).

> Prosecutors have charged Xu Zhiyong with tax evasion, his attorney said on Tuesday [18 August] … Mr Xu is a founder of the Open Constitution Initiative, known in Chinese as *Gongmeng*, a non-profit group that has often taken on high profile cases involving ordinary citizens' civil rights. The government shut down the organization's legal centre on 17 July, three days after accusing it of tax violations, and the police seized Mr Xu on 29 July … Mr Xu was formally charged on 12 August. Mr Xu could face seven years in prison if he is tried and convicted. The prosecutors now must seek an indictment, but that is widely considered a formality. The government's main accusation is that Mr Xu's group failed to pay taxes on a $100,000 grant from Yale that was earmarked for the legal centre … Mr Xu, a professor at Beijing's University of Posts and Telecommunications, has been an elected member of a local governing body, the People's Congress in Beijing's Haidian district, since 2003.
>
> (www.iht.com, 18 August 2009; *IHT*, 19 August 2009, p. 4)

> The incarceration of Xu Zhiyong … comes amid a nationwide crackdown before the sixtieth anniversary of the founding of communist rule on 1 October. Mr Xu is one of the few elected members of the Beijing branch of the National People's Congress.
>
> (www.thetimes.co.uk, 18 August 2009)

> Authorities unexpectedly released three political activists from detention on Sunday [23 August], including one whose case had drawn worldwide attention. Officials offered no reason for the releases, but they occurred one day after the new American ambassador to China, the former Utah governor Jon Huntsman, arrived in Beijing. The government did not say whether it has also suspended criminal tax-evasion charges that were made last week against one of the freed men, Xu Zhiyong, a well known public-interest lawyer, that could result in a prison sentence of seven years were he convicted … Mr Xu and a co-worker, Zhuang Lu, were released more than three weeks after they were seized in their homes on 29 July … Beijing authorities also released Ilham Tohti, an economist, internet activist and

ethnic Uighur who has been detained after deadly riots erupted in Xinjiang in early July ... Mr Tohti ran a website called Uighur Online, a popular forum for ethnic Uighurs ... to discuss issues important to them. After the July rioting Xinjiang's governor, Nur Bekri, charged that the site had helped foment the violence by spreading rumours.

(www.iht.com, 23 August 2009)

'Xu Zhiyong ... and Zhuang Lu, his assistant, were released on bail yesterday [23 August] ... Ilham Tohti ... who was detained shortly after the 5 July riots in Urumqi ... also returned home' (*FT*, 24 August 2009, p. 4).

A Chinese dissident active in the underground China Democracy Party has been sentenced to thirteen years for subversion. Xie Changfa was arrested after trying to organize the party's first national congress in the city of Changsha, Hunan province ... The China Democracy Party was set up in 1998, but has never been approved ... Chinese prosecutors accused Xie of plotting to overthrow China's socialist system and subvert state power ... Xie previously served two years in a reeducation through labour camp for inciting the spread of anti-revolutionary propaganda ... As well as the communist grouping, China has eight other political parties, although these do not seek power for themselves. They are supposed to advise the Chinese leadership, which uses their existence to claim that China is a democratic country.

(www.bbc.co.uk, 2 September 2009)

[Globally] more [journalists] are in jail than at any time since the Committee to Protect Journalists, a New York-based advocacy group, began keeping records ... [Currently] 174 [are being] held ... Iran now holds at least twenty-seven journalists, almost as many as China (thirty), and more than Cuba (twenty-five).

(*The Economist*, 5 September 2009, p. 70)

Harry Wu was condemned to life imprisonment when aged just twenty-one. He was sent to a *laogai*, a Chinese labour camp, for being a 'rightist counter-revolutionary'. He was incarcerated for nineteen years ... In 1957 came the events which defined his life. At the time the government was running the so-called One Hundred Flowers Campaign. Mao said: 'Letting a hundred flowers bloom and a hundred schools of thought contend is the policy for promoting the progress of the arts and the sciences and a flourishing culture in our land' ... But it was a disguised way of finding out who was for, and who was against, the communist revolution ... There are still 3 million inmates in China's labour camps.

(www.independent.co.uk, 20 September 2009)

A Chinese academic who launched a campaign for multi-party democracy has been sentenced to ten years in jail for 'subversion of state power' ... Guo Quan ... who founded a political party two years ago ... was sentenced on Friday [16 October] Mr Guo had published criticism of the government on the internet. He had also focused on the plight of peasants dispossessed in land conflicts and of laid-off factory workers.

(*FT*, 19 October 2009, p. 9)

Guo Quan [is] a former associate professor at Nanjing Normal University and a former judge ... [He] wrote a series of articles in 2007 and 2008 that discussed social problems in China. He also founded the New Democracy Party of China.

(*IHT*, 20 October 2009, p. 8)

Huang Qi has been sentenced to three years in prison for 'illegally holding state secrets'. Mr Huang was arrested after helping families whose children died during the earthquake in Sichuan in May last year [2008] ... Mr Huang was taken into custody in Chengdu in June 2008 and has been held in custody ever since ... Huang Qi has championed the rights of ordinary people for a decade and has previously been prosecuted.

(www.bbc.co.uk, 23 November 2009)

'Huang Qi received the maximum sentence for "illegally holding secret documents"' (www.cnn.com, 23 November 2009).

Liu Xiaobo was indicted Thursday [10 December] on charges of trying to subvert the state ... When President Obama visited China last month [November] ... US officials have given Chinese leaders a list of 'cases of concern' that included Mr Liu and eleven other political and religious activists who are currently imprisoned or facing charges.

(www.iht.com, 11 December 2009)

Charter '08 signers have tried to demonstrate their continued solidarity by issuing joint letters of protest. The most recent one, signed by 165 people, states that 'if Liu Xiaobo is found "guilty" that means each one of us is guilty and we have to shoulder the punishment together with Liu Xiaobo'.

(*IHT*, 12 December 2009, p. 7)

'The charge is "agitation activities, such as spreading of rumours and defaming of the government, aimed at subversion of the state and overthrowing the socialism system"' (www.iht.com, 18 December 2009).

'Liu Xiaobo ... has been charged with "inciting subversion" ... Last week 165 of the original [Charter '08] signatories on the mainland issued a further letter, headed "We are willing to share responsibility with Liu Xiaobo"' (www.guardian.co.uk, 13 December 2009).

'The EU and the United States have called for the immediate release of Liu Xiaobo ... Prosecutors decided to try [him] ... on charges of "inciting subversion of state power"' (www.bbc.co.uk, 15 December 2009).

A Chinese court on Friday [25 December] sentenced ... Liu Xiaobo ... to eleven years in prison for subversion ... The eleven-page verdict, largely a

> restatement of his indictment, was read out Friday … In addition to his prison term, Mr Liu will be deprived of his political rights for an additional two years, a penalty that will prevent him from writing or speaking out on a wide range of issues … Although Mr Liu had faced a fifteen-year sentence, legal experts and human rights advocates said the punishment was very harsh … Mr Liu's sentence was the longest for subversion charges in more than a decade … The trial on Wednesday [23 December] lasted two hours and was closed; his wife, Liu Xia, and more than two dozen diplomats from the United States, Canada and the EU were barred from the courtroom … In addition to helping create Charter '08, Mr Liu's charge for 'inciting subversion of state power' was based on six articles he wrote that were published on the internet outside of China … On Friday officials allowed the defendant and his wife to meet for ten minutes in a small room, although they were divided by a glass barrier.
>
> (www.iht.com, 25 December 2009; *IHT*, 26 December 2009, pp. 1, 5)

'Diplomats from Germany and Australia were among the two dozen people allowed to observe the "public" trial … [but] no one from the American embassy was admitted' (www.iht.com, 29 December 2009).

'It was the longest sentence … since the crime of inciting subversion was established in 1997' (www.thetimes.co.uk, 25 December 2009).

> Nearly a year after he was taken by the authorities, the only news of one of China's most tenacious civil rights lawyers has been that he 'went missing' after his arrest, friends and relatives said Friday [15 January 2010]. They say they have not seen or heard from the lawyer, Gao Zhisheng, a Nobel Peace Prize nominee, whose plight has been taken up by the US Congress, since he was taken from his home last February [4 February 2009]. When his brother inquired about his whereabouts in September [2009] a police official in Beijing explained he had gone missing, according to those who have spoken to the brother … Last January [2009] his wife and two children made a dramatic escape from China … The family … has since been granted asylum in the United States.
>
> (www.iht.com, 15 January 2010; *IHT*, 16 January 2010, p. 5)

> Gao Zhisheng … has been judged by the legal authorities and is 'where he should be' said a foreign ministry official making China's first public comment on the case … At a regular news conference Thursday [21 January] the foreign ministry spokesman indicated that Mr Gao was in custody.
>
> (*IHT*, 23 January 2010, p. 3)

'The Dui Hua Foundation, a US-based human rights group, said it had been told by the Chinese embassy in Washington that Gao Zhisheng was working in Urumqi, the capital of Xinjiang region' (www.guardian.co.uk, 14 February 2010).

Liaoning province ... in north-eastern China ... has become the first to execute convicts by injection rather than gunshot, state-run media reported Friday [11 December] ... China adopted injection as an alternative form of capital punishment in 1997, but gunshot is still predominantly used ... According to Amnesty International ... at least 2,390 people were executed around the world in 2008 ... [including] at least 1,718 executions in China ... Iran was second with 346. Saudi Arabia followed with 102 and the United States was fourth with thirty-seven.

(www.cnn.com, 11 December 2009)

China has intensified efforts over the past year to control what the media can say, a report by the International Federation of Journalists says. It says hundreds of regulations have been introduced since the Beijing Olympics in 2008 to restrict reporters writing on social unrest or scandals ... Foreign journalists encountered violence and their equipment was destroyed in some cases.

(www.bbc.co.uk, 31 January 2010)

Security agents in Sichuan province detained Liao Yiwu, a prominent author and critic of the government, as he prepared to fly on Monday [1 March] to a literary festival in Germany ... It was the thirteenth time Mr Liao had been prevented from leaving the country ... A poet, screenwriter and novelist, Mr Liao is one of China's best known and most outspoken writers. Many of his works tell stories of ordinary Chinese people, from prostitutes to a grave robber and a lavatory attendant, who have been left behind in the nation's rush to economic and political prominence. His 2008 book *The Corpse Walker* ... was published to international acclaim. His works are banned in China, but he has gained a large underground following, and pirated versions of his works can be found in some Chinese bookstores. Mr Liao was imprisoned for four years in the early 1990s after writing an epic poem, 'Massacre', which denounces the Chinese government's suppression of the 1989 Tiananmen Square protests.

(www.iht.com, 2 March 2010)

Releasing its annual report on human rights worldwide for 2009, the State Department said ... that practices in China were 'poor and worsening'. In reply, China accused Washington of hypocrisy, saying the US human rights record was 'terrible'. China said: 'It is also the main source of many human rights disasters worldwide ... [The United States should concentrate on] improving its own human rights.'

(*IHT*, 13 March 2010, p. 4)

Foreign minister Yang Jiechi (16 March): 'Gao Zhisheng has been sentenced on the charge of subverting state power' ... But it was not immediately clear whether that referred to an old charge, or a new one brought against Mr Gao ... Mr Gao was given a three-year prison sentence – suspended for five years – for inciting subversion in 2006, but Mr Yang's comment did not make it clear if new charges had since been brought.

(www.bbc.co.uk, 16 March 2010)

Religion: a chronology of developments since 3 May 2006

3 May 2006. 'The state-controlled Catholic Church in China installed on Wednesday [3 May] a second bishop over the objections of the Vatican' (www.iht.com, 3 May 2006).

> Pope Benedict XVI issued a condemnation of the official Chinese Catholic Church for having consecrated two bishops against the Vatican's wishes. The Vatican underscored its anger by noting that the act is punishable by excommunication, the church's severest censure … [The Pope made] it unusually clear that the church would not accept appointment of bishops by any institution other than the Vatican. He left no doubt in raising the possibility of excommunication, a rare and serious step that has not been carried out for such an offence since 1988 … Excommunication essentially exiles the guilty party from the church. In the case of clerics excommunication bans them from saying Mass and administering sacraments … For China the dispute is about retaining control over a potentially powerful institution with mass appeal at a time of rising social unrest. Though the number of Catholics in China is relatively small, China has a long history of protests that religious movements have helped bind together against the rule of fading dynasties … Most bishops in the official church in recent years have informally obtained the Vatican's blessing The Pope's spokesman: 'The Holy Father has learned of the news with profound displeasure. It is a grave wound to the unity of the church, for which, as it is noted, there are severe canonical sanctions … According to information received bishops and priests have been subjected to – on the part of entities external to the Church – strong pressure and to threats so that they would take part in the Episcopal ordinations' … Relations between Beijing and the Vatican deteriorated on Sunday [30 April], when the Chinese Catholic Patriotic Association arranged for the consecration of one of its senior officials, Ma Yinling, as the bishop of Kunming in south-western China, despite objections from the Vatican over whether he had the spiritual preparation for such a post. But the biggest blow seems to have been the consecration of Liu Xinhong on Wednesday [3 May] as bishop of Wuhu in Anhui province in eastern China, again after the Vatican had objected to whether Liu was a suitable choice.
> (www.iht.com, 4 May 2006; *IHT*, 5 May 2006, pp. 1, 7)

7 May 2006.

> The official Chinese Catholic Church named a new bishop on Sunday [7 May] – reportedly with papal approval … China's Catholics were forced to cut ties to the Vatican after the communist revolution in 1949. But the Holy See and China's church communicate informally and most Chinese bishops have received papal endorsement … The State Administration of Religious Affairs defended the earlier ordinations, saying that Beijing had informed the Vatican in advance but got no response – an apparent reference to the practice of agreeing on bishops through unofficial contacts … In Vietnam

> bishops are appointed [by the Vatican] after consultation with the government ... A US State Department report last week ranked China among eight 'countries of particular concern' that deny religious openness.
>
> (www.iht.com, 7 May 2006)

> Another Catholic bishop was consecrated in China on Sunday [7 May] in a ceremony approved by the Vatican ... For several years a tacit understanding has existed between the Vatican and Beijing under which candidates for becoming bishops have been vetted by both sides. At least five bishops have been approved since 2004 with such dual consent. The consecration on Sunday of Pei Junmin, a priest trained in Philadelphia, was a by-product of that system.
>
> (*IHT*, 8 May 2006, p. 8)

> Though the Vatican has no formal relations with China, the two sides have had an unspoken agreement in recent years under which Beijing has not objected when prospective bishops quietly sought approval from Rome ... On Sunday [14 May] the authorities in Fujian province are expected to hold an 'installation' ceremony for a bishop consecrated several year ago without Papal approval.
>
> (*IHT*, 13 May 2006, pp. 1, 6)

> [Ma Yinglin's] application and that of Liu Xinhong ... had been sent through back channels to Rome and, in a rare move, had even included a scheduled date for a February consecration. But the consecrations were rescheduled when Rome asked for a delay ... Rome apparently had doubts.
>
> (www.iht.com, 12 May 2006)

14 May 2006.

> [On 14 May China] installed a third bishop ... in defiance of Rome. Zhan Silu became bishop of the Mindong diocese in Fujian province ... His appointment ... has not been blessed by Pope Benedict ... Relations deteriorated in February when Pope Benedict elevated the Bishop of Hong Kong, Joseph Zen, an outspoken advocate of democracy for China, to cardinal ... There have been Christians in China since the eighth century. They form between 2 per cent and 4 per cent of the population.
>
> (*The Times*, 15 May 2006, p. 30)

'Like the two other bishops appointed in past weeks, Zhan Silu lacks the blessing of Pope Benedict XVI ... In the past five years Beijing and the Holy See reached an understanding that allowed prospective bishops to seek Vatican approval' (www.iht.com, 14 May 2006).

> The conflict between the Chinese state and the Holy See long predates the communist takeover in 1949 and Mao Zedong's edict two years later isolating the Chinese Catholics. It has, in fact, been simmering for centuries, ever since the first Papal envoy visited the Forbidden City in 1705 ... While the moral and political terms of the struggle are vastly different than what they

were 300 years ago, the fate of the 12 million Catholics in China still hangs in the balance.

(Liam Brockey, www.iht.com, 17 May 2006)

Buddhism ... has been established in China for more than 2,000 years ... [and] has a loose organizational structure and limited record of engaging in politics. It is estimated to have 100 million adherents but in China has a wider presence as it is also often intermixed with Taoism and folk deities.

(*IHT*, 29 May 2006, p. 6)

The fastest growing churches are the underground ones – usually evangelical without any specific denomination – that are independent of the government. The total number of Chinese Christians today probably exceeds 40 million and some estimates go far higher ... The government cracks down on the underground church, but inconsistently and not nearly as harshly as it prosecutes Falun Gong ... The security authorities do not normally bother to raid ordinary house churches or even spy on them much, but the police do apply pressure on those that are considered potential troublemakers.

(Nicholas Kristof, *IHT*, 26 June 2006, p. 6)

25 June 2006.

For the first time in more than five years an official Vatican delegation is visiting China and meeting with government officials, experts here [in Rome] said Wednesday [28 June] ... The Vatican delegation now in Beijing consists of two relatively senior officials ... They arrived last Sunday [25 June] and will remain until Saturday [1 July], meeting with 'mid-level' government officials ... The Vatican and China broke off diplomatic ties in 1951.

(www.iht.com, 28 June 2006)

Since the Regulation on Religious Affairs law was introduced in March 2005 provincial and local governments have begun a series of crackdowns on underground churches across China. The vaguely worded new rules call for local governments to 'standardize' the management of religion nationwide. The Chinese crackdown, which affects other faith [apart from Protestantism], especially Buddhism in Tibet and Islam in the far western Xinjiang province, comes at a time of booming growth in underground churches across the country. The right to practise any of the five recognized faiths – Buddhism, Catholicism, Taoism, Islam and Protestantism – is enshrined in the Chinese constitution ... Under Chinese law, however, all recognized faiths must be registered and approved by the government, and all are closely monitored and required to follow strict and frequently changing regulations.

(www.iht.com, 18 August 2006)

8 October 2006.

The Archbishop of Canterbury, Rowan Williams, has begun his first trip to China ... After Shanghai he will visit four other cities during his two-week stay ... Previous Archbishops of Canterbury, Robert Runcie and George Carey, visited China in 1983 and 1994 respectively ... The visit is being jointly hosted by the Three-Self Patriotic Movement/China Christian Council and the State Administration of Religious Affairs. The Archbishop is set to meet leaders of other registered religions .. including the Chinese Catholic Church ... Communist authorities in China only allow Christians to worship in state-sanctioned churches which come under strict government supervision. These churches have an estimated membership of about 16 million.

(www.bbc.co.uk, 8 October 2006)

November 2006.

The leader of a Christian sect and at least eleven of his subordinates have been executed for ordering the murder of members of a rival religious group, as authorities sought to suppress big underground churches that they deemed cults ... The founder of the Three Grades of Servants Church was put to death last week ... A crackdown on the secretive Protestant sect began in 2004. The case exposed internecine strife among underground churches as well as the determination of the authorities to crush religious groups that do not abide by the rules imposed on officially sanctioned religious organizations. Underground religious movements have become an enormously sensitive issue for the leadership since the Falun Gong spiritual group ... which espouses an idiosyncratic mix of traditional Chinese qigong, or self-healing, exercises and meditation ... organized a mass nationwide movement that Communist Party officials viewed as a threat to their hold on power in the late 1990s. Since that time police have condemned many churches, including Christian churches, as cults ... The relative backwardness of the countryside ... has proven fertile ground for religious groups that offer a mix of religious teaching, communal support, employment opportunities and even health care. Three Grades and another quasi-Protestant sect, Eastern Lightning, were among the largest charismatic and evangelical church groups ... [They] became archrivals in the early part of the decade as they competed to sign up adherents across north-eastern China ... There is a bull market in sects and cults competing for souls ... Government-sanctioned churches operate mainly in cities, where they can be closely monitored, and priests and ministers by law can preach only to those who come to them ... [In] government-licensed churches parishioners [must] be at least eighteen years old ... church members [must] register [and there is a] stipulation that Communist Party officials forswear Christianity.

(www.iht.com, 29 November 2006; *IHT*, 30 November 2006, p. 5)

30 November 2006.

China installed a new bishop Thursday [30 November] over the objections of the Vatican, prompting Cardinal Joseph Zen here [in Hong Kong] to issue a blistering statement accusing the mainland authorities of having threatened and kidnapped bishops to make them participate in the ritual. Zen, who is also the bishop of Hong Kong, said in a statement Thursday that the ordination was more serious than China's consecration of two bishops last spring [2006], because the Holy See specifically warned Beijing against further unapproved ordinations of bishops … Zen, granted considerable discretion by Pope Benedict XVI to speak out on issues involving the church on the mainland, also disclosed the existence of a secret delegation from the Vatican to Beijing after the spring ordinations. The cardinal said that the Chinese government had invited the delegation and had promised that it would not conduct any additional ordinations without Vatican approval.

(*IHT*, 1 December 2006, p. 4)

China's state administration for religious affairs, while describing Rome's objections as 'unreasonable', said in a statement on Sunday [3 December] that it favoured further dialogue to resolve differences over how to choose bishops to run the ninety-seven Roman Catholic dioceses in China … The government agency said: 'The Chinese government has a positive attitude toward improving relations with the Vatican, and we want a constructive dialogue on the issue of the consecration of bishops' … The Vatican said in a statement on Saturday [2 December] that Pope Benedict XVI was 'deeply pained' … [When] two other Chinese bishops [were consecrated in spring 2006] … a statement at the time said that the Pope 'has learned of the news with profound displeasure'.

(www.iht.com, 4 December 2006)

20 January 2007.

The Vatican has issued a measured statement on its future relations with China, saying it wants a 'respectful and constructive dialogue' to rebuild diplomatic ties but still noting the 'suffering' of Chinese Catholics … The statement spoke of 'following the road of a respectful and constructive dialogue with the governing authority to overcome the misunderstandings of the past' … The statement was issued Saturday [20 January 2007] after two days of high level talks at the Vatican on rebuilding relations with China. The statement said Pope Benedict XVI intended to write a special letter to Catholics in China, though it did not say when or hint at any message … The statement strongly praised the bravery of Catholics in China who are still loyal to Rome, rather than to the Chinese authorities. An 'official church' of 5 million Catholics, presided over by the government, exists alongside an underground church of 10 million. The Vatican statement 'noted, with deep recognition, the luminous testimony offered by bishops, priests and the faithful, who without ceding to compromises, have maintained their faith to the Seat of St Peter, at times even at the price of grave suffering.'

(www.iht.com, 21 January 2007)

The Pope himself did not attend [the meeting] … China welcomed the Vatican's new move to resolve their differences, calling it 'a step forward' …

China's state-sanctioned church has 4 million followers with millions more in groups loyal to the Vatican. China's state-run Chinese Patriotic Catholic Association welcomed the meeting and especially Pope Benedict XVI's decision to write a letter to China's 10 million Catholics. Association vice chairman Liu Bainian said: 'This is beneficial for China–Vatican relations. It is a step forward but we still have to see the concrete actions.'

(www.bbc.co.uk, 22 January 2007)

7 February 2007.

The number of religious believers could be three times higher than official estimates, according to a survey reported by state media. A poll of 4,500 people by Shanghai University professors found 31.4 per cent of people above the age of sixteen considered themselves religious. This suggests 300 million people nationwide could be religious, compared to the official figure of 100 million ... The official *China Daily* called their work the 'country's first major survey on religious beliefs'. The survey found that Buddhism, Taoism, Catholicism, Christianity and Islam are the country's five major religions – China considers Catholicism as separate to Christianity, which covers Protestantism. About 200 million believers 'are Buddhists, Taoists or worshippers of legendary figures such as the Dragon King and God of Fortune', the *China Daily* reported. The survey also found a significant rise in Christianity – accounting for 12 per cent of all believers, or 40 million, compared with the official figure of 16 million in 2005 ... [The survey found that] the average age of religious believers had fallen, with two-thirds of those in the polls who considered themselves religious aged between sixteen and thirty-nine. This is markedly different from the previous decade, when most religious believers were in their forties or older.

(www.bbc.co.uk, 7 February 2007)

[There has been] a resurgence of religious or quasi-religious activity across China that – notwithstanding occasional crackdowns – is transforming the social and political landscape of many parts of the countryside. Religion is also attracting many people in the cities, where the party's traditional atheist ideology has traditionally held sway. The resurgence encompasses ancient folk religions and ancestor worship, along with the organized religions of Buddhism, Taoism, Islam (among ethnic minorities) and most strikingly ... Christianity ... In the face of this onslaught the party is beginning to rethink its approach to religion. It now acknowledges that it may even have its uses ... Officially the party regards folk religion as superstition, the public practice of which is illegal. But in many rural areas officials now bend the rules ... Government officials are often fearful of triggering unrest by enforcing unpopular policies that are not vital to the party's interests ... Demonstrations in an official's jurisdiction can do far more damage to his career than turning a blind eye to popular religion – so long as such activity does not directly challenge the party ... Temples applying for official registration

> typically have to treat local officials to banquets. Officials … support temples that pay them respect and tribute; they also gain from taxes levied on merchants who do business at temple fairs. Policemen invited to maintain order at these occasions are paid with cash, good food and liquor … Officially there are more than 100 million religious believers in China … but experts say the real number is very much higher … In the far western province of Xinjiang the government worries that Islam in intertwined with ethnic separatism and keeps tighter rein … Some religions – Tibetan Buddhism, Islam as practised in Xinjiang, Catholicism and 'house church' Protestantism, which involves informal gatherings of believers outside registered churches – are still subject to tight controls … A seven-year crackdown on Falun Gong … is still being pursued with ruthless intensity … Officials are now encouraging a revival of Confucianism.
>
> (*The Economist*, 3 February 2007, pp. 23–5)

Official statistics published in 1997 provide the following figures for adherents: Buddhism, 100 million; Islam, 20 million; Taoism, not available; Protestantism, 16 million; Catholicism, 5 million (p. 24).

> The head of Hong Kong's Roman Catholic Church has urged the Vatican to end its search for a compromise with Beijing. Cardinal Joseph Zen told the BBC the ordinations last year [2006] of three bishops without Vatican approval were 'illegitimate' and 'acts of war'. Beijing's refusal to recognize the Vatican's authority has overturned two decades of compromise efforts, he said … The cardinal said China was waging an undeclared war against Catholics … Cardinal Zen: 'These three illegitimate ordinations … are acts of war against the church. So how can you say that we opt for confrontation? They are waging a war; they want to destroy the church' … He has previously said he has offered to resign from his position to help the Vatican establish ties with China … Pope Benedict XVI is due to make his position clear in the coming months … [A] letter [is] expected from the Pope by early April. The letter was promised after a Vatican meeting held in late January which Cardinal Zen attended.
>
> (www.bbc.co.uk, 9 February 2007)

> A recent poll by East China Normal University estimated that 31.4 per cent of Chinese aged sixteen or older are religious, putting the number of believers at roughly 400 million. In recent years official estimates had placed the number of believers at around 100 million.
>
> (*IHT*, 5 March 2007, p. 2)

> Cardinal Joseph Zen said this weekend that the Vatican had turned down his offer to retire as bishop of Hong Kong and focus most of his energies on mainland China. Cardinal bishops traditionally offer their resignations when they turn seventy-five, as Zen did in January [2007] … Zen also explained the Hong Kong diocese's decision not to allow clergy to fill the church's seven positions as electors in the election on Sunday [25 March] to choose the next

chief executive of Hong Kong, even though there is no specific Vatican policy against priests serving on the body. The diocese allowed parishioners to apply to fill the seven spots, but gave no indication on how to vote.

(www.iht.com, 25 March 2007)

30 June 2007.

Pope Benedict XVI on Saturday [30 June] invited all Roman Catholics in China to unite under his jurisdiction and urged Beijing to restore diplomatic ties and permit religious freedom. He called China's state-run Catholic Church 'incompatible' with Catholic doctrine but nevertheless made unprecedented overtures toward it ... In an eagerly awaited letter to the faithful in China, Benedict insisted on his right to appoint bishops, but said he trusted that an agreement could be reached with the Beijing authorities on nominations ... Significantly, Benedict revoked previous Vatican-issued regulations on both underground and official priests and bishops, and recognized that some Chinese faithful have no choice but to attend officially recognized masses ... Benedict referred repeatedly to the 'Catholic Church in China', without distinguishing between the divisions – an indication of his aim to see the two united and in communion with Rome. On several occasions Benedict also called the [China] Patriotic Association 'incompatible with Catholic doctrine' because it named its own bishops and sought to guide the life of the church. At the same time, however, Benedict made an unprecedented gesture, revoking 1988 guidelines issued by the Vatican's evangelization office that sought to limit contacts with the official church and declared that any bishops ordained by the official church would incur an automatic excommunication. Benedict also revoked special Vatican-approved allowances made to underground bishops to ordain new priests and perform other duties without following traditional norms. They had been granted in the past because the normal way of celebrating the rites could have resulted in retaliation by Chinese authorities ... Benedict stressed that he alone must appoint bishops to ensure apostolic succession – the method by which bishops can trace their succession back to Christ's original apostles. But he said he was willing to compromise ... The Vatican would like to have a formula similar to the one it has with Vietnam, where the Vatican proposes a few names and the government selects one ... [There are] up to 12 million Catholics in China who are divided between an official church – the China Patriotic Association – and an underground church that is not registered with the authorities.

(www.iht.com, 30 June 2007)

The Papal letter mentioned Saturday [30 June] that 'the Catholic Church which is in China does not have a mission to change the structure or administration of the State' ... Pope Benedict XVI has acknowledged the suffering experienced by Catholics under communist rule but also concluded that it was time to forgive past wrongdoings and for the underground and state-sponsored

> Catholic churches in China to reconcile … [There are] an estimated 12 million Catholics, the majority of whom worship in underground churches … Pope Benedict revoked instructions issued by his predecessor, John Paul II, in 1988. Those gave priests and bishops in China 'emergency powers' that allowed them to operate without communication with the Vatican and to modify Catholic practices for their own protection, for example saying a condensed mass … Over the last ten years the practices of the official state churches and underground churches have converged to some extent, depending in part upon the tolerance of the local authorities. It is not unusual to find official 'Patriotic' churches where the Pope is openly revered and that hang pictures of him near the altar. An increasing number also get money from Catholic charities abroad to pay for church building, schools and hospitals.
>
> (www.iht.com, 1 July 2007; *IHT*, 2 July 2007, p. 3)

> Pope Benedict … gave individual bishops in China's underground churches the right to decide whether they should seek formal recognition from Beijing – provided church principles were observed … According to an informal arrangement dating back to 2000, the Holy See is given time to review and tacitly endorse bishopric candidates before their appointment by the Chinese Communist Party. But that truce was broken last year [2006] when Beijing ordained two of its own bishops.
>
> (*FT*, 2 July 2007, p. 6)

> The Pope's letter said Catholics could worship in state churches, even if their priests had no links with the Pope, if finding Vatican-approved clergy caused 'great inconvenience' … The Pope's letter … said some bishops who had been ordained under pressure without the Vatican's approval had subsequently asked for the Pope's acknowledgement. He said he had granted this, taking into account 'the sincerity of their sentiments and the complexity of the situation'. The letter said the 'very small number' of bishops who had not asked for or received the Pope's blessing were 'illegitimate'. But they were still considered 'validly ordained' as long as it was by validly ordained bishops … Last year [2006] China made three appointments without Vatican clearance. Many believed that this was partly prompted by Pope Benedict's decision to make Joseph Zen [of Hong Kong] a cardinal in February 2006 … The state-sponsored church was established in 1957, six years after China severed ties with the Vatican and expelled foreign priests. Many local priests were imprisoned. Several are still in jail because of their opposition to the government church. China says it now has about 5 million Catholics, but there are believed to be millions more who worship in 'underground' churches with priests not recognized by the state.
>
> (*The Economist*, 7 July 2007, p. 60)

'The state-run Chinese Catholic Church has 4 million followers. But it is thought that millions more belong to underground organizations loyal to the Vatican' (www.bbc.co.uk, 2 July 2007).

'Sixty out of the approximately 100 Chinese Catholic bishops are currently over the age of eighty and about half of their present number have died during the past seven years' (www.bbc.co.uk, 30 June 2007).

16 July 2007.

> China's state-controlled Catholic Church has reportedly nominated a new bishop for Beijing ... Members of the Beijing diocese elected Father Joseph Li Shan in a poll on Monday [16 July] ... His nomination is being submitted to the state-controlled Bishops' Conference for approval ... The result needs approval from church officials, but it is not clear if the Vatican's approval will also be sought ... China's state-run Catholic Church has 4 million followers ... The estimated 8 million to 12 million Catholics are currently split between the Beijing-approved Patriotic Church and an underground church which remains loyal to Rome.
>
> (www.bbc.co.uk, 18 July 2007)

> The Reverend Joseph Li Shan is to be installed as the Roman Catholic bishop of Beijing on Friday [21 September] ... Whether in Beijing or in Rome no observers are describing Li's elevation as a fundamental breakthrough in relations, but many voices could be heard saying that the discreet way the appointment has been handled and, above all, the avoidance of any open dispute bodes well for the future relations ... The appointment of Li ... was the result of a delicate back and forth between China and the Vatican whose details neither side is eager to publicize or acknowledge. According to several observers, this has meant the Vatican signalling the identities of a number of Chinese Catholics with whom it is comfortable and Beijing choosing a bishop from among them. A variation on this process might have involved Beijing's producing a list of candidates with the Vatican subsequently signalling its approval. Officials on neither side will say ... In recent weeks, though, the Vatican has quietly signalled that this ordination has its approval and it has notably not spoken out against it.
>
> (*IHT*, 21 September 2007, p. 2)

> China's state-controlled Catholic Church installed a cleric well regarded by the Vatican as bishop of Beijing on Friday [21 September], in a move that officials say should help ease relations ... Joseph Li Shan ... replaces Bishop Fu Tieshan, a Communist Party supporter and hard-liner toward the Vatican ... When Li was named as Fu's replacement in July, Vatican officials praised him.
>
> (www.iht.com, 21 September 2007)

'A new Roman Catholic bishop of Beijing has been consecrated in the Chinese capital, the first for over fifty years to have tacit approval of the Pope' (www.bbc.co.uk, 21 September 2007).

4 December 2007.

> China's state-run Catholic Church has installed a bishop who is said to have been approved by the Vatican. Joseph Gan Junqiu was installed as Bishop of Guangzhou … Both his appointment and that of Lu Shouwang last week as Bishop of Yichang were backed by the Vatican.
>
> (www.bbc.co.uk, 4 December 2007)

'Authorities at the officially approved Protestant and Catholic churches put the size of China's Christian population at around 30 million. But that does not include the tens of millions more who worship in private at underground churches' (*The Times*, 8 December 2007, p. 43).

'In 1949 there were less than a million Protestants in China. Today their number is close to 100 million' (www.iht.com, 17 April 2008).

> The China Philharmonic Orchestra will perform this week for Pope Benedict XVI, the latest indication that Beijing and the Vatican are making progress in improving their often strained ties. The performance at the Vatican on Wednesday [7 May], featuring Mozart's Requiem, was initiated by the Chinese and arranged rather quickly, the conductor [said] … This will be the orchestra's first appearance at the Vatican.
>
> (www.iht.com, 5 May 2008)

> The China Philharmonic Orchestra performed Mozart's Requiem along with the Shanghai Opera House Chorus for Pope Benedict XVI on Wednesday [7 May] … The concert was a last-minute addition to a scheduled tour of Europe, said … the orchestra's artistic director … A spokesman for the Chinese embassy in Rome said the concert was an 'unofficial cultural initiative', not promoted by the government, which could nonetheless 'improve relations between the two states'.
>
> (*IHT*, 8 May 2008, p. 2)

20 September 2008.

> Repression of religious freedom in some parts of China has intensified over the past year, the US government says. The State Department's annual report on religious freedom around the world criticized Beijing's actions in remote Xinjiang province and Tibetan areas … The lengthy report has individual sections dealing with each country separately and covers the period from July 2007 to July 2008. In China the report highlighted the treatment of the Uighur period – a Moslem group living mainly in Xinjiang. The report said: 'The government reportedly continued to detain Uighur Moslem citizens for possession of unauthorized religious texts, imprison them for religious activities determined to be "extremist", and prevent them from observing certain sacred religious traditions' … It was also critical of the Beijing government's handling of protests by Tibetans in March [2008] – particularly of the use of 'patriotic education campaigns' in a bid to stifle dissent. The report is used to compile a blacklist of 'countries of particular

concern', which the State Department announces towards the end of each year. China, Saudi Arabia, Iran, Eritrea and Burma are among those who appear on the blacklist for 2007.

(www.bbc.co.uk, 20 September 2008)

The government says there are 21 million (16 million Protestants, 5 million Catholics). Unofficial figures … [range from] about 70 million [to as many as] … 130 million in early 2008 … [Communist] Party membership is 74 million [by way of comparison] … In 1949, when the Communists took power, less than 1 per cent of the population had been baptized, most of them Catholics. Now the largest, fastest growing number of Christians belong to Protestant 'house churches' … House churches are small congregations who meet privately – usually in apartments … House churches have an unclear status, neither banned nor fully approved of. As long as they avoid neighbourly confrontation and keep their congregations below a certain size (usually about twenty-five), the Protestant ones are mostly tolerated, grudgingly. Catholic ones are kept under closer scrutiny, reflecting China's tense relationship with the Vatican … Formally, the Communist Party forbids members to hold a religious belief, and the churches say they suffer official harassment … The state's attitude seems ambivalent. In December 2007 President Hu Jintao held a meeting with religious leaders and told them that 'the knowledge of religious people must be harnessed to building a prosperous society'.

(*The Economist*, 4 October 2008, pp. 74, 76)

A secret meeting between Chinese officials and leaders of the banned underground Protestant Church has marked the first significant step towards reconciliation on decades. The discussion, which were held in an office in Beijing, were the first time that members of the government and stalwarts of the outlawed 'house churches' had sat down as negotiators rather than foes … Protestants are supposed to worship under the aegis of the official religious body, the Three-Self Patriotic Movement – standing for self-governing, self-teaching and self-supporting. Catholics can worship in churches run by the Chinese Patriotic Catholic Association … The two breakthrough meetings [took place] late last year [2008]. The first involved about a dozen academics and lawyers, many known to be members of the unofficial church. The second brought together six church leaders. No representatives of the underground Catholic Church were invited.

(*The Times*, 26 January 2009, p. 29)

Leo Yao Liang, a Roman Catholic bishop who spent twenty-eight years in Chinese prisons during Mao's rule for his refusal to renounce his allegiance to the Vatican, died on 30 December [2009] … [He] was eighty-seven … [He was] released from prison in 1984 … Millions of Chinese are believed to remain loyal to the Vatican and attend so-called underground churches like those that Bishop Yao led … After Pope Benedict XVI made improved relations between the Vatican and Beijing a priority, Bishop Yao began working to repair relations with the government. The mourners at his week-long funeral, which concludes with his burial on Wednesday [6 January 2010], have included a number of local government officials … In 2006 the authorities ordered Mr Yao to spend two-and-a-half years in isolation from outsiders, studying Chinese religious laws … Bishop Yao's death, not quite a year after he was released from detention, leaves mainland China with ninety-four Vatican-approved bishops.

(www.iht.com, 6 January 2010)

The use of the internet and mobile phones

'The first full internet connection in China was recorded on 17 May 1994' (*The Times*, 10 February 2006, p. 40).

'China has the second largest number of internet users in the world, 130 million, second only to the United States' (*IHT*, 31 May 2006, p. 14).

> The authorities have announced their intention to greatly increase efforts to police and control the internet, along with other communications technologies, like instant messaging and mobile telephones … The new measures being contemplated for tightening control of mobile telephone use reportedly include mandatory user registration. Currently users can easily buy mobile phone cards at any convenience store, instantly obtaining a new telephone number without identifying themselves … According to … Tsinghua University in Beijing, China has 36.82 million Chinese blog sites and 16 million individual bloggers; the number of bloggers is projected to reach 60 million this year [2006].
>
> (www.iht.com, 30 June 2006; *IHT*, 1 July 2006, p. 2)

> The number of people using the internet in China grew by over 30 per cent over the last year to 132 million, state media reports … China already has the world's second largest population of internet users after the United States.
>
> (www.bbc.co.uk, 29 December 2006)

> The China Internet Network Information Centre told state media [that] China had 137 million internet users by the end of 2006, an increase of 23 per cent from the year before … [Some] 10 per cent of the population – and more than 30 per cent of people in Beijing – [are] now online … About 210 million of America's 300 million people now use the internet.
>
> (www.bbc.co.uk, 24 January 2007)

> China will not allow any new internet cafés to open this year [2007] state media reported on Tuesday [6 March]. Xinhua News Agency said fourteen government departments, including the ministry of culture and the ministry of information industry, had issued a notice saying that 'in 2007 local governments must not sanction the opening of new internet bars'. It said there

are about 113,000 internet cafés in China. Many are smoke-filled rooms with rows of computers set up for online gaming ... In January [2007] President Hu Jintao ordered internet regulators to promote a 'healthy online culture' ... China's online population grew by 23.4 per cent last year [2006] to 137 million, about 10 per cent of its 1.3 billion population, the China internet information centre reported last month [February]. The figure puts China on track to surpass the United States in the next two years as the nation with the most internet users, the government had said.

(www.cnn.com, 7 March 2007)

China banned new internet cafés yesterday [6 March 2007], ostensibly to curb soaring addiction to the web among children ... The decision [was made] not to approve any new licences for 'net bars' ... The notice reiterated rules that already prohibited internet cafés from admitting anyone under eighteen and required anyone using computers to register with their identity card. These rules are widely ignored ... China has about 113,000 internet bars, although that number may exclude unregistered cafés ... China's internet population swelled last year [2006] by 23.4 per cent, to 137 million.

(*The Times*, 7 March 2007, p. 47)

'With youngsters becoming too easily addicted to the internet, the government has banned any new internet cafés this year [2007]' (*Independent*, 8 March 2007, p. 32).

China has issued restrictions on the use of 'virtual money' from internet games, warning such currencies could threaten real-world financial stability. The ban on using virtual money to buy 'material products' is part of a wider tightening of controls that includes a crackdown on the cafés frequented by many of China's estimated 137 million internet users ... A formal notice issued quietly to officials last month [February] by the Communist Party and government departments, including the central bank, has ordered 'strict differentiation' between virtual exchanges and 'online commerce in material products' ... Virtual money can be used to buy only virtual products and services the companies provide themselves. Issuance will be limited and users are 'strictly forbidden' from trading it into legal tender for a profit, says the notice ... [China has an] estimated 113,000 internet cafés.

(*FT*, 7 March 2007, p. 9)

Combining sympathy with discipline, a military-style boot camp near Beijing is at the front line of China's battle against internet addiction, a disorder affecting millions of the nation's youth. The Internet Addiction Treatment Centre in Daxing county uses a blend of therapy and military drills to treat the children of China's nouveau riche addicted to online games, internet pornography, cybersex and chats ... [The government is] concerned by a number of high-profile internet-related deaths and juvenile crime ... The government-funded Daxing centre, run by an army colonel under the Beijing Military Hospital, is one of a handful of clinics treating patients with

> internet addiction ... Patients [are] overwhelmingly male and aged fourteen to nineteen ... The centre's tough-love approach to breaking internet addiction is unique to China, but necessary in a country with over 2 million teenage internet addicts, according to the facility's staff ... The centre has treated 1,500 patients since opening in 2004 ... A stay costs about 10,000 yuan, or $1,290, a month, nearly a year's average disposable income in China. But the centre takes on *pro bono* cases for poor families ... At the end of 2006 China had 137 million internet users ... Of users under eighteen an estimated 13 per cent, or 2.3 million, are internet addicts, according to a 2006 study ... Addiction to the internet is blamed for most juvenile crime in China, a number of suicides, and deaths from exhaustion by players unable to tear themselves away from marathon game sessions.
>
> (www.iht.com, 12 March 2007)

> China will intensify controls of the growing number of bloggers using the internet to lay bare their thoughts, politics and even bodies, the country's chief censor has announced. The director of China's general administration of press and publication, Long Xinmin, said the administration was forming rules to further regulate internet publishing, including the legions of bloggers ... Long singled out bloggers as one challenge ... By last September [2006] the number of blog sites reached 34 million, a thirtyfold increase from four years before ... Last year [2006] the ministry of information industry issued rules on internet news content that analysts said were aimed at extending regulations governing licensed news outlets to blogs and internet-only news sites.
>
> (www.iht.com, 13 March 2007)

> China will back away from a proposal that would have required bloggers to use their real names when registering on web logs, following an outcry in the internet industry, the official media reported Tuesday [22 May]. The government said that it would instead promote a 'self-discipline code' on the internet, to encourage, rather than mandate, bloggers to register under their own names ... China has 140 million internet users.
>
> (*IHT*, 23 May 2007, p. 12)

'[There are an] estimated 20 million bloggers' (*The Economist*, 26 May 2007, p. 6).

> China should not punish people for expressing their political views on the internet, Yahoo Inc. said on Monday [11 June] – one day after the mother of a jailed Chinese reporter announced she was suing the US company for helping officials imprison her son ... Shi Tao ... The company said in a statement that: 'Yahoo is dismayed that citizens in China have been imprisoned for expressing their political views on the internet' ... [The company has told China that it condemns] punishment of 'any activity internationally recognized as free expression' ... Shi's legal challenge, filed on 29 May in US District Court, is part of a lawsuit filed earlier by the World Organiza-

> tion for Human Rights USA. The group is suing Yahoo Inc. and its subsidiary in Hong Kong. Also named is Alibaba.com Inc., a Yahoo partner that runs Yahoo China ... Plaintiffs in the American case also include imprisoned dissident Wang Xiaoning and his wife, Yu Ling. Wang was sentenced in September 2003 on the charge of 'incitement to subvert state power' ... The Chinese government said Wang distributed pro-democracy writings authored by him and others by email and through Yahoo Groups, an online email community.
>
> (www.iht.com, 11 June 2007)

('Yahoo has asked a US court to dismiss a lawsuit ... The firm filed a motion for dismissal saying its Chinese subsidiary had no choice but to comply with local laws ... [and] argued that there was little connection between the information the firm gave and the ensuing arrests and imprisonment of its users ... Yahoo is being sued by the World Organization for Human Rights for sharing information about its users with the Chinese government. The information has led to the arrests of writers and dissidents ... The human rights group brought the case on behalf of several plaintiffs, including the Chinese journalist Shi Tao and another named Wang Xiaoning': www.bbc.co.uk, 28 August 2007. 'Yahoo settled a lawsuit Tuesday [13 November] with two Chinese journalists ... Shi Tao and Wang Xiaoning ... who were jailed after the company provided Chinese authorities with information about their online activities ... Neither side disclosed the terms of the settlement other than to agree that Yahoo would pay the attorney fees of the two journalists and the family member who sued. The three were represented by the World Organization for Human Rights in Washington ... [The case] has also been the subject of US congressional hearings, where lawmakers accused the company of collaborating with an oppressive communist regime ... The Yahoo chief executive, Jerry Yang, and its general counsel, Michael Callahan, offered apologies to Shi's mother at a congressional hearing last month [6 November]. Callahan was summoned before the House Foreign Affairs Committee last week to explain testimony he gave to Congress last year [2006]. He said then that Yahoo had no information about the nature of China's investigation when the company handed over details that ended up being used to convict Shi. Callahan subsequently has acknowledged that Yahoo officials had received a subpoena-like document that made reference to suspected "illegal provision of state secrets" – a common charge against political dissidents': *IHT*, 14 November 2007, p. 17.)

> A city where residents recently held mass protests against a planned chemicals plant is preparing to tighten controls on the internet and force users to use their real names when posting messages on local websites. The decision by the south-eastern city of Xiamen appears to be a response to the role played by the internet in the organization of demonstrations last month [June] that forced suspension of plans to build a $1.4 billion plant to produce paraxylene (PX), a chemical feedstock, in the city ... The central government has been considering rules to force users of blogs and message boards

> to use real names, but appears to have postponed the attempt after industry protests and technical difficulties … Xiamen's draft rules are a highly unusual effort by an individual city to go beyond the sweeping internet controls imposed by the central government … The rules would be the first of their type imposed at a city level in China … [There are] more than 100,000 websites registered in Xiamen. Residents wishing to post messages without using their real names would still be able to do so on websites registered in other cities.
>
> (*FT*, 9 July 2007, p. 7)

> The government has launched a campaign to clamp down on under-aged internet gaming, requiring operators to install software that discourages teenage players from spending more than three hours online. Under government rules that went into effect Monday [16 July] Chinese internet gaming companies must implement a screening programme that requires users to enter their identification card numbers … The software monitor slashes by half the points of under-age players if they keep playing beyond three hours, and wipes their points out completely if they stay on more than five hours … About 10 per cent of China's more than 30 million internet gamers were under-age as of the end of 2006, according to [official figures] … President Hu Jintao ordered regulators in January [2007] to promote a 'healthy online culture' to protect the government's stability … He was quoted in state media in April as urging Communist Party leaders to 'curb the spread of decadent and backward ideological and cultural material online' … The government has banned local authorities from approving new internet cafés this year [2007].
>
> (www.iht.com, 17 July 2007; *IHT*, 18 July 2007, p. 11)

'[There were] 162 million estimated internet users by the end of June [2007]' (*FT*, 12 October 2007, p. 15). 'The internet arrived in China in the mid-1990s' (*FT*, 13 November 2007, p. 19).

'China was home to 162 million internet users at the end of June [2007], second only to the United States, according to the government-backed China Network Information Centre' (www.iht.com, 7 November 2007).

> A cyber-dissident has been sentenced to four years in jail after he was convicted of 'inciting the government's overthrow', a press freedom group said Friday [17 August]. Chen Shuqing, an outspoken critic of the government and advocate of democratic reforms, was arrested last year [2006] on charges of inciting subversion against the state … Chen, who is a founding member of the banned China Democracy Party, was arrested last September. Police searched his home and seized his computer disc drives … Chen was sentenced on Thursday … Reporters Without Borders: 'Courts taking their orders from the Communist Party continue to crack down on cyber-dissidents. We reiterate our appeal for the release of Chen and the fifty other cyber-dissidents and internet users held in China.'
>
> (www.iht.com, 17 August 2007)

> Starting 1 September [2007] cartoon alerts will appear every half an hour on thirteen of China's top portals, including Sohu and Sina, and by the end of the year will appear on all websites registered with Beijing servers, the Beijing public security ministry said in a statement [on 28 August] … Virtual police … animated beat officers … [will] pop up on a user's browser and walk, bike or drive across the screen warning them to stay away from illegal internet content … China has the world's second largest population of internet users, with 137 million people online, and is on track to surpass the United States as the largest online population in two years.
>
> (www.iht.com, 28 August 2007)

'China is now the world's second largest online population, with more than 160 million web users' (www.guardian.co.uk, 10 October 2007).

'The number of Chinese cell-phone users has boomed from 140 million to more than 600 million since 2001, while the number of Chinese internet users has soared from 17 million to 162 million since 2000' (*Foreign Policy*, November–December 2007, p. 95).

> One of the more striking end-of-year [2007] statistics pumped out by the government was an update on the number of internet users in the country, which had reached 210 million. It is a staggering figure, up by more than 50 per cent on the previous year and more than three times the number for India … Within a few months, according to Morgan Stanley, an investment bank, China will have more internet users than America, the current leader. And because the proportion of the population using the internet is so low, rapid growth is likely to continue for some time … More than 70 per cent of Chinese internet users are under thirty, precisely the opposite of America.
>
> (*The Economist*, 2 February 2008, p. 69)

> A Chinese scholar who has challenged the government by setting up a democratic opposition party has vowed to sue US internet company Google for excising his name from its local search results … Guo Quan [is] a former Nanjing University professor … He announced late last year [2007] the creation of the New Democracy Party dedicated to ending China's 'one-party dictatorship' … Baidu.com, the Nasdaq-listed Chinese search company, and the locally controlled Chinese arm of US portal Yahoo have also blocked all searches for Mr Guo's name … Analysts say Beijing has been tightening controls on local media and the internet, apparently in an effort to ensure political stability ahead of the Olympics in August.
>
> (*FT*, 2 February 2008, p. 8)

'At the end of 2007 … the country had 210 million internet users' (*Guardian*, 14 March 2008, p. 26).

> [China's] web population is about to overtake the United States to become the world's largest internet market. The United States has 215 million users

in a mature market where around 71 per cent of the population is online. Only about 15 per cent of China's population is online.

(www.guardian.co.uk, 25 March 2008)

Some 229 million people have internet access in the country and usage in China is growing by 30 per cent a year ... Cellphone text messaging is ubiquitous, with more than 98 per cent of the country's 400 million cellphone owners regularly using text messages. Another 300 million people are registered on instant messaging networks like MSN and QQ.

(www.iht.com, 20 April 2008)

They have been called the 'Fifty Cent Party', the 'red vests' and the 'red vanguard'. But China's growing army of web commentators – instigated, trained and financed by party organizations – have just one mission: to safeguard the interests of the Communist Party by infiltrating and policing a rapidly growing Chinese internet. They set out to neutralize undesirable public opinion by pushing pro-Party views through chat rooms and web forums, reporting dangerous content to authorities. By some estimates these commentary teams now comprise as many as 280,000 members nationwide ... In March 2005 a bold new tactic emerged ... [at] Nanjing University ... [where a] team trawled the online forum for undesirable information and actively argued issues from a Party standpoint ... Rumours travelled quickly across the internet that these Party-backed monitors received 50 mao, or roughly seven cents, for each positive post they made. The term 'Fifty Cent Party' was born. The push to outsource web controls to these teams of pro-government stringers went national on 23 January 2007, as President Hu Jintao ... stressed the Party needed to 'use' the internet as well as control it.

(www.feer.com, 16 July 2008)

'The country's army of censors dipped anonymously into the internet debate by paying part-time writers 5 mao, or about 7 cents, per posting to steer public opinion and monitor the tone of the debate online' (*IHT*, 7 August 2008, p. 5).

'By the end of June 2008 China had more than 253 million internet users, [news agency] Xinhua reported' (www.cnn.com, 6 January 2009).

China says its fast growing population of internet users has surpassed the United States to become the world's biggest, with 253 million people online at the end of June [2008] ... The China Internet Network Information Centre [CNNIC] said Friday [25 July] the latest figure is a 56 per cent increase over the same time last year [2007]. According to Nielsen Online, a research firm, the United States had an estimated 223.1 million internet users in June. According to CNNIC, China's internet penetration is still low at just 19.1 per cent.

(www.cnn.com, 25 July 2008)

'In 2001 China had 26.5 million internet users. Today the figure is 253 million, the most in the world' (*IHT*, 7 August 2008, p. 5).

The China Internet Network Information Centre in Beijing … operates under the government-controlled Chinese Academy of Sciences … The new estimate of internet users from the information centre … based on a national survey … only represents about 19 per cent of people in China … By contrast, the United States is estimated to have about 220 million internet users, or about 70 per cent of its population, according to the Nielsen Company, with similarly high percentages in Japan and South Korea … The survey released Thursday [24 July] found that nearly 70 per cent of China's internet users are thirty years old or under, and that in the first half of this year [2008] high school students were by far the fastest growing segment of new users.

(www.iht.com, 25 July 2008; *IHT*, 26 July 2008, p. 17)

A group of Canadian human rights activists and computer security researchers has discovered a huge surveillance system in China that monitors and archives certain internet text conversations that include politically charged words. The system tracks text messages sent by customers of Tom-Skype, a joint venture between a Chinese wireless operator and eBay, the web auctioneer that owns Skype, an online phone and text messaging service … The activists … discovered the surveillance operation last month … The list … of restricted words … also serves as a filter to restrict text conversations … eBay created the joint venture with the Tom Group [founded in October 1999], which holds the majority stake, in September 2005.

(www.iht.com, 2 October 2008; *IHT*, 3 October 2008, p. 20)

A Canadian researcher has discovered that a Chinese version of eBay Inc.'s Skype communications software snoops on text chats that contain certain key words, including 'democracy' … law enforcement and intelligence agencies in other countries … have been bothered by the growing use of Skype, which claims 338 million users across the world … Skype routes calls and chats between computers over the internet, avoiding traditional phone networks. And the contents are supposedly encrypted, raising concerns in law enforcement that Skype could let criminals communicate without fear of eavesdropping … On Wednesday [1 October] Nart Villeneuve at the University of Toronto revealed that a Chinese version of Skype's application is being used for wholesale surveillance of text messages. The software is distributed by Skype's Chinese partner, Tom Online Inc. Skype has acknowledged since 2006 that this version looks for certain sensitive words in text chats and blocks those messages from reaching their destination. The issue appears only to affect people using the Chinese software. What Villeneuve found was that the Tom-Skype programme also passes the messages caught by the filter to a cluster of servers on Tom's network. Because of poor security on those servers he was able to retrieve more than a million stored messages. The filter appears to look for words like 'Tibet', 'democracy' and 'milk powder' – China is in the throes of a food scandal involving tainted milk. This directly contradicts a blog posting

> on Skype's website, which says that the software discards the filtered messages and neither displays nor transmits them anywhere. On Thursday [2 October] Skype president Josh Silverman said the company learned of the message diversion only on Wednesday. It alerted Tom that the messages were insecurely stored, which was quickly fixed.
>
> (www.cnn.com, 3 October 2008)

> Researchers found that the software was scanning messages for ... politically ... sensitive words or phrases such as 'Taiwan independence' and, if they were present, uploading the data to insecure servers in China ... Majority investor Tom Online declined to comment on the report other than to say that the joint venture acted in accordance with local regulations.
>
> (*FT*, 3 October 2008, p. 12)

'Skype ... on Thursday [2 October] accused its joint venture partner in China of keeping it in the dark about a censorship programme that involved the monitoring of politically sensitive terms on the service' (www.ft.com, 3 October 2008).

'Microsoft launched an anti-piracy tool to combat the widespread sale of fake software. Software piracy as a whole [is] said to stand at over 90 per cent' (www.guardian.co.uk, 22 October 2008).

> China has surpassed the United States as the world's biggest online market, with 253 million web users at the end of June [2008], according to the government-backed China Internet Information centre. The country also had 624.1 million cellphone subscribers by the end of September [2008], according to the ministry of industry and information technology.
>
> (www.iht.com, 18 November 2008)

> The Chinese media's increasing reporting of protests over land, labour and investment issues reflects an attempt by the government to manage the impact of bad news by acknowledging it, according to two well-placed sources. An academic close to the propaganda authorities who declined to be identified: 'The Chinese government has started to loosen its control on the negative information. They are trying to control the news by publicizing the news' ... The central government has permitted the local authorities to publicize negative news themselves, with no need to report to upper governments any more. They have a principle of "report the facts quickly, but be cautious on the causes behind the facts"' ... A Communist Party official confirmed that the policy on the dissemination of news had gradually changed this year [2008]. The official (who was not identified because he was not allowed to speak to the media): 'It is almost impossible to block anything nowadays when information can spread very quickly on the internet. We also noticed that it will benefit us if we report the news first' ... The propaganda authorities have issued an order authorizing new organizations to report on unrest, rather than allowing rumours to take hold among Chinese worried about the effects of the global financial crisis on the mainland's economy.
>
> (www.iht.com, 20 November 2008; *IHT*, 21 November 2008, p. 13)

China's internet search giant Baidu has promised to overhaul its operations after state media accused it of allowing unlicensed medical services to buy high research rankings. The search engine dominates the market in the world's largest internet population with about 60 per cent of users – well ahead of Google, which leads the field internationally ... The case ... [has] highlighted users' complaints about the way ... [Baidu] allows companies to buy their way up the list of research results ... State-run China Central Television reported this month [November] that the search rankings had steered people to unlicensed and expensive hospitals or medicines that failed to cure them.

(*Guardian*, 29 November 2008, p. 31)

The government has quietly begun preventing access again to websites that it had stopped blocking during the Olympic Games in August, internet experts said on Tuesday [16 December] ... A spokesman for China's foreign ministry said ... that the government has a right to censor websites that violate the country's laws ... [adding] that 'some websites' [not specified] ... had violated China's law against secession by suggesting that there are two Chinas – a reference to [Taiwan] ... *Asiaweek*, a Hong Kong-based publication, reported this week that the Chinese-language version of its website, as well as those of the BBC, Voice of America and *Ming Pao*, a Hong Kong newspaper, had been blocked since early December.

(www.iht.com, 16 December 2008; *IHT*, 17 December 2008, p. 15)

In a news conference [a] foreign ministry spokesman ... refused to confirm that the government was behind the censorship. But he said some websites violated Chinese law: 'For instance, if a website refers to "two Chinas" or refers to mainland China and Taiwan as two independent regions, we believe that violates China's anti-secession law, as well as other laws' ... In a statement the BBC said it was disappointed that Chinese-speaking audiences in China were denied access to BBCChinese.com. It said that except during the 2008 Games the website had been blocked since its inception nearly a decade ago, and Mandarin radio broadcasts had been 'subject to persistent frequency interference for decades'.

(www.bbc.co.uk, 16 December 2008)

In the first case involving cyberviolence and a 'human flesh engine' in China, a court has fined a website and an internet user for posting personal and intimate details about an unfaithful husband, his mistress and a spurned wife who committed suicide ... The husband soon began receiving death threats, harassing calls at work and vilification on the internet ... The fines in the case were small ... the equivalent of $440 plus court fees ... [One earlier case involved] Grace Wang, a Chinese freshman at Duke University in North Carolina ... [She] was seen trying to mediate a campus standoff in April between pro-Tibetan activists and pro-Beijing Chinese students. She was identified and then vilified on the web as a traitor to her country.

(www.iht.com, 19 December 2008)

[There has been] a recent rise in online vigilantism ... The court ruling, which was announced Friday [19 December], specifically mentioned 'cyber-violence' and the possibilities for abuse by human flesh search engines, which the three-judge court called 'an alarming phenomenon'. The term comes from a widely used compiler of blogs and search engines in China called Renrou, which in Mandarin means human flesh. Renrou searches have been used by countless bloggers to hunt down otherwise-anonymous Chinese citizens in cases ranging from love triangles to political outrage to cold-case murders.

(*IHT*, 20 December 2008, p. 4)

The Chinese authorities have begun blocking access from mainland China to the website of *The New York Times* even while lifting some of the restrictions they had recently imposed on the websites of other media outlets. When computer users in cities like Beijing, Shanghai and Guangzhou tried to connect on Friday morning [19 December] to the site, nytimes.com, they received a message that the site was not available ... The *International Herald Tribune* is the global edition of *The New York Times*. The Chinese-language websites of the BBC, Voice of America and *Asiaweek*, all of which had been blocked earlier in the week, were accessible by Friday. The website of *Ming Pao*, a Hong Kong newspaper, was blocked earlier in the week and still restricted on Friday.

(www.iht.com, 20 December 2008)

The government unblocked the website of *The New York Times* on Monday [22 December], allowing internet users in mainland China to view the site after access had been stopped for more than three days. Last Thursday night [18 December] Chinese authorities began blocking the site without giving any explanation.

(www.iht.com, 22 December 2008)

After years of delay the government said late Wednesday [31 December] that it would issue licences for next-generation 3G wireless services, which could fuel growth in what is already the world's biggest market for wireless services. China's State Council, or cabinet, made the announcement on its website, saying the government would back three standards, including one chiefly developed in China [based on technology developed by the German firm Siemens]. The move has been expected for much of the year ... China said it would issue licences for each of the three major standards, the home-grown TD-SCDMA standard, as well as two international 3G standards that are favoured in the United States [CDMA 2000] and Europe [WCDMA] ... To prepare for the move to 3G, China restructured its telecommunications industry into three major players earlier this year [2008] ... The country now has more than 600 million cellphone subscribers, by far the largest number in the world ... China's telecommunications industry is still not fully open to competition. International telecommunications equipment makers and cellphone producers are thriving here [in China], but only Chinese state-controlled companies can offer telephone services to regular customers.

(www.iht.com, 1 January 2009)

China's government is stepping up internet scrutiny by equipping its web censors with more advanced software that allows them to spot risks of subversion much earlier and root it out more efficiently, according to the country's internet security market leader. The revelation [came from] Beijing's TRS Information Technology, China's leading provider of search technology and text mining solutions ... Traditionally, so-called internet cops look for subversive content via keyword searches on Google or Baidu ... [But TRS says it] is increasingly selling advanced text mining solutions enabling censors to monitor and forecast public opinion rather than take down dangerous talk after it happened.

(*FT*, 5 January 2009, p. 7)

The authorities have launched a fresh campaign to get rid of unhealthy, vulgar and pornographic content on the internet. The authorities have also published the names of nineteen websites that have failed to heed requests to get rid of unsuitable material. These include Google and China's top internet search engine, Baidu. These websites could be closed down if they do not delete the offending material, according to one official ... One of the websites that has been publicly criticized, Tianya, is popular with people who post their criticisms of the government.

(www.bbc.co.uk, 5 January 2009)

China's government has accused the country's leading internet search engines and web portals, including Google, of threatening public morals by a carrying pornographic and vulgar content. While Beijing regularly launches web censorship campaigns, the new crackdown is the first in which the government has targeted heavyweights such as Google and Baidu, the local rivals that lead the Chinese search market. During the last campaign about a year ago, the authorities listed only small and little known websites as responsible for spreading unhealthy content.

(www.ft.com, 5 January 2009)

In the previous campaign, a year ago, officials accused only small and little known sites of carrying unhealthy content ... A senior official at the State Council Information Office said some websites had exploited legal loopholes. He warned of stern punishment.

(*FT*, 6 January 2009, p. 8)

The government broadened its recent effort to limit pornography on the internet by criticizing nineteen companies by name on Monday [5 January], including the two market leaders in the country, Google and Baidu. A statement posted Monday ... said the Ministry of Public Security and six other

> government agencies would work together 'to purify the internet's cultural environment and protect the healthy development of minors'. A similar statement had been issued on 5 December but attracted little attention. The statement Monday went a step further, saying nineteen companies had failed to do enough to stop the spread of pornography … In issuing its warning China appeared to be focusing on large companies that provide search engines, blog hosting and chat forums.
>
> (www.iht.com, 5 January 2009)

'Google and Baidu [are] the providers of the two most popular search engines in the country' (*IHT*, 6 January 2009, p. 11).

> Baidu … has apologized for providing links to pornographic content … Baidu: 'We apologize to the netizens at large for the negative impacts brought upon our society … [We feel] deeply guilty … [for any] negative effects … [We have deleted the] obscene content and links concerned [and improved our regulatory system]' … China's two leading gaming operators, NetEase and SINA Corp., have also issued apologies … The [nineteen] sites have been told to clean up or face possibly being shut down.
>
> (www.bbc.co.uk, 7 January 2009)

> The most popular search engine in China, Baidu, apologized Wednesday [7 January] for hosting links to pornographic content … Baidu: 'Besides deleting the obscene content and links concerned, we have improved our regulatory system. We apologize to the netizens at large for the negative impacts we brought upon the society' … A note in Chinese on its Google China blog late Tuesday said it had fixed links that contained 'vulgar content' … The two companies [Baidu and Google] had failed to take 'efficient' measures after receiving notices from the country's internet regulator, the government said … The popular Chinese web portal Sohu, and Tencent, the company that owns China's most instant messaging system, QQ, as well as an internet portal, apologized separately late Tuesday … Seven government agencies began a one-month campaign against internet content deemed offensive … While distributing pornography is punishable under China's law and banned in the country, with foreign pornographic web sites blocked, distribution of 'vulgar' materials is not so clearly defined … [It was reported] that the authorities were working on a punishment framework for the more vague charge of spreading vulgar images.
>
> (*IHT*, 8 January 2009, p. 11)

> Chinese intellectuals have signed an open letter calling for a boycott of state television news programmes. The letter says China's Central Television (CCTV) has turned its news and historical drama series into propaganda to brainwash its audience … This open letter accuses CCTV of systematic bias in its news coverage. The letter – signed by more than twenty academics and lawyers – lists six broad categories of bias and brainwashing. It says the state television monopoly has ignored many stories of social unrest and

riots, and whitewashed serious events like the recent milk contamination scandal. The letter's author, Ling Cangzhou, told the BBC that its signatories were fed up with the positive spin on domestic news from the central television station and the negative tone on international events. He said that the letter should at least alert the public to the problem, though the state television broadcaster is too pervasive to be boycotted effectively. Media controls meant the letter had to be published on a US-based website, but it has been picked up widely by Chinese websites.

(www.bbc.co.uk, 12 January 2009)

The number of internet users in China has reached 298 million, nearly equal to the population of the United States, according to official figures. Although only 23 per cent of Chinese use the web – compared with 73 per cent in the United States and 22 per cent worldwide – about 88 million went online in China for the first time last year [2008], a 42 per cent increase over 2007, the official China Internet Information Centre said on Tuesday [13 January]. China surpassed the United States as the biggest user of the internet last June [2008]. In 2008 there was also a spike in mobile phone web surfing, with 117.6 million users, a 113 per cent increase over the previous year.

(www.iht.com, 15 January 2009)

[By] the end of 2008 ... China's online population, already the world's largest, had expanded to 298 million. This marked a 41.9 per cent increase on the previous year and is still growing fast, said the government-linked China Internet Information Centre ... [But] China's internet penetration is still low at just 22.6 per cent ... The study also showed huge increases in the number of people accessing the internet through mobile phones. The report also noted that internet use in the countryside was increasing faster than in the cities ... Users in the countryside surged by 60.8 per cent year-on-year to 84.6 million, compared with much more modest growth of 35.6 per cent in the urban areas ... The report said 117.6 million people accessed the internet using their mobile phones last year, up 133 per cent from 2007 ... With 633.8 million mobile phone users, last week China issued long-awaited licences for third-generation (3G) mobile phones to China Mobile, China Telecom and China Unicom. 3G phones enable faster data transmission and services such as watching television, playing online games, wide-area wireless calls and web surfing ... The number of bloggers hit 162 million by the end of 2008.

(www.bbc.co.uk, 14 January 2009)

'China has extended a crackdown on electronic pornography to cellphones after closing 1,250 websites because of explicit content' (*IHT*, 22 January 2009, p. 1).

Rebecca MacKinnon ... said the government uses the internet as a pressure valve that allows aggrieved citizens to blow off steam before their fury comes to a head. She said: 'One can make the argument that the internet

> enables the Communist Party to remain in power longer because it provides a space for people to air grievances without allowing real change.'
>
> (www.iht.com, 5 February 2009; *IHT*, 6 February 2009, p. 11)

'[On 31 March 2009 it was announced that Google had begun] a service in China that provides links to 1.1 million free, legal music downloads in the hope of boosting its share of the Chinese internet-search market' (www.economist.com, 2 April 2009).

> The government has blocked YouTube, the video-sharing website run by Google. Beijing originally blocked YouTube in late March, then lifted the block for a brief period around 27 March. At that time residents of Beijing could use the site. But in recent weeks the site has been inaccessible without going through proxy servers, according to people in several Chinese cities.
>
> (www.iht.com, 24 April 2009)

> A Chinese academic has successfully sued an internet company for closing his website after he posted articles on subjects including corruption and environmental issues. Hu Xingdou, Professor of Economics at the Beijing Institute of Technology, said he hoped his case would encourage other users to protect their rights and net censors to make decisions more responsibly.
>
> (www.guardian.co.uk, 25 May 2009)

> China has issued a sweeping directive requiring all personal computers sold in the country to include sophisticated software that can filter out pornography and other 'unhealthy information' from the internet. The software, which manufacturers must install on all new PCs starting 1 July, allows the government to update computers regularly with an ever-changing list of banned websites. The rules [were] issued last month [19 May] … Free-speech advocates say they fear the new software could make it even more difficult for China's 300 million users to access uncensored news and information … Called 'Green Dam' – green being a foil to the yellow smut of pornography – the software is designed to filter out sexually explicit images and words, according to the company that designed it. Computer experts, however, warn that once installed the software could be directed to block all manner of content or allow the government to monitor internet use and collect personal information … Jinhui Computer System Engineering helped create Green Dam.
>
> (www.iht.com, 8 June 2009; *IHT*, 9 June 2009, p. 15)

'Chinese authorities had earlier assured manufacturers that the software would only be required for computers sold in schools' (www.iht.com, 10 June 2009).

> All computers sold in China – even those imported – will have to be pre-installed with the 'Green Dam-Youth Escort' software … Critics fear this new software could be used by the government to enhance its internet censorship system, known as the Great Firewall of China … Jinhui Computer System Engineering … [is] one of the companies that developed the software.
>
> (www.bbc.co.uk, 9 June 2009)

'Green Dam's designers say the programme … is not capable of acting as spyware. Most importantly, they say the programme can be disabled or erased by computer owners who do not want to use it' (*IHT*, 11 June 2009, p. 17).

> A designer of filtering software that is required to be installed on computers sold in China has been ordered by the Chinese government to fix potential security breaches in the software … Some computer experts who have studied the software said last week that the software is so flawed that it can allow hackers to monitor a user's internet activity, steal data or plant viruses.
>
> (www.iht.com, 15 June 2009)

'One expert … said last week that it had taken only a few hours for him and his students to infiltrate a computer loaded with Green Dam and force it to crash' (*IHT*, 16 June 2009, p. 14).

'China appeared to cave in to public pressure yesterday [16 June] by announcing that computer users were not required to install internet-filtering software although it will still come with all PCs sold on the mainland' (*FT*, 17 June 2009, p. 7).

> State media said yesterday [16 June] the package would now be optional … The *China Daily* said: 'The users have the final say on the installation of the Green Dam-Youth Escort, so it is misleading to say the government compels PC users to use the software … the government's role is limited to having the software developed and providing it free' … Green Dam has been developed by a company called Jinhui, a military-backed software firm.
>
> (*Guardian*, 17 June 2009, p. 16)

'American computer makers say the Chinese government has not backed down from a requirement that internet filtering software be installed on all computers sold in China after 1 July, despite reports this week that the rule had been relaxed' (www.iht.com, 18 June 2009).

'The city of Beijing is planning to hire thousands of internet censors … The city will seek to employ at least 10,000 "internet volunteers" before the end of the year [2009] to monitor "harmful" websites' (www.ft.com, 17 June 2009).

'The city of Beijing wants to recruit 10,000 volunteers by the end of the summer to monitor internet content' (www.iht.com, 18 June 2009).

'The Chinese government disabled some search functions on the Chinese language website of Google Friday [19 June], saying the site was linking too often to pornographic and vulgar content' (www.iht.com, 19 June 2009).

> Beijing has ordered Google to stop users of its Chinese-language service accessing overseas websites … On Thursday [18 June] … the government announced it was ordering the company to suspend foreign searches and automated keywords … Baidu, a domestic search engine, holds 59 per cent market share … Google has been growing aggressively in China over the past year and its market share exceeded 30 per cent for the first time in the first quarter of this year [2009].
>
> (*FT*, 20 June 2009, p. 19)

> [The United States] lodged a formal protest on Wednesday [24 June] with the Chinese government over its plans to force all computers sold in China to come with software [Green Dam-Youth Escort] that blocks access to certain websites ... In part the American officials' complaint framed this as a trade issue, objecting to the burden put on computer makers to install software with little notice. But it also raised broader questions about whether the software would lead to more censorship of the internet in China and restrict freedom of expression.
>
> (www.iht.com, 25 June 2009)

> The health ministry has ordered that most internet users be barred from seeing medical research papers on sexual subjects, the latest move in what it calls the anti-pornography campaign that many China experts see as a harbinger of a broader crackdown on freedom of expression and dissent ... The health ministry posted regulations this week requiring medical information providers to restrict access to articles on sexual subjects.
>
> (www.iht.com, 25 June 2009; *IHT*, 26 June 2009, p. 2)

> Global business groups have made an unusual direct appeal to Chinese premier Wen Jiabao to scrap an order for PC makers to supply internet filtering software, citing security and privacy concerns ... The letter dated Friday [26 June] said: 'The Green Dam mandate raises significant questions of security, privacy, system reliability, the free flow of information and user choice' ... The letter [came] from twenty-two chambers of commerce and trade groups representing the world's major technology suppliers ... The letter was signed by leaders of the American, European and Japanese chambers of commerce in China, the US National Association of Manufacturers and trade groups representing the world's major technology suppliers ... Such a direct appeal to Chinese leaders is highly unusual. Companies usually avoid commenting publicly on government policy for fear of retaliation ... Manufacturers say they are still trying to obtain details of the plan ... Analysts who have reviewed the programme say it contains code to filter out material the government considers politically objectionable ... A California company ... says parts of its own filtering software were used by Green Dam, raising questions about possible violations of intellectual property rights.
>
> (www.iht.com, 27 June 2009)

'The Chinese government announced today [30 June] that it will delay the launch ... Xinhua: "China will delay the mandatory installation of the Green Dam-Youth Escort filtering software in new computers"' (www.guardian.com, 30 June 2009).

> China has agreed to delay today's [1 July] deadline ... The ministry of industry and information technology said last night [30 June] in a statement issued through Xinhua: 'Depending on the concrete situation, they [personal computer makers] can pre-install [the programme] later.'
>
> (*FT*, 1 July 2009, p. 21)

> The ministry of industry and information technology ... announced via Xinhua ... the mandatory installation would be delayed ... to give computer producers more time to put the order into effect. The government will, however, equip school and internet café computers with the software after 1 July, as well as provide a free download of the software for those who want it in China ... Green Dam works only on computers that use the Windows operating system. So far, no version has been released for Macintosh and Linux systems. Nor will the software be required in Hong Kong or Macao ... [On Thursday 25 June] the EU protested saying the software was clearly designed to limit free speech.
>
> (www.iht.com, 30 June 2009)

'As a practical matter, the abrupt postponement bows to reality, because most Chinese computer retailers have large stocks of machines, manufactured months before the decree was announced' (*IHT*, 1 July 2009, p. 1).

> Internet users in China denounced the plan as an attempt to stifle free speech ... But public opinion alone probably would not have derailed the requirement, analysts here [in China] say. Instead, foreign companies and governments mounted an unusually unified protest, arguing that the software was riddle with bugs and threatened to compromise the security of companies that were responsible for much of China's foreign investment. The United States threatened to file a protest alleging that the requirement violated free-trade agreements.
>
> (*IHT*, 2 July 2009, pp. 1, 5)

> The EU Chamber of Commerce said in a statement [on 25 June] that the new software requirement 'raises serious concerns for us and poses significant questions in relation to security, privacy, system reliability, the free flow of information and use choice'.
>
> (www.cnn.com, 1 July 2009)

> Yesterday [14 July] the ministry of health moved to ban the use of electric shocks to cure chronic internet dependency ... The move follows growing concern in the country about young people's compulsive use of chat rooms, websites and online gaming – but also the methods used to wean them offline ... The ban follows reports that ... [a] psychiatric hospital in Shandong province was using electroconvulsive therapy ... The ministry of health asked Shandong's health department to stop the use of 'electrical stimulation' for internet addiction while experts investigated ... There are about 300 million net users in China and 200 million of them are young people.
>
> (www.guardian.co.uk, 14 July 2009; *Guardian*, 15 July 2009, p. 17)

> Police are investigating a boot camp for internet addicts after a teenage [fifteen-year-old] boy died, apparently following a severe beating, just hours after checking in, Xinhua said on Wednesday [5 August] ... There are over

> 200 organizations offering treatment for internet disorders in China. Many of the camps are imbued with a military atmosphere ... China in July banned electro-shock therapy as a treatment for internet addiction after media reports about a controversial psychiatrist who administered electric currents to nearly 3,000 teenagers.
>
> (www.independent.com, 6 August 2009)

('A teenage boy [fourteen] is in a serious condition after being repeatedly beaten at a boot camp to treat internet addicts in China, state media have reported ... China's ministry of health said there was no scheme to register – or monitor – camps that treat internet addiction': www.bbc.co.uk, 19 August 2009.)

> Chinese officials retreated on Thursday [13 August] from a plan to install so-called anti-pornography software on every computer sold here, saying instead that internet cafés, schools and other public places must use the programme, but that individual consumers will be spared. The industry and information technology minister, Li Yizhong, said the notion that the programme, called Green Dam-Youth Escort, would be required on every new computer was a 'misunderstanding' spawned by poorly written regulations ... The information ministry had previously suspended the Green Dam pre-installation mandate on 30 June ... The Thursday statement by Mr Li appeared to make that suspension permanent. Mr Li said the government would neither require the programme to come pre-installed on new computers or force computer makers to include the programme on a CD with optional software. A few Asian computer manufacturers, led by China-based Lenovo and Taiwan's Acer, nevertheless include the software on computers sold in China ... The software remains mandatory in schools, internet cafés and other sites used by scores of millions of people. The government already takes extraordinary steps to monitor computer use in internet cafés, which remain common in a nation where owning a computer remains a comparative luxury.
>
> (www.iht.com, 13 August 2009; *IHT*, 14 August 2009, p. 14)

'The government has now said that citizens can choose whether they use the programme, although installations in public computers will still go ahead' (www.bbc.co.uk, 13 August 2009).

> Individual computer users in China may choose whether to install a controversial content filtering system, but the system will be installed on computers in any public place, China's minister of industry and information technology said Thursday [13 August] ... Li Yizhong: 'Installation is intended to block violent and pornographic content on the internet to protect children.'
>
> (www.cnn.com, 14 August 2009)

> News websites in China, complying with secret government orders, are requiring that new users log on under their true identities to post comments, a shift in policy that the country's internet users have fiercely opposed in the

past. Until recently users could weigh in on news items on many of the affected sites more anonymously, often without registering at all, though the sites were obligated to screen all posts, and the posts could still be placed via internet protocol addresses. But in early August [2009], without notification of change, news portals like Sina, NetEase, Sohu and scores of other sites began asking unregistered users to sign in under their real names and identification numbers, said top editors at two of the major portals affected. A Sina staff member also confirmed the change. The editors said the sites were putting into effect a confidential directive issued in late July by the State Council Information Office, one of the main government bodies responsible for supervising the internet in China. The new step is not foolproof, the editors acknowledged … But the requirement adds a critical new layer of surveillance to mainstream sites in China, which were already heavily policed. Further regulations of the same nature also appeared to be in the pipeline … Government internet regulators have been trying to usher in real name registration controls since 2003, when they ordered internet cafés around China to demand that customers show identification, nominally to keep out minors. Last year [2008] lawmakers and regulators began discussing legislation on a more extensive 'real name system', as it is known. But such proposals have aroused heated debate over the purview of the state to restrict China's online community, which is the largest in the world at about 340 million people and growing … In 2006 internet users and the news media rebuffed an official proposal to require real name registration on blog hosting sites … Central authorities have gone to new lengths to tame online activity in 2009, a year peppered with politically delicate anniversaries.

(www.iht.com, 5 September 2009)

'[There were] 338 million internet users in June 2009' (www.cnn.com, 1 October 2009).

The ministry of health has moved to ban the use of physical punishment to treat teenagers addicted to the web, according to draft guidelines. There are dozens of treatment centres offering to wean youths, mostly boys, from spending hours on the web. Many of them are military-style boot camps that rely on tough programmes of physical exercise and counselling. Two boys were beaten at separate camps earlier this year [in August]; one died and the other was severely injured. The ministry said in a draft guideline: 'When intervening to prevent improper use of the internet we should … strictly prohibit restriction of personal freedom and physical punishments' … In July [2009] the ministry of health formally banned the use of electroshock therapy as a treatment option … Some estimates suggest up to 10 per cent of the country's 100 million web users under the age of twenty could be addicted and a growing number of rehabilitation centres have sprung up to deal with the problem. Some define an internet addict as anyone who is online for at least six hours a day and has little interest in school.

(www.bbc.co.uk, 5 November 2009)

Tighter controls had been expected in a sensitive year for the authorities – the anniversaries of a Tibetan uprising and its subsequent suppression; of the 1989 Tiananmen student democracy movement and ensuing military crackdown; and the sixtieth anniversary of Communist Party rule on 1 October. But more than a month after National Day the restrictions, thought to be temporary, are still in place.

(www.ft.com, 6 November 2009)

China has banned individuals from registering internet domain names and launched a review of millions of existing personal websites in the toughest censorship drive so far on the internet. As of Monday [14 December] people applying to register a domain name in China must present a company chop and a business licence … Internet service providers said they had started to review their client base for potentially fraudulent or 'harmful' individually owned sites … China had 16.3 million domain names as of June this year [2009] … Last week the State Administration of Radio, Film and Television closed down a number of video sharing websites, citing copyright violations and lewd content … Last week the editor of *Southern Weekend* … was demoted after censors expressed dissatisfaction with a story speculating about personnel changes in the Communist Party.

(www.cnn.com, 16 December 2009)

China has banned individuals from registering domain names in Beijing's toughest move to tighten online censorship. From Monday [14 December] people registering a domain name in China would have to present a company seal and a business licence … Officials said the measure was part of a campaign to rein in pornographic content … Beijing said that more than 3,000 people had been arrested nationwide for alleged involvement in posting pornographic content online.

(*FT*, 16 December 2009, p. 8)

Government censors have taken fresh aim at the internet, rolling out new measures that limit ordinary citizens' ability to set up personal websites and to view hundreds of other websites offering films, video games and other forms of entertainment. The authorities say that the stricter controls are intended to protect children from pornography, to limit the piracy of films, music and television shows, and to make it hard to perpetuate internet scams … Under the new initiative, unveiled over the past month, more than 700 websites have been shut down, including many that offered free movies, television dramas and music downloads … Individuals have been banned from registering websites using China's country code domain, .cn. That domain is now limited to registered businesses … Individuals can still register websites in other domains, such as .com and .net … The government has also intensified pressure on cellphone companies to prevent transmissions of online pornography.

(www.iht.com, 17 December 2009; *IHT*, 18 December 2009, p. 18)

China has issued regulations that expand its internet controls by tightening procedures for domain name registration. The Ministry of Industry and Information Technology posted the new rules over the weekend, part of what it called a three-step plan against pornography accessible through cell-phones. The regulations require internet service providers and other tele-communications companies to carry out 'complete and thorough' checks to determine if websites are officially registered. Any websites that have not registered with the ministry should be taken down, the order says. The order also tightens the registration process for domain names. It requires that any website have a business licence or be registered, which would appear to prohibit sites set up by individuals.

(*IHT*, 23 December 2009, p. 17)

Google said Tuesday [13 January] the company and at least twenty others were victims of a 'highly sophisticated and targeted attack' originating in China in mid-December [2009], evidently to gain access to the email accounts of Chinese human rights activists ... Google said: 'Based on our investigation to date we believe the attack did not achieve that objective ... These attacks and the surveillance they have uncovered – combined with the attempts over the past year to further limit free speech on the web – have led us to conclude that we should review the feasibility of our business operations in China. We have decided we are no longer willing to continue censoring our results on google.cn, and so over the next few weeks we will be discussing with the Chinese the basis on which we could operate an unfiltered search engine within the law, if at all. We recognize that this may well mean having to shut down google.cn, and potentially our offices in China' ... A Google spokesman said the targeted human rights activists were in the United States, Europe and China.

(www.cnn.com, 13 January 2010)

Google starting operating in China in 2006 ... Beijing-based Baidu was claiming it had 77 per cent of the market share in the third quarter of last year [2009] ... with Google pulling about 19 per cent. Analysts said less than 2 per cent of Google's revenue comes from China ... The mobile phone market was opening up for its Android operating system and studies show Google has been earning more, per search, than Baidu.

(www.cnn.com, 14 January 2010)

Google said Tuesday [13 January 2010] that it would stop co-operating with Chinese internet censorship and consider shutting down its operations in the country altogether, citing assaults from hackers on its computer systems and China's attempts to 'limit free speech on the web' ... Since arriving in 2006 under an arrangement with the government that purged its Chinese research results of banned topics, Google has come under fire for abetting a system that increasingly restricts what citizens can read online ... The company, however, has repeatedly said it would monitor restrictions in China ...

> Google linked its decision to sophisticated cyber-attacks on its computer systems that it suspected originated in China and that were aimed, at least in part, at the Gmail user accounts of Chinese human rights activists … Many Chinese dissidents used Gmail because its servers are hosted overseas and … it offered extra encryption … Those attacks, which Google said took place last week, were directed at some thirty-four companies or entities, most of them in Silicon Valley, California … The attackers may have succeeded in penetrating elaborate computer security systems and obtaining crucial corporate data and software source codes, though Google said it did not itself suffer losses of that kind. While the scope of the hacking and the motivations and identities of the hackers remained uncertain, Google's response amounted to an unambiguous repudiation of its own five-year courtship of the vast China market … Google said it would try to negotiate a new arrangement to provide uncensored results on its search site, google.cn … Google said it would otherwise cease to run google.cn and would consider shutting its offices in China, where it employs some 700 people … and has an estimated $300 million in annual revenue … Despite a costly investment, the company has a much smaller share of the search market there than it does in other major markets, commanding only about one in three searches by Chinese. The leader in searches, Baidu, is a Chinese-run company that enjoys a close relationship with the government … While Google's business in China is now small, analysts say that the country could soon become one of the most lucrative internet and mobile markets, and a withdrawal would significantly reduce Google's long-term growth … In the past year Google has been increasingly constricted by the Chinese government … Since its entry into China the company has steadily lost market share to Baidu.
>
> (www.iht.com, 13 January 2010)

'Google's software engineers quickly tracked the source of the attack to seven servers in Taiwan, with footprints back to the Chinese mainland' (*IHT*, 26 January 2010, p. 1).

> Baidu … has 300 million users … It is the market leader in China by a wide margin, with a commanding 63 per cent share to Google's 33 per cent … [China] has the world's largest internet population – estimated to be 338 million users.
>
> (www.iht.com, 13 January 2010)

> Perhaps 50 million internet users rely on Google, less than half the number of regular Baidu users, and the advertising that Google sells on its site is proportionately smaller. Still, surveys show that Google's users are the cream of China's web surfing class – more educated, wealthier and better informed than others. Users also rated Google superior to Baidu in finding web pages … perhaps because Google censors fewer web sites than do most Chinese search engines.
>
> (www.iht.com, 14 January 2010)

> Google entered China in 2006, and then sold its $60 million stake in Baidu … Baidu was founded in 1999 by Robin Li, a graduate of one of the top Chinese schools, Peking University. He later studied computer science at State University of New York at Buffalo … [He] returned to China to co-found Baidu with a biochemist … Google made some inroads against Baidu last year [2009] under Lee Kai-fu, a former Microsoft executive who took over the company's Chinese operations in 2006. But Mr Lee announced his departure from Google last September [2009], saying he was forming a company that would help Chinese start-ups.
>
> (*IHT*, 14 January 2010, p. 15)

> Google has gained significant market share since it formally entered China five years ago, but almost all of that has come from smaller rivals. Baidu has also gained market share in that time … Google set up its China business in 2006, after it invested in Baidu and then reportedly tried and failed to buy it outright. Baidu, founded in 2000 when the Chinese internet was beginning to bud, carved out a strong presence by offering something that Google, at first, would not: easy links to download pirated songs, television shows and movies from Chinese websites. Baidu claimed this was legal because the media files were not on its own computers. Google finally introduced a free online music service in China in 2009, with the permission of the music labels … Searching for music is what people did early on in China.
>
> (www.iht.com, 16 January 2010)

'Google may rank a distant second to the Baidu search engine, but its estimated 80 million users are comparatively better educated and wealthier. Surveys show that roughly two-thirds are college educated' (www.iht.com, 16 January 2010).

> Google says it may end its operations in China after hackers targeted the email accounts of Chinese human rights activists. It said it had found a 'sophisticated and targeted attack on our corporate infrastructure originating from China' … David Drummond (senior vice president of corporate development and chief legal officer for Google): 'A primary goal of the attackers was accessing the Gmail accounts of Chinese human rights activists' … The search engine market was worth more than $1 billion in 2009, with analysts expecting Google to make about $600 million from China in 2010.
>
> (www.bbc.co.uk, 13 January 2010)

> Google believes that the attack was mostly blocked and that only minor information, such as creation dates and subject lines, were stolen from two accounts. It said the investigation showed that accounts of dozens of Chinese human rights activists using Gmail in Europe, China or the United States had been 'routinely accessed' using malware (malicious software) … Google have been investigating the cyber-attack since mid-December last year [2009]. Internet analysts believe the attacks had been launched from at least six internet addresses in Taiwan, a method used by Chinese hackers to mask their origin.
>
> (www.thetimes.co.uk, 13 January 2010)

> Google … had long been troubled by the limits imposed by operating behind the Great Firewall of China, a term coined in 1997 by Geremie Barmé, a prominent Chinese historian at the Australian National University. Since then it has become a synonym for the controls imposed by tens of thousands of busy censors protecting China's people from content their leaders deem objectionable or threatening … [Google's] market share is 31.8 per cent, compared with 60.9 per cent for Baidu.
>
> (www.thetimes.co.uk, 14 January 2010)

'Several Chinese rights campaigners said their email accounts, including Gmail, had often been targeted by "phishing" attacks; deceptive emails [attempting to] gain access to the user's information' (www.independent.co.uk, 13 January 2010).

'Google … got only up to 17 per cent of the queries and 33 per cent of the income, the rest going to Baidu' (www.guardian.co.uk, 14 January 2010).

'While links to China's government or military have never been proved, cyber-security experts believe both the government and the security apparatus use hackers as freelance cyber-war experts' (www.ft.com, 13 January 2010). '[Google is] allowing uncensored searches in Chinese for the first time' (*FT*, 16 January 2010, p. 8). 'Baidu has more than 60 per cent of the domestic market in online research' (*FT*, 20 January 2010, p. 11).

> The Alibaba Group of China on Saturday [16 January] criticized Yahoo, one of its largest shareholders, for siding with Google after a cyber attack on that company … A spokesman for Alibaba said executives at the company were angry because Yahoo, which owns 40 per cent of the Chinese internet company, appeared to follow Google in suggesting the Chinese government was behind the cyber-attacks. Alibaba's statement reads: 'Alibaba Group has communicated to Yahoo that Yahoo's statement that it is "aligned" with the position Google took last week was reckless given the lack of facts in evidence. Alibaba doesn't share this view' … Alibaba called the Yahoo statement premature and 'reckless' because Google had not released any proof to support its announcement … On Wednesday [13 January] Yahoo issued a statement supporting its internet rival: 'We condemn any attempts to infiltrate company networks to obtain user information. We stand aligned with Google that these kinds of attacks are deeply disturbing and strongly believe that the violation of user privacy is something that we as internet pioneers must all oppose.' Yahoo is one of the companies that was targeted in the attacks, according to several people with knowledge of the situation. The company has declined to confirm that it was a victim … In September [2009] Yahoo cashed out its investment in Alibaba.com, the publicly traded ecommerce site which is partially owned by Alibaba Group … Yahoo paid Alibaba $1 billion and gave Alibaba control of Yahoo China in exchange for a 40 per cent stake in the Chinese company … Alibaba, one of China's best known technology companies, operates a series of popular websites, including Alibaba.com, Taobao.com and Yahoo China. The company, based

in Hangzhou, is led by Jack Ma, a former English teacher who has transformed himself into one of the country's wealthiest and most admired entrepreneurs. Mr Ma is a celebrity because of his success in forcing eBay to retreat from the Chinese market, and taking over Yahoo's operations after they lost significant market share. Alibaba went public in 2007 with a huge stock offering in Hong Kong and is now valued at $12.5 billion.

(www.iht.com, 16 January 2010; *IHT*, 18 January 2010, p. 18)

'Alibaba Group … in which Yahoo has a 39 per cent stake … runs Taobao, China's largest online retailer, as well as the country's largest e-commerce site, Alibaba.com' (www.bbc.co.uk, 17 January 2010). 'Microsoft admitted that its Internet Browser was a weak link in the recent attacks on Google's systems' (www.bbc.co.uk, 19 January 2010).

Chinese hackers are believed to have attempted to penetrate India's most sensitive government office … India's National Security Adviser said his officer and other government departments were targeted on 15 December [2009], the same date that US companies reported cyber-attacks from China … This was not the first instance.

(*The Times*, 18 January 2010, p. 32)

Google said it was looking at whether any of its staff in China were involved in last month's cyber-attack as a routine part of its investigation. Google is investigating whether one or more of its employees in China helped launch the cyber-attack against it … According to reports, figures released this week showed the number of China's internet users leapt almost 30 per cent in 2009, to 384 million.

(www.iht.com, 18 January 2010)

The number of internet users in China has nearly tripled in the last three years – to 384 million users in December 2009 compared to 137 million in December 2006 … The number one search engine is Baidu, which has a market share of nearly 60 per cent of Chinese users, compared to about 36 per cent for Google.

(www.cnn.com, 22 January 2010)

Google email accounts of least two foreign journalists in Beijing have been compromised, a journalists' advocacy group in China said Monday [18 January 2010], adding that hackers changed Gmail settings so that all messages would be forwarded to unfamiliar addresses … The two foreign journalists were among a large number of Gmail users in China who discovered that their accounts had been compromised after Google made its announcement. In many of those cases it was unclear exactly when the hackers had broken into the accounts. The attacks on email accounts were separate from those weeks ago aimed at the security infrastructure and of Google and more than thirty other companies and entities, most of them based in Silicon Valley in California. One of the two journalists is a television reporter in the

Beijing bureau of The Associated Press, which has one of the largest foreign news operations in China. Email messages in the reporter's account were being forwarded to an email address that the reporter did not recognize. The reporter said that other people the reporter knew in Beijing had suffered the same kind of attack ... It is not known who was behind the email attacks or whether the Chinese government ... had any involvement. The journalists' advocacy group, the Foreign Correspondents' Club of China, said in its announcement concerning the compromised Gmail accounts: 'We remind all members that journalists in China have been the particular targets of hacker attacks in the last two years' ... Several well known rights advocates in China said last week that their Gmail accounts had been hacked recently. The advocates include Ai Weiwei, the rebellious artist, and Teng Biao, a lawyer ... People in the United States briefed on the investigation of the infrastructure attacks said Google was exploring all options, including the possibility that employees in China or elsewhere could have been involved. But that possibility did not appear to be central to the inquiry. The people noted that the attacks were highly sophisticated and probably would have been successful whether or not Google had employees in China.

(www.iht.com, 18 January 2010 and 19 January 2010)

Google says it has postponed the launch of two Android-based mobile phones in China ... The formal launch was due on Wednesday [20 January] ... A Google spokesman said: 'The launch we have been working on with China Unicom has been postponed ... China Unicom is a network provider in the country ... Google had planned to launch two handsets running its Android operating system in co-operation with Samsung and Motorola.

(www.bbc.co.uk, 19 January 2010)

Google today [19 January] postponed the launch in China of a mobile phone incorporating its email and web services ... Informed observers said that Google had decided it could not launch a handset which relies on Google's services – particularly its web and email services ... at a time when it could not be sure whether those will continue to be available in China ... Google has still not yet set a date when it will stop censoring its search results inside China.

(www.guardian.co.uk, 19 January 2010)

Google on Tuesday [19 January] postponed the planned launch of its mobile phone in China ... Also Tuesday a foreign ministry spokesman said the search giant must obey China's laws and traditions ... It was the government's first direct comment on Google since the US company said on 12 January it would no longer censor search results in China and might shut down its China-based site Google.cn.

(www.iht.com, 19 January 2010)

Chinese foreign ministry spokesman Ma Zhaoxu: 'Foreign firms in China should respect China's laws and regulations, and respect China's public customs and traditions, and assume the corresponding social responsibil-

> ities, and of course Google is no exception' ... Until now the foreign ministry had avoided mentioning Google's name in comments on the dispute ... Ma said: 'China is the biggest victim of hacking' ... [He added] that eight out of ten personal computers in China connected to the internet had been hacked. This figure apparently included the many computers infected with viruses spread online.
>
> (www.independent.co.uk, 19 January 2010)

'An American computer security researcher ... Joe Stewart ... has found what he says he believes is strong evidence of the digital fingerprints of Chinese authors in the software programs used in attacks against Google' (www.iht.com, 20 January 2010).

> With 384 internet users, China already accounts for more than one-fifth of the 1.73 billion global internet population ... Chinese people use the web differently from their counterparts in other markets. Simply put, they tend to roam the web like a huge playground, whereas Europeans and Americans are more likely to use it as a gigantic library. Recent research by the McKinsey consultancy suggests Chinese users spend most of their time online on entertainment while their European peers are much more focused on work. Behind this difference is the fact that Chinese internet users are comparatively young, poor and less educated ... As the government is encouraging rural computer and handset sales, and mobile operators move beyond saturated urban markets in search of new subscribers, even larger numbers of low-income users are expected to join in the years ahead.
>
> (*FT*, 20 January 2010, p. 11)

Edward Yu (chief executive of Analysis):

> When eBay first entered the market they were definitely a dominant player, but they just migrated their business model to China. That strategy ignored a key difference in the Chinese consumer – they don't like buying used goods. Taobao was quick to recognize that people wanted to buy new products rather than second-hand goods.
>
> (www.cnn.com, 22 January 2010)

> Expanding what the government says is a campaign against pornography, cellular phone companies in Beijing and Shanghai have been told to suspend text-messaging services to cellphone users who are found to have sent messages with 'illegal or unhealthy content', state-run media reported Tuesday [19 January]. China Mobile, one of the nation's largest cellular providers, reported that text messages would automatically be scanned for 'key words' provided by the police ... Messages will be deemed 'unhealthy' if they violate undisclosed criteria established by the central government ... The increased surveillance of text messages is the latest in a series of government initiatives to tighten control of the internet and other forms of communications. Since November [2010] the government has closed hundreds of

> websites in the name of rooting out pornography and piracy … China Mobile will suspend the text-messaging function for phone numbers whose users are suspected of transmitting unhealthy content while the police evaluate the messages.
>
> (*IHT*, 20 January 2010, p. 17)

> China has signalled a change of approach to the Google crisis, with state media describing the company's threat to pull out of the country as a political conspiracy by the US government. Accusations in two newspapers that Washington was using Google as a foreign policy tool were echoed by Chinese government officials on Wednesday [20 January]. This comes before a policy speech by US Secretary of State Hillary Clinton on Wednesday … *Global Times*, a nationalist tabloid owned by the *People's Daily*, the Communist Party mouthpiece, ran an editorial with the headline: 'The World Does Not Welcome the White House's Google' … *China Youth Daily* said in its Tuesday [19 January] edition that some US politicians were trying to promote human rights issues under the guise of a commercial dispute … In the past week the government has tried to avoid a political fallout by treating the issue as a strictly commercial affair.
>
> (www.cnn.com, 21 January 2010)

'Chinese press have labelled the America research engine "White House's Google"' (www.cnn.com, 22 January 2010).

'*The Global Times*, a nationalist tabloid owned by the *People's Daily*, ran an editorial headlined: 'The World Does Not Welcome the White House's Google"' (www.bbc.co.uk, 22 January 2010).

'A commentary on the English-language *Global Times* website, which is state-run, hit out at the "information imperialism" of the West' (*Guardian*, 23 January 2010, p. 23).

He Yafei (vice foreign minister; on 21 January): 'The Google incident should not be linked to relations between the two governments and countries; otherwise it is an over-interpretation' (www.cnn.com, 22 January 2010).

US Secretary of State Hillary Clinton (21 January):

> Countries that restrict free access to information or violate the basic rights of internet users risk walling themselves off from the progress of the next century … [The United States and China] have different views on this issue and we intend to address those differences candidly and consistently … No nation, no group, no individual should stay buried in the rubble of repression … Countries or individuals that engage in cyber-attacks should face consequences and international condemnation. In an inter-connected world, an attack on one nation's networks can be an attack on all. By reinforcing that message, we can create norms of behaviour among states and encourage respect for the global networked commons … We look to Chinese authorities to conduct a thorough investigation of the cyber intrusions that led Google to make its announcement. We also look for that investigation and its results to

be transparent ... I hope that refusal to support politically motivated censorship will become a trademark characteristic of American technology companies. It should be part of our national brand. And when their business dealings threaten to undermine this freedom, they need to consider what's right, not simply the prospect of quick profits ... A new information curtain is descending across much of the world. In the last year we've seen a spike in threats to the free flow of information. China, Tunisia and Uzbekistan stepped up their censorship of the internet. In Vietnam access to popular social networking sites has suddenly disappeared. And last Friday in Egypt thirty bloggers and activists were detained. Last year in Saudi Arabia a man spent months in prison for blogging about Christianity.

(www.thetimes.com, 21 January 2010; www.bbc.co.uk, 21 January 2010; www.iht.com, 21 January 2010; www.independent.co.uk, 21 January 2010; www.cnn.com, 22 January, 2010)

US Secretary of State Hillary Clinton said ... the United States intended to address issues of internet freedom within its relationship with Beijing ... She named Tunisia, Uzbekistan, Vietnam and Egypt, as well as China, where the 'free flow of information' was threatened.

(www.bbc.co.uk, 21 January 2010)

US Secretary of State Hillary Clinton: 'A new information curtain is descending across much of the world' ... [She was] describing growing curbs on the internet as the modern equivalent of the Berlin Wall. She cited China, Iran, Saudi Arabia and Egypt among countries that censored the net or harassed bloggers.

(*Independent*, 22 January 2010)

US Secretary of State Hillary Clinton likened online censorship by countries such as China, Vietnam and Iran to the rise of communist Europe, warning that a new 'information curtain' threatened to descend on the world unless action to protect internet freedoms was taken.

(*Guardian*, 22 January 2010, p. 15)

US Secretary of State Hillary Clinton ... cited China as among a number of countries where there has been 'a spike in threats to the free flow of information' over the past year. She also named Tunisia, Uzbekistan, Egypt and Vietnam ... Mrs Clinton made her remarks in a wide-ranging speech in Washington about internet freedom and its place in US foreign policy ... Mrs Clinton called on China to conduct a thorough and transparent investigation into the recent cyber-attacks on Google which also targeted dozens of other US companies.

(www.thetimes.co.uk, 21 January 2010)

'About 30 per cent of the world's internet users had restricted access, she said ... She warned that China's economy ... would ultimately be harmed by its attempts to control information' (www.thetimes.co.uk, 22 January 2010).

Foreign ministry spokesman Ma Zhaoxu (22 January 2010):

> The United States has criticized China's policies to administer the internet and insinuated that China restricts internet freedom. This runs contrary to the facts and is harmful to China–US relations. We urge the United States to respect the facts and cease using so-called internet freedom to make groundless accusations against China ... We are firmly against this statement that goes against truth and damages the US-Sino relationship. China has its own national conditions and cultural traditions. China regulates the internet according to laws, which is consistent with worldwide norms ... [Chinese laws forbid internet hacking and violation of privacy] ... China encourages cracking down on internet hacking by strengthening international co-operation and protecting internet security and citizen privacy according to the laws.
>
> (www.thetimes.co.uk, 22 January 2010; www.cnn.com, 22 January 2010)

> In its editorial [of Friday 22 January] the English language edition of *The Global Times* said ... US Secretary of State Hillary Clinton ... had raised the stakes in Washington's clash with Beijing over internet freedom. The American demand for an unfettered internet was a form of 'information imperialism', the newspaper said, because less developed nations cannot possibly compete with Western countries in the area of information flow. The newspaper said: 'The US campaign for uncensored and free flow of information on an unrestricted internet is a disguised attempt to impose its values on other cultures in the name of democracy. The US government's ideological imposition is unacceptable and, for that reason, will not be allowed to succeed.'
>
> (www.iht.com, 23 January 2010)

Editorial, *Global Times* (22 January):

> With her seemingly impassioned speech, US Secretary of State Hillary Clinton may be said to have raised the stakes in Washington's clash with Beijing over internet freedom ... The US campaign for uncensored and free flow of information on an unrestricted internet is a disguised attempt to impose its values on other cultures in the name of democracy ... The free flow of information is a universal value treasured in all nations, including China, but the US government's ideological imposition is unacceptable and, for that reason, will not be allowed to succeed. China's real stake in the "free flow of information" is evident in its refusal to be victimized by informational imperialism.'
>
> (www.bbc.co.uk, 22 January 2010)

A White House spokesman (22 January): 'As the president [Barack Obama] has said, he continues to be troubled by the cyber-security breach that Google attributes to China. All we are looking for from China are some answers' (www.bbc.co.uk, 22 January 2010).

> The United States used 'online warfare' to stir up unrest in Iran after last year's elections, the Chinese Communist Party newspaper claimed today

[24 January] ... An editorial in the *People's Daily* accused the United States of launching a 'hacker brigade' and said it had used social media such as Twitter to spread rumours and create trouble ... The editorial said: 'Behind what America calls free speech is naked political scheming. How did the unrest after the Iranian election come about? It was because online warfare, launched by America via YouTube video and Twitter microblogging, spread rumours, created splits, stirred up and sowed discord between the followers of conservative reformist factions.'

(www.guardian.co.uk, 24 January 2010; *Guardian*, 25 January 2010, p. 16)

An editorial in *People's Daily*, the newspaper of the Chinese Communist Party, accused the United States on Sunday [24 January] of mounting a cyber-army and a 'hacker brigade' and of exploiting social media to foment unrest in Iran ... China has blocked YouTube since March and Twitter since June [2009].

(*IHT*, 25 January 2010, p. 8)

A spokesman for the Ministry of Industry and Information Technology (25 January): '[Any] accusation that the Chinese government participated in cyber-attacks, either in an explicit or inexplicit way, is groundless and aims to denigrate China. We are firmly opposed to that. China's policy on internet safety is transparent and consistent' ... He also noted China has launched internet safety campaigns against such attacks.

(www.cnn.com, 25 January 2010)

A spokesman for the Ministry of Industry and Information Technology (25 January): 'Any accusation that the Chinese government participated in cyber-attacks, either in an explicit or indirect way, is groundless and aims to denigrate China. We are firmly opposed to that. China's policy on internet safety is transparent and consistent' ... The spokesman added that China was the biggest victim of such attacks, with hackers targeting more than 42,000 websites last year [2009]. Using figures from the Internet Society of China, he said cyber-attacks from overseas increased 148 per cent from 2007 to 2008, affecting 'sectors of finance, transportation and energy, which posed severe harm to economic development and people's lives' ... A spokesman for the State Council Information Office (25 January 2010): '[China] bans using the internet to subvert state power and wreck national unity, to incite ethnic hatred and division, to promote cults and to distribute content that is pornographic, salacious, violent or terrorist. China has an ample legal basis for punishing such harmful content, and there is no room for doubting this. This is completely different from so-called restriction of internet freedom' ... The State Council information office is the cabinet arm of China's propaganda apparatus and one of several agencies that control the internet.

(www.guardian.co.uk, 25 January 2010)

On Monday [25 January] ... the Ministry of Industry and Information Technology said the country's anti-hacking policy is transparent and consistent

> … The Communist Party's official *People's Daily* newspaper, meanwhile, accused the US government of strictly controlling the internet at home while urging other countries to build an 'internet freedom utopia' … A Chinese internet security official … Zhou Yonglin … said the team logged attacks on 262,000 Chinese computers last year [2009] by hackers implanting malicious software such as Trojans, which can allow outside access to the target's computer. More than 16 per cent of the attacks came from computers located in the United States.
>
> (www.iht.com, 25 January 2010)

> Zhou Yonglin, the deputy operations chief of China's national Computer Network Emergency Response Technical Team, is quoted as saying that China was the world's largest target for hackers, with more than 262,000 internet addresses under assault last year [2009], and that the greatest share of attacks – one in six – originated in the United States. Mr Zhou also questioned Google's claim that attacks on its computers had been traced to Chinese soil, saying that other American companies had sought his agency's help after previous attacks, but that it 'has not been alerted to any specific report on the issue submitted by Google'. He said: 'We have been hoping that Google will contact us so that we could have details on this issue and provide them help if necessary' … Separately, an identified spokesman for the State Council Information Office defended as 'totally correct' China's censorship on internet sites that the government deems harmful. The spokesman said: 'We are resolutely against those who make an issue of things without referring to actual facts by needlessly accusing China, ignoring Chinese laws and interfering in Chinese internal politics.'
>
> (www.iht.com, 25 January 2010; *IHT*, 26 January 2010, p. 15)

'Chinese Human Rights Defenders said its website and four other activist sites were hit by denial of service attacks on 23–24 January. It called the Chinese government the most likely culprit' (www.iht.com, 25 January 2010).

'As this newspaper reported last week, thirty-four American corporations have recently been targets of hacking attacks traceable to China' (www.iht.com, 3 February 2010).

> Imitation websites of Google and YouTube have emerged in China … YouTubecn.com offers videos from the real YouTube, which is blocked in China. The Google imitation is called Goojje and includes a plea for … Google … not to leave China.
>
> (*IHT*, 29 January 2010, p. 19)

> In addition to independent criminals … computer security specialists say there are so-called patriotic hackers who focus their attacks on political targets. Then there are the intelligence-orientated hackers inside the People's Liberation Army, as well as more shadowy groups that are believed to work with the state government … Because it is difficult to trace hackers, exactly who is behind any specific attack and how and where they operate remains

to a large extent a mystery, technology experts say … Computer hacking is illegal in China. Last year [2009] Beijing revised and stiffened a law that made hacking a crime, with punishments of up to seven years in prison … The law … is not strictly enforced.

(www.iht.com, 2 February 2010; *IHT*, 3 February 2010, p. 13)

[The UK's] security service MI5 has accused China of bugging and burgling UK executives and setting up 'honey-traps' in a bid to blackmail them into betraying sensitive commercial secrets. A leaked MI5 document says that undercover intelligence officers from the People's Liberation Army and the Ministry of Public Security have also approached UK businessmen at trade fairs and exhibitions with the offer of 'gifts' and 'lavish hospitality'. The gifts – cameras and memory sticks – have been found to contain electronic Trojan bugs which provide the Chinese with remote access to users' computers. MI5 says the Chinese government 'represents one of the most significant espionage threats to the UK' because of its use of these methods, as well as widespread electronic hacking … The 'restricted' report describes how China has attacked UK defence, energy, communications and manufacturing companies in a concerted hacking campaign. It claims China has also gone much further, targeting the computer networks and email accounts of public relations companies and international law firms … In 2007 Jonathan Evans, the director-general of MI5, had written privately to 300 executives of banks and other businesses warning them that their IT systems were under attack from 'Chinese state organizations'. There have been other unconfirmed reports that China has tried to hack into computers belonging to the Foreign Office, nine other Whitehall departments and parliament. Last year [2009] a report of Whitehall's Joint Intelligence Committee said China may be capable of shutting down critical services such as power, food and water supplies. But the latest document is the most comprehensive and explicit warning to be issued by the UK authorities on the new threat. Entitled *The Threat from Chinese Espionage*, it was circulated to hundreds of City and business leaders last year.

(www.thetimes.co.uk, 31 January 2010)

Britain's powerful Joint Intelligence Committee, responsible for analysing and co-ordinating policy between MI5 and MI6, the Secret Intelligence Service that is responsible for Britain's foreign intelligence activities, warned last year [2009] that China's growing sophistication in cyber-espionage could enable it to shut down critical services, including power, food and water supplies.

(www.iht.com, 1 February 2010)

'A distinct shift toward more comprehensive controls began nearly two years ago and has hardened over the past six months, analysts say' (*IHT*, 10 February 2010).

In China an estimated four-fifths of computer software is pirated … New government procurement rules require state buyers to give preference to

> Chinese-made computers and communications products, among other supplies and services. James Mulvenon, director of the Center for Intelligence Research and Analysis, a Washington-based consulting firm, said such orders were typically ignored.
>
> (www.iht.com, 12 February 2010)

> China has closed down what is believed to be the country's biggest training website for hackers, state media has reported. They say the site, Black Hawk Safety Net, gave lessons in hacking and sold downloads of malicious software. The reports say three people were arrested ... The hacker training operation openly recruited thousands of members online and provided them with cyber-attack lessons and Trojan software ... Trojans, which can allow outside access to a computer when implanted, are used by hackers to illegally control computers. Black Hawk Safety Net recruited more than 12,000 paying subscribers and collected more than 7 million yuan ($1 million) in membership fees, while another 170,000 people had signed up for free membership.
>
> (www.bbc.co.uk, 8 February 2010)

'Black Hawk Safety net ... collected more than 7 million yuan ($1.02 million) in membership fees ... Authorities were tipped off to its existence while investigating a cyber-attack in 2007. Some suspects arrested in that case were members of Black Hawk' (www.cnn.com, 8 February 2010).

> China has not shut down the well known servers that have been used in these attacks ... [on] Google and other Western companies ... or arrested their operators ... The Black Hawk Safety Net ... [is] said to be used to raise more than $1 million in membership fees from 12,000 paying members ... The website was started in 2005 and had another 170,000 free members, Xinhua reported on Monday [8 February] ... The *Wuhan Evening Post* reported on Sunday [7 February] that the police had actually arrested three people associated with Black Hawk Safety Net last November [2009] ... Xinhua did not mention in its report on Monday that the arrests had taken place in November, giving the impression that they were very recent ... China amended its criminal code last year [2009] to make it a crime to make computer hacking tools available to others. The National Computer Network Emergency Response Co-ordination Centre of China has calculated that hackers caused losses of $1.11 billion last year ... [Wuhan is the capital of Hebei province].
>
> (www.iht.com, 8 February 2010)

> Wuhan happens to be home to the Communication Command Academy, which trains hackers, according to US Congressional testimony by cyber expert James Mulvenon in 2008 ... The popularity of hacking in China, and hackers' use of multiple addresses and servers, in Taiwan and elsewhere, makes it hard to prove how or by whom they are co-ordinated.
>
> (www.independent.co.uk, 8 February 2010)

'A spokesman for the Ministry of Industry and Information Technology has described China as the biggest victim of the practice, saying hackers tampered with more than 42,000 websites last year [2009]' (www.guardian.co.uk, 8 February 2010).

> Google has sent a cease and desist letter to the operators of a Chinese search website whose logo bears a close resemblance to its own. Goojje's home page is adorned with a Google-style logo and the familiar paw print logo of ... Baidu ... Google's logo is protected by trademark.
>
> (www.independent.co.uk, 9 February 2010)

> A series of online attacks on Google and dozens of other American corporations have been traced to computers at two educational institutions in China, including one with close ties to the Chinese military, say people involved in the investigation. They also said the attacks, aimed at stealing trade secrets and computer codes and capturing email of Chinese human rights activists, may have begun as early as April [2009], months earlier than previously believed. Google announced on 12 January [2010] that it and other companies had been subjected to sophisticated attacks that probably came from China ... Until recently, the trail had led only to servers in Taiwan ... The Chinese schools involved are Shanghai Jiatong University and the Lanxiang Vocational School ... Jiatong has one of China's top computer science programmes ... Lanxiang, in east China's Shandong province, is a huge vocational school that was established with military support and trains some computer scientists for the military ... Independent researchers who monitor Chinese information warfare caution that the Chinese have adopted a highly distributed approach to online espionage, making it almost impossible to prove where an attack originated ... The Chinese government often involves volunteer 'patriotic hackers' to support its policies.
>
> (www.iht.com, 19 February 2010; *IHT*, 20 February 2010, p. 8)

> Security experts caution that it is hard to trace online attacks and that the digital footprints may be a 'false flag', a kind of decoy intended to throw investigators off track. But those with knowledge of the investigation say there are reliable clues that suggest the highly sophisticated attacks may have originated at Jiatong and the more obscure campus, Lanxiang Vocational School in Shandong, an institution with ties to the military. Last weekend the two schools strongly denied any knowledge of the attacks, which singled out corporate files and the email accounts of human rights activists ... Lanxiang ... was founded in 1984 by a former military officer on land donated by the military.
>
> (www.iht.com, 22 February 2010; *IHT*, 23 February 2010, p. 15)

> US analysts believe they have identified the Chinese author of the critical programming code used in the alleged state-sponsored hacking attacks on Google and other Western companies ... A freelance security consultant in his thirties wrote the part of the programme that used a previously unknown

security hole in the Internet Explorer web browser to break into computers and insert the spyware … The man who wrote code to take advantage of the browser flaw is not a full-times government worker, did not launch the attack, and in fact would prefer not to be used in such offensive efforts, according the US team that discovered his role.

(*FT*, 22 February 2010, p. 1)

The United States and the EU are pushing China to soften or drop plans for compulsory certification of a range of technology products, as foreign IT companies warn that Beijing's regulatory requirements are pushing them out of the market … Rules set to take effect on 1 May [2010] will exclude suppliers of encryption-related products such as firewalls, secure routers or smart-cards from government tenders unless they undergo testing and certification to meet Chinese standards. In some cases this will require submitting software source codes and other confidential information. Foreign businesses fear the authorities could pass information on to their state-owned competitors. They also argue their products could become unsafe if Beijing used its knowledge of software architecture to install 'backdoors' for surveillance.

(*FT*, 22 February 2010, p. 4)

For a decade Beijing has been making steadily stricter demands on producers of information security products such as encryption software, smart-cards and secure routers. Compulsory certification and domestic technology standard requirements in effect force suppliers to share their technology with the government … Foreign companies complain they will have to operate 'bifurcated product lines' for different markets which benefit local rivals. The rules even include outright prohibitions on non-Chinese suppliers for some security products. Then there is the reasonable fear Beijing may pass the technology it certifies on to Chinese companies. The more insidious implication is political. The better Beijing's mastery of encryption technology, the more easily its censors can circumvent them.

(*FT*, editorial, 23 February 2010, p. 14)

The Chinese government has denied that Google Gmail accounts were hacked into from school computers … Foreign ministry spokesman Ma Zhaoxu branded the accusation 'groundless'. He added that it was 'irresponsible' to blame the government for the attacks … Meanwhile, Google and China are set to resume talks about Google's wish to operate an unfiltered search engine in the country, according to *The Wall Street Journal* … At the moment Google is still censoring search results in China.

(www.bbc.co.uk, 23 February 2010)

Google's assertion that its computers were attacked by hackers based in China was 'groundless', Beijing said today [23 February] … The remarks from foreign ministry spokesman Qin Gang were the first direct rejection of the firm's allegations. China had previously defended its right to censor content on the internet and brushed aside the hacking accusations, saying Google must abide by Chinese law ... The prestigious Shanghai Jiaotong University and previously unknown Lanxiang Vocational College, a high school-level institution, have both denied any role in the attacks. The foreign ministry's Qin Gang said the schools' comments showed the reports were false, as were claims of a link with Beijing ... Qin Gang: 'Google's statement from 12 January is groundless, and we are firmly opposed to it ... China administers its internet according to law, and this position will not change. China prohibits hacking and will crack down on hacking according to law ... Reports that these attacks came from Chinese schools are totally groundless and the accusation of Chinese government involvement is also irresponsible and driven by ulterior motives' ... Xinhua said the stories were 'arbitrary and full of bias'. Chinese people know little about online security, and so their computers can easily be taken over by hackers to give the impression that the hackers are based in China, it said. Google's Chinese language search engine is still censoring results, but talks between the firm and the Chinese government, on whether the firm might be able to run an unrestricted search service within Chinese law, have restarted, *The Wall Street Journal* reported today [23 February].

(www.independent.co.uk, 23 February 2010)

China has tightened controls on internet use, requiring anyone who wants to set up a website to meet regulators and produce identity documents. The technology ministry said the measures were designed to tackle online pornography ... A number of websites are now being registered overseas in an attempt to avoid controls ... The Ministry of Industry and Information Technology on Tuesday [23 February] lifted a freeze introduced in December [2009] on registration for new individual websites. But the technology ministry said would-be operators now have to submit identity cards and photos of themselves, as well as meeting regulators before their sites could be registered ... The Chinese authorities have launched a number of campaigns against online pornography, with the government saying thousands of people were detained last year [2009] alone.

(www.bbc.co.uk, 23 February 2010)

The computer attack which led Google to threaten leaving China ... appears to have been deployed by amateurs, according to an analysis by a US technology firm ... Gunter Ollman (vice president of research at Damballa, an Atlanta-based company that provides computer network security): 'I would say this particular botnet group was not well funded, in which case I would not conclude they were state sponsored, because the level of the tools used would have been far superior to what it was' ... However, Ollman points out that the attackers – who emanated from China – could have been contracted by outside parties to launch the attack. And while the deployment of the attack was not sophisticated, the Internet Explorer software vulnerability

> it exploited to infiltrate Google was ... McAfee Security insights blog called the Google incident a 'sophisticated, multi-vector attack'.
>
> (www.cnn.com, 3 March 2010)

Study abroad

> A new study found that seven out of every ten students who enrol in an overseas university never return to live in their homeland ... The Chinese Academy of Social Science revealed 1.06 million Chinese had gone to study overseas since 1978, but only 275,000 had returned ... In 2005 118,500 students left China to study overseas. By 2010 the forecast is 200,000.
>
> (*Guardian*, 2 June 2007, p. 22)

'Thirty years ago there were no Chinese students studying in American universities; this academic year there are 67,000, while there are 11,000 Americans studying on China's campuses' (www.iht.com, 6 January 2009).

> While India was, for the eighth consecutive year, the leading country of origin for international students [studying in the United States] – sending 104,260 students, a 9 per cent increase over the previous year – China is rapidly catching up, sending 98,510 last year [2008], a 21 per cent increase ... Overall, the number of international students at colleges and universities in the United States increased by 8 per cent to an all-time high of 671,616 in the 2008–9 academic year – the largest percentage increase in more than twenty-five years ... The number of international students exceeded the past peak enrolment years, 2002–3, by 14.5 per cent. In 2008–9 undergraduate enrolment rose 11 per cent, compared with only a 2 per cent increase in graduate enrolment ... Last year China sent 26,275 undergraduates and 57,451 graduate students to the United States – compared with 8,034 undergraduates and 50,976 graduate students five years earlier.
>
> (www.iht.com, 16 November 2009)

Direct elections at the local level

'The party is experimenting with multiple candidates and contested election campaigns for local party committees at the village level. Eighty per cent of village-level governments already have this practice and party committees are now moving in the same direction' (*IHT*, 7 July 2007, p. 4).

> Shortly after he came to power Hu Jintao abrogated experiments, conducted in a few provinces in the last years of Jiang Zemin's tenure, of one-person-one-vote elections to pick the heads of towns and rural townships. Right now Beijing only allows polls at the village level, which were begun by Deng Xiaoping in 1979.
>
> (Willy Lam, *FEER*, November 2007, p. 29)

Earlier this year [2008] Shenzhen's leaders seemed eager to use the anniversary of the [December 1978] political meeting … known as Third Plenum … to position the city as a pioneer for a new era of political reform. Guangdong's new governor, Wang Yang, had encouraged experimentation in better governance, and Shenzhen officials published a reform proposal that advocated some local elections and more independence for local legislatures and courts. But those plans, later tempered by provincial leaders, now seem derailed as officials are focused on staunching the economic damage and maintaining social stability in the face of sporadic protests from workers from shuttered factories.

(*IHT*, 19 December 2008)

Grassroots elections, specifically letting peasants pick village-level administrators through the ballot box, were begun by Deng Xiaoping thirty years ago. In the late 1990s farmers in a dozen-odd towns and townships, which are one rung higher than villages in the Chinese hierarchy, were permitted on a temporary basis to elect the heads of their local administrations. Then President Jiang Zemin reportedly also harboured plans to experiment with other forms of elections at the township, and even county, levels. All such innovations have been stopped in the past year.

(Willy Lam, 'Hu Jintao's Great Leap Backward',
FEER, January–February 2009, p. 21)

7 Health issues

SARS and EV71

Officials in southern China are cracking down on illegal trade in civet cats to prevent an outbreak of SARS in the coming months, state news media said Monday [19 February 2007]. About 7,000 health inspectors have been mobilized in Guangdong province, where severe acute respiratory syndrome first emerged in 2002, and have checked 10,000 restaurants for civet cats … Civet cats, mongoose-like animals, are considered a delicacy in southern China and are suspected of spreading SARS to humans, although the original source of the virus has not been determined. In January 2004 Guangdong banned the raising, selling, killing and eating of civet cats. But health departments have been receiving increasing reports of illegal trade in the animals since November [2006] … During recent inspections a live civet cat and several frozen ones were confiscated and eighteen restaurants were fined … The disease that was eventually identified as SARS was first reported in Guangdong in November 2002. It was spread by travellers to dozens of countries and killed 774 people worldwide before subsiding in June 2003. There were 349 deaths reported on the Chinese mainland. China was heavily criticized for being slow to release information on its outbreak and has since been trying to co-operate in investigating emerging diseases like SARS and bird flu.

(www.iht.com, 19 February 2007)

As Typhoon Krosa barrelled toward eastern China over the weekend every level of the Chinese government was whipped into action, evacuating 1.4 million people from the two coastal provinces on which Krosa set its sights … Analysts and observers said China's ability to move hundreds of thousands of people out of harm's way speaks to the country's exceptional ability to mobilize resources and people to deal with disasters … The efficiency cannot be entirely attributed to a central communist regime and obedient populace, said … the American Red Cross … [which argues that] the situation really dramatically changed after the SARS scare … in 2003 and 2004 … [which] really highlighted the gaps.

(www.cnn.com, 9 October 2007)

A fast-spreading viral outbreak in eastern China has killed twenty-one children, sickened nearly 3,000 others and caused panic among parents in an impoverished corner of Anhui province, state news media reported Friday [2 May 2008]. The intestinal virus, commonly known as hand, foot and mouth disease, has been spreading in the city of Fuyang since early March, but local officials only announced the outbreak last week, raising questions of whether they were trying to conceal word of the growing problem.

In recent days the Chinese media have heavily criticized the government response, offering comparisons to the SARS epidemic of 2003, which drew widespread attention to China's shaky public health system and official attempts to cover up the outbreak. On Thursday [1 May 2008] the WHO warned that the disease, which thrives in warm weather, could spread in the coming months ... The virus, which has no relation to the foot-and-mouth disease that infects livestock, is easily passed between children. The illness begins with a fever and often leads to mouth ulcers and blisters on the hands, feet and buttocks. There is no vaccine or cure ... Health officials in Fuyang say that 700 children remain hospitalized, thirty-six of them in serious condition. All of the fatalities have been in children younger than six, the majority of them under two ... Fuyang is perhaps best known as the epicentre of a powdered milk scandal four years ago that sickened infants, killing thirteen of them ... In recent days the Chinese media have not been shy about lambasting health officials for waiting a month to sound the alarm bells. In mid-April [2008], they noted, local officials who were confronted by reporters denied there was a problem. Two weeks later, after more than a dozen children had died, they were forced to acknowledge that an outbreak was well under way ... During the SARS outbreak Chinese officials withheld information from the WHO, restricted media reporting and undercounted the cases of those stricken. After the disease spread beyond China's borders and provoked worldwide panic, the government apologized and pledged to confront future health emergencies with greater openness.

(www.iht.com, 2 May 2008)

China has issued a nationwide health alert in an effort to control the outbreak of a virus which has killed twenty-two children in the east of the country. A statement from the health ministry said it was taking urgent measures to prevent the spread of the infection, known as Enterovirus 71 (EV71). The highly contagious intestinal virus can cause fever, blisters in the mouth and a rash on the hands and feet. Officials fear the virus has spread from eastern provinces to the south. Health authorities across the country have been told to report all cases of the virus within twenty-four hours ... The outbreak emerged in Fuyang city in March, but was only reported last week. The delay has led to accusations of a cover-up by local authorities. The Chinese health ministry has rejected charges that it has failed to handle the situation properly, arguing that medical teams had been trying to work out what the illness was. The number of children infected

> with EV71 has risen sharply since the outbreak was disclosed. Public health experts think cases will keep rising before peaking around June or July [2008], the WHO said … Almost 1,000 children are currently receiving hospital treatment, fifty-eight of whom are in a critical or serious condition, the health ministry said.
>
> (www.bbc.co.uk, 3 May 2008)

> China's health ministry strengthened surveillance and dispatched specialists to eastern China's Anhui province as the death toll from a virulent disease climbed to twenty-two, the country's Xinhua news agency reported. As of Friday [3 May] there were 3,321 reported cases of the virus in children. The illness – known as Enterovirus 71 – can cause hand, foot and mouth disease (HFMD). A total of 978 children are hospitalized, an Anhui province official told Xinhua. Forty-eight of them are in critical condition … [The health ministry issued] a nationwide order … The order said preventing infectious diseases was needed 'to guarantee the smooth staging of the Beijing Olympics and Paralympics and to practically preserve social stability'. As well as hand, foot and mouth disease, the order targeted other infectious diseases including hepatitis A and measles.
>
> (www.cnn.com, 3 May 2008)

'The death toll from a common illness that typically causes little more than a fever has risen to twenty-four children and health officials fear the worst may be yet to come as outbreaks occur in neighbouring countries' (*IHT*, 5 May 2008, p. 4).

> Cases of a virus that has killed twenty-four children … may continue despite efforts to contain it, the WHO warned yesterday [Sunday 4 May]. Enterovirus 71 (EV71), which causes a severe strain of hand, foot and mouth disease, normally peaks in June and July. Experts fear that infections could increase as the weather becomes warmer … In Fuyang, eastern Anhui province, twenty-two deaths have occurred … WHO China representative Hans Troedsson: 'I do not see it at all as a threat to the Olympics or any upcoming events' … There is no vaccine or cure for hand, foot and mouth disease … It is a common illness among infants and children and it is not usually fatal. However, the virus EV71 can result in a more serious form of the illness and complications including meningitis and heart problems can prove fatal … Two more children were reported dead this weekend, in Guangdong province, 1,000 miles south of Anhui. But Troedsson said the virus had probably come from different sources rather than spread, as had small outbreaks reported in Shaanxi and Hubei … This weekend's order from the health ministry warned that anyone covering up or delaying disclosure of outbreaks faced punishment. The virus EV71 was first identified in the 1960s. But the past decade has witnessed several large outbreaks across Asia.
>
> (*Guardian*, 5 May 2008, p. 14)

The toll from an intestinal virus ... is continuing to rise ... A child died in Zhejiang province bringing the number of deaths from Enterovirus 71 to twenty-six. According to state media, more than 8,500 cases have now been reported, with 5,151 of these in Anhui province. EV71 is highly contagious, causing fever, blisters in the mouth and a rash on the hands and feet. The outbreak emerged in Fuyang city in March, but was only reported in mid-April ... Twenty-two have died in the province [Anhui] and three deaths have also been reported in Guangdong province. The delay in reporting the outbreak has led to accusations of a cover-up by local authorities ... But on Sunday [4 May] the WHO's representative in Beijing, Hans Troedsson, defended the authorities. He said: 'The reason why there was a delay in the reporting at the provincial level was that they did not know what the causes for these different cases were.'

(www.bbc.co.uk, 5 May 2008)

China on Monday [5 May] reported a sharp increase in the number of children affected by hand, foot and mouth disease, saying that more than 9,700 cases had been reported. At least twenty-four deaths in Anhui and Guangdong provinces have been attributed to EV71, one of several viruses that cause the disease ... Two other children, one in Guangdong province and one in Zhejiang province, also died from the disease, but it was not clear by which strain.

(*IHT*, 6 May 2008, p. 4)

Hand and mouth disease [HFMD] has struck 11,905 people and has proved fatal in twenty-six cases, all of them children, China's state-run news agency Xinhua reported Monday [5 May]. The official count has increased dramatically in recent days, the result of an order issued Friday by the ministry of health mandating that all cases be reported ... the worst hit province, Anhui in rural eastern China, where twenty-two of the fatalities have occurred, all of them blamed on EV71, one of the most common causes of HFMD ... HFMD can be caused by a number of intestinal viruses, of which EV71 and Coxsackie A16 are among the most common ... All the deaths in Anhui occurred in Fuyang city and 1,314 of the 4,496 children infected in the city were hospitalized ... Of the total 5,840 child infections in the province, 689 were registered Sunday [4 May] ... Fuyang officials have been accused of sitting on information of the outbreak last month [March] even as children were dying. But a WHO official said weeks passed between the outbreak in mid-March and the first reports because they did not know what they were dealing with. Local officials say they are doing all they can. Though the case fatality rate has dropped from 11 per cent during March to 0.2 per cent during April, according to the WHO, the number of people infected shows no signs of decreasing. Zhejiang province in east China has reported 1,198 infections among children this year [2008]; a five-year-old boy died last month [April]. It reported 101 cases in 2005, 793 cases in 2006 and 1,607 cases last year [2007] ... Guangdong province reported 1,692 cases ...

> Cases have been identified in … Chongqing municipality … Beijing … Hebei province … [and] in the provinces of Jiangsu, Hunan, Shaanxi, Jiangxi and Henan … A large outbreak of HFMD occurred in Taiwan in 1998 with seventy-eight deaths, and smaller outbreaks recurred there in 2000 and 2001.
>
> (www.cnn.com, 6 May 2008)

> The death toll from China's outbreak of HFMD has climbed to twenty-eight – all of them children, Xinhua reported Wednesday [7 May]. The latest deaths were reported by the health bureaus in central China's Hunan province and the Guangxi Zhuang Autonomous Region in the south-west … Authorities reported 15,799 cases of the disease on Tuesday [6 May].
>
> (www.cnn.com, 7 May 2008)

'China last year [2007] saw a total of 80,000 cases and seventeen deaths' (*The Economist*, 10 May 2008, p. 80).

> Beijing … recorded its first death from hand, foot and mouth disease on Wednesday [14 May] … The illness has sickened tens of thousands of children across the country and killed at least forty-two people. A child died Sunday [11 May] on the way to hospital … Another child died of the illness in Beijing, but the death was counted in the victim's home province of Hebei, which neighbours Beijing. A twenty-one-month boy also died of the virus Monday [12 May] in Hubei province … The three newly reported deaths raise the countrywide death toll to forty-two since late March. Hand, foot and mouth disease has sickened more than 24,934 children in seven Chinese provinces plus Beijing … Xinhua said 3,606 infections had been reported in Beijing as of Monday [12 May] … Cases have been reported from Guangdong province in the south to Jilin province in the north-east, and in major cities like Beijing and Shanghai … The death rate has gone down drastically since early May [according to the WHO] … Most cases in China this year [2008] have been blamed on EV71.
>
> (www.iht.com, 14 May 2008)

Bird flu

> The flocks of migratory birds that winged their way south to Africa last autumn [2005] and then back over Europe in recent weeks did not carry the H5N1 flu virus or spread it during their annual journey, scientists have concluded, defying officials' dire predictions … It is quiet now in terms of cases, which is contrary to what many people had expected … In thousands of samples collected in Africa this winter, H5N1 was not detected in a single wild bird, officials and scientists said. In Europe there have been only a handful of cases detected in wild birds since 1 April, at the height of the northward migration. The number of cases in Europe has decreased so dramatically compared to February, when dozens of new cases were found

daily, that experts believe the northward spring migration played no role. There was one grebe in Denmark on 28 April – the last case – as well as a falcon in Germany and a few swans in France, according to the World Organization for Animal Health ... The February cases in Europe were attributed to infected wild swans that travelled west to avoid severe cold in Russia and Central Asia but apparently never carried the virus to Africa ... Worldwide ... the H5N1 bird virus ... has killed about 200 humans, almost all people who were in extremely close contact with sick birds ... While avian influenza has become a huge problem in domestic poultry on farms in a few African countries, like Egypt, Nigeria and Sudan, experts increasingly suspect that it was introduced there through imported infected poultry and poultry products ... Farm-based outbreaks of avian influenza are still occurring constantly in a number of countries, although not in Europe. The Ivory Coast had its first outbreak of bird flu, on a farm, last week.

(www.iht.com, 10 May 2006; *IHT*, 11 May 2006, pp. 1, 7)

Even as it crops up in the far corners of Europe and Africa, the virulent bird flu that raised fears of a human pandemic has been largely snuffed out in the parts of South-east Asia where it claimed its first and most numerous victims ... said David Nabarro, chief pandemic flu co-ordinator for the United Nations. Vietnam, which has had almost half of the human cases of A(H5N1) flu in the world, has not seen a single case in humans or a single outbreak in poultry this year [2006]. Thailand, the second hardest hit nation until Indonesia recently passed it, has not had a human case for five months [correction in *IHT*, 17 May 2006, p. 3] or one in poultry in six months. Encouraging signs have also come from China, though they are harder to interpret ... Confounding expectations, birds making the spring migration north from Africa have not carried the virus into Europe. David Nabarro and other officials warn that it would be highly premature to declare any sort of victory. The virus has moved rapidly across continents and is still rampaging in Myanmar and other countries nearby. It could still hitchhike back in the illegal trade in chicks, fighting cocks or tropical pets, or in migrating birds ... Very different tactics led to success in ... Thailand and Vietnam ... While Vietnam began vaccinating all its 220 million chickens last summer [2005], Thailand did not because it has a large poultry export industry, and other nations would have banned its birds indefinitely. (Vaccines can mask the virus instead of killing it.) Instead, Thailand culled wide areas around infected flocks, compensated farmers generously and deputized a volunteer in every village to report sick chickens. It vaccinates fighting cocks, which can be worth thousands of dollars, and even issues them passports with their vaccination records so they can travel ... Thailand and Vietnam also delivered the antiviral drug Tamiflu to even the smallest regional hospitals and told doctors to treat all flu patients even before laboratory diagnoses could be made ... Hints suggest that the disease is being beaten back in China, the country where it is assumed to have begun. International officials tend to

> greet official public health reports from China sceptically, in part because it concealed the outbreak of the SARS virus there for months. It did not officially report any bird cases for years, even though many scientists contend the virus incubated there between its first appearance in humans in Hong Kong in 1997 and the current outbreak, which began in Vietnam in 2003 … China's reported human cases have remained low: eight last year [2005] and ten this year [2006]. Perhaps more important, its poultry cases … seem to be dropping … China said it had outbreaks in sixteen provinces in 2004. In 2005 it reported outbreaks in only twelve provinces, but one in November [2005] was so large that 2.5 million birds were culled to contain it. After that the agriculture minister announced that it would vaccinate every domestic bird in China … In Cambodia and Laos, which separate Thailand and Vietnam, the situation is vague. Laos has reported no human cases and last reported outbreaks two years ago. Cambodia's reported human cases dropped to two this year [2006], from four last year [2005]. No poultry outbreaks were reported, but surveillance is so spotty that some must have occurred and gone unnoticed … because the country's six human victims were infected by poultry … Where the South-east Asian governments have taken action, however, the risk of the virus returning is ever present, David Nabarro said. For example, he said, it probably exists in Vietnam in Muscovy ducks, which can harbour the virus but do not get sick, and it has turned up in isolated birds in open-air markets near the Chinese border. (Single birds do not constitute an outbreak.) Since Chinese farmers can get three times as much for a chicken in Vietnam as they can at home, the temptation to smuggle persists.
>
> (Donald McNeil, *IHT*, 15 May 2006, p. 4)

> The number of confirmed human deaths from bird flu for 2003, 2004, 2005 and 2006 (as of 12 May), respectively, are as follows: Thailand: zero, twelve, two and zero; Cambodia: zero, zero, four and two; Vietnam: three, twenty, nineteen and zero.
>
> (ibid.)

'A fifth member of an Indonesian family has died of bird flu, according to local tests – it was announced [on 14 May] … Samples from the patients have been sent to the WHO' (*Guardian*, 15 May 2006, p. 22).

> WHO officials said Thursday [18 May] that the five avian flu deaths confirmed this week on Sumatra were probably not a result of human-to-human infection and did not suggest that the virus had mutated into a more deadly form. Five family members were confirmed dead from the H5N1 strain of avian influenza by the WHO on Wednesday, the largest such cluster yet recorded. A sixth family member died of flu-like symptoms but was not tested for the virus … [The WHO said] the number of deaths raised eyebrows but that so far … the recent cluster … is similar to other outbreaks in Indonesia, which were caused by close contacts with infected poultry …

Indonesia's toll has now reached thirty, second only to Vietnam, which has recorded forty-two. Indonesia, however, has been recording bird flu deaths at a much higher rate than any other country in recent months ... A woman died of bird flu in Egypt on Thursday, the sixth death from the disease in that country.

(www.iht.com, 18 May 2006; *IHT*, 19 May 2006, p. 5)

Reacting to the death Monday [22 May] of an Indonesian man, the WHO said that the case appeared to be the first example of the avian flu jumping from human to human to human. But the health agency quickly cautioned Tuesday that this did not necessarily mean that the virus had mutated into a strain that could start a pandemic by jumping rapidly between people as ordinary flu does. It is a 'definite possibility' that the virus jumped more than once inside a family, said ... a spokeswoman for [the WHO] ... In the past there have been at least three cases of suspected human-to-human transmission of the H5N1 strain of bird flu; all were between family members who spent hours in close contact and would have inhaled large amounts of virus-contaminated droplets. The virus is known to attach itself to receptors deep in the lungs, not in the nose and throat as seasonal flu does ... The man who died was thirty-two and became sick on 15 May. He is believed to have caught the flu while caring for his ten-year-old son, who died of the disease on 13 May.

(www.iht.com, 24 May 2006)

The WHO says it is extremely worried about a cluster of recent human deaths from the virulent H5N1 strain of bird flu. Seven people from the same family in northern Sumatra [Indonesia] died from the disease this month [May] ... [The WHO] said there was no sign of diseased poultry in the immediate area. Investigators are looking into the possibility that the virus spread from human to human ... [but it was] emphasized that there was no indication the virus had mutated ... The Sumatran cases ... [are] the largest cluster of human cases to date ... All seven who died were members of the same family. An eighth family member is also thought to have the disease ... The initial victim was a woman, who became ill at the end of April. She died in early May and was buried before laboratory tests could be carried out. The subsequent six victims – all of whom were positively identified as having the virus – had close and prolonged exposure to either her or other family members with the disease ... The H5N1 virus has already killed more than 120 people worldwide since 2003.

(www.bbc.co.uk, 24 May 2006)

'To date there have been 218 infections and 124 human deaths from the virus' (*FT*, 25 May 2006, p. 9).

Preliminary tests have found that bird flu killed two more siblings in Indonesia, officials said Friday [26 May], as the country grappled with a separate outbreak involving the largest cluster ever reported within one family ...

> International health officials so far have confirmed thirty-three human deaths from bird flu in Indonesia, out of 124 worldwide … The newest cases came as Indonesia investigated a separate family cluster in northern Sumatra in which six of seven family members died of bird flu, the most recent Monday. An eighth family member who died was buried before tests could be done, but she was also considered to be among those infected … Similar isolated cases of transmission among humans are believed to have occurred in four or five other family clusters.
>
> (*IHT*, 27 May 2006, p. 2)

'[The brother] has died from bird flu, the thirty-sixth death in Indonesia, according to the WHO' (*The Times*, 30 May 2006, p. 35).

> Wild birds carry only part of the blame for spreading the deadly strain of bird flu and experts said Tuesday [30 May] that they should not be killed but rather studied to understand how the virus spreads … Scientists [were] at an international conference … organized by the Animal Health Service at the United Nations Food and Agriculture Organization … and the World Organization for Animal Health … Migratory birds brought the disease into Russia and Eastern Europe, but in the case of the recent outbreaks in Africa there is little evidence pointing to wild birds … The H5N1 virus has killed at least 127 people worldwide.
>
> (*IHT*, 31 May 2006, p. 3)

> The 300 experts in attendance made little new headway … concluding that far more basic research was needed to understand basic questions, like which species of wild bird are vulnerable to the virus … Wild migrating birds could introduce bird flu into a new country, but it was probably human commerce in poultry that moved it from village to village and from farm to farm. While wild birds have been implicated in spreading the disease to many European nations, their role in Africa has not been established.
>
> A number of countries in the throes of serious bird flu outbreaks are under-reporting the extent of the problem, generally because they do not have the money, veterinary expertise or health systems to track the disease adequately, international health experts said … Countries might be under-reporting, but they do not do it deliberately … African nations give inadequate reports, as well as China and Indonesia … Forty-eight people in Indonesia have now been diagnosed with the disease and thirty-six have died, nearly half of them in the past month – a sign that bird flu is widespread in the country.
>
> (*IHT*, 1 June 2006, p. 8)

> In the wake of a cluster of avian flu cases that killed seven members of a rural Indonesian family, it appears likely that there have been many more human-to-human infections than the authorities have previously acknowledged. The numbers are still relatively small and they do not mean that the virus has mutated to pass easily between people – a change that could touch

off a worldwide epidemic. All the clusters of cases have been among relatives or in nurses who were in long, close contact with patients. But the clusters – in Indonesia, Thailand, Turkey, Azerbaijan, Iraq and Vietnam – paint a grimmer picture of the virus's potential to pass from human to human than is normally described by public health officials, who usually say such cases are 'rare'. Until recently WHO representatives have said there were only two or three such cases … [For example] on 30 May Maria Cheng, a spokeswoman for the UN health agency, said there were 'probably about half a dozen'. She added: 'I don't think anybody's got a solid number' … Most clusters are hard to investigate because they may not even be noticed until a victim is hospitalized and are often in remote villages where people fear talking about it … The WHO is generally conservative in its announcements and, as a UN agency, is sometimes limited by member states in what it is permitted to say about them. Still, several scientists have noted that there are many clusters in which human-to-human infection may be a more logical explanation than the idea that relatives who fell sick days apart got the virus from the same dying bird … Henry Niman, a biochemist in Pittsburgh … has argued for weeks that there have been twenty to thirty human-to-human infections … Niman also said that clusters were becoming more frequent, especially in Indonesia. On 2 June two more emerged there, one including a nurse whose infection has not yet been confirmed. With thirty-six deaths Indonesia is expected to eclipse Vietnam soon as the world's worst-hit country.

(www.iht.com, 4 June 2006)

Avian influenza was first identified over 100 years ago; since then the disease has been reported at irregular intervals in all regions of the world In addition to the current outbreak in Asia, recent epidemics have occurred in Hong Kong in 1997–8 and 2003, in the Netherlands in 2003 and in the Republic of Korea in 2003. Once domestic birds are infected avian influenza outbreaks can be difficult to control and may cause major economic damage to poultry farmers in affected countries, since mortality rates are high and infected fowl generally must be destroyed – the technical term is 'culled' – in order to prevent the spread of the disease. The outbreak is caused by the highly pathogenic H5N1 strain of the virus … East and South-east Asia has suffered significant human and economic losses owing to the present outbreak. Small and medium-sized farmers, whose stocks are often not insured and who have no alternative sources of income, have been the hardest hit. Overall, 140 million birds have been destroyed so far. Poultry meat imports from affected areas were prohibited in many countries. As the size of the poultry industry ranges from 0.6 per cent of GDP in Thailand and Vietnam to over 2 per cent of GDP in the Philippines, a fall in poultry output by 15 per cent, as has already been the case in Vietnam, can imply a reduction in GDP by up to 0.3 per cent. Across the region the total losses from the damaged poultry sector amounted to about $10 billion by the end of 2005. The estimates of deaths from a possible global pandemic of highly pathogenic avian influenza depend on several factors … The economic losses associated with an avian influenza pandemic could well amount to $200 billion in just one quarter, with the Economic and Social Commission for Asia and the Pacific region bearing most of the brunt. This corresponds to 2 per cent of world GDP. The impact on some specific sectors, however, could be catastrophic. Tourism, one of the industries to be potentially affected by an outbreak, accounts for over 9 per cent of GDP in East Asia and about 11 per cent in South-East Asia.

(United Nations 2006, p. 113).

Bird flu was found in a north-eastern Ukrainian village … bordering Russia … officials said Monday [12 June], the first confirmation of the virus's spread beyond the nation's Black Sea regions … The news media reported it was the H5N1 strain … An outbreak of the H5N1 strain hit Ukraine in December [2005], but the cases were confined to Crimea and other Black Sea regions. No human cases have been recorded in Ukraine.

(*IHT*, 13 June 2006, p. 10)

Confirmation of the thirty-eighth death from avian flu in Indonesia has indicated that the situation in the country is continuing to worsen. Indonesia is now in second place after Vietnam, which has forty-two deaths, but none this year [2006], while Indonesia's caseload is climbing rapidly and includes many family clusters … [Indonesia] said Thursday [15 June] that the 1 June death of a seven-year-old girl … was the country's thirty-eighth from avian flu. The girl's ten-year-old brother died on 29 May, but he was buried before specimens were taken, so he was not included in the count. Chickens in the family's household had died earlier … The outbreak in Indonesia has a very high death rate: of the fifty known cases thirty-eight have died … [Indonesia] said Friday [16 June] that a fourteen-year-old had died Wednesday … local tests indicated he was infected with the H5N1 strain of the virus but … an international laboratory would confirm the diagnosis. If the case is confirmed it would raise Indonesia's death toll to thirty-nine … The World Bank said Monday that the country was mounting a disorganized and underfinanced response to the flu.

(www.iht.com, 16 June 2006)

[On 20 June it was announced that WHO] tests confirmed that a fourteen-year-old boy had died from the disease, bringing the death toll [in Indonesia] from the disease to at least thirty-nine people … An Asian Development Bank report in April said that Indonesia's 2006 budget allocated just $14 million to combat the disease, despite the government's own estimate that at least thirty times that amount is needed … At least 120 people have died worldwide since the virus began ravaging Asian poultry in late 2003.

(www.iht.com, 20 June 2006)

An Indonesian man who died after catching the H5N1 bird flu virus from his ten-year-old son represents the first laboratory-confirmed case of human-to-human transmission of the disease, a WHO investigation of an unusual family cluster has concluded, the agency said Friday [23 June]. The WHO investigators also discovered that the virus had mutated slightly when the son had the disease, although not in any way that would allow it to pass more readily among people ... In previous cases where human-to-human transmission was suspected, researchers could not test from the patients, or the virus in the patients was the same as that in poultry in the area ... International health officials have been in Indonesia for much of the past month, investigating a family outbreak that affected seven relatives ... Six of the seven died ... The family had no known direct contact with sick birds, although the first death was a woman who sold vegetables in a market that also sold birds.

(www.iht.com, 23 June 2006; *IHT*, 24 June 2006, p. 3)

A Chinese man who died of pneumonia in November 2003 and was at first classified as a SARS victim might have died of avian influenza – two years before Beijing reported any human bird flu infections on the mainland to the WHO, Chinese researchers reported. The case of the death in Beijing raises the possibility that others attributed to SARS may have actually been caused by the deadly H5N1 flu. But in a confusing development at least one of the researchers asked Wednesday [21 June] that the letter reporting the case be withdrawn from publication.

(www.iht.com, 22 June 2006)

Did China have a death from avian flu two years before it admitted having any human cases? The mystery has deepened and the possibility has been raised that someone had tried to block the publication of that event from a prestigious American medical journal. The *New England Journal of Medicine* on Friday [23 June] reversed an announcement it had made two days before, saying that, in fact, the eight Chinese authors of a letter describing a man's death in 2003 from avian flu had insisted that they really did want it printed. The timing of the death is important because scientists believe that the H5N1 virus had circulated among China's chickens for many years, but it was not until last November [2005] that the government admitted to having a human case. To date it has officially reported nineteen cases and twelve deaths. In 2003 China covered up dozens of cases of SARS deaths for months after the epidemic began there. The journal had gone to press Wednesday [21 June] when the editors received several email messages asking that the letter describing the 2003 death not be printed ... The letter said that doctors initially thought the twenty-four-year-old man had SARS, but tests on his lung tissue proved negative.

(www.iht.com, 25 June 2006)

Four people have died after catching avian flu from infected swans, in the first confirmed cases of the disease being passed from wild birds ... The victims, from a village in Azerbaijan, are believed to have caught the lethal

H5N1 virus earlier this year when they plucked the feathers from dead birds to sell for pillows. Three other people were infected by the swans but survived ... Almost all of the 220 other confirmed human cases of bird flu, including 130 deaths, have been linked to domestic poultry. A handful are believed to have caught the disease directly from humans.

(*Guardian*, 26 June 2006, p. 15)

Spain yesterday [7 July] detected its first case of bird flu after carrying out an autopsy on a dead great crested grebe ... The dead bird was found in northern Spain ... The government said ... there are no poultry farms in the area ... Spain lies on a main migration route for birds flying between Europe and Africa.

(*FT*, 8 July 2006, p. 7)

Only a fraction of nearly $1.9 billion pledged by international donors in January to help the developing world prepare for a bird flu pandemic has been paid out so far, the United Nations said Monday [10 July]. In a joint report with the World Bank, the UN bird flu co-ordinator, David Nabarro, said donor countries had allocated $1.5 billion for bird flu aid in their budgets by the end of April, but had transferred just $331 million to recipients ... The donor funds were designated for improving veterinary systems, vaccination drives and education about animal hygiene, Nabarro said more money was needed to ensure that poorer countries in Africa, Latin America and elsewhere were ready for a resurgence of the bird flu threat later this year.

(*IHT*, 11 July 2006, p. 3)

Vietnam has not recorded any new human deaths this year [2006], thanks in part to an aggressive campaign to slaughter all birds in infected areas. Indonesia has been criticized by some for not carrying out widespread culling ... [Indonesia] has an estimated 2 billion chickens and the virus is endemic in twenty-seven of its thirty-three provinces. Culling all the birds would require a huge amount of compensation to farmers and backyard chicken owners ... [Indonesia has] 230 million people spread across 17,000 islands ... [On 17 July Indonesia said] a WHO laboratory had confirmed the bird flu death of a three-year-old girl, bringing the country's total from the virus to at least forty-two, tying it with Vietnam for the most deaths worldwide. The WHO, however, does not recognize one of Indonesia's bird flu deaths because of the testing method used. The agency, which is co-ordinating the world's fight against the virus, still lists forty-one bird flu deaths in Indonesia. Bird flu has killed at least 132 people worldwide since it started ravaging Asian poultry stocks in late 2003, according to the WHO.

(www.iht.com, 17 July 2006)

Indonesia is poised to surpass Vietnam as the country hardest hit by avian flu. And while Vietnam has not had a single human case or poultry outbreak this year [2006], public health officials and experts say the situation in Indonesia is likely to get worse. Indonesia received word from a Hong Kong laboratory that a forty-four-year-old man who died last week near Jakarta had tested positive for the H5N1 virus, the Indonesian health ministry said Thursday [20 July]. That brought the number of confirmed bird flu cases in Indonesia to forty-two since the first human case was confirmed a year ago, equal to the toll in Vietnam. The flu is ubiquitous in thousands of Indonesian backyard flocks, and appears to be killing more birds every month, increasing the likelihood of human cases … Although the H5N1 flu came relatively late to Indonesia, it soon spiralled out of control and deaths have mounted quickly. Unlike Thailand, which quenched outbreaks by killing millions of chickens, or Vietnam, which used mandatory vaccination, Indonesia has tried a mix of limited culling and vaccination in rings around the cull – so far with little success … The biggest obstacle to beating the disease, international flu experts say, is the decentralized Indonesian government … The country is not only slow to report human cases, but it no longer even reports poultry outbreaks to the World Organization for Animal Health in Paris … Shortages of trained veterinarians and slow compensation of farmers have also been major obstacles to crushing the outbreak … Given the huge population … 245 million Indonesians, living on about 6,000 populated islands [Vietnam has 84 million people] … avian flu remains a relatively rare disease … But Indonesian cases have clustered.

(www.iht.com, 20 July 2006)

Thailand on Wednesday [26 July] confirmed that a sixteen-year-old boy who died this week [on 24 July] was infected with bird flu … The boy became Thailand's fifteenth bird flu fatality and the country's first confirmed case in humans this year … Agriculture officials on Tuesday had confirmed the H5N1 bird flu virus in chickens [in a northern province] … The new cases were the first to be found in Thai poultry in more than eight months … The Thai authorities culled millions of chickens and ducks when a wave of bird flu struck Asia in 2004. Thailand, one of the world's biggest chicken exporting countries, has since conducted regular surveys to check for bird flu among poultry. The last bird flu fatality was a five-year-old boy in December [2005].

(www.iht.com, 26 July 2006)

Last week Indonesia announced its forty-third human death from bird flu. It has now recorded more fatalities than any other nation and, in stark contrast to all other countries, its death toll is climbing regularly … [Among the reasons is the fact that] farmers are being compensated … well below the market price … per bird … thereby discouraging farmers from reporting outbreaks … Pledges to vaccinate hundreds of millions of birds have not been met … SARS [was a] threat in 2003 that never materialized.

(*The Economist*, 29 July 2006, p. 60)

A bird flu vaccine for humans that uses only a very low dose of its active ingredient has proved effective in clinical tests and could be mass produced in 2007, the drugmaker GlaxoSmithKline said Wednesday [26 July] … While Glaxo's vaccine offers protection against the H5N1 virus now circulating, its impact on any mutated strain of the virus is not certain.

(www.iht.com, 26 July 2006; *IHT*, 27 July 2006, p. 3)

Vietnam … is an example of how determined, comprehensive efforts can check the potentially lethal virus. After culling 51 million birds, or more than 17 per cent of the domestic poultry population, and conducting a comprehensive vaccination campaign, Vietnam has not registered any avian influenza cases since mid-November [2005], nor any outbreaks in birds since mid-December … [Vietnam has used a] combination of aggressive culling, vaccination and intensive surveillance … Bird flu spread widely in Vietnam before authorities recognized the threat in early 2004 and moved into battle mode … When outbreaks persisted through mid-2005 Hanoi raised the compensation for dead and culled birds to 50 per cent of the market value, up from 10 per cent, encouraging more co-operation from farmers. Then in October Vietnam launched an expensive, logistically complicated campaign to vaccinate domestic poultry. The measures appear to have checked the virus … [But] Vietnam's battle against bird flu is far from over … Hanoi is worried about bird flu in China and the uncontrolled cross-border poultry trade … Public complacency poses another risk … Agricultural experts caution that the lethal H5N1 virus is almost certainly present in migratory birds, waterfowl and ducks … Small disease outbreaks could be passing unnoticed … Hanoi has asked the international community for $266 million in aid to boost veterinary services and disease control, restructure its poultry industry and improve health services.

(*FT*, 2 August 2006, p. 7)

'A dead swan at a zoo in eastern Germany has tested positive for H5N1 … The bird was found in a pond at the Dresden Zoo on Monday [31 July]' (*The Independent*, 5 August 2006, p. 26).

Beijing confirmed on Tuesday [8 August] that the country's first human case of the H5N1 bird flu virus in 2003 was two years earlier than originally reported … The case has spurred questions about whether there might have been other human H5N1 infections in mainland China before what had been its first reported human case, near the end of 2005 … A spokesman [for China]: 'Although this human infection confirmed in the mainland was two years earlier than previous figures, it has no indication that China had an outbreak of bird flu in 2003' … Eight Chinese researchers published a letter in the *New England Journal of Medicine* in June saying a twenty-four-year-old soldier, who was admitted to a hospital in November 2003 for respiratory distress and pneumonia, had been infected with H5N1 … China's health ministry confirmed the case on Tuesday by 'parallel laboratory tests' carried out in co-operation with the WHO … [The WHO] said the health ministry had told the WHO that military scientists first tested the man and found he was infected with the H5N1 virus but did not tell the health ministry until much later … Experts in Hong Kong have long suspected that the virus has always been present in mainland China, but the Chinese authorities have denied that. Even after several members of a Hong Kong family contracted the virus in Fujian province in southern China, the incident was swept under the carpet.

(www.iht.com, 8 August 2006; *IHT*, 9 August 2006, p. 4)

A new technique for making human vaccines against H5N1 avian influenza produces inoculations that are effective at very low doses, potentially solving the vexing problem of how the world will make adequate numbers of shots in the event of a flu pandemic. In research being published by the journal *The Lancet*, a team of Chinese researchers at the Sinovac Biotech Company in Beijing described how they had made a vaccine using a slightly altered whole bird flu virus, and then enhanced its effect with another chemical, called an adjuvant. The researchers inoculated 120 volunteers and found that nearly 80 per cent given two shots at the optimal dose developed immunity to avian influenza … The study was small, but the results are more encouraging than with previous attempts to create a vaccine.

(*IHT*, 7 September 2006, p. 4)

In an emergency enough could be produced for 675 million people. The Chinese vaccine consists of the H5N1 avian flu virus inactivated so that it cannot cause disease, combined with an additive (adjuvant) that enhances the immune response … The manufacturer is Sinovac Biotech, a Beijing-based pharmaceutical company, which jointly developed it with the Chinese Science and Technology Ministry and the country's Centre for Disease Control and Prevention.

(*The Times*, 7 September 2006, p. 25)

Avian flu kills in much the same way the 1918 flu did, by drowning victims in fluid produced in their own lungs, a new study has found. The study also suggests that immediate treatment with antiviral drugs is crucial … Because the body's own immune response does part of the damage, doctors should consider giving anti-inflammatory drugs along with antivirals like Tamiflu. Although the results of the relatively small study … eighteen people with the H5N1 avian flu in 2004 and 2005 … are precisely what flu experts had predicted from laboratory work … [one expert] called it a major advance because so little clinical information had previously been gleaned from the 241 known cases of the disease.

(*IHT*, 11 September 2006, p. 2)

A fifty-nine-year-old man who bred and raised fighting cocks in north-eastern Thailand contracted the H5N1 bird flu virus and has died, bringing the country's death toll from the disease to seventeen, health official said yesterday [26 September] … He died on 10 August.

(*FT*, 27 September 2006, p. 8)

> An eleven-year-old Indonesian boy has died of bird flu, an official … said yesterday [15 October] … 'so confirmed cases [in Indonesia] are now seventy-one, fifty-three of whom died' [he said] The boy, from south Jakarta, died on Saturday [14 October].
>
> (*FT*, 16 October 2006, p. 6)

'Vietnam has the highest number of bird flu cases recorded by the WHO since 2003 and the highest number of fatalities after Indonesia' (www.iht.com, 26 October 2006).

> The WHO's new plan for ramping up the production of flu vaccine is a measure of how unprepared the world is to cope with an onslaught of pandemic influenza. The plan, conceived by a group of more than 120 experts, lays out a sensible path toward vaccine sufficiency – but it will take years to complete and cost up to $10 billion … So far it has infected only 256 people in ten countries – mostly people in close contact with chickens in Asia – but the highly lethal pathogen has killed some 60 per cent of those.
>
> (Editorial, *The New York Times*, in *IHT*, 30 October 2006, p. 8)

> Margaret Chan, a bird flu expert, won the nomination Wednesday [8 November to become the world's top health official, a position that would make her the first Chinese national to hold a top United Nations post … The executive board of the WHO chose Chan to be its next director-general over four other candidates in a tight race to fill the post vacated by the death in May [2006] of Lee Jong Wook … Anders Nordstrom has been acting director-general … The board set Chan's term to start on 4 January [2007] and to last until the end of June 2012 … Chan's nomination must be approved by a two-thirds majority at a special session of the agency's governing World Health Assembly, comprised all 193 member countries. The World Health Assembly has never rejected a recommendation from the executive board.
>
> (www.iht.com, 8 November 2006)

> Margaret Chan of China [is the WHO's] top official on bird flu … She is a former director of the department of health in Hong Kong whose career has been focused on public health … She had been the frontrunner to replace Lee Jong Wook of South Korea, who died unexpectedly in May from a blood clot in the brain, three years into his five-year term as director-general … Chan stepped aside from her job as the WHO's assistant director-general for communicable diseases to run for the top job in global health … China has recently been criticized for dragging its feet in reporting outbreaks of bird flu to the WHO and supplying virus samples to the global health community for analysis.
>
> (*IHT*, 9 November 2006, p. 5)

> China agreed Friday [10 November] to share its sample of the bird flu virus … from 2004 and 2005 … with international health authorities, after rejecting scientists' findings that a new, vaccine-resistant strain was circulating in

the country ... The decision came after China rejected findings in a paper published ... in *The Proceedings of the National Academy of Scientists* ... last week by Hong Kong and US scientists that reported they had detected a new strain of H5N1 in the southern Chinese province of Fujian last year [2005] ... [China said that when it] had co-operated in the past, the samples had been misused and had encroached upon intellectual property rights ... H5N1 has caused twenty-one human infections in China since late 2003, killing fourteen people.

(www.iht.com, 10 November 2006)

Studies published Thursday [23 November] ... [by] a mix of experts from Indonesia, the WHO and the Centers for Disease Control and Prevention in Atlanta ... were of family clusters of flu cases in Turkey and Indonesia ... The studies followed clusters in three separate families in Indonesia in 2005 and in what appears to have been one extended family near Dogubayazit, in eastern Turkey, in January [2006]. Case clusters particularly worry public health officials because they raise the possibility that the flu is mutating to spread faster between people. In the Indonesian cases the authors ... concluded that human-to-human transmission had probably taken place in two of the three family clusters. In one case a thirty-eight-year-old government auditor appeared to have caught the flu from his eight-year-old daughter or her one-year-old sister. All three died; his wife and two sons did not become ill. No one in the family had any known contact with poultry, wild birds, animals or sick people, so the source was a mystery ... 'But you cannot tell what a young child has done,' said [one of the authors] ... The Dogubayazit cluster was a cause célèbre for some internet flu-watchers following Turkish media reports in January. They argued that widespread human-to-human transmission seemed to be taking place, and that it may have begun at a banquet in late December [2005] attended by members of two related families ... The Turkish government and the WHO did not link the cases or families and tentatively blamed all transmission on birds ... Only eight were confirmed by a WHO laboratory. All were children; four died and four survived ... The lead author ... said he believed there had been no human-to-human transmission because all the children had been in close contact with poultry within seven or fewer days before they fell ill and because none of their parents or the hospital staff that treated them had become sick.

(www.iht.com, 24 November 2006; *IHT*, 25 November 2006, p. 8)

South Korean quarantine officials on Sunday [26 November] began slaughtering ... poultry after an outbreak of the virulent H5N1 form of bird flu at a chicken farm ... The outbreak occurred last week ... South Korea killed 5.3 million birds during the last known outbreak of bird flu in 2003. The H5N1 virus began ravaging Asian poultry stocks in late 2003 and has killed at least 153 people worldwide. So far the disease remains hard for people to catch and most human cases have been traced to contact with birds.

(www.iht.com, 27 November 2006)

Having killed millions of chickens and geese, the bird flu epidemic is now claiming the lives of pet dogs and cats in South Korea … Confirmed cases of bird flu in humans [number] 258 … At least 153 people have died of the H5N1 virus in ten countries since [2003] … Most of those who have died from H5N1 have been in South-east Asia, especially in Indonesia and Vietnam. Nearly all the infections have occurred in people who lived on farms or villages in close daily proximity to chickens or ducks … A mutation of a virus is believed to have created the Spanish flu, which killed between 20 million and 100 million people across the world in 1918 and 1919. Human-to-human infections may have occurred during outbreaks of bird flu in Hong Kong and Europe in 1997, which remained under control.

(*The Times*, 28 November 2006, p. 38)

South Korea will cull more than half a million fowl … having already killed 150,000 chickens … Last week South Korea confirmed it had its first outbreak of the deadly strain in about three years … Between December 2003 and March 2004 about 400,000 poultry on South Korean farms were infected. In that outbreak 5.3 million birds were destroyed.

(*FT*, 1 December 2006, p. 8)

Several cases of avian flu have spread from poultry to humans in the Nile Delta, the Egyptian health authorities said this week as they worked to halt the outbreak among chickens and ducks. A fifteen-year-old girl died Monday [25 December], a day after the death of a woman in her thirties whose family members showed symptoms of infection. Egypt has reported nine confirmed human deaths from H5N1 avian flu since it was first found in birds in February and in a person in March.

(*IHT*, 28 December 2006, p. 3)

An outbreak of the lethal H5N1 strain was found on a poultry farm [in Vietnam] in December [2006], the first in almost a year. New WHO chief Margaret Chan has warned that bird flu remains a global threat … [She] said reports of bird flu had started to surface in recent weeks after a lull and that the danger was particularly severe in poor countries.

(www.bbc.co.uk, 5 January 2007)

Indonesia has the world's highest human death toll from the H5N1 virus and registered more bird flu deaths in 2006 than any other nation … Two women in Indonesia have died after contracting bird flu … raising the country's total number of human deaths to sixty-one … The latest deaths are the third and fourth fatalities of 2007 in Indonesia … Criticism over the country's handling of the disease has led to fresh attempts over the past year to raise awareness.

(www.bbc.co.uk, 13 January 2007)

The deadly H5N1 strain of avian influenza is making a seasonal resurgence in Asia and could easily spread to Europe again this year [2007], the WHO warned yesterday [14 January 2007]. The alarm follows four human deaths in Indonesia in the last five days, the first human case in China for six months (though the infected man has since recovered) and new poultry outbreaks in Vietnam – despite a huge campaign against it – and northern Nigeria … [The WHO said it was] convinced that we are in a repeat of last year and the year before when the virus began to get very active again [in the northern hemisphere winter] and spread from Asia into the Middle East and beyond. Indonesia, where sixty-one people have died, remained the 'biggest flashpoint' … The strain detected in Asia is a mutation of last year's, but it is not showing any sign of moving to a strain that would be more dangerous to humans or have a great likelihood of human-to-human transmission … All four human fatalities in Indonesia contracted the virus from infected birds … The latest outbreak in Vietnam, in six southern provinces despite a widespread poultry cull and tight controls on birds that had resulted in no human cases since 2005.

(*FT*, 15 January 2007, p. 7)

Thailand has suffered an outbreak of the deadly H5N1 strain of bird flu, its first for six months … Vietnam says bird flu has reached a seventh province in the Mekong Delta region … Health officials across Asia are on alert as a growing number of countries have reported cases in both birds and humans in recent weeks … Japan is culling 12,000 birds after an outbreak at a farm south-west of Tokyo at the weekend. It is not clear if the virus is the deadly H5N1 strain … Bird flu has claimed more than 150 lives since it began ravaging Asian poultry farms in late 2003.

(www.bbc.co.uk, 15 January 2007)

Officials in Japan have confirmed that a recent outbreak of bird flu at a poultry [chicken] farm was the deadly H5N1 strain of the virus … There were a number of H5N1 outbreaks in Japan in early 2004, but there have been no human deaths from the virus.

(www.bbc.co.uk, 16 January 2007)

History's most virulent influenza strain, the 1918 Spanish flu, killed millions of previously healthy young adults by sending their immune system into fatal overdrive, a study of monkeys infected with the virus shows … The 1918 virus was reconstructed by generic engineering from human victims of the great epidemic. All the animals were dead within a week, their lungs overwhelmed by an excessive immune response … The experiment … helps explain why so many of the 50 million killed by Spanish flu were healthy men and women in the prime of life … Many of the 161 human deaths from H5N1 infection since 2003 showed symptoms of an excessive immune reaction similar to that in the monkeys killed by the 1918 virus.

(*FT*, 18 January 2007, p. 9)

Hungary yesterday [24 January] confirmed that the … H5 virus killed domestic fowl that died over the weekend, raising the prospect of a new

> outbreak of bird flu in Europe ... Preliminary laboratory results suggested it was the N1 strain, in what would be the first outbreak of H5N1 since August last year [2006].
>
> (*FT*, 25 January 2007, p. 9)

> The EU has confirmed that the deadly H5N1 strain of bird flu has been found on a farm in Hungary ... A flock of 3,000 geese on the infected farm has been destroyed. It is the EU's first case of bird flu for about six months ... The virus first appeared in the country in February last year [2006] in wild geese, swans and domestic poultry.
>
> (www.bbc.co.uk, 29 January 2007)

> So far only 163 people worldwide have died from the virus – mostly in Indonesia, Vietnam, Thailand and China ... In 2006 the virus became deadlier, killing 70 per cent of the people who caught it ... The UN's Food and Agriculture Organization (FAO) reckons H5N1 has cost South-east Asia's poultry farmers $10 billion since 2003.
>
> (*The Economist*, 27 January 2007, p. 57)

'The number of cases among humans is also rising – by the end of 2006 the number of human deaths from the disease had more than doubled in a year, with a noticeably higher mortality rate of almost 60 per cent' (www.bbc.co.uk, 26 January 2007).

The World Health Organization (WHO) has provided information on the number of human cases (total 269) and deaths (total 163) as of 22 January 2007. The respective figures for countries (in alphabetical order) are as follows: Azerbaijan, 8 and 5; Cambodia, 6 and 6; China, 22 and 14; Djibouti, 1 and 0; Egypt, 19 and 11; Indonesia, 80 and 62; Iraq, 3 and 2; Thailand, 25 and 17; Turkey, 12 and 4; Vietnam, 93 and 42 (www.bbc.co.uk, 27 January 2007).

> Officials in Japan have confirmed that a recent outbreak of bird flu at a poultry farm was the deadly H5N1 strain of the virus ... The earlier outbreak occurred in mid-January at a farm in the same region ... There have been a number of H5N1 outbreaks in Japan since early 2004.
>
> (www.bbc.co.uk, 27 January 2007)

'Japan has confirmed only one human H5N1 infection and no human deaths' (www.iht.com, 26 January 2007).

> Nigeria's first human fatality from bird flu has been confirmed by the WHO. Tests in London confirmed that a twenty-two-year-old woman [from Lagos] who died on 17 January was infected with the deadly H5N1 strain. Nigeria reported several human cases last Wednesday [31 January] ... Nigeria reported Africa's first cases of H5N1 about a year ago. Other cases have been reported in Egypt and Djibouti, which have suffered human deaths, and also in Cameroon, Djibouti, Niger, Ivory Coast, Sudan and Burkina Faso.
>
> (www.bbc.co.uk, 3 February 2007)

'It is understood that the dead woman bought the infected chickens from a local farmer' (www.bbc.co.uk, 31 January 2007).

> The British authorities confirmed on Saturday [3 February] that bird flu among turkeys at a poultry farm in the east of the country has been caused by the potentially deadly H5N1 strain that has killed humans in other parts of the world. It was the biggest outbreak of that strain reported in Britain … The virus had been found in only one of the farm's twenty-two turkey sheds … The outbreak near Lowestoft has killed 2,500 turkeys … and a further 160,000 birds will now be culled … It is the first time the H5N1 strain had been found on a British farm. The virus was identified as the highly pathogenic Asian strain, similar to that found in Hungary in January … The outbreak is the first known instance of H5N1 in Britain since an infected wild swan was found … washed up … in Scotland [in April 2006] … Government scientists said it had probably carried the infection from Germany … Turkeys and chickens are more susceptible to H5N1 than wild birds, which can carry the virus over long distances without showing symptoms … Since 2003 164 people, most of them in Asia, have died of the disease.
>
> (www.iht.com, 3 February 2007; *IHT*, 5 February 2007, p. 3)

> The avian flu virus which killed 2,600 turkeys at a Bernard Matthews farm in Suffolk has been confirmed as the Asian strain of the H5N1 virus … A spokeswoman for the [UK] Department for the Environment, Food and Rural Affairs [Defra] … said the flu was the 'highly pathogenic' Asian strain, similar to the virus that was found in Hungary in January. In that incident, the first time bird flu had re-occurred in the EU since August 2006, a flock of 3,000 geese were killed … It is the first case on a UK commercial farm of an H5N1 infection … The strain has killed 164 people – mainly in South-east Asia – since 2003 … Britain's deputy chief veterinary officer said an investigation was under way but the most likely source of the outbreak was wild birds … Professor John Oxford, a virologist, said: 'The most likely explanation is that a small bird has come in through a ventilation shaft. One good thing about this virus is that it's easily destroyed. You can kill it with a bit of detergent' … In [April] 2006 a wild swan found dead in Fife [Scotland] was found to have the H5N1 strain of the virus.
>
> (www.bbc.co.uk, 3 February 2007)

'Officials [in the UK] were uncertain how the virus entered the turkey shed at the Bernard Matthews farm, but there were suspicions that faeces or other matter from waterfowl were carried in by a contaminated worker, feed or equipment' (*FT*, 5 February 2007, p. 1).

> To date there have been 270 human cases and 164 deaths, but only a few reports of human-to human transmission … [The H5N1 virus has] got a huge mortality rate, around 61 per cent, but it is very hard to catch.
>
> (www.bbc.co.uk, 5 February 2007)

> The H5N1 virus remains primarily a disease of birds ... Turkeys are particularly vulnerable because stocks are so inbred, meaning they are all genetically similar ... It has killed or forced the slaughter of more than 200 million birds. But it does occasionally infect people. There have been 271 confirmed bird flu cases in humans worldwide and 165 deaths since 2003, according to the WHO ... The latest death, that of a twenty-two-year-old Nigerian woman, was the first known human fatality from the H5N1 virus in sub-Saharan Africa.
>
> (www.iht.com, 5 February 2007)

> The bird flu outbreak at a Bernard Matthews farm in Suffolk may be linked to imports from the firm's plant in Hungary, a government vet has said. The pathogenic H5N1 strain was found on a Hungarian geese farm in January ... [The deputy chief vet] said imported 'poultry product' was a possible route of infection. Meanwhile, tests on culled turkeys from three sheds on the Suffolk farm, near the shed in which the virus was first found, also showed strains of H5N1 ... Defra said preliminary tests showed the Hungary and UK viruses 'may well be identical' ... Defra confirmed 'partly processed' turkey had been transported by lorry from Hungary to the Suffolk farm each week up to the time of the Suffolk outbreak. The turkeys were taken to a processing plant next to the premises which became infected ... [The vet] said the 'working hypothesis' was that the infection came into the farm through such an import. He said the latest tests 'seem to indicate that this is an infection that has been passed from poultry to poultry', rather than from wild birds ... [A spokesman for Bernard Matthews said that] 'we don't move live birds between Hungary and the UK'.
>
> (www.bbc.co.uk, 8 February 2007)

> The poultry company at the centre of the avian flu outbreak admitted yesterday [5 February] that lorries from Hungary had made regular visits to its Holton [Suffolk, UK] plant ... Government vets are investigating urgently possible links between the Bernard Matthews firm and the outbreak of the H5N1 virus on a goose farm in Hungary ten days ago ... A possible link through the movement of human beings from Hungary is being investigated.
>
> (*The Times*, 6 February 2007, p. 6)

'Experts discounted suggestions that the virus might have been brought to Suffolk on a lorry or the boots of a worker from Hungary ... Bernard Matthews owns Saga poultry, the largest poultry producer in Hungary' (*Independent*, 6 February 2007, p. 4).

> Turkish officials have confirmed that there has been an outbreak of avian influenza [among chickens] in the country's south-east ... Turkey saw the first human deaths from H5N1 outside Asia, in January 2006, when twelve people were infected, four of whom later died.
>
> (www.bbc.co.uk, 8 February 2007)

> The deadly H5N1 strain of bird flu has been found close to the Pakistani capital, Islamabad. All the chickens in the infected flock died from the flu or were slaughtered … Last March [2006] H5N1 was found in north-west Pakistan, India and Afghanistan.
>
> (www.bbc.co.uk, 6 February 2007)

> Indonesia has signed a preliminary deal with a US drug manufacturer to jointly develop a human bird flu vaccine in a move that has stirred controversy. Under the memorandum of understanding Indonesia will provide samples of the bird flu virus to Baxter International. In return, Baxter will offer Indonesia technical help to produce a vaccine … [The WHO] said Indonesia had not shared samples since the start of the year [2007] … [Indonesia] says it wants to maintain intellectual property rights over the strains of the H5N1 virus that are discovered in the country … [and that it] cannot share (virus) samples for free.
>
> (www.bbc.co.uk, 7 February 2007)

> Indonesia decided to act after a foreign company announced work on a vaccine that would be based on its samples. Indonesia stopped co-operating with the WHO and started negotiations to send future samples to another vaccine maker in return for technology that would allow Indonesia to make its own vaccine.
>
> (www.iht.com, 16 February 2007)

('Indonesia agreed yesterday [16 February] to resume sharing samples of the deadly bird flu virus with the WHO, but only after steps were taken to ensure developing countries get fair and equitable access to vaccines … Indonesia [said it] would wait until the new mechanisms were in place … Indonesia stopped sharing in mid-January after learning that the Australian pharmaceutical group CSL had developed a vaccine using the Indonesian H5N1 human strain without permission. It blamed the WHO for providing drug companies with free access to the samples … Last week Jakarta signed a deal with Baxter International that gave the American company commercial rights to the Indonesian bird flu strain in return for supplyinng Indonesia with cheap vaccines … Indonesia wants intellectual property rights over its bird flu strain': *FT*, 17 February 2007, p. 7. 'Indonesia will resume sending avian flu samples to the WHO as soon as it is guaranteed access to affordable vaccines against the disease … A meeting of Asian nations to work out the guarantee, announced late Friday [16 February], was scheduled for next month [March] … Indonesia stopped sending virus samples to the health organization early last month [January], complaining that it and many other poor countries did not want their flu strains made into patented vaccines that only rich countries could afford … [The WHO] said that a fund to buy vaccines for poor countries could be discussed at the March meeeting and that the agency would help Indonesia to eventually develop its own vaccine factories … Baxter Healthcare said it had not asked Indonesia to stop co-operating with the health organization': www.iht.com, 18 February 2007; *IHT*,

19 February 2007, p. 7. '[Indonesia said the Baxter] deal would go ahead despite Friday's agreement with the WHO': www.bbc.co.uk, 16 February 2007.)

> [UK] government inspectors are investigating whether an outbreak of avian flu at a turkey farm in Suffolk owned by Bernard Matthews last week was caused by the importation of infected meat from Hungary. After previously discounting a Hungarian connection, officials have discovered that the H5N1 virus identified in Suffolk is the same strain as one found on a goose in Hungary in January. Officials are looking into movements of lorries of partly processed infected carcasses to and from a Bernard Matthews-owned processing plant near to the Suffolk farm. They do not know from where in Hungary the infected meat might have originated ... Bernard Matthews has fifteen farms in Hungary and owns Saga Food, the country's largest poultry exporter ... Bernard Matthews said it had voluntarily agreed to suspend the movement of poultry products temporarily to and from Hungary until the investigation was complete 'as a precautionary measure'.
>
> (*FT*, 9 February 2007, p. 3)

'[On 8 February] Turkey said it was culling birds after new infections were discovered in the south-east of the country' (*FT*, 9 February 2007, p. 6).

> [UK] government scientists ... now believe ... the infection ... was most likely imported into the [Suffolk] factory from infected meat it acquired in Hungary ... The nearby meat processing plant has continued to operate and only last Thursday [8 February] stopped using meat from Hungary. Officials believe infected meat carcasses from the Suffolk processing plant may have been dumped in skips left open to the air, which may have allowed rats or seagulls to contract the virus and then spread it by gaining access to sheds where turkeys were being raised nearby ... Defra ... said it was continuing to investigate the lorry transport of 'partly processed meat' ... The British Food Standards Agency is considering the withdrawal of processed turkeys from shops across the UK.
>
> (*FT*, 10 February 2007, p. 2)

> Health workers in South Korea have begun to cull thousands of chickens after a new bird flu outbreak was discovered near Seoul. Chickens began dying on Tuesday [6 February]. The outbreak is the country's sixth since bird flu reappeared there three months ago, after a three-year absence. It is not yet known whether it is the H5N1 strain of the virus.
>
> (www.bbc.co.uk, 10 February 2007)

> The outbreak [in South Korea] ... was caused by the H5 strain of the virus, but further tests are needed to determine whether it has been caused by the N1 type ... In January South Korean officials said that the deadly H5N1 strain of the virus had been transmitted to a human being during a recent outbreak among poultry, but the person showed no symptoms of the disease as the poultry farm worker had developed natural immunity to the disease.
>
> (www.iht.com, 9 February 2007)

A twenty-year-old woman from West Java who had tested positive for bird flu died Sunday [11 February] ... Her death raised Indonesia's overall avian flu to sixty-four fatalities, the highest of any country in the world. After a lull last year [2006] concern has grown since the virus flared in Asia in recent months, spreading through poultry flocks in South Korea, Japan, Thailand and Vietnam. Also over the weekend the deadly H5N1 flu strain was confirmed in chickens at a home in Islamabad, the third case in Pakistan in a week, an official said Saturday.

(*IHT*, 12 February 2007, p. 4)

Hungary said Bernard Matthews exported turkey meat last week to the country, where the UK outbreak may have begun ... [Hungary said] that meat had left the Holton plant and arrived at Bernard Matthews' Hungarian site on either Wednesday [7 February] or Thursday [8 February] ... [The] farm at Holton, where bird flu was detected, was shut down after the outbreak was first suspected – but a processing unit on the same site continued to operate ... Reports on Sunday [11 February] said Bernard Matthews imported turkey from Hungary in the days after the outbreak ... [Defra] said exporting cooked poultry from an exclusion zone was allowed under European rules.

(www.bbc.co.uk, 12 February 2007)

The Suffolk farm ... is resuming the slaughtering and processing of turkey ... The government has now given the go-ahead to restart operations ... The first consignment arrived on Tuesday [13 February] ... A spokeswoman for the [Bernard Matthews] company said turkeys were arriving from more than fifty Bernard Matthews farms around Britain not affected by the exclusion zone in Suffolk.

(www.bbc.co.uk, 13 February 2007)

The strains of H5N1 bird flu found in the UK and Hungary are 'essentially identical', [UK government] scientists said. They found the virus that killed turkeys at the Bernard Matthews plant at Holton, Suffolk, was 99.96 similar to one that infected geese in Hungary. The deputy chief vet [in the UK] ... said the most likely transmission route for the outbreak was from poultry to poultry but investigations were continuing. No evidence of 'illegal' movements of poultry products has been found ... [Hungary] denied reports claiming that geese in Hungary infected with bird flu had been culled at the same plant in the city of Kecwskemet that had processed turkeys exported to England.

(www.bbc.co.uk, 13 February 2007)

Most of the scattered bird flu outbreaks so far this year [2007] can be traced to illegal or improper trade in poultry, scientists believe. This probably includes recent outbreaks in Nigeria and Egypt as well as the large outbreak on a turkey farm in England. Last winter wild migrating birds were deemed the primary culprit in the bird flu infestations that hopscotched across

Europe and Africa. Dead swans and ducks were found in many countries, including Austria, France and Italy … No outbreaks have been attributed to wild birds so far this season and not a single infected wild bird has been detected in Europe or Africa, despite a heightened surveillance system developed in the wake of the crisis last year. In most of the world there have been fewer outbreaks compared to a similar period in 2006 … Partially processed meat was routinely shipped from the [Bernard Matthews] company's Hungarian farm to the one in Suffolk for final processing. Although the avian influenza virus is killed by cooking, it survives well in raw meat and such shipments may have been brought into England and onto the property. It could have been transported from the processing plant into the animal pens on workers' shoes or farm equipment … Scientists are unsure why wild birds have not been implicated in spreading bird flu this year, although they speculate it might have to do with warmer weather. Last year extremely cold weather in areas in central Asia where bird flu is endemic might have forced birds like swans that normally do not migrate very far to travel longer distances across Europe … Globally 272 people are known to have contracted bird flu.

(*IHT*, 13 February 2007, pp. 1, 8)

The bird flu virus … killed more people in 2006 than it did in 2005 or 2004, and its fatality rate is rising – 61 per cent now, up from 43 per cent in 2005… The disease is out of control in birds in more locations than ever, including places like the Nile Delta and Nigeria … the 1918 virus had a 2 per cent fatality rate and yet still killed 50 million to 100 million because it was so transmissible … The virus is out of control in poultry in three countries – Indonesia, Nigeria and Egypt – with combined populations of 447 million people. A year ago it was out of control only in Indonesia, and Thailand and Vietnam had stifled outbreaks, though the virus returned. China remains a mystery; despite official denials there is evidence that it is circulating there, too … Eighty per cent of all Indonesian households keep poultry … For unknown reasons, possibly weather patterns and better poultry vaccination in northern China, not as many migrating swans and geese carried the virus up to Siberia, across Western Europe and down into Africa this winter as they did last winter. The main culprit now in spreading the virus seems to be illegal or improper trade in poultry, health officials say.

(*IHT*, 15 February 2007, p. 2)

A thirty-year-old Egyptian woman has died of bird flu, bringing the number of confirmed deaths from the virus in Egypt to thirteen … Egypt has the largest known number of human cases of bird flu outside Asia. Most of those who have contracted the disease have died.

(www.bbc.co.uk, 16 February 2007)

Bernard Matthews was warned about hygiene lapses at its Suffolk turkey farm before the bird flu outbreak. Defra says gulls were seen taking meat

> waste from open bins ... The report says poultry imported to the UK from Hungary is the 'most plausible' cause of the bird flu outbreak ... There were holes in the houses that could have allowed birds or rodents in.
>
> (www.bbc.co.uk, 16 February 2007)

'[The Defra report also said that] water was leaking from roofs into sheds, meaning infection could spread' (*Guardian*, 17 February 2007, p. 6).

> The UK's chief scientist ... [says that] bird flu does not appear to have infected the UK's wild bird population ... He confirmed that it was likely that the virus had spread to poultry at the Bernard Matthews factory through infected meat or on the boots of a worker.
>
> (*FT*, 24 February 2007, p. 4)

('No definitive source has been found for a bird flu outbreak on a British farm earlier this year, but it was probably caused by poultry meat imported from Hungary, a [UK] government report said Thursday [19 April]. Defra said the H5N1 bird flu strain ... was essentially identical to the strain that had earlier infected geese in southern Hungary': *IHT*, 20 April 2007, p. 8.)

'[On 16 February Russia reported that] the H5N1 strain of bird flu has killed poultry in the Moscow region for the first time' (*FT*, 17 February 2007, p. 7).

> Tests have confirmed the presence of the H5N1 bird flu strain in poultry found dead in two suburban Moscow districts ... west and south of Moscow ... It was the first such outbreak to be recorded so close to the Russian capital ... No human cases of bird flu have been reported in Russia. Bird flu cases were registered in ninety-three towns or settlements in Siberia and southern Russia last year [2006] ... The country's first outbreak this year was registered last month [January] in the Krasnodar territory, an agricultural region near the Black Sea.
>
> (www.iht.com, 18 February 2007)

> Russian officials traced dead domestic poultry in several suburban Moscow districts to a single market just outside the city limits Sunday [18 February] as experts reported new outbreaks and tightened quarantines following confirmation of the presence of the H5N1 avian flu strain. The presence of the deadly strain, confirmed by tests Saturday [17 February], was the first such outbreak to be recorded so close to the Russian capital.
>
> (*IHT*, 19 February 2007, p. 7)

> The outbreaks of avian flu that shut down farms and markets in the suburbs of Moscow over the weekend are a sign that the virus is moving westward along migratory bird routes, as it did last winter. The Russian authorities confirmed Sunday [18 February] that the H5N1 avian influenza virus had been found on at least six farms within 50 kilometres, or 30 miles, of the capital ... Since December [2006] related deaths have been reported in domestic and wild birds in other countries bordering the Black Sea, including Turkey, Azerbaijan and Georgia, the same countries to which migrating

birds brought the flu in the winter of 2005–6. Although it is too early to be certain, the pattern of the Moscow outbreak indicates that it could have been caused by poultry trucked north, rather than by migrating birds.

(*IHT*, 21 February 2007, p. 5)

China's southern Guangdong province is the source of the dangerous H5N1 avian flu virus, according to a genetic analysis of the virus published on Monday [5 March]. And Guangdong appears to be the source of renewed waves of the H5N1 strain … the team at the University of California Irvine reported … The researchers' maps show China's north-west Qinghai province to be another source of bird flu's spread … In contrast to China the researchers found that Indochina – Thailand, Cambodia and Vietnam – appeared to absorb strains of the virus. They said H5N1 spreads there but does not spread from there to anywhere else … Since 2003 H5N1 has spread to more than fifty countries as far away from China as Nigeria and Britain … So far it has infected 277 people and killed 167 of them, according to the WHO.

(www.cnn.com, 6 March 2007)

Officials in southern China are cracking down on illegal trade in civet cats to prevent an outbreak of SARS in the coming months, state news media said Monday [19 February 2007]. About 7,000 health inspectors have been mobilized in Guangdong province, where severe acute respiratory syndrome first emerged in 2002, and have checked 10,000 restaurants for civet cats … Civet cats, mongoose-like animals, are considered a delicacy in southern China and are suspected of spreading SARS to humans, although the original source of the virus has not been determined. In January 2004 Guangdong banned the raising, selling, killing and eating of civet cats. But health departments have been receiving increasing reports of illegal trade in the animals since November [2006] … During recent inspections a live civet cat and several frozen ones were confiscated and eighteen restaurants were fined … The disease that was eventually identified as SARS was first reported in Guangdong in November 2002. It was spread by travellers to dozens of countries and killed 774 people worldwide before subsiding in June 2003. There were 349 deaths reported on the Chinese mainland. China was heavily criticized for being slow to release information on its outbreak and has since been trying to co-operate in investigating emerging diseases like SARS and bird flu.

(www.iht.com, 19 February 2007)

A forty-two-year-old woman has become the first person to die from avian influenza in Laos, officials have said. Authorities said they were awaiting further tests to see if the woman was infected with the H5N1 strain … On Thursday [1 March] the country confirmed a fifteen-year-old girl … had been infected with H5N1. She is being treated in Thailand.

(www.bbc.co.uk, 4 March 2007)

A thirty-two-year-old Indonesian man has died of bird flu, officials said yesterday [16 March], raising the death toll in the country worst hit by the virus to sixty-five. The victim died on Thursday [15 March] ... In Laos health authorities confirmed that a woman who died this month had contracted the H5N1 virus.

(*FT*, 17 March 2007, p. 7)

Bird flu virus has been found among dead crows in Islamabad, the Pakistani capital, a government official said [on 22 March] ... At least two have tested positive for the H5N1 virus among six to eight samples of more than fifty that died.

(*FT*, 23 March 2007, p. 9)

[It was announced on 22 March that] the deadly H5N1 strain has been found ... in a poultry farm ... 25 kilometres from Dhaka ... Many experts will be worried by the news that Bangladesh has its first case. Many residents live in close proximity to farmed birds and the country has one of the highest human population densities in the world ... Bangladesh is also situated on major migratory routes for wild birds and this particular outbreak is close to a wild bird sanctuary ... The virus has been found in Pakistan, India and Afghanistan in the last year.

(www.bbc.co.uk, 23 March 2007)

Indonesian health officials continued to project a defiant tone Monday [26 March] at the start of a three-day meeting with the WHO over Indonesia's refusal to share its H5N1 bird flu samples with the organization's researchers unless it is guaranteed affordable access to vaccines. Indonesia's announcement in February was criticized by researchers as a major departure from a fifty-year-old worldwide system of free virus sharing, one that would severely limit the ability of the WTO to monitor the ever-changing virus. But the country has stood firm on the need to change a system that it says keeps life-saving pharmaceuticals out of the reach of poor countries ... Indonesia has had the most human cases of the H5N1 strain of bird flu. Of 281 cases worldwide, eighty-one were recorded there and sixty-three were fatal ... Countries now send samples of the virus to research centres accredited by the WHO in the United States, Britain, Japan and Australia. Those centres develop potential vaccines that are freely shared with pharmaceutical countries, which then manufacture vaccines that are often too expensive for most developing nations.

(www.iht.com, 26 March 2007)

[Indonesia] reached agreement with the WHO on Tuesday [27 March] to resume sharing samples of the bird flu virus for research ... After two days of talks WHO officials said they had 'struck a balance' between the need to continue sharing virus samples and addressing the concerns of poorer nations. Under the deal drug companies will require the consent of countries to access their virus samples.

(www.bbc.co.uk, 28 March 2007)

> At the close of an emergency meeting … [in Jakarta] on Tuesday [27 March] … the Indonesian health minister announced that she had reached an agreement on vaccines and would begin sharing samples of bird flu viruses again immediately … The agreement stipulates that until a new system of sharing is developed the WHO will not hand over potential vaccines developed from samples taken from Indonesia to pharmaceuticals companies without the consent of the Indonesian government … [The WHO] said a complete revision of the virus sharing system would not be finalized for at least three months.
>
> (www.iht.com, 27 March 2007)

'[On 26 March] Indonesia recorded two more deaths from the H5N1 strain of bird flu, bringing the total number of deaths to sixty-eight' (www.iht.com, 27 March 2007).

'Three people in Indonesia have died from bird flu, taking the country's death toll to sixty-nine … [One died] on Saturday [24 March] … [one] on Sunday [25 March] … [and one] on Wednesday [28 March]' (www.bbc.co.uk, 28 March 2007).

> Indonesia announced two more deaths from H5N1 bird flu yesterday [29 March] … bringing the country's confirmed human death toll from the H5N1 virus to seventy-one … China said a teenage boy had died from the virus. The virus has spread to more than fifty countries.
>
> (*FT*, 30 March 2007, p. 5)

'The deadly H5N1 strain of bird flu has spread to Ghana, the WHO has confirmed … This is the first time it has been confirmed in Ghana' (*Independent*, 3 May 2007, p. 27).

'A twenty-six-year-old pregnant woman has become the nineteenth person to die from bird flu in Indonesia this year [2007]' (*The Times*, 15 May 2007, p. 35).

> Indonesia said yesterday [15 May] it had resumed sharing samples of the H5N1 bird flu virus from infected humans with the WHO. But it warned it would not allow pharmaceutical companies to use the samples for vaccines unless they were swiftly and affordably made available to the developing world … The country's health minister told delegates at the annual World Health Assembly in Geneva that … any vaccine producers must pledge preferential pricing, technology transfer and distribution to countries based on need not wealth … Indonesia introduced a resolution on sharing viruses that would require 'the transparent, fair and equitable sharing of benefits' from vaccines developed from virus samples. It said vaccines must be 'affordable and readily available in developing countries' … Indonesia is the country worst affected by bird flu with seventy-six deaths.
>
> (*FT*, 16 May 2007, p. 8)

> China has confirmed a new outbreak of the deadly H5N1 strain of the bird flu virus in the central province of Hunan [where] poultry died … China's

last reported case was in March, when chickens died at a poultry market near the Tibetan capital, Lhasa ... A total of fifteen people have died in China from the H5N1 virus ... Officials are working to vaccinate billions of domestic poultry by the end of May in preparation for the northward migration of wild birds in the summer.

(www.bbc.co.uk, 19 May 2007)

The H5N1 strain of bird flu – which appeared in Asia in 2003 and has led to the death of 185 people – is infecting fewer wild birds, indicating it may be dying out in the wild, The World Organization of Animal Health said yesterday [21 May]. But a form of the bird flu virus which can be transmitted between domestic flocks remained unchanged, the OIE said.

(*FT*, 22 May 2007, p. 8)

'On Tuesday [22 May] Ghana reported that it had found a second confirmed case of the H5N1 virus in the centre of the country, some distance from the first case, discovered at the beginning of May' (www.bbc.co.uk, 23 May 2007).

Vietnam confirmed its first human bird flu case in a year and a half on Wednesday [23 May] as the virus continued to spread through its poultry stocks ... Relatives said he [the man concerned] had helped prepare chickens for a wedding reception before falling ill. It is the country's first human infection of H5N1 since November 2005 and comes as bird flu outbreaks have been reported across Vietnam ... No poultry outbreaks were reported in 2006, but cases of the virus emerged again early this year ... The H5N1 virus has killed forty-two people in Vietnam and 185 worldwide, according to the WHO. Meanwhile a five-year-old Indonesian girl has died of bird flu, according to the country's health ministry. Her death brings the number of confirmed human fatalities in Indonesia to seventy-seven, the highest in the world.

(www.iht.com, 23 May 2007)

'The WHO says it has reached a framework agreement to ensure all countries share samples of the deadly H5N1 strain of the virus' (www.bbc.co.uk, 23 May 2007).

Bird flu [striking on Friday 25 May] has spread to two more provinces in Vietnam, as the country's first human case in eighteen months began to improve in health, officials said Monday [28 May] ... [The cases bring] the number of provinces and cities hit by the virus to ten over the past month ... At least forty-two people have died of bird flu in Vietnam, but none since November 2005.

(www.iht.com, 28 May 2007)

'An Indonesian girl has died of bird flu ... bringing the national death toll from the H5N1 virus to seventy-nine, a health ministry spokeswoman said Sunday [3 June] ... Bird flu has killed at least 187 people worldwide since 2003' (www.iht.com, 3 June 2007).

> A man has died of bird flu in Vietnam, in the first confirmed human death from the virus there since 2005, health officials said … [He] died of the H5N1 strain of the virus on 10 June … Bird flu has killed forty-three people in Vietnam and officials have warned of more human cases as the virus spreads rapidly in poultry in many provinces. None of the country's five recent human bird flu cases has been confirmed by the WHO … In May Vietnam announced its first human case of the deadly H5N1 virus after containing a previous outbreak since November 2005. The H5N1 strain has killed more than 190 people [worldwide] since 2003, according to WHO figures. Indonesia has been the hardest hit, with eighty deaths.
>
> (www.bbc.co.uk, 16 June 2007)

'Two swans and a duck have died of the H5N1 strain of bird flu … at a lake in Nuremberg in southern Germany' (*The Times*, 25 June 2007, p. 33).

'Czech authorities have culled thousands of birds at a poultry farm in the east of the country following the discovery of the H5N1 avian influenza virus, A similar outbreak was discovered last week at a nearby turkey farm' (*FT*, 29 June 2007, p. 1).

> Tests have confirmed that three swans found dead in eastern France died from the H5N1 bird flu virus, France's first cases of the disease in more than a year, the agriculture ministry said Thursday [5 July] … Germany said it was raising its assessment of the risk of bird flu following the French announcement and after officials Wednesday [4 July] discovered more birds that had died of the H5N1 virus in the eastern state of Thuringia … This year's outbreaks probably spread through the migration of infected water birds. Last year [2006] thirteen EU states confirmed bird flu cases – Germany, Austria, Denmark, Italy, Greece, Britain, the Czech Republic, Poland, Slovakia, Slovenia, Sweden, France and Hungary. In France the virus was found in more than sixty wild birds and at a farm with 11,000 turkeys. It has not been detected in the country since April 2006 … The large flu epidemic that appeared after World War I, also known as Spanish flu, was of avian origin … Since 2003 the [H5N1] virus has sickened 317 people in a dozen countries, killing 191 of them, according to the WHO.
>
> (*IHT*, 6 July 2007, p. 3)

> The German authorities have discovered the H5N1 bird flu virus in domestic poultry for the first time this year [2007]. A goose … in the state of Thuringia was found to be infected with the virus … The infected bird lived on a small farm in a remote area.
>
> (*IHT*, 7 July 2007, p. 6)

'Bird flu has killed its first human victim on the Indonesian island of Bali … The twenty-nine-year-old woman died on Sunday [22 August] … Indonesia has now confirmed eighty-two human deaths from bird flu' (www.bbc.co.uk, 13 August 2007).

'Only 308 people have succumbed to bird flu worldwide' (*IHT*, 24 August 2007, p. 4).

'An outbreak of bird flu on a poultry farm in Bavaria was identified yesterday [26 August] as the pathogenic strain of the H5N1 virus … Officials described [it] as the largest culling action in recent German history' (*FT*, 27 August 2007, p. 5).

'Officials confirmed the first H5N1 bird flu outbreak [in China] since May [2007] … [The] outbreak [was] in Guangzhou' (*FT*, 19 September 2007, p. 14).

> A woman has died from … the deadly H5N1 strain of … bird flu … on the Indonesian island of Sumatra … bringing the country's toll from the disease to eighty-seven … [Indonesia] has confirmed 108 human cases of the virus, eighty-seven of whom have died.
>
> (www.bbc.co.uk, 8 October 2007)

> The type of bird flu found in turkeys on a Suffolk [free-range] farm is the virulent strain, according to [UK] government vets. The virus was discovered on Sunday [11 November] … All 6,500 birds … at the affected premises – including approximately 5,000 turkeys, 1,000 ducks and 500 geese – will be slaughtered.
>
> (www.bbc.co.uk, 13 November 2007)

'[This] is the fourth case of avian influenza in the UK this year [2007] and the H5N1 virus has been found in the UK, the Czech Republic, Hungary, France and Germany this year' (www.guardian.co.uk, 13 November 2007).

> [The] free-range turkeys … [were] reared outdoors … Wild swans and ducks regularly gather at the [Suffolk] farm. There is also a lake within a mile from the family farm that is another favourite gathering place for birds … Tests on wild birds are being stepped up … To date, however, there has not been one positive test for avian flu on birds in the UK.
>
> (www.thetimes.co.uk, 13 November 2007)

> An outbreak of bird flu in a poultry farm in Bavaria, southern Germany, was identified Sunday [11 November] as the pathogenic strain of the H5N1 virus … The culling [of] 160,000 ducks and other birds on the farm … [was] described as the largest such culling action in recent German history.
>
> (www.ft.com, 13 November 2007)

> Around 24,000 birds on four [more] premises are being culled as a precaution … The five premises shared the same farming staff … Acting chief vet Fred Landeg … said his department [Defra] was keeping an 'open mind' about how the virus reached the farm, but added that early indications were that it was related to outbreaks in the Czech Republic and Germany – which suggested a wild bird source. The affected birds were free-range – meaning they had access to the outdoors and were located near a lake used by a number of wild fowl … There was an H5N1 outbreak at a turkey farm … in Suffolk in February.
>
> (www.bbc.co.uk, 14 November 2007)

> A cull of poultry suspected of having bird flu is under way at a second Suffolk farm [one of the four] ... Defra says 5,500 turkeys are ... being 'slaughtered on suspicion' of having the disease ... Precautionary culls are also under way at three additional farms ... Defra ordered the culling of a total of 22,000 free-range turkeys at these three farms.
>
> (www.bbc.co.uk, 15 November 2007)

'[The second] farm where turkeys were being slaughtered on suspicion ... has been given the all-clear, the owners say' (www.bbc.co.uk, 16 November 2007).

> The 200th death [worldwide] occurred in September 2007. The first human deaths from H5N1 outside Asia ... in Turkey ... [occurred] in January 2006 ... In June 2007 Indonesia became the first country to have 100 confirmed cases of H5N1 among humans ... The first outbreaks in the EU were recorded in January 2006 when cases were confirmed in wild swans in Italy, Greece, Germany and Austria.
>
> (www.bbc.co.uk, 14 November 2007)

As of 12 November 2007, according to the World Health Organization, there were 335 human cases of H5N1 and 206 deaths. The number of deaths by country was as follows: Indonesia (91); Vietnam (46); Thailand (17); China (16); Egypt (15); Cambodia (7); Azerbaijan (5); Turkey (4); Iraq (2); Laos (2); Nigeria (1) (www.bbc.co.uk, 14 November 2007).

> A second case of the virulent H5N1 strain of bird flu has been confirmed at a farm by Defra ... nearby [the original farm where the first outbreak occurred] ... The new infected premises is operated by the same company as the site of the first outbreak ... The cull of poultry on four sites suspected of being infected ended on 18 November.
>
> (www.bbc.co.uk, 19 November 2007)

'A second case of the deadly H5N1 strain has been found in turkeys ... The farm was one of the four where culls were taking place because of fears of "dangerous contact" with the initial case' (www.independent.co.uk, 20 November 2007).

> Indonesia's health minister reiterated Sunday [25 November] that she would not send bird flu specimens to the WHO, saying poor nations needed assurances that any pandemic vaccines developed from the virus would be affordable. Siti Fadilah Supari made the comments on her return from Geneva, where the WHO held an intergovernmental conference aimed at rebuilding a global system for sharing flu viruses following a months-long standoff with Indonesia ... Siti Fadilah Supari: 'The meeting failed to come up with a material of transfer agreement. So we have no obligation to send bird flu virus samples to the WHO' ... Indonesia has been harder hit by the H5N1 bird flu virus than any other country in the world, accounting for ninety-one of the 206 known human deaths from the virus. Vietnam ranks second with forty-six deaths and Thailand third with seventeen. Though Indonesia has been reluctant to share bird flu samples with the WHO, saying it was worried

the virus would be used to make vaccines that would be affordable only to the rich, it made exceptions following several human deaths on the Indonesian island of Bali. That appeared, however, to be an attempt to lure tourists back to the resort island, which has been hit by a string of terrorist attacks in recent years. Supari wants to change its fifty-year-old virus-sharing system so that developing countries that hand over samples retain the rights over their biological resources, saying this was not the time for 'safety'.

(www.iht.com, 25 November 2007)

[On 27 November] a man in China's eastern province of Jiangsu died from the deadly H5N1 strain of bird flu ... [It was] said he had no known contact with dead poultry and no outbreaks of bird flu were reported nearby. A total of seventeen people have died in China from the H5N1 virus and millions of birds have been killed.

(www.bbc.co.uk, 3 December 2007)

The father of a Chinese man who died of bird flu has also been infected with the virus ... The WHO said it could not rule out the possibility that the H5N1 virus had spread from the son ... [who died] on 2 December ... to the father ... Of the twenty-six cases confirmed to date in China, seventeen have been fatal. Suspected human-to-human transmission of H5N1 has been reported in Hong Kong, Vietnam and Indonesia, but none of the cases have been proven.

(www.bbc.co.uk, 7 December 2007)

A second woman from Egypt's Nile Delta region died of bird flu on Monday [31 December], the health ministry said, bringing the week's toll from the virus to four. The deaths are thought to have resulted from exposure to poultry infected with the H5N1 strain ... Nineteen people have now died of bird flu in Egypt in the past two years. The government says the large number of people who keep poultry at home makes it difficult to eradicate the disease. Egypt has the largest known number of human cases of bird flu outside Asia and most of those who have contracted the virus have died. Most of the Egyptians who have died have been women. Women and girls are often responsible for looking after poultry in Egypt. The WHO announced earlier this year [2007] that some of those who had died in Egypt had been infected with a strain of the virus that showed moderate resistance to the antiviral drug Tamiflu. More than 213 people have died of H5N1 bird flu since the disease's resurgence in December 2003 – most in South-east Asia. Experts point out that cross-infection to humans is still relatively rare and usually occurs where people have been in close contact with infected birds. But they say if the H5N1 strain mutates so it can be passed between humans, it could become a global pandemic.

(www.bbc.co.uk, 31 December 2007)

Three mute swans in Dorset [a county on the south coast of England] have been found dead with the virulent H5N1 strain of bird flu. Other birds are being tested at Abbotsbury Swannery, near Weymouth ... The swans' carcasses were found following routine surveillance ... Culling of wild birds has been ruled out because experts fear this may disperse birds further ... Defra has set up two restricted areas – a wild bird control area and a larger wild bird monitoring area.

(www.bbc.co.uk, 10 January 2008)

[The] Abbotsbury Swannery holds 600 swans ... Ornithologists say mute swans rarely migrate so it is most likely the virus got into the colony from a passing wild bird. This is not a major migration season, but wintry weather could have prompted some birds to fly to Britain from Europe in search of food ... Dorset is not an area of extensive poultry production.

(www.bbc.co.uk, 11 January 2008)

A fourth swan has tested positive for the virulent H5N1 strain of bird flu ... The fourth swan was one of four found dead at the swannery on Friday [11 January]. Tests on the other three proved negative ... Defra said there was currently no evidence to suggest the disease was widespread among wild birds in the area.

(www.bbc.co.uk, 16 January 2008)

As of January 2008 the WHO had confirmed 348 cases of H5N1 in humans in Azerbaijan, Cambodia. China, Djibouti, Egypt, Indonesia, Iraq, Lao People's Democratic Republic, Myanmar, Nigeria, Pakistan, Thailand, Turkey and Vietnam, leading to 216 deaths ... Scientists studying a case in Vietnam found the virus can affect all parts of the body, not just the lungs ... After bird flu claimed its first human victim – a three-year-old boy in Hong Kong in May 1997 – the disease was not detected again until February 2003, when a father and son were diagnosed with H5N1, again in Hong Kong. Since then it has spread westwards through Asia, the Middle East, Europe and Africa ... The mortality rate presently stands at around 50 per cent of confirmed cases.

(www.bbc.co.uk, 11 January 2008)

Health and veterinary workers are culling thousands of chickens in the Indian state of West Bengal after an outbreak of bird flu was confirmed ... Nearly 10,000 chickens were found dead in the area in the past week ... The birds were found to be carrying the deadly H5N1 virus ... Several outbreaks of bird flu in India in recent years have all been brought under control ... India faced a major outbreak of bird flu [in 2007].

(www.bbc.co.uk, 16 January 2008)

Last year [2007] for the first time since avian flu emerged as a global threat, the number of human cases was down from the year before ... There were eighty-six confirmed human cases compared with 115 in 2006, according to the WHO, and fifty-nine deaths compared with seventy-nine. Experts assume that the real numbers are several times larger, because many cases are missed ... David Nabarro, the senior United Nations co-ordinator for human and avian flu, recently conceded that he worried somewhat less than he did three years ago: 'Not because I think the threat has changed, but because the response to it has gotten so much better' ... The world is clearly more prepared. Vaccines have been developed. Stockpiles of Tamiflu and masks have grown. Many countries, cities, companies and schools have written pandemic plans ... In the worst-hit countries – all poor – laboratories have become faster at flu tests. Government veterinarians now move more quickly to cull chickens. Hospital wards for suspect patients, and epidemiologists trace contacts and treat all with Tamiflu – a tactic meant to encircle and snuff outbreaks before the virus can adapt itself to humans ... The most worrisome aspect of H5N1, virtually all scientists agree, is that it persists in birds without becoming less lethal to them ... David Nabarro: 'This is the most serious bird flu that has ever been known. By 2007 it was in sixty countries. It must be dealt with' ... Despite the culling of hundreds of millions of birds and the injection of billions of doses of poultry vaccine, the virus is out of control in some of the most populous countries – though exactly which ones are in dispute, because some are touchy about conceding that they cannot rid their flocks of it. Bernard Vallat, director-general of the World Organization for Animal Health, has named three countries where it [H5N1] is now endemic in local birds: Egypt, Indonesia and Nigeria. Nabarro added Bangladesh, Vietnam and parts of China. Reports of recurrent outbreaks also persist in parts of India, Myanmar and Pakistan. Last week villagers in India were reported to be killing and eating their flocks before government cullers, who paid less than a third of market value, could seize them ... In December [2007] dying birds were found in Poland and Russia, in Saudi Arabia and even a kindergarten petting zoo in Israel. On 8 January [2008] it reached one of England's most famous swan breeding grounds, the Abbotsbury Swannery, which has been around since the eleventh century ... Pakistan had its first human cases last year [2007], as did Laos, Myanmar and Nigeria.

(www.iht.com, 22 January 2008; *IHT*, 23 January 2008, p. 2)

Three people died of bird flu this week, pushing the number of deaths in Indonesia to 101 – nearly half of all the bird flu deaths in the world. The other countries with the highest reported death tolls are Vietnam (with forty-eight), Egypt (with nineteen) and China and Thailand (each with seventeen). The mortality rate in Indonesia is also the highest in the world. Only twenty-four of the 125 people reported to have been infected have survived. The virus is known to have infected 358 people around the world in fourteen countries, killing 224 of them, according to the WHO. Experts say that because of poor reporting of infections and deaths, the true number could be much higher.

(*IHT*, 1 February 2008, p. 5)

Aviaries at a popular Hong Kong theme park were closed to the public for three weeks beginning Thursday [31 January] after tests indicated that a wild heron found dead in the park may have been killed by bird flu, agriculture officials said … Last year [2007] Hong Kong discovered twenty-one wild birds infected with H5N1, but it has not suffered a major outbreak of the disease since 1997, when the virus killed six people, prompting the government to slaughter the territory's entire poultry population of about 1.5 million birds.

(www.iht.com, 31 January 2008)

An Indonesian woman died of bird flu [on 2 February] … bringing the country's death toll from the disease to 103, the health ministry said … A spokesman said: 'Her death raised the Indonesian death toll to 103 out of 126 cases.'

(www.iht.com, 4 February 2008)

The bird flu epidemic has spread to over half of Bangladesh's sixty-four districts … Officials in the Indian state of West Bengal – which neighbours Bangladesh – said the virus has been detected in thirteen of the state's nineteen districts … But so far no cases of human infection have been reported either in India or Bangladesh. Bird flu has also been reported recently in Pakistan … Last month [January] the UN's Food and Agriculture Organization said that the virus 'appeared to be endemic' in [Bangladesh].

(www.bbc.co.uk, 4 February 2008)

'A forty-year-old man died of bird flu and another man was infected after coming into contact with infected chickens. The latest death was the second in Vietnam this year [2008] and brings the toll to forty-nine' (*The Times*, 15 February 2008, p. 43).

Health authorities [in Hong Kong] tightened surveillance measures against avian influenza Monday [25 February] following the fourth death in mainland China suspected to have been caused by the virus since late last year [2007 … Her death follows several confirmed cases of bird flu infection since 2 December [2007] … The WHO has reported 232 deaths worldwide in the past four years, twenty-nine of them in China. Almost all the reported cases have been as a result of close contact between humans and infected birds.

(www.iht.com, 25 February 2008)

'Two more people have died of bird flu in Indonesia, bringing the death toll in the country worst hit by the virus to 107, the health ministry said Monday [31 March] … Both died last week' (www.iht.com, Monday 31 March 2008).

Beijing has given the go-ahead to a Chinese drug maker to begin large-scale production of a human bird flu vaccine, after a second clinical trial [in November 2007] showed the vaccine was safe and effective, the company said Thursday [3 April]. The vaccine uses an inactivated H5N1 virus from Vietnam, said an official for Sinovac Biotech, which developed the vaccine along with the Chinese Centres for Disease Control … The virus has infected 376 people in fourteen countries since late 2003 and killed 238 of them, or 63 per cent. An eventual vaccine to protect people against a flu pandemic would probably be made only four to six months after the start of such a disaster, after the culprit virus strain had been identified. But some form of protection would still be needed for the initial months of a pandemic, and drug companies, including Sinovac, are in a race to design what are known as 'pre-pandemic' vaccines. Sinovac is conducting tests to see if its bird flu vaccine offers cross protection against other strains of the virus found in Indonesia, Turkey and Abhui province in China ... On 2 March [2008] GlaxoSmithKline company said a vaccine it had designed to protect people against H5N1 might be effective in warding off a few different subtypes of the virus.

(www.iht.com, 3 April 2008)

Japan is to become the first country in the world to vaccinate thousands of officials against bird flu. Six thousand health workers and other staff will be inoculated over the next few months and the programme might be extended to cover millions more. Although bird flu has caused 240 deaths since 1993, none has been in Japan. But there are fears that an outbreak elsewhere in Asia could spread quickly in Japan, which has some of the world's most densely populated areas ... Japan has already stockpiled 20 million doses of so-called 'pre-pandemic' bird flu vaccine for use after a major outbreak. The vaccine has been made using the deadly H5N1 strain of the disease collected in Vietnam and Indonesia ... The plan is to initially use 6,400 doses of vaccine to inoculate doctors, quarantine inspectors and other health and immigration officials. If successful, the government aims to expand the programme to others ... [an additional] 10 million people who are in medical occupations or other key jobs such as in utilities ... By taking this action Japan is taking bird flu precautions to levels not seen anywhere else in the world ... Japan is probably the only Asian country which has the resources to do this ... The WHO does not sound convinced that it would improve the chances of Japan weathering a major bird flu outbreak ... WHO spokesman Gregory Harti: '[The planned vaccinations are] a big roll of the dice. Obviously, the Japanese think there's some benefit to be had from this and we are not going to prevent an individual country from using their resources.'

(www.bbc.co.uk, 16 April 2008)

Chinese officials have reported that the country's fifth outbreak of the H5N1 avian flu this year [2008] is killing chickens in poultry markets in the southern city of Guangzhou. Although this particular outbreak is not known to have infected humans, China has already reported three human avian flu deaths this year. Far more worrisome is the 3 April confirmation by the government of Pakistan and the WHO of three cases in a family cluster in Pakistan's North West province late last year [2007], suggesting limited human-to-human transmission ... China's prodigious effort to vaccinate 14 billion chickens annually has been chaotic, compromised by the appearance of significant amounts of counterfeit vaccines and the absence of protective gear for vaccination teams – who might actually spread the disease by carrying faecal material on their shoes from one farm to another.

(www.feer.com, 30 April 2008)

'A three-year-old boy has died of bird flu in Indonesia, raising the death toll from the disease there to 108, the health ministry said yesterday [30 April]' (*FT*, 1 May 2008, p. 10).

South Korean officials say they have killed the entire poultry population of Seoul to curb the spread of bird flu … The cull began just hours after the authorities recorded Seol's second outbreak of the virus in a week … Tests are being carried out to determine if the South Korean outbreak was the deadly H5N1 strain. The virus was detected in southern parts of the country last month [April] … [For] the first time the virus has been found in Busan – South Korea's second largest city … The outbreaks brought the number of confirmed detections of the virus in South Korea to twenty-eight.

(www.bbc.co.uk, 12 May 2008)

European medical regulators have approved the first human vaccine against bird flu intended for use before or in the early stages of a pandemic, GlaxoSmithKline, its maker, said Monday [19 May]. The vaccine, Prepandrix, activates an immune response to the H5N1 strain of bird flu … The company has previously announced plans to donate 50 million doses of the prepandemic vaccine to the WHO … The official licence comes from the European Commission, the executive arm of the EU.

(*IHT*, 20 May 2008, p. 19)

The Hong Kong government ordered a mass cull of all poultry on Wednesday [11 May] in a bid to stop the spread of the H5N1 virus among birds in hundreds of markets scattered across the territory. Last week officials found the bird flu virus at a poultry stall in one of the city's many so-called wet markets and ordered the culling of 2,700 birds during the week. On Wednesday government officials said that the virus had since spread among the island's poultry population and mass cullings were now necessary as a precaution. Cheng Siu-hin (director of agriculture, fisheries and conservation): 'We have not found any dead chickens – not yet. We have not had any human cases' … Since the H5N1 virus resurfaced in Asia in 2003 it has killed 241 people in a dozen countries, according to the WHO. The largest number of human fatalities has been in Indonesia, with at least 108 confirmed deaths.

(www.iht.com, 11 June 2008)

The government [of Hong Kong has] decided to preclude future problems with its drastic decision to end live-chicken trade … The government has offered $128 million to put the whole business out of its misery. That is the cost of a plan unveiled on 20 June to buy back all the licences allowing live

> chickens to be sold. The latest bout of bird flu was first detected in four wet markets in Hong Kong on 11 June [2008].
>
> (*The Economist*, 28 June 2008, pp. 76–7)

'Authorities in Brussels yesterday [10 October] confirmed two "risk areas" had been set up in Germany to contain a new outbreak of avian flu on a poultry farm in Saxony' (*FT*, 11 October 2008, p. 9).

'The WTO says there have been 246 confirmed cases of the disease in humans since 2003 [including seven in Cambodia]' (www.iht.com, 12 December 2008).

> More than 370,000 chickens have been culled in China's eastern province of Jiangsu after an outbreak of the H5N1 strain of bird flu … The outbreak is thought to be the first in mainland China since June. Meanwhile a man has reportedly contracted the virus in Cambodia, while Taiwan is investigating suspected infection among birds. The death of a teenage girl from H5N1 was announced in Egypt on Tuesday [16 December] and a bird cull is also underway in India. More than 200 people in a dozen countries have died of the virus since it resurfaced in Asia in 2003 … China's ministry of agriculture said it received notification that the H5N1 virus had been found in two areas of Jiangsu on Monday [15 December] … Officials say they think migrating birds might have been the source of the disease … China is among a number of countries experiencing a return of the virus this season. Authorities in the Indian state of West Bengal are implementing a cull after tests on poultry from two villages yielded positive results. In Cambodia another cull is under way after the WTO and government confirmed a young man had the virus … Authorities in Taiwan say they are investigating the cause of the sudden death of poultry in Luzhu, Kaohsiung county … Earlier in the week Egyptian authorities announced the death of a sixteen-year-old girl from the virus. The discovery of infected birds in Hong Kong last week sparked a cull of more than 80,000 birds.
>
> (www.bbc.co.uk, 17 December 2008)

> A woman suspected of being infected with bird flu has died in Beijing, the local health bureau said today [6 January 2009]. It would be the first bird flu death in the country in almost a year. The woman died yesterday [5 January] … Xinhua news agency said the woman, from eastern Fujian province, had bought nine ducks at a market in Hebei province, which surrounds Beijing, and then gutted the birds … The last known reported fatality in China was in February last year [2008] when a forty-four-year-old woman died in the southern province of Guangdong. At least twenty people have died of bird flu in China to date.
>
> (www.independent.co.uk, 6 January 2009)

> A [nineteen-year-old] woman has died from bird flu in a Beijing hospital, the government reported Tuesday [6 January], but the WHO said the case did not appear to signal a new public health threat … Tests confirmed she

> had the H5N1 bird flu virus … [She] became ill after buying and cleaning nine ducks in December at a market in Hebei province, which borders Beijing. It was the first reported death in China from the illness in nearly a year … According to the latest WHO tally, bird flu has killed 248 people worldwide since 2003, including twenty-one in China … In northern Vietnam an eight-year-old girl has tested positive for the disease – the first human case reported there in almost a year, health officials said Tuesday. The girl from Thanh Hoa province was admitted to a hospital on 27 December with a high fever and other symptoms after eating a sick goose raised by the family … The H5N1 bird flu virus continues to devastate poultry stocks around the world. China, which raises more poultry than any other country, has vowed to aggressively fight the virus.
>
> (www.iht.com, 7 January 2009)

'China has issued an alert against bird flu following the death of a nineteen-year-old woman from the disease … Since the outbreak of bird flu in 2003 twenty-one people in China have died. Worldwide 247 people have died' (www.bbc.co.uk, 7 January 2009).

'Nepal said that it had found the H5N1 bird flu in poultry, the first time the deadly virus has surfaced in the Himalayan nation, prompting widespread culling operations in the country's south-east region' (*The Times*, 17 January 2009, p. 46).

> A two-year-old girl in northern China is in critical condition after testing positive for bird flu, state media said Sunday [18 January]. It is China's second confirmed case of the virus this month. The girl fell ill on 7 January in the central Hunan province and was taken to her home province of Shanxi in northern China … Since the end of 2003 the H5N1 virus has infected numerous species of birds in more than sixty countries in Asia, Europe and Africa. It has not been found in North or South America, including the Caribbean, according to the Food and Agriculture Organization … [China] reported its first human infection case in 2005. So far thirty cases have been confirmed. Twenty of them have been fatal, Xinhua said. China announced it was setting up a nationwide network to test for the virus.
>
> (www.cnn.com, 18 January 2009)

> A Chinese woman has died from bird flu in the eastern Shandong province … Aged twenty-seven … [she] died at the weekend after becoming infected with the H5N1 strain of avian influenza … The three new cases are the first to be reported in China in almost a year … The toll from bird flu in China is now reported by the state media as twenty-two since 2003 … The ministry of agriculture said on Sunday [18 January] … [that] China now faces 'a grim situation' in bird flu prevention, threatened by frequent outbreaks in neighbouring countries … Bird flu often resurges in the winter months in China, but not every case is fatal … [The] H5N1 [strain] resurfaced in Asia in 2003, killing at least 247 people.
>
> (www.bbc.co.uk, 19 January 2009)

China has recorded its third bird flu death this year [2009] after a sixteen-year-old boy died in central China on Tuesday [20 January] ... On Saturday [17 January] a twenty-seven-year-old woman from eastern China died of bird flu, making her the second person to die this year ... On 5 January a nineteen-year-old woman died of bird flu after handling poultry.

(www.cnn.com, 20 January 2009)

Shu Yulong, from the National Centre for Disease Control and Prevention ... said that the country is likely to experience an epidemic of human flu cases in the next month or two ... Winter and spring are prime bird flu seasons, when more than 70 per cent of cases occur. Millions of Chinese people are heading home for Chinese New Year, increasing the chances of infection ... and in spring birds carry the virus over great distances ... A two-year-old toddler reported to have been in critical condition with the H5N1 virus has now recovered and is described as 'stable' ... In Hong Kong consumers have been told not to eat poultry brought in from the Chinese mainland.

(www.bbc.co.uk, 20 January 2009)

A woman from China's far north-west ... in Xinjiang Uighur Autonomous Region ... has died from bird flu, health authorities said Saturday [24 January], making her the country's fourth fatality from the deadly avian influenza so far this year. The thirty-one-year-old woman ... died Friday morning [23 January] ... Tests were positive for H5N1, the department said.

(www.cnn.com, 24 January 2009)

A twenty-nine-year-old man in south-west China is in critical condition after testing positive for bird flu, making him the country's sixth confirmed case of the virus this month, state media said Sunday [25 January] ... The man fell ill on 15 January.

(www.cnn.com, 25 January 2009)

A twenty-one-year-old woman in central China has been infected by the H5N1 strain of bird flu in the country's eighth reported case of the disease this year [2009], the health ministry said Sunday [1 February], as Hong Kong reported that three birds found at local beaches had died of bird flu ... China has reported seven other cases of H5N1 since January, five of which were fatal ... Hong Kong said the carcasses of a goose and two ducks found in the city had tested positive for bird flu ... [but] said it was not clear yet which strain the fowl carried. There are several subtypes of H5 bird flu, including the H5N2 strain, which is not known to be harmful to humans. The more virulent H5N1 strain has killed 254 people worldwide since 2003, including twenty-five in China, according to the WHO. While the disease remains hard for humans to catch, scientists have warned that if outbreaks among poultry are not controlled, the virus may mutate into a form more easily passed between people, possibly triggering a pandemic that could kill millions worldwide ... India has reported no human infections ... [but] the latest outbreak of the virus in poultry is the sixth since 2007 in West Bengal, where more than 4 million birds were culled early last year [2008] in what the WHO called India's worst bird flu outbreak ... Hundreds of thousands of birds were also culled in the north-east of India after the virus was detected there in November [2008].

(www.iht.com, 1 February 2009)

Bird flu is becoming less deadly ... [but] scientists fear that this is the very thing that could make the virus more able to cause a pandemic ... This paradox – emerging from Egypt, the most recent epicentre of the disease – threatens to increase the disease's ability to spread from person to person by helping it achieve the crucial mutation in the virus ... The WHO is to back an investigation into a change in the pattern of the disease in Egypt, the most seriously affected country outside Asia. Although infections have been on the rise this year [2009] ... they have almost all been in children under the age of three, while twelve months ago it was mainly adults and older children who were infected. And the infections have been much milder than usual; the disease normally kills more than half of those infected; all of the eleven Egyptians so far infected this year are still alive. Experts say that these developments make it more likely that the virus will spread. Ironically, its very virulence has provided an important safeguard. It did not get much chance to infect other people when it killed its victims swiftly, but now it has much more of a chance to mutate and be passed on ... [An expert who works with the WHO in Egypt] stressed that there was still no evidence of the disease passing from person to person.

(www.independent.co.uk, 12 April 2009)

AIDS

Xinjiang [is] an overwhelmingly Moslem region close to the rich poppy fields of Afghanistan and near the border with Kyrgyzstan and Tajikistan. With a population of about 20 million and an officially estimated 60,000 infections, Xinjiang has one-tenth of China's AIDS cases and the highest HIV infection rate in the country. The Chinese authorities estimate that Kashgar prefecture, with a population of about 3 million, has 780 cases, but public health experts here say the real figure is probably four times that and rising fast.

Since 2005 the authorities in Xinjiang have been trying everything from needle exchanges and drug substitution programmes – approaches that first became popular in the West in the 1960s – to community programmes, often involving imams and mullahs.

(www.iht.com, 12 November 2006)

This year [2006] China issued a statute banning discrimination against people with HIV/AIDS, but it has yet to do the same for hepatitis B, which kills many more people in China than does AIDS ... Early last year [2005] the central government declared that [hepatitis B] carriers would no longer be barred from government posts.

(*The Economist*, 18 November 2006, p. 66)

China's reported cases of HIV/AIDS jumped nearly 30 per cent in the first ten months of 2006 ... the health ministry said Wednesday [22 November 2006]. The hefty rise in reported cases shows how China is doing a better job testing and tracking the disease, said Joel Rehnstrom, co-ordinator for the UNAIDS China office. But, he said, it also shows 'that the epidemic continues to grow in many parts of the country'. State media reported that the country's drug users still share dirty needles and more than half of sex workers do not use condoms. The reported number of HIV cases grew more than 28 per cent to 183,733 by 31 October this year [2006], up from 144,089 at the end of last year [2005], the health ministry said. Of the reported cases more than a fifth (40,667) have developed into AIDS. During the same period there were 4,060 AIDS deaths, bringing the total number of reported deaths in China due to the disease to 12,464 since it was identified in China in the early 1990s. Rehnstrom said reported HIV cases have been steadily increasing at a rate of about 30 per cent annually since 1999 but with testing still inadequate for such a large country the real figure is likely to be four to five times the reported figure. After years of denying that AIDS was a problem Chinese leaders have dramatically shifted gears in recent years, confronting the disease more openly, promising anonymous testing, free treatment for the poor and a ban on discrimination against people with the virus ... Despite greater openness the government often harasses the more outspoken AIDS activists and ill treatment of HIV sufferers remains common ... The health ministry said in its report that 37 per cent of the cases reported this year were linked to drug use and 28 per cent to unsafe sex ... The ministry said 5.1 per cent of the cases were caused by people selling blood illegally or receiving infected blood from hospitals. HIV gained a foothold in China largely due to unsanitary blood plasma-buying schemes and tainted transfusions in hospitals. China has cracked down harshly on such schemes and declared last year that the problem of tainted blood supplies was under control though new cases still emerge sporadically, often in rural areas ... [Globally] an estimated 39.5 million people are now living with HIV ... Of that total 4.3 million became infected this year [2006]. There have been 2.9 million AIDS deaths in 2006, the highest number reported in any year ... In China some programmes focused on sex workers had led to increases in condom use and decreases in rates of sexually transmitted infections. Also programmes for injecting drug users have shown progress in some areas.

(www.iht.com, 22 November 2006; *IHT*, 23 November 2006, p. 7)

China's estimate [is that] total infections, including unreported cases, have reached 650,000. Health officials warned that HIV/AIDS appears to be spreading from high-risk groups to the general public ... HIV first became a

problem in China in the 1980s and 1990s, owing largely to blood-selling schemes and unsanitary transfusions ... Experts warn that the actual figure for those infected with HIV/AIDS is much higher than the official statistics report – and that many people do not know they have the virus, or choose not to report it. At the end of 2005 both the health ministry and the United Nations estimated that the total number of HIV cases in China was actually about 650,000 and that another 75,000 people were living with AIDS.
(www.bbc.co.uk, 22 November 2006)

The number of people newly infected with HIV (the virus that causes the disease) in the past twelve months is estimated at 4.3 million. In the same period 2.9 million have died from the disease. The total number of people now infected stands at somewhere between 34 million and 47 million, the range reflecting the fact that it is, indeed, an estimate rather than a proper census.
(*The Economist*, 25 November 2006, p. 112)

Gao Yaojie ... a retired doctor acclaimed for helping people with AIDS has been placed under house arrest to stop her travelling to an awards ceremony in the United States [on 14 March 2007] ... [She] has been confined to her apartment [since 1 February 2007] ... Gao gained international attention after she helped expose a blood-selling programme in central China that infected tens of thousands of farmers with HIV during the 1990s ... She is among a handful of advocates whose work is credited with helping to force the government to confront the spread of HIV ... In 2001 she was forbidden from going abroad to receive an international award for her work on AIDS.
(www.iht.com, 5 February 2007)

'[In addition the authorities] have barred non-family visits [to Gao Yaojie's apartment]' (*FT*, 6 February 2007, p. 5).

'Gao Yaojie [has] said her restrictions have been loosened a bit. Her family can now visit her. She can step outside her building for some air' (www.iht.com, 15 February 2007).

The authorities are to allow ... Gao Yaojie ... to visit the United States to receive an award from a rights group ... Gao Yaojie exposed corrupt blood selling deals that infected thousands of people with HIV in the 1990s. She blew the whistle on commercial blood operations in Henan province, often run by officials, which spread HIV among farmers who sold their plasma.
(www.bbc.co.uk, 17 February 2007).

'Estimated at around one in 2,000, HIV prevalence among the general population is still low by international standards. But infections are increasing by 11 per cent a year' (*The Economist*, 21 April 2007, p. 70).

'An estimated 40 million people worldwide are infected with HIV, the vast majority in the developing world' (*IHT*, 2 June 2007, p. 8).

HIV, the virus that causes AIDS, [is] a disease that has killed some 25 million people in the past quarter century ... There is still some uncertainty about its origin … [There is the suggestion] that the virus jumped to humans from a Cameroonian population of chimps early in the last century. The virus probably made the leap twice more since … [the second involving] a separate group of chimps in Cameroon … Wild gorillas … are probably responsible for a third form of the virus.

(www.economist.com, 24 June 2007)

A doctor who exposed the cover-up of the SARS outbreak in 2003 has been barred from travelling to the United States to collect a human rights award … The doctor, Jiang Yanyong, a retired surgeon in the People's Liberation Army, was awarded the Heinz R. Pagels Human Rights of Scientists Award by the New York Academy of Sciences … Jiang rose to prominence in 2003, when he disclosed in a letter circulated to international news organizations that at least 100 people were being treated in Beijing hospitals for SARS. At the time the Chinese medical authorities were acknowledging only a small number of cases on the mainland and maintaining that the disease was under control there … SARS eventually killed more than 800 people worldwide … Jiang was initially hailed as a hero in Chinese and foreign news media. He used his new prestige in 2004 to press the ruling Politburo Standing Committee to say that the leadership had erred in ordering the military to shoot unarmed civilians staging pro-democracy demonstrations in Tiananmen Square in June 1989. Jiang, who treated Beijing residents wounded in the 1989 assault, contended that the official line that the crackdown had been necessary to suppress a rebellion was false.

(www.iht.com, 13 July 2007)

China's state media says unsafe sex has, for the first time, become the main means of transmission of HIV/AIDS, overtaking intravenous drug use. Infected blood transfusions also caused many of the early cases … An official report says China saw 70,000 new cases of HIV in 2005 – and almost half were contracted from sexual intercourse … The news raises fresh concerns that HIV infections are moving from high risk groups to the mainstream population. China estimates that about 650,000 people are HIV positive, but it is thought that widespread under-reporting makes accurate figures hard to come by.

(www.bbc.co.uk, 20 August 2007)

An estimated 650,000 people have HIV in China, according to the most recent government statistics, dating from 2005 … The country has made more open efforts to tackle … HIV/AIDS … in recent years but still clamps down on some AIDS-aware activists who are critical of the government's policies on the spread of the virus.

(www.iht.com, 13 November 2007)

China will relax a long-standing rule that bars foreigners with HIV from entering the country, according to the ministry of health. The law will be revised but a date has not yet been set, a spokesman said [on 12 November].

> Under a 1994 law, foreigners applying for a residence permit in China must take an HIV test. Visitors to the country are asked whether they have the virus, and can be refused entry or deported if they do. The law also affects those with other sexually transmitted diseases or tuberculosis.
>
> (*IHT*, 14 November 2007, p. 8)

> The United Nations AIDS-fighting agency … UNAIDS … plans to issue a report Tuesday [20 November] acknowledging that it overestimated the size of the epidemic and that new infections … have been dropping each year since they peaked in the late 1990s … UNAIDS will lower the number of people it believes are infected worldwide to 33.2 million from the 39.5 million it estimated late last year [2006] … Although new infections have dropped, the number of people with the disease is growing because more AIDS victims are living longer, thanks to antiretroviral drugs … Better surveys, particularly a household survey in India, have driven the figures down.
>
> (www.iht.com, 20 November 2007)

> The total of 33.2 million by major regions was as follows: sub-Saharan Africa, 22.5 million; Asia, 4.9 million; North America/West and Central Europe, 2.1 million; Eastern Europe/Central Asia, 1.6 million; Latin America, 2.1 million. '[Critics say that] because the vast majority of people who are infected with HIV do not know it, there is actually no way to know if this new WHO figure is any more reliable than the previous estimation.
>
> (www.bbc.co.uk, 20 November 2007)

'UNAIDS said on Tuesday [20 November] that many fewer people have HIV than it thought before … This drop is a result of better counting' (www.economist.com, 20 November 2007).

> The number of people estimated to be living with HIV in China has risen to 700,000, says a report by the United Nations and the Chinese government. The government had previously estimated that 650,000 people were living with HIV, the virus that causes AIDS. There were 50,000 new cases in 2007 … China's HIV epidemic remains one of low prevalence overall, but with pockets of high infection among specific sub-populations … The report also notes that the number of HIV cases officially reported still remained at 223,501 – far lower that the estimated total in part because of people's reluctance to seek testing in China. The officially reported figure includes those who developed AIDS and those who died from the disease … After years of denying that AIDS was a problem, China's leaders have shifted gears dramatically in recent years, confronting the disease more openly and promising anonymous testing, free treatment for the poor and a ban on discrimination against people with the virus. But the topic remains sensitive and the authorities regularly crack down on activists and patients who seek more support and rights. In 2004 China scaled back the estimated number of people infected with HIV to 840,000 people, from nearly one million. It

> lowered the figure to 650,000 in 2005. Experts have said the figures were probably accurate because they were in line with a change in the way data were collected … [China says] the amount spent in 2007 … fighting HIV/AIDS … had risen to 944 million yuan ($126 million) from 854 million yuan in 2006.
>
> (www.iht.com, 29 November 2007)

'The health ministry estimated that China would have 50,000 new HIV cases this year [2007], with about 700,000 infected in total, including 85,000 with full-blown AIDS. Its figures are endorsed by the WHO, but independent estimates are far higher' (*Guardian*, 1 December 2007, p. 32).

> New cases of HIV/AIDS soared by 45 per cent last year [2007] compared with 2006, the health ministry has revealed. The staggering rise was put down to changing social attitudes and an improvement in data collection. The government had said late last year that 700,000 people were living with the virus, an increase from an earlier estimate of 650,000. The year before China lowered its estimate to 650,000 from 840,000, despite warnings from international experts that the disease was spreading … The disease is now mainly sexually transmitted; before it had been mostly caused by intravenous drug use. The United Nations has warned that China could have 10 million cases of HIV by 2010 unless it takes steps to educate the public and fight the epidemic … About 70,000 had been infected by contaminated [blood] transfusions.
>
> China's 200 million migrant workers are among the high risk groups … [Since] 2006 no organization or individual is allowed to discriminate against AIDS patients or their families, and AIDS patients will be entitled to free treatment.
>
> (*Independent*, 23 February 2008, p. 38)

'The Joint UN Programme on HIV/AIDS estimates there were around 700,000 HIV-positive people in China at the end of 2007' (*Guardian*, 18 April 2008, p. 25).

> There were an estimated 700,000 HIV/AIDS cases as of October 2007, up 8 per cent compared to 2006 … Some 38 per cent of cases were attributed to heterosexual contact, more than triple the 11 per cent in 2005. Cases among gay and bisexual men jumped to 3.3 per cent in 2007 from 0.4 per cent in 2005 … Researchers warned the disease was moving from high risk communities into the wider population … The AIDS virus has been circulating among people for about 100 years, decades longer than scientists thought, a new study suggests. Genetic analysis pushes the estimated origin of HIV back to between 1884 and 1924, with a more focused estimate at 1908. Previously scientists had estimated the origin at around 1930. AIDS was not recognized formally until 1981, when it got the attention of public health officials in the United States … Scientists say HIV descended from a chimpanzee virus that jumped to humans in Africa, probably when people

butchered chimps. Many individuals were probably infected that way, but so few other people caught the virus that it failed to get a lasting foothold, researchers say. But the growth of African cities may have changed that by putting many people close together and promoting prostitution.

(www.iht.com, 2 October 2008)

Infection with the AIDS virus in China is spreading beyond the country's original high risk groups – heroin addicts in the south and blood sellers in rural central counties. A new study finds that the virus has spread to all provinces, and cases are rising quickly among gay men and female prostitutes. Heterosexual transmission in increasing … Although the number of estimated cases – 700,000 – is low for a population of 1.3 billion, it has risen 8 per cent since 2005 … Scientists believe AIDS entered in the 1980s with drug traffickers in Yunnan, which borders South-east Asia's opium 'Golden Triangle'. It grew in Henan, where illegal banks pooled blood from indigent farmers, spun it to remove clotting factors and returned mixed red cells to all sellers. Tracking HIV subtypes suggests the virus has moved along drug trafficking routes, creating an outbreak in western Xinjiang.

(www.iht.com, 7 October 2008)

Chinese officials have said that HIV/AIDS was the leading cause of death last year [2008], compared with other infectious diseases. It is thought to be the first time this has happened. A report by the country's state media said HIV/AIDS had led to the deaths of almost 7,000 people in the first nine months of 2008. The number of deaths caused by tuberculosis and rabies fell back into second and third place. The numbers are increasing dramatically – China's ministry of health says that until three years ago fewer than 8,000 people altogether had died from HIV/AIDS. By last year the total had risen to five times that many … But there are still concerns that officials at local and provincial level are under-reporting, either by mistake or because they think it is not in their interest to show rises. This latest news comes as the spread of HIV in China has entered a dangerous new phase. Initially it was concentrated in high risk populations, injecting drug users in particular. Infection from contaminated blood transfusions was also common. But now the main cause of transmission is thought to be unsafe sex.

(www.bbc.co.uk, 18 February 2009)

It is estimated that some 700,000 people are living with HIV in China and there are about 50,000 new infections every year, according to the Chinese government and UNAIDS. The UN agency believes a significant number of those new infections include sex workers … About one in 200 sex workers currently has HIV [according to UNAIDS] … As China's economy grows, it is likely the sex industry will as well. Current estimates show that some 30 million to 50 million people are at risk for HIV infection … When HIV initially began to spread in China, infections were concentrated among people who injected drugs … Campaigns among this group have been effective, while infections among other groups have risen … A majority of the infections are concentrated among drug users, men having sex with men, and sex workers and their clients.

(www.cnn.com, 22 June 2009)

Although the government pays for HIV medication, AIDS is so widely feared that many hospitals refuse to admit people with the disease. In Beijing, for example, only a handful of surgeons will operate on those who are positive … Compared to other developing countries, the prevalence of HIV in China is relatively low, with fewer than a million people thought to be carrying the virus, according to government figures issued last week.

(*IHT*, 1 December 2009, p. 2)

Pig disease

A disease killing millions of pigs has sharply lifted the price of pork, the country's staple meat … China's 500-odd million pigs are the country's most important source of affordable meat … While the price of feed, such as corn, has risen, the main culprit is an epidemic of a mysterious illness known as 'blue ear' disease as well as the more common foot-and-mouth affliction. 'I have heard it has killed as many as 20 million hogs,' an industry executive said. The government has not issued any estimate of how many pigs have been struck by the disease.

(*FT*, 29 May 2007, p. 7)

'Blue ear [is] a contagious disease which may have killed 18,000 or 20 million, depending on whom you believe' (*The Economist*, 9 June 2007, p. 66).

'"Blue ear" disease is also known as porcine reproductive and respiratory syndrome … The disease is estimated to have killed nearly 40,000 pigs in the first half of this year [2007]' (*FT*, 25 July 2007, p. 6).

So far the mysterious virus, believed to be an unusually deadly form of an infection known as blue ear pig disease, has spread to twenty-five of the country's thirty-three provinces and regions. The government in Beijing acknowledged that in the past year the virus had decimated pig stocks in southern and coastal areas. But animal virus experts said that the Chinese authorities were playing down the gravity and spread of the outbreak and had refused to co-operate with international scientists … No one knows for sure how many of the country's 500 million pigs have been infected by the virus … The government in Beijing said that about 165,000 pigs had contracted the virus this year [2007]. But in a country that on average loses 25 million pigs a year to disease, few believe the figures … Health experts said China had declined to send tissue samples to testing labs outside the country for independent verification by a lab affiliated with the World Organization for Animal Health in Paris. The government insisted that the disease was under control and that a vaccine had been developed and distributed …

> Chinese scientists said the virus first struck last year [2006], infecting ten provinces and 2 million pigs; 400,000 died of the disease. This year the virus has spread to twenty-five provinces but up until recently the government had insisted the disease was under control.
>
> (*IHT*, 16 August 2007, p. 12)

> There are reports that the Chinese government is withholding information on a fast-spreading virus decimating its pig population … So far there are no signs that this virus is a threat to humans … Chinese officials claim that the disease is an infection called blue-ear disease. But that diagnosis has not been confirmed by any outside agencies and China has not shared tissue samples yet that would allow confirmation … The disease, which may be the result of mutating pathogens, is spreading rapidly. And the effects are more lethal than those usually associated with blue-ear pig disease, a relatively common ailment. The number of pig deaths has not been reliably reported so far, but the epidemic appears to be widespread … A similar virus has already been seen in Vietnam and Myanmar.
>
> (*IHT*, 18 August 2007, p. 4)

> With pigs dying all over the country and the price of pork soaring, China has come under suspicion of attempting to cover up a dangerous outbreak of an infectious disease … As a health threat, the current outbreak of Porcine Reproductive and Respiratory Syndrome (PRRS), also known as 'blue ear pig disease', is nothing like the earlier cases, where human lives were at stake. Avian influenza has appeared in pockets in China in recent years and has occasionally spread to – and even killed – humans, but PRRS can affect only pigs … International health officials have for months been wondering what to make of anecdotal reports of massive numbers of infected pigs … A technical adviser to the United Nations Food and Agriculture Organization … [said] it would be helpful if China shared tissue samples with international organizations … Infected pigs have also been found in one other country, China's neighbour Vietnam. The FAO and other authorities want more information about the vaccine that China claims to be using so successfully. Vaccines have hitherto not been known to be effective against the disease, which tends to mutate quickly … [China's] chief veterinary officer, Jia Youling, called a press conference on 20 August to report that PRRS had been brought under 'preliminary control'. The disease had affected 257,000 pigs in twenty-six provinces, of which 68,000 died and 175,000 were destroyed. But through a massive vaccination programme 100 million pigs were already protected … He admitted that some local officials had indeed covered up the disease in their jurisdictions.
>
> (*The Economist*, 25 August 2007, p. 58)

'Blue ear disease, which can lead to infertility and stillbirths in hogs, has killed 68,000 animals in twenty-six Chinese provinces and led to the culling of an additional 175,000, the newspaper *People's Daily* reported last week' (*IHT*, 27 August 2007, p. 13).

> Chinese inflation has hit its second ten-year high in two months, led again by a further sharp rise in meat prices. China's rate of consumer price inflation hit 6.5 per cent in the year to August, up from 5.6 per cent in July ... Meat prices have risen 49 per cent over the past year, caused by a shortage of pork after a series of disease outbreaks ... China, the world's biggest consumer of pork, has seen its pig population decline by 10 per cent over the past year due to major outbreaks of blue ear disease.
>
> (www.bbc.co.uk, 11 September 2007)

The increase in meat prices has been blamed on a shortage of pigs and higher feed costs for poultry and cattle farmers ... The sharp rise in prices for pork, China's staple meat, has been blamed on farmers' reluctance to raise pigs due to high feed prices and an outbreak of blue ear disease that prompted authorities to destroy thousands of animals. Beijing has promised free vaccination for the disease and other aid to farmers to raise pork output.

(www.iht.com, 11 September 2007)

Swine flu

'Swine flu is a contagious respiratory disease that affects pigs and can jump to humans' (www.cnn.com, 30 April 2009). 'Mexico is the epicentre of the outbreak' (www.cnn.com, 3 May 2009).

> Hong Kong, the epicentre of a SARS outbreak six years ago, announced some of the toughest measures anywhere on Sunday [26 April] in response to a swine flu outbreak in Mexico and the United States ... One legacy of SARS is that Hong Kong may now be better prepared for a flu pandemic than practically anywhere else in the world. Fearing that SARS might recur each winter, the city embarked on a building programme to enlarge its capacity to isolate and treat those affected with communicable respiratory diseases. The city has also expanded its flu research labs, already the best in the world and leaders in tracking the H5N1 avian flu virus. The so-called bird flu virus ... is different from the H1N1 flu virus causing illnesses in Mexico and the United States.
>
> (www.iht.com, 27 April 2009)

'Pork producers question whether the term "swine flu" is appropriate, given that pigs so far do not seem to be falling ill' (*IHT*, 29 April 2009, p. 5). 'The strain, scientists say, is a mixture of swine, human and bird viruses' (*IHT*, 9 May 2009, p. 3).

> China has banned imports of pork products from Mexico and several US states as part of attempts to prevent a deadly flu virus entering the country. Japan, Hong Kong, Singapore, Malaysia and Indonesia announced plans to screen travellers for symptoms of swine flu. Asian governments are on high alert after the WHO warned of a possible pandemic ... Beijing has banned pork imports from Mexico and the US states of Texas, Kansas and California ... China's

> ministry of health has warned its citizens to be vigilant although it also noted that so far there is no evidence that the new flu virus can be spread through food … In Hong Kong … all travellers will be screened on arrival and any ill person will be quarantined. Japan, Singapore, Malaysia and Indonesia have announced similar plans, with many airports using devices that were put in place to monitor SARS and bird flu over the last few years. H1N1 is the same strain that causes seasonal flu outbreaks in humans but the newly detected version contains genetic material from versions of flu which usually affect pigs and birds.
>
> (www.bbc.co.uk, 27 April 2009)

('A declaration from the WHO [stated] that "there is no risk of infection from this virus from consumption of well-cooked pork and pork products"': *IHT*, 29 April 2009.)

'China and Russia are moving to quarantine visitors with suspicious symptoms. Asian airports have turned on their heat-sensing equipment to detect sick incoming passengers – kit they had installed after earlier scares resulting from outbreaks of avian flu and SARS' (www.economist.com, 27 April 2009).

> New Zealand on Tuesday [28 April] became the first country in the Asia-Pacific to confirm cases of swine flu … In China Hans Troedsson, the WHO representative in China, said he believed a school in the province of Shaanxi has been closed down after several students had shown symptoms of respiratory infections … Earlier on Tuesday the State Council said it would strengthen supervision of and public information about swine flu … Local media reported over the weekend that up to 100 students of a primary school in northern Shaanxi province suffered from flu symptoms and the school had been shut … On Monday [27 April] the WHO increased its alert on the H1N1 virus to an unprecedented phase 4, saying that it posed a 'significant risk', intensifying fears that the flu could become a global pandemic. Aside from Mexico, from where the disease spread, there have been confirmed cases of swine flu in the United States, Canada, Spain and the UK.
>
> (www.ft.com, 28 April 2009)

'Chinese officials said on Wednesday [29 April] they would work with Taiwan in controlling any spread of swine flu' (www.ft.com, 29 April 2009).

'On 29 April the WHO upgraded the status of swine flu's spread to grade five [Phase 5] out of six, indicating that a global pandemic is thought to be imminent' (www.baltictimes.com, 30 April 2009).

'The level five designation means infection from the outbreak that originated in Mexico has been jumping from person to person with relative ease' (www.cnn.com, 30 April 2009).

> Phase 6, the highest level in the WHO's alert system, is a pandemic … The term describes the geographic spread of a disease, not its severity. There can be a pandemic of a mild disease … Phase 5 means that the disease is spreading in communities – not just within households or in returning travellers – in two countries in one of the WHO's six regions, in this case the United

> States and Mexico. Phase 5 also means a pandemic is imminent. To move up to Phase 6 community spread would have to occur in at least one other country in another region.
>
> (www.iht.com, 3 May 2009)

'To reach Phase 6 there would need to be evidence that the virus was spreading in a sustained way in a country outside the Americas' (*IHT*, 9 May 2009, p. 3).

> In the clearest sign yet of how seriously China is taking swine flu, President Hu Jintao convened a meeting on Thursday morning [30 April] of the Standing Committee of the Politburo – the nine men who run China – and the meeting was immediately announced. It is rare for China's authorities to disclose any meeting of the Standing Committee, and particularly to do so as soon as the meeting ended … After struggling to cope six years ago with an outbreak of SARS, the Chinese leadership is taking a much more visible approach now to swine flu … Government officials hid the [SARS] outbreak for four months, even concealing patients at closed military hospitals, before the disease spread to Hong Kong and then around the world … On Tuesday morning [28 April] … President Hu Jintao announced that China was stepping up its inspection and quarantine procedures for people and imports of pigs and pork products … East Asia, Central Asia and South Asia have not yet had a laboratory-confirmed case of swine flu, although suspected cases are being tested, notably in South Korea and Hong Kong. But flu experts predict that the disease will arrive in the region soon, if it has not already … The novel form of flu now moving around the globe is politically more palatable for China because it made its first appearance far from China's shores. The new flu does have a genetic segment that has been identified as coming from pigs in Eurasia, prompting the Mexican ambassador to China to suggest that his country should not be blamed for the disease. But flu specialists say that the disease appears to have jumped to people in Mexico. China's agriculture ministry said on Wednesday that swine flu had not been found in the country's pigs and that China had not been the origin of the virus … [There has been] heavy media attention to the issue in Hong Kong.
>
> (www.iht.com, 30 April 2009)

'The first case of swine flu in Asia was confirmed by the Hong Kong government today … A Mexican citizen who had flown to the territory with a stopover in Shanghai had developed a fever after arriving yesterday [30 April]' (www.iht.com, 1 May 2009).

> Hong Kong authorities quarantined the man at a local hospital … [and] immediately quarantined the hotel where the traveller had stayed on Thursday night [30 April] … The man did not leave the airport while in Shanghai … Hong Kong has begun requiring all travellers to fill out health declarations before entering the territory.
>
> (*IHT*, 2 May 2009, p. 5)

> Six years after SARS paralysed this city and killed 299 of its citizens, Hong Kong is not taking chances with swine flu. Within minutes of the

> confirmation on Friday evening [1 May] of Asia's first swine flu case – a twenty-five-year-old traveller from Mexico – the police had cordoned off the hotel where the young man stayed for fewer than seven hours on Thursday afternoon and evening [30 April]. More than 200 guests will be quarantined in the building for a week … Roughly 100 hotel staff members will also be quarantined for at least one night at the hotel, and then at government vacation camps that are being converted into quarantine centres. Everyone who sat in the five rows closest to the Mexican traveller on a flight from Shanghai to Hong Kong at midday on Thursday is being contacted and will be quarantined for a week, along with the aircraft's flight crew … Hong Kong has fifteen times as many beds for severe respiratory illnesses as it uses for those illnesses on an everyday basis … In Beijing authorities suspended all regularly scheduled flights between mainland China and Mexico until further notice. Hong Kong does not have direct flights to Mexico … Even before lab tests confirmed Friday evening [1 May] that the traveller had swine flu, Hong Kong authorities sent vans of police officers and health workers to the hotel.
>
> (www.iht.com, 2 May 2009)

'China says it will quarantine all those who travelled on a flight from Mexico with a man suffering from swine flu … Beijing said it would put his fellow passengers under week-long observation. It also suspended flights from Mexico' (www.bbc.co.uk, 2 May 2009).

> On Saturday [2 May] Canadian health officials said that the virus has been found in sick pigs on one farm in Alberta, the first report of the swine flu actually being found in swine. Previously there has been heated debate about whether the virus could infect pigs, even though its genetic makeup clearly points to its having originated in swine at some point. But people were infecting each other, and, until Saturday, no pigs had been found with the virus – a fact that the pork industry used to bolster its argument that the virus should not even be named for swine. The news from Canada changes things. But it has a somewhat unexpected shift: a person appears to have spread the disease to pigs, and not the other way around. A worker at the farm had travelled to Mexico, fallen ill there and unknowingly brought the disease back to Canada last month [April]. The worker has recovered. About 10 per cent of the 2,200 pigs on the farm got sick … All recovered without treatment. The entire herd remains under quarantine as a precaution.
>
> (www.iht.com, 3 May 2009)

On Sunday … [Mexico] said that the virus appeared to have peaked between 23 April and 28 April … [Mexico has] 101 suspected deaths, twenty-two confirmed … Outside Mexico the effects of the virus do not appear to be severe … More than 100 people, including many Mexicans, have been quarantined in China … Mexican officials say more than seventy Mexican citizens have so far been isolated … About fifty are being held in quarantine in Shanghai … with ten in Beijing. Mexican nationals are also being held in the city of Wenzhou.

(www.bbc.co.uk, 4 May 2009)

The WHO reported Monday [4 May] that the disease had widened globally, with twenty countries reporting 985 laboratory confirmed cases, compared to 898 confirmed cases in eighteen countries on Sunday [3 May] ... [Mexico has] 60 per cent of the world's total confirmed cases and the United States 23 per cent of the total ... Twenty-five deaths from the disease have been confirmed in Mexico ... In the United States there has been one death, a toddler from Mexico City who died in Texas. No deaths have been reported in other nations.

(www.iht.com, 4 May 2009)

'On Sunday [4 May] a group of twenty-five Canadian exchange students were confined to a hotel in the northern city of Changchun' (*IHT*, 5 May 2009, p. 4).

The Mexican and Chinese governments sent chartered flights to each other's countries on Tuesday [5 May] to pick up their respective nationals stranded or quarantined because of the global swine flu outbreak. By Tuesday the number of confirmed cases stood at 1,085 in twenty-one countries, according to the WHO. Twenty-five people have died of the virus in Mexico; one died in the United States. An Aeroméxico flight was making several stops throughout China to collect nearly seventy citizens who were being held in quarantine ... As a result of the flight suspensions 200 Chinese citizens were stranded in Mexico City and Tijuana. A China Southern Airlines flight was expected to fetch them Tuesday ... Mexican officials have bitterly criticized China for putting Mexican citizens in isolation. They said Mexicans were being singled out because of their passports, despite showing no signs of the virus. China has denied discriminating against Mexicans, saying it is exercising proper precautions to prevent the spread of the virus.

(www.cnn.com, 5 May 2009)

'[A Chinese] foreign ministry spokesman denied there was any discrimination: "The measures concerned are not targeted at Mexican citizens. This is purely a medical quarantine issue" ' (www.bbc.co.uk, 5 May 2009).

'Key developments on swine flu outbreaks: deaths, twenty-six in Mexico and one in the United States, a toddler from Mexico who died in Texas; confirmed sickened worldwide 1,447 (802 in Mexico; 380 in the United States)' (www.iht.com, 5 May 2009).

'A Texan with H1N1 flu died this week, only the second death outside Mexico ... The Texan woman [was] in her thirties ... US health officials said she had chronic health problems' (www.independent.co.uk, 6 May 2009).

An aircraft carrying ninety-eight Chinese stranded in Mexico by the flu outbreak arrived in Shanghai today [6 May] and all appeared healthy but will have to spend a week in quarantine. An Aeroméxico plane had arrived in Shanghai a day earlier to pick up dozens of Mexicans ... None of the forty-three Mexicans that China had quarantined showed symptoms of H1N1, prompting Mexico to accuse China of discrimination.

(www.independence.co.uk, 6 May 2009)

> More than 2,000 people in twenty-three countries worldwide now have confirmed cases of the new strain of the H1N1 flu, the WHO said on Thursday [7 May 2009]. Over half of the 2,099 laboratory confirmed cases are in Mexico … where forty-two people are confirmed to have died of the disease … Thirty per cent of the WHO confirmed cases are in the United States, where authorities say the virus is now widespread and two deaths have been reported … Serious cases of the virus have particularly struck young people for reasons that are still not fully understood … In Shanghai on Thursday [7 May] travellers from Mexico began to be released after spending a week in quarantine, while some 350 guests of a quarantined hotel in Hong Kong were due to be released Thursday night.
>
> (www.iht.com, 7 May 2009)

'Hong Kong officials isolated 286 guests and staff at a hotel there after a Mexican guest fell ill' (www.iht.com, 11 May 2009).

> The WHO is considering an overhaul of its pandemic ratings system … The WHO's system of pandemic alerts provides no indication of the danger of the virus. Even if the A(H1N1) virus in Mexico proves no more lethal than a typical seasonal flu, it could soon trigger the highest level 6 WHO pandemic alert once it has been identified as spreading widely between humans in different parts of the world.
>
> (www.ft.com, 7 May 2009)

> Nearly 300 guests and staff at a hotel in Hong Kong have been released after being held in quarantine for a week … Although critics called the quarantine an over-reaction, officials were keen to avoid a repeat of the 2003 SARS epidemic. That outbreak killed 300 people in Hong Kong and 800 worldwide after a single carrier spread the disease in a city hotel. The Mexican man who sparked the scare is in a stable condition at a hospital in Hong Kong. It is not clear when he will be released.
>
> (www.bbc.co.uk, 8 May 2009)

> According to the latest WHO tally, 2,384 people in twenty-four countries have been infected with the strain … Mexico [on Friday 8 May] confirmed another death from swine flu, bringing the national death toll to forty-five … [while] the total number of people made ill by the virus [rose] to 13,179. The United States has 1,639 cases of the H1N1 flu in forty-three states, with two deaths.
>
> (*IHT*, 9 May 2009, p. 3)

'Canada reported its first death linked to swine flu on Friday [8 May] … She died on 28 April … [but it was] not clear to what extent H1N1 may or may not have contributed to her death' (www.iht.im, 9 May 2009).

> China, Indonesia, Russia and a dozen more countries … [have banned] imports of pork products from the United States and others touched by the virus … Even before the flu outbreak China had deployed several arguments to keep out American pork.
>
> (www.iht.com, 10 May 2009; *IHT*, 11 May 2009, p. 8)

There have been few more dramatic moments at the WHO than the late-night gathering on 29 April, when Dr Margaret Chan, its powerful director-general, declared: 'It really is all of humanity that is under threat during a pandemic' ... In her announcement on 29 April Dr Chan made clear that she alone had decided to raise the pandemic level ... In the days since her announcement, concerns about the swine flu outbreak have eased around the globe ... Coverage of the flu outbreak no longer dominates cable news shows ... But Dr Chan has yet to relax the alert level of the organization, the public health arm of the United Nations. That is because the warning system is based on how far the virus has spread, not its lethality. While most praise the actions of Dr Chan and the WHO in the current outbreak, some have said that the organization needs to adjust its warning system to reflect what is known about the severity of the spreading illness ... Dr Chan said she had been guided in her recent decisions by her experiences during the 2003 SARS outbreak in Hong Kong, where she led the health department. Rules adopted in 2005 by the WHO, based in Geneva, have made Dr Chan perhaps the most powerful international health official in history. She no longer must beg for co-operation from national authorities but can demand information about threats to global health ... In 2005 rules adopted by the WHO gave the director-general complete authority to change the global pandemic alert level ... She faced a terrible decision in 1997 when an outbreak of avian influenza threatened the population. Fresh poultry is a Hong Kong staple, but Dr Chan ordered the region's population of 1.4 million chickens and ducks slaughtered. The outbreak ended. Public health experts who witnessed her handling of SARS gave her high marks ... Dr Chan was later criticized by some in Hong Kong for failing to respond quickly enough to the 2003 SARS epidemic, although a panel of experts supported her leadership. Her rapid and urgent response to an infectious threat from Mexico last month grew out of that experience, several who knew her said ... Initial reports from Mexico suggested that swine flu was both lethal and highly infectious. Only when the disease spread to the United States did it become clearer that it was not as dangerous as feared.

(www.iht.com, 10 May 2009; *IHT*, 11 May 2009, pp. 1, 4)

WHO experts say it is not possible to create a scale giving a scientific assessment of the severity of the outbreak, on the lines of hurricane warnings or the Richter scale for earthquakes. That is because the new flu affects people differently in various countries, depending on their stage of development, healthcare systems and experience in dealing with epidemics.

(www.iht.com, 14 May 2009)

A Chinese man returning from studying at a US university has become the first suspected case of swine flu in mainland China, the health ministry said Sunday [10 May]. The ministry identified the patient as a thirty-year-old student ... He was being treated in a hospital in Chengdu and has been placed in isolation ... Twenty-nine countries have now officially reported

> 4,379 cases of swine flu, The WHO said Sunday … Mexico has reported 1,626 confirmed human cases, including forty-five deaths, while the United States has reported 2,254 laboratory-confirmed cases, including two deaths. A third swine-flu-related death was confirmed in the United States over the weekend.
>
> (*IHT*, 11 May 2009, p. 4)

> Chengdu city officials said they had located and quarantined more than 130 of the estimated 150 other passengers who had travelled with the infected man on a connecting flight from Beijing to Chengdu, the capital of Sichuan province … His father and girlfriend, who met him at Chengdu airport, have been placed in quarantine, as has the taxi driver who took him to the hospital … All three reported deaths in the United States to this point have involved victims with health problems, as has the single fatal case in Canada.
>
> (www.iht.com, 11 May 2009)

> China has confirmed the first case of swine flu on the Chinese mainland and is searching for people who could have had contact with the infected man … The authorities say he travelled from St Louis [in the United States] to Tokyo, then to Beijing and finally landed in Chengdu on Saturday [9 May] … About 130 people from the patient's flight to Chengdu have already been quarantined.
>
> (www.bbc.co.uk, 11 May 2009)

> Mexico has complained that the Chinese measures unfairly target its citizens, and announced Sunday [10 May] that thirty Mexican companies would boycott an international food industry event in Shanghai next week at which they were to have been guests of honour.
>
> (www.iht.com, 11 May 2009)

'The WHO reported Monday [11 May] that thirty countries have officially confirmed 4,694 cases of the new influenza infection. The United States, with 2,532 cases, has now surpassed Mexico with 1,626 cases. Mexico has reported forty-eight deaths from swine flu' (www.iht.com, 11 May 2009).

> The number of confirmed cases of the new influenza A(H1N1) flu has climbed to 6,497, including sixty-five deaths, the WHO said on Thursday. The number of countries reporting confirmed cases remains at thirty-three … Other countries with confirmed cases but no deaths … [include] China (four).
>
> (www.iht.com, 14 May 2009)

> As of 17 May 2009: deaths: global total of seventy-five … [including] sixty-eight in Mexico, five in the United States … Confirmed cases: the WHO says thirty-nine countries have reported more than 8,480 cases, mostly in the United States and Mexico.
>
> (www.iht.com, 17 May 2009)

'As of 18 May China had three confirmed cases and one suspected case of swine flu and Hong Kong had three, all in people travelling from the United States, Mexico and Canada' (*IHT*, 20 May 2009, p. 2).

'There have been no reports of deaths from H1N1 flu in China. Among nearly 19,000 infections worldwide 117 people have died' (www.bbc.co.uk, 8 June 2009).

> The WHO raised its alert on swine flu to the highest level [Phase 6] on Thursday [11 June], in its first designation of a global pandemic in forty-one years ... But the pandemic is 'moderate' in severity ... with the overwhelming majority of patients experiencing only mild symptoms and a full recovery, often in the absence of any medical treatment ... The WHO released a report Wednesday [10 June] saying that seventy-four countries had reported 27,737 cases of the disease and 141 deaths since April ... The last pandemic, the Hong Kong flu of 1968, killed about 700,000 people worldwide. Ordinary flu kills 150,000 to 500,000 people each year ... On Wednesday a fifty-five-year-old man became the first person to contact the case locally in Hong Kong, according to health officials. So far the city has had no fatalities ... China confirmed ten new flu cases on Thursday [11 June], bringing the total number of infections on the mainland to 111. Health officials say all of the country's flu cases have involved people returning from abroad.
>
> (www.iht.com, 11 June 2009)

> The WHO ... emphasized that it was acting because of the geographic spread of the virus to seventy-four countries, not because it had proved particularly lethal ... According to WHO rules, the organization should declare a pandemic upon finding evidence of widespread 'community transmission' – meaning beyond travellers, schools and immediate contacts – on two continents ... Since the outbreak started in Mexico in April, the virus has been heavily concentrated in the Americas, but the rise in cases in Australia and elsewhere appears to indicate community-wide spread in other regions.
>
> (*IHT*, 12 June 2009, p. 5)

'The WHO [said that] ... increasing the alert to Phase 6 does not mean that the disease is deadlier or more dangerous than before, just that it has spread to more countries' (www.cnn.com, 11 June 2009).

'The last pandemic in 1968 killed about 1 million people' (www.bbc.co.uk, 11 June 2009).

> Contrary to the popular assumption that the new swine flu pandemic arose on factory farms in Mexico, [US] federal agriculture officials now believe that it most likely emerged in pigs in Asia, but then travelled to North America in a human. But they emphasized that there was no way to prove their theory and only sketchy data underpinning it.
>
> (www.iht.com, 24 June 2009)

H1N1 swine flu has killed more than 700 people around the world since the outbreak began four months ago, says the WHO … This represents a jump of at least two-thirds from the last official death toll of 429, published by the WHO on 6 July.

(www.bbc.co.uk, 21 July 2009)

More than 1,000 people worldwide have died from swine flu since it emerged in Mexico and the United States in April, according to the latest figures from the WHO. As of 31 July the total number of victims killed by the H1N1 virus, also known as swine flu, stood at 1,154 – an increase of 338 since the WHO's previous update on 27 July. The virus has spread around the world with unprecedented speed, spreading as widely in six weeks as common influenza viruses spread in the six months, according to the WHO.

(www.cnn.com, 5 August 2009)

Chinese health authorities have approved a vaccine that they say prevents swine flu with a single dose … More than 5,000 cases of swine flu have been confirmed in China. The WTO says the situation in the country is 'quite stable'.

(www.bbc.co.uk, 3 September 2009)

The new H1N1 flu virus has killed at least 2,837 people [globally] but it is not causing more severe illness than initially feared and has not mutated, the WHO said Friday [4 September] … About a quarter of a million cases have been laboratory-confirmed worldwide, but this is far fewer than the true number, according to the WHO, which has stopped requiring its 193 member states to report individual cases. Its previous update of 28 August showed at least 2,185 deaths … The virus could eventually infect 2 billion people, or a third of the world's population, according to WHO estimates.

(*IHT*, 5 September 2009, p. 2)

China's health minister says the nation is facing a grim situation as it tries to contain a rapid surge in swine flu. Chen Zhu said a vaccination programme would start this week, prioritizing those taking part in events to celebrate National Day on 1 October … China is the first country in the world to use swine flu vaccines, after conducting successful clinical trials … About 6,000 people have fallen ill with swine flu.

(www.bbc.co.uk, 8 September 2009)

China has developed a vaccine for swine flu and is set to become the first country in the world to begin mass inoculations … The single-shot vaccine has been approved … More than 5 million doses will be ready by the end of September … Health minister Chen Zhu … [has said] that some 200,000 people taking part in the [1 October] anniversary celebrations will be the first to receive the vaccine … Chen said on Tuesday [8 September] that there have been 5,592 recorded cases of H1N1 in China's thirty-one inland provinces, but no one has yet died from the illness. He said: 'Due to the

> rising number of cases, especially since late August, we have indeed started seeing some serious cases' ... There are plans to vaccinate 65 million people before the end of the year [2009].
>
> (www.cnn.com, 10 September 2009)

'Four women have died of swine flu, in the first confirmed deaths from the H1N1 virus in Russia ... Russia has recorded 1,349 confirmed cases of swine flu' (*The Times*, 28 October 2009, p. 39).

> China is fighting a rapid rise in the number of swine flu cases after initially appearing to have the outbreak under control. The ministry of health says there have been seven deaths and nearly 50,000 confirmed cases. China tried to prevent the virus entering the country by employing strict quarantine measures for people arriving with flu-like symptoms. But it has now turned its efforts to controlling the virus inside China. Chan Zhu (health minister): 'The epidemic has entered a period of high incidence earlier that we expected and the infected cases are rapidly increasing' ... The WHO in China said: 'In the first few months they were trying to stop the virus at the borders because they were mostly seeing imported cases ... They then shifted focus to controlling it inside the country' ... The number of cases has risen rapidly over recent days ... The ministry of health reported nearly 4,000 new cases over just three days until Monday [2 November] ... China has developed its own vaccine to battle the virus and hopes to produce 100 million doses by the beginning of next year [2010] ... The WHO has classified the H1N1 outbreak as a pandemic.
>
> (www.bbc.co.uk, 3 November 2009)

> Quarantines and medical detentions are among the aggressive measures that Chinese officials have taken to slow the transmission of H1N1, which quickly spread worldwide after being first diagnosed in North America ... China was virtually alone in taking such harsh measures, which continued throughout most of the summer ... The State Council did not decide to relax the quarantine policy until July ... China has not had to cope with a crush of cases, and it began administering a vaccine for swine flu in early September [2009], the first country to do so ... On 5 September China became the first country to declare that it had discovered a vaccine, and by late October it had produced nearly 53 million doses ... Foreign officials also say China demonstrated an unusual openness to sharing information about H1N1 with its citizens and other governments, in contrast to its secretive approach to the near pandemic of SARS a few years ago ... That is not to say that China has been spared. On Tuesday [11 November] health ministry officials reported that there had been an 'explosive' growth of H1N1 infection on the mainland because of the onset of winter, with 5,000 new cases in the previous three days pushing the total to more than 59,000. At least thirty people have died after contracting H1N1 ... The Indian health ministry has reported 505 deaths. The United States ... has reported more than 2 million cases and

about 4,000 deaths in a population of 300 million ... Chinese and Western officials say Chinese leaders put in place a comprehensive plan for a pandemic outbreak after the disastrous experience of SARS. This includes, at least in the first stages, some of the strongest quarantine measures of the SARS era, but also emphasizes educating the population about the disease.

(www.iht.com, 11 November 2009; *IHT*, 12 November 2009, p. 2)

In the United States on Thursday [12 November] ... new estimates [were released] of the number of American swine flu deaths: about 3,900, or more than three times the number authorities had previously used. The earlier number, about 1,200, represented laboratory-confirmed cases; the new numbers represent estimates that include people who ultimately died of other conditions, like pneumonia, but whose illnesses were triggered by the flu.

(www.iht.com, 13 November 2009)

China has detected eight cases of swine flu mutation, a health official said Wednesday [25 November] ... Last week the WHO said it was investigating samples of swine flu variant linked to two deaths in Norway. But the director of the Chinese National Influenza Centre told Xinhua that the mutated swine flu virus found in China had shown an 'isolated' spread in the mainland, was not resistant to drugs and further infection could be prevented by vaccines.

(*IHT*, 26 November 2009, p. 10)

North Korea on Wednesday [9 December] acknowledged an outbreak of swine flu, as relief officials in South Korea reported that the virus had killed dozens of people in [North Korea] ... North Korea's official news agency, KCNA, said nine cases had been confirmed in the capital of Pyongyang and in Sinuiju, a town near the border with China. It did not say whether there had been any deaths. But the Seoul-based aid group Good Friends said about forty people had already died after swine flu broke out in the North last month [November]. Such reports compelled the South Korean president, Lee Myung Bak, on Tuesday [8 December] to offer to send swine flu medication to North Korea ... Good Friends, which gleans information on North Korea through inside informants, also said that the North Korean government was strengthening customs inspections on the border with China in an apparent attempt to contain the virus. It also said the authorities were instructing schools to start a winter vacation earlier than usual.

(www.iht.com, 9 December 2009)

On Thursday [10 December], in a rare admission of a domestic problem and a sign of new openness, North Korea accepted a South Korean offer to ship swine flu medication, South Korean officials said. A day earlier the North had acknowledged nine cases of H1N1 influenza in Pyongyang and Sinuiju, a town on the Chinese border. But Good Friends, a relief agency based in Seoul, reported that the outbreak was far more serious and has caused dozens of deaths. The South Korean president. Lee Myung Bak, offered Tuesday [8 December] to send vaccine, and on Thursday South Korea's unification minister, Hyun In Taek, said the country was prepared to ship enough Tamiflu and other medications to treat 500,000. It was unusual for the North to accept Mr Lee's offer so quickly. Pyongyang has denounced him for his tough stance against its nuclear programme.

(www.iht.com, 10 December 2009; *IHT*, 11 December 2009, p. 9)

A convoy of South Korean trucks crossed the border into North Korea on Friday [18 December] to deliver medicine to combat swine flu ... North Korea acknowledged for the first time last week that swine flu had broken out in the country after Seoul offered unconditional aid to help contain the spread of the virus. North Korean officials did not mention any virus-related deaths, but a civic group in Seoul said the disease had killed about fifty people in the North since early November. South Korea sent enough doses of the antiviral drugs Tamiflu and Relenza for 500,000 North Koreans.

(www.iht.com, 18 December 2009)

South Korea has sent medicine for swine flu to North Korea, after the North said it had nine cases of the virus ... The shipment of Tamiflu and Relenza, worth $15 million and enough to treat 500,000 people, was taken over the border to the North's town of Kaesong in refrigerated trucks ... [South Korean] officials say they believe the flu virus to be more widespread in the North than reported so far and do not want to see it spread further with the onset of winter.

(www.bbc.co.uk, 18 December 2009)

Pneumonic plague

Officials have sealed off an isolated town of 10,000 people in rural west-central China after an outbreak of pneumonic plague killed two residents, Xinhua reported on Monday [3 August] ... Ziketan is a remote, ethnically Tibetan town in eastern Qinghai province, one of the largest and least populated regions of China ... The first victim, a thirty-two-year-old herdsman, died last Thursday [30 July 2009], and the second, a neighbour who was also a herdsman, died on Sunday [2 August] ... The World Health Organization [WHO] said that ... experts were monitoring the outbreak but were not especially concerned by it ... Pneumonic plague ... is closely related to bubonic plague, the so-called Black Death that killed scores of millions worldwide in the 1300s.

(www.iht.com, 3 August 2009)

The WHO said an outbreak such as this was always a concern, but praised the Chinese for reacting quickly and for getting the situation under control ... This was the third outbreak of the disease in Qinghai within the last ten

> years … Pneumonic plague is cause by the same bacteria that occur in bubonic plague – the Black Death that killed an estimated 25 million people in Europe during the Middle Ages.
>
> (www.bbc.co.uk, 3 August 2009)

'Pneumonic plague is one of the deadliest infectious diseases … In 2004 eight villagers in Qinghai province died of plague' (www.independent.co.uk, 3 August 2009).

> The authorities killed rats and fleas Tuesday [4 August] as they disinfected a remote farming town in north-western China that was sealed off after three people died of pneumonic plague … The police set up checkpoints around Ziketan in Qinghai province after the outbreak was first detected Thursday [30 July].
>
> (*IHT*, 5 August 2009, p. 5)

> A blockade around Ziketan … where pneumonic plague killed three people and sickened nine … was lifted after no new infections were reported, an official said Sunday [9 August]. The blockade ended Saturday night [8 August] after ten days … [The] nine patients were recovering.
>
> (*IHT*, 10 August 2009, p. 5)

Food contamination and defective goods

> A syrupy poison, diethylene glycol, is an indispensable part of the modern world, an industrial solvent and prime ingredient in antifreeze. It is also a killer … Over the years the poison has been loaded into all varieties of medicine – cough syrup, fever medication, injectable drugs – a result of counterfeiters who profit by substituting the sweet-tasting solvent for a safe, more expensive syrup, usually glycerine, commonly used in drugs, food, toothpaste and other products. Toxic syrup has figured in at least eight mass poisonings around the world in the past two decades. Researchers estimate that thousands have died. In many cases the precise origin of the poison has never been determined. But records and interviews show that in three of the last four cases it was made in China, a major source of counterfeit drugs … Beyond Panama and China, toxic syrup has caused mass poisonings in Haiti, Bangladesh, Argentina, Nigeria and India … A Chinese company is already being accused by the US authorities of exporting wheat gluten with an industrial chemical, melamine, that ended up in pet food and animal feed. Washington recently banned imports of Chinese-made wheat gluten after it was linked to pet deaths in the United States … In China the government is vowing to clean up its pharmaceutical industry, in part because of criticisms over fake drugs flooding the world markets. In December [2006] two top drug regulators were arrested on charges of taking bribes to approve drugs. As well, 440 counterfeiting operations were closed down last year [2006], the WHO said.
>
> (www.iht.com, 6 May 2007; *IHT*, 7 May 2007, pp. 1, 3)

> Officials in Hong Kong as well as at the WHO and the FAO ... said Monday that they had received little information from mainland Chinese officials about a mysterious ailment killing pigs in south-eastern China or about Chinese wheat gluten contaminated with plastic scrap, raising questions again whether Beijing is willing to share data on global health issues ... [They said] they had received practically no information [from mainland China] about the latest pig deaths and limited details about wheat gluten contamination ... Pigs can catch many of the same diseases as people, notably bird flu ... The most popular scientific model for how avian influenza viruses cause pandemics in humans is that human and avian influenza viruses exchange genetic material when they infect a pig at the same time ... The presence of melamine in pet food has been linked to the deaths of as many as 4,000 cats and dogs in the United States and prompted the culling of chickens that ate contaminated feed ... The official Xinhua press agency [in mainland China] briefly reported a month ago that the mainland had begun nationwide testing of wheat gluten for melamine.
>
> (www.iht.com, 7 May 2007)

'Regulators in the United States suspect that Chinese companies mix melamine into animal feed because it is high in nitrogen and can be used to bolster protein levels artificially' (www.iht.com, 8 May 2007).

> A second industrial chemical that regulators have found in contaminated pet food in the United States may also have been intentionally added to animal feed by producers seeking larger profits, according to interviews with chemical industry officials. Three Chinese chemical makers said that animal feed producers often purchase, or seek to purchase, the chemical, cyanuric acid, from their factories to blend into animal feed ... [Cyanuric acid is] high in nitrogen, enabling feed producers to lift the protein reading of the feed artificially.
>
> (www.iht.com, 8 May 2007)

> China acknowledged Tuesday [8 May] that two Chinese companies had illegally exported contaminated wheat gluten and rice protein for pet food blamed for a spate of animal deaths in the United States ... China had [previously] denied the US Food and Drug Administration's assertions that melamine ... had been added to wheat gluten and rice protein exported from China as pet food ... The Chinese government said Tuesday that a Chinese company that sold a batch of diethylene glycol, a chemical cousin of antifreeze that killed fifty-one people in Panama, had no licence to sell pharmaceuticals ... The brief comments marked Beijing's first public acknowledgement that it had investigated claims that one of its manufacturers was to blame for the deaths.
>
> (*IHT*, 9 May 2007, p. 11)

> China's drug regulation agency has confirmed that the company linked to counterfeit medicine that caused at least 100 deaths in Panama was not

> licensed to be engaged in the pharmaceutical business … A foreign ministry spokeswoman said Tuesday [8 May] that the State Food and Drug Administration conducted an investigation last year [2006] in response to a request by officials at the US Food and Drug Administration … Cough medicine in Panama was tainted with a poisonous industrial solvent, diethylene glycol, that was traced to a factory in eastern China.
>
> (www.iht.com, 9 May 2007)

> Diethylene glycol, a poison, has been found in 6,000 tubes of toothpaste in Panama, and customs officials there said Friday [18 May] that the product appeared to have originated in China … Some of the toothpaste … was reexported to the Dominican Republic … [and] Australia … Diethylene glycol is the same poison that the Panamanian government inadvertently mixed into cold medicine last year [2006], killing at least 100 people. Records show that in that incident the poison, falsely labelled as harmless syrup, also originated in China … A factory not certified to make pharmaceutical ingredients sold barrels of syrup containing diethylene glycol that had been falsely labelled as 99.5 per cent pure glycerine. That syrup passed through several trading companies before ending up in Panama, where it was mixed into bottles of cough medicine. At least 100 people died as a direct result … Counterfeiters have found it financially advantageous to substitute diethylene glycol, a sweet tasting syrup, for its chemical cousin glycerine, which is usually much more expensive.
>
> (www.iht.com, 19 May 2007)

'China is investigating whether two companies from this coastal region of China … Danyang … exported toothpaste laced with a poisonous chemical, diethylene glycol. A team of government investigators arrived Sunday [20 May]' (www.iht.com, 22 May 2007).

> The Food and Drug Administration will begin testing samples of all toothpaste imported into the United States from China … There is no evidence that the tainted toothpaste is in the United States or that anyone has been harmed by it. Even so, the FDA decided to issue the order out of caution.
>
> (www.iht.com, 24 May 2007)

> China has been facing persistent consumer and safety problems. In 2004 China punished ninety-seven government officials over the sale of fake milk powder with no nutritional value that caused the deaths of at least thirteen babies in the eastern province of Anhui. In recent months there have been complaints in the United States about pet deaths from tainted wheat gluten and rice protein imported from China … More than 20 per cent of Chinese-made toys and baby clothes are below standard, the country's consumer watchdog has said. An investigation by the General Administration of Quality Supervision and Quarantine found some were even dangerous … China will ban the sale of toys that fail to pass a national compulsory safety certification beginning 1 June [2007] … About half of all goods withdrawn

from sale in the EU in 2006 were Chinese, according to figures from the European Commission.

(www.bbc.co.uk, 28 May 2007)

'Last year [2006] a sub-standard antibiotic, Xinfu, which was not properly sterilized, caused the deaths of eleven people. Thirteen babies died of malnutrition in 2005 after being fed powdered milk that contained no nutritional value' (www.bbc.co.uk, 29 May 2007).

The former head of China's top food and drug safety agency was sentenced to death Tuesday [29 May] after pleading guilty to corruption and accepting bribes ... The court accused him of accepting about $850,000 in bribes in exchange for approving drug-production licences ... Zheng Xiaoyu, who served as commissioner of the Food and Drug Administration from its founding in 1998 until mid-2005, was detained in February as part of a government investigation into corruption at the agency. The unusually harsh sentence for the sixty-two-year-old former commissioner came at a time of heightened concern about the quality and safety of China's food and drug system, following a series of scandals involving tainted food and counterfeit drugs ... While tales of heavy metals in vegetables, poisonous dyes in eggs and fake drugs have been a staple diet of the Chinese media for the past few years, it has taken pet deaths in the United States to draw world attention to the problem ... Every year thousands of people are sickened or killed [in China] because of rampant counterfeiting and phoney or tainted food and drugs. Last year [2006] eleven people died in China after being treated with an injection tainted by a fake chemical. Also, six people died and eight fell ill after taking an antibiotic that was produced with what regulators later said was a 'substandard disinfectant'. Small drug makers have long been accused of manufacturing phoney or substandard drugs and marketing them to the nation's hospitals and pharmacies. Mass food poisonings involving tainted food products are common. This week the state-controlled media in Shanghai said the city's food and drug regulator had recalled drugs made by three companies that were not registered as drug makers ... On Tuesday government officials said they were preparing to release the first regulations on nationwide food recalls.

(www.iht.com, 29 May 2007; *IHT*, 30 May 2007, p. 6)

The sentence is unusually harsh for a senior figure, but Zheng Xiaoyu could have his sentence reduced to life on appeal. The verdict came as the government announced plans for the first ever recall system of unsafe food products ... The government said a new recall process targeting 'potentially dangerous and unapproved food products' would be brought in by the end of the year.

(www.bbc.co.uk, 29 May 2007)

Businesses in Panama not China were 'mainly responsible' for passing off an industrial chemical as a medical ingredient leading to the deaths of at least fifty-one people, a senior official in China's product inspection agency said Thursday [31 May] … China admits it was the source of the deadly chemical that ended up in cough syrup and other treatments but insists the chemical was originally labelled as for industrial use only … [The official] acknowledged that the Chinese manufacturer … and the Chinese distributor … 'engaged in some misconduct' because they used the name TD glycerine for a mix of 15 per cent diethylene glycol and 'other substances' … [The official] also dismissed concerns about exported Chinese toothpaste made with diethylene glycol … saying there was 'no sound evidence' to indicate that the chemical was dangerous in very low concentrations.

(www.iht.com, 31 May 2007)

US officials said Wednesday that a manufacturing plant in Ohio was using the banned substance melamine to make binding agents that ended up in feed for farmed fish, shrimp and livestock … Melamine is not permitted in food or pet food products.

(www.iht.com, 31 May 2007)

[On 2 June] China rejected a warning by the US Food and Drug Administration urging customers to avoid using Chinese toothpaste because it may contain a poisonous chemical … diethylene glycol … China's general Administration of Quality Supervision, Inspection and Quarantine said … that low levels of the chemical have been deemed safe for consumption … A slew of Chinese exports have recently been banned or turned away by US inspectors including wheat gluten tainted with the chemical melamine that has been blamed for dog and cat deaths in North America; monkfish that turned out to be toxic pufferfish; drug-laced frozen eel; and juice made with banned colour additives.

(www.iht.com, 3 June 2007; *IHT*, 4 June 2007, p. 11)

China announced [on 5 June] that it was overhauling its food and drug safety regulations and would introduce nationwide inspections … On 17 April the State Council approved a new food and drug safety guarantee system … By 2010 the government plans to place new controls on food and drug imports and exports, to step up random testing on medicines and have inspection information on 90 per cent of all food products. There are also plans for safety checks on a large majority of food makers and for regulators to crack down on the sale of counterfeit drugs and medical devices … Chinese regulators have stepped up safety inspections and shut down companies accused of producing unsafe food or counterfeit drugs … A few weeks ago the government announced that for the first time it was planning to set up a food-recall system … The challenges facing China are enormous because its regulatory system is weak and enforcement is particularly difficult.

(www.iht.com, 6 June 2007; *IHT*, 7 June 2007, p. 12)

The government published a five-year plan on Tuesday [5 June] to increase inspections and tests on exported food … In the future 'illegal activities behind production and sale of fake and shoddy foods and pharmaceuticals will be effectively contained', the five-year plan says ... Singapore has become the latest country to take action against Chinese toothpaste ... Singapore has banned three brands of toothpaste imported from China, after tests showed they contained diethylene glycol ... On Thursday [31 May] Nicaraguan health authorities seized 40,000 tubes of Chinese-made toothpaste after they were found to contain diethylene glycol. The Dominican Republic, Panama and Costa Rica have already removed thousands of tubes of toothpaste from store shelves.

(www.bbc.co.uk, 6 June 2007)

The release by the State Council, or cabinet, of the first 'five-year plan' specifically addressing food and drug safety is intended to focus bureaucratic efforts on improving and more strictly implementing supervision of the two industries ... It sets targets such as an increase in coverage of sample inspections of pharmaceuticals to 80 per cent from the current 30 per cent.

(*FT*, 7 June 2007, p. 10)

[On 6 June China released] its first five-year plan to improve food and drug safety standards ... However, the implementation of the plan is likely to be difficult ... The plan calls for more inspections of food exports, improved procedures for recalling faulty or tainted products, more pollution monitoring in food producing areas, as well as an improved structure for monitoring – and blacklisting – food trading companies. According to the Chinese state media, the plan also aims to implement a system of special inspections for 90 per cent of food producers. It also calls for more stringent controls on the use of additives and pesticides, and for nationwide monitoring of the ill effects of medication. However, despite the plan's laudable aims, corruption and inefficiency will continue to leave doors wide open for companies wanting to cut corners ... The US pet deaths ... were not all that different from many past cases in China. However, the massive scale of the pet food recall, involving thousands of retail products, was unprecedented ... Investigations into such cases have thrown light on the tangled morass of the Chinese regulatory system. The State Food and Drug Administration, the General Administration of Quality Supervision, Inspection and Quarantine and other agencies have a tendency to pass the buck between each other, denying responsibility for mistakes. That allows producers and traders to get on with business as usual. In many cases a lack of regulatory clarity and co-ordination prevents the authorities from tackling abuses. In others, businesses simply buy the required documentation ... Investigative programmes exposing factories, farms and restaurants engaged in various nefarious practices with food are a stomach-churning staple of Chinese television. Yet Chinese officials' reflexive response to more serious cases remains the cover-up.

(www.economist.com, 12 June 2007)

'The Chinese authorities are investigating the widespread sale of fake blood protein to hospitals and pharmacies … Thousands are sickened or die every year from bad drugs and mass food poisonings' (www.iht.com, 11 June 2007).

> Investigators say nearly sixty hospitals and pharmacies in north-east China have been using fake blood protein in patients' drips. Albumin, or plasma protein, is used to treat patients suffering from shock and burns and during open-heart surgery … The scandal is the latest to expose weaknesses in China's regulation of food and drug standards.
>
> (www.bbc.co.uk, 11 June 2007)

> After a drug ingredient from China killed dozens of Haitian children a decade ago, a senior American health official sent a cable to her investigators: find out who made the poisonous ingredient and why a state-owned company in China exported it as safe, pharmaceutical-grade glycerine … Officially at least eighty-eight children died, nearly half under the age of two. But those eighty-eight were only the ones doctors remembered or for whom hospital records could be found … 'The United States imports lots of Chinese glycerine and it is used in ingested products such as toothpaste,' Mary Prendergast, then deputy commissioner for the Food and Drug Administration, wrote on 27 October 1997. Learning how diethyene glycol … ended up in Haitian fever medicine might 'prevent this tragedy from happening again,' she wrote … The FDA's mission ultimately failed … . Chinese companies said they bore no responsibility for the mass poisoning … Ten years later it happened again, this time in Panama. Chinese-made diethylene glycol … was mixed into medicine … China itself was a victim of diethylene glycol poisoning last year [2006] when at least eighteen people died after ingesting poisonous medicine made there … Beyond the three incidents linked to Chinese diethylene glycol, there have been at least five other mass poisonings involving the mislabelled chemical in the past two decades – in Bangladesh, Nigeria, Argentina and twice in India … A prominent physician in Bangladesh said the foreign suppliers of diethylene glycol were never prosecuted for the deaths of thousands of children from 1982 to 1992 … In Argentina a court official said no one had been prosecuted for supplying the diethylene glycol that ended up in a health supplement, killing twenty-nine people in 1992.
>
> (www.iht.com, 16 June 2007)

> China's regulatory standards chief pledged Wednesday [20 June] to update and enhance enforcement of food safety rules … [It was said that] China will speed up revisions to national and industry standards on farm produce and process food products … Reports of food poisonings or tainted food are almost daily occurrences in China. In the latest food safety scare a company was ordered to stop production after it was found to be repackaging the filling from two-year-old rice dumplings.
>
> (www.iht.com, 20 June 2007)

Every one of the twenty-four [types of] toys recalled for safety reasons in the United States so far this year … was manufactured in China … The latest recall, announced last week, involves … train and rail sets … coated at a factory in China with potentially poisonous lead paint … Toys made in China make up 70 per cent to 80 per cent of the toys sold [in the United States] … Overall, the number of products made in China by the Consumer Product Safety Commission has doubled in the last five years … China today is responsible for about 60 per cent of the overall product recalls, compared to 36 per cent in 2000 … China is also the source of 81 per cent of the counterfeit goods seized last year [2006] at ports of entry in the United States.

(*IHT*, 19 June 2007, pp. 1, 16)

US officials have told a small New Jersey importer to recall 450,000 radial tyres for pickup trucks, sport utility vehicles and vans after the company disclosed that its Chinese manufacturer had stopped including a safety feature that prevented the tyres from separating … [The Chinese manufacturer] sold the tyres to at least six other importers or distributors in the United States …[but] has denied they were defective … The defective tyres join a growing list of problematic products with origins in China.

(www.iht.com, 26 June 2007; *IHT*, 27 June 2007, p. 12)

After weeks of insisting that food here is largely safe, regulators said [on 26 June] that they had recently closed 180 food plants and that inspectors had uncovered more than 23,000 food safety violations. The nationwide crackdown began in December [2006] … China has strongly denied that its food exports are hazardous and has seemingly retaliated in recent weeks by seizing American and European imports … Experts here say that the country's food regulations are not being enforced and that small businesses go to extraordinary lengths to make a profit. Corruption and bribery have also infected the food and drug industry. The former head of the food and drug regulator was recently sentenced to death for accepting bribes and approving the licensing of substandard drugs. A ministry of agriculture official is now on trial in Beijing for accepting bribes in exchange for endorsing food products. But not all the problems stem from corruption or malfeasance … One cause of food safety problems is a lack of cold storage and logistics systems.

(www.iht.com, 27 June 2007; *IHT*, 28 June 2007, p. 12)

A government spokesman guaranteed the safety of Chinese exports Thursday [28 June] … The guarantee came a day after the US authorities disclosed that tainted toothpaste imported from China had been distributed more widely than earlier believed … On Wednesday [27 June] three Japanese importers recalled millions of Chinese-made travel toothpaste sets.

(*IHT*, 29 June 2007, p. 14)

[On 26 June] Chinese officials said they had closed 180 food manufacturing businesses that had used industrial additives including formaldehyde, paraffin and dyes in food products … The companies had been closed during inspections held between December [2006] and May [2007]' … Chinese officials have argued that such levels of … diethylene glycol [in toothpaste] … do not pose a threat to human health.

(*FT*, 29 June 2007, p. 12)

In the latest move against Chinese imports, the [US] Food and Drug Administration Thursday [28 June] effectively blocked the sale of five types of farm-raised seafood from China because of repeated instances of contamination from unapproved animal drugs and food additives … [The FDA] stressed that the seafood posed no immediate health threat, though long-term consumption could result in health problems … China [is] the world's largest producer of farm-raised fish. The country is also the biggest foreign supplier of seafood to the United States, accounting for 22 per cent of the total imports. The seafood named in the FDA's 'import alert' are shrimp, catfish, eel, basa (which are similar to catfish) and dace (similar to carp). Some of the contaminants cited have been found to cause cancer in laboratory animals, while others may increase antibiotic resistance. Under the import alert the seafood can be sold in the United States only if importers provide independent testing that shows seafood does not contain the contaminants … The banned substances, primarily antifungals and antibacterials, have been used by some Chinese farmers to prevent disease among their seafood … The problems with contaminated Chinese seafood imports date back at least six years … In May [2007], for instance, the agency turned away 165 shipments from China, forty-nine of them seafoods.

(www.iht.com, 29 June 2007; *IHT*, 30 June 2007, p. 13)

The US Food and Drug Administration said it had found that Chinese seafood tested between October 2006 and May 2007 was repeatedly contaminated with antimicrobial agents … In what is thought to be a response to the US move, Chinese authorities this week seized two shipments of American food, saying they were substandard.

(www.bbc.co.uk, 30 June 2007)

The US Food and Drug Administration announced Thursday [28 June] it would detain three types of fish – catfish, basa and dace – as well as shrimp and eel after repeated testing turned up contamination with drugs unapproved in the United States for use in farmed seafood … The safety scandals have put at risk surging Chinese agricultural exports to the United States, which reached $2.26 billion last year [2006], led by poultry products, sausage casing, shellfish, spices and apple juice … Earlier this week China announced it had seized shipments of US-made orange pulp and dried apricots containing high levels of bacteria and preservatives.

(www.cnn.com, 30 June 2007)

Big American companies are increasing their scrutiny of thousands of everyday products they receive from Chinese suppliers, as widening recalls of items like toys and toothpaste force them to focus on potential hazards that were overlooked in the past ... Chinese agricultural exports to the United States reached $2.26 billion in 2006.

(*IHT*, 2 July 2007, p. 13)

In May of this year [2007] alone, a lengthy list of Chinese seafood shipments was blocked from entering the United States because of safety violations. Regulators tagged 'filthy frozen scallops', catfish, eel and shrimp laced with banned chemicals, unsafe additives, pesticides and cancer causing agents. EU officials say they have also noticed a rise this year in the number of Chinese seafood turning up with banned chemicals, despite strict procedures, including food safety test certificates presented by the Chinese government.

(*IHT*, 3 July 2007, p. 10)

The US government is grappling with realities exposed by a string of Chinese imports that slipped through its inspection system and turned out to be dangerous, from poisoned pet food and toothpaste to defective tyres and Thomas the Tank Engine toys painted with lead. As Congress and federal agencies consider how to ensure the safety of imports from a nation rife with counterfeiting and corner-cutting, product safety experts point to fireworks as a model. Most of the US fireworks trade voluntarily contributes to a consortium, established in 1989 in response to safety complaints, that employs about fifty inspectors to test and certify every shipment to member companies before it leaves Chinese factories. US regulators and fireworks importers agree that the consortium, called the American Fireworks Standards Laboratory, uses standards that exceed federal mandates and has boosted safety compliance ... People familiar with these issues could not think of another US industry that so scrutinizes Chinese consumer products at the source ... The largest companies formed the standards lab in 1989 and adopted standards stricter than the government's. The lab covers an estimated 80 per cent of fireworks in the United States ... Overseas testing began in 1994 ... China is usually credited with the invention of fireworks more than 1,000 years ago. US manufacturers never really blossomed, and have faded in an era of globalization.

(www.iht.com, 3 July 2007)

A seasoning made with Chinese ingredients and used in recalled snacks was contaminated with salmonella, the head of a US company said [on 3 July]. The snacks sickened dozens of people ... The seasoning's ingredients came primarily from China, the company said. Separately, nearly one-fifth of products made in China for domestic consumption failed quality and safety standards, the Chinese government said Wednesday [2 July] ... In the first half of 2007 19.1 per cent of products made for domestic consumption were found to be substandard, the Chinese General Administration of Quality Supervision, Inspection and Quarantine said ... Canned and preserved fruit and dried fish were the most problematic, primarily because of excessive bacteria and additives, the agency said. Meanwhile, China was devising new safety rules for oral care, the state media reported, apparently impelled by international alarm over use by toothpaste producers of a potentially toxic chemical found in antifreeze.

(www.iht.com, 4 July 2007; *IHT*, 5 July 2007, p. 10)

China said Wednesday [4 July] that nearly a fifth of the food and consumer products that it checked in a nationwide survey this year [2007] were found to be substandard or tainted … Regulators said the broad survey of foods, agricultural tools, clothing, women's and children's products and other types of goods turned up sizable quality and safety failure rates for products that are sold domestically. The government said, for instance, that canned and preserved fruit and dried fish contained excessive bacteria; that 20 per cent of the fruit and vegetable juice surveyed was deemed substandard, and that some of the children's products were defective or laced with harmful chemicals … The survey, conducted in the first half of this year [2007], showed quality and safety improvements compared with conditions in the period a year earlier … The government said 80.9 per cent of the food and other products checked in a nationwide survey met safety standards and that this rate was higher than a year earlier, when about 78 per cent of the goods surveyed were deemed safe … The government said that baby formula and baby clothing did not meet the safety standards, that animal feed, fertilizer and agricultural equipment were defective and that many food items were mislabelled or heavily coloured by additives … Regulators said, in effect, that goods sold in China were far more hazardous than the exports … A regulatory official … [said in June] that '99 per cent of the food exported to the United States was up to safety standards over the past two years' … During the last month [June] regulators and quality inspectors say they have discovered candied fruit with sixty-three times the permitted amount of sweetener; excessive additives and preservatives in nearly 40 per cent of the children's snacks surveyed in western Guangxi province; fake human blood protein at hospitals; and food tainted with formaldehyde, illegal dyes and industrial wax … Experts say aggressive and opportunistic entrepreneurs continue to take advantage of the country's chronically weak enforcement of regulations.

(www.iht.com, 5 July 2007)

About 19 per cent of products sold locally in the first half [of 2007] did not meet Chinese standards, according to a survey of 7,200 types of food, farm products and consumer goods from 6,362 companies, posted yesterday [4 July] on the website of the General Administration of Quality Supervision, Inspection and Quarantine.

(*FT*, 5 July 2007, p. 10)

In 2004 bogus baby formula killed dozens of infants … For the first time in decades the government has gone so far as to appoint respected professionals who are not members of the Communist Party to run the ministries of science and health. Both of the ministers concerned have studied and worked in Europe.

(*The Economist*, 7 July 2007, p. 67)

For the second time in three months a former high ranking official at China's top food and drug watchdog agency has been sentenced to death for corruption and approving bogus drugs ... Cao Wenzhuang, who until 2005 [2002–5] was in charge of drug registration approvals at the State Food and Drug Administration, was accused of accepting over $300,000 in bribes from two pharmaceutical companies and helping undermine the public's confidence in an agency that is supposed to be safeguarding the nation's health ... he was charged with neglecting his duties in approving drugs ... Cao was given the death sentence with a two-year reprieve, a lighter penalty [than Zheng Xiaoyu] that may allow the forty-five-year-old to have his sentence commuted to life imprisonment ... Such suspended sentences are usually commuted to life in prison if the convict is deemed to have reformed ... Four other senior food and drug agency officials were also sentenced to long prison terms on Thursday [6 July] ... Last November [2006] another high ranking drug agency official, Hao Heping, was sentenced to fifteen years in prison for bribery ... In 2002 the former director of the Zhejiang Provincial Drug Administration was sentenced to death with a two-year reprieve ... Cao and Hao had both at one time served as close aides to Zheng Xiaoyu, the former agency director ... Under Zheng's 1998–2005 tenure as top drug regulator, his agency approved six medicines that turned out to be fake, and the drugmakers used falsified documents to apply for approvals ... China's drug industry boom also worries global drug makers, who say the world is inundated with fake and potentially deadly counterfeit drugs that are being exported from China.

(www.iht.com, 6 July 2007; *IHT*, 7 July 2007, pp. 1, 4, 13, 14)

'Cao Wenzhuang was given a two-year reprieve, which often results in commutation to life in prison' (www.iht.com, 10 July 2007).

[On 6 July] US regulators ordered a recall of three more Chinese-made products deemed dangerous to children ... The US Consumer Product Safety Commission announced Thursday [6 July] three recalls, covering jewellery that the agency said could cause lead poisoning. They also covered a magnetic building set and plastic castles with small parts, which it said could choke children.

(www.iht.com, 6 July 2007)

China may now have to cope with another consumer product disaster: exploding mobile phone batteries. Chinese regulators in the southern Guangdong province ... said this week that they had found Motorola and Nokia mobile phone batteries that failed safety tests and were prone to explode under certain conditions. The batteries were said to be manufactured by Motorola and the Sanyo operation in Beijing, and were being distributed by companies based in Guangdong province … In June a twenty-two-year-old man in western China was killed after his Motorola cellphone exploded … Motorola and Nokia – two of the world's biggest mobile phone makers – immediately denied links to the distributors of the problem batteries, suggesting that they were counterfeit.

(www.iht.com, 6 July 2007; *IHT*, 7 July 2007, pp. 1, 14)

To spur economic growth in the 1980s top leaders gave local officials more power … Regulatory power was also scattered. Growth surged … but safety, as well as labour and environmental standards, fell by the wayside … Perhaps the most sensational cases occurred in 2004, when small factories in central China produced cheap infant milk formula that lacked protein. Some fifty infants in Anhui province died from malnutrition after their parents and some doctors mistook their symptoms – bloated faces and hands – as a sign of overfeeding. Since then regulatory efforts have been strengthened, but often with mixed results. As many as seventeen bureaucracies have overlapping responsibilities in the food and drug sphere alone, and they jealously guard their power. The ministry of health, the ministry of agriculture, the State Administration of Industry and Commerce and the General Administration of Quality Supervision, Inspection and Quarantine have all vied for monitoring fees. The reason: they wanted to collect fees and fines to supplement their measly budgets. No less significantly, inspectors and their bosses could collect bribes in exchange for favours … Realizing they had created a muddle of competing bureaucracies, top leaders in 2003 formed the State Food and Drug Administration, named after its US counterpart, that on paper had 'superministerial authority' to co-ordinate all the other agencies that monitored the potentially sensitive food and drug sphere. But the agency quickly fell victim to infighting and lost clout in 2005, when its first director, Zheng Xiaoyu, was forced out. He was later convicted of taking bribes to speed approval of new drugs. After the latest string of safety scandals erupted, Zheng was sentenced to death. Blurred lines of responsibility and weak investigative powers partly explain why Chinese regulators gave little help to their US counterparts in the deadliest example of China's safety problems reaching foreign shores … The diethylene glycol was made in Chinese chemical factories but ended up in pharmaceutical products. This meant it fell into a regulatory void. No agency wanted to take control … Mao Shoulong [a public policy expert at People's University in Beijing]: 'Competition inside our bureaucracy has led to a diffusion of power and a tendency to shirk responsibility' … President Hu Jintao has pushed through a series of measures under the slogan of 'scientific development' meant to strengthen central regulators and economic planners, reduce abuses of low-wage workers and protect the degraded environment. He has met with plenty of resistance, and it remains unclear how much he will pull back from China's fast-growth model … The state-run media has given unusual latitude to expose shoddy goods. One of the most popular shows on China Central Television, *Weekly Quality Report*, investigates accidents, poisonings and cheap fakes. Recent topics include defective motorcycles, a fake rabies vaccine, faulty tyres and toxic food additives.

(Joseph Khan, *IHT*, 9 July 2007, pp. 1, 6)

For weeks, as questions have multiplied over the safety of China's exports of food and other consumer goods, the Chinese news media have had a constant refrain. American complaints about China's products are part of a mounting trade war. They are the expression of efforts by Westerners to keep China down, to invent what the newspaper media here [in China] have called a 'China threat' to manipulate public opinion. Exceptions can be found to this line, particularly regarding safety issues involving Chinese-made toothpastes … After an initial spate of attacks on the foreign coverage, many Chinese media outlets have belatedly come to accept that the country's toothpaste standards – which hold that the chemical [diethylene glocol] in small amounts is not harmful – need to be refined … Such commentary, however, has been rare. And that is remarkable, given that for years Chinese consumers have been bombarded with reports about problems with domestic food safety and fraud … The food safety crisis has revealed major weaknesses in China's emerging civil society, which for all its booming, frontier capitalist ethos has never developed anything like a consumer movement or citizen advocacy groups … The government has announced that it would rewrite food safety regulations, introduce a national recall system and overhaul the nation's top drug watchdog … The news … [of a] government survey showing that nearly 20 per cent of consumer goods on sale in China were substandard … drew scant commentary here … [There are] few prominent consumer advocates … [They say that] faults in the consumer safety system … include the lack of responsibility in the main watchdog agencies for food and drug quality. The food safety crisis also underscores persistent shortcomings in the Chinese news media, which … sometimes manage to be feisty and surprisingly investigative. The best example came recently, when a Chinese television reporter … uncovered longstanding practices akin to slave labour in the brick-making industry in Shanxi province. What China's emerging media outlets are less willing to do is directly criticize the government for failures in basic responsibilities, like ensuring the safety of food, medicine and other widely used products. As hard questions are being raised by outsiders, the Chinese news media have fallen back on the old formula of defensive nationalist posturing … The common story line of an American-driven plot to discredit China and Chinese products has run into difficulty, however, as Japan, the EU, certain South-east Asian countries and even Hong Kong … have all announced tightened controls or stricter inspections of Chinese consumables. In contrast to coverage of American bans on Chinese toothpaste, dog food ingredients and fish, reports about the international concerns on food safety here have been sparse.

(Howard French, www.iht.com, 8 July 2007; *IHT*, 9 July 2007, p. 5)

Following a series of scares in the United States and elsewhere over the safety of goods made in China, potentially toxic consumer products have now turned up in Europe in the form of tubes of toothpaste … officials confirmed Monday [9 July] … Tens of thousands of tubes of toothpaste have been seized in Spain and Italy on suspicion of being tainted, the European Commission said … More than half of all imported products notified for recall in the EU in 2006 originated in China … A Panamanian prosecutor has said tests show at least ninety-four people died from taking medicine contaminated with diethylene glycol since July 2006 and 293 more deaths are under investigation … Tainted products have also been found in Japan and Canada. Because of these discoveries the European Commission sent an official warning on 29 May to authorities in thirty European countries that participate in an information-sharing rapid alert system on non-food dangerous products, prompting the discoveries.

(www.iht.com, 9 July 2007; *IHT*, 10 July 2007, pp. 1, 15)

The former head of China's State Food and Drug Administration, Zheng Xiaoyu, has been executed [on 10 July] … He was convicted of taking $850,000 in bribes and of dereliction of duty at a trial in May. The bribes were linked to substandard medicines, blamed for several deaths … Following Zheng's sacking in 2005 the government announced an urgent review of about 170,000 medical licences that were awarded during his tenure at the agency.

(www.bbc.co.uk, 10 July 2007)

Zheng Xiaoyu became China's top drug regulator in 1994, when he was named to the top position of what was then called the State Pharmaceutical Administration. In 2003 the agency became the State Food and Drug Administration and acquired responsibility for overseeing the nation's food supply as well, in an attempt by the government to consolidate regulatory authority into one agency. He was removed in June 2005 for reasons that were not specified at the time. His ouster followed a period of bureaucratic infighting over the powers of the food and drug regulator, whose expanded responsibilities encroached on the purview and revenue sources of rival departments … [He] was sentenced to death in May … His agency approved 137 drugs that had not submitted proper applications … Six of those drugs turned out to be entirely fake. The list of drugs approved by Zheng included an antibiotic blamed for at least ten deaths in China … [He] became the first ministerial-level official put to death since 2000 and only the fourth since China opened its doors to the outside world nearly thirty years ago … The authorities said that inspectors would start shifting posts more often to

> prevent corruption and that they would check a wide range of goods more frequently to ferret out fakes … Officials acknowledge that responsibility for food and drug safety involves as many as seventeen government agencies, ranging from the ministry of health, which sets hygienic standards, to the Public Security Bureau, which has power to investigate criminal cases … On Tuesday [10 July] officials asserted that the five agencies that have the most direct, front-line responsibility for food and drug safety have stepped up their co-ordination.
>
> (www.iht.com, 10 July 2007; *IHT*, 11 July 2007, pp. 1, 8)

'Zheng Xiaoyu is the most senior official to be executed since 2000 … The government [said it] is now rotating officials in key positions on a regular basis to prevent them from forging too close ties with companies' (www.ft.com, 10 July 2007).

> Zheng Xiaoyu … had started out as an idealistic reformer. Concerned about the unsafe drug supply in China, he lobbied for the creation of the State Food and Drug Administration. Yet in the end, according to friends and associates, he was corrupted by the very system he had sought to change, even enlisting his wife … and son … to solicit bribes.
>
> (*IHT*, 13 July 2007, p. 1)

> China banned manufacturers from making toothpaste with diethylene glycol [it was officially reported on 11 July] … Chinese regulators said diethylene glocol in small amounts is safe, particularly since toothpaste is meant to be spat out, not consumed. But the US Food and Drug Administration disagreed, saying children might swallow it. Some Chinese brands were aimed at children, with flavours like bubblegum and strawberry.
>
> (www.iht.com, 12 July 2007)

> The army is to take steps to ensure the safety of its food supply, due to fears unsafe products could harm combat capacity … The People's Liberation Army's 2.3 million troops grow around 10 per cent of their own food but depend on suppliers for the other 90 per cent … Troops will also be banned from sharing communal dishes to prevent the spread of disease.
>
> (www.bbc.co.uk, 13 July 2007)

> China said late Friday [13 July] that it was suspending imports of some chicken and pork produced in the United States after inspectors found shipments that were contaminated with chemicals or bacteria. The government said it would immediately block imports from some of the biggest US meat producers, including Tyson Foods and Cargill, and also strengthen inspections of American meat to guard against health risks.
>
> (*IHT*, 16 July 2007, p. 12)

> China's top quality control official on Monday accused foreign media of raising unnecessary alarm about the safety of the country's food and drug exports, complaining in particular about US reports … Li Changjiang,

> minister of the General Administration of Quality Supervision, Inspection and Quarantine, said that more than 99 per cent of Chinese exports to the United States in the past three years had met quality standards, the same or better than the amount of US food exports to China.
>
> (*IHT*, 17 July 2007, p. 11)

> The government has defended a national tyre maker accused in the United States of exporting faulty products. Hangzhou Zhongce Rubber is being sued by the US firm Foreign Tire Sales (FTS), which has called on the Chinese firm to recall 450,000 of its truck tyres. The New Jersey firm said in May it had stopped buying Zhongce van and truck tyres owing to safety worries. But China's top quality control body … the General Administration of Quality Supervision, Inspection and Quarantine … said tests on the tyres showed they were 'qualified to be sold in the United States' … The Chinese company has also denied there were any problems with its tyres. FTS is being sued by the relatives of two men killed last year [2006] in a crash involving a vehicle said to have used Zhongce tyres … The United States imports more than 30 million tyres from Chinese producers.
>
> (www.bbc.co.uk, 18 July 2007)

'Beijing regulators say they tested several similar models of the tyre and that all tyres met US safety standards. The company, Hangzhou Zhongce Rubber, said that the fatal accident was caused by misuse of the tyres' (www.iht.com, 20 July 2007).

> Last month [June] the US authorities ordered a recall of up to 450,000 tyres made by Hangzhou Zhongce after its US distributor, Foreign Tire Sales Inc., said they lacked a gum strip, an important safety feature that binds the belts of a tyre. From 1 September [2007] all exports will bear a seal indicating that they have been inspected by the Chinese quality administration and importers will be able to trace the producer using a code.
>
> (*IHT*, 19 July 2007, p. 12)

> China has closed down three companies and arrested several people involved in food and drug scandals that have caused alarm both at home and abroad. Two of the firms exported contaminated wheat protein to the United States that eventually led to the deaths of cats and dogs. Another firm was shut down after being linked to the deaths of a number of people in Panama … Minister Li Changjiang, in charge of food and drug safety, personally oversaw the publication of some of the results. One found that a firm in Jiangsu province and another in Shandong province had together exported more than 1,300 tonnes of contaminated wheat protein to the United States. They avoided detection at customs by labelling their products as chemical ingredients. These products were contaminated with melamine, a chemical usually used in the production of plastics. They were used to make pet food. A glycerine factory in Jiangsu province has also been closed down in connection with the deaths in Panama. Those occurred after a chemical called

TD glycerine, which should be used only for industrial purposes, found its way into cough syrup.

(www.bbc.co.uk, 20 July 2007)

Li Changjiang, who heads the General Administration for Quality Supervision, Inspection and Quarantine, said officials were also focusing on stricter market access requirements for companies, conducting random checks, and beefing up product testing ... Li's administration said it had pulled the business licence of Taixing Glycerine Factory, which has been accused of selling what is called 'TD glycerine', a mix of 15 per cent diethylene glycol and other substances ... Chinese quality officials have said 'TD glycerine' is a misleading label because it could be mistaken for glycerine. But they have also said the bulk of the blame lies with Panamanian merchants, who fraudulently mislabelled the 'TD glycerine' as medical glycerine and for altering the use-by date of the already expired product. It eventually ended up in Panamanian cough syrup and other medicines that killed at least ninety-four people. It was the first time action against the company had been publicly announced ... The statement also detailed punishments against Xuzhou Anying Biologic Technology Development Co. Ltd and Binzhou Futian Biology Technology Co. Ltd, the two companies linked to the melamine-tainted wheat gluten blamed for the deaths of dozens of dogs and cats in North America. Xuzhou Anying, also in Jiangsu province, had its licence revoked, its offices and workshops closed and it rights to import and export taken away ... The business licence for Binzhou Futian, headquartered in neighbouring Shandong province, was also revoked and its offices and workshops closed ... Melamine, used in plastics, fertilizers and flame retardants, has no nutritional value but is high in nitrogen, making products to which it is added appear to be higher in protein – a way to cut costs for the manufacturer. China has also accused the companies of illegally mislabelling their exported products to avoid inspections. All have been banned from exporting. Legal action was being taken against managers of the companies ... Li said one of the biggest problems in food safety is the regulatory nightmare of countless small and illegal food manufacturers throughout the country ... However, he added that 'the quality of Chinese food is going up' and said 85 per cent of food manufactured in China passed recent random quality tests. Additionally, random tests on exports in the first half of 2007 showed a passing rate of 99.1 per cent for foods going to the United States and 99.8 per cent for those going to the EU. Conversely, 99.3 per cent of imports from the United States and 98.8 per cent of imports from the EU passed Chinese inspections in the same period.

(www.iht.com, 20 July 2007)

On Friday [20 July] the government acknowledged that several Chinese companies had exported seafood tainted with banned chemicals to the United States. Regulators said they had not caught the problem because several seafood suppliers were not registered with the government's quality

> inspectors. Regulators in Beijing also said they had revoked the licences of three companies that had exported tainted pet food ingredients and mislabelled drug ingredients to the United States and other parts of the world ... This month [July] Beijing ... began offering foreign journalists tours of government safety labs and Chinese factories that the government says it believes meet international standards.
>
> (*IHT*, 21 July 2007, p. 11)

'The food scare highlights China's inability to regulate a fragmented food supply system of about 200 million small farms and 448,000 food processing companies' (www.iht.com, 31 July 2007).

'Toymaker Fisher-Price is to recall more than one-and-a-half million Chinese-made toys over fears that their paint contains too much lead ... Mattel Inc. owns Fisher-Price' (www.bbc.co.uk, 2 August 2007).

> Mattel, the maker of Barbie dolls and Hot Wheel cars, is widely considered the most conscientious toy maker operating in China. It has sophisticated testing labs and independent audits of its facilities [in China] ... and the company requires contract manufacturers to follow stringent quality and safety guidelines. But despite those checks Mattel said Wednesday [1 August] it was recalling 1.5 million toys globally, many featuring Sesame Street and Nickelodeon characters, because the products might be coated with toxic levels of lead paint ... [The] recall involves over eighty products ... All the toys, Mattel said, were made by a contract manufacturer in China. Nearly a million were sold in the United States, the rest mainly in Europe and Canada ... [Mattel said that]: 'This is a vendor [contract manufacturer] plant with whom we have worked for fifteen years' ... Earlier this year RC2, a US-based company, was forced to recall 1.5 million of its popular Thomas & Friends toy railway sets because those products were coated with lead paint. The company was also using a Chinese contract manufacturer ... Mattel is the only big toy maker that still owns factories in China and recently started operating a new post-production testing system in the country to ensure quality ... Analysts say Mattel is widely admired in the toy industry because it has hired an independent auditor who is allowed to post his findings on the internet ... While the company owns five factories [in China] ... that produce its core products, like Barbie dolls and Hot Wheels cars, a large percentage of its China-made products are produced by thirty to fifty contract manufacturers. Mattel, the world's biggest toy manufacturer, also says that it has over 1,000 licensees, who can produce goods based on its brands, and that those companies operate about 3,000 factories in China ... According to some estimates, China has over 10,000 toy factories, many of them small operations.
>
> (*IHT*, 3 August 2007, p. 10)

'Mattel issued a safety recall for 1.5 million of its Fisher-Price toys (a million of which are in America) because they may contain hazardous levels of lead paint' (*The Economist*, 4 August 2007, p. 7).

'[This] is the biggest such problem to face the US toymaker in more than a decade … Mattel said it was able to retrieve two-thirds of the toys before they reached the stores' (*FT*, 3 August 2007, p. 8).

> Mattel has identified the Chinese vendor that made nearly a million Fisher-Price toys that were recalled … Mattel said Tuesday [7 August] that Lee Der Industrial Company in Guangdong province made the 967,000 toys in question, sold under the Fisher-Price brand in the United States between May and August … China will spend more than $1 billion improving food and safety by 2010 and its regulator will be given stronger oversight powers … [It was said that] $1.16 billion has been earmarked for food and drug safety under the current five year plan, which runs to 2010.
>
> (www.iht.com, 8 August 2007)

'As part of the five year plan to boost product safety, the government will … introduce rules that allow the regulator to shut factories suspected of making sub-standard goods' (*FT*, 9 August 2007, p. 4).

> China said Thursday [9 August] that it had suspended the export licences of two factories that were blamed for using lead paint in toys that were made for American companies … Last week Mattel, the world's largest toy maker, said it would spend about $30 million to recall 1.5 million Fisher-Price brand toys … In June [2007] RC2 recalled 1.5 million Thomas & Friends wooden toy railroad sets … Products coated with paints that have high levels of lead can sicken or poison children.
>
> (*IHT*, 10 August 2007, p. 12).

> China stripped export licences from Hansheng Wooden Products Factory and Lida Toy Company, both in the southern province of Guangdong … Hansheng, based in Dongguan, was the producer of 1.5 million wooden vehicles, buildings and other train-set toys sold in the United States from January 2005 through June 2007, which were then voluntarily recalled by the US toy maker RC2 that imports the popular 'Thomas & Friends' train toys. About 1.5 million preschool toys made by Lida Toy, a contract manufacturer in Foshan for a Mattel-Price unit, were recalled across the globe by Mattel last week … China has also put on trial five drug company managers accused of killing patients with a tainted medicine … The medicine killed thirteen patients in the southern city of Guangzhou, where the trial began on Wednesday [8 August]. The same Chinese-made chemical has been linked to dozens of deaths in Panama, where it was used as cough syrup … A US tyre importer, Foreign Tire Sales, said Thursday [9 August] it would recall 255,000 Chinese-made tyres that it claims were defective because they lack a safety feature that prevents tread separation.
>
> (www.iht.com, 9 August 2007)

> [On 6 August] Wang Wei, a vice president with Beijing's Olympic organizing committee, said a monitoring system was being created to ensure the

safety of food and medicine for the more than 10,000 athletes participating in the Games ... The elaborate monitoring system is a response to growing international concerns about the quality and safety of many Chinese exports, particularly food and pharmaceutical supplies. Wang said that global positioning satellites would be used to track trucks delivering food to the Olympic village and inspections would also be conducted at farms and slaughterhouses. Deliveries will even be labelled with electronic bar codes as a safeguard ... Wang emphasized that Beijing had staged numerous events without any problems of food contamination.

(www.iht.com, 6 August 2007)

The head of a Chinese toy manufacturing company [Lee Der Industrial] at the centre of a huge US recall [by Mattel] committed suicide [on 11 August] ... [He was] the co-owner of Lee Der ... [and] a supplier, his best friend, sold Lee Der the paint that was used in the toys ... Lead poisoning can cause vomiting, anaemia and learning difficulties. In extreme cases it can cause severe neurological damage and death.

(www.iht.com, 13 August 2007).

While paint containing lead has long been restricted from being used in toys made for the United States, Europe and even China, it remains much cheaper than lead-free paint. Companies here [in China] say paint containing lead is sometimes preferred because it offers richer colours and is easier to apply ... High levels of lead have also been found in Chinese-made jewellery and trinkets.

(www.iht.com, 14 August 2007)

Mattel announced Tuesday [14 August] its second major recall in a month of defective toys that were made in China. The company said it was recalling a total of 436,000 marketed in the United States and elsewhere that had 'impermissible levels of lead'. The toy is a die-cast vehicle featuring the Sarge character from the movie *Cars*. In addition, the company said it was expanding a recall of toys that have small powerful magnets that could become loose and be ingested by children ... Mattel began an advertising campaign Tuesday in an effort to reassure consumers about its commitment to product safety ... Many international toy industry officials say that while the recalls are serious the problem with defective toys made in China is being grossly exaggerated ... 'There are something like 30,000 different toy products on sale at any one time,' says Ian Anderson, the Asia-Pacific director at SGS, a consumer testing company that works with Mattel and other toy makers in China.

(www.iht.com, 14 August 2007)

The latest move [by Mattel] involves toys from a different Chinese contractor than the one that produced toys recalled earlier this month. The separate action Tuesday [14 August] involving 18.2 million magnetic toys, about half of them sold in the United States, expanded a recall initiated last year

> after reports of deaths and injuries to children who ingested magnets that had come loose. Mattel said the recall covered sixty-three different toys, made since 2002 and sold before January of this year [2007] ... The US Consumer Product Safety Commission said Tuesday that all ... the magnetic-based toys ... were from China ... [Mattel] said Tuesday that 65 per cent of its toys are made in China.
>
> (*IHT*, 15 August 2007, pp. 1, 11)

'About 80 per cent of the toys sold in the United States [are] manufactured in China' (www.iht.com, 15 August 2007). '[About] 80 per cent of the $22.3 billion worth of toys sold in the United States were made in China' (www.iht.com, 21 August 2007). 'Mattel has certified only eight paint suppliers. Lee Der bought lead-tainted paint from an uncertified company. Hong Li Da, the subcontractor, used uncertified paint when a tub provided by Early Light ran out' (*IHT*, 29 August 2007, p. 10).

> Mattel has recalled more than 18 million toys worldwide, the second recall in two weeks ... The [US] Consumer Product Safety Commission (CPSC) said it had no reports of any injuries from the recalled products ... Mattel has recalled 253,000 Sarge toy cars in the United States and 183,000 from the rest of the world ... The CPSC said that there had been 400 reports of magnets coming loose since Mattel recalled 2.4 million magnetic play sets in November 2006 ... Mattel is recalling 18.2 million magnetic toys worldwide, 1.9 million of which were sold in the UK.
>
> (www.bbc.co.uk, 14 August 2007)

'Some 80 per cent of the world's toys are made in China' (www.independent.co.uk, 16 August 2007).

'A reported 80 per cent of the world's toy production is in China' (*FEER*, September 2007, p. 15).

'Nokia, the world's largest cellphone maker [based in Finland], warned customers on Tuesday [14 August] that 46 million of its handsets contained defective batteries made in China that could in rare cases overheat and even dislodge during the recharging' (*IHT*, 15 August 2007, p. 1).

'Certain vinyl bibs sold at Toys 'R' Us stores appear to be contaminated with lead, laboratory tests have shown, making inexpensive bibs another example of a made-in-China product that may be a health hazard to children' (*IHT*, 16 August 2007, p. 12).

> Chinese government authorities are prepared to require that every shipment of food being exported to the United States and other countries be inspected for quality by the government, starting 1 September [2007] ... All types of food would be inspected, with at least one box in each shipment checked, and each package or shipment would be affixed with a government seal ... The enhanced food inspections will not mean that every box of food will be inspected by a government official. Instead, every shipment will be checked at some point along the production line and a higher percentage of the food

> in individual shipments will be physically checked … [It was said that the Chinese] government would oppose any mandate that importers hire independent safety laboratories to test all of the Chinese toys destined for the United States. It would also oppose deploying US government toy inspectors to China.
>
> (www.iht.com, 16 August 2007; *IHT*, 17 August 2007, p. 11)

'A global search by John & Jahnson has tracked to China counterfeit versions of an at-home diabetes test used by 10 million Americans to measure blood sugar levels' (www.iht.com, 17 August 2007).

> On Friday [17 August] Thailand's health ministry said about 10 per cent of 11,500 Chinese food products entering its northern border were not up to standard. And Beijing said nearly 15 per cent of Chinese food products had failed a recent quality check.
>
> (www.iht.com, 17 August 2007)

'Thailand this week … [announced] that about 10 per cent of 11,500 Chinese food products coming into the country across its northern borders had been rejected because they contained "hazardous residues of chemicals and pesticides"' (*FT*, 18 August 2007, p. 6).

> More than 99 per cent of China's food exports meet US, EU and Japanese standards, according to a report released by the information office of China's cabinet. The government named deputy prime minister Wu Yi to head a working group on food safety and product quality … China's 2006 food exports rose 13.3 per cent to 24.2 million tonnes, valued at $26.7 billion. Imports rose 7.9 per cent to 20.3 million tonnes, valued at $13.4 billion … In the report Friday the government reiterated previously released figures that 99.2 per cent of Chinese food export shipments last year [2006] to the United States met American standards. That compares with the 99.9 per cent pass rate for exports to the EU and 99.4 per cent to Japan, the report said. To improve quality the Chinese government plans to force small producers to combine into larger, better financed groups that can afford to increase quality and safety measures. Almost 80 per cent of China's food producers are small shops employing fewer than ten workers, according to the report. Up to 30 per cent of the small producers failed quality standards last year, the report said.
>
> (www.iht.com, 17 August 2007)

'The report also cited Japanese data that showed that Chinese food products shipped to Japan were more widely sampled and had a higher acceptance rate in that country than exports from the EU and the United States' (www.iht.com, 23 August 2007)'

'Japanese companies always exported primarily under their own brand names, so the premium market value of branded quality was fundamental to their success. China, by contrast, has developed its export base behind the relative anonymity of an outsourced manufacturing model' (Ken DeWoskin, 'The "made in China" stigma shock', *FEER*, September 2007, p. 10).

Wu Yi [is] a vice premier ... The appointment of Ms Wu, who has long been used by the government as a troubleshooter in trade disputes and health issues, is both a sign of the seriousness of the issue and a convenient way to co-ordinate a response across the government ... The authorities [in China] estimate that 80 per cent of the country's 450,000 food manufacturers have fewer than ten staff, which means they have few resources to spend on safety but are harder to monitor. The government said yesterday [17 August] that 15 per cent of food products had failed quality checks in the first six months of the year [2007].

(*FT*, 18 August 2007, p. 6)

'Deputy prime minister Wu Yi [is] a tough bureaucrat who negotiated the entry of China into the WTO ... Wu, who some analysts regard as a government troubleshooter, was also drafted to lead the fight against the 2003 SARS outbreak' (www.iht.com, 23 August 2007).

Britain's biggest toy store and the high street fashion chain Monsoon have been selling children's jewellery imported from China containing levels of lead that can potentially cause brain damage and even kill. Of twenty-four items of children's jewellery bought in London and Birmingham, eight tested positive for high levels of lead. Six items had one or more components with more than 80 per cent lead, compared with a recommended international safety limit of 0.06 per cent. Among the items that had high levels of the metal were two from Hamleys in Regent Street, central London, including a bracelet with heart shapes containing more than 93 per cent lead and two from Monsoon Accessorize, including a pink skull and crossbones that contained more than 59 per cent lead ... Senior figures in the jewellery industry say one of the reasons for the use of lead in children's trinkets in the UK is there are no specific regulations on the level permitted. Levels are strictly controlled in toys and even a watch should not contain more than 0.1 per cent lead.

(*The Sunday Times*, 19 August 2007, p. 1)

'*The Sunday Times* exposed [the problem] ... [For example] a P-shaped pendant was found to have 27 per cent lead ... There are no regulations [in the UK] stipulating levels in children's jewellery' (www.bbc.co.uk, 19 August 2007).

Last year [2006] there were about twelve US recalls of Chinese-made jewellery because of excessive levels of lead. In the first eight months of this year [2007] – possibly because of heightened regulatory scrutiny – there have already been twenty-two recalls of children's jewellery, twenty-one of which were products made in China. All told, of the approximately thirty-nine lead-related US recalls this year, thirty-eight were of Chinese-made goods.

(www.iht.com, 11 September 2007)

> [On 19 August] Li Changjiang, director of the general administration of quality supervision, inspection and quarantine, said he believed there was a 'new trend in trade protectionism' … China is the source of close to half of all problem consumer goods – excluding food – seized by the EU last year [2006]. To some extent this reflects trade flows, since over a quarter of all goods the EU imports are from China.
>
> (*IHT*, 21 August 2007, p. 10)

'State controlled media on Sunday [19 August] began broadcasting a week-long television series, "Believe in made in China"' (*IHT*, 24 August 2007, p. 10).

> China, the world's biggest buyer of soybeans, said Wednesday [22 August] that it had recently found 'substantial' quality-related problems with imports of the US oilseed and urged Washington to investigate and improve its procedures … The problems with the soybeans indicate there are 'holes' in the US production, transportation, export inspection and quarantine processes, the Beijing statement said. It did not list specific shipments or companies … In the past the practice was to destroy the problematic shipments on arrival under the supervision of inspectors.
>
> (www.iht.com, 22 August 2007)

> The General Administration of Quality Supervision, Inspection and Quarantine said it had found 'numerous quality problems' with soybeans imported from the United States. The quality watchdog said it had found pesticides, poisonous weeds and dirt in the US exports … Mattel, which recalled 19 million Chinese-made items contaminated with lead paint, is partly to blame for the problems, said the executive vice chairman of the Guangdong provincial toy industry association … Blankets made in China and found to contain high levels of formaldehyde have been recalled across Australia and New Zealand, the distributor said Wednesday, as retailers sought urgent testing of clothing imports from China.
>
> (*IHT*, 23 August 2007, p. 11)

'Senior Chinese officials say that foreign companies, including Mattel … should also shoulder some of the blame for failing to detect defective or dangerous products' (www.iht.com, 23 August 2007).

> Two more US firms have recalled Chinese-made toys, saying they include paint with dangerous levels of lead … The recall of about 300,000 toys comes a week after US firm Mattel recalled 18.5 million toys … Ohio firm Martin Designs and Schyllings Associates of Massachusetts issued the recall through the US Consumer Product Safety Commission.
>
> (www.bbc.co.uk, 22 August 2007)

'In the latest toy recall the US Consumer Product Safety Commission issued a notice Wednesday [22 August] covering more than 300,000 Chinese-made products for children because they may contain excessive levels of lead' (www.iht.com, 23 August 2007).

Lead paint is cheaper ... Paint with higher levels of lead often costs a third as much as paint with low levels of lead ... A [toy] company in Shantou, in southern China, said leaded paint was about 30 per cent cheaper than non-leaded paint ... In addition to importing lead-containing waste ... [e.g.] from electronic waste shipped from the United States ... China is the world's largest miner and producer of lead, much of which goes into battery production ... On the books China's paint standards are stricter than those in the United States, requiring that paint intended for household or consumer-product use contain no more than ninety parts per million. By comparison, US regulations allow 600 parts per million. Those regulations are supposed to safeguard health, particularly in children, as ingesting lead has been linked to everything from the retardation of physical and mental development to behavioural problems. But enforcement of the regulations in China is lax ... Another problem in China is the abundant supply of industrial paint, used on everything from buildings, bridges and cars to sidewalks, railings and other outdoor surfaces. Several paint companies said the government [in China] has no restrictions on lead in industrial paint. As a result a lot of cheap industrial paint may be finding its way into toy factories and even households. While the United States still allows paint with higher levels of lead to be used outdoors and in many industrial settings, such paint is slowly being phased out of even industrial use ... partly because it can pose dangers to work crews who apply or remove it ... Heavy exposure to environmental lead has serious health effects. It can linger in the air, leech into water supplies and crops, and coat outdoor surfaces. It is those dangers that have led much of the world to move away from the leaded products that China still uses.

(www.iht.com, 11 September 2007)

China had launched a four-month 'war' on tainted food, drugs and exports, state media reported on Friday [24 August] ... Vice premier Wu Yi told officials the campaign, to run to the end of the year [2007], would focus on problem products that have badly dented domestic and foreign consumers' confidence in the 'Made in China' label ... Wu Yi: 'This is a special battle to protect the health and personal interests of the public and to protect the reputation of Chinese goods and the national image ... In some businesses the management level is low, production conditions are poor, quantity levels and standards are low, and reliability is weak' ... Wu blamed lax inspection and enforcement and failure of officials in rival agencies to co-operate. She vowed to whip them into line with a list of eight tasks and twenty specific goals.

(www.cnn.com, 24 August 2007)

China hit back on Monday [27 August] after Mattel's massive toy recall, saying designers and importers should also take responsibility for product safety, but promised to punish its own manufacturers who flout standards. The world's largest toymaker recalled more than 18 million Chinese-made toys this month because of hazards from small magnets that can cause injury if swallowed … Li Changjiang (head of China's General Administration for Quality Supervision, Inspection and Quarantine): 'I myself looked at some of the samples of these problematic toys and I found that there is a serious problem with the design. The design is seriously defective. In my view, no matter where those toys were sold there would be a recall because it is highly likely they are dangerous for children. While we recognize that Chinese producers should be blamed for those problematic toys, what kind of responsibility should the US designers and the US importers take in this respect?' … On Monday he blamed differing national standards, misleading statistics and lack of communication for some of the product safety scares … 'For some products, the two countries enforce different standards,' Li said of China and the United States, also citing 'inaccurate statistics'. But he said the latest Chinese campaign to improve product safety would focus on creating a chain of supervision across the entire production process for both industrial products and food. Monitoring and inspection of drug manufacturers would also be strengthened, and celebrities banned from endorsing drugs in advertising, Li said. The country's certification body also plans to strengthen controls of export permits for toys, the official Xinhua agency said on Monday. Li acknowledged the vast challenge China faces in overseeing its hundreds of thousands of tiny, often family-run producers, a task compounded by lack of communication between myriad government agencies overseeing production and safety standards, and between central and local authorities. But he defended the 'made in China' label … Li Changjiang: 'In China about 3 million workers are working in the toy industry, providing toys to children all across the world. It is because of their hard work that children in other parts of the world are having fun in their daily life.'

(www.cnn.com, 27 August 2007)

[In late August a] poll found that 57 per cent of America consumers are either 'not too confident' or 'not at all confident' in the safety of products made in China. And while 65 per cent said they felt the US government was not doing enough to assure the safety of such imports, about the same number, 64 per cent, laid 'a lot of blame' for the problem with the Chinese manufacturers.

(*FEER*, September 2007, p. 9)

Toys 'R' Us, the biggest US toy store chain, recalled 27,000 crayon and paint box sets made in China because ink on the wooden cases contains lead … Some of the black watercolour paint also contained 'excessive' levels of lead … the US Consumer Product Safety Commission said.

(*FT*, 31 August 2007, p. 8)

'[On 1 September] the authorities implemented a nationwide recall system for consumer goods' (*FT*, 5 September 2007, p. 10).

'China's General Administration of Quality Supervision and Quarantine announced that all major food exports produced from 1 September onward must carry labels to show they have passed inspection' (www.iht.com, 3 September 2007).

> Beijing introduced a new food and toy recall system last week and also announced what it called a 'special war' to crack down on poor quality products and unlicensed manufacturers ... Beginning last weekend regulators also said food packages that did not contain a quarantine label certifying them as safe were blocked from being exported ... Two weeks ago New Zealand said it was investigating reports about what some called 'chemical pyjamas', Chinese-made clothing that some scientists said contained dangerous levels of toxic formaldehyde. And late last week Canada announced it was recalling thousands of pencils made in China because of fears they were coated with too much lead. Beijing, however, has made food safety one of its first initiatives. The government says it plans to spend $1.1 billion to improve food and drug safety by 2010. The government also said that under the new recall system announced last week producers would be held accountable for products that posed a danger to public safety. The government even issued a lengthy 'white paper' on food safety and said it would begin offering rewards to those who blow the whistle on bad producers ... White mice will be used to test most food served to athletes [during the Olympics] and pigs are already being bred organically in secret locations. Global position, or GPS, technology is being employed to track the whereabouts of some animals.
>
> (*IHT*, 5 September 2007, p. 9)

> Mattel announced a global recall of 848,000 toys last night [4 September], the company's third recent recall because of hazardous levels of lead paint on toys. The recall includes three toys sold by Fisher-Price [including toy trains] and eight Barbie accessories, though no Barbie dolls. Most of the units recalled are Barbie accessories, and 530,000 of the toys were sold in the United States, according to Mattel ... Mattel has stepped up testing of toy production and has nearly concluded its testing of recently made toys, the company said last night ... Mattel, long known for its rigorous safety checks, has quickly become the best known company announcing recalls of Chinese products ... The US Consumer Product Safety Commission announced that 773,900 toys in the United States were being recalled. Mattel, standing by its figure of 530,000, said that figure was incorrect.
>
> (www.iht.com, 5 September 2007)

'Mattel announced that it was recalling 800,000 toys, including 675,000 accessories for one of the company's biggest sellers, the Barbie doll ... In July Hasbro recalled Chinese-made Easy Bake ovens on reports of second- and third-degree burns to children' (*IHT*, 6 September 2007, p. 12).

'Mattel said that 522,000 of the recalled toys were sold in the United States, 2,500 in the UK and 320,000 in the rest of the world' (www.guardian.co.uk, 5 September 2007).

> *The Wall Street Journal* reported this week that Mattel ... has delayed reporting defects to the government because it thinks the reporting rules are unreasonable. The Consumer Product Safety Commission, which requires companies to report potential hazards within twenty-four hours of their discovery, has fined Mattel twice for such delays since 2001: once because it waited about two years before reporting a fire hazard in its Power Wheels motorized mini-cars and on another occasion because it took months to report loose screws on its Little People Animal Sounds Farm. The commission is now investigating Mattel's recent handling of toys containing tiny magnets that, if swallowed, could puncture a toddler's stomach lining. Though the company recalled 2 million Polly Pocket figurines with these magnets last November [2006] it wasn't until August that it recalled another 18 million toys that were studded with the magnets ... The commission's fines ... [are] puny ... [being] capped at less than $2 million.
>
> (*IHT*, 7 September 2007, p. 4)

> The largest US toy makers have taken the unusual step of asking the federal government to impose mandatory safety-testing standards for all toys sold in the United States ... The industry is asking that safety tests be required of toy companies big and small ... The proposal, approved by the board of the Toy Industry Association at a meeting last week, does not envision a broad federal inspection programme. Instead, companies would be required to hire independent laboratories to check a certain portion of their toys, whether made in the United States or overseas. Leading companies already do such testing, but industry officials acknowledge that it has not been enough ... The proposal calls for uniform standards for frequency of testing, to determine at what point during production the test would be conducted and what specific hazards, whether lead paint or small parts, must be checked for. The uniform standards would also establish global requirements for laboratories that do this testing ... Small companies that currently do little or no testing would be required to pay for testing as well. Europeans already require that toys and certain other products undergo such testing, and they affix a certification mark to products before they are sold. The United States has no such pre-market requirement ... The Consumer Product Safety Commission has extremely limited capacity to test toys: it employs only one full-time toy tester at its laboratory in Maryland.
>
> (*IHT*, 8 September 2007)

'The Consumer Product Safety Commission has a $63 million budget and a full-time staff of about 400 people to monitor billions of dollars' worth of goods' (www.iht.com, 9 September 2007).

> China signed an agreement yesterday [11 September] to prohibit the use of lead paint on toys exported to the United States ... The agreement was

> unveiled during the second US–China summit on consumer product safety … Beijing also pledged to step up inspections of its exports and to take steps to ensure those products met US standards.
>
> (*FT*, 12 September 2007, p. 6)

'Beijing has rejected consignments of pork from the United States and Canada because they contain a banned additive, in spite of a shortage of China's staple meat … The discovery [was made] of ractopamine residue' (*FT*, 17 September 2007, p. 6).

> On Saturday [15 September] Beijing said it rejected 18.4 tonnes of American pork because it contained ractopamine, a drug that is used by US hog farmers to produce leaner meat but is banned in China … China has sharply increased inspections of imported US food, escalating its spat with Washington over product safety and leaving American beef piling up in warehouses and delaying shipments of black pepper and other goods. Authorities who used to inspect as little as 5 per cent of imported goods now check every shipment of American poultry, snack foods and other goods, companies and trade groups say … The Administration for Quality Supervision, Inspection and Quarantine said in June it would step up inspections of US food for chemical or biological contamination. It cited the discovery of excessive bacteria and sulphur dioxide in raisins, dried oranges and health care products from several American companies … There was no immediate impact on shipments of soybeans, the biggest US agricultural export to China … Chinese grocery stores and importers said that so far they have seen little impact on their business from the increased inspections.
>
> (www.iht.com, 17 September 2007)

> Mattel … issued an extraordinary apology to China on Friday [21 September] over the recall of Chinese-made toys, taking the blame for design flaws and saying it had recalled more lead-tainted toys than justified. The gesture by Thomas Debrowski, Mattel's executive vice president for worldwide operations, came in a meeting with the Chinese product safety chief, Li Changjiang, at which Li upbraided the company for maintaining weak safety controls … Mattel ordered three high-profile recalls this summer involving more than 21 million Chinese-made toys, including Barbie doll accessories and toy cars, because of concerns about lead paint and tiny magnets that could be swallowed. The recalls have prompted complaints from China that manufacturers were being blamed for design faults introduced by Mattel … Tests had found that lead levels in paint in recalled toys were as high as 110,000 parts per million, or nearly 200 times higher than the accepted safety ceiling of 600 per million … China has become a centre of the world's toy-making industry, exporting $7.5 billion worth of toys last year [2006].
>
> (www.iht.com, 21 September 2007)

> Mattel has been in China for twenty-five years and about 65 per cent of its products are made in China. Debrowski said the company was committed to

> manufacturing in China and was also investing $30 million in a Barbie store in Shanghai … The official Xinhua news agency quoted Li as saying that police had detained four Chinese nationals accused of having supplied one of Mattel's contract manufacturers, the Lida Toy Company, with the substandard paint behind the first recall in August. The head of Lida, Zhang Shuhong, a Hong Kong businessman in his fifties, killed himself after the recall.
>
> (*IHT*, 22 September 2007, pp. 1, 22)

Thomas Debrowski (Mattel's executive vice president for worldwide operations):

> Our reputation has been damaged lately by these recalls. And Mattel takes full responsibility for these recalls and apologizes personally to you, the Chinese people, and all of our customers who received the toys … It is important for everyone to understand that the vast majority of these products that we recalled were the result of a flaw in Mattel's design, not through a manufacturing flaw in Chinese manufacturers … We understand and appreciate deeply the issues that this has caused for the reputation of Chinese manufacturers.
>
> (www.iht.com, 21 September 2007; www.bbc.co.uk, 21 September 2007)

The Mattel statement:

> Mattel is committed to applying the highest standards of safety for its products. Consistent with this, Mattel's lead-related recalls were overly inclusive, including toys that may not have had lead in paint in excess of US standards. The follow-up inspections also confirmed that part of the recalled toys complied with the US standards.
>
> (www.ft.com, 21 September 2007; www.iht.com, 21 September 2007)

> Mattel's statement comes after a recent report by Professor Paul Beamish from the Richard Ivey School of Business, and Hari Bapuji from the University of Manitoba, indicating that fewer than 10 per cent of product recalls since 1988 in the United States have been due to manufacturing defects, and that more than 75 per cent stemmed from design flaws.
>
> (www.ft.com, 21 September 2007)

'Unlike the lead paint, the magnets recall was due to a design fault, not the result of Chinese factories cutting corners' (*FT*, 22 September 2007, p. 14).

'Mattel admitted that of 21 million products recalled, 87 per cent were for design faults and only 13 per cent because of the lead paint' (*The Times*, 22 September 2007, p. 47).

'Simplicity, a US-based baby products manufacturer, yesterday [21 September] recalled 1 million Chinese-made cots over a design flaw that has been blamed for the deaths of two infants' (*FT*, 22 September 2007, p. 15). 'One million Chinese-manufactured cots were recalled … although this was due to a design fault' (p. 14).

The apology was late, reluctant and was no sooner made than it was partly retracted ... A few hours later Mattel said that the nature of the meeting had been 'mischaracterized'. The apology in Beijing was not a kowtow to the Chinese, it said, but merely an elaboration of the apology it had already made to consumers all over the world. Thomas Debrowski had not intended to talk to Li Changjiang in the presence of journalists, but Chinese officials made it a condition for the meeting ... On 5 September Mattel had told an American Congressional committee that its recall of 17.4 million toys containing a small magnet that could be swallowed by children was due to a flaw in the toys' design, rather than production flaws in China. As for some other toys recalled because of allegedly hazardous levels of lead in their paint, Mattel admitted that it had been overzealous and is likely to have recalled toys that did not contravene American regulations on lead content.

(*The Economist*, 29 September 2007)

China has sponsored quality control training for more than 1,000 people in the country's toy industry in an effort to ensure the safety of exports, state media said Sunday [14 October] ... The two-day sessions began Thursday [11 October] ... China is the world's largest toy manufacturer, exporting 22 billion toys last year [2006], about 60 per cent of the world's total.

(www.iht.com, 14 October 2007)

A slew of products made in China, ranging from children's jewellery to cake decorations, were recalled because they contain excessive amounts of lead. The recall of roughly 665,000 items [was] announced by the [US] Consumer Product Safety Commission ... Mattel is also recalling 12,000 toys in Britain and Ireland due to excessive levels of lead paint found in the products.

(*IHT*, 26 October 2007, p. 13)

China said Monday that it had arrested 774 people over the past two months as part of a nationwide crackdown on the production and sale of tainted food and agricultural products ... [The government undertook] a four-month campaign to root out bad food and drug producers and sellers ... But the government acknowledged Monday [29 October] that as of earlier this month [October] only 82 per cent of the food tested in medium and large cities in China met food safety standards, and that nearly 30 per cent of the restaurants surveyed by regulators had failed food safety inspections ... Trade statistics, though, show that with few exceptions Chinese exports to the rest of the world continue to soar, even toys, seafood and agricultural products.

(www.iht.com, 29 October 2007)

China has approved new legislation aimed at improving national standards in food production ... New laws will standardize food production and clamp down on illegal activity in the industry ... The new law replaces the existing patchwork of rules which are overseen by several government agencies ...

> China announced this week that 774 people have been arrested so far during investigations into the manufacture and sale of substandard food and drugs.
>
> (www.bbc.co.uk, 31 October 2007)

> Chemical manufacturers that sell drug ingredients fall into a regulatory hole. Pharmaceutical companies are regulated by the food and drug agency. Chemical companies that make products as varied as fertilizer and industrial solvents are overseen by other agencies.
>
> (www.iht.com, 31 October 2007)

> Chinese regulators said Thursday [1 November] that they had suspended the export licences of more than 700 toy companies because of quality control problems … The government also said that another 690 toy factories in southern China were ordered to improve their facilities or face similar punishment … More than 5,000 toymakers [are] believed to be operating in southern China, the world's largest toy manufacturing centre.
>
> (*IHT*, 2 November 2007, p. 9)

> Poisonous toy beads from China were not under suspicion when an Australian biochemist began trying last month [October] to figure out why a two-year-old boy had fallen into a shallow coma with seizure-like movements and been rushed to hospital … What he [the doctor] found was gamma hydroxybutyrate, or GHB, a banned 'date rape' drug that can be life threatening … [The doctor concluded] that the boy had eaten Bindeez toy beads coated with a glue compound that the boy's digestive system had converted into GHB. At least four other children have been temporarily hospitalized in Australia and New Zealand in the past three weeks after eating the beads. The toy's distributor Moose Enterprise of Australia ordered a recall this week [6 November] of Bindeez … Australia's toy of the year … Toy stores in Australia, New Zealand, Hong Kong, Malaysia and Singapore have begun taking beads off their shelves.
>
> (*IHT*, 8 November 2007, p. 1)

'US safety officials have recalled about 4.2 million Chinese-made Aqua Dots bead toys that contain a chemical that has caused some children to vomit and become comatose after swallowing them' (www.cnn.com, 8 November 2007).

> China's government has suspended exports of toys covered with a toxic chemical that have been subject to recalls from Australia to the United States after sickening children … The government's quality control administration issued the export ban … Millions of units of the popular toys, which are sold as Aqua Dots in the United States and as Bindeez in Australia, were recalled in those countries as well as in Britain, Malaysia, Singapore and elsewhere this past week after children began falling sick from swallowing the toy's bead-like parts. Test showed they were coated with the industrial chemical 1,4-butanediol. When ingested the chemical metabolizes into the 'date-rape' drug gamma hydroxybutyrate, and may cause breathing

problems, loss of consciousness, seizures, drowsiness, coma and death. At least nine children in the United States and three in Australia have taken sick ... Companies worldwide have increasingly outsourced manufacturing, often choosing Chinese factories for their cost and quality. But heated competition among factories and the rising cost of labour, land and fuel have sometimes put pressure on profits, causing some to cut corners. In the latest case the Aqua Dots or Bindeez were supposed to have been coated with non-toxic 1,5-pentanediol ... But that chemical generally sells for three to four times the price of the toxic compound found on the tainted toys, 1,4-butanediol.

(www.iht.com, 11 November 2007)

The Chinese government announced that it had confirmed the presence of poison on toy beads exported around the world, while in the United States the Consumer Product Safety Commission said that seven more children had been sickened. The Chinese government's General Administration of Quality Supervision. Inspection and Quarantine also identified the factory that manufactured the beads, the Wangqi Product Factory in the south-eastern city of Shenzhen. It said that the factory's export licence had been suspended. The Chinese response to the poisonous toy beads, which came late Saturday [10 November], represents an unusually swift reaction ... The US Consumer Product Safety Commission said that the number of children in the United States sickened by Aqua Dots had risen to nine from two in the past week ... The bead toys are distributed in about forty countries across Asia and Europe.

(www.iht.com, 11 November 2007)

The Hong Kong company that manufactured millions of poisonous toy beads in mainland China issued a public apology Thursday [29 November], with the chairman saying that it had not occurred to anyone to check whether an inexpensive glue ingredient on the beads would be dangerous for children to eat. The beads ... were recalled this month [November] after at least fourteen children became sick when they ate the beads. Several of the children briefly fell into comas ... [The company chairman said it] had chosen a glue ingredient for the beads that cost only half as much as the glue ingredient that the Australian distributor of the beads, Moose Enterprise, thought was being used to soften the plastic beads. But he insisted that the choice of the inexpensive but hazardous ingredient, which is also needed to soften the plastic beads, had not been made for cost reasons.

(www.iht.com, 29 November 2007; *IHT*, 30 November 2007, p. 10)

A toy face-and-body paint made in China that the authorities ... in Hong Kong ... say poses a high risk of poisoning was withdrawn from the market Wednesday [5 December] ... The toy, marketed in Hong Kong as Six Colours face-and-body makeup colour paint, was found by a government laboratory to contain dangerous levels of lead, chromium and barium ...

> A spokeswoman for the Hong Kong Customs and Excise Department … said it was not known where outside Hong Kong the mainland-manufactured product had been sold. She declined to name the manufacturer.
>
> (www.iht.com, 5 December 2007)

'The tainted pet food scare is believed to have caused the death of at least 300 dogs and cats this year' (*IHT*, 22 December 2007).

> China said that it would introduce new production standards, including several measures aimed at improving product safety and guarding against the use of illegal veterinary drugs. The ministry of agriculture said … that the new standards would cover more than 100 categories, including breeding fish, seafood products, disease prevention and drug controls … China is the world's largest producer and exporter of seafood … The ministry of agriculture said this week that the agency would strengthen law enforcement in the industry with certificates, drug usage sales and production licences. The government also said it would work to produce a more environmentally friendly mode of seafood production.
>
> (www.iht.com, 27 December 2007; *IHT*, 28 December 2007, p. 12)

> In August [2007] the government undertook its most extensive public safety campaign since it mobilized to fight the 2002 outbreak of SARS. The new campaign's goal: to shore up China's battered reputation as a manufacturer of quality goods. The four-month initiative … ended in December and experts say that China has taken significant steps toward addressing product quality and safety problems. But they also note the risk of backsliding in a country with a convoluted bureaucracy and a well-documented history of local leaders ignoring edicts from the top … While the high profile campaign has ended, the government is continuing work on several fronts, including developing the first food safety law in China … [China's] top problem solver, vice premier Wu Yi, [was appointed] to head a cabinet-level panel overseeing the campaign … One month into the product safety campaign Wu set out to randomly inspect shops and restaurants in the eastern province of Zhejiang … Thousands of unlicensed manufacturers were reportedly shut down. Teams of inspectors were dispatched and labels showing that the quality of export food products had been checked became mandatory.
>
> (*IHT*, 8 January 2008, p. 12)

> The ministry of agriculture said a recent nationwide crackdown on the use of illegal veterinary drugs had already significantly improved the quality and safety of the country's seafood production … But officials from the ministry's fisheries bureau also said that pollution and water quality problems had become the biggest challenges facing China's fish farming or aquaculture industry, something they have rarely acknowledged in public … China is now the leading producer and exporter of seafood in the world and an important supplier to the United States and Japan … After years of spec-

tacular growth this country's booming seafood industry is being threatened by water shortages, contaminated water supplies and illegal veterinary drug use ... Experts in Beijing say fish farmers often turn to illegal veterinary drugs because they can help keep fish alive in overcrowded fish ponds that are sometimes contaminated by sewage, agricultural run-off and industrial chemicals ... But China has also lashed out at the United States and other countries that have blocked its food exports, insisting that the vast majority are safe and meet quality standards and that media coverage has often been sensational and distorted ... China said its seafood exports grew to a record $8.7 billion in the year through November [2007], although the rate of growth slowed to about 4 per cent from 19 per cent a year earlier.

(www.iht.com, 17 January 2008; *IHT*, 18 January 2008, p. 15)

A huge state-owned Chinese pharmaceutical company that exports to dozens of countries, including the United States, is at the centre of a nationwide drug scandal after nearly 200 Chinese cancer patients were paralysed or otherwise harmed last summer [2007] by contaminated leukaemia drugs. Chinese drug regulators have accused the manufacturer of the tainted drugs of a cover-up and have closed the factory that produced them. In December [2007] the Chinese State Food and Drug Administration said the Shanghai police had begun a criminal investigation and that two officials, including the head of the plant, had been detained ... Shanghai Hualian is a division of one of China's largest pharmaceutical companies, the Shanghai Pharmaceutical Group, which owns dozens of factories ... In the last two years scores of people around the world have died after ingesting contaminated drugs and drug ingredients produced in China. Last year [2007] China executed its top drug safety official for accepting bribes to approve drugs ... Hualian is the latest in a string of tainted medicine cases ... In 2006 at least eighteen Chinese died after an intravenous drug used to treat liver disease was laced with diethylene glycol, a toxic chemical used in some antifreeze. Also in 2006 at least fourteen Chinese died after taking a Chinese antibiotic which was not properly sterilized during production. And more than 100 people died in Panama after taking cold medicine containing a mislabelled and toxic chemical from China.

(www.iht.com, 31 January 2008; *IHT*, 1 February 2008, p. 14)

Dozens of Japanese people say they have fallen ill after eating Chinese-made dumplings ... Japanese officials said they contained traces of pesticide, probably added in production or packaging in China. China said no traces of pesticide had been found in pre-export inspections, but ordered a halt to production.

(www.bbc.co.uk, 31 January 2008)

The [Japanese] government said Friday [1 February] that at least 175 people in Japan were sickened by the insecticide-tainted dumplings from China, prompting supermarkets to pull Chinese-made meat products from their shelves while Tokyo pressed Beijing to improve food safety. Newspaper headlines warned of a national panic as hundreds more people complained of dizziness and nausea after eating dumplings and other Chinese-made foods. As of Friday, a dozen Japanese food processing companies said they had issued recalls for at least fifty-nine meat products imported from China, from beef jerky to pork chops. All those products came from the same Chinese company that produced the tainted dumplings, Tianyang Food Processing in Hebei province ... While pesticide has only been found in the dumplings, the [Japanese health] ministry said it had halted sale of all the Chinese company's products ... [The] agricultural pesticide, methamidophos, is used in China but is not common in Japan.

(www.iht.com, 1 February 2008)

Pesticide-laced Chinese dumplings that sickened at least ten people in Japan and triggered a nationwide scare were probably poisoned deliberately, Japan's health minister said Tuesday [5 February] ... Investigators found traces of the pesticide on the outside of the dumplings, rather than in the filling. The poison was also found in much higher concentrations than would be expected from residue from pesticides sprayed on vegetables.

(www.iht.com, 5 February 2008)

'Opponents of Chinese government relations with Japan may have contaminated Chinese-made dumplings that sickened ten people in Japan ... a senior Chinese food safety official said Wednesday [6 February]' (*IHT*, 7 February 2008, p. 19).

The Chinese authorities spoke yesterday [28 February]: 'After careful investigation and tests, we believe there is little chance that methamidophos [the pesticide] was put into dumplings in China ... We conclude that the dumpling poisoning is an individual contrived case instead of a case of food safety resulting from pesticide residue.'

(*FT*, 29 February 2008, p. 8)

Two Chinese companies and an American importer have been indicted [in the United States] on charges on intentionally defrauding and misleading American manufacturers about poisonous ingredients used in pet food last year [2007]. Tainted wheat gluten, used as an ingredient in moist pet food, killed at least sixteen dogs and cats, sickened thousands of others and led to one of the biggest pet food recalls in US history ... It was a prelude to scores of other recalls of Chinese-made products last year, including tyres, fish, children's jewellery and toys. The US federal indictment on Wednesday [6 February], citing email traffic between the Chinese manufacturer and the American importer, says the importer of the tainted ingredient knew it was being mislabelled to avoid inspection ... Melamine [was added] to make the wheat gluten appear higher in protein ... Melamine, which can be toxic when ingested, is used in many industrial products like glues, inks and fertilizers, but has no approved uses in food in the United States. The US

Food and Drug Administration found the melamine in the wheat gluten in late March [2006] and determined that it had been used in the wheat gluten ... shipped from November 2006 to February 2007.

(www.iht.com, 7 February 2008)

The Chinese processor is charged with lacing the product with melamine, an inexpensive additive that can make the wheat gluten look like it contains more protein than it actually does. The export broker is accused of mislabelling the shipments with an inaccurate product code to escape mandatory inspections in China ... [The US importer] is accused of knowing that the shipments had been miscoded – and would not be inspected in China – yet failed to disclose that to American manufacturers who bought the gluten.

(www.iht.com, 10 February 2008)

'Last year [2007] 800 tonnes of wheat gluten from China tainted with melamine was sold to US pet food makers, triggering millions of recalls there and killing over 200 cats and 100 dogs' (*IHT*, 18 March 2008, p. 15).

'Last spring [2007] hundreds if not thousands of pets died or were sickened in the United States by a Chinese pet food ingredient that contained lethal levels of melamine' (www.iht.com, 30 March 2008).

An unusual coalition of scientists, public health workers and police investigators used an innovative form of pollen analysis to help track down the source of ... [the counterfeit] anti-malarial medicine, artesunate ... Artesunate, developed by the Chinese and derived from a plant called sweet wormwood, is part of a therapy that has become a cornerstone in the fight against malaria ... More than a million people [worldwide] are believed to die each year from the disease ... [The investigation led] to the arrest of an organized crime ring that funnelled the fake drugs from China into South-east Asian countries ... [The] fake drugs [were traced] to an illegal factory on the outskirts of Puning, a city in Guangdong province ... The investigation was coordinated by Interpol, the World Health Organization and the Wellcome Trust, a medical research charity based in Britain ... Using forensic palynology, the analysis of pollen and powdered minerals, investigators traced some of the fake drugs to southern Russia, close to the border with Vietnam, Laos and Myanmar ... Late last month [January] deputy prime minister Wu Ti and China's top regulator Shao Mingli said separately that, partly because of concerns about counterfeiting, the government intended to crack down on chemical companies illegally producing drugs.

(*IHT*, 13 February 2008, p. 15)

Panamanian investigators have concluded that at least 174 people were poisoned. 115 of them fatally, by counterfeit cold medicine linked to an unlicensed Chinese chemical plant. The report was the government's first effort to offer a precise toll of those killed and disabled in the mass poisoning in 2006. But the head of the agency that prepared the report ... said the number of victims was bound to be much higher because many in remote areas of the country were unlikely to report their cases … Previously the government had estimated the death toll at 100 … In 128 cases the government said it lacked enough information to reach a definitive conclusion.

(www.iht.com, 14 February 2008)

A Chinese factory that supplies much of the active ingredient for a brand of a blood thinner that has been linked to four deaths in the United States is not certified by China's drug regulators to make pharmaceutical products … Because the plant, Changzhou SPL, has no drug certification, China's drug agency did not inspect it. The United States Food and Drug Administration said this week that it had not inspected the plant either – a violation of its own policy – before allowing the company to become a major supplier of the blood thinner, heparin, to Baxter International in the United States. Baxter announced Monday [11 February] that it was suspending sales of its multidose vials of heparin after four patients died and 350 suffered complications … China provides a growing proportion of the active pharmaceutical ingredients used in drugs sold in the United States. And Chinese drug regulators have said that all producers of those ingredients are required to obtain certification by the State Food and Drug Administration. However, some of the active ingredients that China exports are made by chemical companies, which do not fall under the Chinese drug agency's jurisdiction. In December [2007] American and Chinese regulators signed an agreement under which China promised to begin registering at least some of the thousands of chemical companies that sell drug ingredients. Some of these companies are the source of counterfeit or diluted drugs, including those used to treat malaria … The heparin plant in China has not been accused of providing a harmful product. The American owner of the plant, Scientific Protein Laboratories, also owns a plant in Wisconsin that produces the active ingredient in heparin for Baxter.

(www.iht.com, 17 February 2008)

Amid indications that more people may have died or been harmed after being given a brand of the blood thinner heparin, US federal drug regulators said Thursday [29 February] that they had found 'potential deficiencies' at a Chinese plant that supplied much of the active ingredient for the drug … The Food and Drug Administration emphasized that it had yet to identify the root cause of the problem and that it had not concluded that the Chinese plant was responsible … [A US] company is the majority owner of the Chinese plant … The Chinese heparin market has been in turmoil over the last year, as pig disease has swept through the country, depleting stocks, leading some farmers to sell sick pigs into the market and forcing heparin producers to scramble for new sources of raw material. As a result, even big companies have been turning increasingly to small village workshops, which are often unsanitary.

(www.iht.com, 29 February 2008)

> US government drug regulators have discovered that a crucial blood thinner that has been linked to at least nineteen deaths and whose raw components are produced in China contained a possibly counterfeit ingredient that mimicked the real drug. Routine tests failed to distinguish the contaminant from the drug, heparin. Only sophisticated magnetic resonance imaging tests uncovered that as much as 20 per cent of the product's active ingredient was a heparin mimic blended in with the real thing ... The US Food and Drug Administration: 'At this point we do not know whether the introduction was accidental or whether it was deliberate.'
>
> (www.iht.com, 6 March 2008)

> Concerns about the safety of the blood thinner heparin have spread to Germany after drug authorities there received reports of patients being sickened after getting the drug ... Germany has reported fewer than 100 cases of patients suffering severe allergic reactions and shock, and no deaths ... Meanwhile, US Food and Drug Administration officials also announced Thursday [6 March] that they were asking all companies in the United States that produce heparin to test it with two new procedures ... Federal officials said they could not yet say that the contaminant, which mimics real heparin, caused the reactions ... FDA officials declined to say whether the raw ingredients for the suspect heparin came from China ... Most of the world's heparin supply is from China.
>
> (www.iht.com, 7 March 2008)

'German authorities confirmed Friday that they had recalled German-manufactured products containing heparin' (*IHT*, 8 March 2008, p. 3).

> China and the United States are working together to investigate the blood-thinner heparin, which has been linked to nineteen American deaths, the Chinese State Food and Drug Administration said Sunday [16 March] ... [It said that] US and Chinese officials have been investigating heparin samples but have reached no conclusions.
>
> (www.iht.com, 16 March 2008)

> Scientists investigating a mystery contaminant in the blood thinner heparin are closing in on what they believe is a counterfeit substance, most likely made in China from animal cartilage, that was chemically altered to act like the real drug ... Even so researchers said they were not certain that the contaminant, constituting between 5 per cent and 20 per cent of the drug, is what is causing the allergic reactions, nor do they know precisely how or when it was mixed into the active ingredient.
>
> (www.iht.com, 19 March 2008)

'The Chinese drug safety regulator ... has ordered the local authorities to tighten controls on production of heparin' (*IHT*, 22 March 2008, p. 18).

> More than 500 plants in China export drug ingredients to the United States but the United States Food and Drug Administration inspected only thirteen

of them last year [2007]. One of the plants not inspected was the one that made the contaminated heparin ingredient. That plant, Changzhou SPL, blames someone else further upstream in the supply chain for selling tainted raw materials.

(www.iht.com, 30 March 2008)

Heparin … has been found in drug supplies in eleven countries and federal officials said Monday [21 April] they had discovered a clear link between the contaminant and severe reactions now associated with eighty-one deaths in the United States. But a Chinese official disputed the assertion that the contaminant found in the drug caused any deaths and insisted that his country's own inspectors be allowed to inspect the American plant where the finished heparin vials were made. He said any future agreement to allow American inspections of Chinese firms should be reciprocal … [US] officials have discovered heparin lots that included the cheap fake additive manufactured as early as 2006, although a spike in illnesses associated with contaminated heparin began in November [2007] and persisted through February [2008], officials said … The Food and Drug Administration has announced plans to open inspection offices in three Chinese cities, but the agency has yet to get permission from the Chinese government.

(www.iht.com, 22 April 2008)

China said no other countries have had a problem with heparin … [It] said there was no evidence that the contaminant – a chemical called oversulphated chondroitin sulphate – was to blame for the deaths in the United States … [It] pointed out that the chemical had been found in heparin stocks in other countries, but that no deaths has been reported outside of the United States … In addition to the United States and Germany, more than ten other countries also use the heparin ingredient that contained [the contaminant].

(www.bbc.co.uk, 23 April 2008)

The EU says China supplied half of all dangerous products seized by the European authorities last year [2007] … The EU's executive office says in a report released Thursday [17 April] that the EU's rapid alert system flagged 1,605 dangerous products last year – up 53 per cent from 1,051 the previous year. The national authorities in the EU's twenty-seven nations use the system to share information on toxic goods and product recalls.

(www.iht.com, 17 April 2008)

The number of fake cosmetics, medicines and toys seized coming into Europe has soared, according to EU statistics released yesterday [19 May] … China remained the largest single source of seized goods, accounting for almost 60 per cent of the total … China is the most common country of origin for seized clothing, shoes, computer equipment, CDs/DVDs, jewellery, toys and cigarettes … [EU] officials say China is becoming more co-operative.

(*FT*, 20 May 2008, p. 12)

> A new report [by the European Commission says there was] ... soaring ... number of cases of fraudulent goods seized last year [2007] ... The amount of times customs officials intercepted dodgy products at EU borders rose 17 per cent last year with cases of counterfeit medicines alone up 50 per cent. The European Commission remained the main source of counterfeit goods, accounting for 60 per cent of all items.
>
> (www.bbc.co.uk, 20 May 2008)

'According to EU figures ... the proportion of counterfeit goods seized at EU borders that originate in China fell to 60 per cent last year [2007] from 80 per cent in 2006' (*IHT*, 16 September 2008, p. 13).

> Manufacturers who produce substandard food could be jailed for life under a draft law ... The law also covers a new scheme to identify and track products ranging from food to cosmetics to boost consumer confidence. Under the draft legislation ... producers whose goods are not up to scratch could be fined, have their incomes confiscated or their production certificates revoked. In serious cases they could face between three years and life imprisonment ... [It was] initially said that by the end of June [2008] products in nine categories – including food, cosmetics and home appliances – must carry a code allowing consumers to trace their place and time of origin ... The deadline has now been extended until the end of the year [2008] ... The US Food and Drug Administration announced last week that it was to open an office in China.
>
> (*Guardian*, 22 April 2008, p. 22)

> The deaths of six hospital patients who received a blood-based drug at a hospital in the south-central province of Jiangxi has prompted an unusually swift and vigorous response from regulators, the first sign that the government may be following through on promises of tighter security of the pharmaceutical industry ... The speed of the government's response appeared to reflect a new system put in place for responding to reports of unsafe drugs.
>
> (www.iht.com, 3 June 2008)

> According to investigators based in Beijing and Hong Kong, who refused to speak on the record because they fear government reprisals, visitors might consider steering clear of military-owned hospitals where they could run the risk of being treated with substandard or counterfeit medicines ... The Chinese military operates outside of the law, running counterfeiting networks even though such profit-making military enterprises are technically illegal. Such operations are tolerated by the Beijing regime.
>
> (www.feer.com, 6 August 2008)

> One of China's highest ranking food safety officials committed suicide earlier this month [August] during a government corruption investigation ... The official, Wu Jianping, the head of food production supervision at the General Administration of Quality Supervision Inspection and Quarantine,

died jumping from a building on 2 August ... Several other high ranking officials in the State Food and Drug Administration have also been found guilty of corruption and sentenced to long prison terms.

(www.iht.com, 15 August 2008)

The Chinese health ministry on Friday [12 September] ordered a nationwide investigation of milk powder linked to a rash of kidney stones in infants and one death ... The major Chinese dairy that produced the formula ... Sanlu Group Co. ... has recalled 700 tonnes of the product and said it was contaminated with melamine, a chemical used in plastic ... In one province, Gansu in the north-west, doctors have reported a total of fifty-nine cases of kidney stones in infants, compared with none in 2006 or 2007 ... Many of those babies were fed the Sanlu formula. Fonterra, a New Zealand dairy co-operative that owns 43 per cent of Sanlu, said it was advised the company has a 'quality issue in its products' as a result of receiving defective milk in China ... The contaminated powder was produced before 6 August ... Melamine is the chemical involved in a massive pet food recall last year [2007]. It is not supposed to be added to any food ingredients, but suppliers in China sometimes mix it into food to make it appear to be high in protein. Melamine is nitrogen rich and standard tests for protein in bulk food ingredients measure levels of nitrogen. In Washington the US Food and Drug Administration warned customers to avoid infant formula from China. Authorities said Chinese formula was not legally approved for importation into the United States, but might be sold at ethnic grocery stores ... Sanlu, based in Shijiazhuang, south-west of Beijing, is the biggest Chinese producer of milk powder, with 18 per cent of the market ... The company produces 6,800 tonnes of milk a day ... In 2004 more than 200 Chinese infants suffered malnutrition and at least twelve died after being fed phoney formula that contained no nutrients. Some forty companies were found to be making phoney formula.

(www.iht.com, 12 September 2008)

China began a nationwide inquiry into the safety of all infant formulas on Friday as investigators from six government agencies descended on a milk powder factory ... China's health ministry ... [said] the majority of the babies who have fallen sick had definitely consumed the Sanlu formula ... China reported the problem to the WHO ... Sanlu ordered its recall and promised its own investigation after determining that batches of its formula manufactured before 6 August had been contaminated ... There have been reports of babies developing kidney stones and kidney failure in at least seven provinces. A cluster of cases in Gansu province in western China triggered the recall ... [In] a scandal four years ago thirteen infants died after drinking substandard formula by counterfeiters under the Sanlu brand.

(www.iht.com, 12 September 2008)

State media said the [nationwide] inquiry would seek to discover if the tainted formula led to the baby's death and caused kidney stones in dozens of other babies. The new scare revived memories of a fake formula scandal four years ago in which at least thirteen babies died ... A fake milk powder scandal in 2004 killed at least thirteen babies in the eastern province of Anhui.

(www.bbc.co.uk, 12 September 2008)

Melamine is a toxic chemical used in plastics, fertilizers and cleaning products ... It was linked to the formation of kidney stones and kidney failure in pets in the United States last year [2007], leading to thousands of deaths and illnesses.

(www.bbc.co.uk, 13 September 2008)

'The product was contaminated with tripolycyanamide, a chemical believed to cause kidney stones ... Officials will also check milk powders made by other companies' (www.cnn.com, 12 September 2008).

A Chinese dairy that sold baby milk powder linked to kidney stones in infants and one death knew weeks before it ordered a recall that the product contained a banned chemical, the health ministry said Saturday [13 September], as the number of sick babies rose to 140 ... The number of infants suffering kidney stones after being fed Sanlu formula has risen to 140 ... Some fifty-nine were in Gansu, a poor province in the north-west, where one child died ... In August Sanlu's testing 'revealed melamine in the baby milk powder and showed it was contaminated', a ministry statement said. It was not known when Sanlu alerted authorities about its findings ... Kidney problems in infants were reported as early as mid-July but authorities failed to launch a food safety investigation, the official Xinhua news agency said. Another news report said the dairy received complaints as early as March ... Xinhua cited a Gansu provincial health department spokesman as saying he received reports on 16 July that sixteen infants under a year old, all of whom drank Sanlu milk, were suffering a rare kidney ailment ... A Sanlu manager quoted by the newspaper *Beijing News* said the dairy received complaints in March and June but could not track down the problem ... The contamination occurred when dairy farmers added melamine to milk, possibly to make its protein appear higher ... Sanlu buys milk from a nationwide network of suppliers that includes 60,000 family farms ... In 2004 more than 200 infants suffered malnutrition and at least twelve died after being fed phoney formula that contained no nutrients. Some forty companies were found to be making phoney formula ... In China shoddy or counterfeit products are common.

(www.cnn.com, 13 September 2008)

A Chinese dairy that sold milk powder linked to kidney stones in infants and one death knew it contained a banned chemical before ordering a recall, the health ministry said Saturday [13 September], as the number of sick babies rose to 432 ... Investigators have detained nineteen people ... Officials said ... some tainted powder was exported to Taiwan but none was sent to other

> … overseas markets … Chinese officials … said authorities were only told of the contamination Monday [8 September], even though Sanlu received complaints as early as March and its tests found melamine in August … Investigators were [said to be] looking into whether dairy farmers added the chemical … [It was said that] it might have been done to fool quality tests after water was added to fraudulently increase the milk's volume. Melamine is rich in nitrogen and standard tests for protein in food ingredients measure nitrogen levels … Authorities have seized 2,176 tonnes of Sanlu formula and ordered a recall totalling 8,218 tonnes … That was far more than the 700 tonnes in Sanlu's initial recall announcement … Beijing has launched an emergency inspection of all 175 companies in China that produce infant formula … In Taiwan [it was said that] … the Chinese shipment of milk powder, which arrived in June, was 55,115 lb (25,000 kg) … Only 21,660 lb (9,825 kg) had been recovered … [Xinhua reported] a Gansu provincial health official saying he received reports on 16 July that sixteen infants, all of whom drank Sanlu milk, were suffering a rare kidney ailment. He said the health ministry launched an epidemic survey … [but] it seemed no food and safety survey had been done … A Sanlu manager quoted by the newspaper *Beijing News* said the dairy received complaints in March and June but could not track down the problem. The manager: 'We finally imported foreign equipment and finally found the milk powder contained melamine.'
>
> (www.iht.com, 13 September 2008)

> On Saturday the provincial government of Hebei, where Sanlu is based, ordered that Sanlu shut down all of its milk powder production … Beijing's highest government agencies ordered a 'first class national food emergency response' Saturday, calling for a thorough investigation into the causes of the contamination and offering aid to infants suffering from kidney stones … The government said it thought the melamine had been intentionally added to the powder to make it seem to have more protein. Last year [2007] the same chemical was found in animal feed from China that was then sold to pet food makers in the United States, sickening hundreds of cats and dogs … In interviews with melamine producers and sellers last year several acknowledged that melamine was commonly used to artificially raise the protein count in a variety of foods, fish feeds and even dairy products. Melamine, which can be made from coal, is high in nitrogen and for decades has been used by farmers to bolster protein counts in food and feed. Food safety officials in Beijing said Saturday that dairy farmers could have used cheap melamine filler to make the infant formula powder seem far richer … On Sunday [14 September] … the New Zealand dairy giant Fonterra said it had known since August that the Chinese firm in which it holds a 43 per cent stake was selling contaminated milk but that it had sought a recall.
>
> (www.iht.com, 14 September 2008)

> The manufacturer has already recalled more than 8,200 tonnes of the tainted formula … Sanlu group has also sealed off more than 2,100 tonnes of con-

taminated product and another 700 tonnes need to be recalled, the news agency [Xinhua] said ... Testing by Sanlu found tripolycyanamide, also known as melamine, in 700 tonnes of its product, the news agency reported ... Health experts say ingesting melamine can lead to kidney stones, urinary tract ulcers, and eye and skin irritation. The chemical is commonly used in coatings and laminates, fabric coatings, ceiling tiles and flame retardants.

(www.cnn.com, 13 September 2008)

New Zealand-based dairy giant Fonterra said it had urged China's Sanlu group to recall the tainted powder six weeks before Sanlu took adequate action ... In a statement released on Sunday [14 September] Fonterra said it had urged Sanlu's board to recall the milk powder as soon as it learnt of the contamination – on 2 August. The statement said: 'From the day we were advised of the product contamination issue in August, Fonterra called for a full public recall of all affected products and we have continued to push for this all along.'

(www.bbc.co.uk, 15 September 2008)

Chinese state media on Monday [15 September] reported that a second infant has died after ingesting contaminated baby powder in what has become a rapidly expanding food safety scandal with nearly 500 babies sickened by tainted milk powder. The death of a second infant in western China's Gansu province comes after regulators last week ordered one of China's leading dairy producers, the Sanlu Group, to halt production of its baby formula and advising stores to stop selling it ... The death of the second infant came as officials in Gansu province announced that another forty-three sickened babies had been discovered. Nearly all the patients in Gansu are from poorer, rural areas and are aged three or younger ... Last year [2007] the United States ordered a recall of Chinese pet food ... Chinese regulators responded with a high profile crackdown and banned the mixing of melamine into vegetable protein for export or domestic food use ... On Monday New Zealand's prime minister said that local officials in China refused to take action until the New Zealand government contacted the central authorities in Beijing. Helen Clark: '[Fonterra has] been trying for weeks to get official recall and the local authorities in China would not do it. I think the first inclination was to try and put a towel over it and deal with it without an official recall' ... By last weekend Chinese investigators were inspecting Sanlu's production chain ... Inspectors discovered melamine at two dairy producers that provided milk powder to the Sanlu Group.

(www.iht.com, 15 September 2008)

China's ministry of health on Monday [15 September] announced that two babies have died in recent months and that 1,253 others have been sickened by contaminated milk powder in a rapidly expanding food scandal that became public only last week. More than 340 infants remain hospitalized, including fifty-three in serious condition. Meanwhile, inspection teams are now visiting dairy farms and processing centres in the country's four main milk producing provinces to ensure that producers are not violating safety standards ... At a Monday afternoon conference health officials said physicians had examined 10,000 infants who had been fed the Sanlu formula and found that 1,253 had been sickened. Most of those infants were not considered dangerously ill, though 340 remained in hospital, including the fifty-three in serious condition ... Many of the ailing children are from poorer areas, including north-west China's Gansu province ... Li Changjiang, minister of the general Administration of Quality Supervision, Inspection and Quarantine ... said the result of the investigation would be announced later this week but suggested that the problem occurred at milk processing centres rather than on farms. These milk stations collect milk from farmers and then pool it together to be sold to larger dairy concerns.

(www.iht.com, 15 September 2008)

More than 10,000 tonnes of baby powder have been seized or recalled, the health ministry said, and the authorities have also ordered the company to halt production ... Investigators are trying to determine how the formula became contaminated and whether Sanlu intentionally covered up the problem before announcing the recall.

(*IHT*, 16 September 2008, p. 2)

Cases of contamination have also been reported in the provinces of Hebei and Jiangsu ... New Zealand prime minister Helen Clark said her government learned of the contamination problem on 5 September, then three days later decided to inform Beijing after local Chinese officials refused to act ... New Zealand's Fonterra Co-operative [is] the country's biggest dairy producer ... Fonterra's chief executive [is] Andrew Ferrier ... He said Fonterra had known of the contamination in early August and wanted an immediate recall but that Sanlu had had to abide by Chinese rules. Ferrier said: 'We together with Sanlu have done everything that we possibly could to get the product off the shelf.'

(www.bbc.co.uk, 15 September 2008)

New Zealand prime minister Helen Clark: '[Fonterra] have been trying for weeks to get an official recall and the local authorities in China would not do it' ... Andrew Ferrier (Fonterra's chief executive): 'As a minority shareholder [Fonterra] had to continue to push Sanlu. Sanlu had to work with their own government to follow the procedures that they were given.'

(*FT*, 16 September 2008, p. 12)

The health ministry warned Tuesday [16 September] of a possible rise in the number of babies affected by the contaminated milk powder that has already been linked to the deaths of two infants [on 1 May and 22 July] and to health problems in more than 1,200 others ... [The ministry said] that 1,253 infants had become sick – mainly after developing kidney stones – more than twice the number acknowledged the previous week. Of those 913

> infants were only slightly affected, while 340 remained hospitalized and fifty-three cases were considered especially severe ... Sanlu said that the suppliers of the raw milk used in the product were responsible for adding the chemical ... The milk formula scandal is embarrassing for China's product safety system, which was recently overhauled in an attempt to restore consumer confidence and preserve export markets after a string of recalls and warnings abroad over tainted toothpaste, faulty tyres and other goods.
>
> (www.iht.com, 16 September 2008)

'Hong Kong authorities announced Tuesday [16 September] that traces of melamine had been discovered in frozen yoghurt made by the Inner Mongolia Yili Industrial Group' (www.iht.com, 17 September 2008).

> China's health minister said Wednesday [17 September] that tainted milk formula has killed three babies and sickened 6,200 in a spreading scandal that prompted three additional companies – including China's biggest dairy – to recall products. About 20 per cent of the dairy companies tested nationwide had sold products tainted with melamine ... The companies included Mengniu Dairy, China's biggest milk company, which said Wednesday it was recalling its baby formula ... Health minister Chen Zhu ... [said] that 6,244 babies had been sickened after being fed tainted milk formula, and that 158 were suffering from acute kidney failure. Chen reported the death of a third baby in eastern Zheliang province ... The two earlier deaths had been reported in Gansu province ... Free medical care will be provided to all affected infants and a hot line is being set up ... More than 1,300 infants remain hospitalized ... Four Hebei provincial officials have been fired ... The general manager of Sanlu group was also fired ... The head of China's quality control watchdog, Li Changjiang, said that in addition to the company at the heart of the food scandal, Sanlu Group, and Mengniu, two other companies, Guangdong-based Yashili and Qingdao-based Suncare, were recalling their products after melamine was found in their milk powder. Yashili and Suncare export their products to Bangladesh, Yemen, Gabon, Burundi and Myanmar ... The General Administration of Quality Supervision, Inspection and Quarantine had already reported that its inspectors had found melamine 'in sixty-nine batches of milk powder manufactured by twenty-two companies'. The nationwide inspection took test samples from 109 companies that produce milk powder in China. Li said another sixty-six companies had stopped production before the melamine problem emerged. The highest concentration of melamine was found in Sanlu's milk powder ... Starting immediately, 1,400 teams with 5,000 inspectors will be stationed at all companies producing baby milk to strictly oversee the process ... Li said the government is seeking more information after Hong Kong inspectors ordered the recall of an ice cream bar made by Shanghai Yili AB Foods because melamine was found.
>
> (www.iht.com, 17 September 2008)

> Initially the contamination problem was thought to be confined to baby formula produced by the Sanlu group, one the country's largest dairy companies. But investigators have since discovered traces of melamine in some batches of powdered formula produced by twenty-one other dairy companies, including China's biggest outfit, Mengniu Dairy … A nationwide inspection examined 491 batches of formula selected from the 109 companies that produce baby formula in China. Testing found that the Sanlu brand contained the highest levels of melamine, while levels of contamination differed in other brands … In all twenty-two companies were found to have produced some batches of bad formula. Two of these, Yashili, which is based in Guangdong, and Suncare, which is based in Qingdao, export to Asian and African countries, but it was unclear whether there was melamine in those products.
>
> (*IHT*, 18 September 2008, p. 2)

'Of China's 175 baby milk powder production companies, sixty-six have already stopped production … Investigators are testing samples at the rest' (www.cnn.com, 17 September 2008).

> The government has labelled the poisonings a 'level one' food safety incident and formed an emergency team to grapple with the fallout … Rising public anger, expressed on China's active internet forums, is prompting reports of a crackdown by the government on reporting of the scandal.
>
> (www.bbc.co.uk, 17 September 2008)

> [The] head of the state quality supervision body AQSIQ [General Administration of Quality Supervision, Inspection and Quarantine] … Li Changjiang … said China would adjust its baby formula standards to allow for poisonous substances such as melamine. He said tests for the substance had not been made before, because it was banned from food products.
>
> (www.bbc.co.uk, 17 September 2008)

> China says it will launch nationwide testing of all dairy products … More than 6,200 babies have fallen ill after drinking milk tainted with the toxic chemical melamine … The government described the dairy market as 'chaotic' and said its supervision is flawed
>
> In a statement the Chinese cabinet said: '[The incident reflects] chaotic industry conditions and loopholes in the supervision and management of the industry' … The giant milk company Mengniu Dairy … says it is recalling three batches of formula made in January, after government tests found melamine in its product … [The government said that] two companies – Yashili and Suncare – exported milk powder and they were recalling their products.
>
> (www.bbc.co.uk, 18 September 2008)

> The mayor of a city whose officials have been accused of failing to deal with reports of tainted milk powder was dismissed Thursday [18 September] and the Chinese government announced that a fourth infant had died after

drinking contaminated milk and that the police had arrested a dozen more people in a widening investigation. The mayor of Shijiazhuang, Ji Chintang, was the most senior official to be fired so far … Shijiazhuang, in the northern province of Hebei, is the location of the headquarters of Sanlu Group … The latest death took place in a Mongolian area of Xinjiang, in China's far west … Sanlu received complaints months ago about suspected problems in the milk, but waited until 2 August to tell the Shijiazhuang city government, Hebei's deputy governor said Wednesday [17 September], City officials waited until 9 September to tell provincial officials, who did not inform the central government until the next day. Some people are accusing officials of hiding reports of bad milk so as not to mar the Olympic Games in Beijing, which ran from 8 August to 24 August, and the Paralympics, which ended Wednesday [17 September] … The central government's department in charge of quality inspection said Wednesday that it was no longer exempting any companies from product testing … Previously, major companies with a long track record of making quality products could get an exemption … On Thursday [18 September] Hong Kong ordered the recall of the dairy products of Yili Industrial Group based in Inner Mongolia, after tests found melamine in eight of the company's products … The recall covers milk, yoghurt, ice cream and all other products … It is the second time Hong Kong food inspectors called back Yili products. On Tuesday [16 September] one sample of yoghurt-flavoured ice bar was found to contain melamine.

(www.iht.com, 18 September 2008)

This year [2008] … to improve monitoring … the country's food and drug safety agency … was put under the ministry of health … The central government has boasted it was quick to react to the latest problem. But the chronology revealed so far suggests otherwise. It has fuelled speculation of a delay to make sure the Olympic Games were not marred by a food scare. The government of Gansu province in China's west says it told the ministry of health on 16 July about an unusual upsurge of kidney stones among infants who had all drunk the same brand of milk. It was not until 1 September that the ministry says its experts tentatively concluded that the powder had caused the sickness. Still, nothing appeared to happen. Prodding from the government of New Zealand may have been what eventually goaded the Chinese authorities into action. On 8 September it told them what it had learnt from Fonterra, a New Zealand dairy company that owns 43 per cent of Sanlu. Fonterra says it was told by Sanlu of a problem with the powder on 2 August, six days before the Games. Helen Clark, New Zealand's prime minister, said Fonterra had tried 'for weeks' to persuade local officials to allow a public recall. Fonterra has defended its decision to keep its information under wraps for so long … A government investigation found smaller traces of melamine in milk powder from twenty-one other companies, including leading brands such as Inner Mongolia Yili Industrial Group

> (an Olympic sponsor, though the government says no melamine got into the dairy supply for the Olympics or the Paralympics).
>
> (*The Economist*, 20 September 2008, pp. 69–70)

'Police in China today [18 September] arrested twelve more people as part of their investigation. There were already eighteen suspects being held and another eighty-seven summoned for questioning' (www.guardian.co.uk, 18 September 2008).

> China today [18 September] tried to calm jitters about exports of tainted baby milk powder to five poor developing countries, saying no problems had been reported so far ... The government has already announced that five countries – Yemen, Bangladesh, Myanmar, Gabon and Burundi – have imported milk powder made by two Chinese firms whose products were found to be contaminated. A Chinese foreign ministry spokeswoman: 'Though there has been no bad reaction, the quality watchdog has demanded that these companies take action to recall the products.'
>
> (www.independent.co.uk, 18 September 2008)

> China's latest tainted product crisis widened Friday [19 September] after tests found the chemical melamine in liquid milk by three of the country's leading dairy companies ... About 10 per cent of liquid milk samples taken from the Mengniu Dairy Group and Yili Industrial Group – China's two largest dairy producers – contained melamine ... Milk from the Shanghai-based Bright Dairy showed contamination ... On Friday regulators for consumer product safety in the United States, the EU and China met to announce a joint initiative that would allow for direct co-operation between the three parties on consumer safety issues ... About 1,300 babies, mostly newborns, remain hospitalized, with 158 suffering from acute kidney failure.
>
> (www.iht.com, 19 September 2008)

> Milk product samples from three Chinese dairies have tested positive for a chemical [melamine] that has already killed four babies ... The chemical showed up in testing done on milk and yoghurt ... The Chinese State Administration of Quality Supervision, Inspection and Quarantine said the amount of the chemical found in the milk would not cause ill effects in adults who drank less than 2 litres a day.
>
> (www.cnn.com, 19 September 2008)

'Chinese officials sought to allay panic by insisting most milk was safe to drink' (www.bbc.co.uk, 19 September 2008).

> Despite assurances that no one had fallen ill from drinking liquid milk, the news prompted shop owners in China and elsewhere to clear their shelves. The issue has provoked a worldwide reaction, with both the EU and the United States asking for an explanation, and Singapore and Malaysia banning Chinese milk imports.
>
> (www.bbc.co.uk, 20 September 2008)

'Chinese officials have ordered an all-out effort to save babies made ill by contaminated milk products. A cabinet statement said all affected children should get free check-ups and treatment and called for more screening in remote areas' (www.bbc.co.uk, 20 September 2008).

> China sought Saturday [20 September] to shore up public confidence weakened by a milk safety scandal, with the president scolding officials for negligence and government agencies promising adequate supplies of uncontaminated milk ... Many leading brands of powdered and liquid milk and other dairy products have been pulled from store shelves ... The ministry of health ordered all thirty-one provinces and major cities nationwide to set up separate twenty-four-hour crisis hot lines to meet surging public calls and help arrange care for the sick. The order followed a barrage of instructions late Friday from the State Council, China's cabinet, requiring hospitals to provide free medical care ... The top economic agencies promised to monitor markets for supply disruptions and for any price gouging in sales of powdered milk – a staple in rural China ... The commerce ministry said: 'Market supplies of powdered milk not tainted with melamine are sufficient' ... State-run newspapers and national China Central Television ran lists of brands and products that were clear of safety violations and deemed safe. In Beijing and Shanghai grocery stores where dairy sections were emptied by recalls Friday [19 September] displayed thinly stocked shelves by Saturday afternoon, mostly imported or from China operations of Nestlé SA and other foreign-owned dairies ... President Hu Jintao (Friday 19 September): 'Some officials have ignored public opinion and turned a blind eye to people's hardships, even on major problems that affect people's lives and safety. We must all learn a painful lesson' ... Last year [2007] the government promised to overhaul safety regimes after medicines, toys and pet food killed and sickened people and pets in North and South America and other export markets. On Saturday Japan joined Singapore and Hong Kong in recalling Chinese-made dairy products ... Questions have been raised about whether officials sought to cover up contamination of powdered milk, in part to avoid a scandal around the 8–24 August Olympics ... A vice governor of Hebei province, where Sanlu is located, told reporters this week that two suppliers detained this month admitted they had been adding melamine to milk for three years.
>
> (www.iht.com, 20 September 2008)

> A three-year-old Hong Kong girl has been diagnosed with a small kidney stone after drinking Chinese-produced milk contaminated with an industrial chemical, but is in good condition and does not require surgery, a hospital official said Sunday [21 September]. It is the first sickness reported outside mainland China in a scandal involving dairy products containing melamine ... The Hong Kong government and individual retailers and dairy companies have also tested local inventories and issued recalls in [Hong Kong] ... On Sunday the Hong Kong government said its tests have found

> melamine in Chinese-made Nestlé brand milk and ordered the product recalled. The government said in a statement that the chemical was found in Nestlé Dairy Farm milk for catering use. It said the milk was made by Nestlé Qingdao Ltd, located in the Chinese coastal city of Qingdao. The test found only a small amount of melamine and the milk does not pose a serious health risk, the government said. However, it recommended that it not be fed to young children. Nestlé said in a statement last Wednesday [17 September] that none of its infant formula and milk powder products contained melamine.
>
> (www.cnn.com, 21 September 2008)

> Beijing has begun high-profile efforts to show it is on top of the crisis, with prime minister Wen Jiabao appearing on state-run television Sunday [21 September] to say dairy companies had to show more 'social responsibility'. Wen was shown visiting a Beijing hospital where children were having health checks. He also stopped at a supermarket to look at dairy products … Japan and Singapore have recalled Chinese-made dairy products, and the governments of Malaysia and Brunei announced bans on milk products from China though neither country currently imports Chinese dairy items … On Sunday a World Health Organization [WHO] official said delays in releasing critical information about the contamination of milk supplies hampered Beijing's ability to deal with the problem rapidly and warn consumers.
>
> (www.iht.com, 21 September 2008)

'Regulators have revoked exemptions that previously allowed many top companies to police themselves. China alerted the WHO to the contamination' (www.iht.com, 21 September 2008).

'Premier Wen Jiabao: "We absolutely cannot exchange people's health for industrial development and economic growth"' (*FT*, 22 September 2008, p. 11).

> Nearly 13,000 children in China have been hospitalized due to tainted Chinese milk powder … China's health ministry said [on Sunday 21 September] 104 out of 12,892 babies showed serious symptoms … Officials from the health ministry said 12,892 infants were currently being treated in hospitals around the country. They said that 1,579 babies had been treated and discharged, adding that hospitals had checked nearly 40,000 baby patients.
>
> (www.bbc.co.uk, 22 September 2008)

'[The government] said 12,892 children, most of them under the age of two, had been admitted to hospital and nearly 40,000 more had been examined or treated in hospital and released' (*FT*, 23 September 2008, p. 13).

> In recent weeks 12,892 infants have been hospitalized across China, most two years old or younger, the ministry reported … The ministry of health reported that none of the infants, as yet, had been linked to contaminated liquid milk. Of the nearly 13,000 sickened, officials said, 1,579 had already recovered and been released from hospital … The ministry said nearly 40,000 infants had been examined.
>
> (www.iht.com, 22 September 2008)

Beijing for years has encouraged children to drink more milk as part of a national health campaign ... [China has a] fast-growing $18 billion [dairy] industry ... [Beijing has] allowed extensive media coverage ... In the EU imports of dairy products, including formula, are banned because of a lack of procedures to guarantee their safety.

(*IHT*, 23 September 2008, p. 2)

As the number of Chinese infants reported sickened by tainted milk increased to 53,000, premier Wen Jiabao called manufacturers 'heartless' and promised stricter laws to protect the public ... The Chinese premier visited Beijing hospitals and a supermarket Sunday [21 September]. He said: 'What we need to do now is to ensure that nothing like this happens in the future, not only in dairy products, but in all foods. Manufacturers and owners of dairy companies should show more morality and social responsibility in these cases. They are heartless, so we have to create strict laws and legislation. I am sorry' ... The Hong Kong centre for Food Safety announced Sunday [21 September] that a sample of Nestlé Dairy Farm Pure Milk, sold in one-litre packs for catering use only, had tested positive for melamine. But the Swiss company said in a news release it is 'confident' none of its milk products made in China contains the chemical. The officials asked that retail sales of the milk for catering be halted and that Nestlé recall the product. The level of melamine detected in the Nestlé sample was ... low. However, small children should not consume the product, the centre said. The other sixty-four samples were free from the toxic substance ... [On its website] Nestlé did not address the report regarding its Dairy Farm Pure Milk ... [But] Nestlé said: 'Following press reports in Hong Kong earlier today claiming that traces of melamine had been found in a Nestlé growing-up milk, Nestlé is confident that none of its products in China is made up from milk adulterated with melamine.'

(www.cnn.com, 22 September 2008)

More than 80 per cent of the 12,892 children hospitalized in recent weeks are two years or younger ... The [health] ministry says another 39,965 children have received outpatient treatment at hospitals and are considered 'basically recovered' ... In all at least eleven countries have banned ... importing Chinese dairy products.

(www.cnn.com, 23 September 2008)

The head of China's quality watchdog resigned [on Monday 22 September] ... Li Changjiang stepped down 'with the approval of the State Council', China's cabinet ... He is the first central government official to lose his job over the scandal ... Mr Li, whose agency is responsible for ensuring that China's food supply chain is safe, will be replaced by Wang Yong, senior cabinet official ... Authorities in Singapore, Malaysia, Hong Kong, Taiwan, Japan, the Philippines, Vietnam and elsewhere have been testing Chinese-made dairy products or pulling them from the shelves altogether.

(www.bbc.co.uk, 22 September 2008)

> The resignation of Li Changjiang, head of the General Administration of Quality Supervision, Inspection and Quarantine … was announced Monday [22 September] … The government has arrested nineteen people … The government in Hong Kong said Monday that a second child in the territory had been diagnosed with a kidney stone. The government said the child, a four-year-old boy, was in a stable condition.
>
> (www.iht.com, 22 September 2008)

> Countries across Asia are testing Chinese dairy products as fears spread over melamine-tainted milk – and some have banned these products outright … Four children in Hong Kong have now been diagnosed with kidney stones after drinking milk from the mainland … Sanlu began receiving complaints about sick children as early as last December [2007], but did not report the issue to the authorities until early September [2008], according to a CCTV report citing an official investigation.
>
> (www.bbc.co.uk, 23 September 2008)

> China vowed to prevent toxic milk from reaching processors and export markets after an infant powder scandal that has made more than 54,000 children sick … Two more Hong Kong children who drank milk with melamine have been diagnosed with kidney stones, bringing the total to four, the Hong Kong government said Tuesday [23 September] … Vietnam stopped sales of milk products from unidentified sources.
>
> (www.iht.com, 23 September 2008)

> Sanlu Group … received consumer complaints about its baby milk formula as early as December 2007 – much earlier than previously thought and nine months before the producer ordered a nationwide recall … state media said Tuesday [23 September] … Baby milk formula in China tainted by melamine has already sickened more than 53,000 infants and killed four children nationwide … Recalls [have taken place] of Chinese-made dairy products in China and other parts of Asia, devastating this nation's huge dairy industry and casting a renewed pall over the quality of Chinese food production … China's dairy industry has been booming for more than a decade, with the aid of a government initiative to get Chinese to drink more milk … The government announced Tuesday that more than 7,000 tonnes of dairy products had been removed from store shelves. Also on Tuesday the ministry of health said the nation's dairy collection system was 'out of control'.
>
> (www.iht.com, 24 September 2008)

'In Hong Kong Nestlé, the world's largest food company, said it had recalled a UHT pure milk product after a local watchdog discovered samples containing a tiny amount of the chemical melamine' (www.guardian.co.uk, 23 September 2008).

> China has brought under control a tainted milk scandal … a senior official said Wednesday [24 September], as prime minister Wen Jiabao vowed

tougher monitoring ... Xiang Yuzhang, the national quality monitor's chief inspection official, said that consumers could now rest easy after a widespread recall of tainted products and increased testing of dairy goods. He said: 'The Chinese government has taken a series of very strong measures to get to the bottom of this matter. I have just returned from an inspection trip to the regions. At present there is basically no melamine problem any more in the Chinese market, including for producers. There is no problem. It has been brought under control, more or less. As far as I know, there will be no more bad news' ... [Prime minister] Wen Jiabao said that China would seize the crisis as an opportunity to overhaul product safety controls. He said: '[The country will] strengthen institutional development and take seriously supervision and inspections in every link of production, truly ensuring the interests of consumers' ... The New Zealand dairy export giant, Fonterra Co-operative Group, slashed the value of its big investment in China's Sanlu Group by nearly 70 per cent on Wednesday ... More than a dozen countries in Asia and Africa have banned China dairy products and several others had recalled products by Wednesday.

(www.iht.com, 24 September 2008)

Several of China's big internet portals have been accused of filtering out information about tainted milk from as long ago as December [2007] in order to protect China's reputation during the run-up to the Olympics ... Foreign companies have been concerned about the possibility of a scandal for some time. Unilever dumped its joint ventures years ago, to ensure it had full control of all domestic Chinese operations. McDonald's had created its own closed supply chain, spanning beef, fries, bread and pickles. Coca-Cola imposes stringent rules on suppliers of sugar, water and carbon dioxide.

(*The Economist*, 27 September 2008, pp. 86, 88)

The fallout from a tainted milk scandal in China continues to spread around the globe with tainted crackers found in South Korea, two more illnesses reported in Hong Kong and a grocery chain in Great Britain pulling Chinese products. The United States said inspectors would expand testing for Chinese products that may contain high levels of milk or milk protein ... In South Korea the government banned the importation of all Chinese products containing milk after Chinese biscuits tainted with melamine were discovered in the country, a government spokesman said Wednesday [24 September]. A formal announcement was expected on Thursday, but the ban went into effect Wednesday night ... In Hong Kong health officials reported two new cases of kidney stones in children who have consumed melamine-tainted dairy products. A pair of boys from mainland China – ages two and nine – were diagnosed with the condition at local hospitals, the government [said on Tuesday 23 September]. The latest cases of kidney stones bring to four the confirmed number of illnesses in Hong Kong caused by the consumption of contaminated milk products ... In the United Kingdom the supermarket chain Tesco said Wednesday [24 September] that it had pulled the children's sweets from store shelves over fears they may contain melamine. A Tesco representative said: 'As a precautionary measure we have withdrawn White Rabbit Candies from the very small number of UK stores that sell them as part of our ethnic range' ... Health experts say that ingesting melamine can lead to kidney stones, urinary tract ulcers, and eye and skin irritation ... It also robs infants of much-needed protein.

(www.cnn.com, 25 September 2008)

The famed White Rabbit Creamy Candy [was] invented in 1943 by a Chinese businessman impressed by a similar English milk candy ... The candy has for five decades been a staple treat for every Chinese child ... Tesco said that it had withdrawn the white rabbit candies from its UK stores on Tuesday [23 September] as a 'precautionary measure'. The sweets had been on sale in 100 of its supermarkets for the past six months. They were also sold in Tesco's stores in China and Malaysia.

(www.thetimes.co.uk, 25 September 2008)

The European Commission is imposing a ban on EU imports of Chinese baby food that contains any trace of milk, while other Chinese food will undergo tests ... The commission says all imported products from China containing more than 15 per cent milk powder will be tested. Random testing will be done on all such products already on sale in the EU. The EU does not import milk or other dairy produce from China, but processed foods such as biscuits and chocolates might have traces of milk powder ... No food contaminated with melamine had been found in the EU so far ... The European Food Safety Authority said on Thursday [25 September] that there could be a risk for children who consumed above-average amounts of biscuits and chocolates contaminated with melamine.

(www.bbc.co.uk, 25 September 2008)

The World Health Organization [WHO] and Unicef said in a joint statement (25 September): 'Deliberate contamination of foods intended for consumption by vulnerable infants and young children is particularly deplorable ... We are confident that swift and firm actions are being taken by China's food safety authorities to investigate this incident fully. We also expect that following the investigation and in the context of the Chinese government's increasing attention to food safety, better regulation of foods for infants and young children will be enforced' ... The WHO and Unicef also urged mothers to breast-feed their infants, a need further underscored by 'alarming examples' of tainted formula scandals in China and around the world ... India became the largest and most populous country to announce a ban on Chinese milk and milk products on Thursday [25 September], with the ban to remain in force for three months. Vietnam and Nepal halted sales of all Chinese milk products and would now increase testing of such imports. Vietnam health officials warned tainted Chinese milk may have been sold in its remote, impoverished central region ... Three baby animals at the

> Hangzhou Safari Park near Shanghai have kidney stones after being fed milk powder for more than a year … The powder was made by the Sanlu Group … The two orangutans and a lion cub were found with kidney stones Wednesday [24 September].
>
> (www.iht.com, 25 September 2008)

> The maker of White Rabbit Creamy Candies announced Friday [26 September] that it would stop selling in China the popular confection … Guanshengyuan, the manufacturer, had already recalled its exports of the widely distributed Chinese candy because they contained unacceptable levels of the chemical melamine … Food safety authorities in a rapidly growing list of countries, including Australia, New Zealand and India, have pulled the candies from shelves … Nearly 53,000 children in China, including five in Hong Kong, have been sickened by baby formula or other products contaminated with melamine. Four babies have died. More than a dozen countries, from Asia to Africa to Europe, have banned or recalled Chinese milk products.
>
> (www.cnn.com, 26 September 2008)

> Guanshengyuan … has stopped domestic sales of … the popular White Rabbit candy … Canada's food safety regulator has recommended a recall of White Rabbit sweets, while authorities in Singapore said they found melamine in samples of the product imported from China. The Philippines has also ordered Chinese-made dairy products off the shelves … The WHO's China representative said the scandal may have peaked but said there could be more deaths.
>
> (www.bbc.co.uk, 26 September 2008)

'The harm caused by melamine is related to weight' (*IHT*, 276 September 2008, p. 3).

> Koala-shaped cookies from a major Japanese confectioner were the latest products caught up in China's tainted milk scandal Friday [26 September], while Taiwan reported three babies with kidney stones in the island's first cases possibly linked to the crisis. But the WHO said it did not expect the number of victims to grow dramatically … The government in the Chinese territory of Macao said late Thursday [25 September] they had found levels of melamine at twenty-four times the safety limit in Koala's March cookies made by Lotte China Foods. The company is a member of Lotte Group, a Tokyo conglomerate. An official at Lotte China Investment in Shanghai said Friday that previous inspections had not shown any problems … A company spokeswoman in Tokyo said that products sold in Japan were not made with Chinese dairy ingredients … Three Taiwanese children – two three-year-old girls and a one-year-old boy – who had been consuming Chinese formula were found to have kidney stones. A mother of one of the girls also has kidney stones, said [a health chief in eastern Taiwan] … He said: 'They have all consumed Chinese milk, but more tests are needed to establish the link to their kidney stones.'
>
> (www.iht.com, 26 September 2008).

The list of problematic products continues to grow ... The Hong Kong government said the contaminated baby vegetable formula cereals were made by Heinz. It also said melamine was found in steamed potato wasabi crackers produced by Silang House. Both were made in China.

(*IHT*, 27 September 2008, p. 5)

Recent disclosures have shown that parents who tried to act as whistleblowers were thwarted by an unresponsive bureaucracy, while Chinese journalists were blocked by censorship edicts banning coverage of politically touchy subjects during the prelude to the Olympics. Officials now acknowledge that China's leading dairy companies, including the Sanlu group, the worst offender in the scandal, were exempted from mandatory government inspections ... Last May [2008] the government's top food quality agency rated dairy companies among the safest producers in China's food industry, reporting that 99 per cent of them passed safety inspections for their infant milk formula ... There were early warnings that were not publicized because of censorship ... [One] news weekly discovered cases of sickened children in July ... but could not publish articles so close to the Games ... A mother in Hunan province wrote a detailed letter on 30 June, pleading for help from Beijing's top food quality agency ... The mother said she had already complained in vain to Sanlu and local officials ... The health bureau in Gansu province said his agency sent an urgent report to the ministry of health in July ... Some dairy farmers interviewed this week in Hebei province said it was an open secret that milk was adulterated, although many claimed they did not know that melamine was being used ... [One dairy farmer] said quality testers at Sanlu took bribes in exchange for looking the other way on milk adulterated with melamine ... Analysts said the lack of a truly independent regulatory system means that high profile gestures, like executing or firing officials, have limited impact, especially since local industries are so often intertwined with local officials.

(*IHT*, 27 September 2008, pp. 1, 5)

In the United States the Food and Drug Administration [FDA] said Friday [26 September] that some instant coffee and tea drinks, all containing a non-dairy creamer made in China, had been recalled for fear of contamination. It is the first recall in the United States growing out of the melamine scare. The FDA said the King Car Food Industrial Company of Taiwan had called back seven products ... mostly sold in stores specializing in Asian foods. The company's tests in Taiwan had determined that its non-dairy creamer, which was made in China, was contaminated by melamine, the FDA said. No contaminated products have actually been found on American shelves. The FDA also said that it had extensively tested milk-based products imported from China into the United States in recent weeks ... Exports of food ingredients from China have boomed in recent years ... Supermarket shelves in China are still largely empty of domestic dairy brands.

(www.iht.com, 28 September 2008)

'Officials in a number of provinces are pressurizing lawyers to pull out of a volunteer legal advice group set up to help the families of thousands of children who were poisoned by contaminated milk, according to people involved in the group' (*FT*, 29 September 2008, p. 13).

'British candy maker Cadbury has recalled eleven types of its Chinese-made chocolate as a precaution, the Hong Kong government said … Cadbury Asia Pacific … [said] the chocolates were made in Cadbury's factory in Beijing' (www.iht.com, 29 September 2008).

> Two US foodmakers were investigating Indonesian claims Monday [29 September] that high traces of melamine were found in Oreo wafers, M&Ms and Snickers imported from China … Kraft Foods Inc. and Mars Inc. said they were adhering to a recall order but stressed the same products were cleared of melamine in other Asian countries. They were looking into explanations, including the possibility that the goods were counterfeit.
>
> (www.cnn.com, 29 September 2008)

> Cadbury, the British candy maker, said Monday [29 September] that tests had 'cast doubt on the integrity of a range of our products manufactured in China' … Myanmar added its name to the list Monday, saying dairy items from China would be barred from entering its military-ruled country.
>
> (www.iht.com, 29 September 2008)

> Cadbury said Monday that it was recalling eleven kinds of Chinese-made chocolates after tests found that they contained the industrial chemical melamine. Cadbury said in a statement that it had recalled eleven chocolate products made at its factory in Beijing that are distributed in Taiwan, Hong Kong and Australia. The company said, however, that all its dairy suppliers had been cleared by government milk testing. A spokesman for Cadbury said it was too early to say how much of the chemical was in the chocolates … The police raided dairy farms and milk purchasing stations in northern China, detaining twenty-two people accused of involvement in a network that produced, sold and added melamine to milk … Police officers in Hebei province seized more than 220 kg, or 485 lb, of melamine in the raids.
>
> (*IHT*, 30 September 2008, p. 8)

> British confectioner Cadbury has recalled all of its Chinese-made candy products over fears they may be contaminated with the chemical melamine, a company statement said Monday [29 September] … Some or all of the products were exported to Taiwan, Hong Kong, Australia, the Pacific island of Nauru and Christmas Island in the Indian Ocean … Chinese police have arrested forty people in the tainted milk scandal, including twenty-two announced Monday in northern China's Hebei province. Nineteen of those were managers of pastures, breeding farms and milk-purchasing stations … Eighteen arrests were announced earlier. They include two brothers who

face charges of selling contaminated milk. The brothers could face death if convicted.

(www.cnn.com, 28 September 2008)

Cadbury had earlier recalled eleven chocolate types from mainland China, Hong King, Taiwan and Australia because of fears of contamination … [Cadbury] emphasized that the only goods affected were those made in the company's Beijing factory, and not those produced in the UK or elsewhere … In mainland China lawyers and local rights groups are seeking to support families affected by the scandal, possibly by suing dairies or officials who failed to disclose the problem. But many say they are facing pressure from the authorities to abandon their efforts.

(www.bbc.co.uk, 29 September 2008)

Police have arrested twenty-two people … Police said the melamine had been produced in underground plants and then sold to breeding farms and purchasing stations … China's dairy industry is on the brink of collapse and importers of food products containing any Chinese milk products are being recalled from shops around the world … More than a dozen Asian and African countries, plus the twenty-seven-member EU, have taken steps to ban or otherwise limit consumption of Chinese milk product imports. Laos, Mali and Niger on Monday [29 September] became the latest to order such measures. Besides the toll in mainland China, five children in Hong Kong, one in Macao and four people in Taiwan have reportedly developed kidney stones after drinking tainted milk.

(www.bbc.co.uk, 30 September 2008)

China said Monday [29 September] that it had detained twenty-two people suspected of operating an underground network that intentionally adulterated milk with melamine. The contamination has led to the nation's worst food safety crisis in decades. The announcement was the third regarding a mass detention of suspects in the contamination … On 14 September the government said nineteen people had been detained, and on 19 September it reported the detention of twelve more. The government did not explain in the Monday announcement how many suspects in all had been detained in the investigation, or whether some had been included in the earlier announcements … The government accused the group of operating as a kind of criminal syndicate, producing melamine in underground factories and then marketing it to dairy farms and milking stations in Hebei province to adulterate the milk for profit … In China the milk scare has set off a minor panic. In Hebei province alone, where the scandal is centred because it is the location of the headquarters of the Sanlu Group, the country's biggest maker of infant milk formula, more than 200,000 children had been brought into hospitals to be checked for melamine contamination or kidney stones over the past few weeks. Since announcing last week that about 53,000 children had been affected by melamine-tainted dairy goods, the Chinese government has not updated the number of victims nor has it held a news conference in recent days detailing its findings. But in recent days the government has tried to reassure consumers that the country's dairy supply is safe, reporting that hundreds of tests conducted after 14 September and involving some of the biggest dairy makers had not detected melamine.

(www.iht.com, 30 September 2008)

New testing has found melamine tainting in another thirty-one brands of Chinese milk powder ... In all the State Administration of Quality Supervision, Inspection and Quarantine tested samples from 265 brands produced before 14 September. Nine of those found tainted were produced by the company at the centre of the scandal, Sanlu ... Hong Kong authorities [on Tuesday 30 September] said the amount of melamine found in samples of chocolate made at Cadbury's Beijing factory was legally acceptable for human consumption ... Hong Kong's Centre for Food Safety said it ran tests on six Cadbury products, two of which had been made in Beijing and had been recalled, and found them to have melamine levels lower than the territory's legal limit ... It did not say whether it was testing the other nine products being recalled. Cadbury said the Hong Kong test results did not change their decision to recall the products from the Beijing plant ... The state-run China News Service says twenty-seven people have been arrested so far ... The Dutch food safety watchdog announced Tuesday it had found slightly elevated levels of melamine in cookies imported from China and sold under the 'Koala' brand. The cookies have been pulled from shelves in the Netherlands and the chance they have made anybody sick is 'extremely small', the agency said ... Also Tuesday Anglo-Dutch food giant Unilever said it was recalling its Lipton-brand 3-in-1 milk tea powder in Hong Kong and Macao after it was found to contain melamine. Last week Unilever recalled Lipton Milk Tea from the Taiwan market because the product used Chinese-made milk ... Hong Kong authorities also said they had found high levels of melamine in Pocky Men's coffee cream coated biscuit stick, produced by Japan's Ezaki Glico Co. Ltd ... Two samples of coconut and walnut cakes manufactured by Tian Le Foods Co. Ltd in southern China were also found to contain unacceptably high levels of melamine, authorities said ... Melamine has now been found in six products imported to South Korea, and the country has banned imports of all Chinese-made food products containing powdered milk.

(www.ccn.com, 1 October 2008)

Sanlu ... is reported to have asked for government help to cover up the extent of the problem. The official *People's Daily* said the Sanlu Group asked Shijiazhuang city government to help 'manage' the media response to the case. It made the request in August, weeks before the contamination of milk with melamine became public knowledge. It comes as a new list of tainted milk products is published. Fifteen more Chinese companies have been identified as having produced milk products contaminated with the industrial chemical. It brings to twenty the number of companies named as producing goods with melamine … The Chinese authorities have already acknowledged that the Shijiazhuang government sat on a report from Sanlu about milk contamination for more than a month while Beijing hosted the Olympic Games. It now says that in a letter to the city government Sanlu asked for help to 'increase control and co-ordination of the media, to create a good environment for the recall of the company's problem products', the *People's Daily* reported.

(www.bbc.co.uk, 1 October 2008)

A city government implicated in attempts to cover up China's widening scandal over contaminated milk has admitted 'lacking political sensitivity' in its handling of the case, but it also sought to shift blame to a local dairy producer it says requested controls on media coverage … The Communist Party's *People's Daily* newspaper yesterday [1 October] quoted the deputy party secretary of northern Shijiazhuang city as saying Sanlu Group had asked in a letter in early August for 'strengthened management' of news media. It had done so in order to prevent reports 'creating negative influences on society by stirring up this issue'. The deputy party secretary insisted that the city government had worked hard to deal with the milk contamination through increased testing and a trade recall but said it delayed reporting to higher authorities because of a lack of political sensitivity that prevented its understanding of the overall situation … Fonterra Dairy Co-operative of New Zealand owns 43 per cent of Sanlu … Fonterra has had to write down the book value of its Sanlu investment by 70 per cent to reflect the cost of product recalls and brand damage … It says it advised Sanlu on quality testing but did not independently check any of its partner's products. Fonterra had three members on the Sanlu board but only one of them spoke Mandarin – and only one Fonterra quality control specialist worked permanently at Sanlu. Andrew Ferrier, Fonterra chief executive, argues … that if his company had not blown the whistle the milk powder scandal might not have become public … At the [2] August board meeting Fonterra demanded an immediate public recall. By the end of the month there had been at least three meetings with local government officials, but they pursued a quieter 'trade recall' from wholesalers … For nearly six weeks nothing was done. Fonterra eventually went over the heads of local officials and got Wellington to alert Beijing … Fonterra could have gone public nearly six weeks earlier, but Mr Ferrier insists that the wiser course was to work within the system. He says: 'It was a very tough call and one we revisited many times. The risk of going against the will of the local government is that we would have been shut out of the process altogether' … Sanlu is majority owned by the local government in Shijiazhuang [in Hebei province] … Central government approval would have been required to get recall advertisements into the Chinese press.

(*FT*, 2 October 2008, p. 13)

This week the *People's Daily*, the authoritative newspaper of the Communist Party, carried an unusual article in which a spokesman in Shijiazhuang apologized but also accused officials at Sanlu of asking for a cover-up of the problem in August, shortly before the beginning of the Olympics ... The article never addressed whether city officials participated in a cover-up but stated that they did not inform higher officials in the province of the probe until a month later ... In China a couple filed a lawsuit against [Sanlu] ... despite efforts by the authorities to keep it out of the courts ... The parents of a one-year-old boy have sued the Sanlu Group because the infant developed kidney stones after drinking the company's powdered baby formula. The parents, who reside in Henna province in central China, are asking for $22,000 in compensation. However ... [it was] reported that the local court had yet to accept their lawsuit.

(www.iht.com, 2 October 2008)

The parents of a baby allegedly sickened by tainted infant formula are suing [Sanlu] ... [but it would not be known] until next week if the court in Henna province would take the case ... China's State Council has ordered hospitals to provide free treatment for sick infants, but the one-year-old baby is at Beijing's Children's Hospital, which will only offer free treatment to children diagnosed after 12 September, when the scandal broke ... One lawyer suggested his profession was under pressure to not accept lawsuits connected with the scandal ... Other lawyers told the Associated Press they had not come under pressure to reject such cases.

(www.cnn.com, 2 October 2008)

Melamine has been found in milk powder from fifteen more Chinese dairies, the authorities said Wednesday [1 October] and Hong Kong's food safety agency said its tests had found melamine in a Japanese-brand cheesecake that is made in China ... Thirty-one new batches of Chinese milk powder were found tainted with melamine. Of the twenty companies on the list, fifteen have not been named in previous tests ... In the most recent tests nine of the batches containing melamine were produced by Sanlu ... The new batches being tested were mostly milk powder for adults ... The new figure brings to at least 100 the number of tested batches of milk powder found to contain melamine. Tests have also found melamine in twenty-four batches of milk produced by three of China's best known dairies ... The State Administration of Quality Supervision, Inspection and Quarantine ... tested 265 batches produced by 154 different companies before 14 September. China has 290 companies making powdered milk.

(www.iht.com, 1 October 2008)

More contaminated Chinese candy was discovered in the United States on Wednesday [1 October], this time in Connecticut, where consumer protection officials issued a public warning against eating the sticky sweet ... Testing found traces of melamine ... Last month the Food and Drug

Administration warned consumers about White Rabbit candy and in California health officials found traces of melamine after testing samples of White Rabbit. The American distributor of the candy has already ordered a recall but some candy may still remain in stores … White Rabbit Creamy Candy is made in Shanghai and has already been pulled from stores in Britain and many Asian countries.

(www.iht.com, 2 October 2008)

Officials in the United States on Wednesday [1 October] reported finding tainted White Rabbit candies for sale in Asian food markets in the state of New Jersey, after finding them earlier in California and Hawaii. Officials in Germany said they had discovered them in the southern state of Baden Württemberg. The Shanghai-based maker of the candy, Guan Sheng Co., said last week it was halting production of the sticky, taffy-like confection, an iconic brand beloved by generations of Chinese.

(www.cnn.com, 2 October 2008)

Taiwan's health minister says its tests have found minor doses of melamine in milk powders produced in China by the Switzerland-based Nestlé … [and that] they will be taken off shelves on Thursday [2 October] as a temporary measure. He says Taiwan will discuss with food safety experts from the United States, Japan, Europe and the WHO to decide whether to permit milk products containing minor doses of the chemical.

(www.iht.com, 2 October 2008)

Austria's health ministry says a non-threatening amount of melamine has been found in a milkshake at a Chinese restaurant in Graz. The ministry says a small amount of the substance was found during a random sampling of Chinese products. It says the milkshake was not sold to customers and that no one has been sickened by it. The ministry said Thursday [2 October] the tainted product came from a Chinese store in Vienna and is off the market.

(www.cnn.com, 2 October 2008)

Taiwan's health minister has been admitted to hospital after being allegedly attacked by opposition MPs over the tainted Chinese milk scandal … The opposition, which is angry at the government's response to the milk scandal, denies its MPs attacked him … Yeh Ching-chuan became health minister last week after his predecessor resigned amid accusations that he had been too lax about products from China contaminated with the chemical melamine … The opposition Democratic Progressive Party … has accused the government of wavering over food safety standards.

(www.bbc.co.uk, 3 October 2008)

Russian food inspectors have found nearly 2 tonnes of Chinese dry milk believed to be contaminated with melamine … [it was] reported Friday [3 October] … the same day that the list of tainted products grew … The Vietnamese health ministry has discovered the industrial chemical in eighteen food products imported from China and three other countries, and has ordered them recalled and destroyed ... Health officials in the Philippines found melamine in two of thirty milk products from China tested for the chemical. The Philippine government has halted imports and sales of Chinese milk products pending inspections last week. Australian food regulators recalled Chinese-made Kitin Milk Tea after tests found that the drink contained melamine. It is the fourth product withdrawn from the country's stores as a result of the tainted milk scandal ... The [US] Food and Drug Administration said Friday [3 October] that trace amounts of melamine are safe in most foods, except for baby formula.

(www.iht.com, 4 October 2008)

South Korea's food watchdog has ordered four more Chinese-made food products [made by Mars, Nestlé and Lotte Confectionery Co.] to be destroyed after they were found to contain melamine ... The test results raise the number of known melamine-tainted food products imported into South Korea from China to ten. About 430 Chinese-made products using dairy ingredients have already been pulled from store shelves and put into storage pending testing.

(www.cnn.com, 4 October 2008)

'Chinese food manufacturers still do not routinely test for the product' (www.feer.com, 3 October 2008).

Dairy farmers say they have been squeezed as price controls on food went into effect, creating incentives to dilute the milk among farmers and big companies alike. Many farmers here insist they never used melamine, and that the real culprits are the dairy companies and the milking stations they operate in villages like the ones near Shijiazhuang. Regulatory loopholes and corruption are believed to be part of the problem. Many dairy farmers in the region said bribery was common at milking stations. And dairy experts say local regulators are also known to take bribes or favour companies that are partly owned by a local government entity, which sometimes means the regulator and the regulated are virtually one and the same ... Sanlu's decision to lower its prices this year [2008] was the first blow to local farmers, many of whom took out huge loans to purchase cows just two or three years ago and moved here to work as dairy farmers. Sanlu and other major dairy companies were responding to government price controls that were supposed to help fight inflation and rising food costs around the nation. But here in Hebei province the policy hurt farmers who were already struggling to cope with soaring animal food costs, driven up by the global surge in grain prices ... 'Sanlu has a monopoly here,' said [one farmer] ... Zhang Guanong [of Juangnan University] ... says the 1986 code regulating the quality of milk is outdated ... He said: 'In 2004 I was one of the drafters of the China Dairy Products Quality Inspection report. I found adulteration widespread: urea, soap powder, starch are very popular additives. We suggested new inspection methods targeted on these additives should be written into the regulation. But on the other hand we feared that once these were written into the regulation more dairy makers would know these tricks or even innovate by creating new tricks' … Xiang Zhikong (Renmin University): 'The problem was and still is that anyone can become a dairy supplier and anyone can own or invest in third party dairy stations. There are no licensing requirements or any other sort of quality regulatory standards.'

(www.iht.com, 4 October 2008)

On Saturday [4 October] China announced that a test of 607 batches of liquid milk from twenty-seven cities found the samples to be melamine-free. The tests were the sixth Chinese officials have carried out since melamine was discovered in powdered infant formula last month [September]. Authorities have promised to subsidize farmers hit by the shrinking demand for milk. Among them is the northern Hebei province, which has earmarked 316 million yuan ($46.1 million) for subsidies. That translates to giving a farmer 200 yuan ($29) per cow.

(www.cnn.com, 5 October 2008)

Hong Kong authorities Sunday [5 October] announced that two recalled candy products made by British confectioner Cadbury had high levels of melamine … The company stresses that its products manufactured at its Beijing plant are only exported to Taiwan and Hong Kong, with one product – Cadbury Éclairs – sent to Australia, Nauru and Christmas Island … Hong Kong's Centre for Food Safety tested 104 samples of products made by a variety of manufacturers, including Cadbury, Nestlé and some US and Chinese companies. Only two of the samples showed unsatisfactory levels of melamine – Cadbury Dairy Milk Cookies Chocolate (bulk pack 5 kg) and Cadbury Dairy Milk Hazelnut Chocolate (bulk pack 5 kg).

(www.cnn.com, 5 October 2008)

Hong Kong said Sunday that its health inspectors had found two Cadbury chocolate products containing considerably more melamine than the city's legal limit … In another blow to China's food industry, Iran banned imports of all dairy products from China … The health ministry said the ban on imports of dairy products from China would be in place until further notice … The latest tests of 129 batches of baby formula and 212 batches of other kinds of milk powder showed they were free from melamine contamination, the General Administration of Quality Supervision, Inspection and Quarantine said.

(www.iht.com, 6 October 2008)

China pledged on Monday [6 October] to improve food safety, and officials detained six more people … Police detained six suspects for allegedly mixing melamine into raw milk … The move brings the number of people being held in connection with the scandal to thirty-two … Wang Yong (the director of the General Administration of Quality Supervision, Inspection and Quarantine): 'Food safety concerns not only the health of the public, but also the life of business' ... Wang replaced Li Changjiang, who resigned last month [September] in the wake of the scandal ... Part of the agency's clean-up effort was the deployment in mid-September of more than 5,000 inspectors to check dairy factories. Wang said the inspections covered all dairy producers across the country to monitor the entire production process around the clock.

(www.iht.com, 6 October 2008)

[It was reported on Tuesday 7 October that] China's iconic White Rabbit candy is back in production after being pulled out of stores around the world last month [September] ... The popular, vanilla-flavoured sweets are sold in more than fifty countries ... Production stopped last month [September] ... The White Rabbit announcement was made after the cabinet promised to overhaul its 'chaotic' dairy industry and acknowledged China suffered from a lack of oversight ... Testing continues on milk and milk-related products in China, and the maker of White Rabbit candy said its new batches of candy will undergo government quality testing ... Guan Sheng Yuan Co. said White Rabbit candy production has resumed because the company is now using a safe supply of powdered milk, but ... the company did not say where the raw milk for the powder came from ... Guan Sheng Yuan did not say when White Rabbit candy would go on sale again.

(www.iht.com, 7 October 2008)

The health ministry announced on Wednesday [8 October] new limits set by the government on the amount of melamine to be permitted in dairy products, but it refused to provide updated statistics on the number of people who have died or fallen ill from ingesting melamine-tainted dairy products ... Health officials said that traces of melamine are found in many food products because melamine is used to make plastic and can seep into food from packaging. A certain amount of melamine can be tolerated, they said. The government has now set melamine limits at 1 milligramme per kilogramme of infant formula and 2.5 milligrammes per kilogramme of liquid milk, milk powder and food products that contain more than 15 per cent milk. Any dairy products with higher levels are banned. The new limits are supported by assessments by the Hong Kong government, the WHO and the UN, the officials said. When asked what the previous standards were, the official declined to give an answer and implied that there had been no limits before the milk scandal erupted last month [September] ... The new limits act as guidance for how much unintentional seepage of melamine into food can be permitted by inspectors. People who purposefully add melamine to food will be prosecuted ... In late September the ministry reported the figures on the deaths and illnesses from drinking tainted milk products. At the time 13,000 children were hospitalized, it said. Since then the government has not released any new statistics. Before that announcement

Xinhua reported that an infant in the western region of Xinjiang had died from melamine ingestion, but the ministry has not confirmed it. The latest news reports from Xinhua put the number of deaths at three. A scan by *The New York Times* of statistics on the websites or official news media outlets of eight of China's more than thirty-two provinces and provincial-level administrative areas shows that in those eight territories about 52,000 people have fallen ill from tainted milk. Some of the numbers were published in early October and others in late September. Extrapolating from those statistics, the number sickened across all of China would be much higher than the 53,000 announced by the health ministry in late September.

(www.iht.com, 8 October 2008)

Under health ministry guidelines released Wednesday [8 October] melamine is limited to one part per million for infant formula and 2.5 parts per million for liquid milk, milk powder and food products that contain more than 15 per cent milk ... Any items containing higher levels will be prohibited from sales ... Levels of melamine discovered in batches of milk powder recently registered as much as 6,196 parts per million. Guidelines in Hong Kong and New Zealand say melamine in food products is considered safe at 2.5 parts per million or less. Hong Kong meanwhile has lowered the level for children under three and pregnant or lactating women to one part per million. In the United States the Food and Drug Administration says its experts have concluded that eating 2.5 parts per million of melamine – a miniscule amount – would not raise health risks, even if a person ate food every day that is laced with it.

(www.cnn.com, 9 October 2008)

Nearly 1,700 infants and children were still in hospital ... the health ministry said. It last updated the figures on 21 September, when it said that 12,892 children were being treated for kidney problems caused by drinking milk tainted with melamine ... No more infants have died from the contaminated milk ... leaving the death toll at four. Eight of the 10,666 children still in hospital Wednesday [8 October] were in serious condition ... Altogether 36,144 had left hospital after being treated. It did not give an overall figure for the number of children affected so far, but reports from local media across the country complied by Reuters suggest the number of affected children has risen to nearly 94,000. While the number of children in hospital is declining, 539 children were admitted after drinking melamine-laced milk, while 2,067 others checked out after being treated.

(www.iht.com, 9 October 2008)

On Wednesday [8 October] alone 539 children were admitted to hospitals. On Thursday [9 October] the finance ministry announced that it would give the equivalent of $44 million in subsidies to dairy farmers hit hard by the downturn in milk sales. Many farmers have had to dispose of vast quantities of suspect milk. Most of the money will go to farmers in the main dairy producing regions and provinces of Inner Mongolia, Hebei, Liaoning, Shanxi and Shandong.

(www.iht.com, 9 October 2008)

The government announced that it has banned the sale of a herbal medicine after three people died and three others fell seriously ill. The warning about the medicine, called Ciwujia, was posted on the website of the State Food and Drug Administration late Wednesday [8 October]. It said six people had been severely affected after being injected with the herbal formula ... It is sold in various forms, including capsules and herbal teas ... Toxic drugs have long been a problem in China.

(www.iht.com, 9 October 2008)

China's food exports have increasingly suffered, with more than thirty countries restricting Chinese dairy imports and in some cases all Chinese food products. At a meeting of the WTO in Geneva, Chinese officials sought to limit the damage Thursday [9 October], saying Beijing was making enormous efforts to deal with the problem and maintaining no new cases of contamination had been detected since 30 September. The official also contended the contamination has been accidental, contradicting a WHO assessment that the chemical was added deliberately ... Until this week there had been no standards in China for the amount of the chemical allowed in food products.

(www.iht.com, 10 October 2008)

France has recalled sweets and biscuits made with Chinese dairy products after finding high levels of melamine ... The agriculture ministry said: 'The first results of tests conducted in France have shown a melamine level above the warning level set by the European Commission at 2.5 mg per kilo' ... The EU banned imports of Chinese baby food containing traces of milk ... The recall of White Rabbit sweets and Koala biscuits is the first such order to be made by a European country.

(www.bbc.co.uk, 11 October 2008)

Chinese companies are major suppliers of common ingredients and additives, like citric acid and many types of vitamins. The country is the world's largest exporter of seafood, most of it from fish farms, and a major exporter of chicken, fruits and vegetables. In the medical field China sells large quantities of penicillin and paracetamol, an aspirin alternative, overseas ... In the EU alone: Chinese fish and shrimp were rejected because they contained fungicides, antibiotics or other banned drugs; dried fruit and vegetables were found to have more than the allowable level of preservative sulphite; peanuts had excessive levels of fungus-related toxins; and packaged foods tested positive for heavy metals that leached from their packaging. Although only the world's eighth largest exporter of food, China ranked in first place last year [2007] for the number of hazardous imports detected by regulators in the EU. China has 352 notifications, its highest level ever, compared with 191 for the United States, which is the world's largest agricultural exporter … [But] the EU's annual report on food safety found contamination in foods exported from well over 100 countries. It is also working with Chinese regulators to improve their monitoring techniques … [and] the European Commission said it had recorded a decline in quality problems with Chinese food imports in the second half of last year … As of April 2007 China had the third highest rate of import refusals in the United States, after Mexico and India. Fruit, vegetables and most meat in China are not required to go through a cold distribution chain … In July 2007 the government carried out the execution of the head of the food and drug safety agency who was convicted of taking bribes in return for approving drugs. Regulators also closed 180 food manufacturers that it said had been using banned dyes, hydrochloric acid and formaldehyde in candies, seafood, pickles and cookies … On Friday [10 October] the Chinese government announced measures intended to improve the quality and safety of dairy products as well as new regulations on the breeding of cows and the production and sale of dairy products. It also called for tougher penalties for people who violate safety standards … Fonterra, a New Zealand company that owns a large stake in [Sanlu] … says it never occurred to them to check for melamine. A spokeswoman said: 'Melamine is not something you would reasonably expect to find in milk. We have only recently become aware of one dairy company in the world who routinely tests for melamine' … The Food and Drug Administration in the United States only has the capacity to examine 1 per cent of all shipments into the country, according to a report [by Congress] last year [2007] … In Asia governments are also sometimes afraid to anger Beijing.

(www.iht.com, 12 October 2008)

The Chinese government ordered a recall on Tuesday [14 October] of all milk products produced before 14 September and still on the shelves so the products can be tested for melamine … Melamine has led to the deaths of at least three babies; at least 53,000 other children have fallen ill. The government announced limits for allowable traces of melamine last week. If the recalled products meet the new standards, they will be put back on the market … A lawyer based in Shanghai has filed a lawsuit in Gansu province on behalf of a family whose six-month-old son died in May after drinking tainted baby formula.

(www.iht.com, 14 October 2008)

China has ordered the withdrawal of all liquid and powdered milk made more than a month ago to help restore confidence … It is the first time the government has issued a blanket recall of products since the tainted milk scandal emerged last month [September] … The order requires shops across China to take off the shelves all liquid and powdered milk produced before 14 September, the day before a countrywide inspection of milk-producing facilities was launched. Even those brands that have previously passed the government's quality tests are not exempt ... [The BBC] says the order has so far not been strictly heeded and some stores are still selling dairy products without quality checks or new labels.

(www.bbc.co.uk, 14 October 2008)

China ordered all milk products more than a month old pulled from store shelves for emergency testing ... It is not clear why the cut-off date for the latest notice is 14 September, but China launched a countrywide inspection of dairy-producing facilities focusing on milk collecting centres on 15 September ... Also Tuesday [14 October] Hong Kong's government said a two-year-old boy developed two kidney stones after consuming melamine-laced milk and cookies ... One of Thailand's most popular bakery chains, S&P, said Tuesday that it was recalling all its packaged cookies from stores nationwide after Swiss authorities said they found high concentrations of melamine in the Thai biscuits.

(www.cnn.com, 15 October 2008)

Taiwanese and Chinese officials have agreed to set up a hot line to inform each other of food safety emergencies ... In Vietnam state media said Wednesday [15 October] that the health ministry had banned all products for human consumption that are contaminated with melamine.

(www.iht.com, 15 October 2008)

Japanese health officials warned residents on Wednesday [15 October] not to eat a variety of frozen green beans imported from China that are contaminated with an extremely high concentration of pesticides ... more than 34,000 times the acceptable limit ... Several people have been sickened, but there were no reports of serious injuries from the pesticides.

(www.cnn.com, 15 October 2008)

The baby died on 1 May ... he was six months old. The parents filed a lawsuit Monday [13 October] in the arid north-west province of Gansu where the parents live, to try to wrest more than $152,000 in compensation from the Sanlu Group, the maker of the baby formula ... [the baby] had been drinking ... But as in two other courts dealing with such lawsuits, the judge has so far declined to hear the case ... Tainted infant formula is the latest in a long string of food and drug safety problems that have exposed corruption and inefficiency among regulators. Scandals have followed one after the other not only because regulators often fail to do their jobs, but also because companies that produce shoddy goods almost never face financial penalties from the Communist Party's legal system ... Government officials are quietly pressurizing everyone involved, from the parents to the lawyers to the judges, to drop the issue, say legal scholars and lawyers who have volunteered to help the parents ... [The parents of the baby who died on 1 May] are among only a handful of Chinese who have filed against a dairy company. The plaintiffs are all individual families and lawyers say there is almost zero chance that any judge would consider a class-action lawsuit since those are

> highly discouraged … [One argument is that the government does not] want to see so many people getting involved in one lawsuit [since] this might threaten social stability … More than 100 lawyers across the country have put themselves on a list of volunteers willing to give legal advice to anxious parents, but local government officials have put pressure on some to not take on any cases, several lawyers say. More than twenty lawyers have since removed themselves from the list … Government officials have told parents and lawyers in the milk cases that their complaints can be resolved through out-of-court compensation payments … A lawyer in Beijing who is collecting material for a possible class-action lawsuit … [says that] to prevent a public airing of grievances the government will pressure complainants to sign individual compensation agreements … In the milk scandal judges are trying to decide whether to accept three lawsuits that have been filed in the provinces of Gansu, Henan and Guangdong. Lawyers in Henan, a poor, backward province, have faced more harassment from local officials than lawyers elsewhere. Most of the lawyers who have dropped off the volunteer list are from Henan. On 27 September officials from the province's judicial bureau met with lawyers to discourage them from taking on the cases. A working brief issued on 7 October by the national volunteer group said the officials had directly told the lawyers not to give any legal aid to the parents.
>
> (www.iht.com, 16 October 2008; *IHT*, 17 October 2008, p. 4)

> Premier Wen Jiabao has said that the government is partly responsible for the tainted milk scandal … He said that while the problems were with a private company, the government had not properly supervised the dairy industry. He said: 'We feel that although problems occurred at the company, the government also has a responsibility' … Mr Wen said that clear standards and testing requirements were needed in all the steps of making milk – the production of raw milk, collection, transportation, processing and making formula.
>
> (www.bbc.co.uk, 18 October 2008)

> Journalists had to be mindful of long-standing, but mostly secret, orders from the Propaganda Department about reporting food safety issues. *The Economist* has seen a directive issued by a provincial propaganda bureau. Circulated in January 2005 it bans the media from naming any suspect food product until a 'clear verdict' has been reached by the authorities. There are to be no exposés of safety problems concerning famous Chinese food brands or food products for export without official approval. For imported food approval must come from Beijing. If it causes poisoning only Xinhua, the official news agency, may break the news and even its reports must be approved by the Propaganda Department and the foreign ministry.
>
> (www.economist.com, 23 October 2008)

'On Monday [20 October] Australia said it had ordered a recall of a milk drink and cake after tests showed they were contaminated with melamine' (www.iht.com, 20 October 2008).

> Some 1,500 dogs in north-east China have died after eating animal feed tainted with melamine … a veterinarian said Monday [20 October] … The raccoon dogs – a breed native to east Asia that is raised for its fur – were fed a product that contained melamine and developed kidney stones … All of the dogs died on farms in just one village … A [newspaper] report said … the deaths … had occurred over the past few months … An [inspection] official tested one sample of animal feed and found that it contained about 500 parts per million of melamine. China's health ministry recently capped the amount of melamine permissible in milk, milk powder and food products that contain more than 15 per cent dairy to 2.5 parts per million.
>
> (www.iht.com, 20 October 2008)

'The dogs died at farms in the north-eastern Liaoning province … The name of the company that supplied the feed [was not given] … but tests had shown it had been tainted' (www.bbc.co.uk, 21 October 2008).

> China's legislature began reviewing a draft law on Thursday [23 October] that would strictly limit food additives … The health ministry already ordered more restrictive food safety regulations on 8 October. State media also reported that six people had been arrested in Inner Mongolia on suspicion of mixing melamine powder with milk products.
>
> (www.iht.com, 24 October 2008)

> Prime minister Wen Jiabao said the crisis involving tainted dairy products will spur the introduction of China's first major food safety law and will ensure food exports meet international standards … The state-run *China Daily* newspaper said the law will impose safety standards on food additives and ban all harmful chemicals. It will also allow the government to recall unsafe food if companies fail to do so … The draft law was submitted for review by the National People's Congress on Thursday [23 October] at the beginning of a six-day session.
>
> (www.cnn.com, 25 October 2008)

'The state-run *China Daily* newspaper said the new law would impose safety standards on food additives and ban all harmful chemicals. It would also allow the government to recall unsafe food if companies fail to comply' (www.iht.com, 26 October 2008).

> The discovery of excessive levels of the industrial chemical melamine in Chinese eggs has prompted the Hong Kong authorities to expand health tests to include meat products imported from China, a senior official said Sunday [26 October]. The move follows the announcement late Saturday [25 October] that Hong Kong testers had found 4.7 parts per million of melamine in imported eggs … the legal limit for melamine in foodstuffs in Hong Kong is 2.5 ppm.
>
> [Hong Kong] said the melamine may have come from feed given to the chickens that laid the eggs … In an earlier egg-related food safety scare in

Hong Kong and China the banned cancer-causing industrial dye, Sudan Red, was used to colour egg yolks … The Hong Kong government also said it found excessive amounts of melamine in … crackers made by [a] Philippine company … More than 3,600 children remain sick in China from contaminated milk, with three in serious condition, the ministry of health said last week.

(www.cnn.com, 26 October 2008)

Scientists in China worry that in addition to being used to adulterate dairy supplies, melamine may have been intentionally added to animal feed in China, according to a report published on Sunday [26 October] in the *South China Morning Post*. Tainted chicken and possibly fish and hog feed could result in poisonous meat and seafood. There were also indications over the weekend that the contamination may have reached far more children in China than reported. Health officials said Sunday that a broad survey of homes in Beijing had found that nearly a quarter of the 300,000 families with children younger than three, about 74,000 families, had a child who had been fed with melamine-tainted milk. The government said it was a door-to-door survey conducted between late September and late October, but did not say how many of those children had fallen ill … Late last year [2007] Beijing announced a crackdown on shoddy and unsafe food producers and ordered the closing of thousands of slaughterhouses and food factories. During that time several Chinese melamine suppliers admitted in newspaper interviews to selling melamine to animal feed operations and fish feed providers in China. The government, however, never reported finding melamine-tainted fish or animal feed in China's food supply.

(www.iht.com, 27 October 2008)

Health authorities in Hong Kong have found more eggs contaminated with melamine [it was reported on 28 October] … Although much lower in melamine content than … [the previous ones they] were still above the legal limit … Health officials in Hong Kong say that there is little risk to human health – and that a child would have to eat perhaps twenty eggs a day for the melamine to have an effect … Experts say melamine's health risks are not well known … Food exports from China were worth $27 billion in 2006.

(www.cnn.com, 29 October 2008)

Nine families with babies suffering kidney problems … have filed separate lawsuits against one of China's largest milk companies … The lawsuits were filed on Wednesday [29 October] in the northern city of Shijiazhuang, the location of the headquarters of the Sanlu Group … The lawsuits demand compensation from Sanlu … The families are asking for at least 14,000 yuan, or about $2,000 … Each family had an infant that had to go to hospital because of kidney stones and six are still in hospital … The lawyers did not file a class-action lawsuit on behalf of all the parents because each case had different details … Both product liability lawsuits and class-action lawsuits are rare in China … Class-action lawsuits are highly discouraged in the Chinese legal system. Technically they can be filed, but onerous rules put in place in recent years by official legal bodies have made it difficult for lawyers to file such lawsuits. Some Chinese legal scholars say the government views class-action lawsuits as a threat to social stability … In the first weeks of the scandal more than 100 lawyers put themselves on a list of lawyers volunteering to dispense legal advice to the families. But at least two dozen have since dropped their names from the list; most of them are from Henan province, where lawyers have complained of subtle pressure put on them by local officials … At least three other lawsuits had already been filed before Wednesday.

(www.iht.com, 30 October 2008)

Melamine is probably being routinely added to Chinese animal feed, state media has reported … Several state newspapers carried reports on Thursday [30 October] suggesting that the addition of melamine to animal feed was widespread. The state-run *China Daily* said in an editorial: 'The feed industry seems to have acquiesced to agree on using the chemical to reduce production costs while maintaining the protein count for quality inspections. We cannot say for sure if the same chemical has made its way into other types of food' … The practice of mixing melamine into animal feed is an 'open secret' in the industry, the *Nanafang Daily* reported … Analysts say that Friday's news reports [31 October] are an unusual departure for Chinese officials.

(www.bbc.co.uk, 31 October 2008)

Chinese regulators said Friday [31 October] that they were widening their investigation into contaminated food amid growing signs that melamine has leached into the nation's animal feed supplies … The announcement came after food safety tests this week found that eggs produced in three provinces in China were contaminated with melamine … China is one of the world's largest exporters of food and food ingredients, including meats, seafood, beverages and vitamins … Interviews Friday and during the past year with several chemical dealers who sell melamine suggest that melamine scrap, the substantially cheaper waste left after producing melamine, has been added to animal and fish feed in China for years … Melamine was banned as an animal feed additive in July 2007 … State-run newspapers are publishing editorials in China calling for a full investigation into the use of melamine in food and feed.

(www.iht.com, 31 October 2008)

Regulators said over the weekend that they had confiscated and destroyed more than 3,600 tonnes of animal feed tainted with melamine … In what appears to be the biggest food safety crackdown in years, the government also said Saturday [1 November] that it had closed 238 illegal feed makers in a series of nationwide sweeps that involved more than 369,000 government inspectors … But government officials also said that China's animal feed had improved in recent years. They insisted that only a small number of rogue operators had deliberately added melamine to feed.

(www.iht.com, 2 November 2008)

Hong Kong food inspectors have found fish feed imported from China contaminated with high levels of melamine … The Hong Kong government finding [was] reported late Tuesday [11 November] … Inspectors said fish feed imported from Fujian province in southern China was found to have more than twice the level of melamine deemed to be safe for food, 6.6 parts per million. The acceptable level in Hong Kong and the United States is 2.5 parts per million. But Hong Kong officials also said in an announcement that melamine-tainted fish feed would probably not pose serious health problems for people who consumed fish because consumers would not be directly eating the melamine. As a precautionary measure, however, inspectors asked Hong Kong fish farms not to use feed contaminated with melamine. In late October newspapers in Vietnam reported that tests on 240 tonnes of fish feed imported from China found traces of melamine, but not high levels.

(www.iht.com, 12 November 2008)

[An] area of agricultural concern is animal feed. Chinese eggs seized last month [October] in Hong Kong, for instance, contained elevated levels of melamine-laded wheat gluten used in the feed for the chickens that produced the eggs … The United States imports most of its wheat gluten.

(www.iht.com, 16 November 2008)

Candy, snacks, cereal and any other products from China that contain milk will be detained at the border until tests prove that they are not contaminated, the US government announced Thursday [13 November] … Chinese products that contain milk or milk powder will be detained until the manufacturer or its customer has the product tested and found to be free of contamination, or they show documentation indicating that the product does not contain milk or milk-derived ingredients … The alert also noted that inspectors in thirteen other countries had discovered melamine in Chinese products including milk, yoghurt, frozen desserts, biscuits, chocolates and cookies.

(www.iht.com, 14 November 2008)

The EU and the United States on Monday [17 November] sought to bind China into international controls on product safety when the three trading partners discussed consumer scares ranging from contaminated Chinese milk to dangerous toys. At a meeting in Brussels Beijing officials signed a new agreement with the EU promising to strengthen the exchange of information over faulty products, improve the ability to trace dangerous goods, and increase co-operation in taking them out of circulation … The accord coincided with the release of figures showing a significant rise in dangerous goods from China entering the European market. As a percentage of products taken off the EU market, those from China have increased to 56 per cent in the first nine months of this year [2008] from 47 per cent a year earlier. Officials advised caution over the statistics, arguing that the increase may reflect improved detection rates. However, the figures also show that, of around 200 faulty products of which the Chinese authorities are notified each year, only around eighty are investigated. This resulted in corrective action in 51 per cent of cases investigated. China is the biggest exporter to the EU and around 85 per cent of toys on the European market are made in China. At the meeting on Monday the United States also agreed to work more closely with the EU on converging regulatory standards and exchanging information. Last year [2007] ... [the EU] complained to Washington that it learned of the mass recall of Mattel products only from newspaper reports. US product safety legislation enacted in August now permits advance notice of such moves ... The US Food and Drug Administration also announced it will open three offices in China this week in an unprecedented effort to improve the safety of exports headed to America ... The new FDA offices are the first outside of the United States ... Chinese officials say they support the goal ... [of] toy standard harmonization ... since it is difficult to meet two different sets of export standards.

(www.iht.com, 17 November 2008)

'The EU and the United States on Monday [17 November] sought to bind China into international controls on product safety when the three trading partners discussed consumer scares ranging from contaminated Chinese milk to dangerous toys' (*IHT*, 18 November 2008, p. 14).

Officials from China, the United States and the EU yesterday [17 November] agreed to work towards synchronizing safety standards for children's toys in the first trilateral summit on product safety ... The three parties have resolved to work towards merging their product tracing systems so dangerous items can be identified and tracked back to the manufacturer as quickly as possible.

(*FT*, 18 November 2008, p. 11)

The United States opened a branch of the Food and Drug Administration in Beijing on Wednesday [19 November], the first of several offices that will seek to regulate the safety of food and medicine bound for America ... Later this week the agency will open inspection stations in Shanghai and Guangzhou; in the coming months it plans to establish offices in India, Latin America and Europe ... Overseas offices would ensure the safety and quality of goods that make up 15 per cent of the food Americans consume ... The United States imported more than $321 billion worth of goods from China last year [2007] ... All three outlets will work with Chinese counterpart agencies to inspect products bound for the United States. They will also certify third-party inspectors who can approve the quality of exports ...

The US Department of Agriculture is charged with monitoring the safety of imported meat, poultry and eggs, which make up about 20 per cent of the American food supply. The FDA is responsible for the other 80 per cent – virtually all other foods, vitamins, supplements and pharmaceuticals, as well as medical equipment … The opening of the offices comes less than a week after the FDA ordered a wide range of Chinese products held at the US border … Beijing has objected to the FDA measures, saying the products have been certified by the Chinese inspectors under new, stricter measures.

(www.iht.com, 19 November 2008; *IHT*, 20 November 2008, p. 4)

The Chinese government … announced a wide range of food safety measures on Thursday [20 November] aimed at reining in abuses in the dairy industry. The State Council issues several new rules it says will govern all aspects of the industry, from cow breeding and animal feed to the packaging and sale of the milk … The government said it would issue new laws and standards by next October [2009] and that by 2011 'the goal is to have well-bred cows and a mass-producing industry' … The government said it would also provide loans and grants to dairy farmers and milk producers struggling to survive the crisis.

(www.iht.com, 20 November 2008)

Officials on Monday [2 December] issued new figures for the number of children affected by tainted dairy products, saying that as many as six babies may have died and more than 300,000 were sickened after drinking contaminated milk power. The government had previously set the death toll at three infants, with 50,000 others made ill after consuming milk laced with melamine … The ministry of health issued a statement saying that 860 babies who drank tainted milk were still hospitalized with kidney or urinary tract problems; 154 of those were described as being in serious condition … On Monday *China Daily* said milk exports have dropped by 92 per cent since September, when news of the scandal emerged … The melamine scandal has devastated China's dairy industry … the world's third largest … [In 2007] China's fast growing dairy industry was worth $18 billion … On Tuesday [2 December] the private equity firm of Kohlberg Kravis Roberts & Co. would spend $100 million to buy a minority stake in China Mengniu Dairy, the country's largest milk producer.

(www.iht.com, 2 December 2008; *IHT*, 3 December 2008, p. 4)

The health ministry had until now said four infants had died after consuming the toxic compound … The health ministry … said 294,000 were now known to have fallen ill as a result, five times more than had been originally thought … A total of 294,000 infants are reported to have suffered 'urinary system abnormalities' such as kidney stones due to the tainted milk. Some 51,900 were taken to hospital and 861 are still admitted … Four of the deaths were recorded in the provinces of Jiangxi, Zhejiang, Guizhou and Shaanxi, and the other two in Gansu.

(www.bbc.co.uk, 2 December 2008)

Hong Kong authorities have found the toxic chemical melamine in another Chinese brand of eggs ... The eggs came from a farm in Dehui City, in China's north-eastern Jilin province ... The centre for Food Safety said it had tested 307 egg samples and four of them were found to have almost twice the legal limit of melamine. Scientists had set an allowable limit of 2.5 parts per million of melamine in food, but the latest tests showed the eggs had 4.7 parts per million.

(www.bbc.co.uk, 3 December 2008)

EU regulators have banned imports of Chinese soy-based food products for infants and young children after melamine was found in Chinese soy-bean meal, the European Commission said Wednesday [3 December] ... Rich in nitrogen, melamine is fairly inexpensive and can be added to sub-standard or watered-down milk to fool quality checks, which often use nitrogen to measure protein levels in milk ... Only feed and food containing less than 2.5 milligrammes of melamine per kilogramme, or 2.3 pounds, will be allowed into EU markets. The ban is expected to come into force by the end of this week. All Chinese shipments of baking powder, or ammonium bicarbonate, will also be tested at EU points of entry after high levels of melamine were found.

(*IHT*, 4 December 2008, p. 12)

The ministry of health is preparing a blacklist of dangerous food additives, 'especially toxic or harmful substances, which are likely to be used in food products' ... The ministry also said it would be establishing stricter food labelling requirements and quality standards, starting with the dairy sector.

(www.iht.com, 5 December 2008)

The Chinese dairy company at the forefront of the tainted milk scandal in China has been declared bankrupt, according to a New Zealand company that is a major investor in the firm. Fonterra, the New Zealand firm, said Wednesday [24 December] that a Chinese court in Hebei province had issued a bankruptcy order against Sanlu, the Chinese dairy, in response to a petition from a creditor. A court-appointed receiver will take over Sanlu to sell off its assets and pay creditors, Fonterra said in a statement ... [Fonterra said it had] elected to write down the full value of its investment in Sanlu ... Fonterra's 43 per cent stake in Sanlu was reported to be $113 million.

(www.iht.com, 24 December 2008)

Sanlu Group has filed for bankruptcy. A court in Shijiazhuang, where the company is based, told CNN Wednesday [24 December] it has received the bankruptcy application ... Sanlu could be taken over by Beijing Sanyuan Food Company or Wandashan Dairy, Xinhua reported.

(www.cnn.com, 25 December 2008)

'A dealer of a toxic chemical and a producer went on trial Friday [26 December] ... accused of illegally devising and selling a so-called "protein powder" that was largely constituted on malt dextrin and the chemical melamine' (www.cnn.com, 26 December 2008).

> Six people accused of contaminating milk powder … went on trial today [26 December] … Those accused appeared before four separate courts in the northern province of Hebei, charged with producing or selling a supposedly protein-rich additive for powdered milk which contained melamine … A court in Shijiazhuang, Hebei's capital, is trying two of the principal suspects. One is charged with producing 775 tonnes of the tainted powder … the other accused man bought 230 tonnes of the powder and resold it to others. Four other suspects went on trial in three smaller courts in the province accused of adding smaller amounts of the tainted powder to milk, which was then sold on to Sanlu … The Sanlu company knew the milk was tainted months before it told local officials, allowing it to be sold in the meantime.
>
> (www.guardian.co.uk, 26 December 2008)

> Among those in court Friday [26 December] was the owner of a workshop that was allegedly the country's largest source of melamine … producing 776 tonnes of the additive powder from October 2007 through August 2008 … In the same case a second man was accused of buying and selling 230 tonnes … Four other men were being tried in three separate courts across Hebei province for adding the chemical to raw milk and then selling it to Sanlu Group … Xinhua reported Thursday [26 December] that Sanlu has 1.1 billion yuan of net debt and that a branch of the Shijiazhuang City Commercial Bank was the creditor that applied to a court to have Sanlu declared bankrupt. It said the intermediate court in Shijiazhuang had accepted the filing. Xinhua said Sanlu owes a creditor 902 million yuan that it borrowed this month [December] to pay for the medical treatment of children sickened after drinking the company's infant formula and for compensation of the babies' families … The issue of compensation for the families of the children sickened or killed has become a sensitive one, with courts so far not accepting any lawsuits filed by the families … [It was] reported that Tian Wenhua, Sanlu's chairwoman and general manager, would go on trial Wednesday [31 December] in Shijiazhuang for 'selling fake and shoddy products'. Sanlu, like a number of major Chinese dairies, had been exempt from government inspections because it was deemed to have superior quality controls – until high levels of the industrial chemical melamine were found in its baby formula and other products in September. Several other dairies were also found to have sold tainted goods.
>
> (www.iht.com, 26 December 2008)

> The legal proceedings are increasing fears among victims that they could be left without compensation … According to the Shijiazhuang city government, Sanlu borrowed more than renminbi 900 million ($132 million) to pay for medical tests and treatment for infants harmed by its baby milk powder.

Those funds had already been transferred to the China Dairy Association to deal with the claimants, a city government spokesman said ... Some parents now oppose the plan to fight for compensation in the courts ... [One] father of a melamine victim ... [said]: 'I am worried that after the bankruptcy there will be no more than renminbi 900m for the victims, but that is never going to be enough. Therefore, this is no longer the responsibility of Sanlu; it is the responsibility of the government, and one it cannot push away.'

(*FT*, 27 December 2008, p. 17)

Chinese dairy firms involved in the tainted milk scandal are to compensate the families of the nearly 300,000 affected children, state media said. Twenty-two companies will make an undisclosed one-off cash payment, Xinhua reported quoting the China Dairy Industry Association ... The firms have also agreed to create a fund to cover the medical bills for any potential after-effects of the poisoning, it said.

(www.bbc.co.uk, 27 December 2008)

The country's Dairy Industry Association ... said Saturday [27 December] victims will receive a one-time cash payment, but did not provide the amounts ... No date for the payments was given. The twenty-two dairies also raised money to cover medical bills for any after-effects suffered ... Six children died from what the ministry of health said was likely melamine contamination. About 294,000 infants also suffered from urinary problems such as kidney stones ... At least eighteen people were arrested ... As of 27 November 861 babies remained hospitalized, Xinhua reported, citing the ministry of health. The news agency said it had requested updated numbers but they were not immediately available.

(www.cnn.com, 27 December 2008)

Four more people linked to the scandal have gone on trial on Monday [29 December] ... This brings the number before the courts to ten ... On Friday six people suspected of involvement in the scandal went on trial, and face sentences of at least 10 years, lawyers said.

(www.bbc.co.uk, 29 December 2008)

A group of nine people accused of intentionally tainting dairy supplies went on trial Monday [29 December] on northern Hebei province, charged with endangering public security ... the nine people are part of a larger group of dairy industry suppliers who government prosecutors say sold some of the poisoned milk that killed at least six children and sickened nearly 300,000 children nationwide. In a related case six other people went on trial Friday [26 December] in Hebei province.

(*IHT*, 30 December 2008, p. 8)

A group of dairy companies accused of selling contaminated milk ... has agreed to pay $160 million in compensation to the victims ... a spokeswoman for the China Dairy Industry said Tuesday [30 December] ...

The settlement would amount to about $550 per victim, which is the equivalent of about three months' salary for the typical factory worker in southern China.

(*IHT*, 31 December 2008, p. 4)

Four executives working for the Sanlu Group … went on trial Wednesday [31 December] … The trial [was held] at Shijiazhuang Intermediate People's Court in northern Hebei province … Tian Wenhua, Sanlu's former board chairwoman and general manager, and the other executives were accused by prosecutors of producing and selling fake or substandard products … The three other executives are [two] former deputy managers … and a former executive heading Sanlu's milk division … The ministry of health has said the contamination likely caused the deaths of at least six babies. Another 294,000 infants suffered from urinary problems, such as kidney stones.

(www.cnn.com, 31 December 2008)

Tian Wenhua, former board chairwoman and general manager of Sanlu Group Co., pleaded guilty to charges of producing and selling fake or substandard products … [She] testified Wednesday [31 December] that she began investigating product quality issues in May but did not notify authorities until August … [She] could face the death penalty … [A] former deputy general manager at Sanlu used a wheelchair because he lost use of his legs during a suicide attempt … Seventeen others have gone on trial over the past few days … The defendants included people accused of producing melamine and marketing it to milk producers, as well as milk collectors who mixed the chemical into raw milk sold to major dairies … Details [were released] of a 1.1 billion yuan ($160 million) compensation plan … Some families have said the planned payout by dairies was too low, and their lawyers pledged to continue attempts to sue for more compensation … The twenty-two Chinese dairy companies found to have sold tainted products would contribute to the 1.1 billion yuan ($160 million) compensation fund. Children who suffered kidney stones would get 2,000 yuan ($290), while sicker children would be paid 30,000 yuan ($4,380) … The one-time cash payments total 900 million yuan ($131 million), while another 200 million ($29 million) will go to a fund set up to cover bills for lingering health problems. The fund would pay medical costs related to tainted milk until victims turn eighteen … Sanlu, which filed for bankruptcy and faces 1.1 billion yuan ($160 million) in debt, has leased its plants to a subsidiary of Beijing Sanyuan Foods Co. Ltd … Production will start soon at the plants which have been shut down since 12 September, shortly after news of the baby formula contamination broke. Sanyuan emerged from the scandal with its reputation largely intact because its products were never found to contain melamine … China's top product quality watchdog said it was testing tableware made of melamine after reports that the products could be toxic when heated, Xinhua said late Tuesday [30 December]. The utensils were sold in domestic supermarkets and wholesale markets, the report citing the General Administration of Quality Supervision, Inspection and Quarantine.

(www.iht.com, 31 December 2008)

Tian Wenhua is one of the highest ranking corporate executives to go on trial in China and could face life imprisonment or even the death sentence if convicted ... [She] pleaded guilty to selling tainted powdered formula ... Tian's plea Wednesday [31 December] came on the first day of a trial that involves three other Sanlu executives. The court said that consumer complaints about Sanlu's milk came in as early as December 2007. Tian said she knew the company was selling contaminated formula by May 2008 but did not report the problem to local government officials until August. Between May and September, when Sanlu stopped production, prosecutors said the company made more than 900 tonnes of melamine-contaminated powdered formula. Until Wednesday company officials had maintained that they learned of the problem only in August. That is when executives at the Fonterra Group of New Zealand, which owns a large stake in Sanlu, said they became aware of a problem and pushed Sanlu to issue a recall. The Fonterra executives said they believed that their warnings, on the eve of the Beijing Olympics, had reached government officials in the capital. But so far investigations have focused mostly on local officials, though the head of the country's product safety watchdog, the General Administration of Quality Supervision and Quarantine, resigned ... According to media reports, Tian said she was told in August 2008 that European standards allowed up to 20 milligrammes of melamine per kilogramme, or 2.2 pounds, to be present in food products. In September some Sanlu products were found to have more than 2,000 milligrammes per kilogramme ... Several high ranking Shijiazhuang government officials have been fired for not guarding public safety.

(www.iht.com, 1 January 2009)

Tian Wenhua, the sixty-six-year-old former general manager of the new bankrupt Sanlu Group ... told the court she learned of the tainted milk complaints from consumers in mid-May ... The company set up a working team led by Tian to handle the case, but did not submit a written report about the milk powder to the Shijiazhuang city government until 2 August. Tian said. The Shijiazhuang government did not report the case to higher government authorities until a month later, prompting speculation authorities sought to avoid a scandal upsetting Beijing's Olympic Games in August ... Terms, which include a 2,000 yuan ($293) one-off payment for victims with 'mild symptoms', have been greeted with scepticism ... More than 1,500 boxes of Chinese biscuits exported to Hong Kong and Singapore had also tested positive for melamine, local media reported yesterday [30 December].

(www.independent.co.uk, 31 December 2008)

'Sanlu stopped production on 12 September … the company itself is also a defendant' (www.bbc.co.uk, 1 January 2009).

'[A parent] could receive 200,000 yuan in compensation for the death of a child … Children who suffered kidney stones would get 2,000 yuan, while sicker children would be paid 30,000 yuan' (www.thetimes.co.uk, 31 December 2008).

> Tian Wenhua … has argued that the country's lack of regulations regarding a toxic chemical contributed to a tainted milk scandal … In a statement distributed by her attorney on Thursday [1 January 2009] Tian said China should consider the standards of the EU regarding the chemical melamine. She also said other independent companies under the Sanlu umbrella produced some of the 'tainted milk powder' and their leaders should also shoulder some responsibility. Tian said she did not intentionally sell tainted products and had taken several steps aimed at making up for the harm caused. In her closing statement Tian apologized … Wang Yuliang appeared in court in a wheelchair after he broke his leg in a suicide attempt … He said: 'I apologize to Sanlu's faithful consumers. When I think of the children who were harmed … I feel extreme inadequacy towards these sick children and their parents' … The trial ended after a fourteen-hour session.
>
> (www.cnn.com, 2 January 2009)

> [Twenty-two] dairy companies involved in the tainted milk scandal have apologized in a New Year text message sent to millions of mobile phone subscribers: 'We are deeply sorry for the harm caused to the children and society. We sincerely apologize for that and we beg your forgiveness' … A group of parents whose children drank the tainted milk have reportedly been detained by police. A father of one ill child said Beijing police tried to block them from holding a news conference, and added that some of the group – including him – were detained for a while and are now under house arrest. But a small press briefing did go ahead on a Beijing pavement, with parents complaining about lack of government support … One man from Sichuan province told Reuters: 'The government said all the medical care is free, but when it comes to the local level things change. I have already paid more than 50,000 yuan [$7,300]' … One mother said: 'Our babies have been diagnosed with kidney stones, but we do not know what other diseases they will contract when they grow up … We are asking for research on how much damage melamine can wreak.'
>
> (www.bbc.co.uk, 2 January 2009)

> Police detained the father of a child sickened by tainted milk apparently to prevent him and other parents from holding a news conference to complain that proposed compensation for their ill children is too low … Under the plan families whose children died would receive 200,000 yuan, or about $29,000, while others would receive 30,000 yuan for serious cases of kidney stones and 2,000 yuan for less severe cases … An additional 200 million yuan would go to a fund to cover bills for lingering health problems.
>
> (www.iht.com, 2 January 2009)

Authorities [say they] have arrested sixty people in connection with the country's tainted milk scandal ... The arrests have been made over the past several months ... Twenty-one of them went on trial between 26 and 31 December, including four executives of Sanlu Group.

(www.cnn.com, 12 January 2009)

A brand of imported pet food is being pulled off store shelves in China after reports of dogs being sickened by it, a company official said Tuesday [13 January]. Natural Pet Corporation, which is the distributor for Optima dog food from Australia, has ordered a recall, according to ... the company's general manager in Shanghai ... Dogs [have been] poisoned by aflatoxin after eating Optima products ... Chinese media reports detail dozens of poisonings ... Aflatoxin attacks the liver in several animal species. Although rare in many parts of the world, the fungi that produce aflatoxin can contaminate cereal grains often used in pet foods ... Natural Pet Corporation [said it is] fully aware of the reports of sick dogs and that the products are being tested.

(www.cnn.com, 13 January 2009)

A group of parents whose children were poisoned by tainted domestic dairy products said they would reject a government-sanctioned compensation passage. Instead, they would press for long-term health care for the victims and demand medical research into the illnesses that still afflict tens of thousands of children ... The $160 million compensation plan announced last month was [considered to be] inadequate and failed to address the medical needs of children whose health had been profoundly damaged ... The current offer, which is to be financed by twenty-two dairy companies, provides about $29,000 for each family that lost a child and about $4,400 for each child who suffered serious kidney damage. The families with relatively minor health problems would receive about $290. That is about three months of the average worker's salary ... Among the parents' complaints is a rule that withholds compensation for children over three years old ... [In addition] the package provides no assistance to the families that incurred tens of thousands of dollars in hospital bills.

(www.iht.com, 14 January 2009)

The parents of a baby who died last May [2008] from drinking milk formula have accepted a cash payment from [Sanlu] ... a lawyer representing the parents said Friday [16 January] ... The parents are the first to receive compensation for the death of a child from tainted milk. They accepted more than $29,200 from Sanlu Group ... Their six-month-old son ... is believed to have been the first baby to die from drinking a tainted milk product. As part of the compensation deal the parents have agreed to drop a lawsuit they filed in October against Sanlu ... The court, the Lanzhou Intermediate People's Court, did not accept the case ... The milk scandal has become a politically sensitive issue because Communist Party officials were involved in covering up the deaths and illnesses of the victims and judges and lawyers in parts of China have been under pressure from officials not to take on any milk-related cases. So far no court has agreed to hear a case … Xinhua, the state news agency, reported that more than 3,000 families in Shijiazhuang, the capital of Hebei province, where Sanlu is based, have accepted compensation payments. But some parents are vocally rejecting the payment offers, including a group that has gathered 250 signatures from victims' families and is demanding long-term health care for victims and medical research into their continuing illnesses.

(www.iht.com, 16 January 2009)

A group of lawyers said Tuesday [21 January] that they had filed a lawsuit against twenty-two dairy companies to seek compensation for the deaths or illnesses of hundreds of children who consumed milk products tainted with a toxic chemical. The filing is a rare instance in which Chinese lawyers are proceeding with a class-action product liability case. The lawsuit was filed Friday [16 January] with the Supreme People's Court in Beijing on behalf of the families of 213 children … said … an administrator for a group of lawyers who have volunteered to represent the victims' families … It was unclear whether the court intended to accept the lawsuit. Two class-action suits filed in lower courts last month [December 2008] on behalf of the melamine victims were rejected … The 213 victims in the latest lawsuit include four dead children who have not been included by the government in the official death toll … The lawyers are also preparing a lawsuit concerning a fifth unacknowledged dead child … Product liability cases and class-action lawsuits are extremely uncommon in China … The lawyers' group filed the two earlier class-action lawsuits … The current lawsuit includes plaintiffs from those filings. In the first the lawyers sued in Hebei Province High Court on behalf of sixty-three victims. In the second 111 victims were represented in a suit filed in Shijiazhuang Intermediate Court. In both previous cases the only defendant named was the Sanlu Group … In the class-action suit filed Friday parents were asking for compensation totalling more than $5.2 million. The compensation amounts being demanded vary case by case, with the largest being $73,000 for a dead child.

(www.iht.com, 21 January 2009)

Two men have been given the death penalty for their involvement in China's contaminated milk scandal … The court sentenced Zhang Yujun and Geng Jinping to death. Zhang Yujun was accused of running an illegal workshop in Shandong province in eastern China, producing 600 tonnes of the fake protein powder – the largest source of melamine in the country. Geng Jinping was convicted of producing and selling toxic food to dairy companies. His associate Geng Jinzhu was given eight years in prison. Zhang Yanzhang, who was accused of selling on protein powder produced by Zhang Yujun, was given a life sentence. Gao Junjie received a suspended death sentence … Tian Wenhua … was general manager of the Sanlu

> Group, which sold tainted baby milk powder. She had already pleaded guilty to the charges of producing and selling fake or substandard produce, and was given a life sentence by the Intermediate People's Court in Shijiazhuang ... They are among twenty-one sentences handed down by the court in northern China, where Sanlu is based.
>
> (www.bbc.co.uk, 22 January 2008)

> Tian Wenhua ... [was also] ordered to pay a fine of $2.9 million. Sanlu itself was fined $7.3 million ... even though the firm has been declared bankrupt. Earlier the court sentenced cattle farmer Zhang Yujun and milk trader Geng Jinping to death ... Kidney damage was reported in hundreds of thousands of people. At least six babies were killed because of ... tainted milk.
>
> (www.bbc.co.uk, 22 January 2009)

> Gao Junjie received a death sentence with a two-year reprieve, which means he could be spared execution. Tian Wenhua was sentenced to life imprisonment for her failure to stop producing and selling the tainted goods even after her company learned that the products were flawed. She was the highest ranking corporate executive brought to trial last year [2008] ... Three other former executives of Sanlu were sentenced to prison terms ranging from five to fifteen years. She pleaded guilty to the charge of failing to act properly in the case. She was also fined about $3 million. The other five defendants received jail sentences ranging from five years to life ... Foreign journalists have been barred from attending some of the court sessions.
>
> (www.iht.com, 22 January 2009)

> Tian Wenhua had pleaded guilty to charges of producing and selling fake or substandard products, which state media said did not carry a death sentence ... A third man was handed down a suspended death sentence, which usually means life in prison on good behaviour.
>
> (www.independent.co.uk, 22 January 2009)

'Three people were sentenced to death and two others to life imprisonment for their roles, while three others received prison terms of five to fifteen years each' (www.cnn.com, 22 January 2009).

> Sanlu Group Co. was declared bankrupt by a court in its north China base of Shijiazhuang, the capital of Hebei, on Thursday [12 February] ... Fonterra, a New Zealand farmer-owned co-operative that owns 43 per cent of Sanlu, has already written off its $139 million investment.
>
> (www.iht.com, 16 February 2009)

'In its bankruptcy filing, executives said their company was crippled by $161 million in debt, much of that medical costs for hospitalized children sickened by Sanlu products' (www.iht.com, 12 February 2009).

> An agency of the Shanghai government said over the weekend that an infant formula made by a subsidiary of Danone, the large French food and

> beverage company, was not contaminated with melamine … The announcement by the Shanghai government came after Chinese newspapers published reports last week quoting parents accusing Danone of selling contaminated dairy products.
>
> (www.iht.com, 16 February 2009; *IHT*, 17 February 2009, p. 8)

> At least seventy people have fallen ill after eating pork products contaminated with an illegal animal feed additive … The tainted pig organs contained the steroid clenbuterol, which is used to prevent animals gaining fat … The pork was brought last week from markets in Guangzhou, the provincial capital of Guangdong, and came from farms in the neighbouring Hunan province … Clenbuterol is banned as a food additive because it can be fatal for humans. The drug is given to treat asthma and has been used illegally by athletes to build muscle.
>
> (www.bbc.co.uk, 23 February 2009)

> Seventy residents of south-eastern China have been sickened by a banned nervous system agent, state media reported on Monday [23 February] … [Because clenbuterol] burns fat and increases muscle mass, it is illegally used to produce animals with lean meat … Clenbuterol has been used illegally by athletes to shed fat and build muscle, and it is also touted as a quick, if illegal, weight-loss drug.
>
> (*IHT*, 24 February 2009, p. 5)

> Clenbuterol can prevent pigs from accumulating fat but is harmful to humans and can be fatal. One of the largest food poisoning cases involving clenbuterol happened in Shanghai in September 2006, when 336 people were hospitalized after eating pig meat or organs contaminated with the additive.
>
> (www.cnn.com, 23 February 2009)

> China has passed a strict new food safety law … The law, five years in the making, consolidates hundreds of separate regulations and statutes covering China's 500,000 food processing firms. The law pays special attention to food additives, which were at the centre of a tainted milk scandal last year [2008]. No additives will be allowed unless proven safe, the new law declares. It will go into effect on 1 June [2009] … The new law will also include a system for monitoring and supervision of a set of national standards for food safety, severe discipline for offenders and a system for food recall. Just last week at least seventy people fell ill after eating pork products contaminated with an illegal animal feed additive.
>
> (www.bbc.co.uk, 1 March 2009)

'Victims of last year's tainted baby milk scandal will be allowed to seek redress in court, a senior judicial official has announced … China's Supreme

People's Court said ... such lawsuits ... would now be accepted' (www.ft.com, 3 March 2009).

> China said Friday [20 March] that eight senior regulators were fired last week for 'slack supervision' in a tainted milk scandal that killed at least six children and sickened over 300,000 last year [2008]. The government said high ranking regulators in the country's major food supervisory agencies, including the ministries of health and agriculture and the top food safety watchdog, were stripped of their positions and their membership of the Communist Party.
>
> (www.iht.com, 22 March 2009)

'A court in Shijizhuang has agreed to hear the first lawsuit seeking compensation for last year's tainted milk scandal ... The case has been brought by a parent of one of the sick children against the Sanlu Group' (*The Times*, 26 March 2009, p 41).

> The European Commission said [that] ... customs authorities across the [EU] ... seized 178 million fake items in 2008, up 125 per cent from 79 million in 2007 ... Pirate DVDs and CDs were the most prevalent fake goods ... The European Commission said China remained the main source of counterfeit goods coming into the EU, accounting for 54 per cent of the total in 2008.
>
> (www.bbc.co.uk, 11 July 2009)

> This month [October] the US Consumer Product Safety Commission, whose investigation into Chinese drywall ... or plasterboard, used for interior walls or ceilings ... is the largest in its history, will release the results of a study to determine why the drywall might be causing problems and what kind of remediation programme might be effective.
>
> (*IHT*, 9 October 2009, p. 19)

> Federal investigators [in the United States] reported on Monday [23 November] that a 'strong association' exists between chemicals in Chinese drywall installed in thousands of homes during the housing boom and electrical problems in those homes. In addition, investigators said that the drywall was a possible cause of respiratory problems reported by homeowners, brought on by hydrogen sulphide gas emitted from imported drywall in combination with formaldehyde, which is common in new homes. The finding, released by the Consumer Product Safety Commission, is the second in a series of progress reports on a widespread investigation into complaints by homeowners that their newly built homes were giving off a rotten egg odour and causing respiratory problems, and that appliances and electrical systems were failing quickly ... An estimated 60,000 homes may have been built with Chinese drywall, but the commission said that not all Chinese-made drywall was tainted ... The commission also said that no new Chinese drywall had entered the United States since 2009, although stockpiles of uninstalled Chinese drywall had been located.
>
> (www.iht.com, 24 November 2009)

China has executed two people for their role in a scandal involving tainted milk powder … Zhang Yujun and Geng Jinping were the only people to have been executed over the scandal … Zhang Yujun was convicted of producing and selling more than 770 tonnes of the tainted milk powder from July 2007 to August 2008 … Geng Jinping, who managed a milk production centre, was convicted of supplying milk containing melamine to dairies.

(www.bbc.co.uk, 24 November 2009)

China on Tuesday [24 November] executed two people for their roles in a tainted milk powder scandal in which at least six children died and more than 300,000 became sick … Their sentences were upheld in March by an appellate court in the northern city of Shijizhuang. China requires death sentences to receive final approval from the Supreme People's Court in Beijing, after which most are carried out by lethal injection … Both had been convicted of producing and selling a phoney protein powder containing melamine … No public investigation was ever made into accusations that news of the melamine tainting was suppressed ahead of last year's Beijing Olympic Games because the government did not want to see it overshadowing the prestigious event.

(www.iht.com, 24 November 2009)

Dairy industry officials said last summer that the farmers and producers had largely recovered from the scandal, but some parents are still seeking redress, arguing that many of those punished so far are only scapegoats. One group filed suit in the spring. Others have tried to wage a public campaign to hold more officials accountable but say they have been harassed by the authorities.

(www.iht.com, 24 November 2009)

A Chinese court is hearing the first civil compensation claim by a parent whose child fell ill during last year's tainted milk scandal … [The parent] is suing Sanlu and a supermarket for $8,000 … As well as the [original] compensation … [the parent] wants his son's medical expenses to be paid by the state-administered milk compensation fund until the boy reaches adulthood … [A] Beijing-based lawyer is handling about 200 such cases … He said that the cases were being handled individually because the courts had rejected an attempt to sue for compensation as a group. So far six cases have been accepted by courts across the country … The trial began on Friday [27 November] at a court in Beijing and continues on 9 December.

(www.bbc.co.uk, 29 November 2009)

The dairy company, the Sanlu Group, and Longhua, a supermarket chain based in Beijing, both said they should not have to pay compensation to … [the parent] because his son should be covered under a fund set up by the government … A lawyer for Sanlu also argued that there were no medical records linking the boy's kidney problems to drinking tainted milk.

(www.iht.com, 29 November 2009)

The Chinese police arrested three people on Tuesday [8 December], accusing them of selling milk powder contaminated with melamine, the same toxic chemical that was blamed last year [2008] for killing six children and sickening over 300,000 others ... The three men, all of whom worked for Jinqiao Dairy Company in north China's Shaanxi province, were accused of producing and selling toxic food ... The three men were initially detained on 2 December and formally arrested this week ... The police accused three men of selling more than 5 tonnes of melamine-tainted milk powder in September to the Nanning Yueqian Food Additive Company in southern China's Guangxi province. A spokesman for Nanning Yueqian, which produces milk powder for big cities like Shanghai and Nanjing, said they discovered the milk powder was contaminated in September and informed the government. The spokesman said: 'We contacted Jinqiao immediately to inform them about the problem, but they denied it and sent us a report saying that the milk powder was already tested and turned out to be safe. We did not trust them because last year's Sanlu case was so heartbreaking' ... Investigators said the milk powder was confiscated in November [2009] before it could reach stores. There is no indication that Jinqiao Dairy's products are exported ... This is the third consecutive year that regulators have caught food producers selling goods that were apparently intentionally doctored with melamine.

(www.iht.com, 11 December 2009)

Municipal health authorities have shut down the Shanghai Panda Dairy, charging it with producing milk products containing the industrial chemical melamine ... Three top executives of the firm were arrested ... The arrests and the closure of the dairy [were] reported Friday [1 January 2010] ... The Shanghai Bureau of Quality and Technical Supervision found high levels of melamine in high calcium milk powder that was marketed toward middle-aged and elderly consumers. Batches of condensed milk also had elevated levels of melamine ... The Shanghai Panda Dairy was one of twenty-two firms implicated in the 2008 scandal in which six Chinese children died and hundreds of thousands were sickened and hospitalized. The case rocked China's dairy industry and caused nationwide and global recalls of Chinese-made infant formula, cookies, cakes and dairy goods ... Shanghai Panda Dairy was allowed to resume production. Investigators found that some of its tainted dairy products came from milk provided by the Ningxia Panda Dairy in north-central China ... Three weeks ago three senior executives of the Jingqiao Company in north China's Shaanxi province were arrested and charged with producing and selling milk powder laced with melamine ... Investigators said the milk powder was confiscated in November before it could reach stores.

(www.iht.com, 1 January 2010)

Shanghai municipal inspectors closed Shanghai Panda Dairy on Thursday [31 December] for producing milk that had 'unacceptably high levels' of melamine ... Shanghai Panda Dairy produces milk for a large number of provinces in China and exports to Africa and South-east Asia ... Chinese law allows 2.5 milligrammes of melamine to be present in a kilogramme (2.2 pounds) of food product ... The government said Shanghai Panda Dairy was one of the companies on the government's melamine blacklist after the 2008 scandal, recording some of the highest levels of contamination. But the company was allowed to resume production after promises to strengthen its safety procedures ... A website lists Shanghai Panda as a subsidiary of Zhejiang Panda, though the relationship could not be confirmed ... A sister company, Ningxia Panda, was also being investigated because it was believed to have supplied some of the raw material for the milk powder and condensed milk.

(*IHT*, 2 January 2010, p. 13)

On 31 December [2009] ... regulators announced they had arrested three executives and shut down the Shanghai Panda Dairy Company ... But Wednesday [6 January 2010] a government official [at the prosecutor's office in Shanghai] acknowledged that: 'In February 2009 the Shanghai Fengxian prosecutor found that these products were contaminated and started the investigation. On 28 April the three executives from Panda Dairy were arrested' ... [He] declined to comment on why the announcement was delayed until January 2010 and why the public was not alerted to the dangers of Shanghai Panda milk last year [2009], before or shortly after the company was shut down. Last June [2008] China passed a new food safety law that required food producers to alert consumers and other business people of serious food safety problems. The prosecutor's office statement came a day after the *21st Century Business Herald*, a Guangzhou-based newspaper, first reported the investigation into Shanghai Panda may have been conducted months earlier ... The government did not say whether the contaminated milk from Shanghai Panda had sickened anyone, only that regulators believed they had confiscated dangerous milk during the investigation ... Shanghai officials said Wednesday that executives at Shanghai Panda held a meeting in December 2008, after a nationwide recall of melamine-tainted milk powder, and decided to resell contaminated milk that had been returned to the company in the earlier recall of melamine-tainted goods. Panda Dairy decided to mix the contaminated, condensed milk with standard products and resell it, [the statement said] ... Shanghai Panda products were found to have some of the highest levels of contamination.

(www.iht.com, 6 January 2010)

The Shanghai prosecutor's office: 'The case was not allowed to be released to the public' ... The General Administration of Quality Supervision, Inspection and Quarantine ... [said] that the case was withheld because it was under criminal investigation by police ... [The general administration] denied that such materials [tainted products that were recycled and sold again illegally] were involved in the new case, saying local governments had overseen the destruction of all recalled products ... [The spokesman] said both the administration and the Shanghai government were informed immediately after the case was found, and all harmful products were seized. It was not clear when officials began recalling them.

(www.guardian.co.uk, 6 January 2010)

Three dairy executives will be prosecuted this week for selling melamine-tainted milk ... stirring memories of a tainted milk scandal in 2008. But this case has nothing to do with the 2008 scandal said ... the General Administration of Quality, Supervision, Inspection and Quarantine.

(www.cnn.com, 7 January 2010)

Health officials in southern China have swept frozen confectioneries and other dairy products from stores after discovering they contained melamine ... news reports said on Monday [25 January] ... It was the third time in a month that Chinese authorities have uncovered dairy products with melamine ... In interviews this month with the Chinese press ... former head of the Guangdong Provincial Dairy Association Wang Dingmian ... was quoted as saying that officials had failed to monitor a large batch of melamine-tainted products left on the market after the 2008 scandal, and that word of the lapse had been kept quiet 'to safeguard the good image of the dairy industry' ... In the latest incident ... in Guizhou province ... food companies from Hebei, Liaoning and Shangong provinces and the city of Shanghai had produced the tainted products in March and April 2009. The companies' officials were reported to have said that the melamine was in milk powder they bought elsewhere to use as an ingredient in their product ... [It was] reported Monday that the three companies were banned from selling products in Guizhou.

(www.iht.com, 25 January 2010; *IHT*, 26 January 2010, p. 3)

China has begun an emergency nationwide inspection of dairy products after reports that tainted foodstuffs the government had ordered destroyed in 2008 were still being sold, according to a report Tuesday [2 February] ... Melamine was discovered in a wide range of dairy products as a huge food safety scandal erupted in September 2008 ... A global recall ensued, and officials ordered all products suspected of containing melamine to be destroyed. But some 'unscrupulous' companies have taken the recalled products and repackaged them to be sold in stores ... The products still being sold are largely 'processed foods like ice cream and condensed milk' ... As recently as late January three Chinese companies were found to be selling dairy products tainted with melamine that authorities said were leftovers from a wave of bad products discovered in 2008.

(www.iht.com, 2 February 2010)

China has ordered a ten-day emergency examination of tainted milk products after several were found back on the market ... It was unclear how many tainted products were still on the market ... The national food safety office has sent eight inspection teams to check products in sixteen provinces, an official said Tuesday [2 February] ... The review started Monday.

(*IHT*, 3 February 2010, p. 8)

China launched a ten-day emergency crackdown yesterday [1 February] on tainted milk after several products were found to be creeping back on to the market despite the 2008 scandal ... The crackdown comes after the milk products tainted with the melamine were pulled from shelves in Shanghai and the provinces of Shaanxi, Shandong, Liaoning and Hebei ... Some had been recalled in the previous scandal and repackaged ... Health concerns peaked again early this year [2010] after authorities in Shanghai said they secretly investigated a dairy for nearly a year before announcing it had been producing contaminated milk products.

(www.guardian.co.uk, 2 February 2010)

The scandal over tainted products ... resurfaced. This week official media called for an intensive sweep to identify tainted products after it emerged that some of the companies involved in the 2008 scandal had reused tainted milk powder in other dairy products rather than destroying it as ordered by Beijing ... Products laced with [melamine] ... have been found in foods in several provinces. Xinhua reported on Monday [1 February] that dairy products from at least five manufacturers had been removed from shelves because of melamine contamination. Some of the seizures took place months ago but have only now come to light.

(*FT*, 3 February 2010, p. 12)

Three dairy plant managers and a milk powder dealer in central China have been arrested on accusations of selling milk products tainted with melamine, shortly after the government began a ten-day crackdown. The managers, who work at Lekang Dairy in Shaanxi, have been charged with manufacturing and selling tainted milk power.

(*IHT*, 4 February 2010)

A widening national toxic food scandal that has its roots in this tropical island resort area in the South China Sea has set off a rare case of public sniping between officials. The scandal, which has been reported by official news organizations in the last few days, is centred on a cowpea – an ancient species of legume that includes the black-eyed pea. Since late February [2010] batches of cowpeas from the lush Sanya area of the island of Hainan have tested positive for a highly toxic pesticide, isocarbophos, that is banned from use on fruits and vegetables, according to a report on Tuesday [2 March] in *China Daily*, the official English language newspaper. Tainted cowpeas from here have been found in the provinces of Hubei, Guangdong, Anhi and Jiangsu. The pesticide was banned in Hainan in 2004 but can still be found in remote parts of the island ... Some farmers still use it because it is much cheaper than legal pesticides ... The outrage over the Hainan cowpeas ... erupted on 21 February, when the agriculture bureau of Wuhan,

> the capital of Hebei, announced that it had destroyed 3.5 tonnes of toxic cowpeas from Hainan. An urgent nationwide warning was issued by the central government's ministry of agriculture, and within days cowpeas tainted with the banned pesticide were discovered in three other provinces. Officials in Sanya have criticized the Wuhan officials for breaking an 'unspoken rule' that officials in different cities and provinces report problems to one another rather than telling the public.
>
> (www.iht.com, 3 March 2010; *IHT*, 4 March 2010, p. 4)

'China will step up food safety efforts following a major dairy scandal, expanding efforts to reach more of the country's countless small farms, an agriculture official said Wednesday [10 March]' (*IHT*, 11 March 2010, p. 6).

8 Developments, congresses and Central Committee sessions since May 2006

9 May 2006.

> Beijing has scrapped plans for a 'green measure' of GDP ... A National Bureau of Statistics official said a planned 'green measure' of national economic output that took into account the effect on the environment had been dropped because of problems over its calculation. Chinese leaders asked the NBS three years ago to draw up the index.
>
> (*FT*, 10 May 2006, p. 6)

16 May 2006.

> The Cultural Revolution was launched on 16 May 1966 ... It ended with Mao Zedong's death in 1976 ... The Gang of Four were accused of persecuting 700,000 people and held directly responsible for 35,000 deaths. Most foreign scholarship puts the killings at between 300,000 and 800,000. In their biography of Mao, Jung Chang and Jon Halliday estimate the toll at 3 million.
>
> (*Guardian*, 16 May 2006, p. 17)

> The Communist Party's unwillingness to confront the horrors of the Cultural Revolution ... means that for Chinese historians as well as for millions of victims that entire period is, in effect, off-limits for debate. The passage of time does not appear to be helping. Chinese scholars say the government has been even more intent on stopping public commemoration of this week's anniversary than it was a decade ago. No mention of it has appeared in the state-controlled media ... Officials fear that closer scrutiny of the Cultural Revolution could destabilize the country by inflaming long suppressed antagonisms. Many scholars now believe that well over 1 million were killed or driven to suicide in political struggles between 1966 and 1976. The lives of almost all urban residents were profoundly disrupted. Schools and universities were closed. Educated people were forced to leave cities and work on farms. Family members turned on one another. Many of those now in their fifties belong to a 'lost generation' whose education and careers were permanently blighted by the Cultural Revolution. In 1981 the party leadership issued a long denunciation of the Cultural Revolution, as well as

other 'mistakes' made by Mao, though these were portrayed as secondary to his contributions. The Gang of Four led by Mao's wife, Jiang Qing, who were deemed responsible for the Cultural Revolution's atrocities, were given lengthy prison terms (the last of the four died in December [2005]). Most of those persecuted were officially 'rehabilitated' by the early 1980s. There is, however, no official memorial to the victims.

(*The Economist*, 20 May 2006, pp. 69–70)

20 May 2006.

A ceremony was set on Saturday [20 May] to mark the end of construction ... of the Three Gorges Dam ... though the hugely controversial project is not fully completed. The government-backed company that runs the dam said earlier this week that the final twelve of the dam's twenty-six generators would be installed over the next two years, finishing the project in 2008, a year ahead of schedule. Begun in 1993 the project has steamed ahead with the backing of the communist leadership despite objections to its $22 billion cost and environmental and social impact. More than 1.3 million people have been relocated to make way for the dam and its reservoir.

(www.iht.com, 19 May 2006)

On 20 May a topping-out ceremony was held ... after thirteen years of work – and a few months ahead of schedule ... The origins ... [of] the Three Gorges Dam on the Yangtze ... go back to ... Sun Yat-sen early in the twentieth century. With unusual candour the official media said the task had cost the lives of more than 100 workers ... Officials say 1.13 million people have been removed from towns and villages upriver for a reservoir that will stretch for 660 kilometres. These figures are conservative. Many people living upstream without long-term permits have not been counted or compensated. Many others complain that corrupt officials have siphoned off resettlement funds. Numerous protest leaders have been arrested or jailed over the years.

(*The Economist*, 27 May 2006, p. 71)

24 May 2006. The US Defence Department annual report *Military Power of the People's Republic of China*:

China's leaders have yet to adequately explain the purposes or desired end-states of their military expansion ... Estimates place Chinese defence expenditure at two to three times officially disclosed figures ... The United States welcomes the rise of a peaceful and prosperous China. US policy encourages China to participate as a responsible international stakeholder by taking on a greater share of responsibility for the health and success of the global system from which China has derived great benefit.

(www.iht.com, 24 May 2006)

The International Institute for Strategic Studies ... [published its] annual military balance report [on 24 May 2006] ... [The report says that] China

> spends 70 per cent more on its military than its official budget suggests … The IISS estimates China's total military related expenditures in 2003 were $39.6 billion at market exchange prices, about 1.7 times the official budget. This means its total spending was 2.7 per cent of GDP in 2003, compared with 3.7 per cent in the United States, 2.4 per cent in South Korea and the UK and 1 per cent in Japan. Using purchasing-power parity figures from the World Bank the figure expands to $75.5 billion. That puts China well behind the United States, which spent $456 billion in that year, but ahead of Russia in third place. The report warns, however, that the PPP figures should be used with caution. According to the IISS, the official budget ignores a number of big spending items. These include overseas weapons procurement, defence industry subsidies and research and development spending.
>
> (*FT*, 25 May 2006, p. 5)

'China … committed $35 billion to its military last year [2005] or 1.5 per cent of GDP, using official Chinese figures' (*IHT*, 1 June 2006, p. 2).

> Villagers detained after a clash with the authorities, in which the police opened fire on protesters and killed at least three people, have been sentenced to prison … Twelve people from the village of Dongzhou in Guangdong province were given sentences up to seven years for their role in the 6 December [2005] protest over land seizures. Nine others were acquitted … The villagers were sentenced on Wednesday [24 May] for illegal assembly, disturbing public order and illegally manufacturing explosives used against the police … The government said three people were killed but residents put the toll as high as twenty.
>
> (www.iht.com, 25 May 2006)

4 June 2006.

> Cardinal Joseph Zen … the highest official of the Roman Catholic Church in China … marked the seventeenth anniversary of the Tiananmen Square killing … strongly criticized the Chinese government and called on it to hold a full and open review of the killings … The Roman Catholic Church in Hong Kong has marked each anniversary of the Tiananmen Square killings since 1990. Zen, the bishop of Hong Kong since 1996 [and a cardinal since March 2006] … has been especially vocal at the anniversaries since 2003 … An annual survey of attitudes in Hong Kong toward the student protests in Beijing in 1989 and the government's suppression of them found that public support for the students remains strong here [in Hong Kong], although many also believe that the Chinese government's human rights record has improved since then. The Hong Kong University poll found that 53 per cent believed that the students 'did the right thing' and 63 per cent believed the government 'did the wrong thing'.
>
> (www.iht.com, 4 June 2006)

> Cardinal Joseph Zen did not attend the Sunday [4 June] vigil, which was not organized by the church. The vigil's supporters, a group that has supported

> the students' cause ever since 1989, estimated the crowd at 44,000 people. But the Hong Kong police put the crowd at 19,000.
>
> (*IHT*, 5 June 2006, p. 5)

'Several hundred people gathered at a Hong Kong park Sunday to mark seventeen years since Chinese troops crushed a pro-democracy protest at Beijing's Tiananmen Square, killing at least hundreds' (www.cnn.com, 4 June 2006).

5 June 2006.

> The mouthpiece of China's Communist Party yesterday [5 June] urged that members 'unwaveringly uphold reform', in a call seen as an attempt by Beijing's top leaders to silence opposition to wider foreign and private involvement in the economy. A *People's Daily* newspaper article that received extensive attention from other state media and was clearly intended to represent party policy, said China had no choice but to deepen market reforms and open further to the outside world … The article stated: 'If we do not drive ahead with reform, not only will we be unable to win new achievements, we will also find it hard to maintain the progress we have made in the past' … Its publication follows unusually open and heated criticism during the past year of government policies on issues such as foreign takeovers of Chinese companies and management buy-outs of state-owned companies, all set against a backdrop of rising social inequality … The *People's Daily*, nevertheless, took care to stress that the state sector should maintain its 'guiding' role in the economy. It also quoted former president Jiang Zemin on the importance of retaining a commitment to socialism … The newspaper quoted Mr Jiang as saying: 'In creating the socialist market economy we cannot miss out the word "socialist". It is not superfluous, like "adding legs to a picture of a snake".'
>
> (*FT*, 6 June 2006, p. 10)

The *People's Daily's* article stated:

> The glorious achievements in the past twenty-eight years demonstrated that reform is the only road for China to achieve prosperity. Without reform China could not make further progress, nor could it keep the achievements that have been scored … The urgency and complexity of reforms calls for absolute determination to advance the reform. A balance should be realized between reform, development and social stability. Reform should be the driving force, development the goal, and stability the prerequisite.
>
> (*The Times*, 6 June 2006, p. 40)

6 June 2006.

> China's efforts to field an early-warning aircraft that could help it project power far beyond its borders and challenge American intervention in any conflict with Taiwan were dealt at least a temporary blow by the crash of a surveillance aircraft Sunday [4 June] … In addition to the loss of the

aircraft, one of four China has built, experts said the deaths of forty people on board, including thirty-five electronics and avionics technicians, could hinder one of China's most pressing military modernization programmes.

(www.iht.com, 6 June 2006; *IHT*, 7 June 2006, p. 7)

A Japanese government panel has approved the resumption of aid loans to China ... Japan halted the aid loans in March ... The panel's decision must still be approved by the cabinet ... [but it was said] that cabinet approval would come soon ... Loans of $660 million [would be provided] retroactively for fiscal 2005 ... The aid focuses on environmental and energy issues and regional stability ... There was no change in Japan's policy to terminate aid to China by 2008 ... [the idea being] to phase out the China loans over the next three years ... Japan's loans to China date back to 1979, seven years after the two Asian neighbours established diplomatic relations, but the annual sum has been dwindling since 2000.

(www.iht.com, 6 June 2006)

'The Yasukuni Shrine hosts a museum defending Japan's past militarism' www.iht.com, 2 July 2006).

As for the 'Class A' war criminals of Yasukuni, the term referred not to the magnitude of the crimes, but to 'crimes against peace', a broad term aimed mainly at political figures. Actual 'war crimes' and 'crimes against humanity' (such as the Nanjing massacre) were in other categories.

(www.iht.com, 1 October 2006)

11 June 2006.

A Beijing vice-mayor with a central role in the capital's preparations for the 2008 Olympics has been fired for alleged corruption ... 'because of his corrupt and degenerate ways' ... The surprise dismissal of Liu Zhihua, head of the Beijing city government commission responsible for Olympics-related construction, marked one of the highest level graft scandals to hit the capital since the toppling of former mayor Chen Xitong in the mid-1990s ... No details have been released of Mr Liu's alleged offences, but the official Xinhua news agency said he was under investigation over violations of Communist Party and government employee rules ... Less than two years ago a senior Beijing official in charge of road building was toppled for allegedly taking 'enormous bribes many times' to help others win advantage from public works.

(*FT*, 12 June 2006, p. 7)

Right up to his detention by party investigators on 9 June, Liu Zhihua had been portrayed by official media as a staunch supporter of anti-corruption efforts. He is the most senior official in the capital to be accused of corruption since the arrest of a former city party chief, Chen Xitong, in the mid-1990s.

(*The Economist*, 17 June 2006, p. 68)

13 June 2006.

> Germany has protested strongly to China over the severe beating of a prominent human rights activist who was attacked after criticizing corruption in the controversial Three Gorges Dam project on German television. The activist Fu Xiancai, who appeared in an ARD German state-funded television programme on 19 May, was attacked on 8 June after he had given evidence at a police station in Hubei province. He was badly injured and partly disabled.
>
> (*FT*, 14 June 2006, p. 6)

> Fu Xiancai ... lies paralysed with a broken neck ... He has lost control of all bodily functions except the ability to speak ... Mr Fu has lobbied provincial governments and local officials since the 1990s to secure compensation for some of the million people resettled to make way for the dam ... He has gathered evidence over the years, including sworn testimonies by people who have received no compensation from the local government.
>
> (*Independent*, 14 June 2006, p. 23)

('Fu Xiancai, an activist who campaigned for the rights of farmers displaced by the Three Gorges Dam ... was left paralysed after an attack last month [8 June] ... He has regained only the use of his arms ... A report by local police investigators said: "No injury was found being caused by someone else; therefore, no case can be established" ': *Independent*, 28 July 2006, p. 20.)

14 June 2006.

> Eight out of ten Chinese say they are satisfied with the way things are going in China, according to survey results, in a sign that robust economic growth is outweighing social tensions over the income gap between rich and poor. The 81 per cent satisfaction rate is an increase from the 72 per cent recorded in 2005, the Pew Global Attitudes Project said in a public opinion poll of fifteen countries. Those Chinese who were unhappy with the state of the nation dropped to 13 per cent, from 19 per cent a year ago, according to results released Tuesday [14 June]. Aside from China, citizens of only two other countries – Egypt and Jordan – were content with national conditions, said the survey, which covered a range of topics, from national attitudes to global warming, bird flu and the Iran crisis ... The survey ... interviewed 2,180 people between the ages of eighteen and sixty and was skewed toward urban China, with the interviews mostly conducted in the cities of Beijing, Shanghai, Guangzhou, Xinjiang, Jinzhong and Luzhou.
>
> (www.iht.com, 14 June 2006; *IHT*, 15 June 2006, p. 8)

16 June 2006.

> The authorities tried to slow the spread of a toxic spill by building fifty-one makeshift dams along the tainted Dasha river and using fire trucks to pump out polluted water before it reaches a reservoir that serves a city of 10 million people. The spill of 60 tonnes of coal tar into the river in Shanxi

> province was the latest in a series of mishaps fouling China's already polluted waterways. In a separate incident Thursday [15 June] a series of explosions rocked the Longxin chemical plant in the city of Longquan in Zheijiang province, destroying two factories and threatening to contaminate the Oujiang river, which empties into the East China Sea.
>
> (*IHT*, 17 June 2006, p. 6)

18 June 2006. '[A] seven-country [eight-day] tour of Africa by [prime minister] Wen Jiabao … began at the weekend' (*FT*, Monday 20 June 2006, p. 1).

> Wen Jiabao, prime minister, has just completed the third top-level tour of Africa in less than six months, following visits by Li Zhaoxing, foreign minister, and Hu Jintao, president … China is sensitive enough to charges of ignoring human rights abuses to have omitted Sudan and Zimbabwe – countries with which it has particularly cosy relationships – from top-level tours. It has, however, rolled out the red carpet in Beijing for Robert Mugabe, Zimbabwe's president … and more recently his deputy … as well as a senior Sudanese delegation.
>
> (*FT*, 26 June 2006, p. 18)

19 June 2006.

> China and India have agreed to reopen border trade at the historic Nathu-la Pass after more than forty years, a symbol of rapprochement between Asian giants who fought a Himalayan war in 1962. The pass, at an altitude of 4,300 metres, or 14,100 feet, will open on 6 July … [it] was reported Monday [19 June] … and handle trade between the tiny north-east Indian state of Sikkim and southern Tibet.
>
> (*IHT*, 20 June 2006, p. 14)

('China and India reopened an ancient Himalayan border pass Thursday [6 July] … The Nathu-la Pass, once part of the ancient Silk Road that linked China and India, was reopened for local trade forty-four years after it was shut during a brief but fierce border war [in 1962] … The mountain pass … connects … Tibet with the north-eastern Indian state of Sikkim … The dispute over this once-independent principality, which was annexed by India in 1975 and subsequently claimed by China, represented a thorn in bilateral relations until last year [2005] when Beijing finally recognized the Indian annexation … After painstaking negotiations Beijing and New Delhi have resumed trade at three remote passes along their 3,500 kilometre or 2,100 mile frontier, although major sections of the border remain in dispute … The date of the opening of the Nathu-la Pass was fixed by the Chinese … [and there is the theory that this was timed to coincide with] the seventy-first birthday of the Dalai Lama': www.iht.com, 6 July 2006.)

27 June 2006.

> Chinese media outlets will be fined if they report on 'sudden events' without prior authorization from government officials, under a new draft law [Law

> on Response to Contingencies] being considered by … the Standing Committee of the National People's Congress … While the state media did not offer a definition of 'sudden events', in the past the term has included natural disasters, major incidents and events leading to public health and social safety.
>
> (www.iht.com, 27 June 2006)

('An official involved in preparing the legislation said Monday [3 July] … [that the] draft law that threatens to fine news media for reporting "sudden incidents" without permission applies to foreign as well as domestic news organizations': *IHT*, 4 July 2006, p. 4.)

30 June 2006.

> President Hu Jintao said Friday [30 June] that his political concept of maintaining the 'advanced nature' of the Communist Party was the key to its survival, while warning that corruption threatened to undermine its hold on power … Hu used a nationwide televised address on the eve of the eighty-fifth anniversary of the party's founding on 1 July to elevate his vague but now omnipresent notion of *xianjinxing*, which translates literally to 'advanceness' or 'advanced nature' to the status of official doctrine. He said the essence of Marxist thought was to maintain an 'advanced nature' and that the success of China's communists in fighting Japan, toppling the Nationalists, rising to power in 1949 and creating economic prosperity in the past three decades can all be attributed to the same idea.
>
> (*IHT*, 1 July 2006, p. 2)

1 July 2006. China celebrates the eighty-fifth anniversary of the founding of the Communist Party, the tenth anniversary of the return of Hong Kong to Chinese sovereignty and the opening of the Beijing–Lhasa railway.

> China this weekend [1 July] is opening the world's highest railway, a 1,140 kilometre line that crosses the vertiginous Tibetan Plateau … Mao proposed extending a railway to Tibet after the People's Liberation Army invaded the territory … in 1951 … The first section, extending from Beijing to Golmud in Qinghai province, was completed in 1984. But the 710-mile section connecting Golmud to Lhasa was put on indefinite hold. It would have to cross the Tibetan Plateau, survive extreme temperatures and stay fixed in the shifting permafrost of the highlands. The plan was revived in 2001 … The official price tag of $4.1 billion … [compares with] Tibet's GDP in 2005 of $3.12 billion.
>
> (*IHT*, 1 July 2006, p. 2)

('The railway ministry said it was stepping up monitoring and maintenance work to reinforce its rail link to Tibet, after reports by state media that the train track had developed cracks and other problems. Temperature changes can cause shifts in the permafrost on which about 550 kilometres of the Tibet rail link is built … The railway is running normally [China said] … The ministry estimates that the railway will handle three-quarters of Tibet's inward and outbound cargo shipments by 2010': www.iht.com, 21 August 2006.)

'[The] journey from Beijing to ... Lhasa ... [covers] 4,000 kilometres (2,500 miles) ... Previously, the journey from Beijing to Lhasa would have taken days, if not weeks, by road and rail. It can now be completed in forty-eight hours' (*The Times*, 4 July 2006, pp. 38–9).

> Connecting the last rail-free region of China to the railway network has been a mission of enormous political importance to the [Chinese] leadership ... Only one or two freight trains a day in each direction are currently planned. Most goods will therefore continue to be transported by truck along the four highways that connect Lhasa to the rest of China ... Even without the railway, tourism – the mainstay of Tibet's economy – has been booming, thanks to growing interest among China's newly affluent urbanites.
>
> (*The Economist*, 8 July 2006, p. 62)

10 July 2006.

> A three-volume set of his [Jiang Zemin's] 'Selected Works' went on sale on 10 August, a week before his eightieth birthday. Its release puts him in the company of Deng Xiaoping and Mao Zedong as a leader worthy of the honour. State media urged careful study of the opus and carried gushing, if improbable, reports of frenzied queues at bookstores as far afield as Tibet.
>
> (*The Economist*, 26 August 2006, p. 50)

13 July 2006.

> [On 13 July China] announced the results of an eighteen-month re-education campaign for party members to ensure they retained their position as the most 'advanced' or 'progressive' force in society. The campaign was the 'largest centralized Marxist educational activity' since the party's founding in Shanghai in 1921 ... The success of the campaign [it was said] was confirmed by an opinion poll of 6.3 million people and party members, showing more than 97 per cent of respondents approved of the party's work ... The country has 70.3 million party members.
>
> (*FT*, 14 July 2006, p. 9)

20 July 2006.

> Prime minister Junichiro Koizumi [of Japan] pays his respects to the Yasukuni Shrine every year ... and says he will continue even though the late Emperor Hirohito, greatly revered in Japan, apparently believed such visits were inappropriate ... The revelation [was] first published Thursday [20 July] ... The diaries, kept by a former steward of the Imperial Household Agency, which manages Japan's imperial family, are said to contain transcripts of private conversations with Hirohito, who died in 1989. The emperor ... is recorded as saying that he stopped visiting ... the Yasukuni Shrine after it began honouring convicted war criminals in 1978. In that year

> Yasukuni, which honours Japan's modern war dead, added to the honourees the fourteen World War II leaders convicted of crimes against humanity. Hirohito last visited the shrine in 1975 ... Koizumi's annual visits to the shrine ... have been deeply divisive in Japan ... The visits have outraged the victims of Japanese aggression in Asia in the 1930s and 1940s ... Emperor Hirohito's son, Emperor Akihito, has not visited the shrine since taking the throne. Chief cabinet secretary Shinzo Abe, the front-runner to succeed Koizumi, has visited the shrine in the past and defended his pilgrimage when asked about the Hirohito remarks.
>
> (www.iht.com, 21 July 2006; *IHT*, 22 July 2006, p. 2)

'Emperor Hirohito ... stopped visiting Yasukuni in 1975, when the shrine first became politically touchy. Three years later, when Yasukuni's head priest enshrined Hideki Tojo and other wartime officials, Hirohito's stance became a matter of personal policy' (*IHT*, 10 August 2006, p. 2).

15 August 2006.

Prime minister Junichiro Koizumi [of Japan] prayed at the Yasukuni Shrine on Tuesday [15 August], choosing the most politically sensitive and diplomatically explosive day, the anniversary of the end of World War II, for his last visit in office to the war memorial ... He said in a news conference later that he had avoided this date for his visits until now because of pressure ... In Japan, where opposition to the visits has been rising, the visit was also criticized by Koizumi's finance minister, Sadakazu Tanigaki, who is running to succeed Koizumi as prime minister, and Takenori Kanzaki, the leader of New Komeito, the junior partner to the governing Liberal Democrats ... Koizumi, who in the past had argued that he went to Yasukuni as a private citizen, left fifteen minutes later after recording his visit with his name and title ... Koizumi [was] in formal attire ... The visit ended months of speculation about whether Koizumi, who is retiring next month [September], would visit the shrine on this symbolically laden day ... When he ran for office as leader of the Liberal Democratic Party more than five years ago, Koizumi had promised to visit the shrine on this anniversary. But until Tuesday he had avoided it.

(www.iht.com, 15 August 2006; *IHT*, 16 August 2006, p. 2)

'Ironically, the name Yasukuni, adopted in 1879, comes from Chinese classical literature and means "to bring peace to the nation"' (www.iht.com, 15 August 2006). 'Yasukuni [is] a private Shinto memorial ... Foreign minister Taro Aso last week called for turning Yasukuni into a state memorial' (*IHT*, 16 August 2006, p. 7).

> So bitter has the shrine stand-off been that Junichiro Koizumi has been unable to visit Beijing for talks with his Chinese counterpart throughout his five-year tenure – an astonishing freeze in relations given that China has pipped the United States as Japan's biggest trading partner.
>
> (*FT*, 15 August 2006, p. 4)

> 'Junichiro Koizumi ... paid a sixth visit to the controversial Yasukuni Shrine ... Polls show that most Japanese no longer favour such visits' (*The Economist*, 19 August 2006, p. 6). 'When he was running for office in 2001 ... [he] promised to visit Tokyo's Yasukuni Shrine every year and to do so on 15 August, the anniversary of the emperor's admission that Japan had lost the war ... Only this week did he fulfil the second [promise]. In formal morning coat ... he spent only ten minutes at the shrine ... A connected museum paints Japan in its wars of 1937–45 as a liberator of Asia, a victim of Western belligerency ... This week it could not be plainer that he came as prime minister, the first visit on 15 August in two decades.
>
> (p. 10)

'China says that 300,000 Chinese people were slaughtered by Japanese soldiers in Nanjing, but the 1948 Tokyo war crimes tribunal found that Japanese troops killed 155,000 people' (*The Independent*, 15 August 2006, p. 27). '[In] Nanjing in 1937 ... up to 20,000 women may have been raped by Japanese troops' (*The Independent*, 16 August 2006, p. 27).

23 August 2006.

> The Venezuelan president, Hugo Chavez ... began the first day of an official visit [on 23 August] ... a six-day tour ... to win lucrative energy contracts for his country ... Talks with President Hu Jintao, set for Thursday [24 August], are expected to produce an agreement to increase Venezuelan oil exports to China ... Chavez, making his fourth trip to China [since 1999], suggested that it could be the most important one so far. In particular, Chavez said, he hopes for greater participation by Chinese enterprises in exploiting the resources in the Venezuelan region of Orinoco, which has one of the world's richest oil reserves. The visit is also expected to yield contracts to build eighteen tankers to transport crude oil to China and twelve drilling rigs to help Venezuela increase its oil production capacity.
>
> (www.iht.com, 23 August 2006)

> Venezuela plans to increase oil exports to China six-fold before 2019. President Hugo Chavez of Venezuela said Thursday [24 August] after holding talks with President Hu Jintao ... Chavez said joint venture agreements would be signed with two of China's state-owned oil giants, Sinopec and CNPC, to extract and export crude from the Orinoco river basin in Venezuela.
>
> (*IHT*, 24 August 2006, p. 11)

> Hugo Chavez, Venezuela's president, is due to meet China's leaders in Beijing today [24 August] as he seeks to divert Venezuelan oil exports for the United States to Asia, but experts are sceptical that it will lead to a significant impact on oil flows. One of Mr Chavez's policy goals is to weaken ties with the United States, Venezuela's main trading partner ... Venezuela [is] the world's fifth largest oil exporter.
>
> (*FT*, 24 August 2006, p. 9)

'Mr Chavez announced plans for a six-fold increase in sales to China over the next decade ... It currently imports only about 2 per cent of its oil needs from Venezuela' (*FT*, 25 August 2006, p. 12).

9 September 2006. The thirtieth anniversary of the death of Mao Zedong, who died on 9 September 1976.

10 September 2006.

> Xinhua, Beijing's official news agency, yesterday [10 September] issued rules demanding international counterparts censor news and information distributed in China and barring them from dealing directly with local clients. The rules, which take effect immediately, mark a dramatic resumption of Xinhua's efforts to regulate the Chinese operations of foreign news agencies tightly. They appear to pose a serious threat to the China businesses of agencies such as Reuters, Dow Jones and Bloomberg, and could limit Chinese financial institutions' timely access to market-moving news and data ... Xinhua [made clear it] was targeting Reuters in particular ... Criticism is likely to centre on the news agency's dual role as regulator and powerful participant in the news and financial data industry. In the late 1990s Xinhua was forced largely to abandon an effort to impose controls and lucrative fees on foreign agencies after strong opposition from US trade negotiators. Yesterday's ban on the distribution of any agency content that 'harms China's national security or honour' or 'disturbs the Chinese economy or social order' matches other recent moves by Beijing to tighten media censorship. However, foreign news agencies are already able to distribute their English and Chinese news and financial data only to approved clients, while Xinhua has made no secret of its determination to win a greater share of their business ... Xinhua can suspend or revoke the licence of any agency found to have had contact with its subscribers or which distributes news that contravenes vaguely worded bans on topics ranging from 'promoting superstition' to 'hurting ethnic feelings'.
>
> (*FT*, 11 September 2006, p. 7)

> Under the new rules that were said to take effect immediately Xinhua, China's main state-run news agency, said it would become the gate-keeper for foreign news agencies, photographs and graphics entering China. The agency announced in its own dispatch that it would censor content that 'endangers national security'. If enforced as drafted the regulations could have a major effect on news agencies like the Associated Press, Reuters and Bloomberg, which sell news-related products to a wide range of Chinese clients ... Xinhua has long played a dual role in China's media world. It acts as the official distributor of state news and information, selling its products as any Western news agency would do. But it also regulates outside news agencies, a power that Western news providers say it seeks to use to enhance its own bottom line. A decade ago Xinhua sought to take control of the lucrative business of providing live news and data feeds to banks and

financial firms in the country, determining pricing, policing content and collecting the revenue. The industry, dominated by big Western agencies like Reuters and Bloomberg, successfully fought those restrictions. They have continued to market their products directly to traders in China rather than providing all services through Xinhua.

(*IHT*, 11 September 2006, p. 11)

The new rules require that foreign news agencies conduct their business through Xinhua and they bar foreign news outlets from selling their information directly to customers. Western media like Bloomberg News and Reuters sell financial data and news to banks, trading houses and websites in China, a lucrative business that ... the president of Xinhua publicly vowed to capture in a speech this year [2006] ... Selling financial information in China is a business that is growing even faster than the Chinese economy ... [There is the view that] ultimately the effort by Xinhua backfired in the 1990s because of pressure from those in China who were worried that Xinhua would slow down the flow of financial information.

(*IHT*, 12 September 2006, p. 17)

The measures ... ban foreign agencies from distributing their content except through Xinhua or its authorized entities. Xinhua said reports that disrupted economic and social order would be banned. Also prohibited is news that endangers national unity, sovereignty and territorial integrity. While the latest rules do not specify economic reports, they resemble similar regulations issued ten years ago, when Xinhua tried to muscle in on such financial news providers as Reuters, Bloomberg and Dow Jones by requiring registration of all contracts and a 15 per cent fee ... The news agencies, backed by the EU and the United States, succeeded in watering down the 1996 measures through two years of tortuous negotiations ... Xinhua finally gave up trying to take a share of foreign agencies' revenues because the row was having an impact on China's delicate negotiations to join the WTO.

(*The Times*, 11 September 2006, p. 31)

The new rules do not affect foreign newspapers or broadcasters in China, which are subject to different regulatory regimes ... The rules state that foreign agencies must work through a Xinhua-approved agent that is 'legally qualified', has an appropriate service network and 'means of transmission', and meets other undefined 'administrative regulations'.

(*FT*, 12 September 2006, p. 14)

[China] gave the state-run Xinhua news agency monopoly control over the lucrative financial news business and the power to administer broad censorship rules for all foreign news entering China ... Foreign agencies have long been barred from selling general news directly to the Chinese media ... Xinhua listed ten categories of news covering politics, religion and national unity – code for Taiwan – that could not be released into China. For the last decade financial news providers received better treatment and were allowed to sell their less politically sensitive information directly to banks and brokers. Now, under the new rules, they will have to distribute their wares through a designated agent of Xinhua – a fine way to get Xinhua, which is eager to sell its own financial news, a guaranteed cut of the multimillion-dollar action.

(*IHT*, 14 September 2006, p. 6)

The regulations threaten to disrupt a business that major Western financial news providers ... value at about $100 million a year. Most of the revenue comes from banks and brokerages that subscribe to Western providers of news and data services to keep abreast of developments affecting stock, bond and currency markets ... In 1996 Xinhua issued similar rules and demanded a 40 per cent share of revenue from subscriptions ... Xinhua retreated from those demands a decade ago under heavy international pressure. It subsequently sought to build its own financial information services, but it has failed to capture more than a small slice of the Western agencies' revenue in China. Xinhua said Thursday [14 September] that it was acting now purely as a regulatory agency and that it would seek profit from the rules it was imposing ... The agency insisted that it was mainly acting as a censor of news and financial information to ensure that news coming into China would not threaten national security, provoke social or ethnic unrest or promote the spread of religious cults.

(www.iht.com, 14 September 2006)

18 September 2006.

Member states of the IMF ... voted Monday [18 September] to adopt a plan to modify the fund's power structure and take steps to amplify the voices of fast-developing countries like China ... The modification of the IMF ... was widely described as the biggest step since the fund was established in the 1940s ... China's share of the votes at the IMF, which has 184 members, would go up slightly from 2.98 per cent to 3.719 per cent. The shares of South Korea, Turkey and Mexico, the other countries that gained more power from the vote Monday [18 September], was similarly modest ... The United States has about 17 per cent of the vote and Europe in aggregate about 23 per cent ... Japan has 6.1 per cent ... The change in the fund governance was advocated by the United States and many European countries as a way of getting China and other developing countries to feel more invested in the international economic system ... Another objective of the United States [is] to engage China in the fund as it expands its role in monitoring currency flows and exchange rates. Washington hopes that the fund will become another voice urging China to let its currency fluctuate more freely in relation to the dollar.

(www.iht.com, 18 September 2006; *IHT*, 19 September 2006, p. 13)

Prime minister Wen Jiabao confirmed on Monday [18 September] that his country would increase its UN peacekeeping presence in Lebanon to 1,000

> ... China had contributed 187 troops to the previous 1,900-strong peacekeeping force in Lebanon ... China has become increasingly involved in UN peacekeeping operations since 2000. A Chinese observer for the United Nations was among those killed when Israel bombed and invaded south Lebanon after Hezbollah guerrillas captured two Israeli soldiers in July. The conflict killed nearly 1,200 people in Lebanon, most of them civilians, and 157 Israelis. A UN-brokered ceasefire halted the war on 14 August.
>
> (www.iht.com, 18 September 2006)

> Before the reinforcement of its Lebanon contingent, China had about 1,650 soldiers and police officers serving with peacekeeping missions ... Since it first deployed a peacekeeping force to Cambodia in 1992, China has sent military or police teams to such trouble spots as the Democratic Republic of Congo, Liberia, East Timor, Kosovo, Haiti, Afghanistan and Bosnia-Herzegovina. This year [2006], before the Israeli invasion, China sent more than 180 peacekeepers, mostly engineers expert at mine clearing, to join a 2,000-strong UN force in Lebanon. That was China's first mission to the Middle East.
>
> (*IHT*, 20 September 2006, p. 3)

20 September 2006. 'The United States and China ... on Wednesday [20 September] established high level teams of officials in both countries to conduct a "strategic economic dialogue" to be led on the American side by Treasury Secretary Henry Paulson Jr' (*IHT*, 20 September 2006, p. 11).

'The discussion [on the Chinese side] ... will be led by ... Wu Yi, China's vice-premier for trade and foreign investment policy' (*FT*, 21 September 2006, p. 8).

> Treasury Secretary Henry Paulson Jr of the United States, winding up a four-day visit to China, met Friday [22 September] with President Hu Jintao and prime minister Wen Jiabao ... The secretary's fifty-minute session with Hu and fifty-five minute session with Wen were highly unusual for a Treasury Secretary. Paulson's predecessor, John Snow, met with Hu for only a couple of minutes when he was Treasury Secretary ... Paulson's visit began Tuesday [19 September].
>
> (www.iht.com, 22 September 2006; *IHT*, 23 September 2006, p. 4)

(Henry Paulson Jr ... [was] formerly the chairman and CEO of Goldman Sachs [and had visited China on a number of occasions on behalf of the company]': *IHT*, 22 September 2006, p. 17.)

21 September 2006.

> A Chinese factory worker has been released after serving seventeen years in jail for setting fire to a military vehicle during the Tiananmen Square protests. Zhang Maosheng was twenty-one when he was jailed on a charge of counter-revolutionary arson. According to the Hong Kong-based Information Centre for Human Rights and Democracy, 15,000 people were sen-

tenced to death or jail terms following the pro-democracy riots. At least 200 remain in prison. Many of the harshest sentences were given not to the protest leaders but to workers such as Mr Zhang who resisted the military assault.

(*Guardian*, 22 September 2006, p. 20)

24 September 2006.

The administrator of NASA began a tour of space agency sites in China on Sunday [24 September], making him the most senior space official to go to China to discuss possible co-operation between the countries' programmes. The official, Michael Griffin, has cautioned that the tour ... is an exploratory visit that will not result in any bilateral space agreement or formal partnerships ... China is the third country, after the United States and Russia, to have sent humans into space. It has been seeking more international co-operation in aerospace projects, but the United States has been reluctant. Much of China's programme is run by the military, raising concerns about possible technology transfer or other national security issues for any such co-operation ... When Chinese space officials invited the previous NASA administrator ... to visit their operations two years ago, nothing came of the overture ... China has major space agreements with Russia, Europe and most other nations with space programmes.

(www.iht.com, 24 September 2006)

On Sunday [24 September] security forces put Chen Liangyu ... the Communist Party boss of Shanghai ... fifty-nine ... under a form of house arrest. State media reported Monday [25 September] that he had lost his political posts and might face criminal charges ... As an heir of the influential Shanghai-centred political machine built by Jiang Zemin, Chen never won the trust of Hu ... Chen's political machine has long been considered one of the strongest and most corrupt in the country ... At least half a dozen other officials and many prominent local deal makers have also been arrested in recent weeks ... As the Shanghai boss, a post that controls great wealth and enjoys considerable autonomy in many policy matters, Chen became an important figure in Chinese politics. He joined the twenty-four-man Politburo and, given his relatively young age, was viewed as a possible contender for higher positions down the road ... The last time a sitting Politburo member lost his post for corruption was in 1995, when Jiang Zemin, then the top Chinese leader, purged Chen Xitong, the Beijing party chief Jiang considered a formidable rival. Hu's corruption crackdown began last spring and picked up pace during the summer months. It has so far resulted in the arrests of lower level officials and well-connected businessmen in Shanghai, Beijing, Tianjin, Jujian and most other areas. Most of the people implicated are viewed as old loyalists of Jiang or members of the Politburo not considered among the core supporters of Hu, leading to suspicions that Hu has used the fight against corruption as a tool to eliminate opponents.

(*IHT*, 26 September 2006, pp. 1, 7)

President Hu Jintao moved decisively to cement his political authority and that of the Beijing central government in economic affairs by sacking Chen Liangyu, the Communist Party secretary in Shanghai for alleged corruption. A scandal involving the Shanghai pensions system erupted into a national political struggle after Mr Hu used the allegations to dismiss Mr Chen. As a member of the national Politburo, from which he has also been suspended, Mr Chen is the most senior Chinese official to be dismissed for corruption in at least a decade … The official Xinhua news agency announced, in an unusually strong statement, that Mr Chen had been sacked because of his role in mismanagement of the Shanghai pension fund … He was accused of illegally enriching relatives, protecting staff who broke the law and 'creating malign political influences'. Mr Chen has been detained under a form of house arrest while under investigation … Jiang Zemin served as mayor of Shanghai.

(*FT*, 26 September 2006, p. 9)

The arrest in August [2005] of Qin Yu, a district chief in Shanghai and a former aide to Chen Liangyu, suggested the noose was tightening. Mr Qin was accused of involvement in the misappropriation of $400 million of the city's social security funds. Now investigators say Mr Chen himself played an unspecified part in the scandal. He is also accused of 'seeking benefits for a number of unlawful enterprises owners', protecting law-breaking aides and seeking illegitimate gains for his relatives … Mr Chen … was appointed as party leader and a member of the Politburo … at the same time as Hu Jintao became the party's general secretary … There is little sign that Mr Hu's leadership has been seriously threatened by Chen Liangyu. It appears more likely that Mr Hu has moved against Mr Chen in order to demonstrate his resolve in the face of a more general threat: that of provincial and lower level leaders blithely ignoring the central government's efforts to tame the economy. With the help of compliant local banks, many are investing in lavish new projects and encouraging speculation in real estate. The central government fears this is creating bubbles in the property market that could threaten social and financial stability … The party has just announced that its Central Committee will hold its annual session from 8 to 11 October … During the meeting Mr Chen is likely to be expelled from the Politburo – his duties have been suspended … In the build-up to the five-yearly party congress due to take place in late 2007, many local officials will end their terms. Mr Hu wants them replaced with loyalists … Apart from a centrally managed fund … China's social security funds … are currently in the hands of local officials who have a tendency to invest them rashly or to pocket them … An official [has been quoted] as saying that from next year [2007] the funds might be supervised centrally and entrusted to 'independent fund managers'.

(*The Economist*, 30 September 2006, pp. 77–8)

26 September 2006. Shinzo Abe becomes the new prime minister of Japan, succeeding Junichiro Koizumi. Shinzo Abe is to visit Beijing on 8 October and

Seoul on 9 October. (President Roh Moo Hyun of South Korea is to visit Beijing on 13 October.)

28 September 2006.

> China's cabinet has ordered high level investigations into property dealings in a dozen cities and provinces, the government said Thursday [28 September] ... Chen Liangyu, the chief of the Communist Party in Shanghai, was dismissed and removed from the party Politburo on Monday, following accusations of corruption and illicit investments of pension funds in real estate and other projects. Chen is also being investigated for having allegedly provided assistance to illegal businesses, shielding corrupt colleagues and abusing his position to benefit family members. The investigation into alleged misuse of Shanghai pension funds and other abuses widened Thursday, with the city's personnel chief joining the list of those implicated in the corruption scandal.
>
> (www.iht.com, 28 September 2006; *IHT*, 29 September 2006, p. 70)

('The corruption scandal in Shanghai that had already taken down one of China's most powerful officials claimed two smaller scalps last week. The chief of the national statistics bureau was fired and an official with the Formlua One racing circuit was hauled in for questioning ... The latest World Bank governance survey found that China had seriously backslid in the category of "containing corruption" when much of the rest of the world, if not improving, was basically unchanged on the issue ... The ministry of commerce has estimated that 4,000 officials have fled overseas in recent years with roughly $50 billion in embezzled money. In 2005, an expert in the national audit office found, $35 billion in state assets was misappropriated': www.iht.com, 22 October 2006.)

> A sweeping anti-corruption investigation is aimed at revamping the country's political leadership and bolstering the power of the ruling Communist Party's two main leaders, party officials and Chinese political analysts said. The investigation, the largest of its kind since China first pursued market-style changes to its economy more than a quarter of a century ago, was planned by Zeng Qinghong, China's vice president and the day-to-day manager of Communist Party affairs, people informed about the operation said. They said Zeng had used the investigation to eliminate provincial opposition to central party directives, sideline remaining loyalists to Jiang Zemin and strengthen his own hand as well as that of President Hu Jintao.
>
> (www.iht.com, 4 October 2006)

> Over the last month the reformist camp has scored a number of notable victories, with the passage of long-awaited bankruptcy regulations and, more significantly, approval of a draft property law. The property law was delayed at the February meeting of the National People's Congress after a prominent law professor raised concerns that it could facilitate the theft of state property. The latest draft makes a rhetorical gesture to such complaints, saying

that private and public property will have equal status, while suggesting that theft of state assets will be considered the 'gravest violation'.

(*FT*, 20 September 2006, p. 8)

President Hu Jintao won the blessing of ... Jiang Zemin before toppling ... Chen Liangyu ... sources said on Thursday [28 September] as a corruption investigation in the city deepened. Beijing party sources say that Jiang ... was consulted before Chen Liangyu was dismissed.

(www.iht.com, 28 September 2006)

Festivities to commemorate Confucius will culminate today [28 September] with ceremonies in Qufu to mark the 2,557th birthday of the sage ... A decision [was taken] yesterday [27 September] to recognize women for the first time as descendants of the ancient Chinese sage ... Kong Fuzi [his name in Chinese] was born in 551 BC and died in 479.

(*The Times*, 28 September 2006, p. 38)

[There is] a growing move to reinterpret and apply the ancient teachings ... Confucian temples are being rebuilt, school textbooks include increasing references to the teachings, at least eighteen universities have started offering courses in Confucian studies, and the government is using the sage's name to project China overseas through a $10 billion programme to establish 100 Confucius Institutes worldwide by 2010 ... [There is] a big push [in China itself] to strengthen Confucian values among the population ... During the Cultural Revolution Confucianism was scorned as a backward philosophy, but in recent years it has made a strong comeback with the full support of a communist-one-party government that has now every reason to embrace the sage's emphasis on harmony and benevolent dictatorship. President Hu Jintao has been the most obvious convert. At a keynote speech last year [2005] he eschewed Marxist rhetoric for some words of wisdom from the sage: 'Confucius said "harmony is something to be cherished"', he observed. Since that moment the government's central goal has been the construction of a 'harmonious society'. Its moral basis was outlined by Mr Hu earlier this year [2006] with a lecture on ethics that owed more to Confucius than Mao Zedong. The sermon on the 'socialist concept of honour and disgrace' extolled ... eight virtues, which include obedience, hard work, plain living, patriotism and public service. The eight disgraces include lawlessness, the embrace of chaos and the pursuit of profit and luxury at the expense of others ... Posters in trains, military barracks and Communist Party offices throughout the nation now remind people of these honours and disgraces.

(*Guardian*, 28 September 2006, p. 23)

8 October 2006. 'Japanese prime minister Shinzo Abe flew to China ... the first visit by a Japanese prime minister in five years ... [He was to travel] to South Korea on Monday [9 October]' (www.iht.com, 8 October 2006). (Shinzo Abe became prime minister on 26 September 2006, succeeding Junichiro Koizumi.)

> President Hu Jintao and prime minister Shinzo Abe said Sunday [8 October] they were 'deeply concerned' over a possible North Korean nuclear test ... Abe put the North Korean issue at the top of his agenda following Pyongyang's announced intention to conduct a nuclear test. The Japanese leader met separately with prime minister Wen Jiabao.
>
> (www.iht.com, 8 October 2006)

> China and Japan said Sunday [8 October] that they had made progress addressing historical animosities and territorial tensions, as Shinzo Abe devoted his first overseas trip to mending ties with Asian neighbours ... Abe broke a tradition among Japanese prime ministers of making Washington the inaugural overseas destination ... The main results of the meetings appeared to be a commitment to step up dialogue. Abe said he had invited Hu and Wen to Japan and that they planned to visit soon. The two sides agreed to set up a panel of experts to study history and to engage in talks about reforming the United Nations, including Japan's desire to join the Security Council. Abe said they would advance co-operation on managing exploration in the East China Sea, as well as on broader energy and environmental issues ... Abe has declined to say whether he will visit the Yasukuni Shrine, calling it a policy of ambiguity.
>
> (*IHT*, 9 October 2006, pp. 1, 8)

> The visit to Beijing by Shinzo Abe [means that he is] the only postwar Japanese prime minister to make China his first destination as premier ... The joint communiqué referred to 'grave concern' over the threat of nuclear tests and an attempt to deal with the issue through the six-party talks ... Mr Abe has not said whether he will visit the Yasukuni Shrine or not, but told both leaders he would deal with the issue 'appropriately'.
>
> (*FT*, 9 October 2006, p. 5)

'The last bilateral summit between Japan and China took place on October 2001, when Junichiro Koizumi visited Beijing. The last meeting between the two countries' leaders came in April 2005, on the fringes of an Asia-African summit in Indonesia' (www.bbc.co.uk, 8 October 2006).

'Since his recent election victory Shinzo Abe has so far refused to comment on whether he plans to visit the Yasukuni Shrine' (www.bbc.co.uk, 8 October 2006).

'[According to opinion polls run in Japan on 26–27 September 2006] a slim majority – 51 per cent – said Shinzo Abe should not visit Yasukuni as prime minister' (www.iht.com, 27 September 2006).

> The Central Committee ... nearly 350 members ... opened an annual meeting Sunday [8 October] that will focus both on policies for spreading the nation's newfound prosperity more evenly and on President Hu Jintao's attempts to further consolidate his power ... The official Xinhua press agency said that the party members would discuss 'building a harmonious society' before adopting a resolution on the matter ... Hu and his cohorts

have promised to increase spending in rural areas and on health care and education ... Xinhua said the richest 10 per cent of the population controls 40 per cent of the nation's wealth, while the poorest 10 per cent have 2 per cent.

(www.iht.com, 8 October 2006)

On Wednesday [11 October] ... the Central Committee ... endorsed a new doctrine of harmony that puts more emphasis on tackling the severe side-effects of unrestrained growth ... The annual meeting of the Central Committee formally adopted President's Hu Jintao's proposal to 'build a harmonious socialist society' ... The leadership declared that a range of social concerns, including the surging wealth gap, corruption, pollution and access to education and medical care, must be placed on a par with economic growth in party theory and government policy ... The party shows no signs of attempting to sharply reduce the rate [of economic growth] soon ... The Central Committee statement: 'There are many conflicts and problems affecting social harmony. Our party has to be more proactive in recognizing and dissolving these contradictions ... A harmonious society above all needs development' ... [China has been transformed] from one of the most egalitarian societies to one of the most unequal, with an urban–rural gap that measures among the biggest in the world ... The Central Committee statement did not commit the leadership to specific targets in reducing the wealth gap beyond stating that it would need to see improvement by the year 2020.

(*IHT*, 12 October 2006, pp. 1, 6)

[On 11 October a] decision [was made] by the Communist Party to build a 'socialist harmonious society', in which peasants prosper and corruption fizzles ... The full text of the document, published on 18 October, prescribes many ways to make China harmonious. They include political reform (how is not said) and cracking down on domestic and foreign 'hostile forces'. Another element, officials say, is creating a 'new socialist countryside', as distinct from the present one where corruption is rampant, health care and education are becoming prohibitively expensive and incomes are falling further behind those in booming cities ... The government says ... a new health insurance scheme ... will be available in 80 per cent of rural counties by 2008. For now they [villagers] have to pay market rates at private clinics. But even when insurance becomes available they will still have to pay between 35 per cent and 60 per cent of treatment costs themselves ... The Central Committee document establishes ambitious goals. The environment is to get 'conspicuously better'. The widening gap between urban and rural areas is to be narrowed. Wealth is to be spread more evenly. Pensions are to be made available for everyone, not just those enjoying the privileged status of registered urban residents ... The committee has set a date for achieving harmony in China. It is to happen by 2020 ... President Hu Jintao and other party leaders remain focused on the party's paramount objective: maintaining social stability. Although corruption, rural poverty and damage to the

> environment threaten this, party leaders are still more concerned about the danger of unemployment ... At a meeting this week of China's top advisory body senior members said that job creation should be a 'priority' in the building of a harmonious society. This year [2006] the urban job market is expected to provide work for only 11 million of 25 million job seekers.
>
> (*The Economist*, 21 October 2006, pp. 75–6)

9 October 2006. North Korea says that it has carried out its first test of a nuclear weapon. (For details, see Jeffries 2009.)

22 October 2006.

> President Hu Jintao appealed on Sunday [22 October] to 70 million members of his ruling Communist Party to show solidarity ... Hu Jintao: 'We should consciously resist money worship, hedonism and extreme individualism and other negative decadent erosion of ideology and culture' ... Hu made the call in his first joint public appearance with Jiang Zemin since the 24 September dismissal of Chen Liangyu as party boss of Shanghai ... [Hu Jintao was addressing] a gathering at the Great Hall of the People marking the seventieth anniversary of the end of Mao Zedong's epic Long March during China's long civil war. State television ... showed footage of both Hu and Jiang, but not of them standing together.
>
> (www.iht.com, 22 October 2006)

27 October 2006.

> Russia surpassed the United States in 2005 as the leader in weapons deals with the developing world, and its new agreements included selling $700 million in surface-to-air missiles to Iran and eight new aerial refuelling tankers to China, according to a new [US] congressional study ... delivered to members of Congress on Friday [27 October] ... Those weapons deals were part of the highly competitive global arms bazaar in the developing world, which grew to $30.2 billion in 2005, up from $26.4 billion in 2004. It is a market that the United States has regularly dominated. Russian agreements with Iran are not the biggest part of its total sales – India and China are its principal buyers ... Among other arms transfers described in the study was a statistic that a single, unnamed nation – but one identified separately by Pentagon and other administration officials to be North Korea – shipped about forty missiles to other nations in the four-year period ending in 2005, the only nation to have done so. Transfers of these weapons are prohibited under international agreements to control the trade of ballistic missiles ... The report, *Conventional Arms Transfers to Developing Nations*, found that Russian arms agreements with the developing world totalled $7 billion in 2005, an increase from its $5.4 billion in sales in 2004. That figure surpassed the United States' annual sales agreements to the developing world for the first time since the collapse of the Soviet Union. France ranked second in arms transfer agreements to developing nations, with $6.3 billion,

and the United States was third, with $6.2 billion. The leading buyer in the developing world was India, with $5.4 billion in weapons purchases, followed by Saudi Arabia with $3.4 billion and China with $2.8 billion. The total value of all arms sales deals worldwide, counting both developing and developed nations, was $44.2 billion in 2005 ... Russia agreed in 2005 to sell China eight of the IL-78M aerial refuelling tankers ... In 2005 the United States led in total arms transfer agreements, when deals to both developed and developing nations are combined. The total was $12.8 billion, down from $13.2 billion in 2004 ... France ranked second in total sales, with $7.9 billion, up from $2.2 billion in 2004. Russia was third when total sales were considered, with $7.4 billion, up from $5.6 billion in 2004.

(www.iht.com, 29 October 2006; *IHT*, 30 October 2006, pp. 1, 7)

Russia captured almost a quarter of the arms market in the developing world in 2005 ... The report named China, India and Iran as the Kremlin's best customers ... The report ... entitled *Conventional Arms Transfers to Developing Nations* ... covered government arms deals but excluded agreements by commercial dealers. France, the United States and the UK [$2.4 billion] took second, third and fourth place respectively ... The biggest arms dealer [in total] remains the United States. It made arms deals last year [2005] worth a total of $12.8 billion and was involved in almost a third of all transactions.

(*The Independent*, 31 October 2006, p. 20)

3–5 November 2006.

All forty-eight countries invited to the summit ... have agreed to send representatives ... Most have confirmed that their heads of state will attend. The five nations in the fifty-three-strong African Union that still recognizes Taipei ahead of Beijing have also agreed to send observers ... China had invested about $6.3 billion in Africa up to the end of last year [2005], about 10 per cent of all its overseas investment ... Two-way trade has jumped from about $10 billion in 2000 to an expected $50 billion this year [2006]. The trade balance between the two is slightly in Africa's favour. Angola, which has overtaken Saudi Arabia as China's largest oil supplier, and South Africa are the two biggest bilateral trading partners.

(*FT*, 27 October 2006, p. 5)

Leaders of forty-eight of the fifty-three African countries, including forty heads of state, plan to arrive this weekend. The official purpose of the three-day China–Africa forum is to expand trade, allow China to secure the oil and ore it needs for its booming economy, and help African nations improve roads, railroads and schools ... The forum's slogan – 'Peace, Friendship, Co-operation, Development' – underscores China's pledge not to discriminate or intervene. Beijing even invited the four remaining African nations that still extend diplomatic recognition to Taiwan, though none of them agreed to attend ... China buys timber from Brazzaville in the Congo Republic, iron ore from South Africa and cobalt and copper from Zambia. There are an estimated 80,000 Chinese expatriates living in Africa, selling shoes, televisions and everything else the world's factory produces.

(www.iht.com, 2 November 2006; *IHT*, 3 November 2006, pp. 1, 8)

'To date forty-eight African countries have paid due obeisance to Beijing; Chad, Senegal and Liberia are the latest to have abandoned their recognition of Taiwan' (*The Economist*, 28 October 2006, p. 73).

> Trade between China and Africa has soared from $3 billion in 1995 to over $32 billion last year [2005] ... [although] Africa makes up only 2.3 per cent of the total [of China's foreign trade] ... According to China's statistics, it invested $900 million in Africa in 2004, out of the $15 billion the continent received.
>
> (pp. 71–2)

'China also invited Taiwan's diplomatic allies in Africa – Burkina Faso, Swaziland, Malawi, Gambia and São Tome and Principe – to attend, although it is not clear whether they have taken up the offer or not' (*The Independent*, 1 November 2006, p. 31).

> [At] a two-day China-African Co-operation Summit forty-five African heads of state and government are to discuss economic and development issues ... China runs a trade deficit with most of the developing world [as a whole], a far cry from its relationships with major markets like the United States, Europe and Japan. But developing countries are vital to China's growth, supplying the raw materials and energy it desperately needs.
>
> (www.iht.com, 1 November 2006)

> Beijing will host African leaders at the Third Forum on China-African Co-operation ... Since January [2006] President Hu Jintao, prime minister Wen Jiabao and foreign minister Li Zhaoxing have all travelled to Africa, visiting a total of fifteen countries ... Two-way trade has quadrupled in the last five years to $40 billion in 2005, making China Africa's third largest trading partner after the EU and the United States ... While China's voracious demand for commodities has driven investment priorities, it is diversifying into apparel, food processing, telecommunications and construction. At $1.2 billion, Chinese foreign direct investment in Africa is small compared with the $29 billion total recorded last year [2005], but if the flux of Chinese firms is any guide – a tenfold increase since 2003 – future capital inflows will likely multiply.
>
> (www.iht.com, 1 November 2006; *IHT*, 2 November 2006, p. 8)

> More than forty African heads of state and ministers are in Beijing for a summit on trade and investment ... The three-day summit celebrates fifty years of diplomatic relations between China and Africa ... Trade between China and Africa has increased tenfold since 1995 ... Taiwan has called on

the five African countries with whom it has diplomatic relations … Gambia, Malawi, Burkina Faso, Swaziland and São Tome … not to attend the summit … China has said that the five countries are welcome to send observers to the Sino-African summit, though they remain ineligible to join the Sino-African strategic economic partnership.

(www.bbc.co.uk, 3 November 2006)

The three-day summit is concentrating on the rapidly expanding economic ties between the two sides … China has pledged to double its aid to Africa and provide $5 billion in loans and credits over the next three years … President Hu Jintao made the announcement as he opened the summit … The summit is focusing on business with more than 2,000 deals under discussion. African leaders welcome their booming trade links with China, but critics accuse Beijing of dealing with repressive regimes … Hu said that China would double its aid to Africa from its 2006 level by 2009, although he gave no figures. Beijing will offer $3 billion in preferential loans and $2 billion in export credits over the next three years, President Hu said. It will more than double the number of goods which do not attract tax when imported to China from Africa. China will train 15,000 African professionals and set up a development fund to help build schools and hospitals. China's drive to buy African oil and other commodities has led to a big increase in two-way trade, worth $42 billion in 2005. Africa is also a growing market for Chinese goods, but critics say Beijing is stifling African manufacturing … Some critics have voiced concerns over how Chinese-owned firms treat African workers. Protests broke out in Zambia in July about the alleged ill-treatment of workers at a Chinese-owned mine, and there have been reports of pay disputes in Namibia.

(www.bbc.co.uk, 4 November 2006)

China and African nations reached sixteen trade and investment deals valued at $1.9 billion on Sunday [5 November] … The business deals with eleven African countries announced on Sunday [5 November] covered infrastructure, telecommunications, insurance and mineral resources … President Hu Jintao [on Saturday 4 November] also pledged to extend $5 billion in loans and credits to Africa, to forgive past debts and double foreign aid to the continent … Hu unveiled a wide-ranging aid package that included loans, debt relief and technical assistance. He said Beijing would provide $3 billion in preferential loans and $2 billion in preferential credits over the next three years and that by 2009 China's annual aid to Africa will be double the level this year [2006] … Though China supported socialist, post-colonial African leaders in Mao's time, it had largely withdrawn its attention from Africa in the 1980s and 1990s as it accelerated market-orientated growth at home. More recently Hu has made cultivating new economic and diplomatic ties to Africa a major foreign policy priority even as the United States concentrates on combating terrorism. Analysts say the main purpose is to secure supplies of natural resources, especially oil, iron ore and copper

> ... China's push has been criticized by some Western critics because Beijing has ignored large-scale human rights violations or serious corruption in countries that it has courted, including Sudan, Zimbabwe and Angola ... Hu and Wen Jiabao, the prime minister, did say they would take steps to encourage greater commercial two-way trade with Africa. They said China would increase to 440 from 190 the number of African exports that can enter China tariff free. They did not specify the items on that list, but if the exports include more manufactured goods the offer could dampen criticism that China does not do enough to promote African manufactured goods. Wen predicted that bilateral trade would top $100 billion by 2010. Trade between China and Africa increased tenfold over the past decade, reaching almost $40 billion last year [2005], and is expected to reach $50 billion this year [2006].
>
> (www.iht.com, 5 November 2006; *IHT*, 6 November 2006, p. 11)

> Chinese companies have signed agreements with eleven African nations for investments worth $1.9 billion in areas such as telecoms and technological equipment, infrastructure, raw materials, banking and insurance ... China's renewed interest in a continent with which it established close ties in the 1960s has provoked criticism that Beijing is trampling over initiatives to combat corruption.
>
> (*FT*, 6 November 2006, p. 9)

> Sudan, which was an oil importer before the Chinese arrived, now earns $2 billion in oil exports each year, half of which goes to China ... China has come under criticism from the World Bank and the IMF for its unrestricted lending and investment in Africa, and for undermining Western attempts to improve governance and cut down on corruption in Africa.
>
> (*The Times*, 6 November 2006, p. 39)

20 November 2006.

> At the start of a symbolic [four-day] visit [to India] President Hu Jintao and Indian prime minister Manmohan Singh introduced a ten-point plan that aims to double bilateral trade to $40 billion by 2010. They also pledged co-operation in the field of civilian nuclear energy ... Just days before the start of the state visit – the first by a Chinese president to India in ten years – China's ambassador to India reiterated Beijing's claim to the north-eastern state of Arunachel Pradesh.
>
> (*IHT*, 22 November 2006, p. 15)

'Bilateral trade has surged to $17.6 billion in 2005–2006 from $260 million in 1990, albeit with a growing surplus in China's favour' (*FT*, 22 November 2006, p. 10).

23 November 2006. President Hu Jintao began a four-day visit to Pakistan.

'President Hu Jintao signed a five-year trade pact with Pakistan on Friday [24 November]' (*IHT*, 25 November 2006, p. 8).

24 November 2006.

> China said Friday [24 November 2006] that a government audit had found that more than $900 million was misappropriated from the nation's $37 billion social security fund, in the latest massive government fraud to be uncovered in the past two years ... The government said that most of the money had been siphoned off for foreign investments, building projects and commercial loans. The country's social security fund was created in 2000 to help the government cope with its massive aging population. It is also meant to provide a cushion in a country where the gap between the rich and the poor has widened dramatically ... A large number of retirees and unemployed workers live on the money ... The national audit office report comes at a time when China has embarked upon one of its most serious crackdowns on government corruption in decades. In September the government fired Chen Liangyu, the Shanghai party secretary and a member of the Politburo. A government investigation determined that he was implicated in the misuse of social security funds in Shanghai. Since then several other government and business leaders have been arrested or called in for questioning in a widening inquiry into official wrongdoing involving bribery or stealing government funds. Some experts have said that the corruption investigations are being used as a political weapon to remove government officials who are not loyal to President Hu Jintao. But most analysts also note that corruption is endemic and that it is threatening the country's prosperity ... [and] stability ... The national audit office for the past few years has been systematically scrutinizing the books of government agencies and institutions and then releasing its findings to the public. The 'audit storm' ... has uncovered a stunning degree of corruption in the biggest Chinese banks, hospitals, ministries and even in smaller departments like the lottery division of the national sports body. Last year [2005], for instance, the national audit office said that more than $35 billion of government money had been misused. The government also said it had handled 147,000 corruption cases last year and that regulators had uncovered over $60 billion in 'irregularities' at the big four state-owned banks ... Local governments managed about half of all social security funds in 2005, the report said. Last year the social security fund managed to cover only about 43 million people in China, a country that today has more than 220 million people over the age of sixty. By 2040 that figure is expected to nearly double to about 400 million, according to the United Nations.
>
> (*IHT*, 25 November 2006, p. 15)

3 December 2006.

> Muhammad Yunus, the Nobel Peace Prize laureate, said Sunday [3 December] that he was working with the Chinese government to bring his Grameen Bank lending system to rural China within a year ... [He] said China had invited him to begin a trial of the 'microcredit' system, which specializes in making loans of $100 or less, in one of three remote locations. The test

could lead to expansion of the programme throughout the country. In Yunus's native Bangladesh Grameen Bank has provided collateral-free loans to 5 million people – 96 per cent of them women – since 1976. Yunus and Grameen were awarded the Nobel in October for their achievements in reducing poverty. At the same time Grameen is noted for its loan repayment rate of more than 98 per cent. China already has more than 100 microcredit programmes, Yunus said, but they have attracted only about 100,000 customers over the past twelve years.

(*IHT*, 4 December 2006, p. 11)

13–15 December 2006.

China will waive tuition fees in 2007 for 150 million rural residents in an effort to narrow the great wealth gap between the affluent coast and the impoverished countryside, the state news media reported Wednesday [13 December]. The students would be exempt from tuition and incidental fees over the course of their nine-year compulsory education, starting in the 2007 spring semester. The measure will cost the government 15 billion yuan, or $1.9 billion, per year ... Annual *per capita* disposable income for rural residents was 2,762 yuan after the third quarter of 2006, compared with 8,799 yuan for urban dwellers.

(www.iht.com, 13 December 2006)

US Treasury Secretary Henry Paulson ... arrived Wednesday [13 December] with Commerce Secretary Carlos Gutierrez, Labor Secretary Elaine Chao, Health and Human Services Secretary Michael Leavitt, Energy Secretary Samuel Bodman, the trade representative Susan Schwab and Stephen Johnson, head of the Environmental Protection Agency.

(www.iht.com, 13 December 2006; *IHT*, 14 December 2006, p. 11)

A high level array of the most senior cabinet officials from China and the United States, opening an unusual two-day [14–15 December] dialogue behind closed doors on economic issues, promoted clashing visions Thursday [14 December] of how quickly Beijing should move to modernize its economic policies to resolve tensions with Washington.

(*IHT*, 15 December 2006, p. 1)

Top officials from China and the United States concluded two days of talks on economic disputes on Friday [15 December] by setting up several study groups and making general pledges ... Another session of the talks ... has been scheduled for May [2007] in Washington.

(www.iht.com, 15 December 2006)

Two days of economic talks ended inconclusively ... US Federal Reserve chairman Ben Bernanke in the text of a speech called the undervalued currency an 'effective subsidy' of exports ... though Bernanke did not say 'effective subsidy' when he delivered the speech.

(*IHT*, 16 December 2006, p. 15)

'The Federal Reserve chairman dropped the phrase ... "effective subsidy" ... from a speech to the Chinese Academy of Social Sciences, using instead the less inflammatory term "distortion"' (*FT*, 16 December 2006, p. 6).

17 December 2006.

> Japan and China have agreed to hold annual ministerial-level talks on energy as they seek to repair relations strained by territorial disputes over oil and gas fields, a senior Japanese official said Sunday [17 December] ... the talks came a day after the two countries took part in an energy meeting of [consuming countries] in which Beijing announced that it was awarding a multibillion-dollar nuclear reactor to Westinghouse Electric, which is part of Toshiba Corporation. The meeting [on 16 December] included ministers from the United States, India, Japan and South Korea, countries that together consume nearly half the world's oil.
>
> (*IHT*, 18 December 2006, p. 11)
>
> [On 16 December China decided] to buy four Westinghouse nuclear reactors ... [the United States and China signing] a memorandum of understanding ... The deal calls for China National Nuclear to buy the reactors from Westinghouse Electric, a company acquired by Toshiba, of Japan, this year [October 2006].
>
> (p. 12)

24 December 2006.

> Parliament has taken up measures ... [to protect] private property and equalize taxes for foreign and domestic companies. The proposed property law is the most controversial measure to come before parliament in recent years. Earlier versions prompted an outcry by leftists ... The property law, first proposed five years ago, was withdrawn during parliament's last full meeting in March ... The National People's Congress began considering a seventh draft Sunday [24 December] that 'strikes a balance between private property and state ownership', according to Xinhua, the state-run press agency. It said backers hoped to pass it when parliament held its next full meeting in March [2007] ... Xinhua said the opposition faded after a new draft enshrined government ownership 'at the heart of the economic system' ... Also Sunday lawmakers took up a proposed law to equalize tax rates paid by Chinese and foreign companies, as many foreign companies qualify for lower taxes because of incentives intended to attract investment ... The proposed law would unify tax rates at 25 per cent.
>
> (www.iht.com, 25 December 2006)

26 December 2006.

> Japanese and Chinese experts are beginning an ambitious project to try to resolve arguments over the two countries' shared past. Ten government-appointed academics from each country are holding their first two-day

meeting in Beijing … They hope to complete the task in 2008 … Groups of historians from both countries have collaborated to produce textbooks before but these are not widely used, at least in Japan. This initiative is being promoted by the two countries' foreign ministers.

(www.bbc.co.uk, 26 December 2006)

27 December 2006.

President Hu Jintao has called on top military commanders to build a powerful navy … as China continues to spend heavily on a modern, blue-water fleet. In a speech to navy officers at a Communist Party meeting Wednesday [27 December] Hu said China was an important maritime nation and the navy should be ready to protect the country's interests 'at any time' … Hu Jintao: 'We should endeavour to build a powerful people's navy that can adapt to its historical mission during a new century and a new period … In the process of protecting the nation's authority and security and maintaining our maritime rights, the navy's role is very important. It is a glorious task' … Hu is also chairman of the Central Military Commission … Hu's speech also suggested that … he was continuing efforts to consolidate his leadership over the country's 2.3 million-strong military. In the early decades of communist rule China's navy was little more than a coastal defence force with obsolete ships and weapons. But after double-digit increases in annual defence outlays over much of the past fifteen years, most analysts believe China is on track to become a major naval power. Over that period Beijing spent heavily on potent surface ships, submarines and weapons from Russia … In the longer term some experts believe that China will add aircraft carriers to its fleet to protect its merchant shipping on distant sea lanes.

(www.iht.com, 28 December 2006; *IHT*, 29 December 2006, p. 6)

29 December 2006.

China said Friday [29 December] that it would strengthen its military ability to block Taiwan from pursuing independence, complaining about US arms sales to the self-ruled island, while also trying to quell foreign unease about Beijing's rapid build-up. In its latest military policy paper the government said it would also focus on strengthening its ability to police its borders and territorial waters, cracking down on terrorism and modernizing its weapons … The white paper said: 'China will not engage in any arms race or pose a military threat to any other country. China is determined to remain a staunch force for global peace, security and stability … [The United States] continues to sell advanced weapons to Taiwan, and has strengthened military ties with Taiwan' … Its reported 2006 budget is $36 billion, but the Pentagon maintains that the true figure, which does not include weapons purchases and other critical items, is several times higher. By comparison President George W. Bush has signed a bill authorizing $532.8 billion in defence spending for the 2007 fiscal year that began on 1 October.

(www.iht.com, 29 December 2006)

> In a defence white paper the government said it would focus its spending on strengthening the country's naval and air forces ... The document, which is published every two years, says military spending in 2006 is set to reach $36 billion, up from $32 billion last year [2005], although the United States believes the true figure to be much higher.
>
> (www.bbc.co.uk, 29 December 2006)

('For two decades China has laboured to build its first state-of-the-art jet fighter as part of its drive to become a leading military power. In December ... it revealed that its new fighter, the J-10, had entered service in the air force ... Chinese engineers ... [had] help from Israel and Russia': *IHT*, 9 February 2007, p. 1.)

1 January 2007.

> [In Japan the] Yasukuni [Shrine] yesterday [1 January 2007] unveiled small tweaks to its history exhibition. The museum still presents a view that Japan was reluctantly forced into war, both with China and with the Allies, but it has softened some of the words relating to such episodes as the colonization of Manchuria and the reasons behind the US embargo on Japan.
>
> (*FT*, 2 January 2007, p. 6)

10 January 2007.

> Hu Jintao has been urged to cede the presidency ... Political allies of Vice President Zeng Qinghong have urged that he be promoted to state president at parliament's annual session in 2008, the sources with close ties to the top leadership said ... The presidency and the top party and military jobs [are] all currently held by Hu ... [In] the late 1950s and early 1960s ... power was shared by four national leaders. The practice continued under the paramount leader Deng Xiaoping in the early 1980s, with Hu Yaobang as party chief, Zhao Ziyang as prime minister and Li Xiannian as president. After Hu's political demise, Zhao took the top party post. In a departure from that practice Jiang Zemin was given the presidency and the top party and military posts to bolster his relatively weak position as he rose to power after the Tiananmen Square crackdown. Jiang ruled for thirteen years until 2002, when he handed the party general secretary post to Hu, who replaced Jiang as president in 2003 and military chief the following year.
>
> (www.iht.com, 10 January 2007)

11 January 2007.

> The murder of an untested reporter for an obscure publication on 11 January has become a watershed event ... Lan Chengzhang had decided to take on what everyone knew could be a most dangerous subject: illegal coal mines ... That Lan's death has become a national event was helped in no small measure by Hu Jintao, who in an unusual statement a few days afterward demanded that justice be done. But it also highlighted the culture of corruption that many journalists acknowledge pervades the industry, particularly

> the practice among some reporters of demanding money from subjects to avoid damaging articles ... In Datong, the city where Lan was killed, he was quickly labelled an impostor, the implication being that he had visited an illegal coal mine to shake down its owner, promising not to write about him in exchange for a payment ... After several days of intense commentary about the killing in the international media and on Chinese blogs and websites, Hu may have been moved to protect his country's image.
>
> (*IHT*, 1 February 2007, p. 2)

11–12 January 2007.

> China successfully carried out its first test of an anti-satellite weapon last week ... China made no public or private announcements about the test ... The launching was detected by the United States in the early evening of 11 January, which would have been early morning on 12 January in China ... Only two countries – the Soviet Union and the United States – have previously destroyed spacecraft in anti-satellite tests, most recently the United States in the mid-1980s ... Arms control experts called the test, in which the weapon destroyed an aging Chinese weather satellite, a troubling development that could foreshadow an anti-satellite arms race. Alternatively, however, some experts speculated that it could precede a diplomatic push by China to prod the Bush administration into negotiations on a weapons ban ... Despite its protest, the Bush administration has long resisted a global treaty banning such tests because it says it needs freedom of action in space.
>
> (www.iht.com, 19 January 2007; *IHT*, 20 January 2007, pp. 1, 6)

> China's success ... reportedly came after three earlier tests failed ... The Chinese test, which Beijing has not acknowledged but was tracked by intelligence agencies, destroyed an aging communications satellite some 500 miles, or 800 kilometres, above the Earth. The [ground-based] missile [using kinetic force] smashed the satellite into hundreds of pieces large enough to pose a danger to spacecraft or satellites that pass through the debris for a decade or more ... American satellites [are] used to conduct military reconnaissance, spot nuclear tests and direct smart weapons ... A [US] national space policy issued in October [2006] declared that 'freedom of action in space is as important to the United Sates as air power and sea power'.
>
> (www.iht.com, 21 January 2007)

> US government and private experts say early estimates of 800 pieces of detectable debris from the shattered satellite will grow to nearly 1,000 ... At either number it is the worst such episode in space history ... Experts say China's test ... means the chain reaction ... a slow cascade of collisions that would expand for centuries ... will most likely start sooner.
>
> (*IHT*, 7 February 2007, p. 2)

12 January 2007. '[It is reported that] syphilis, which was largely eliminated in China in the 1960s, has returned with a vengeance and urgent intervention is needed to curb the epidemic, according to researchers in China and the United States' (www.iht.com, 12 January 2007).

14 January 2007.

> [On 14 January China signed] a new trade-in-services agreement with the ten … [Asean] countries … Conference delegates billed the trade and services deal, which emphasizes high-technology services, energy and construction, as a major step forward in establishing a comprehensive free trade pact between Asean and China … China and Asean began lowering barriers to trading in 2005. Since then tariffs on more than 7,000 products from China and Asean have been lowered … Two-way trade volume last year [2006] amounted to more than $160 billion, up 23 per cent from 2005 … Asean leaders and [China's prime minister] Wen Jiabao also iterated a 2002 agreement pledging to resolve the dispute over claims by China, the Philippines, Vietnam, Malaysia, Brunei and Taiwan to the Spratly Islands in the South China Sea … The pleasant words exchanged on Sunday [14 January] between China and Asean over the Spratlys – a chain of islands scattered along a major shipping lane that are believed to be rich in oil and mineral resources – were not matched by any substantive new agreements beyond the 2002 accord … which commits the claimants to resolve disputes peacefully.
>
> (*IHT*, 15 January 2007, p. 11)

'The accord comes into force in July … [Asean] countries should get greater access to rapidly growing Chinese sectors – such as banking information, information technology, real estate, health, engineering, education, transport and construction' (*FT*, 15 January 2007, p. 8).

15 January 2007.

> Bo Yibo, the last of the 'Eight Immortal' Communist Party leaders who steered China through a politically volatile shift from Maoism to the market-orientated economic boom of today, died Monday [15 January] … He was ninety-eight … Bo helped Deng Xiaoping overcome elite opposition to capitalist-style economic reforms … Bo threw his weight behind the [Tiananmen Square] crackdown … He is the father of Bo Xilai, the commerce minister.
>
> (*IHT*, 17 January 2007, p. 10)

23 January 2007.

> China has confirmed it carried out a test that destroyed a satellite … A foreign ministry spokesman: '[China has notified] other parties and … the American side [of the test] … But China stresses that it has consistently advocated the peaceful development of outer space and it opposes the arming of space and military competition in space. China has never, and will never, participate in any form of space arms race' … China has con-

> firmed that it has destroyed a satellite with a ballistic missile ... In 2002 China and Russia proposed a treaty banning the use of weapons in space, but the United States opposes such a treaty ... US policy, authorized by President Bush on 31 August last year [2006], included the statement: 'The United States will oppose the development of new legal regimes or other restrictions that seek to prohibit or limit US access to or use of space' ... The Outer Space Treaty of 1967, ratified by the major powers, does ban nuclear weapons in space ... But significantly it does not mention other weapons, although space has so far been free of weapons.
>
> (www.bbc.co.uk, 23 January 2007)

> The first confirmation appeared to have come when Christopher Hill, a US Assistant Secretary of State, visited his counterparts in Beijing over the weekend to discuss reviving six-nation negotiations on North Korea's nuclear weapons programme ... Independent experts on the Chinese military said that China has sought a workable anti-satellite weapon since the 1980s. It has experimented with using lasers and kinetic force, such as missiles or other satellites, to disable or destroy satellites in orbit ... China has long feared that the United States might intervene in the event of a military conflict with Taiwan, and it has invested heavily in weapons that experts say are geared toward giving it the power to attack Taiwan while keeping American forces at bay ... Over the summer [of 2006] President George W. Bush authorized a new space policy that seeks to preserve 'freedom of action' in space, and he said that the United States reserves the right to use force against countries that seek to disrupt American satellites.
>
> (www.iht.com, 23 January 2007; *IHT*, 24 January 2007, p. 10)

'[China used] a missile-launched "kinetic kill vehicle" [to destroy the satellite]' (*FT*, 5 February 2007, p. 6).

> Trash from the destruction of a Chinese satellite in a missile test has spread widely in space, creating a debris cloud that could jeopardize spy satellites and commercial imagery satellites in low orbits around the Earth, US officials said. Even the manned International Space Station is vulnerable to being hit by some of the thousands of pieces created when China slammed a ground-based medium-range ballistic missile into an aging Chinese weather satellite ... [It has been estimated] that more than 120 satellites were orbiting in the area.
>
> (www.iht.com, 23 January 2007)

'Over 800 satellites orbit the Earth in all' (www.bbc.co.uk, 23 January 2007).

30 January 2007.

> President Hu Jintao left for an eight-nation tour of Africa on Tuesday [30 January] ... Hu's twelve-day journey will take him to Cameroon, Liberia, Zambia, South Africa, Mozambique, the Seychelles and Sudan ... Trade between China and Africa has soared fourfold this decade to $40 billion in

> 2005. Beijing has also become a major supplier of aid, last year [2006] announcing $10 billion in assistance from 2006 to 2009 … China's official Xinhua News Agency … said $3 billion in preferential loans was to be dispersed over the next three years to help African countries with infrastructure projects, buy technological equipment and set up production facilities. China will also send young volunteers to do aid work in Africa, build hospitals, provide anti-malarial medicine to thirty-three countries, and help build 100 new primary schools by 2009 … China has recently raised expectations that it is heeding the message by calling on Sudan to co-operate with the world body [the United Nations] in finding a solution to the civil strife … [in Darfur where] more than 200,000 people have died and 2.5 million people have been displaced as a result of a four-year-old conflict between rebels and government-backed militias … Xinhua said Hu will inaugurate an economic co-operation zone during his stop in Zambia … In South Africa, which has complained the influx of cheap Chinese clothes could devastate the textile industry, Xinhua said China will make a donation of $2.6 million 'as part of efforts to help the country in skill training and poverty alleviation'.
>
> (www.iht.com, 30 January 2007)

'Trade between China and Africa jumped 40 per cent to $55.5 billion in 2006, with the balance of trade $2.1 billion in Africa's favour, according to [China]' (*IHT*, 1 February 2007, p. 12).

> China will lend African nations $3 billion in preferential credit over three years and double aid and interest-free loans over the same period, Beijing announced yesterday [29 January] ahead of President Hu Jintao's eight-nation tour to Africa, starting today [30 January] … The loans would be mainly for basic infrastructure, power projects and joint enterprises.
>
> (*FT*, 30 January 2007, p. 8)

31 January 2007. '[China] said Wednesday [31 January] that it would support a joint UN–Africa Union peacekeeping mission to Darfur' (*IHT*, 1 February 2007, p. 12). 'During the China–Africa summit meeting in Beijing in early November [2006] when Hu Jintao raised the issue with President Omar al-Bashir of Sudan' (*IHT*, 2 February 2007, p. 7).

2 February 2007. 'President Hu Jintao on Friday [2 February] urged the leader of Sudan, Omar al-Bashir, to work harder to bring more Darfur rebels into the nation's peace process … Hu's visit was the first by a Chinese president to Sudan' (*IHT*, 3 February 2007, p. 6).

3 February 2007.

> China has announced a new investment worth $800 million in Zambia … [flowing] into mining, manufacturing and farms … A special economic zone would be created in Zambia's copper mining area. Chinese companies will be able to operate there without having to pay import or value-added taxes

... Beijing also agreed to write off part of Zambia's debt to China ... A decision by Chinese owners to close Zambia's largest textile firm prompted unrest last month [January].

(www.bbc.co.uk, 3 February 2007)

The foundation stone for the Mulungushi textile factory [was laid] three decades ago ... It grew to become the biggest textile mill in the country ... [There have been complaints that] textile factories cannot compete with cheap Chinese imports ... But last month [January] the factory shut down production ... Hostility is such in some quarters that Hu Jintao ... cancelled plans to launch a $200 million smelter at a Chinese-owned Zambian copper mine at the weekend because of miners' anger at working conditions. He also faced protests from the sacked Mulungushi factory workers ... Two years ago forty-nine miners were blown up in an explosives factory at the Chinese-owned Chambishi mine in an accident blamed on lax safety. Last year [2006] the police shot five miners at Chambishi in a riot over working conditions ... [There are] large numbers of Chinese traders and labourers who have become an increasing source of agitation for taking business and jobs.

(*Guardian*, Monday 5 February 2007, p. 21)

5 February 2007.

President Hu Jintao capped a two-day visit to Zambia on Monday [5 February] by inaugurating a massive mining investment partnership that has been heralded as a model for Beijing's growing business interests in Africa. Hu and President Levy Mwanawasa of Zambia said the new economic partnership zone would be the first of several throughout the continent ... Hu Jintao: 'The Zambia–China Economic Trade and Co-operation Zone is the first of its kind established by China in Africa' ... Mwanawasa and Hu on Sunday [4 February] initiated an economic partnership zone centred around the Chambishi copper mine in Copperbelt province. The partnership is designed to draw $800 million in mining investment from scores of Chinese companies and to create 60,000 jobs.

(*IHT*, 6 February 2007, p. 4)

6 February 2007.

President Hu Jintao headed Tuesday for South Africa, Beijing's biggest trade partner on the continent ... South African trade unions have complained that Chinese textile imports are devastating domestic industry, forcing the two governments to sign a memorandum of understanding last year [2006] aimed at restricting imports.

(www.iht.com, 6 February 2007)

'Last year [2006] President Thabo Mbeki warned that Africa needed to guard against allowing ties with China to develop into a "colonial relationship"' (www.iht.com, 7 February 2007).

('At the end of an eight-country tour of Africa [on 9 February] ... President Hu Jintao said he would try to cut his country's $3 billion trade surplus with the continent': *The Economist*, 10 February 2007, p. 8. 'China imports less African oil, invests less money and spends less on aid than does the United States or Europe. As an African trading partner China ranks third behind the United States and France, and much of that trade is in oil purchased from Sudan, Angola and Nigeria, not in goods made by African workers': *IHT*, 10 February 2007, p. 5. '[According to official figures, in 2006] of Africa's total oil exports China took 8.7 per cent. Europe took 36 per cent and the United States 33 per cent': www.iht.com, 12 March 2007.)

8 February 2007.

> The government has said it will review the licences granted to around 170,000 medicines approved during ... [the tenure of] Zheng Xiaoyu, the head of the ... State Food and Drug Administration ... [who] was sacked in 2005 over allegations that he received large bribes to approve drugs ... According to Chinese media, corruption at the drug agency runs so deep that Beijing is considering closing it down entirely. Dozens of people across the country have died from illegally produced or fake drugs in recent years.
>
> (www.bbc.co.uk, 9 February 2007)

> The government said it has detained Zheng Xiaoyu, the head of the State Food and Drug Administration from the time of its founding in 1998 until he left in June 2005. Beijing is investigating whether Zheng accepted bribes from Chinese pharmaceutical companies in exchange for approving drug production licences ... China has ordered a thorough investigation into the government agency that is supposed to be the national watchdog ... The move comes amid a widening investigation into corruption in the country's fast-growing pharmaceutical industry ... For the past few years there have been widespread reports of illnesses and deaths caused by dangerous foods or fraudulent drugs ... The government said Thursday [8 February] that it would review over 170,000 production licences issued by the agency over the past decade, particularly those issued between 1999 and 2002. The state-run media also reported that drug supervision authorities had already revoked the business licences of 160 drug manufacturers and retailers in 2006.
>
> (www.iht.com, 9 February 2007)

13 February 2007.

> China said Tuesday [13 February] that ... 97,260 members of the Communist Party ... were punished for corruption last year [2006] ... and that more than 80 per cent of them 'took bribes and violated the party's financial and economic rules' ... The cases include China's former top statistician, Qiu Xiaohua, who is accused of taking bribes and having more than one wife ... Besides Qiu the other high profile case was the arrest last year of Shanghai's

former Communist Party chief, Chen Liangyu, who was detained in a pension fund scandal that has ensnared more than a dozen officials and business executives ... Other prominent officials under investigation include Zheng Xiaoyu, the former head of the State Food and Drug Administration, accused of taking bribes to approve shoddy drugs blamed in a string of deaths ... Another high profile case was the arrest on bribery charges of Beijing's former vice mayor, Liu Zhihua, who was in charge of overseeing Olympic construction projects. Beijing officials have said that Liu's alleged misdeeds did not involve Olympic projects.

(www.iht.com, 13 February 2007)

[China] said the government was 'actively preparing to establish a special national-level agency to guard against corruption' ... The new agency [was announced on 13 February] ... a day after state media reported the detention of He Minxu, former vice governor of Anhui province, on charges of receiving at least $1.03 million in bribes and selling official positions.

(*FT*, 14 February 2007, p. 7)

9 March 2007.

Several people were injured as up to 20,000 people clashed with 1,000 police in Hunan province on Friday [9 March] ... The clash was sparked by rising public transport costs ... [with] the rising cost of bus prices ... They were also unhappy about official corruption ... Sporadic incidents continued on Monday [12 March].

(www.bbc.co.uk, 12 March 2007)

An estimated 20,000 people clashed with police in Hunan province ... as a protest over rising transportation costs escalated into a riot ... The protests were said to have been set off by concern about the inflated prices charged for public transportation during the Lunar New Year holiday in February ... On Monday [12 March] truckloads of armed police officers descended on an area of rural Hunan near the village of Zhushan to restore order ... Several protesters and police officers were injured. The *South China Morning Post* reported that one protester had been killed in a skirmish.

(www.iht.com, 13 March 2007)

China sent in the army to restore order yesterday [13 March] after a student [schoolboy] was killed and dozens were hurt when police in a remote town used batons to beat back 20,000 residents demonstrating against a steep rise in bus fares ... As the demonstrations in the mountainous town of Zhushan entered a fourth day, the government deployed a regiment ... and 400 special police ... Residents began to mass around a government building last Friday [9 March] to protest against the new price of tickets for buses running along the main route linking the village to the nearest town. They continued to gather throughout the weekend. They were angered after the price doubled over the Chinese New Year holiday ... plus an additional ... [charge] for a

> bag … and then remained there after the festival ended on 4 March. The protest turned violent on Monday … Five police vehicles were set on fire and the car of the local contractor who had taken over the bus company and its route to a district in Yongzhou city was also burnt … Further fuelling their rage was a view among farmers that the businessmen who had taken over the bus route was colluding with local officials to make money.
>
> (*The Times*, 14 March 2007, p. 35)

> The official Xinhua News Agency reported on Wednesday [14 March] that calm had been restored to the village of Zhushan in Hunan after what it described as a 'mass incident' that began when villagers, upset at higher bus fares, destroyed some buses. The police detained those responsible for the damage and there were no reports of any deaths, Xinhua said. Overseas news reports and witnesses said a student was killed and about sixty protesters injured when police clashed with about 20,000 protesters in Zhushan on Monday [12 March]. In Dongzhou village in Guangdong province last Sunday [11 March] the police broke up a protest of about 1,000 people, the Human Rights Watch report said. People in Dongzhou have been involved in a long-standing dispute over land with the local government … China has mounted a violent crackdown on protests and arrested political activists in a bid to curb dissent during the annual session of its parliament, Human Rights Watch said in a report on Wednesday. The human rights group said protests in the central province of Hunan and another in Guangdong province in the south had been violently suppressed earlier this week. In Beijing, the report said, the authorities rounded up hundreds of petitioners this month [March], while dozens of activists around the country were under house arrest or close surveillance.
>
> (www.iht.com, 14 March 2007)

> The protest in Hunan was apparently sparked by a sudden doubling of public bus fares during the Chinese Lunar New Year holiday, when many people travel to visit their families … As in previous cases, the ostensible reason for the Hunan protest seems disproportionate to the scale and violence of the incident, pointing to deeper discontent that was only waiting for a trigger to manifest in major unrest. Local officials have reportedly acknowledged that the protest was an expression of underlying resentment against corruption … The protest is the most recent manifestation of widespread discontent in the countryside, which is being fuelled by poverty, inequality, corruption, rising healthcare costs and illegal land requisition. According to one official source, there were around 23,000 'mass incidents' in 2006, down from 26,000 in 2005 … Other official sources put the number of mass incidents in 2005 at 87,000.
>
> (www.economist.com, 15 March 2007)

'Security is tight in … Zhushan town … But the protesters believe they have won because the bus company has since brought its prices back down … Complaints [were] initially brought from the parents of secondary school children' (www.bbc.co.uk, 15 March 2007). 'The bus company was forced to abandon its fare rise' (www.bbc.co.uk, 16 March 2007).

13 March 2007.

> Yesterday [13 March] Tian Chengping, minister of labour and social security, gave a warning that the government would be able to find work for only half the 24 million people expected to join the labour market ... The government will be able to find jobs for only half the 24 million who will be looking for jobs this year [2007] ... Those seeking employment will include almost 5 million university graduates and people made redundant by moribund state enterprises, as well as the rural labourers flooding towards the cities.
>
> (*The Times*, 14 March 2007, p. 35)

5–16 March 2007. The annual session of the National People's Congress is held.

'The National People's Congress is constitutionally China's supreme body. But it is controlled by the Communist Party through its choice of members' (*The Telegraph*, 6 March 2007, p. 19). '[In attendance were] 2,985 deputies of the National People's Congress' (*The Times*, 8 March 2007, p. 38). '[There were] 2,889 legislators attending the National People's Congress' (www.bbc.co.uk, 16 March 2007).

> On the eve of the opening of the annual ... two-week ... session of the National People's Congress [on 4 March], a spokesman for the congress ... said defence outlays would increase by 17.8 per cent to 350.92 billion yuan, or $45 billion, this year [2007]. The budget represents the largest increase in military spending in five years ... [following] a 14.7 per cent budget increase in 2006 ... Some foreign military experts said they believed China was actually spending up to three times more on its military than the official figure ... Defence planners are continuing to downsize the world's largest standing army. Since 2003 the military's manpower has been cut by 200,000 to 2.3 million, according to government figures, and the military is now spending heavily on improving training and equipment for this leaner force.
>
> (www.iht.com, 4 March 2007; *IHT*, 5 March 2007, pp. 1, 4)

> China's official defence budget for 2007 rose 18 per cent to $45.3 billion ... Even at that level ... China's defence budget in 2007 exceeds that of Japan and is fast approaching the budgeted levels of defence spending in Britain and France, the largest military spenders after the United States.
>
> (*IHT*, 17 March 2007, p. 6)

'China says its military budget rose by 14.7 per cent last year [2006] to $36.6 billion, but the US and other observers believe the actual figure may be two to three times that amount' (www.bbc.co.uk, 4 March 2007).

> The newly allocated funds for the People's Liberation Army will be about 7.5 per cent of the nation's total budgeted spending for the year, according

> to [the spokesman] ... The real spending figure is believed to be much higher, however, since the official number probably does not include large procurements and other costs. In the past the Pentagon has said that China's real military spending could be as much as three times the stated sum ... In a rare white paper on defence released last December [2006] China estimated that its military spending in 2005 was only 6.2 per cent of total US spending and just over half that of the UK.
>
> (*FT*, 5 March 2007, p. 9).

> [The] spokesman for the National People's Congress said that even with the increase of China's military budget was less than a tenth of the Pentagon's. The US defence department has asked for $481 billion this year [2007], not including operations in Iraq and Afghanistan.
>
> (*Guardian*, 5 March 2007, p. 14)

('The [Bush administration has made a] request for $100 billion for Iraq and Afghanistan': *IHT*, 12 March 2007, p. 6. '[The] recently unveiled Pentagon total for 2008 [was] of more than $620 billion': *IHT*, 13 March 2007, p. 6.)

> The government has set a target of reducing by a fifth the amount of energy consumed to generate each unit of GDP by 2010 and of reducing the emission of harmful pollutants by 10 per cent. In 2006 China met less than a third of its energy-saving goals for the year. China is the world's number two oil importer and is expected to surpass the United States, the leading importer, as the top producer of greenhouse gases.
>
> (www.iht.com, 9 March 2007)

> Prime minister Wen Jiabao ... making the annual address on the state of China ... conceded Monday [5 March] that China was failing on important energy and pollution goals ... The most recent five-year plan calls for a 20 per cent reduction in energy consumption per unit of GDP. But Wen acknowledged that China had already failed to meet reduction goals in the first year of that programme. It also failed to meet a goal of reducing the overall discharge of pollutants last year [2006], he said ... [Wen Jiabao described] plans to shut down 'backward' steel and iron foundries and inefficient, polluting power plants. He said new development projects would have to meet national environmental standards ... Wen: 'We must make conserving energy, decreasing energy consumption, protecting the environment and using land intensively the breakthrough point and main fulcrum for changing the pattern of economic growth' ...[Wen Jiabao] pledged more government spending on education and health care, particularly for poorer residents in rural areas ... [He] emphasized past themes like social equality and the need to reduce the income gap between rural and urban residents ... [He] described serious structural problems in the economy [but said]: 'The most important task for us is to promote sound and fast economic development' ... He warned that illegal land confiscation had to be stopped. He praised the real estate industry as an essential part of the national economy,

but he called on developers ... to also focus on building affordable housing and to not threaten 'primary farmland'. The prime minister also announced that the government would stop collecting tuition fees from all rural students. He said the government would expand pilot projects to build a rural co-operative health care system and would begin establishing the equivalent of a welfare programme for the poorest people.

(www.iht.com, 5 March 2007; *IHT*, 6 March 2007, p. 5)

Premier Wen Jiabao opened the annual session of the country's legislature with a call for more sustainable growth ... [He gave a] two-hour address to nearly 3,000 delegates in the Great Hall of the People ... Wen Jiabao: 'We should ... avoid seeking only faster growth and competing for faster growth ... The pattern of economic growth is inefficient. This can be seen most clearly in excessive energy consumption and serious environmental pollution. We must attach greater importance to saving energy and resources, protecting the environment and using land intensively.'

(www.bbc.co.uk, 5 March 2007)

Wen Jiabao said 'many backward production facilities' had not been shut as planned and local governments and enterprises had failed to comply with laws ... Mr Wen confirmed that a target in the last five-year economic plan to cut energy consumption per unit of output by 4 per cent a year and reduce the discharge of pollutants by 2 per cent was not met last year [2006] ... The key programmes in the government's push to try to stem the rising rich–poor divide are the introduction of a rural medical insurance system and a guarantee of free basic education ... Mr Wen said land would not be allowed for individual houses, golf courses or training centres for the party.

(*FT*, 6 March 2007, p. 6)

[China] is now on course to overtake the United States as the biggest producer of greenhouse gases by 2009. It is also making slow progress on reducing waste. According to the latest five-year plan, China should use 20 per cent less energy per unit of economic output by 2010. Last year [2006], however, it managed to improve energy efficiency by only 1 per cent. Wen Jiabao said these failures were partly the fault of local governments which failed to abide by national environmental laws. 'We must make conserving energy, decreasing energy consumption, protecting the environment and using land intensively the breakthrough point and main fulcrum for changing the pattern of economic growth,' he said ... Mr Wen announced an 8 per cent economic growth target for this year [2007].

(*Guardian*, 6 March 2007, p. 22)

'Prime minister Wen Jiabao told the opening session of the National People's Congress ... [that]: "We should avoid seeking only faster growth and competing for faster growth. We must put people first"' (*The Telegraph*, 6 March 2007, p. 19).

From this year [2007], said Wen Jiabao, schools would no longer charge tuition or other fees for children having their compulsory education (up to the end of junior high school. A medical insurance scheme, launched in 2003, is to cover 80 per cent of rural areas by the end of this year [2007], up from 50 per cent at present. The aim is to have complete coverage by 2010 ... Even the health insurance scheme in the countryside is not all it is cracked up to be. The programme requires contributions from peasants and provincial governments as well as the central government. The peasant has to pay only a dollar or two a year. But he still has to pay a considerable proportion of expenses for hospital treatment.

(*The Economist*, 10 March 2007, p. 27)

[On 16 March] prime minister Wen Jiabao ... [gave] a news conference [to end the session] ... Wen stressed that his focus remained squarely on overcoming what he termed 'hidden crises' that threaten to undermine China's economy, which, he said, remained 'unbalanced, uncoordinated, unstable and unsustainable', even as it grew rapidly. He said the country must also address the 'over-concentration of power' that has fuelled rampant corruption and that it must do more to help the poor ... 'The two great tasks are first to develop the productive forces of society, and second to advance social justice and fairness' ... The prime minister said that China needed to pursue 'political reform' to combat corruption, which he acknowledged had infiltrated the 'top ranks' of the Communist Party.

(*IHT*, 17 March 2007, pp. 1, 6)

Premier Wen Jiabao admitted yesterday [16 March] that corruption was rife and was the result of too much power in the hands of government officials ... Wen Jiabao: 'There are many reasons behind corruption, but the most important one is because of the over-concentration of power that cannot be effectively checked and supervised' ... He admitted that corruption was becoming increasingly serious, was occurring continuously and involved top officials.

(*The Times*, 17 March 2007, p. 56)

In a televised press conference yesterday Mr Wen said candidly that the chief cause of China's 'increasingly serious' corruption 'is the over-concentration of power', with no 'efficient restriction'. His remedy is further liberalization, on the sound premise that fewer official licences would mean fewer opportunities for the corrupt. He talked about 'building a law-governed country' and 'Chinese democracy'.

(p. 20)

At a news conference ... Wen Jiabao ... said that corruption had been getting 'more and more serious', a departure from the party's usual line that its clean-up is having some success ... [But] in the official transcript published by the Chinese press his remarks were more cautious: corruption was only 'quite serious' in some places and departments ... [In March 2007

> Vietnam] issued a decree requiring legislators and senior officials to declare their assets. China imposes no such burden on legislators; officials are subject only to patchily and secretly enforced requirements to report their incomes.
>
> (*The Economist*, 21 April 2007, pp. 69–70)

The property law was finally approved. '[When the property bill was put to the vote on 16 March] 99.1 per cent of the 2,889 legislators attending the National People's Congress backed the property law' (www.bbc.co.uk, 16 March 2007).

> Originally scheduled for March 2006 the passage of the [property rights] law was delayed after Peking University law professor Gong Xiantian issued an open letter arguing that the draft law violated Article 12 of the constitution (which declares that state property is inviolable) and basic principles of socialism. This appeal, which was published on the internet, ignited considerable controversy. In late 2006 Professor Gong issued a second letter, this one signed by hundreds of scholars and former officials, again attacking the draft law.
>
> (*FEER*, May 2007, p. 17)

> Old-style Marxists oppose the property rights bill, which they warned would worsen inequalities in society and legitimize the theft of state assets by corrupt officials ... In a survey by the Chinese Academy of Social Sciences, half of the respondents believed the rich had acquired their wealth through illegal means. Critics of the bill say it will legitimize what they see as a mass theft from the people ... Most representatives in the National People's Congress [they say] are high-level officials from the provinces. They have personally benefited from privatization so they support the new law ... Although details [of the bill] have yet to be made public, it is expected to include a passage that states: 'Ownership rights of the state, groups and individuals are protected by law, and no individual or organization may violate these rights' ... Building owners are expected to be offered an automatic extension of their leases.
>
> (*Guardian*, 5 March 2007, p. 14)

'The law ... has drawn criticism from lawmakers and some senior officials who fear it could protect the gains of those who misappropriate state-owned assets' (*IHT*, 5 March 2007, p. 1).

> Perhaps the most important clause is the one that gives urban residents full effective ownership of their homes. City housing must currently be bought under a seventy-year lease that has to be reregistered. Yin Tian, a professor at Peking University and one of those who drafted the law, said that ownership would be extended automatically. 'Before this there was no legal answer in China as to what would happen to your property after the seventy years' [he said].
>
> (*The Times*, 8 March 2007, p. 38)

> Parliament began debating a landmark private property measure on Thursday [8 March] that would ensure that all forms of property, including the assets of individuals, the state and collectives, have protection under the law ... would be given equal protection under the law ... At a news briefing on Sunday [4 March], before the opening session, the parliamentary spokesman, Jiang Enzhu, said: 'No matter if it is state, collective or private property', it should be protected equally ... The introduction of the proposed law to the National People's Congress follows a rare and long public consultation ... In a speech introducing the draft law, Wang Zhaoguo, vice chairman of the Standing Committee, told delegates Thursday that protecting people's property rights was aimed at 'stimulating their vigour to create wealth' and enhancing social stability. 'As the reform and opening-up and the economy develop, people's living standards improve in general and they urgently require effective protection of their own lawful property accumulated through hard work,' Wang said ... While all land in China remains the property of the state, legal experts consulted in drafting the law said it would automatically extend the leases that farmers and landowners hold over the land they occupy. But experts say the new law is unlikely to curb the forced reallocation of farming land for commercial or industrial use that has led to widespread unrest and protests in rural areas ... A leading Chinese Marxist economist, Gong Xiantian, has been a key figure in rallying opposition to the draft law. After a government call for public comment in 2005 Gong wrote an open letter to the chairman of the Standing Committee, Wu Bangguo, warning that putting private property on the same legal basis as public assets would 'undermine the legal foundation of China's socialist economy'. 'This means that people who become rich by preying on state-owned assets and bribes could be shielded from prosecution,' Gong wrote in the letter, which included the signatures of 3,274 people, including retired senior officials and military officers. 'Such a law would pose a serious violation against China's constitution, which stipulates that socialist public property is deemed sacrosanct and shall be free from encroachment,' he wrote ... Some economists warn that the law's passage would not significantly enhance the rights of property owners while government officials exerted influence or even outright control over the courts ... Advocates of farmers' rights unsuccessfully urged the authorities to include provisions in the property law that would make it more difficult for local governments to seize farms and sell the rights to use this land to private developers or industry. Under existing law local governments have the power to convert agricultural land to other uses if it is deemed to be in the public interest.
>
> (www.iht.com, 8 March 2007; *IHT*, 9 March 2007, pp. 1, 8)

'It is not clear whether the current version will adequately address the expropriation of collectively owned land from peasants for development – one of the biggest sources of rural unrest' (www.iht.com, 14 March 2007).

> [The] new property law ... is the first piece of legislation to cover an individual's right to own assets ... The latest text of the bill states that: 'The property of the state, the collective, the individual and other obligees is protected by law, and no units or individuals may infringe upon it.' But it adds that: 'The nation is in the first stage of socialism and should stick to the basic economic system in which public ownership predominates, co-existing with other kinds of ownership' ... The bill also seeks to address the often illegal land seizures that are taking place, and the government transfer of farmland to developers, frequently without farmers being given adequate compensation ... The bill will also reportedly boost protection against land seizures, which have become a major source of unrest among farmers in rural areas.
>
> (www.bbc.co.uk, 8 March 2007)

> Wang Zhaoguo, a vice chairman of the National People's Congress, introducing the bill yesterday [8 March]: 'Effective property of private citizens is not only stipulated by China's constitution ... but is also the general aspiration and urgent demand of the people' ... The wording of the final bill ... includes lengthy references to the primacy of the 'socialist system' and 'state ownership' ... The bill also explicitly rejects any change to the system of 'collective' ownership of rural land, where farmer occupiers have only usage rights over limited contract periods rather than any title that can be bought and sold. Properties in cities, by contrast, can be bought and sold under leases of between fifty and seventy years.
>
> (*FT*, 9 March 2007, p. 7)

'Experts say ... the new property rights bill ... will not give farmers much more protection against unscrupulous officials' (*FT*, 4 April 2007, p. 13).

> Living up to one's name poses something of a problem for the Communist Party ... whose name in Chinese literally means 'the public property party' ... Should an underdog try to use the new law to enforce his rights, the corrupt and pliant judiciary would usually ensure he was wasting his time.
>
> (*The Economist*, 10 March 2007, p. 11)

> [The] new law on property rights is mainly intended to reassure the country's fast-growing middle class that their assets are secure. Three years ago China added a clause to its constitution saying that private property was 'not to be encroached upon' ... A vocal body of intellectuals and retired officials has denounced the property law as a betrayal of the country's socialist principles. It will, they say, protect the fortunes of corrupt officials and the ill-gotten gains of crooked businessmen. Further, it will hasten the demise of China's remaining state-owned industries and the creation of a plutocracy ... Among the more than 3,200 signatories ... [of] a recent petition to the NPC ... are seven former government ministers or deputy ministers, five former provincial leaders, a sprinkling of retired senior military officers and about fifty professors at the party's Central School, an academy for top

officials ... Ownership could be challenged, but critics worry that it would be difficult to do so for former state-owned assets or for land-use rights that had been sold off in shady deals. The timing of the earlier draft's publication in 2005 was bad for the bill's supporters. It followed an upsurge of debate about the frequent sale of state-owned enterprises at rock-bottom prices to their managers. In response, the government banned management buy-outs of large state enterprises. But there was also concern about its sales of strategic stakes in state-owned banks to foreign investors ... The leadership itself invited discussion by publishing a draft of the law in 2005 – a very unusual move in a country that normally keeps its legislative processes shrouded in secrecy ... Sweeping privatization of housing since the late 1990s has radically changed the social and political fabric of urban China. Property rights have become a topic of critical interest to urban residents anxious to protect their new assets from the whims of the state ... Farmers ... have something to gain ... The good news is that the latest draft, unlike the 2005 version, gives farmers the right to renew their land-use rights after they expire. Unlike urban land, which is state-owned with usage rights granted for periods of between forty and seventy years, rural land is 'collectively' owned. Farmers are given thirty-year leases (though often no supporting documents) to use plots of land. But the law will put no new limits on the government's powers to appropriate land. It also says that village committees represent the collective. These are supposedly democratically elected but party regulations still give unelected party officials the final say over village affairs. Most important, the ban on mortgaging farmland will remain.

(pp. 25–7)

Land-use conversion regulations have been tightened in an effort to reduce unrest provoked by unfair seizures of land. For example, local governments must now record land sales as 'on-budget' income and certain types of projects – such as golf courses and theme parks – have been banned on undeveloped land. Enforcement efforts have been strengthened by sending out teams of auditors to review land rezoning arrangements by local governments. The NPC will also pass a new private property law which, while stopping short of reforming the rural land-tenure system, reiterates the legal requirements to compensate farmers adequately for the expropriation of their land.

(www.economist.com, 15 March 2007)

China on Friday [16 March] enacted its first law to protect private property ... [There was] a ban on news media discussion of the proposal ... When one popular financial magazine, *Caijing*, defied the propaganda department's ban on reporting on the matter and published a cover story on the law last week, it was ordered to halt distribution and reprint the magazine without the offending story ... [Neither Hu Jintao or Wen Jiabao] has spoken publicly about [the property law]. Wen Jiabao's two-hour address to

> the nation on the opening day of the annual two-week session did not mention property rights ... The leadership did not so much overcome opposition to the property law as forbid it. Unlike in 2005, when leaders invited broad discussion about property rights, the latest drafts of the law were not widely circulated. Several left-leaning scholars ... said they had come under pressure from their universities to stay silent ... Hundreds of scholars and retired officials signed a petition in February against the law, which they said 'overturns the basic system of socialism'. The petition claimed the law did too little to distinguish between private property gained legally through hard work and public property that falls into private hands through corruption. They also argued that China could not give state-owned property and private property the same legal status and still call itself socialist ... Supporters of the law dispute the assertion that it will protect the ill-gotten gains of corruption, arguing that it protects only legally held property ... China's urban middle class has fuelled a real estate boom, even though all land is owned by the state and purchasers trade only the right to use property on it for up to seventy years. The disposition of property after that term expires is one of many unsettled issues that the property law is intended to address, but the details have yet to be publicized ... The final wording of the law remains unclear – as does the nature of any compromises that may have been necessary to build a consensus within the party to pass it.
>
> (www.iht.com, 16 March 2007; *IHT*, 17 March 2007, p. 6)

'Farmers will be able to renew their leases, but they will neither be allowed to mortgage land nor to acquire the individual title that would give them property protection against forcible acquisition' (*The Times*, 17 March 2007, p. 20).

Legislation was passed to standardize tax rates levied on foreign and domestic companies. '[When the property bill was put to the vote on 16 March] 99.1 per cent of the 2,889 legislators attending the National People's Congress backed the property law. The tax legislation ... was passed with only slightly less support' (www.bbc.co.uk, 16 March 2007).

> Chinese companies [currently] pay 33 per cent tax, while foreign investors pay as little as 15 per cent ... Many of the supposedly foreign investors profiting from tax concessions are ... Chinese investors 'round-tripping' their money via the British Virgin Islands and other tax havens.
>
> (*FT*, 5 March 2007, p. 18)

> China ended nearly three decades of favourable treatment for foreign companies yesterday [8 March] with the introduction of a measure to equalize tax rates paid by local and overseas enterprises. The long-awaited law ... will see a single tax rate of 25 per cent levied on all companies. Under the current system Chinese companies have been taxed at up to 33 per cent while foreign enterprises have paid as little as 15 per cent ... The biggest winners will be China's large state banks, according to [the company]

> J.P. Morgan, because income and revenue tax – the last of which only banks have to pay – now eat up nearly 50 per cent of their pre-tax profit … [J.P. Morgan] expected the 5 per cent revenue tax to be gradually phased out … The new law, to start next year [2008], also targets so-called 'fake' foreign companies – local companies that move money out of and back into China to earn a tax break. The bill enacting the changes may not affect foreign companies already operating in China fully for up to five years. Because of the way it was being phased in, China would also continue to offer concessionary tax rates to 'low profit enterprises' and to investors offering high-tech projects.
>
> (*FT*, 9 March 2007, p. 7)

'On Sunday [4 March] lawmakers said they would unify China's income tax rate at 25 per cent, cutting the rate on local companies from 33 per cent and raising it from 15 per cent on overseas firms, [the] legislature spokesman said' (*IHT*, 5 March 2007, p. 11).

> China's plan to unify tax rates for foreign and domestic companies should raise the total annual tax bill for foreign investors by about $5.5 billion, finance minister Jin Renqing said Friday [9 March] … If the bill is confirmed next week it will take effect next 1 January [2008]. A measure being considered by China's legislature would end nearly three decades of blanket tax breaks for foreign investors. It would unify tax rates for foreign and Chinese companies at 25 per cent, up from the average of 15 per cent that the government says foreign companies pay now. That increase [is] to be phased in over five years.
>
> (www.iht.com, 9 March 2007)

> Tax paid by foreign and domestic firms will be unified at 25 per cent … Domestic firms currently pay income tax of 33 per cent, while foreign-funded businesses pay between 15 per cent and 24 per cent … A controversial 50 per cent tax break for foreign firms that focus on exports – which the United States had said was anti-competitive – will be scrapped. High technology will be taxed at 15 per cent under the reforms.
>
> (www.bbc.co.uk, 8 March 2007)

> China is creating an investment company to get better returns of its foreign currency reserves worth $1 trillion … Finance minister Jin Renqing gave no details when the fund would be set up or how it would manage the money. However, he pointed to Singapore's state investment firm Temasek as a possible model.
>
> (www.bbc.co.uk, 9 March 2007)

> People close to the state administration of foreign exchange, which is controlled by the People's Bank of China and manages the country's reserves, estimated that the agency already held about $100 billion worth of American mortgage-backed securities … The People's Bank of China discloses

few details about its holdings. But experts estimate that it holds another $600 billion or so worth of US Treasury securities that it lends actively to generate extra profit, as well as at least $200 billion worth of Euro-denominated bonds. The remainder is thought to be held in bonds denominated in yen and other currencies.

(*IHT*, 6 March 2007, p. 14)

Finance minister Jin Renqing … announced the formation of a new agency on Friday [9 March] to oversee investment of the country's massive $1 trillion in foreign currency reserves … [although] he offered no specifics about how much of China's currency reserves would be made available to the investment agency. China already has the world's largest foreign exchange holdings and they are growing at a rapid pace … The government said one of the models for the new agency is Temasek Holdings, the Singapore government's hugely successful investment agency, which manages an $84 billion global portfolio of investments. China's currency exchange reserves are now held by … the People's Bank of China and most of the reserves are expected to continue to be held there in safe, conservative investments in government securities. But a large sum is expected to be shifted to the new agency or investment group, which could … invest it for higher returns … Jin Renqing said the new agency would answer directly to the State Council.

(www.iht.com, 9 March 2007)

China's currency exchange reserves are now held by the People's Bank of China and most of the reserves are expected to continue to be held there, in safe, conservative investments in government securities … Jin Renqing: 'The biggest priority is safety and under the principle of security we will try to increase the efficiency of management and the investments' returns.'

(*IHT*, 10 March 2007, pp. 1, 17)

'The State Council has already made research into separating the management of normal foreign exchange reserves and a portion allocated for investment,' Jin Renqing said … 'This company is now under construction' [he said] … Mr Jin said the aim of the new agency was to manage the reserves prudently, but also more 'profitably' and 'efficiently'. The government is under increasing pressure over managing the reserves, which reached $1,966 billion by the end of last year [2006] and have risen by about $20 billion a month, fuelled mainly by China's trade surplus … Mr Jin said the new agency would report to the State Council, China's cabinet, but he shed no light on its structure, which has been the subject of extensive debate. Nor did he give any detail on how much of the reserves would be put under the management of the new agency. Chinese officials and local press reports have suggested a sum of up to $300 million. However, this amount is unlikely to be transferred in a single tranche for immediate investment, either domestic or offshore … The bulk of the reserves will continue to be managed by the present custodian, the state administration for foreign currency, an agency under the central bank. The make-up of the investment portfolio is secret, but its mandates for foreign banks investing money on its behalf have generally been conservative, focusing on Treasury bills and mortgaged-backed securities. About three-quarters of the reserves are believed to be in US dollar-denominated assets. In recent years the state administration for foreign currency has also given mandates to foreign mutual funds but they are relatively small compared to the huge amounts of money under its management.

(*FT*, 10 March 2007, p. 9)

Prime minister Wen Jiabao said Friday [16 March] that China's creation of a new company to invest a portion of its $1 trillion in foreign exchange reserves would have no impact on Beijing's holdings of US dollar-denominated assets … Wen Jiabao: 'Our purchases of US dollars are mutually beneficial. Setting up of the new agency won't affect the value of the US dollar assets' … China is believed to keep as much as 70 per cent of its reserves in US Treasuries and other dollar-denominated assets.

(www.iht.com, 16 March 2007)

Wen said that even as China explored new ways to invest more than $1 trillion in foreign currency reserves in overseas assets, Beijing still amounted to a small player in world financial markets and would 'not have any impact on US dollar-denominated assets' globally.

(*IHT*, 17 March 2007, p. 6)

Wen Jiabao … said at the press conference to close the National People's Congress [on 16 March] that investments by the … new state investment agency … 'would not have any impact on US dollar-denominated assets'. Mr Wen's comments were reinforced by the People's Bank of China, which said in a report hours later that it would not make 'frequent, major adjustments to the structure of the reserves in response to market movements' … Chinese leaders have been cautious in what they say about the reserves, especially regarding the US dollar, for fear of encouraging speculation that Beijing is reducing its holdings of the currency. Mr Wen's reassurance on the US dollar is also in China's self-interest, since any dollar sell-off would leave huge capital losses for Beijing's existing holdings. The precise make-up of China's holdings is a state secret, but about 75 per cent are believed to be held in dollar-denominated assets. Mr Wen said: 'I can assure you that by instituting such a foreign exchange reserve investment company, it will not have any adverse impact on US dollar-denominated assets'. He acknowledged that China held the majority of its reserves in US dollar instruments, which he said had been purchased 'on the basis of mutual benefit'.

(*FT*, 17 March 2007, p. 5)

24 March 2007.

[On 24 March the] Communist Party appointed Xi Jinping as the top leader [party secretary] of Shanghai … [He] is regarded by political analysts as favouring deeper market-orientated reforms ... His appointment ... follows the removal last autumn [2006] of Chen Liangyu, the Shanghai party chief and member of the Politburo ... Xi Jinping is the son of a former top government official, Xi Zhongxun. As a result he is seen as part of a class of officials known as 'princelings', whose political influence stems from elite connections ... He is considered a close ally of Zeng Qinghong, the Vice President, who is also known as a princeling.

(www.iht.com, 25 March 2007)

25 March 2007.

Mao Zedong's last surviving son, Mao Anqing, who suffered from mental illnesses but worked as a Russian translator, has died in Beijing at the age of eighty-four ... Analysts have said that Mao planned to name his eldest son ... Mao Anying ... his heir before he was killed in the Korean War and that Mao Anqing's mental problems thwarted plans for a dynastic leadership.

(www.iht.com, 25 March 2007)

'Unlike the children of many other top officials, none have become powerful political or economic figures' (www.cnn.com, 25 March 2007).

26 March 2007.

Japan's prime minister Shinzo Abe has apologized in parliament for the country's use of women as sex slaves during World War II. The apology comes after Mr Abe was criticized by Asian neighbours for previous comments casting doubt on whether the women were coerced ... Shinzo Abe: 'I apologize here and now as prime minister.'

(www.bbc.co.uk, 26 March 2007)

Prime minister Shinzo Abe, under fire for denying government involvement in forcing women to serve as sex slaves during World War II, said Monday [26 March] that he was 'apologizing here and now as the prime minister'. However, he did not retract a statement he made earlier this month [March] that there was no proof that the Japanese army or government had kidnapped the 'comfort women' as the wartime sex slaves are known in Japan. He also stood by a 1993 apology known as the Kono Statement that acknowledged official involvement in the brothels. But he has said that there would be no apology even if US lawmakers adopted a resolution seeking one. 'I am apologizing here and now as the prime minister, and it is stated in the Kono Agreement,' Abe told a parliamentary committee in response to a question by an opposition lawmaker. 'As I frequently say, I feel sympathy for the people who underwent hardships, and I apologize for the fact that they were placed in this situation at the time.'

(www.iht.com, 26 March 2007)

Facing increasing criticism for denying that Japan coerced women into sex slavery during World War II, prime minister Shinzo Abe repeatedly refused

> Monday to acknowledge state responsibility in recruiting so-called comfort women, but offered an apology to them. In a debate in parliament, under intense questioning by an opposition lawmaker, Abe refused to withdraw a recent statement in which he said that there was no evidence that the military had forcibly recruited women to work in so-called comfort stations established throughout Asia ... Abe said: 'I express my sympathy for the hardships they [comfort women] suffered and offer my apology for the situation they found themselves in' ... Abe said he would adhere to a 1993 statement by a government spokesman that acknowledged Japan's role in managing the wartime comfort stations, as well as forcibly recruiting sex slaves.
>
> (www.iht.com, 26 March 2007)

(Prime minister Shinzo Abe of Japan on a visit to the United States [27 April 2007]: 'I feel sympathy from the bottom of my heart to former comfort women. I feel deeply sorry that they were forced to be placed in such extremely painful situations. I believe my remarks and true intentions were not conveyed accurately [in March]': www.bbc.co.uk, 27 April 2007. 'Prime minister Shinzo Abe ... offered an apology, but used pointedly vague language to sidestep the issue of Japan's responsibility toward the sex slaves, known euphemistically as comfort women ... Abe said that he had "deep-seated sympathies that the people who had to serve as comfort women were placed in extreme hardships" and expressed his "apologies for the fact that they were placed in that sort of circumstance" ... [Critics] said that Abe's comments reflected both the vagueness of the Japanese language and a carefully worded script ... What Abe said does not acknowledge the issue of coercion': www.iht.com, 29 April 2007).

> President Hu Jintao is starting a three-day visit to Russia ... Mr Hu's talks with Russian counterpart Vladimir Putin are expected to focus on possible oil and gas deals ... China bought tens of billions of dollars worth of Russian military technology and would like to buy a lot more Russian oil and gas. But bilateral trade of around $40 billion a year is still only 20 per cent of China's overall trade and a fraction of that of the United States.
>
> (www.bbc.co.uk, 26 March 2007)

> President Hu Jintao and President Vladimir Putin pledged to expand economic co-operation, which has lagged behind thriving military and security ties ... Trade between the ... neighbours is far outstripped by China's commercial ties to the United States, Japan and South Korea. Bilateral trade hovers around $30 billion annually, just about 2 per cent of China's total trade volume. Hu and Putin issued a joint communiqué on Monday [26 March], pledging support for joint projects in the oil and gas spheres but offering no specifics ... They called for an international agreement to bar the deployment of weapons in space ... Residents of some sparsely populated regions are concerned about the growing number of Chinese migrants.
>
> (www.iht.com, 27 March 2007)

'The two countries announced a joint effort to explore Mars and one of its moons in 2009' (*The Economist*, 31 March 2007, p. 8).

28 March 2007.

> China has found a huge offshore oil field that could become the ... biggest new oil source in a decade, a state news agency said Wednesday [28 March] ... PetroChina found the field in Bohai Bay off China's east coast ... The biggest recent domestic oil discovery, also made by PetroChina, was a field found in the mid-1990s in the Tarim Basin in China's desert northwest. Chinese oil companies have been spending heavily on exploration in the north-western and coastal areas but results have been disappointing.
>
> (www.iht.com, 28 March 2007)

30 March 2007.

> In another sign that Japan is pressing ahead in revising its history of World War II, new high school textbooks will no longer acknowledge that the Imperial Army was responsible for a major atrocity in Okinawa, the government has announced. The ministry of education on Friday [30 March] ordered publishers to delete passages stating that the Imperial Army ordered civilians to commit mass suicide during the Battle of Okinawa, as the island was about to fall to American troops in the final months of the war ... 'There were some people who were forced to commit suicide by the Japanese Army,' one old textbook explained. But in the revision ordered by the ministry, it now reads: 'There were some people who were driven to mass suicide' ... As with Abe's denial regarding sexual slavery, the ministry's new position appeared to discount overwhelming evidence of coercion, particularly the testimony of victims and survivors themselves.
>
> (*IHT*, 2 April 2007, p. 8)

> On the Battle of Okinawa ... one of the textbooks in question at present says: 'The Japanese army gave hand grenades to residents, making them commit mass suicide and kill each other' ... After the screeners took issue with the statement the textbook was revised to say: 'Mass suicides took place among the residents using hand grenades given them by the Japanese army.'
>
> (*FT*, 2 April 2007, p. 8).

6–11 April 2007.

> Zhai Jun, an assistant foreign minister, met Omar al-Bashir, the Sudanese president, during a four-day trip which began on Friday [6 April] ... [Zhai Jun] said China hopes Khartoum will show flexibility over a UN plan to stop the fighting in Darfur.
>
> (*Independent*, 10 April 2007, p. 23)

> For the past two years China has protected the Sudanese government as the United States and Britain have pushed for UN Security Council sanctions

> against Sudan for the violence in Darfur ... where at least 200,000 people – some say as many as 400,000 – mostly non-Arab men, women and children, have died and 2.5 million have been displaced, as government-backed Arab militias called the janjaweed have attacked the local population ... President Omar Hassan al-Bashir of Sudan has repeatedly refused America, African and European demands that he allow a UN peacekeeping force to supplement an under-equipped and besieged African Union force of 7,000 soldiers ... But in the past week things have happened. A senior Chinese official, Zhai Jun, travelled to Sudan to push the Sudanese government to accept a UN peacekeeping force ... Non-government organizations and other groups appear to have scored a surprising success in an effort to link the Olympics ... to the killings in Darfur ... During a news conference on Wednesday [11 April] Zhai called activists who want to boycott the games 'either ignorant or ill natured'. But he added: 'We suggest the Sudan side show flexibility and accept' the UN peacekeepers.
>
> (www.iht.com, 13 April 2007; *IHT*, 14 April 2007, p. 2)

'China urged Sudan in unusually strong terms to accept UN peacekeepers in Darfur. Sudan's government, hitherto with China's support, had been resisting the replacement of a weak African Union force by a 20,000-strong UN one' (*The Economist*, 14 April 2007, p. 8).

'Premier Wen Jiabao officially appointed Donald Tsang as Hong Kong's leader on Monday [9 April] ... [The] five-year term begins on 1 July' (www.iht.com, 9 April 2007).

> Gao Zhisheng, one of the most outspoken dissidents in China until his conviction on sedition charges last year [2006], said in a recorded statement made available over the weekend that, while his confession had resulted in a light sentence, it had been made under mental and physical duress. Gao's remarks, recorded by a close friend ... were his first public statement since he was convicted in December [2006]. He was given a suspended sentence.
>
> (*IHT*, 11 April 2007, p. 8)

11–13 April 2007.

> Wen Jiabao arrives in Tokyo on Wednesday [11 April] for the first visit by a Chinese premier to Japan since 2000 ... [He] was scheduled to give a speech to parliament ... on Thursday ... before returning to China [on 13 April] ... Japan's trade with China surged 11.5 per cent in 2006 to $211 billion ... China is poised to become Japan's top trading partner this year [2007], accounting for 17.2 per cent of Japanese trade in 2006 – just a shade short of the US share of 17.4 per cent.
>
> (www.iht.com, 10 April 2007)

('China is Japan's second largest trading partner after the United States, while Japan is China's third largest trade partner after the EU and the United States': www.economist.com, 12 April 2007.)

> Wen Jiabao and Shinzo Abe ... signed a series of agreements ... [One was] an environmental accord ... The other committed Japan and China to co-operate on developing energy resources. In the joint statement the two vowed to seek ways to jointly develop gas deposits in disputed waters, pursue the denuclearization of the Korean Peninsula and work together on intellectual property rights. The two powers also agreed to strengthen defence co-operation, setting up a visit by Chinese defence minister Cao Gangchuan later this year [2007], as well as reciprocal visits by the countries' battleships ... The visit was a high profile follow-up to Abe's landmark summit with Chinese leaders in Beijing in October [2006] ... China, including Hong Kong, is Japan's number one trading partner ... The Chinese premier arrived hours after the two countries signed an accord lifting Beijing's four-year ban on Japanese rice imports. China banned imports in 2003, claiming Japanese rice did not qualify for its tightened quarantine system.
>
> (www.iht.com, 11 April 2007)

'The joint statement said that China and Japan agreed to "look at history frankly and jointly to build a beautiful future" ... China has opposed Japan's bid for a permanent seat on the United Nations Security Council' (*IHT*, 12 April 2007, p. 4).

'[On 12 April Wen Jiabao spoke] in a rare address to the Japanese parliament by a Chinese leader ... the first in twenty-two years by a Chinese leader' (www.iht.com, 12 April 2007).

> Wen Jiabao ... thanked Japan for its 'support and assistance' in China's reform and modernization, in a nod to Japanese officials who have long complained that Japan's massive aid over the past two decades has been continually played down by Beijing ... Wen Jiabao: 'The Japanese government and Japanese leaders have stated many times their stance on history-related problems, publicly acknowledged their invasion and expressed their deep remorse and regret to victimized nations. That is something that the Chinese government and people regard positively. We sincerely hope that Japan will show in concrete ways their expressed attitudes and promises' ... The last comment appeared to be a warning against Shinzo Abe not to visit the Yasukuni Shrine.
>
> (*IHT*, 13 April 2007, p. 2)

> Wen's trip was heavy on broad statements of good will and atmospherics, but short on concrete solutions to the countries' enduring conflicts over wartime history and maritime territory ... In his speech ... Wen urged lawmakers not to forget Japan's past aggression ... At the same time Wen appeared more conciliatory over the war, while urging Tokyo to turn that contrition into concrete actions ... A more contemporary spat, over undersea gas and oil deposits in disputed waters in the East China Sea, also dogged the trip. While Wen and Abe declared intentions to work out a solution, China's foreign ministry in Beijing asserted exploration rights in the

> area. Tokyo expressed concern on Thursday [12 April] over a report by state-controlled China National Offshore Oil Corporation that said it had begun producing oil and gas from a disputed field between the two countries. Japanese officials have asked China for more details.
>
> (www.iht.com, 13 April 2007)

'[Wen Jiabao's] was the first ever Diet address by a Chinese premier' (www.bbc.co.uk, 12 April 2007).

> Japan's lower house of parliament approved guidelines for amending the pacifist constitution on Friday [13 April], a key step in prime minister Shinzo Abe's push to give the military a larger global role … The US-drafted constitution, which dates from 1947, has never been amended.
>
> (www.iht.com, 13 April 2007)

27 April 2007.

> China's government abruptly replaced its foreign minister Friday [27 April], elevating former ambassador to the United States Yang Jiechi to the post in an early reshuffling of top positions ahead of political meetings. The removal of Li Zhaoxing as foreign minister had been widely expected – but not until much later this year, when the ruling Communist Party convenes a once-every-five-years congress to reapportion top jobs. At sixty-six Li was already a year past the customary retirement age for cabinet ministers. Along with Li the ministers of land resources and science and technology also retired Friday … Two of the departing ministers, foreign minister Li and science and technology minister Xu Guanhua were closely associated with Jiang Zemin … More pugnacious than charming, Li often struck an undiplomatic posture internationally … The fifty-seven-year-old Yang is more low-key in approach.
>
> (www.iht.com, 27 April 2007)

'Yang Jiechi was ambassador to Washington from 2001 to 2005 … [and was] formerly a deputy foreign minister … Yang studied at Bath University in Britain and the London School of Economics from 1973 to 1975' (*IHT*, 28 April 2007, p. 6).

> The clean-out of ministers displays a determination by Hu Jintao to put his personal stamp on the administration ahead of the party conference held every five years … Wan Gang was appointed as minister for science and technology – the first non-party member appointed to the cabinet since the mid-1950s … Mr Wan studied and lived overseas for fifteen years – in Germany, where he gained a PhD and then worked for Audi … Mr Wan has been a member of the Public Interest Party, one of China's eight registered democratic parties, since 2005 … These parties are subservient groupings whose role is to give the political system a veneer of diversity … A few non-communists were ministers in the early years of communist rule, but they were purged in an 'anti-rightist' movement in 1958. No non-party member

has held a cabinet rank since … In other moves Xu Shaoshi replaced Sun Wensheng as the land and resources minister, and Chen Lei was appointed to handle the water resources portfolio, in place of Wang Shucheng.

(*FT*, 28 April 2007, p. 5)

4 May 2007. 'China's biggest oil firm, PetroChina, says it has made the country's largest crude discovery in a decade … The find [is] off China's north-east coast' (www.bbc.co.uk, 4 May 2007).

8 May 2007.

> Prime minister Shinzo Abe of Japan made a ceremonial offering to … [the] Yasukuni Shrine … last month [April], but did not go himself, a shrine official said Tuesday [8 May] … The plant was offered during an annual spring ceremony at the shrine that was held on 21–23 April … Abe sent a small plant as a type of compromise … The top government spokesman later told reporters that the government could not comment because the offering was made by Abe as a private citizen and not in his capacity as Japanese leader … The South Korean foreign ministry reacted angrily to the move … The last prime minister to make that type of offering was Yasuhiro Nakasone in 1985. Nakasone also visited the shrine.
>
> (www.iht.com, 8 May 2007)

'Prime minister Shinzo Abe offered a potted masakaki tree, accompanied by a card that read "the prime minister", to mark Yasukuni's spring festival on 21–23 April' (www.bbc.co.uk, 8 May 2007).

> China has named a senior diplomat as its first special envoy to Africa, with a brief to focus on the crisis in Darfur, in a sign of Beijing's mounting concern about a global backlash against its close ties to the Sudan regime. The appointment of Liu Guijin, who has served as ambassador in South Africa and Zimbabwe during fifteen years on the continent, was announced by the foreign ministry … [China] buys about 60 per cent of Sudan's oil output, much of it extracted by China National Petroleum Corp … Beijing also announced this week that it would send a 275-strong team of military engineers to join any peacekeeping force in the region.
>
> (*FT*, 11 May 2007, p. 11)

'[There have been] threats of an Olympic backlash unless Beijing makes greater use of its influence to stop the slaughter in Darfur' (*Guardian*, 11 May 2007, p. 27).

> A group of 108 members of the US House of Representatives sent a letter to the Chinese government in the past week declaring that China must use its influence with Sudan's government to improve the situation in Darfur or face a possible backlash against its serving as host of the Olympic Games. Leading Hollywood personalities have also warned China that it could face a boycott of the Games unless it puts more pressure on Sudan.
>
> (www.iht.com, 19 May 2007)

16 May 2007. '[On 16 May] the African Development Bank ... [started its three-day meeting] in Shanghai ... It is the first time the bank's annual meeting has taken place in Asia' (www.bbc.co.uk, 16 May 2007).

'[This is] only the second time the African Development Bank's annual meeting ... has taken place outside Africa' (*FT*, 17 May 2007, p. 12).

('The [official Chinese] Xinhua press agency recently estimated there were at least 750,000 Chinese working or living for extended periods on the continent, a reflection of burgeoning economic ties between China and Africa that reached $55 billion in trade in 2006, compared with less than $10 million a generation earlier': www.iht.com, 17 August 2007.)

17 May 2007.

> China's economic alliance with Sudan has not prevented Beijing from exerting pressure on Khartoum to accept deployment of peacekeepers to Darfur, according to ... Jan Eliasson, special UN envoy to Darfur ... Eliasson, speaking late Thursday [17 May], said it was Chinese pressure that had helped persuade Sudanese officials to lift their opposition to the deployment of 3,000 UN peacekeepers in Darfur. The force will give way for an additional 17,000 peacekeepers, who would protect the 2.5 million Darfurians in refugee camps and ensure safe delivery of humanitarian supplies.
>
> (www.iht.com, 17 May 2007)

('China has appointed a special envoy to Sudan, Lui Guijin, who returned from a recent trip to Darfur disputing reports from the United Nations and international aid groups ... Lui Guijin: "I did not see a desperate scenario of people dying of hunger there"': www.iht.com, 31 May 2007.)

('The Chinese special envoy on the Darfur issue, Liu Guijin, said that his country would seriously consider sending troops for a peacekeeping mission ... He said that China was instrumental in a diplomatic breakthrough this month [June] when the Sudanese government finally agreed to let a major force of UN and African Union peacekeepers deploy in Darfur. Sudan has accepted this hybrid operation "without any reservation", Liu said, adding that Beijing had advised the Sudanese regime to "be more flexible" regarding the force ... China has not received a formal request to send soldiers for the 19,000-strong peacekeeping mission but is "open and sincere to making its contribution", Liu said. "We will study the request carefully and seriously," he said, adding that it was "a strong sign" that China has already committed 275 military engineers to the current UN force in Darfur': www.iht.com, 22 June 2007.)

('Last week China launched a communications satellite for Nigeria in a project that serves as a tidy case study of how space has become another arena where China is trying to exert its soft power. Not only did China design, build and launch the satellite for oil-rich Nigeria – it also provided a huge loan to help pay the bill ... In recent years China has managed to attract customers with its less expensive satellite launching services. Yet it had never demonstrated the technical expertise to compete for international contracts to build satellites. The Nigeria deal changed that': www.iht.com, 23 May 2007; *IHT*, 24 May 2007, p. 1.)

17–19 May 2007.

> An intensive campaign to enforce strict population-control measures prompted violent clashes between the police and local residents in ... several regions of Guangxi autonomous region ... in south-western China ... An escalating series of confrontations began Thursday [17 May] and continued through the weekend ... There were inconsistent reports of deaths and injuries ... Villagers and visitors gave varying accounts of injuries and deaths, with some asserting that as many as five people were killed, including three officials responsible for population-control work ... A local official in one of the counties affected confirmed the rioting ... but ... denied reports of deaths or serious injuries.
>
> (www.iht.com, 21 May 2007; *IHT*, 22 May 2007, p. 4)

'[There have been] unconfirmed reports of two fatalities' (*Guardian*, 22 May 2007, p. 23).

> Thousands of villagers have rioted in south-western China ... The villagers in Guangxi province reportedly attacked government offices after officials imposed heavy fines on families who had too many children. The rioting allegedly took place on Friday and Saturday [18–19 May].
>
> (www.bbc.co.uk, 21 May 2007)

> The police in south-western China arrested twenty-eight people for instigating riots over family planning controls last weekend, but officials were dispatched to affected areas to 'deal with complaints' about the area's strict measures to enforce birth control measures, state media said on Wednesday [23 May]. Seven towns in a rural part of the Guangxi autonomous region erupted in violence over heavy fines and other measures to impose tighter family planning controls in the area, the official Xinhua press agency said. In its first report about the unrest that began late last week, the agency said as many as 3,000 people had stormed government offices, overturned vehicles, burned documents and confronted officials. It did not mention whether there had been deaths or injuries ... Residents said in earlier telephone conversations that tens of thousands of people had participated in riots and that as many as five people had died, including several officials involved in family planning work.
>
> (www.iht.com, 23 May 2007)

25 May 2007. 'In its annual report on Chinese military developments the Pentagon said the People's Liberation Army was building a greater capacity to launch pre-emptive strikes. It cited as examples China's acquisition of submarines, unmanned combat aircraft and precision-guided air-to-ground missiles' (*IHT*, 26 May 2007, p. 4).

> China is modernizing its military in ways that give it options for launching surprise attacks, potentially far from its borders, the US Defence Department said Friday [25 May] ... The report outlined areas of perceived

> ambiguity in Chinese strategy, including its declared policy of never starting a nuclear war; it concluded that Beijing may be exploring 'new options' provided by its force modernization … The Pentagon said China's short-term focus remains the Taiwan Straits, where it continues to position more short-range ballistic missiles. But more broadly the People's Liberation Army is pursuing a strategy that appears designed to give China a capability to fight wars farther from its shores and to thwart any US advances … In a section entitled 'Is China Developing a Pre-emptive Strategy?' the report cited the fact that the People's Liberation Army has been acquiring long-endurance submarines, unmanned combat aircraft, additional precision-guided air-to-ground missiles and long-distance military communications systems. Chinese military training that focuses on no-notice, long-range air strikes 'could also indicate planning for pre-emptive military options in advance of regional crises', the report said … 'This logic suggests the potential for China to engage in military pre-emption, perhaps from its borders, if the use of force protects or advances core interests, including territorial claims,' the report said … A prominent theme in the Pentagon report is a perceived lack of transparency in Chinese military activities and plans. As it has in the past, the Pentagon said China's true defence spending is two or three times the publicly announced defence budget, which this year [2007] was put at the equivalent of $45 billion. The Pentagon report said actual defence spending, including funds from sources other than the defence budget, is $85 billion to $125 billion.
>
> (www.iht.com, 25 May 2007)

> The report cited what it called the unexpectedly speedy development of a new Jin-class submarine equipped to carry missiles with a range of more than 5,000 miles, or 8,000 kilometres. The report also said that China was preparing to deploy a new land-based intercontinental ballistic missile, called the DF-31, that had the range to target parts of the United States. Both Jin-class submarines and the DF-31 missile are part of China's nuclear forces and the Pentagon raised the possibility that with enhanced capabilities China may seek to overhaul its longstanding policy of maintaining only a minimal nuclear deterrent. Analysts have said that Washington's efforts to develop a comprehensive nuclear missile defence system have prompted China to improve the manoeuvrability and survivability of its nuclear forces. China has repeatedly said that its policy of 'no first use' of nuclear weapons remains unchanged.
>
> (*IHT*, 28 May 2007, p. 4)

'"The People's Liberation Army appears in a sustained effort to develop the capability to interdict, at long ranges, aircraft carrier groups and strike groups that might deploy to the western Pacific," the report stated' (www.iht.com, 2 June 2007).

> China is modernizing and expanding its arsenal of nuclear weapons giving it an enhanced nuclear strike capability, according to a new Pentagon report on the Chinese military. The Pentagon said China was developing mobile,

land-based intercontinental ballistic missiles in addition to long-range, submarine-launched ballistic missiles that would be employed on a fleet of nuclear submarines ... The Chinese navy is developing five Jin-class submarines that would carry the JL-2 submarine-launched ballistic missile, which has an estimated range of more than 8,000 kilometres ... The report said: 'China is pursuing long-term comprehensive transformation of its military forces to improve its capabilities for power-projection, anti-access and areas denial. China's actions in certain areas increasingly appear inconsistent with its declaratory policies' ... China's recent focus on increasing its naval power, including attack submarines, is believed to be partly aimed at protecting sea routes for transporting energy resources.

(*FT*, 26 May 2007, p. 7)

The annual report says Beijing is moving towards a more pre-emptive defence strategy with the focus on its border areas ... The Pentagon report highlights concerns about China's preparations to deploy a mobile, land-based ballistic missile, with a range that reportedly covers the entire United States. The development of a new fleet of nuclear-powered submarines, equipped with ballistic missiles with a range of more than 8,000 kilometres (5,000 miles) is also cited. Experts say the Jin-class vessels are capable of carrying twelve missiles, with one armed with three nuclear warheads. One of these Chinese-built submarines is currently undergoing tests and five more are planned ... Previously China had one nuclear-powered submarine, which was so unreliable it rarely travelled far from its base ... The Pentagon report describes a successful anti-satellite weapon test in January as posing a threat to 'all space-faring nations'.

(www.bbc.co.uk, 25 May 2007)

'The Pentagon report ... said that Beijing was building up its capabilities with an eye on "regional contingencies, such as conflict over resources or territory", in addition to its traditional focus on Taiwan' (www.bbc.co.uk, 27 May 2007).

28 May 2007.

China has called on Western countries to put aside fears about the death penalty and sign extradition treaties, state media reported Monday [28 May], as the Communist Party seeks the return of suspected corrupt officials and criminals who have fled overseas. In March [2007] France became the third developed country after Spain and Portugal to sign an extradition treaty with China ... In its agreements with these three countries Beijing guaranteed that suspects returned to China for trial will not face the death penalty ... The *China Daily* newspaper reported Monday that twenty-nine countries had now signed extradition treaties with China ... The *China Daily* reported that about 800 suspects wanted for economic crimes were at large overseas ... In earlier reports state media said that up to 4,000 officials have pocketed a total of $50 billion and escaped overseas in recent years ... The absence of an extradition treaty does not automatically prevent the return of suspected or convicted criminals. This month [May] Japan, which lacks such a treaty with China, for the first time repatriated a Chinese official accused of corruption ... The United States also co-operated with China to return Yu Zhendong, a fugitive wanted for his part in the embezzlement of at least $485 million from 1992 to 2001 from the Bank of China in Guangdong province.

(www.iht.com, 28 May 2007)

2 June 2007.

Vice premier Huang Ju ... died [on 2 June] aged sixty-eight ... Huang was in charge of financial and economic policy-making in the Politburo ... He had not attended official functions since March 2006, when it was announced he was ill, reportedly with cancer ... Huang was one of the closest allies of ... Jiang Zemin and formed part of Mr Jiang's so-called 'Shanghai Gang' ... When Jiang Zemin stepped down and was succeeded by President Hu Jintao, Huang remained in place ... He became mayor of Shanghai in 1991 ... From 1995 until 2002 Huang served as both chief of the Communist Party in Shanghai and a member of the Politburo ... In 2002 Huang was promoted to the Politburo's nine-member Standing Committee ... Huang's final appointment came in March 2003, when he became one of the State Council's four vice premiers. His main responsibility was to formulate financial and economic policies. The vice-premier's last public appearance was at the National People's Congress in March 2006, when he urged delegates from Shanghai to support President Hu's anti-corruption drive. The crackdown led to Huang's successor as Communist Party chief in Shanghai, Chen Liangyu, being sacked for corruption. Shortly afterwards the state announced he was ill and would not attend all official functions.

(www.bbc.co.uk, 2 June 2007)

Huang Ju ranked sixth in the Communist Party hierarchy ... Huang Ju would serve as Shanghai's party secretary from 1995 to 2002 and then join the Politburo Standing Committee in Beijing. He also served as a vice prime minister in the State Council ... Huang Ju's portfolio on the Standing Committee was dominated by financial affairs. He presided over reforms to the banking system and was the leadership's designated point person in efforts to modernize the financial system ... His public appearances had become infrequent during the past year and rumours swirled that he might be toppled as part of a sweeping corruption investigation in Shanghai ordered by Hu. Last year [2006] speculation circulated in Beijing that Huang and another Politburo member, Jia Qinglin, might be stripped of power.

(www.iht.com, 3 June 2007)

Huang Ju had been ranked sixth on the Politburo Standing Committee ... Another vice premier, Wu Yi, had already taken over his roles ... [He became mayor of Shanghai] in 1991 and Communist Party boss there in 1994 ... He was promoted in 2002 to the Politburo Standing Committee.

(www.ft.com, 3 June 2007)

19 June 2007.

> About 100 Japanese governing party lawmakers denounced the Nanjing Massacre as a fabrication on Tuesday [19 June 2007], contesting claims that Japanese soldiers killed hundreds of thousands of people after seizing the Chinese city in 1937. The members of prime minister Shinzo Abe's Liberal Democratic Party said there was no evidence to prove mass killings by Japanese soldiers in the captured Nationalist capital, then known as Nanking. They accused Beijing of using the alleged incident as a 'political advertisement' ... The group created to study World War II historical issues and education said documents from the Japanese government's archives indicated that about 20,000 people were killed – about one-tenth of the more commonly cited figure of 150,000 to 200,000 – in the 1937 attack. China says that as many as 300,000 people were killed. Nanjing suffered a rampage of murder, rape and looting by Japanese troops that became known as 'the Rape of Nanking'. Historians generally agree that the Japanese army slaughtered at least 150,000 civilians and raped tens of thousands of women.
>
> (www.iht.com, 19 June 2007)

25 June 2007.

> President Hu Jintao ... used a major address to the party, government and military elite in Beijing on Monday [25 June] to promote a gradualist vision of political and economic change ... The address at the Communist Party's Central Party School in Beijing was attended by members of the Central Committee of the Communist Party, to central government and provincial leaders and senior military and security officials, marking it as one of Hu's most important speeches since he became China's top leader in 2002 ... President Hu Jintao said that attempts to modernize the country's political system must not jeopardize one-party rule, setting a conservative tone ahead of an important Communist Party conclave in the autumn ... The event was closed to Chinese and foreign journalists. The published text of his speech broke little new ground. He stressed his now well-worn ideological formulas of promoting a 'harmonious society' and 'scientific development' ... He said 'socialist democracy' and 'grassroots democracy' were long-term goals of the party and that it should make 'active and safe' efforts to develop it. He also said that such changes must proceed in an orderly fashion, without diminishing the party's 'leading role'.
>
> (www.iht.com, 26 June 2007)

'A "harmonious society" ... means reducing the social tensions created by rapid economic change' (*The Economist*, 22 September 2007, p. 74).

> President Hu Jintao pledged to continue his policy of 'scientific development', a phrase now used by all government officials and which local scholars say is code for a commitment to a new model of development. Instead of growth at all costs, 'scientific development' stipulates that environmental

> and social costs should be given greater weight ... Mr Hu called for greater efforts to overcome endemic corruption. Party committees at all levels must recognize the 'long-term nature, difficulty and complexity' of the struggle, he said.
>
> (*FT*, 27 June 2007, p. 12)

> In a much publicized speech ... President Hun Jintao ... acknowledged the growing public demand for a say in politics. Efforts to reform the country's political system, he said, should match these aspirations ... In recent months he has tolerated an unusually open debate about the country's political options. Calls for a multi-party democracy remain taboo, but not much else ... As Mr Hu prepares for a crucial five-yearly party congress around October [2007] he appears a bit more open to ideas. His speech set clear boundaries. The party's leadership must be upheld; reform must adhere to the 'correct political orientation'. This means no Western-style parliamentary democracy or balance of power between executive, legislature and judiciary. But his reference to 'political participation' suggests he faces some pressure to set a clearer agenda. He said scope for participation should be expanded, but in an 'orderly' way.
>
> (*The Economist*, 30 June 2007, p. 67)

President Hu Jintao:

> The reform of our nation's political system must maintain a correct political direction, must unrelentingly keep pace with economic and social development, and must endeavour to adjust to the active political participation of our nation's people ... [Changes should] advance the self-perfection in the development of the socialist political system ... We must maintain the party's leadership, empower the people and rule the country by law ... We should develop [the country] for the people and by the people and the fruits of our development should be shared by the people ... [The aim is a] basically well-off society [by 2020] ... This is where the interests of all the nation's ethnic groups lie.
>
> (www.iht.com, 26 June 2007; www.bbc.co.uk, 26 June 2007; *FT*, 27 June 2007, p. 12)

29 June 2007.

> [The] government has appointed a second non-communist cabinet minister ... Chen Zhu, a French-trained scientist, was named health minister ... But Gao Qiang, the outgoing minister, was retained both as a vice president and secretary of the ministry's party meetings – meaning he will continue to outrank Mr Chen ... Mr Chen's appointment follows that of Wan Gang, a German-trained engineer, who was made science minister this year [2007]. As the party and its 70 million members control every other significant government post, these two ministerial appointments represent a symbolic rather than a substantive change.
>
> (*FT*, 30 June 2007, p. 10)

In addition to the ruling Communist Party, China has eight other so-called 'democratic parties' – which are represented in the People's Political Consultative Congress, or CPPCC. Significant efforts are being made by Communist Party leaders to meet with these non-communist politicians. China's new health and science and technology ministers both come from the CPPCC and are not Communist Party members.

(*IHT*, 7 July 2007, p. 4)

7 July 2007.

Hundreds of veterans and students gathered for a low-key ceremony Saturday [7 July] at the Marco Polo Bridge just outside Beijing, where Japanese and Chinese troops exchanged fire on 7 July 1937, starting an eight-year conflict that ended in Japan's surrender in World War II ... People gathered for exhibitions, memorials and anti-Japanese songs in more than ten cities across the country ... Historians generally agree that Japanese troops killed at least 150,000 civilians and raped tens of thousands of women in the rampage in the city of Nanjing in 1937, an incident that became known as 'the Rape of Nanking' – the name by which the city was known in the West at that time ... Dozens of veterans attended Saturday's commemoration in the northern Taiwan city of Hsinchu.

(*IHT*, 9 July 2007, p. 5)

17 July 2007.

The most important document signed by the parties [on 17 July] was a contract between Turkmenistan's State Agency for Hydrocarbon Resources and the China National Petroleum Corporation (CNPC) on production-sharing at the Bagtiyarlyk gas field along the right bank of the Amu Darya River. The field will supply the resources that will be transported by the future Central Asian gas pipeline from Turkmenistan to China. The CNPC also signed a thirty-year contract with Turkmengaz for the delivery of 30 billion cubic metres of gas each year beginning in 2009 ... Turkmenistan currently produces approximately 70 billion cubic metres a year. Of that amount 42 billion goes to Russia, another 8 billion is supplied to Iran, and 7 billion to 15 billion is consumed in the domestic market.

(*CDSP*, 2007, vol. 59, nos 28–9, pp. 21–2)

24 July 2007.

The former Communist Party boss of Shanghai, Chen Liangyu, has been stripped of his membership in the parliament, signalling that he will probably face criminal charges soon ... Chen, who had served on the ruling Politburo as well as leading China's east coast financial centre, was dismissed from his party post last year [2006] in the biggest political shake-up in more than a decade. Shanghai's municipal parliament removed Chen from the National People's Congress, essentially stripping him of the legal immunity granted to members of the party-run legislature ... the investigation into misuse of pension funds eventually implicated more than a dozen officials.

(www.iht.com, 25 July 2007)

26 July 2007.

The former Communist Party leader in Shanghai has been expelled from the party, state media reports. Chen Liangyu was also sacked from all his government positions ... The case has also led to the removal and detention of several other officials, including the city's social security and labour chief, Mr Chen was the first member of the Politburo ... to be dismissed for corruption since 1995.

(www.bbc.co.uk, 26 July 2007)

27 July 2007.

[On 26 July] Chen Liangyu ... was expelled from the party and handed over to judicial investigators ... [On 27 July] Xia Zanzhong, a deputy head of the party's Central Commission of Discipline Inspection, told the official Xinhua press agency that Chen's downfall should serve as a warning ... Xia Zanzhong: 'Chen Liangyu's behaviour totally betrayed the party principles and ideals that a Communist Party member and leading official should have. His outlook on the world, life and values gravely degenerated. When leading officials drop the ideological weapon of fighting corruption and upholding clean government, their capacity to resist drops and even collapses, and they are finally trapped in an abyss of corruption' ... Chen has been accused of abusing power to give cronies access to city social welfare funds, helping them illegally buy state-owned businesses and 'dallying with women and trading power for sex'. Xinhua reported ... Felled last September [2006], Chen was the first member of the party's Politburo to be purged for corruption since 1995. A dozen other officials and business people have since been implicated by a spreading inquiry.

(www.iht.com, 27 July 2007; *IHT*, 30 July 2007, p. 3)

30 July 2007.

The [US] House of Representatives approved a resolution Monday [30 July] urging Japan to formally apologize for forcing thousands of women to work as sex slaves for its military during World War II. The non-binding resolution is symbolic, but it has caused unease in Japan ... The House resolution, which has no companion in the Senate, urges Japan to 'formally acknowledge, apologize and accept historical responsibility in a clear and unequivocal manner' for the suffering of 'comfort women' ... . Lawmakers want an apology to match the one the US government gave to Japanese-Americans forced into internment during World War II. That apology was approved by Congress and signed into law by President Ronald Regan in 1988.

(www.iht.com, 30 July 2007)

'On Monday the House unanimously passed a non-binding resolution demanding that the Japanese government "formally acknowledge" and "apologize" for its military's "coercion of women into sexual slavery"' (www.iht.com, 1 August 2007).

'[On 1 August] prime minister Shinzo Abe said: "The resolution approval was regrettable"' (www.iht.com, 1 August 2007).

3 August 2007.

> Almost 1,800 officials confessed to corruption in June ... The officials are taking advantage of a month-long leniency offer that began on 30 May, the Central Commission for Discipline Inspection. Over the month 1,790 people confessed to corruption totalling $10.2 million.
>
> (www.bbc.co.uk, 3 August 2007)

> Nearly 1,800 officials confessed to their involvement in hundreds of acts of 'misconduct' after a nationwide 'discipline' campaign ... launched in May ... Inspectors were sent across the country to investigate corruption at local party offices, state-owned enterprises and banks, and the buying and selling of government positions ... The cases are passed to the courts to decide on, but guilt is already presumed.
>
> (*Guardian*, 4 August 2007, p. 28)

6 August 2007.

> Wang Wei, a vice president with Beijing's Olympic organizing committee, said a monitoring system was being created to ensure the safety of food and medicine for the more than 10,000 athletes participating in the Games ... The elaborate monitoring system is a response to growing international concerns about the quality and safety of many Chinese exports, particularly food and pharmaceutical supplies. Wang said that global positioning satellites would be used to track trucks delivering food to the Olympic village and inspections would also be conducted at farms and slaughterhouses. Deliveries will even be labelled with electronic bar codes as a safeguard ... Wang emphasized that Beijing had staged numerous events without any problems of food contamination.
>
> (www.iht.com, 6 August 2007)

8 August 2007.

> Wednesday [8 August] marks the one-year countdown to the Olympics ... Chinese authorities have violated pledges made when bidding for the Olympic Games by heightening abuse and surveillance of political and religious dissidents, jailing journalists and closing publications focusing on social development, human rights group Amnesty International said in a new report [published on 7 August] ... Under a regulation announced last year [2006] foreign reporters can travel and conduct interviews in China without asking for government approval from 1 January until

> mid-October 2008. The temporary freedoms do not extend to local Chinese journalists ... Amnesty's report comes on the heels of one issued last week by Human Rights Watch, which also said the Chinese government had failed to live up to promises of greater human rights, instead clamping down on domestic activists and journalists. Amnesty's release came as six activists [from Canada, the United States and the UK] were detained Tuesday [7 August] after scaling down a part of the Great Wall with a large banner that read 'One World, One Dream, Free Tibet 2008', the London-based Free Tibet Campaign and Students for a Free Tibet said ... On Monday [6 August] police detained journalists ... with the advocacy group Reporters Without Borders ... at a rare protest in Beijing staged by a free-press advocacy group that accused the Chinese government of failing to meet pledges for greater media freedom. The detentions, which came during a visit to Beijing by International Olympics Committee president Jacques Rogge, followed the unfurling of posters depicting the Olympic rings made from handcuffs by members of Reporters Without Borders on a pedestrian bridge outside the headquarters of the Beijing Olympics planning committee. The Paris-based group said China continues to restrict press freedoms and lock up journalists, political dissidents and activists who publish on the internet – despite pledges to liberalize made when bidding to stage the Games ... A recent survey of Beijing-based foreign correspondents found that harassment and numerous obstacles still existed ... A group of Chinese scholars, journalists and lawyers wrote an open letter to President Hu Jintao and other national leaders calling for the release of political prisoners, including jailed Chinese reporters and inmates convicted on religious grounds. The group wrote that China's Olympic slogan, 'One World, One Dream', should instead be 'One World, One Dream, Same Human Rights'.
>
> (www.iht.com, 7 August 2007)

'In April the Chinese authorities arrested four pro-Tibetan independence protesters who had climbed to the Mount Everest base camp and hung a banner to protest plans to take the Olympic torch through the Tibetan Himalayas' (*IHT*, 14 August 2007, p. 2).

> At the Great Wall, on the outskirts of Beijing, a group of Tibetans from Britain, Canada and America displayed a huge banner proclaiming 'One World. One Dream, Free Tibet 2008'. The slogan plays on Beijing's official Olympic motto 'One World, One Dream'. A similar protest was mounted (and a similar banner unfurled) in April [2007] at the Mount Everest base camp in Tibet ... In a brave open letter, a group of prominent Chinese activists and intellectuals – former political prisoners among them – took their own liberties with the official slogan. Entitled 'One World, One Dream, Universal Human Rights', the letter was addressed to China's leaders, as well as heads of international organization, including the United Nations and the International Olympic Committee ... The dissidents wrote: 'We find

no consolation or comfort in the rise of grandiose sports facilities, or a temporary beautified Beijing city, or the prospect of Chinese athletes winning medals. We know too well how these glories are built on the ruins of ordinary people.'

(*The Economist*, 11 August 2007, pp. 46–7)

> Wednesday starts the one-year countdown to the Olympics opening ceremony ... Advocacy groups want to use the milestone to attract attention to their cause ... The police are sweeping up vagrants and other Beijing residents under a controversial policy that allows officers to detain people for up to four years without trial. The Amnesty report described the detentions as part of the citywide cleanup operation to prepare for the Olympics ... People [are being] evicted in Beijing to make way for construction projects directly or indirectly related to the Olympics.
>
> (*IHT*, 8 August 2007, p. 5)

'A recent study by a European research institute estimated that 1.5 million people would be evicted or displaced in Beijing by the opening of the Olympics – a figure very difficult to verify' (*IHT*, 10 August 2007, p. 2).

'The Geneva-based Centre on Housing Rights and Evictions reckons 1.5 million will have been relocated for Olympics-related projects. Government estimates put the figure at just over 6,000' (*Independent*, 13 August 2007, p. 22).

> China was yesterday [8 August] put on notice that if it did not address air pollution before the 2008 Beijing Olympics, organizers could order some endurance events ... like the cycling race ... to be rescheduled. The warning [came from] Jacques Rogge, president of the International Committee ... The IOC later indicated events would be postponed for a matter of hours rather than days.
>
> (*FT*, 9 August 2007, p. 7)

'One historical comparison studied by the Communist Party and its critics is Seoul 1988. There the Olympics reshaped political history when public anticipation of the Games fed demonstrations that toppled an authoritarian regime and ushered in democracy' (Jim Yardley, *IHT*, 14 August 2007, p. 2).

15 August 2007.

> Veterans, relatives of war dead and lawmakers crowded a Tokyo war shrine Wednesday [15 August] as Japan marked the sixty-second anniversary of its World War II surrender. But prime minister Shinzo Abe and all but one member of his cabinet stayed away. The one member who visited Yasukuni Shrine was ... [the one] whose portfolio includes affairs related to Okinawa, which suffered heavy casualties during the war ... Separately, forty-six members of parliament offered their prayers at the shrine, down from sixty-two last year [2006] ... Abe's predecessor, Junichiro Koizumi, paid a visit to Yasukuni on Wednesday ... Earlier, at a war ceremony near Yasukuni also attended by Emperor Akihito, Abe expressed his contrition for the

> suffering Japan caused during its military conquests in Asia ... Shinzo Abe: 'Japan caused great damage and pain to people in many countries, especially Asia. I express sympathy to these victims on behalf of the people of Japan' ... [Shinzo Abe] regularly prayed at Yasukuni before he became prime minister in September [2006], but he has not gone since.
>
> (www.iht.com, 15 August 2007)

16 August 2007.

> Leaders of China, Russia and the Central Asian states of Kazakhstan, Kyrgyzstan, Tajikistan and Uzbekistan gather for this year's SCO [Shanghai Co-operation Organization] in Bishkek [Kyrgyzstan] tomorrow [16 August] ... There is a military exercise, a first for the forum.
>
> (*FT*, 15 August 2007, p. 8)

'The SCO states are holding joint military exercises in Russia's Urals. Sergei Lavrov, Russia's foreign minister, said the exercises would be an annual event' (*FT*, 17 August 2007, p. 5).

'The presidents of China, Russia, Iran and Afghanistan are meeting their Central Asian counterparts ... [during] the annual meeting of the Shanghai Co-operation Council' (www.bbc.co.uk, 17 August 2007). 'The SCO was created eleven years ago to address religious extremism and border security issues in Central Asia ... Iran, Pakistan and Mongolia ... [have signed] on as observers' (www.iht.com, 17 August 2007).

17 August 2007.

> Russian and Chinese forces on Friday [17 August] held their first joint manoeuvres on Russian land ... The war games in the southern Ural mountains involved some 6,000 troops from Russia and China along with a handful of soldiers from four ex-Soviet Central Asian nations that are part of the SCO ... President Vladimir Putin, Chinese leader Hu Jintao and other leaders of the SCO nations attended the exercise, which followed their summit Thursday [16 August] in the Kyrgyz capital Bishkek ... Friday's military exercise involved dozens of aircraft and hundreds of armoured vehicles and other heavy weapons that countered a mock attack by terrorists and insurgents striving to take control of energy resources.
>
> (www.iht.com, 17 August 2007)

'Russian and Chinese forces completed major war games exercises for the first time on Russian turf ... The Russian–Chinese war games ... took place in the Ural mountains' (*IHT*, 18 August 2007, p. 3).

18 August 2007.

> Kazakhstan and China have agreed to build pipelines to carry oil and gas from fields near the Caspian Sea to China. 'The Caspian will be linked to western China,' Nursultan Nazarbayev., the president of Kazakhstan, said

> after a meeting with Ju Jintao, the Chinese leader, in Astana, the Kazakh capital, on Saturday [18 August] … Last year [2006] Kazakhstan and China completed a pipeline from a field owned by Chinese National Petroleum Corporation (CNPC) in the central part of the republic to Xinjiang province, China. That pipeline will now be connected with another CNPC field and pipeline in western Kazakhstan … Mr Nazarbayev said the pipeline from Kazakhstan to China would also carry supplies from Turkmenistan. The pipeline … will provide Central Asia with a first large non-Russian route for gas exports.
>
> (*FT*, 20 August 2007, p. 8)

'It was announcd that an additional oil pipeline would be built from Kazakhstan to China; and that a new gas pipeline linking Turkmenistan with China would run through Kazakhstan' (*The Economist*, 25 August 2007, p. 61).

28 August 2007. '[The] Communist Party has announced it will hold its … Seventeenth National Congress … [beginning] in Beijing on 15 October' (www.bbc.co.uk, 28 August 2007).

> About 2,200 delegates [will attend] the party's Seventeenth National Congress … The congress will be the first presided over by Hu Jintao, who became leader just after the last one in 2002. It is a chance for him to promote his preferred successors and rewrite the party's charter to enshrine his notion of 'scientific development' – meaning a bigger emphasis (largely rhetorical, say critics) on the poor and the environment. There are often high profile job losses before congresses.
>
> (*The Economist*, 1 September 2007, p. 48)

29 August 2007. 'The Chinese defence minister … Cao Gangchuan … kicked off a five-day visit to Japan on Wednesday [29 August], the first such visit in nearly a decade' (www.iht.com, 29 August 2007).

> [On 29 August] President Hu Jintao denounced a lack of integrity among financial officers … Hu Jintao: '[There is need to] comprehensively improve the ideological and political qualities of financial personnel, especially leading officers at all levels … [to] promote a new spirit of integrity, oppose malign trends and notorious influences and create a healthy professional ethos.'.
>
> (www.ft.com, 30 August 2007)

30 August 2007.

> Chinese finance minister Jin Renqing has resigned for 'personal reasons', the government said Thursday [30 August] … He has been finance minister since 2003 … [It was announced that] Xie Xuren, fifty-nine, director of the state administration of taxation, had replaced Jin … The State Council has transferred Jin to a government think-tank, where he will be deputy chief … 'For personal reasons Jin Renqing requested to resign. The central

> government agreed to his request and approved appointing him to be deputy director of the development research centre of the State Council,' a spokesman for the State Council [said] … Jin, sixty-three, is still two years below the official retirement age for officials at the central government level … [It was] also announced that Zhang Qingwei had been appointed minister in charge of the state commission of science, technology and industry for national defence. He replaces Zhang Yunchuan.
>
> (www.iht.com, 29 August 2007)

> The government replaced the finance minister Thursday and appointed four other ministers … [There have been reports in Hong Kong newspapers that Jin Renqing] has been linked to a prostitution scandal … involving a handful of senior officials, including Chen Tonghai, the former board chairman of the state-owned energy company Sinopec … Left unclear is whether Jin's dismissal is related to job performance or connected to corruption allegations … Other personnel moves announced Thursday included [the following]: a new head of the ministry of state security, Geng Huichang; a new minister of personnel, Yin Weimin; a new minister of supervision, Ma Wen; and a new defence industry minister, Zhang Qingwei.
>
> (www.iht.com, 30 August 2007)

'There has been speculation over Jin Renqing's private life. Hong Kong newspapers have linked him with a sex scandal involving a disgraced party official' (www.bbc.co.uk, 30 August 2007).

> In late June [2007] it was suddenly announced that Chen Tonghai, chairman of China Petroleum & Chemical Corporation, a giant state-owned oil company, had resigned, also for 'personal reasons'. Widespread speculation, including in China's press, has linked his departure to corruption investigations. Some reports have made a connection with the cases of Chen Liangyu.
>
> (*The Economist*, 1 September 2007, p. 48)

> China removed four officials accused of corruption from its legislature Thursday [30 August] … Chen Liangyu, a former boss of Shanghai who has been jailed and is awaiting trial on corruption charges, was stripped of his last official post as a deputy to the National People's Congress. Chen was kicked out of the party last month [July] and fired from all government positions after he was dismissed as Shanghai party secretary in 2006. He is the highest-level Chinese official to be dismissed in a decade … Also kicked out of the People's Congress were Duan Yihe, head of the city council in Shandong's capital, Jinan, Sun Shengchang, a former mayor in north-east China's Heilongjiang province; and Bao Jianmin, former director of the Henan provincial bureau of quality supervision … Sun, who had been mayor of the city of Qitaihe since 2002, was expelled from the party on Wednesday [29 August].
>
> (www.iht.com, 30 August 2007)

China's new spy chief is an expert on commercial intelligence whose appointment signals a shift of emphasis to obtaining and protecting trade secrets, a monitoring group said Friday [31 August]. Gen Huichang, fifty-five, was promoted from vice minister to minister of state security on Thursday [30 August] as part of a major cabinet reshuffle ahead of a twice-a-decade Communist Party Congress in October. The ministry has long been regarded as China's version of the former Soviet Union's KGB. However, to allow it to focus more on commercial intelligence, some of its duties will now be shifted to the military or the public security ministry, which is in charge of police, the Hong Kong-based Information Centre for Human Rights reported.

(www.iht.com, 31 August 2007)

2 September 2007.

China said Sunday [2 September] that it would submit information about its military spending and weapons trading to the United Nations ... The foreign ministry announced that the country would begin providing basic data about its military budget and also resume annual accounts of imports and exports of conventional weapons. China had ceased providing the arms trade data in 1996 ... The [US] Pentagon argues that China's real military spending exceeds the published military budget by a factor of two or three, which, if accurate, would mean that China spends more on its armed forces than any country except the United States.

(*IHT*, 3 September 2007, p. 5)

[A foreign ministry spokeswoman] said China had stopped reporting details to the register on conventional arms after a 'certain country', which she did not name, had begun providing details to the United Nations of its arms sales to Taiwan in 1996 ... She said that: 'As the country concerned has stopped [this] behaviour, the Chinese government has decided to resume providing data annually on imports and exports of conventional arms in the seven categories to the register from this year [2007].'

(*FT*, 3 September 2007, p. 8)

3 September 2007.

The Chinese military hacked into a Pentagon computer network in June [2007] in the most successful cyber attack on the US defence department, say American officials. The Pentagon acknowledged shutting down part of a computer system serving the office of Robert Gates, defence secretary, but declined to say who it believed was behind the attack. Current and former officials have told the *Financial Times* that an internal investigation has revealed that the incursion came from the People's Liberation Army. One senior US official said the Pentagon has pinpointed the exact origins of the attack. Another person familiar with the event said there was a 'very high level of confidence ... trending towards total certainty' that the PLA was

> responsible … One person with knowledge of the attack said most of the information was probably 'unclassified' … Angela Merkel, Germany's chancellor, raised reports of Chinese infiltration of German government computers with Wen Jiabao, China's premier, in a visit to Beijing, after which the Chinese foreign ministry said the government opposed and forbade 'any criminal acts undermining computer systems, including hacking'.
>
> (*FT*, 4 September 2007, p. 1)

4 September 2007. 'China yesterday [4 September] strongly denied that its military was behind a hacking attack on the Pentagon computer network … A foreign ministry spokeswoman: "The criticism is unfounded, which represents Cold War thinking"' (*FT*, 5 September 2007, p. 10).

'China has denied reports that its military hacked into the computer networks of the US Department of Defence. A foreign ministry official said the claims "reflected Cold War mentality"' (www.bbc.co.uk, 4 September 2007).

> A foreign ministry spokeswoman: 'The Chinese government has always opposed any internet-wrecking crime, including hacking, and cracked down on it according to the law … Some people are making wild allegations against China and wantonly saying the Chinese military attacked the Pentagon's computer network. These are totally groundless and also reflect a Cold War mentality' … Officially the United States has not accused Beijing of cracking into the military email system that serves Defence Secretary Robert Gates and hundreds of other State Department employees. But behind the scenes a senior Bush administration official told CNN that China is the number one suspect in the June hacking incident. On Monday [3 September] the *Financial Times* of London also reported that Washington believed China was responsible … The cyber attack led the Pentagon to shut down its unclassified email for nearly three weeks. US government sources said the unclassified email system is not connected to other email networks that contain sensitive military secrets. Pentagon officials said none of their operations were disrupted.
>
> (www.cnn.com, 5 September 2007)

'Chinese hackers, some believed to be from the People's Liberation Army, have been attacking the computer networks of British government departments, the *Guardian* has learned' (*Guardian*, 5 September 2007, p. 1).

> There is mounting evidence that cyber-operations emanating from China have apparently been underway for at least four years. The story first came to light in 2003 when sources within the [US] Department of Defense leaked information on a successful Chinese cyber-attack operation code named 'Titan Rain', aimed at widespread exploitation of United States government and defence industry computer networks. The finger was pointed directly at China's People's Liberation Army, but there is speculation as to the identity of the perpetrators and whether or not the Chinese military leadership sanctioned this kind of operation.
>
> (*Newsbrief*, October 2007, p. 113)

6 September 2007.

> President George W. Bush said Thursday [6 September] that he had accepted an invitation from President Hu Jintao to attend the 2008 Summer Olympics in Beijing ... He extended the invitation – reiterating an offer he has made before – during a ninety-minute private session with Bush [in Australia] on the eve of an economic summit of Asian nations ... Bush had told aides privately that he would like to attend the 2008 games, but Thursday was the first time he said so publicly. Aides said the president would attend as a sports fan, and not to make any political statement ... Hu and Bush also agreed to create a new hotline that will link the two countries' militaries, a move that evokes memories of the Cold War era hotline that tied the United States to the former Soviet Union. Details of the hotline have not yet been worked out.
>
> (www.iht.com, 6 September 2007; *IHT*, 7 September 2007, p. 7)

'[The two presidents attended the] summit meeting of twenty-one Asia-Pacific Economic Co-operation leaders' (*FT*, 7 September 2007, p. 12).

8 September 2007.

> Pacific Rim leaders agreed Saturday [8 September] to curb global warming by improving energy use and expanding forest, laying out a plan they hope will influence future climate change talks but that critics described as too timid ... Under the platform Apec members will reduce 'energy intensity' – the amount of energy needed to produce a dollar of GDP – 25 per cent by 2030. They pledge to increase forest cover in the region by at least 20 million hectares (50 million acres) by 2020 ... President George W. Bush, President Vladimir Putin, President Hu Jintao and leaders of other Asia-Pacific economies adopted the programme at an annual summit after officials struck a deal between richer and developing nations over targets. The programme's centrepieces are two modest goals – one on energy efficiency, the other on forests. Unlike the contentious UN-backed Kyoto Protocol, it does not set targets on the greenhouse gases emissions which cause global warming, and its goals are voluntary ... The group accounts for more than half the world's economy and contains most of its biggest polluters.
>
> (www.iht.com, 9 September 2007)

> Asia-Pacific leaders meeting in Sydney have agreed an 'aspirational' goal to restrain the rise of greenhouse gas emissions to tackle climate change ... The Apec statement included a non-binding goal of reducing 'energy efficiency' – the amount of energy used to produce a dollar of GDP – by at least 25 per cent by 2030. The leaders also called for increased forest cover in the Asia-Pacific region of at least 20 million hectares (50 million acres) by 2020. And they agreed greenhouse gas reduction strategies should reflect 'differences in economic and social conditions' in each country ... Apec's twenty-one members, which also include Russia and Japan, together account for about 60 per cent of annual greenhouse gas emissions.
>
> (www.bbc.co.uk, 8 September 2007)

'The world needs to slow, stop and then reverse the growth of global greenhouse gas emissions,' the leaders said in a joint statement on the climate. But the agreement is vague, adopting non-binding targets for slowing the increase in carbon emissions. They hope that by 2030 for every 1 per cent of growth in national output, the increase in carbon emissions will be held to 0.75 per cent. The statement brought a swift response from environmental campaigners, who say cuts in emissions are needed and that concrete targets are the only solution.

(www.iht.com, 10 September 2007)

9 September 2007.

A leading French national security official said French government computers were targeted by hackers linked to China ... Francis Delon (secretary-general for national defence): 'We have proof that there was involvement with China. But ... that is not to say the Chinese government.'

(*FT*, 10 September 2007, p. 8)

26 September 2007.

[It is reported that] China has replaced the head of its air force ... appointed in 2002 under Jiang Zemin and two years away from the usual retirement age for all but top leaders ... and other top military leaders ahead of a major Communist Party congress next month [October] at which President Hun Jintao is expected to fill several top posts with younger leaders loyal to his rule ... Other recent announcements include the heads of five of the seven main military regions, including the one surrounding Beijing and the Nanjing military district tasked with making war preparations against Taiwan ... Wednesday's report [26 September] comes just days after China publicized the appointment of a new chief of general staff in charge of day-to-day operations for its 2.3 million-member armed forces, the world's largest standing army ... Hu, who is also party leader and head of the eleven-member commission that exercises ultimate control over the military, has been manoeuvring quietly to place allies in key positions ahead of the ruling party's twice-a-decade congress starting on 15 October ... While servicemen and women make up just a fraction of the party's 70 million members, they will account for 296, or 13.3 per cent, of the 2,220 delegates to attend the congress.

(www.iht.com, 26 September 2007)

[The] Three Gorges Dam threatens to become an environmental catastrophe if the government does not act quickly, senior government officials have warned in an unusual public nod to the massive project's ecological impact. The comments, carried in state media yesterday [26 September], mark a rare Chinese admission that dire predictions of ecological predictions from international experts and domestic opponents of the world's largest dam are coming true. Landslides, silting and erosion above the dam are creating environmental and safety hazards that cannot be ignored, Wang Xiaofeng, director of the State Council Three Gorges Construction Committee, was

> quoted as saying … He said: 'We cannot exchange environmental destruction for short-term economic gain' … The unusual criticism of such a symbolic project could be politically motivated in the lead up to the Seventeenth Communist Party Congress … Construction began under … Jiang Zemin … [There have been] fifteen years of construction.
>
> (*FT*, 27 September 2007)

'Hu Jintao … stayed away from the completion ceremonies a year ago' (www.thetimes.co.uk, 27 September 2007).

'The dam's head of construction, Wang Xiaofeng, said ecological problems like soil erosion, landslides and water pollution could not be ignored … The $25 billion project … is due to be completed by the end of 2008' (www.bbc.co.uk, 26 September 2007).

> The website of the *People's Daily*, the Communist Party's newspaper … quoted senior officials as saying: 'There are many new and hidden ecological and environmental dangers concerning the Three Gorges Dam. If preventative measures are not taken, the project could lead to a catastrophe' … Wang Xiaofeng [a senior member in charge of building the dam]: 'We cannot win by achieving economic prosperity at the cost of the environment' … The $2.3 billion Three Gorges Dam … [was] begun in 1993 … [leading to] the forced relocation of 1.4 million residents from areas flooded by its vast reservoir. The left bank of the dam began generating power in 2005, and turbines on the right side of the dam started sending their first trickle of electricity to the power grid this month [September]. The project is scheduled to be fully operational by 2009.
>
> (www.iht.com, 27 September 2007)

'The official Xinhua news agency said the size of the reservoir behind the Three Gorges Dam had started to erode the Yangtze's banks in many places, which "together with frequent fluctuations in water levels, had triggered a series of landslides"' (*IHT*, 28 September 2007, p. 6).

('The government has announced that it will relocate an additional 3 to 4 million people from the banks of the Yangtze river because of the construction of the Three Gorges Dam … The relocations will take place over a period of ten to fifteen years. They are required because of mounting concerns about pollution in a new lake created by the dam and because of the proliferation of unforeseen landslides as the riverbank's walls collapse in many places … Chongqing, which is one of China's largest and fastest growing cities, sits at the western end of the dam's 400-mile-long reservoir and will absorb many of the displaced people … Already 1.4 million people have been moved to make way for the construction, many of them more than once, as understanding of the project's impact on the river has evolved. The … $22 billion … Three Gorges Dam, which was begun in 1994 and is nearing completion, is the world's largest hydroelectric dam … In recent weeks Chinese officials have been unusually blunt in speaking about problems arising from the dam's construction. These include heavy silting of the riverbed, which could eventually cripple the dam, the accumulation of heavy metals and other pollutants in the waters, and now riverbank erosion': www.iht.com, 12 October 2007. 'At least 4 million people are to be moved from the area around China's Three Gorges Dam amid warnings of an "environmental catastrophe" … Critics have long warned the dam … could cause huge environmental damage … The problems include landslides caused by erosion on the steep hills around the dam, conflicts over land shortages, deteriorating quality of drinking water and pollution seeping from submerged industrial sites. Landslides crashing into the reservoir have produced huge waves that have damaged the shoreline … [Critics also say that there are] now homeless labourers [and that] many people were not provided with the land they were promised or compensation they were promised … The $25 billion project … is due to be completed by the end of 2008': www.bbc.co.uk, 12 October 2007. 'In September Xinhua … said that frequent landslides had been triggered by changes in water level': *The Economist*, 3 November 2007, p. 74. 'The project's official tally [is] of 1.13 million displaced people … Officials want to begin a new relocation programme that would be bigger than the first … On 12 October the Xinhua news agency disclosed an unexpected bombshell: at least 4 million people in Chongqing municipality would have to be moved by 2020, including at least 2 million living in the reservoir region': www.iht.com, 19 November 2007; *IHT*, 20 November 2007, pp. 1–2. 'Water pollution, soil erosion and landslides are becoming increasingly frequent as water continues to rise and inundate more land in the reservoir behind the mammoth dam': *IHT*, 22 November 2007, p. 4. 'The higher water level places greater weight on the shoreline and seeps into crevices of existing rock formations and mountains': www.iht.com, 27 November 2007. 'China has announced plans to confront environmental and geological problems around the Three Gorges Dam … On Tuesday [20 November 2007] state media announced a host of new measures from the Three Gorges Project Committee of the State Council, the highest executive body in the government. Specifics were scarce, but state media described "seven projects" focused on guaranteeing safe drinking water, curbing municipal and industrial dumping, and instituting an environmental monitoring system. The proposal announced Tuesday appeared to be the same basic plan that was discussed privately in late September [2007] by select officials and experts at a closed forum': *IHT*, 22 November 2007, p. 4. 'China sought Thursday [22 November] to head off rising concern about the environmental impact of the Three Gorges Dam, playing down a deadly landslide this week and saying that any damage had been foreseen by planners. The comments in state-run media marked a stark reversal from recent warnings by officials who said China faced a catastrophe if it failed to stop riverbank erosion and other environmental problems caused by the dam, the world's largest hydropower project': *IHT*, 23 November 2007, p. 3. 'This week Chinese officials have been making a major public relations push to play down problems at the dam. The *China Daily*, the official English language newspaper, ran a banner article across the front page beneath the headline: "Dam Impact Less than Predicted"': www.iht.com, 23 November 2007. 'The officials overseeing the Three Gorges Dam defended the project's environmental record Tuesday [27 November], asserting that rising waters in the dam's reservoir were not to blame for any major geological incidents or disasters in the region … Wang Xiaofeng [is] director of the government's Three Gorges Project Construction Committee … Li Yongan [is] general manager of the China Yangtze River Three Gorges Project Development Corporation … Last week at least thirty-one people were killed in a landslide … On Tuesday Wang and two other officials spent nearly two hours fielding questions at a news conference in Beijing that represented the government's most concerted effort to tamp down the controversy around the dam. The officials said that the project remained critical for flood control and power generation and that the dam's benefits outweighed its "disadvantages". The upbeat assessment contrasted with a September forum held in the city of Wuhan … On Tuesday Wang described his speech at the forum as an analysis of potential problems that could arise, but he said that he considered the overall environmental situation to be stable and, in some cases, better than expected': www.iht.com, 27 November 2007.)

29 September 2007.

> Burma's [Myanmar's] closest ally, China, has made its most strident call yet for the military regime to end a violent crackdown on pro-democracy protesters … Prime minister Wen Jiabao: 'China hopes all parties concerned show restraint, resume stability through peaceful means as soon as possible, promote domestic reconciliation and achieve democracy and development.'
>
> (www.bbc.co.uk, 29 September 2007)

> China has said repeatedly that Myanmar's troubles are its own internal affair, and last year [2006] it blocked an American move to place Myanmar's violations of human rights on the agenda of the UN Security Council. But it has recently taken small public steps to press for democratic reform in Myanmar. In June it arranged a highly unusual meeting in Beijing between representatives of Myanmar and the United States at which the Americans pressed for the release of Aung San Suu Kyi … the pro-democracy leader … who has been under house arrest for twelve of the past eighteen years … Earlier this month [13 September], as the demonstrations built in Myanmar, a senior Chinese diplomat, Tang Jiaxuan, told the visiting Myanmar foreign minister, Nyan Win, that 'China wholeheartedly hopes that Myanmar will push forward a democracy process that is appropriate for the country.'
>
> (*IHT*, 25 September 2007, p. 3)

> Demonstrations … started tentatively on 19 August after a fuel price increase raised the costs of transportation and basic goods … Huge demonstrations [have been] led by Buddhist monks … The military junta … [has] crushed a peaceful pro-democracy uprising [with loss of life].
>
> (*IHT*, 1 October 2007, p. 8)

> Aung San Suu Kyi … led the National League for Democracy Party in elections in 1990 … Although the party won by a landslide, she was by that point under arrest and the election result was never recognized by the military.
>
> (www.bbc.co.uk, 27 September 2007)

> Since September 1988 the country [Burma] has been run by a corrupt and repressive military junta (which renamed the country Myanmar). Soon after taking power ... the junta ... placed Aung San Suu Kyi ... under house arrest. In 1990 it allowed national elections, but then ignored the National League for Democracy's landslide victory and clung to power.
>
> (www.iht.com, 1 October 2007)

'In 1989 the Burmese junta renamed the country Myanmar' (www.iht.com, 2 October 2007).

11 October 2007.

> China turned against the Burmese government last night [11 October] and supported a UN Security Council statement rebuking the military regime for its suppression of peaceful protests and demanding the release of all political prisoners. The Security Council statement, which also calls for 'genuine dialogue' with the opposition leader, Aung San Suu Kyi, marked the first time that Beijing had agreed to UN criticism of the junta. The statement did not threaten sanctions, but ... [there was] unanimous support by all fifteen members of the Security Council ... The statement had to be diluted from earlier drafts to win Chinese approval, dropping a demand for the Burmese government to account for what happened to detained demonstrators and a call for a transition to democracy ... The [Burmese] government has said that ten people were killed ... in the course of last month's street demonstrations.
>
> (www.guardian.co.uk, 12 October 2007)

('Burma's military authorities killed at least thirty-one people ... from 26 to 29 September ... a UN human rights envoy has said ... Paulo Sergio Pinheiro said he gave Burma a list of sixteen named individuals who were killed, in addition to fifteen others confirmed as dead by the state ... Earlier Human Rights Watch ... [a] New York-based group ... said at least twenty people died ... but concluded that the total must be much higher': www.bbc.co.uk, 7 December 2007.)

15–21 October 2007. The Seventeenth Communist Party Congress is held in Beijing, with 2,235 delegates in attendance.

'The founding meeting [of the Communist Party took place in 1921 in Shanghai] ... Thirteen delegates [attended], including Mao Zedong' (*The Times*, 15 October 2007, p. 33).

'The congress delegates will "elect" a new Central Committee from a pre-approved list of candidates only slightly bigger than the number of seats to be filled' (www.economist.com, 16 October 2007).

'The internal election of the Central Committee was marginally more democratic than at the 2002 Congress, with 8 per cent of the nominees eliminated, compared with 5 per cent last time' (*FT*, 22 October 2007, p. 6).

'The party nominated 221 candidates to fill 204 seats on the Central Committee, meaning that 8.3 per cent of those deemed eligible did not get a seat' (*IHT*, 23 October 2007, p. 6).

'This year is the first time in the party's history that it has published the names of delegates' (*The Times*, 15 October 2007, p. 33).

'Ex-President Jiang Zemin as well as two former premiers, Li Peng and Zhu Rongji, will attend the congress as special delegates' (www.bbc.co.uk, 14 October 2007).

Developments prior to the congress:

> China has promoted [in September] senior military officers with experience in planning for war over Taiwan ahead of … the Seventeenth Party Congress scheduled to open on 15 October … at which the Communist Party has said it will adopt a new strategy to stop the island moving toward independence … The proportion of officers holding key command positions with first-hand experience in planning for a conflict over Taiwan has been increasing in recent years.
>
> (www.iht.com, 9 October 2007)

> The Communist Party … [has] 73.4 million members … The party presides over large and cash-rich state businesses, a control exercised by monopolizing the selection of senior executives … In the past five years the party has sought to add another set of strings to its bow by bringing the private sector … firmly into its purview through the establishment of member committees inside non-state companies … Ouyang Song, vice minister of the Organization Department of the powerful party body in charge of top level appointments to ministries and state enterprises, said last year [2006] that 85 per cent of private companies eligible to have a committee had established one. Companies qualify to form a committee if at least three employees are party members. By the end of June this year [2007] about 3.2 million party members were working in private companies … Entrepreneurs, in turn, have been officially welcomed as party members since the 2002 congress … The 2002 Communist Party Congress officially accepted private entrepreneurs as party members.
>
> (*FT*, 12 October 2007, p. 15)

> After intensive bargaining, China's Communist Party has approved a new leadership line-up that denies President Hu Jintao the decisive consolidation of power that his supporters hoped would allow him to govern more assertively in his final five-year term as China's top leader. The party's Central Committee agreed to elevate four senior officials to the ruling Politburo Standing Committee, but only one of them, Li Keqiang, the party secretary of Liaoning province, clearly owed his rise in the hierarchy to Hu's patronage, people told about the results of a Central Committee meeting said Friday [12 October]. Xi Jinping, the party boss of Shanghai, is also expected to join the Standing Committee. He would outrank Li and become the most likely successor to Hu as part chief, head of state and top military official in 2012, the people said. Xi, whose father was a senior party official under Mao, is viewed as a compromise choice,

acceptable to Hu but also to his now-retired predecessor as top leader, Jiang Zemin, who party officials say exercised broad sway over the reshuffling. Xi moved to Shanghai from Zhejiang province just six months ago to replace the now disgraced Chen Liangyu, who was ousted in China's biggest corruption scandal of the past decade. Two other members of the Standing Committee, He Guoqiang, a party organization official, and Zhou Yongkang, China's top law enforcement officer, are widely viewed as close allies of China's vice president, Zeng Qinghong, who will step down from the Standing Committee. Personnel shifts in the party are decided in secret and the final leadership line-up will not be made public until the conclusion of a party congress, which convenes on Monday [15 October] ... The Central Committee issued a public statement Friday [12 October] that offered no information about personnel changes but praised Hu lavishly ... The committee said the party would amend its constitution. That suggests that Hu's concept of 'scientific development', a catch phrase for his policies to promote more balanced, equitable and sustainable development, will be enshrined in the constitution alongside the political slogans of Mao, Deng Xiaoping and Jiang Zemin ... Hu will still have to work to build a consensus among the nine members of the Standing Committee, a majority of whom owe their rise more to the support of Jiang or Zeng than to Hu. Party members said Hu had hoped to reduce membership in the Standing Committee to seven from nine, and to elevate more members of his political base, the Communist Youth League, to the top body ... After years of careful cultivation, Hu did not succeed in positioning Li Keqiang, fifty-two, the Liaoning party boss, as his successor, party officials said. Instead, Li will probably assume the position of prime minister, now held by Wen Jiabao, when Hu and Wen retire in five years. Xi, fifty-four, is expected to succeed Zeng as vice president and as the day-to-day manager of Communist Party affairs at this congress as the first step toward succeeding Hu as number one leader when the next congress convenes in 2012. Just as Hu owed his designation in 1992 as the party's future leader to Deng rather than to Jiang, who was party chief at the time, Xi's rise came mainly at the behest of Jiang and Zeng, the people told about the deliberations said. Xi is not likely to be identified publicly as Hu's successor. The semi-official China News Service said Thursday [11 October] in a report that Hu would not follow Mao's or Deng's lead in picking a successor, but would rely on 'collective discussion and collective decisions' within the party ... Some political observers have suggested that by having two younger members of the Standing Committee the choice of a future leader could become competitive, permitting the 190 members and the 152 alternate members of the Central Committee to choose among candidates rather than ratifying decisions made at the very top. But party officials said Friday that the party leadership had decided the matter ... Wang Qishan, the technocratic mayor of Beijing, is now slated to succeed Zeng Peiyan as China's top economic planner ... Zhang Dejiang, the party secretary of Guangdong

> province, will assume Wu Yi's portfolio as the country's trade policy maker and troubleshooter who co-ordinates responses to medical and safety problems.
>
> (www.iht.com, 13 October 2007)

'Li Keqiang worked his way up from humble peasant origins' (*Guardian*, 15 October 2007, p. 17).

> The highest placed newcomer in the ... Standing Committee of the Politburo is expected to be Xi Jinping, the Shanghai party boss. He has a revolutionary pedigree but emerged as a strong candidate only in recent months ... Standing Committee members are expected to retire at the age of sixty-eight. Except for Li Keqiang, fifty-two, and Xi Jinping, fifty-four, all other members will be at least sixty-eight when Hu Jintao is due to step down in 2012.
>
> (*FT*, 15 October 2007, p. 7)

> At a five-yearly congress due to begin on 15 October the party, at Hu Jintao's request, will rewrite its own character to give the president's theory about the need for 'scientific development' (meaning pro-poor and pro-environment) the same sanctity as the philosophies of Mao, Deng Xiaoping and Jiang Zemin.
>
> (*The Economist*, 13 October 2007, p. 27)

' "Scientific development" seeks a more environmentally sustainable and socially harmonious model of economic development' (*Guardian*, 15 October 2007, p. 17).

> [The concept of] 'scientific development' ... calls for more balanced economic development that does not lead to problems such as pollution or a widening wealth gap between rich and poor. The constitution was also changed in 2002 to include previous President Jiang Zemin's contribution to political thought – the Three Represents. That idea reflected the former president's desire to bring a wider range of people into the party, most notably China's newly rich business class.
>
> (www.bbc.co.uk, 14 October 2007)

' "Scientific development" ... broadly translates to what is known in the West as sustainable development' (www.ft.com, 15 October 2007).

> The party charter will now feature Hu Jintao's vows to create a 'harmonious society' cleansed of conflict and a 'scientific outlook on development' promising to balance economic growth with efforts to clean up pollution and create a more equal society ... Hu has been able to elevate his key ideas with many years still in office ... Hu's predecessor, Jiang took thirteen years before he was able to push his trademark notions into the party charter shortly before his retirement in 2002.
>
> (www.iht.com, 21 October 2007)

> Hu Jintao succeeded in inserting his signature political theory, 'the scientific outlook on development', into the party constitution five years before he retires. Jiang Zemin managed only to write his equivalent 'three represents' into the party constitution when he was leaving the helm in 2002.
>
> (www.iht.com, 23 October 2007)

'Today one-third of provincial party secretaries and governors are from the Communist Youth League, Hu Jintao's primary power base since he served as its secretary-general in the early 1980s' (www.iht.com, 23 October 2007).

> PLA [People's Liberation Army] members were heavily represented at the congress, accounting for about 13 per cent of the 2,217 delegates attending, even though the armed forces make up just 2.2 per cent of the party's 73 million members. About 1.6 million members of the PLA and the paramilitary People's Armed Police are party members ... China says spending for the PLA grew 17.8 per cent last year to about $44.94 billion.
>
> (www.iht.com, 15 October 2007)

Developments at the congress:

'[On 15 October] Hu Jintao ... appeared on a rostrum with all the other members of the Politburo Standing Committee and the Central Committee arranged in precise hierarchical order. They were joined by party elders, including Jiang Zemin' (www.iht.com, 16 October 2007).

Hu Jintao (excerpts from the speech given on 15 October):

> Contemporary China is going through a wide-ranging and deep-going transformation. This brings us unprecedented opportunities as well as unprecedented challenges. On the whole the opportunities outweigh the challenges.
>
> [Economic development is of] decisive significance to build moderately prosperous society ... and socialist modernization ... Rapid development represents the most remarkable achievement [of the last five years].
>
> [One of the main goals is to build a] moderately prosperous society [by 2020] ... [The aim is to quadruple *per capita* GDP by 2020].
>
> During this period China's overall strength grew considerably and the people enjoyed more tangible benefits. China's international standing and influence rose notably.
>
> [A] scientific outlook on development [is necessary] ... Our economic growth is realized at an extremely high cost of resources and the environment ... We must adopt an enlightened approach to development that results in expanded production, a better life and sound ecological and environmental conditions. We need to correctly handle the major relationships between urban and rural development, economic and social development and man and nature ... There are still a considerable number of impover-

ished and low-income people in both urban and rural areas, and it has become more difficult to accommodate the interests of all sides ... To realize social equity and justice is the Chinese Communists' consistent position ... Balanced and sustainable [development is necessary].

To stop or reverse [economic] reform and opening up would only lead up a blind alley.

[Public ownership will remain] dominant ... [but] all economic sectors [can] compete on an equal footing and reinforce each other.

While recognizing our achievements we must be well aware that they still fall short of the expectations of the people ... The governance capability of the party falls somewhat short of the need to deal with the new situation and task ... A small number of party cadres are not honest and upright ... [Their] extravagance, waste and corruption and other undesirable behaviour are still serious problems with them ... Resolutely punishing and effectively preventing corruption bears on the popular support of the party and its very survival ... We must guard against arrogance and rashness, preserve plain living and struggle hard.

[We must] expand socialist democracy ... Citizens' participation in political affairs will expand in an orderly way ... [Citizens will have] more extensive democratic rights [by 2020] ... Power must be exercised in the sunshine to ensure that it is exercised correctly ... [There is need to] explore various ways to expand intra-party democracy at the grassroots level ... We will expand intra-party democracy to develop the people's democracy.

[There is need for] solidarity and unity ... All party members must firmly uphold the centralized and unified leadership of the party ... [Members must] conscientiously abide by the party's political discipline, always be in agreement with the Central Committee and resolutely safeguard its authority to ensure that its resolutions and decisions are carried out effectively.

[The forces of] Taiwan independence [are stepping up their efforts] ... [We] will never allow anyone to separate Taiwan from the motherland in any name or by any means ... We would like to make a solemn appeal: On the basis of the One China principle let us discuss a formal end to the state of authority between the two sides, reach a peace agreement.

The trend toward a multi-polar world is irreversible.

We must build strong armed forces through science and technology. In keeping with the new trends in world military affairs and the new requirements of China's development, we must promote innovation in military theory, technology, organization and development. We are determined to safeguard China's sovereignty, security and international integrity and make contributions to maintaining world peace. We will adjust and reform the systems of defence-related science, technology and industry and of weapons

> and equipment procurement, and enhance our capacity for independent innovation in research and development of weapons and equipment.
>
> (Sources for Hu Jintao's speech: www.bbc.co.uk, 15 October 2007; www.iht.com, 15 October 2007; *IHT*, 16 October 2007, p. 5; www.guardian.co.uk, 15 October 2007; *Guardian*, 16 October 2007, p. 17; www.ft.com, 15 October 2007; *FT*, 16 October 2007, p. 8; www.cnn.com, 15 October 2007; *The Times*, 16 October 2007, p. 33)

Hu Jintao (21 October): '[The party has recommitted itself to the] basic line of taking economic development as its central task ... [and] building a moderately well off society in all respects' (www.iht.com, 21 October 2007).

'The government believes that its top priority is to continue economic growth, albeit in a more balanced fashion' (Minxin Pei, www.ft.com, 28 October 2007).

Personnel changes:

The Central Committee (204 full members and 167 alternate members; announced on 21 October): those who ceased to be members included the following: Zeng Qinghong (sixty-eight; vice president); Luo Gan (seventy-two; oversaw national security affairs as head of the party's politics and law committee); Wu Guanzheng (sixty-nine; head of the party's disciplinary committee); Wu Yi (vice premier); Zeng Peiyan (vice premier); Cao Gangchuan (defence minister).

> [The] new Central Committee does not include Zeng Qinghong or two other members of the nine-man Politburo Standing Committee, Luo Gan and Wu Guanzheng ... all of whom owed their positions in the hierarchy mainly to Jiang Zemin ... Zeng Qinghong is considered the most powerful party official after Hu Jintao himself and his retirement allows a new, younger official to manage the ruling party's day-to-day affairs as head of its secretariat.
>
> (*IHT*, 22 October 2007, p. 2)

'Zeng Qinghong ranked fifth in the party hierarchy ... Mr Zeng belonged to the elite group of China's "princelings", the children of veteran Communist Party revolutionaries' (www.bbc.co.uk, 21 October 2007).

'Zeng Qinghong [was] the fifth ranked leader [in the Standing Committee]' (www.ft.com, 22 October 2007).

'Hu Jintao was the top vote-getter in the tightly controlled ballot for the committee, winning all but two of the 2,235 votes' (www.iht.com, 21 October 2007).

> Jia Qinglin, sixty-seven, a long-time ally of Jiang, remained. He has long been shadowed by claims he let corruption run rampant in coastal Fujian province in the 1990s ... Jia resided over Fujian province in the south during one of the biggest corruption scandals in the history of Communist Party rule, when several officials close to Jia, as well as his wife, were investigated for receiving large gifts from a corrupt businessman ... [Jia Qinglin is] a member of the Standing Committee who heads the organization that co-ordinates the Communist Party's relations with other political, ethnic and commercial interests in China.
>
> (www.iht.com, 21 October 2007)

'Huang Ju died in the summer [of 2007]' (www.bbc.co.uk, 21 October 2007).

'Hu Jintao was able to fill 20 per cent of the Central Committee with veterans of the Communist Youth League, his major power base' (*FEER*, November 2007, p. 28).

The New Standing Committee in order of rank (announced on 22 October; nine members, five old and four new ones): Hu Jintao; Wu Bangguo (speaker of the National People's Congress); Wen Jiabao; Jia Qinglin (chairman of the Chinese People's Political Consultative Conference, a body that co-ordinates the party's relations with other political, ethnic and commercial interests); Li Changchun (in charge of party propaganda); Xi Jinping (new; new head of the party's secretariat, with day-to-day command of party affairs, assuming the position formerly held by Zeng Qinghong); Li Keqiang (new; executive vice premier); He Guoqiang (new; the party's organization chief, a department in charge of investigating officials before they are promoted; head of the party's anti-corruption Central Discipline Inspection Committee); Zhou Yongkang (new; minister for public security).

'Committee member Huang Ju died in the summer [of 2007]' (www.bbc.co.uk, 22 October 2007).

> The Committee walked out onto the stage in order of rank, with Xi Jinping at the head of the [four] new appointees. Chinese Communist tradition dictates that the first new face of the new generation becomes the heir apparent ... Li Keqiang ... won plaudits for his work to revitalize the economy in the north-eastern province of Liaoning ... Liaoning [is] an industrial province that has suffered following China's economic reforms ... Mr Xi's position in the Committee – he is ranked sixth compared with Mr Li's seventh – also suggests he will become China's next president in 2012 ... But it is impossible to say for sure who will get the top job ... While Mr Xi's elevation to the Committee was widely predicted last week, few people were linking him with such a promotion several months ago.
>
> (www.bbc.co.uk, 22 October 2007)

'Hu Jintao said: "Xi Jinping, fifty-four, and Li Keqiang, fifty-two, are comrades who are relatively younger" ' (www.guardian.co.uk, 22 October 2007).

> The roster adheres precisely to a list submitted secretly to the party elite at the opening of the congress ... During the extended bargaining for positions in the Standing Committee over the summer and into the fall, Hu Jintao had sought to reduce the number of members from nine to seven, several people told about the deliberations said. He had also worked for years to position Li Keqiang [fifty-two] as his successor. He did not succeed on either count, though it remains possible that Li could eventually become the number one if Xi Jinping [fifty-four] stumbles or loses support ... Both Xi and Li ... are considered moderate, pro-business leaders ... While there was no formal announcement of succession in 2012, the arrangement strongly suggests that Xi will inherit Hu's positions as China's number one leader, while Li is in

> line to replace Wen Jiabao as prime minister, both after five years ... He Guoqiang [sixty-three] is considered an ally of Zeng Qinghong ... Zhou Yongkang [sixty-four] has close ties to both Jiang Zemin and Zeng ... Party officials and political observers informed about the party's debates said Hu had hoped to remove two other officials, Jia Qinglin [sixty-seven] and Li Changchun [sixty-three], who were promoted mainly by Jiang Zemin.
>
> (www.iht.com, 22 October 2007)

'Xi Jinping is less beholden to Hu Jintao and emerged in recent weeks as a compromise candidate for leaders who feared giving Hu too much sway' (www.cnn.com, 22 October 2007).

> Judging by their background, they [Xi Jinping and Li Keqiang] appear to be very talented party insiders, with a broad range of experience in various fields. The consensus among analysts is that Mr Xi is a candidate with the broadest scope of support from various groups inside the party. Unless something dramatic happens in the next five years, it is almost certain that these two individuals will assume the two top positions in China, the general secretary of the party and the premier of the State Council.
>
> (Minxin Pei, www.ft.com, 28 October 2007)

'Li Changchun, who was party chief of Henan province during the outbreak and attempted cover-up of the HIV-contaminated blood scandal, retains his grip on the powerful propaganda department' (www.guardian.co.uk, 22 October 2007).

The Politburo: the nine Standing Committee members; Bo Xilai; Liu Yandong; and others.

> No 'competitive elections' were allowed when the 204 Central Committee members chose from among themselves members of the Politburo and the Politburo Standing Committee ... The average age of the twenty-five-member Politburo is 61.7, or 1.1 years older than that of the previous one.
>
> (*FEER*, November 2007, pp. 27–8)

'Wang Qishan, the mayor of Beijing, was elevated to the Politburo and is expected to become the vice premier next year [2008] in charge of the financial sector' (www.ft.com, 22 October 2007).

> The nine members of the Standing Committee of the Politburo ... appointed after the 2002 congress were all engineers ... Xi Jinping and Li Keqiang have degrees in social sciences and education, and law and economics, respectively. In the broader Politburo itself three-quarters of its members in 2002 were engineers, compared with just half in the latest group.
>
> (*FT*, 23 October 2007, p. 5)

'Xi Jinping is a Doctor of Law, while Li Keqiang is a Doctor of Economics ... Li Keqiang studied law at the elite Peking University after the Cultural Revolution' (www.independent.co.uk, 23 October 2007).

'Xi Jinping is ... an engineering and law graduate of Tsinghua University' (www.guardian.co.uk, 24 October 2007). '[Xi Jinping had] two degrees from the elite Tsinghua University. Unlike most recent Politburo members he has a doctorate in law and ideological education' (*Guardian*, 26 October 2007, p. 23).

> Some twenty entrepreneurs were included in the Central Committee of 204 full and 167 alternate members ... To be sure, the great majority of the committee members are still senior officials of the party, government and military. Yet not a single genuine peasant or worker – whom President Hu Jintao has vowed to serve under his much-cited 'putting people first' policy – was inducted into the Central Committee ... Members of what critics have called the new party aristocracy include the chief executives of government-controlled conglomerates that are listed on the Shanghai and Hong Kong stock exchanges. The top brass of China Telecom, the State Grid Corporation of China, PetroChina and China Construction Bank, among others, were all elevated. There was one representative from the private sector, the chairman of Haier, the largest Chinese maker of home appliances. The theoretical justification for the businessmen's ascent up the party hierarchy is former President Jiang Zemin's so-called 'Theory of the Three Represents', which says, among other things, that the party must recruit elite members of the 'new classes' who represent 'the highest productivity and the foremost culture'. The controversial theory was enshrined in the party constitution at the Sixteenth Party Congress in 2002, which also endorsed Hu Jintao as Jiang's successor. Since 2003 Hu and his ally prime minister Wen Jiabao have seldom mentioned the 'Three Represents'. Instead, they have focused their public campaigns on their so-called 'scientific theory of development', which underscores the need to give peasants and workers a bigger share of the fruits of economic growth, as well as to promote social justice and equal opportunities for all. In reality, however, the Hu–Wen leadership has faithfully followed Jiang's strategy of injecting new blood into the Communist Party by including 'new social sectors' such as Western educated businessmen, professionals and experts. Other disadvantaged sectors of society have remained barred from the corridors of power ... [But] there was a groundswell of discontent against the 'favouring of the rich', which was evident from the voting patterns of Congress delegates ... Most of the 'red delegates' scored poorly: six of the twelve alternate members who garnered the least number of ballots were state entrepreneurs and managers of government investment houses. It is probably because of the leadership's anxiety over alienating the leftist members and cadres, several hundred of whom wrote a petition to the Congress protesting the rise of businessmen, that these bosses only qualified as alternate members ... Hu stated for the first time that it was imperative to 'deepen the reform of monopolistic enterprises by introducing competitive mechanisms and boosting government supervision and social scrutiny' ... [The party leadership has] successfully

> persuaded more of the nation's estimated 11 million private bosses to join the Communist Party.
>
> (Willy Lam, *IHT*, 27 October 2007, p. 4)

'The latest annual "rich list", published just weeks before the congress by the *Hurun* group, said China had 106 $ billionaires, up from fifteen last year [2006] and only seven in 2005' (*FT*, 23 October 2007, p. 5).

> When China's 'rich list' [*Hurun* China Rich List] was launched in 1999 … [by] Rupert Hoogewerf, the young British accountant … it had just one US dollar billionaire. 'Red Capitalist' Rong Yiren, the former China vice president, who founded the sprawling state-controlled Citic conglomerate, topped the list with an estimated wealth of $1 billion, up from only fourteen last year [2006] … A third of the 800 on this year's rich list are members of the Communist Party, according to *Hurun*, and thirty-eight are delegates to the National People's Congress.
>
> (p. 16)

'China now has 106 $ billionaires, second only to the United States. There were none in 2002' (*IHT*, 7 November 2007, p. 5).

> The United States has more billionaires than any other country: 415 by *Forbes*'s last count. Number two … is China. A year ago there were fifteen billionaires in China. Now there are more than 100, according to the *Hurun* survey, and sixty-six according to *Forbes*.
>
> (*IHT*, 7 November 2007, p. 1)

'Japan has only twenty-four billionaires' (p. 17).

> When the *Forbes* magazine … [published the list in March 2007] 415 of this year's 746 billionaires were from the United States, twenty from China. By November the number of Chinese billionaires had grown to sixty-six. At the same time the Shanghai-based *Hurun Report* was listing 106 billionaires – up from fifteen the year before … Both the *Forbes* and *Hurun* reports inserted disclaimers that their ranking of Chinese billionaires may not be complete because of the lack of transparency in the stock holdings of China's 'state-owned' companies. China may in fact currently have as many as 200 billionaires.
>
> (Peter Kwong, www.iht.com, 16 November 2007)

24 October 2007.

> China has launched its first lunar orbiter, on a planned year-long exploration mission to the moon … The unmanned satellite … *Chang'e* … is named after a Chinese goddess who flew to the moon. Analysts say it is a key step towards China's aim of putting a man on the moon by 2020.
>
> (www.bbc.co.uk, 24 October 2007)

> China launched its first lunar probe Wednesday [24 October], the first step in an ambitious ten-year plan to send a rover to the moon and return it to

> earth ... The launch marks the first step of a three-stage moon mission. In about 2012 there will be a moon landing with a moon rover. In the third phase about five years later another rover will land on the moon and be returned to earth with lunar soil and stone samples.
>
> (www.cnn.com, 24 October 2007)

'The orbiter is the first phase of a lunar programme that aims to land an unmanned rover on the surface by 2012 and put a man on the moon before 2020' (www.guardian.co.uk, 24 October 2007).

> Only last month [September] Japan became the first Asian nation to send a satellite to orbit the moon. China had wanted to send its satellite, *Chang'e 1*, up in April but unspecified technical difficulties prevented that ... India is hoping to launch a similar orbiter next year (as is America).
>
> (*The Economist*, 27 October 2007, p. 78)

(Sun Laiyan, head of the China National Space Administration, on 26 November: 'I have heard reports which say that China will put a man on the moon by 2020, but I do not know of such a plan ... But I am confident that one day we will put an astronaut on the moon': www.bbc.co.uk, 26 November 2007.)

9 November 2007.

> A government panel announced plans Friday [9 November] to revamp the country's holiday schedule to reemphasize traditional festivals at the expense of the Marxist May Day celebration. The news schedule aimed to address the severe overloading of China's air, rail and road links during nearly a week around the Chinese New Year, in the first week of May and the first week of October, periods when virtually the entire country goes on vacation ... These national holidays frequently produce transportation gridlock. The panel's plans were posted on the internet for public comment Friday and in theory could be changed. But Xinhua reported that the plan was ready to be in place early next year [2008] ... The plan calls for trimming the 1 May holiday to one working day from three. At the same time three traditional Chinese festivals will each become one-day public holidays. The new holidays are Tomb-Sweeping Day in April, the Dragon Boat Festival in June and the Mid-Autumn Festival in September. The exact date of each festival varies on Western calendars because each is calculated according to a lunar calendar. Chinese New Year, which usually falls in late January or early February, and China's National Day, which falls on 1 October, will each retain three days of national holidays. These holidays typically expand to seven days through the practice of rearranging weekends: if the national holidays fall on Monday, Tuesday and Wednesday, for example, the Thursday and Friday frequently become holidays as well, while the following Saturday and Sunday become workdays ... Mao Zedong tried to erase many traditional Chinese celebrations, but their popularity has reemerged as communist ideology has lost most of its influence in contemporary Chinese society.
>
> (www.iht.com, 11 November 2007)

21 November 2007.

> A Chinese warship sailed Wednesday [21 November] for the first port visit to Japan since the end of World War II ... The warship will visit Tokyo and the port of Yokosuka ... The warship's departure follows a warm meeting Tuesday [20 November] between prime minister Wen Jiabao and Yasuo Fukuda, Japan's prime minister, on the sidelines of an Asean meeting in Singapore, the first since the Japanese leader took office in September ... Fukuda's late father, Takeo Fukuda, signed the landmark Treaty of Peace and Friendship between the two countries when he was Japan's prime minister in 1978.
>
> (www.iht.com, 21 November 2007)

> A Chinese warship dropped anchor off Tokyo in the communist nation's first military visit to Japan since World War II ... The port call ... was part of an exchange that will bring a Japanese warship to China on a later visit. It was the first ever visit to Japan by China's People's Liberation Army ... The Chinese warship ... [is on a] four-day visit.
>
> (*IHT*, 29 November 2007, p. 2)

24 November 2007.

> Rebels in Darfur have demanded that peacekeepers from China pull out of the Sudanese region just hours after the arrival of 135 Chinese engineers ... tasked with building roads and bridges and digging wells ahead of the deployment of the joint peacekeeping force planned for January ... The army engineers arrived on Saturday [24 November] to prepare for a joint UN and African Union peacekeeping force of 26,000. The key Justice and Equality Movement (JEM) rebel group accuses China of being complicit in the Darfur conflict ... An estimated 200,000 people have died during four-and-a-half years of fighting in Darfur, with a further 2 million people displaced.
>
> (www.bbc.co.uk, 24 November 2007)

30 November 2007.

> A property tycoon has been jailed for sixteen years on corruption charges, including bribery and forging tax receipts ... Zhou Zhengyi was once named China's eleventh richest man with an estimated fortune of more than $320 million. He had been released from prison in May last year [2006] after serving a three-year sentence for manipulating the stock market and fraud ... Zhou was arrested in October 2006 after an investigation of a Shanghai social security fund scandal ... The probe led to the downfall of Shanghai Communist Party leader Chen Liangyu.
>
> (www.bbc.co.uk, 30 November 2007)

'A judge announced ... Zhou Zhengyi ... guilty on five charges including misappropriation of funds, bribery and forging tax receipts ... His company was fined $450,000 ... By 2002 *Forbes* magazine estimated his wealth at $320 million' (*IHT*, 1 December 2007, p. 7).

1–2 December 2007.

> China and Japan began talks on trade and economic issues Saturday [1 December] ... On the agenda were macroeconomic policies, disputes over the value of the Chinese yuan, co-operation on energy and the environment, investment policies and world trade talks ... The weekend of meetings brings together the largest number of cabinet officials from the two countries since they opened diplomatic relations thirty-five years ago and is modelled after similar dialogues China holds with the United States and the EU ... Only two modest agreements were struck ... One [was] on a $420 million Japanese loan to China to fund six environmental projects, the last Japan will provide under a twenty-eight-year-old development assistant programme that provided China with $30 billion in loans at low interest rates ... The other [agreement was] a treaty to allow the countries' police and prosecutors to work directly on criminal extradition ... No breakthroughs were reached in a morning meeting of the foreign ministers on Japan's chief issue, China's exploitation of a gas field that straddles a contested part of the East China Sea ... Tokyo and Beijing have held eleven rounds of talks on the issue, agreeing to jointly develop the field, but little else ... The foreign ministers agreed to more exchanges among the countries' militaries and defence officials.
>
> (www.iht.com, 1 December 2007)

> China and Japan wrapped up their first high level trade and economic talks Sunday [2 December] by pledging greater overall co-operation, but they left the touchy issue of natural gas exploration in the East China Sea unresolved. Prime minister Wen Jiabao described the two-day meeting as successful and the two sides issued a joint statement promising to strengthen efforts to form a regional free-trade zone, promote energy efficiency and improve protection of intellectual property rights. They also agreed to participate in a framework to help counter global warming and replace the Kyoto Protocol and to work on measures to combat money laundering, terrorism financing and smuggling.
>
> (*IHT*, 3 December 2007, p. 13)

('Economic talks between Beijing and Tokyo threatened to turn ugly after Japan accused China of deleting a phrase from a joint statement calling for Beijing to further relax controls on its currency': www.iht.com, 27 December 2007.)

> In an unprecedented alert, the director-general of MI5 ... Jonathan Evans ... sent a confidential letter to 300 chief executives and security chiefs at banks, accountants and legal firms this week warning them that they were under attack from 'Chinese state organizations'. It is believed to be the first time

that the [UK] government has directly accused Russia of involvement in web-based espionage … [One commentator considers that one motive may be to find out] exactly how much money a British company … trying to buy a company in China … is prepared to spend.

(*The Times*, 1 December 2007, p. 1)

Computer experts have blamed hackers linked to the Chinese military for cyber attacks on the US Pentagon, the British parliament and the German Chancellery … Hackers in China were believed responsible for four out of five major cyber attacks on government targets in 2007.

(www.iht.com, 2 December 2007)

A cyber attack reported last week by one of the federal government's nuclear weapons laboratories … Oak Ridge National Laboratory in Tennessee … may have originated in China … However, such links did not prove that the Chinese government or Chinese citizens were involved in the attacks. In the past intruders have compromised computers in China and then used them to disguise their true location … The original email and first potential corruption occurred on 29 October 2007.

(www.iht.com, 9 December 2007)

13 December 2007.

Thursday [13 December 2007, marked] the seventieth anniversary of Japan's notorious massacre of civilians in the Chinese city of Nanjing … The city reopened a vastly expanded memorial to the victims of the massacre long known in the West as 'the Rape of Nanking' … Japanese troops began a rampage that many historians generally agree ended with the slaughter of at least 150,000 civilians and disarmed soldiers and the rape of tens of thousands of women in Nanjing, then the capital of China's Nationalist government. China puts the number killed at 300,000.

(www.iht.com, 13 December 2007)

Although last Thursday [13 December] marked the seventieth anniversary of the beginning of the notorious Nanking massacre, political activists in both Japan and China have been notable – so far at least – for their restraint … The massacre, which began on 13 December 1937 and continued for six weeks, was one of the worst atrocities in military history … On conservative estimates at least 150,000 people were annihilated.

(*IHT*, 18 December 2007, p. 4)

While the seventieth anniversary is being marked in Nanjing, it has taken on a relatively low profile in the country as a whole and senior leaders are not attending the main events … The city fell [after] three days [on 13 December] … Up to 80,000 women and girls of all ages were raped … The Chinese say the invaders killed 300,000 civilians, while many in Japan say it is far less. A wartime tribunal put the figure at 142,000.

(*Independent*, 13 December 2007, p. 38)

China yesterday [13 December] marked the seventieth anniversary of the Nanjing Massacre by opening a memorial hall that blends commemoration of atrocities inflicted by invading Japanese with a message of peace ... Estimates of the number killed by mainstream Japanese historians range from around 13,000 to more than 100,000, with totals depending in part on whether deaths before the city's fall and in nearby regions are included. China has sought to prevent debate on the scale of the killings being included in government-sponsored discussions launched last year [2006].

(*FT*, 12 December 2007)

Over six long weeks between December 1937 and January 1938 troops of the Japanese Imperial Army captured Nanjing, then the Chinese capital, and killed, looted and raped in an orgy of destruction. In the summer of 1937 the Japanese invasion had begun and, much to Tokyo's surprise, the Chinese armies had responded vigorously. By the time the Japanese had arrived in Nanjing their soldiers were frustrated at the resistance they encountered and their behaviour went out of control ... The official Chinese total is 300,000 dead, the highest number possible. Revisionists on the Japanese extreme right try to argue that only a few thousand died ... Objective historians who have looked into the question rarely place the number of deaths below the tens of thousands ... Nanjing had been the Chinese capital under the Ming Dynasty.

(www.bbc.co.uk, 27 May 2008)

19 December 2007.

A new website created by China's anti-corruption bureau crashed after barely a day because too many visitors had tried to log on to register complaints, state media reported Wednesday [19 December]. The National Bureau of Corruption Prevention was formed in September to tackle mounting corruption scandals involving government and Communist Party officials. On Monday [17 December] the bureau unveiled a website that allowed the public to leave comments about its work, but the strain of too many visitors brought down the site Tuesday ... The site was back on line Wednesday.

(www.iht.com, 19 December 2007)

20 December 2007.

India and China have begun a landmark joint military exercise, the first of its kind between the two largest armies in the world. The exercise is taking place between 20 and 28 December in China's south-western province of Yunnan. It involves a company – just over 100 officers and men – from each side. India and China fought a brief but bloody war in 1962.

(www.bbc.co.uk, 1 December 2007)

21 December 2007.

China has held a ceremony to inaugurate its first home-grown commercial aircraft ... Its maiden flight [will take place] in March [2008] and then go

> into mass production in 2009 … China wants to grab 60 per cent of the medium-sized jet market currently dominated by firms such as Bombardier [Canada] and Embraer [Brazil].
>
> (www.bbc.co.uk, 21 December 2007)

26 December 2007.

> The Japanese education ministry announced Wednesday [26 December] that it would partly reinstate references in textbooks to the Japanese military's role in forcing civilians to commit mass suicide during the Battle of Okinawa in the final months of World War II. Faced with protests from Okinawa, the ministry said it would acknowledge the military's 'involvement' in the mass suicides in high school textbooks to be used in the next academic year. The ministry stopped short, however, of putting back original references to the military's 'coercing' or 'forcing' Okinawans into committing mass suicides, saying that no supporting documents had been found. In April, under the administration of Shinzo Abe, education officials said textbooks would be cleansed of longtime references to the military … The contents of Japan's history textbooks have long been a source of tension with China and South Korea … But the ministry plan to revise explanations about the Battle of Okinawa was the first time that the issue of textbooks had become a political problem domestically.
>
> (www.iht.com, 27 December 2007)

27–30 December 2007. Prime minister Yasuo Fukuda visits China.

'Yasuo Fukuda has said he will not visit the controversial [Yasukuni] shrine while he is prime minister' (www.bbc.co.uk, 27 December 2007).

'China is Japan's number one trade partner' (www.iht.com, 27 December 2007).

> Japan urged China to do more to fight global warming and pledged to help the country reduce runaway pollution during high level talks Friday [28 December]. Prime minister Yasuo Fukuda made energy and environmental issues the centrepiece of his four-day visit to China … Japan uses less energy per dollar of economic output than any other developed country. It has cut its carbon emissions sharply, partly by outsourcing manufacturing to China and other Asian countries … China has displaced Japan as Asia's largest manufacturing country … Fukuda, seventy-one, whose father signed a historic peace treaty with Beijing in 1978, vowed not to visit Yasukuni while in office.
>
> (www.iht.com, 28 December 2007)

'Fukuda said the two countries should put more of a joint effort into fighting climate change, and promised to increase aid and technology sharing to help China improve energy efficiency and reduce emissions' (*IHT*, 29 December 2007, p. 3).

'Under a new arrangement about fifty Chinese researchers will be invited to Japan every year for the next four years to train in the science of combating climate change' (www.bbc.co.uk, 29 December 2007).

Yasuo Fukuda's visit to China was his first since taking office in September … The two men agreed to co-operate on climate change and trade, and to increase youth exchanges between their countries. But despite eleven previous rounds of talks, no agreement was reached on the two countries' territorial dispute over lucrative gas fields in the East China Sea. China does not accept the maritime border which Japan has proposed as a starting point for negotiations. The two leaders agreed only to raise discussions to vice-ministerial level.

(www.bbc.co.uk, 30 December 2007)

Yasuo Fukuda has a family legacy to enshrine. Three decades ago his father was also prime minister … [His father] reopened Japan's relations with China and assured the region that his country had forever renounced force against its neighbours. This became known as the Fukuda Doctrine and the son warmly embraced it.

(www.economist.com, 26 March 2008)

1 January 2008.

Foreign journalists working in China face continued harassment despite new reporting rules brought in for the Olympic Games, a report by the Beijing-based Foreign Correspondents Club of China [FCCC] said Tuesday [1 January 2008]. The authorities relaxed restrictions on foreign journalists at the beginning of 2007, exempting them from having to apply for permission to travel and conduct interviews … But the journalists' organization said it received more than 180 reports of interference in journalists' work in 2007, including beatings and intimidation by local plainclothes thugs in Beijing and other places like central Hubei province. Sensitive areas like Xinjiang province, home to China's Uighur minority, and Tibet still remain difficult places in which to work due to official obstruction and harassment, the FCCC said. Before the rule change reporters had to apply for permission to travel outside of the major cities, as well as to conduct interviews … [The FCCC says that] while the year-old regulations have improved overall reporting conditions for foreign journalists … [it is] particularly troubled by repeated violations in several areas … Journalists working in Tibet and Xinjiang were followed or detained, or their sources were intimidated, the FCCC said. The government decree announcing the relaxed reporting rules said they would expire on 17 October [2008] after the Summer Games and the Paralympics that follow.

(www.iht.com, 1 January 2008)

Basic questions remain over how food safety will be assured during the Olympic Games, not least the safety of meat, which has been a focus of concern over the possibility that residual drugs could cause positive doping tests. The use of antibiotics and growth stimulants to increase yields is common in food production globally, including in China where it is poorly regulated.

(www.iht.com, 9 January 2008)

3 January 2008.

> A sports magnate credited with bringing Formula One to China has been jailed for four years for corruption ... Yu Zhifei, ex-manager of the Shanghai International Circuit, was convicted of embezzling more than $137,500 during the late 1990s. The charges related to his time as head of Shanghai Shenhua Football Club. He is one of a number of the city's top officials arrested and expelled from the Communist Party for corruption ... He helped to organize the country's first Grand Prix in September 2004. But Yu came under investigation in 2006 in a wide-ranging probe of Shanghai's officials.
>
> (www.bbc.co.uk, 3 January 2008)

10 January 2008. The onset of unusually severe snow storms in parts of China.

> The worst winter weather in fifty years ... an unrelenting snow storm ... is expected to pummel the country for at least another three days ... Brutal winter weather has pounded China's central, eastern and southern sections since 10 January [2008] ... Crops destroyed by snow have resulted in increased food prices, while the inability to transport goods around the country has further inflated prices and led to shortages in stores. The price of cabbage and other vegetables is up more than 50 per cent at markets – in a country that's already battling its highest inflation rate in a decade.
>
> (www.cnn.com, 31 January 2008)

> Acute electricity shortages across a swathe of central and southern China after winter blizzards disrupted coal deliveries have exposed the fragility of transport networks ... [Coal accounts for] more than 80 per cent of the country's electricity ... Food prices are increasing in major cities including Beijing as distribution bottlenecks and bad weather hamper deliveries of vegetables and meat ... The authorities have capped the prices utilities can charge for power at a time when coal prices have been soaring. Without the incentive of adequate profits, power producers have been reluctant to increase output.
>
> (www.iht.com, 31 January 2008; *IHT*, 1 February 2008, p. 14)

> On Wednesday [30 January] prime minister Wen Jiabao ... took the extraordinary step of flying to the southern city of Guangzhou to address a crowd of hundreds of thousands of migrant workers who were desperate for seats on trains that were not coming ... He voiced an apology for the difficulties.
>
> (*IHT*, 2 February 2008, p. 2)

'Wen Jabao, the premier, has visited crowded railway stations to appeal for calm and reassure frustrated passengers that everything possible is being done to help them' (*FT*, 2 February 2008, p. 10).

'[The severe weather has caused] the government to order a ceiling on food prices' (*Guardian*, 31 January 2008, p. 24).

'The authorities have ordered coal production to be increased and imposed emergency price controls' (www.bbc.co.uk, 1 February 2008).

> Power companies – caught between rising coal costs and fixed prices for their output – have been haggling with the coal suppliers, and found themselves short of coal stocks when the snowstorms hit ... China has ordered financial institutions to provide emergency loans to businesses and individuals hit by the snow storms and power cuts that have paralysed swathes of central and southern China.
>
> (*FT*, 2 February 2008, pp. 8, 10)

> A flawed reform has freed fuel prices but left power producers unable to pass on the rising cost of coal to consumers, because electricity prices are fixed. Many producers responded by letting their stocks fall to dangerously low levels, in the hope prices would fall when the weather warms up in the spring ... Power plants that normally stock eighteen to twenty days' worth of coal had in some cases run their reserves down to as little as three days' worth ... Electricity prices are fixed and, unable to pass on costs; power producers had been waiting for seasonal price cuts in March before stocking up.
>
> (www.economist.com, 7 February 2008)

> Snowstorms that have battered many parts of China over the past three weeks have killed at least sixty people and caused 53.8 billion yuan in damage, the civil affairs ministry said Friday [1 February]. Besides the $7.5 billion in damage, the freakish weather, the worst in China in five decades, has already crippled transportation during the biggest holiday travel season of the country, paralysed the densely populated central and eastern regions just as millions were seeking to return home for the Lunar New Year holiday ... More bad weather was forecast, with snow still falling in four central and eastern provinces.
>
> (www.iht.com, 1 February 2008)

> China's top leaders donned hard hats and anoraks to visit some of the millions of people stranded by the worst ice and snow in fifty years, as water, food and fuel dwindled ... Keeping coal output high and food moving has become a priority as seventeen provinces experienced electricity blackouts. The national stockpile of coal to generate power has fallen to a mere six days ... President Hu Jintao [has been] travelling the country to encourage relief workers [coalminers and dockworkers] ... Premier Wen Jiabao has also been on the road for the past three days [visiting railway stations and coal mines] ... After months of keeping a tight rein on lending by banks in an effort to curb runaway economic growth, China's central bank has ordered provincial banks to speed up loans issued in the worst-hit areas.
>
> (*Independent*, 2 February 2008, p. 37)

'Fallen transmission lines, frozen equipment and coal shortages caused power cuts across seventeen provinces; at least eleven electricians died making repairs' (www.economist.com, 7 February 2008).

Travellers stampeded train stations in their thousands as rail service resumed Friday [1 February] … The winter storm – China's worst in fifty years – has already been blamed for at least sixty-three deaths around the country, including at least twenty-five when a bus plunged off a slippery mountain road … For an estimated 200 million people the annual trek is sometimes the only opportunity to see family that they have left behind and the vast majority travel by train. This year the holiday begins 6 February.

(www.cnn.com, 1 February 2008)

Many of the worst effects have been in parts of east-central and southern China, which are largely unaccustomed to serious snowfall … As many as 100 million people have been directly affected … In the last week the government has worked as hard at public relations as at crisis management, with both of the country's top leaders travelling to some of the worst-affected areas. Prime minister Wen Jiabao, who has moved about China almost nonstop during this period, travelled early last week to the southern city of Guangzhou, where as many as 800,000 people had gathered at the train station at one point seeking to begin their annual leaves. President Hu Jintao travelled later in the week to a coal mine in northern Shaanxi province to encourage miners to redouble their efforts, including forgoing New Year celebrations, in order to spare the country's power grid from further brownouts. Hu, known for his circumspection in public, was quoted as saying he was unable to sleep because of the scale of the emergency … One migrant worker died Saturday [2 February], crushed as a crowd surged to board a train … According to some estimates, the country's coal reserves at power plants had dwindled to a historic low, with only a two-day supply remaining in many places … One of the worst-hit areas of the power emergency has been Chenzhou, a city of 4 million on Guangdong province's northern border, where many have gone without water, electricity, heating or commercial food supplies for ten days.

(www.iht.com, 3 February 2008)

The National Development and Reform Commission stated that certain previously closed mines would be allowed to reopen to meet demand … [raising] questions about whether the government was signalling that unsafe mines could be reopened. China has the world's most dangerous mines and the government has closed thousands of small ones since 2006 in an effort to reduce fatalities by consolidating the industry into more efficient operations. Last year [2007] the number of mining fatalities dropped by one-fifth to 3,786 deaths, still the highest figure in the world.

(*IHT*, 9 February 2008, p. 6)

Chenzhou, a city of 4 million in southern Hunan, has been without electricity for nine days … Wen Jiabao, China's premier, briefly visited Chenzhou on Saturday [2 February] … In the latest official estimate of the immediate impact of the weather, the government said the cost of damage was $7.5 billion.

(*FT*, 4 February 2008, p. 6)

Snow storms that have stranded millions of travellers are a 'severe disaster' that will continue for several days, top leaders have warned ... More snow is expected and heavy fog has also hit central provinces ... Residents of some central provinces have been without power and water for days.

(www.bbc.co.uk, 4 February 2008)

At Guangzhou train station Monday [4 February] authorities sought to control crowds with the vigour of a wartime military exercise after a young woman was trampled to death Friday [1 February] during a stampede by frantic travellers ... China's state-run Xinhua news agency said Friday that 95 per cent of rail traffic had 'returned to normal'. But Guangzhou's train station remained packed with a backlog of hundreds of thousands of travellers hoping to get home for the holiday ... The Lunar New Year starts Wednesday [6 February].

(www.cnn.com, 4 February 2008)

The head of the Chinese meteorological administration, Zheng Guoguang, said on 4 February that: 'In northern China we have quite a good emergency plan to cope with unusual weather conditions. But in southern parts of China the mechanism and emergency plan to cope with such weather needs to be improved.'

(www.bbc.co.uk, 4 February 2008)

Zheng Guoguang said the severe weather was a product of a periodic cooling of waters in the Pacific Ocean that has also brought unusually heavy snowfall to parts of the western United States ... Zheng Guoguang: 'This was a historic event. We did not foresee temperatures dropping so low.'

(www.iht.com, 4 February 2008)

China's main north–south national highway ... the Zhuhai–Beijing highway ... reopened Monday [4 February] after weeks of ice and snowstorms that throttled transport and disrupted fuel supplies during the country's peak holiday season ... Rail service was also slowly returning to normal ... Some areas have seen the worst winter storms in more than half a century, with ice and snow storms that began on 10 January causing power lines to snap and pylons to topple. Electric locomotives stopped on the tracks, forcing the cancellation of hundreds of trains, while parts of central China have been without electricity for ten days. While the weather has not been exceptionally harsh by northern standards, many temperate parts of the country have little experience in dealing with snow. Houses are poorly insulated and many communities lack snowploughs and other winter equipment ... On Monday [4 February] the police were dividing the huge crowd [in Guangzhou railway station] into groups ... As one group was allowed to enter the train station the other waves were allowed to advance further ... The new measures follow the crushing to death of a woman at the station on Saturday [2 February] ... Damage has been estimated at $7.5 billion.

(www.iht.com, 4 February 2008)

> Ice that formed on power lines was up to six times thicker than the cables had been designed to withstand ... The Chinese meteorological administration said Monday [4 February] that the weather was the coldest in 100 years in central Hubei and Hunan provinces ... [On 5 February] the central city of Chenzhou entered the twelfth day of a blackout ... The city remained almost entirely without power ... Power was temporarily restored to some parts of Chenzhou on Monday but failed again after just three hours.
>
> (www.iht.com, 5 February 2008)

'Hundreds of [coal] mines were kept running through the Lunar New Year holiday' (*IHT*, 12 February 2008, p. 12).

> [The] transport gridlock is easing as roads and railways are being cleared ... The Hunan Electric Power Company said that services would resume soon ... In Guangzhou, where numbers of stranded passengers were highest, the railway service is back to normal, and crowds at stations around the country are much reduced, according to Xinhua news agency.
>
> (www.bbc.co.uk, 6 February 2008)

'The World Bank says that China's railways carry 25 per cent of the world's railway traffic on just 6 per cent of its length' (*The Economist*, 16 February 2008, p. 30).

> Chenzhou, a city in the central province of Hunan and the worst hit, began its twelfth day without power on Wednesday [6 February] after a short-lived resumption ... The vice general manager of Hunan Electric Power said: 'Power supply will be restored gradually for citizens in Chenzhou starting today [6 February]' ... About 1,000 pylons and poles had collapsed under the weight of ice and snow, which means the local grid, which took decades to build, had effectively been destroyed, Xinhua said.
>
> (www.iht.com, 6 February 2008)

> On Wednesday [6 February], which was New Year's Eve, top leaders visited some of the areas hardest hit by the severe weather ... President Hu Jintao visited Guangxi in the south, while premier Wen Jiabao met residents in Jiangxi's province's Fuzhou city, where power has been out for twenty days ... Electricity [has been] restored in 162 of 170 worst hit counties ... But problems remain in many areas, including Chenzhou in Hunan province, where about half of the 4 million residents remain without electricity after nearly two weeks ... The weather is believed to have affected more than 100 million people and has so far caused $11 billion of damage. More than eighty people are thought to have been killed.
>
> (www.bbc.co.uk, 7 February 2008)

> China's mines could face a wave of accidents as collieries shut by the freezing weather resume operations, the country's top safety agency has warned. Many mines lost power and had to close because of snow that hit much of China in January and early February. They could face gas build-up, unstable

> power supply and flooding as they start up again, the State Administration of Work Safety said … Unusually severe blizzards hit large areas of central and southern China at the beginning of the year, blocking transport links and causing widespread chaos … [The safety agency said] more than 2,000 mines were facing problems. Gas had built up in about 1,800 mines in the provinces of Jiangxi, Hunan, Guizhou and Yunnan because of power cuts and another 600 mines had been flooded … On Sunday [17 February] the government said that power had been restored to some 23 million people – or almost 90 per cent of those who had been hit by blackouts during the winter weather. Direct economic losses from the snow and ice amounted to $15.4 billion, Xinhua news agency said.
>
> (www.bbc.co.uk, 18 February 2008)

> China will spend $9 billion to help farmers hit by brutal January snowstorms recover for spring planting, a state news agency said Friday [22 February] … The government last week promised $1.25 billion in aid to stricken areas to rebuild houses and help the poor pay for food and heat. Chinese banks have been ordered to lend more to help farmers recover. Xinhua said: 'The government is striving to give preferential policies to the farming sector, those who plant grain crops and industrial agricultural equipment will get direct subsidies on time.'
>
> (www.iht.com, 22 February 2008)

'[Some] 800,000 passengers at the Guangzhou train station [had been stranded]' (www.iht.com, 25 February 2008).

13 January 2008.

> Prime minister Manmohan Singh of India arrived in Beijing on Sunday [13 January] for a three-day visit to China … When President Hu Jintao visited India in 2006 the two countries pledged to double trade to $40 billion by 2010 – a goal they nearly reached last year [2007] and are likely to surpass this year [2008]. Both sides are expected to continue the trade this week. Singh is bringing a large business delegation and is keen to correct a trade imbalance that tips in China's favour.
>
> (www.iht.com, 13 January 2008)

> Their talks are expected to focus on territorial disputes and increasing bilateral trade, worth $37 billion … Manmohan Singh's trip to China [is] the first by an Indian prime minister in nearly five years … India's trade deficit with China has risen from around $4 billion to $9.6 billion since 2006.
>
> (www.bbc.co.uk, 13 January 2008)

> China and India have pledged to increase economic and military ties … Indian prime minister Manmohan Singh and Chinese prime minister Wen Jiabao signed a broad agreement to expand trade between their countries to $60 billion by 2010 … Trade between them has risen rapidly in recent years, reaching over $30 billion in 2007 … The leaders also agreed to co-operate

on further joint military exercises … [agreeing] to stage a second round of joint military exercises, following the first ever such manoeuvres in December 2007 … Prime minister Singh: 'Both sides reiterated their mutual commitment to maintaining peace and tranquillity in the border areas.'

(www.bbc.co.uk, 14 January 2008)

Both governments would work to create an environment for closer economic ties, Manmohan Singh said … 'This has to include creating a level playing field' [he said], citing the need for Chinese action on issues such as non-tariff barriers, intellectual property rights and for 'market-related' currency exchange rates … The value of Sino-Indian trade soared 56 per cent to $38.7 billion last year [2007], according to Chinese data … With a trade deficit it put at $9 billion last year, New Delhi is becoming more assertive in pushing China to act to balance trade … India's commerce and industry minister … [said] India was pushing for greater access to the Chinese markets for fruits and vegetables, aviation and entertainment products and for the removal of non-tariff barriers to pharmaceuticals.

(*FT*, 15 January 2008, p. 11)

On Monday [14 January] Indian prime minister Manmohan Singh signed a joint statement with the Chinese prime minister, Wen Jiabao, that focused on broad themes but also touched on a handful of specific issues. One potentially substantive section dealt with Indian aspirations for a permanent seat on the UN Security Council, an ambition some analysts say China has not encouraged. The document stated that: 'The Indian side reiterated its aspirations for permanent membership of the UN Security Council. The Chinese side understands and supports India's aspirations to play a greater role in the United Nations, including in the Security Council' … The joint agreement also called for new negotiations to begin a regional trade agreement.

(www.iht.com, 15 January 2008)

16 January 2008.

Tackling corrupt practices that have become widespread among Chinese officials will be a very tough task, President Hu Jintao has acknowledged. Addressing the problem would be a 'long-term, complicated and difficult struggle', he told the Communist Party's anti-corruption watchdog … Hu warned that the party's 'very survival' depended on how it tackled the issue … Mr Hu said that tackling corruption required stronger measures and a more resolute attitude. Better education and more checks and balance were needed, as well as tough punishments for corrupt officials … Hu Jintao: 'The party must seriously deal with major corruption cases that greatly infringe on public interests' … Earlier this month [January] Chinese authorities published a list of 'ten taboos' for officials, ahead of a provincial employment reshuffle, banning bribery, lobbying for promotion and dirty tricks.

(www.bbc.co.uk, 16 January 2008)

17 January 2008.

> An official obituary praised a late Communist Party city boss on Thursday [17 January] for 'maintaining stability' during the 1989 Tiananmen Square protests in a rare mention of a subject that remains taboo to this day. Publication of the obituary of Zhang Lichang, the former party boss of the port city of Tianjin [who died on 10 January] ... coincided with the third anniversary of the death of Zhao Ziyang. Zhao was toppled as national party chief in 1989 for opposing a decision by Deng Xiaoping, then paramount leader, to send in troops to crush the student-led protests. Hundreds, perhaps thousands, were killed. Families of victims and dissidents are kept under tight police surveillance and have had no success in petitioning the government to reverse the official verdict that the protests were 'counter-revolutionary' ... Zhang, who presided over the party in Tianjin for almost ten years until last March [2007], did not play a direct role in the crackdown in nearby Beijing on 3–4 June 1989. The obituary read: 'During the political disturbance that occurred when spring was changing into summer in 1989, he resolutely supported the Party Central's major decisions and policies ... [His efforts] maintained social stability and guaranteed the livelihood of city residents.'
>
> (www.iht.com, 17 January 2008)

18 January 2008. British prime minister Gordon Brown starts a three-day visit to China.

> Gordon Brown and prime minister Wen Jiabao agreed to increase trade between the two countries by 50 per cent by 2010 ... Trade between China and the UK was worth an estimated $40 billion (£20.2 billion) last year [2007] ... [The British prime minister] is being accompanied on the trip by more than twenty leading British and European business figures ... Mr Brown's five-day visit [to Asia] will also take him later this week to India [for a two-day visit].
>
> (www.bbc.co.uk, 18 January 2008)

> The two leaders agreed to expand trade to a value of $60 billion by 2010, compared with about $40 billion last year [2007] ... British prime minister Gordon Brown: 'Britain will welcome substantial new investment from China in our country in the years to come. We want Britain to be the number one destination of choice for Chinese business as it invests in the rest of the world. I believe by 2010 we will see new Chinese companies investing in the UK, we will see 100 partnerships between our universities and Chinese universities and we will double the number of firms listed on the London stock exchange and thousands of jobs will be created' ... Brown added that he welcomed investment from the huge Chinese sovereign wealth fund ... Britain has been the biggest EU investor in China over the past few years but it has been less successful than European rivals in exporting to China.
>
> (www.iht.com, 18 January 2008)

Gordon Brown urged China's new £100 billion sovereign wealth fund to use London as a hub for its international operations ... He hopes the China Investment Corporation (CIC) will soon open an office in London and told business leaders that it would be 'welcome' in Britain ... Wen Jiabao pledged that the fund would operate on 'a totally corporate basis, without intervention from the government' ... He said CIC would be 'entirely commercial' and 'transparent and open' ... [Gordon Brown] called on his hosts to lift restrictions on Chinese companies raising capital abroad and set a target of doubling to more than 100 the number of Chinese companies listed in London ... Mr Brown believes providing technical help to China to develop clean energy is more useful than hectoring Beijing to set carbon reduction targets.

(*FT*, 19 January 2008, p. 2)

[On 19 January] Gordon Brown arrived in Shanghai on the second day of his trip to China. The prime minister has been focusing on green issues – visiting a 'clean' power station outside Beijing before heading to Shanghai to see a new 'eco-city' ... the Dongtan eco-city outside the city ... The Taiyang Gong power station, fuelled by natural gas instead of coal, is the first of its kind in China and has been developed with the help of a UK firm ... Mr Brown has offered China £50 million to help the country tackle climate change.

(www.bbc.co.uk, 19 January 2008)

21 January 2008.

Germany and China agreed Monday [21 January] to heal a rift that opened after Beijing suspended most high level contacts to protest Chancellor Angela Merkel's meeting last year [2007] with the Dalai Lama and her human rights policies. The thaw was announced after it was confirmed that Frank-Walter Steinmeier, Germany's foreign minister, had secretly met with his Chinese counterpart, Yang Jiechi, late last year to pledge that Berlin fully supported the One China policy that stipulates that Tibet and Taiwan are part of China ... Yang is expected in Berlin on Tuesday [22 January] for a meeting of the foreign ministers of the five permanent UN Security Council members ... Merkel never challenged the One China policy, but in her talks with Chinese officials in Beijing last summer and her meeting in September with the Dalai Lama in Berlin, she stressed the importance of defending human rights, supporting non-governmental organizations and meeting dissidents ... Steinmeier, a Social Democrat, who was recently appointed Vice Chancellor, joined Germany's business community in assailing Merkel for her meeting with the Dalai Lama and her direct foreign policy style. They accused her of seeking publicity about her human rights policy at the expense of trade ... Merkel brushed aside the criticism, insisting that human rights and trade are 'two sides of the same coin' ... She said: 'I think that friendly relations can withstand differences of opinion.'

(www.iht.com, 21 January 2008)

25 January 2008.

> China has begun making payments to personnel involved in nuclear tests as part of its efforts to improve benefits for former military veterans ... China's minister of civil affairs, Li Xueju, said the government had begun paying 'subsidies' to nuclear test veterans last year [2007] in the first public acknowledgement of the new benefit ... Li said that the government paid 15.12 billion yuan, or $2.07 billion, last year to more than 8 million veterans and families of service personnel killed in combat or while performing public services, an increase of 34.8 per cent over outlays in 2006. This included payments to 'some military personnel and civilians' who took part in nuclear tests ... China conducted forty-five nuclear tests at its remote Lop Nur site in the western region of Xinjiang, twenty-three of these in the atmosphere, between 1964 and 1996, when it signed the Comprehensive Nuclear Test Ban Treaty ... In recent years Chinese military veterans and demobilized soldiers have been increasingly assertive in pressurizing the authorities for improved benefits, employment opportunities and retraining. Li said the government provided more than 1 billion yuan last year for housing for handicapped veterans and to assist former military personnel find civilian jobs.
>
> (www.iht.com, 27 January 2008)

5 February 2008. 'The World Bank named Justin Lin as its chief economist, the first time the post has gone to someone outside Europe and the United States. Taiwan-born Mr Lin defected to the mainland in 1979' (*FT*, 6 February 2008, p. 10.

11 February 2008.

> The United States yesterday [11 February] announced a series of arrests involving alleged spying by the Chinese government, including one where a Pentagon official was alleged to have helped Beijing obtain secret information ... The FBI arrested Gregg Bergersen, a Pentagon employee with top secret security clearances, on charges of handing over classified information about US weapons sales to Taiwan. In a separate case the justice department charged Chung Dongfan, a former Boeing employee, with economic sabotage involving US military programmes ... Mr Chung is a naturalized US citizen.
>
> (*FT*, 12 February 2008, p. 6)

'The FBI arrested Tai Shen Kuo, a Chinese-born New Orleans businessman, and Yu Xin Kang, also of New Orleans, along with Gregg Bergersen' (*The Times*, 12 February 2008, p. 28).

> Federal officials arrested a Defence Department official in Virginia on Monday [11 February] and charged him with passing to agents of China classified defence documents about Taiwan's arms purchases. About the same time officials arrested a former Boeing engineer in California on

> charges of economic espionage, specifically stealing trade secrets from Boeing about the space shuttle and other projects on behalf of the Chinese government. There was no direct connection between the arrests, but the Justice Department announced them together, which seemed to underline what officials described as continuing Chinese efforts to obtain commercial and military secrets ... Kenneth Wainstein (assistant attorney-general for national security): 'While there are entities from over a hundred different countries trying to get access to our secrets or our controlled technology, there are a number of countries that have proven themselves particularly determined and methodological in their espionage efforts. The People's Republic of China is one of those countries ... [Regarding China] in the last six months we have filed charges in a half-dozen cases involving efforts to acquire different types of [military] technology' ... The authorities charged Gregg Bergersen ... [with] receiving payments for providing information about the projected sales of weapons and military equipment to Taiwan. The court documents said he was befriended by Tai Shen Kuo of New Orleans, a Taiwanese native and naturalized American citizen who was working for the People's Republic of China ... Kuo [was] identified as a furniture salesman ... Kuo used an associate, Yu Xin Kang, to communicate with a Chinese government official ... The former Boeing engineer arrested Monday, Dongfan Chung, was indicted last week.
>
> (www.iht.com, 12 February 2008)

> Gregg Bergersen was charged with selling classified information about US military sales to Taiwan to a Taiwanese-born American citizen, Tai Shen Kuo. Kuo was charged with conspiracy to deliver defence information to the Chinese government. A Chinese citizen, Yu Xin Kang, was the third person charged in the case. Prosecutors allege that Kang was the conduit for passing the material to China. In a separate case a former Being engineer, Dongfan Chung, was charged with stealing secrets from the military contractor for the Chinese government ... German and British intelligence officials have also warned in recent months that China has intensified its clandestine efforts to collect military secrets and advanced technology.
>
> (www.iht.com, 14 February 2008)

('China denied Thursday [14 February] that it was conducting espionage operations in the United States': www.iht.com, 14 February 2008.)

('Gregg Bergersen ... pleaded guilty to delivering classified information about US and Taiwanese military relations to a New Orleans furniture salesman who turned out to be working with the Chinese government ... Prosecutors alleged he [Bergersen] divulged military secrets to a Louisiana businessman, Tai Kuo, who turned the information over to a Chinese foreign agent. In a plea hearing Monday [1 April] Bergersen pleaded guilty to a single count of conspiring to communicate national defence information to a person not entitled to receive it. He faces up to ten years in prison when sentenced in June. According to a statement of facts, Bergersen thought Kuo was aligned with the Taiwan ministry of defence. Bergersen was unaware, though, that Kuo maintained regular contact with a foreign official from Beijing, to whom Kuo was relaying the secret information': www.iht.com, 1 April 2008.)

12 February 2008. 'Taiwan said Tuesday [12 February] it was trying to ascertain whether an alleged Chinese spy arrested in the United States provided Beijing with information on the island's new air defence system' (www.iht.com, 12 February 2008).

'Taiwan's defence ministry said it was trying to establish whether Tai Shen Kuo had also spied on Taiwan' (*FT*, 13 February 2008, p. 8).

> Russia and China have proposed ... at a disarmament conference in Geneva ... a new international treaty to ban the use of weapons in outer space ... The draft treaty would prohibit the deployment of weapons in space and the use of threat of force against satellites or other craft ... The United States has long opposed being bound by such an agreement ... The 1967 Outer Space Treaty bans the stationing of weapons of mass destruction in space.
>
> (www.bbc.co.uk, 12 February 2008)

'The latest Russian–Chinese draft treaty to ban weapons in space ... would not cover ground- or sea-based weapons' (*IHT*, 19 February 2008, p. 6).

> [Russian] foreign minister Sergei Lavrov presented a joint Russian–Chinese draft of a treaty banning weapons in space Tuesday [12 February] to the United Nations Conference on Disarmament, calling for action from a body that has not produced an agreement since 1997 ... [namely] an arms control measure on chemical weapons ... Lavrov submitted a draft on 'the prevention of the placement of weapons in outer space, the threat or use of force against outer space objects'.
>
> (*IHT*, 13 February 2008, p. 3)

13 February 2008.

> US film director Steven Spielberg has withdrawn as artistic adviser at the 2008 Olympics in Beijing. In a statement he accused China of not doing enough to pressure Sudan to end the 'continuing human suffering' in the troubled western Darfur region. At least 200,000 people have been killed and 2 million forced from their homes in the five-year conflict. Beijing has not yet responded to the move, which correspondents say is its first big setback in staging the Games ... Mr Spielberg had been brought in as artistic adviser for the opening and closing ceremonies of the Games ... Earlier on Tuesday [13 February], as part of a 'Global Day of Action' focusing on Darfur, an open letter signed by Nobel Peace Prize laureates [including Archbishop Desmond Tutu and Elie Wiesel] and former Olympians was sent to China's president. Actress Mia Farrow signed the letter ... Sudan sells some two-thirds of its oil to Beijing ... Beijing sells weapons to the Sudanese government.
>
> (www.bbc.co.uk, 13 February 2008)

> Steven Spielberg said he had not signed his contract to serve as an artistic adviser to the Games' opening and closing ceremonies in hopes that dialogue with China would produce results … China buys two-thirds of the country's oil exports while selling the regime weapons.
>
> (www.iht.com, 13 February 2008)

> Movie director Steven Spielberg has said he is withdrawing as an artistic adviser … after almost a year of trying to prod President Hu Jintao to do more to try to end Sudan's attacks in the Darfur region … Spielberg had written to Hu about Darfur twice in the past two months … Steven Spielberg: 'Sudan's government bears the bulk of the responsibility for these ongoing crimes but the international community, and particularly China, should be doing more to end the continuing human suffering there. China's economic, military and diplomatic ties to the government of Sudan continue to provide it with the opportunity and obligation to press for change' … Spielberg has come under increasing pressure from activists working on Darfur, including a campaign by the actress Mia Farrow, to drop his association with the Beijing Olympics … Farrow [is] a good-will ambassador for Unicef who helped start a campaign last year [2007] to label the games in Beijing the 'Genocide Olympics'.
>
> (www.iht.com, 13 February 2008)

'Steven Spielberg had previously warned Beijing that he would withdraw unless it did more to distance itself from the violence [in Darfur]' (www.guardian.co.uk, 13 February 2008).

> Earlier this week a coalition of Hollywood stars, Nobel Peace Prize winners, politicians and athletes sent an open letter to President Hu Jintao calling on China to do more to ease the suffering in Darfur. The petition was delivered to the Chinese mission to the UN in New York by the actress Mia Farrow and other activists.
>
> (www.guardian.co.uk, 14 February 2008)

> [In the 1988 Seoul Olympic Games] the host nation, South Korea, displaced 720,000 residents to build facilities … According to an advocacy group, the Centre on Housing Rights and Evictions, China has more than doubled that figure to an estimated 1.5 million displaced for its Games.
>
> (www.iht.com, 13 April 2008)

17 February 2008.

> Russia has accused the United States of using a plan to shoot down a broken spy satellite as a cover for testing an anti-satellite weapon … Russia's defence ministry said the United States planned to test its 'anti-missile defence system's capacity to destroy other countries' satellites' … A Russian defence ministry statement said: 'Speculations about the danger of the satellite hide preparations for the classical testing of an anti-satellite weapon. Such testing essentially means the creation of a new type of stra-

> tegic weapon' ... [The United States] said that blowing the satellite up would disperse the hydrazine ... toxic fuel ... in space, leaving only small-scale satellite debris to fall harmlessly to earth.
>
> (www.bbc.co.uk, 17 February 2008)

18 February 2008.

> In response to a US plan to shoot down a malfunctioning satellite, China has warned against threats to security in outer space, without mentioning its own successful anti-satellite missile test last year ... [when in January 2007 it destroyed] a defunct weather satellite ... The Chinese government also stopped short of linking the planned US strike with Beijing's repeated calls for a complete ban on space weapons ... [The Chinese foreign ministry] said the government was highly concerned about the US plan ... noting the target satellite was loaded with toxic fuel ... The United States opposes treaties or other measures to restrict space weapons ... The United States shot down a satellite with a missile fired from a fighter aircraft in a 1985 test ... China has been devoting considerable resources to building and deploying its own communications, navigation and weather satellite in recent years. Some analysts have suggested that Beijing ultimately wants to deploy an independent navigation satellite constellation with similar capabilities as the Global Positioning network.
>
> (www.iht.com, 18 February 2008)

20 February 2008.

> A missile interceptor launched from a US Navy warship struck a dying American spy satellite orbiting 130 miles [210 kilometres] over the Pacific Ocean ... [It was] the first time an interceptor designed for missile defence was used to attack a satellite ... China objected to the strike on the satellite, warning that the action could threaten security in outer space.
>
> (*IHT*, 22 February 2008, p. 3)

'The satellite went out of control shortly after it was launched in December 2006' (www.bbc.co.uk, 22 February 2008).

24 February 2008.

> Pollution turned part of a major river system in central China red and foamy, forcing authorities to cut water supplies to as many as 200,000 people ... The Han River [is] a branch of the Yangtze ... The pollution was discovered Sunday [24 February] ... Tests showed the polluted waters contained elevated levels of ammonia, nitrogen and permanganate, a chemical used in metal cleaning, tanning and bleaching ... A paper mill dumped wastewater directly into the Han in September 2006, forcing authorities to cut water supplies for a week in some areas.
>
> (www.iht.com, 27 February 2007)

'Officials in Hubei initially blamed high levels of pollutants ... But last night [27 February] water supplies for most residents resumed, with the authorities saying non-toxic algae bloom due to weather changes was to blame' (*Guardian*, 28 February 2008, p. 24).

> The Chinese special envoy for Darfur has arrived in the Sudanese capital, Khartoum, for a five-day visit … Liu Guijin will travel to Darfur on Tuesday [26 February], the fifth anniversary of the start of the conflict which has left 200,000 people dead and 2.5 million homeless … Liu Guijin: 'What China is pursuing is to realize peace in Darfur as soon as possible and to help Sudan achieve stability and development as soon as possible. China's devotion to solving the Darfur issue is for the sake of peace rather than for expediency' … This week it [China] will provide $11 million of humanitarian assistance … Mr Liu told the BBC on Friday [22 February] that only 8 per cent of weapons imported by Sudan came from China in 2006 … Mr Liu also said he would co-operate on the deployment of the new UN–African Union peacekeeping force in Darfur. The UN mission to Darfur, Unamid, began deploying in January, but the force still lacks most of the 26,000 personnel planned for the mission.
>
> (www.bbc.co.uk, 24 February 2008)

26 February 2008.

> China has settled on a new leadership team for the finance industry, headed by Wang Qishan, an incoming vice premier with a strong track record in forcing through reforms in the banking and securities sector … [His] appointment as vice premier will be formalized at the annual session of the National People's Congress in early March, which will oversee the inauguration of a new government … Mr Wang is expected to maintain a stable set of regulators under him in the finance sector. Most important is the retention of Zhou Xiaochuan as the governor of the People's Bank of China, defying widespread speculation in recent months he would be shifted … He and the central bank appear to have got their way in recent months on one key issue, the currency, which has been strengthening at a faster rate, something the bank has long sought.
>
> (*FT*, 27 February 2007, p. 12)

3–4 March 2008.

> The Beijing Olympics [8–24 August], rising inflation and a plan to streamline the central government were highlighted Monday [3 March] as government goals at the opening of China's legislative season. More than 2,200 members of the Chinese People's Political Consultative Conference, the legislature's top non-Communist advisory body, gathered [in Beijing] … Party members account for only about 40 per cent of the conference's delegates, who are drawn from among businesspeople, religious figures, academics, celebrities and athletes.
>
> (www.iht.com, 3 March 2008)

> The Chinese military is increasingly developing capabilities, including counter space programmes, to conduct military operations beyond any con-

flict in the Taiwan Strait, the Pentagon said yesterday [3 March]. In its annual report on the Chinese military, the Pentagon said China appeared focused in the short term on Taiwan ... but added that the People's Liberation Army [PLA] was building a force of other operations unrelated to Taiwan ... The Pentagon and the PLA last week finally agreed to set up a telephone hot line.

(*FT*, 4 March 2008, p. 6)

China says it plans to increase military spending by nearly 18 per cent this year [2008] ... Japan's defence ministry said in a statement ... [that] this year's rise in military spending 'will mark the twentieth consecutive year that the Chinese military budget has increased by double digits' ... In an annual Pentagon report released hours before China's defence spending announcement, the United States highlighted particular concern over Chinese activities in both space and cyberspace ... The report said that China was developing weapons that would disable its enemies' space technology – such as satellites – in the event of a conflict ... In its report the Pentagon estimated that China's total military spending in 2007 was between $97 billion and $139 billion. Last month [February] the Bush administration requested $515 billion for the next fiscal year, not including extra spending for the wars in Iraq and Afghanistan ... There has recently been some progress in US–Chinese military relations, including the installation of a joint telephone hotline.

(www.bbc.co.uk, 4 March 2008)

China said Tuesday [4 March] that spending on its military this year [2008] will jump by 17.8 per cent compared with 2007. The increase follows a similar one last year [2007]. China has had double-digit increases in military spending every year since the early 1990s ... [China] said spending would total $59 billion in 2008 ... Other countries say ... the real figure could be three times as much as the publicly released figure. China has said spending grew 17.8 per cent during 2007, to nearly $45 billion. It was the largest annual increase in more than a decade. The 2007 figure put China roughly in the same neighbourhood as Japan, Russia and Britain in defence spending, although it is less than one-tenth of what the US military costs.

(www.iht.com, 4 March 2008)

[China's] 2.3 million-strong military [is] the world's biggest standing force. Foreign security experts in the United States and elsewhere say that Beijing's real defence spending is two or three times the announced figure ... In its annual report to Congress on the Chinese military, released Monday [3 March], the Pentagon said the international community had limited knowledge of the motivation behind China's accelerating build-up and the capabilities it was developing ... China and the United States agreed last Friday [29 February] to set up a telephone hot line between the two militaries ... By November 2007 the Chinese military had deployed about

> 1,000 short-range missiles opposite Taiwan and was adding 200 missiles to this force each year, it [the Pentagon report] said.
>
> (www.iht.com, 4 March 2008)

5 March 2008. The National People's Congress begins its 11-day session. '[In attendance are] 2,987 congress delegates' (*FT*, 6 March 2008, p. 8).

Prime minister Wen Jiabao (opening address):

> The current price hikes and increasing inflationary pressures are the biggest concern of the people ... Governments at all levels must give high priority to keeping prices stable because price stability has a direct bearing on the quality of people's lives ... Last year's price increases are still exerting a fairly strong influence and quite a few factors are creating inflationary pressure. We have to take into consideration the ability of individuals, enterprises and all sectors of society to tolerate price increases ... [The government will try to keep consumer price inflation in 2008 to] around 4.8 per cent ... The primary task for macroeconomic regulation this year [2008] is to prevent fast economic growth from becoming overheated growth and keep the structural price increases from turning into significant inflation ... [The government will prevent valuable farmland being used for construction and control the amount of grain exported].
>
> (www.iht.com, 5 March 2008; www.bbc.co.uk, 5 March 2008; *FT*, 6 March 2008, p. 8).

> Prime minister Wen Jiabao ... said China would improve its exchange rate protocol and make it more flexible ... Wen said Beijing would continue efforts to rebuild the education and health infrastructure. He said compulsory education would be free for all students in rural and urban areas. He said tuition in urban schools would be waived beginning this fall. He also said the government would continue expanding basic medical coverage for urban workers. Expectations have been focused on proposals to restructure the government bureaucracy, by creating super-ministries intended to allow Beijing greater control in deciding and implementing policies. Wen equated administrative restructuring with political reform and described a plan that 'explores ways to establish larger departments that organically integrate' smaller bureaucracies. He offered no details but said a plan would be presented to the legislative session.
>
> (www.iht.com, 5 March 2008)

'No major pieces of legislation are pending this year because the Communist Party is also focused on preparing to play host to the Summer Olympics in Beijing in August' (*IHT*, 6 March 2008, p. 5).

> Prime minister Wen Jiabao laid out a government reform agenda that combined efforts to tame prices and a 'prudent' fiscal policy with more generous spending on health and social sectors. Education spending alone will rise 45 per cent this year [2008] ... But the premier said the political priority was to

tame consumer price inflation ... Subsidies for the poor would be increased and provincial governors and mayors held responsible for ensuring basic food supplies ... Mr Wen set a new routine annual 'target' of 8 per cent expansion in GDP.

(*FT*, 6 March 2008, p. 8)

7 March 2008.

China has expressed 'grave concerns' to the Sudanese government about the violence in western Darfur and is actively working to resolve delays in establishing an international peacekeeping force to Darfur, China's special envoy to Darfur said Friday [7 March] Liu Guijin recently returned home from his fourth visit to Sudan ... He also expressed surprise at the film director Steven Spielberg's public withdrawal as artistic director of the Beijing Olympics last month [February] because he said the relationship had effectively ended months earlier. Liu said he and Spielberg had met for an hour in September [2007] in New York. He said Spielberg had missed the deadline to sign a formal contract and so he told the director that he assumed this meant that any professional ties were severed. He said he did not try to convince Spielberg to change his mind ... He said he was surprised when Spielberg announced that he had resigned from the post because he said he had never formally held it.

(www.iht.com, 7 March 2008)

A spokesman for Steven Spielberg said that Spielberg had left his contract unsigned during the time he was working as an artistic adviser, a point that he said was made clear when Spielberg withdrew from his position last month [February] ... [The spokesman] insisted that this had never diminished his role and that he had still been working as an artistic adviser until he stepped down ... China, like Iran, Russia and others, sells weapons to Sudan ... While China says it abides by a United Nations embargo on sending weapons directly to Darfur, a panel of United Nations experts found that Chinese weapons were making their way to Darfur. Liu said that China could not control what happened to weapons that were legally sold to the Sudanese government but might end up in the hands of janjaweed militias.

(*IHT*, 8 March 2008, p. 5)

9 March 2008.

China is facing a very severe unemployment problem, says labour minister Tian Chengping. He said 20 million new workers entered the labour market each year, chasing only 12 million jobs. He said employers were complaining about a lack of skilled workers and China had to provide more training. Speaking on the sidelines of the annual National People's Congress in Beijing, Mr Tian said the aim was to keep urban unemployment at or below 4.5 per cent. China is aiming to create 10 million new jobs this year [2008] and find work for 5 million sacked workers, he added ... The authorities

> also face pressure from large numbers of university graduates entering the labour market. Some employers have said new labour legislation is worsening the problem … The new legislation makes it easier for workers to obtain continuing contracts and also requires companies to contribute more to pension and insurance funds.
>
> (www.bbc.co.uk, 9 March 2008)

'The new law mandates contracts for all employees, open-ended contracts for long-term employees, and health insurance and other benefits. Unlike past labour laws, it provides more channels for workers to bring complaints against employers' (*FEER*, March 2008, p. 32).

10 March 2008.

> One of the world's top long-distance runners has said he will not compete in the marathon at the Beijing Olympics because China's air pollution would pose an unacceptable risk to his health and future career … The world record holder, Haile Gebrselassie of Ethiopia, said he still intended to participate in the 10,000 metres … [He] suffers from asthma.
>
> (*Independent*, 11 March 2008, p. 36)

11 March 2008.

> China announced Tuesday [11 March] that it would reorganize the central government by creating five so-called 'super ministries', including one charged with improving environmental protection. But the plan stopped short of creating a single agency to oversee the contentious issue of energy policy. The plan submitted Tuesday during the annual session of the National People's Congress is intended to streamline an overlapping array of government agencies, commissions and ministries around core issues like [the following]: environmental protection; social services; housing and construction; transportation; and industry and information … Chinese state media quickly framed the plan, which is expected to be endorsed this week by the legislature, as a major bureaucratic reform that would improve implementation of national policies … China's economy is still heavily shaped by the government's central planning agency, the National Development and Reform Commission. Some analysts had argued that the government could become more efficient by stripping away some of the commission's responsibilities, including over energy policy. Speculation had centred on whether an independent ministry would be established. But the new plan divides authority over energy. A new 'high level' energy commission would develop national energy strategies. But an energy bureau under the central planning agency would control administration and oversight of the energy sector … The central planning agency would no longer have final approval on major construction projects … The expanded ministry over transportation would oversee civil aviation and urban road transportation but would not include the current railway ministry, which lobbied strenuously to

remain autonomous ... [There is a] new environment ministry ... Environmentalists have complained that the State Environmental Protection Administration was easily steamrollered in bureaucratic turf battles because it did not rank as a full government agency. The new plan elevates the agency to ministry status ... Yet it is unclear if this new status will also include an expanded budget for more staff to carry out regulatory policies. Currently the agency has only a few hundred employees to co-ordinate and regulate environmental protection ... Xie Zhenhua, vice chairman of the National Development and Reform Commission, said the country was steadily lowering its energy usage but still not meeting the target of annual 4 per cent reductions. Last year [2007] China's energy consumption per unit of GDP dropped by 3.27 per cent ... [China's has a] five-year goal of reducing energy usage per unit of GDP by 20 per cent by 2010.

(www.iht.com, 11 March 2008; *IHT*, 12 March 2008, p. 4)

China has announced five new 'super ministries' as part of an effort to streamline a bloated bureaucracy and clarify conflicting responsibilities that stymie top-level decision-making ... Plans to create a new energy ministry have been put off because of strong opposition from influential state companies in the oil and power sectors. A new 'energy commission' will be established but it will report through the National Development and Reform Commission [NDRC], the chief economic co-ordination body, which already has overall responsibility for energy issues. But the NDRC, which contains the remnants of China's old 'planned economy' functions, lost out elsewhere, with local authorities taking some investment approval decisions away from the central agency ... The super ministries will eventually lay the ground for further reforms to separate policymaking and regulatory functions, and also force government agencies out of business ... The reorganization includes the creation of a potentially powerful new ministry with responsibility for general industrial policy and development of the IT sector. The new body, to be called the Ministry of Industry and Informatization, will absorb the current Ministry of Information Industry (MII), parts of the NDRC and most of the Commission of Science, Technology and Industry for National Defence (Costind) ... The ministry will retain the MII's dual role as both policymaker and regulator for the telecoms sector ... [There was] a similar ministerial shake-up in 1998 ... The reform announced yesterday [11 March] is the sixth such administrative restructuring since 1982, when the number of ministries under the State Council, or cabinet, was cut from 100 to sixty-one ... After the latest shake-up there are now twenty-seven ministries under the State Council.

(*FT*, 12 March 2008, p. 10)

[There was] a long-mooted reordering of the central government's structure, folding separate bureaucracies into five 'super ministries'. Human Resources and Social Security, for example, are now one ministry, as are Housing and Construction. The former Environmental Protection Agency was upgraded to ministerial status and a new National Energy Commission was established. The Ministry of Health, as expected, was handed oversight of food and drug safety ... Comparably ambitious reorderings have been undertaken half a dozen times over the past two decades only to bog down in the inertia and turf battles they were meant to overcome.

(*The Economist*, 22 March 2008, p. 74)

15 March 2008.

Hu Jintao has been elected for another five-year term as president, after a near-unanimous vote in the National People's Congress. The Congress also voted to elect Mr Hu as chairman of China's Central Military Commission ... Xi Jinping won election as vice president ... He has been given the high profile job of masterminding China's preparations for the Olympics.

(www.bbc.co.uk, 15 March 2008)

16 March 2008. 'The European Parliament ... has sold its share in PetroChina/CNPC ... a firm accused of being one of the chief bankrollers of the Sudanese government. The move follows revelations that MEPs' pension funds continued to be invested in the company' (*Independent*, 17 March 2008, p. 22).

17 March 2008.

Chinese legislators appointed new officials Monday [17 March], the second-to-last day of their annual session. The four vice premiers picked included Li Keqiang ... Hu Jintao and Wen Jiabao were earlier appointed to their second five-year terms by the session. Other appointments approved by the 2,987 members of the National People's Congress included top officials overseeing foreign trade and overseas relations, as well as governor of the People's Bank of China ... The delegates also approved the appointment of Ma Kai, Dai Bingguo, Liang Guanglie and Meng Jianzhu as state councillors, or members of the government cabinet. Meng, sixty, is also minister of public security in charge of the police, while Liang, sixty-seven, is the minister of defence ... The appointments are the largest reorganization of China's government ranks since 2003, as Wen and Hu prepare to hand over the reins of power to a generation of younger leaders. Nearly 60 per cent, or twenty-two, of the cabinet's thirty-seven positions, were new appointments ... Li Shenglin was named the minister of communications and transportation, responsible for highways and civil aviation. Zhou Shengxian was named as leader of a new Ministry of Environmental Protection.

(www.iht.com, 17 March 2008)

18 March 2008.

On the issue of whether he would sacrifice economic output to bring down inflation, at the risk of increasing unemployment, prime minister Wen Jiabao indicated that growth remained the overarching priority ... Wen Jiabao: 'We must ensure that our economy will grow ... in order to ensure employment. China is a developing country with 1.3 billion people. We

> have to maintain a certain degree of fast economic growth to provide enough jobs' ... He said China needed to add about 10 million jobs a year for the next five years, a lower figure than in the past when the aim was growth of 15 million to 20 million jobs a year.
>
> (*FT*, 19 March 2008, p. 10)

Wen Jiabao: 'As long as we come up with appropriate policies and effective measures, we are fully confident that we can control the situation of excessive price rises' (*IHT*, 20 March 2008, p. 13).

25 March 2008.

> A Chinese-born engineer found guilty last year [2007] of conspiring to export sensitive US defence technology to China has been jailed for 24.5 years. The court in California had also convicted Chi Mak, sixty-seven, of acting as a foreign agent and of making false statements to federal agents ... Mak [is] a naturalized US citizen ... He was not formally charged with espionage as the information was not officially deemed to be classified.
>
> (www.bbc.co.uk, 25 March 2008)

11 April 2008.

> The former Communist Party chief in Shanghai has been sentenced to eighteen years in jail ... Chen Liangyu [was] found guilty of taking bribes and abusing his position ... He was ousted from office two years ago after being accused of misusing a multi-million dollar pension fund. He is the most senior Chinese official to be convicted of corruption in more than a decade ... Chen was found guilty of offering illegal loans to favoured businessmen. He was also found to have taken bribes ... In 1998 Beijing mayor Chen Xitong was jailed for corruption. In 2000 scores of officials were implicated in a smuggling scandal in Xiamen. In 2001 the mayor of Shenyang and his deputy were sentenced to death for land deals.
>
> (www.bbc.co.uk, 11 April 2008)

> Chen Liangyu, who before his arrest in late [September] 2006 as also a member of the country's ruling Politburo, is the highest ranking government official to be stripped of power in more than a decade ... The pension fund scandal rocked Shanghai in late 2006 and early 2007, leading to the arrests of a group of powerful politicians and businessmen, including Zhang Rogkun, once one of the country's wealthiest men. Zhang was sentenced earlier this month [April] to nineteen years in prison for stock manipulation, financial fraud and his role in the city pension fund scandal. Prosecutors said Chen had helped Zhang acquire land and other holdings by illegally lending him money from the city's pension fund ... Last October [2007] Chen was stripped of his Communist Party post ... Chen had served in various city posts, including vice mayor, mayor and Shanghai party secretary, the highest position. The government said he was guilty of accepting $300,000 in bribes.
>
> (www.iht.com, 11 April 2008)

20 April 2008.

> Police opened fire on about 100 villagers, killing one ... in a remote south-western village after protests against land seizures ... The unrest was sparked when farmers in Saixi village in Yunnan province staged a demonstration on Sunday [20 April] to protest against the construction of a tungsten mine ... The Ziling Mining Group went ahead with the work despite a failure to agree on compensation. The local government, in a rare move, released the news that lethal force had been used to quash the protests and said that warning shots were fired initially. Officers of the People's Armed Police, a paramilitary force with the task of maintaining domestic order, had been brought in by the state-owned mining company to contain the protests, the Chinese Human Rights Defenders network said.
>
> (*The Times*, 23 April 2008, p. 35)

> New visa restrictions are causing mounting anxiety among the 250,000 foreign citizens who have settled in the capital in recent years. The rules, which were introduced last week with no warning and little explanation, limit new visas to thirty days, making it difficult, if not impossible, for long-term residents to hold down jobs and maintain uncomplicated lives. The restrictions are also infuriating business leaders in Hong Kong who have become used to crossing the border with ease ... [e.g.] the president of the American Chamber of Commerce in Hong Kong ... Residents who in the past could easily extend year-long tourist or business visas have been instructed to reapply at Chinese embassies in their home countries; even if their applications are approved officials are only giving out thirty-day visas ... In the past few years China has had a fairly lax attitude toward foreign residents, many of whom live and hold down jobs without proper work visas.
>
> (*IHT*, 24 April 2008, p. 4)

> A crucial issue facing thousands of foreign businessmen based in Hong Kong [is] the pre-Olympic refusal of Beijing to issue multiple re-entry visas. The issue is of major concern to the foreign chambers of commerce whose members must cross the border frequently to meet suppliers and visit factories.
>
> (www.iht.com, 1 May 2008)

30 April 2008.

> Police have rescued more than 100 village children sold to work as slave labourers in the booming southern province of Guangdong. The children, from the ethnic Yi minority, came from poor families in Sichuan about 600 miles (960 kilometres) away. The *China Daily* said 167 children had been rescued from the factory in the industrial city of Dongguan so far and several arrests have been made ... According to unconfirmed media reports, there may be more than 1,000 child labourers in at least one city in southern China. Local newspapers said ... that two of the rescued girls appeared

reluctant to leave because of the hardships of their home village. Hong Kong's *Wei Po* paper reported that 107 boys and sixty girls had been taken into care by police.

(www.bbc.co.uk, 30 April 2008)

China said Wednesday [30 April] that it was investigating whether hundreds or perhaps thousands of children from poor areas in the south-west part of the country were sold to work as slave labourers in booming coastal factory cities. Authorities in southern Guangdong province, near Hong Kong, said they had 'rescued' over 100 children from factories in the city of Dongguan, a huge manufacturing centre known for producing and exporting toys, textiles and electronics. The children, mostly between the ages of thirteen and fifteen, were often tricked or kidnapped by employment agencies working in an impoverished part of western Sichuan province and then sent to factory towns in Guangdong, where they were often forced to work as much as 300 hours a month for little money … The authorities in southern China said Wednesday that they had arrested several people involved in the case and that they were now trying to determine the identities of the children … China said Wednesday that it had broken up a child labour ring that provided children from poor, inland areas with work in booming coastal cities, acknowledging that severe labour abuses extended into the heart of its export economy … The child labour scandal, which was uncovered by *Southern Metropolis*, a crusading newspaper based in Guangzhou, in southern China, comes less than a year after the authorities said they had rescued hundreds of people, including children, from working as 'slave labourers' in brick kilns in the north and central part of the country … [This] earlier case, which local officials initially sought to keep quiet, set off a national uproar … Local officials in Guangdong may have moved quickly to acknowledge the latest incident to keep it from becoming a running scandal as the Olympics approach … The newspaper alleged that when the children were paid they received about 3 renminbi per hour, or about 42 cents, far below the local minimum wage of about 64 cents an hour … By law overtime pay is much higher … *Southern Metropolis* said some children were threatened with death if they tried to escape … Young people can legally go to work at age sixteen … The newspaper did not identify the coastal factories where the children worked, but the report said that one was a toy factory in Dongguan … Hu Xingdou (Beijing Institute of Technology): 'The Liangshan child labour case is quite typical. China's economy is developing at a fascinating speed, but often at the expense of laws, human rights and environmental protection. Most of the work force comes from underdeveloped or poverty stricken areas. Some children are even sold by their parents, who often do not have any idea of the working conditions' … Last August [2007] Beijing revoked the licence of a factory accused of using child labour to produce Olympic merchandise.

(www.iht.com, 30 April 2008 and 1 May 2008; *IHT*, 2 May 2008, p. 12)

4 May 2008.

> This weekend China will be commemorating an event seen as pivotal in its long revolution – the protests on 4 May 1919 against the humiliation of China by the Versailles Treaty, which bequeathed German 'concessions' in China to Japan. The Communist Party had roots in that movement.
>
> (*The Economist*, 3 May 2008, p. 17)

6 May 2008.

> President Hu Jintao has begun a five-day state visit to Japan, the first such trip in a decade ... Mr Hu's visit will be the longest he has made to a single country ... China has overtaken the United States as Japan's top trading partner, with bilateral trade increasing 12 per cent last year [2007] to $236.6 billion.
>
> (www.bbc.co.uk, 6 May 2008)

> Before President Hu Jintao's arrival [in Japan] about 500 people protested in Tokyo. Some of the demonstrators held banners calling for a 'Free Tibet'. There were no reports of arrests. More protesters scuffled with the police outside of the French restaurant where President Hu Jintao and prime minister Yasuo Fukuda dined Tuesday night [6 May] ... Ties between the two nations were strained in 1998 when President Jiang Zemin travelled to Tokyo expecting an apology over Japan's 1931–45 occupation of much of China. Rebuffed, Jiang lectured Japanese politicians about China's historical grievances ... Ling Ling, the beloved twenty-two-year-old giant panda at Tokyo's largest zoo and a symbol of friendship with China, died last week of heart failure.
>
> (www.iht.com, 6 May 2008)

> Hu Jintao [is] the first Chinese president to visit Japan since Jiang Zemin in 1998 ... As Hu arrived hundreds of demonstrators in Japan marched against China's policy in Tibet and thousands of riot police were mobilized to ensure his safety.
>
> (www.iht.com, 7 May 2008)

> Hundreds of marchers carrying 'Free Tibet' banners did take to the streets before Hu's visit and Japanese right-wing groups circled the capital in convoys of black trucks with Rising Sun flags and loudspeakers blaring martial music, but no arrests were reported.
>
> (www.iht.com, 7 May 2008)

'[Hu Jintao's] arrival was greeted by ... pro-Tibetan activists and members of the Japanese far right' (*Guardian*, 7 May 2008, p. 22).

> On Tuesday [6 May] Hu Jintao began a state visit, the first trip to Japan by a Chinese president in a decade; at five days it will also be the longest for Mr Hu ... The two countries' militaries have embarked on measures to improve confidence, including port visits by naval ships. Elsewhere diplomats point

> to the way a food scare in Japan involving tainted Chinese dumplings was handled calmly by the authorities on both sides, even as hysteria was whipped up by Japan's mass media ... The temperature began to plunge in 1998, with the visit to Japan – the first ever by a Chinese head of state – of Mr Hu's predecessor, Jiang Zemin. Mr Jiang had come demanding a fulsome written apology for Japan's wartime past, yet as he delivered hectoring lectures on the subject the apology never came.
>
> (www.economist.com, 6 May 2008)

> China acknowledged for the first time Tuesday [6 May] that it is tightening its visa policies ahead of the Olympic Games ... The policies ... a foreign ministry spokesman said ... would 'be maintained for a period of time' ... Travel agents in Hong Kong, a major gateway to mainland China, reported last month [April] that the government visa office told them multiple-entry business visas would not be available from mid-April until mid-October. In the past such visas were easily obtainable ... However ... the foreign ministry spokesman ... said it was not true all multiple-entry visas had been suspended ... More rules including additional documentation for business visas and hotel bookings and plane tickets for tourist visas have also been reported ... Both the American and European chambers of commerce in Hong Kong sent letters to the Chinese government last month, citing several cases of visa denials and raising concerns over the impact on businesses.
>
> (www.iht.com, 6 May 2008)

7 May 2008.

> Hu Jintao [7 May]: 'We hope that the Dalai will express his sincerity through his acts. We hope the Dalai will stop acting to separate the homeland, stop orchestrating the inciting of violent acts and stop undermining the Beijing Olympics, so as to create the conditions for further discussions. We hope that the contacts will have a positive result' ... China says twenty-two people died in the riots in Lhasa in Tibet, while overseas Tibet supporters say many times that number died in protests and a subsequent crackdown.
>
> (www.iht.com, 7 May 2008)

'Prime minister Yasuo Fukuda said that during the talks he urged the Chinese leader to address world concerns about the situation in Tibet ... He also praised Beijing's decision to meet with representatives of the Dalai Lama' (*IHT*, 8 May 2008, p. 5).

> [Fukuda spoke] frankly about Tibet last month [April] with the Chinese foreign minister, Yang Jiechi, who was in Tokyo to prepare for Hu's visit ... According to a Japanese foreign ministry statement: 'Prime minister Fukuda stated that there was a need to face up to the reality that the matter has become an international issue' ... In a meeting with the Japanese foreign minister, Masahiko Komakura ... the *Mainichi Shimbun* newspaper reported [that] ... Yang countered with a warning over Tibet: 'If you say anything

further on this matter, it will consist of an infringement on our domestic affairs' … To this, Komakura replied: 'I am annoyed to be told of an infringement on domestic matters while I am advising you as a friend' … [In China] the editor of *Southern Metropolis Weekly* … was fired for reflecting on the lack of honesty in Chinese reporting on Tibet.

(www.iht.com, 8 May 2008)

Prime minister Yasuo Fukuda said Beijing's hosting of the Olympics is much like Tokyo's hosting of the 1964 games, which he said marked Japan's emergence on the world stage after its defeat in World War II. Fukuda, however, said he had not decided whether to attend the opening ceremony … Hu said Beijing is willing to loan Tokyo a pair of pandas. The twenty-two-year-old giant panda Ling Ling recently died at Tokyo's largest zoo.

(www.iht.com, 7 May 2008)

China and Japan signed a historic deal agreeing a 'new starting point' in relations after summit talks in Tokyo … A joint statement after the summit read: 'The two nations agreed that Japan and China both share larger responsibilities for the world's peace and development in the 21st century. Leaders of the two states will develop ways for regular exchanges, with one leader visiting the other in principle every year.'

(www.bbc.co.uk, 7 May 2008)

'Yasuo Fukuda … has long criticized politicians' visits to Yaskuni … the Tokyo shrine that honours not just Japan's war dead but also executed war criminals … and believes that good relations with Japan's Asian nations are paramount' (*The Economist*, 10 May 2008, p. 80).

8 May 2008.

President Hu Jintao … urged the two Asian powers to look to the future as partners instead of rivals, but [there were] protests outside the venue where he was speaking. As Hu spoke about 200 protesters waved signs outside the university gate saying 'Free Tibet' and 'No Pandas, No Poison Dumplings' … About fifty Chinese students held their own rally … [calling, among other things, for] 'Sino-Japanese Friendship'.

(www.iht.com, 8 May 2008)

The earthquake of 12 May 2008

A powerful earthquake struck western China on Monday [12 May] … the country's worst natural disaster in three decades … The quake was China's biggest natural disaster since another earthquake levelled the city of Tangshan in 1976, leaving 240,000 people dead and posing a severe challenge to the Communist Party, which initially tried to cover up the catastrophe … The powerful initial quake struck at 2.28 p.m. near Wechuan country … The relatively vigorous flow of information and the fast response from top officials and rescue workers stood in stark contrast to the way China handled the Tangshan earthquake.

(www.iht.com, 13 May 2008)

The 7.8 magnitude earthquake hit Sichuan province on Monday afternoon ... [In] the Tangshan earthquake of 1976 more than 240,000 people died ... Tangshan [is] more than 110 kilometres from Beijing ... Many of China's biggest cities are in high risk earthquake zones.

(*IHT*, 13 May 2008, pp. 1, 8)

Prime minister Wen Jiabao flew to Sichuan hours after the earthquake struck ... Local leaders may also face intense scrutiny of their compliance with building codes. Since the Tangshan earthquake China has required that new structures withstand major quakes. But the collapse of schools, hospitals and factories in several different areas around Sichuan may raise questions about how rigorously such codes have been enforced during China's recent, epic building boom.

(www.iht.com, 13 May 2008)

'Wen Jiabao ... jumped on a jet bound for Sichuan province less than two hours after the earthquake struck' (www.iht.com, 21 May 2008). 'Several parents wanted an investigation into the construction quality of school buildings in Dujiangyan. They say six schoolhouses collapsed in the city, even as other government buildings remain standing' (www.iht.com, 15 May 2008). 'An earthquake struck the north-eastern city of Tangshan, killing at least 240,000 people – a quarter of its population – in one of the deadliest natural disasters in modern history' (www.iht.com, 16 May 2008).

The 7.8 magnitude quake struck on Monday [12 May] at 14.28 local time and was felt as far away as Beijing and the Thai capital Bangkok ... [Chemical plants and schools were among the buildings that collapsed] ... Several strong aftershocks have been reported since the quake, China's worst since 1976 when 242,000 people were killed in Tangshan ... [The BBC's correspondent said] it was one of the most open and speedy responses to an emergency ever seen from Chinese state media.

(www.bbc.co.uk, 13 May 2008)

'China's worst earthquake in thirty years ... [struck] south-western Sichuan province ... The earthquake was the most deadly since 1976 when a tremor levelled the northern city of Tangshan, killing at least 270,500 people' (*FT*, 13 May 2008, p. 7). 'The devastating 1976 tremor in the north-eastern city of Tangshan killed up to 300,000 people' (www.ft.com, 16 May 2008). ('The 1976 earthquake in the north-eastern city of Tangshan killed up to 300,000 people': www.independent.co.uk, 18 May 2008.)

The last major earthquake in the region occurred in the north-western margin of the Sichuan basin when a 7.5 magnitude quake killed more than

> 9,300 on 25 August 1933 … An earthquake with 7.5 magnitude struck the northern city of Tangshan in 1976, killing 255,000 people – the greatest death toll from an earthquake in the last four centuries and the second greatest in recorded history Tangshan is roughly 995 miles (1,600 kilometres) from Chengdu, the nearest major city to the epicentre of Monday's quake. Monday's quake shook the ground in Beijing, 950 miles (1,528 kilometres) away. At least seven more earthquakes – with magnitude between 4.0 and 6.0 – were recorded nearby during the four hours after the initial quake.
>
> (www.cnn.com, 13 May 2008)

> The quake struck at 14.28 local time on Monday [12 May], when children were at school and many workers were in their offices and factories. The epicentre was in Wenchuan county, some 90 kilometres north-west of the provincial capital of Chengdu. Measured at a magnitude of 7.8 by Chinese authorities and at 7.9 by the United States Geological Survey … rattled tall buildings in many of China's largest cities, including Beijing and Shanghai, several hundred kilometres away. Tremors registering at a magnitude of 3.9 were felt in Beijing … Prime minister Wen Jiabao flew to Sichuan within hours of the earthquake … Officials were quick to report that the city's dozens of Olympic venues were built to withstand earthquakes and that none had suffered damage. Authorities also said that no damage was observed at the massive Three Gorges Dam, located on the Yangtze River, several hundred kilometres east of the epicentre … But with so many other buildings collapsing particular scrutiny may fall on China's system for setting and enforcing construction codes in earthquake-prone zones such as Sichuan … China has moved quickly to mobilize, but has yet to respond to offers of foreign aid.
>
> (www.economist.com, 13 May 2008)

> Mr Wen has remained at the scene to direct relief operations … Some residents are angry, but their resentment is directed at local officials rather than the central government … Even the state-owned media have said shoddy construction may have exacerbated the impact … The Chinese media note that the government's decision to allow prompt coverage follows the implementation on 1 May of new rules on 'government information transparency'. Under these rules the authorities are supposed to make public any information involving the 'vital interests of citizens' … The regulations still allow information to be withheld if it relates to 'state secrets'.
>
> (*The Economist*, 17 May 2008, pp. 71–2)

'The Tangshan earthquake of 1976 … left an estimated 250,000 dead' (www.feer.com, 13 May 2008).

> Premier Wen Jiabao, a geologist by training, was at the scene of the earthquake in Dujiangyan, fifteen miles from the epicentre, within six hours. It took President George W. Bush four days (approximately ninety-six hours) to visit the devastation of Hurricane Katrina … The 1976 Tangshan earth-

quake claimed 240,000 lives ... Geologist Yang Yong ... [claims] that China's construction of numerous dams in the region destabilized the fault line and directly led to the earthquake.

(www.feer.com, 14 May 2008)

Western governments and aid agencies offering to send teams of rescue workers to China were rebuffed yesterday [13 May] by a senior Chinese official. The head of China's civil affairs ministry said that foreigners would not be allowed into the country because travel conditions were too difficult in the Sichuan region. Wang Zhenyao (head of the ministry's relief department): 'Transportation in affected areas is obstructed and it is impossible for our rescue teams to reach the disaster-hit areas. So the conditions are not yet ripe for us to allow international teams into China.'

(*The Times*, 14 May 2008, p. 9)

'Beijing politely rebuffed offers of help on Tuesday [13 May] from international earthquake rescue teams, saying conditions were "not yet right" to let them travel to the disaster area' (www.ft.com, 14 May 2008).

Wang Zhenyao [the civil affairs ministry's top relief official]: 'We welcome funds and supplies. We cannot accommodate personnel at this point' ... Soldiers and medics spent the day [13 May] clambering over landslides and the remnants of a mountain highway before breaking through to Wenchuan, a city of 100,000 and the epicentre of the quake.

(www.iht.com, 14 May 2008)

[China decided] Tuesday [13 May] to downscale the [Olympic] torch's route through quake-battered Sichuan ... China will observe one minute's silence at the start of each day of the Olympic torch relay ... The one minute will start on Wednesday [14 May] in Ruijin, with the celebrations scaled down for all future stops ... The torch will pass through Sichuan from 15–18 June as scheduled on a route altered by the crisis ... Charity donation boxes would be placed along the path of the flame each day.

(*IHT*, 14 May 2008, pp. 1, 8)

Late on Tuesday [13 May] a few hundred soldiers finally reached the epicentre in Wenchuan county, where an estimated 60,000 people remain missing ... Aftershocks have struck regularly ... Olympic Games organizers say they will scale down the route of the torch through the county [Sichuan] and there will be a minute's silence when the next leg starts in the south-eastern city of Ruijin on Wednesday [14 May].

(www.bbc.co.uk, 14 May 2008)

The only complaint we [CNN] heard was questioning why the government did not give a warning that the quake was coming, the way officials did in 1976, when an earthquake virtually destroyed the city of Tangshan, north-east of Beijing, killing at least 240,000 people.

(www.cnn.com, 14 May 2008)

> Chinese state media reported that 'extremely dangerous' cracks had appeared in a dam upriver from the earthquake-hit city of Dujiangyan … Thousands of soldiers rushed on Wednesday [14 May] to repair a dam badly cracked by the massive earthquake. China's top economic planning body said the quake had damaged 391 mostly small dams. It left 'extremely dangerous' cracks in the Zipingpu Dam upriver from Dujiangyan and some 2,000 soldiers were sent to repair the damage.
>
> (www.iht.com, 14 May 2008)

> [On 14 May] the government released a report that said nearly 400 dams had suffered damage … Most of them were small dams … The government said Wednesday [14 May] that experts had inspected the Zipingpu Dam and declared it safe.
>
> (*IHT*, 15 May 2008, p. 1)

> One state news media report said late Wednesday that inspectors had declared the Zipingpu Dam safe, while China National Radio said that soldiers would, in fact, release some water … According to Xinhua: '[The earthquake] caused cracks on the surface of the dam of the Zipingpu Hydropower station. Some walls of the plant and other buildings have collapsed and some are partly sunk.' Experts from China's earthquake bureau raised concerns about the station's location near a fault zone before it was built in 2000, according to … a group that opposed construction of the dam.
>
> (www.iht.com, 15 May 2008)

> On Thursday [15 May] officials from the largest Chinese power company warned that two dams were at risk of crumbling, threatening to drown more than 100 people still trapped in the ruins of a hydropower plant in the town of Huaneng.
>
> Officials warned … an additional 391 dams were in 'dangerous condition', posing an imminent risk to thousands of people downstream … A report in the *Beijing Times* said that a dam along the Jian River in Beichuan county was also in a fragile state.
>
> (www.iht.com, 15 May 2008)

'A probe revealed that the [Zipingpu] Dam is stable and safe, Xinhua reported' (www.cnn.com, 15 May 2008).

'The [Zipingpu] dam was completed less than two years ago despite concerns raised at the time about building it so close to a seismic fault line' (*The Economist*, 17 May 2008, p. 72).

> Huaneng Power, one of the country's largest power producers, said [on 15 May] that two dams upstream of its hydropower station in Sichuan could collapse 'at any time' … The government warned on Wednesday [15 May] that as many as 391 dams had been damaged by the earthquake, which measured 7.9 on the Richter scale.
>
> (www.ft.com, 15 May 2008)

> Relief organizations in Taiwan are sending two plane loads of relief materials and volunteers to south-west China. Around 150 tonnes of goods – including tents, sleeping bags and blankets – are being sent in the first two cargo flights, donated by several Taiwanese religious and charity groups.
>
> (www.bbc.co.uk, 15 May 2008)

> The government issued a rare public appeal for assistance, asking for donations of rescue equipment, including cranes, concrete-cutting tools, body-heat detectors and rubber boats [plus hammers]. Fifty thousand more shovels were also required. The authorities have also begun to ask for assistance from overseas disaster experts to help the relief effort, having so far only accepted offers of money or supplies on the grounds that it was logistically difficult for foreigners to work in the disaster area. Japan said it would send two groups of thirty rescue workers on Thursday [15 May] to China, who are expected to bring sniffer dogs and heat-sensing equipment ... Taiwan's Red Cross is sending a team of disaster relief experts, while the Taiwanese government is also sending a planeload of supplies to Sichuan, including tents and medicines.
>
> (www.ft.com, 15 May 2008)

'Japan has extensive earthquake-rescue expertise, suffering large tremors throughout its history ... The Red Cross for Taiwan said it is being allowed to send a twenty-man team' (www.cnn.com, 15 May 2008).

> Taiwan is sending a cargo plane to Chengdu with tents and medical supplies. The Air Macau plane will make a brief stop in Macao ... Taiwan and China have banned regular direct links ... The International Federation of Red Cross and Red Crescent Societies [have] issued an emergency appeal for medical help, food, water and tents.
>
> (www.iht.com, 15 May 2008)

'Taiwan's largest private carrier, China Airlines, was given permission to ferry relief supplies on charter flights ... The quake zone is home to several military installations and China's nuclear-weapons design programme' (www.iht.com, 15 May 2008).

> Officials asked Japan to send sixty earthquake rescue experts, the first such team it has taken from a foreign country during the current crisis and one of the few relief missions China has ever accepted from abroad. They also accepted help from two private rescue teams from Taiwan ... The two Taiwanese groups invited to participate in rescue operations are both Buddhist organizations without official government ties, and one of them, Tzu Chi, has been granted permission for two relief flights directly into Chengdu, the capital of Sichuan province ... China and Taiwan do not have regular direct air connections ... Both Japan and Taiwan have extensive experience with earthquakes ... Many of the troops involved in rescue efforts appear to have little training in disaster relief and lack proper tools and equipment. Prime

> minister Wen Jiabao issued a detailed request for heavy equipment needed to clear mountain roads. The request included thousands of pieces of earth-moving equipment, mechanized hammers, shovels and cranes, as well as satellite communications technology.
>
> (www.iht.com, 16 May 2008)

> One of the first aid groups to arrive was Tzu Chi, a Buddhist charity from Taiwan. Tzu Chi was replicating a pattern that over the past decade has earned it a reputation among the global disaster relief community as a rapid responder to tragedies such as the 2004 Indian Ocean tsunami ... Tzu Chi in March [2008] became the first foreign relief group to be registered as a local charity in China ... The group has been active ... in Taiwan ... since 1991... The group demands that its members abstain from politics.
>
> (*FT*, 20 May 2008, p. 14)

('[Tzu Chi's] aid workers are trained volunteers who pay their own way to disaster zones. Master Cheng Yen, a Buddhist nun who founded the organization in 1966, teaches that charitable givers must thank those they help in person, preferably with a bow. That is not just a wonderful bit of courtesy. It is also a way to make sure that aid reaches its recipients, rather than ending up in the hands of an unworthy government': *The Economist*, 31 May 2008, p. 71.)

> State television has said that the death toll ... could reach 50,000. The official death toll in south-western China has now topped 19,500, Sichuan provincial government officials said Thursday [15 May]. More than 4.3 million homes have now collapsed or sustained damage from the 7.9 magnitude quake, according to the Chinese embassy in Washington. Authorities say nearly 400 dams were damaged ... A probe revealed that the [Zipingpu] Dam is stable and safe, Xinhua reported. The waters at Zipingpu are now being lowered to decrease pressure on the structure ... International Rivers, a US-based group ... alleges that experts at China's earthquake bureau warned eight years ago that Zipingpu Dam was at risk due to closeness to a significant geographic faultline.
>
> (www.cnn.com, 15 May 2008)

> Officials say about 10 million people have been affected ... International Rivers told the BBC that China had a poor record concerning collapsed dams. A report on the group's website said the government had been warned of earthquake risks to the project before it was built.
>
> (www.bbc.co.uk, 15 May 2008).

'More than 4 million [houses] have been damaged in some way' (www.bbc.co.uk, 16 May 2008).

> The earthquake, which had a magnitude of 7.0, devastated entire counties, destroying an estimated 4 million homes, rendering roads impassable and leaving as many as 10 million people dependent on relief aid ... Untold numbers of smaller towns and villages have still not been reached in a

> mountain region of Sichuan considered one of the most remote and rugged in China. The scale of the devastation is so great that even as the government has mobilized a mammoth rescue effort, much of the manpower is focused on the most populated places, like Wenchuan and Beichuan.
>
> (www.iht.com, 16 May 2008)

'China warned [on 15 May] the death toll could soar to 50,000 ... with 10 million directly affected by Monday's tremor ... The confirmed death toll reached 19,509 ... More than 130,000 soldiers and police [have] joined the relief operation' (www.iht.com, 15 May 2008).

'By late Thursday afternoon [15 May] state television was reporting that the death toll could rise above 50,000 ... Officials said more than 130,000 emergency personnel, including soldiers and medics, were working in the quake zone' (www.iht.com, 15 May 2008).

'After an initial deployment of 5,000 troops the number was ramped up to 100,000 within three days' (*The Economist*, 17 May 2008, p. 71).

> President Hu Jintao has flown to south-western Sichuan province ... The first foreign rescuers have now arrived ... Thirty-one Japanese experts arrived on Friday morning [16 May] ... and a second team with sniffer dogs was due there later in the day. Russia, South Korea and Singapore are also sending teams to help in the rescue effort ... China has announced an investigation into why so many schools have collapsed.
>
> (www.bbc.co.uk, 16 May 2008)

'Premier Wen Jiabao said the quake was the most destructive and widespread since the People's Republic was founded in 1949. Its scale was greater than that of the Tangshan earthquake in 1976 which left 240,000 dead, he said' (www.bbc.co.uk, 17 May 2008).

'Premier Wen Jiabao ... calling the quake "the biggest and most destructive" since before the communist revolution of 1949 ... said the quick response had helped to reduce casualties' (www.independent.co.uk, 18 May 2008).

> A 5.6 magnitude quake rattled the eastern Sichuan province on Friday [16 May]. It was just the latest in dozens of tremors ... Xinhua reported 135,000 Chinese troops and medics are involved in the rescue effort – now in fifty-eight counties and cities ... More than 4.3 million homes collapsed or sustained damage because of the quake, according to the Chinese embassy in Washington.
>
> (www.cnn.com, 16 May 2008)

> An official at state-owned Huaneng Power – which had earlier been quoted as saying that two up-stream dams in the area could collapse 'at any time' – said yesterday [16 May] that one had indeed been damaged but 'the problem is not big'. The situation of some dams and reservoirs in the area remained unclear, however.
>
> (*FT*, 17 May 2008, p. 10)

The government says more than $200 million has been donated to relief efforts, including large donations from corporations around the world. The French retailer Carrefour, just weeks ago the target of nationalist anger in China [see the section on the Olympic torch relay], was one of them … [Carrefour said] the firm had so far donated 3 million yuan, or $430,000, in cash and 220,000 yuan in goods to the relief effort … [and that] the company had also contributed to relief efforts after previous disasters, including the crippling snowstorms that hit southern and central China in January.

(*IHT*, 17 May 2008, p. 7)

For multinational companies doing business in China, the devastating earthquakes that struck the country last week offer a chance to turn around their image after weeks of nationalistic anger directed at foreigners … [owing to] the anti-Chinese protests that trailed the international leg of the Olympic torch relay … Scores of Western companies have contributed cash and goods to the aid effort … The change in atmosphere may matter most to Carrefour, the French supermarket chain that bore the brunt of the anti-foreigner sentiment … Carrefour was one of the first companies to pledge aid … Many of the Western and Japanese companies that have contributed to relief efforts have joined their Chinese counterparts in taking out large advertisements in local newspapers to express condolences and make known that they are helping … Carrefour and other foreign companies noted that they had long contributed money to humanitarian causes in China.

(www.iht.com, 19 May 2008)

Can earthquakes be predicted? Most scientists would say no. But if some insistent Chinese bloggers are to be believed, nature provided enough warning to have saved many of those who perished Monday [12 May]. In the days before the deadly earthquake shook much of mountainous Sichuan province, their stories go, ponds unexpectedly drained, cows flung themselves against their enclosures and swarms of toads invaded the streets of a town that was later decimated by the quake … Some bloggers … say that alerts by a local seismology bureau were brushed off by provincial officials … In China the belief in omens and portents, often rooted in ancient cosmology, is widespread, even by the worldly and well educated … Even the Communist Party decided to inflect the Beijing Olympics with as many lucky eights as possible, starting them on 8 August, or 8.08.2008, with a start time of 8.08 p.m.

(www.iht.com, 16 May 2008)

China's main centres for designing, making and storing nuclear arms lie in the shattered earthquake zone … China began building the plants in the 1960s, calculating that their remote locations would make them less vulnerable to enemy attack … China's main complex for making nuclear warhead fuel, codenamed Plat 821, is beside a river in a hilly, forested part of the earthquake zone ... It is unclear if the plutonium-production reactor at Plant 821 has operated recently. Hans Kristensen of the Federation of American Scientists said China was expanding its nuclear forces to 240 warheads in its overall stockpile from around 200 ... Closer to the epicentre of the quake that struck Monday [12 May] is Mianyang, a science city whose outskirts house the primary laboratory for the design of nuclear arms. It is considered the Chinese equal to Los Alamos [in the United States] ... North, in an even more rugged and inaccessible region, nuclear experts said, China maintains a hidden complex of large tunnels in the side of a mountain where it stores nuclear arms ... The exact location of the secret complex has never been publicly disclosed.

(www.iht.com, 16 May 2008)

Almost 5 million people have been left homeless by Monday's devastating earthquake in China's south-western Sichuan province ... [It was said that] 4.8 million people were now in 'temporary shelter' ... So far 22,069 deaths have been confirmed ... China has announced an investigation into why so many schools collapsed. Further aftershocks – one measuring 5.9 – continued to strike the area, causing landslides that buried vehicles and knocked out communications only just restored.

(www.bbc.co.uk, 16 May 2008)

'[A] 5.5 magnitude earthquake rattled Sichuan province shortly after President Hu Jintao arrived in the quake zone on Friday [16 May] ... More than 4.3 million homes collapsed or sustained damage' (www.cnn.com, 16 May 2008).

The government said Friday [16 May] that it was investigating why so many school buildings had collapsed ... Beijing promised to mete out harsh punishment if any wrongdoing was involved ... The government said two dams around Chuanbei were destroyed ... [The condition of] one of China's biggest dams, the Dujian Dam, is still unknown.

(www.iht.com, 16 May 2008)

'Rumours have spread fast that officials were bribed to overlook shoddy construction practices' (www.independent.co.uk, 18 May 2008).

The government has undertaken a plan to find homes for orphans of the disastrous earthquake, repeating a similar plan that was instituted in 1976 after 240,000 people were killed by a massive earthquake in the city of Tangshan. The government said adoption applications have risen this week and have included an offer from an orphanage in Tangshan to take up to 200 children.

(www.iht.com, 16 May 2008)

Thousands of Chinese earthquake victims and rescuers are fleeing areas near the epicentre over fear of floods from a river blocked by landslides. The stampede of thousands of people on Saturday afternoon [17 May] came as Chinese officials said the official death toll from the earthquake had risen to 28,881 ... Landslides caused by Monday's quake had blocked the Qingzhu

> River in Beichuan county, creating two lakes with fast-rising water levels ... Officials, worried that one or both of the lakes could burst, forced the evacuation of ten villages and townships downriver ... Beijing has allocated until now nearly $5 billion for the rescue relief fund ... This weekend the United States will send two US Air Force C-17s carrying supplies, which include tents and generators ... Earlier the United States pledged $500,000 ... and the money has been delivered by the US Red Cross ... Saudi Arabia, the UK, Germany, Vietnam and Poland were among the countries providing humanitarian assistance ... The EU has said it will give initial emergency aid of $3.1 million to cover supplies including food and blankets.
>
> (www.ccn.com, 17 May 2008)

> There has been panic in Beichuan after reports a river had burst its bank sparked fears the entire city could be flooded. The whole city has been evacuated, forcing the suspension of all rescue efforts ... The authorities said that though the river had burst its banks the city was not under threat from the water, but the majority of people are remaining on the surrounding hillsides ... Rescue teams from South Korea, Singapore and Russia have joined Japanese and Taiwanese experts taking part in the operation.
>
> (www.bbc.co.uk, 17 May 2008)

> There was a stampede ... in Beichuan ... as thousands of people fled to higher ground ... The city went from a scene of rescue and relief into mayhem ... The Xinhua news agency warned that a lake, formed by landslides blocking a river, 'may burst its bank at any time'. However, the authorities later said the city was not under threat from the water.
>
> (www.bbc.co.uk, 17 May 2008)

'Rescue efforts resumed in Beichuan ... The city – that lies near the epicentre of the quake – was reduced to ruins' (www.bbc.co.uk, 18 May 2008).

'In Beichuan rescue work resumed later in the day [Saturday 17 May] and experts were monitoring the blocked river above' (www.ccn.com, 18 May 2008).

'Government officials said Saturday [17 May] that the death toll had risen to 28,881 ... Officials said Saturday that 12.5 million homes had been damaged and 3.1 million had collapsed' (www.iht.com, 18 May 2008).

> President Hu Jintao has voiced his gratitude for the international aid ... Offers of help in the relief effort from home and abroad have now surpassed $800 million ... The number of confirmed deaths in the south-western Sichuan province has now risen to 28,881 ... The region shuddered again as a strong aftershock – measured by the US Geological Survey at 6.0 – struck at 01.18 Sunday [18 May] local time (15.08 GMT Saturday). There have been hundreds of aftershocks since Monday's quake, causing landslides which have made conditions even more difficult ... Rescue teams from South Korea, Singapore and Russia have joined Japanese and Taiwanese experts taking part in the massive search. The specialist teams are equipped

> with sniffer dogs, and fibre-optic cameras and heat censors to detect people buried under the rubble … The authorities have resorted to burying the bodies in mass graves in an effort to prevent disease.
>
> (www.bbc.co.uk, 18 May 2008)

> A strong aftershock – the second in two days and measured by the US Geological Survey at magnitude 5.7 – shook the area early Sunday [18 May] … [The government] said 28,881 deaths have been confirmed so far … The number of security forces helping victims rose to almost 150,000 and the government added cash payments to victims to its response. The government would give $715 in compensation to each family that lost a member in the earthquake, National Radio reported Saturday [17 May]. At a State Council meeting hosted by premier Wen Jiabao in Beijing the government decided it would also hand out a daily ration of food and $1.4 to survivors, the report said … Soldiers who first arrived with little but shovels were better supplied.
>
> (www.cnn.com, 18 May 2008)

'An aftershock measuring 6.1 on the Richter scale shook Sichuan province' (www.independent.co.uk, 18 May 2008).

> Government officials said that more than 3 million homes had been destroyed … and more than 12 million had been damaged … the United Nations announced that it would provide a grant of $7 million from an emergency response fund 'to help meet the most urgent humanitarian requirements' … The gravest threat of flooding came from a lake in the far north of Sichuan province that had already begun to overflow because of a blockage in the Qingzhu River … Early on Sunday [18 May] a tremor with a magnitude of 6.0 struck northern Sichuan, one of the largest quakes since last Monday [12 May]; other tremors over the past several days have cause new landslides … Landslides continue to pose one of the greatest threats across the mountainous terrain of Sichuan. Daily aftershocks and tremors – at least 168 significant ones since Monday – set off new slides. At least thirteen rivers and lakes have been dammed up by the lake, the state-run China National Radio reported Saturday [17 May]. On Thursday [15 May] the top economic planning body issued a report saying the quake had damaged 391 reservoirs … Experts outside China say many of the threatened dams and reservoirs were built along the well-recognized Longmen Shan fault and that the dams might have sustained damage that could cause them to fail weeks later.
>
> (www.iht.com, 18 May 2008)

> China has announced three days of national mourning … By Sunday evening [18 May] the official death toll rose to 32,477 … Chinese officials said the three-day period of mourning will begin at 2.28 p.m. [14.28 local time or 06.28 GMT] on Monday [19 May], exactly one week after the quake struck the south-western Sichuan province. During that period the torch

> relay will be suspended … The torch was going to be in the eastern cities of Ningbo and Jiaxing in Zhejiang province on Monday, then in Shanghai on Tuesday and Wednesday. China's state-run news agency Sunday announced that … [the China Seismological Bureau had] … increased the magnitude of the quake from 7.8 to 8.0. The US Geological Survey measured the tremor at 7.9 … [That] figure remained unchanged as of Sunday … So far almost sixty organizations from thirteen countries were assisting … [including] India, France, Singapore, the Philippines and the United States. Two US military planes landed in Chengdu Sunday with blankets, water and other relief supplies … Early Sunday a strong aftershock rattled areas, while fears of flash flooding and landslides hindered rescue efforts. Sunday's 6.0 magnitude aftershock shook the region near the border of Sichuan and Gansu provinces just after 1 a.m. … Thousands of aftershocks have plagued the area since Monday [12 May].
>
> (www.cnn.com, 18 May 2008)

> Offers of help in the relief efforts from home and abroad have now surpassed $860 million … A British rescue team standing by in Hong Kong is returning home after being refused permission to travel to the earthquake zone … Three giant pandas are missing from the Wolong Nature Reserve … All the pandas at the reserve were initially reported safe … Nuclear facilities in the affected area have been confirmed to be safe … China has a research reactor, two nuclear fuel production sites and two nuclear weapons facilities in Sichuan, all between 60–145 kilometres (40–90 miles) from the epicentre.
>
> (www.bbc.co.uk, 18 May 2008)

'Strong aftershocks are continuing to shake the region, hampering the rescue effort. On Sunday [18 May] a tremor with a magnitude of 6.0 killed three people … in Jiangyou city in Sichuan province's Mianyang county' (www.bbc.co.uk, 19 May 2008).

> The mourning period will … include three minutes of silence observed by citizens nationwide … while air raid sirens and horns of vehicles, trains and ships will wail in grief. All national flags will fly at half-mast at home and at Chinese diplomatic missions abroad, and public recreational activities will be halted … Flood threats from rivers blocked by landslides from the quake appeared to have eased after three waterways near the epicentre overflowed with no problems … County officials diverted the released water as a precaution. The quake damaged some water projects, such as reservoirs and hydroelectric stations, but no reservoirs had burst … On Sunday officials from the China Seismological Bureau revised the earthquake's magnitude to 8.0 from 7.8. According to the United States Geological Survey, earthquakes of that magnitude are occurring worldwide on average once a year … Officials said [Sunday 18 May] a 78 metre, or 230 foot, high wall of water that had formed behind a landslide on the Qingzhu River had subsided … Officials said that

> more than 21,000 people had been saved from the rubble, including sixty-three on Saturday [17 May] … In all 205,000 people have been evacuated from the quake zone … Government officials said they were providing 4.8 million people with temporary shelter. With 10 million people in need of food, prime minister Wen Jiabao announced that Beijing would provide quake survivors with a daily cash allowance of 10 yuan, or $1.40, for at least three months. The government appealed for more public donations in a live telethon Sunday evening … Before the telethon China had received 8.9 billion yuan ($1.3 billion) in civic donations from home and abroad … Three giant pandas were missing from the world's most famous reserve for the endangered animals. Panda houses at the reserve were severely damaged and five staff members were killed … The sixty other giant pandas at the Wolong Nature Reserve were safe … There are roughly 1,600 pandas living wild in China, most spread across forty-four nature reserves in Sichuan.
>
> (www.iht.com, 18 May 2008)

'A group of British recovery experts was denied entry visas Sunday [18 May] after waiting four days in Hong Kong. Chinese officials told the ten-member International Rescue Corps that … [they were] worried about their safety' (*IHT*, 19 May 2008, p. 8).

> A government official said today [18 May] that the quake had blocked rivers and streams in twenty-one places … In the days following the earthquake the area has suffered 145 aftershocks measuring 4.0 or higher on the Richter scale. In the early hours of this morning a 6.1 magnitude shock centred in Sichuan's Jiangyou city killed a further three people.
>
> (www.thetimes.co.uk, 18 May 2008)

'A team of volunteers from Britain … got only as far as Hong Kong. The Chinese government denied visas to the ten specialists of International Rescue Corps, arguing that it lacked the resources to manage their work' (*The Times*, 19 May 2008, p. 33).

International Rescue Corps … [said its ten members] left on Saturday [17 May] after the Chinese government said it did not have the resources to manage their work' (www.guardian.co.uk, 19 May 2008).

> China on Monday [19 May] began three days of national mourning … The national flag was lowered to half-staff [half-mast] at 4.58 a.m. (8.58 p.m. Sunday GMT) at Beijing's Tiananmen Square … officials said three minutes of silence would begun at 2.28 p.m. local time on Monday … It was the first time China had formally commemorated the victims of a natural disaster in a period of national mourning … So far almost sixty aid organizations from thirteen countries were assisting … [including] India, France, Singapore, the Philippines and the United States … [A US seismologist] said a civil engineer in China told him that the country has no centralized, uniform code for earthquake-resistant public buildings such as schools or hospitals.
>
> (www.cnn.com, 19 May 2008)

> The national mourning period was the first in modern China for anyone other than a national leader ... The national flag in Tiananmen Square, solemnly raised every morning at dawn, was flown as half-staff [half-mast] ... The government order for the mourning period said all internet entertainment and game sites had to be taken off-line and users redirected to sites dedicated to commemorating earthquake victims ... The confirmed death toll stood at 32,476, said the State Council, China's cabinet.
>
> (www.iht.com, 19 May 2008)

> On Monday [19 May] Xinhua, the official news agency, said the confirmed death toll had risen to more than 33,570 ... Xinhua reported that more than 200 relief workers had been buried in mud flows over the past three days while trying to repair broken roads in the earthquake areas. The brief report did not indicate how many of these workers had been rescued from the mud flows or whether any of the workers were injured or killed.
>
> (www.iht.com, 19 May 2008)

> The death toll ... rose to at least 34,073 ... government officials said Monday [19 May] ... The government said Monday that companies affected by the quake had suffered $9.5 billion in damage ... Independent estimates suggest the final cost to the economy could reach $20 billion.
>
> (www.cnn.com, 19 May 2008)

'Beijing today [19 May] appealed to the international community for more tents for the estimated 4.8 million survivors left homeless' (www.thetimes.co.uk, 19 May 2008).

> In an indication of the challenge in dealing with millions of homeless and injured survivors, China said it would accept foreign medical teams and issued an international appeal for tents ... [A] foreign ministry spokesman said in a statement that tents were a priority 'because many houses were toppled in the quake and because it is the rainy season'.
>
> (www.independent.co.uk, 19 May 2008)

> The total number of confirmed dead rose to 34,073, the government [State Council] said ... The media said mudslides had buried 200 relief workers in the last three days. A local official said there had been some fatalities, but the numbers dead and injured were not known. The workers were said to have been repairing damaged roads ... The government said the country was expected to make direct economic losses of $9.5 billion, approximately 0.27 per cent of GDP.
>
> (www.bbc.co.uk, 19 May 2008)

'Companies suffered damage put at $9.6 billion ... Independent estimates have put losses at up to $20 billion after lost future output is taken into account' (*FT*, 20 May 2008, p. 14). 'Economists expect the overall impact on the economy to be relatively small, in large part because the stricken area is one of the nation's poorest ... Beijing has ordered price freezes in the disaster zone' (*FT*, 21 May 2008, p. 12).

'The reconstruction cost is projected to amount to about 1 per cent of GDP ... J.P. Morgan estimates' (*IHT*, 5 June 2008, p. 17).

> China has long pushed major infrastructure and even military developments in the area despite the quake risk. The mountainous region outside Chengdu became a major military production base in the 1960s, when China feared the possibility of an attack from the Soviet Union or the United States. Nuclear design, plutonium and fighter jet production facilities were located not far from the Longmenshan belt, largely because the region, deep in central China, was far from the country's borders and considered relatively safe from aerial assault. Under Mao's Third Front policy major industrial and military facilities were located in the Chinese heartland rather than in coastal areas viewed as more vulnerable.
>
> (www.iht.com, 5 June 2008)

> The government said that over the past three days landslides killed 158 relief workers, burying them in mud as they tried to repair roads in some of the worst hit areas ... The nation hangs on stories of remarkable rescues by more than 140,000 relief and medical workers involved in the rescue ... Huge donations have poured in, totalling over $1.2 billion.
>
> (www.iht.com, 19 May 2008)

> Near midnight ... panic erupted in the Sichuan provincial capital city [Chengdu] ... on Monday [19 May] ... after provincial television issued a warning of the possibility of a severe aftershock of as much as 6.7 magnitude ... In Mianyang ... guests were evacuated from hotels, joining the masses in the streets.
>
> (www.iht.com, 19 May 2008)

> Tens of thousands of people in Sichuan province rushed from their homes after a government warning of a possible major aftershock. People slept on the streets or drove to open ground after the warning was broadcast on television ... On Monday [19 May] a statement from the National Seismological Bureau was read out on television. People in cities across the quake-hit area rushed out of their homes carrying pillows and blankets. Roads out of Sichuan's provincial capital, Chengdu, were jammed as people headed for the open ground of the province's agricultural plains. The US Geological Survey reported an aftershock of magnitude 5.2 in the region on Monday night ... Dozens of aftershocks have rattled the region; the strongest has measured 6.1 ... To help raise money for the long-term relief effort, the government is to sell special stamps starting next month [June]. Thirteen million of the stamps, featuring three interlocking hearts on a red background, will be sold, potentially raising as much as $4 million.
>
> (www.bbc.co.uk, 20 May 2008)

> The Sichuan Seismological Bureau warned residents that a strong aftershock was likely to happen ... State media showed people camping on the streets

and in city squares after the government-issued aftershock warning … Chinese seismologists measured a 5.4 magnitude tremor at 2.06 p.m. Monday [19 May].

(www.ccn.com, 20 May 2008)

An unexpected mobilization has come outside official channels as thousands of ordinary people have streamed into the quake region or donated record sums of money in a striking and unscripted public response … Exact figures change daily, but donations from Chinese citizens and companies have already surpassed the $500 million allocated by the government, according to state media … Citing safety concerns, officials have asked individuals and small groups of private volunteers to stop coming to earthquake zones. During past natural disasters the government created little room for non-governmental volunteer efforts … The groundswell of compassion has also produced a very different type of national pride from the nationalist anger that erupted in response to the Tibetan unrest and foreign protests against the Olympic torch relay.

(*IHT*, 20 May 2008, pp. 1, 4)

Beijing tends to favour 'government-organized NGOs' (known as 'gongos') as a way of encouraging contributions from wider society without sacrificing political influence. Because of lack of flexible regulation for true NGOs, many still operate in a legal grey area that means they can be shut down at any time … [There] has been a wave of complaints on Chinese websites and text messages that foreign companies were not doing enough to support the relief effort – gossip that inspired at least one protest outside a McDonald's restaurant in China. The rumours prompted Chen Deming, the commerce minister, to go on national television last night [22 May] to thank multinationals, which have donated $245 million to earthquake projects.

(*FT*, 23 May 2008, p. 11)

The death toll … has risen to 40,075, officials said [on 20 May]. .. Japan's foreign minister criticized China for not accepting foreign aid workers sooner. Masahiko Komura: 'It would have been better if the decision was quicker' … On Monday [19 May] premier Wen Jiabao ordered troops to reach every single town and village in the earthquake zone within twenty-four hours.

(www.bbc.co.uk, 20 May 2008)

'When China began a three-day national mourning period, people across the country quietly understood it as marking an unofficial end to the search and rescue phase of recovery … On Tuesday the government raised the confirmed death toll to 40,075' (www.iht.com, 20 May 2008).

Qin Gang, the foreign ministry spokesman, said: 'China is willing to work closely [with outside doctors]. But, given the situation and difficulties in the area, including transportation and telecommunications, it is not possible for us to accept all of the rescue and medical teams to engage in relief work' … A Russian medical team arrived with a mobile hospital today in Chengdu … The Taiwan Red Cross had sent a thirty-seven-member medical team to the disaster zone, Japan had sent a twenty-three-member disaster relief team and medical crews had been sent by the United States, Germany and Italy … A giant panda was returned safely after going missing from the Wolong giant panda reserve. Two others remained unaccounted for, but a forestry officer said they were 'very likely to be alive'.

(www.guardian.co.uk, 20 May 2008)

In a circular the Communist Party's graft watchdog told local agencies to deal 'swiftly and severely' with any official corruption linked to relief work, Xinhua reported … The Communist Party's anti-corruption commission said any action that hampered progress or wasted supplies would be swiftly dealt with … The source, destination and quantity of relief supplies should be made public, it said, and police should crack down on any fraudulent collection of donations for earthquake victims. There have already been reports of scam text messages calling for donations to help survivors … In the earthquake zone many residents have been sleeping outside because of continued fear of aftershocks.

(www.bbc.co.uk, 21 May 2008)

The official death toll … has risen to 41,353. State media reported that medical teams had now reached all affected villages in remote regions of south-western Sichuan province … A Chinese military source said rescuers had reached all of the 1,044 quake-damaged villages in Sichuan province by Tuesday evening [20 May] … A shipment of specialized recovery equipment and a team of specialists from the United States was expected to arrive in south-western China Wednesday [21 May] … The US Agency for International Development (USAID) announced Tuesday it was sending more than $815,000 worth of additional assistance to China. That brings the total USAID assistance to China to more than $1.3 million.

(www.iht.com, 21 May 2008)

The impact on China's economy will be small and on the global economy negligible … Direct economic losses in Sichuan will amount to about $9.6 billion, the equivalent of 0.27 per cent of China's GDP in 2007, the government said this week … The eleven quake-stricken counties in Sichuan collectively account for less than 0.4 per cent of national grain, edible oil and meat output and only 0.17 per cent of industrial production.

(*IHT*, 22 May 2008, p. 17)

The government ordered budgets slashed to free money for relief efforts. State agencies were told to cut planned spending by 5 per cent this year [2008], which will go to create a $10 billion reconstruction fund, the State Council said … The government planned to rebuild Beichuan, one of the hardest hit cities, in a new location … State-owned companies suffered

> losses worth $4.29 billion in the disaster … Officials said this week that all companies had been hit with $9.5 billion in losses from the quake … The State Council said in a statement Wednesday [21] that the country's top anti-corruption office would deal sternly with officials who misuse or delay distribution of relief money. Officials have said they will make public the information on where relief money comes from and where it goes … The Tibetan government-in-exile called for a temporary stop to anti-Chinese protests 'to express our solidarity' with quake victims, according to a Tuesday evening, [20 May] statement.
>
> (p. 6)

'Private donations have already raised more than $500 million' (www.iht.com, 22 May 2008). 'China's police announced that they had punished seventeen earthquake "rumour mongers" last week, with penalties of up to fifteen days in jail' (www.iht.com, 22 May 2008).

> Sichuan accounts for about 4 per cent of China's GDP, 2.5 per cent of industrial production and only about 0.2 per cent of exports. These sort of figures are simply too small for the earthquake to make more than a minor difference to China's total economy. But the quake can have an effect in other areas. Sichuan produces 6 per cent of China's agricultural output and 7 per cent of its rice. So it is likely that disruption in Sichuan will add to Chinese food inflation. Food takes up about 35 per cent of Chinese household expenditure (and even more for lower income rural households).
>
> (www.feer.com, 28 May 2008)

> The government said yesterday [21 May] that donations had reached $1.8 billion, mostly to official charities … Many young Chinese are keen to help the victims but want to avoid going through the government … Private charities are the product of widespread scepticism about how the government would distribute donations … Aware of the political backlash if the relief efforts were tarred by corruption, the State Council announced yesterday that any officials caught misappropriating earthquake funds would receive severe punishments … Private charities still have an ambiguous status, however. Although China has thousands of NGOs, in theory they are required to have a government institution as a partner … The appearance of new private groups has put pressure on China's official charities to be more transparent about their operations and spending. The Red Cross Society of China, which has been inundated with donations, has said it will soon publish a list detailing how it is spending money in Sichuan.
>
> (*FT*, 22 May 2008, p. 10)

> [There have] been massive donations from China's new class of wealthy … Within a week of the earthquake *Hurun Report*, a group which complies lists of the wealthiest people in China, estimated that the top 100 richest people in the country had already contributed $120 million collectively … [The contributors included Zhang Xin of property developer Soho China,

> Zhang Jindong of the Suning electronics retail chain and Huang Guangyu of electrical goods company Gome] ... A few years ago China's entrepreneurs were almost completely uninvolved in private philanthropy. But even before the earthquake there were signs that the idea was starting to take hold.
>
> (*FT*, 'Wealth, Issue Two', Summer 2008, pp. 32, 35)

'[There is] an army of 150,000 volunteers' (*Guardian*, 10 June 2008, p. 15).

'[The] earthquake has created more than 4,000 orphans, a Chinese official said Wednesday [21 May] ... [although] it will take time to determine the real number of parentless children' (www.cnn.com, 22 May 2008).

> The death toll ... has leaped to 51,151 – an increase of almost 10,000 – government officials reported on Thursday [22 May] ... As of mid-day Thursday domestic and international donations ... had reached $3 billion ... China's central government has announced it will allocate $10 billion to the country's reconstruction fund ... Premier Wen Jiabao said government spending will be cut by 5 per cent this year [2008] ... Beijing will also allocate $3.6 billion for rescue and relief efforts ... Foreign Ministry spokesman Qin Gang said 'We need more than 3.3 million tents' ... adding that 400,000 tents had already been delivered ... The two-day [torch] relay through Sichuan province ... will start on 3 August ... The relay had been scheduled for 15 June.
>
> (www.cnn.com, 22 May 2008)

'The death toll ... was raised to 55,740, government officials reported on Friday [23 May]' (www.ccn.com, 23 May 2008).

> The vice governor of Sichuan province ... Li Chengyun ... set a three-year goal to rebuild towns and infrastructure in the region ... More than 5.47 million people were homeless and 5.46 million buildings had collapsed ... On Friday premier Wen Jiabao paid his second visit to the region, visiting the temporary site of Beichuan middle school.
>
> (www.bbc.co.uk, 23 May 2008)

('The prime minister, Wen Jiabao, appears to have earned considerable kudos by rushing to the scene and staying there for five days to direct relief operations, at one point in tears': *The Economist*, 24 May 2008, p. 85. 'Chinese leaders are not known for making themselves available to the public, even since the internet opened the door to governments around the world. But prime minister Wen Jiabao has jumped into the online social networking world with a page on Facebook, one of the most popular of its kind': www.iht.com, 28 May 2008. 'Wen Jiabao [is] widely known in China as "Grandpa Wen" ... The first message on the "wall" was posted by the page creator on 14 May': *IHT*, 29 May 2008, p. 14. 'Wen Jiabao's Facebook profile was created two days after the 7.9 magnitude quake': www.cnn.com, 28 May 2008.)

'All nuclear facilities in the quake area were safe; however, experts were still trying to secure some fifteen "sources" of radiation, said Wu Xiaoqing, vice minister for environmental protection' (www.iht.com, 23 May 2008).

'As of midday Friday [23 May] domestic and international donations ... had reached $3.6 billion' (www.cnn.com, 23 May 2008).

> Chinese banks were told Friday [23 May] to forgive debts owed by earthquake survivors ... and the government warned it was cracking down on price gouging by merchants in the disaster area ... The China Banking Regulatory Commission said banks should forgive debts owed by survivors of the 12 May quake who lack insurance. It gave no indication how much that might cost. But state-owned Agricultural Bank of China, the country's main rural lender, says it expects borrowers in the area to default on $850 million in loans. The bank agency's announcement said: 'For borrowers who have suffered a great loss in the earthquake and had no insurance, or if they have insurance but still cannot repay their debts, their borrowing should be counted as bad loans and the banks should cancel them' ... The government put business losses at $9.5 billion. As little as 5 per cent of losses are believed to be covered by insurance ... Banks should also forgive credit card debts owed by people killed in the quake, the bank agency said ... Also Friday the deputy governor of Sichuan said authorities are taking action against price gouging in earthquake areas after finding sixty cases of overcharging.
>
> (www.iht.com, 23 May 2008)

> The earthquake ... seems to have had only a limited effect on China's overall economy. Only 1 per cent of China's population lives in the hardest hit quake-affected area, in northern Sichuan province. These residents account for an even smaller share of China's economic output, because many of them are impoverished farmers ... The China Banking Regulatory Commission has ordered banks to write off many loans to residents of the quake-affected region. Chinese insurance companies face claims on property and casualty policies and life insurance. But lending and insurance in the quake region were so meagre before the earthquake that bank and insurance analysts say the effect will be negligible. Add together all the bank loans outstanding in the three provinces hit by the quake – Sichuan and neighbouring Gansu and Shaanxi – and the total is less than in Shanghai alone [according to one estimate] ... The earthquake has disrupted road and rail links from Sichuan province, a big producer of pork and grain ... Though Sichuan province mines less than 1 per cent of China's coal, one of the country's main rail arteries for distributing coal runs through the quake-affected area and was temporarily blocked by quake debris.
>
> (www.iht.com, 4 June 1008)

> As well as a short-term effect on economic output as reconstruction begins, there is a chance that the outpouring of civic spirit in response to the disaster may not only reshape Chinese politics but also strengthen its economic foundations. The idea of social capital as a long-term driver of economic growth is well known to academics ... Francis Fukuyama identified social

> cohesion as one reason Japan and Germany recovered so quickly after World War II. Chinese people, wary of working together for common purposes in groups beyond the family, appeared on Fukuyama's list of 'low-trust societies'. The reaction to the quake challenges that appraisal. Donations of money, goods and blood poured in. An efficient relief operation seems to have strengthened the social contract between the citizenry and a leadership often seen as aloof ... Increased social cohesion may also be the main outcome of the Beijing Olympics. China is likely to be able to take collective pride in a well run Games.
>
> (Alan Wheatly, www.iht.com, 9 June 2008)

> Earthquake survivors living downstream from lakes formed by blocked rivers were being evacuated Friday [23 May] over fears that aftershocks could loosen the debris and cause flooding ... Nearly three dozen new lakes were formed after the quake threw down debris, which formed barriers across rivers ... Russia sent rescue crews and a mobile hospital to the disaster area.
>
> (www.iht.com, 23 May 2008)

'Jiang Li, deputy minister of civil affairs, said ... [that] the family of each victim would be paid $725' (*IHT*, 24 May 2008, p. 8).

> Chinese officials said yesterday [23 May] said it would take three years to rebuild the area of Sichuan devastated by last week's earthquake, as first indications of unrest among the millions of people affected began to surface. Television cameras captured images of a large protest outside a supermarket in Deyang after residents suspected earthquake aid had been diverted to the store ... There have also been reports of relief trucks held up by survivors desperate for food and water ... The government has so far distributed 400,000 [tents] but believes it needs more than 3 million ... Li Chengyun, vice governor of Sichuan province ... estimated that as many as 200,000 people had volunteered to help.
>
> (*FT*, 24 May 2008, p. 8)

> The death toll ... has passed 60,000 and could rise to 80,000 or more, premier Wen Jiabao said. Mr Wen was speaking in the town of Yingxiu, which was reduced to rubble in the 12 May quake, as he visited with UN General Secretary Ban Ki Moon ... Thirty-four lakes were created in the province when landslides blocked rivers, Xinhua said.
>
> (www.bbc.co.uk, 24 May 2008)

'Mr Ban praised China's "extraordinary leadership" in dealing with the earthquake and said the UN was ready to provide further support in the relief effort' (www.bbc.co.uk, 25 May 2008).

> Secretary-general Ban Ki Moon of the United Nations visited one of the hardest-hit towns in China's earthquake zone ... Yingxiu ... Saturday [24 May] as the guest of prime minister Wen Jiabao, who said the [death] toll

> may climb to 80,000 or more. The State Council, China's cabinet, said the latest confirmed death toll for the quake was 60,560 … Wen Jiabao: 'It may further climb to a level of 70,000, 80,000 or more … Previously our main priority was the search and rescue of affected people. Our priority now is to resettle the affected people and to make plans for the post-quake reconstruction' … The quake destroyed more than 15 million homes, Wen said. He said the government had begun an urgent effort to reconstruct temporary housing, complete with schools and trash collection. Some 10,000 medical workers have been dispatched to prevent outbreaks of disease, Wen said. Vice governor Li Chengyun of Sichuan said the province would aim to rebuild roads and cities within three years … Ban Ki Moon, who came to China directly from another Asian disaster zone, cyclone-stricken Myanmar, promised that the United Nations would help with reconstruction and was waiting for China's assessment of what it needed … Also on Saturday eight pandas arrived safely in Beijing after a long journey from their damaged reserve near the epicentre of the quake … Experts searched for fifteen radiation sources buried in the rubble and survivors moved out of possible danger areas downstream from rivers dammed by landslides … The environmental protection ministry said experts from the National Nuclear Safety Administration were trying to contain fifteen unspecified 'sources' of radiation. Some fifty potential radiation sources were buried by the quake, environmental vice minister Wu Xiaoqing said Friday [23 May] in Beijing. While thirty-five have been secured, fifteen remained buried under buildings and houses and, though located, were inaccessible, he said. Wu said the radiation was not leaking. But the number of unsecured sources was higher than the two the agency reported days earlier. China has said all nuclear facilities are safe and foreign experts have said the unsecured radiation material was likely used by hospitals and factories or for research.
>
> (www.iht.com, 25 May 2008)

> A global network of sensors has found no evidence that China's complex of nuclear facilities in the earthquake zone let any radioactivity escape, its operators reported Wednesday [21 May] … [It was] reported Monday [19 May] that China's National Nuclear Safety Administration had ordered all reactors operating in Sichuan to shut down … The Chinese government will allow Sichuan's reactors to restart only after authorities have been reassured that the plants 'meet minimum national nuclear seismic standards'.
>
> (www.iht.com, 25 May 2008)

('Some 134,000 Burmese are now dead or missing – over 40 per cent of whom are believed to be children. The United Nations reports that only 42 per cent of the storm's 2.4 million affected victims have received any humanitarian relief': www.iht.com, 28 May 2008. 'No one has good numbers, but it is estimated that Cyclone Nargis killed about 120,000 people and left about 2.5 million needing some form of assistance. For comparison, the Indian Ocean tsunami in December 2004 killed about 190,000 and left more than 3 million needing help in six countries': Tony Banbury, Asia regional director of the United Nations World Food Organization, *IHT*, 6 June 2008, p. 6. 'Cyclone Nargis, which struck [Myanmar] on 2 May, has left 134,000 people dead or missing and another 2.4 million clinging to survival ... The regime has been under fire for stalling foreign aid destined for the cyclone victims': www.bbc.co.uk, 28 May 2008. 'According to official [Burmese] figures, 78,000 people were killed and another 56,000 are missing': www.bbc.co.uk, 7 June 2008. 'Cyclone Nargis killed as many as 140,000 and displaced as many as 2.5 million': www.feer.com, 24 May 2008.)

> Authorities [on Sunday 25 May] revised up the death toll to 62,664 ... A powerful magnitude 5.8 aftershock hit the area killing at least one person ... China's water ministry on Sunday warned that sixty-nine dams were close to bursting their banks ... The central government estimates that 45 million people, mostly in Sichuan province, were affected ... and that 5 million were left homeless.
>
> (www.cnn.com, 25 May 2008)

> A 5.8 magnitude aftershock hit the area on Sunday [25 May] and was felt in Beijing ... It was one of the strongest of about 8,000 aftershocks detected since the 7.9 quake on 12 May. The tremor thought to be the biggest, measuring 6.0, came six days after the quake and killed three people ... There have been no reports of any dams breaking. Thirty-four lakes were created in the province when landslides blocked rivers, Xinhua said.
>
> (www.bbc.co.uk, 25 May 2008)

'On Sunday six people died ... About 270,000 more houses were destroyed or severely damaged' (www.bbc.co.uk, 26 May 2008).

> The central government has said the quake affected 391 dams, mostly small ones ... Mudslides since the quake have killed 200 rescue workers ... The first of eight Russian military transport planes carrying tents, medicine and food landed today [25 May] in Chengdu, with other flights expected tomorrow ... Two pandas are unaccounted for after the quake.
>
> (www.guardian.co.uk, 25 May 2008)

> There is no official figure on how many children died ... but the number of student deaths seems likely to exceed 10,000, possibly much higher, a staggering figure that has become a simmering controversy in China as grieving parents say their children might have lived had the schools been better built ... Angry parents are beginning to stage small demonstrations. On Wednesday [21 May] more than 200 Xinjian parents demonstrated at the temporary tents used by Dujiangyan's education bureau, demanding an investigation and accusing officials of corruption and negligence ... Parents at the [Xinjiang primary] school posted an online petition on Wednesday. They demanded justice for their children. Local police officials have promised an investigation, but the parents are not satisfied. They intend to protest again

... Prime minister Wen Jiabao said Saturday [24 May] that construction materials used in schools and hospitals that had collapsed should be collected 'for reference in future construction' ... Schools collapsed during the earthquake, killing over 10,000 students, causing anger among parents about shoddy construction.

(www.iht.com, 25 May 2008)

The government has previously said the earthquake left 5 million people homeless, but on Sunday [25 May] Xinhua quoted a top official in Sichuan province, Huang Yanrong, as saying that there are over 11 million homeless ... By Saturday [24 May] 448,140 tents had been sent to disaster areas, according to Xinhua.

(www.iht.com, 25 May 2008)

Last week President Hu Jintao visited factories that manufacture tents and temporary buildings, pressing them to step up production ... The government is planning a massive reconstruction project that includes building more than 1.5 million temporary homes, which are expected to last two to three years. Beijing has pledged more than $9 billion for the reconstruction effort and says that it has received another $4 billion in donations of food, money and supplies from around the world.

(www.iht.com, 26 May 2008)

Soldiers set to work Monday [26 May] trying to unblock a debris-clogged river threatening to flood homeless survivors ... The 1,800 soldiers marched into the new Tangjiashan lake in Beichuan county carrying explosives to blast through the debris ...

A powerful aftershock Sunday [25 May] destroyed tens of thousands of homes. On Monday Xinhua said the death toll in the aftershock had risen to six, including deaths in neighbouring provinces ... The magnitude 6.0 aftershock was among the most powerful recorded since the initial 12 May quake, according to the US Geological Survey. The China National Seismic Network said the aftershock was the strongest ... in the nearly two weeks after the disaster.

(www.iht.com, 26 May 2008)

The water in the lake ... [raised] the possibility of flash flooding that could threaten the lives of 70,000 people downstream ... A senior official in Beijing warned that sixty-nine dams ... could present 'dangerous situations' and risked some danger of collapsing.

(www.iht.com, 26 May 2008)

The official death toll from the original quake has now risen to 65,080, China's civil affairs ministry said Monday [26 May] ... A strong aftershock on Sunday [25 May] killed at least eight people ... and destroyed more than 70,000 homes in Sichuan, Gansu and Shaanxi provinces ... The aftershock damaged more than 200,000 other homes ... At a news conference Sunday

> [25 May] a civil affairs ministry official said rescue workers had pulled 6,537 people alive from the rubble of the earthquake. An official from the ministry of water resources said at the same briefing that sixty-nine dams damaged by the quake were in danger of bursting in Sichuan province. The government estimates that 45 million people, mostly in Sichuan province, were affected by the earthquake and that 5 million were left homeless.
>
> (www.cnn.com, 26 May 2008)

> China is relaxing its one-child policy for earthquake survivors … Couples whose only child was killed, severely injured or disabled in the quake can get a certificate allowing them to have another child, the Chengdu population and family planning committee, which oversees the policy in the capital of Sichuan province, said Monday [26 May] … The 12 May earthquake killed many children during a single school day … The announcement affects the city of Chengdu, which has 10 million people, as well as two of the hardest hit cities nearby, Dujiangyan and Pengzhou. It was not clear whether other cities in the quake zone, including Qingchuan, would make similar announcements … The announcement says that if a child born illegally was killed in the quake, the parents will no longer have to pay fines for that child – but the previously paid fines will not be refunded. If a couple's legally born child was killed and the couple is left with an illegally born child under the age of eighteen, that child can be registered as the legal child – an important move that gives the child previously denied rights including nine years of free compulsory education. Many Chinese have shown interest in adopting earthquake orphans and the announcement says there are no limits on the number a family can adopt.
>
> (www.iht.com, 26 May 2008)

'Qualified parents could apply for legal permission to have another child' (www.iht.com, 27 May 2008).

'Officials announced that couples who adopt earthquake orphans will still be allowed to have a biological child. It is estimated that 4,000 children have been left without parents, some of whom have no other family' (www.guardian.co.uk, 27 May 2008). ('The overall pupil death count … is 4,737': *FT*, 30 May 2008, p. 6.)

('China is sending medics to offer reverse sterilization operations to parents who lost their only children in last month's quake … The family planning authorities say the team will provide counselling, surgery and in-vitro fertilization treatment. Under China's one-child policy, parents who lose a child or have one with disabilities are allowed a second baby … China's one-child policy limits urban couples to one child and rural couples to two … The authorities in Sichuan province estimate about 7,000 of those killed in the 12 May quake were only children … Parents of the estimated 16,000 only children injured in the tremor may also be included under the scheme': www.bbc.co.uk, 8 June 2008.)

Authorities Tuesday [27 May] evacuated … around 100,000 people … in Sichuan province as engineers prepared to dynamite a potentially dangerous lake

[Tangjiashan] formed when landslides dammed a river' (www.cnn.com, 27 May 2008).

> The State Council said Tuesday [27 May] that 67,183 people were confirmed killed … and 20,790 were still missing … Also Tuesday health officials said that higher-than-normal rates of stomach pains and fever had been reported among the millions of quake survivors, but that no major disease outbreaks had occurred. About 5 million people were left homeless by the quake. Many of them are living in tents or makeshift communities that are clustered throughout the disaster area … Officials rushed Tuesday to evacuate another 80,000 people from the path of potential floodwaters building up behind a dam [the Tangjiashan lake] … Emergency workers would try to complete the evacuation by midnight on Tuesday, taking the number of people moved out of the threatened valley to almost 160,000 from more than thirty townships … In Qingchuan county in northern Sichuan 1,300 people were evacuated from Guanzhuang because of landslide worries … Plans were being drawn up to evacuate all 23,000 people in the area if needed.
>
> (www.iht.com, 27 May 2008)

> The authorities have ordered the evacuations of 150,000 people threatened by possible flooding from [Tangjiashan lake] … and military engineers struggled Tuesday to dig sluiceways to drain the water safely … As fears about the lake intensified the earthquake zone was struck by another powerful aftershock Tuesday … magnitude 5.4 … Thirty minutes later a 5.7 magnitude tremor was registered in Sichuan province.
>
> (www.iht.com, 27 May 2008)

> Another 80,000 people are being evacuated near a lake [Tangjiashan] formed by landslides … About 70,000 people have already been moved from nearby Mianyang city in Sichuan province … Emergency workers aim to evacuate the 80,000 people by midnight on Tuesday [27 May] … Two further aftershocks have destroyed more than 420,000 houses in the region hit by a massive earthquake … One of the aftershocks measured magnitude 5.7, according to the US Geological Survey … [Qingchuan] province was strongly shaken on Sunday [25 May], wrecking 300,000 more homes … [and] killing eight people.
>
> (www.bbc.co.uk, 27 May 2008)

> [Xinhua] today [27 May] said 420,000 houses had collapsed in aftershocks from the Sichuan earthquake … Emergency workers hope to move around 160,000 people by the end of the day … If it appeared the entire [Tangjiashan] dam would burst 1.3 million would be moved.
>
> (www.guardian.co.uk, 27 May 2008)

> The official death toll from the quake rose to 68,109 on Wednesday [28 May] … with 19,851 missing … Vice premier Hui Liangyu: 'The Tangjiashan quake lake should be our most urgent task. It is threatening mil-

lions of lives in the area downstream and any negligence will cause new disasters to people who have already suffered the quake' ... Engineers are attempting to create a spillway to relieve water pressure as the Jianjiang River fills in behind the massive pile of rock and soil ... Authorities have evacuated 158,000 people from 170 communities, but that number could swell to 1.3 million if engineers become convinced a catastrophic release of water is about to occur ... Sichuan province suffered through four after-shocks Tuesday, injuring at least sixty-three people – six of them critically – and causing the collapse of more than 420,000 homes ... All of them measured between magnitude 4.5 and 5.5, according to the US Geological Survey.

(www.cnn.com, 28 May 2008)

Government officials on Wednesday [28 May] raised the confirmed death toll to 68,109, with 19,851 people still missing ... In recent days at least 160,000 people have been evacuated, although hundreds of thousands of others are still living downstream [of the dam], most of them in temporary camps that are proving a formidable challenge for the government as it struggles to provide food, water and shelter for more than 15 million displaced people ... In several towns parents continued to agitate for a speedy government investigation into why so many schools collapsed during the earthquake, killing thousands of students and teachers. In Shifang more than 300 parents whose children died at the Jiandi Middle School protested at the gates of the local government ... In Dujiangyan a group of 500 parents gathered at a tent temporarily housing the city's education bureau and demanded that officials open a provincial-level investigation into why the Xinjian school fell, killing at least 300 children ... Parents planned to stage a 'mourning rally' on 1 June, which is Children's Day in China, a national holiday.

(www.iht.com, 28 May 2008)

Before the dust had settled from China's devastating earthquake, residents in the disaster zone were already asking why so many schools collapsed, while most government offices seemed to survive intact ... Over recent weeks there has been intense scrutiny of building ruins across northern Sichuan ... Most of the focus has been on schools, many of which were the only structures in their immediate area to suffer a total collapse ... Protests are occurring on an almost daily basis, as parents demand explanations for why the school collapsed – and justice for their children ... The ministry of education has promised an investigation into school construction and premier Wen Jiabao urged officials to spend less on business travel, banquets and entertainment and suspended approval for all new government or party-related office buildings.

(*FT*, 31 May 2008, p. 7)

On Wednesday [28 May] Japanese officials said they were considering a Chinese request to provide tents and blankets to the homeless ... Nobutaka

Machimura, Japan's chief cabinet secretary, said it was unclear whether China would allow the Japanese Air Force to deliver aid. If it did it would mark the first time that the Japanese military touched down on Chinese soil since World War II.

(www.iht.com, 28 May 2008)

China has asked Japanese soldiers to deliver earthquake relief aid in what would be the first significant military dispatch between the two countries since World War II … It would involve Japanese defence forces airlifting tents and other relief supplies to quake-hit areas in central China … Chief cabinet secretary Nobutaka Machimura said Japan is considering using a military plane and surplus tents and blankets. He said: 'Our understanding is that the request is to fly a plane belonging to the Self Defence Forces to deliver its tents and blankets to a Chinese airport. A decision should not take too long and we are working on it now' … Earlier a foreign ministry official in charge of China affairs said officials were considering whether to use Self Defence Forces aircraft or civilian chartered planes … Japan was the first foreign nation that China turned to for help after the 12 May quake. Tokyo sent a sixty-member civilian emergency rescue team days after the quake struck Sichuan province, followed by a medical team last week … Japan invaded China and set up a puppet regime in Manchuria in 1932, then conquered larger areas of the country.

(www.iht.com, 28 May 2008)

Tomohiko Taniguchi (a Japanese foreign ministry spokesman): 'The Chinese government, through diplomatic channels, did request … rescue materials, tents and medical gear, and wondered if it would be possible to send them by aircraft of the Air Self Defence Force' … No aircraft operated by Japan's Air Self Defence Force … has ever visited China, where memories of Tokyo's 1931–45 invasion and occupation still run deep … Less than two weeks ago, when Japan sent rescue workers to search for victims of the earthquake, they flew by commercial aircraft via Beijing. At the time Osama Saakashita, deputy cabinet secretary, described as 'too sensitive' the suggestion that Japan could send them directly to the disaster area in military aircraft … Chinese media have given appreciative coverage to the efforts of the Japanese earthquake teams – the first foreign rescuers allowed into the country after Beijing dropped initial reluctance to accept such assistance. Many Chinese were particularly touched by a widely published photograph of a rescue team bowing in silent prayer to a corpse that they had retrieved from the rubble.

(*FT*, 29 May 2008, p. 6)

China has begun talks with Tokyo about what would be the first significant military dispatch involving the two countries since World War II … [it was] reported Thursday [29 May]. Foreign ministry spokesman Qin Gang: 'Given the magnitude of this disaster, if some countries or militaries are ready to provide us with material in urgent need, we will express our welcome' …

The Kyodo news agency said Japan plans to dispatch Self Defence Forces aircraft to transport tents and other relief supplies to main airports, but the troops will not be allowed to go into the affected areas.

(www.iht.com, 20 May 2008)

China did not confirm results on Wednesday [28 May] that it had requested aid from Japan. Foreign ministry spokesman Qin Gang: 'If the Japanese Self Defence Forces are ready to provide assistance, the specifics will be discussed at the defence departments of the two countries' ... Qin Gang said South Korean President Lee Myung Bak would visit Sichuan on Friday [30 May].

(www.iht.com, 29 May 2008)

Japan plans to dispatch a military plane with relief supplies for the victims of the earthquake ... Television stations in Japan ... say the planned dispatch of an Air Self Defence Force C-130 cargo plane will be the first flight into Chinese airspace by the Japanese military since hostilities ended more than sixty years ago. Japanese ministers are stressing that China asked for tents, blankets and other supplies and accepted they would be brought in by the military. It appears, though, that the Japanese will not be asked to transport the aid around the country.

(www.bbc.co.uk, 29 May 2008)

[On Wednesday 28 May] the head of Taiwan's ruling party met with President Hu Jintao, the highest level encounter since the two sides split in 1949. Kuomintang (Nationalist Party) chairman Wu Poh-hsiung is in China for a six-day landmark visit ... Hu Jintao: 'The love for compatriots shown by the whole Chinese people in time of disaster will become the power to drive co-operation between the compatriots across the strait and create the future together. We cannot guarantee there won't be any natural disasters ... but through our mutual efforts we can ensure there is no war.'

(www.bbc.co.uk, 28 May 2008)

President Hu Jintao:

For half a month people from all circles in Taiwan have expressed their concern, love and generous support. The love for compatriots shown by the whole Chinese people in time of disaster will become the power to drive co-operation between the compatriots across the strait and create the future together. As long as both sides across the strait are concerned about each other and make exchanges with each other, a peaceful and stable development of relations across the strait can be expected.

(www.iht.com, 28 May 2008)

Sharon Stone (US actress):

I'm not happy about the way the Chinese are treating the Tibetans because I don't think anyone should be unkind to anyone else. I've been concerned about how we should deal with the Olympics, because they are not being nice to the Dalai Lama, who is a good friend of mine. And then all this earthquake and all this stuff happened, and I thought is that karma – when you're not nice that bad things happen to you?

(www.independent.co.uk, 28 May 2008; www.guardian.co.uk, 28 May 2008)

Sharon Stone is facing an escalating consumer boycott from cinema-goers in China … The founder of one of China's biggest cinema chains said yesterday [28 May] that his company would no longer show her films in its theatres … The comments were made on the red carpet at Cannes last week [during the film festival], but have since reached a worldwide audience on YouTube … Later in the interview the actress conceded that her hard-line attitude had softened after she received a letter from the Tibetan Foundation asking her to go and help quake victims.

(*Independent*, 29 May 2008, p. 26)

Christian Dior was yesterday [28 May] scrambling to avoid a Chinese consumer backlash after the actress Sharon Stone, who is a model for the group, suggested the Sichuan earthquake might have been retribution for Beijing's policies in Tibet. The luxury goods group has apologized to its Chinese customers … In a statement Dior said: 'We absolutely disagree with her hasty comments and we are also deeply sorry about them … We will never support any opinion that hurts the feelings of the Chinese people' … A Beijing newspaper reported yesterday that photographs of the actress had been taken down from Dior branches in several of the city's malls … Two companies operating cinema chains in mainland China and Hong Kong said they would not show any films featuring the actress, while the Shanghai International Film Festival said it would withdraw her invitation.

(*FT*, 29 May 2008, p. 6)

Facing the possibility of a boycott of its products, the luxury company … Christian Dior, the French fashion brand … said Thursday [29 May] that it had dropped the American actress Sharon Stone from its advertising in China … An official at Dior's Shanghai office said the ads featuring Stone would no longer appear in China. And Dior released a statement in which Stone apologized, saying: 'Due to my inappropriate words and actions during the interview, I feel deeply sorry and sad about hurting Chinese people. I am willing to take part in the relief work of China's earthquake and wholly devote myself to helping affected Chinese people.'

(www.iht.com, 29 May 2008)

Sharon Stone claims Dior distorted her words in apology … Dior, which has a modelling contract with Stone for a face cream, removed her from advertising in China, fearing a backlash. Dior's Shanghai office issued a statement in which Stone was quoted apologizing: 'I am deeply sorry and sad about hurting Chinese people.' [In an interview held on Thursday 29 May] Stone … insisted her comments had been taken out of context. She also said that

> she resisted Dior's efforts at damage control and that the apology issued in her name distorted her words. Early last week, Stone said, she received a call from Sidney Toledano, the chief executive of Dior ... Sharon Stone: 'I talked to Sidney and I said let's get serious here. You guys know me very well. I'm not going to apologize for something that isn't real and true – not for face creams' ... Stone said that she told Toledano of Dior that since she didn't believe she had done anything wrong, why didn't Dior let her clarify her remarks with a statement?. That statement said, in part: 'I am deeply saddened that a ten-second poorly edited film clip has besmirched my reputation of over twenty years of charitable services on behalf of international charities. My intention is to be of service to the Chinese people' ... She expressed sympathy for the earthquake victims and said she regretted if her comments in Cannes were misunderstood ... She said: 'I misspoke for four seconds and it's become an international incident' ... Sharon Stone (watching a video of her remarks in Cannes): 'Clearly I sound like an idiot ... I had absolutely no intention of saying that, which I did say and now, looking at it on the tape, I look a complete ding-dong.'
>
> (www.iht.com, 1 June 2008)

('Actress Sharon Stone said in a statement Saturday [31 May]: "I could not be more regretful. Yes, I misspoke. I could not be more regretful of that mistake. It was unintentional. I apologize. Those words were never meant to be hurtful to anyone. They were an accident of my distraction and a product of news sensationalism" ': www.cnn.com, 1 June 2008.)

'The official death toll from the quake climbed to 68,516 on Thursday [29 May] ... [with] 19,350 missing' (www.ccn.com, 29 May 2008).

> Five thousand tonnes of dangerous chemicals and heavy rain are adding to the mix of threats from one of China's 'quake lakes' in danger of bursting its banks, a newspaper said Thursday [29 May] ... About 5,000 tonnes of chemicals, including sulphuric and hydrochloric acid, were trapped downstream from the Tangjiashan lake and had to be moved to safe ground, the *Beijing News* said.
>
> (www.iht.com, 29 May 2008)

> The official death toll from the quake stands at 68,858 as of Friday [30 May], with another 18,618 people missing ... An additional 40,000 people in Beichuan county have been ordered to leave at-risk areas downstream from the so-called quake lake, bringing the total to nearly 200,000. A report that China had ordered the evacuation of 1.3 million people, however, turned out not to be true. The report appeared Friday in Xinhua. The Chinese authorities say they actually are planning a drill to make sure they are prepared in case they have to evacuate 1.3 million. That is an estimate of the number of people who would be evacuated if the dam breaks completely.
>
> (www.cnn.com, 30 May 2008)

Japan said Friday [30 May] that it had withdrawn an offer to send tents and other material to China by military aircraft and would dispatch it by civil planes instead. Japanese officials said the abrupt shift came about in deference to Chinese sensitivities to strong lingering resentment of Japan because of that country's invasion of China in the 1930s. A military airlift would have marked the first mission by Japan's Self Defence Forces to China since the end of World War II. Nobutaka Machimura [Japan's chief cabinet secretary]: 'Currently we have no plan to use aircraft of the Self Defence Force. This is not something that should be done if it creates friction' ... Shigeru Ishiba [Japan's defence minister]: 'The country has different memories of Japan than it does of other nations. We have to continue making every effort in an honest way to establish firm relations of trust' ... In speaking publicly of the talks on aid between the two countries for the first time, Chinese officials would not say whether Beijing had requested a Japanese airlift or whether the offer had come from Japan. 'If the Japanese Self Defence Forces are ready to provide assistance, then the specifics will be discussed by the two countries' defence departments,' a foreign ministry spokesman, Qin Gang, said Thursday [29 May] before the Japanese offer was modified. The diplomatic wording appeared to reflect official Chinese concern over widespread animosity toward Japan. Reports of the possible military airlift prompted swift criticism among many online commentators in China.

(www.iht.com, 30 May 2008)

Japan's defence minister Shigeru Ishiba said he was aware that 'a backlash and aversion to Japan has been posted on websites', but added that the decision would not derail plans for future defence exchanges. The chief cabinet secretary, Nobutaka Machimura, said Tokyo would instead send civilian planes to the affected region. He said: 'As there were concerns in China, Japan and China had discussions and decided to shelve the idea of Self Defence Force planes providing transport' ... Russian and US military planes have already visited the devastated region.

(www.guardian.co.uk, 30 May 2008)

Yesterday [30 May] Nobutaka Machimura, Japan's chief cabinet secretary, said: 'Considering, among other things, cautious views emerging in some quarters in China and, after discussions between Japan and China, we have decided to forgo transportation using aircraft from the Self Defence Forces' ... Commenting on the change of plan, Shigeru Ishiba, Japan's defence minister, cited 'something close to a backlash' on Chinese websites ... In a rare statement to the media, China's defence ministry insisted that Beijing has 'never suggested' the use of military aircraft. China's foreign ministry, which had previously appeared open to the idea of Air Self Defence Force [ASDF] flights, declined to comment ... Tokyo announced on Wednesday [28 May] that Beijing had requested aid and had 'wondered if it would be possible' to deliver it with ASDF planes. Japanese newspapers said Tokyo

> had planned to fly tents and medical equipment in ASDF C-130 transport planes to south-west China.
>
> (*FT*, 31 May 2008, p. 7)

'The confirmed death toll ... was raised today [31 May] to 68,977 ... Another 17,974 were still missing' (www.guardian.co.uk, 31 May 2008).

> Authorities had evacuated nearly 200,000 people by early Saturday [31 May] and warned more than 1 million others to be ready to leave quickly as a lake [Tangjiashan] ... threatened to breach its dam ... Xinhua said 'a total of 197,477 people were evacuated to safe ground as of 8 a.m. (00.00 GMT) Saturday' ... Tan Li, the Communist Party chief of Mianyang, had issued another order that calls for all 1.3 million people in the area to be evacuated if 'the barrier of the quake lake fully opens' and floods the area ... Saturday's drill would involve testing the command system of various levels of government officials to ensure that any order to evacuate – if it comes – would be passed on quickly to everyone in the valley ... Tangjiashan is the largest of more than thirty lakes that have been formed behind landslides caused by the quake, which has also weakened man-made dams in the mountainous parts of the disaster one ... Xinhua reported that President Hu Jintao arrived Saturday to check on relief efforts in Shaanxi province. Just to the north of Sichuan, Shaanxi also suffered damage in the 12 May earthquake.
>
> (www.cnn.com, 31 May 2008)

> On Saturday [31 May] a military helicopter carrying nineteen people, many of them injured in China's earthquake, crashed in fog and turbulence. The Russian-designed Mi-171 transport helicopter crashed in Wenchuan county ... Xinhua reported. Xinhua said late Sunday [1 June] that the aircraft was carrying five crew and fourteen other people, including some with quake injuries.
>
> (www.iht.com, 1 June 2008)

> A new official toll put the number of people killed ... at 69,016, with another 18,830 missing ... Many of those who died were children, killed when their schools were destroyed. Almost 7,000 classrooms are reported to have collapsed, killing more than 11,000 children and teachers, triggering complaints that the schools were badly built. On Sunday [1 June] many parents marked International Children's Day by gathering at the sites of collapsed schools to mourn their offspring ... Troops battling to stop a lake [Tangjiashan] formed in the quake from flooding the city of Mianyang are reported to have finished digging a diversion channel ... If dams burst water could reach Mianyang within hours.
>
> (www.bbc.co.uk, 1 June 2008)

'The confirmed death toll on Monday [2 June] was 69,019 ... Another 18,627 are still missing' (www.cnn.com, 2 June 2008).

> In Dujianyang about 200 parents and relatives of pupils killed in the quake gathered on Sunday [1 June] for a Children's Day commemoration in the rubble-strewn grounds of what used to be Xinjian primary school … Angry and tearful they [parents] wore white T-shirts with the name of the school on the front and, in huge red characters on the back, the slogan 'Severely Punish Corrupt Tofu Dregs Construction' – in reference to the remnants left after tofu is made, and a Chinese term for shoddy workmanship and poor materials … China's cabinet has ordered appraisals of all school buildings in the quake zone, according to Xinhua. It quoted a construction ministry investigator … as saying that steel concrete reinforcement rods in the Juyuan Middle School – where 900 students were buried – 'were too thin'.
>
> (www.iht.com, 1 June 2008)

> In the town of Wufu they [parents] shouted slogans about corrupt politicians. In Mianzhu they staged a sit-in. And at Juyuan they were shooed away by soldiers who sealed off the grounds of a middle school so workers could search for the bodies of six children. By the evening one of them had been recovered … At Xinjian primary school in the city of Dujiangyan about 600 people put on white T-shirts that bore red lettering on the front and back. 'We Firmly Ask for Justice for the Dead Students', said the characters on one side. The other side read: 'Severely Punish the Corruption in the Tofu Construction', a reference to flimsily constructed buildings. More than 400 children died at the school … Last week a team of government inspectors visited Juyuan middle school, where 900 died, and after a cursory inspection pronounced the building structurally deficient … After an initial spate of coverage the state-run media have been largely silent on the issue of poorly built schools … At the Xinjian primary school the parents who organized an unofficial bereavement ceremony … blocked off entry to the schoolyard and required all those who entered to write down their names; journalists were asked to show credentials. The organizers said both measures were aimed at keeping out officials, who they accused of trying to subvert previous gatherings … In Sichuan province a local official resigned, saying he felt responsible for the large death toll of students and teachers, thought to be in excess of 10,000.
>
> (*IHT*, 2 June 2008, p. 7)

'In Mianyang the parents whose children died at the Fuxing primary school decided to head to the city government's offices after their ceremony' (www.iht.com, 2 June 2008).

'The government has instructed the country's media to rein in coverage of the schools that collapsed … A notice was sent to media outlets across the country last week' (*FT*, 2 June 2008, p. 6).

> The confirmed death toll … was raised Tuesday [3 June] to 69,107, with 18,230 people listed as missing … The police on Tuesday [3 June] dragged away more than 100 parents who were protesting the deaths of their children

in poorly constructed schools that collapsed in last month's earthquake. The parents, many of them holding pictures of their dead children, were pulled down the street, away from a courthouse in Dujiangyan ... [They] had been kneeling in front of the courthouse. The children attended a high school in Juyuan, near Dujiangyan, where 270 students died ... The protest happened while Li Changchun, one of the country's most senior leaders [the country's fifth-ranked ruler], was touring other parts of the city and reportedly checking on damaged heritage sites ... Xinhua reported that the authorities have delayed for two days an attempt to divert water from a 'quake lake' ... With little rain forecast, Xinhua reported, workers were not likely to start draining off water until Thursday [5 June].

(www.iht.com, 3 June 2008)

[In Dujiangyan] police officers surrounded more than 100 parents protesting Tuesday [3 June] against shoddy school construction ... The police dragged away several crying mothers and harassed journalists ... The standoff between parents ... and officers in black uniforms last for several hours and ended with parents walking off feeling both intimidated and frustrated, said those involved in the protest.

(www.iht.com, 4 June 2008)

Parents are thought to have been prevented from filing a lawsuit against the principal of one collapsed school where hundreds died. And officials seem to be attempting to tone down public expressions of grief ... On Tuesday [3 June] scores of parents went to Dujiangyan People's Court. They went to file a lawsuit, reportedly against the headmaster of the city's Juyuan Middle School, which collapsed killing hundreds of pupils. Eyewitnesses say they were prevented from handing over their document and were dragged away by police officers. Police denied the report when the BBC visited the court later in the day, but about 100 officers were stationed inside the building ... Grieving parents say wreaths left on the rubble at Xinjian Primary School were taken away by officials ... The wreaths were put back after an outcry, but banners, calling for a thorough investigation into why the school collapsed were not. Nationally, state-controlled media outlets have been told to rein in coverage of the schools issue.

(www.bbc.co.uk, 3 June 2008)

Engineers built the spillway to drain water from the lake [Tangjiashan] in a controlled way once it tops the lowest levels of debris blocking the river ... They finished work on the channel Sunday [1 June]. Thirty-five so-called quake lakes were created by the 7.9 magnitude quake.

(www.cnn.com, 4 June 2008)

Anguished Chinese parents said Wednesday [4 June] that they would press ahead with complaints against the officials they blame for collapsed schools, a day after the police sought to silence one protest ... Many parents of the 9,000 or more children killed blame flimsy schools and the officials they say

> spurned building safety rules. In Dujiangyan … some parents vowed to keep up their complaints a day after the police prevented about 150 of them from trying to lodge a lawsuit over a collapsed middle school … Officials have said 278 children at the school died, but parents say 400 or more may have perished and pointed out that apartments nearby stood upright while the school building fell … In Dujiangyan on Wednesday troops guarded the area around the school and police officers patrolled the town … In past days Chinese newspapers and magazines have reported on the many schools that fell, citing experts who blamed brittle concrete, thin or non-existent reinforcement and improperly positioned pillars … In Beijing lawyers have held meetings on the rights of quake victims and issued calls for a full inquiry into the schools.
>
> (www.iht.com, 4 June 2008)

'This week a sweeping law was introduced requiring strict building standards for public structures like schools and hospitals' (*IHT*, 6 June 2008, p. 2).

'About 1,869 children were orphaned by the tremor and another 9,000 were killed in collapsed schools' (*The Times*, 5 June 2008, p. 35).

'Beijing estimates that aid from its private citizens amounted to at least $192 million' (www.iht.com, 4 June 2008; *IHT*, 5 June 2008, p. 8).

> A smaller crowd than usual turned out … in Hong Kong … on Wednesday evening [4 June] for the usual candlelight vigil commemorating the 1989 crackdown on pro-democracy protesters in Tiananmen Square … The vigil attracted thousands of people, but the crowd appeared smaller than last year's [2007], estimated by organizers at 55,000 and by the police at 27,000 … Human Rights Watch, the advocacy group, called on Monday [2 June] for the release of 130 people that it described as having still been in prison in China in 2004 after being improperly arrested or tried in connection with the crackdown. More up-to-date figures for the number of detainees are not available, Human Rights Watch said.
>
> (www.iht.com, 4 June 2008)

'This year [2008] organizers put the crowd at 48,000, while the police put the figure at 15,700' (*IHT*, 5 June 2008, p. 10).

> The event … the annual rally and vigil in Hong Kong … is organized by the Hong Kong Alliance in Support of the Patriotic Democratic Movement in China. Its spokesman, Cheung Man-kwong, said both the victims of Tiananmen and Sichuan would be remembered. He said: 'Of course, we are concerned about the Sichuan earthquake, so that is why we agree and decide to donate all the money from the 4 June rally in Victoria Park.'
>
> (www.bbc.co.uk, 5 June 2008)

'The official death toll … has risen to 69,127, China's civil affairs ministry reported on Thursday [5 June] … and 17,991 remain missing' (www.cnn.com, 5 June 2008).

Prime minister Wen Jiabao said efforts to ease a swollen lake had reached a 'critical moment', as he flew to oversee the relief work ... A magnitude 5.3 aftershock hit Sichuan as workers prepared to drain the lake [Tangjiashan] through a long, specially dug channel ... Plans are in place to quickly evacuate an estimated 1.3 million people who live in the surrounding area if the lake bursts. More than 250,000 people downstream have already been moved to higher ground. The level of the lake – which is on the Jian River just above Beichuan – is still rising, although the water had begun seeping out through the debris ... The number of special police in the quake zone has nearly doubled to 5,000. Xinhua reported ... Correspondents say Beijing is becoming increasingly nervous over the grieving parents' protests.

(www.bbc.co.uk, 5 June 2008)

Four more earthquakes measuring between magnitude 4.5 and 5.3 rattled the region during a twenty-four-hour period, ending Thursday [5 June]. Engineers were anxiously watching as water rising behind the dam neared a spillway designed to relieve the pressure on it ... Engineers built the spillway to drain water from the lake in a controlled way once it tops the lowest levels of debris blocking the Jianjiang River.

(www.cnn.com, 5 June 2008)

Workers have already dug a 400 metre channel that is intended to help drain the water and relieve pressure on the [Tangjiashan] dam. But water has to overflow the dam before it can drain along the channel and as of Friday morning [6 June] the water level was still two feet below the lowest point at the top of the dam. The government has ordered soldiers to deepen the channel in hopes of starting the draining earlier ... The dam showed signs of weakening – seepage was already occurring in parts of it, signalling that the dam could burst ... Prime minister Wen Jiabao flew over Tangjiashan by helicopter Thursday [5 June] to survey the scene.

(*IHT*, 7 June 2008, p. 2)

The earthquake killed 69,127 people ... with 17,918 still missing, according to the latest government figures [6 June]. As of 20 May authorities recorded 4,700 unclaimed children whose parents were presumed to have died in the quake ... Domestic and foreign donations had reached $6.33 billion as of midday Thursday [5 June], Xinhua said.

(www.iht.com, 6 June 2008)

Soldiers were ordered to deepen a diversion channel to speed the draining of ... the Tangjiashan 'quake lake' ... More than 250,000 people in low-lying areas about 50 kilometres, or 30 miles, downstream had been evacuated as of Thursday [5 June].

(www.iht.com, 6 June 2008)

More than 250,000 people downstream ... [of the] dangerously swollen quake lake at Tangjiashan ... have already been moved to higher ground ...

> Plans are in place to quickly evacuate an estimated 1.3 million people who live in the surrounding area.
>
> (www.bbc.co.uk, 6 June 2008)

'A court has jailed a man for over seven years for looting buildings which collapsed' (www.bbc.co.uk, 6 June 2008).

'The quake death toll inched upwards Friday [6 June] to 69,130 with another 17,824 people missing, the government said' (www.bbc.co.uk, 8 June 2008).

> [On Saturday 7 June] troops began draining a 'quake lake' at Tangjiashan … Water started draining through a sluice and channel built to release some of the water threatening to break through makeshift dam … [Xinhua quoted a military commander as saying]: 'Emergency work is still proceeding urgently, but in the foreseeable future there is no risk of the dam collapsing' … Work crews are trying to dig a secondary channel to improve the flow … Plans are in place to quickly evacuate an estimated 1.3 million people who live in the surrounding area of the lake, just above the town of Beichuan.
>
> (www.bbc.co.uk, 8 June 2008)

'The official death toll crept up Saturday [7 June] to 69,134 people, with 17,681 still missing' (www.cnn.com, 8 June 2008).

'The official death toll from the quake crept up Sunday [8 June] to 69,136 people, with 17,868 still missing' (www.iht.com, 8 June 2008).

> Soldiers blew up wooden houses and other debris Sunday [8 June] in the lake … to speed the flow of water into a spillway and ease the threat of flooding … The Tangjiashan lake … the largest of more than thirty created by last month's quake … continued to swell even as water gushed down the diversion channel built after two weeks of frantic work by engineers and soldiers … Authorities were still on high alert, although the draining operation was progressing smoothly … Government experts, quoted by state media, played down the threat of imminent flooding, saying Tangjiashan's dam should hold. But state media and officials estimated it would be a week before the evacuees could return home, even if all goes well.
>
> (www.cnn.com, 8 June 2008)

> A 'relatively strong' aftershock shook a massive quake-formed lake Sunday [8 June] that had been threatening to flood more than 1 million people, sending landslides tumbling down surrounding mountains … The effects of the twenty-second tremor on the Tangjiashan lake was not immediately known … Its magnitude was not immediately known … Though water had been draining from a hastily dug diversion channel for nearly two days, the lake continued to swell. Soldiers blew up wooden houses, boulders and other debris Sunday to speed the flow of water into the spillway. Other troops were deepening the channel and digging a second spillway on the other side of the dam … The rising water levels of the Tangjiashan lake … created when a landslide damned the Tongkou River … underscored the

persisting threat to quake survivors, even before the aftershock. Though water began draining from the diversion channel early Saturday [7 June] the effect was hardly noticeable in some downstream communities. The turquoise waters of the Tongkou flowed placidly past the village of Jiuling, about 45 kilometres, or 28 miles, downstream.

(www.iht.com, 8 June 2008)

The magnitude of yesterday's [7 June] twenty-second tremor was unknown, although the United States Geological Survey reported a 5.0 magnitude earthquake at the exact same time ... A number of the lakes burst their banks weeks after powerful earthquakes hit the same area in 1786 and 1933, both killing several times more people than those who died directly from the tremors.

(*Independent*, 9 June 2008, p. 23)

'The twenty-second magnitude five aftershock caused landslides on mountains near the Tangjiashan lake ... The lake's water level was continuing to rise dangerously on Sunday [8 June] despite the drainage channel, Xinhua reported' (www.bbc.co.uk, 8 June 2008). 'Rainfall and further landslides caused by a 4.8 magnitude aftershock on Sunday afternoon [7 June] have made the situation harder still' (www.bbc.co.uk, 9 June 2008).

A further aftershock was felt at 11.00 a.m. (03.30 GMT) on Monday [9 June] ... The water level in [the Tangjiashan dam] ... is still rising, despite the creation of a drainage channel. By early Monday the water level was more than 6 feet (2 metres) higher than the man-made channel created to ease the problem ... Soldiers are using short-range missiles to blast away rocks and mud preventing the water from getting to the channel. Experts are warning that the lake could burst at any time ... Soldiers have managed to make the run-off channel wider and deeper ... and are now working on a second drainage channel.

(www.bbc.co.uk, 9 June 2008)

'Latest government figures put the quake death toll at 69,136 with another 17,686 people missing' (www.bbc.co.uk, 9 June 2008).

'The death toll from the quake was increased Monday [9 June] to 69,142, with 17,551 people still missing' (www.iht.com, 9 June 2008).

Soldiers today [9 June] cleared the way for a third drainage channel from a giant lake [Tangjiashan] ... Despite efforts to cut through the dam and let the water drain away, levels of the lake rose nearly a metre in the twenty-four hours to this morning ... Tremors with a magnitude of 5 hit the area today and yesterday [8 June]. The army is battling to reduce the lake before the rainy season begins.

(www.guardian.co.uk, 9 June 2008)

Soldiers used anti-tank weapons to blast away rocks and mud holding back waters in [the Tangjiashan lake] ... [Troops] were sent Monday [9 June] to the lake to continue the draining operation, which included deepening the diversion channel and digging a second spillway. Troops were carving a third drainage channel … The level of the water continued to rise … The water level was more than 2 metres, or 6 feet, above the mouth of the spillway … Rising water levels indicated the outflow was not fast enough … Another magnitude 5 aftershock rattled parts of the quake zone Monday afternoon, including the Tangjiashan lake.

(www.iht.com, 9 June 2008)

Engineers made progress Tuesday [10 June] in relieving pressure on [the Tangjiashan lake] … Authorities in Sichuan province were concerned that the Tongkou River would top the dam unless they could increase the drainage rate from the vast lake forming behind it, but that has begun to change. Three spillways created by engineers during the past several weeks boosted the outflow so that it now exceeds the amount of water coming in … The increased drainage pushed the Jianjiang River out of its banks, but officials hoped minor flooding now would prevent a catastrophic flood later on, if the dam were to collapse … A pair of magnitude 5.0 quakes have rattled eastern Sichuan province over the last twenty-four hours.

(www.cnn.com, 10 June 2008)

A torrent coursed through … Beichuan … Tuesday [10 June] after soldiers blasted away debris holding back [water in the Tangjiashan dam] … Xinhua said the water level fell by more than 40 feet after the soldiers detonated 'two massive blasts on Monday evening [9 June] which broke through the bottleneck'. The flow of water increased tenfold, Xinhua said, leaving the top of the dam unstable and cracking. Soldiers and civilian engineers on top of the dam were plucked to safety by helicopter … Television footage showed a surge of muddy water sweeping trees and vehicles before it as it flowed through lower lying parts of Beichuan in a broad loop, spilling into sidestreets. Authorities have told former residents of Beichuan that the town will be abandoned and rebuilt elsewhere. It was one of the worst hit in the quake and some 15,000 people died there … Witnesses downstream from Beichuan said the water flowing from the dam had turned into a broad, fast-flowing stream hundreds of yards wide at Mianyang, which is home to some of those evacuated from Beichuan. Authorities insisted that the situation had not slipped out of control.

[A spokesman for the lake relief operation:] 'The flow downstream has increased dramatically, but the dam has not collapsed. The channel has widened but this is not a collapse. So far everything is happening within expectations. As things are we do not expect to have to evacuate any more' … But many former residents took the torrent as the final confirmation that they would never return to homes, stores and other businesses.

(www.iht.com, 10 June 2008)

Low-lying areas in [Beichuan] … were flooded Tuesday [10 June] as a torrent of water surged [from Tangjiashan dam] … the gushing water dislodged wrecked homes, cars and corpses ... Trees, refrigerators and the occasional corpse [were seen] ... The flooding of parts of Beichuan, once the home of 2,000 people, is contributing to the total destruction of the town ... Government officials said in May that they wanted to preserve part of the ruined town ... as a memorial to the victims of the quake ... It was unclear how the flood Tuesday might affect any plans for a memorial ... Many victims were buried too deep in the rubble to be pulled out. In Beichuan, as in other devastated towns, those corpses that were dug out were mostly buried later in anonymous mass graves after forensic scientists collected tissue or teeth samples for DNA testing ... Besides Beichuan parts of several towns downstream from the lake were affected by floodwaters Tuesday. Across the region quake relief efforts were continuing, but corruption remained a major concern. The government announced Tuesday that at least fifteen officials in Sichuan province had been removed from their jobs for mishandling quake aid and thirteen others had been punished in other ways ... The government also announced Tuesday that the wreckage of an army helicopter that crashed on 31 May had been discovered north-west of the town of Yingxiu, at the quake's epicentre. Five crew members and fourteen quake survivors that the Russian-designed Mi-171 transport helicopter were carrying all died in the crash ... Staff workers at the Wolong Panda Reserve buried a nine-year-old panda killed in a landslide during the earthquake ... The body was found on Monday [9 June]; she is the only panda confirmed to have been killed in the quake. One other panda is still missing.

(www.iht.com, 10 June 2008)

A torrent of muddy water and debris roared down from the mountains of Sichuan today [10 June] after soldiers used anti-tank rockets and dynamite to drain a dangerously instable 'quake lake'. Local media said dead bodies, cars and household goods were swept downstream as the controlled flood rushed through Beichuan and other communities ... The measures appeared to work today as the water level of the lake dropped by 13 metres ... Elsewhere, however, the reconstruction effort is in full swing. According to the government, relief workers have completed 57,100 temporary homes and materials have arrived for 88,600 more. Almost a million tents have been sent to the region. Refugees say the government has promised to build permanent homes for all the homeless survivors within five years, though it remains unclear who will pay ... According to the *China Daily* newspaper, fifteen Sichuan provincial officials have been fired for malpractice in quake relief operations.

(www.guardian.co.uk, 10 June 2008)

The controlled release of water with no major flooding was exactly the result the authorities wanted. In the city of Mianyang, one-and-a-half hours downstream from Tangjiashan lake, the river is usually wide and water levels low. In just a few hours that changed dramatically ... There was little chance the river would burst its banks ... Much of the town of Beichuan, just below the lake, was flooded in rushing water … The authorities have called the successful draining of the lake a 'defining victory'. There are other, smaller quake lakes that may still cause problems.

(www.bbc.co.uk, 11 June 2008)

Evacuees hauled mattresses and carts down from temporary camps in the hills [above Mianyang] on Wednesday [11 June] after authorities declared the flood threat over from an earthquake-formed lake that was drained the day before … China has ordered government departments to free up reconstruction funds for the estimated 5 million people made homeless, few of whom had insurance.

(www.iht.com, 11 June 2008)

[On Thursday 12 June] police cordoned off schools destroyed [in the earthquake] … apparently on alert for protests by parents demanding investigations into whether shoddy construction played a role in their children's deaths. Police barred entry to at least two towns [Juyuan and Dujiangyan] where schools collapsed … The security measures underscore how public anger over the deaths of so many children has unnerved authorities … Planning experts have recommended that more than thirty towns … including Beichuan … be rebuilt elsewhere.

(www.cnn.com, 12 June 2008)

Chinese police blocked access to several collapsed schools today [12 June] as distraught parents tried to mark the one-month anniversary of the Sichuan earthquake with ceremonies for their dead children. The clampdown [was] near schools in Dujiangyan and Juyuan … The regime is worried the destroyed schools could become a focus for anti-government sentiment … Central government investigation teams have visited the sites but will not release their findings until 20 June at the earliest … Damaged schools in other areas – such as Beichuan and Mianzhu – are still open. A provincial government official said the restrictions were not ordered by higher authorities … Ninety-five per cent of the buildings in Wenchuan county, near the epicentre, have been destroyed or condemned.

(www.guardian.co.uk, 12 June 2008; *Guardian*, 13 June 2008, p. 26).

The students lined up row by row on the outdoor basketball courts of Sangzao Middle School in the minutes after the earthquake. When the head count was complete, their fate was clear: all 2,323 were alive … Sangzao is a farming town of 30,000 … The school principal, Ye Zhiping … [had been nervous] about the shoddiness of the school building. Ye scraped together more than 400,000 yuan, or about $60,000, over three years to renovate. He had workers widen concrete pillars and insert iron rods into them. He demanded stronger balcony railings. He demolished a bathroom that had been weakened by water … Ye not only shored up … the building's structure but also had students and teachers prepare for a disaster. They rehearsed an emergency evacuation plan twice a year, Because of that, students and teachers say, everyone managed to flee in less than two minutes on 12 May ... From 1996 to 1999 Ye oversaw a complete overhaul. He said he pestered county officials [from a poor county] for money. Eventually the education department gave him about 400,000 yuan ... Ye said in a recent interview that 'The standards now are still not enough' ... The building codes that Ye criticized had been set by the central government in Beijing ... Ye said that construction codes improved after 2000 and that buildings were now supposed to be rated a 6 or 7 for earthquake preparedness. 'But we see from this earthquake that the standard should be lifted to 11 or 12,' he said ... Ye said it [the Sangzao Middle School] would be torn down, never again used for classes ... Structural engineers and earthquake experts outside China who have examined photographs of collapsed schools point to two critical flaws: a lack of adequate iron reinforcing rods and poorly built hollow concrete slab floors.

(www.iht.com, 15 June 2008)

'A landslide in northern China buried a brick factory, killing nineteen workers ... One worker was rescued Friday [13 June]' (www.cnn.com, 14 June 2008).

'In Shanxi a landslide buried a brick factory, killing nineteen workers' (www.bbc.co.uk, 14 June 2008).

'By Saturday afternoon [14 June] the official death toll from the quake had risen to 69,170 ... Another 374,159 people were injured and 17,428 are still missing' (www.cnn.com, 15 June 2008).

Flooding has killed fifty-five people and forced more than 1 million to flee their homes across a stretch of south-western China, including the earthquake-ravaged Sichuan province, state media reported Sunday [15 June]. Authorities said that torrential rains were expected to pound the region for another ten days, raising water levels further ... The flood hit nine provinces the hardest – including Sichuan.

(www.cnn.com, 15 June 2008)

At least fifty-five people have died and seven are missing in flooding across a broad stretch of southern China, state media reported Sunday [15 June]. More than 1.2 million people have been forced to flee their homes across nine provinces, including Sichuan ... Heavy rain in Sichuan, Guizhou and Yunnan provinces will further raise water levels downstream, especially in the coastal manufacturing powerhouse of Guangdong ... Most of those areas are expected to receive more heavy rain over the next ten days.

(www.iht.com, 15 June 2008)

Massive flooding across a broad stretch of southern China killed almost sixty people and forced 1.3 million others from their homes, state media reported Monday [16 June]. People were forced to flee their homes across nine provinces, including Sichuan ... At least fifty-seven people died and eight were missing ... Heavy rain is expected to pummel the southern region over the next few days ... Heavy rain in Sichuan, Guizhou and Yunnan provinces will further raise water levels downstream, especially in the coastal manufacturing powerhouse ... Most of those areas are expected to receive more heavy rain over the next ten days ... The worst hit province was Guangdong, where twenty people died and eight were missing ... Streets and houses along the Fijian River in Guangdong were submerged in the worst flooding to hit the Pearl River Delta region in fifty years.

(www.cnn.com, 16 June 2008)

Two human rights groups expressed concern on Sunday [15 June] over the fate of Huang I, a Chinese activist who friends fear was detained for offering support to families of children who died in the Sichuan earthquake. Huang lives in Chengdu, capital of Sichuan province ... New York-based Human Rights in China said it had confirmed his detention on 10 June in Chengdu, but that police did not disclose the grounds. Huang was previously jailed on a charge of subversion of state power ... PEN, which champions writers' freedoms, expressed alarm over Huang's detention and said two of his associates, Huang Xiaoping and Zhang I, were detained on 16 May after declaring their intention to join the rescue efforts. Huang Xiaoping was released after fifteen days, but Zhang was still being held, the group said. In a separate case, PEN reported that Zeng Hong ling, a fifty-three-year-old retired worker from the quake-hit area of Mianyang, was detained on 9 June on suspicion of 'illegally providing information overseas'. Zeng, who published a series of articles entitled 'The accounts of my personal experiences during the earthquake' on an overseas website, was being held at a detention centre in Mianyang, PEN said.

(www.iht.com, 15 June 2008)

At least sixty-three people have died in the past month ... China's overall flood deaths for the year stood at 171 ... The central government Tuesday [17 June] ordered inspectors to be on alert for price gouging in food markets in areas ravaged by some of the worst flooding in five decades. More torrential rain fell Tuesday ... Provinces on the lower and middle parts of the [Yellow] River ... the nation's second longest after the Yangtze River ... including Shanxi, Shaanxi, Henan and Shandong were in the most danger. At least sixty-three people have died in ten provinces and thirteen more were missing in the flooding triggered by heavy rainfall that began last month [May] ... So far this year [2008] flooding in twenty provinces and the western Xinjiang region has already killed 171 people ... At least 1.27 million people have been relocated ... the hardest hit provinces include Guangxi. Jiangxi, Hunan, Hubei, Guangdong, Guizhou, Yunnan, Shavian and Anhui. The most recent flooding has not been as severe as in 2005, when at least 536 people died nationwide. In 1998 flooding during China's summer season claimed 4,150 lives.

(www.iht.com, 17 June 2008)

The government said the storms and floods had killed at least sixty-three people over the past week, left thirteen missing and affected more than 17 million people in nine southern provinces. The high waters have also inundated ... cropland, set off landslides, damaged roads and bridges and forced more than 1.5 million people to flee their homes in southern and central provinces ... The government said that about twenty provinces were affected by heavy rains and flooding that began early this month [June] and that some areas were experiencing the worst flooding in 100 years. Forecasters were saying that heavy rain could cause further damage over the next five days. China Central Television reported Tuesday afternoon [17 June] that about 200 people had been killed or were missing because of floods in recent weeks.

(www.iht.com, 17 June 2008)

The death toll in southern China flooding has risen to more than 100 ... Media reports varied Tuesday [17 June] on the death toll from the flooding. The China News Agency reported that 112 people have died, citing the China ministry of civil affairs. The *China Daily*, also citing government sources, reported that 169 people have died. The floods have displaced 1.27 million people, according to both sources, with the deaths occurring in twelve provinces in the area. Hardest hit provinces are Guangxi, Guangdong, Hunan and Jiangxi.

(www.cnn.com, 17 June 2008)

'In total the floods have affected approximately 18 million people' (www.cnn.com, 17 June 2008).

Floodwaters began to recede in parts of southern China today [17 June] after killing at least sixty-three people ... But heavy rain forecast for the next few days in central China had officials worrying about flooding on the Yellow River, the country's second longest, which flows through some of the most populous and poorest provinces ... At least 1.66 million people were evacuated from their homes.

(www.independent.co.uk, 17 June 2008)

For weeks after the devastating earthquake that struck Sichuan province last month [May] ... the Chinese government provided precise daily updates on the rising numbers of dead and missing. In the past few days the updates have all but stopped, frozen now with grim precision at the figure of 69,172. Behind this seeming clarity, however, lies a far messier reality. Officials involved in the data collection process quietly acknowledge that the publicly available death toll is little more than a rough guess of numbers of people killed in the 12 May earthquake ... Methods of tallying the two categories ... [of] dead and missing ... varied widely from place to place. In some localities the toll was ascertained through body counts, other direct physical evidence or witness accounts, while in other areas mostly guesswork prevailed.

(www.iht.com, 18 June 2008; *IHT*, 19 June 2008, p. 4)

China has fired twelve officials for dereliction of duty and misuse of earthquake relief supplies, a top anti-corruption official said Monday [23 June]. Supervision Minister Ma Wen: 'Quite a number of the reports exposed the misuse of tents, food and other relief supplies. Some revealed the slow reaction and poor ability of a few cadres' ... Administrative punishments had been handed out to forty-three officials, twelve of whom were removed from office. She said ... Ma, who also heads the National Bureau of Corruption Prevention, also repeated promises to investigate possible graft in the construction of schools, large numbers of which collapsed in the quake ... Engineers and parents of students killed have pointed to weak cement, a lack of iron reinforcement, and the favouring of flashy designs over solid construction as signs that building funds may have been siphoned off ... Vice finance minister Liao Xiaojun said the central government has earmarked nearly $7.3 billion for disaster relief and rebuilding. Central government departments have been told to cut spending by 5 per cent to free up additional funds, something Liao said would bring in another $218 million.

(www.iht.com, 23 June 2008)

Twelve officials have been fired by the government for their handling of the earthquake ... They were sacked for dereliction of duty and misuse of relief supplies ... The anti-corruption department received 1,178 complaints exposing 'misuse of tents, food and other relief supplies', said supervision minister Ma Wen. A further thirty-one officials were reprimanded by the department.

(www.bbc.co.uk, 23 June 2008)

Supervision minister Ma Wen said her department had received 1,178 complaints involving officials' response to the 12 May quake in Sichuan province and had dealt with more than 1,000 of them ... While no major quake-related corruption scandals have been revealed, shortages of tents and other temporary housing have led to frequent allegations of favouritism.

(www.cnn.com, 23 June 2008)

The death toll from last month's massive earthquake in south-western China is expected to exceed 80,000, state media reported Tuesday [24 June]. Officially 69,181 people are dead with another 18,498 missing, according to authorities. Vice premier Hui Liangyu: 'Because it is presumed that the missing people are already dead, the total death toll of this disaster is likely to exceed 80,000' ... If all the missing are dead then the death toll would top 87,000.

(www.cnn.com, 24 June 2008)

In Chengdu, Sichuan province, the provincial education bureau warned schools to be on the look-out for trouble-makers. 'Schools must set up an effective plan to ensure stability,' read the notice, which called for twenty-four hours' surveillance in order to 'absolutely prevent petitioners from going to Beijing' ... [which] is making its final preparations for the Olympic Games, which will open on 8 August.

(www.iht.com, 26 June 2008)

[US] Secretary of States Condoleezza Rice praised China's post-quake recovery efforts during a visit to the disaster zone on Sunday [29 June], saying it contrasted with Myanmar's reluctance to allow outside aid after a cyclone devastated the country. Rice was the highest ranking American to inspect damage from the 12 May quake ... She stopped in Dujiangyan, a badly hit city of 250,000, where officials said 3,000 people died and 90 per cent of the buildings were now uninhabitable ... Rice said China's efforts contrasted with that of Myanmar's ruling junta, which faced worldwide criticism after Cyclone Nargis hit in May for failing to speed aid to survivors and initially barring foreign aid workers from the hardest hit area, the Irrawaddy Delta. The government's official death toll this week was more than 84,500 ... Grieving parents in Dujiangyan, about an hour's drive by car from the provincial capital of Chengdu, have unsuccessfully tried to file a lawsuit demanding compensation along with an explanation and apology from the government for the large number of students killed. But officials have refused to accept their papers.

(www.iht.com, 29 June 2008)

Security forces are putting pressure on angry parents to abandon demands for a full investigation into why so many schools collapsed in the May earthquake in Sichuan province and have rounded up human rights workers in the earthquake-ravaged region ... Beijing ordered a nationwide crackdown on dissent over the weekend, calling on officials to ensure 'zero mass petitions to Beijing, zero petitions to provincial capitals and no mass incidents during the Olympic Games period'.

(*FT*, 2 July 2008, p. 1)

Approximately 130,000 troops from the army, navy, air force and 2nd Artillery scrambled to the mountains of Sichuan, China's broadest deployment of its armed forces since it fought a border war with Vietnam in 1979 ... Seven weeks later 137,000 troops remain deployed in Sichuan, pitching tents for the homeless, feeding people, repairing roads and clearing and moving ... debris ... [In June the military claimed it] had saved 3,336 people.

(*IHT*, 2 July 2008)

An outspoken pro-democracy lawmaker in Hong Kong was barred Friday [4 July] from travelling to south-west China to visit areas damaged in a massive earthquake. Leung Kwok-hung, a member of the territory's Legislative Council, received word that Chinese authorities had rejected his application for the necessary travel documents shortly before he was to board a plane to the mainland Friday afternoon. Like many pro-democracy activists, he has been refused a 'home-return permit', the document that lets Hong Kong Chinese travel to the mainland without a visa ... the maverick lawmaker, also known as 'Long Hair', was among a twenty-member delegation scheduled to pay a three-day visit to Sichuan to survey the damage from the

12 May earthquake and meet with local officials. Four other pro-democracy lawmakers, however, received approval to travel minutes before they boarded the plane ... Leung was turned back at the mainland border last year [2007] in a bid to petition in Beijing for direct elections in Hong Kong.

(www.iht.com, 4 July 2008)

China has launched a massive campaign to ensure earthquake relief funds are not misused by local officials. Nearly 10,000 auditors have been dispatched to areas of Sichuan hit by the disaster in May, to guarantee money is spent on those who actually need it ... China says there have been no major cases of embezzlement ... Chinese leaders ... recently unveiled a five-year plan to fight [corruption] ... Ordinary people have donated about $7.4 billion ... Foreign donors have so far provided about $218 million worth of cash and goods for the relief effort ... Officials recently said they had received nearly 1,200 complaints from the public about the misuse of earthquake funds. So far twelve officials have been sacked, with thirty-one others punished, according to Ma Wen, head of the National Bureau of Corruption Prevention ... problems have occurred, but these are small said Ms Ma. They include accounting irregularities and exaggerating relief needs. This favourable view is backed up by the International Federation of Red Cross and Red Crescent Societies.

(www.bbc.co.uk, 8 July 2008)

Three weeks after the earthquake in Sichuan province five bereaved fathers whose children died in collapsed schools sought help from a local human rights activist named Huang Qi. The fathers visited Huang at the Tianwang Human Rights Centre, an informal advocacy organization in the provincial capital of Chengdu, where he worked and lived ... A week later plainclothes officers intercepted Huang on the street outside his home and stuffed him into a car. The police have informed his wife and mother that they are holding him on suspicion of illegally possessing state secrets ... Huang, who was detained on 10 June [2008], has not yet been formally charged with any crime ... Activists who tried to gather and publish information about school construction were detained.

(www.iht.com, 12 July 2008)

Hundreds of parents protesting shoddy school construction that they say led to the deaths of their children in the May earthquake were harassed by riot police and criticized by local government officials, the parents said Wednesday [16 July]. Local officials were also trying to buy the silence of the parents by offering them 60,000 yuan, or $8,700, if they signed a contract agreeing not to raise the school issue further ... The confrontation between grieving parents and the police erupted Tuesday morning [15 July] as 200 parents protested outside the government offices in the city of Mianzhu in Sichuan province ... It was the latest in a series of protests held by grieving parents, many of whom lost their only child in the quake ... The authorities have ordered the police to crack down on the rallies. Chinese news organizations have also been told by the central government not to report on the schools, and all journalists are barred from approaching the sites of the collapses. The parents in Mianzhu were demanding Tuesday that the government offer a full report on why the Dongqi Middle School collapsed, killing at least 200 of the school's 900 students. The government has reported that a total of 7,000 classrooms collapsed during the 12 May earthquake, and some people estimate that 10,000 of the nearly 70,000 confirmed deaths were schoolchildren. In the aftermath of the quake many local governments promised to formally investigate the school collapses, but parents across Sichuan complain they have yet to receive any reports … [One protester] said the parents of Dongqi students were asked to sign a contract agreeing to receive 60,000 yuan from the government of Sichuan province, but most of the parents involved in the protest refused to sign … [The protester] said the parents from Dongqi Middle School would petition their case at higher levels of government. Many of the parents are farmers or self-employed small businesspeople … Hundreds of parents also held a rally on Tuesday [15 July 2008] in the city of Shifang to protest government attempts to give them compensation in return for their silence … A report from Radio Free Asia … said the local government was offering to hand out 100,000 yuan to each household.

(www.iht.com, 16 July 2008; *IHT*, 17 July 2008, p. 5)

China began withdrawing the first batch of 40,000 troops on Monday [21 July] from the three provinces hit by the 12 May earthquake, as the authorities shifted the focus from rescue work to reconstruction. The order, signed by President Hu Jintao, who also heads the Central Military Commission, went into effect Monday … China mobilized about 130,000 troops and armed police officers to help with relief and reconstruction in Sichuan, Gansu and Shaanxi after the 7.9 magnitude earthquake. The quake destroyed a massive swathe of Sichuan as well as the two neighbouring provinces, leaving nearly 70,000 confirmed dead and another 18,000 missing. An estimated 5 million people were left homeless. The first group of soldiers, about 500 paratroopers, left the Sichuan capital of Chengdu by train on Monday … The remaining troops will continue their work in road repair and disease prevention … As of 18 July the troops and armed forces had repaired more than 14,600 kilometres, or 9,100 miles, of roads, installed 220,000 shelters and relocated more than 1.4 million people.

(www.iht.com, 21 July 2008)

Local governments in south-west China's Sichuan province have begun a co-ordinated campaign to buy the silence of angry parents whose children died during the earthquake. Officials coerce the parents into signing the compensation contract by threatening that the parents will receive no money at all if they refuse the agreements, the parents say … The amount of the payments vary slightly depending on the local government. Parents in

> Hanwang said they were being offered 60,000 yuan, or $8,800, in immediate cash and a permanent pension of nearly 38,000 yuan ... Local governments have begun to bulldoze the remains of some of the schools.
>
> (*IHT*, 24 July 2008, p. 1)

'Three earthquakes struck western China, killing one person ... in the same region where a 7.9 magnitude tremor [struck on 12 May]' (*IHT*, 26 July 2008, p. 6).

> A Chinese teacher ... from Guanghan Middle School in Deyang city [in Sichuan province] ... has been detained for posting images on the internet of schools that collapsed in the Sichuan earthquake, a rights group has said. Human Rights in China said Liu Shaokun had been ordered to serve a year of 'reeducation through labour'. Liu was detained for 'disseminating rumours and destroying social order', the group said ... The 'reeducation through labour' system allows police to incarcerate a crime suspect for up to four years without the need for a criminal trial or a formal charge.
>
> (www.bbc.co.uk, 30 July 2008)

> The system of 'reeducation through labour' ... in place since 1957 ... allows the police to incarcerate a crime suspect for up to four years ... [It is] an extrajudicial system that sidesteps the need for a trial or formal charges ... Critics say it is misused to detain political or religious activists and violates suspects' rights.
>
> (*IHT*, 31 July 2008, p. 11)

'The government quickly required all volunteers to register with the authorities and operate through an approved organization. Soon it became clear that some types of volunteers were unwelcome' (*FT*, 4 August 2008, p. 7).

'A 6.1-strength aftershock on Friday [1 August] ... one of the largest ... [in the] Sichuan region ... since the main tremor on 12 May – injured 231 people' (www.guardian.co.uk, 3 August 2008).

> An earthquake with a magnitude of 6.0 has struck Sichuan province, the US Geological Survey said. The quake struck just before 18.00 (10.00 GMT) 48 kilometres (30 miles) north-west of Guangyuan city ... [Since 12 May] thousands of aftershocks have rattled the region ... The quake came a few hours after the Olympic torch was paraded through Sichuan's provincial capital, Chengdu, the last leg of its journey before it returns to Beijing for the opening ceremony. The state media agency Xinhua said the tremors were felt in Chengdu.
>
> (www.bbc.co.uk, 5 August 2008)

'A 6.0-magnitude earhquake struck Sichuan province on Tuesday [5 August], killing at least one person and seriously wounding five others' (www.cnn.com, 5 August 2008).

'Three people were killed by ... the 6.0 quake [which] struck near Guangyuan city on Tuesday [5 August]' (www.bbc.co.uk, 6 August 2008).

> China's government estimates it will cost $147 billion to rebuild from the massive earthquake ... The National Development and Reform Commission's draft rebuilding plan published this week includes new homes for more than 3 million rural households, as well as the creation of jobs for about 1 million people, the *China Daily* newspaper reported Wednesday [13 August] ... The quake caused more than $122 billion in direct economic losses, Xinhua reported. Sichuan officials have said they want to rebuild communities within three years and premier Wen Jiabao has said rebuilding in the other two provinces should be complete by 2010. Soon after the quake China set up a $10 billion reconstruction fund – compared with the $40 billion spent on the Olympic Games.
>
> (www.iht.com, 14 August 2008)

> China says almost $150 billion is needed to rebuild the region devastated by the 12 May Sichuan earthquake. The sum is equivalent to over one-fifth of government tax revenue in 2007 ... Three million houses are needed in rural areas and almost 1 million urban apartments, the report said.
>
> (www.bbc.co.uk, 14 August 2008)

'An earthquake in south-western China killed twenty-two people ... The 6.1 magnitude earthquake struck ... close to the town of Panzhihua in Sichuan province, near the border with Yunnan' (www.bbc.co.uk, 31 August 2008).

> An earthquake that hit Sichuan and Yunnan provinces in south-western China killed twenty-seven people ... state media said Sunday [31 August]. The epicentre of the quake Saturday [30 August] was about 30 kilometres, or almost 20 miles, south-east of Panzhihua, near Sichuan's border with Yunnan, according to the US Geological Survey. It put the quake at 5.7, while China's official Xinhua news agency said it measured 6.1.
>
> (*IHT*, 1 September 2008, p. 6)

> A weekend earthquake killed at least thirty-eight people ... Xinhua said on Monday [1 September] ... [The quake] Saturday ... struck along the same fault line as a 12 May earthquake that killed nearly 70,000 ... At least 660,000 school buildings had been destroyed and the tremors were felt as far away as Chengdu, the provincial capital, and Kinming, the capital of Yunnan province, to the south ... [the quake] destroyed 258,000 homes ... A 5.6 magnitude aftershock struck just one minute later, the US Geological Survey said ... The Sichuan provincial seismological bureau said the region was hit by about 300 aftershocks on Sunday morning [31 August].
>
> (www.iht.com, 1 September 2008)

'Aftershocks continued in the day following the earthquake, with one later on Sunday [31 August] measuring 5.6 magnitude, China's Earthquake Administration recorded' (www.bbc.co.uk, 1 September 2008).

> Premier Wen Jiabao ... [visited] near the epicentre of the devastating 12 May quake. During the visit on Tuesday [2 September] marking 110 days

> since the tremor ... Wen said the number of people known to have died in the disaster had passed 80,000 ... The region has suffered hundreds of smaller but alarming tremors in past months.
>
> (www.iht.com, 3 September 2008)

> A Chinese government committee said Thursday [4 September] that a rush to build schools during the country's economic boom might have led to shoddy construction that resulted in the deaths of thousands of children in a devastating earthquake in May. The statement by Ma Zongjin, chairman of an official committee of experts assessing damage from the 12 May quake, was the first time a representative of the government acknowledged that poor construction may have led to the collapses ... In all nearly 70,000 people died in the quake and 18,000 are considered missing. Officials say those still missing are almost certainly dead ... At a news conference in Beijing on Thursday [4 September]. Ma said more than 1,000 schools suffered from at least one of two major problems: they were built on the fault line and collapsed like many other buildings around them. Or they were poorly built. Ma said: '[The second problem involved] the construction quality of the building itself – its structure is not completely sound or its materials are not very strong, which is possible. Recently we have built school buildings relatively fast, so some construction problems might exist' ... Ma also acknowledged how important the issue had become to the public and said the government had sent 2,000 experts to the quake zone to examine the schools ... When the central government teams showed up in the quake zone, some local officials tried to overstate the intensity of the quake so that poor construction or corruption would not be blamed for the building collapses, Ma said. Some officials also tried to report greater financial losses in their areas than actually occurred to get more aid money, he added. Shi Peijun, vice chairman of the earthquake committee, said at the news conference that the total direct financial loss from the earthquake was $123 billion. Ma did not give further details on the experts' findings or say when the government would release a final report. Some Chinese news organizations are once again taking a more aggressive approach to the issue of the school collapses, even though the central government ordered the media to stop such reporting shortly after the earthquake.
>
> (www.iht.com, 4 September 2008)

'Previously officials in Beijing and in south-west Sichuan province, which suffered the most damage, said the sheer force of the 7.9 magnitude quake caused the [school] collapses' (*IHT*, 5 September 2008, p. 2).

> In response to a question about the schools he [Ma Zongjin] said: 'The structures were not necessarily reasonable and the materials were not necessarily strong enough. Both are possibilities ... There were some buildings in the earthquake fault zone that were not able to resist the earthquake. So it did not matter whether it was a building for children, a school, a govern-

ment building or a residential block. They were all destroyed ... There were possibly some construction problems because we have built schools relatively quickly in recent times.'

(www.bbc.co.uk, 4 September 2008)

> A Chinese government scientist has said a rush to build schools in recent years likely led to construction flaws that caused many of them to collapse in May's devastating earthquake – the first official admission that low building standards may have been behind the deaths of thousands of children ... Ma Zongjin (a geologist who is chairman of an official committee of experts): 'In recent years a lot of buildings have been built in China and in this process of rapid development some problems may exist. The structure of the school buildings may not be reasonable enough and the related construction materials may not be strong enough' ... Often schoolhouses were the only buildings in the area to fully collapse and experts say China's problem, similar to that in many other parts of the world, was a lack of commitment by governments to safe schools. Local communist leaders have seemed eager to suppress the matter as they tried to provide for the 5 million people left homeless. Parents and volunteers who questioned authorities were often subjected to detention, intimidation and financial inducements to silence them ... The government has said about 7,000 classrooms were destroyed, but has so far not released a tally of how many school children died in the quake.
>
> (www.cnn.com, 5 September 2008)

'At least thirty people have died after two earthquakes struck the Himalayan region of Tibet ... The US Geological Survey said the first quake's magnitude was 6.6 and the second's magnitude was 5.1' (www.bbc.co.uk, 6 October 2008).

'Strong earthquakes hit China's remote western regions of Tibet and Xinjiang today [6 October], but both appear to have struck sparsely populated mountainous areas and caused only limited damage' (www.independent.co.uk, 6 October 2008).

'An earthquake struck western China on Monday [6 October] ... killing thirty people ... The earthquake jolted Lhasa ... about 80 kilometres, or 50 miles [from the epicentre]' (www.iht.com, 7 October 2008).

> China will spend 1 trillion yuan over the next three years to rebuild areas ravaged by an earthquake in Sichuan province in May, local media reported Thursday [6 November] ... The funds, which total $147 billion, would have the goal of making 'basic living standards and economic development match or exceed pre-quake levels' ... The budget, allocated to fifty-one of the hardest hit counties, would include 120 billion yuan for health, education and other basic services.
>
> (*IHT*, 7 November 2008, p. 10)

'A 6.5 magnitude earthquake shook Qinghai province Monday [10 November], the US Geological Survey reported' (www.cnn.com, 10 November 2008).

In China's first official acknowledgement of the scope of children's deaths in the massive Sichuan earthquake in May, a senior government official said Friday [21 November] that more than 19,000 children had perished. The 7.9 magnitude quake left more than 88,000 people dead or missing ... Wei Hong, the executive vice governor of Sichuan, the province hardest hit by the quake, said the children's death toll was 19,065. He noted that the toll was incomplete and that officials were still tallying the final numbers. Ma Zongjin, chairman of an official damage assessment committee, said in September that more than 1,000 schools had suffered from poor construction or being built on fault lines ... Beijing has put the total financial loss from the earthquake at $123 billion.

(www.iht.com, 21 November 2008)

The news conference Friday [21 November] was meant to explain how far the government has come in helping victims of the earthquake that devastated Sichuan province last May. More than 200,000 homes have been rebuilt, 650,000 others are under construction, and $441 billion will be spent in the coming years to help make Sichuan whole again, Wei Hong, the provincial vice governor said. But a garbled translation of Wei's words ended up shifting attention from valiant reconstruction efforts to unresolved questions about how many children perished beneath the rubble of their poorly built schools. Asked about the final student death toll by a foreign reporter, Wei gave a lengthy answer that ended with the figure of 19,065 – more than double previous estimates and one that would suggest that a quarter of earthquake victims were children ... The figure seemed a stunningly frank admission that the quake's toll on children had been even more horrific than anyone imagined. Later, however, the government issued a clarification, insisting that Wei's remarks had been flubbed by his translator. The 19,065 figure applied to the number of positively identified victims, it said, not the number of dead students. For now the official toll stands at 69,227, with 18,222 missing. A government spokesman said the authorities were still working on a final tally of students ... During his news conference Wei was eager to move on to other issues, pointing out that 2 million people still remain homeless and vulnerable as winter approaches.

(www.iht.com, 21 November 2008; *IHT*, 22 November 2008, p. 6)

Parents whose children died in the collapse of an elementary school during the May earthquake have filed a lawsuit against government officials and a construction contractor. The lawsuit is the first filed by grieving parents ... The lawsuit was filed on 1 December in a court in the city of Deyang in Sichuan province ... The parents who brought the lawsuit said in interviews last weekend that they were waiting to hear whether the court would allow the case to go forward ... One of the plaintiffs said that the parents were demanding compensation equivalent to $19,000 per dead child. Over the summer the local government had offered parents the equivalent of $8,000 in cash and several thousand more in post-retirement pension payments if the parents agreed to drop the issue of the collapsed schools ... [Another plaintiff] said that parents of fifty-seven dead children were taking part in the lawsuit ... At least 127 students were crushed to death ... in the collapse of Fuxin No. 2 Primary School ... One parent said a court official met with several parents on 8 December to say that the court would not accept the case. No formal answer has come yet.

(www.iht.com, 22 December 2008; *IHT*, 23 December 2008, p. 2)

The suit, dated 1 December, asked for $1.1 million in damages and a public apology ... But last week a judge at the Intermediate People's Court in the city of Deyang rejected the lawsuit ... The parents have said they would pursue the case to the nation's highest court.

(www.iht.com, 26 December 2008)

Government officials have acknowledged that many schools across the country are poorly constructed and that 20 per cent of primary schools in one south-western province may be unsafe ... The ministry of education report ... was published by the state media on Friday [26 December] ... Nearly 2.5 per cent of all primary and middle schools in China have structural problems ... [with] 90 per cent of these schools in rural areas and the earthquake-prone zone west of the country. The report singled out Yunnan province, just south of Sichuan, as having some of the most structurally unsound schools, including 20 per cent of the province's primary schools and 11 per cent of its middle schools ... On Friday morning a 4.9 magnitude earthquake shook Yunnan province, injuring nine people.

(www.iht.com, 26 December 2008)

On Saturday [27 December] the government took on ... shoddy construction by creating stricter codes to make schools and other public buildings more resistant to earthquakes ... The regulations, passed by the National People's Congress, impose new requirements on both new and existing schools. They also cover hospitals and shopping centres ... The rules ... would be carried out largely by local governments.

(www.iht.com, 28 December 2008)

President Hu Jintao visited a region of south-west China over the weekend that was hard hit by the earthquake last May, according to a report on Monday [29 December] by Xinhua. It was Hu's second visit to the area since 16 May, when he flew to Sichuan province to check on rescue efforts ... Hu has made his trips in the footsteps of prime minister Wen Jiabao, who has travelled to the earthquake region a half-dozen times ... Many survivors are still living in prefabricated homes with little heating in the depths of winter.

(www.iht.com, 30 December 2008)

'Quake reconstruction is a central plank of the government's stimulus plan for the ailing Chinese economy. It is set to take one quarter of a promised spending increase of 4 trillion yuan ($586 billion)' (www.iht.com, 30 December 2008).

> Parents who were trying to travel secretly from south-west China to Beijing this week to ask the central government for a full investigation into deadly school collapses during the May earthquake were stopped by the local police and forced to return to their homes ... A leader of the grieving parents ... was detained overnight and released only after more than sixty parents gathered at the gates of the town government to demand that the authorities free him ... Many parents have said they want to make their case to the central government in Beijing, in the belief that those authorities will help rather than hinder them in their quest for justice. The parents who tried to leave for Beijing on Tuesday [6 January] are from the town of Fuxin in Sichuan province, where the No. 2 Primary School collapsed, killing at least 126 children. Nearly sixty sets of parents from Fuxin joined together to file a lawsuit on 1 December against government officials and a construction contractor, but the court has declined to hear the case. The parents said in interviews in late December that going to Beijing would be a last resort.
>
> (www.iht.com, 9 January 2009)

> A human rights activist who tried to help grieving parents push for an official investigation into a school that collapsed during last May's earthquake in Sichuan province has been charged with illegal possession of state secrets, a legal step Chinese officials take when they intend to punish a dissident. The advocate, Huang Qi, runs an informal organization called the Tianwang Human Rights Centre in the city of Chengdu, the capital of Sichuan, in south-west China. Huang's wife, Zeng Li, said she was told Monday [2 February] the charge against her husband and that a closed-door trial would be held soon ... Huang has been held since 10 June without being indicted ... Huang was detained on 10 June after posting an article on his centre's website ... relating the demands of five parents whose children had died in the collapse of Dongqi Middle School in the town of Hanwang. The parents wanted compensation, an investigation into the school's construction and the responsible parties to be held accountable if fault was found ... Huang and Zeng started their human rights organization in 1998 to focus on human trafficking. In 2000, after Huang wrote on his website about a member of the banned Falun Gong spiritual movement who had been beaten to death in police custody, the local police blocked his site. Huang then moved his content to a server in the United States. He later wrote about a fifteen-year-old boy who was detained in Chengdu during the 1989 student-led protests in Beijing and died in police custody. The police detained Huang after that and a court eventually found him guilty of inciting subversion. Huang was sentenced to prison for five years. When he got out he started his website again and asked for human rights advocates to contribute articles.
>
> (www.iht.com, 2 February 2009; *IHT*, 3 February 2009, p. 5)

Pressure from a dam … Zipingpu Dam, the area's biggest … its reservoir's heavy waters weighing on geologic fault lines, may have helped trigger China's devastating earthquake last May, some scientists say … The quake cracked Zipingpu, forcing the draining of the reservoir … [One Chinese engineer] said Wednesday [4 February] that the immense weight of Zipingpu's waters … probably affected the timing and magnitude of the quake. Though earthquakes are not rare in the area, one of such magnitude had not occurred for thousands of years … Many scientists are unconvinced that the Zipingpu Dam caused the Sichuan quake, even if it may have been a factor.

(www.iht.com, 5 February 2009)

A growing number of US and Chinese scientists are questioning whether the calamity was triggered by a four-year-old reservoir erected close to the earthquake's geological fault line … The authorities have steadfastly denied any notion that reservoir building either helped trigger the earthquake or placed citizens at a risk of a burst dam, as some scientists have contended … Although a reservoir cannot by itself cause an earthquake, some scientists contend that it can hasten its occurrence if geological conditions for a quake exists … [One US scientist] said the stress of the water's weight might have hastened the Sichuan earthquake by a few hundred years … Controversy quickly followed the start of construction in 2001 … A retired senior engineer from the provincial seismological authorities argued that major fault lines occurred in the area and officials were underestimating the potential for a major earthquake.

(*IHT*, 6 February 2009, pp. 1, 4)

A vice governor of the province hardest hit by the earthquake last May said Sunday [8 March] that many schools collapsed then because of the strength of the 7.9 magnitude quake, and not because of shoddy construction. Wei Hong, one of the eight vice governors of Sichuan province, also declined to make public the number of schoolchildren killed, asserting that the exact tally had still not been calculated almost ten months later.

(*IHT*, 9 March 2009, p. 2)

One of the most prominent and provocative artists in China is challenging the government to end what he calls its 'cover-up' on the devastating earthquake last May … Ai Weiwei, an internationally acclaimed artist who helped design the Olympic National Stadium known as the Bird's Nest, is creating a sensation in China by posting angry commentaries about government incompetence on his popular blog … On his blog the artist has published his own list of children killed in the 7.9 magnitude earthquake, having already gathered over 1,500 names … Nearly ten months after the earthquake the government still says it is unclear how many children died in the rubble … Although he participated in the design process on the National Stadium, he vowed to stay away from the Beijing Olympics opening ceremony, saying he believes in freedom, not autocracy.

(www.iht.com, 19 March 2009; *IHT*, 20 March 2009, p. 4)

'When the city of Tangshang was hit by an earthquake in 1976 240,000 people died, but that toll was classified for three years and foreign journalists were excluded for seven. Yet after last year's Sichuan earthquake coverage began in hours' (*Guardian*, 21 March 2009, p. 23).

> Police have arrested a man who was investigating whether poor construction caused schools to collapse during last year's massive earthquake. The detention of Tan Zuoren is part of a crackdown in Sichuan province just weeks ahead of the first anniversary of the quake … [said] the Centre for Human Rights and Democracy … Mr Tan was detained on 28 March on charges of subversion of state policies … Tan Zuoren had asked internet users and people who lost their children in the quake to help compile a detailed database of the victims. He also asked volunteers to detail any evidence of poor construction at the schools … Mr Tan was the latest of several government critics to be detained or summoned for questioning in recent weeks.
>
> (www.bbc.co.uk, 1 April 2009)

> Amnesty International has called on the Chinese government to stop intimidating parents and relatives of the child victims, who face harassment and arrest as they seek justice for the dead and injured … The number of children who perished has never been released, but some estimates put it at around 10,000 – out of a death toll of 80,000. More than 80,000 families lost their only child in the disaster, with angry parents blaming shoddy building – or 'tofu construction' – for their loss … The Amnesty report, entitled *Justice Denied: Harassment of Sichuan Earthquake Survivors and Activists*, outlines how officials in the province detained parents and relatives for up to three weeks for simply trying to get answers about how their children died.
>
> (*Independent*, 4 May 2009, p. 15)

> Parents who lost their children in China's earthquake fear they will not be allowed to properly commemorate the disaster's first anniversary. Many parents want to return to the site of the schools in Sichuan that killed their children when they collapsed. But the authorities have previously stopped them going to the schools, and are said to be monitoring the parents ahead of 12 May … Amnesty International this week released a report saying the authorities continued to intimidate and detain parents who had lost children in the earthquake. It is particularly targeting parents who are seeking answers about why so many schools collapsed during the earthquake, the rights group said.
>
> (www.bbc.co.uk, 6 May 2009)

> As public attention focuses again on Sichuan for the first anniversary of the earthquake, the Chinese government has ramped up its campaign to stifle discussion of the school collapses. Local security officers have threatened restive parents with imprisonment … Ai Weiwei, a prominent artist who often criticizes the government, has, with the help of volunteers,

painstakingly collected the names of 5,161 dead students and posted them on his blog.

(*IHT*, 6 May 2009, p. 2)

Foreign journalists trying to conduct interviews in the Sichuan earthquake zone in western China are being attacked and detained ... In separate incidents on Tuesday [5 May] a Finnish television crew and a *Financial Times* reporter were attacked near Fuxin Number Two primary school while trying to interview parents of the 126 children killed when the school collapsed. In another incident yesterday [6 May] a correspondent for the *Irish Times* was detained by police for almost an hour for trying to meet parents of hundreds of children who died in another school collapse in the town of Juyuan. He was released but told that foreign reporters were forbidden from interviewing grieving parents during the 'sensitive period' around the ... first anniversary of the quake on 12 May ... Several other media organizations said their staff had been harassed and detained in the earthquake zone ... Following Tuesday's confrontation an *FT* correspondent was attacked by local officials again yesterday while trying to interview earthquake survivors waiting to make complaints outside a government building in Mianyang city.

(*FT*, 7 May 2009, p. 14)

Provincial officials on Thursday [7 May] released the first official tally of student deaths from the earthquake last May, saying that 5,335 children had been either killed or remain missing [in Sichuan]. Another 546 were left disabled, they said. Previous estimates placed the number of students who died in the collapse of school buildings as high as 9,000. Overall, government officials say that 70,000 people died during the 12 May Sichuan quake, and another 18,000 are listed as missing but are presumed dead ... Many of the parents of those who died in the rubble of classrooms say the buildings were poorly constructed. The government has largely quashed the issue by harassing or detaining parents who insisted on pressing the matter ... According to the official media, 7,000 schools collapsed during the quake and another 14,000 were damaged. Although the central government initially promised to investigate why so many schools fell while surrounding buildings remained intact, they have yet to release any results ... More than 5 million people were left homeless by the quake, although the government says most of those are now living in temporary or permanent housing.

(www.iht.com, 7 May 2009)

The Chinese authorities on Thursday released the first official tally of student deaths from the earthquake in Sichuan province last May ... Previous estimates placed the number of dead in the collapse of school buildings as high as 10,000. Government officials say that a total of 68,712 people died in the earthquake on 12 May 2008. Another 17,921 are listed as missing and presumed dead ... The new numbers did little to quell critics. Ai Weiwei, an artist who is one of China's best-known gadflies, said the

> figures were 'meaningless' because they lacked specifics like names, ages and places of death ... Mr Ai's inquiry has yielded the names of 5,205 students, although he estimates the final figure could be as high as 8,000. Parents who have been agitating for a public accounting into the school collapses have reported intense intimidation in recent days ... Foreign journalists trying to interview parents have been detained and have had equipment broken by security officers ... A reporter for the *Financial Times* was punched Tuesday [5 May] ... possibly [by] a plainclothes security officer.
>
> (*IHT*, 8 May 2009, p. 4)

> The figures ... [5,335 schoolchildren dead or missing] do not include casualties from surrounding provinces ... The official number is far lower than other independent estimates ... News reports at the time of the disaster said 9,000 children and teachers died, while independent surveys put the figure closer to 7,000 ... A disproportionate number of school buildings collapsed ... The government has admitted that nearly 14,000 schools were damaged or collapsed.
>
> (www.bbc.co.uk, 7 May 2009)

> In an open letter released Thursday [7 May] and addressed to Chinese leaders, a group of more than 140 Chinese writers, intellectuals and human rights activists welcomed the tally of student deaths but said it was not enough. [The letter:] 'We wish the authorities will do more, not just to investigate the identities of the student-victims but also to find out the factors that caused these massive deaths and injuries, which could have been avoided, in order to prevent similar occurrences. At the same time we ask that you stop the persecution of citizens who are investigating the incident and that you allow citizens to participate in the investigation of the deaths and in post-quake reconstruction' ... The Foreign Correspondents' Club said it had 'received several reports of journalists being harassed and detained in Sichuan province' in the lead up to the anniversary ... Some parents pointed to poor design and use of substandard building materials as some of the reasons why many schools – described as 'beancurd dregs buildings' – collapsed in areas where other buildings were not badly affected.
>
> (www.cnn.com, 11 May 2009)

'The dearth of funds led to what critics called the construction of "three without" schools in rural areas – classrooms built without standardized design, without construction supervision and without quality control' (www.iht.com, 11 May 2009).

> China says it has found no evidence that human negligence caused schools to collapse during last year's earthquake ... Tang Kai, a senior planning official, said there was no evidence that human negligence led to the collapse of any school – or any other building. He said: 'Up to now we have not found that anybody caused or did anything to make the buildings vulnerable so that they collapsed.'
>
> (www.bbc.co.uk, 8 May 2009)

> Hou Xiangfei … vice head of the Sichuan Communist Party committee's propaganda department … denied that any reporters had been harassed or detained in recent weeks and said the government had not received any complaints … He said: 'A very small number of [foreign] media and journalists did not go to the earthquake zone to conduct interviews but to incite trouble and we have proof of this. [They] did not go to interview the masses in the earthquake zone but to ask [the people]: "Why don't you organize yourselves and fight the government?" ' … This week alone journalists from organizations including the *Irish Times*, Finnish Broadcasting Company, Agence-Presse and *Financial Times* reporters were physically attacked by government officials in separate incidents while trying to interview bereaved parents who are calling for an investigation into why so many schools collapsed in the quake.
>
> (www.ft.com, 8 May 2009)

> China has announced a series of measures aimed at improving its response to natural disasters … The new policy calls for bigger relief stocks, satellite forecasting, and training for thousands of officials. The government says more than 70 per cent of China's cities, and more than half the population, are vulnerable to serious natural disasters.
>
> (www.bbc.co.uk, 11 May 2009)

> [On the first anniversary of the 12 March 2008 earthquake] the government said that 160 nations and assorted international organizations had donated more than $11 billion to quake relief efforts, and that their rescue teams had given medical care to 10,000 survivors and saved one victim who had been buried in the wreckage.
>
> (www.iht.com, 12 May 2009)

'Ai Weiwei, an artist and architect who has organized a campaign to count the number of dead children, said that twenty of his volunteers had been attacked or detained and that his blog postings were frequently deleted' (www.iht.com, 13 May 2009).

'An earthquake [has] struck south-west China … The quake hit Yunnan province in south-west China Thursday evening [9 July] … Xinhua reported the quake having a 6.0 magnitude, while the US Geological Survey gave a figure of 5.7' (www.cnn.com, 10 July 2009).

> Thousands camped in tents in south-western China on Saturday [11 July] after a magnitude 6.0 earthquake destroyed thousands of homes, killed one person and injured 320, state media reported … The quake displaced some 250,000 people, the report said, sharply revising downward an initial estimate of 400,000 … Yunnan is part of a quake-prone region bordered on the north by Sichuan province.
>
> (www.iht.com, 11 July 2009)

> A Chinese activist who questioned why so many schoolchildren died in 2008's massive earthquake has been charged with subversion and will stand

trial in mid-August … Tan Zuoren tried to investigate the collapse of school buildings in the quake and the number of schoolchildren killed, estimating at least 5,600 students were victims … he was detained in late March … In May the government finally released its own account of students killed in the disaster, putting the official toll at 5,335 … The charges appear to be linked to Tan's quake investigation as well as essays he wrote about the 1989 student-led demonstrations in Tiananmen Square that ended in a deadly military crackdown.

(www.iht.com, 31 July 2009)

When the American film-makers Jon Alpert and Matthew O'Neill travelled around Sichuan province last year [2008] to document the anger of parents whose children had died in school collapses during the earthquake in May, they ran into a chilly reception from officials. The police officers harassed the two men and their co-workers, detained them and interrogated them for eight hours, they said. Now the Chinese government has denied both of them visas, blocking them from presenting their documentary, *China's Unnatural Disaster: The Tears of Sichuan Province*, at the Beijing Independent Film Festival … The Sichuan documentary was shown on HBO in May [2009], one year after the earthquake … A Chinese film-maker, Pan Jianlin, was tracked by security officials after his documentary (*Who Killed Our Children?*) was shown last year at the Pusan International Film Festival in South Korea.

(www.iht.com, 1 September 2009)

Late last year [2008] the national government strengthened building codes for school buildings. New schools are now required to meet higher earthquake standards than ordinary buildings … This year [2009] the central government allocated more than $1.1 billion to reinforce existing schools.

(www.iht.com, 23 November 2009; *IHT*, 24 November 2009, p. 7)

A moderate, magnitude 5.2 earthquake in Sichuan … has brought down at least 100 homes, killing one person … The National Audit Office reported this week that reconstruction after the 2008 quake was nearly complete. By the end of last October [2009] eleven of seventy-two major reconstruction projects had been completed and fifty-four launched … A total of 480 of the 753 schools to be reconstructed had been completed and 238 were under construction. Repair of 797,900 rural houses and 212,900 urban houses had also been completed, with repairs on 54,400 other homes in progress.

(www.bbc.co.uk, 31 January 2010)

A Chinese activist who had investigated whether shoddy construction contributed to deaths in the Sichuan earthquake in 2008 has been sentenced to five years in jail. Tan Zuoren was formally charged in connection with the bloody suppression of pro-democracy protest in Tiananmen Square in 1989. But human rights groups say the real reason for the action taken against him was his investigations ... Mr Tan was arrested while preparing a report into the collapse of school buildings during the Sichuan quake.

(www.bbc.co.uk, 9 February 2010)

A Chinese activist who sought to document shoddy construction that he contended had contributed to deaths in China's devastating 2008 earthquake has been sentenced to five years in prison for subversion, his lawyer said Tuesday [9 February]. The charges against Tan Zuoren had nothing directly to do with his efforts on behalf of those killed in the earthquake. Instead, he was accused of inciting subversion of state power because of comments he made in email messages about the crackdown on 4 June 1989 ... But Mr Tan's supporters and Amnesty International say he had planned to issue an independent report on the collapse of school buildings during the earthquake in Sichuan, in which more than 80,000 people died. And that, they argue, was the reason for his arrest and conviction ... [His lawyer] said Mr Tan was the first person in a decade to be sentenced for actions related to the Tiananmen Square crackdown.

(www.iht.com, 9 February 2010)

Tan Zuoren was sentenced Tuesday by a court in Chengdu ... for criticizing the Communist Party by writing and protesting recently against the Tiananmen Square massacre of 1989, when soldiers killed hundreds and perhaps thousands of civilians ... Mr Tan was detained in March 2009.

(www.iht.com, 9 February 2010)

The conviction of inciting subversion of state power was based on Tan Zuoren's activities in recent years to draw attention to the student-led demonstrations in Tiananmen Square ... Tan estimated at least 5,600 students were among the dead, while a figure released by the government last May [2009] put the count at 5,335 ... Tan started his investigation in December 2008 and hoped to complete it before the 12 May anniversary of the quake the following year, but he was detained in late March.

(www.independent.co.uk, 9 February 2009)

The Olympic Games

10 June 2008.

China has banned all fireworks from Beijing ahead of and during the Olympics for safety reasons, state media reported today [10 June]. 'The ban on firecrackers and fireworks will be extended to areas beyond the fifth ring road,' the *China Daily* said, referring to a major motorway six miles outside the city centre. The firework ban will last from 1 July to 8 October. The Games begin on 8 August. The sale of firecrackers would also be banned and all stocks will be stored in warehouses specially designated by the city's safety officials ... People living within the area of the permanent ban are only allowed to use fireworks or firecrackers on special occasions, such as the Lunar New Year and other festivals ... Officials also introduced safety measures for petrol stations. Those within 300 yards of the Olympic Games venues must install video surveillance equipment and explosion-prevention devices ... China has already introduced a host of safety measures ahead of the Olympics ... Security has been stepped up at airports where passengers are banned from carrying lighters on to planes, and smoking has been partly banned in the capital ... The Olympics run from 8–24 August, followed by the 6–17 September Paralympic Games, also taking place in Beijing.

(www.guardian.co.uk, 10 June 2008)

13 June 2008.

An explosion a coalmine in northern China has killed at least twenty-seven miners with rescuers still working to free another seven people who are trapped ... The explosion [occurred] on Friday morning [13 June] in Shanxi province. China's coalmines are the deadliest in the world, with an average of ten miners killed every day last year [2007].

(www.bbc.co.uk, 14 June 2008)

'Nearly 3,800 miners died in China last year [2007], an average of about ten a day, making the country's mining industry the most dangerous in the world' (www.iht.com, 13 June 2008).

16 June 2008.

Japan and China are close to a deal that would ease a long-running dispute over gas fields in the East China Sea, reports from Japan say. The two sides were 'working out final details', top government spokesman Nobutaka Machimura said. His comments came after Japanese media said an agreement on joint exploration of disputed areas had been reached. China will allow Japan to invest in drilling projects in return for a share of the profits ... Under the deal China and Japan would conduct joint exploration of several gas fields in offshore areas each side claims ... The deal would allow undersea oil and gas resources to be accessed while putting to one side the wider issue of overlapping territorial claims ... An official announcement could come as early as this week.

(www.bbc.co.uk, 16 June 2008)

Japan's prime minister said that his country and China were close to resolving a dispute over offshore natural gas fields ... Prime minister Yasuo Fukuda told reporters Tuesday [17 June] that the two sides were close to an agreement on developing a string of natural gas fields in a contested part of the East China Sea. While he did not provide details, Japanese newspapers said the agreement would allow Japanese investment in Chinese companies that would drill in the area, which sits roughly midway between Shanghai and the Japanese island of Okinawa ... By allowing Japanese companies to invest in Chinese development of the gas fields, the agreement would allow Japan to share the profits from their development ... The two nations have been in negotiations over drilling rights since 2004 ... The contested gas reserves in the East China Sea are not believed to be particularly large ... [They] are estimated at the equivalent of about 93 million barrels of oil, or enough to meet just three weeks of Japan's energy needs ... Parts of the gas fields sit in waters over which both Tokyo and Beijing claim exclusive economic rights. These claims have stirred strong emotions, as they touch on issues of national sovereignty. Four years ago tensions over the disputed gas fields rose to the point that both sides sent in naval vessels and planes to patrol the area. Chinese patrol boats stopped a Norwegian ship hired by Japan from surveying the sea floor ... In another sign of improving ties Japan's defence ministry said Tuesday [17 June] that one of its warships would visit a Chinese port for the first time since World War II.

(www.iht.com, 18 June 2008)

Japan and China have struck a deal for the joint development of a gas field in the East China Sea ... Japanese private sector firms will take part in China's project to develop the Chunxiao gas field, which is known as Shirakaba in Japan. A small crowd of Chinese protesters denounced the deal outside the Japanese embassy in Beijing ... China started drilling in Chunxiao in 2003 ... China contends that the gas field falls easily within its maritime zone, but Japan contests this. In 2004 a Chinese submarine intruded into Japanese waters near the gas fields ... There are three other gas fields still in dispute and Japanese media said the two sides had also agreed to cooperate on a second area ... The dispute flared four years ago when China began unilaterally drilling in one of the fields. Japan responded with a rare show of force for the normally pacifist nation, sending in naval ships and aircraft to patrol the area, sometimes coming within sight of the Chinese drilling platforms. Tensions seemed to escalate when Chinese patrol boats stopped a Norwegian ship hired by Japan from conducting undersea surveys ... A small crowd of Chinese protesters outside the Japanese embassy on Wednesday [18 June] denounced the natural gas deal, saying it could betray national interests.

(www.bbc.co.uk, 18 June 2008)

China and Japan reached an agreement on Wednesday [18 June] to end a long-running dispute over control of offshore natural gas fields ... The agreement, announced by the Japanese foreign ministry, clears the way for joint development of two gas fields in disputed waters of the East China Sea. The two sides compromised by allowing China to take a leading role in the fields' exploration, with Japanese companies investing in and sharing the profits from the Chinese development ... Still, the Wednesday accord left important issues unresolved. In particular, it sidestepped a broader territorial dispute at the centre of the gas field issue, in which both countries hold competing claims to exclusive economic rights over a broad stretch of the East China Sea. Japan has said it has economic control up to a line about midway between the two nations. China has drawn that boundary much closer to Japan, claiming waters up to the edge of Asia's undersea continental shelf.

(www.iht.com, 18 June 2008; *IHT*, 19 June 2008, p. 4)

In the Chunxiao field Japan will form a joint venture with two Chinese state-owned companies, with profits split in proportion to their investment. Both sides have agreed that the Longjing field, which more certainly extends across the median line, will in future also be developed jointly, with costs and profits split. Agreement has yet to be reached on other fields … The Chinese have cheekily suggested to the Japanese the joint development of possible gas fields around the Senkakus, too – which would be sure to rile Taiwan … The island is keen to be on friendly terms with Japan, one of the few countries to grant Taiwanese visa-free entry. But over the Senkakus Taiwanese show an emotional side.

(*The Economist*, 21 June 2008, p. 83)

20 June 2008.

Beijing officials announced a temporary measure on Friday [20 June] to unsnarl the city's traffic and reduce its chronic and sometimes choking air pollution. The temporary policy, which Chinese media outlined months ago but the government waited to announce until Friday, will be enforced from 20 July through 20 September during the Olympic and Paralympic Games. It will restrict owners of private cars to driving on alternate days, depending on whether the last number of their licence plate is even or odd … Operating hours for public transportation will be extended during the two-month period … [Some] 70 per cent of the estimated 300,000 cars registered to the government will be taken off the roads starting in late July … Trucks and other vehicles with poor emissions standards will be forbidden from entering Beijing during the day, starting 1 July, and will have to reroute around the city.

(www.iht.com, 20 June 2008)

With the Olympics less than two months away, China has been restricting foreign visitors from entering the country in the hope of guarding against terrorist threats or unruly visitors who might plot to disrupt the Games, which begin on 8 August. The government appears to be approving fewer tourist visas. Business executives say they face new bureaucratic hurdles to visiting the city. And hotels are being asked to give the government detailed information about foreign guests … Business executives, particularly from the United States, Hong Kong and Taiwan, have complained that new visa restrictions have crimped deal-making in the run-up to the Olympics. Many Hong Kong executives, for example, say visa rules were tightened in April [2008], forcing them to apply more frequently for visas, and often required proof of a hotel booking, round-trip airline tickets, and, in some cases, a letter of invitation.

(www.iht.com, 20 June 2008)

24 June 2008.

> A Japanese warship is due to arrive in southern China for a five-day port call, the first such visit to the country since World War II. The *Sazanami* will be led into port in the city of Zhanjiang by the *Shenzhen*, the Chinese naval vessel that visited Japan last year [2007] ... The reciprocal calls were agreed at a meeting last year between senior military figures from the two nations ... The *Sazanami*, a destroyer, is carrying relief supplies for the victims of last month's [May's] Sichuan earthquake.
>
> (www.bbc.co.uk, 24 June 2008)

'The warship visit was originally intended to take place early this month [June] ... but was postponed, ostensibly because of political sensitivities' (www.iht.com, 24 June 2008).

> China and Japan agreed to conduct the naval exchange in 2000 ... They postponed it ... The two sides agreed to resurrect the plan last November [2007] ... [The relief supplies represent] the first aid to be delivered to China by Japan's armed forces.
>
> (*The Times*, 25 June 2008, p. 33)

28 June 2008.

> Angry villagers set fire to police and government offices and overturned vehicles in south-west China to protest how officials had handled the death of a teenage girl ... The violence erupted Saturday afternoon [28 June] in Wengan, a county in Guizhou province. Thousands of people [about 10,000], including many middle school students, converged around the buildings and started attacking them ... The unrest was provoked by the death of a sixteen-year-old student who [protesters claimed] was raped and killed ... after being called away by three young men, two of whom were related to officials in the county's security bureau ... One person died.
>
> (www.iht.com, 29 July 2008)

> Local residents were angered after a police report concluded that the girl, found dead in a river earlier in June [22 June], had committed suicide. Her family accused the son of a local official of raping and killing her ... Riots had erupted on Saturday [28 June] when the girl's uncle was pronounced dead in hospital after seeking justice for his niece ... Order began to return after crowds dispersed early on Sunday morning [29 June].
>
> (www.bbc.co.uk, 29 June 2008)

('Police will reopen an investigation into the death of a teenage girl after accusations of a cover-up led to rioting in Wengan ... a state agency reported Tuesday [1 July]. The widespread protests ... stemmed from the official report about the death of a high school student and allegations that a suspect was related to a local officer ... An initial police report found that the girl drowned, prompting

30,000 people to swarm to the streets in anger on Saturday [28 June], Xinhua reported. Xinhua then reported Tuesday [1 July] that the investigation would be reopened. Officials have rounded up 300 people accused of taking part in the riot Saturday, the Hong Kong-based Information Centre for Human Rights and Democracy said': www.iht.com, 1 July 2008.)

('Residents torched a police headquarters and many vehicles … after claims spread that police had covered up as a suicide the rape and murder of a seventeen-year-old girl … The police have promised a fresh autopsy … With officials now acknowledging that the anger reflected broader lapses in policing, the provincial authorities announced the dismissal of the public security chief of Wengan and the chief of the county's legal affairs committee. The Communist Party secretary of Guizhou said officials had mishandled public tensions over mining development, housing demolitions and resident resettlement': www.iht.com, 4 July 2008.)

4 July 2008.

> The White House has announced that President George W. Bush will attend the opening ceremonies of the Beijing Olympics … The leaders of Britain and Germany have said they will skip the opening ceremonies. For some time the White House has said that Bush will attend the Games but had refused to provide further details … On Thursday [3 July] … the state newspaper *China Daily* said (citing an internet survey by Sina.co.cn): 'Chinese people do not want the French president, Nicolas Sarkozy, to attend the opening ceremonies of the Beijing Olympics.'
>
> (www.iht.com, 5 July 2008)

'President George W. Bush will attend the opening ceremony of the Beijing Olympics … While it was understood that Mr Bush would go to the Games, no firm plans for the opening had been revealed' (www.bbc.co.uk, 5 July 2008). 'Germany's Angela Merkel is not attending and UK prime minister Gordon Brown will be in Beijing for the closing ceremony only' (www.bbc.co.uk, 6 July 2008).

'The French media reported yesterday [4 July] that Nicolas Sarkozy, French president, would join his US counterpart George W. Bush in attending the opening ceremony' (*FT*, 5 July 2008, p. 1).

('[On 6 July Japanese prime minister Yasuo Fukuda announced he would] join President George W. Bush at the opening ceremony of the Olympic Games': www.iht.com, 6 July 2008. 'Prime minister Gordon Brown of Britain [has] said he would [only] attend the closing ceremony, to receive the torch on behalf of London, the host of the next Summer games, in 2012': *IHT*, 1 August 2008, p. 7.)

Yang Huanning (vice minister of public security responsible for the Olympics): 'As the Beijing Olympic Games draw near a range of anti-China forces and hostile forces are striving by any means and redoubling efforts to engage in troublemaking and sabotage' (www.iht.com, 4 July 2008).

5 July 2008.

China has ordered the closure of forty factories in a city close to Beijing in the run-up to the Olympic Games. The plants in the eastern port city of Tianjin have been ordered to stop production from late July. The move is the latest attempt by China to minimize air pollution in the capital during the Games in August … On Friday [4 July] similar action was taken in the city of Tangshan, 150 kilometres (90 miles) east of Beijing where 300 factories will suspend their operations. Beijing is one of the most polluted cities in the world and officials have been making extensive efforts to improve air quality before the Games. But correspondents say that pollution in the city is as bad as ever and it is often shrouded in heavy smog.

(www.bbc.co.uk, 5 July 2008)

With Beijing struggling to clear polluted skies before the Olympics in August, the nearby industrial port of Tianjin … about 110 kilometres, or 70 miles, south-east of Beijing … has ordered forty factories to suspend some operations for two months as part of a broader effort to improve air quality during the Games … The planned shutdowns in Tianjin are one piece of a regional plan that is expected to bring temporary factory closures or slowdowns across a large swathe of northern China during the Games … Beijing's air quality remains a major concern for the Games as the city continues to struggle with pollution, despite a $20 billion government clean-up campaign. Beijing is also a victim of its neighbourhood: pollution blows in from surrounding regions, which are dotted with coal mines, coal-fired power plants, steel mills, cement factories and other clusters of heavy industry. The Olympic opening ceremony is 8 August and meteorologists have said that officials must begin closing factories a few weeks in advance to make a difference. The suspensions in Tianjin will begin on 25 July and continue until 30 September, after the conclusion of the Paralympics in Beijing … Tianjin is a host city for the Olympic soccer competition and work at twenty-six construction sites near the city's Olympic stadium will be suspended. Meanwhile, one of the busiest steel centres in China is ordering 267 firms to shut down operations by 8 July … The city of Tangshan, about 150 kilometres from Beijing, is closing sixty-six smaller steel mills, coking operations, cement factories and smaller power generators … The companies could reopen only on an unspecified date after undergoing an environmental review … [Beijing] will begin alternate-day driving restrictions on 20 July to ease traffic and reduce pollution.

(www.iht.com, 6 July 2008)

With a month remaining before the Beijing Olympics, the International Olympic Committee praised the city's preparations Tuesday [8 July] but also cited two remaining 'open issues' of whether Beijing can deliver good air quality and fulfil promises to allow television networks to broadcast from non-Olympic venues.

(www.iht.com, 8 July 2008)

'The government has reversed its ban on live broadcasts by the foreign media from Tiananmen Square … But it is insisting on limited hours and no invited guests' (www.economist.com, 17 July 2008).

11 July 2008.

> A former Pentagon analyst who passed military secrets to a Chinese spy has been sentenced to almost five years in prison by a US court. Gregg Bergersen pleaded guilty in March [2008] to disclosing defence information to a New Orleans businessman, Tai Shen Kuo. Much of the information was about US military sales to Taiwan. Mr Bergersen admitted accepting gifts from Mr Kuo, along with cash payments and money for gambling trips to Las Vegas. A court in Virginia sentenced Mr Bergersen to fifty-seven months' imprisonment, and a further three years' supervision upon release. He had faced a maximum sentence of ten years in prison. Mr Bergersen had been unaware that Mr Kuo was passing the information on to the Chinese government. Mr Kuo, who was arrested in February [2008], will go on trial next month [August].
>
> (www.bbc.co.uk, 13 July 2008)

('A Taiwan-born US national who admitted passing US military secrets to China has beens sentenced to fifteen years in a US prison … Tai Shen Kuo [is] a naturalized US citizen … YuXin Kang, who helped in the handover of the documents, was sentenced to eighteen months in jail on 1 August, after pleading guilty to charges of aiding a foreign government agent': www.bbc.co.uk, 9 August 2008.)

13 July 2008.

> The BBC has found the first evidence that China is currently helping Sudan's government militarily in Darfur. The *Panorama* television programme tracked down Chinese army lorries in the Sudanese province that came from a batch exported from China to Sudan in 2005. The BBC was also told that China was training fighter pilots who fly Chinese A5 Fantan fighter jets in Darfur. China's government has declined to comment on the BBC's findings, which contravene a UN arms embargo on Darfur. The embargo requires foreign nations to take measures to ensure they do not militarily assist anyone in the conflict in Darfur, in which the UN estimates that about 300,000 people have died. More than 2 million people are also believed to have fled their villages in Darfur, destroyed by pro-government Arab Janjaweed militia.
>
> (www.bbc.co.uk, 13 July 2008)

> On Monday [14 July] the BBC's *Panorama* programme revealed evidence that China had sent military trucks to Sudan, which were used in attacks on civilians in Darfur. It also said China was training fighter pilots who fly Chinese A5 jets there. But China's special envoy for Darfur, Liu Guijin, says his country has never violated a UN ban on arms to Darfur … China

has said in the past that it told Sudan's government not to use Chinese military equipment in Darfur.

(www.bbc.co.uk, 15 July 2008)

14 July 2008.

Beijing authorities have ordered firms, shops and other organizations to stagger work times to cut traffic volumes during the Olympics. City officials say state-run businesses should not start work until 09.00 – up to an hour later than usual. They are also encouraging as many people as possible to work from home ... Government departments, organizations providing essential services and schools will operate as normal.

(www.bbc.co.uk, 14 July 2008)

Hundreds of migrant workers angry over the mistreatment of a fellow worker rioted for three days in eastern China, surrounding a police station and smashing cars and motorbikes, a human rights organization based in Hong Kong said Monday [14 July]. The riot began Thursday [10 July] in Kanmen, a town in Zhejiang province, reported the Information Centre for Human Rights and Democracy. Three hundred military police officers arrived Sunday [13 July] and thirty migrant workers were detained, the group said. No injuries were reported ... The rights group said the unrest was centred on a migrant worker who was alleged to have been beaten by a security guard while trying to get a temporary residence permit ... Also on Monday Xinhua said that the police in Guizhou province had detained 100 people, including thirty-nine members of what it said were local gangs, for involvement in the protest last month [June] over the death of the student in the town of Wengan.

(www.iht.com, 14 July 2008)

17 July 2008.

China will ban all entertainers from overseas, Hong Kong and Taiwan who have ever attended activities that 'threaten national sovereignty', the government said Thursday [17 July], after an outburst by the Icelandic singer Björk ... Earlier this year [2008] Björk shouted 'Tibet! Tibet!' at a Shanghai concert having performed her song 'Declare Independence' ... The ministry of culture said: 'Any artistic group or individual who have ever engaged in activities which threaten our national sovereignty will not be allowed in' ... During performances entertainers who 'threaten national unity', 'whip up ethnic hatred', 'violate religious policy or cultural norms' or 'advocate obscenity or feudalism and superstition' will also be banned, the rules say. The new rules come on top of Beijing banning pop festivals and tightening approvals for outdoor events in the months leading up to the Olympics.

(www.iht.com, 17 July 2008)

Foreign entertainers who have taken part in activities that China deems a threat to its sovereignty will not be allowed to perform, according to new rules posted Thursday [17 July] ... The rules say that the background credentials of performers from foreign countries, Hong Kong, Macao and Taiwan will be scrutinized. The rules say: 'Those who used to take part in activities that harm our nation's sovereignty are firmly not allowed to perform in China' ... They also call for barring performers who promote ethnic hatred or 'advocate obscenity or feudalism and superstition'. The rules are the latest attempt by China to clamp down on any political dissent before the Beijing Olympics ... Government officials have set up security checkpoints throughout Beijing, deported some foreigners or refused to renew visas and shut down protests by grieving parents whose children died in schools in the 12 May earthquake ... In Taiwan some entertainers advocate formal independence for Taiwan.

(www.iht.com, 19 July 2008)

Authorities said her [Björk's] outburst 'broke Chinese law and hurt Chinese people's feelings' and vowed to be stricter on foreign performers ... [The ministry of culture said on Thursday 17 July]: 'The content of the performance [by a foreigner] should not violate the country's law, including situations that harm the sovereignty of the country ... [The performance should also not harm] national security, or incite racial hatred and ruin ethnic unity.'

(www.cnn.com, 18 July 2008)

18 July 2008.

Workmen have torn down the home of a Beijing family that was refusing to move to make way for redevelopment ... Hundreds of 'nail houses' have sprung up across China. These are houses whose owners refuse to budge to make way for redevelopment projects. Families often complain that they are forced out of their homes and are not given enough compensation. Earlier this week a Swiss-based organization estimated that up to 1.5 million people have been moved from their Beijing homes because of the Olympics. The centre on Housing Rights and Evictions said this had taken place over an eight year period leading up to this summer's games. It said: '[The] authorities have used tactics of harassment, repression, imprisonment and even violence against residents and activists' ... China disagrees with these figures. It says that just 6,000 families have been moved to make way for Olympic building projects.

(www.bbc.co.uk, 18 July 2008)

20 July 2008.

Beijing started its drastic traffic control plan Sunday [20 July] in a last-minute push to clear the capital's pollution-choked skies in time for the August Olympics. Under the two-month plan half of Beijing's 3.3 million cars will be removed from city streets on alternate days, depending on whether the licence plate ends in an odd or even number ... To further ease vehicle emissions, one of the city's chief sources of pollution, employers have been asked to stagger work schedules and public institutions will open an hour later than normal. Two new subway lines and an airport link should also bring relief. All three lines opened Saturday [19 July] – a month behind schedule. In addition to the traffic plan, chemical plants, power stations and foundries have to cut emissions by 30 per cent beginning Sunday. Dust-spewing construction in the capital was to stop entirely. It is unclear how the effectiveness of the plan will be gauged. The government has not made public a specific target for emissions levels or said how it will measure air quality … A World Bank study found China is home to sixteen of the twenty worst cities for air quality. Three-quarters of the water flowing through urban areas is unsuitable for drinking or fishing. International Olympic Committee president Jacques Rogge has repeatedly warned that outdoor endurance events lasting more than an hour will be postponed if the air quality is poor … Under the two-month plan vehicles will be allowed on the roads every other day depending on even–odd registration numbers. In addition 300,000 heavy polluting vehicles – ageing industrial trucks, many of which operate only at night – were banned beginning 1 July. Five days after Sunday's traffic ban goes into effect special Olympic lanes will begin operating until 25 September, a plan that has been used in previous Games. Beijing is setting aside 165 miles of roadway on which certified Olympic vehicles will be allowed to move from hotels, Olympic venues and Athletes' Village … To further ease congestion employers are being asked to stagger work schedules. Public institutions will open an hour later than normal and two new subway lines scheduled to open Sunday should also bring relief … The plan to clean the grey air seems to match the high security tone of the Games, which will be policed by 100,000 officials. Razor-wire barriers and soldiers standing to attention guard the outskirts of the Olympic Green area and the Chinese have even installed ground-to-air missiles near one Olympic venue to protect it from possible attacks. Security, tight visa rules and inflated hotel prices seem to be keeping foreigners away. Many nightspots near Olympic venues are being closed by security officials, who say the Games are under threat from Moslem extremists in China's western Xinjiang region … Beijing organizers are also in protracted showdown with television broadcasters, who are seeking free movement and reporting during the Games. China's government seems to fear being embarrassed during the Games by pro-Tibet, local dissidents or critics of China's human rights policies.

(www.cnn.com, 20 July 2008)

'[Offending] drivers caught by the surveillance network will be fined 100 yuan ($15) … The International Olympic Committee has said it could postpone endurance events of more than one hour when the pollution is too bad' (www.bbc.co.uk, 20 July 2008).

Despite architecturally adventurous venues and $40 billion spent on improving infrastructure, China's greatest challenge has been keeping the city's air clean for the world's greatest athletes participating in the 8–24 August Games. Instead of blue skies, Beijing's skyline is normally shrouded with a thick grey haze. Already many competitors are choosing to train away from Beijing ... The world's greatest distance runner, Haile Gebrselassie of Ethiopia, has decided not to run the marathon event because the city's pollution irritates his breathing ... The government has beefed up public transportation options for the estimated 4 million extra people who will be off the roads because of the traffic plan ... The city plans to add up to 3,000 more buses by the time the Olympics start, raising the daily capacity for passengers from 12.5 million to 15 million ... On 25 July special Olympic traffic lanes will begin operating and will stay in place until 25 September ... Experts say the city cleanup measures could still go wrong because unpredictable winds might blow pollution into Beijing, or the lack of wind – generally a feature of August – could enable local pollution to build up.

(www.iht.com, 20 July 2008)

On many days Beijing's skyline can barely be seen because of a thick, grey-brown haze that hangs over the city. Already many competitors in the 8–24 August Olympics are choosing to train outside of Beijing and International Olympic Committee president Jacques Rogge has said outdoor endurance events lasting more than an hour will be postponed if air quality is poor ... The government has improved public transportation options for the estimated 4 million extra people who will not be able to use private vehicles because of the traffic plan.

(www.iht.com, 21 July 2008)

The Chinese organizing committee ... [has said] that broadcasters that have paid for rights to the Games, like the US network NBC, will be able to transmit live from the square [Tiananmen] – but only for six hours a day ... After months of uncertainties, officials said on 9 July that all applications for live broadcasting would be approved throughout Beijing and other cities where Olympic competitions could take place. Furthermore, the committee said all broadcasters would be allowed to tape reports from Tiananmen Square ... Journalists and viewers could be facing the most restrictive environment for an Olympics in modern times.

(*IHT*, 21 July 2008, pp. 1, 14)

Hackles have been raised in Taiwan by a reference by China's state-run news agency to the 'China, Taipei' Olympic team, Taiwan says the correct term should be 'Chinese Taipei', supposedly suggesting a merely cultural link with China – not belonging to it.

(*The Economist*, 26 July 2008, p. 64)

China [is] already the world's second largest advertising market after the United States ... A record sixty-three companies have become sponsors or partners of the Beijing Olympics ... The avalanche of Olympic television advertising is compounded by so-called ambush marketing, in which non-sponsors – often rivals of official sponsors – try to grab some Olympic glory without paying the high sponsorship fees. The proliferation of such ads is not going unchecked: China is scrutinizing the ads of non-sponsors, trying to give prime billboard space to the official sponsors ... Further blurring the line between official and unofficial, some competing companies have been allowed as sponsors: three beer makers – Budweiser, Tsingtao and Yanjing – will be Olympic sponsors, authorized not by the International Olympic Committee but by the Beijing Olympic Committee.

(www.iht.com, 20 July 2008)

21 July 2008.

China and Russia signed an agreement Monday [21 July] to end a long-running dispute over the demarcation of their eastern border ... The tug-of-war over the eastern part of their 4,300 kilometre, or 2,700 mile, border reaches back centuries to their competition for territory as imperial China and Czarist Russia expanded toward each other. The struggle resulted in violent clashes in the 1960s and 1970s ... The *China Daily*, reported that Russia will return Yinlong Island (known as Tarabarov Island in Russian) and half of Heixiazi Island (Bolshoi Ussuriysky) to China. The 174 square kilometres of territory are on the northeast border with China ... Former Russian President Vladimir Putin signed a border agreement with China in 2004. But it is not clear how far that accord went to resolve the dispute over the stretch of river and islands along China's north-eastern border with Russia's Far East.

(www.iht.com, 21 July 2008)

The latest treaty involves a dispute over the eastern part of the [China–Russia] border ... However, China still has outstanding border issues with Japan and South Korea to the east, Vietnam to the south and India to the south-west. It has trumpeted its treaty with Russia as a new approach to border disputes. But analysts say that with energy reserves behind many of the territorial disputes, it will be many more years before China can hope to settle its borders with all its neighbours.

(www.bbc.co.uk, 21 July 2008)

'The [China–Russia] agreement settles the status of four islands in the Amur River ... The agreement itself was signed three years ago ... In 1969 a dispute over the Amur islands flared into a brief war' (*FT*, 22 July 2008, p. 6).

After decades of dispute China and Russia have at last reached agreement on where the entire length of their common border lies. On 21 July the two countries signed an accord on the last small stretch that had yet to be formally settled ... In recent years they have been tidying up the remaining odds and ends along their 4,300 kilometre (2,670 mile) frontier. The latest agreement ... resolves the niggling matter of a couple of islands at the confluence of the Amur and Ussuri rivers near the city of Khabarovsk in

Russia's Far East. The two countries reached an initial accord on this problem in 2004. The deal was that Russia would hand over one of the islands, Tabarov (Yinling, as China calls it) and half of Bolshoi Ussuriysky island (Heixiazi or Bear Island) ... The outcome is a compromise. Since the 1960s China had been demanding the islands in their entirety. They had been illegally taken over, they insisted, by the then Soviet Union in 1929. The Russians, who had settled on Bolshoi Ussuriysky, did not want to abandon it. Now the Chinese have got the all-but-uninhabited parts, where, according to rumours in the Chinese media, officials are examining the potential for tourism.

(*The Economist*, 26 July 2008, pp. 64–5)

Two public buses exploded during the Monday morning [21 July] rush hour on the south-western city of Kunming, killing at least two people ... in what the authorities described as deliberate attacks ... The two blasts struck city buses at 7.05 a.m. and 8.10 a.m. ... Public security officials in Kunming, the capital of Yunnan province, provided no information about whether the two explosions were co-ordinated or were separate attacks. Nor did the authorities say whether the explosions were the work of terrorist groups or disgruntled individuals ... The explosions came as China has experienced a spate of riots and public protests in recent weeks ... Last month as many as 30,000 people rioted in Wengan county in Guizhou province in response to allegations that the local police had mishandled the death investigation of a teenage girl. Last week a mob of 100 angry protesters attacked a village police station in Guangdong province in another uprising over allegations of police malfeasance. Last weekend the police in a rural region of Yunnan province killed two people after a violent clash with 500 rubber farmers. The farmers, armed with knives, wounded forty-one police officers and damaged several police cars in a confrontation rooted in a long-running dispute between farmers and a local rubber company.

(www.iht.com, 21 July 2007; *IHT*, 22 July 2008, p. 8)

Two explosions on buses in the south-western city of Kunming have left at least two people dead ... Police said the blasts seemed to have been deliberate ... Police said the blasts were believed to have been due to 'sabotage' ... In the latest incident of unrest in Yunnan, on Saturday [19 July], rubber farmers clashed with police in Menglian county, in the south-west of the province close to the border with Burma (Myanmar). Police shot dead two farmers in the clash, which also reportedly left dozens of police officers injured.

(www.bbc.co.uk, 21 July 2008)

China's largest city [Shanghai] and the host of a dozen Olympic soccer matches started tightening security this past weekend at airports and train stations ... Work to install surveillance systems on every subway train has started, but it is not clear how long it will take ... Also on Monday [21 July]

> Olympics security chief Ma Zhenchuan [was quoted] as saying that a radical Islamic group [the East Turkestan Islamic Group or ETIM] based in China's predominantly Moslem Xinjiang region 'poses a real threat to the Beijing Olympics' ... China has prepared an anti-terror force of nearly 100,000 commandos, police and troops for the Olympics.
>
> (www.cnn.com, 21 July 2008)

'Chinese leaders are mobilizing an army of security many times greater than previous Olympics – 110,000 police, riot sqads and special forces, augmented by more than 300,000 Olympic volunteers and neighbourhood watch members' (www.cnn.com, 29 July 2008).

23 July 2008.

> Beijing will set up specially designed zones for protesters during next month's Olympics, a security official said Wednesday [23 July] ... Worries about terrorists attacks, both from international groups and Moslem separatists from western China, and about protests of any kind have prompted one of China's broadest security clampdowns in years ... Liu Shaowu, director for security for the Beijing Olympic Organizing Committee, said Wednesday that areas in at least three public parks near outlying sporting venues have been set aside for use by demonstrators ... The special protest areas are not near the Olympic Green where most venues and medal ceremonies are concentrated, but rather in outlying parks ... Liu also reiterated that Chinese regulations require that all protesters apply and receive permission in advance, though he sidestepped questions about whether that includes the special zones.
>
> (www.cnn.com, 23 July 2008)

'The authorities have named three city parks where demonstrations, in theory, will be allowed (five days' notice required)' (*The Economist*, 26 July 2008, p. 64).

> Liu Shaowu ... was hazy about how potential protesters would apply for permission and on whether spontaneous demonstrations would be allowed ... [Earlier he] made it clear no activities involving ethnic, political or religious activities would be allowed inside Olympic venues.
>
> (www.bbc.co.uk, 23 July 2008)

> Beijing will permit public protests inside three designated city parks during next month's Olympics, but demonstrators must first obtain permits from the local police and also abide by Chinese laws that usually make it nearly impossible to legally picket over politically charged issues ... Liu Shaowu (director for security for Beijing's Olympics organizing committee): 'The police will safeguard the right to demonstrate as long as protesters have obtained prior approval and are in accordance with the law' ... Under Chinese law citizens must apply to the local public security bureau five days in advance of a scheduled protest. Applicants must appear in person and

> offer detailed information about their topic, any possible slogans and the expected number of demonstrators. The law prohibits protests that are deemed harmful to national unity and social stability or that agitate for ethnic separation. These prohibitions can be interpreted so broadly that most legal protests are not approved.
>
> (www.iht.com, 23 July 2008; *IHT*, 24 July 2008, p. 2)

> Among residents whose neighbourhoods face demolition, the chief objections are a lack of compensation from the government or developers and having to move far from the city centre to find an affordable place to live. Few see the hutong areas ... narrow alleyways or hutongs ... as treasured historical landmarks.
>
> (Nicolai Ouroussoff, *IHT*, 24 July 2008, p. 2)

(Hutongs ... [are] urban courtyards': www.iht.com, 24 August 2008.)

24 July 2008. 'China has issued new restrictions on business visas for the next two months' (*IHT*, 25 July 2008, p. 8).

'[Owing to a fall in the number of foreign visitors, it has been reported that] hotels are cutting prices by 10 per cent to 20 per cent' (*Guardian*, 28 July 2008, p. 17).

'City tourism officials say four-star hotels are only 50 per cent booked during the 8–24 August Olympic Games' (www.independent.co.uk, 3 August 2008).

24 July 2008.

> A tabloid newspaper was withdrawn from news-stands ... and part of its website was blocked ... after running a photograph from the 1989 crackdown on Tiananmen Square protesters. The photo – of two wounded young men being taken away on a rickshaw – was carried in Thursday's *Beijing News* [24 July]. The picture was simply captioned 'The Wounded' and no mention of the protests was made in the text ... The photograph was printed alongside an interview with the Hong Kong-born American photographer Liu Xiangcheng as an example of his work ... It seems most likely to have been a mistake by staff who did not realize the significance of the photo ... Last year [2007] the authorities sacked three editors on a provincial newspaper for printing an advert praising the mothers of the Tiananmen victims for their campaign of justice.
>
> (www.bbc.co.uk, 25 and 27 July 2008)

26 July 2008.

> China said it is examining a statement from a separatist group which is threatening to attack the forthcoming Olympic Games. The group, calling itself the Turkestan Islamic Party, also claimed to have carried out bomb attacks on buses. The blasts, in the port of Shanghai and the western province of Yunnan, happened over the last three months. China has previously denied the explosions were the work of militants but has warned of threats to the Games ... The Washington-based IntelCenter, which monitors terror-

ism communications, said the group had released a video entitled *Our Blessed Jihad in Yunnan*. In it the group's leader, Commander Seyfullah, claimed credit for several attacks and threatened next month's Olympics. IntelCenter quoted him as saying: 'Despite the Turkestan Islamic Party's repeated warnings to China and international community about stopping the 29th Olympics in Beijing, the Chinese have haughtily ignored our warnings. The Turkestan Islamic Party volunteers who had gone through special preparations have started urgent actions' ... China's foreign ministry said it was examining the claims.

(www.bbc.co.uk, 26 July 2008)

Chinese authorities have dismissed claims by a militant Islamist group that it was responsible for recent explosions on buses. The Turkestan Islamic Party said that it had blown up buses in Shanghai and Yunnan, killing five people ... In Yunnan province two explosions on buses last Monday [21 July] left two people dead ... In Shanghai three people died in an explosion in May [2008] ... It also said it was planning attacks on the Olympic Games ... But a public security official in Yunnan ... said no evidence had been found linking the explosions with terrorism. In Shanghai police also denied a link to terrorism.

(www.bbc.co.uk, 27 July 2008)

The Turkestan Islamic Party released a video dated 23 July featured a statement by a Commander Seyfullah. He said, according to a translation by IntelCenter, a terrorism research firm in Washington, which obtained the video: 'We will try to attack Chinese cities severely, using tactics that have never been employed' ... It is unclear whether the Turkestan Islamic Party, which released the video, is part of the East Turkestan Islamic Movement, which advocates an independent state in the Xinjiang region. Turkestan is a region of central Asia from the Caspian Sea to the Gobi Desert, extending through a number of countries, including China. In the video, Commander Seyfullah, speaking mostly in the Uighur language, says his group attacked public buses in Kunming on 21 July, bombed two buses in Shanghai on 5 May and was responsible for blasts in Wenzhou and Guangzhou. In Kunming, capital of Yunnan province, two buses exploded on 21 July, killing two people ... Investigators are still searching for suspects and have tripled a reward to 300,000 yuan, or about $43,500. But on Saturday [26 July] the authorities played down any terror links. A spokesman for the Yunnan province department of public security: 'We have noticed media reports about the claims, but so far no evidence has been found to indicate the explosions were connected with terrorists and their attacks, or with the Beijing Olympics.'

(www.iht.com, 27 July 2008)

28 July 2008.

All tickets to Olympic events in Beijing have been sold, organizers said Monday [28 July], putting the Summer Games on course to be the first to sell out although tickets that went to sponsors and the national Olympic committees of participating counties may not all get used. In all 6.8 million Olympic tickets have been available for domestic and foreign sales. The release of the final batch of 250,000 tickets sparked chaotic scenes in Beijing on Friday [25 July], as a crowd of 30,000 swarmed a Beijing ticketing centre. Police shoved and kicked them and used metal barricades to prevent a stampede among people who had stood in line for up to two days. Another 570,000 tickets went on sale for preliminary soccer matches in the cities of Tianjin, Shanghai, Shenyang and Qinhuangdao, where some tickets remained available. There were no reports of major problems at the other sites … An official with the organizers' ticketing centre said organizers expected those matches to eventually sell out also … The high demand has put massive pressure on the ticketing system and organizers had to suspend one round of domestic sales in November [2007] after overwhelming demand crashed the computerized ticketing system, prompting a switch to a lottery system. Ticket sales for past Olympics have varied widely. The 2004 Athens games sold only about two-thirds of 5.3 million tickets available, and there were many empty seats. The most expensive tickets in Beijing are for the 8 August opening ceremony, which cost $645. Organizers said 58 per cent of all tickets would cost $12.90 or less, in line with efforts to make them affordable to average Chinese citizens.

(www.cnn.com, 28 July 2008)

Chinese media are playing down reports of a third bus blast in south-western Kunming tonight [28 July] – exactly a week after two explosions killed two people in the city. A witness said he heard a loud blast shortly before 9 p.m. local time and saw police and ambulance staff gathered around a damaged vehicle only 200 metres from the scene of the previous incidents. But a police officer … dismissed reports of an attack as 'rumours' and Xinhua said it was not terrorism-related. A local news site for Yunnan province blamed mechanical problems, adding that the engine of the bus appeared to have exploded … The Chinese authorities dismissed a Uighur separatist group's claims of responsibility for last Monday's incidents [21 July]. Officials said those explosions were deliberate but that there was no evidence of terrorism … In a video obtained by a terrorism watchdog this weekend, the little-known Turkestan Islamic Party – thought by some analysts to be another name for the East Turkestan Islamic Movement – claimed responsibility for last week's explosions and several other incidents. They included a bus blast in Shanghai in May [2008], in which three people died … It was blamed on a passenger carrying 'flammable materials'.

(www.guardian.co.uk, 28 July 2008)

'Police said the bus explosion in Shanghai in which three people died was caused by an oil fire and the Wenzhou explosion by a debt-ridden gambler, while there is no evidence to connect the Kunming bus bombings to terrorism' (www.cnn.com, 29 July 2008).

Chinese and Western terrorism experts say ... [that] the Turkestan Islamic Party ... is an offshoot of a secessionist group from China's Central Asian frontier with ties to al-Qaeda ... The East Turkestan Islamic Movement was based in Afghanistan before the US invasion and is listed as a terrorist organization by the United States. After its leader was killed in 2003 members reorganized into similar groups, including the Turkestan Islamic Party and received training from al-Qaeda in Pakistan's tribal area abutting Afghanistan [according to] terrorism experts.

(www.cnn.com, 29 July 2008)

The East Turkestan Islamic Movement (ETIM) was listed as a terrorist group by the United States in 2002. Rohan Gunaratna, a terrorism expert based in Singapore, said one branch of ETIM had been based for a number of years in the border region between Pakistan and Afghanistan, where it had received 'ideology, training and financing' from al-Qaeda. Its numbers had been reduced from several thousand to a few hundred as a result of Pakistani military operations, he said.

(*FT*, 30 July 2008, p. 8)

Chinese officials say the greatest risk of an attack comes from a shadowy group called the East Turkestan Islamic Movement, or ETIM, which promotes independence for the region's Uighurs ... Some outside experts say the organization is fairly small and includes a group called the Turkestan Islamic Party, which released a video on 23 July ... claiming responsibility for recent bus explosions in Kunming and Shanghai that killed five people ... Chinese officials say the explosions were acts of disgruntled individuals and not terrorist attacks, though several outside terrorism experts suspect the East Turkestan Islamic Movement was involved.

(www.iht.com, 4 August 2008)

29 July 2008.

The human rights situation in China has deteriorated in the run-up to its hosting of the Olympic Games this year, Amnesty International says. It documents the use of 'reeducation through labour', the suppression of rights activists and journalist, and the use of arbitrary imprisonment ... The report says that Chinese activists have been locked up, people have been made homeless, journalists have been detained, websites blocked, and the use of labour camps and prison beatings have increased. Roseann Rife [a deputy programme director for Amnesty International]: 'We've seen a deterioration in human rights because of the Olympics. Specifically we've seen crackdowns on domestic human rights activists, media censorship and increased use of reeducation through labour as a means to clean up Beijing and surrounding areas.'

(www.bbc.co.uk, 29 July 2008)

The report by Amnesty International, entitled 'The Olympics Countdown: Broken Promises', was released Tuesday [29 July] and outlines particular

> areas of concern, including the death penalty, detention without trial, the persecution of rights activists and the lack of media freedom … Roseann Rife (Asia-Pacific deputy director): 'By continuing to persecute and punish those who speak out for human rights, the Chinese authorities have lost sight of the promises they made when they were granted the Games seven years ago' … Despite new media regulations that were supposed to allow for freer reporting for foreign journalists, Amnesty says they continue to be prevented from covering 'sensitive issues', including talking to those who suffer human rights violations. It says foreign correspondents in China reported more than 250 instances of interference with their work since the start of last year [2007] … One example given by Amnesty is housing rights activist Ye Guozhu, who continues to serve a four-year sentence for 'picking quarrels and stirring up trouble' because of his opposition to the seizure and demolition of property to make way for new construction projects for next month's Games. Ye Guozhu's prison sentence was due to expire on 26 July. Instead, the Chinese authorities say he will remain imprisoned until at least 1 October, after the end of the 2008 Olympic Games.
>
> (www.cnn.com, 29 July 2008)

'Amnesty International said that the Chinese government's preoccupation with security and stability in the run-up to the Games had contributed to a deterioration rather than an improvement in human rights across the country' (www.ft.com, 29 July 2008).

> President George W. Bush has held private talks with five prominent Chinese dissidents and has urged China's foreign minister [Yang Jiechi] to relax restrictions on human rights … Bush received the dissidents – Harry Wu, Wei Jingsheng, Rebiya Kadeer, Sasha Gong and Bob Fu – on Tuesday [29 July] in the White House residence … The dissidents told Bush that an estimated 80 million to 100 million Chinese are worshipping in underground churches.
>
> (www.iht.com, 30 July 2008)

> The White House said President George W. Bush had expressed 'concerns' to the group about the human rights situation in China. The president also told the Chinese foreign minister that the Olympics were an 'opportunity to demonstrate compassion on human rights and freedom'.
>
> (www.guardian.co.uk, 31 July 2008)

30 July 2008.

> Chinese officials say foreign journalists covering the Beijing Olympic Games will not have completely uncensored access to the internet. A top spokesman said sites relating to spiritual movement Falun Gong would be blocked. Another said other unspecified sites would also be unavailable … A senior International Olympic Committee (IOC) member confirmed that while journalists would have free range over the games, the IOC was aware

some sites would be blocked ... More than 20,000 foreign media personnel are due in the Chinese capital to cover the Olympic Games ... Many are already moving into the press and broadcast centres in Beijing. On Tuesday [29 July] they were reportedly unable to access the website of Amnesty International as it released a critical report on China's human rights record. Some international news pages and sites that dealt with issues such as Tibet were also inaccessible.

(www.bbc.co.uk, 30 July 2008)

Officials of the International Olympic Committee have negotiated an agreement with China to allow the blocking of sensitive websites to the news media during the Beijing Games, a senior IOC official said Wednesday [30 July]. The official, Kevan Gosper, who heads the IOC press commission, previously said internet access for the 21,500 news media representatives accredited for the Games would be 'open'. Gosper, a former Olympic runner from Australia, said he now understood 'that some IOC officials negotiated with the Chinese that some sensitive sites would be blocked on the basis they were not considered Games related'.

(www.iht.com, 30 July 2008)

Kevan Gosper (chairman of the IOC's press commission): 'I also now understand that some IOC officials negotiated with the Chinese that sensitive sites would be blocked on the basis they were not games-related' ... Jacques Rogge, IOC head, this month [July] cited free internet access as an achievement of his 'silent diplomacy' with Chinese officials. He said: 'For the first time foreign media will be able to report freely and publish their work freely in China. There will be no censorship on the internet' ... However, BOCOG, the Beijing Games Organizing Committee, insisted yesterday [30 July] it had never promised full freedom.

(*FT*, 31 July 2008, p. 8)

Officials announced an emergency plan to deal with Beijing's persistent pollution problem ... The plan, announced on Wednesday [30 July], calls for more factory closings, a complete halt to all construction projects and further reduction of the number of vehicles on the streets at any one time. The measures would be implemented if forecasters see stagnant weather conditions forty-eight hours in advance. The environment ministry drafted the plan in conjunction with the cities of Beijing and Tianjin and Hebei province ... The emergency plan would close an additional 105 factories in Beijing and more than 106 others outside the city. The plan would further restrict driving by preventing vehicles from being in operation if the last digit of the licence plate number corresponds with the day of the month. The plan would also institute odd/even driving days for Tianjin city. Odd/even driving days would also be put into effect in Hebei province, but only between the hours of 7 a.m. and 10 p.m.

(www.cnn.com, 31 July 2008)

The capital and surrounding areas of north-eastern China have the world's worst nitrogen dioxide levels, according to satellite images taken by the European Space Agency in 2005. The US Environmental Protection Agency says the chemical can cause eye, nose and throat irritation. It may also cause impaired lung function and increased respiratory infections. Most days Beijing is a city shrouded in grey.

(www.cnn.com, 3 August 2008)

The measures would be invoked during the Games only in the case of 'extremely unfavourable weather conditions' – for example, hot, humid air without winds to disperse pollution ... The plan unveiled Thursday [31 July] ... maintains the odd–even restrictions but adds a new prohibition that bans driving on days that match the last number on a motorist's licence plate. (Anyone with a plate ending in 9 could not drive on 9 August or 19 August, while other motorists with odd-numbered plates could still do so.) This would remove another 10 per cent of all vehicles from the streets. The plan would also suspend production at 105 more factories in Beijing and at another fifty-six coal-fired power plants, chemical plants and other industries in nearby Tianjin. In Tianjin, a municipality with more than 11 million people, motorist would also be subjected to the odd–even restrictions. Meanwhile, in Hebei province motorists in major cities would face odd–even driving restrictions in the daytime and early evening. The province would also suspend or reduce operations at another sixty-one factories.

(www.iht.com, 31 July 2008)

The BBC's Chinese language website appears to have been unblocked ahead of the Olympic Games ... Some journalists arriving to cover the Games complained when they found a number of websites at Olympic media centres were blocked.

[On Wednesday 30 July] the IOC promised to take the matter up with the Organizing Committee of the Beijing Games (Bocog). The BBC's Chinese language website was among many websites that were blocked by the authorities, but it now appears to have been made accessible ... The BBC's English language website was unblocked in March [2008] ... The website for the Chinese language version of Wikipedia [an online encyclopaedia] also appears to be available. It was unobtainable at Olympic sites on Wednesday, but available in China on Thursday [31 July]. An IOC spokeswoman told the BBC that the Olympic organization had been in talks with Bocog since Wednesday about blocking journalists' access to the internet.

(www.bbc.co.uk, 31 July 2008)

31 July 2008.

A South Korean television station has broadcast a secret dress rehearsal for the opening of Beijing's Olympics, irking the Chinese organizers of the Games. The SBS network aired just over a minute of footage, saying it had recorded the event legitimately. A staff reporter said: 'We went and nobody stopped us. So we just shot' ... But China has complained about it ... The ceremony has been a closely guarded secret.

(www.bbc.co.uk, 31 July 2008)

In 1932 Liu Changchun [the first Chinese to take part in the Olympics], a sprinter, made his way to Los Angeles from his home in north-eastern China, then under Japanese occupation ... China sent teams to the Olympics in 1936, 1948 and 1952, but then stayed away until the Winter Games of 1980. Four years after that [in Los Angeles] ... Xu Haifeng, a pistol shooter, won China's first gold medal.

(*The Economist*, Survey [on the business of sport], 2 August 2008, p. 3)

Using a Chinese number associated with fortune and prosperity, the Olympics are to start on the eight day of the eighth month ... With China third in the Sydney 2000 table [of medals], then second in Athens 2004, the big question is whether it can go one better this time. Its Soviet-style training system plucks physically promising athletes from an early age and sends them to special schools with an eye to maximizing medal hauls.

(www.iht.com, 4 August 2008)

With total spending expected to exceed $40 billion, Beijing's Olympic Games may be the most expensive in history. China has spent the money on new stadiums, infrastructure projects and cleaning up the capital's polluted atmosphere ... According to the Beijing Organizing Committee (Bocog), the city has spent $1.9 billion building twelve new stadiums and refurbishing others. Many of these have been built with money from both government and the private sector ... Beijing organizers estimate they will also spend $2.1 billion on operational costs, such as hosting the opening ceremony and staging sporting events. Part of this money comes from the International Olympic Committee, which gets its money by selling sponsorship and television rights. In addition to these costs, the city has spent $20.5 billion over the past ten years on environmental projects, according to Bocog. There have been improvements to the city's water supply, its sewage system and projects directed at cleaning up its polluted air. Beijing has spent billions more dollars on new infrastructure projects, including a new airport [the terminal costing $4 billion to build] ... and extra subway lines ... According to Xinhua, these infrastructure projects mean the total bill is just over $42 billion. By comparison, Athens four years ago cost about $16 billion. But the Beijing organizers argue that some projects would have been carried out anyway and so are not really Olympic costs.

(www.bbc.co.uk, 2 August 2008)

Tens of thousands of middle-age and elderly residents wearing red armbands ... now patrol neighbourhoods looking for even a slightly suspicious act or person ... The Security Industry Association, a Washington-based trade group for security companies around the world, said in a study last year [2007] that from 2001, when Beijing was awarded the Olympics, China

> spent as much as $6.5 billion on security in the Beijing area alone. The bulk of the spending is for extensive video monitoring systems that will stay in place after the Games. The surveillance system deployed by China for the Olympics includes key pieces of Western technology … Largely separate from the Olympics, China is moving to install video monitoring systems in its 600 largest cities, and some, from Shenzhen in south-eastern China to Lhasa in Tibet, are already far along. The United States Commerce Department has begun a review of whether to tighten enforcement of legislation involving crime-control equipment, enacted by Congress after the Tiananmen Square massacre. The legislation bars the sale of such equipment to China, but the department has allowed the transfer of American-made anti-terrorism gear.
>
> (www.iht.com, 4 August 2008)

'Television rights will bring in $1.8 billion … In Beijing there will be some 70,000 volunteers, plus 100,000 police and military on security duty' (www.independent.co.uk, 3 August 2008).

1 August 2008.

> Olympic organizers unblocked some internet sites at the main press centre and media venues Friday [1 August] while others remain off limits for journalists covering the Beijing Games … Senior International Olympic Committee officials met late into the night Thursday [31 July] with their Chinese counterparts and said they reached an agreement to unblock sites, although the IOC statement said the details were still being formulated … Amnesty International's site was open on Friday, but links to the banned spiritual movement Falun Gong remained closed. Some websites dealing with Tibet were open, but others tied to the restive region in the west of China were blocked. The BBC's Chinese language site was open at times, but frequently unavailable. Searches for Falun Gong turned up only blank web pages and searching for sensitive phrases like 'Tiananmen Square' turned up sites that could not be accessed.
>
> (www.cnn.com, 1 August 2008)

'The BBC's Chinese language website appeared to be unblocked on Thursday [31 July]. Other Chinese language sites, such as Voice of America and Hong Kong newspaper *Apple Daily*, also now appear accessible' (www.bbc.co.uk, 1 August 2008).

> The Chinese authorities, bowing to pressure from Olympic officials, foreign journalists and Western political leaders, have lifted some of the restrictions that blocked sites at the main press centre for the Summer Games, although politically sensitive sites remained inaccessible Friday [1 August]. The government made no announcement about the partial lifting of its firewall and it was unclear if the change would be temporary. The International Olympic Committee also sought Friday to counter statements by its top press official,

who had suggested that IOC negotiators had quietly acquiesced to the government's restrictions ... Access to sites the government normally blocks expanded through the day Friday. The first sites unblocked included those of Amnesty International, Human Rights Watch, Radio Free Asia and the Chinese language service of the BBC. By early evening reporters at the press centre could read about topics that have long been taboo here: Taiwanese independence, jailed Chinese dissidents and the 1989 crackdown on protesters in Tiananmen ... Kevan Gosper, the chief of the IOC's press commission and a former Olympic runner from Australia, maintained his position that high-level IOC colleagues had bowed to China's internet restrictions. He accused the organization of secretly agreeing to the policy change and then continuing to publicize the idea that China would not censor the internet for reporters covering the Games. Gosper: 'It has dented my reputation quite seriously. People take me at my word, so I expect the information I am giving to be consistent.'

(www.iht.com, 1 August 2008)

2 August 2008.

Yesterday [2 August] the president of the IOC, Jacques Rogge, was accused of backtracking on promises to safeguard press freedom after some internet sites remained blocked. He denied that the IOC had agreed to accept the situation, saying: 'There has been no deal whatsoever to accept restrictions ... [The media] must have the fullest access possible to report on the Olympic Games. I'm not going to make an apology for something the IOC is not responsible for. We are not running the internet in China. The Chinese authorities are running the internet.'

(www.independent.co.uk, 3 August 2008)

Jacques Rogge, IOC head, had last month [July] cited free internet access as an achievement of his 'quiet diplomacy', but on Saturday [2 August] merely said the committee required 'that different media have the fullest access possible to report on the Olympic Games'.

(*FT*, 4 August 2008, p. 7)

Kevan Gosper, head of the IOC's press commission, described the changes as 'a work in progress', but acknowledged that some restrictions would remain. Gosper: 'The IOC put in place a working group with Bocog [the Beijing Organizing Committee for the Games of the XXIX Olympiad] to start examining those sites that the international media thought should be unblocked' ... But he added that every country censored sites that it judged to be subversive or dangerous to national interests. He said: 'The line between what could be considered as a national interest issue might be a bit blurred, but we will work on it and deal with any potential grievances.' ... The IOC agreed yesterday [2 August] to donate £2 million to the earthquake-hit Sichuan region.

(www.guardian.co.uk, 3 August 2008)

3 August 2008.

> The Olympic torch began an emotional tour of Sichuan on Sunday [23 August] ... Sichuan is the last stop for the Olympic flame before it heads to Beijing for Friday's opening ceremony of the Games. The segment had originally been scheduled for mid-June.
>
> (www.guardian.co.uk, 3 August 2008)

> The Chinese authorities have laid out strict guidelines for protesters wishing to speak out during the Olympics yesterday [3 August], telling them to avoid harming 'national interests' and requiring them to apply in writing five days in advance. The authorities have designated three protest zones in parks around Beijing during the Games ... Games organizers said yesterday that the police would maintain tight control over which groups were allowed to protest. Chinese and foreign applicants would have to submit a proposal to the local police five days in advance, together with their identification documents. Liu Shaowu (the Beijing organizing committee's security chief): 'Assembling to march and protest is a citizen's right. But citizens must respect and not harm others' freedoms and rights and must not harm national, social and collective interests' ... One group of housing activists who have been campaigning against the demolition of their property ahead of the Olympics said they have been refused permission to demonstrate during the Games.
>
> (*FT*, 4 August 2008, p 7)

4 August 2008.

> Assailants armed with grenades and knives killed sixteen policemen in a restive western region of China on Monday [4 August] ... The attackers drove up and tossed explosives at a border barracks in the remote Xinjiang region near the old Silk Road city of Kashgar, Xinhua reported. They also hacked policemen. Sixteen officers were injured in the attack that Chinese police called 'suspected terrorism'. Xinhua: 'Rioters drove two vehicles into the border patrol armed police division.'
>
> (www.iht.com, 4 August 2008)

'Two men armed with knives and grenades ambushed a military police unit in Kashgar ... before being subdued and arrested ... The assault in Kashgar ... ranks as one of the deadliest outbursts of violence since the early 1990s' (www.iht.com, 4 August 2008).

> The assault in Kashgar took place just before dawn as a brigade of the border patrol police was jogging outside its barracks in the centre of the city. According to official media accounts, two men driving trucks rammed their vehicles into the soldiers ... Last month [July] the authorities executed two men and meted out heavy sentences to fifteen others who they claimed were members of the East Turkestan Islamic Movement.
>
> (www.iht.com, 4 August 2008)

Two men armed with knives and explosives ambushed a military police unit ... killing sixteen officers and wounding sixteen others before being arrested in what the state media called the deadliest terrorist attack in China since the early 1990s ... The assault took place at dawn in the oasis city of Kashgar, as a brigade of border control officers jogged outside their barracks near the city centre. Two men driving a dump truck rammed their vehicle into the jogging soldiers ... The attackers jumped out of the truck, stabbing the soldiers with knives, and then lobbed homemade bombs at the barracks, although they exploded outside the compound, Xinhua said. The police arrested the attackers ... described as Uighurs, twenty-eight and thirty-three years old ... The police later discovered ten more such devices and what it described as a 'home-made gun' in the dump truck ... Last month [July] the authorities executed two men and meted out heavy sentences to fifteen others who said they were members of the East Turkestan Islamic Movement [ETIM]. The men were seized during a raid on what officials described as a terrorist training camp ... Some outside experts say the organization is fairly small and includes a group call the Turkestan Islamic Party, which released a video on 23 July Rohan Gunaratna ... considers ETIM the biggest threat ... Gunaratna estimated that the group had about forty members based in the mountainous tribal areas of Pakistan who intend to carry out operations. Uighurs trained in Afghanistan before the US invasion in 2001, although their affiliations with terrorist groups are unclear. ETIM now survives in Pakistan under the protection of al-Qaeda and the Pakistani Taliban, and in recent years adopted the ideology of global jihad espoused by al-Qaeda, Gunaratna said ... China has girded Beijing with soldiers, missile launchers and sidewalk cameras.

(www.iht.com, 5 August 2008)

Sixteen Chinese policemen were killed in an attack on a border post in the restive Moslem region of Xinjian ... Two attackers reportedly drove up to the post in a rubbish truck and threw two grenades, before moving in to attack the policemen with knives ... Fourteen died at the scene and two on the way to hospital. Another sixteen were injured ... Last week a senior Chinese army officer warned that Islamic separatists were the biggest threat to the Olympics. Colonel Tian Yixiang of the Olympics security command centre ... [said] the main threat came from the 'East Turkestan terrorist organization'.

(www.bbc.co.uk, 4 August 2008)

Xinhua said the attack happened at about 08.00 (00.00 GMT) as the policemen were jogging outside the compound ... Since the 9/11 attacks in the United States China has increasingly portrayed its Uighur separatists as auxiliaries of al-Qaeda. It has accused them of receiving training and indoctrination from Islamic militants in neighbouring Afghanistan. However, little public evidence has been produced in support of these claims. More than twenty Uighurs were captured by the US military after its invasion of

> Afghanistan. Though imprisoned at Guantanamo Bay for six years, they have yet to be charged with any offence.
>
> (www.bbc.co.uk, 5 August 2008)

'The men [who attacked the Chinese police officers were] a taxi driver and a vegetable seller from the local area, according to Chinese media' (www.bbc.co.uk, 5 August 2008).

> According to the state Xinhua news agency, two attackers drove one of two lorries into a police station in the far western city of Kashgar, an oasis town of the ancient Silk Road ... Senior Colonel Tian Yixiang, the military officer in charge of Olympic security, said last week that 'East Turkestan terrorist groups' represented the greatest threat to the Games, ahead of Tibetan separatists and the religious group, Falun Gong. But on the same day a vice governor of Xinjiang, Kuerxi Maihesuti, pooh-poohed the threat: 'We see that these terrorist groups are not that capable of instigating massive sabotage activities, as some hostile forces have hoped to see. If there had been such major incidents, no government could cover them up because the media would release the information very quickly. There are only a very small number of sabotage activities in Xinjiang and many were nipped in the bud.'
>
> (www.thetimes.co.uk, 4 August 2008)

> Local officials in Xinjiang have become increasingly concerned about the reach of an international Sunni group, the Hisz-ut-Tahrir, or Party of Liberation, whose aim is to set up an Islamic caliphate across Asia and which organized protests in the western city of Khotan in March [2008].
>
> (www.thetimes.co.uk, 4 August 2008)

> At least sixteen police officers were killed and sixteen more were wounded after an attack on a border police station in western China on Monday morning [4 August], the state-run Xinhua news agency reported. A pair of attackers crashed a heavy truck into a group of police officers who were jogging near the station and then threw at least five homemade bombs into a police barracks, setting off an explosion ... The attackers also hacked some of the police with knives ... The incident happened in Kashi, in the Xinjiang Uighur Autonomous Region, which is also known as East Turkestan. Both attackers were arrested. Police suspect a terrorist plot behind the raid. The regional public security department said it received clues suggesting the East Turkestan Islamic Movement planned to make terrorist attacks between 1 August and 8 August [the start of the Olympic Games] ... The Xinjiang Uighur Autonomous Region is home to a Sunni Moslem ethnic minority.
>
> (www.cnn.com, 4 August 2008)

'State television gave a different account, saying the police were attacked while marching in front of a hotel on morning drills' (www.guardian.co.uk, 4 August 2008).

> Few incidents involving the ETIM [East Turkestan Islamic Movement] have been reported by the Chinese authorities in recent years. Early last year [2007] the Chinese police said that they had raided an ETIM training camp on the Xinjiang border, killing eighteen suspects and arresting seventeen others … A group called the Turkestan Islamic Party (possibly another name for ETIM) last month [July] claimed responsibility for bombing buses in Shanghai and Kunming in May and July, but the government rejected the claim. Last week a Xinjiang official, Kuerxi Maihesuti, said that there had only been three or four cases of 'terrorist schemes' foiled by the police this year, he also suggested that terrorists in Xinjiang were 'not that capable of instigating massive sabotage as some hostile forces have hoped to see'.
>
> (www.economist.com, 5 August 2008)

> A small group of dislocated residents staged a brief demonstration near Tiananmen Square on Monday [4 August] to protest the lack of compensation they were given to make way for a redevelopment project. The protest, which drew a swarm of police and caused a traffic jam, was promptly broken up.
>
> (www.iht.com, 4 August 2008)

'[There was] a small protest near Tiananmen Square on Monday by people who said they had not been compensated after their homes were demolished for a redevelopment project, but a swarm of police officers rapidly broke it up' (www.iht.com, 5 August 2008).

> President George W. Bush was leaving Monday [4 August] for a trip to Asia that will include four days in Beijing … Aides organizing President George W. Bush's trip to China for the Olympics considered having him worship at a house church, one of the underground religious institutions that routinely face harassment, but the Chinese refused. Pastors, lawyers and other political activists that Bush considered meeting in Beijing as a powerful signal of support have instead been ordered by the authorities to leave the city during the president's visit. Scores of others have been arrested … Bush is the first sitting president to attend the Games overseas … Last month [July] Chinese officials announced they would refer to the Taiwan Olympic delegation by its official name, Zhonghua Taipei, rather than Zhongguo Taipei, the name favoured by people on the mainland. Zhongguo Taipei implies that Taiwan is part of the mainland, and Taiwanese officials are threatening to boycott the Games if China uses it.
>
> (www.iht.com, 5 August 2008)

5 August 2008.

> A day after two men attacked a military police unit … Chinese officials sought Tuesday [5 August] to portray the ambush as an act of terrorism and said the men were members of an outlawed organization they contend has links to al-Qaeda … A photographer for Agence France-Presse said the police had forced him to erase photographs taken at the scene. Two Japanese

journalists said they were roughed up and detained by the authorities … Officials have suggested that the attack was part of a 'holy war' orchestrated by the East Turkestan Islamic Movement, or ETIM, a group they contend is seeking to create 'East Turkestan', an independent nation that would take in Xinjiang and parts of central Asian countries like Kazakhstan, Kyrgyzstan and Uzbekistan. In the past the Chinese authorities have claimed that 1,000 ETIM members received training from al-Qaeda. Terrorism experts outside China, however, have called such claims highly inflated … On Tuesday [5 August] Shi Dagang, the Communist Party Secretary of Kashgar, said the police had found evidence linking Monday's incident with ETIM. A gun and explosives discovered at the scene, he said, resembled weapons found during a raid on an ETIM training camp in south-west Xinjiang last year [2007]. In addition to seizing twenty-two handmade tank grenades and 1,500 unfinished ones during that raid, the authorities said they killed and wounded scores of 'terrorists'. Officials offered no evidence at the time. In addition to finding nine unexploded devices, a gun and four knives at the scene, Shi said, a note left by one of the assailants indicated a desire to die during 'jihad' and said that religion was more important than family or life itself. He said that the two men, a thirty-three-year-old cabdriver and a twenty-eight-year-old fruit vendor, had planned the attack for a month. Sunday night [3 August], Shi said, the pair stole the dump truck they used to plough into the soldiers as they were lining up for morning exercises. Shi said one of the assailants lost an arm when an explosive device detonated in his hand. He said the attack Monday was part of an effort by the group to disrupt the Olympics by unleashing monthly attacks.

(www.iht.com, 5 August 2008)

A Chinese official said yesterday [5 August] that eighteen members of a separatist terrorist group in the course of this year [2008] had been trained outside China … However, the authorities offered conflicting accounts of the attack [on 4 August], with one official describing it as the act of a 'jihadi' terrorist group, and another saying there was no link yet to terrorism … The head of the Communist Party in Kashgar said the attack bore the fingerprints of the East Turkestan Islamic Movement (ETIM), an organization that has been labelled a terrorist group by both the US State Department and the United Nations. Shi Dagang: 'Religion is more important to them than their own life, and so they set out to perform jihad' … Mr Shi said eighteen suspected terrorists arrested this year had received training outside China … However, at a separate press conference in the provincial capital of Urumqi, the head of the Xinjiang public security department played down the evidence of links to terrorist groups. Liu Yaohua: 'No sufficient evidence has been found to say for sure that ETIM was behind Monday's attack [4 August]' … Analysts also said the primitive weapons used, such as homemade grenades and machetes, did not indicate that the attackers had received organized training.

(*FT*, 6 August 2008, p. 8)

> Outside scholars also raise doubts that this was a terrorist attack, and they say the Chinese are waving the banner of their own 'war on terror' to tighten Beijing's hold on the area ... [Some] scholars suggest that the attack was probably carried out by disgruntled individuals and not as an act of terrorism ... Attacks on the police have been on the rise across China.
>
> (*IHT*, 6 August 2008, pp. 1, 3)

('Fresh accounts told to the *New York Times* by three foreign tourists who happened to be in the area challenge central parts of the official Chinese version of the events of 4 August in Kashgar ... One tourist took twenty-seven photographs. Among other discrepancies the witnesses said that they heard no loud explosions and that the men wielding the machetes appeared to be paramilitary officers who were attacking other uniformed men': www.iht.com, 29 September 2008.)

> China has apologized for the beating of two Japanese journalists. The journalists, a reporter and a photographer, were detained near the site of Monday's attack in Kashgar [4 August]. Police held them for two hours and punched them, they said ... Officials and police in Kashgar also apologized for the incident, but accused the two men of breaking rules.
>
> (www.bbc/co.uk, 5 August 2008)

'The police apologized. They explained that they could not immediately identify [the Japanese photographer] ... because of the language barrier ... Furthermore, the police said they were angry and short-tempered due to Monday's attack [4 August]' (www.cnn.com, 5 August 2008).

6 August 2008.

> Euphoric crowds cheered the Olympic flame through Tiananmen Square on Wednesday [6 August] ... One of China's most famous sportsmen, 7 ft 6 in basketball player Yao Ming, held the flame ... China's first man in space, Yang Liwei, started the Beijing torch relay ... the start of the flame's passage through Beijing took place under smog-filled skies. Some $18 billion of cleanup measures have reduced contamination to safe levels, according to Olympics chiefs ... Foreign protesters ... unfurled 'Free Tibet' banners from electricity poles near the main 'Bird's Nest' venue [the National Stadium with its latticed construction]. Police rushed to detain the two Britons and two Americans ... Team Darfur, a coalition of athletes seeking to draw attention to the conflict in western Sudan, said Beijing had revoked the visa of its co-founder and Olympic gold medallist [in Turin in 2006 for speed skating] Joey Cheek ... Cheek had planned to fly to Beijing on Wednesday ... Team Darfur is a group of athletes, including seventy-two current Olympians.
>
> (www.iht.com, 6 August 2008)

> Jill Savitt ... executive director of Dream for Darfur ... was also denied a visa. Savitt works with American actress Mia Farrow, who will be

broadcasting from a Sudanese refugee camp in neighbouring Chad during the first week of the Beijing Olympics.

(www.iht.com, 7 August 2008)

Four Tibet activists unfurled Tibetan flags and pro-independence banners near the National Stadium in Beijing early Wednesday [6 August] ... Two men in the group scaled electric poles shortly after dawn to display banners nearing pro-Tibetan independence slogans and the flag of the Tibetan government in exile. Police rushed to the scene and took away 'four foreigners' – three men and a woman – shortly after the protest, which is believed to be the first at a venue of the Games. Students for a Free Tibet, a Tibetan activist group, said in a statement that those involved in the demonstration were from the United States and Britain. The group said the signs – which carried English and Chinese slogans including: 'One World, One Dream: Free Tibet', 'Tibet Will Be Free' and 'Free Tibet' – were on display for about an hour. Police said it was only about twelve minutes. The demonstrators entered China on tourist visas, police said.

(www.ccn.com, 6 August 2008)

Other protests today [6 August] included a low-key demonstration by three Americans, who stood in Tiananmen Square – well after the torch passed through – to shout a denunciation of China's population control policies. Police allowed them to leave the area after questioning them briefly.

(www.guardian.co.uk, 6 August 2008)

In the afternoon three Americans denouncing China's population control policies protested at Tiananmen Square ... [They] shouted against Chinese population control measures that sometimes impose force abortions on women who violate the rule, and held up a banner reading 'Jesus Christ is King' ... One yelled: 'To those who are forced to go through forced abortions and have no voice: we are your voice.'

(www.iht.com, 6 August 2008)

Pakistan's President Pervez Musharraf cancelled plans to visit China for the Olympic opening ceremony ... Musharraf, who has struggled to retain a grip on power in Pakistan during months of recent political turmoil, scrapped the plans 'due to developments at home', the foreign office [said].

(www.cnn.com, 6 August 2008)

Pakistani President Pervez Musharraf has cancelled a planned trip to China to attend the opening ceremony of the Beijing Olympics. The move comes as the country's governing alliance is discussing his possible impeachment ... China is one of the country's closest allies.

(www.bbc.co.uk, 6 August 2008)

Pakistani President Pervez Musharraf will attend Friday's opening ceremony of the Olympic Games, despite an earlier report saying that he scrapped the trip amid a brewing political standoff in his home country ...

> Hours [after the initial announcement] ... another report [was put out] saying Musharraf had postponed his departure by a day and will leave on Thursday [7 August].
>
> (www.cnn.com, 6 August 2008)

7 August 2008.

> The head of the International Olympic Committee, Jacques Rogge, has praised Beijing's 'extraordinary' efforts to cut pollution ahead of the Games. He said there would be no danger to the health of athletes, despite continuing concerns about pollution levels ... He said there was 'absolutely no danger' to the health of athletes taking part in events that last less than one hour. But he said if the pollution was bad, events which lasted more than that could be shifted or postponed. Mr Rogge urged reporters to distinguish between fog and pollution – a point often made by Chinese authorities ... A day before the Games a BBC reading suggested Beijing's air quality was far below World Health Organization (WHO) standards ... Mr Rogge said athletes would be prevented from making any political statements or protests in official venues – in accordance with rule 51 of the Olympic Charter, which forbids athletes from making political, religious, commercial or racial propaganda.
>
> (www.bbc.co.uk, 7 August 2008)

'A BBC reading suggested Beijing's air quality was far below WHO standards. It put particulate matter (PM10) at 191 micrograms per cubic metre. This exceeds the WHO target for developing countries of 150 [and for developed countries of 50]' (www.bbc.co.uk, 8 August 2008).

> More than forty athletes taking part in the Beijing Olympics have today [7 August] signed an open letter addressed to China's government urging it to respect human rights and freedom of religion, particularly in Tibet ... Signatories to the letter include the men's 110m hurdles world record holder, Dayron Robles of Cuba, well known to Chinese fans as the main rival to their most famous track athlete, Liu Xiang, the reigning Olympic champion ... The letter calls on President Hu Jintao 'to protect freedom of expression, freedom of religion and freedom of opinion in your country, including Tibet'. It asks Hu 'to ensure that human rights defenders are no longer intimidated or imprisoned' and to end the death penalty.
>
> (www.guardian.co.uk, 7 August 2008)

> As President George W. Bush flew into Beijing for the Olympic ceremony, three US Christian demonstrators were dragged away from Tiananmen Square by plainclothes police ... Patrick Mahoney (director of the Christian Defence Coalition): 'We come here to speak out against the human rights abuses of the Chinese government. We are the voice of those with no voice. We are the voice of the Falun Gong practitioners.'
>
> (www.guardian.co.uk, 7 August 2008)

> A second protest, by three Americans in Tiananmen Square, was stopped by security agents … A day earlier the three, including an anti-abortion activist, the Reverend Patrick Mahoney, spent almost a hour in the square criticizing the government's handling of issues like forced abortions and the 1989 pro-democracy demonstrations.
>
> (www.iht.com, 7 August 2008)

> At least two women who have protested being evicted from their homes ahead of the Olympics were rounded up and taken to a police station … Also Thursday [7 August] a Hong Kong lawmaker said immigration officials deported three US-based Chinese pro-democracy activists after denying them entry to the territory, which is hosting the Olympic equestrian events … The protest groups so far have been small and police have acted with relative restraint … In Hong Kong immigration officials denied Yang Jianli, Wang Min and Zhou Jian entry when they arrived on Wednesday [6 August].
>
> (www.iht.com, 7 August 2008)

'At least two women who protested their forced evictions ahead of the Olympic Games were taken from their homes by Chinese police Thursday [7 August] … [They] were rounded up late Wednesday [6 August] and early Thursday morning' (www.cnn.com, 7 August 2008).

> Thousands of … itinerant workers … [have] been forced to leave town [Beijing] by a lack of work and an unwritten government policy encouraging migrant workers to clear out until the dignitaries and journalists have gone home … No one knows for sure how many of Beijing's 17 million residents are migrants, but they are thought to number around 4 million.
>
> (www.iht.com, 7 August 2008)

> President Nicolas Sarkozy of France, who will attend the opening ceremony of the Beijing Olympics despite domestic criticism, announced on Thursday [7 August] that he would not meet the Dalai Lama later this month in France. Instead, his office said, Sarkozy's wife, Carla, would meet with the exiled Tibetan leader, taking part in a religious ceremony to open a Buddhist temple in southern France on 22 August. Sarkozy's political party, however, said that the French president would meet the Dalai Lama before the end of the year [2008] … Sarkozy's office, in a carefully worded statement, suggested that it was the Dalai Lama who decided the time was not right for a meeting this month.
>
> (www.iht.com, 7 August 2008)

> Responding to a speech by President George W. Bush on Thursday [7 August], in which he praised China's modernization but expressed 'deep concern over restrictions on faith and free speech', the Chinese foreign ministry issued a curt statement that bristled with anger over 'any words or acts that interfere in other countries' internal affairs' … President George W. Bush rebuked China over political and religious freedoms for a second day

> on Friday [8 August], though he tempered his criticism with effusive praise for the country's history and embraced its hosting of the Olympic Games ... Bush described relations with China as 'constructive, co-operative and candid' and he echoed criticisms of his speech on Thursday in Bangkok [Thailand] in which he urged China's leaders not to fear faith or free expression, though he did so in Beijing in a mild tone ... Bush: 'We must ... continue to be candid about our belief that all people should have the freedom to say what they think and worship as they choose. We strongly believe societies which allow the free expression of ideas tend to be the most prosperous and the most peaceful' ... Bush will hold formal meetings with Hu Jintao and other senior Chinese leaders on Sunday [10 August].
>
> (www.iht.com, 7 August 2008)

> A terrorist group ... has released a video threatening an attack on the Olympic Games, according to an American organization that tracks terrorist internet posts ... A man holding an assault rifle, who identifies himself as Abdullah Mansour, says in the Uighur language: 'We, members of the Turkestan Islamic Party, have declared war against China. We oppose China's occupation of our homeland of East Turkestan, which is part of the Islamic world.'
>
> (*IHT*, 9 August 2008, p. 5)

8 August 2008. The Olympic Games opened in Beijing at 08.08 on 8 August 2008.

'Beijing on Friday [8 August] endured more smoggy skies' (www.iht.com, 8 August 2008).

> The $100 million budget for the opening ceremony, which is directed by China's most famous film director, Zhang Yimou, is only a fraction of the estimated $43 billion that China has spent in building roads, stadiums, parks and subway lines in an attempt to transform Beijing into an Olympic city.
>
> (www.iht.com, 8 August 2008)

'Eight, which sounds like the word for wealth, is a lucky number in China' (www.independent.co.uk, 8 August 2008).

'An estimated global audience of 4 billion people will watch the opening ceremony' (www.bbc.co.uk, 8 August 2008). 'Some 10,000 performers took part in the [opening] ceremony, watched by an estimated 1 billion people' (www.bbc.co.uk, 9 August 2008).

'The International Olympic Committee estimated that the global television audience for the opening ceremony could surpass 1 billion' (www.iht.com, 8 August 2008).

'The global television audience was estimated to surpass 4 billion viewers' (*IHT*, 9 August 2008, p. 1).

> In Ankara [Turkey] a member of China's Uighur minority drenched himself in gasoline and set himself alight before fellow demonstrators rushed to extinguish the flames and he was taken to hospital ... Exiled Tibetans took

> their grievances to the street in Nepal and India. And three American activists were reportedly detained in Beijing. Demonstrations also took place in London, Madrid, Berlin, Stockholm, Lisbon and Amsterdam, with further marches in Washington and Toronto ... The initiative that received perhaps the most attention was in Beijing itself, where a group advocating media freedom pirated a radio frequency and broadcast criticism of China in Mandarin, French and English. The twenty-minute broadcast, organized by Reporters Without Borders, began about 8 a.m., twelve hours before the Olympic opening ceremony ... Students for a Free Tibet said that three American activists had been detained after trying to protest near the opening ceremony in Beijing ... In Hong Kong a lone British activist dubbed Spiderman by the local media scaled a bridge and hung a banner that read: 'The people of China want freedom from oppression'. The police later removed the banner. Several groups of activists organized a small demonstration outside the site in Hong Kong where Olympic dressage and show jumping events will be held over the next two weeks ... In Kathmandu, Nepal, the police arrested about 1,000 people who gathered outside the visa office of the Chinese embassy despite a ban on protests ... In New Delhi almost 3,000 Tibetans chanting anti-China slogans marched outside the Indian parliament, and a group of monks tried storming a Chinese visa office during the opening ceremony. Hundreds more marched in the Indian city of Dharamsala, where the exiled Tibetan leadership is based.
>
> (www.iht.com, 9 August 2008)

'On Saturday [9 August] five activists staged a "peaceful protest" in Tiananmen Square ... Students for a Free Tibet said the protesters draped themselves in Tibetan flags and lay down in the square' (www.cnn.com, 9 August 2008).

> A knife-wielding Chinese man attacked the two relatives of a coach for the US Olympic men's volleyball team at a tourist site in Beijing, killing one and injuring the other on the first day of the Olympics on Saturday [9 August] ... Their Chinese tour guide was also injured ... [The assailant] then committed suicide by throwing himself from the second storey of the site, the thirteenth-century Drum Tower just five miles from the main Olympic site.
>
> (www.iht.com, 9 August 2008)

> The dead American was Todd Bachman, a sixty-two-year-old businessman whose son-in-law is the head coach for the men's volleyball team. His wife, Barbara, sixty-two, was critically wounded in the assault, as was a Chinese guide, whose name has not been released ... [The assailant was] Tang Yongming ... forty-seven ... [an unemployed man from] the eastern city of Hangzhou.
>
> (www.iht.com, 10 August 2008)

'Several explosions rocked a county in north-western China early Sunday [10 August]' (www.cnn.com, 10 August 2008).

A series of bomb attacks targeted a police station in Xinjiang, state media reported. The explosions were followed by gunfire ... Two policemen were injured and five attackers killed in the pre-dawn violence in southern Kuqa county ... Kuqa county is almost exclusively populated by Uighurs ... Xinhua reported: 'The lawbreakers drove a taxi to the local security office, industry and business administration and other sites and tossed homemade explosives, destroying two police vehicles.'

(www.bbc.co.uk, 10 August 2008)

Five people were killed early Sunday morning [10 August] after a violent confrontation in Xinjiang region in which police fired on assailants who had attacked a police station with homemade bombs, state media reported ... The blasts that happened Sunday took place in Kuqa county in a succession of explosions between 3.20 a.m. and 4 a.m. ... Witnesses told Xinhua of seeing 'flashes of fire' and also hearing 'sporadic gunshots' after the explosions. Xinhua said that a group of 'criminals' held a drive-by attack against a public security office in Kuqa and another building, tossing homemade explosives that destroyed two police cars. Initial accounts indicated that two officers were killed, though later accounts suggested that two officers were wounded. Officers shot dead five of the assailants ... Kuqa [is] a city of about 400,000 people that is located in the southern part of Xinjiang ... One obscure militant group, the Turkestan Islamic Party, has released videos taking responsibility for previous explosions in China ... The IntelCenter, a private group in Washington that monitors terrorism activity, has concluded that this group is the same as ETIM [East Turkestan Islamic Movement].

(www.iht.com, 10 August 2008)

[In Xinjiang on] Sunday morning [10 August] eight suspects were killed by the police after a series of bomb attacks that began with a pre-dawn assault against a police station, state media reported ... In all, the authorities say, twelve explosive devices were detonated in attacks against at least four local government buildings ... Xinhua described a series of attacks that began at 2.30 a.m. when a vehicle was driven into the yard outside a public security bureau and exploded. A security guard was killed ... Police returned fire, shooting and killing one suspect and capturing another, as one assailant reportedly committed suicide. Roughly six hours later assailants began hurling homemade bombs at different government buildings in Kuqa ... The police shot dead two more attackers and said three others committed suicide. One captured suspect told the police that fifteen people were involved in the attack ... Wang Wei, vice president of the Beijing Olympic Organizing Committee, blamed ETIM for the attacks ... IntelCenter, a private group based in [the United States] ... that monitors militants' internet postings ... sent by email a photograph of ETIM's supposed founder, Hasan Mahsum, who was killed by the Pakistani army in 2003 ... According to IntelCenter, the name ETIM has been used by China, the United Nations and other organizations, but the Turkestan Islamic Party never called itself that. It originally called itself the East Turkestan Islamic Party, or ETIP, but after a transformation from 1998 to 2000, it removed the 'East' from its name, IntelCenter said.

(www.iht.com, 10 August 2008)

The death toll reported by the state media was inconsistent and changed several times. By late Sunday [10 August] the authorities were quoted as saying that eight suspects had been fatally shot by the police and that at least two others had died as suicide bombers ... The deaths of a security guard and at least ten suspects [were reported] ... Xinhua described the suspects in Sunday's attack as 'terrorists', though the authorities have not attributed the attack to any terrorist group.

(www.iht.com, 11 August 2008)

According to Xinhua, police in Xinjiang said there was not enough evidence yet to pin the latest attacks on terror groups in the region, notably the East Turkestan Islamic Movement, which has been labelled a terrorist group by the United States and the United Nations. However, Wang Wei, an official with the Beijing Olympic Organizing Committee, said the attack was the work of 'East Turkestan terrorists'.

(*FT*, 11 August 2008, p. 6)

Three security officers were killed and one wounded Tuesday [12 August] at a road checkpoint near Kasgar ... The attackers used knives ... The attack is the third in nine days against Chinese security forces in the Xinjiang Uighur Autonomous Region ... It is unclear whether the attacks are part of a broader pattern or whether the assailants were acting separately.

(www.iht.com, 12 August 2008)

'Although analysts both within and outside of China allege that the ETIM has strong links with al-Qaeda, there is little evidence to support this claim' (*Newsbrief*, August 2008, p. 67).

[It is reported that] Hua Huiqi, a religious dissident who was detained by the authorities Sunday [10 August] as he made his way to a church service where President George W. Bush was scheduled to pray, has escaped from the police, according to human rights advocates and family members. Hua slipped away from his guards Sunday night after they fell asleep at a makeshift detention centre.

(www.iht.com, 12 August 2008)

Five activists protesting on behalf of Tibet, including three Americans, were arrested Thursday [14 August] for what Chinese police called 'activities against Chinese law' and will be deported ... The five, who were part of the group Students for a Free Tibet, hung a pro-Tibetan banner ... near the construction site of new buildings to house CCTV.

(www.iht.com, 15 August 2008)

'Despite ugly scenes in July when thousands of people queued for hours, pushed and shoved and tussled with police to buy the last available Olympic tickets, many seats were vacant during the first week of competition' (*The Economist*, 16 August 2008, p. 54).

> Officials say one-fifth of rooms in the city's 120-odd designated Olympic hotels were unoccupied after the Games started on 8 August … But no figures have been published for the 700 others. Price cutting at many hotels suggests there may be a glut of rooms.
>
> (p. 53)

> A former land use official in Shanghai was sentenced to death [on 14 August] as an investigation into bribe-taking in return for real estate approvals winds down in [Shanghai] … However, the court ordered the actual execution be 'suspended' for two years … Such sentences are usually commuted to life imprisonment.
>
> (www.iht.com, 15 August 2008)

> Air quality remained poor during the run-up to the Games, with four days in late July violating China's national pollution standards. Chinese officials blamed poor weather conditions, especially a lack of dispersing winds and rainfall to clear the smoggy haze. Those rains have come sporadically since the opening ceremony, including a deluge last Sunday night [10 August] and subsequent showers … As of Sunday [17 August], halfway through the Olympics, the Beijing Games were operating smoothly and pollution levels have remained low, with previous days seeing either bright sunshine or clouds with sporadic showers. Friday [15 August] and Saturday [16 August] brought two of the clearest summer days in recent memory in Beijing, including miniscule pollution levels for a city that often ranks among the worst in the world when it comes to air quality.
>
> (www.iht.com, 17 August 2008)

> China has confirmed … [Beijing's] air quality has been good. Environmental officials say pollution levels have met expected standards on every day of the Olympics so far. They say this is down to measures brought in to reduce emissions during the Olympics and Paralympics. But one [Italian] pollution expert says Beijing has also benefited from favourable weather conditions … such as rain … According to our [BBC] data, Beijing met the strictest WHO standard for particulate matter in six out of the first eleven days of the Games.
>
> (www.bbc.co.uk, 19 August 2008)

> Customs officials confiscated more than 300 [315] Bibles on Sunday [17 August] from four American Christians who arrived in a south-western city [Kunming] with plans to distribute them … [One of the Americans said] the customs officers had told him they could each have [only] one Bible for

> personal use ... [and that the Americans] had to apply ahead of time for permission ... to bring the [other] Bibles in.
>
> (www.iht.com, 17 August 2008)

'Public Security has arrested at least a half-dozen people who have shown up to apply for protest permits ... The government set aside three "protest zones"' (www.iht.com, 17 August 2008).

> Authorities have received seventy-seven applications from people who want to hold protests ... in three designated areas ... during the Beijing Olympics, but all were withdrawn, suspended or rejected, state media said Monday [18 August] ... Xinhua said the seventy-seven applications received since 1 August were submitted by 149 people, including three from overseas. The complaints ranged from labour and medical disputes to inadequate welfare ... Xinhua said seventy-four of the applications were withdrawn because the problems 'were properly addressed by relevant authorities or departments through consultations'. Two other applications were suspended because they did not provide sufficient information and one was rejected because it violated laws against demonstrations and protests ... There have been no demonstrations in the areas since the Games started, though small unregulated protests have occurred at other places in the city. Most of them have been conducted by foreigners who have been swiftly deported after unfurling 'Free Tibet' banners. Human rights groups and families of people who have applied to protest in the parks say some were taken away afterward by security agents, prompting critics to accuse officials of using the plan as a trap to draw potential protesters to their attention. Under the protest park rules applications must be filed five days in advance and a response would be provided forty-eight hours before the requested rally time. Liu Shaowu, the Beijing Olympics security chief, also warned that protests must not harm 'national, social and collective interests'.
>
> (www.iht.com, 18 August 2008)

> Demonstrations are not illegal in China, but they require advance government approval, a prospect that often dissuades citizens, daunted by excessive bureaucracy or potential retaliation. Posters and slogans must be submitted by the police and each participant must apply in person. Any rally deemed a threat to 'social stability and public order' can be denied permission, and most are.
>
> (www.iht.com, 18 August 2008)

> The IOC called the Beijing Olympics a 'success' even though the Games are only halfway through ... [The IOC said that] things were going so well that a key meeting between the Chinese Olympic organizers and senior IOC officials had been postponed until Saturday [23 August].
>
> (www.bbc.co.uk, 18 August 2008)

'An American artist who planned to use laser beams to flash "Free Tibet" on buildings in Beijing was detained Tuesday [19 August]' (*IHT*, 20 August 2008, p. 5).

> In their latest confrontation with pro-Tibetan protesters during the Olympics, Chinese authorities arrested five Americans on Tuesday [19 August] after they spelled out 'Free Tibet' with blue LED lights near the National Stadium. Three other people, including a New York artist who fashions giant displays with lasers on buildings, were detained for a separatist protest ... Since 8 August members of the organization ... Students for a Free Tibet ... have staged seven protests involving thirty-seven people. All of those who were detained were promptly deported. On Tuesday five protesters hoisted a banner near the National Stadium ... and projected their message in Chinese and English using blue lights ... Students for a Free Tibet ... [said it] was more concerned with the plight of protesters in Tibet. In recent days ... [it said] at least three people have reportedly been killed in the city of Ganzi after protesting on the street.
>
> (www.iht.com, 20 August 2008)

> Two elderly woman [seventy-nine and seventy-seven] have been sentenced to a year of 'reeducation through labour' after they repeatedly sought a permit to demonstrate in one of the official Olympic protest areas, according to family members and human rights advocates ... The women had made five visits to the police this month [August] in an effort to obtain permission to protest what they considered inadequate compensation for the demolition of their homes in Beijing ... At least a half-dozen people have been detained by the authorities after they responded to a government announcement late last month [July] designating venues in three city parks as 'protest zones' during the Olympics. So far no demonstrations have taken place ... Human rights advocates have long criticized the [reeducation through labour] system because punishment is handed down by officials without a trial or means of appeal. Last year [2007] the government briefly grappled with revamping the system but backed off in the face of opposition from public security officials.
>
> (www.iht.com, 20 August 2008)

'Two women in their seventies who wanted to complain about inadequate compensation for being relocated from their homes ... [were both sentenced] to a year in labour camp, though the sentences are suspended as long as they behave well' (www.economist.com, 28 August 2008).

> Six Americans who were taken into custody on Tuesday [19 August] as they tried to protest against China's rule in Tibet have been given ten-day detentions, the Chinese police said Friday [22 August]. But other members of their organization, the New York-based Students for a Free Tibet, said that they had no information about four other protesters who were detained early Thursday [21 August] during a protest near the National Stadium. The four

> are two Americans, a German and a British citizen. Although a common form of punishment for Chinese dissidents, extrajudicial detentions are rarely handed out to foreigners, who are often deported almost immediately after being taken into custody. Members of Students for a Free Tibet have staged eight protests involving fifty-five people since the Olympics began on 8 August ... Public security bureau officials ... [explained] that the six Americans had been 'apprehended for upsetting public order' ... The Foreign Correspondents' Club of China has received dozens of complaints from foreign journalists who have been detained, trailed or had equipment damaged by the police.
>
> (www.iht.com, 22 August 2008; *IHT*, 23 August 2008, p. 3)

'The Foreign Correspondents' Club of China said at least fifty-nine reporters were harassed while trying to do their jobs' (www.bbc.co.uk, 28 August 2008).

('Eight Americans arrested for planning or staging protests in Beijing were deported to the United States on Sunday [24 August] ... Chinese law allows police to hold foreign nationals in jail for up to two weeks before pressing formal charges': www.cnn.com, 25 August 2008. 'China deported a British woman and a German man who had taken part in a protest during the Olympic Games, officials said Monday [25 August], hours after eight American activists were sent home during the closing ceremony ... Prime minister Gordon Brown of Britain, who attended the closing ceremony Sunday [24 August], had urged the Chinese authorities to release the woman ... [The two] were part of a group of four who unfurled a Tibetan flag last week and shouted "Free Tibet" south of the National Stadium ... [The other two] were among eight Americans sent home late Sunday after Washington expressed disappointment that the Olympics had not brought more "openness and tolerance" in China ... Mostly foreign activists staged a series of small illegal demonstrations near Olympic sites and at Beijing landmarks ... A few journalists trying to cover the protests were roughed up by authorities, then released ... [The US ambassador to China] had pressed the Chinese government Saturday [23 August] to release the eight ... A US embassy statement said Sunday: "We are disappointed that China has not used the occasion of the Olympics to demonstrate greater tolerance and openness" ... Several members of another group that sought permission to protest about corruption during the Games were detained in a room for forty-eight hours by the Chinese authorities before being deported home to Hong Kong, a group spokesman said': www.iht.com, 25 August 2008. 'Security agents detained the elderly bishop of an underground Catholic church in northern China before the closing of the Olympic Games, a US-based monitoring group said Monday [25 August]. Bishop Julius Jia Zhiguo, seventy-three, of Zhengding, a city in northern Hebei province, was taken by six government officials from his cathedral Sunday morning [24 August], the group, the Cardinal Kung Foundation, said ... Jia has been repeatedly detained by security forces ... The Games ended Sunday night ... Jia's diocese ... is a traditional stronghold of Catholic sentiment in northern China': www.iht.com, 25 August 2008.)

The Beijing Games draw to a close on Sunday [24 August] after what many have described as one of the best Olympics ever held. China, having beaten the United States to top the medals table, will hand the Olympic flag to the 2012 hosts London at a closing ceremony from 13.00 BST ... The sporting action has been enthralling ... [with] 302 gold medals awarded.

(www.bbc.co.uk, 24 August 2008)

Worries over pollution and its impact on athletes seemed to fade away. Distance running events ran smoothly and while the air was thick with smog on many days during the Games, media did not report widespread health concerns by the tens of thousands of foreigners attending the Games.

(www.cnn.com, 24 August 2008)

China concluded its debut as Olympic host Sunday [24 August] after sixteen days of nearly flawless logistics and superlative athletic achievement that co-existed awkwardly with the government's wariness of dissent and free speech ... Its athletes topped the gold medal standings for the first time ... Two athletes gave some of the greatest performances in Olympic history – Michael Phelps [of the United States] with his eight gold medals in swimming; Jamaica's Usain Bolt with three golds and three world records in the sprints [100 metres, 200 metres and 4 x 100 metres relay] ... Led by Phelps and Bolt athletes broke forty-three world records and 132 Olympic records during the Games ... Athletes shied away from making political statements and 'protest zones' established in Beijing went unused as the authorities refused to issue permits for them ... China invested more than $40 billion in the Games ... Olympic telecasts achieved record ratings in China and the United States, and the Games's presence online was by far the most extensive ever ... Smog that enveloped the city early in the Games gave way to mostly clear skies, easing fears that some endurance events might be hazardous for the athletes ... Jacques Rogge (IOC committee president) contended that media restrictions had been looser during the Olympics than beforehand 'and so we believe the Games had a good influence' ... Rogge, who visited every venue, said the most touching moment for him came after the 10-metre air pistol event, when the gold medallist, Nino Salukvadze of Georgia, embraced the runner-up, Natalia Paderina of Russia, even as their two countries' armies fought back in Georgia.

(www.iht.com, 24 August 2008)

[China won 100 medals in total] ... [China] finished with fifty-one [gold medals], the highest figure for any nation at an Olympics in twenty years, and they won them across a wider range of sports than any team in Beijing ... The United States finished with 110 [medals in total] ... The Russians won thirty-six gold medals and eighty-eight overall in 2000; they won twenty-seven golds and ninety-two overall in Athens. This time the final tallies were twenty-three [coming third after China and the United States] and seventy-two.

(www.iht.com, 24 August 2008)

The medal count for the top four countries was as follows (gold, silver, bronze, total): China (51, 21, 28, 100); United States (36, 38, 36, 110); Russia (23, 21, 28, 72); Britain (19, 13, 15, 47) (*IHT*, 25 August 2008, p. 18).

> [The] $43 billion price tag for the Games was almost completely absorbed by the state. China's fifty-one gold medals, easily the most of any nation, were the product of a state-controlled sports machine … Critics say that the Olympics have underscored the deep resistance within the Communist Party to becoming more tolerant of dissent.
>
> (*IHT*, 25 August 2008, p. 15)

'China won its first Summer Olympic gold medal in 1984' (www.cnn.com, 24 August 2008).

'China won thirty-two gold medals in Athens in 2004' (www.iht.com, 6 August 2008).

'Although the organization of the Games has been widely praised, rights groups have criticized the Beijing government throughout' (www.bbc.co.uk, 24 August 2008).

> After the Olympic party … many in China are likely to wonder whether it was all really worth it. Wang Yang, a member of the ruling Politburo and one of the more outspoken leaders (a rare breed), has called for tolerance of public grievances. Attempting to suppress people's views might create an 'opinion quake lake', he said recently, referring to the perilously unstable lakes that were formed by landslides during the Sichuan earthquake.
>
> (*The Economist*, 2 August 2008, p. 3)

> What many outside China saw during the Olympics was a clampdown on dissent and a disdain even for the spontaneous street-party exuberance of previous Games … Officially the Games cost $2.2 billion, compared with an original estimate of $1.6 billion. Beijing also spent $40 billion on preparing the infrastructure and cleaning up the environment … [For] Vice President Xi Jinping … the Games were his first big political test since he emerged as China's leader-in-waiting after a Communist Party congress in October last year [2007]. Mr Xi took charge of preparations for the Games … Officially a lower-ranking Politburo member, Beijing's party chief, Liu Qi, remained the top organizer. Organizationally the Games went well.
>
> (*The Economist*, 30 August 2008, p. 63)

> Chinese athletes who won gold medals at this summer's Beijing Olympics are to be paid about $51,000 each … The payments are an increase on the $29,000 that China paid its gold medallists after the 2004 Games. China came top of the medals table at this year's Games, winning 100 medals in twenty-five sports, including fifty-one golds. China spends about $117 million each year on sports, according to China's sports chief, Liu Peng.
>
> (www.bbc.co.uk, 26 August 2008)

> The country's gold medallists will each get a tax-free bonus of $51,000, about $22,000 more than the bonus Chinese gold medallists received after the 2004 Athens Games. In the 1984 Los Angeles Games, the first modern Summer Olympics in which China took part, the gold medallists received bonuses of less than $900 each. China won fifteen medals that year ... The Paralympics [are] scheduled for 6–17 September. About 4,500 athletes with disabilities are expected to compete.
>
> (www.iht.com, 28 August 2008)

'The massive effort to clear the skies over Beijing for the Summer Olympics paid off, the city's environmental authority said Monday [1 September], with the capital seeing its cleanest air in a decade' (www.iht.com, 1 September 2008).

> Beijing Environmental Protection Bureau announced last month [August] that it had fulfilled its Olympic pledges, but on Monday [1 September] it gave more details. It said air pollution during the Olympics was down by 50 per cent – a ten-year record. Not only do Beijing residents like their cleaner city, they also appear more willing to fight to keep it that way. There are reports that Beijing residents protested outside a rubbish incineration plant on Saturday [30 August]. Residents, who claim the site gives off noxious fumes, staged their demonstration when the site opened again after being closed during the Olympics.
>
> (www.bbc.co.uk, 2 September 2008)

> Protesters took to the streets of Beijing yesterday [30 August] in an escalating campaign against the city's biggest dump site, which they claimed was polluting the air with a foul stench and dangerous dioxins ... Residents of the affluent Changying district of east Beijing have complained for more than three years about the nearby Gaoantun landfill and waste incineration facility.
>
> (www.guardian.co.uk, 31 August 2008)

The Paralympic Games took place from Saturday 6 September to 17 September 2008. 'China topped the medal table, winning an astonishing eighty-seven golds out of a total of 207, after investing heavily in Paralympic sport and bolstering their squad' (www.bbc.co.uk, 18 September 2008).

> A legal advocate who was arrested after applying to hold a legal protest in Beijing during the Olympics in August has been sentenced to three years in prison ... Ji Sizun was sentenced on 7 January [2009] ... for forging official seals and documents ... He arrived in Beijing planning to hold a protest against government corruption ... [He applied] for a permit to hold a protest.
>
> (www.iht.com, 15 January 2009)

> A woman and her sisters, who came to Beijing from southern China during the Paralympics in September to protest property seizures but were arrested, have been sentenced to one year of detention for vandalism, the woman said

> on Thursday [30 July]. The woman had already been held for nearly a year in a hotel – known as a 'black jail' – while awaiting trial ... [She] was released from the hotel ... on 17 July. She said she expected to remain under a form of house arrest for one year in her home town, under police surveillance.
>
> (www.iht.com, 31 July 2009)

' "Black jails" [are] illegal holding cells that some officials use to silence persistent critics' (www.iht.com, 10 August 2009).

> Before last year's Olympics the government imposed a regimen based on even and odd licence-plate numbers that effectively banned half of all private automobiles from the road on weekdays. Officials – and the public – liked it so much that a modified version, banning one in five cars, is now a permanent rule.
>
> (www.iht.com, 17 October 2009)

'The 2010 World Expo will run from May until October [2010] ... China is lavishing as much money on the World Expo and accompanying makeover of Shanghai ($45 billion) as it did on the Olympics and sprucing up Beijing' (www.economist.com, 3 December 2009; *IHT*, 5 December 2009, p. 70).

> No one expects China to dominate the 2010 Winter Olympics [in Vancouver] the way it ruled the 2008 Summer Games in Beijing. But its Olympic officials are hoping for a breakthrough that could bring perhaps five or more gold medals and about fifteen overall – a significant number given that China has won only four previous golds and thirty-three cumulative medals since it began participating in the Winter Games in 1980 in Lake Placid, NY.
>
> (www.iht.com, 15 February 2010)

China actually won eleven medals in total (five gold, two silver and four bronze) (*IHT*, 1 March 2010, p. 13).

> The United States won the highest number of medals in total, thirty-seven (nine gold, fifteen silver and thirteen bronze). Germany was second, with a total of thirty medals (ten gold, thirteen silver and seven bronze). Canada was third, with a total of twenty-six medals (fourteen gold, seven silver and five bronze).
>
> (www.bbc.co.uk, 1 March 2010)

General developments from 20 August 2008 onwards

20 August 2008.

> Hua Guofeng, handpicked by Mao Tse-tung (Zedong) in 1976 to succeed him as Communist Party chairman but pushed aside by Deng Xaioping ... died Wednesday [20 August] at the age of eighty-seven ... Hua took power

after Mao's death in September 1976 but saw his powers erode until Deng Xiaoping took control two years later. He was forced out as Communist Party chairman in 1981 and slipped into obscurity ... Hua remained part of the inner circle as a member of the party's Central Committee ... Deng had been purged in Mao's final years but was restored to his official posts in July 1977. Hua was effectively stripped of his powers at a party meeting in December 1978. The same gathering approved Deng's 'reform and opening' policy legalizing small-scale private farms, the first step in what became a successful programme of capitalist changes. Hua resigned as prime minister in September 1980 and was replaced by Zhao Ziyang ... The following year Deng had Hua replaced as party secretary by Hu Yaobang. Both Zhao and Hu would later be dismissed by Deng – Hu in the mid-1980s after he was blamed for allowing student protests and Zhao after the 1989 Tiananmen Square pro-democracy demonstrations.

(www.iht.com, 20 August 2008)

Hua was chairman of the Communist Party and prime minister when security forces arrested the Gang of Four a month after Mao's death ... [Hua] became acting prime minister only in January 1976, succeeding Zhou Enlai. Mao confirmed him as prime minister three months later, when Hua also became deputy party chairman. He succeeded Mao as chairman when Mao died five months later ... Having lost most of his influence by the end of 1978, Hua lost the post of prime minister to Zhao Ziyang in September 1980. Hua was forced to relinquish his position as chairman of the Central Military Commission in June 1981, and stepped down from his top positions in the Communist Party, including his Politburo membership, in September 1982.

(*IHT*, 21 August 2008, p. 5)

After Hua Guofeng took over, the members of the so-called Gang of Four – including Mao's widow Jiang Qing – were arrested and blamed for the excesses that accompanied the decade-long Cultural Revolution. Hua also allowed the rehabilitation of Deng Xiaoping, who was restored to the post of vice premier, which he had held before losing favour with Mao.

(www.bbc.co.uk, 20 August 2008)

26 August 2008. On 26 August Russia recognized the independence of the South Ossetia and Abkhazia, breakaway regions within Georgia's internationally recognized sovereign territory. Georgia had tried to regain control of South Ossetia by force on 7 August and this led to a brief war between Georgia and Russia, which the former lost. But China did not support Russia's recognition.

'China addressed the crisis ... by expressing "concern" about developments in the region and urging dialogue. The comments came as Chinese President Hu Jintao met President Dmitri Medvedev in Tajikistan ahead of a regional summit' (www.bbc.co.uk, 28 August 2008).

In a joint statement [issued on 28 August in Dushanbe, the capital of Tajikistan] the SCO [Shanghai Co-operation Organization] gave their

> support for Russia's 'active role' in resolving the conflict in Georgia by 'assisting in peace and co-operation in the region'. The statement said: 'The SCO members express their deep concern over the recent tensions surrounding the South Ossetia question and call for the sides to resolve existing problems through dialogue' ... The SOC – which includes China, Kazakhstan, Kyrgyzstan, Russia, Tajikistan and Uzbekistan – was established in 2001 ... Russian President Dmitri Medvedev said the grouping's united position would have 'international resonance'. He said: 'I hope it will serve as a serious signal to those who try to turn black into white and justify this aggression.'
>
> (www.bbc.co.uk, 28 August 2008)

'Russia failed to get strong backing from [the SCO] ... The group did not follow Russia in recognizing the independence of South Ossetia and Abkhazia. Russian President Dmitri Medvedev insisted he had the backing of the nations over Moscow's actions' (www.bbc.co.uk, 28 August 2008).

> China and other Asian nations expressed concern about mounting tensions in the region. The joint declaration from the Shanghai Co-operation Organization, or SCO ... said the countries hoped any further conflict could be resolved peacefully through dialogue. The declaration said: 'The presidents reaffirmed their commitments to the principles of respect for historic and cultural traditions of every country and efforts aimed at preserving the unity of a state and its territorial integrity. Placing the emphasis exclusively on the use of force has no prospects and hinders a comprehensive settlement of local conflicts' ... President Dmitri Medvedev told the group support for Russia would serve as a 'serious signal for those who are trying to justify aggression'.
>
> (www.cnn.com, 28 August 2008)

> Russia's hopes on winning international support for its actions in Georgia were dashed Thursday [28 August] when China and other Asian nations expressed concern about tension in the region. The joint declaration from the SCO ... said the countries hoped any further conflict could be resolved peacefully.
>
> (www.cnn.com, 28 August 2008)

> The summit's closing statement said: 'The SCO states express grave concern in connection with the recent tensions around the South Ossetian issue and urge the sides to solve existing problems peacefully, through dialogue and to make efforts facilitating reconciliation and talks' ... Even China ... issued a veiled criticism of Moscow's actions, saying it was 'concerned about the latest changes in South Ossetia and Abkhazia'. Kazakhstan said it was too early to consider recognition ... No other country has recognized the territories.
>
> (www.iht.com, 28 August 2008).

'A group of Asian allies led by China failed to follow Russia's lead on independence for [South Ossetia and Abkhazia]' (www.iht.com, 28 August 2008).

> The leaders of the Shanghai group did endorse some aspects of Russian involvement in the Caucasus, saying that the organization approved of 'the active role of Russia in assisting in peace and co-operation in the region' … The Shanghai organization was created seven years ago to foster co-operation and combat terrorism … The group conducts joint military exercises.
>
> (*IHT*, 29 August 2008, p. 3)

'The Shanghai Co-operation Organization … also includes Iran, Mongolia and India as observers' (www.iht.com, 29 August 2008).

'China was urging Russia and Georgia to resolve their conflict through "dialogue and consultation", [the Chinese foreign ministry said on 2 September]' (www.bbc.co.uk, 2 September 2008).

> The executive board of the Asian Development Bank, representing countries from Japan and China to Turkmenistan and Uzbekistan, unanimously approved a $40 million loan to Georgia at the lowest possible interest rate on Friday [12 September] … Juan Miranda, director-general of the bank's Central and West Asia Department, said the loan had been scheduled for board consideration on Friday before Russian troops moved into Georgia a month ago. But the Russian military action strengthened support at the bank for helping Georgia, he said … The bank is also studying the possibility of making an emergency loan to Georgia to help it cope with budget problems after the brief war with Russia … China names one of the twelve directors of the Asian Development Bank … Russia has been seeking membership of the Asian Development Bank since 1997. It has been blocked by the United States … The bank does not proceed on the admittance of new members until a consensus has emerged on the board. The United States, China and Japan each name a director to the board. The other members, including seventeen European nations, share representation by the remaining nine directors. Georgia, the newest member of the Asian Development Bank, joined last year [2007]. The loan approved Friday is for the Municipal Development Fund of Georgia, which in turn will relend the money for municipalities to pay for sewage works, clean water supplies and other basic services.
>
> (www.iht.com, 12 September 2008; *IHT*, 13 September 2008, p. 3)

28 August 2008.

> Central government departments misused more than 46 billion yuan ($6.73 billion) last year [2007], including using disaster relief money to build government offices and diverting funds to speculate in stocks, the National Audit Office said … An audit of fifty-three central government departments and their subsidiary units found the misuse or embezzlement of 4.52 billion yuan in 2007, down from 7 billion yuan the year before [2006].
>
> (www.ft.com, 28 August 2008)

Ten central government departments, including the ministry of finance, 'misused or embezzled' more than 4.52 billion yuan, or $660 million, last year [2007], according to a report from China's top auditor. The report also said that fourteen officials were referred for prosecution, eighty-eight people in all were arrested and an additional 104 government employees were punished for their roles in mismanaging or embezzling what amounted to billions of dollars of additional government funds, state media reported Thursday [28 August]. Even the State Administration of Taxation was accused of fraud. Liu Jiayi, the nation's top auditor, said in the report that another 41.7 billion yuan in government funds was 'mismanaged' last year, and that fraud had been detected in dozens of government bureaus, including the Ministry of Education, the National Bureau of Statistics, the Ministry of Health, the Chinese Academy of Sciences and the State Administration of Radio, Film and Television … Since 1999 the national audits, dubbed the 'audit storm', have resulted in the discovery of billions of dollars' worth of fraud and mismanagement in everything from state-owned banks to the country's social security fund. In 2006 the government said $900 million had been misappropriated from the nation's $37 billion social security fund. And in 2005 the auditor said that $35 billion in government funds had been misused … In the latest report fraud was also uncovered in railway projects [and] government housing funds and auditors said that the Agricultural Bank of China had illegally used about 14.2 billion yuan in funds.

(www.iht.com, 28 August 2008)

Government departments misused, embezzled or mismanaged more than 46 billion yuan (6.7 billion) in 2007, the state auditor said in an annual report. China's national audit office said offences included using disaster relief funds to build government offices … In this latest report to parliament Auditor-General Liu Jiayi said an audit of more than fifty government departments and their subsidiaries had discovered that 4.5 billion yuan ($660 million) had been misused or embezzled in 2007. He said the offences included diverting public funds to speculate in stocks and using disaster relief money to build government offices. The report also found 'managerial irregularities' in the use of another 41.7 billion yuan ($6 billion) of public money. It said the country's education and commerce ministries, along with the statistics and tax offices, were among the major offenders.

(www.bbc.co.uk, 28 August 2008)

1 September 2008.

Prime minister Yasuo Fukuda of Japan abruptly announced his resignation on Monday [1 September], ending a short-lived and unpopular government marred by political paralysis. Fukuda's sudden departure … seemed to catch his country by surprise … [The resignation came] after the equally sudden resignation last year [2007] of Fukuda's predecessor, Shinzo Abe.

(www.iht.com, 1 September 2008)

The surprise announcement means the seventy-year-old ... Yasuo Fukuda ... is resigning less than a year after he took office. His government has suffered chronic unpopularity. Lost pension records, a controversial healthcare scheme and a sliding economy have added to his woes ... The upper house of parliament is controlled by the opposition.

(www.bbc.co.uk, 1 September 2008)

5 September 2008.

The government is reported to have sent thousands of soldiers and police to quell unrest in the central province of Hunan. Up to 10,000 people took to the streets in Jishou to demand money back from an allegedly fraudulent fund-raising firm, a Hong Kong-based rights group said. In another protest in the eastern port of Ningbo 10,000 workers clashed with police, the group added. Social unrest is common in China, but rarely on this scale. The Hong Kong-based Information Centre for Human Rights and Democracy said that in both protests violent clashes erupted between angry crowds and local authorities ... According to Xinhua, the protesters ... in Jishou ... blocked roads and trains to demand that the government take action after a fund-raising company 'failed to pay them back as promised' ... In the second incident thousands of migrant workers confronted police in Ningbo to protest about the injury of a man in a local factory.

(www.bbc.co.uk, 5 September 2008)

8 September 2008.

The governor of Shanxi province in northern China resigned Sunday [14 September] in the wake of a mud and rock slide that has killed at least 254 people ... The vice governor has been removed from his post as well ... More than 1,000 rescue workers have combed through 99 per cent of the inundated area – digging through tons of slush, mud and rocks around a mine in Xiangfen county ... Crews have begun a new search round a 330-yard ditch filled with silt ... Earlier authorities detained thirteen people. Among them are the board chairman of the Xinta Mining Company, the mine manager, a vice manager and accountant. The deaths occurred after torrential rain on 8 September at the unlicensed Tashan Mine, which operated illegally. The amount of iron ore waste in a holding pond exceeded the pond's capacity ... and intense rain triggered a flow of mud and rocks that roared down a valley Monday [8 September].

(www.cnn.com, 15 September 2008)

The governor ... Meng Xuenong ... and deputy governor of Shanxi province lost their jobs Sunday [14 September] after at least 254 villagers were killed when their homes were engulfed in a cascade of muddy iron ore waste from the reservoir of an unlicensed mine ... Even by the standards of China's mining industry, the most dangerous in the world with more than 5,000 deaths a year, the mudflow was an especially horrible and deadly accident. Heavy rains caused the retaining wall of a reservoir of iron ore waste to collapse ... The latest death toll, 254, included bodies pulled from the muck through Saturday evening [13 September] ... Meng Xuenong was a rising star when he was named mayor of Beijing in January 2003. He was removed three months later for covering up the spread of SARS to the capital. His next post was a big demotion, to deputy director of China's biggest water project. But he retained his position as one of the roughly 300 members of the Communist Party's Central Committee and ended up being named governor of Shanxi province in January [2008].

(www.iht.com, 14 September 2008)

22 September 2008.

Taro Aso, an outspoken conservative who has advocated a return to old-style government spending to stimulate Japan's economy, was chosen Monday [22 September] by the governing Liberal Democratic Party to become the nation's next prime minister Aso [is] a former foreign minister ... The party's control of the lower house of parliament virtually ensures he will replace prime minister Yasuo Fukuda in a parliament session Wednesday [24 September] ... Aso's propensity for verbal gaffes ... has angered Asian neighbours in the past by stirring up bitter memories of Japan's prewar imperial expansion ... As prime minister he is expected to continue to seek improvement of Japan's often testy ties with China and South Korea. He has also said he favours close ties with Washington.

(www.iht.com, 23 September 2008)

24 September 2008.

The lower house of Japan's parliament, the Diet, has elected Taro Aso as the country's new prime minister. He will be Japan's third leader in just two years and replaces Yasuo Fukuda, who resigned earlier this month. Mr Aso's nomination as prime minister now goes to Japan's upper house before it is officially confirmed. The upper house is controlled by the opposition, but Mr Aso's appointment is not in doubt as the lower house can overrule the upper house when they disagree.

(www.bbc.co.uk, 24 September 2008)

Yasuo Fukuda's popularity plummeted after he introduced a medical plan that raises premiums for people over seventy-five and deducts health care expenses from pension payments. The government has said the plan is unavoidable in a country with one of the largest ageing populations ... Aso, a former Olympic sharpshooter, is a Catholic in a country where only 1 per cent of the population is of that faith.

(www.cnn.com, 24 September 2008)

Two years ago Taro Aso ... suggested Japan – whose pacifist constitution forswears war – should have a debate on whether to acquire nuclear weapons ... Aso once described ... China's growing economic and military clout ...

> as a 'major threat' ... He recently ... [compared] the top opposition party to the Nazis. In 2001 he was forced to apologize after saying the ideal country would be one that attracts 'the richest Jewish people' ... Aso, a former Olympic skeetshooter and Japan's first Catholic leader, will inherit a government paralysed by gridlock ... The economy has stalled in recent months.
>
> (www.iht.com, 24 September 2008)

> Taro Aso, a veteran politician who had fought for years to win Japan's top political post, was officially named the country's fourth prime minister in two years Wednesday [24 September] by the lower house of parliament. In his first news conference, Aso, sixty-eight, said his priority was to revive the economy, which economists say may have already slipped into a recession ... The main opposition Democratic Party seized the less powerful upper house of parliament last year [2007].
>
> (www.iht.com, 24 September 2008)

> Taro Aso is well known by Japan's neighbours as a pugnacious nationalist. As foreign minister from 2005 to 2007 Aso soured relations with China and South Korea and raised tensions throughout the region, praising the achievements of prewar Japanese colonialism, justifying wartime atrocities and portraying China as a dangerous military threat ... Aso is expected to focus on stimulating Japan's stagnant economy.
>
> (*IHT*, 26 September 2008, p. 4)

'As foreign minister ... [Taro Aso] praised the compulsory education Japan imposed on Taiwan during its colonial rule of the island before World War II' (www.feer.com, 29 September 2008).

('Japan's transport minister resigned Sunday [28 September] after a string of gaffes ... The resignation of Nariaki Nakayama marked an embarrassing and rocky start for Taro Aso, who took office on Wednesday [24 September] with the lowest public support of any newly appointed prime minister in eight years. The latest newspaper polls had shown his approval rating at just below 50 per cent ... The resignation follows remarks by Nakayama on Saturday [27 September], when he called Japan's largest teachers' union "a cancer" ... He also said the Japan Teachers' Union should be abolished ... [In addition] Nakayama said last week that "Japan is ethnically homogeneous", drawing criticism from the Ainu, the indigenous people of northern Japan ... He angered China last year [2007] by claiming that the death toll in the "Rape of Nanking" massacre was grossly inflated. Nakayama, who headed a group of about 100 Japanese governing party lawmakers, said documents from the Japanese government's archives indicated that about 20,000 people were killed in the 1937 massacre – far below the more commonly cited figure of 150,000 to 200,000': www.iht.com, 28 September 2008.)

25 September 2008.

> A Chinese Shenzhou 7 spaceship was scheduled to lift off Thursday evening [25 September] on the nation's third manned space mission, one that

> includes China's space walk. The three-day mission will include China's first space walk if all goes according to plan ... In [October] 2003 China became the third country to send people into space, when military pilot Yang Liwei circled the earth for twenty-one hours. Its second mission – in 2005 – had two crew members and lasted five days.
>
> (www.cnn.com, 25 September 2008)

> The spacewalk is expected to help China master the technology for docking two orbiters to create China's first orbiting space station in the next few years ... The two astronauts who don spacesuits for the Shenzhou 7 spacewalk will be supported by Russian experts throughout the mission. Only one will actually leave the orbiter module to retrieve scientific experiments placed outside. One of the astronauts will wear China's homemade Feitian suit, while the other will wear a Russian-made suit. Fighter pilot Zhai Zhigang ... has been touted to carry out the spacewalk.
>
> (www.cnn.com, 25 September 2008)

> If all goes to plan the event will be shown live on national television ... One of the crew will walk in space. And he will be wearing a Chinese-made suit ... Just in case he needs any help, another astronaut wearing a Russian suit will be standing by in the airlock ... For the first time since China began its manned space flights, the authorities have allowed foreign journalists (albeit only a handful) to witness the launch ... Another programme, which began last October [2007] with the launch of a lunar probe called *Chang'e*, aims to put an unmanned rover on the surface of the moon around 2017 and return it to earth with samples ... Japan launched a lunar probe shortly before China did last year ... Japan's parliament, or Diet, in May [2008] rescinded a 1969 resolution mandating that Japan only pursue peaceful uses of space. The new policy allows space technologies to be used for 'national security' as well ... Chian has drawn extensively on ... [Russia's] expertise to get its manned space programme going. It has even sent its astronauts for training by Russians. In October next year [2009] a Russian rocket will launch a Chinese probe to Mars.
>
> (*The Economist*, 27 September 2008, p. 80)

> The Shenzhou 7 capsule will go into orbit atop a Long-March II-F rocket from the Jiuquan spaceport in Gansu province in the north-west of China. The flight is expected to last in the region of seventy hours and will include the first spacewalk, undertaken by forty-two-year-old fighter pilot Zhai Zhigang. Mr Zhai is joined on the mission by two other *yuhangyuan* (astronauts) – Liu Boming and Jing Haipeng.
>
> (www.bbc.co.uk, 25 September 2008)

'In 1970 China launched its first satellite, which circled the earth broadcasting the communist song "The East is Red". In 1999 [the] successful launch of a Shenzhou-series spaceship paved the way for the manned space programme' (*FT*, 25 September 2008, p. 7).

> The three-day mission is part of Project 921, China's ambitious unmanned space programme, and was expected to include the country's first attempt at a space walk, which would make China only the third country to accomplish the feat, after Russia and the United States ... [One] of the experienced fighter pilots ... is expected to walk in space for thirty minutes on Saturday [27 September] ... The three *taikonauts* – the Chinese term for astronauts – plan to take samples from space and launch a small satellite monitoring station ... [China hopes it will] establish a space station by 2020 and eventually put a man on the moon ... [China] is now aggressively launching commercial satellites, putting men in space and even shooting down ageing satellites ... China is only the third nation to launch a man into space. India and Japan are now aggressively developing their own space programmes ... On Wednesday [24 September] the US Federal Bureau of Investigation arrested a Chinese-born physicist ... on charges of illegally exporting space launch technical data and services to China beginning in January 2003. The physicist, Shu Quan-Sheng, sixty-eight, was born in China but was a naturalized US citizen ... Shu was said to be involved in China's 'systematic effort to upgrade their space exploration and satellite technology capabilities by providing technical expertise and foreign technology acquisition', according to an FBI press release.
>
> (www.iht.com, 25 September 2008)

> One astronaut is wearing what the state-run news media has dubbed 'the most complicated, advanced and expensive suit in the world', a $4.4 million space suit designed and produced in China ... China says its space programme is speeding along, often with Chinese technology.
>
> (www.iht.com, 26 September 2008)

'Russia and the United States accomplished their first space walks in 1965 and the United States put a man on the moon in 1969' (*IHT*, 26 September 2008, p. 2).

> China has launched its third manned space mission ... The rocket lit up the darkness as it blasted off from Jiuquan at 21.10 Beijing time (13.10 GMT) ... Zhai Zhigang will retrieve an externally mounted experiment and oversee the release of a satellite.
>
> (www.bbc.co.uk, 25 September 2008)

> A Chinese astronaut has become the first in his country's history to take a walk in space. In an operation broadcast live on national television, fighter pilot Zhai Zhigang emerged from the capsule orbiting the Earth to wave a Chinese flag. Mr Zhai stayed outside the capsule for fifteen minutes ... Mr Zhai began his manoeuvre just after 16.30 Beijing time (08.30 GMT) on Saturday [27 September] and completed it about fifteen minutes later ... His colleague. Liu Boming, also briefly got his head out of the capsule to hand him the flag. Mr Zhai wore a Chinese-made spacesuit thought to have cost between $10 million and $40 million for the space walk ... Mr Zhai retrieved an externally mounted experiment. The third *yuhangyuan*

> (astronaut) on the mission is Jing Hipeng ... The ship is to release a 40 kilogramme (90 pound) satellite which will circle the orbiter and beam back images to mission control ... According to the Associated Press news agency, Xinhua ... the state-run news agency ... posted an article on its website prior to lift-off that was written as if the Shenzhou 7 had already been launched into space. The article reportedly carried a date of 27 September and came complete with a dialogue between the astronauts. Chinese media report that this latest mission is the 'most critical step' in the country's 'three step' space programme. These stages are: sending a human into orbit, docking spacecraft together to form a small laboratory and, ultimately, building a large space station. The Shenzhou 8 and 9 missions are expected to help set up a space laboratory complex in 2010. China launched an unmanned Moon probe last year [2007] about one month after rival Japan blasted its own lunar orbiter into space.
>
> (www.bbc.co.uk, 27 September 2008)

'Zhai Zhigang returned to the interior of his capsule and closed the hatch after less than twenty minutes outside ... Fellow astronaut Liu Boming also emerged briefly from the capsule to hand Zhai the Chinese flag' (www.cnn.com, 27 September 2008).

> Three Chinese astronauts returned to Earth Sunday [28 September], completing a three-day mission that included China's first ever spacewalk. The Shenzhou 7 re-entry capsule parachuted to a landing on the Inner Mongolia steppe at about 5.39 p.m. (09.39 GMT). The highlight of the mission came Saturday [27 September] when astronaut Zhai Zhigang emerged from the hatch of the Shenzhou 7 spaceship for a thirteen-minute excursion outside ... the astronaut stayed close to the spacecraft, linked by tethers and always keeping one hand on railings.
>
> (www.cnn.com, 28 September 2008)

> Zhai Zhigang's sole task was to retrieve a rack attached to the outside of the orbital module containing an experiment involving solid lubricants ... Zhai appeared to struggle with the hatch and a fire alarm was triggered in the orbiter as he began the spacewalk ... A faulty sensor [was blamed] for the fire alarm.
>
> (www.iht.com, 28 September 2008)

'The mission commander, wearing a $4.4 million Chinese-made suit ... floated out of the Shenzhou 7's orbital module for about thirteen minutes ... The Soviet put Sputnik, the first satellite, into orbit in 1957' (www.guardian.co.uk, 28 September 2008).

'The Shenzhou 7 mission comes just three days before the fiftieth anniversary of the US space agency, Nasa' (www.independent.co.uk, 28 September 2008).

> Three Chinese astronauts who returned to earth safely on Sunday [28 September] have been given a hero's welcome in Beijing ... The celebrations kicked off a week when the government marks National Day ... Events to

celebrate the establishment of the communist state began on Sunday, with a reception and concert in the Great Hall of the People. The official date, 1 October, will be marked by more ceremonies, in Hong Kong and Macao as well as the mainland.

(www.bbc.co.uk, 29 September 2008)

30 September 2008.

Beijing is preparing to reinstate certain traffic restrictions, after rules enforced during the Olympic Games helped clean the city's polluted air ... The response from Beijingers was overwhelmingly positive ... Although there is no formal system for public consultation in China, internet forums and letters to the media conveyed genuine satisfaction. Now the authorities have responded by bringing in a milder set of restrictions, which are to be trialled until April 2009 and made permanent if found to be working. Beginning Wednesday [1 October] the government is setting an example by keeping 30 per cent of its vehicles off the streets at any one time. Later in October all cars will be banned from the roads on one day a week, depending on their number plates. Employers are meantime being asked to stagger working hours to reduce peak traffic. In just one generation Chinese cities have turned from virtually car-free environments into traffic-choked ones.

(www.bbc.co.uk, 30 September 2008)

3 October 2008.

About 450 people have fallen ill in southern China after drinking contaminated water ... Four of the sick, in two villages in Guangxi province, have arsenic poisoning ... Residents began to show symptoms of facial swelling, vomiting and blurred vision on 3 October ... Industrial waste from a metal company has been blamed ... Torrential rain caused waste water containing arsenic from the Jinhai Metallurgy Chemical Company to overflow and pollute nearby ponds and wells ... The local government and the company agreed to share the medical costs of the villagers ... The company was closed after the contamination was discovered.

(www.bbc.co.uk, 11 October 2008)

8–9 October 2008.

The police have beaten and detained protesters holding a rally in southern China to seek compensation for damaged property, an activist group said Thursday [9 October] ... Human Rights in China said that more than 500 police and paramilitary police officers clashed Wednesday [8 October] with hundreds of village protesters in rural Sanjiang town in Guangdong province's Xinhui district ... The protest followed a typhoon that collapsed the local dam, damaging farmland, fish ponds and farm property. Villagers blamed government officials for illegally selling and removing trees around the dam, which may have caused it to collapse, the group said.

(www.iht.com, 9 October 2008)

10 October 2008.

> The Norwegian Nobel Committee awarded its 2008 peace prize on Friday [10 October] to Martti Ahtisaari, the former Finnish president who has been associated over decades with peace efforts and quiet, cautious diplomacy from Asia to Africa and Europe … Specifically, the committee mentioned his work in ending South African domination of Namibia, the former South-West Africa, from the 1970s to the late 1990s [Namibia becoming independent in 1990], and peace efforts in the Indonesian province of Aceh, as well as Kosovo [being special envoy of the UN Secretary-General in Kosovo from 2005 until early 2008], Northern Ireland, Central Asia, the Horn of Africa and, most recently, in Iraq … There had been wide speculation before the winner of the prize was announced that it could be awarded to the Chinese human rights activist Hu Jia.
>
> (www.iht.com, 10 October 2008)

'Chinese dissidents Hu Jia and Gao Zhisheng were also leading contenders, prompting Beijing to issue a veiled warning that the prize should go the "right person"' (www.iht.com, 10 October 2008).

('China has said it hopes the Nobel peace prize will reward what it called "the right person", amid reports that jailed dissidents top the list of favourites … The Chinese foreign ministry said some past choices had gone against the prize's original purpose of promoting world peace and human progress. The award went to the Dalai Lama nineteen years ago, and dissidents Hu Jia and Gao Zhisheng are on this year's list': www.bbc.co.uk, 7 October 2008.)

13 October 2008.

> Traffic restrictions have been reintroduced in Beijing in an attempt to bring back the clear skies seen during the Olympics … Each car must spend one day a week off the road, in a scheme based on registration numbers … It is expected to reduce Beijing's average road traffic flow by 6.5 per cent … During periods of heavy pollution the restrictions will be increased so that half of Beijing's 3.4 million cars will be taken off the roads … The new restrictions will be implemented on a trial basis for six months until April [2009].
>
> (www.bbc.co.uk, 13 October 2008)

17 October 2008.

> The official Chinese news agency said Friday [17 October] that the country was easing restrictions on foreign journalists. Xinhua said the new rules would allow foreign correspondents to interview citizens without special permission from the government. Such permission – lifted during the Olympics – had been required in the past.
>
> (*IHT*, 18 October 2008, p. 5)

> Special Olympic regulations that had allowed foreign journalists to report freely in most of China for nearly two years expired yesterday [17 October],

although local governments across the country said they would continue to follow the rules in the short term.

(*The Independent*, 18 October 2008, p. 30)

> China introduced the rules in January last year [2007] for foreign journalists who wanted to report on Olympic-related issues. They expired on 17 October. They allowed correspondents to travel around China without first getting permission from the authorities – as they had to do previously. The regulation stated: 'To interview organizations or individuals in China, foreign journalists need only to obtain their prior consent' ... In practice foreign reporters did have more freedom to do their work, but were not completely left alone by the authorities. Certain sensitive areas, such as Tibet, were off limits, and correspondents continued to be detained by the authorities.
>
> (www.bbc.co.uk, 17 October 2008)

'Foreign journalists will be allowed to travel freely across most of the country for reporting, though access to Tibet remains tightly controlled' (www.iht.com, 19 October 2008).

> Some restrictions remain: sensitive areas such as Tibet and military installations will still be off limits without official permission ... The old rules were formalized in 1990, one year after the Tiananmen crackdown ... Implementation has been the big issue ... In its most recent ranking of press freedom by countries, Reporters Without Borders ranked China 167th, just behind Iran.
>
> (www.cnn.com, 24 October 2008)

'The new rules continue to restrict journalists' access to certain parts of the country, most notably Tibet. Instead, correspondents who wish to go there must submit to a lengthy and onerous application process, and permission to visit rarely eventuates' (www.feer.com, 31 October 2008).

18 October 2008.

> Pakistan said Saturday [18 October] that China will help it build two more nuclear power plants, offsetting Pakistani frustration over a recent nuclear deal between archrival India and the United States ... [which] allows American businesses to sell nuclear fuel, technology and reactors to India in exchange for safeguards and UN inspections of India's civilian – but not military – nuclear installations ... [The United States has said that it] would help Pakistan ... develop its huge coal reserves, expand hydroelectric power generation and build wind farms on its Arabian Sea coast ... China, a major investor and arms supplier for Pakistan, has already helped it build a nuclear power plant ... Work on a second nuclear plant is in progress and is expected to be completed in 2011 ... [Pakistan] did not say when they [the two new plants] would be built or what assistance China would provide ... [Nor did Pakistan] discuss any measures to prevent nuclear materials from the new plants from being diverted to Pakistan's atomic weapons

programme. Pakistan has placed several other reactors under IAEA safeguards … Pakistan detonated its first nuclear charges in 1998 in response to a similar test by India … [There followed] the revelation in 2004 that the architect of Islamabad's nuclear programme, Abdul Qadeer Khan, had passed nuclear secrets to Iran, Libya and North Korea … Pakistan, the Islamic world's only known nuclear weapons state, began operating its first nuclear power station with Canadian assistance in 1972.

(www.cnn.com, 18 October 2008)

Pakistan has not signed the Nuclear Non-proliferation Treaty, the main international agreement meant to stem the spread of nuclear weapons technology. However, it has placed several of its civilian reactors under IAEA safeguards … [China] said Thursday [16 October] that China, which signed the NPT in the 1990s, was willing to continue its co-operation with Pakistan on nuclear programmes – provided they are peaceful, in line with its international commitments and supervised by the IAEA.

(www.iht.com, 18 October 2008)

A Chinese foreign ministry spokesman:

We are ready to continue our co-operation with Pakistan in this field on the basis of equality and mutual benefit. China–Pakistan co-operation in the civilian application of nuclear energy is, firstly, entirely for peaceful purposes, secondly, in keeping with each other's international obligations, and, thirdly, subject to IAEA's safeguards and supervision.

(www.bbc.co.uk, 18 October 2008)

[Pakistan did not receive] a commitment for cash needed to shore up Pakistan's crumbling economy … Pakistani officials said they had received promises from China to help build two nuclear power plants, and pledges for business investment in the coming year. But Pakistan had also hoped China would deposit $1.5 billion to $3 billion in its central bank … The infusion of cash would have helped with payments for oil and food as currency reserves dwindle.

(www.cnn.com, 19 October 2008)

A former vice mayor of Beijing has received a suspended death sentence for corruption … Liu Zhihua was convicted by a court … of taking $1,020,000 in bribes while in charge of building venues for the Olympic Games. Liu abused his power to give contracts, loans and promotions to others in return for the money … When sacked as vice mayor in 2006 Liu was also accused of having bad morals. He was believed to have kept several mistresses, some of whom he reportedly helped become rich through his illegal activities … A suspended death penalty in China is normally commuted to life imprisonment on condition of good behaviour … Correspondents say reporting on Liu's prosecution was restricted in the months leading up to the Olympics in order to avoid tarnishing the state's image.

(www.bbc.co.uk, 19 October 2008)

> [The court] ordered the death sentence Saturday [18 October] after finding Liu Zhihua guilty of taking bribes ... However, the sentence was 'suspended' for two years ... The reprieve means that if Liu shows good behaviour his sentence will be commuted to life imprisonment ... Liu was elected to his post as vice mayor of Beijing in 1999 and dismissed and kicked out of the Communist Party in 2006. Liu faced ten charges for accepting bribes totalling about $1 million and gifts in return for favours to property development companies ... The government squelched all reporting on Liu's prosecution in the months leading up to the August Olympic Games to avoid tarnishing its image on the global stage.
>
> (www.cnn.com, 19 October 2008)

22 October 2008.

> India launched its first unmanned spacecraft to orbit the moon early Wednesday [22 October] ... The Indian mission is scheduled to last two years ... The spacecraft will not land on the moon, though it is supposed to send a small 'impactor' probe to the surface ... The launch ... comes about a year after China's first moon mission. Talk of a space race with China could not be contained.
>
> (www.iht.com, 22 October 2008)

27 October 2008.

> Kidnappers killed five of nine Chinese oil workers they had been holding hostage in central Sudan for more than a week, the Sudanese foreign ministry said Monday [27 October]. The ministry blamed ... a Darfur rebel group for seizing and killing the Chinese workers. Five were murdered. Two were able to escape ... The kidnappers were still holding the remaining two hostages ... The nine workers were captured near a small oil field where they were doing contract work for the Greater Nile Petroleum Operating Company, a consortium led by CNPC of China that also includes ONGC of India, Petronas of Malaysia and the state-owned Sudanese company Sudapet ... [Sudan] said the kidnappers had demanded that Chinese oil companies leave the region ... China is the biggest foreign investor in Sudan and one of Khartoum's strongest allies.
>
> (www.iht.com, 28 October 2008)

('Sudanese authorities say they have found one of two missing Chinese oil workers from a group of nine kidnapped thirteen days ago. The Chinese ambassador to Sudan said the worker was alive and in an "acceptable condition"': www.bbc.co.uk, 1 November 2008.)

28 October 2008.

> The kidnappers of nine Chinese oil workers in Sudan panicked when they saw a military aircraft fly overhead and killed five of their hostages, a Sudanese government official said Tuesday [28 October], contradicting Chinese claims ... China said the kidnappers killed five of the nine hostages during a

Sudanese rescue operation ... A [Chinese] foreign ministry spokeswoman said Tuesday that China was involved in the rescue attempt ... Two hostages escaped and a third was handed over Tuesday to local tribal chiefs, leaving the ninth Chinese oil worker unaccounted for [Sudan said] ... The kidnapping occurred on 18 October ... China buys nearly two-thirds of Sudan's oil.

(www.iht.com, 28 October 2008)

Russian prime minister Vladimir Putin and Chinese prime minister Wen Jiabao at an economic forum in Moscow yesterday [28 October] agreed to extend an oil pipeline from Siberia to the Chinese border ... Oil companies could receive 'considerable' loans from China in return for increased supplies.

(*FT*, 29 October 2008, p. 1)

Russian oil companies are negotiating multi-billion dollar lines of credit from [China] A potential loan-for-oil deal would be backed by future exports to China ... Plans for a pipeline to China, a spur off a trans-Siberian pipeline that is currently under construction, specify that it could carry about 300,000 barrels of oil a day ... The two countries agreed Tuesday [28 October] to build the spur [oil] pipeline, which will run from the Russian town of Skovorodino to the Chinese border ... But in reality the pipeline project had never really been in much doubt ... [There is] a crushing need for cash by Russian oil companies that are no longer able to draw credit from Western banks ... Rosneft, for example, has about $21 billion in debt and some of its creditors are demanding early payment ... The Russian government, which has a healthy cash reserve, has pledged $9 billion in loans to oil companies ... China has $1.9 trillion in currency reserves, the largest in the world.

(*IHT*, 29 October 2008, p. 3)

18 November 2008.

President Hu Jintao has arrived in Cuba – his second visit since 2004 ... [for a] two-day visit ... China is now Cuba's biggest trading partner after Venezuela, with bilateral trade at $2.3 billion in 2007. China has seen its trade with Latin American nations climb from $13 billion in 2000 to more than $100 billion in 2007 ... Mr Hu arrived in Cuba from Costa Rica, which last year [2007] switched diplomatic allegiance from Taiwan to China. Costa Rican officials said at the time that the move was designed to attract Chinese investment.

(www.bbc.co.uk, 18 November 2008)

'He will travel on from Cuba to Peru, where he will attend the Apec (Asia-Pacific Economic Co-operation) summit in Lima on 21 and 22 November' (www.bbc.co.uk, 19 November 2008).

Peru and China have concluded a free-trade agreement. Peru is the second Latin American country to complete such a deal with China, after Chile in

2005. But many small businesses and workers in Peru are concerned about the deal with China, fearing floods of cheaper imports that could put Peruvians out of work. Peruvian products such as textiles, clothing and shoes were left out of the deal, while only Chinese wood and tobacco were excluded ... Xinhua reported this month that exports to Latin America grew 52 per cent in the first nine months of 2008.

(www.bbc.co.uk, 20 November 2008)

[Trade between China and Latin America] still amounts to much less than [Latin America's] trade with the United States ($560 billion) or the EU ($250 billion), but the trend is significant. China is buying more and more Latin American commodities like oil, minerals and soya ... Chinese direct foreign investment in the region is far less than that of the United States or the EU. The official [Chinese] figure is more than $20 billion, but critics say much of this goes into offshore tax havens. According to figures from the Chinese embassy in Washington in early 2008, only about $2 billion is direct investment in extractive industries like oil and minerals ... Chile was the first non-Asian country to sign a free-trade agreement with China in 2005 ... Hu Jintao's visit to Peru [was] the first ever by a Chinese president ... Eleven of the remaining twenty-three countries that still recognize Taiwan are found in Central America and the Caribbean ... Costa Rica was being rewarded with a presidential visit (and a new football stadium) for its decision last year [2007] to recognize China. It is the only Central American country to do so.

(www.bbc.co.uk, 23 November 2008)

China's presence in Latin America has grown quietly but dramatically in recent years, paralleling China's growing roles in Africa and the Middle East ... Trade [between China and Latin America] soared eightfold from $12.6 billion in 2000 to $102.6 billion in 2007 ... China has emerged as the region's third largest trading partner, and is especially important for Argentina, Brazil, Chile, Peru and Venezuela ... China's regional investments totalled a cumulative $1.89 billion by 2007 ... Just two weeks ago Beijing became a full member of the Inter-American Development Bank, and it has had observer status in the Organization of American States (OAS) since 2004.

(www.iht.com, 20 November 2008)

China today [18 November] denied that it was stealing American space technology after a scientist admitted selling the information to the communist state. Physicist Quan-Sheng Shu, a naturalized American citizen born in Shanghai, pleaded guilty in a district court in Norfolk, Virginia, yesterday [17 November] to selling rocket technology to China and bribing Chinese officials to secure a lucrative contract for his high-tech company.

(www.guardian.co.uk, 18 November 2008)

21 November 2008.

The International Campaign to ban landmines ... said Friday [21 November] ... [that] Greece, Turkey and Belarus have all violated an international treaty by not destroying land mine stockpiles, and fifteen countries (including Britain) will miss their 2009 clearance targets ... Greece and Turkey have a combined stockpile of 4.2 million anti-personnel mines, and Belarus has 3.4 million remaining to destroy under the [treaty] ... also known as the Ottawa Convention ... China, Russia and the United States – the countries with the largest mine stockpiles – remain outside the pact. Myanmar and Russia, neither of which are signatories to the treaty, were the only two governments reported to have used anti-personnel mines in the past year.

(www.iht.com, 22 November 2008)

24 November 2008.

President Hu Jintao is due to begin a three-day state visit to Greece for talks expected to focus on trade ... President Hu is due to finalize a deal worth an estimated $5.4 billion which will see China's Ocean Shipping Group (COSCO) taking control of container operations at Piraeus for the next thirty-five years. Dockworkers' unions at the state-owned port are opposed to the deal and staged a long strike earlier this year.

(www.bbc.co.uk, 24 November 2008)

30 November 2008.

Beijing said Monday [1 December] that it had already reached its target number of 256 'blue sky days' this year with the help of ambitious environmental measures the city imposed to cut emissions for the Olympic Games. The notoriously polluted city of 17 million reached the clean air day target on Sunday [30 November], thirty-one days ahead of schedule ... [Beijing said the] city's air has shown constant improvement over the last ten years ... Beijing had only 100 blue sky days in 1998, when it introduced a clean air campaign and began investing more than $15 billion to improve air quality ... China's air pollution index, which ranges from 1 to 500, uses a standard calculation derived from levels of major pollutants. A reading below 50 is considered good and 51 to 100 is moderate. Below 100 is considered a blue sky day. Only fifty-six days have measured 'good' so far this year ... But environmentalists say a blue sky is still more polluted than what is considered healthy by the WHO ... [Critics also claim that] the city has moved monitoring stations to less polluted areas and has varied the way it measured pollutants since 1998.

(www.iht.com, 1 December 2008)

3 December 2008.

The first of more than 100 countries have begun signing a treaty to ban current designs of cluster bombs, at a conference in Oslo, Norway ... But some of the biggest stockpilers, including the United States, Russia and China, are not among them ... [The treaty] allows for the development of cluster bombs with greater precision and lower failure rates – an approach the United States in particular says it is already pursuing.

(www.bbc.co.uk, 3 December 2008)

Some 111 countries were due to adopt the Convention on Cluster Munitions at an all-day signing conference in Oslo. But four of the biggest cluster bomb makers – Russia, China, Israel and the United States, which claims the devices are a vital part of its defence strategy – stayed away ... The agreement requires the destruction of stockpiles of the weapons within eight years.

(www.ccn.com, 3 December 2008)

[The United States says it is] developing advanced cluster munitions that were less likely to harm civilians and despite providing nearly half of all global funding for the clearance of unexploded ordnance ... The only concession to the United States was a paragraph permitting treaty signers to conduct military operations with allies that have not signed ... In a June 2008 memo Defence Secretary Robert Gates ordered the United States military services to gradually replace their least reliable cluster bombs. He said that by 2018 only munitions with a dud rate of less than 1 per cent would be employed, referring to the unexploded bombs that can be left over from an attack and explode later ... The convention will not enter into force until six months after the thirtieth nation has officially ratified it – a milestone that Norwegian organizers said could be achieved by 2009 ... The cluster munitions treaty was negotiated outside the United Nations system, under Norway's guidance. But it won praise from the UN Secretary-General Ban Ki Moon and will be administered through the United Nations ... The treaty permits cluster-type weapons containing fewer than ten bomblets as long as each of them is advanced enough to independently engage a specific target and to automatically deactivate in case it fails to explode as designed.

(www.iht.com, 3 December 2008)

9 December 2008.

Companies from emerging economies such as Russia and China are more likely to pay bribes when doing business in other countries, a survey claims. Anti-corruption body Transparency International interviewed 2,742 senior business executives to see which firms would pay bribes in foreign countries. Russia, China, Mexico, India, Brazil and Italy were the worst of the twenty-two economies ranked in the survey. Firms in Belgium and Canada were seen as least likely to pay bribes. The United States ranked ninth, while Britain, Germany and Japan were in joint fifth place [with the Netherlands third and Switzerland fourth] ... In the previous Bribe Payers Index (BPI), published in 2006, India was named as the worst, followed by China and Russia, while Switzerland, Sweden and Australia got the highest scores

... Russia, India and China are among the countries which have not signed the OECD's convention against bribery.

(www.bbc.co.uk, 9 December 2008)

13 December 2008.

The leaders of China, Japan and South Korea held their nations' first three-way summit Saturday [13 December] in a meeting [held in Japan] intended to overcome political animosities that instead focused on a joint Asian response to the global economic crisis ... The three leaders – prime minister Wen Jiabao of China, prime minister Taro Aso of Japan and President Lee Myung Bak of South Korea – also discussed regional political issues such as ending North Korea's nuclear weapons programme ... The leaders ... promised new stimulus spending to lift domestic demand and pick up the slack in global growth left by the US slowdown. Japan and China also agreed to open lines of foreign currency credit to South Korea, whose economy has been hit hardest by the crisis ... The summit meeting was originally planned months ago, before the turmoil in financial markets began in September, with the vague goals of building good will and establishing political dialogue. The nations' leaders have held three-way meetings in the past, but only on the sidelines of larger international conferences ... The leaders agreed to increase dialogue by holding three-way summits on a regular basis. The statement said the nations will hold a second summit meeting next year [2009] in China, and a third in South Korea ... Prime minister Taro Aso of Japan: 'It is the first time historically for the three countries to hold an independent summit. It is epoch-making progress for the leaders of the three countries to hold meetings regularly and strengthen ties' ... Among the summit's few concrete results were agreements by Japan and China to lend foreign currency to South Korea to shore up the won, which has dropped by one-third against the dollar since the current crisis began. The agreements will expand so-called currency swap deals in which the South Korean central bank is allowed to borrow foreign currency from the other nations' central bank using won as collateral. Tokyo promised to make available the equivalent of $20 billion, while Beijing pledged $26 billion. Seoul has sought the agreements after depleting its foreign currency reserves trying to defend the won ... There were also signs of tension, such as when Aso raised concerns with Wen about Chinese ships that entered waters off a disputed group of islands in the past week. The islands, called Senkaku by the Japanese and the Diaoyu by the Chinese, are claimed by Tokyo, Beijing and Taipei.

(www.iht.com, 13 December 2008; *IHT*, 15 December 2008, p. 14)

18 December 2008.

President Hu Jintao praised the achievements made by his country during thirty years of reforms ... The president made his keynote speech at a special event ... organized to celebrate the thirtieth anniversary of the reforms, begun by Deng Xiaoping ... Mr Hu ... [said] China would never adopt a Western political system. The economy had grown by an annual rate of 9.8 per cent, and nearly 240 rural people had escaped poverty, he said. Mr Hu praised the country for responding to the global economic downturn ... He said: '[The] path of socialism with Chinese characteristics, led by the party, its policies and its theories, is correct' ... One recent Chinese news report quoted an official as saying more than 10 million migrant workers have lost their jobs.

(www.bbc.co.uk, 18 December 2008)

President Hu Jintao ... has vowed to continue the economic reforms ... Speaking on the thirtieth anniversary of China's decision to open itself up to the outside world, President Hu Jintao told a crowd of 6,000 at Beijing's Great Hall of the People: 'Standing still and regressing will lead only to a dead end' ... The first policies were approved on 18 December 1978. Hu said: 'Reform and opening up are the fundamental causes of all achievements and progress we have made ... [Deng Xiaoping's vision three decades ago was] completely correct' ... Over the past thirty years China has averaged an average annual growth rate of 9.8 per cent – triple the world average – China's Xinhua news agency reported ... Chinese GDP soared from $53 billion in 1978 to $3.7 trillion in 2007, making China the world's fourth largest economy, according to Xinhua. However, Hu warned the Chinese people not to grow complacent, especially in the midst of the global economic crisis. He said China must continue to concentrate on economic development and diversification. Hu Jintao said: 'We must adhere to the correct direction of reform and opening up so as to build a system that is full of vigour, highly efficient, more open and has a favourable environment for scientific development.'

(www.cnn.com, 18 December 2008)

President Hu Jintao: 'We must be clearly aware that development is of overriding importance and stability is our overriding task. If there is no stability, then nothing can be achieved, and what achievements we have made will be lost ... [China has] achieved positive results in responding to the international financial crisis. We must earnestly implement various measures to further boost domestic demand and promote economic growth, properly address the global financial crisis and other risks from the international economic world and do our best to keep relatively fast and stable growth' ... The World Bank estimates China's plans to cut taxes and boost spending on infrastructure will add up to 3 percentage points of GDP in genuine fiscal stimulus.

(*FT*, 19 December 2008, p. 8)

'Hu Jintao: "We must draw on the benefits of humankind's political civilization. But we must never copy the model of the Western political system" ... The 1978 political meeting [is] known as the Third Plenum' (*IHT*, 19 December 2008, p. 7).

China plans to send a fleet of ships to help patrol pirate-infested waters off the Horn of Africa, Chinese media reported Thursday [18 December]. The move would be rare for Beijing, which has not sent military ships far from its shores in centuries. But China, along with other countries, has seen its commercial ships repeatedly falling prey to pirate attacks that have ramped up dramatically in recent months. The news came a day after the UN Security Council passed a resolution allowing members of an international coalition force to pursue pirates onto land. China is the only permanent member of the council that has yet to commit forces to the effort ... Vice foreign minister He Yafei said Tuesday that Beijing 'is seriously considering sending naval ships to the Gulf of Aden and waters off the Somali coast for escorting operations in the near future' ... China's navy is considered a 'brown water fleet' – designed to operate almost exclusively along its coast. But the country has reportedly been working to rapidly modernize its fleet for the past several years.

(www.cnn.com, 18 December 2008)

The mission, which is expected to begin in about two weeks, would be the first modern deployment of Chinese warships outside the Pacific ... A Beijing newspaper, *The Global Times*, reported that the navy was likely to deploy two destroyers and a supply ship ... The Chinese navy, officially known as the People's Liberation Army Navy, has long concentrated on coastal defence and regional manoeuvres. But in recent years it has embarked on an ambitious modernization plan.

(www.iht.com, 18 December 2008)

China will send two navy destroyers and a supply vessel to the Gulf of Aden to protect merchant ships from attacks by Somali pirates, state media have said ... The three ships will set sail from the port of Sanya on 26 December ... The three ships, part of the country's South Sea Fleet, will leave Sanya on Friday [26 December] for the Gulf of Aden and the waters off Somalia ... [China said] their main mission would be to protect the safety of Chinese vessels and their crews in the region, as well as protecting vessels delivering humanitarian aid [sent by] international organizations ... [China said] the ships would abide strictly to the relevant UN Security Council resolutions and international law, and would be willing to co-operate with other convoy protection ships from concerned countries. They will also participate in humanitarian assistance missions. At a news conference on Thursday [18 December] ... [China] said 20 per cent of Chinese ships passing through the region between January and November this year [2008] had been attacked by Somali pirates ... Correspondents say the deployment will be the first of its kind for a country that has traditionally followed a doctrine of non-interference in other nations' affairs ... The Chinese taskforce will join warships from the EU, the United States, India, Russia, Malaysia and others which are already patrolling in the area. Earlier an Iranian vessel began patrolling in the Gulf, where two Iranian vessels have been hijacked recently.

(www.bbc.co.uk, 20 December 2008)

23 December 2008.

> In the clearest indication yet that China could soon begin building its first aircraft carrier, a military ministry spokesman said Tuesday [23 December] that the country was seriously considering 'relevant issues' in making its decision about whether to move ahead with the project … China has been expanding its navy at a fast pace. The government has built at least sixty warships since 2000 and its fleet of 860 vessels includes about sixty submarines … Last month [November] a senior military officer hinted in an interview with the *Financial Times* that China would like to build an aircraft carrier … the United States has eleven aircraft carriers, but only a handful of other nations – including Britain, France, Italy and Russia – have carriers; none have more than a few.
>
> (www.iht.com, 24 December 2008)

24 December 2008.

> Burma's military government has signed a deal with a consortium of four foreign firms to pipe natural gas into neighbouring China … The firms – from South Korea and India – will pipe the gas from the fields off Burma's north-western coast. The deal was signed in a ceremony in Rangoon on 24 December … [South Korea's] Daewoo holds the leading 51 per cent stake in the deal … Reports from China suggest construction will start in the new year [2009] … [There have been] energy investments from nearby countries, including China, India and Thailand, all hungry for its [Burma's] reserves of oil and gas.
>
> (www.bbc.co.uk, 29 December 2008)

26 December 2008.

> Three naval ships set sail for waters off Somalia to protect Chinese vessels from pirate attacks. Two destroyers and a supply ship left the port of Sanya on Hainan Island to join warships from other nations already patrolling the area. It will be the Chinese navy's first operation beyond the Pacific … The Chinese military says there have been seven attacks this year [2008] on Chinese vessels in the area. It says its forces will board and inspect suspected pirate ships, try to rescue those who are attacked and amount a vigorous defence if they themselves come under attack … The Chinese will work with other members of the international task force in the area. China has no bases in the region so keeping its forces well supplied during what is expected to be a lengthy deployment is a major challenge.
>
> (www.bbc.co.uk, 26 December 2008)

> In its first modern deployment of battle-ready warships beyond the Pacific, a naval task force set out Friday [26 December] to begin escorts and patrols in the pirate-infested Gulf of Aden … The Piracy Reporting Centre in Kuala Lumpur, Malaysia, said Friday that 110 ships have been attacked in the gulf this year, and forty-two have been hijacked. Fourteen ships are still being

> held for ransom … [China] said 1,265 Chinese commercial vessels had passed through the gulf so far this year [2008] and seven have been attacked. A Chinese fishing trawler and eighteen crew members were still being held by pirates … An EU flotilla has begun patrolling the gulf in recent days, joining naval ships from India, the United States, Iran and Russia … About 60 per cent of China's imported oil comes from the Middle East, and most of that passes through the gulf, along with huge shipments of raw materials out of Africa … China has not sent warships out of its region since the fifteenth century, under the Chinese Moslem admiral Zheng He.
>
> (www.iht.com, 26 December 2008)

'On Friday [26 December] two destroyers and a supply vessel departed on China's first long-range naval expedition since 1433 … Warships from EU nations, the United States, India, Russia and even Malaysia are already on patrol' (www.iht.com, 28 December 2008).

('The fleet began escorting four ships – one from Hong Kong and three from mainland China – through the gulf on Tuesday afternoon [6 January 2009]': www.cnn.com, 7 January 2009.)

29 December 2008.

> A new military hotline between Beijing and Moscow has been used for the first time, according to reports in the Chinese state media … This first historic call was not urgent … There is still no hotline between China's armed forces and the Pentagon in Washington. The two countries' presidents first agreed to set one up nearly three years ago. A further deal was signed between the two defence departments in February, but since then progress on establishing it appears to have stalled.
>
> (www.bbc.co.uk, 29 December 2008)

> The party's Central Commission for Discipline Inspection issued its annual broadside to government and party officials … The warning this year focuses on illegal business deals … Xinhua quoted the party commission's new circular that reminds officials: 'Live a frugal life and rule out extravagance and waste … Feasts, sightseeing and gift-giving with government money are absolutely forbidden' … That advisory was followed by a report Monday [29 December] in *China Daily* that forty government officials in Nanjing are under investigation over accusations that they accepted gifts worth $21,000 from a local toy company during the last New Year holiday … The party announced last week that nearly 151,000 government officials had been penalized in the year ending in November on various corruption and bribery charges … At a news conference last Friday [26 December it was announced that] 4,960 of these were senior officials … Among those [were] … a deputy mayor of Beijing, the former general manager of the oil and chemical giant Sinopec, the vice chairman of the Communist Party in Henan province, and the vice chairman of the Guangxi Zhuang autonomous region. Cai Wenlong, a senior government official and board chairman of

several state-owned companies in Anhui province, received a suspended death sentence last week for embezzlement. State media reported that Cai had stolen or mishandled about $5 million, and that he had lost more than $43.8 million investing state funds in the stock and futures market. Two senior Communist Party members have been expelled from the party for overstaying their visas in France ... One of the officials has returned to China; the other has not. In addition, Huang Songyou, a former vice president of the Supreme People's Court, also remained under investigation, said the discipline inspection commission. Huang was removed in October for taking bribes, Xinhua reported, making him the highest-ranking judicial official to be fired for corruption since 1949.

(www.iht.com, 30 December 2008)

31 December 2008.

China and Vietnam say they have resolved a long-running border dispute. The two countries announced they had completed the demarcation just hours before a midnight deadline. Government teams from both sides had worked for years planting stones to mark the line of the frontier which stretches 1,350 kilometres (840 miles) ... Neither side mentioned any progress on a separate unresolved maritime dispute. The Spratly Islands, a strategic string of rocky outcrops in the middle of the South China Sea, is claimed by several nations including China and Vietnam ... The two countries normalized relations in 1991.

(www.bbc.co.uk, 31 December 2008)

Vietnam and China have completed the demarcation of their long-disputed land border ... The two countries signed a land border agreement in 1999, but it took them nine years to demarcate the 1,350 kilometre, or 840 mile, frontier ... China backed the Vietnamese communists during the Vietnam War but sent troops to invade Vietnam in early 1979 for ousting the Khmer Rouge from Cambodia. The Khmer Rouge was backed by Beijing. Vietnam and China normalized relations in 1991 and have since maintained annual high-level visits. The two sides, however, did not resolve their dispute over the Spratly Islands, the largely uninhabited islands and surrounding waters that are believed to have large oil and natural gas reserves. They straddle busy sea lanes and are rich fishing grounds. Taiwan, the Philippines, Malaysia and Brunei also claim sovereignty over all or some of the Spratlys. The dispute touched off a rare anti-China street protest in Vietnam late last year.

(www.iht.com, 1 January 2009)

The settlement of the dispute – which covered the land border between the two countries – came during a 28–31 December meeting in Hanoi ... The border dispute arose after China ... invaded its southern neighbour in February 1979 – two months after Vietnam invaded Cambodia and ousted the pro-Beijing Pol Pot regime. The twenty-nine-day incursion ended with the last Chinese troops leaving on 19 March – and without having forced the

Vietnamese out of Cambodia. During the next two decades both sides stationed hundreds of thousands of troops along the border until the 1999 China–Vietnam land boundary treaty.

(www.cnn.com, 2 January 2008)

1 January 2009.

1 January [2009] marked the thirtieth anniversary of the establishment of diplomatic relations between the People's Republic of China and the United States. While President Richard Nixon and Mao Zedong opened the door, it was President Jimmy Carter's secret negotiations with Deng Xiaoping that normalized relations thirty years ago.

(*IHT*, 7 January 2009, p. 6)

[On 12 January] American and Chinese leaders ... [attended the opening of] a two-day conference to celebrate the thirtieth anniversary of the normalization of relations between the United States and China. Jimmy Carter was president when the American government restored diplomatic relations with mainland China on 1 January 1979.

(www.iht.com, 12 January 2009; *IHT*, 13 January 2009, p. 2)

14 January 2009.

A group of the biggest state-controlled media organizations in China is planning to spend billions of dollars to expand overseas as part of a government effort to improve the country's image abroad and to create respected international news organizations, people briefed on the proposal said Wednesday [14 January] ... Media giants are looking to acquire international media assets, to open more news bureaus outside the country and to publish and broadcast more broadly in English and other languages ... The plan also envisions creating a twenty-four-hour news channel ... with correspondents around the world ... Among the media outlets looking to expand overseas are China Central Television, Xinhua (the official state-run news agency), *People's Daily* (the official news organ of the Communist Party) and the Shanghai Media Group.

(*IHT*, 15 January 2009, p. 11)

20 January 2009. Barack Obama is sworn in as the forty-fourth US president.

China Central Television, or CCTV, the main state-run network, broadcast the speech live until the moment Barack Obama mentioned 'communism' in a line about the past defeat of ideologies. After the off-screen translation said 'communism' in Chinese, the audio faded even as Obama's lips continued to move. CCTV then showed an anchor asking an analyst about the economic challenges that Obama faces. The analyst was clearly caught off-guard by the sudden question. The offending line was this: 'Recall that earlier generations faced down fascism and communism not just with missiles and tanks, but with sturdy alliances and enduring convictions.' Later the president said: 'To those who cling to power through corruption and

> deceit and the silencing of dissent, know that you are on the wrong side of history, but that we will extend a hand if you are willing to unclench your fist' ... Chinese translations of the speech published Wednesday [21 January] omitted the line and the earlier one on communism. The government, however, has allowed the full English text to be published.
>
> (www.iht.com, 21 January 2009)

> Chinese state media have urged Barack Obama not to ignore the 'hard-earned progress' in ties made by George W. Bush, his predecessor as president. The *China Daily* praised Bush for laying 'a decent foundation for one of the world's most influential relationships', between the United States and China, which it described as a fine bequest. The *China Daily* said: 'To many former President Bush's eight years at the helm of US foreign policies were full of disappointments ... Yet let us be fair and honest – the Bush years were not devoid of merits. Anchoring the relationship between the world's single superpower and the largest developing country is no easy job. But the Bush administration managed it.'
>
> (*FT*, 22 January 2009, p. 7)

> A White Paper on national defence [was] released Tuesday [20 January] by the State Council, the Chinese equivalent of the cabinet ... The White Paper did not give a number for a defence budget for next year. The government had said it expected to spend $61 billion on the military in 2008, a nearly 18 per cent increase over 2007. Some foreign analysts say the actual figure is much higher. The Chinese military has about 2.3 million members. The White Paper made no mention of construction of an aircraft carrier, which Chinese military officials have said is a project under consideration. It did say, though, that in regards to the navy 'efforts are being made to build new types of submarines, destroyers, frigates and aircraft'.
>
> (www.iht.com, 20 January 2009)

'The report [is] entitled "China's National Defence in 2008" ... In 2007 Chinese military spending was just 1.4 per cent of GDP. That figure was 4.5 per cent in the United States and 2.7 per cent in the UK, according to China' (www.bbc.co.uk, 20 January 2009).

> Premier Wen Jiabao is due to travel to Europe next week, the foreign ministry announced – but his trip will pointedly exclude France. Mr Wen will visit Germany, Spain and Britain, as well as the EU in Brussels and the World Economic Forum in Davos. Correspondents say Beijing continues to snub Paris because of a meeting between President Nicolas Sarkozy and the Dalai Lama late last year [2008].
>
> (www.bbc.co.uk, 20 January 2009)

Prime minister Wen Jiabao is to travel to Switzerland, Germany, Spain, Britain and the EU headquarters in Brussels on the 27 January–2 February trip ... Wen's itinerary does not include France, which prompted questions about whether Paris was excluded due to Chinese anger over French President Nicolas Sarkozy's meeting with the Dalai Lama last month [December 2008] in Poland … [A Chinese spokesman] blamed Wen's tight schedule but said only France can resolve 'difficulties' in their relations.

(www.iht.com, 22 January 2009)

31 January 2009. Prime minister Wen Jiabao arrives in the UK for a three-day visit.

'Wen Jiabao is on a three-day visit to Britain focusing on building economic ties and fighting the global downturn' (www.iht.com, 1 February 2009).

> [On 1 February] five protesters were arrested after trying to approach premier Wen Jiabao during a Free Tibet Group demonstration. Several people vaulted barriers as he arrived outside the Chinese embassy in London amid a noisy demonstration … A group of around 100 were chanting pro-Tibetan slogans and brandishing placards from behind barriers … A dozen or so protesters vaulted over the barriers and made their way across the road … Supporters of Mr Wen were also outside the [Chinese embassy].
>
> (www.bbc.co.uk, 1 February 2009)

> Five of the pro-Tibetan demonstrators were arrested when they tried to take the Free Tibet flag to the doors of the embassy … One protester had concealed himself with the pro-Chinese group of about 100 people, who were gathered opposite a bigger crowd of people, many of whom were from the Free Tibet organization … The police presence quickly quelled the rebellion and the majority of the protest passed off peacefully without violence.
>
> (www.thetimes.co.uk, 1 February 2009)

'A spokesman for the group of about 200 demonstrators said a small number of them were trying to take the Free Tibet flag to the doors of the building … The protests passed off largely peacefully' (www.guardian.co.uk, 1 February 2009).

'Police detained several pro-Tibetan protesters … Police soon confined the rest of the 200 or so protesters' (www.iht.com, 1 February 2009).

'Approximately 150 Chinese counter-demonstrators were also at the demonstration chanting pro-Chinese slogans' (www.cnn.com, 1 February 2009).

> As prime minister Wen Jiabao arrived at the university he was met by both pro-China supporters and people demonstrating against China's human rights record in its own country and in Tibet … A twenty-seven-year old man has been charged after a shoe was thrown at the prime minister during a visit to Cambridge University … The shoe was thrown at Mr Wen and he was called a 'dictator' as he gave a speech on the global economy on Monday [2 February]. The premier, on a three-day UK visit, described the incident as 'despicable'. The protest was similar to an event in December [2008] when US President George W. Bush was forced to duck to avoid [two] shoes thrown at him by an Iraqi journalist in Baghdad … Throwing shoes is an insult in the Middle East.
>
> (www.bbc.co.uk, 3 February 2009)

> Witnesses said the protester shouted: 'How can the university prostitute itself with this dictator? How can you listen to the lies he is telling?' … Prime minister Wen Jiabao continued with his speech after the incident, telling the audience: 'We come in peace. This is not going to obstruct China–UK relationships. History shows harmony will not be obstructed by any force, so would you let me continue?'
>
> (www.guardian.co.uk, 3 February 2009)

'The shoe missed prime minister Wen Jiabao and landed about a metre away from him … He said: "This despicable behaviour cannot stand in the way of friendship between China and the UK"' (*IHT*, 3 February 2009, p. 1).

'The shoe lobbed in his direction [was thrown] by a protesting German student' (www.economist.com, 19 March 2009).

15 February 2009.

> President Hu Jintao has granted $22 million in aid to Tanzania as he continues his tour of Africa … Mr Hu has visited Mali and Senegal and will end his tour in Mauritius. China's trade with Africa has boomed in recent years but has stalled recently … On his fourth visit to Africa President Hu has stayed away from the resource-rich nations that China has previously courted. China is getting oil from Angola and Sudan, and minerals from Zambia, Congo and many others … Prime minister Wen Jiabao has already pledged that China will not cut aid to Africa or backtrack its promise to waive debts owed by more than thirty poor African countries.
>
> (www.bbc.co.uk, 15 February 2009)

'Last year [2008] China overtook the United States as Africa's top trading partner' (*IHT*, 19 August 2009, p. 14).

20 February 2009.

> US Secretary of State Hillary Clinton: 'Our pressing on those issues [human rights, Taiwan and Tibet] can't interfere with the global economic crisis, the global climate change crisis and the security crises. We have to have a dialogue that leads to an understanding and co-operation on each of those.'
>
> (www.bbc.co.uk, 21 February 2009)

> Speaking en route to Beijing on Friday night [20 February]: 'That doesn't mean that questions of Taiwan, Tibet, human rights, the whole range of challenges that we often engage on with the Chinese, are not part of the agenda. But we pretty much know what they're going to say. We have to continue to press them. But our pressing on those issues can't interfere with the global economic crisis, the global climate change crisis and the security crisis. We have to have a dialogue that leads to an understanding and co-operation on each of those.'
>
> (www.ft.com, 21 February 2009)

21 February 2009.

US Secretary of State Hillary Clinton broached the issue of human rights with Chinese leaders Saturday [21 February], but emphasized that the world economic and other crises are more pressing and immediate priorities. Clinton said in talks with China's foreign minister [Yang Jiechi]: 'Human rights cannot interfere with the global economic crisis, the global climate change crisis and the security crises' ... Clinton made China the last and most crucial stopover in her Asia trip [Japan, Indonesia, South Korea and China] ... She met President Hu Jintao on Saturday and discussed the framework for further high-level and mid-level discussions ... Earlier Saturday Clinton met with premier Wen Jiabao ... Foreign minister Yang Jiechi: 'Although differences exist China is willing to conduct dialogues with the United States to push forward the human rights situation on the premise of mutual respect and non-interference in each other's internal affairs' ... Mid-level military discussions will resume this month [February], Clinton announced Saturday. Last October [2008] the Bush administration notified Congress of its plan to sell $6.5 billion in arms to Taiwan which caused China to suspend military talks with the United States ... President Hu Jintao and US President Barack Obama are scheduled to meet at the G20 meeting in London in April.

(www.cnn.com, 21 February 2009)

In 1995, when Hillary Clinton, then first lady, gave a speech in Beijing at a United Nations conference in which she catalogued abuses against women ... Secretary of State Hillary Rodham Clinton invited China to join the United States in an ambitious effort to curb greenhouse gases, as she toured an energy-efficient power plant in Beijing on Saturday [21 February] ... The gas-fired power plant ... the Taiyanggong Thermal Power Plant ... uses sophisticated turbines made by General Electric ... She introduced her special envoy for climate change, Todd Stern, who noted that the United States and China accounted for 40 per cent of the world's emissions ... So far the United States and China are mainly collaborating on research projects and ventures like the power plant.

(www.iht.com, 22 February 2009; *IHT*, 23 February 2009, p. 7)

22 February 2009.

US Secretary of State Hillary Clinton ... started the third and final day of her stay in China by attending a church service. She then met academics, journalists and entrepreneurs ... Her week-long Asian tour has included stops in Japan, Indonesia and South Korea. Mrs Clinton began her last day in China by attending a service at the government-approved Haidian Church. She then headed to the US embassy to host a forum with a small group of female academics, non-governmental organizations, journalists and entrepreneurs.

(www.bbc.co.uk, 22 February 2009)

> US Secretary of State Hillary Clinton ended her visit to China on Sunday [22 February] by attending services at a state-sanctioned church, having a conversation with women's rights activists and doing a brief web chat … Clinton said she met about two dozen women's rights activists at the US embassy. She warmly praised the activists, who included legal rights advocates, environmentalists and an eighty-two-year-old doctor, Gao Yaojie, who exposed official complicity in the spread of AIDS in central China … Gao received an award in Washington two years ago after Clinton wrote to President Hu Jintao asking that he intervene with local officials who had sought to prevent the elderly doctor from travelling … China and the United States are both dependent on the revival of the US economy and will rise or fall together, she [said] … China is the world's biggest holder of US treasuries and Clinton said continuing to invest in them was 'a very smart decision'.
>
> (www.independent.co.uk, 22 February 2009)

28 February 2009.

> Two days of military consultations between the United States and China ended Saturday [28 February] with glowing reviews from the senior Pentagon official at the talks … Under Secretary of Defence David Sedney … who said that high level meetings between the nations on military issues, suspended last year, would resume soon … Dozens of American military experts accompanied Sedney to Beijing for the annual meeting, known as the Defence Policy Co-ordination Talks … The Chinese suspended senior level military contacts with the United States in October [2008], protesting the Bush administration's approval of a record $6.5 billion arms sale to Taiwan. This week's discussions, while long scheduled, were the first top level talks to occur since [then] … Both nations' navies had cooperated in recent months to combat piracy in the Gulf of Aden, off the coast of Somalia.
>
> (www.iht.com, 1 March 2009; *IHT*, 2 March 2009, p. 7)

1 March 2009.

A Chinese space probe smashed into the moon on Sunday [1 March] as part of a controlled crash at the end of a sixteen-month mission … Named for a moon goddess, the *Chang'e 1* orbited the earth's satellite thousands of times to map its surface in preparation for a mission to land a vehicle there in 2012.

(*IHT*, 2 March 2009, p. 6)

> China's first lunar probe landed on the moon in a controlled collision Sunday [1 March], marking the first phase of the nation's three-stage moon mission … The second stage involves sending a second probe to practise soft landings … The mission will culminate with the launch and landing of a rover on the moon to collect mineral samples in 2012. The probe … [was] launched into space on 24 October 2007. China became only the third

> nation, after the United States and Russia, to send a manned spacecraft into orbit. It did so in October 2003.
>
> (www.cnn.com, 2 March 2009)

5–13 March 2009. A session of the National People's Congress is held.

'Already the Beijing authorities have rounded up hundreds of would-be petitioners who travelled from other cities, many hoping to present grievances personally to the National People's Congress delegates' (www.iht.com, 5 March 2009).

> As Beijing hosts ten days of political pageantry known as the National People's Congress, tens of thousands of desperate citizens are trying to seek redress by lodging formal complaints at petition offices … 'Black houses' … also called 'black jails' … are unofficial jails for the hordes of petitioners who flock to the capital seeking justice … the newest weapon local officials use to prevent these aggrieved citizens from embarrassing them in front of central government officials. Officially these jails do not exist … A successfully filed petition … is considered a black mark on the bureaucratic record of the local officials accused of wrongdoing … The police in Beijing have done little to prevent such abuses. They are regularly accused of turning a blind eye or even helping local thugs round up petitioners. This raises suspicions that the central government is not especially upset about efforts to undermine the integrity of the petition system … Over the past year rights workers have been gathering evidence of what they say is an underground network of jails, first established in 2005, that was aggressively expanded in the months leading up to the Olympics … China's petition system originated in the Ming Dynasty, from the fourteenth to the seventeenth centuries, when commoners wronged by local officials sought the intervention of the imperial court. Since the Communist Party came to power, the right to petition the central government has been enshrined in the constitution.
>
> (www.iht.com, 9 March 2009; *IHT*, 10 March 2009, p. 5)

'The session will last for only nine days, making it the shortest in recent years. Mainland Chinese delegates will be barred from staying in five-star hotels and their food budget will be capped at 100 yuan per day per person' (www.cnn.com, 3 March 2009).

'China's parliament was convened for only nine days instead of the usual two weeks' (www.economist.com, 19 March 2009).

> China says it will increase military spending by a 'modest' 14.9 per cent this year [2009] to 480.6 billion yuan ($70.2 billion) … Official spokesman Li Zhaoxing: 'There is no such thing as the so-called hidden military expenditure in China' … Analysts say the increase marks the nineteenth double-digit boost in defence spending by China in the last twenty years … The US military budget for 2009 has been pegged at $515 billion, a 7.5 per cent increase from 2008. That figure does not include billions of dollars for the wars in Iraq and Afghanistan.
>
> (www.bbc.co.uk, 4 March 2009)

'Prime minister Wen Jibao called again Thursday [5 March] for closer political and economic relations with Taiwan' (www.iht.com, 5 March 2009). 'Wen Jiabao: "We are ready to hold talks on cross-straits political and military issues and create conditions for ending the state of hostility and concluding a peace agreement between the two sides of the Taiwan Straits"' (www.iht.com, 6 March 2009).

'Premier Wen Jiabao ... [said] that the nation was ready to end "a state of hostility" with Taiwan' (www.cnn.com, 5 March 2009).

'The delegates will consider a bill that would pour $124 billion into health care reform, setting up a national insurance programme and overhauling the medical care system' (www.iht.com, 5 March 2009).

The global financial crisis dominated the session of the National People's Congress and so details are to be found in that section of the companion volume, *Economic Developments in Contemporary China*.

8 March 2009.

> The Pentagon said Monday [9 March] that Chinese ships harassed a US surveillance ship Sunday [8 March] in the South China Sea ... while it was conducting routine operations in international waters ... in the latest of several instances of 'increasingly aggressive conduct' in the past week ... The Pentagon cited three previous instances of what it described as harassment, the first of which occurred Wednesday [4 March involving another US surveillance ship].
>
> (www.cnn.com, 9 March 2009)

'The *Impeccable* is one of six [US] surveillance ships that perform military survey operations, according to the [US] navy. It is an oceanographic ship that gathers underwater acoustic data, using sonar' (www.cnn.com, 10 March 2009).

> Five Chinese ships have manoeuvred dangerously close to an unarmed US navy vessel in the South China Sea, the US government has said. US officials said the incident came after days of 'increasingly aggressive' acts by Chinese ships ... A protest was expected to be delivered.
>
> (www.bbc.co.uk, 9 March 2009)

'China and America have been drawn into a rare confrontation on the high seas, it emerged today [9 March], when the Pentagon accused Chinese ships of manoeuvring dangerously close to a US navy vessel' (www.guardian.co.uk, 9 March 2009).

> The [US] Defence Department said Monday [9 March] that five Chinese ships manoeuvred dangerously close to a US navy vessel [on 8 March] in an apparent attempt to harass the American crew ... American officials said a protest was lodged with the Chinese government over the weekend and that it was to be repeated [Monday] ... [The ship] was one of five [US] surveillance ships that gather underwater acoustical data ... Pentagon officials said the encounter came after several other incidents involving ... [the ship] and

> another US vessel Wednesday [4 March], Thursday [5 March] and Saturday [7 March] ... China views almost the entirety of the South China Sea as its territory.
>
> (*IHT*, 10 March 2009, p. 5)

> China says a US navy ship involved in a confrontation with its vessels off the southern island of Hainan violated international law ... The United States said the incident happened as the USNS *Impeccable* was on routine operations in international waters 75 miles (120 kilometres) south of Hainan Island.
>
> (www.bbc.co.uk, 10 March 2009)

> The boundaries of China's exclusive economic zone remain disputed, while Beijing and Washington differ on which activities are permitted by law within a nation's exclusive economic zone. China says that any intelligence gathering by foreign governments within its exclusive economic zone is illegal – but the United States does not agree with this. The *Impeccable* is used to map the ocean floor with sonar. The information is used by the US navy to steer its own submarines or track those of other nations.
>
> (www.bbc.co.uk, 11 March 2009)

> [China said] the *Impeccable* has 'conducted activities in China's special economic zone in the South China Sea without China's permission'. Although the United States and other nations consider most of the South China Sea to be international waters, China claims an economic exclusion zone extending 200 nautical miles, or 230 miles, from its coastline.
>
> (www.iht.com, 10 March 2009)

'Under the UN Convention of the Law of the Sea activities in China's exclusive economic zone would be illegal only if they were aimed at researching or prospecting natural resources' (*FT*, 11 March 2009, p. 8).

'China has ratified ... the 1982 United Nations Convention Law of the Sea ... The United States has not, although it maintains that most of it is binding customary law' (www.iht.com, 13 March 2009).

'[The unarmed] *Impeccable* [is] under naval supervision but with a civilian crew ... the Chinese say the *Impeccable* was on a spy mission. Detecting submarines is indeed one of her roles, and Hainan Island is home to Chinese submarine bases' (*The Economist*, 14 March 2009, p. 59).

> Hans Kristensen ... a military analyst ... with the Federation of American Scientists said the US ship *Impeccable* was probably monitoring China's new nuclear-powered attack submarine ... Kristensen said the US navy has been 'busy collecting data on the submarines and sea floor to improve its ability to detect the submarines in peacetime and more efficiently hunt them in case of war' ... The *Impeccable* had been towing an underwater listening and mapping device known as a Surtass array. At one point the Chinese tried to snag the tow-line with a long grappling hook ... China claims an

> 'exclusive economic zone', which extends out 200 nautical miles from its coastline, with exclusive rights to oil and gas exploration, drilling and fishing. For other activities and normal sea passage, international waters are typically defined as twelve miles offshore.
>
> (www.iht.com, 12 March 2009)

'Chinese navy officers reacted with annoyance today [13 March] when it emerged that the United States had sent a destroyer to back up a surveillance vessel in the South China Sea' (www.thetimes.com, 13 March 2009).

'America later sent a guided-missile destroyer to protect the *Impeccable*' (www.economist.com, 19 March 2009).

> China has deployed a large fisheries patrol boat to a group of disputed islands in the South China Sea, a state newspaper said Sunday [15 March] ... The vessel would reach the Paracel Islands on Sunday to patrol China's exclusive economic zone and strengthen fishery administration in the South China Sea.
>
> (*IHT*, 16 March 2009, p. 8)

> The United States says its military surveys do not require Chinese permission; China says they do. Analysts note that the United States would never allow similar activity off its coast ... On 11 March Xinhua, the official Chinese news agency, reported that China had dispatched a 4,450-ton fisheries patrol boat to protect its interest in the South China Sea, which includes the disputed – and potentially oil-rich – Spratly Islands ... In the past few weeks the Philippines and Malaysia have restated conflicting claims to the Spratlys, where, in 1995, the Philippines and China came to the brink of open conflict over alleged Chinese military installations on Mischief Reef.
>
> (www.iht.com, 25 March 2009)

25 March 2009.

> [On 25 March] a report called the 'Military Power of the People's Republic of China' ... the Pentagon's annual report to Congress ... [was] released by the Pentagon ... [The report said that] China's military is developing longer-range ballistic and anti-ship missiles that are 'shifting the balance of power in the region' and could help Beijing secure resources or settle territorial disputes ... China also continues to build up short-range missiles and increase its 'coercive capabilities' against Taiwan ... In citing China's cyber warfare the report notes that US government computers were the target of 'intrusions that appear to have originated' from China, although they were not confirmed to be from the military.
>
> (www.cnn.com, 26 March 2009)

'In its annual report to Congress the Pentagon said China was developing "disruptive" technologies for nuclear, space and cyber warfare' (www.bbc.co.uk, 26 March 2009).

> China is seeking technology and weapons to disrupt the traditional advantages of American forces, and secrecy surrounding its military creates the potential for miscalculation on both sides, according to a Pentagon study ... From 2003 to 2007 China sold nearly $7 billion of conventional weapons around the world, mostly to Pakistan, the report said.
>
> (www.iht.com, 26 March 2009)

1 April 2009.

> [On 1 April] US president Barack Obama and Chinese President Hu Jintao met in London ahead of the G-20 economic summit ... Mr Obama accepted an invitation to visit China this year [2009] ... The two leaders agreed to establish a Strategic and Economic Dialogue Group to tackle the global financial crisis and strengthen the world's financial systems. The White House said Secretary of State Hillary Clinton and Treasury Secretary Timothy Geithner would represent the United States at those talks.
>
> (www.bbc.co.uk, 1 April 2009)

> The two [leaders] agreed to set up a high level Strategic and Economic Dialogue Group chaired by ... Secretary of State Hillary Clinton and Secretary of the Treasury Timothy Geithner for the United States, and State Councillor Dai Bingguo and vice premier Wang Qishan for China ... The White House statement: 'The two sides agreed to resume the human rights dialogue as soon as possible' ... China did not immediately confirm the details of the US announcement.
>
> (www.cnn.com, 1 April 2009)

'Some analysts speak of a "G-2", referring to the first meeting between the new US president and his Chinese counterpart on the sidelines of the G-20' (www.cnn.com, 2 April 2009).

15 April 2009.

> The twentieth anniversary of the death of reformist Chinese leader Hu Yaobang has passed without being marked in China. The anniversary is seen as the start of an ultra-sensitive period for Beijing, in the run-up to the twentieth anniversary of the 1989 Tiananmen Square protests. It was Hu's death that set in motion the chain of events leading to the 4 June crackdown. Meanwhile students in Hong Kong are holding a vote on whether China should apologize for the Tiananmen killings ... Mr Hu was ousted as Communist Party chief in 1987 for his perceived weakness during protests the previous December, and his attempts at reform. When he died on 15 April 1989 mourners gathered and called for his rehabilitation. By the eve of his funeral on 21 April 200,000 students rallied in Tiananmen Square, demanding fresh political reforms. China's leadership dithered, but eventually declared martial law. Protests grew throughout May 1989 until early June, when troops were sent in killing hundreds, perhaps thousands, of protesters.
>
> (www.bbc.co.uk, 15 April 2009)

23 April 2009.

> China is staging a military parade to celebrate its navy's sixtieth anniversary – and show the world its latest warships ... Twenty-one foreign naval vessels from fourteen countries are also taking part, including the United States [two ships], France and Russia ... A total of twenty-five ships and thirty-one aircraft from the People's Liberation Army Navy were involved in the event ... Joining President Hu Jintao on the destroyer were military officials from nearly thirty countries.
>
> (www.bbc.co.uk, 23 April 2009)

> The parade [was] in the port city of Qingdao ... [China] invited foreign navies to take part, including America's Seventh Fleet, which sent a guided-missile destroyer ... Among the vessels inspected by President Hu Jintao from on board a Chinese-made destroyer were two nuclear-powered submarines ... These are not China's very latest models, but showing them at all was rare ... China has said nothing about its new Jin-class submarines armed with long-range nuclear missiles. The Pentagon reported that the first of these had been deployed ... Officials have dropped several recent hints that China is close to announcing it will acquire its first ... aircraft carrier.
>
> (*The Economist*, 25 April 2009, pp. 63–4)

'A total of fifty-two navy vessels and aircraft were shown taking part in manoeuvres off the eastern port of Qingdao. As naval delegations from twenty-nine countries watched, President Hun Jintao also reviewed twenty-one foreign naval vessels' (*FT*, 24 April 2009).

> The celebration began on Monday [20 April] and includes delegations from twenty-nine countries. Of those fourteen countries will be showing twenty-one vessels ... tensions with the Philippines rose in March over the disputed Nansha Islands, which the Filipino government claimed as its territory in a law passed on 10 March.
>
> (www.iht.com, 21 April 2009)

'The naval review included vessels from the United States and thirteen other nations. It was hosted by the People's Liberation Army Navy and included the first known public display of two Chinese nuclear-powered submarines' (www.iht.com, 24 April 2009).

> The Chinese government denounced Japanese prime minister Taro Aso on Thursday [23 April] for ... [making] an offering [on Tuesday 21 April] of a potted tree worth about $500 to commemorate a spring festival at the Yasukuni Shrine ... On Wednesday [22 April] dozens of Japanese lawmakers visited the shrine ... Mr Aso prepares to travel to China next week for a two-day meeting ... Mr Aso, who took office in September 2008, has not stated publicly his views on shrine visits.
>
> (www.iht.com, 23 April 2009)

1 May 2009.

> The Pentagon has accused Chinese fishing boats of 'dangerous' manoeuvres near a US navy surveillance ship in the Yellow Sea last week. Two boats came within 30 yards (27 metres) of the USNS *Victorious* in an 'unsafe and dangerous' fashion on Friday [1 May], a statement said ... The vessels did not leave until the *Victorious* radioed a nearby Chinese military vessel for help ... There have been four incidents in the past month in which Chinese-flagged fishing vessels manoeuvred too close to two unarmed ships staffed by civilians and used by the Pentagon for underwater surveillance and submarine-hunting missions.
>
> (www.bbc.co.uk, 5 May 2009)
>
> China said Wednesday [7 May] that it was concerned after a stand-off in the Yellow Sea ... The incident, the fifth of its kind in two months, occurred Friday [1 May] in international waters about 275 kilometres (170 miles) from the Chinese mainland ... [China] said in a statement that the [US] ship was operating in China's exclusive economic zone without permission and had not respected Chinese or international rules and laws.
>
> (*IHT*, 7 May 2009, p. 8)

16 May 2009.

> President Barack Obama on Saturday [16 May] selected one of the nation's leading Republican governors to serve as ambassador to China, nominating Jon Huntsman of Utah for a diplomatic post that Mr Obama called 'as important as any in the world' ... Mr Huntsman, forty-nine, learned to speak Mandarin Chinese from his time as a Mormon missionary in Taiwan ... [He has] seven children, one of whom was adopted from China ... [the] Mandarin-speaking former US trade official [has] deep personal and family business ties to China ... Mr Huntsman is the son of billionaire and philanthropist Jon Huntsman, and his family founded chemical company Huntsman Corp., which has operations in China including a factory in Shanghai ... In a 2006 speech at Shanghai Normal University he urged bilateral co-operation to foster peace and economic prosperity on both sides of the Pacific, but also had some stern words about how environmental damage in Asia hurt wildlife in his home state of Utah ... He said at the time: 'As leading stakeholders in the international community, the United States and China must be good examples and stewards of the Earth. We must match economic progress with environmental stewardship. The effects of industrialization are felt worldwide.'
>
> (www.iht.com, 16 May 2009 and 17 May 2009)

22 May 2009.

> A factory boss and nine foremen have been arrested in eastern China after the police raided a brick kiln late last month [April] and found thirty-two mentally disabled people working in what were described as slave-like con-

ditions, according to state-run news media … The police say the factory boss said he had bought the workers from a taxi driver in Shandong province.

(www.iht.com, 23 May 2009)

The police said Friday [22 May] that eighty officers had carried out the raid last month and rescued the workers, some of whom had been beaten. The brick kiln was operating in … Anhui province, one of China's poorest regions. Similar raids in 2007 led to the rescue of more than 1,300 people – about 350 of them mentally retarded – from working as modern-day slaves in brick kilns in the northern province of Shanxi.

(*IHT*, 23 May 2009, p. 5)

Less than a year after Beijing hosted the Summer Olympics, Shanghai is gearing up for its own mega-event: the 2010 World Expo. Although the World Expo may have lost much of the lustre it had when it was better known as the World's Fair, and though the global financial crisis drags on … the city is planning to spend $45 billion, more than was spent on the Beijing Olympics, to upgrade Shanghai's infrastructure, build new transportation links and create what organizers promise will be the biggest and most extravagant Expo ever … The exposition is held every five years … Following Beijing's example, Shanghai is asking residents to study English and vowing to teach etiquette to 1 million local families. The city also plans to ban smoking in public places and curtail pollution during the event.

(www.iht.com, 31 May 2009; *IHT*, 1 June 2009, p. 15)

4 June 2009. The twentieth anniversary of Tiananmen.

Thousands have marched in Hong Kong to mark the forthcoming twentieth anniversary of the Tiananmen killings … Police said at least 4,700 people had gathered, and tens of thousands more were set to attend a candlelit vigil later on Sunday [31 May].

(www.bbc.co.uk, 31 May 2009)

'The Hong Kong government has refused entry to a former leader of the democracy movement centred around Tiananmen Square in 1989. Xiang Xiaoji [is] now a US citizen' (www.bbc.co.uk, 3 June 2009).

'In the run-up to the twentieth anniversary of the Tiananmen Square massacre, China is censoring foreign media and the internet to an extent not seen since the crackdown that preceded the Beijing Olympics' (*FT*, 3 June 2009, p. 7).

The Chinese government has taken extraordinary steps in advance of the Tiananmen anniversary to avert protests and any other public displays related to the military crackdown. Censorship of the internet, television and printed matter, already strict, has been increased, and human rights groups say that a number of well-known political dissidents have been detained, apparently until Thursday's [4 June] anniversary has passed. Among them is Zhou Dou

> … Wu Gaoxing was seized on Saturday [31 May] … Mr Wu was among five men who released a letter last weekend charging that former prisoners have been targeted for economic hardship after their prison terms ended.
>
> (www.iht.com, 2 June 2009)

'Former dissidents from the protest were denied entry to Macao and Hong Kong' (*IHT*, 4 June 2009, p. 2).

'Xinang Xiaoji, a dissident who took part in the 1989 demonstrations, was denied entry to Hong Kong on Wednesday [3 June] … [He is] now an American citizen' (www.iht.com, 4 June 2009).

> Chinese censors blocked access to Twitter and other popular online services on Tuesday afternoon [2 June] … The move came as authorities detained a leading dissident and ordered another to leave Beijing … The free blogging site Blogger.com was blocked last month [May] and access to YouTube, owned by Google, has been blocked since March.
>
> (www.guardian.co.uk, 2 June 2009)

'The [Chinese] government has rounded up and detained or confined to their homes hundreds of dissidents and outspoken family members of people killed in the 1989 crackdown' (*FT*, 5 June 2009, p. 10).

> There was not a flicker of protest. Other than the intense police presence and the government's blockage of some popular internet services, the scorchingly hot day passed like any other in the capital … US Secretary of State Hillary Clinton urged China to publish the names of the dead, missing or detained … She also called on the Chinese authorities to release all prisoners still jailed for taking part in the demonstrations and to stop harassing bereaved relatives, who have formed a group called Tiananmen Mothers.
>
> (www.iht.com, 4 June 2009)

> Throngs of men, women and children gathered at a park in Hong Kong on Thursday evening [4 June] for an enormous, sombre candlelight vigil to mark the twentieth anniversary of the Tiananmen Square killings. The organizers said that 150,000 people joined the vigil, tying the record set by the first anniversary vigil in 1990 and dwarfing every vigil since then … The peaceful assemblage spilled into nearby streets … Even before the vigil began at 8 p.m. the tens of thousands assembled represented the largest crowd for the annual event in recent years. The only crowd since the early 1990s that came remotely close was in 2004, when the fifteenth anniversary of the military crackdown coincided with a surge in pro-democracy sentiment in Hong Kong … In 2004 organizers estimated the crowd at 82,000, though the police gave a lower estimate of 48,000. That had been the largest vigil since 1991, when 100,000 attended … When a large crowd showed up in 2004 it was after public pressure had forced the government to retreat from plans to impose stringent security legislation sought by Beijing. The local government has not sought since then to reintroduce the legislation …

> Hong Kong is the only place in China where large public gatherings are allowed to mark the anniversaries of the 1989 killings.
>
> (www.iht.com, 4 June 2009)

> The organizers of the vigil in and around Hong Kong's Victoria Park said that 150,000 people took part, tying the record set by the first anniversary vigil in 1990 and dwarfing every vigil held since then. The police estimated the crowd at 62,800, their largest estimate for any vigil except in 1990, which they put at 80,000.
>
> (*IHT*, 5 June 2009, p. 7)

> An estimated 150,000 people gathered in Victoria Park for the annual event, which was addressed by one of the 1989 leaders, Xiong Yan ... Now a chaplain for the US army ... [He] thanked the crowd for Hong Kong's support in helping him escape after 1989 ... Other Tiananmen veterans were banned from entering the territory ... Some [of the people] wore T-shirts saying 'Donald Tsang you don't represent me' in a rejection of recent remarks by Hong Kong's chief executive. He had tried to argue that history could be forgotten as economic development was more important.
>
> (www.bbc.co.uk, 4 June 2009)

'Organizers put the turnout at 150,000, while police estimated that 65,000 had gathered in the park' (*The Times*, 5 June 2009, p. 43).

> China has never released a death toll from the suppression on what it says was a counter-revolutionary conspiracy. Hundreds are believed to have died in and around the square ... As the anniversary of what China calls the '4 June incident' gets closer, the Communist Party appears to be in a particularly vigilant mood.
>
> (www.bbc.co.uk, 2 June 2009)

'The number [killed in Tiananmen] is disputed, but the government figure of 241 is widely believed to be too low' (*The Times*, 30 May 2009, p. 41).

'[Estimates of those] killed range from hundreds to more than 2,500' (*FT*, 4 June 2009, p. 11).

'Human Rights Watch estimates that about thirty of the hundreds who were imprisoned after the Tiananmen protests remain in jail' (www.iht.com, 2 June 2009).

'The San Francisco-based rights group Dui Hua estimates that thirty people remain in prison for offences related to the Tiananmen crackdown' (*Independent*, 4 June 2009, p. 28).

'The human rights group Amnesty International says as many as 200 people remain in detention for their involvement in the 1989 pro-democracy protests' (www.bbc.co.uk, 2 June 2009).

8 June 2009.

> World governments spent $1.46 trillion on upgrading armed forces last year [2008] ... with China climbing to second place, behind the United States, as

> the top military spender, a Swedish research group said Monday [8 June]. Global military spending was 4 per cent higher in 2008 than in 2007, and 45 per cent higher than a decade ago, the Stockholm International Peace Research Institute said in its annual report. American military spending increased nearly 10 per cent in 2008 to $607 billion and accounted for about 42 per cent of global arms spending, the institute said. The United States was followed for the first time by China, which increased its military spending to an estimated $84.9 billion.
>
> (www.iht.com, 9 June 2009)

'As of January [2009] Russia had a total of 3,909 [nuclear] warheads, while the United States had 5,576 warheads, according to the US State Department. The Russian foreign ministry has not published its own figures' (www.iht.com, 10 June 2009).

12 June 2009. 'The mayor of Shenzhen, Xu Zongheng, has been sacked for disciplinary offences' (www.bc.co.uk, 12 June 2009).

15–16 June 2009. 'The Shanghai Co-operation Organization's ninth summit [opened on 15 June in Russia] ... The SCO was formed in 2001 ... India, Pakistan and Mongolia later joined as observer members' (www.bbc.co.uk, 15 June 2009).

> The first major summit of the so-called BRIC group – Brazil, Russia, India and China [was held in Russia] ... The BRIC countries comprise about 15 per cent of the world economy and have about 40 per cent of global reserves [gold and hard currency reserves] ... Only about 2 per cent of China's trade last year [2008] was with Russia.
>
> (*IHT*, 16 June 2009, pp. 1, 3)

> Leaders of the four largest emerging market economies ... held their first formal summit meeting Tuesday [16 June] ... The term BRIC was coined by a Goldman Sachs economist [Jim O'Neill] in 2001 ... Leaders of Brazil, Russia, India and China have met before, on the sidelines of a Group of Eight [G-8] meeting, but never in a summit meeting ... President Hun Jintao pledged $10 billion in aid to central Asian countries, in a group [the Shanghai Co-operation Organization] which consist of China, Russia and ... Kazakhstan, Kyrgyzstan, Tajikistan and Uzbekistan.
>
> (*IHT*, 17 June 2009, p. 3)

> BRIC countries account for 40 per cent of the world's population and 15 per cent of its economy, President Hu Jintao told the summit of the Shanghai Co-operation Organization ... that Chinese credit [$10 billion] would help Central Asian countries 'make their own efforts to counter the shock of the international financial crisis'.
>
> (*FT*, 17 June 2009, p. 8)

24 June 2009.

> Chinese and American officials on Wednesday [24 June] gave a positive assessment of their military talks aimed at addressing the growing nuclear

threat from North Korea and a series of naval skirmishes that have marred relations between the two countries ... The two days of dialogue were the first military talks since December 2008, when China broke off annual military exchanges to protest a $6.5 billion arms deal between the United States and Taiwan ... Both sides agreed to another round of high level military talks next month.

(www.iht.com, 24 June 2009)

25 June 2009.

China yesterday [25 June] signed a thirty-year agreement to buy natural gas from Turkmenistan ... Turkmenistan said it would increase the amount of gas it sells to Beijing annually by 30 per cent ... Work on a 4,000-mile pipeline to China is likely to be completed this year [2009] ... Russia reduced its gas imports from Turkmenistan this year because of falling prices and demand from Europe.

(*Guardian*, 26 June 2009, p. 25)

15 July 2009.

The former chairman of Sinopec was convicted of corruption by a court in Beijing on Wednesday [15 July] ... Chen Tonghai was given a suspended death sentence for taking $28.7 million in bribes ... He is expected to serve a life term in prison.

(www.iht.com, 15 July 2009; *IHT*, 16 July 2009, p. 17)

24 July 2009.

The privatization of a steel company has been scrapped after an executive was beaten to death by workers angry at the threat to their jobs from a takeover of their firm ... The violent riot in north-east China late last week involved up to 30,000 workers ... The government laid off about 50 million workers in state enterprises in the 1990s ... Tonghua Iron and Steel, a traditional state enterprise, has about 50,000 workers and has struggled to make consistent profits in recent years, making it a prime target for restructuring by its owner, Jilin province. The privately held Jianlong Group, one of China's largest steel companies, had first proposed taking over Tonghua in 2005, backed out of the deal when the economy slowed last year [2008], but re-entered negotiations recently when industrial demand picked up ... The interim general manager sent by Jianlong to run Tonghua ... had infuriated the workers with his high-handed attitude ... He had reportedly said that he would re-establish Tonghua ... and lay off nearly all the employees ... With Tonghua Steel's retired workers each receiving only 200 renminbi a month for living expenses ... [the general manager] was paid an annual salary of 3 million renminbi.

(www.ft.com, 26 July 2009; *FT*, 27 July 2009, p. 7)

'About 100 people were hurt in violence in the north-eastern city of Tonghua after workers heard that Jianlong Steel would buy a majority share ...

[An estimated] 30,000 steel workers clashed with riot police on Friday [24 July]' (www.bbc.co.uk, 26 July 2009).

> About 30,000 disgruntled steelworkers clashed with riot police officers in Jilin province to protest a takeover deal, resulting in the death of an executive ... News that Jianlong Steel Holding would buy a majority stake in Tonghua Iron and Steel Group set off the protest Friday [24 July] The general manager of Jianlong was beaten to death by workers who were angry over his high salary ... [He] was paid about 3 million renminbi (nearly $440,000) last year [2008] ... Local television announced that the deal would be shelved permanently.
>
> (*IHT*, 27 July 2009, p. 5)

> On the day of the Tonghua incident, the provincial government ordered Jianlong to abandon its plan to buy out the steel plant ... China introduced a series of labour laws that improved mediation and set up an arbitration process to give workers better formal recourse for their grievances, both individual and collective ... But only a small share of disputes are taken up, whereas discontents are multiplying.
>
> (*The Economist*, 1 August 2009, p. 50)

('A provincial government on Sunday [16 August] halted the privatization of a state-owned steel mill where thousands of workers protested last week and took an official hostage, in the latest sign of increasing labour activism in the steel industry. The apparent capitulation of the government of Henan province in central China came three weeks after rioting workers beat to death the executive overseeing the sale to a private business of another state-owned steel company, Tonghua Iron and Steek Works, in the north-eastern province of Jilin ... The global economic downturn has severely hurt the sector ... Faced with a glut of steelmaking capacity and many small steel companies vying to buy iron ore, Beijing officials on Thursday [13 August] ordered a three-year moratorium on the construction of any new steel mills or the expansion of existing ones': www.iht.com, 16 August 2009; *IHT*, 17 August 2009, p. 16.)

25 July 2009.

> Chinese state television has begun broadcasting an Arabic-language channel for the Middle East and Africa ... The twenty-four hour channel began operating on Saturday [25 July] ... China Central Television [CCTV] already broadcasts in English, French and Spanish as well as in Mandarin ... CCTV announced plans last month [June] for a Russian channel.
>
> (www.iht.com, 26 July 2009)

19 August 2009.

> The government has issued a new regulation to stop petitioners from travelling to the capital, Beijing. Legal officials from Beijing will now visit people with complaints in the provinces in order to hear their cases. Petitions can also

be filed online and a response or solution is to be given within sixty days. Officials have previously tried to stop the thousands who go to the capital with complaints about land grabs, police beatings and legal abuses. It is the first time the highest level of the Communist Party has taken such measures in order to deal with the issue ... The phenomenon has been attributed to China's imperial past, when people sought the emperor seeking justice. But it reflects a growing distrust of the local courts and officials ... The Communist Party says it will send legal officials to areas with a high number of petitioners, to review cases on the spot. Officials in every province, city and county have also been told to set aside one day every month on order to deal with petitions locally. People who make repeated trips to Beijing have been warned that if they persist in doing so, their cases may be dismissed without review. The move is part of a drive to maintain social harmony and stability ahead of the sixtieth anniversary of the People's Republic of China [on 1 October]. Beijing has tightened security and ordered hotels and private landlords not to provide accommodation for petitioners before the celebrations in October.

(www.bbc.co.uk, 19 August 2009)

China's Communist Party has ordered local officials to meet regularly with people complaining of injustices in a bid to stop them travelling to petition the central government. The party also promised to send legal experts to the provinces to hear the cases, state media reported Wednesday [19 August], the first such proposal from senior party officials aimed at dealing with the regular deluge of petitioners.

(*IHT*, 20 August 2009, p. 4)

27 August 2009.

Senior members of China's legislature approved a new law on Thursday [27 August] detailing the authority of the People's Armed Police, a large paramilitary force that played a key role in putting down the riots in Xinjiang last month [July]. The law is the first to explicitly govern the force, whose members serve as border guards, security details for government officials, fire-fighters and disaster relief, among other duties, but are best known outside China for their role in suppressing political and social unrest. President Hu Jintao, in Xinjiang on Tuesday [26 August], told armed police troops there that ensuring social stability was 'the most urgent task' they faced. After the riots the force was criticized in some quarters as unprepared and slow to respond to the violence. The new law should address those concerns by clarifying how and when the troops may be deployed. Estimates of the size of the People's Armed Police have ranged as high as 1.5 million troops, but the government pegged the number in 2006 at 660,000. Once seen as corrupt and ill-trained, the armed police have become more professional in recent years. But they are sometimes regarded as unaccountable by ordinary Chinese and human rights advocates have accused the troops of brutality and insensitivity to the law in handling civil disorders. The troops' contact with average Chinese citizens has grown in recent years as China's transformation – and dislocation – has led to an increasing number of spontaneous street protests. The new law was ordered by the Standing Committee of the National People's Congress … It gives the troops authority in 'handling rebellion, riots, large-scale serious criminal violence, terror attacks and other social safety incidents' … The legislation also apparently removes the authority of county-level officials to summon the force to handle disorders. Ordinary Chinese have complained that the armed police are sometimes enlisted by low-level officials to abusively bolster their powers, sometimes with excessive force.

(www.iht.com, 27 August 2009)

31 August 2009.

Japanese voters Sunday [31 August] cast out the Liberal Democratic Party for only the second time in postwar history, handing a landslide victory to the … opposition Democratic Party of Japan … The only previous non-Liberal Democratic Party government, in 1993, collapsed in just eleven months because of infighting and defections.

(*IHT*, 31 August 2009, pp. 1, 8)

Yukio Hatoyama is expected to be the next prime minister … [He has made a] pledge not to visit the Yasukuni Shrine, a symbol of Japan's wartime past. Visits by some of his predecessors stirred tensions with China and South Korea.

(*IHT*, 2 September 2009, p. 6)

September 2009.

Despite a recession that knocked down global arms sales last year [2008], the United States expanded its role as the world's leading weapons supplier, increasing its share to more than two-thirds of all foreign armaments deals, according to a new Congressional study. The United States signed weapons agreements valued at $37.8 billion in 2008, or 68.4 per cent of all business in the global arms bazaar, significantly up from American sales of $25.4 billion the year before [2007]. Italy was a distant second, with $3.7 billion in worldwide weapons agreements in 2008, while Russia was third with $3.5 billion in arms sales last year – down considerably from the $10.8 billion in weapons deals signed by Moscow in 2007 … The value of global arms sales in 2008 was $55.2 billion, a drop of 7.6 per cent in 2007 and the lowest total for international weapons agreements since 2005 … The report notes that while Moscow continues to have China and India as its main weapons client, Russia's new focus is on arms sales to Latin America, in particular to Venezuela.

(www.iht.com, 6 September 2009)

15–18 September 2009. 'China's Communist Party will convene its annual policy meeting Tuesday [15 September] … [namely] the annual plenary session of the party's Seventeenth Central Committee' (*IHT*, 15 September 2009, p. 8).

'The festivities at Tiananmen Square on 1 October will commemorate the sixtieth anniversary of National Day ... The Chinese will enjoy eight days off, from 1 October to 8 October – both for the National Day and the Mid-Autumn Festival' (www.cnn.com, 21 September 2009).

> The four-day session [15–18 September] is widely expected to promote Vice President Xi Jinping to the powerful [Central] Military Commission ... [which is] in charge of the 2.3 million-strong People's Liberation Army ... The Central Committee full session, or plenum, will meet behind closed doors ... A regulation requiring party cadres to reveal their family wealth and assets is reportedly up for discussion ... According to Xinhua, the 204-member committee will discuss a draft document on 'party building' which covers everything from the battle against corruption to recruitment for the 75 million-member party.
>
> (www.bbc.co.uk, 15 September 2009)

> Following its four-day summit, the Communist Party announced it intended to: 'Effectively prevent and resolutely crack down on ethnicity-related separatist activities. Under the new circumstances, we should continue to promote the progress of ethnic unity to ensure the country's long-term social stability and harmony' ... The Communist Party also repeated its commitment to tackling corruption, building its power base and strengthening the economy ... It vowed to continue to promote economic growth, warning that the foundations of the recovery were 'not stable, not solid and not balanced' ... The Communist Party recommended strengthening intra-party democracy at a grassroots level as a way of ensuring unity ... But no reference was made to Xi Jinping, the man believed to be being groomed to succeed President Hu Jintao ... No announcement was made of Mr Xi's widely predicted promotion to a powerful military commission ... Analysts say the announcement could come after National Day celebrations in early October, marking sixty years of communist rule in China.
>
> (www.bbc.co.uk, 18 September 2009)

> The Communist Party elite has issued the first specifics of an annual strategy session, a summary of an anti-corruption directive that would force officials and their families to disclose to Beijing their property holdings and investments, including assets overseas ... That rule [was] issued Saturday [19 September] ... Communiqués [were] issued Friday and Saturday ... The communiqué stressed a well-known position, the need to crack down on ethnic separatists to keep China unified and relations between its ethnic groups harmonious ... The Central Committee [did not] act, as many had expected, to appoint Vice President Xi Jinping to a key military post ... Mr Xi could still win the appointment, as vice chairman of the Central Military Commission, at a later date ... But the initial reports of the plenum, which was largely devoted to the Communist Party's internal challenges, suggests that the Central Committee's members were either reluctant to make major

> changes, or disagreed over how those changes might be made ... Communist leaders had billed the four-day meeting ... as an attack on 'acute problems' that threatened the party's political standing, from official corruption to the lack of democracy within the party's own ranks ... The party's internal bureaucratic workings were in need of reform, the communiqué stated.
>
> (*IHT*, 21 September 2009)

'Party leaders ... outlined an anti-corruption directive that would compel officials and their families to disclose their property holdings and investments' (www.cnn.com, 22 October 2009).

'At the party's meeting in September President Hu Jintao said: "Inner-party democracy is the life of the party. Centralism and unity are the guarantee of its strength"' (*The Economist*, 19 December 2009, p. 104).

16 September 2009. Yukio Hatoyama is sworn in as Japan's prime minister.

22 September 2009.

> President Hu Jintao committed his country to reducing carbon emissions, but only as a percentage of its economic output, saying that the size of the cuts would depend on the growth of his nation's economy, rather than an absolute number. Mr Hu said China would develop nuclear power and increase the use of renewable energy to 15 per cent of the power used in China. But he also emphasized his country's position that the world should address the needs of developing countries by providing financing and technology to help them reduce emissions. Mr Hu promised to set a target for reducing the rate at which China's greenhouse gas emissions are rising. The pledge to reduce China's so-called carbon intensity means total emissions will still grow ... Mr Hu failed to set a figure, or a date, by which China's emissions would peak.
>
> (www.iht.com, 22 September 2009)

'President Hu Jintao said: "Developing countries need to strike a balance between economic growth, social development and environmental protection"' (*IHT*, 23 September 2009, p. 1).

'President Hu Jintao ... promised to reduce the amount of greenhouse gases produced for each dollar of national economic output by a "noticeable margin" by 2020 from 2005 levels. He gave no specific "carbon intensity" targets' (www.thetimes.co.uk, 22 September 2009).

> China will increase efforts to improve energy efficiency and cut CO_2 emissions, President Hu Jintao has told a UN climate change summit in New York. Mr Hu said CO_2 emissions would be cut by a 'notable margin' by 2020, but gave no overall figure ... The Chinese president said his country's cuts would be measured by units of GDP. He also pledged to 'vigorously develop' renewable and nuclear energy. He restated China's position that developed nations needed to do more than developing nations to fight climate change because they were historically responsible for the problem. He said:

> 'China fully appreciates the importance and urgency of addressing climate change. First, we will intensify our effort to conserve and improve energy efficiency. We will endeavour to cut carbon dioxide emissions per cent of GDP by a notable margin by 2020 from the 2005 levels. Second, we will vigorously develop renewable energy and nuclear energy. We will endeavour to increase the share of non-fossil fuels in primary energy consumption to around 15 per cent by 2020. Third, we will energetically increase forest carbon sink. We will endeavour to increase forest coverage by 40 million hectares and forest stock volume by 1.3 billion cubic meters by 2020 from the 2005 levels. Fourth, we will step up our efforts to develop a green economy, a low carbon economy, and a circular economy and enhance research, development and dissemination of climate friendly technologies. Developed countries should fulfil the task of emission reduction set in the Kyoto Protocol, continue to undertake substantial mid-term quantified emission reduction targets and support developing countries in countering climate change' ... About 100 leaders are attending the talks [in New York], ahead of the [December 2009] Copenhagen summit which is due to approve a new treaty ... Negotiators for the Copenhagen summit are trying to agree on a replacement for the [1997] Kyoto Protocol to limit carbon emissions ... China and the United States each account for about 20 per cent of the world's greenhouse gas pollution from coal, natural gas and oil. The EU is responsible for 14 per cent, followed by Russia and India with 5 per cent each.
>
> (www.bbc.co.uk, 22 September 2009)

> The new climate treaty being negotiated by the UN Framework Convention on Climate Change would succeed the Kyoto Protocol, the world's first major climate change treaty, which expires in 2012 ... The overarching and generally accepted goal [is one of] limiting the rise of Earth's temperature to within 2 degrees Fahrenheit above its temperature before the industrial revolution.
>
> (www.cnn.com, 22 September 2009)

'The main hurdle is coming up with a plan over the next decade that would keep the temperature rise to no more than 2 degrees Celsius (or 3.6 degrees Fahrenheit) above pre-industrial levels' (*IHT*, 23 September 2009, p. 6).

> In less than three months negotiations will begin in Copenhagen for a new agreement to replace the 1997 Kyoto protocol. The hope is these talks will produce commitments from each nation that, collectively, would keep temperatures from rising 2 degrees Celsius (or 3.6 degrees Fahrenheit) above pre-industrial levels.
>
> (www.iht.com, 23 September 2009)

24 September 2009.

> A rare meeting of UN Security Council heads of state, led for the first time by a US president, adopted a resolution Thursday [24 September] focused on stopping the spread of nuclear weapons ... It was the first Security

> Council summit chaired by a US president, and only the fifth time that Security Council heads of state have met. President Barack Obama led the meeting because the United States holds the revolving presidency of the Security Council in September … The resolution, which was adopted unanimously [fifteen to zero], calls for tighter controls on nuclear materials to prevent them from being stolen or used for military purposes. It also encourages enforcement of international treaties and UN resolutions regarding nuclear non-proliferation, particularly when nations such as Iran and North Korea are in violation.
>
> (www.cnn.com, 24 September 2009)

> The UN Security Council has unanimously adopted a resolution calling for nuclear disarmament … The resolution calls for further efforts to stop the spread of nuclear arms, to boost disarmament and to lower the risk of 'nuclear terrorism' … The resolution commits member nations to work toward a world without nuclear weapons, and endorses a broad framework of actions to reduce global nuclear risks. It also urges states to: join and comply with the Nuclear Non-proliferation Treaty; refrain from testing nuclear weapons and ratify the Comprehensive Test Ban Treaty; ensure safeguards of nuclear material and prevent trafficking.
>
> (www.bbc.co.uk, 24 September 2009)

'The UN Security Council voted unanimously for a resolution on disarmament and non-proliferation … The resolution, however, is non-binding' (*Guardian*, 25 September 2009, p. 18).

'The resolution set a practical target by urging states to secure all vulnerable nuclear materials within four years' (*IHT*, 26 September 2009, p. 8).

1 October 2009.

> Amid tight security, China marked its National Day on 1 October with an extravaganza showing off a rapidly growing arsenal of sophisticated made-in-China weaponry … Unlike at the parade in 1999, which featured Russian-made SU-27 fighter jets streaking overhead, this parade, marking the sixtieth anniversary of the founding of communist China, involved only Chinese-built equipment … Chinese state-run television noted that the parade was the first through Beijing to feature cruise missiles.
>
> (*The Economist*, 3 October 2009, p. 76)

> The display of armour included a number of pieces, including a cruise missile and an aerial refuelling tanker, that are relatively new to the Chinese arsenal. But analysts say there was nothing that had not been known to foreign military observers.
>
> (www.iht.com, 1 October 2009)

'China held such a parade on each of the eleven National Days from 1949 to 1959, then again in 1984 … The last was in 1999' (www.thetimes.co.uk, 1 October 2009).

('China is planning to spend billions of dollars over the next few years to dramatically restructure its media, entertainment and culture industries, some of the most tightly controlled parts of its economy. The plan, set forth in regulations issued last week by the State Council, or cabinet, would wean those industries off government funding and make them more market-orientated. Analysts say the government also wants to create media giants like Walt Disney, New Corp., Time Warner or Viacom ... In its announcement last week Beijing said it would "lend both policy and financial support to the growth of the culture sector", which includes the Chinese media, and that state-owned groups would be restructured as market-orientated enterprises, "to live on their own rather than being attached to government departments as parasites" ... The regulations are being released at a time when China's state-run news media are trying to upgrade or create foreign language publications, wire services and television programmes to reach readers and viewers overseas': *IHT*, 5 October 2009, p. 19.)

13 October 2009.

> Russia and China looked to steady their close but increasingly imbalanced relationship on Tuesday [13 October] when visiting Russian prime minister Vladimir Putin ushered through trade deals said to be worth $3.5 billion ... Russian and Chinese companies signed deals worth $3.5 billion on Tuesday, the second day of Putin's visit to Beijing ... The Kremlin said last week the two sides would sign commercial deals worth $5.5 billion during Putin's visit ... There were about forty deals made, including a pair of $500 million bank deals.
>
> (www.iht.com, 13 October 2009)

> The main Russian gas exporter signed a general trade agreement with China's largest state-run energy company on Tuesday, but failed to work out pricing details and other mechanisms that would actually put the agreement into effect ... Gazprom made the deal with the China National Petroleum Corp., China's largest oil and gas producer. The deal calls for the supply of up to 70 billion cubic metres of gas per year via two potential routes originating from Siberia ... Gazprom said in 2006 that Russia would supply natural gas to China via two pipelines, but no contract has been signed because the state-run enterprises in the two countries have failed to agree on pricing. The agreement reached Tuesday appeared to be an affirmation of the deal from 2006, but did not contain the crucial mechanisms needed for the actual trade to start.
>
> (www.iht.com, 13 October 2009)

'Russia is building a trans-Siberian oil pipeline to supply China, and this year [2009] The Russian state oil company, Rosneft, accepted a $25 billion Chinese loan secured by future oil exports' (*IHT*, 14 October 2009, p. 1).

'The deals included two $500 million banking deals – one involving Russia's Vneshkombank (VEB) and the China Development Bank, and the other between

Russia's VTB bank and the Agricultural Bank of China' (www.cnn.com, 13 October 2009).

> The annual *Hurun Report* ... a luxury publishing and events group ... said that China has 130 known billionaires [the richest $5.1 billion], up from 101 last year [2008]. The number in the United States is 359, while Russia has thirty-two and India twenty-four, according to *Forbes* magazine ... One-third of the people on the 1,000-name *Hurun* list are estimated to be Party members.
>
> (www.iht.com, 13 October 2009)

'Rupert Hoogewerf compiles the annual *Hurun* list of China's richest' (*FT*, 28 October 2009, p. 10).

18 October 2009.

> After years of delicate preparations, China was the 'honoured guest' this past week at the Frankfurt Book Fair [which ended on 18 October], the largest and most influential book trade event, based on the number of publishers represented. But what Beijing hoped would be a celebration of its cultural achievements turned into a tug of war between control and free speech, as much as a showcase for Chinese dissidents as the state's approved writers.
>
> (www.iht.com, 19 October 2009; *IHT*, 20 October 2009, p. 4)

> The Frankfurt Book Fair ... has fired its project manager after yet another embarrassing refusal to let Chinese dissidents speak ... Two Chinese dissident writers, the journalist Dai Qing and the poet Bei Ling, were not allowed to address the closing ceremony, despite what they said were invitations to do so ... Fair organizers ... blamed him for 'persistent co-ordination problems in connection with this year's guest of honour, China'.
>
> (*IHT*, 22 October 2009, p. 4)

27 October 2009.

> China will search for the remains of victims from a US Air Force bomber that crashed nearly sixty years ago, the state media said Tuesday [27 October], a gesture made just weeks ahead of President Barack Obama's first visit to the country, planned for 15–18 November. China yielded last year [2008] to a long-standing US request to provide access to military records that might resolve the fate of thousands of US servicemen missing from the Korean War and other Cold War-era conflicts.
>
> (*IHT*, 28 October 2009, p. 7)

28 October 2009.

> Police in China say they have recovered over 2,000 children in a six-month campaign against human trafficking ... Of the 2,008 children recovered, some have already been reunited with their parents. Criminal gangs steal the children and sell them to childless couples.
>
> (www.bbc.co.uk, 28 October 2009)

31 October 2009.

Qian Xuesen, a brilliant rocket scientist who single-handedly led China's space and military rocketry after he was drummed out of the United States during the redbaiting of the McCarthy era, died on Saturday [31 October] in Beijing. He was ninety-eight years old ... In the United States in the 1930s and 1940s he was no less valuable as a pioneer in American jet and rocket technology ... [He] was born in 1911 in Hangzhou in eastern China ... In 1955 Mr Qian was sent back to China ... The loyalty allegations have never been fully resolved.

(www.iht.com, 3 November 2009)

2 November 2009.

Facing rising criticism over the quality of schools and a crush of jobless college graduates, China's legislature announced Monday [2 November] that it had removed the minister of education after six years on the job and replaced him with a deputy ... Zhou Ji had become a prime target for critics of China's education system.

(www.iht.com, 2 November 2009)

3 November 2009.

The spectacle taking place in Chongqing is one of the most lurid, sprawling and avidly followed campaigns against criminality in recent memory. It involves more than 9,000 suspects, fifty public officials, a billionaire and what prosecutors describe as 104 criminal organizations that dabbled in drug trafficking, illegal mining, real estate and random acts of savagery, the most notable of which was the killing of a man for his loud karaoke voice.

Among those on trial this week is Li Qiang, a local legislature and billionaire ... The uncontested star of the drama is Bo Xilai, a charismatic figure and Chongqing's Communist Party chief whose war on malfeasance has earned him lavish praise ... But the adoration does not extend through the ranks of the party elite, many of whom view the crackdown as a self-serving performance aimed at raising his profile among the mandarins in Beijing ... Mr Bo's swagger, which includes boastful comments on the news media, has ruffled many a feather. Largely unsaid is the fear that his campaign, if unchecked, could spread far and wide, taking down public officials whose private dealings might not pass the smell test ... Mr Bo, sixty, was the popular mayor of Dalian, a north-eastern coastal city known for eco-friendly development, before becoming a member of the Politburo.

(*IHT*, 4 November 2009, pp. 1,8)

A woman called the 'godmother' of a mafia-style gang in Chongqing was sentenced to eighteen years in prison Tuesday [3 November] for running underground casinos and bribing government officials. The trial of Xie Caiping is part of a months-long crackdown in the city that has exposed widespread government and police involvement in providing cover to numerous local gangs, or 'black societies'. It has also riveted China's state-controlled media with tales of a violent underworld. Twenty-one others were sentenced to between one and thirteen years in prison … The crackdown in Chongqing has been extensive, netting more than 1,544 suspects – gangsters, prominent businessmen and fourteen high-ranking officials. Six gang members in the city have already been sentenced to death for crimes including murder and blackmail, the first among hundreds expected to go on trial. Xie is the sister-in-law of the city's long-serving deputy police chief, who was detained for investigation by the Communist Party in August. He is regarded as being the centre of an extensive network of protection of local gangs for over a decade.

(www.iht.com, 3 November 2009)

The court said Xie Caiping, forty-six, ran gambling dens, protected drug users and bribed police to turn a blind eye … Hundreds of people have been arrested in Chongqing in recent months in a sweeping crackdown on criminal gangs. Among them was Wen Qiang, Xie's brother-in-law and former head of the judiciary, who was arrested in August on serious corruption charges … Xie is reported to have earned more than 2 million yuan ($292,000) from her criminal activities and was fined 1.02 million yuan in addition to her jail term … The gang and corruption crackdown in Chongqing has been running since June and has seen the arrest of several high-profile official figures, including at least six district police chiefs. Xie's brother-in-law, Mr Wen, will be prosecuted later this month on charges including rape, money laundering, bribery and illegal money lending … The details emerging have revealed just how corrupt the city of 30 million people is.

(www.bbc.co.uk, 3 November 2009)

A massive crackdown, which began in China's Chongqing municipality in June, has implicated millionaires, gangsters and even police officers. Known as *dahei* or 'combat triads', the campaign put the spotlight on organized crime and how it has infested local bureaucracy and businesses through bribery, blackmail and violence. Police operations have led to the arrest of more than 4,800 suspected gangsters and the confiscation of 1,700 illegal firearms. Investigations led to many city officials, including police officers. More trials are expected as the city fights at least fourteen mafia-style gangs … The trials are being extensively covered by the Chinese media … Chongqing … in Sichuan province … became the world's largest city in 1997 when the central government incorporated a huge area adjacent to the city … The city of 31 million has been at the centre of an economic boom. But the economic boom has also led to the resurgence of local gangs engaged in human and drug trafficking, illegal gambling, prostitution, extortion and protection rackets. Gangsters were blamed for heinous crimes of murder and kidnapping. Local officials were accused of 'economic crimes' – bribery, profiteering and corrupt behaviour in public office, involving public funds and property.

(www.cnn.com, 3 November 2009)

8 November 2009.

China has pledged to give Africa $10 billion in concessional loans over the next three years, premier Wen Jiabao has said at a summit in Egypt. The Chinese leader is attending a two-day forum on China–Africa co-operation attended by officials from fifty nations ... China pledged $5 billion of assistance at the last co-operation summit in Beijing in 2006, and signed agreements to relieve or cancel the debt of more than thirty African countries.

(www.bbc.co.uk, 8 November 2009)

Prime minister Wen Jiabao of China on Sunday [8 November] offered Africa $10 billion in concessional loans over the next three years ... In addition to the loans, Mr Wen said China would help Africa develop clean energy and cope with climate change, encourage Chinese financial institutions to lend to smaller African firms and expand African products' market access ... China's friendship with Africa dates from the 1950s, when Beijing backed some of the liberation movements fighting colonial rule.

(www.iht.com, 8 November 2009)

Prime minister Wen Jiabao [pledged] China would grant African countries $10 billion in low-interest development loans over the next three years, establish a $1 billion loan programme for small and medium-sized businesses, and forgive the remaining debt on certain interest-free loans that China has granted less-developed African nations in the past ... Forty-nine African nations [were] in attendance ... Besides the financial assistance, Mr Wen also promised to form a partnership to address climate change in Africa, including building 100 clean-energy projects across the continent. Beijing will also remove tariffs on most exports to China from least developed African nations that do not have diplomatic relations with Taiwan, and to sponsor an array of other programmes in health, education, culture and agriculture ... Trade [between Africa and China] has soared from about $10 billion in 2000 to $106.8 billion last year [2008]. Chinese direct investment in Africa leaped 81 per cent in the first six months of this year [2009] to $552 million.

(*IHT*, 9 November 2009, p. 5)

9 November 2009.

'The pioneering editor' of the top Chinese business magazine has left her post with plans to start anew, after a tussle for control involving much the same mix of political and financial intrigue that she made her mark uncovering. Hu Shuli, fifty-six, resigned Monday [9 November] from *Caijing*, the magazine she built into a thriving print and web outlet that specialized in investigating government corruption and corporate fraud ... senior editors and most of *Caijing*'s journalists had either already resigned or were preparing to as well ... For months Ms Hu, the editor in chief, and the business managers of the magazine had been locked in a stalemate with the owners of *Caijing* over the breadth of the magazine's coverage and the budgeting of its operations ... The owners of the magazine had come under pressure from Communist Party officials to rein in *Caijing*'s aggressive journalism ... The managers had been seeking to create a more independent publication by changing the magazine's shareholding structure, seeking outside investors and pressing the owners to allow more employees to own a stake in the magazine. In a well-publicized exodus earlier this autumn [2009] nearly seventy business employees resigned. Ms Hu held on until Monday. She has now accepted a new post as the dean of journalism school at Sun Yat-sen University in Guangzhou, a job she had been offered before it became clear that she would leave *Caijing*. At the same time she, along with a large contingent of editors and executives departing *Caijing*, was working to secure new licences and open a new venture ... *Caijing*'s parent company, the State Exchange Executive Council (SEEC), had already recruited a new team from another progressive publication, *The Economic Observer* in Beijing ... In eleven years at *Caijing* editorials by Ms Hu pinpointed interest groups and bottlenecks that she said blocked economic overhauls. And exclusives by *Caijing* hastened the demise of some of the more notorious felons in China ... After a run-in with a *Caijing* reporter covering the ethnic riots in Xinjian in July, officials leaned harder on Ms Hu's superiors to curb her coverage ... At one point the SEEC was ordered to fire Ms Hu ... The pressures brought the infighting over editorial and financial control of *Caijing* to a boil ... Under her current plan, her new publishing sponsor would be the province-level Zhejiang Daily Press ... Her proposed new publication's title has a familiar ring: *Caixin* short for *Caijing Newsweek* ... *Caijing* now generates about half of the group's revenue, but the SEEC has reinvested a considerably smaller percentage ... The authorities have reprimanded the magazine for at least eight articles this year [2009], including the China Central Television inquiry [involving a corruption investigation] and directed it to 'return to positive reporting on finance and economics' ... In September *Caijing*'s general manager and other executives led a walkout of more than sixty business staff members. As of last month [October] dozens who resigned had already started working at what several said were *Caijing*'s new offices ... New publishing licences [are required].

(www.iht.com, 9 November 2009)

As the central authorities lavish official media giants with support to grow and compete globally, they have also made moves to tighten their chain of command over muckrakers like Ms Hu ... She has become an unrivalled celebrity, and counts senior economic officials as friends from her reporting days at state-owned newspapers ... The organization that sponsors *Caijing*'s publishing licence [is] the All-China Federation of Industry and Commerce.

(*IHT*, 10 November 2009, p. 15)

Caijing's management ... [also wanted a larger share of the magazine's profits to be invested in new operations, including an English language website. But the magazine's owner, the SEEC, a partially state-owned, par-

> tially private entity, has apparently refused to surrender control or restructure its operations. Ms Hu [is] a former propaganda writer for *Workers' Daily*, the Communist Party publication. She helped found *Caijing* in 1998.
>
> (www.iht.com, 12 October 2009)

'SEEC has close links to high-ranking officials but is only loosely affiliated with the stock exchange. The rupture comes amid attempts by Beijing to create commercially strong groups while reinforcing its control over the media' (*FT*, 10 November 2009, p. 12).

'President Barack Obama said on Monday [9 November] that he plans to raise the issue of the yuan with Chinese officials when he meets with them in Beijing next week' (www.iht.com, 10 November 2009). 'Obama said he would talk to the Chinese about revaluing the yuan, as well as encouraging Chinese consumers to spend more and opening Chinese markets further to US goods' (www.iht.com, 12 November 2009).

'The Obama administration's approach towards China, known as "Strategic Reassurance", builds on a Bush administration effort to ease mistrust between Washington and Beijing and encourage China to become a responsible stakeholder in global affairs' (www.iht.com, 12 November 2009).

> In a speech this fall [2009] … James Steinberg, the Deputy Secretary of State … argued that China needed to adopt a policy of 'strategic reassurance' to the rest of the world, a phrase that appeared intended to be the successor to the framework of the Bush era, when China was urged to embrace a role as a 'responsible stakeholder' … James Steinberg: 'Strategic reassurance rests on a core, if tacit, bargain. Just as we and our allies must make clear that we welcome China's "arrival" … [China] must reassure the world that its development and growing global role will not come at the expense of security and well-being of others.'
>
> (www.iht.com, 14 November 2009)

'[In 2008 the US] military budget was $607 billion, representing almost half of the world's total military spending. The military budget of China … is less than one-seventh of that' (*FT*, 12 November 2009, p. 13).

'Beijing already trains Afghan anti-drug forces in China' (*FT*, 13 November 2009, p. 6).

12 November 2009.

> China is running a number of unlawful detention centres in which its citizens can be kept for months, according to Human Rights Watch. It says these centres – known as 'black jails' – are often in state-run hotels, nursing homes or psychiatric hospitals. Among those detained are ordinary people who have travelled to Beijing to report local injustices … China regularly denies such claims, but even state-run media outlets have reported the existence of 'black jails'.
>
> (www.bbc.co.uk, 12 November 2009)

> China should abolish secret jails used to unlawfully detain citizens who travel to the capital and other major cities to file complaints, Human Rights Watch says … For the past six years citizens have been held without communications in so-called 'black jails', according to a new report from the human rights group.
>
> (www.cnn.com, 12 November 2009)

> Human Rights Watch … accused China's national government on Thursday [12 November] of tolerating an extensive network of secret jails in Beijing which are operated by provincial and municipal governments to prevent their citizens from complaining to national officials … Provincial and municipal officials in China are subject to a national civil service evaluation system in which they are penalized based on the number of complaints received in Beijing about their management. So local and provincial officials have a strong incentive to prevent petitioners from reaching the central government … A foreign ministry spokesman said in Beijing on Thursday [12 November]: 'There are no "black jails" in China.'
>
> (www.iht.com, 12 November 2009)

13 November 2009.

> Unusually early snowstorms in north-central China have claimed forty lives, caused thousands of buildings to collapse and destroyed almost 500,000 acres of winter crops, the civil affairs ministry said Friday [13 November]. Nineteen of the deaths resulted from traffic accidents related to the storms, which began on 9 November … State media reported that at least two deaths were caused by the collapse of buildings, including a school cafeteria. The snowfall is heaviest in the northern and central provinces of Hebei, Shanxi, Shaanxi, Shandong and Henan since recordkeeping began after the establishment of the communist state in 1949 … Chinese state media said some of the snow was induced through cloud seeding, a measure intended to ease lingering dry conditions … The storms caused the collapse of more than 9,000 buildings … an unwelcome reminder of weaknesses in China's infrastructure … School buildings [collapsed] in the devastating 2008 earthquake in Sichuan province.
>
> (www.iht.com, 15 November 2009)

> Police in China are reported to have detained dozens of citizens in a crackdown ahead of President Barack Obama's visit … Human rights campaigners said that at least thirty activists who were expected to apply for the right to hold protests directed at the government during the US president's visit were arrested.
>
> (www.bbc.co.uk, 15 November 2009)

'Campaigners have reported that dozens of dissidents and activists have been detained ahead of President Barack Obama's arrival [on 15 November]' (www.guardian.co.uk, 16 November 2009).

'Chinese officials have rounded up dozens of Beijing's tiny coterie of activists and petitioners in case any dissident tries to approach President Barack Obama' (www.thetimes.com, 16 November 2009).

'Police have detained dozens of dissidents and human rights activists to stop them from staging protests or trying to meet President Barack Obama, who has requested personal meetings with at least one prominent human rights lawyer' (www.ft.com, 16 November 2009).

15–18 November 2009. President Barack Obama's visit to China.

> President Barack Obama held a town hall meeting with university students in Shanghai on Monday [16 November], but unlike previous such gatherings with other American presidents, Mr Obama's question-and-answer session was not broadcast live on China's official state network. Instead, according to the official news agency Xinhua, the live broadcast inside China was to be on the agency's website ... Edited portions were expected to be available later on China Central Television (CCTV), the state network ... The White House offered live streaming of the event on its website, which is not blocked or censored in China, and a simultaneous Chinese translation was offered ... Previous town hall gatherings with visiting American leaders were shown live on CCTV: Bill Clinton spoke at Beijing University and took questions during a visit in 1998, and George W. Bush met with students at Tsinghua University in Beijing in 2002.
>
> (www.iht.com, 16 November 2009)

> The students – some 500 – in the audience seemed handpicked by the government and many were members of the Communist Youth League ... Unlike previous town hall gatherings in China with other American presidents, Mr Obama's question-and-answer session was not broadcast live on China's official state network. Instead ... live broadcasts inside China were carried on the agency's website and on local Shanghai stations.
>
> (www.iht.com, 16 November 2009)

'China's government ... allowed the Twitter question and Mr Obama's answer to stay up on websites for several hours after the town hall meeting' (*IHT*, 17 November 2009, p. 4).

> Most of those who attended the event at the Museum of Science and Technology turned out to be members of the Communist Youth League ... Some Chinese bloggers whom the White House had tried to invite were barred from attending. Even then the Chinese government took no chances, declining to broadcast the event live to a national audience – or even mention it on the main evening newscast of state-run China Central Television ... Beijing vetoed the White House's attempt to invite a group of popular bloggers.
>
> (www.iht.com, 17 November 2009)

> Chinese officials rejected US proposals that 1,000 people should attend and that it should be broadcast live. It was streamed on the White House site,

> broadcast live on a local Shanghai television channel and transmitted in text form on state news agency Xinhua's website.
>
> (www.guardian.co.uk, 16 November 2009)

'The Xinhua news agency posted a translated running transcript of the event on its website. The United States also streamed the forum ... Chinese censors did not block the event to those with internet access' (www.cnn.com, 16 November 2009).

> Responding to a question that came via the internet during a town hall meeting with Shanghai students – 'Should we able to use Twitter freely?' ... President Barack Obama said: 'I should be honest, as president of the United States, there are times when I wish information didn't flow so freely because then I wouldn't have to listen to people criticizing me all the time ... [But] because in the United States information is free, and I have a lot of critics in the United States who can say all kinds of things about me, I actually think that makes our democracy stronger and it makes me a better leader because it forces me to hear opinions that I don't want to hear.'
>
> (www.iht.com, 16 November 2009)

'Asked about China's "Great Firewall" Obama described himself as "a big supporter of non-censorship" and said criticism enabled by freedom of expression in the United States made him a better president' (www.guardian.co.uk, 16 November 2009).

'China kept in place its block on Facebook, a social networking site on which the White House invited internet users to join a live discussion of the meetings' (www.economist.com, 16 November 2009).

> The courteous but rigidly formal reception afforded President Barack Obama stood in sharp contrast to that given ... President Bill Clinton in 1998. Chinese television aired an interview with Mr Clinton and gave live coverage to his meeting with Chinese students and to a joint press conference with President Jiang Zemin ... What the Americans described as a 'town hall' meeting with young Chinese ... was shown only on Shanghai television, along with a painfully slow feed relayed through the internet ... Chinese participants were coached beforehand on how they should pose their questions. They were also carefully selected. Many were members of the Communist Youth League ... [The meeting was] open only to handpicked young Communists ... Later, in Beijing, Mr Obama held a ritual meeting with reporters alongside President Hu Jintao. But unlike in 1998 no questions were allowed.
>
> (www.economist.com, 19 November 2009)

> Standing next to President Hu Jintao, President Barack Obama ... said China should resume talks with representatives of the Dalai Lama to resolve differences about the Himalayan region ... President Hu said the two sides would hold talks about human rights and religious freedom [and] that their

> two countries must shun protectionism. President Hu said the two sides would 'continue to have consultations on an even footing to properly resolve economic and trade frictions'.
>
> (www.bbc.co.uk, 17 November 2009)

'President Hu Jintao: "Our two countries need to oppose and reject protectionism and all its manifestations" ' (www.iht.com, 17 November 2009).

> President Barack Obama ... revealed that the two had agreed to resume early next year [2010] a human rights dialogue that has been stalled since 2004. He stressed his 'bedrock' belief that human rights were universal and should be available to all and to 'all ethnic and religious minorities' ... President Hu stood beside him impassive when he referred to the Dalai Lama. Washington, Mr Obama said, supported 'the early resumption of talks between Beijing and the Dalai Lama to resolve any concerns or differences the two sides may have' ... President Hu Jintao: 'I stressed to President Obama that under the current circumstances our two countries need to oppose and reject protectionism and all its manifestations in an even stronger stance.'
>
> (www.thetimes.co.uk, 17 November 2009)

'President Barack Obama held a ritual meeting with reporters alongside President Hu Jintao ... No questions were allowed ... [The] joint "press conference" ... [was] confined to statements from the leaders with no questions allowed' (www.economist.com, 19 November 2009).

> There was general agreement on climate change, with both leaders saying that their nations – the two biggest emitters of greenhouse gases – were vital to hopes of a deal to slow global warming ... President Barack Obama: 'Our aim there [in Copenhagen] is ... not a partial accord or a political declaration but rather an accord that covers all the issues in the negotiations and one that has immediate operational effect.'
>
> (www.thetimes.co.uk, 17 November 2009)

> President Barack Obama ... said after a meeting with President Hu Jintao Tuesday [17 November] that he wanted an all-encompassing agreement in Copenhagen, even if it falls short of a legal treaty. And he said he wants something 'that has immediate operational effect'.
>
> (www.iht.com, 17 November 2009)

'In a joint communiqué the leaders said an accord in Denmark should include emission reduction targets for rich nations and a declaration of action plans to ease greenhouse gas emissions in developing countries' (www.guardian.co.uk, 17 November 2009).

'A lengthy joint statement outlined measures to step up co-operation on developing clean energy' (www.economist.com, 19 November 2009).

('The United Nations body in charge of managing carbon trading has suspended approvals for dozens of Chinese wind farms amid questions over the country's use of industrial policy to obtain money under the scheme. China has been by far the biggest beneficiary of the so-called Clean Development Mechanism [CDM], a carbon trading system designed to direct funds from wealthy countries to developing nations to cut greenhouse gases. China has earned 153 million carbon credits, worth more than $1 billion and making up almost half of the total issued under the UN-run programme in the past five years ... Projects only qualify for credits if the applicants prove they would not have been built anyway, a condition known as 'additionality' ... The CDM's board in Bonn began refusing approval for Chinese wind projects mid-year [2009], over concerns that Beijing had deliberately lowered subsidies to make them eligible for funding': *FT*, 2 December 2009, p. 1.)

> President Barack Obama urged Beijing to allow the yuan to rise in value ... He said: 'I was pleased to note the Chinese commitment, made in past statements, to move towards a more market orientated exchange rate over time ... Doing so based on economic fundamentals would make an essential contribution to the global rebalancing effort.'
>
> (www.thetimes.co.uk, 17 November 2009)

> The Obama team offered an exclusive interview to *Southern Weekend*, China's most feisty newspaper, based in Guangzhou. Once again journalists were programmed and the paper censored. In protest, the paper prominently displayed vast white spaces on the first and second page of the edition that carried the interview. Propaganda officials are investigating this act of defiance.
>
> (www.iht.com, 24 November 2009)

> The top editor of *Southern Weekly*, one of China's most influential newspapers, has apparently been demoted, just weeks after his interview with President Barack Obama ... Although the interview with Mr Obama at the end of his visit to China did not yield any significant news, or even include unusually tough questions, it seemed to bother propaganda officials by putting the spotlight on the feisty, liberal-leaning news agency, Xinhua, or its main broadcaster, China Central Television.
>
> (www.iht.com, 16 December 2009)

'President Barack Obama met premier Wen Jiabao on the last day of his visit [Wednesday 18 November]' (www.bbc.co.uk, 18 November 2009).

'The president met briefly Monday [16 November] in Beijing with his half-brother, Mark Okoth Obama Ndesandjo, who lives in southern China' (www.iht.com, 18 November 2009).

24 November 2009.

> A magazine has revealed details about a system of secret detention centres in Beijing where Chinese citizens are forcibly held and sometimes beaten to prevent them from lodging formal complains with the central government. The report appeared on Tuesday [24 November] in *Liaowang* (Outlook), a

state-run magazine that is written for the government elite and published by Xinhua … [The] problem has long [been] denied.

(*IHT*, 27 November 2009, p. 5)

Secret, illegal 'black jails' exist in China, a state-run weekly has confirmed, despite official denials otherwise … The report by the state-run weekly magazine *Outlook* – detailing a 'grey industry' of illegal detention centres – was published online by its parent company, the official Xinhua news agency. It was a rare reference to illegal detention centres in official Chinese media … Human rights activists and petitioners call them 'black jails' because they operate outside the sanctioned institutions … According to *Outlook*, local governments send officials to Beijing to set up *ad hoc* offices to handle the petitioners from their regions … [Petitioners are locked up] in run-down hotels, rented houses and nursing homes … Xinhua referred to a report from an 'authorized department' saying that there are seventy-three temporary 'petitioner-reception offices' in Beijing, among which fifty-seven, or 78 per cent, are set up by local cities. There are forty-six illegal petitioner-reception centres, such as houses rented from farmers.

(www.cnn.com, 30 November 2009)

'A guard at an unofficial detention centre ['black jail'] in Beijing was sentenced Friday [11 December] to eight years in prison for raping a young woman detainee' (*IHT*, 12 December 2009, p. 10).

25–26 November 2009.

President Barack Obama announced Wednesday [25 November] that he would attend the … UN climate change summit … which is to run 7–18 December 2009 in Copenhagen … The world's top economic powers acknowledged earlier this month [November] that there was no hope of a major breakthrough over climate change by year's end … Next month's climate talks aim to strike a deal on a successor to the Kyoto Protocol, the 1997 pact that has legally binding targets for reducing greenhouse gas emissions. The United States has never ratified it, though more than 200 nations did.

(www.cnn.com, 26 November 2009)

On Wednesday 25 November the White House announced that President Barack Obama will appear during the first week of negotiations … [at] the Copenhagen climate talks … with a specific American promise: to cut greenhouse gases by 17 per cent from 2005 levels by 2020, by 30 per cent by 2025, by 42 per cent by 2035 and by 83 per cent by 2050 … Mr Obama and other leaders have already conceded that Copenhagen will not produce a full schedule of legally binding emissions targets for all the world's countries, a successor to the Kyoto protocol that expires in 2012 … [The] EU promises [cuts of] 20 per cent or 30 per cent on 1990 ones.

(www.economist.com, 26 November 2009)

> [President Barack Obama's offer] to cut US emissions by 17 per cent from 2005 levels by 2020 … is much less than the EU's pledge of a 20 per cent cut over the same period, or a 30 per cent cut if there is a global deal; and much less than the 25 per cent to 40 per cent figure that developing countries are demanding.
>
> (www.bbc.co.uk, 26 November 2009)

> In Copenhagen President Barack Obama will tell the delegates that the United States intends to reduce its greenhouse gas emissions 'in the range of' 17 per cent below 2005 levels by 2020 and 83 per cent by 2050 … President Obama pledged a provisional target for reductions in greenhouse gas emissions in the United States, the first time in more than a decade that an American administration has offered even a tentative promise to reduce production of climate-altering gases … The figures released by the White House on Wednesday [26 November] were based on targets specified by legislation that passed the House of Representatives in June but is stalled in the Senate. Congress has never passed legislation that includes firm emissions limits or ratified an international global warming agreement with binding targets … The house bill aims at greenhouse gas reductions of 17 per cent below 2005 levels by 2020 and sharper cuts in the following decades, through a cap-and-trade system that includes most of the nation's major sources of carbon dioxide emissions.
>
> (www.iht.com, 26 November 2009)

> Chinese officials announced Thursday [26 November] that prime minister Wen Jiabao would attend the climate talks … a day after US officials said President Barack Obama planned to take part at an early stage of the twelve-day meeting [in Copenhagen] himself.
>
> (*IHT*, 27 November 2009, p. 1)

'Prime minister Wen Jiabao will attend the Copenhagen climate talks next month, the government said today [26 November], as it unveiled targets for reducing the world's biggest carbon footprint' (www.guardian.co.uk, 26 November 2009).

> [On Thursday 26 November] China unveiled its first firm target for limiting greenhouse gas emissions … Beijing said it would aim to reduce its 'carbon intensity' by 40 per cent to 45 per cent by the year 2020, compared with 2005 levels. Carbon intensity, China's preferred measurement, is the amount of carbon dioxide emitted for each unit of GDP.
>
> (www.bbc.co.uk, 26 November 2009)

> The Chinese propose, by 2020, to reduce so-called carbon intensity – or the amount of carbon dioxide emitted per unit of economic output – by 40 per cent to 50 per cent compared with 2005 levels. By that measure emission would still increase, though the rate would slow. That falls far short of what many in Europe and other nations had hoped for – an increase in energy

efficiency of at least 50 per cent ... Michael Levi, director of the climate change programme at the Council on Foreign Relations, called the target announcement disappointing because it did not move the country much faster along the path it was already on. Mr Levi said: 'The Department of Energy estimates that existing Chinese policies will already cut carbon intensity by 45 per cent to 46 per cent.'

(www.iht.com, 27 November 2009)

In November China announced its pollution reduction target and said it would enforce it with domestic law. US officials privately said the target was too low and raised questions about the reliability of Beijing's reporting methods, saying that some form of international monitoring would be necessary. China protested and declared it would not sacrifice its sovereignty to an outside verification scheme.

(*IHT*, 21 December 2009, p. 7)

China has rejected demands to announce an absolute reduction in carbon emissions, arguing that environmental concerns must be balanced with economic growth and that developed countries must first demonstrate a significant commitment to reducing emissions ... As part of national civil service reviews, provincial and even municipal officials are now assessed partly on how they have improved energy efficiency ... A draft amendment this autumn [2009] to China's renewable energy law would require the grid companies to build connections to all renewable energy projects, and allow companies to sue the grid companies for losses if the connections are not built ... Under the draft, which is still being discussed in Beijing, the grid companies could seek compensation from a national energy fund for the extra cost of building the extra high-power lines.

(www.iht.com, 26 November 2009)

In September [2009] President Hu Jintao announced at the United Nations that China would reduce carbon intensity by 2020 but ... [did not give] a number. Earlier China had set a goal of reducing by 2010 the amount of energy needed to produce every 1,000 yuan (about $146) of GDP, compared with 2005 levels. By choosing a base line of 2005 in improving carbon dioxide emitted, China is including considerable improvements that it has already made. The current five year plan, which runs from 2006 through 2010, calls for an improvement of 20 per cent in overall energy efficiency.

(*IHT*, 27 November 2009, p. 3)

On Thursday [26 November] the State Council announced plans 'to reduce the intensity of carbon dioxide emissions per unit' of GDP in 2020 by 40 per cent to 45 per cent, compared with its 2005 level ... Thursday's announcement by China marks the first time it has issued numerical targets for plans to curb the growth of greenhouse gas emissions.

(www.bbc.co.uk, 26 November 2009)

> China has not yet set a target date for its carbon emissions to peak. There has been speculation that negotiators would make a commitment in Denmark. Developed countries would like China to set a date of 2025 or before. China is understood to have discussed dates around 2035. In public China has only said its emissions would peak before 2050, which developed country negotiators regard as too late.
>
> (*FT*, 27 November 2009, p. 8)

> International scholars are meeting in Vietnam to discuss territorial disputes in the South China Sea … China and six other nations (Vietnam, Malaysia, Indonesia, Brunei, Singapore and the Philippines) claim sovereignty to areas in the South China Sea … Smaller claimants have been especially alarmed by recent developments such as the establishment of a Chinese submarine base on Hainan Island and increasing Chinese naval activities. Beijing always maintains that territorial disputes in the South China Sea are bilateral issues that should be dealt with by individual countries. But the two-day meeting in Hanoi is sending out clear signals that smaller claimants may have embarked on a different approach.
>
> (www.bbc.co.uk, 26 November 2009)

27 November 2009. 'China will launch a second lunar probe … named *Chang'e-2* … next October [2010], state-run media reported Friday [27 November]' (www.cnn.com, 27 November 2009).

30 November 2009.

> Ten journalists and forty-eight officials have been charged with taking bribes to cover up a mining disaster … in Hebei province … last year [2008], according to a report Monday in *China Daily*, an official English language newspaper … Thirty-four miners and a rescuer were killed in an explosion … on 14 July 2008, almost a month before the Beijing Olympics … The cover-up kept the incident out of the public eye for eighty-five days. In September 2008 someone reported the cover-up in an internet chat site, and the ensuing clamour forced the central government to step in, firing twenty-five local officials and putting twenty-two of them under criminal investigation … Last year journalists were also accused of helping to cover up at least one other mine disaster in China … Small mines, legal and illegal, accounted for three-fourths of the deaths but only a third of the production.
>
> (www.iht.com, 30 November 2009; *IHT*, 1 December 2009, p. 7)

> The mayor of Chongqing, Wang Hongju, has been fired by the Central Committee of the Communist Party, according to a report Monday [30 November] … Huang Qifan was named mayor and vice party secretary … With a population of more than 30 million, Chongqing is the largest provincial-level municipality in China.
>
> (*IHT*, 1 December 2009, p. 7)

12 December 2009.

> [On 12 December] President Hu Jintao unveiled the Kazakh section of a 7,000-kilometre (4,300-mile) natural gas pipeline joining Central Asia to China ... On Monday [14 December] Mr Hu is due to head to a commissioning ceremony in Turkmenistan where the pipeline actually begins. He is also expected to be joined there by President Islam, the leader of Uzbekistan – the fourth country involved in the project ... The pipeline, which begins near a Turkmenistan gas field being developed by the China National Petroleum Corporation concludes in Xinjiang in western China ... This is Kazakhstan's first export route that does not go through Russia. This segment cost $6.7 billion and was completed within two years. Most of the finance for the project came from the state-run China Development Bank. The whole pipeline is expected to be finished by 2013.
>
> (www.bbc.co.uk, 13 December 2009)

> Supplies stalled following an accident in April [2009] on the main pipeline to Russia. So far the two countries have failed to agree new terms, causing Turkmenistan to lose around $1 billion a month ... Turkmenistan is nearing the completion of another pipeline to Iran, and expressed an interest in supporting the EU-backed Nabucco project.
>
> (www.bbc.co.uk, 14 December 2009)

> The first pipeline bringing Central Asian natural gas to China opened yesterday [14 December], underscoring Beijing's rising importance to the former Soviet republics. President Hu Jintao joined his counterparts from Turkmenistan and Uzbekistan for the ceremony at a Turkmen refinery. Turkmenistan has agreed to supply China with up to 40 billion cubic metres – about half its annual production – through the new pipeline, which begins at the Samandepe gas field and crosses Uzbekistan and Kazakhstan to China. Kazakhstan and Uzbekistan are also considering supplying gas to China. The new gas pipeline breaks Russia's lock over gas exports from central Asia and deals a blow to the EU's plans to win Turkmen supplies for the planned Nabucco pipeline to bring Caspian and central Asian gas to Europe across the Caucasus and Turkey ... China National Petroleum won a contract to develop Samandepe in 2007, becoming the first and only foreign company to gain access to Turkmenistan's vast onshore gas resources. China lent Turkmenistan $3 billion this year [2009] to help develop the giant South Iolotan field in the east of the country, a move that could secure a future role for China National in the project. The opening of the pipeline to China comes at an opportune time for Turkmenistan, which is locked in a gas trading dispute with Gazprom that has halted exports to Russia since April [2009]. Gazprom, facing a decline in gas demand and in prices, said last month [November] it would reduce to 25 billion cubic metres the amount of gas it imported from central Asia in 2010, about half the volume earlier planned. Turkmenistan has refused to accept Gazprom's new terms,

> turning to China and Iran with offers of extra gas supplies and conducting talks with the EU about possibly joining the Nabucco.
>
> (*FT*, 15 December 2009, p. 11)

7–18 December 2009. Conference of the Parties to the United Nations Framework Convention on Climate Change: the fifteenth session of the Copenhagen climate change conference was held 7–18 December 2009. This fifteenth session is the latest in a series which followed a climate change meeting in Rio de Janeiro in 1992.

> President Barack Obama had been planning to attend the early stages of the Copenhagen summit … but the White House announced last week that he would come at the end instead … In June [2009] President Dmitri Medvedev said Russia would reduce emissions levels by 10 per cent to 15 per cent from 1990 levels by 2020. But what this actually means is a 30 per cent rise from the present levels. Using the 1990 figures as a benchmark is a way to gain extra leeway, because emissions in Russia have tumbled since the Soviet Union collapsed and much of its polluting industrial complex went down with it.
>
> (www.independent.co.uk, 7 December 2009)

'Just about all of the growth in greenhouse gases is expected to come from the developing world between now and 2030, half from China' (www.iht.com, 12 December 2009).

'China and the United States together account for 40 per cent of global greenhouse gas emissions' (www.iht.com, 18 December 2009)

'Scientists say 2 degrees Celsius [3.6 degrees Fahrenheit] is the minimum to avoid some of the worst impacts of climate change including several metres sea level rise, extinctions and crop failures' (www.iht.com, 18 December 2009).

> President Barack Obama, shortly after landing in Copenhagen on Friday morning [18 December], delivered a direct challenge to China by calling for a global climate change accord to include a way to monitor whether countries complied with promised emissions cuts. He said: 'These measures need not be intrusive, or infringe upon sovereignty. They must, however, ensure that an accord is credible, and that we are living up to our obligations. For without such accountability, any agreement would be empty words on a page' … The issue of verification has become a chief source of friction between the Americans and Chinese.
>
> (*IHT*, 19 December 2009, p. 1)

> The Copenhagen Accord, reached … on Friday [18 December] … between the United States, China, India, Brazil and South Africa, contains no reference to a legally binding agreement … Neither is there a deadline for transforming it into a binding deal … The Accord was merely 'recognized' by the 193 nations at the Copenhagen summit, rather than approved, which would have required unanimous support … The chairman of the plenary

> session declared: 'The conference decides to take note of the Copenhagen Accord of 18 December 2009' ... The text recognizes the need to limit global temperatures rising no more than 2 degrees Celsius (3.6 degrees Fahrenheit) above pre-industrial levels ... The Accord does not identify a year by which carbon emissions should peak ... Countries are asked to spell out by 1 February next year [2010] their pledges for curbing carbon emissions by 2020 ... The implementation of the Copenhagen Accord will be reviewed by 2015 ... The main opposition to the five-nation Accord had come from the ALBA bloc of Latin American countries to which Nicaragua and Venezuela belong, along with Cuba, Ecuador and Bolivia ... The Sudanese negotiator had said the draft text asked 'Africa to sign a suicide pact'.
>
> (www.bbc.co.uk, 19 December 2009)

'Germany will host the next climate change conference in six months in Bonn ... The final outcome is supposed to be sealed at a conference in Mexico City at the end of 2010' (www.bbc.co.uk, 20 December 2009).

> The Copenhagen Accord 'recognizes' the scientific case for keeping temperature rises to no more than 2 degrees Celsius but does not contain commitments to emissions reductions to achieve that goal ... The Accord ... codifies the commitments of individual nations to act on their own to tackle global warming ... The deal presented Friday evening [18 December] said that the agreement should be reviewed and put in place by 2015 ... The Accord provides a system for monitoring and reporting progress toward those national pollution-reduction goals, a compromise on an issue over which China bargained hard ... It lacked the kind of independent verification of emission reductions by developing countries that the United States and others demanded ... The agreement set up a forestry deal which is hoped would significantly reduce deforestation in return for cash.
>
> (www.iht.com, 19 December 2009)

> After two weeks of delays, theatrics and last-minute deal-making, the United Nations climate change talks concluded early Saturday morning with a grudging agreement by the participants to 'take note' of a pact shaped by five major nations ... The Sudanese delegate likened the effect of the Accord on poor nations to the Holocaust ... Ultimately, all but a handful of countries – Venezuela, Cuba, Sudan and Saudi Arabia among them – went along with the decision to accept the document. Before the parties gathered in Copenhagen, the United States and China had been sniping at each other over various aspects of the proposed agreement, particularly over American demands that Beijing agree to a system of international monitoring, through which its public promise to reduce the carbon intensity of its economy – the rate of emissions per unit of economic activity – could be verified ... Twice during the day [Friday 18 December] prime minister Wen Jiabao sent an underling to represent him at the meetings with President Barack Obama ... Each time it was a lower-level official ... Shortly before the appointed time

> of the meeting with Mr Wen ... [White House officials] were startled to find the Chinese prime minister already meeting with the leaders of three other countries. They alerted Mr Obama and he rushed to the site of the meeting.
>
> (www.iht.com, 20 December 2009)

> China fought hard against strong US pressure to submit to a regime of international monitoring. The Chinese prime minister, Wen Jiabao, walked out of the conference at one point, and sent a lowly protocol officer to negotiate with President Barack Obama.
>
> (www.guardian.co.uk, 20 December 2009)

> A decision at marathon 193-nation talks merely took note of the new accord, a non-binding deal for combating global warming ... The deal would list the countries that were in favour of the deal and those against ... China had resisted international monitoring of its emissions curbs and the final wording took into account Chinese concerns, speaking of the need to protect sovereignty ... The deal sets an end-January 2010 deadline for all nations to submit plans for curbs on emissions to the United Nations. A separate text proposes an end-2010 deadline for reporting back on – but dropped a plan to insist on a legally binding treaty.
>
> (www.independent.co.uk, 19 December 2009)

> The plan does not specify greenhouse gas cuts needed to achieve the 2 degrees Celsius goal ... Sudan, Nicaragua, Venezuela and Bolivia all denounced the plan ... Under the Accord countries will be able to set out all their pledges for the action they plan to take to tackle climate change in an appendix to the document, and will provide information to other nations on their progress ... Further talks are expected at conferences in Germany and Mexico next year [2010].
>
> (www.thetimes.co.uk, 19 December 2009)

'The emissions reductions the Accord enshrines are, at least so far, significantly smaller than is needed to provide any confidence about the 2 degrees Celsius target' (www.economist.com, 19 December 2009).

Copenhagen Accord: Draft Decision, 18 December 2009, United Nations, selected quotations:

> We underline that climate change is one of the greatest challenges of our time ... We shall, recognizing the scientific view that the increase in global temperature should be below 2 degrees Celsius, on the basis of equity and in the context of sustainable development, enhance our long-term co-operative action to combat climate change.

> Annex 1 Parties commit to implement individually or jointly the quantified economy-wide emissions targets for 2020, to be submitted ... to the secretariat by 31 January 2010 ... Annex 1 Parties that are Party to the Kyoto Protocol will thereby strengthen the emissions reductions initiated by the Kyoto Protocol. Delivery of reductions and financing by developed coun-

tries will be measured, reported and verified in accordance with existing and any further guidelines adopted by the Conference of the Parties and will ensure that accounting of such targets and finance is rigorous, robust and transparent.

Non-Annex 1 Parties to the Convention will implement mitigation actions, including those to be submitted to the secretariat by non-Annex 1 Parties ... by 31 January 2010 ... in the context of sustainable development. Least developed countries and small island developing states may undertake actions voluntarily and on the basis of support. Mitigation actions subsequently undertaken and envisaged by Non-Annex 1 Parties, including national inventory reports, shall be communicated through national communications ... every two years ... Those mitigation actions in national communications or otherwise communicated to the Secretariat will be added to the list in Appendix II. Mitigation actions taken by Non-Annex 1 Parties will be subject to their domestic measurement, reporting and verification the result of which will be reported through their national communications every two years. Non-Annex 1 Parties will communicate information on their actions through National Communications, with provisions for international consultations and analysis under clearly defined guidelines that will ensure that national security is respected. Nationally appropriate mitigation actions seeking international support will be recorded in a registry along with relevant technology, finance and capacity building support ... These supported national appropriate mitigation actions will be subject to international measurement, reporting and verification in accordance with guidelines adopted by the Conference of the Parties.

We recognize the crucial role of reducing emission from deforestation and forest degradation and the need to enhance removals of greenhouse gas emissions by forests and agree on the need to provide positive incentives to such actions through the immediate establishment of a mechanism ... to enable mobilization of financial resources from developed countries.

The collective commitment by developed countries is to provide new and additional resources, including forestry investments through international institutions, approaching $30 billion for the period 2010–2012 with balance allocation between adaptation and mitigation. Funding for adaptation will be prioritized for the most vulnerable developing countries, such as the least developed countries, small island developing states and Africa. In the context of meaningful mitigation actions and transparency on implementation, developed countries commit to a goal of mobilizing jointly $100 billion a year by 2010 to address the needs of developing countries.

We call for an assessment of the implementation of this Accord to be completed by 2015.

(Copenhagen Accord: Draft Decision CP.15; FCCC/CP/2009/L.7; 18 December 2009)

> China will treat talks on a binding climate change pact in 2010 as a struggle over the 'right to develop', a Chinese foreign ministry official has said … Yi Xianliang said Monday [21 December]: 'The diplomatic and political wrangling over climate change that is opening up will be focused on the right to develop and space to develop' … China has said it should have the formal right to aid even if the most vulnerable countries are the first in line to receive it.
>
> (*IHT*, 22 December 2009, p. 4)

Opinion:

> China 'systematically wrecked' the Copenhagen climate summit because it feared being presented with a legally binding target to cut the country's soaring carbon emissions, a senior official from an EU country, present during the negotiations, told *The Independent on Sunday* … A timetable for making its commitments legally binding by this time next year was taken out at the last minute at the insistence of the Chinese, who otherwise would have refused to agree the deal. Also removed, at Chinese insistence, was a statement of a global goal to cut carbon emissions by 50 per cent by 2050, and for the developed world to cut its emissions by 80 per cent by the same date. The latter is regarded as essential if the world is to stay below the danger level by a 2 degree Centigrade temperature rise. The '50–50' and '50–80' goals have already been accepted by the G-20 group of nations … The European official said: 'China thinks that by 2050 it will be a developed country and they do not want to constrain their growth.'
>
> (www.independent.com, 20 December 2009)

> Some delegates were openly critical of China for its intransigence. Asked by *The Observer* who was to blame for blocking the introduction of controlled emissions, the director-general of the Swedish environmental protection agency, Lars-Erik Liljelund, replied: 'China. China does not like numbers' … Others have criticized the Americans for pushing China too hard.
>
> (www.guardian.co.uk, 20 December 2009)

> In the words of a UK-based analyst … who has attended climate conferences for more than fifteen years … China wants to weaken the climate regulation regime now 'in order to avoid the risk that it might be called on to be more ambitious in a few years' time'.
>
> (www.guardian.co.uk, 23 December 2009)

'China demonstrated its formidable negotiating skills in bringing about an outcome that suits it better than any other nation' (*FT*, 21 December 2009, p. 4).

> The UK Secretary of State for Energy and Climate Change … claimed [on Monday 21 December] that Beijing 'vetoed' moves to give legal force to the accord and blocked an agreement on global reductions in greenhouse emissions. Its delegates even blocked attempts by advanced industrial countries to set a target of an 80 per cent reduction by 2050 for themselves …

Ed Miliband said: 'Some leading developing countries currently refuse to countenance this. That is why we did not secure an agreement that the political accord in Copenhagen should lead to a legally binding outcome. We did not get an agreement on 50 per cent reductions in global emissions by 2050 or on 80 per cent reductions by developed countries. Both were vetoed by China, despite the support of a coalition of developed and the vast majority of developing countries.'

(www.thetimes.com, 21 December 2009)

Yesterday [Monday 21 December] Ed Miliband openly referred to China's obstructionist tactics – first detailed at the weekend in the *Independent on Sunday* – and accused the Chinese of 'hijacking' the Copenhagen summit. He said: 'We did not get an agreement on 50 per cent reductions in global emissions by 2050, or on 80 per cent reductions by developed countries, as both were vetoed by China, despite the support of a coalition of developed and the vast majority of developing countries.'

(*Independent*, 22 December 2009, p. 11)

British climate change minister Edward Miliband singled out Beijing as the culprit behind the talks' near collapse … Miliband wrote in the *Guardian* newspaper Sunday [20 December] that most countries – developed and developing – supported binding cuts in emissions, but that 'some leading developing countries currently refuse to countenance this' … He said: 'We did not get an agreement on 50 per cent reductions in global emissions by 2050 or on 80 per cent reductions by developed countries. Both were vetoed by China, despite the support of a coalition of developed and the vast majority of developing countries. We cannot again allow negotiations on real points of substance to be hijacked in this way.'

(www.iht.com, 22 December 2009)

China, now the world's largest and fastest growing source of global warming pollution, had privately signalled early last year [2009] that if the United States passed meaningful legislation, it would join in serious efforts to produce an effective treaty. When the Senate failed to follow the lead of the House of Representatives, forcing the president to go to Copenhagen without a new law in hand, the Chinese baulked. With the two largest polluters refusing to act, the world community was paralysed.

(Al Gore, *IHT*, 1 March 2010, p. 8)

A senior member of the Chinese negotiating team at Copenhagen has been shifted from his post, prompting speculation that he has been punished for the debacle of the climate talks. He Yafei, who was at the forefront of China's blocking actions on the final fraught day of the summit, has been removed as vice foreign minister … The Hong Kong newspaper *Sing Tao* suggest He Yafei has been punished with a shift to a post at the United Nations for failing to smooth relations between China, the United States and Europe, particularly as tempers flared in the last hours of the talks …

Privately officials are furious at the public relations disaster of the summit, which ended with Europe blaming China for sinking long-term goals to cut greenhouse emissions … European diplomats accused China of 'systematically wrecking the accord' with leaks and obstructionist tactics … But it would be unusual for a Chinese foreign ministry official to be demoted for having a sharp tongue. Standing up strongly to foreigners is normally considered an asset.

(*Guardian*, 6 January 2010, p. 20)

Chinese negotiators achieved their goal at Copenhagen climate talks in ensuring financial aid for developing countries was not linked to external reviews of China's environment plans. Its top climate envoy said today [9 January] … China would never accept outside checks of its plans to slow greenhouse gas emissions and could only make a promise of 'increasing transparency', Xie Zhenhua, deputy head of the powerful National Development and Reform Commission, said at a forum … Xie also said that China was well on track to meeting its goal of cutting energy intensity – or the amount of energy consumed to produce each dollar of national income – by 20 per cent over the five years through 2010. It had already made a 16 per cent cut as of the end of last year [2009], he said. He said: 'As long as we continue to make efforts, we are likely to achieve the targeted 20 per cent cut this year [2010]' … Xie added that China was drafting tough guidelines for reducing the carbon intensity of its growth in its next five year plan for economic development, which will cover the 2011–2015 period. China has pledged to cut the amount of carbon dioxide produced for each unit of economic growth by 40 per cent to 45 per cent, compared with 2005 levels.

(www.independent.co.uk, 9 January 2010)

China's lead climate change negotiator … Xie Zhenhua … speaking in Delhi at a meeting of envoys from Brazil, China, India and South Africa said: 'It is already a solid fact that the climate is warming. There is one starkly different view, that the climate change or climate warming is caused by the cyclical element of nature itself. I think we need to adopt an open attitude to the scientific research … [It is important to include as many views as possible] to be more scientific and to be more consistent' … At their [two-day] weekend gathering the officials said they would announce by the end of the month [January] their plans to cut emissions. They also agreed to contribute $10 billion this year [2010] to help poor nations combat the effects of climate change.

(www.bbc.co.uk, 25 January 2010)

26 December 2009.

China streaked ahead of its Western and Asian rivals at the weekend by unveiling the world's fastest long-distance passenger train service. The *Harmony* express raced 1,100 kilometres in less than three hours on Saturday [26 December], travelling from Guangzhou, capital of southern Guangdong province, to the central city of Wuhan. The journey previously took at least eleven hours ... The *Harmony* express, which reached a top speed of 394 kilometres per hour in pre-launch trails, travelled at an average rate of 350 kilometres per hour on its debut. This compared with a maximum service speed of 300 kilometres per hour for Japan's *Shuinkansen* bullet trains and France's TGV service ... In total the railways ministry intends to complete 18,000 kilometres of high-speed rail lines by 2012, allowing passengers to travel between most Chinese provincial capitals in eight hours or less.

(www.cnn.com, 28 December 2009)

29 December 2009.

The British government condemned China's execution of a British national Tuesday [29 December] on drug smuggling charges. Prime minister Gordon Brown: 'I condemn the execution of Akmal Shaikh in the strongest terms, and am appalled and disappointed that our persistent requests for clemency have not been granted. I am particularly concerned that no mental health assessment was undertaken' ... Akmal Shaikh was convicted of carrying up to 4 kg (8.8 lb) of heroin at Urumqi Airport in September 2007 ... His family and the British government had asked Chinese leaders for clemency. His supporters argued that Shaikh was mentally ill, and that Chinese officials did not take his mental condition into account when trying him. Shaikh's advocates say he suffered from a bipolar disorder and that he was tricked into carrying heroin into China with promises of a career as a pop singer.

(www.cnn.com, 29 December 2009)

A statement issued after the execution said: 'As for his possible mental illness which has been much talked about, there apparently has been no previous medical record' ... A report from Xinhua said that China's Supreme People's Court had not been provided with any documentation proving that Akmal Shaikh had a mental disorder.

(www.bbc.co.uk, 29 December 2009)

British officials pressed the courts to consider Akmal Shaikh's history and mental disturbance. Britain had called on the courts to allow an independent evaluation of Mr Shaikh's mental state ... [There had been] appeals for clemency from his family, human rights groups and British prime minister Gordon Brown ... Xinhua said he was executed by lethal injection ... [Xinhua] said that government officials had determined that there was insufficient evidence that Mr Shaikh had suffered from mental health problems ... Mr Shaikh was born in Pakistan and moved to Britain at age eleven ... Jerome Cohen ... a professor emeritus at New York University School of Law and a specialist in Chinese law ... [says] that the Chinese courts had ignored their own laws because Chinese law 'exempts from criminal responsibility someone unable to recognize or control his misconduct'.

(www.iht.com, 29 December 2009)

According to Western human rights groups, the last European to have been executed in China was an Italian, Antonio Riva, who was shot by firing squad in 1951, along with a Japanese man, Ruichi Yamaguchi, after being convicted of involvement in what China alleged was an American plot to assassinate Mao Zedong and other high ranking communist officials … Amnesty International estimated that at least 1,700 court-ordered executions were carried out in 2008, more than in any other country. Other human rights groups have put the figure much higher, in some cases as high as several thousand.

(www.iht.com, 25 December 2009)

30 December 2009.

One of China's most independent editors today [30 December] announced that she had taken the reins at a prominent general news magazine … Hu Shuli has become the executive editor of *New Century News*, a statement from her company, Caixin Media, said. Most of the staff from *Caijing*, her former publication, had joined her … Insiders say the content will be similar to that of *Caijing*, a financial news magazine which blazed a trail for other media groups by exposing corruption, the cover-up of the SARS epidemic and the construction flaws that led to the collapse of schools during the Sichuan earthquake … her new publisher [is] the China Institute for Reform and Development think-tank … Today's statement said Hu had been appointed as a senior researcher at the institute.

(www.guardian.co.uk, 30 December 2009)

Many of the employees who resigned from *Caijing* had pledged to follow Hu Shuli to a new media venture she was readying. For now that venture consists primarily of *Century Weekly*, which is being published by an independent think-tank called the China Institute for Research and Development. The institute is based in Hainan province, an island off the coast of China. The magazine's first issue has already been published, dated 4 January 2010, with a cover story on inflation in China. The magazine was formerly called the *News* magazine … Ms Hu was recently named dean of the journalism school at Sun Yat-sen University in Guangzhou … A spokeswoman for Caixin Media, a company Ms Hu formed with a group of investors, said the media group was planning other ventures. At *Caijing* Ms Hu had a reputation for pushing her reporters to expose corporate fraud and government corruption. She also helped *Caijing* form a partnership with *The Wall Street Journal* and created an English language website.

(www.iht.com, 31 December 2009)

Hu Shuli … has joined *New Century News*, a previously little-known publication run by the China Institute for Reform and Development, a think-tank based in Hainan … Chi Fulin [president of the think-tank, said of the new weekly magazine]: 'It will still be a general news magazine, instead of a finance magazine like *Caijing*' ... [The launch] comes amid attempts by Beijing to create commercially strong publishing groups while reinforcing its control over the media.

(*FT*, 2 January 2009, p. 16)

8 January 2010.

A lawyer representing an alleged mob boss has been jailed for two-and-a-half years on charges of fabricating evidence in a case that has raised widespread concerns about the rights of lawyers and their clients ... Li Zhuang was accused of instructing his client ... an alleged gang boss accused of murder, arms possession and loan-sharking ... to tell the court that he was tortured by police and of encouraging other witnesses to lie ... Mr Li's trial was linked to a huge crackdown on organized crime and corruption in Chongqing that has seen more than 1,500 arrested since the summer [of 2009] ... [The alleged gang boss] gave evidence to police that he was instructed by his lawyer to claim that he had made a confession only after being tortured.

(*FT*, 9 January 2010, p. 5)

19 January 2010.

A court has sentenced a former Supreme Court judge to life in prison for taking bribes and other corruption charges ... He was deputy head of the Supreme Court ... He was removed from his position on the Supreme People's Court in 2008 ... Huang Songyou is the most senior judge to have been convicted on such charges ... Huang Songyou is the most senior judicial figure to fall since the Communist Party took power in 1949.

(www.bbc.co.uk, 19 January 2010)

25 January 2010.

China's government is reported to have ordered the closure of thousands of 'regional liaison offices' – in essence, lobbying firms – that local governments and companies operate in Beijing to curry favour with high officials ... Beijing officials have vowed to shutter the liaison offices within six months in an effort to staunch what some analysts call a culture of unalloyed corruption surrounding the institutions ... By some calculations Beijing boasts more than 5,500 local government provincial offices, and perhaps 5,000 more offices representing state-run corporations, associations and other entities. The provincial-level offices alone employ close to 8,000 workers, housed in impressive bureaux designed to convey the power and prestige of the areas they represent. The central government directive would close the offices of state-run firms and governments below the county level. The survivors would be strictly regulated ... Local government corruption is a common subject of attack by local journalists and internet surfers. But, with some exceptions, higher-level corruption has largely been excluded from government campaigns ... China's central government has been talking since at least 2006 about reining in the offices, with little success.

One problem is that offices represent China's provinces, which are also represented on … the Central Committee of the Chinese Communist Party.

(www.iht.com, 25 January 2010)

26 January 2010.

Huge changes in the world's scientific landscape are revealed in an analysis of the output of the four Bric (Brazil, Russia, India and China] countries since 1981, carried out for the *FT* by Thompson Reuters, which indexes papers from 10,500 research journals worldwide … China has experienced the strongest growth in scientific research over the past three decades of any country … and the pace shows no sign of slowing … China's 'awe-inspiring' growth means it is now the second largest producer of scientific knowledge – and is on course to overtake the United States by 2020 if it continues on its present trajectory … Although its quality remains mixed, Chinese research has also become more collaborative, with almost 9 per cent of papers originating in China having at least one US-based author.

(*FT*, 26 January 2010, pp. 1, 3)

27 January 2010. 'On Wednesday [27 January] the government announced the creation of a National Energy Commission composed of cabinet members as a "super-ministry" led by prime minister Wen Jiabao' (www.iht.com, 30 January 2010).

13 February 2010.

The former chairman of one of China's largest electronics companies has been charged with insider trading, offering bribes and running illegal operations … Huang Guangyu's case was sent to the Beijing Municipal Second Intermediate People's Court for trial, and the people accused of being his accomplices have also been indicted, China News Service said Saturday [13 February] without identifying those people. The charges against Mr Huang had long been expected. He has been in detention since November 2008 … The long-standing scandal over Mr Huang's alleged activities has already tarnished the careers of a series of officials. Zhu Ying, the former director of the Shanghai Municipal Public Security Bureau, was expelled from the municipal discipline inspection committee of the Communist Party last December [2009]. The committee issued a statement at the time saying … that he had been stripped of his membership in connection with the investigation of Mr Huang. The investigation of Mr Huang has also resulted in further reviews at the Ministry of Public Security of how the ministry's economic crimes section had handled the affair, according to Xinhua, which is larger than China News Service. Before his arrest Mr Huang had been one of the wealthiest people in China, with *Forbes* magazine estimating his wealth at $2.7 billion and the *Hurun Report*, which also keeps track of the wealth of Chinese business leaders, estimating that he was worth $6.3 billion.

(www.iht.com, 14 February 2010)

Huang Guangyu, founder of Gome, China's largest electronics retail chain and once the country's richest man, has been indicted on charges of bribery, illegal business dealings and insider trading ... The reported charges confirm concerns that Mr Huang could face much harsher treatment than initially expected. The case is being closely watched as a benchmark for the legal position on private entrepreneurs in China. Mr Huang was detained in late 2008 on what was initially identified as suspicions of share manipulation. But over the past year several officials – including a former deputy minister of public security and a former deputy Shanghai police chief – have been unseated as investigators accused them of corruption in relation to Huang's case ... The formal indictment moves the case closer to a trial at a time when China's private entrepreneurs are under increasing political pressure. A recent opinion poll conducted by *People's Daily*, the Communist Party's mouthpiece, said a majority of respondents viewed individuals or families who gained wealth over the past decades of economic reform as 'corrupt'. Only 16 per cent of respondents thought their wealth was a result of wisdom or hard work. Mr Huang has already spent more than fourteen months in prison awaiting formal charges – ending what was one of China's most spectacular rags-to-riches stories. Born the son of a poor farmer in Guangdong, Mr Huang started with his brother, selling batteries and radios bought from factories in the manufacturing base of Beijing. From there he built up Gome, a company that is now China's leading electronics retailer. In 2008 Mr Huang topped the *Hurun* list of the richest people in China with an estimated net worth of $6.3 billion. But in early 2009 Mr Huang and a number of other executives resigned from their posts and have since lost control of the company.

(*FT*, 15 February 2010, p. 21)

24 February 2010.

The Communist Party has issued a new fifty-two-point ethics code, in an attempt to control growing corruption among officials. The code bans members from property speculation, money-making deals and lavish expenditure. The last set of rules was issued thirteen years ago ... Party officials should work hard to serve the people and avoid accepting gifts or using their influence to benefit family members, according to the new ethics code. The guide bans lavish weddings and funerals, and overseas tours. Officials should also stay out of profit-making deals ... Spending lavish amounts on government buildings or flash cars is also banned.

(www.bbc.co.uk, 24 February 2010)

1 March 2010.

The president of the Japanese car company Toyota, Akio Toyoda, has apologized to customers in China, the world's biggest auto market. Mr Toyoda travelled to Beijing after his high profile appearance before angry US lawmakers last month [February] ... Toyota's share of the Chinese car market is small compared to that of most of its rivals, about 5 per cent of the country's total auto sales. It has recalled just over 75,000 vehicles here [in China] because of concerns over faulty accelerators, a tiny fraction of the 8.5 million recalls worldwide ... Worries over quality have damaged Toyota's sales elsewhere. The company's sales here [in China] have held steady in recent weeks.

(www.bbc.co.uk, 1 March 2010)

The president of Toyota, Akio Toyoda, apologized Monday [1 March] to customers in China, the fast growing market that has become increasingly important to automakers as they struggle with weak global sales. The number of Toyota vehicles recalled in China makes up only a small percentage of the 8.5 million pulled worldwide since October [2009] for sticky gas pedals, faulty floor mats and glitches in braking software ... China's state-controlled media have made only muted comment on the recalls, in contrast to the blistering criticism Toyoda faced from American lawmakers. The flood of recalls in the United States has shaken confidence in Toyota's reputation for excellent quality. In China the company announced a recall of 75,552 RAV4 sport-utility vehicles in late January [2010] because of the gas pedal problem ... Toyota got a relatively late start in China after fitful efforts to break into the market using tie-ups between its subsidiary Daihatsu Motor and state-run Tianjin Automobile Industry Holding Co. Toyota rolled out its first made-in-China Camry in May 2006. Sales growth lagged behind other foreign brands last year [2010] because of Toyota's focus on bigger cars while the government promoted smaller vehicles with tax breaks and subsidies. Toyota sales rose 50 per cent, compared with 76 per cent for Volkswagen and 219 per cent for the Chevrolet unit in General Motors [GM]. Toyota is preparing to release a lower cost brand for China in response to demand for smaller cars. In August [2009] its joint venture with FAW recalled nearly 690,000 Camry and Yaris passenger cars after finding problems with electric window controls. There was no apparent effect on sales.

(www.iht.com, 1 March 2010)

2 March 2010.

Identical editorials appeared Monday [1 March] in more than a dozen publications calling for reform of China's household registration system ... that ties government benefits to a person's home town ... The editorials declared: 'China has suffered for a long time under the *hukou* system. We believe in people born to be free and people possessing the right to migrate freely' ... But a few hours later the editorials had largely vanished from the internet ... The short-lived proclamations, published by a mix of thirteen big-city newspapers, financial publications and regional dailies ... [The] issue has bedevilled the Communist Party since Mao established the *hukou* system to prevent famine-stricken peasants from flooding the wealthier cities.

(www.iht.com, 2 March 2010)

> The editorial also said: 'The National People's Congress deputies and Chinese People's Political Consultative Conference National Committee members should press related ministries to provide a clear timetable for a national household registration reform and gradually use personal information to replace household registration and then finally eliminate it ... Reform of this system would not only benefit people's livelihoods, but would also reject more vitality into the Chinese economy. More importantly, it would set up the people-orientated awareness, which would push social progress and harmony.'
>
> (www.cnn.com, 12 March 2010)

'In a highly unusual campaign on 1 March a dozen publications ran identical editorials ... The household registration system discriminates against rural Chinese' (*The Economist*, 6 March 2010, p. 71).

'The government wants to encourage rural dwellers to move to smaller cities in their own provinces' (*Guardian*, 2 March 2010, p. 19).

> In recent years there have been a number of small pilot projects that have experimented with reform [of the *hukou* system] in the cities of Chengdu, Chongqing and Wuhan and parts of Guangdong and Zhejiang provinces. In some cases the schemes have operated a swap where farmers have given up their land in return of a city *hukou* ... These schemes usually apply only to rural residents who move to the nearest town or city ... Beijing said in 2004 that migrant families should get access to city schools, but without any new revenue to pay for this; only a few cities such as Shanghai have implemented this policy.
>
> (*FT*, 5 March 2010, p. 9)

'Most of the roughly 200 million migrants working in the urban centres cannot register as city residents, thus depriving them of schooling for their children, income support and subsidized housing' (*FT*, 8 March 2010, p. 12).

> Pilot programmes are underway in more than ten cities, including Shanghai, Shenzhen and Guangzhou in south China, where governments have started to grant permanent residency and access to social welfare to non-residents working and living in the cities ... Official estimates put the total 'floating population' at around 180 million last year [2009].
>
> (www.cnn.com, 12 March 2010)

3 March 2010.

> The Heavenly Palace, the first module in China's permanent space station, will be launched next year [2011], a senior aerospace official confirmed Wednesday [3 March] ... The craft, an orbiting laboratory known in Mandarin as *Tiangong-1*, would initially serve as a docking station for other spacecraft ... The China National Space Administration said it plans three docking missions with the lab next year. The space agency's long-range plans include a 20-tonne permanent space station that will incorporate

Tiangong-1, as well as a separate lunar mission by 2022. China successfully launched its first satellite in April 1970, a craft called *Dong Fang Hong-1*, or 'The East is Red', which was sent into orbit by a Long March-1 rocket. China's first manned spacecraft went aloft in October 2003 and made fourteen orbits of the Earth. The country's first spacewalk took place eighteen months ago ... [China] tested an anti-satellite system in 2007, using a ballistic missile to shoot down one of its own weather satellites 540 miles up.

(www.iht.com, 3 March 2010; *IHT*, 4 March 2010, p. 4)

4 March 2010.

[On 4 March] China said its military spending will increase by 7.5 per cent in 2010, ending a long run of double-digit growth. It will spend 532.1 billion yuan ($77.9 billion) over the year ... According to Chinese figures, this is the first time in more than twenty years that the military budget increase has dipped below 10 per cent. The spending spree began in the late 1980s, when China embarked on an ambitious programme to update its armed forces. Since then it has bought and produced its own high-tech weapons, and reduced the number of personnel in an attempt to have fewer, but better trained, troops.

(www.bbc.co.uk, 4 March 2010)

China's official military budget will rise by just 7.5 per cent in 2010, a government spokesman said on Thursday [4 March], a rate that is about half the increase in recent years and the first single-digit rise in military spending since 1989 ... A budget report submitted to the legislature said the government had earmarked 531.1 billion renminbi (about $77.9 billion) for the military in 2010, an increase of about $5.4 billion from actual spending last year [2009]. Military spending in 2009 had been forecast to expand by 14.9 per cent over the 2008 total, but Reuters reported that spending grew at a slightly greater rate because the military spent about $2 billion more than anticipated. While China's government has disclosed more information about military spending in recent years, most of its spending plans remain secret. The Pentagon's 2009 report on the Chinese military estimated total spending to be between $105 billion and $150 billion, and said that spending had risen an average of 12.9 per cent annually from 1996 to 2008. Even the highest estimates, however, are dwarfed by US military expenses, which accounted for 48 per cent of the entire world's military spending in 2008, according to the Center for Arms Control and Non-Proliferation. American military spending amounts to about 4 per cent of the nation's GDP, compared to about 1.4 per cent for China ... The growth in China's military spending has swung sharply in recent years – it grew by 11.6 per cent in 2004, but 17.8 per cent three years later, in 2007 – but the 2010 figure marks the first time in twenty-one years that the rate of increase has fallen below double digits.

(www.iht.com, 4 March 2010; *IHT*, 5 March 2010, p. 5)

> A spokesman for the National People's Congress said ... defence spending had accounted for about 1.4 per cent of GDP in recent years, as opposed to more than 4 per cent in the United States and more than 2 per cent in Britain, France and Russia ... The People's Liberation Army [is] the world's largest standing military with more than 2.3 million members.
>
> (*Guardian*, 5 March 2010, p. 22)

'A spokesman for the National People's Congress said ... defence expenditure accounted for 6.3 per cent of the whole budget, suggesting the growth of total government spending would slow compared with last year [2009]' (*FT*, 5 March 2010, p. 9).

> The slower growth in [military] spending surprised international analysts who had forecast a rise in the region of 14.5 per cent, slightly less than last year [2009] ... [According to Western estimates] US spending as a proportion of the world's military budget [is] 45.7 per cent ... China's spending [amounts to] 4.3 per cent.
>
> (*The Times*, 5 March 2010, p. 35)

> The budget report ... said military spending would be 519 billion yuan ($76 billion) this year [2010] ... This year's projected growth would be only 1,2 percentage points higher than the budgeted increase in overall central government spending, a far narrower gap than in previous years ... The Pentagon last year [2009] ... estimated ... that China's actual military spending in 2008 was between $105 billion and $150 billion, compared with an officially declared budget of $60 billion that year.
>
> (www.economist.com, 5 March 2010)

5 March 2010. The opening session of the National People's Congress took place on 5 March. '[There were] 2,987 delegates to the National People's Congress' (*IHT*, 5 March 2010, p. 5).

'Associated Press reported that two dozen people who hoped to petition officials for redress of grievances or who raised suspicion were bundled into a police bus and driven away from the area' (www.guardian.co.uk, 5 March 2010).

'Beijing police have rounded up beggars and out-of-town petitioners who travel to Beijing to seek redress. Dissidents and civil rights activists have been placed under house arrest to pre-empt protests' (www.cnn.com, 6 March 2010).

'The Chinese People's Political Consultative Conference (CPPCC) [is] an advisory body that holds a meeting at the same time as the legislative session' (www.bbc.co.uk, 4 March 2010).

'The Chinese People's Political Consultative Conference (CPPCC) [is an] advisory body ... [with] 2,374 delegates ... China has eight democratic parties, but their leadership, operations and funding are all provided by the Communist Party' (*FT*, 4 March 2010, p. 7).

'The Chinese People's Political Consultative Conference (CPPCC) [is] a 2,252-member body that advises Communist Party leaders' (*IHT*, 4 March 2010, p. 4).

Bo Xilai [is] the popular … mafia-busting Communist Party chief in the south-western city of Chongqing … At sixty, Bo Xilai is comparatively young … He has been a big-city mayor, provincial governor and trade tsar … It is an open secret that Mr Bo is seeking promotion to the powerful nine-member Politburo Standing Committee.

(*Independent*, 8 March 2010, p. 26)

Bo Xilai [is] the Communist Party boss of Chongqing city in central China. For the past six months Mr Bo has been on a crusade that has won him countless headlines and stirred up a political hornets' nest in Beijing. The Chongqing government has been conducting an all-out campaign against organized crime that has led to more than 3,000 arrests – including that of the leading judicial official – and prompted calls for similar action across the country … Last summer [2009] the first arrests were made in a crack-down called an 'anti-Triad tornado' … One of the most high profile arrests was of Xie Caiping, known as the 'godmother of the Chongqing under-world' because of her network of casinos, one of which was based across the road from the supreme court … The trials revealed the extent of alleged ties between gangsters and the local government, especially the arrest of Wen Qiang, a former police chief and head of the city's judicial bureau, who happens to be the brother-in-law of Ms Xie. [He was] the most senior of the more than fifty government officials arrested … [Bo Xilai] became well known in the 1990s as mayor of Dalian city, then governor of Liaoning province, both in the north-east, before moving to Beijing as commerce secretary in 2004 … At a 2007 party congress he saw two members of his own generation ['fifth generation'] promoted to the nine-man Standing Committee … Xi Jinping [is] expected to take over from Hu Jintao in 2012–13; and Li Keqiang [is] expected to become premier. … Mr Bo was appointed party secretary of the fast-growing municipality Chongqing … The Chongqing anti-corruption campaign has embarrassed parts of the political elite. He Guoqiang, a member of the Standing Committee [head of party discipline], is a former Chongqing party boss, as is Wang Yang, now in charge of Guangdong province … Both now face questions about why they let organized crime fester. It has also created problems for President Hu Jintao … Around the country there have been demands for Chongqing-style crack-downs on gangsters and their political allies. Not only has the campaign made Beijing's anti-corruption drives seem toothless, the revelations at Wen Qiang's trial that party promotions are bought and sold has created yet more popular pressure for action … Recent newspaper articles suggest the campaign against Chongqing's gangsters is winding down.

(*FT*, 10 March 2010, p. 13)

In a major speech at the start of China's annual parliamentary session [on 5 March] … premier Wen Jiabao said China must reverse its widening income gap between rich and poor … [He] also said the economy needed restructuring. He wants Chinese firms to improve their ability to innovate, producing high-tech and high quality products ... He said: 'We will not only make the pie of social wealth bigger by developing the economy, but also distribute it well ... [We will] resolutely reverse the widening income gap' ... As part of that project, the premier said China would reform the household registration system that classifies people as either city or rural dwellers ... He said: '[We will] gradually ensure that they [migrant workers] receive the same treatment as urban residents in areas such as pay, children's education, healthcare, housing and social security' ... He said reforms would only be carried out in towns and smaller cities ... Premier Wen said China needed to concentrate on restructuring the economy. He said: 'This is crucial for ... accelerating the transformation of the pattern of economic development' ... He wants future growth to be fuelled by innovation. China should also expand consumer demand by getting people to spend on such things as tourism, fitness and other services ... Many people across China are currently concerned about rising house prices that mean many cannot afford a home. Mr Wen said China would do something about it.

(www.bbc.co.uk, 5 March 2010)

Premier Wen Jiabao promised increased spending on welfare and rural areas, aiming to halt the growth of the gap between rich and poor, maintain stability and spur domestic demand. His annual policy speech set a steady course for the country – with a growth target of 8 per cent, as in previous years – but left the government room for flexibility as he cautioned that the global economic outlook remained uncertain ... The 11.4 per cent increase will take total spending to 8.45 trillion yuan, but is less than half of last year's 24 per cent rise ... He said: 'We must not interpret the economic turnaround as a fundamental improvement in the economic situation. There are insufficient internal drivers of economic growth ... We can ensure that there is sustained impetus for economic development, a solid foundation for social progress, and lasting stability for the country only by working hard to ensure and improve people's well-being' ... In an online chat on Saturday [27 February] he said that a society was 'doomed to instability' if wealth was concentrated in the hands of a few. Today's [5 March] two-hour speech announced increases of 8.8 per cent on social spending and 12.8 per cent on rural programmes – well above the unexpectedly low 7.5 per cent rise in the military budget announced yesterday [4 March] ... He reiterated Beijing's pledge to keep its currency basically steady ... Wen Jiabao also said Beijing would maintain an appropriately easy monetary stance and an active fiscal policy. He set the inflation target at around 3 per cent and said the [budget] deficit would be kept below 3 per cent of national income. He pledged to curb the 'precipitous rises in housing prices' in some cities ... The government will boost funding for low income housing by 14.8 per cent ... The premier said ... a special effort would be made to raise living standards of minority ethnic communities.

(www.guardian.co.uk, 5 March 2010)

> Prime minister Wen Jiabao said Friday [5 March] that the nation would expand social spending, bolster lending, curb inflation and meet its traditional 8 per cent growth target in 2010, but he cautioned that China still confronted 'a very complex situation' in the wake of the global financial crisis ... Mr Wen said that 'destabilizing factors and uncertainties' in the world economy posed a challenge to China's continued growth. But he effectively said that China's plan to ease away from last year's [2009] enormous stimulus programme ... would continue unchanged ... China managed an 8.7 per cent increase in its GDP ... He pledged to clamp down on speculative real estate purchases, which some analysts say are creating a bubble in China's housing market. He also said the state would take measures to rein in an explosive rise in urban land prices. He warned that some Chinese industries ... had developed serious overcapacity problems. And even as he committed to expand the nation's money supply by 17 per cent this year [2010], increasing lending by 7.5 trillion renminbi ($1.1 trillion). Mr Wen warned that 'latent risks in the banking and public finance sectors are increasing' ... Mr Wen said the government would run a budget deficit of $154 billion in 2010, which is in line with economists' expectations. As a share of GDP the projected deficit is unchanged from last year [2009]. Overall, spending will rise about 11.4 per cent this year [2010], half of the increase in spending during the recession last year ... Last year, he said, the government's stimulus measures helped increase auto sales by 46.2 per cent, housing by 42.1 per cent, as measured in square metres, and retail sales of consumer goods by 16 per cent Mr Wen said that China would pour money into strategic industries, increasing research and development and infrastructure spending to 'capture the economic, scientific and technological high ground'. Among the areas he singled out were biomedicine, energy conservation, information technology and high-end manufacturing ... Mr Wen pledged to increase environmental protection measures ... Wen Jiabao: 'At the same time as we keep our reforms orientated toward a market economy, let market forces play their basic role in allocating resources and stimulate the market's vitality, we must make best use of the socialist system's advantages, which enable us to make decisions efficiently, organize effectively and concentrate resources to accomplish large undertakings.'
>
> (www.iht.com, 5 March 2010)

'Premier Wen Jiabao said the government hopes to hold overall consumer price rises to 3 per cent this year [2010]' (www.iht.com, 11 March 2010).

> China's economy, prime minister Wen Jiabao said, in a two-hour speech, had been the first in the world to make a turnaround ... He spoke of socialism's 'advantages': quick decision-making, effective organization and an ability to 'concentrate resources to accomplish large undertakings' ... China's economic planning agency, the National Development and Reform Commission, acknowledged in a report to the National People's Congress that house prices were 'overheating' in some cities, consumer spending was unlikely to grow

significantly this year [2010] and the effect of stimulus measures 'might wear off'. Yet the government says it wants to keep the budget deficit to 2.8 per cent of GDP this year, about the same as last year [2009].

(www.economist.com, 5 March 2010)

Premier Wen Jiabao … said that to meet the target of 8 per cent growth, Beijing would maintain a 'proactive fiscal policy and moderately easy monetary policy' … He said: 'The launching of new projects must be strictly controlled … [Government investment] should be used mainly for carrying on and completing projects' … Mr Wen also warned that 'latent risks in the banking and public finance sectors are increasing' … Mr Wen, who last week referred to property markets in some cities as being like a 'wild horse', said the government would increase spending on low-income housing and rein in property speculation … He said: 'We will resolutely curb the precipitous rise of housing prices in some cities' … The budget deficit is forecast to be 2.8 per cent of GDP this year [2010], compared with 2.2 per cent of GDP in 2009 … [There is] a marked slowdown in the rate of growth of government spending, from 21 per cent last year [2009] to 11 per cent this year.

(*FT*, 6 March 2010, p. 7)

'There was still "insufficient internal impetus driving economic growth"' (*FT*, 8 March 2010, p. 12).

Premier Wen Jiabao … said the exchange rate would remain 'basically stable at an appropriate and balanced level' … The premier announced a series of measures to help small and medium-sized companies, including tax breaks and bank guarantees.

(www.cnn.com, 6 March 2010)

In his annual work report at the National People's Congress session, premier Wen Jiabao pledged to solve employment and living problems that rural residents face in the cities in a 'planned and step-by-step manner'. He also promised to 'ensure that they receive the same treatment as urban residents in areas such as pay, children's education, health care, housing and social security'.

(www.cnn.com, 12 March 2010)

'About 140 million rural migrants are now working in the cities' (*Guardian*, 15 March 2010, p. 21).

[On Saturday 6 March] the central bank head, Zhou Xiaochuan, said China should be 'very cautious' about revaluing the yuan as long as major economies remained mired in slow growth. He called China's practice of pegging the renminbi to the dollar a 'special foreign exchange mechanism' made to respond to the world financial crisis. Such mechanisms will be abandoned 'sooner or later', he said, but 'we must be very cautious and discreet in choosing the timing' … Mr Zhou offered no timetable for allowing the renminbi to resume its rise against the dollar, but he noted that it could take two or three years for global export markets to recover from the financial

> collapse ... A slowdown in exports did shave roughly 4 percentage points off the growth rate of China's GDP last year [2009], economists say. But the currency stabilization and a large stimulus programme kept China's economy on track so that it exceeded the 8 per cent target that the government has set for economic growth in 2009.
>
> (www.iht.com, 7 March 2010; *IHT*, 8 March 2010, p. 19)

> China's central bank chief Zhou Xiaochuan (6 March): 'This is part of our package for dealing with the global financial crisis. Sooner or later we will exit the policies. If we say we withdraw from non-conventional policy and return to conventional economic policy, we must be very cautious and discreet in choosing the timing. This also includes the renminbi exchange rate policy' ... Chen Deming, commerce minister, said the outlook for international trade remained 'uncertain and unstable' and it would take two or three years before Chinese exports recovered to pre-crisis levels.
>
> (*FT*, 8 March 2010, p. 6)

Prime minister Wen Jiabao (speaking on 14 March, the final day of the annual session of the National People's Congress):

> I do not think the renminbi is undervalued. We oppose all countries engaging in mutual finger-pointing or taking strong measures to force other nations to appreciate their currencies. That is not in the interest of reform of the renminbi or the renminbi's exchange rate regime. We will continue to reform the renminbi exchange rate regime and will keep the renminbi basically stable at an appropriate and balanced level. Since the outbreak of the international financial crisis, we have made strong efforts to keep the renminbi exchange rate at a stable level. This has played an important role in facilitating the global economy ... [Protecting the dollar is a matter of] national credibility [for the United States]. Any fluctuation in the value of the US currency is a big concern for us ... We are very concerned about the lack of stability in the US dollar ... In the press conference last year I said I was a bit concerned [about the security of US Treasuries that China holds] ... This year I make the same remark. I am still concerned. We cannot afford any mistake, however slight, when it comes to financial assets ... I hope the United States will take concrete measures to reassure international investors ... It is not only in the interests of the investors, but also the United States itself ... I understand some economies want to increase their exports, but what I do not understand is the practice of depreciating one's own currency and attempting to force other countries to appreciate their own currencies, just for the purpose of increasing their own exports. In my view that is a protectionist measure. All countries should be fully alarmed by such developments.
>
> (www.iht.com, 14 March 2010; www.bbc.co.uk, 14 March 2010; www.guardian.co.uk, 14 March 2010; www.cnn.com, 14 March 2010; www.ft.com, 14 March 2010; www.thetimes.co.uk, 14 March 2010; *IHT*, 15 March 2010, pp. 1, 16; *FT*, 15 March 2010, p. 1)

> Prime minister Wen Jiabao argued that the renminbi is not unfairly valued, citing government calculations that suggested that, measured in real terms, China's currency had actually risen in value at the height of the economic crisis ... Analysts expect Beijing to let the yuan rise against the dollar some time this year [2010]. But they foresee a gradual increase of no more than 5 per cent this year.
>
> (www.iht.com, 14 March 2010; *IHT*, 15 March 2010, p. 16)

> Prime minister Wen Jiabao pointed out that around half of China's exports were processing trade – where imported components are assembled at factories in China – and 60 per cent were made by foreign companies or joint ventures with a foreign partner. He said: 'If you restrict trade with China, you are hurting your own countries' firms.'
>
> (www.ft.com, 14 March 2010; *FT*, 15 March 2010, p. 1)

> Prime minister Wen Jiabao insisted that inflation must be managed while maintaining rapid economic growth and carrying out state-led economic restructuring, a goal that he conceded would be 'extremely difficult' ... Prime minister Wen Jiabao: 'If there is inflation, plus unfair income distribution and corruption, that could be strong enough to affect social stability and even the consolidation of state power ... It will be an extremely difficult task for us to promote steady and fast economic growth, adjust our economic structure and manage inflation expectations all at the same time, but it is imperative for us to accomplish these three tasks' ... Mr Wen said other countries faced the prospect of inflation, which he said was a big factor contributing to the risk of a double-dip global recession. Mr Wen said: 'As a result of inflation expectations, some countries are facing difficulties in making the right policy decisions. Should we encounter setbacks [in China's economic recovery] much is at stake and the cost will be too high ... [China aims to maintain an] appropriate and sufficient money supply, keep our interest rates at a reasonable level and manage inflation expectations.'
>
> (*FT*, 15 March 2010, p. 8)

'Inflation in February was higher than expected but not by enough to force a change in strategy, the central bank governor, Zhou Xiaochuan, said Sunday [14 March]' (*IHT*, 15 March 2010, p. 17).

9 March 2010.

> China and India formally agreed Tuesday [9 March] to join the international climate change agreement reached last December [2009] in Copenhagen, the last two major economies to sign up. The two countries ... submitted letters to the United Nations agreeing to be included on a list of countries covered by the so-called Copenhagen Accord, a three-page non-binding statement reached at the end of the contentious and chaotic ten-day conference. China and India join more than 100 countries that have signed up under the accord, which calls for limiting the rise in global temperatures to

> no more than 2 degrees Celsius (3.6 degrees Fahrenheit) beyond pre-industrial levels. The agreement also calls for spending as much as $100 billion a year to help emerging countries adapt to climate change and develop low-carbon energy systems, accelerated energy technology transfers to the developing world and steps to protect tropical forests from destruction … Virtually all major economies, including China and India, have already submitted emissions reductions targets to be inscribed in the accord, although there is no legal obligation for individual countries to meet them. Analysts who have studied the pledges find that they fall short of the overall goal of the agreement but would make a substantial dent in the greenhouse gas emissions … Negotiators are trying to write an enforceable global climate treaty, but there is little expectation that such an agreement will be reached this year [2010] … The next UN climate summit meeting [is] to be held beginning in late November [2010] in Cancun, Mexico.
>
> (www.iht.com, 9 March 2010)

> A top editor of a weekly newspaper who recently called for the reform of China's household registration system … has been forced out of his job … Zhang Hong had been deputy editor-in-chief of the website of the *Economic Observer*, which is based in Beijing … In a letter published Tuesday [9 March] on the website of *The Wall Street Journal*, Mr Zhang wrote that 'I was punished accordingly; other colleagues and media partners also felt repercussions'. He also wrote in the letter that his editorial had been 'the product of a few editors working behind closed doors, but the stir it created went beyond our initial expectations'. On 1 March Mr Zhang's newspaper and a dozen other Chinese publications published his editorial, asserting that the registration system unfairly restricts the right of Chinese citizens to seek a better life outside their home towns. The editorial proclaimed: 'We believe in people born to be free and people possessing the right to migrate freely' … The editorial vanished from the internet within hours … The editorial on the registration of households [was published] by thirteen big-city newspapers, financial publications and regional dailies.
>
> (www.iht.com, 9 March 2010)

15 March 2010.

> A small group of artists who held a daring protest in the heart of Beijing against forced evictions last month [February] is getting compensation for giving up claims to property, a representative of the artists said Monday [15 March] … The nearly two dozen artists only got 500 yards before security forces broke up the protest, according to Ai Weiwei, a prominent artist who, though not threatened with eviction, was among the protesters … Forced evictions have provoked a growing number of protests across China, especially in rural areas.
>
> (www.iht.com, 15 March 2010; *IHT*, 16 March 2010, p. 2)

('Nearly two dozen artists protesting the forced demolition of their homes and studios marched through the ceremonial heart of the capital before the police intervened and prevented them from reaching Tiananmen Square. The protesters said they decided to take to the streets on Monday [22 February] hours after scores of masked men swinging iron rods swarmed over their community on the northern edge of the city, which has been resisting redevelopment … [It was claimed that] the attackers … had been sent by developers who wanted to clear the area for a large-scale residential project … Ai Weiwei, an artist and dissident who joined the demonstration … [said the march made] only about 500 yards before the police intervened … The course of development threatens at least ten clusters of studios where artists live and work on the fringes of the city … [The] two adjacent art districts that were the scene of the early morning protest [are] known as Zheng Yang and 008 … many artists are furious because they were lured to the villages with long-term leases – some for nearly twenty years – and encouraged to invest their life savings in renovations … The fight over the future of Beijing's artists coincides with soaring real estate values and ugly scuffles over land expropriation, several of which have led to the suicides of those facing eviction': www.iht.com, 23 February 2010.)

Postscript

Taiwan

1 May 2010.

> A scheduled flight from Taipei to Shanghai was diverted to a nearby Chinese airport [Hangzhou] on Saturday [1 May] after a passenger told cabin crew his luggage contained explosives ... Nothing was found ... China and Taiwan began regular direct flights in 2008 after newly inaugurated President Ma Ying-jeou moved to reverse his predecessor's pro-independence policies in favour of closer ties with the mainland. ... There are now some 270 weekly flights between the sides.
>
> (www.iht.com, 1 May 2010)

> A fifty-eight-year-old American man forced a China Airlines jet to divert a flight to Shanghai ... after he told a flight attendant that he had a bomb in his luggage ... A search of the plane and the 297 passengers' luggage turned up no explosives ... The American man ... identified only by his surname Lin ... was travelling on an American passport ... He later told the authorities that he was joking ... Shanghai is hosting a world exhibition [World Expo] ... Chinese authorities have taken extraordinary security measures to avert incidents in Shanghai as the Expo 2010 began on Friday [30 April]. The government even sealed China's borders with ... Kyrgyzstan and. Kazakhstan, ... some 2,300 miles from the Expo site.
>
> (www.iht.com, 2 May 2010)

4 May 2010. 'Taiwan set up its first government office in China yesterday [4 May] ... [namely] a Taiwan tourist office in Beijing' (*The Independent*, 5 May 2010, p. 37).

> In recent years Taiwan has watched as rivals like South Korea have signed free-trade deals in Asia ... Taiwan has been hampered in negotiating similar agreements because Beijing views the island as a part of China and objects to other countries signing formal treaties that could strengthen Taiwan's claims to independence. The island has trade deals with only five Latin American countries, which buy a tiny slice of its exports. The Ma Ying-jeou

administration argues that the ... Economic Co-operation Framework Agreement being negotiated [with China] ... would be a prelude to similar deals with Malaysia, Singapore and, eventually, Japan or the United States ... Taiwan has invested $150 billion in China since the early 1990s, according to a Taiwan government estimate. About 40 per cent of Taiwan's exports go to China, where they face average tariffs of 9 per cent. Half of those exports to China are semi-finished goods that are shipped to factories for assembly and other value-added services and then re-exported, according to Mr Ma ... Mr Ma's government ... [insists] that the deal would not allow mainland workers into Taiwan or remove restrictions on mainland agricultural imports – at least at first.

(www.iht.com, 12 May 2010; *IHT*, 13 May 2010, p. 16)

Hong Kong

A by-election is under way aimed at putting pressure on mainland China to speed up the move to full democracy. Five activists triggered the vote by resigning their posts in the Legislative Council (Lego) in January [2010]. The activists want universal suffrage for the election of Hong Kong's chief executive and representatives. However, correspondents say their move has been rendered almost meaningless by the refusal of pro-Beijing candidates to contest the by-election seats. The five legislators are from two small pro-democracy parties [one being the Civic Party] ... The chief executive and other senior government figures have announced that they will not vote on Sunday [16 May]. But Hong Kong's former deputy leader Anson Chan has backed the election ... Voter turnout is expected to be only about 25 per cent for a poll that has been criticised as a waste of taxpayers' money.

(www.bbc.co.uk, 16 May 2010)

All five pro-democracy lawmakers won reelection on Sunday [16 May] in legislative by-elections in Hong Kong that were marked by a low voter turnout. The five lawmakers, one in each of Hong Kong's five multi-seat geographic constituencies, triggered the by-elections by resigning their seats on the Legislative Council in January. Their goal was to trigger what they described as an informal referendum on democracy, by campaigning during the by-election for the introduction of full democracy in Hong Kong in 2012. But the lawmakers came from only two of the city's pro-democracy parties, with the other three parties – including the largest, the Democratic Party – questioning whether the by-elections were worthwhile. Pro-Beijing parties declined to enter candidates in the by-elections while the Hong Kong government criticised them as an inefficient use of resources ... The voter turnout was 17.1 per cent, as each of the pro-democracy candidates trounced fringe candidates. The Hong Kong government is drafting legislation to adjust electoral procedures in 2012 in ways that may provide some increase in popular participation; it has also promised more democratic procedures

> for the election of the chief executive in 2017 and the legislature in 2010. Democracy advocates have said that the plans for 2012 do not go far enough.
>
> (www.iht.com, 17 May 2010)

> The 17 per cent turnout was way below the 30 per cent the five main candidates wanted. But they still toasted their victory saying 500,000 of the city's people had voted to show they cared about democracy ... Chief Executive Donald Tsang refused to vote in the poll, as did other government leaders ... The only senior figure to openly support the by-election was Catholic Cardinal Joseph Zen.
>
> (www.bbc.co.uk, 17 May 2010)

> A Chinese official on Wednesday [26 May] met with a second group of Hong Kong democracy activists as Beijing stepped up lobbying for its plan to allow only limited political changes in the territory. The meeting between the Chinese official, Li Gang, and the Alliance for Universal Suffrage came two days after the first official contact between Beijing and Hong Kong's leading opposition party, the Democratic Party. Mr Li, deputy director of the Chinese government's liaison office in Hong Kong, met the chairman and deputy chairwoman of the Democratic Party on Monday [24 May] in an unprecedented outreach to a group that Beijing traditionally views as troublemakers.
>
> (*IHT*, 27 May 2010, p. 6)

> Last Friday night [4 June] ... more than 100,000 people gathered in a park in Hong Kong to commemorate the twenty-first anniversary of the crushing of the Tiananmen protests on 4 June 1989 ... The Hong Kong demonstrators lit candles to commemorate the dead of 1989 and, as one speaker put it, 'for all those people on the mainland of China, who cannot demonstrate tonight'.
>
> (*FT*, 7 June 2010, p. 15)

Tibet

'Groups of students in two Tibetan areas of Gansu province in western China have held separate protests after Chinese security forces imposed lockdowns at boarding schools before the anniversaries of previous uprisings' (www.iht.com, 24 March 2010).

> People in Lhasa will have to register their names if they want to make photocopies ... Individuals wanting to photocopy documents will have to show ID cards and have the information recorded. Companies will have to register their names and addresses, the number of copies they want and provide the name of the manager in charge of the work.
>
> (www.bbc.co.uk, 19 May 2010)

> Public security officials intend to more tightly control printing and photocopying shops ... A regulation now in the works will require the operators

of printing and photocopying shops to obtain a new permit from the government ... They will also be required to take down identifying information about their clients and the specific documents printed or copied.

(www.iht.com, 20 May 2010)

A court has handed down a suspended death sentence to a Tibetan man accused of taking part in the riots that ravaged the Tibetan capital more than two years ago ... The same court also sentenced five other people to lengthy prison terms ... three to seven years ... for their role in harbouring the man, Sonam Tsering, who was convicted of 'rioting and inciting the public to riot' ... At least four people have been executed and three others have been given suspended death sentences for their role in the unrest of March 2008.

(www.iht.com, 27 May 2010)

Uighurs

China has replaced the most powerful official in Xinjiang ... Wang Lequan, who had served as secretary of the Communist Party in Xinjiang since 1994, was replaced by Zhang Chunxian ... Mr Wang was appointed to a new post in the Communist Party ... [namely] deputy secretary of the political and legislative affairs of the Central Committee ... Last September [2009] thousands of angry Han Chinese took to the streets of Urumqi to demand his removal and better security after the July riots and a spate of assaults using hypodermic needles. The regional police chief and the Communist Party secretary of Urumqi were sacked after the protests ... As secretary of the regional Communist Party, Zhang Chunxian becomes the most powerful figure in Xinjiang.

(www.bbc.co.uk, 24 April 2010)

Chinese leaders announced Saturday [24 April] that they had replaced Wang Lequan, the ruling official in Xinjiang ... Mr Wang, who served fifteen years as the party secretary of Xinjiang, an extraordinary length of time in such a post, has been replaced by Zhang Chunxian, the party secretary of Hunan province ... Mr Wang has also served since 2002 on the Politburo ... For much of his tenure in Xinjiang, Mr Wang was known as 'the stability secretary' and he occupied a singular position in the hierarchy of power. He devised hard-line policies for governing Xinjiang ... But after last summer's violence support for Mr Wang within the party began to falter ... Last week Chinese leaders decided at a meeting overseen by President Hu Jintao to speed up the economic development of Xinjiang ... Zhang Chunxian has little experience of dealing with ethnic unrest, but has helped manage aspects of China's economic and infrastructure development, notably as communications minister from 2002 to 2005 ... In early September [2009] Mr Wang became the direct target of popular resentment when tens of thousands of Han protesters marched through central Urumqi demanding that the government provide better security. Crowds surrounded the regional government headquarters and chanted 'Wang Lequan, step down!' ... The protesters were outraged over widespread talk that Uighurs were stabbing Han with needles infected with HIV. There was no independent confirmation of the attacks, and the government kept a blackout for weeks on any information, contributing to the paranoia.

(www.iht.com, 25 April 2010)

Full internet service was restored to Xinjiang on Friday [14 may], ten months after it was blocked ... The blockage was the longest and most widespread in China since the internet became readily available throughout the country ... The restoration of internet service comes before a central government meeting this month [May] that is aimed at setting new policy in Xinjiang ... [The new] regional party secretary ... Zhang Chunxian ... is nicknamed the 'internet secretary' for his willingness to use online tools to communicate with ordinary people.

(www.iht.com, 14 May 2010)

The government says internet services have 'fully resumed' in Xinjiang ... because the situation in Xinjiang has stabilized ... Xinhua said the [July 2009] riot was believed to have been orchestrated using the internet, text messages and long distance phone calls.

(www.bbc.co.uk, 14 May 2010)

The new leader of Xinjiang has announced a series of economic measures to bolster confidence in the regional government ... Earlier this month [May] the central government held a high-level policy conference on Xinjiang and announced new steps to invigorate the regional economy and ... ensure 'leapfrog development and lasting stability'. The announcement on Thursday [27 May] by the new Communist Party secretary of Xinjiang, Zhang Chunxian, came on the heels of the national planning session ... Mr Zhang said that a regional work conference this week had drawn up critical development policies ... One was to promote bilingual education in all schools by 2015, especially in southern Xinjiang, so that all students can speak fluent Chinese by 2010. Another was to move 700,000 urban families to 'safer and earthquake-resistant houses' by 2015 and force 100,000 nomads to settle down. Officials will also try to find jobs for the unemployed and ensure that all elderly people in rural areas are covered by social welfare and insurance by 2012 ... The economic policies announced by the central government last week include reforming tax policies in Xinjiang, encouraging foreign and commercial banks to open branches there, releasing more land for construction and easing access for some industries. The goal is to create a 'moderately well off society' in the region by 2010.

(www.iht.com, 28 May 2010)

Human rights

> Gao Zhisheng ... suddenly resurfaced Sunday [27 March], saying he is now living in northern China and wants only to spend time with his family away from media attention. Twitter messages appeared Sunday saying Gao Zhisheng's family had been in touch with him and listed his phone number. It was the first contact that friends, family and reporters have had with Gao since he went missing on 4 February 2009, from his home town in central China ... Contacted briefly on his cellphone, Gao said he is living in Wutai Shan, a mountain range famous as a Buddhist retreat, and that he is 'free at present'. Gao said: 'I just want to be in peace and quiet for a while and be reunited with my family' ... Gao declined to answer further questions, saying he was not allowed by law, nor was he willing, to accept interviews. Bans on interviews are often a condition of parole. Li Heping, a Beijing-based human rights lawyer and friend of Gao's, said he had also reached Gao on his cellphone and they had spoken briefly, and that he believed Gao was being followed by authorities. Li said: 'I believe he does not have freedom. First, when we were speaking, he sounded like he wanted to hang up. He told me that he had friends around him. I am sure that the people around him are limiting what he can say. Secondly, he would not tell me exactly where he is when I suggested visiting him' ... Gao was arrested in August 2006.
>
> (www.iht.com, 28 March 2010)

> Gao Zhisheng said: 'I have been sentenced but released' ... He said he would spend time with his extended family in Shanxi province and that he had no plans to return to his work as a rights defender. He said: 'Right now I just need to calm down and lead a quiet life.'
>
> (*IHT*, 29 March 2010, p. 8)

'A human rights group said he was most likely living under tight surveillance by Chinese scurity forces' (www.iht.com, 30 March 2010).

'Gao Zhisheng said ... he had been released six months ago' (www.bbc.co.uk, 28 March 2010).

'Gao Zhisheng went missing from his home town in Shanxi province on 4 February 2009' (www.guardian.co.uk, 28 March 2010).

> Gao Zhisheng ... said Wednesday [7 April] that he is abandoning his once prominent role as a government critic in hopes he will be allowed to reunite with his family ... Gao's sudden resurfacing on 18 March added to the confusion about him. For a few days he spoke with friends, family and the media by mobile phone, saying he was at Mount Wutai, a well-known Buddhist retreat, and wanted to be left alone. That explanation was so out of character ... that it brought speculation from friends and supporters that he was being pressured by the authorities.
>
> (www.iht.com, 7 April 2010)

> Amnesty International criticised China on Tuesday [30 March] for failing to reveal the number of people it executed last year [2009], which the rights group estimates is more than the rest of the world combined … Eighteen countries executed a total of at least 714 people last year … Amnesty said its figures were conservative and did not include a death count for China, which the rights group believes is in the thousands.
>
> (www.iht.com, 30 March 2010)

> Hu Jia, an internationally known human rights activist who has been imprisoned for more than two years on charges of subverting state power, is seriously ill with a liver disease that may be cancer, his wife said Thursday [8 April] . She said she had asked authorities to grant him parole, but that she and Mr Hu's lawyer had received strong indications from prison officials that the request was unlikely to be granted … In April 2008 he was sentenced to three-and-a-half years in prison. His term ends in June 2011.
>
> (www.iht.com, 8 April 2010)

> [On Monday 12 April his family announced that] Hu Jia … had been denied early release from prison … The prison officials who denied the family's request for medical parole said the growth on Mr Hu's liver was a 'vascular cyst' … It was the second time Mr Hu has been denied medical parole.
>
> (www.iht.com, 12 April 2010)

> Two lawyers who represented a follower of the banned Falun Gong spiritual movement could have their licences permanently removed in an administrative hearing on Thursday [22 April] … The lawyers, Tang Jitian and Liu Wei, said in a written statement that they were accused by the Beijing Municipal Bureau of Justice of having 'disrupted the order of the court and interfered with the regular litigation process' … The lawyers defended Yang Ming, the Falun Gong practitioner, nearly a year ago [in April 2009] … In May 2009 the licences of fifty-three in Beijing were not renewed, making it impossible for the lawyers to work legally. Mr Tang and Ms Liu, who were among them, have still not received the proper stamp that would allow them to resume practising but have so far managed to avoid having their licences permanently revoked.
>
> (www.iht.com, 21 April 2010)

'The lawyers said Monday [10 May] … [that they] have had their licences permanently revoked, a move that prevents them from ever practising law in China' (www.iht.com, 10 May 2010).

> Gao Zhisheng … has again vanished, his friends said Friday [30 April]. Associates said Mr Gao failed to return to a Beijing apartment on 20 April after spending more than a week in Urumqi, the capital of Xinjiang region, where he had been visiting his father-in-law. Mr Gao had telephoned his father-in-law after his plane left Urumqi, saying he would call upon his arrival in Beijing, they said. That was his last contact with the outside world

... The *South Morning Post*, a newspaper based in Hong Kong that first reported Mr Gao's disappearance on Friday, stated in an article that he had been 'quite outspoken' during a 6 April interview in his Beijing apartment, despite the certainty that his conversation was being recorded. However, the article said that he had asked that details of his treatment by authorities while in captivity not be made public. He was quoted as saying: 'If this is reported, I'll disappear again.'

(www.iht.com, 30 April 2010)

China's top judicial and law enforcement bodies have issued new guidelines that seek to halt the use of torture in obtaining confessions or witness testimony, especially in death penalty cases. The rules, issued Sunday [30 May], would nullify evidence gathered through violence or intimidation and give defendants the ability to challenge the validity of confessions presented during their trials. The new regulations come weeks after the authorities conceded that the confession used to erroneously convict a farmer for a murder was based on torture. The case came to light only after the supposed victim turned up alive and the defendant had spent ten years in jail ... Legal experts say it is the first time that Chinese law has explicitly spelled out rules for the admissibility of prosecutorial evidence ... The new regulations [are] part of a larger package of legal reforms that have been in the works for years but have been stalled by powerful interests within the country's public security apparatus ... The regulations require the police to testify in court if they are accused of using torture to extract a confession.

(www.iht.com, 31 May 2010; *IHT*, 1 June 2010, p. 3)

Laws banning torture are already in place, but analysts say they are widely disregarded ... The government has issued two new sets of procedures – the first covers evidence in cases subject to the death penalty, and the second rules on evidence obtained under duress in all criminal cases. For people appealing against the death penalty, testimony given under duress and evidence from unnamed sources are to be excluded. Death penalty defendants have also been given the right for an investigation into whether their testimony was obtained illegally. The regulations banned any evidence of unclear origin, confessions obtained through torture, or testimony obtained through violence and intimidation. Legal expert Zhao Bingzhi: '[It is the first time a] systematic and clear regulation [has been given on the issue] ... Previously we could only infer from abstract laws that illegal evidence is not allowed. But in reality, in many cases, such evidence was considered valid.'

(www.bbc.co.uk, 31 May 2010)

Religion

China's state-backed church has begun to ordain Vatican-approved bishops after a hiatus of more than two years ... At the weekend ... the third bishop ... [was] installed in as many weeks with the approval of both China's government-sanctioned Catholic Patriotic Association and the Vatican ... As many as twenty mutually agreed bishops could be ordained in coming months ... China and the Vatican have not recognized each other since 1951 ... The Vatican is the only country in the developed world that still maintains diplomatic relations with Taiwan rather than China ... [The Catholic Church] claims spiritual leadership over 1 billion Catholics worldwide ... [China] is home to an estimated 11 million Catholics ... Senior diplomatic officials from both sides have been meeting two or three times a year in their ongoing effort to reestablish diplomatic relations. The last summit was held in Rome in February, with the next expected in Beijing this summer.

(*FT*, 10 May 2010, p. 10)

Internet

Google hopes to retain a substantial business presence in China even if its stand-off with China over censorship forces it to close its flagship local search engine, local employees and industry experts say ... The company runs google.cn, its China-registered website, in a joint venture with a domestic partner, as Chinese law bars foreigners from holding controlling stakes in the internet content business. But most of Google's workforce in the country is employed by a separate company, wholly owned by the US parent. An employee at Google Information Technology (China) said: 'Research and Development staff all work with us' ... Google Information Technology (China) [is] a foreign-owned company, according to the Beijing administration for industry and commerce ... Another employee who works in sales said most of Google's sales force in China was employed by the same company and not by the joint venture ... The R&D and advertising sales operations [were] set up well before it launched google.cn.

(*FT*, 20 March 2010, p. 19)

'Google threatened on 13 January to quit obeying China's censorship laws' (www.cnn.com, 22 March 2010).

'[Following the 13 January decision] some internet users laid flowers outside the company's Beijing headquarters' (*The Independent*, 22 March 2010, p. 22).

'Last January, when Google initially threatened to leave China, many young people there placed wreaths at the company headquarters in Beijing as a sign of mourning' (www.iht.com, 22 March 2010).

'In recent days a series of articles in the Chinese media have attacked ... Google' (www.thetimes.co.uk, 22 March 2010).

'Official news outlets have accused Google of acting as an agent of the US government in trying to put pressure on China' (*FT*, 23 March 2010, p. 1).

Google has stopped censoring its search results in China. The US company said its Chinese users would be redirected to the uncensored pages of its Hong Kong website ... google.com.hk ... The company said the Chinese

> government had been 'crystal clear throughout our discussions that self-censorship is a non-negotiable legal requirement' ... Google said it would maintain an R&D and sales presence in China. It said the size of its sales team would depend on how many Chinese people can get at the Hong Kong-based site. Currently about 700 of Google's 20,000-strong workforce are based in China. On Sunday [21 March] state media in China attacked Google for what they described as the company's 'intricate ties' with the US government. Google provided US intelligence agencies with a record of its search engine results, Xinhua said.
>
> (www.bbc.co.uk, 22 March 2010)

> Google said: 'We want as many people in the world as possible to have access to our services, including users in mainland China, yet the Chinese government had been crystal clear throughout our discussions that self-censorship is a non-negotiable legal requirement' ... In addition to search, Google generates revenue from an ad sales business in China, its Android mobile phone operating system and its Chrome browser business. It also runs a host of web services in China, including email service Gmail ... Most of the approximately $300 million of revenue that Google took from its China operations last year [2009] was from the company's other [than search operations] businesses, including its online advertising business, analysts say ... China is the fastest growing cell phone market, with about 700 million customers.
>
> (www.cnn.com, 22 March 2010)

> China accounted for a small fraction of Google's $23.6 billion in global revenues last year [2009] ... Google does not break down revenue by country, but people familiar with the company's business in China said its quarterly sales were in the vicinity of $150 million in the most recent quarter, which ended 31 December [2009]. Globally, it had $6.67 billion in revenue in the same period. Much of Google's revenue in China comes from ads that Chinese companies place on Google's sites in the United States and elsewhere ... Microsoft's search engine, Bing, has a very small market share ... Microsoft's MSN instant messaging service badly trails rival Tencent.
>
> (www.iht.com, 22 March 2010)

'China accounted for a small fraction of Google's $24 billion in annual revenue. Analysts estimate Google brought in $250 million to $600 million from China. It is unclear how much of that amount flowed exclusively from google.cn' (*IHT*, 23 March 2010, p. 16).

> The move follows sophisticated cyber attacks ... David Drummond (chief legal officer of Google): 'These attacks and the surveillance they uncovered – combined with attempts over the last year to further limit free speech on the web in China, including the persistent blocking of websites such as Facebook, Twitter, YouTube, Google Docs and Blogger – had led us to conclude that we could no longer continue censoring our results on google.cn.'
>
> (www.guardian.co.uk, 22 March 2010)

> David Drummond (Google's chief legal officer): 'We very much hope that the Chinese government respects our decision, though we are well aware that it could at any time block access to our services' ... Beijing could block access in China to both Google's local and Hong Kong search sites, just as it blocks many foreign websites on the mainland.
>
> (*FT*, 23 March 2010, p. 1)

'It is thought that the bulk of Google's estimated $300 million revenues in China in 2009 came from export-orientated companies that the company hopes would continue to advertise via the Hong Kong site' (www.thetimes.co.uk, 22 March 2010).

> Google.com.hk [is] an uncensored portal in Hong Kong ... [Google] acknowledged that the Chinese authorities might block access to its site ... Google's decision follows several attempts to hack its email system, ever stronger censorship of its searches, legal complaints tied to its digitization of books, and ... growing vitriol in the state-controlled press ... Over the past decade revenues from digital advertising have grown exponentially, admittedly from a tiny base ... Foreign companies operating in China have been quick to see this potential but largely unable to grasp it. Facebook, Twitter and YouTube are all explicitly blocked. EBay faltered because of its own managerial errors, but also because of delayed approval for PayPal, its online payment system, which this week announced a partnership with a Chinese rival. Yahoo caused a stir by allowing the Chinese authorities to probe its users' emails in a hunt for political dissidents – something it has since pledged not to do. There are now domestic Chinese equivalents of all these sites – Baidu for Google, Taobao for eBay, Renren for Facebook, QQ for instant messaging, games and social networking – and they are doing well.
>
> (www.economist.com, 23 March 2010)

> The State Council Information Office said on 23 March: 'Google has violated the written promise it made when entering the Chinese market by stopping filtering its searching service and blaming China in insinuation for alleged hacker attacks. This is totally wrong. We are uncompromisingly opposed to the politicization of commercial issues, and express our discontent and indignation to Google for its unreasonable accusations and conducts.'
>
> (www.bbc.co.uk, 23 March 2010; www.independent.co.uk, 23 March 2010)

'Supporters left flowers, chocolate and other gifts outside Google's Beijing headquarters this morning [23 March]' (www.guardian.co.uk, 23 March 2010).

'A few passers-by laid flowers or chocolates on a large metal "Google" sign outside the company's office in Beijing' (www.thetimes.co.uk, 23 March 2010).

'At Google's office in northern Beijing on Tuesday [23 March] a few Chinese passers-by laid flowers or chocolates on the large metal "Google" sign outside' (www.iht.com, 23 March 2010).

'The Chinese government moved on Tuesday [23 March] to block access to the Hong Kong site' (www.iht.com, 23 March 2010).

> Beijing is already reportedly disabling searches and blocking search results on Google's site … Its YouTube service, like Facebook and Twitter, is blocked … China Mobile, the biggest cellular company in the country, was expected to cancel a deal to use Google's search engine on its home page. China Unicom was thought to have cancelled plans to create a telephone based on Google's Android system.
>
> (www.iht.com, 24 March 2010)

'Chinese internet users were left with less information from Google as their government appeared to apply an unusually strict filtering system to the US search engine' (www.ft.com, 23 March 2010). 'Internet users using Google have experienced widely divergent search results' (*FT*, 25 March 2010, p. 27).

'There were reports that some Google searches were being filtered' (www.economist.com, 25 March 2010).

> Alan Davidson, director of United States public policy for Google, told a joint Congressional panel [on Wednesday 24 March] that the United States and other democracies should draft trade agreements that incorporate pledges to keep web sites uncensored. He said censorship had become more than a human rights issue and was hurting profit for foreign companies … He said: 'The growing problem for internet censorship is not isolated to one country or one region. No single company and no single industry can tackle internet censorship on its own' … So far, Mr Davidson said, the company had noticed 'intermittent' censorship of the Hong Kong site … The fallout from China's restrictive internet policies widened on Wednesday when an internet services company, the [US] Go Daddy Group, said it would halt registration of Chinese domain names … The commission [was told] that the company was concerned about the privacy of its customers after Chinese officials requested copies of photo identification and signatures for each customer. For the first time Go Daddy had been asked to retrospectively obtain documentation or individuals who had registered a domain name … [Go Daddy] said a central obstacle in China was rampant hacker attacks that local authorities failed to combat.
>
> (www.iht.com, 24 March 2010)

> Go Daddy.com, the world's largest internet domain register, told a US Congressional hearing that it will pull out of China because of concerns over government interference and privacy. The company, which says it manages 27,000 Chinese domain names, said the authorities there had asked it to collect photo headshots, business licence information and signed registration forms from customers and forward them to the government. Christine Jones (Go Daddy's executive vice president): 'The intent of the new

procedures appeared ... to be based on a desire by the Chinese authorities to exercise increased control over the subject matter of domain name registrations by Chinese nationals. There appears to be a recent increase in China's surveillance and monitoring of the internet activities of its citizens' ... Internet analysts played down the significance of Go Daddy's move, pointing out that .cn domains made up les than 1 per cent of the company's business and that many people were simply unwilling to register under the rules ... Some other technology companies have chosen not to enter the Chinese market [e.g. Facebook and Twitter] ... Microsoft, after being criticised when it censored blogs on its MSN service, made careful changes to its policies. For example, its Hotmail email service does not keep any data in mainland China. However, the company continues to self-censor other aspects of its service, and its co-founder, Bill Gates, surprised observers recently by saying that Chinese censorship was 'very limited' ... Rupert Murdoch's News Corporation holds significant interests in the country, not least MySpace China, begun in 2007. The site, which is locally owned, operated and managed, is notorious for censoring users who talk about politics or religion.

(*Guardian*, 26 March 2010, p. 31)

China's second largest mobile operator ... China Unicom ... has announced that it will remove Google's search function from new handsets developed with the US company ... According to official figures, the country has 384 million internet users, but 745 million mobile subscribers, many of them regular users of the internet on their handsets.

(*FT*, 25 March 2010, p. 27)

'Google said Monday [29 March] that its mobile internet services were being partially blocked in China' (www.ft.com, 30 March 2010; www.cnn.com, 30 March 2010).

'Google shifted the blame for widespread unavailability of its search services in China on Tuesday [30 March] to the authorities of the country, after earlier in the day saying a technical flaw in its own systems had caused the problem' (www.ft.com, 31 March 2010; www.cnn.com, 31 March 2010).

Google added to the confusion, saying at first that the problem had been the result of a change it had made to the string of characters it sends along with search requests, which may run foul of China's powerful internet filter. Later in the day Google said that it had actually made that change a week earlier, so the disruption must have been caused by changes on China's end. It also said by early Wednesday morning [31 March] its services appeared to have been restored.

(www.iht.com, 31 March 2010)

'Access [to] ... Google's portal in Hong Kong ... has been patchy' (www.independent.co.uk, 31 March 2010).

> In what appeared to be a co-ordinated assault, the email accounts of more than a dozen rights activists, academics and journalists who cover China have been compromised by unknown intruders. A Chinese human rights organization also said that hackers disabled its website for a fifth straight day. The infiltrations, which involved Yahoo email accounts, appeared to be aimed at people who write about China and Taiwan, rendering their accounts inaccessible ... Most ... of the attacks ... began on 25 March.
>
> (www.iht.com, 31 March 2010)

'Yahoo email accounts of some journalists and other users whose work relates to China were compromised in an attack discovered this week ... Some journalists in China and Taiwan found they were unable to access their accounts beginning 25 March' (www.independent.co.uk, 31 March 2010).

> The Foreign Correspondents' Club of China said ... Friday [2 April] that its website was taken down because of denial-of-service attacks apparently launched over the last two days by computers within China and in the United States ... Yahoo email accounts belonging to foreign journalists in China have also apparently been hacked in recent weeks, and the website of the Hong Kong-based China Human Rights Defenders remained shut down Friday after a denial-of-service attack hit last week ... Service interruptions hit Google's new offshore search service for several hours Tuesday [30 March], rendering it unusable for web users in China.
>
> (www.iht.com, 2 April 2010)

> The Foreign Correspondents' Club of China ... said that it had been rendered inoperable by hackers just days after cyber-attacks compromised the email accounts of more than a dozen reporters in China and Taiwan. The earlier intrusions, which occurred in recent weeks but were publicized Tuesday [30 March], affected users of Yahoo's email service. Some of the users were still unable to gain access to their accounts Friday ... Scott McDonald [the Foreign Correspondents' Club of China president] said Friday that it was nearly impossible to determine the origin of the attacks ... [The] attack ... [on] the website of Chinese Human Rights Defenders ... which began on 25 March, has now entered its second week. The intrusions on Yahoo accounts affected about twenty people, most of them academics, human rights advocates and reporters, based in at least four countries ... [It is claimed that] at least thirteen foreign reporters in China and Taiwan had been affected ... Several said they were still locked out of their email accounts.
>
> (*IHT*, 3 April 2010, p. 13)

> The young people who dominate web use in China are not just searching for information; they are searching for a lifestyle. They are passionate about downloading music, playing online games and engaging in social networking. Richard Ji (an internet analyst at Morgan Stanley): 'Sixty per cent of the internet users here [in China] are under the age of thirty. In the United

> States it's the other way around. And in the United States it's about information. But in China the number one priority is entertainment.'
>
> (www.iht.com, 24 March 2010)

'In the technology sector, Google is viewed as an innovator that has spurred the rapid development of the Chinese web. Its departure will leave some Chinese companies with greater influence, but could also stifle competition, some fear' (www.iht.com, 24 March 2010).

> A Reuters report said Microsoft's Chinese version of Windows sold fewer than 3,000 copies in February 1994, the month before Bill Gates made his first journey to China … That trip came as rancour between the United States and China – and Microsoft – was high over piracy, intellectual property rights and Beijing's fight for the renewal of its most-favoured-nation trade status with Washington … In 2007 *Forbes* estimates Microsoft revenue from China topped $700 million. Gates told the magazine he anticipated China – which is now the world's largest computer market – would be Microsoft's top market by 2017. Moreover, the company's China operations have become an integral part of the company as a whole. The company's total operations in China are the largest in any country outside the United States. Microsoft opened its first research centre in the country in 1998, and now has campuses in Beijing, Shanghai and Shenzhen. In 2008 the company announced plans to invest an additional $1 billion in Chinese research and more than double staff to 3,000 in the next three years.
>
> (www.cnn.com, 29 March 2010)

> Turning the tables on a China-based computer espionage gang, Canadian and US computer security researchers have monitored a spying operation for the past eight months, observing while the intruders pilfered classified and restricted documents from the highest level of the Indian defence ministry. In a report issued Monday [5 April] the researchers, based at the Munk School of Global Affairs at the University of Toronto, provide a detailed account of how a spy operation it called the Shadow Network systematically hacked into personal computers in government offices on several continents … [Included among the material obtained was] a year's worth of the Dalai Lama's personal email messages. The intruders even stole documents related to the travel of Nato forces in Afghanistan … The attacks look like the work of a criminal gang based in Sichuan province, but as with all cyber-attacks it is easy to mask the true origin, the researchers said. Given the sophistication of the intruders and the targets of the operation, the researchers said, it is possible that the Chinese government approved the spying … The new report shows that the India-focused spy ring made extensive use of internet services like Twitter, Google Groups, Blogspot, blog.com, Baidu Blogs and Yahoo!Mail to automate the control of computers once they had been infected … The Canadian researchers co-operated in their investigation with a volunteer group of security experts in the United

States at the Shadowserver Foundation, which focuses on internet criminal activity ... By gaining access to the control servers used by the second cyber gang, the researchers observed the theft of a wide range of material, including classified documents from the Indian government and reports taken from Indian military analysts and corporations, as well as documents from agencies of the United Nations and other governments ... By examining a series of email addresses the investigators traced the attacks to hackers who appeared to be based in Chengdu, which is home to a large population from neighbouring Tibet. Researchers believe that one hacker ... may have been affiliated with the city's prestigious University of Electronic Science and Technology ... The People's Liberation Army operates a technical reconnaissance bureau in the city, and helps finance the university's research on computer network defence ... The Canadian researchers stressed that while the new spy ring focussed on India, there were clear international ramifications ... Even after eight months of watching the spy ring, the Toronto researchers said they could not determine exactly who was using the Chengdu computers to infiltrate the Indian government.

(www.iht.com, 6 April 2010; *IHT*, 7 April 2010, pp. 13, 16)

The Foreign Correspondents' Club of China has shut its website after a burst of hacker attacks ... The club's board said: 'We do not know who is behind the attacks or what their motivation is' ... [The board explained] it had decided to shut down temporarily the site after two days of 'persistent' attacks.

(www.independent.co.uk, 6 April 2010)

China has quietly formed a new bureau expected to help police social networking sites and other user-driven forums on the internet, which are proving harder for the government to monitor and control than ordinary news portals ... The new agency, officially called the internet news co-ordination bureau, is part of the effort to better monitor the communications of Chinese web users, who total nearly 400 million by official estimates ... Both the new and pre-existing bureaux are under the auspices of the State Council Information Office, which acts as a leading daily enforcer over news-related content on the web. For weeks, the head of the newly established bureau has represented it in meetings with foreign diplomats and in official propaganda conferences and training sessions. But public acknowledgements of the addition only came last week after *The New York Times* submitted a question about the overhaul. The next day the Information Office altered a page on its website to reflect the new internet bureau. It also unveiled another new bureau, devoted to regulating foreign news and information outlets that conduct business in China. This week, in a faxed response, the Information Office said the internet news co-ordination bureau, which it also refers to as bureau nine, 'is mainly responsible for guidance, co-ordination and other work related to the construction and management of the web culture' ... China already employs a sprawling bureaucracy of government, party, and industry bodies, and local affiliates down to the neighbourhood level, to screen, filter, and steer public opinion online, and regulate various facets of the industry ... Previously, the Information Office operated a single Bureau of Internet Affairs, referred to as bureau five ... Now two bureaux will divide the labour.

(www.iht.com, 17 April 2010)

Ever since Google disclosed in January that internet intruders had stolen information from its computers, the exact nature and extent of the theft has been a closely guarded company secret. But a person with direct knowledge of the investigation now says that the losses included one of Google's crown jewels, a password system that controls access by millions of users worldwide to almost all of the company's web services, including email and business applications. The programme, code named Gaia for the Greek goddess of the earth, was attacked in a lightning raid taking less than two days last December [2009]. Described publicly only once at a technical conference four years ago, the software is intended to enable users and employees to sign in with their password just once to operate a range services. The intruders do not appear to have stolen passwords of Gmail users, and the company quickly started making significant changes to the security of its networks after the intrusions. But the theft leaves open the possibility, however faint, that the intruders may find weaknesses that Google might not even be aware of, independent computer experts said.

(www.iht.com, 20 April 2010)

China is on the verge of requiring telecommunications and internet companies to detect, stop and report leaks of state secrets by their customers, the latest in a string of moves designed to strengthen the government's control over private communications. The proposed amendments to the state secrets law, reported Tuesday [27 April] by state media, loosely defines a state secret as information that, if disclosed, would damage China's security or interests in political, economic, defence and other realms. The wording of the amendment as cited by the state-run media suggested that internet providers and telecommunications companies would have to take a more active stance in checking emails or text messages for leaked information ... State-run media outlets characterized the new measure as part of a drive to further engage businesses in protecting state security. But several analysts suggested it would have a limited effect. Internet and telecommunications companies are already expected to co-operate fully with state security investigations ... The amendment was submitted Monday [26 April] to the Standing Committee of the National People's Congress for a third reading, the final step before being signed into law ... China has issued rules calling on its state-owned companies to strengthen protection of their commercial secrets, which is defined broadly to include information including acquisitions and technologies ... The State-Owned Assets Supervision and Administration Commission, which oversees more than 120 companies, defined commercial secrets as any practical information that is not publicly available and may potentially bring economic benefits to enterprises. China's definition of commercial secrets has fuelled concern among companies after a Rio Tinto employee and Australian citizen was sentenced to ten years in prison last month [March] for taking bribes and industrial espionage.

(www.iht.com, 27 April 2010)

The wording of the amendment, as cited by the state-run *China Daily*, suggested that internet and telecommunications companies would have to take a more proactive stance identifying leaks of state secrets and their sources. The newspaper said companies must detect, report and delete unauthorized disclosures. But reports by Xinhua seemed less definitive about whether those companies must independently scour online transmissions for forbidden information or simply co-operate with authorities if they suspect transgressions. Xinhua reported that once companies discovered leaks, they must stop them, delete them, report them to the authorities and co-operate with the investigators ... The new regulations define commercial secrets of state-owned firms very broadly. Included is information related to strategic plans, management, mergers, equity trades, stock market listings, reserves, production, procurement and sales strategy, financing and finances, negotiations, joint ventures and technology transfers.

(*IHT*, 28 April 2010, p. 15)

China's legislature has imposed tighter requirements on web and telecommunications companies to shield the nation's state secrets ... The amendments to the state secrets law, adopted Thursday [29 April] and set to take effect on 1 October, obligates operators and service providers to co-operate with the police, state security officials and prosecutors in investigating leaks of state secrets. On discovering a leak, they must promptly block it and report it to higher authorities, according to a final draft distributed at a news conference in Beijing. Regulatory or security authorities would punish those who fail to comply ... [In December 2009] the legislature's Standing Committee passed a liability law that had been amended to permit individuals to ask internet service providers to delete or block posted material infringing on their civil rights or interests, and to sue providers if they do not comply. Liberal critics had argued, unsuccessfully, that the provision would chill online activism. The process of amending the Law on Guarding State Secrets, first enacted in 1988, has been fraught with contention as well ... Officials in charge of controlling state secrets at national and local levels retain highly elastic powers under the law, leaving ample space for the government to grant exceptions or broaden the scope of what is deemed to be classified material in seemingly arbitrary fashion.

(www.iht.com, 1 May 2010)

China has defended its right to censor the internet in a document laying out the government's attitude towards the web ... The white paper [was] released on Tuesday [8 June] ... By the end of last year [2009] the country had 384 million internet users ... The government hopes that nearly half of the population will have access to the internet within five years. That figure is nearly 30 per cent at the moment.

(www.bbc.co.uk, 8 June 2010)

AIDS

Days before travellers worldwide are to begin arriving for Shanghai's world exposition, China has lifted a two-decade ban on travel to the country by people who carry the virus that causes AIDS or who have other sexually transmitted diseases. The action also removed a long-standing ban on travel to China by people with leprosy. The government approved amendments to a 1986 law governing quarantines and a 1989 law regulating entry by foreigners, removing prohibitions related to people with HIV, which causes AIDS, China's State Council reported Tuesday [27 April 2010) ... With the changes, the ban on travel is officially limited only to people with infectious tuberculosis, serious mental disorders and 'infectious diseases which could possibly greatly harm the public health'. China has temporarily lifted the ban on HIV-positive travellers for major events in the past, but the revision of long-standing laws indicates the latest change will be permanent ... A spokesman for the health ministry ... [said] the ministry had been working to permanently remove the prohibition since the 2008 Beijing Olympics ... Between 450,000 and one million Chinese are infected with the HIV virus, according to ... the United Nations health organization. Roughly 75,000 of those have developed AIDS. The proportion of HIV-infected people in China is far below that of neighbouring countries – Vietnam, for example, records about 20,000 AIDS deaths a year – but health exports have worried that China's HIV population may be poised to expand. The infection is most common among sex workers, migrant workers and residents of some border areas, like Yunnan province in south-west China, where drugs are smuggled into the country. In January the United States dropped its own ban on visitors who are HIV positive. The ban had been in effect for twenty-two years.

(www.iht.com, 28 April 2010)

Xinhua reported Tuesday [27 April] that China's State Council decided to repeal the ban after realizing it did little to prevent the spread of disease and caused problems when the country was hosting international events. The revision came days before the opening of the six-month Shanghai World Expo, which organizers expect will draw 70 million people. The government had previously lifted the ban temporarily for other large-scale events, including the 2008 Olympics in Beijing. Xinhua said the health ministry estimates the number of people living with HIV in China had reached 740,000 by October 2009, with deaths caused by AIDS totalling 49,845 since the first case was reported in 1985 ... Until January the United States was one of seven countries with laws barring entry of people with HIV.

(www.cnn.com, 28 April 2010)

Wan Yanhai, the founder of a prominent AIDS activist group in Beijing, has left China for the United States with his family because of increasing pressure from the government, Mr Wan and his supporters said Monday [10 May] ... In recent months the group that Mr Wan led, the Aizhixing Institute, had come under increasing scrutiny from tax officials and even the fire department, he said ... Mr Wan is arguably the most outspoken AIDS campaigner in China. He founded Aizhixing in 1994 to support the cause of AIDS awareness and prevention. At the time the Chinese government was reluctant to speak publicly about AIDS. Mr Wan helped turn an international spotlight on villages in Henan province where residents had become infected with HIV in the 1990s because of poor government oversight of blood transfusions. He was detained for four weeks in 2002 because of that advocacy ... Although Mr Wan and his group had come under pressure before, the latest scrutiny coincides with a wider crackdown on civil society groups and organizations that operate independently of the government. The authorities have been especially wary of groups that receive any financing from abroad and have imposed news restrictions on such financing.

(www.iht.com, 10 May 2010)

Wan Yanhai's departure comes less than a year after another AIDS campaigner moved to America ... Wan said he expects to stay in the United States for two to three years ... Wan had been detained and questioned several times, but said he felt increasing pressure in recent months, following checks by tax, education and propaganda officials, and the state administration for industry and commerce. Tightened regulations on foreign donations have also caused funding problems, he said ... Gao Yaojie, who blew the whistle on Henan province's HIV epidemic, moved to the United States last year [2009]. Hu Jia, another HIV/AIDS activist, is serving a three-and-a-year prison sentence for inciting subversion.

(*Guardian*, 11 May 2010, p. 24)

Food contamination and defective goods

A newspaper article by one of China's best known investigative reporters has reawakened controversy over whether provincial authorities improperly stored vaccines in rooms without air conditioning, rendering them ineffective, and the let them be administered to children. China's health ministry said on Thursday [18 March] that it would look into the report by Wang Keqin in the *China Economic Times*, while cautioning that it had examined the evidence in late 2008 and not found a widespread problem. But Chen Taoan, the former chief spokesman of the Shanxi Province Disease Control and Prevention Centre and still on the centre's staff, said on Thursday that a senior official there had been relieved of all duties at the end of last year [2009] because of improprieties related to the vaccines. Mr Chen said the centre, which is part of the Shanxi health department, had required all hospitals in the province to buy vaccines at steep prices. To monitor compliance by the hospitals, the centre put a sticker on each package of the vaccine to show that it had been approved. But the stickers would not adhere to the packages in air-conditioned rooms, Mr Chen said, so the centre routinely through 2006 and 2007 had vaccines transferred to a warm room where the stickers were attacked … Mr Chen said that he was still on the centre's payroll but had been relieved of his duties because of his objections to the handling of the vaccines. The centre stopped exposing the vaccines to the heat in 2008 but did not recall those that might have already been damaged, he said … The article said that the parents of four children who died and seventy-four children with severe illnesses were blaming the vaccines … [but] provincial health experts [who] had examined some of the children … concluded that their problems were not caused by vaccines.

(www.iht.com, 18 March 2010; *IHT*, 19 March 2010, p. 4)

Regulators are investigating whether restaurants throughout China are creating hazards by cooking with recycled oil, some tainted with food waste, and prominence given to the issue in the state-controlled media suggests that the problem could be widespread. The State Food and Drug Administration issued a nationwide emergency notice telling health bureaux to investigate the sources of cooking oil in mid-March. The notice came shortly after a professor and a group of students at Wuhan Polytechnic University announced that they had found widespread use of recycled oil in their region in an undercover investigation. The professor, He Dongping, asserted that recycled oil was being used to prepare one in ten meals in China. Regulators are now searching for illegal oil recycling mills and some health bureaux have begun releasing the names of restaurants and food establishments that were found to be using questionable oil … This week alone state newspapers have reported finding 'unsafe artificial green peas' in Hunan province and some 20,000 pounds of 'toxic vegetables' in Guangxi Zuhan Autonomous Region. Those vegetables had excessive pesticide residues … In the case of the green peas, two illegal food workshops were caught processing dried snow peas and soybeans with chemicals and bleach to produce the appearance of more expensive green peas.

(www.iht.com, 31 March 2010)

The federal government [in the United States] on Friday [2 April] instructed families with certain Chinese-made drywall to rid their homes of the material and replace electrical wiring, gas pipes and sprinkler systems. The drywall has been linked to respiratory and electrical problems in thousands of new homes, primarily in Florida and Louisiana. Consumer advocates have argued that high levels of hydrogen sulphide in the drywall corrode electrical wires and create health risks … About 3,000 households have complained about the drywall ... [One study] showed that the Chinese drywall emitted hydrogen sulphide at a rate 100 times greater than non-Chinese samples ... The drywall was installed in homes across the South during the housing boom, when the supply of American-made drywall was limited and Chinese materials were cheap. Construction surged after hurricanes devastated many parts of the Gulf Coast ... [Complaints were received] from households in Florida, Louisiana, Alabama, Mississippi and Virginia.

(www.iht.com, 4 April 2010)

Many firms doing business in China agree to use Hong Kong as a forum to resolve legal disputes, in an effort to avoid China's notoriously arbitrary and corrupt courts. Now some of their customers have had a similar idea: the families of four children poisoned in China by tainted milk in 2008 have sued in Hong Kong for compensation. On 27 May Hong Kong's Small Claims Tribunal, which handles claims of HK$50,000 ($6,400) or less without the intercession of lawyers, dismissed the case, largely on jurisdictional grounds ... An appeal is in the works ... The plaintiffs had sued Fonterra, a dairy co-operative based in New Zealand. It has a subsidiary registered in Hong Kong that held a 43 per cent stake, and three out of seven board seats in Sanlu, a dairy firm that adulterated its products with melamine, causing mass illness.

(www.economist.com, 3 June 2010)

Earthquakes

A powerful earthquake in north-west China killed at least 400 people ... on Wednesday [14 April 2010] ... The quake, which struck at 7.49 a.m. in Qinghai province, had a magnitude of 7.1, according to China's earthquake administration ... The earthquake struck in Yushu county, a remote and mountainous area sparsely population by farmers and herders, most of them ethnic Tibetans. The region is pocked with copper, tin and coal mines and rich in natural gas ... The county's population is around 80,000. China National Radio said that more than 80 per cent of the homes in the area had collapsed but that schools and government buildings had largely remained standing ... Last August [2009] Golmud was hit by a 6.2 magnitude earthquake that destroyed dozens of homes but caused no deaths. Qinghai is an ethnic melting pot of Tibetans, Mongols and Han Chinese. It is adjacent to Sichuan province, where at least 87,000 people died in a powerful earthquake in 2008.

(www.iht.com, 14 April 2010)

Among those still missing were twenty children buried in the wreckage of a primary school, and as many as fifty people who were buried in an office building that houses the departments of commerce and industry ... At least eighteen aftershocks measuring more than 6.0 followed the quake throughout the day.

(www.iht.com, 14 April 2010)

The earthquake was of] 6.9 magnitude as measured by the US Geological Survey ... [which] also reported several strong aftershocks – one of magnitude 5.8 – within hours of the initial quake ... [Xinhua reported that] most of the houses in the area were made wood with earthen walls.

(www.cnn.com, 14 April 2010)

The death toll ... rose to at least 617 people on Thursday [15 April] ... Many remained buried under debris ... The dead included at least fifty-six students and five teachers who were crushed in the rubble of collapsing schools or dormitories ... Among those still missing were twenty children buried in the wreckage of a primary school ... The quake centred on Yushu county ... The prefecture that includes Yushu is on the Tibetan plateau, with a population that is more than 96 per cent Tibetan and overwhelmingly poor ... China National Radio ... said that 70 per cent of the school building had collapsed in neighbouring Yushu Tibetan Autonomous Prefecture ... that has a population of 350,000 ... Workers were rushing to release water from a reservoir after cracks were discovered in a dam.

(www.iht.com, 15 April 2010)

Officials say 617 people died ... [while] 313 remain missing ... Several schools collapsed and at least fifty-six students are known to have died, twenty-two of them in a school in Yushu ... According to the US Geological Survey, this was the strongest tremor within 100 kilometres of the area since 1976.

(www.bbc.co.uk, 15 April 2010)

State news agencies reported late Thursday [15 April] that premier Wen Jiabao had arrived in the area to inspect the damage ... Some of the worst casualties occurred at local schools, where Xinhua reported at least sixty-six students and ten teachers dead, including thirty-two at an elementary school ... It was unclear, however, what role construction quality played in collapses in Yushu, where some 70 per cent of buildings were built not of concrete but wood and mud. China has moved to strengthen earthquake resistance in schools and public buildings after the Sichuan quake, but the effort remains a work in progress ... [said] the disaster relief director at the ministry of civil affairs.

(www.iht.com, 15 April 2010)

Premier Wen Jiabao promised to rebuild the quake-hit region ... [He was] visiting Yushu county, the remote Tibetan mountain area at the epicentre. Officials now say 791 people died and 294 are missing, but local people say they believe the toll is much higher ... The quake struck on Wednesday morning [14 April] at the shallow depth of 10 kilometres (6 miles) ... President Hu Jintao announced on Thursday [15 April] he was cutting short his attendance at the BRIC (Brazil, Russia, India and China) summit in Brazil to return home because of the 'huge calamity'.

(www.bbc.co.uk, 16 April 2010)

'Both prime minister Wen Jiabao [Brunei, Indonesia and Mynamar] and President Hu Jintao [Chile and Venezuela] postponed planned foreign trips because of the disaster' (www.cnn.com, 16 April 2010).

> Soldiers, civilians and Tibetan monks combed through rubble in Qinghai province ... Heavy equipment and aid are now arriving in Yushu county, where 791 people are known to have died, with another 294 missing. Local people say they believe the number of dead is much higher ... Ninety-seven per cent of Yushu's population is ethnic Tibetan ... Prime minister Wen Jiabao, who flew to the area on Thursday evening [15 April] to see the rescue efforts, toured it again on Friday.
>
> (www.bbc.co.uk, 16 April 2010)

'The number of people known to have been killed in Qinghai province has risen to 1,144, said officials [on Friday 16 April] ... Another 417 are still missing' (www.bbc.co.uk, 17 April 2010).

'The official government death toll was 1,144 as of Friday evening [16 April], up from 791 in the afternoon' (*IHT*, 17 April 2010, p. 4).

> Prime minister Wen Jiabao spent Friday in the Tibetan high country ... He said: 'No matter whether you are Tibetans or Hans, you are all in one family' ... At the Yushu Ethnic Minority Vocational School, where a section of the girls' dormitory turned into rubble, teachers said more than 200 students might have been lost.
>
> (www.iht.com, 17 April 2010)

> The Dalai Lama ... is seeking to visit the Tibetan region rocked by a deadly earthquake ... In a statement issued Saturday [17 April] ... [he] said the devastated region is where he was born ... The death toll now stands at 1,339 [said Xinhua] ... [while] 332 remain missing ... Ethnic Tibetans have accused Chinese soldiers of not doing enough to help in the immediate aftermath of the quake ... But the Dalai Lama on Saturday praised Chinese authorities for visiting the predominantly Tibetan region. He singled out prime minister Wen Jiabao for offering comfort to people in the region and overseeing the relief efforts. He also said he appreciates the freedom given to the media to report the quake and its aftermath. The Dalai Lama wanted to visit victims of the 2008 earthquake in Sichuan, but he was not allowed to visit China ... Qinghai province is home to about 5 million people ... About half its people are Han Chinese, but the area is home to more than forty ethnic groupings, including Tibetans, Hui and Mongols.
>
> (www.cnn.com, 17 April 2010)

'President Hu Jintao has visited survivors … as the death toll rose to more than 1,700 people … The death toll … in Qinghai province was raised to 1,706 and 256 [are] missing, Xinhua said' (www.bbc.co.uk, 18 April 2010).

> President Hu Jintao flew to the remote and ruined Yushu county to speed relief distribution yesterday [18 April], as Tibetan monks prayed over victims of an earthquake in China's north-west that killed at least 1,706 people. Hu Jintao: 'Saving life remains the first priority. We treasure every life and at the same time we should ensure victims regain a normal life.'
>
> (*FT*, 19 April 2010)

> Chinese state television showed him cradling an injured young Tibetan survivor and assuring her: 'You will have a bright future. Grandpa will be thinking of you' … Hu Jintao cut short an official trip to South America … Although Yushu was not one of the Tibetan areas which saw unrest in 2008, there have been some signs of underlying tensions since Wednesday's quake. Many blamed Chinese mining for causing the disaster, while some monks complained they had not been given sufficient credit for their rescue work.
>
> (www.guardian.co.uk, 19 April 2010)

'President Hu Jintao has promised an all-out effort to rebuild the region. Tibetan monks have been heavily involved in the emergency operation, digging through the rubble for survivors and distributing aid. They have also been collecting bodies and holding funerals' (www.bbc.co.uk, 20 April 2010).

'[On Monday 19 April] the number of people killed in the quake reached 1,944 … [with] 216 people still missing, officials say' (www.bbc.co.uk, 19 April 2010).

'Xinhua reported that at least sixty-six children and ten teachers died' (www.guardian.co.uk, 19 April 2010).

> China is planning a day of mourning … China will suspend all public entertainment and lower flags half mast on Wednesday [21 April] as the nation mourns the 2,039 people killed in last week's earthquake … Another 195 people were still missing … Earlier premier Wen Jiabao said: 'Your suffering is our suffering … The family members you lost are also our family members, and we grieve for them as you do' … The quake shook the region shortly before 8 a.m. Wednesday [7 April], when many residents were still at home and schools were just getting started for the day.
>
> (www.cnn.com, 20 April 2010)

'The death toll from the 14 April quake in Yushu county in Qinghai province rose to 2,064 on Tuesday [20 April] … [while] 175 others are missing' (*IHT*, 21 April 2010, p. 5).

> In an elaborately orchestrated outpouring of grief, China mourned the victims of the earthquake in western Qinghai province by printing monochromatic newspapers, shuttering karaoke parlours and cancelling sporting

events. The quake ... killed more than 2,000 people [and] devastated Jiegu ... As many as 100,000 survivors have been left homeless ... The national day of mourning Wednesday [21 April], not unlike the one staged in 2008 for those killed during a devastating earthquake in Sichuan province, was sweeping and in some cases compulsory. Movie theatres and bars were forced to close for twenty-four hours, video games disappeared from the internet and televised movies and soap operas were abruptly replaced by an emotive news loop produced by the country's central broadcaster ... During a three-hour televised gala Tuesday night [20 April] more than $307 million was donated by state-owned enterprises, army units and ordinary people. A similar telethon for the Sichuan earthquake, by comparison, raised about $214 million ... In recent days Beijing has promised to spend $161 million on relief efforts, and more than 10,000 soldiers, police officers and emergency workers have made the arduous journey to the quake zone ... Relief convoys were so thick earlier this week that they caused a twenty-four-hour jam on the only road that links Jiegu to the provincial capital 500 miles away. Would-be volunteers have been ordered to stay away ... Banners draped across military relief trucks declared: 'Whether Han or Tibetan, we are all one family' ... Domestic media coverage has been tightly controlled, with reporters instructed to focus on heroism of rescue from the trunks of cars. Even the day-long broadcast of mourning Wednesday excluded any images of the monks ... The state-run media has also avoided any discussion of the collapse of at least a dozen school structures that, according to the official tally, left at least 180 students dead or missing. Although some Chinese reporters who raced to Jiegu in the first days after the quake were later instructed to leave, others said they were allowed to work unimpeded ... Foreign reporters who covered the earthquake say they experienced little government interference. In an interview on Wednesday Woeser, an influential Tibetan blogger who is in frequent contact with people in the earthquake zone, said several monks told her that they had been ordered to leave Jiegu in recent days.

(www.iht.com, 21 April 2010)

'China lowered flags to half mast and pulled all entertainment programming from the airwaves' (www.cnn.com, 22 April 2010).

Chinese officials have ordered some monasteries to recall monks from the western town devastated by an earthquake last week. Buddhist lamas have played a crucial role in rescue and relief operations in Jiegu ... Thousands have dug for survivors in the rubble, disposed of bodies and arranged food and shelter for the homeless. More than 2,180 people died in the 14 April earthquake ... Yixi Luoren, the head of Gengqing monastery, said 120 of the 150 monks who went to Yushu county had left on the orders of officials ... He said: 'The authorities did not tell us the reason but we assume they might have worried that there are too many people there and wanted us to come home safely' ... Woeser, a Beijing-based Tibetan poet and activist, said Han and Tibetan acquaintances reported similar orders being given to other monks. She said: 'A clear reason for the order was not given but it was very strict. Local officials told them through translators in Tibetan: "You have done everything already. You have done too much. You have to leave Yushu now; otherwise there will be trouble"' ... Other lamas were still at work ... State media have focussed on the efforts of the military and the armed police in tackling the disaster, leading Tibetans to complain that monks have not received sufficient credit. CCTV, the official broadcaster, is thought to have shown lengthy footage of monks at work on the day of the disaster, but little since. Chinese premier Wen Jiabao praised the work of lamas as he toured a destroyed monastery, although Reuters reported that state media did not cover the visit.

(www.guardian.co.uk, 22 April 2010)

Chinese authorities confirmed Friday [23 April] reports that they had asked Buddhist monks to end their relief work in Qinghai ... where an earthquake last week left at least 2,187 dead. The officials disputed complaints from some monks that they were being expelled for political reasons, saying that better-trained workers were required for tasks like disease prevention and building reconstruction ... The State Council Information Office expressed gratitude for the monks' rescue efforts. But 'it would bring more difficulties to disaster relief work if lots of unprofessional personnel were at the scene', the statement added ... Buddhist monks ran most of the early rescue operations in Jiegu, a city of 100,000 near the quake's epicentre. As rescues of survivors dwindled, the monks have supervised mass cremations and the mandatory three-day period of mourning. For days the monks conducted their work with little of no interference from officials. But some complained this week that Chinese army personnel and other government officials had begun to elbow them out of rescue and relief efforts. They said the government wanted to cast the rescue operations not as an indigenous effort, but as a generous gesture from the central government to the region's ethnic Tibetan population.

(www.iht.com, 24 April 2010)

The government has confirmed that it has asked Tibetan monks to leave Qinghai's earthquake-hit region so as not to hinder relief operations ... The State Council Information Office: 'The duties of rescue workers in the quake zone are basically over, and the focus has moved to disease prevention and reconstruction, which need specialized people. While fully recognizing the positive contributions of the monks that came from other areas, we suggested to them that they return to their monasteries to ensure the high effectiveness and order of quake relief work.'

(www.bbc.co.uk, 24 April 2010)

The death toll rose to 2,203 ... state media reported late Saturday [24 April] ... At least seventy-eight people are missing ... Officials said they would raise the monthly allowance from 600 yuan ($87) to 1,000 yuan ($146) for orphaned children, widowed elderly and disabled people in the wake of the quake. Families of the dead also will receive 8,000 yuan ($1,171) for each death.

(www.cnn.com, 24 April 2010)

Relatives of many victims of the quake in Sichuan province are now able to start registering loved ones as dead, two years after the disaster. Some 18,000 people remain officially designated as 'missing' from the quake, which killed a further 69,000. Chinese law says families must wait two years after an accident before starting to register missing relatives as dead.

(www.bbc.co.uk, 12 May 2010)

Olympics

The International Olympic Committee on Wednesday [28 April] stripped China of a bronze in the women's team event at the 2000 [Sydney] Olympic Games ... after finding one of the team's athletes was underage ... An inquiry showed that ... the gymnast ... was [then] only fourteen ... [whereas] athletes must be sixteen in the year of the Games in order to compete.

(www.cnn.com, 29 April 2010)

Chronology

14 March 2010. 'The National People's Congress adopted an amendment to the main electoral law on 14 March. The amendment reportedly gives rural residents the same rights in selecting representatives to the National People's Congress as residents in cities' (www.iht.com, 21 March 2010).

31 March–13 April 2010.

China announced on Thursday [1 April] that President Hu Jintao will attend a summit on nuclear security in Washington later this month ... Beijing had not committed to attend the 12 April summit ... [The Chinese] foreign ministry spokesman ... [said] the nuclear summit would mainly discuss nuclear terrorism and potential counter-measures ... [The United States] said on Wednesday [31 March] that Beijing had agreed in a conference call to start talks about sanctions against Iran.

(www.ft.com, 1 April 2010)

The security meeting, scheduled for 12–13 April, seeks to limit the proliferation of nuclear materials 'so that they never fall into the hands of terrorists', President Barack Obama said in announcing it in his State of the Nation speech in January [2010] ... [The announcement] came less than a day after the Chinese government appeared to throw its support behind new UN sanctions aimed at pressurizing Iran over its nuclear programme. In recent months the five permanent members of the Security Council have been stymied by China's insistence on diplomacy over sanctions.

(www.iht.com, 1 April 2010)

The US ambassador to the United Nations, Susan Rice, said on Wednesday [31 March] her government, Britain, France, Russia and Germany had agreed with China to begin discussing a proposed UN Security Council resolution with new sanctions on Iran. She said: 'This is progress, but the negotiations have yet to begin in earnest.'

(www.iht.com, 1 April 2010)

On Thursday night [1 April] President Barack Obama spoke with President Hu Jintao for about an hour by telephone ... For now the United States is setting aside potentially the most divisive issue in the relationship, deferring a decision on whether to accuse China of manipulating its currency until well after Mr Hu's visit, according to a senior administration official ... The administration decided not to report on 15 April, one of ten deadlines set by Congress and the Treasury Department to issue a report on possible currency manipulation ... An official said that if China did not take action on its own, the administration could raise the issue again at the G-20 summit meeting in June ... American officials said they expected China to wrangle over the wording of a UN resolution, with a goal of watering down the measures against Tehran.

(www.iht.com, 2 April 2010)

Susan Rice, US ambassador to the United Nations, said this week that China agreed to negotiate possible sanctions against Iran. But Chinese officials were not as bold in their statements Thursday [1 April], again emphasizing the difference in priorities. Foreign ministry spokesman Qin Gang said he hoped the issue could be resolved 'through diplomatic negotiations'. The spokesman added: 'We oppose Iran's possession of nuclear weapons, and at the same time we also believe that as a sovereign state it has the right to peacefully use nuclear technology.'

(www.iht.com, 2 April 2010)

'On Wednesday [31 March] US ambassador to the United Nations, Susan Rice, said China had "agreed to sit down and begin serious negotiations in New York" over possible new sanctions against Iran ... Iran is China's third largest oil supplier' (www.cnn.com, 4 April 2010).

'The US ambassador to the UN, Susan Rice, said ... China had indicated it was ready to hold "serious" talks with Western powers on a new UN resolution' (www.bbc.co.uk, 2 April 2010).

President Hu Jintao will travel to Washington next month for a summit on nuclear issues ... The announcement comes as the United States and France are pushing for sanctions against Iran's nuclear energy programme, and as Iran's top nuclear official was heading to China to discuss his country's nuclear programme ... Chinese foreign ministry spokesman Qin Gang: '[China hopes the issue can be solved] through diplomatic negotiations. We oppose Iran's possession of nuclear weapons, and at the same time we also believe that as a sovereign state it has the right to peacefully use nuclear technology.'

(www.cnn.com, 1 April 2010)

China traditionally opposes sanctions. Although it went along with three earlier UN sanctions against Iran, Beijing has been a vocal opponent of a fourth round, insisting that further negotiations with Tehran were needed. But US officials say a Chinese representative made a commitment in a phone call on Wednesday [31 March] with officials of the United States, Russia, China, Britain, France and Germany to discuss specifics of a potential Security Council resolution ... China depends on oil- and gas-rich Iran for 11 per cent of its energy needs and last year [2009] became Tehran's biggest trading partner, according to Iranian figures.

(www.independent.co.uk, 2 April 2010)

The Obama administration said Saturday [3 April] that it would delay a decision on whether to declare China a currency valuation manipulator, but it vowed to press Chinese leaders on the politically charged issue of currency manipulation during a series of meetings through June ... US Treasury Secretary Timothy Geithner said he had decided to delay the semi-annual exchange rate report to Congress, which was to be due on 15 April ... Timothy Geithner: 'China's inflexible exchange rate has made it difficult for other emerging market economies to let their currencies appreciate. A move by China to a more market-orientated exchange rate will make an essential contribution to global rebalancing. China's continued maintenance of a currency peg has required increasingly large volumes of currency intervention' ... Mr Geithner pledged to raise the issue at a series of forums: a meeting of finance ministers and central banker governors from the G-20 nations later this month [April]; the twice-yearly Strategic and Economic Dialogue between the two countries, expected to be in China in May; and a meeting of G-20 leaders and finance ministers in June. Mr Geithner called these meetings 'the best avenue of advancing US interests at this time' ... China said on Thursday [1 April] that President Hu Jintao would attend a nuclear security summit meeting in Washington this month ... The United States has not found China to be a currency manipulator since 1994. Under successive administrations, officials have tried to persuade China that letting the renminbi appreciate would stimulate domestic demand and reduce reliance on exports ... Within the Chinese government there has been debate about the [exchange rate] issue. The central bank has signalled that a gradual appreciation is in order, but the commerce ministry, which represents the interests of the country's powerful exporters and manufacturers, has argued for maintaining the currency peg.

(www.iht.com, 4 April 2010; *IHT*, 5 April 2010, pp. 1, 15)

> US Treasury Secretary Timothy Geithner has delayed a scheduled 15 April report to Congress ... Timothy Geithner, explaining the delay in a statement Saturday [3 April], said a series of upcoming meetings, including among officials of the G-20 financially influential countries and with China, are 'the best avenue for advancing US interests at this time'.
>
> (www.cnn.com, 4 April 2010)

> White House spokesman Robert Gibbs: 'The president has spoken repeatedly and recently that China's currency must be market-based' ... A congressional aid speaking on condition of anonymity: 'If there's no substantive sign of action, Congress will be forced to act' ... Several Chinese economists quoted in the overseas edition of the *People's Daily*, the official newspaper of the Communist Party, maintained that the yuan was not to blame for the US trade deficit. But Li Daokui, a member of the central bank's monetary policy committee, said China could nonetheless buy more goods to ease pressure from the White House and Congress. Li Daokui (a Harvard-trained economist at Tsinghua University in Beijing): 'China can increase purchases from [US] states facing mass unemployment because of recession in the manufacturing sector.'
>
> (www.iht.com, 5 April 2010)

> President Hu Jintao at the nuclear security summit in Washington (13 April): 'China will firmly stick to a path of reforming the yuan's exchange rate formation mechanism ... [But the move] won't be advanced by any foreign pressure ... Renminbi appreciation would neither balance Sino–US trade nor solve the unemployment problem in the United States' ... Financial markets reacted by lowering expectations for liberalization of the renminbi. Economists said a gradual rise beginning around the middle of the year was still the most likely outcome.
>
> (*FT*, 14 April 2010, p. 7)

'President Barack Obama: "I think China rightly sees the issue of currency as ... sovereign issue. I think they are resistant to international pressure when it comes to them making decisions about their currency policy and monetary policy"' (www.iht.com, 14 April 2010).

> China is facing growing international pressure to begin allowing its currency to appreciate, providing unexpected allies for the United States .... Speaking ahead of a meeting of finance ministers and central bank heads from the G-20 countries which starts today [Thursday 22 April] in Washington, Indian and Brazilian central bank presidents have made the most forceful statements yet by their countries about the case for a stronger renminbi ... Lee Hsien Loong, prime minister of Singapore ... last week ... [said] it was 'in China's interests' with the financial crisis over to have a more flexible exchange rate ... The increase in criticism of China comes at a time of relative calm between Beijing and Washington over the issue, with many US officials and analysts assuming China has already decided to abandon its

> peg with the dollar over coming months ... Although there have been strong signs in recent weeks that China is preparing to shift policy, a number of prominent officials continue to oppose any immediate changes.
>
> (*FT*, 22 April 2010, p. 10)

'Although India and Brazil this week joined calls by the United States for China to allow the value of the renminbi to appreciate, G-20 officials said the topic did not come up in the meetings [held 22–3 April]' (www.iht.com, 24 April 2010).

('The pain of the European debt crisis is spreading, with the plummeting Euro making Chinese companies less competitive in Europe, their largest market, and complicating any move to break the Chinese currency's page to the dollar. Chinese policy-makers reached a consensus last month [April] about dropping the dollar peg. But allowing the renminbi to rise against the dollar now would mean a further increase in the renminbi's level against the Euro, creating even more problems for Chinese exporters to Europe. The Euro has plunged against the renminbi in recent weeks, at one point Monday [17 May] reaching its lowest level since late 2002 before turning higher. The steep rise of the renminbi prompted a commerce ministry official in Beijing to warn on Monday that China's exports could be threatened. The official's comments ... suggest that even China ... is not immune to the crisis that started in Greece and threatens to spread across much of Europe. Yal Jian [the ministry official said]: "The yuan has risen about 14.5 per cent against the Euro during the past four months, which will increase cost pressure for Chinese exporters and also have a negative impact on China's exports to European countries" ... The renminbi is rising along with the dollar against the Euro. The Chinese government has continued to intervene heavily in currency markets in recent weeks to prevent the renminbi from rising against the dollar, maintaining an informal peg of 6.827 renminbi to the dollar, the level since July 2008. Because American companies compete in the Chinese market with European companies in many industries, the Euro's weakness against the renminbi is pitting American companies at a disadvantage just as Gary Locke, the US commerce secretary, is leading the first cabinet-level trade mission of the administration of President Barack Obama this week ... Chinese leaders reached a consensus in April [2010] to break the renminbi's peg to the dollar, ending a dispute that spilled into public view in March when commerce ministry officials warned in speeches and interviews in Beijing and Washington about the dangers of any change in the renminbi's value. The ministry halted those warnings immediately after the consensus was reached, and Chen Deming, the commerce minister, even reversed himself publicly by saying that China's trade deficit in March was nothing to worry about. But events since then have delayed implementation of the consensus, including public attention paid to a visit to Beijing by US Treasury secretary Timothy Geithner, followed by the earthquake in Qinghai province and then the Euro's slide': www.iht.com, 17 May 2010.)

> President Barack Obama said Monday [5 April] that he was revamping American nuclear strategy to substantially narrow the conditions under

which the United States would use nuclear weapons. But the president said in an interview [with *The New York Times*] that he was carving out an exception for 'outliers like Iran and North Korea' that have violated or renounced the main treaty to halt proliferation … North Korea renounced the Nuclear Non-proliferation Treaty in 2003. Iran remains a signatory, but the UN Security Council has repeatedly found it in violation of its obligations … The new strategy renounces the development of any new nuclear weapons, overruling the initial position of his own defence secretary … For the first time the United States is explicitly committing not to use nuclear weapons against non-nuclear states that are in compliance with the Nuclear Non-proliferation Treaty, even if they attacked the United States with biological or chemical weapons or launched a crippling cyber-attack … White House officials said the new strategy would include the option of reconsidering the use of nuclear retaliation against a biological attack, if the development of such weapons reached a level that made the United States vulnerable to a devastating strike … The release of the new strategy, known as the Nuclear Posture Review, opens an intensive nine days of nuclear diplomacy geared toward reducing weapons. Mr Obama flies to Prague to sign a new arms control agreement with Russia on Thursday [8 April] and then will host forty-seven world leaders in Washington for a summit meeting on nuclear security … The strategy to be released on Tuesday [6 April] is months late, partly because Mr Obama had to adjudicate among advisers who feared he was not changing American policy significantly enough, and those who fear that anything too precipitous could embolden potential adversaries … He ended up with a document that differed considerably from the one President George W. Bush published in early 2002, just three months after the 11 September attacks. Mr Bush, too, argued for a post-Cold War rethinking of nuclear deterrence, reducing reliance on those weapons. But Mr Bush's document also reserved the right to use nuclear weapons 'to deter a wide range of threats', including banned chemical and biological weapons and large-scale conventional attacks. Mr Obama's strategy abandons that option – except if the attack is by a nuclear state, or a non-signatory or violator of the non-proliferation treaty. The document to be released Tuesday after months of study by the Defense Department will declare that 'the fundamental role' of nuclear weapons is to deter attacks on the United States, allies or partners, a narrower presumption than the past. But Mr Obama rejected the formulation sought by arms control advocates to declare that the 'sole role' of nuclear weapons is to deter a nuclear attack.

(www.iht.com, 6 April 2010)

Mr Obama on Monday described his policy as part of a broader effort to edge the world toward making nuclear weapons obsolete and to create incentives for countries to give up nuclear ambitions … Mr Obama's strategy … seeks to revamp the American nuclear posture for a new age in which rogue states and terrorist organizations are greater threats than traditional powers like Russia and China. It eliminates much of the ambiguity that has deliberately existed in US nuclear policy since the opening days of the Cold War ... Mr Obama said: 'We are going to want to make sure that we can continue to move toward less emphasis on nuclear weapons ... [and to] make sure that our conventional capability is an effective deterrent in all but the most extreme circumstances.'

(*IHT*, 7 April 2010, pp. 1, 4)

The Nuclear Posture Review said: 'The massive nuclear arsenal we inherited from the Cold War era of bipolar military confrontations is poorly suited to address the challenges posed by suicidal terrorists and unfriendly regimes seeking nuclear weapons. Therefore, it is essential that we better align our nuclear policies and posture to our most urgent priorities – preventing nuclear terrorism and nuclear proliferation.'

(*The Independent*, 7 April 2010, p. 19)

President Obama's administration has unveiled a defence policy to significantly narrow the circumstances in which the United States would use nuclear arms. But its far-reaching Nuclear Posture Review warned countries breaking the rules remain potential targets ... The Nuclear Policy Review, published on Tuesday [6 April], outlines plans for 'achieving substantial further nuclear force reductions' beyond the new [Start] treaty. Every president since 1991 conducts such a review – the last one took place in 2001 at the start of George W, Bush's administration ... For the first time the United States is ruling out a nuclear response to attacks on America involving biological, chemical or conventional weapons. But this comes with a big caveat: countries will only be spared a nuclear response if they comply with the Nuclear Non-proliferation Treaty – this does not include Iran and North Korea ... The document said America would only use nuclear arms in 'extreme circumstances', and committed it to not developing any new nuclear warheads ... The US strategy document also raised concerns about a 'lack of transparency' in China's nuclear programme ... The US defence department document said China's nuclear arsenal remained much smaller than those of Russia and America. It noted: 'But the lack of transparency surrounding its nuclear programmes – their pace and scope, as well as the strategy and doctrine that guides them – raises questions about China's future strategic intentions' ... The White House announced later on Tuesday that President Barack Obama would hold talks with Chinese President Hu Jintao on the sidelines of a nuclear non-proliferation summit ... The two-day conference begins in Washington on Monday [12 April].

(www.bbc.co.uk, 6 April 2010)

The Nuclear Policy Review said: 'The United States and China's Asian neighbours remain concerned about the pace and scope of China's current military modernization efforts, including its quantitative and qualitative modernization of its nuclear capabilities' ... The US report reiterated the

> Pentagon's oft-stated wish to hold a strategic dialogue with the Chinese military that would 'provide a venue and mechanism for each side to communicate its views about the other's strategies, policies and programmes on nuclear weapons and other strategic capabilities. The goal of such a dialogue is to enhance confidence, improve transparency, and reduce mistrust.'
>
> (www.iht.com, 6 April 2010)

> The document released Tuesday [6 April] declares that 'the fundamental role' of nuclear weapons is to deter nuclear attacks on the United States, allies or partners, a narrower presumption than the past. But Mr Obama rejected the formulation sought by arms control advocates that the 'sole role' of nuclear weapons is to deter a nuclear attack … [There are an] estimated 200 tactical nuclear weapons [that] the United States still has stationed in Western Europe. Russia has called for their removal and there is growing interest among European nations in such a move as well. But Mr Obama said he wanted to consult with Nato allies before making such as commitment.
>
> (*IHT*, 7 April 2010, p. 4)

> President Barack Obama … has committed to maintaining the safety and security of America's nuclear stockpile. He has already backed that up with an extra $624 million in next year's budget for the nuclear labs and promised … an additional $5 billion over the next five years to build up their ageing infrastructure. Mr Obama has also promised support for more advanced conventional arms.
>
> (www.iht.com, 7 April 2010)

'President Barack Obama's new strategy marks a break with the Bush administration's more hawkish policy laid out in its 2002 review, threatening the use of nuclear weapons to pre-empt or respond to chemical or biological attack, even from non-nuclear countries' (www.guardian.co.uk, 6 April 2010).

> The Nuclear Posture Review, published after a year's work, marks one of the biggest changes in strategic thinking since the end of the Cold War and reverses policies introduced by the Bush administration. Among the changes is a pledge not to develop any new nuclear weapons, a move pushed through in the face of strong resistance by the Pentagon … The Nuclear Posture Review shifts the focus away from a Cold War strategy that saw the main threat as coming from Russia or China, recognizing the major threat now is from nuclear proliferation or from a terrorist organization. It also regards a huge nuclear stockpile as redundant. The biggest change is recognition that the circumstances in which nuclear weapons could be used had to be narrowed. The key passage in the review says that the strategic situation has changed since the end of the Cold War and the United States has a strong enough conventional capability to deter a biological or chemical attack. As a result, the review says: 'The United States will not use or threaten to use nuclear weapons against non-nuclear weapons states that are party to

the Non-proliferation Treaty and in compliance with their nuclear non-proliferation obligations' ... This contrasts with the Bush administration, which in 2001 declared that nuclear weapons would be used to deter a wide range of threats, including weapons of mass destruction and large-scale conventional military force ... North Korea pulled out of the Non-proliferation Treaty in 2003, while the United States claims Iran is covertly engaged in developing a nuclear weapons capability, which Iran denies ... The review allows the retention of about 200 tactical nuclear weapons held in five European countries.

(www.guardian.co.uk, 6 April 2010)

The Washington Post reported that the Pentagon is developing a weapon to plug the gap left by nuclear warheads: missiles armed with conventional warheads that could strike anywhere in the world in less than an hour. US military officials say the intercontinental ballistic missiles, known as prompt global strike weapons, are a necessary new form of deterrence against terrorist networks.

(www.guardian.co.uk, 8 April 2010)

Russia deploys 2,600 strategic warheads while the United States deploys about 2,100. Both sides have thousands more reserve warheads or tactical warheads ... By contrast, China has an estimated 180 warheads, India and Pakistan each have about seventy or eighty and North Korea just a handful.

(*IHT*, 8 April 2010, p. 4)

In May [2010] the operation of the Nuclear Non-proliferation Treaty will be the subject of review in New York in which nearly all governments in the world will take part. The review that took place in 2005 ended in acrimony and some predicted the end of the treaty. Through adherence to the non-proliferation treaty that was concluded in 1970, states have committed themselves to stay away from nuclear weapons or to move away from these weapons. If all states had joined and fulfilled their commitments, the treaty would have led by now to a world free of nuclear weapons. This has not happened, of course. The number of nuclear weapons, which peaked at more than 50,000 during the Cold War, is still over 20,000 – most of them in the United States and Russia. The number of states with nuclear weapons has gone from five to nine since 1970 ... [There was an] obligation of five nuclear weapons states under the treaty to negotiate toward nuclear disarmament ... Israel has nuclear weapons and has refrained from adhering to the treaty ... Although Iraq and Libya have been brought into compliance, North Korea has not and Iran and perhaps others might be aiming to ignore the treaty ... There are many reasons for suspecting that the aim of Iran's enrichment programme is the development of a nuclear weapon in breach of treaty obligations or, at least, to move closer to the ability to make a weapon ... The Comprehensive Test Ban Treaty has not entered into force because the United States, China and a number of other states have not ratified it.

> The negotiation of a convention prohibiting the production of enriched uranium and plutonium for weapons remains blocked at the Geneva Disarmament Conference. The Additional Protocol of the International Atomic Energy Agency for strengthened safeguards inspections remains unratified by a large number of states, including Iran … In the last few years the appeals have intensified for governments to aim, as the non-proliferation treaty does, to free the world from nuclear weapons. In January 2007 former US Secretaries of State George Schultz and Henry Kissinger, former Secretary of Defence Bill Perry and former Senator Sam Nunn published an article in which they reminded the United States and the world that the Cold War was over. They argued that if the United States, Russia and others continued to see nuclear weapons as necessary for their security, others would see the same thing and proliferation would result. They urged that the United States and Russia take the lead in a long process that would eventually result in a nuclear weapon-free world … [President Barack Obama and President Dmitri Medvedev] jointly espoused the long-term aim of full disarmament in a declaration in London in April 2009.
>
> (Hans Blix, head of the International Atomic Energy Agency from 1981 to 1997 and chief UN arms inspector for Iraq from 2000 to 2003, www.iht.com, 4 April 2010; *IHT*, 5 April 2010, p. 8)

> Dozens of world leaders gather in Washington next week for an unprecedented meeting on nuclear security … Forty-seven countries [will gather] … Two nations excluded form the meeting are Iran … and North Korea … North Korea withdrew from the Nuclear Non-proliferation Treaty in 2003 … Iran rejects Western allegations that its atomic programme is aimed at developing weapons and refuses to stop enriching uranium … A draft communiqué circulated to countries attending the summit … includes a US proposal to 'secure all vulnerable nuclear material in four years'. The draft text will likely be revised before it is adopted at the end of the 12–13 April meeting.
>
> (www.iht.com, 8 April 2010)

'The meeting … seeks ways to better secure existing supplies of bomb-usable plutonium and highly enriched uranium' (www.iht.com, 12 April 2010).

'North Korea and Iran … [have not] been invited to the summit … Syria was also left off the invitation list because the United States believes Damascus also has nuclear ambitions' (www.bbc.co.uk, 12 April 2010).

> Ukraine has agreed to eliminate its entire stockpile of weapons-grade nuclear material, US officials said ahead of a key nuclear security summit. The White House said Ukraine would by 2012 get rid of enough highly enriched uranium to build 'several weapons' … This would be removed with some technical and financial help from the United States … The summit is all about securing stocks of highly enriched uranium and plutonium … It is estimated that there are around 1,600 tonnes of highly enriched

uranium around the world – the type used in nuclear weapons. Experts agree that virtually all of it is held by the acknowledged nuclear weapons states, most of it in Russia. There are also about 500 tonnes of the other key ingredient of nuclear weapons – plutonium. In total that is enough to make 120,000 nuclear weapons. Much international, largely US-funded, effort has attempted to clamp down on the threat of nuclear leakage from Russia in particular, but it remains a concern.

(www.bbc.co.uk, 12 April 2010)

Kiev had agreed to return nuclear warheads on its territory to Russia in 1994, but retained stockpiles of enriched uranium, some of its extracted from those weapons by Russia and returned to Ukraine ... The leaders of forty-seven countries converged on Washington for the summit meeting, the largest such assemblage since Franklin D. Roosevelt organized a meeting in 1945 to create the United Nations.

(*IHT*, 13 April 2010, p. 4)

The Nuclear Threat Initiative, a non-profit group that studies proliferation, has estimated Ukraine's stockpile at 163 kilograms, or roughly enough for seven weapons. According to a senior administration official, under the deal announced Monday [12 April] the United States will pay to secure the highly enriched uranium, which will likely be sent to Russia for conversion into low-enriched uranium for nuclear power plants. As part of the deal, the United States will also supply Ukraine with new low-enriched fuel and a new research facility.

(www.iht.com, 13 April 2010)

The head of the International Atomic Energy Authority, Yukiya Amano, said that nuclear powers needed to do more to protect nuclear materials ... He said: 'On average every two days we receive one new information on an incident involving theft or smuggling of nuclear material.'

(www.bbc.co.uk, 13 April 2010)

Before the talks President Barack Obama and President Hu Jintao agreed to step up pressure on Iran over its atomic plans. A US official ... [said] that Mr Hu had agreed to direct Chinese officials to work with their US counterparts on a UN sanctions resolution against Tehran ... A US spokesman said: 'The two presidents agreed the two delegations should work together on a sanctions resolution in New York.'

(www.bbc.co.uk, 13 April 2010)

President Barack Obama secured a promise from President Hu Jintao on Monday [13 April] to join negotiations on a new package of sanctions against Iran, administration officials said, but Mr Hu made no specific commitment ... The session with Mr Hu came just before the opening of the first summit meeting devoted to the challenges of keeping nuclear weapons and material out of the hands of terrorists ... Mr Obama laid out the details of the sanctions package for Mr Hu ... The Chinese import nearly 12 per cent of their oil from Iran ... Former President George W. Bush [made] three efforts to corral Chinese support for UN Security Council penalties ... In those cases, former American officials said, the Chinese agreed to go along with efforts to address Iran's nuclear ambitions but then used Security Council negotiating sessions to water down the resolutions that ultimately passed.

(www.iht.com, 13 April 2010)

Ukraine, Canada, Mexico and Malaysia have offered individual undertakings to tighten controls, reduce nuclear stocks or move from highly enriched to low enriched uranium fuel ... [On Monday 12 April] Ukraine said it would rid itself of all its highly enriched uranium – reportedly enough for about seven weapons – by 2012 ... President Lee Myung Bak of South Korea said that North Korea would be welcome at the next summit meeting [in Seoul] if it made sufficient progress in the six-nation talks on its nuclear programme.

(*IHT*, 14 April 2010, p. 4)

So far only twenty-one countries have ratified the UN's Convention on Physical Protection of Nuclear Materials – far too few for it to enter into force ... President Barack Obama's goal ... [is to secure] all such material by 2013 ... Russia and the United States signed an agreement yesterday [13 April] to dispose of 34 tonnes of plutonium apiece, breaking a decade-long logjam on how to implement a deal in 2000 to do so ... Despite its record in returning risk material and its continuing nuclear power programme, Belarus ... was also not invited ... Yesterday South Korean President Lee Myung-Bak agreed to hold another nuclear security summit in his country in 2012.

(*FT*, 14 April 2010, p. 7)

Georgian security forces have foiled a criminal plot to sell weapons-grade uranium on the black market ... President Mikheil Saakashvili [said on 13 April] ... Georgian sources said the highly enriched uranium was intercepted in a sting operation carried out in March [2010] ... The Georgian president told the summit: 'The Georgian ministry of interior has foiled eight attempts of illicit trafficking of enriched uranium during the last ten years. Including several cases of weapons-grade enrichment ...' Ukraine and Canada said they would no longer use highly enriched uranium in research reactors. Malaysia announced it had enforced tougher controls on the shipment of nuclear equipment ... The summit's final communiqué affirmed the support of the forty-seven nations for President Barack Obama's goal of securing the stockpiles of fissile materials within four years, and called for more countries to switch from highly enriched uranium to low enriched uranium reactors. It also called on the ratification of UN conventions aimed at setting international standards for nuclear security.

(*Guardian*, 14 April 2010, p. 19)

> Ending an unprecedented forty-seven-nation nuclear security summit, President Barack Obama won pledges from world leaders to take joint action to prevent terrorist groups from getting nuclear weapons … The summit's final communiqué promised greater efforts to block 'non-state actors' like al Qaeda from obtaining the building blocks for atomic weapons for 'malicious purposes' … The summit communiqué included no mechanism to enforce the agreement … South Korea would host the next nuclear security summit in 2012 … [There is an] estimated 2,000 tonnes of plutonium and highly enriched uranium in dozens of countries. Washington and Moscow signed a deal to reduce stocks of excess weapons-grade plutonium. The United States, Canada and Mexico agreed to work together with the International Atomic Energy Agency (IAEA) to convert Mexico's research reactor from the use of highly enriched uranium to low enriched uranium fuel … Today a Japanese expert, Yukiya Amano, leads the IAEA.
>
> (www.iht.com, 14 April 2010)

'On Tuesday [13 April] Russia announced that it would close its ADE-2 reactor, which has been producing weapons-grade plutonium near Krasnoyarsk in Siberia for the past fifty years' (www.economist.com, 14 April 2010).

> The leaders … pledged to secure all vulnerable nuclear material within four years. US president Barack Obama said the joint action plan agreed at a summit in Washington would make a real contribution to a safer world. The plan calls for every nation to safeguard nuclear stocks and keep material out of terrorists' hands. Earlier Russia and the United States signed an agreement to dispose of 68 tonnes of surplus weapons-grade plutonium. The combined stockpiles – 34 tonnes from each country – are said to be enough to make 17,000 nuclear warheads. US officials said it would be used as fuel in civilian reactors to generate electricity. The United States will provide $400 million of the funding for the disposal of Russia's plutonium, which Moscow estimates will cost up to $2.5 billion. Several other countries – including Mexico, Chile and Ukraine – had earlier agreed to give up their stocks of highly enriched uranium … Mexico pledged to eliminate all its highly enriched uranium. The country will work with the United States, Canada and the IAEA to convert the uranium at its research reactor into lower grade fuel … In a joint communiqué the leaders agreed to non-binding measures to 'secure all vulnerable nuclear material in four years' and to 'prevent non-state actors from obtaining the information or technology required to use such material'. They said they would co-operate more deeply with the UN's nuclear watchdog, the International Atomic Energy Agency (IAEA), and share information on nuclear detection and ways to prevent nuclear trafficking. But increased security should 'not infringe upon the rights of states to develop and utilize nuclear energy for peaceful purposes and technology', they added. Progress is to be reviewed at a summit in South Korea in 2012 … Iran has announced that it will hold its own

nuclear summit in Tehran this weekend with the foreign ministers of fifteen countries.

(www.bbc.co.uk, 14 April 2010)

6 April 2010.

China has executed a Japanese man convicted of drug smuggling, Xinhua reported ... He is the first Japanese citizen to be put to death in China since diplomatic ties between the two countries were re-established in 1972 ... Beijing told Japan last week that it plans to execute three more Japanese drug smugglers this week.

(www.bbc.co.uk, 6 April 2010)

9 April 2010.

Three Japanese citizens have been executed for trying to smuggle the drug methamphetamine. This follows the execution of another Japanese drug smuggler on Tuesday 6 April] ... Japan also has the death penalty, but not for drug smuggling.

(www.bbc.co.uk, 9 April 2010)

14 April 2010.

A former senior police officer has been sentenced to death for corruption and rape. Wen Qiang was charged with accepting vast sums of money from criminal; gangs in Chongqing in exchange for protection from the law. He was also found guilty of rape and failing to account for his assets ... Wen is the most senior official to be charged under a major corruption probe in the city ... Three other senior Chongqing police officers received sentences ranging from six months to twenty years.

(www.bbc.co.uk, 14 April 2010)

15 April 2010.

Hu Yaobang ... was the reformist party leader whose death twenty-one years ago helped inspire the pro-democracy protests in Tiananmen Square ... So tens of thousands of Chinese took note on Thursday [15 April] when a long and emotional tribute to Mr Hu – written by prime minister Wen Jiabao – was published Thursday in *Renmin Ribao*, the Communist Party's official newspaper, otherwise known as *People's Daily* ... Since 2005 Communist Party leaders have been rehabilitating the image of Mr Hu, who was forced out as Communist Party General Secretary in 1987, two years before the Tiananmen demonstrations ... Mr Hu helped inaugurate China's early market-orientated economic changes, promoted people purged under Mao and pushed political liberalization as a vital component of economic reform. Once viewed as the most likely successor to Deng Xiaoping as China's leader, he was forced out of power by party conservatives who claimed his 'bourgeois' leanings threatened the country's security. Mr Wen's essay deals with none of that. He recalled Mr Hu's work ethic, stoicism and determination to pierce the pleasing facades created by lower-level officials and grasp the true conditions of the people. He quoted Mr Hu as saying: 'The greatest danger for those who assume leadership is to be removed from reality' ... Analysts poring over that and other parts of Mr Wen's text were divided over their meaning ... What to say about Mr Hu has been an issue within the party since he lost his position as the party's leader in 1987 ... President Hu Jintao took the first steps in elevating the official memory of Hu Yaobang in 2005, when the party organized memorial services and a seminar to discuss his legacy.

(www.iht.com, 15 April 2010)

On 15 April ... the Communist Party's *People's Daily* published an article on the top of its second page by prime minister Wen Jiabao. Its glowing praise for Hu Yaobang, a politically incorrect former party chief whose death triggered the Tiananmen Square protest ... Hu's death on 15 April 1989 prompted thousands of students to take to the streets in mourning. They bore aloft pictures of the late leader, who though still a member of the ruling Politburo when he died, had been forced to resign as the party's General Secretary two years earlier for being too soft on dissent. Because Hu had not been fully purged, the party had no choice but to hold an elaborate funeral for him. This provided cover for the students, who soon switched their attention to demands for democratic reform. Hu's political views have been notable for their absence in recent articles, suggesting that only his affable character is open for discussion ... Tea leaf readers are divided over what, if any, further political message might have been intended [by the Wen Jiabao article].

(www.economist.com, 22 April 2010; *The Economist*, 24 April 2010, p. 58)

18 April 2010.

President Hugo Chavez said over the weekend that China had agreed to extend $20 billion in loans to Venezuela, pointing to deepening ties between the two countries as China seeks to secure oil supplies there. The announcement of the loans follows other financing agreements with China ... including a $12 billion bilateral investment fund. China's ties with Venezuela have grown increasingly warm in recent years, marked by rising Venezuelan oil exports to China, the Chinese launching of a satellite for Venezuela and the sale of Chinese aircraft to Venezuela ... Xinhua said ... the new financing deal ... involved 'soft loans' channelled through the China Development Bank. The linchpin of the loans appears to be China's thirst for oil, with the China National Petroleum Corporation (CNPC) agreeing to form a venture with Venezuela's national oil company to explore for oil in southern Venezuela ... CNPC would need to pay $1 billion to move the venture forward.

(www.iht.com, 19 April 2010)

25 April 2010.

> Members of the World Bank agreed on Sunday [25 April] to support a $5.1 billion increase in its operating capital, the largest increase in general financing since 1988 and give developing countries a greater say in running the anti-poverty institution. Under the changes China will become the World Bank's third largest shareholder, ahead of Germany, after the United States and Japan. Countries like Brazil, India, Indonesia and Vietnam will also have greater representation … The World Bank's 186 members also agreed a reform package that calls for greater openness and disclosure of information and improvements in managing risks and measuring results. The World Bank has made $105 billion in financial commitments since July 2008 in response to the global economic turmoil … The World Bank president … Robert Zoellick … devised the capital increase and voting changes to be adopted together. The $5.1 billion in so-called paid-in capital, which the bank can use for day-to-day operations, will bring the bank's cash on hand to about $40 billion. Of the $5.1 billion, developing countries will contribute $1.6 billion in connection with a shift in representation that will give them 47.19 per cent of voting power, up from 44.06 per cent. The actions fulfil a pledge the bank's members made in Istanbul in October [2009] … In 2008 the bank's members approved a smaller shift of 1.46 per cent of voting power to the developing countries from the wealthy ones … All told, the cumulative shift of 4.59 per cent of voting power amounts to the greatest alignment in representation at the World Bank since 1988 … The bank's members approved on Sunday an $86.2 billion general capital increase, bringing the bank's total subscribed capital, not counting about $26 billion in reserves, to $276.1 billion … Mr Zoellick … said … that the less wealthy countries were leading the global economic recovery.
>
> (www.iht.com, 26 April 2010)

'The United States, which holds the largest voting share in the World Bank at 16.4 per cent, would not seek any increase in that' (www.bbc.co.uk, 26 April 2010).

> The World Bank increased the voting power of developing and transition countries among its 186 members, raising the total for that block to 47.2 per cent, from 44.6 per cent in 2008. China's voting share was raised to 4.42 per cent, vaulting it ahead of European countries and leaving it behind only the United States and Japan … World Bank shareholders (2010): United States, 15.85 per cent; Japan, 6.84 per cent; China, 4.42 per cent; Germany, 4.00 per cent; France, 3.75 per cent; Britain, 3.75 per cent; India, 2.91 per cent.
>
> (www.economist.com, 29 April 2010; *The Economist*, 1 May 2010, p. 8)

26 April 2010.

> A city mayor in north-eastern China has been sacked for mishandling a protest about corruption among local officials, state media says. Sun Ming

> was accused of ignoring hundreds of people who staged a 'kneel down' protest in front of the city hall in Zhuanghe, Dalian province ... on 13 April.
>
> (www.bbc.co.uk, 26 April 2010)

1 May 2010.

> The Shanghai [World] Expo [opened on 1 May] ... and runs until 31 October ... The first Universal Exposition was held at Crystal Palace in London in 1851 ... Shanghai won the bid to put on this year's event back in 2002 ... The cost is estimated at $55 billion – more than twice what Beijing spent on the Olympics ... Official figures range from renminbi 300 billion ($44 billion) to renminbi 400 billion but Jones Lang La Salle, the property services firm, estimates infrastructure investments made or brought forward for Expo boost the total to $95 billion ... Only 5 per cent of Expo visitors are expected to be from overseas.
>
> (*FT*, 29 April 2010, p. 11)

> The renminbi 400 billion ($59 billion) Shanghai World Expo ... [is] more than twice as costly as the 2008 Beijing Olympics ... During the next six months ... Expo will host up to 100 million people, 95 per cent of them from China ... Beijing has set ... 2010 ... [as] the deadline for Shanghai to become a global financial centre.
>
> (*FT*, Survey on Shanghai. 30 April 2010, p. 1)

'Expo's theme ... "Better Cities, Better Life" ... [is that] of better integrating urban life with the natural environment' (*FT*, 30 April 2010, p. 10).

> Fireworks lit up Shanghai last night [30 April] at the launch of the largest World Expo in history, The opening performance, including lasers and neon-lit skyscrapers along a stretch of the city's Huangpu River, was billed as the largest outdoor multi-media show.
>
> (*FT*, 1 May 2010, p. 6)

> World Expos ... are sometimes known [as] ... World's Fairs ... Shanghai is hoping to attract 70 million visitors to its six-month fair ... It says it has spent $4.2 billion on the event alone – more than twice as much as Beijing spent on the Olympic Games in 2008 – plus tens of millions on accelerated improvements to the city's infrastructure.
>
> (www.economist.com, 29 April 2010; *The Economist*, 1 May 2010, p. 55)

'China says the cost is $4.2 billion – others say costs reached $58 billion' (www.bbc.co.uk, 30 April 2010).

> Shanghai is expected to spend $45 billion ... on infrastructure and to host what organizers are calling a six-month 'cultural gala' ... A record 189 countries, including the United States and even North Korea, are participating ... Shanghai has upgraded the city's infrastructure with new roads, bridges, tunnels and airport terminals over the past several years ... Shanghai has now passed New York and London and now has the world's largest

subway system … Shanghai [is] China's second biggest city with 18 million inhabitants.

(*IHT*, 30 May 2010, p. 5)

'"Better Cities, Better Life" … [is] its theme… making the promotion of sustainable urban development practices a key goal' (p. 9).

The city has spent a reported $58 billion on the Expo and related infrastructure to accommodate the 70 million mainly Chinese who will visit during the six-month spectacular … The government had to relocate thousands of people for the Expo, some forcefully, according to rights groups. Activists have been threatened by the police to keep quiet during the festivities.

(www.iht.com, 30 April 2010)

'Foreigners … are expected to account for only 5 per cent of all visitors to the Expo' (www.ihtcom, 17 May 2010).

Shortly after winning the bid to host the event in 2002, Shanghai began clearing an area along the Huangpu River covering 528 hectares (2 square miles). That involved moving 18,000 families and 270 factories, including the hulking Jiangnan Shipyard, which employs 10,000 workers … Last week the police detained 6,000 people they say were involved in street crimes like theft and prostitution during a twelve-day crackdown to prepare for the Expo. Human rights groups say some activists have been detained.

(*IHT*, 30 April 2010, p. 5)

The tradition of Expos and World Fairs began with the Greta Exhibition of 1851 in London, but has lost much of its lustre in recent years. China is hoping to breathe new life into it. It is spending $4.2 billion to host the Expo. A reported $45 billion has been spent overhauling Shanghai for the event – more than Beijing spent for the Olympics – with new airport terminals, hundreds of miles of subway line and a revamp of its historic waterfront, the Bund … But [human rights] campaigners say the event has also brought a crackdown on dissent. The Chinese Human Rights Defenders network said officials have detained, harassed or placed under surveillance activists, intellectuals and petitioners across Shanghai and surrounding areas. One target has been those who have protested over the forced demolition of homes to make way for the Expo site. According to official estimates, 18,000 households have been knocked down … Similar pressure was put on activists ahead of the Olympics.

(www.guardian.co.uk, 30 April 2010)

'More than 6,000 people were detained in a crime crackdown in recent weeks, and 17,000 others have been relocated to make way for the $4 billion Expo grounds' (www.cnn.com, 30 April 2010).

Visitor numbers for the World Expo in Shanghai, in its first three days of opening, have been far lower than the organizers had predicted. Some 70 million visitors – mostly Chinese – are expected to visit the enormous site over the six months that the fair is open. But to achieve this, more than 380,000 people are needed to visit each day. So far, the highest number of visitors in any one day has been about 215,000, according to the organizers' website. The opening of the World Expo was celebrated with a gala that was tightly choreographed and faultlessly executed. But now, the way the fair is run and its appeal to the masses appears less impressive. First there is [the problem of] the queues. At one point this weekend 25,000 people were waiting to go through security at one of the gates. They were stuck there for hours. It is a similar story at the popular pavilions ... To visit the China pavilion you need a special reservation ticket. On day one they were all issued in the first five minutes. On day two the supply lasted longer but ran out just twenty minutes after the park opened ... The problems are affecting turnout. By lunchtime on Monday [3 May] 40 per cent fewer people had entered the park than by the same time on Sunday [2 May] – despite the fact that it is a public holiday.

(www.bbc.co.uk, 3 May 2010)

3 May 2010.

Reporters Without Borders has named the leaders of China, Russia and Rwanda as some of the world's worst 'predators of freedom'. The report, marking World Press Freedom Day, lists what the Paris-based group regards as the forty worst offenders against the freedom of the press. North Korea's leader Kim Jong Il and the head of Burma's military government Than Shwe are also on the list ... Russian prime minister Vladimir Putin has 'promoted a climate of pumped-up national pride that encourages the persecution of dissidents and freethinkers'.

(www.bbc.co.uk, 3 May 2010)

3–28 May 2010. The latest five-yearly review conference of the Nuclear Non-proliferation Treaty is held at the United Nations in New York.

The Iranian president, Mahmoud Ahmadinejad, accused the United States and other nuclear powers on Monday [3 May] of trying to intimidate non-nuclear countries and said the Americans were the 'main suspect' in the stockpiling, spread and threat of nuclear weapons. Mr Ahmadinejad took a defiant posture as the United Nations opened a conference to strengthen the forty-year-old Nuclear Non-proliferation Treaty, arguing that the world's nuclear powers needed to disarm and that there was no credible evidence that his nation was seeking to develop nuclear weapons ... In opening the conference, Secretary-General Ban Ki-moon had called on Iran to prove that its nuclear programme was solely for peaceful purposes and to accept a compromise deal offered to Tehran last fall [2009] ... Mr Ban called on Iran to comply with Security Council resolutions demanding that it stop enriching uranium and to co-operate with the IAEA in answering outstanding questions about whether its programme was peaceful or aimed at developing nuclear weapons. Mr Ban said: 'The onus is on Iran to clarify the doubts and concerns about its programme' … Mr Ban said the conference negotiations should focus on a few central issues: more nuclear arms cuts; greater transparency in national nuclear programmes; getting the three states outside the treaty – India, Pakistan and Israel [Israel's nuclear arsenal being estimated at 100 to 200 warheads] – to sign it; and a nuclear-free zone in the Middle East … Mr Ban said that the need to strengthen the non-proliferation treaty remained as important as ever, given the expanding number of countries with nuclear programmes and the possible threat of nuclear terrorism … Mr Ban also called on North Korea to return to negotiations over its nuclear programme. North Korea, which has tested nuclear devices, withdrew from the non-proliferation treaty in 2003 … Yukiya Amano, the director-general of the IAEA, singled out Iran, North Korea and Syria for their lack of co-operation with the agency. North Korea has refused any co-operation with the agency since April 2009, he said, while Syria has refused to engage since June 2008 over questions about what officials suspect was a nuclear facility imported from North Korea and destroyed by Israel. Mr Amano said Iran needed to comply with the safeguards agreement it had signed with the agency … One emphasis at the review conference is to persuade countries to sign up for additional inspections by the agency. Mr Amano noted that ninety-eight of the 189 parties to the treaty had signed up for the additional inspections. Iran initially accepted them, but changed its mind after its nuclear programme was referred to the Security Council. The Council has passed three rounds of sanctions against Iran and is negotiating a fourth … Iran maintains that its nuclear efforts are for peaceful purposes, but Western nations suspect that Tehran is secretly aiming to develop a bomb … Any agreement reached at the end of the conference on 28 May has to be adopted by consensus of all 189 members … The last time it was held, in 2005, the nuclear non-proliferation review conference collapsed, with non-nuclear states critical of nuclear powers for not sufficiently reducing their arsenals and with extended, ineffectual bickering over how to grapple with the nuclear programmes of Iran and North Korea.

(www.iht.com, 3 May 2010; *IHT*, 4 May 2010, pp. 1, 4)

In his speech Mr Ahmadinejad said that all nuclear powers tried to intimidate countries that had no nuclear weapons, but he called the United States the 'main suspect' in fostering a nuclear arms race … The Pentagon on Monday [3 May] declassified statistics showing that the United States now possesses 5,113 nuclear weapons, down 84 per cent from its peak of 31,255 in 1967 … The statistics' broad outlines have been known, in general terms, for many years. The Pentagon issued gross numbers on Monday, deliberately lumping together deployed weapons, those in storage and 'inactive' warheads. The figures released for the current stockpile … do not include several thousand retired weapons awaiting complete disarmament [waiting to be dismantled].

(www.iht.com, 4 May 2010)

'President Mahmoud Ahmadinejad of Iran accused states with nuclear weapons of threatening those who wanted to develop peaceful nuclear weapons' (www.bbc.co.uk, 4 May 2010).

> The Nuclear Non-proliferation Treaty is the central element of international efforts to halt the spread of nuclear weapons. It comprises a kind of bargain in which those countries which had nuclear weapons when signing the treaty in 1970 – the United States, the former Soviet Union, China, the UK and France – agreed eventually to disarm ... All other treaty signatories agreed never to develop nuclear weapons in return for receiving full access to civilian nuclear technology ... Two nuclear weapons states – India and Pakistan – along with Israel, which has an unacknowledged nuclear arsenal, are not signatories.
>
> (www.bbc.co.uk, 3 May 2010)

> The majority of his [President Mahmoud Ahmadinejad's] thirty-five-minute speech was devoted to criticizing the massive US nuclear arsenal and suggested the US nuclear posture threatened other countries and justified their pursuit of nuclear weapons to protect themselves. He called the provision in the US Nuclear Posture Review retaining an option to use nuclear weapons against countries a non-compliance with the very treaty it accuses Iran of violating. He said: 'Regrettably, the government of the United States has not only used nuclear weapons [in World War II], but also continues to threaten to use such weapons against other countries, including Iran.'
>
> (www.cnn.com, 4 May 2010)

8 May 2010.

> A man has been arrested after allegedly stabbing to death eight people, including three family members ... Police said that ... [he] killed his mother, wife, daughter, four neighbours and a migrant worker in eastern China's Jiangxi province. He was arrested on Saturday evening [8 May] ... China has been on alert after a number of recent knife attacks on children ... Such violent incidents are rare ... Some analysts have suggested that an increase in psychiatric illnesses brought about by rapid social change is behind the attacks.
>
> (www.bbc.co.uk, 9 May 2010)

> China traditionally has had a comparatively low rate of violent crime, but this is no longer the case. Experts quoted in Western media have suggested that the school attacks are a form of revenge on society by individuals with no outlet for their anger. Some Chinese commentators have alluded to the growing gap between rich and poor, and the rapid pace of economic development and social upheaval as possible factors leading to outbreaks of violence. But reports in official media have generally played down any wider causes for the school attacks, portraying them as isolated incidents perpetrated by disturbed individuals.
>
> (www.bbc.co.uk, 12 May 2010)

There has been much speculation on the cause of the attacks, with some blaming inadequate provision for people with mental health issues. Others have suggested the attacks are a form of revenge on society by individuals with no outlet for their anger in a political environment heavily controlled by the Communist Party.

(www.bbc.co.uk, 15 May 2010)

China has been shaken in recent weeks by multiple cases of mass violence, including attacks on children at schools. Some have been blamed on the attackers' mental illness and others on the pressures of a rapidly changing society and a lack of a strong social support system.

(www.iht.com, 9 May 2010)

12 May 2010.

Seven kindergarteners and a teacher were stabbed to death ... in an attack on a school in ... Shaanxi province ... After killing the eight people on Wednesday [12 May] the attacker returned home and committed suicide ... The attack was one of the deadliest a bizarre series of attacks on schoolchildren by apparent lunatics wielding knives and hand tools. The latest attacks are presumably copycat crimes ... Unlike in the United States, school shootings are rare in China because it is difficult to buy guns of any kind ... Sharp objects and tools are the weapons of choice. Although official Chinese news organizations have been quick to release initial reports on the string of attacks, the government has been carefully censoring subsequent stories, perhaps to prevent other copycat murders, or perhaps to diminish any suggestion of dysfunction within Chinese society. In presenting China as a 'harmonious society' – the signature propaganda of President Hu Jintao – the government often deletes dissonant reports from the internet and other media platforms. Some scholars have speculated that the attacks point to the absence of adequate pressure-release valves in a society going through significant economic upheaval, where the gap between the wealthy and the destitute is rapidly widening, and where corruption by local officials heightens frustration among ordinary citizens. Mental illness, too, is rarely acknowledged and thus treatment is in short supply. The first of the recent wave of attacks took place on 23 March [2010] when Zheng Minsheng stabbed eight primary school students to death in Fujian province ... Mr Zheng was executed on 28 April, the same day that sixteen children and their teacher were attacked at a primary school in Guangdong province. The following day in the city of Taixing in Jiangsu province twenty-nine kindergarten children and three adults were injured by an attacker with a knife ... The day after that five kindergarteners and a teacher were injured by a man in Shandong province ... The man beat the children with a hammer, then doused himself with gasoline ... The attacker died ... Mental illness is rarely discussed in China, and thus treatment is often unavailable. In June [2009] the British medical journal [the *Lancet*] published an analysis of

> mental health issues in four Chinese provinces and concluded that an estimated 91 per cent of 173 million Chinese adults who are believed to be suffering mental problems never receive professional help.
>
> (www.iht.com, 12 May 2010)

'A man with a kitchen cleaver rampaged through a kindergarten ... He hacked to death seven children and two adults [the kindergarten owner and a teacher] before returning home and killing himself' (www.iht.com, 12 May 2010).

> The attacker ... was reported to have owned the building in which the privately run kindergarten was held and to have been involved in a rental dispute with its manager ... She and her mother were both killed ... [The police said the attacker] had also been suffering from depression linked to worsening physical illnesses.
>
> (www.bbc.co.uk, 14 May 2010)

14 May 2010.

> Premier Wen Jiabao said a spate of fatal attacks on schools shows the country has 'social tensions' which must be addressed ... Mr Wen said that as well as boosting the security presence, China needed to 'handle social problems. Resolve disputes and strengthen mediation at the grassroots level' ... Wu Heping [minister in charge of public security]: 'The public security bureaux and judicial authorities will severely punish this kind of crime according to the law ... Innovation in the management of society is not only essential but urgent. I have noticed the central government's demand for the public security bureaux, under the leadership of all levels of local government, to properly handle the various conflicts in society.'
>
> (www.bbc.co.uk, 14 May 2010)

'Wu Heping ... added that police would also help resolve soial conflicts, show concern for disadvantaged groups and ensure psychological guidance for people "with extreme thoughts of intolerant characters" ' (www.guardian.co.uk, 14 May 2010).

> Prime minister Wen Jiabao: 'Apart from taking powerful security measures, we also need to solve the deeper reasons behind this issue, including resolving social tensions, reconciling disputes and enhancing mediation at the grassroots level. We are sparing no effort in all of the above works' ... Under orders from the central propaganda department, most of the main Chinese news organizations have declined to run follow-up stories on Wednesday's attack in ... Shaanxi province. *China Daily*, an English-language newspaper aimed at foreigners, was an exception – it ran a front-page headline on Friday [14 May] that said 'School Security Beefed Up' and carried Mr Wen's comments ... Mr Wen did not mention addressing mental illness, a topic that the Chinese often avoid discussing. Interviews by the Associated Press ... indicate that the killer ... was an unbalanced individual – he had tried to commit suicide twice in the last month and believed

the kindergarten administrator … had put a curse on him to prevent his diabetes condition from improving … [They] had frequent arguments over rental of the kindergarten building [which the attacker owned].

(www.iht.com, 14 May 2010)

A recent study, co-financed by the WHO, found that 17.5 per cent of people in China have some kind of mental disorder, and 95 per cent of them have never seen a mental health professional. The study says: 'The combined category of neuropsychiatric conditions and suicide accounted for more than 20 per cent of the total burden of illness in China in 2004, making it the most important category of illness or injury. But only 2.35 per cent of the government's health budget is spent on mental health and less than 15 per cent of the population had health insurance that covered psychiatric disorders.'

(*FT*, 15 May 2010, p. 7)

15 May 2010.

A court in eastern China sentenced a man to death Saturday [15 May] for attacking twenty-nine kindergarten students and three teachers with a knife … No one died in the [29 April] attacks … The Taoxing court found … [him] guilty of intentional homicide … Guns are strictly regulated in China, but until recently large knives were not. Chinese authorities have recently issued a regulation requiring people to register with their national ID cards when they buy knives longer than 15 centimetres.

(www.cnn.com, 15 May 2010)

18 May 2010.

Huang Guangyu, once China's richest man, was sentenced Tuesday [18 May] to fourteen years in prison … Huang, the head of Gome, one of China's leading retail chains, was charged with stock market manipulation, insider trading and bribery … He emerged as a rags-to-riches entrepreneur in the late 1980s … Huang ranked first on *Hurun*'s China Rich List, a local publication, in 2008 with an estimated fortune worth $6.3 billion … Police detained Huang in November 2008 for an investigation into suspected 'economic crimes'. Little was heard of him or of the investigation, but the police dragnet gradually grew wider, ensnaring government and police officials in charge of fighting financial crimes.

(www.cnn.com, 18 May 2010)

Huang Guangyu … was jailed for fourteen years for bribery, insider trading and illegal business dealings … Huang, who made his fortune by founding and building up Gome Electrical Appliances Holdings Ltd, was detained in November 2008 during a police investigation of stock market manipulation allegations. The investigations gradually grew wider, ensnaring government officials and police who had been assigned to fight financial crime … Huang built his fortune from humble beginnings, having been raised in a poor family in Guangdong province. He moved to Beijing in his late teens with his brother and set up a home appliances distribution firm with 30,000 yuan ($4,400) and founded Gome in 1987.

(www.iht.com, 18 May 2010)

The conviction of the former Gome chairman, Huang Guangyu, was among the most significant in a string of recent business-related corruption trials that have brought down top officials in China's oil and nuclear power industries and felled other executives in the airline, beverage, cellphone and securities businesses, among others ... Mr Huang resigned as chairman two months after his detention ... He left school at sixteen and, with his brother, opened the first Gome store in Beijing in 1987 with 4,000 renminbi they had earned as travelling salesmen in Inner Mongolia and a 30,000 renminbi loan ... At its peak, Gome was China's largest retail appliance chain, with 1,350 stores in more than 200 cities. Mr Huang became fabulously wealthy by floating his company on the Hong Kong stock market in 2004, then investing in real estate and stock in mainland China ... Mr Huang's sentencing officially closed a spectacular rise-and-fall saga that had led the Chinese press in 2008 to crown him the nation's richest man, with an estimated net worth of $6.3 billion. *Forbes* magazine's list of the wealthy placed his assets at a more modest $2.7 billion ... In November 2008 Beijing public security officers detained Mr Huang on suspicion of 'economic crimes'. In the ensuing seventeen months investigators accused him of bribing five senior tax and police officials, illegally converting 800 million renminbi ($117 million) into foreign currency and insider trading involving the stock of a company in the city of Shenzhen that was said to have netted him about $45 million. Perhaps a dozen prominent people were reported in the Chinese press to have been caught up in the investigation ... [These included the following]: Xu Zongheng, a one-time mayor of Shenxzhen; the former police chief and the former top anti-corruption official in Guangdong province; the deputy public security chief in Shanghai; and a major investor in Neptune Group, a cruise line and casino operator based in Hong Kong ... Mr Huang's wife, Du Juan, was also convicted of insider trading on Tuesday and was sentenced to three years in prison ... Two of the firms Mr Huang once ran, Gome Electrical Appliances Holdings and Beijing Pengrun Real Estate Development, were fined $730,000 and $176,000, respectively, for paying bribes.

(www.iht.com, 18 May 2010)

The Gome chain of domestic appliance shops was the second largest in the country ... [In November 2008 Huang Guangyu] was arrested. He had been accused of manipulating share trading for two listed companies – Sanlain Commercial Co and Beijing Centergate Technologies Co., Xinhua reported before his trial.

(www.bbc.co.uk, 18 May 2010)

'He is still the company's [Gome's] biggest shareholder' (www.bbc.co.uk, 18 May 2010).

'Centergate's chairman ... was sentenced ... to three years' (www.economist.com, 20 May 2010).

> Nearly 30 billionaires who have appeared on the *Hurun* rich list have been charged with bribery or are at the centre of a police investigation, while nineteen of the 1,330 business tycoons listed in the past ten years are either in jail or awaiting sentencing on bribery charges ... Among the tycoons serving time are Mou Qizhong, who got life for bank fraud, and property developer Zhou Zhengyi who was sentenced in 2008 to sixteen years for bribery, fraud and embezzlement.
>
> (*The Independent*, 19 May 2010, p. 30)

19 May 2010.

> About five to six men, armed with knives and cleavers, rushed into a college dormitory in southern China on Wednesday, wounding nine students – one of them seriously ... The men burst into a dormitory at the Hainan Institute of Science and Technology in Hainan province.
>
> (www.cnn.com, 19 May 2010)

23–25 May 2010. The annual China–US Strategic and Economic Dialogue took place in Beijing on 23–25 May.

> Secretary of State Hillary Clinton and Treasury Secretary Timothy Geithner are leading a delegation that will included nearly 200 policy-makers and advisers, one of the largest groups of Americans ever to travel to a foreign capital for a single set of meetings.
>
> (www.iht.com, 21 May 2010)

'[There are to be] three days of high-level economic and security meetings ... Nearly 200 American officials have descended on Beijing, the largest such groups ever to come to the Chinese capital' (www.iht.com, 23 May 2010).

> China is Boeing's largest market outside the United States, with 450 orders for planes from fast-growing carriers like China Eastern Airlines, which is headquartered in Shanghai. But Boeing, which buys parts from Chinese suppliers, is facing greater competition from Airbus, the European consortium. Airbus opened a final assembly plant, its first outside Europe, in the industrial city of Tianjin in 2009.
>
> (www.iht.com, 23 May 2010)

> President Hu Jintao (24 May): 'China will continue to steadily advance reform of the renminbi exchange rate mechanism following the principles of being independent, controllable and gradual' ... [He] said the two global powers needed to enhance economic policy co-ordination and work together to promote 'full economic recovery' ... He said his government wanted to expand domestic demand to create more balanced growth ... The annual US

trade deficit with China fell to $226.8 billion in 2009, down from a record $280.0 billion in 2008.

(www.iht.com, 24 May 2010)

President Hu Jintao ... praised the 'mutually beneficial and win–win co-operation' between the United States and China. Such co-ordination, he said, had helped the recovery from the 2008 financial crisis ... [As regards the renminbi exchange rate mechanism] Hu said Beijing would move 'under the principle of independent decision-making, controllability, and gradual progress' ... Mr Hu [made a] pledge to 'steadily advance the reform mechanism of the renminbi exchange rate' ... without repeating his previous references to the rate being 'basically stable'.

(www.iht.com, 24 May 2010; *IHT*, 25 May 2010, pp. 1, 4)

China and the United States wrapped up two days of high-level meetings on Tuesday [25 May] with some modest trade and energy agreements but little progress on winning China's backing for international measures against North Korea over the sinking of a South Korean warship. Secretary of State Hillary Clinton said China would take 'a period of careful consideration in order to determine the best way forward in dealing with North Korea as a result of this incident' ... Treasury Secretary Timothy Geithner said: '[President Hu Jintao recognizes that moving China's currency closer to a market rate] is an important part of their broader reform agenda. This, of course, is China's choice' ... The United States did get concessions on two issues of importance to American investors in China: a change in rules governing innovation that now disadvantage foreign companies, and a pledge to submit a revised offer to join the WTO's agreement on government procurement by 2010. The two countries also signed a raft of modest agreements on issues ranging from clean energy and shale gas exploration to trade finance between the export–import banks of the United States and China. They also agreed to co-operate on nuclear safety and on preventing infectious diseases ... The Chinese government has agreed to help pay for 10,000 students to study for doctorate degrees in the United States, while President Barack Obama has set a goal of sending 100,000 American students to China over the next four years.

(www.iht.com, 25 May 2010; *IHT*, 26 May 2010, pp. 1, 8)

'China's current account surplus fell from 11 per cent of GDP in 2007 to 5.8 per cent last year [2009]' (*FT*, 24 May 2010, p. 1).

On North Korea, US Secretary of State Hillary Clinton opted for low-key encouragement of China to back the administration's criticisms of Pyongyang over the sinking of a South Korean warship [a corvette], the *Cheonan* in March [2010]. She said {24 May]: 'I can say that the Chinese recognize the gravity of the situation we face. They understand the reaction by the South Koreans and they understand our unique responsibility for peace and stability on the Korean Peninsula.'

(*FT*, 25 May 2010, p. 12)

'The *Cheonan* sank near the inter-Korean maritime border on 26 March. An international panel says a torpedo fired from a North Korean submarine sent the ship down, but Pyongyang denies this' (www.bbc.co.uk, 25 May 2010). 'The investigation itself was given an added air of impartiality by the presence of twenty-four foreign experts from American, Australia, Britain and Sweden' (www.bbc.co.uk, 24 May 2010).

> South Korean military officials on Thursday [20 May] announced the results of an official investigation into the sinking of the *Cheonan*, which concluded that North Korea fired a torpedo that cut the vessel in half ... The South Korean military group that presented its report on the ship's sinking on Thursday comprises experts from South Korea, Australia, Sweden, the United Kingdom and the United States. Yoon Duk Yong (the group's chairman): 'The evidence points overwhelmingly to the conclusion that the torpedo was fired by a North Korean submarine. There is no other plausible explanation.'
>
> (www.cnn.com, 21 May 2010)

'North Korea has denied responsibility for the sinking of the *Cheonan*, on 26 March, which left forty-six sailors dead. A growing body of evidence assembled by the South has suggested a North Korean torpedo sank the ship' (*IHT*, 25 May 2010, p. 4).

> Prime minister Wen Jiabao met with President Lee Myung Bak of South Korea on Friday [28 May] before the start of three-party weekend talks [in South Korea] with Japan ... Mr Wen told Mr Lee that China will make an 'impartial judgement' on who was responsible for sinking the ship. Wen Jiabao: 'Once we have our conclusion, we will not protect anyone.'
>
> (www.iht.com, 28 May 2010)

'The summit ... was originally meant to focus on regional economic integration' (www.iht.com, 30 May 2010). 'The talks had been scheduled before the *Choeonan* sinking to discuss greater regional co-operation and economic integration' (www.iht.com, 31 May 2010).

> Prime minister Wen Jiabao (after talks in Seoul): 'China objects to and condemns any act that destroys the peace and stability of the Korean Peninsula ... The Chinese government will decide its position by objectively and fairly judging what is right and wrong about the incident while respecting the international probe and responses to it by each nation' ... China has previously called for all sides to show restraint.
>
> (www.bbc.co.uk, 28 May 2010)

'The three-nation summit was meant to focus on trade, but the sinking of the warship overshadowed other issues' (www.bbc.co.uk, 30 May 2010).

> Premier Wen Jiabao said during a visit to Seoul yesterday [28 May] that China would not protect 'whoever sank the warship' ... South Korea has given China the complete technical report on the sinking and has said it

> would welcome a Chinese delegation should they want to inspect the shattered hull and corroded torpedo retrieved from the seabed.
>
> (*FT*, 29 May 2010)

'Prime minister Wen Jiabao offered condolences on Saturday to South Korea for the sinking of one of its warships' (www.iht.com, 29 May 2010).

Premier Wen Jiabao: 'The sinking of the *Cheonan* is an unfortunate incident. We understand the sorrow of the South Korean people, especially the victims' families ... If clashes flare up the worst victim will be South Korea. And China, too, cannot avoid misfortune' (www.cnn.com, 4 June 2010).

Prime minister Wen Jiabao (30 May):

> We must promote peace and stability in the North-east Asian region through every effort. We should be considerate of each other on a grave issue, deal reasonably with a sensitive matter and strengthen political trust ... The urgent task for the moment is to properly handle the serious impact caused by the *Cheonan* incident, gradually defuse tensions over it, and avoid possible conflicts. China will continue to work with every country through aggressive negotiations and co-operation to fulfil our mission of maintaining peace and stability in the region.
>
> (www.cnn.com, 30 May 2010; www.bbc.co.uk, 30 May 2010)

> Prime minister Wen Jiabao [30 May]: 'Most urgent is to dispel the impact of the *Cheonan* incident, gradually ease tension and especially avoid a clash. We must put all our efforts without fail to boost peace and stability in North-east Asia. Without this we cannot talk about development, and the achievements we have made with difficulty will evaporate' ... After Mr Wen's bilateral talks with President Lee Myung Bak on Friday [28 May] Mr Lee's office quoted Mr Wen as saying that Beijing 'will not protect anyone' once it had concluded who was responsible after its own 'impartial judgement' ... Reading from a joint statement from the three leaders, Mr Lee said that Japan and China 'attached importance' to the 20 May report by the South Korean-led international investigative team that blamed North Korea for the sinking.
>
> (www.iht.com, 31 May 2010)

'The three said in a joint statement issued on 30 May: "We share the view that a denuclearized Korean Peninsula would greatly contribute to enduring peace, security and economic prosperity in North-east Asia"' (www.cnn.com, 30 May 2010).

27 May 2010.

> President Barack Obama's first formal National Security Strategy ... calls on China to take on 'a responsible leadership role' and vows to 'monitor China's military modernization programme' while saying that disagreements on human rights 'should not prevent co-operation on issues of mutual interest'.
>
> (*IHT*, 28 May 2010, p. 6)

30 May 2010.

> A man who had been sentenced to death for attacking [on 29 April] twenty-nine children and three teachers at a kindergarten in Jiangsu province [in eastern China] ... was executed Sunday [30 May] ... [All thirty-two victims survived the attack but] the Chinese penal code says a person can be convicted of intentional homicide for acting on an intent to kill.
>
> (www.cnn.com, 30 May 2010)

4 June 2010.

> Deng Xiaoping ordered the military to try to limit injuries when it moved against Tiananmen Square protesters twenty-one years ago, but told them to be ready to 'shed some blood' if necessary, according to an unpublished diary said to document internal decisions that led to the violent crackdown. The death toll from the military action against protesters, the night of 3 to 4 June 1989, remains in dispute. Official estimates at the time said 200 demonstrators died; some rights activists place the toll at 1,000 or more and say anywhere from seventy to 300 protesters remain in prison. The diary, covering some nine weeks before and after the military action, is said to be written by Li Peng, China's premier at the time ... A Hong Kong publisher, New Century Press, plans to release the 279-page manuscript as a Chinese language book [*Li Peng's 4 June Diary*] on 22 June. The same publisher caused a sensation in May 2009 by issuing the secret memoirs of Zhao Ziyang ... Li Peng was said to have been ready to publish his work in 2004 ... but was discouraged by Chinese leaders. Bao Pu, the Hong Kong publisher of both works, said ... that he had received the latest diary from an unidentified source, and so could not unconditionally guarantee its authenticity. Mr Bao said he was unable to contact Mr Li, now eighty-one and reportedly in ill health. But he said a detailed study of the work convinced him and other experts that Mr Li was the author ... Hong Kong's *South China Morning Post*, which reported on Friday [4 June] that it had obtained a copy of the manuscript, said Mr Li wrote in a forward dated 6 December 2003 that he felt bound to record what happened 'to serve as the most important historical testimony' about Tiananmen. The newspaper said he wrote that the protesters threatened to send China into a new era of upheaval akin to the chaos into which Mao periodically plunged the nation during his rule. The newspaper quoted a 2 May 1989 diary entry: 'From the beginning of the turmoil I have prepared for the worst. I would rather sacrifice my own life and that of my family to prevent China from going through a tragedy like the Cultural Revolution' ... Zhao Ziyang's memoir is not legally available on the mainland, and Mr Li's also seems certain to be banned.
>
> (www.iht.com, 4 June 2010; *IHT*, 5 June 2010, p. 4).
>
> Li Peng ... announced martial law in Beijing shortly before troops moved in ... The man behind the project is Bao Pu, the son of Bao Tong, a senior adviser to the Communist Party at the time of the Tiananmen protests ...

The manuscript was handed to Mr Bao by an intermediary ... He admits that there are question about the diary's authenticity ... but added [that] 'even with those remaining doubts, I still believe this is authentic, given the details and how consistent they are with other known records' ... Mr Bao last year [2009] published the memoirs of Zhao Ziyang.

(www.bbc.co.uk, 4 June 2010)

4–5 June 2010.

[On 4 June] US Defence Secretary Robert Gates told reporters travelling with him to an Asian security conference in Singapore: 'Nearly all of the aspects of the relationship between the United States and China are moving in a positive direction, with the sole exception of the military-to-military relationship ... As I'll say in my speech, the Taiwan arms sales issue is far from new in this relationship ... [American arms sales to Taiwan approved by both the Bush and Obama administrations] were carefully calibrated to keep them on the defensive side' ... Mr Gates had considered stopping in Beijing on this trip, making good on an invitation issued by Chinese military leaders who visited Washington last winter. But the invitation was cancelled, or at least put on hold.

(*IHT*, 5 June 2010, p. 6)

[On 5 June] Defence Secretary Robert Gates ... during an Asian security conference in Singapore ... urged China to restore military ties with the United States, saying their suspension was damaging security in Asia ... On China's suspension of military ties, Mr Gates said the policy made 'little sense'. He said: 'There is a real cost to any absence of military-to-military relations' ... He added that China's suspension of ties 'will not change United States policy towards Taiwan'.

(www.bbc.co.uk, 5 June 2010)

Monday's [21 June] 0.42 per cent rise was the biggest one-day move since 2005 and an indication that China had begun to permit a gradual rise in the renminbi against the dollar ... The renminbi [has been pegged] at around 6.827 to the dollar, permitting only the tiniest of moves within a trading band that in theory allowed for fluctuations of up to 0.5 per cent above and below the daily reference rate to the dollar ... [The moves] were widely interpreted as a precursor to a gradual and modest appreciation of the renminbi.

(www.iht.com, 22 and 23 June 2010)

Bibliography

Periodicals and reports

CDSP Current Digest of the Soviet Press (since 5 February 1992 *Post-Soviet*)
EIU Economist Intelligence Unit
FEER Far Eastern Economic Review
FT Financial Times
IHT International Herald Tribune

Books and journals

Aubert, C. (1990) 'The Chinese model and the future of rural–urban development' in K.-E. Wädekin (ed.) *Communist Agriculture: Farming in the Far East and Cuba*, London: Routledge.

Aziz, J. and Dunaway, S. (2007) 'China's rebalancing act', *Finance and Development*, September.

Bai, C., Li, D. and Wang, Y. (1997) 'Enterprise productivity and efficiency: when is up really down?' *Journal of Comparative Economics*, vol. 24, no. 3.

Bergson, A. (1985) 'A visit to China's economic reform', *Comparative Economic Studies*, vol. XXVII, no. 2.

Bideleux, R. and Jeffries, I. (1998) *A History of Eastern Europe: Crisis and Change*, London: Routledge.

—— (2007a) *A History of Eastern Europe: Crisis and Change*, second edition, London: Routledge.

—— (2007b) *The Balkans*, London: Routledge.

Bleaney, M. (1988) *Do Socialist Economies Work? The Soviet and East European Experience*, Oxford: Basil Blackwell.

Bolton, P. (1995) 'Privatization and the separation of ownership and control: lessons from Chinese enterprise reform', *Economics of Transition*, vol. 3, no. 1.

Bowles, P. and White, G. (1989) 'Contradictions in China's financial reforms: the relationship between banks and enterprises', *Cambridge Journal of Economics*, vol. 13, no. 4.

Bramall, C. (1993) 'The role of decollectivization in China's agricultural miracle, 1978–90', *Journal of Peasant Studies*, vol. 20, no. 2.

Broadman, H. (1999) 'The Chinese state as corporate shareholder', *Finance and Development*, September.

Brooks, K., Guash, L., Braverman, A. and Csaki, C. (1991) 'Agriculture and the transition to the market', *Journal of Economic Perspectives*, vol. 5, no. 4.

Cao, Y., Fan, G. and Woo, W. (1997) 'Chinese economic reforms: past successes and future challenges' in W. Woo, S. Parker and J. Sachs (eds) *Economies in Transition: Comparing Asia and Eastern Europe*, London: MIT Press.

Chai, J. (1992) 'Consumption and living standards in China', *China Quarterly*, no. 131.

Chamberlain, H. (1987) 'Party–management relations in Chinese industry: some political dimensions of economic reform', *China Quarterly*, no. 112 (December).

Chan, T. (1986) 'China's price reform in the 1980s', discussion paper no. 78, Department of Economics, University of Hong Kong.

Chang, C. and Wang, Y. (1994) 'The nature of the township-village enterprise', *Journal of Comparative Economics*, vol. 19, no. 3.

Chang, G. and Wen G. (1997) 'Communal dining and the Chinese famine of 1958–1961', *Economic Development and Cultural Change*, vol. 46, no. 1.

Chen, C., Chang, L. and Zhang, Y. (1995) 'The role of foreign direct investment in China's post-1978 economic development', *World Development*, vol. 23, no. 4.

Chen, K., Hongchang, W., Yuxin, Z., Jefferson, G. and Rawski, T. (1988) 'Productivity changes in Chinese industry', *Journal of Comparative Economics*, vol. XII.

Chen, K., Jefferson, G. and Singh, I. (1992) 'Lessons from China's economic reform', *Journal of Comparative Economics*, vol. 16, no. 2.

Cheung, S. (1986) *Will China Go Capitalist?* London: Institute of Economic Affairs (Hobart Papers).

Chow, G. (1997) 'Challenges of China's economic system for economic theory', *American Economic Review*, Papers and Proceedings, vol. 87, no. 2.

Dillon, M. (2002) 'China and the US bases in Central Asia', *The World Today*, vol. 58, no. 7.

Dipchand, C. (1994) 'The interbank market in China', *Development Policy Review*, vol. 12, no. 1.

Dittmer, L. (1989) 'The Tiananmen massacre', *Problems of Communism*, September–October.

Dollar, D. (1990) 'Economic reform and allocative efficiency in China's state-owned industry', *Economic Development and Cultural Change*, vol. 39, no. 1.

Donnithorne, A. (1967) *China's Economic System*, London: Allen & Unwin.

Economist, The (various surveys): 'China', 28 November 1992; 'Asia', 30 October 1993 'Asia'; 'China', 18 March 1995; 'China', 8 March 1997; 'Central Asia', 7 February 1998; 'China', 24 October 1998; 'China', 8 April 2000; 'China's economic power', 10 March 2001; 'China', 15 June 2002; 'Central Asia', 26 July 2003; 'A survey of the world economy: the dragon and the eagle', 2 October 2004; 'India and China', 5 March 2005; 'China', 25 March 2006; 'Hong Kong', 30 June 2007; 'Technology in India and China', 10 November 2007; 'China's quest for resources', 15 March 2008; 'China and America', 24 October 2009.

Economy, E. (2007) 'The Great Leap Backward?' *Foreign Affairs*, vol. 86, no. 5.

Ellman, M. (1979) *Socialist Planning*, London: Cambridge University Press.

—— (1986) 'Economic reform in China', *International Affairs*, vol. 62, no. 3.

Feder, G., Lau, L., Lin, J. and Luo, X. (1992) 'The determinants of farm investment and residential construction in post-reform China', *Economic Development and Cultural Change*, vol. 41, no. 1.

Field, R. (1984) 'Changes in Chinese industry since 1978', *China Quarterly*, December.

Financial Times (various surveys on China): 9 December 1985; 20 August 1986; 5 September 1986; 22 September 1986; 29 September 1986; 30 September 1986; 18 December 1986; 18 December 1987; 12 December 1989; 24 April 1991; 16 June 1992; 2 June

1993; 18 November 1993; 7 November 1994; 20 November 1995; 27 June 1996; 8 December 1997; 19 May 1998 (Shanghai); 16 November 1998; 1 October 1999; 13 November 2000; 15 March 2002 (China and the WTO); 12 December 2002; 8 February 2003 (Asian Finance); 29 April 2003 (Yangtze Delta); 16 December 2003; 20 March 2004; 7 December 2004; 8 November 2005; 12 December 2006; 31 March 2007; 29 June 2007 (Hong Kong); 30 June 2008 (Hong Kong); 24 November 2008; 2 April 2009 (G-20 Summit: China and the World); 1 October 2009.

Fischer, A. (2008) 'Reaping Tibet's whirlwind', *FEER*, March.

Fischer, S. and Sahay, R. (2000) 'Taking stock', *Finance and Development*, vol. 37, no. 3.

Gallagher, M. (2005) 'China in 2004', *Asian Survey*, vol. XLV, no. 1.

Gaynor, M. and Putterman, L. (1993) 'Productivity consequences of alternative land division methods in China's decollectivization', *Journal of Development Economics*, vol. 42, no. 2.

Ge, W. (1999) 'Special Economic Zones and the opening of the Chinese economy: some lessons for economic liberalization', *World Development*, vol. 27, no. 7.

Gelb, A., Jefferson, G. and Singh, I. (1993) 'Can communist economies transform incrementally? The experience of China', *Economics of Transition*, vol. 1, no. 4.

Gold, T. (1989) 'Urban private business in China', *Studies in Comparative Communism*, vol. XXII, nos 2 and 3.

Goldman, M. and Goldman, M. (1988) 'Soviet and Chinese economic reforms', *Foreign Affairs*, vol. 66, no. 3

Gordon, R. and Li, W. (1991) 'Chinese economic reforms, 1979–89: lessons for the future', *American Economic Review*, Papers and Proceedings, May.

Granick, D. (1990) *Chinese State Enterprises: A Regional Property Rights Analysis*, Chicago: University of Chicago Press.

Gregory, P. and Stuart, R. (1990) *Soviet Economic Structure and Performance*, fourth edition, New York: Harper & Row (second edition 1981 and third edition 1986).

—— (1994) *Soviet and Post-Soviet Economic Structure and Performance*, fifth edition, New York: HarperCollins.

Groves, T., Hong, Y., McMillan, J. and Naughton, B. (1994) 'Autonomy and incentives in Chinese state enterprises' *Quarterly Journal of Economics*, vol. CIX, no. 1.

—— (1995) 'China's evolving managerial labour market', *Journal of Political Economy*, vol. 103, no. 4.

Guardian (various surveys on China): 13 October 1986; regional China – Jiangsu and Guangdong, 16 October 1987; Shanghai: 19 November 1987.

Gungwu, W. (1993) 'Greater China and the Chinese overseas', *China Quarterly*, no. 136.

Halpern, N. (1985) 'China's industrial economic reform: the question of strategy', *Asian Survey*, vol. XXV, no. 10.

Harris, P. (2008) 'Tibet's legal right to autonomy', *FEER*, May.

Hartford, K. (1987) 'Socialist countries in the world food system: the Soviet Union, Hungary and China', *Food Research Institute Studies*, vol. XX, no. 3.

Hillman, B. (2008) 'Money can't buy Tibetan's love', *FEER*, April.

Hirschler, R. (2002) 'China's experience with transition: what is behind its stunning economic success?' *Transition*, vol. 13, no. 3.

Holzman, F. (1976) *International Trade under Communism*, New York: Basic Books.

Hsu, R. (1989) 'Changing conceptions of the socialist enterprise in China, 1979–88', *Modern China*, vol. 14, no. 4.

—— (1992) 'Industrial reform in China' in I. Jeffries (ed.) *Industrial Reform in Socialist Countries: from Restructuring to Revolution*, Aldershot: Edward Elgar.

Hu, Teh-wei, Li, Ming and Shi, Shuzhong (1988) 'Analysis of wages and bonus payments among Tianjin urban workers', *China Quarterly*, no. 113.

Hu, Z. and Khan, M. (1997) 'Why is China growing so fast?' *IMF Staff Papers*, vol. 44, no. 1.

Huang Yasheng (1990) 'Webs of interest and patterns of behaviour of Chinese local economic bureaucracies and enterprises during reforms', *China Quarterly*, no. 123 (September).

Huang, Y. and Duncan, R. (1997) 'How successful were China's state sector reforms?' *Journal of Comparative Economics*, vol. 24, no. 1.

Hussain, A. (1992) 'The Chinese economic reforms in retrospect and prospect', LSE, Discussion Paper CP no. 24.

Hussain, A. and Stern, N. (1991) 'Effective demand, enterprise reforms and public finance in China', *Economic Policy*, no. 12.

—— (1993) 'The role of the state, ownership and taxation in transitional economies', *Economics of Transition*, vol. 1, no. 1.

—— (1994) 'Economic transition on the other side of the Wall: China', LSE, Discussion Paper CP no. 29.

Hussain, A. and Zhuang, J. (1996) 'Pattern and causes of loss-making in Chinese state enterprises', LSE, Discussion Paper CP no. 31.

Imai, H. (1994) 'Inflationary pressure in China's consumption goods market: estimation and analysis', *The Developing Economies*, vol. XXXII, no. 2.

International Herald Tribune (various surveys on China): 15 September 1986; 9 July 1986; 11 April 1994; 30 May 1994; 13 March 1995; 24 April 1995; 28 October 1996; 25 November 1996; 12 August 1997; 1 October 1999; 27 June 2002.

Ishihara, K. (1987) 'Planning and the market in China', *The Developing Economies*, vol. XXV, no. 4.

—— (1990) 'Inflation and economic reform in China', *The Developing Economies*, vol. XXVIII, no. 2.

Jackson, S. (1986) 'Reform of state enterprise management in China', *China Quarterly*, no. 107.

Jefferson, G. and Rawski, T. (1994) 'Enterprise reform in Chinese industry', *Journal of Economic Perspectives*, vol. 8, no. 2.

Jefferson, G. and Xu, W. (1991) 'The impact of reform on socialist enterprises in transition: structure, conduct, and performance in Chinese industry', *Journal of Comparative Economics*, vol. 15, no. 1.

—— (1994) 'Assessing gains in efficient production among China's industrial enterprises', *Economic Development and Cultural Change*, vol. 42, no. 3.

Jefferson, G., Rawski, T. and Zheng, Y. (1996) 'Chinese industrial productivity: trends, measurement issues and recent developments', *Journal of Comparative Economics*, vol. 23, no. 2.

Jeffries, I. (ed.) (1981) *The Industrial Enterprise in Eastern Europe*, New York: Praeger.

—— (1990) *A Guide to the Socialist Economies*, London: Routledge.

—— (1992a) 'The impact of reunification on the East German economy' in J. Osmond (ed.) *German Reunification: A Reference Guide and Commentary*, London: Longman.

—— (ed.) (1992b) *Industrial Reform in Socialist Countries: From Restructuring to Revolution*, Aldershot: Edward Elgar.

—— (1993) *Socialist Economies and the Transition to the Market: A Guide*, London: Routledge.

—— (1996a) *A Guide to the Economies in Transition*, London: Routledge.

—— (ed.) (1996b) *Problems of Economic and Political Transformation in the Balkans*, London: Pinter.

—— (2001a) *Economies in Transition: A Guide to China, Cuba, Mongolia, North Korea and Vietnam at the Turn of the Twenty-first Century*, London: Routledge.

—— (2001b) 'Good governance and the first decade of transition' in H. Hoen (ed.) *Good Governance in Central and Eastern Europe: The Puzzle of Capitalism by Design*, Cheltenham: Edward Elgar.

—— (2002a) *Eastern Europe at the Turn of the Twenty-First Century: A Guide to the Economies in Transition*, London: Routledge.

—— (2002b) *The Former Yugoslavia at the Turn of the Twenty-First Century: A Guide to the Economies in Transition*, London: Routledge.

—— (2002c) *The New Russia: A Handbook of Economic and Political Developments*, London: RoutledgeCurzon.

—— (2003) *The Caucasus and Central Asian Republics at the Turn of the Twenty-First Century: A Guide to the Economies in Transition*, London: Routledge.

—— (2004) *The Countries of the Former Soviet Union: the Baltic and European States in Transition*, London: Routledge.

—— (2006a) *China: A Guide to Economic and Political Developments*, London: Routledge.

—— (2006b) *North Korea: A Guide to Economic and Political Developments*, London: Routledge.

—— (2006c) *Vietnam: A Guide to Economic and Political Developments*, London: Routledge.

—— (2007) *Mongolia: A Guide to Economic and Political Developments*, London: Routledge.

—— (2009) *Contemporary North Korea: A Guide to Economic and Political Developments*, London: Routledge.

Jeffries, I., Melzer, M. (eds), and Breuning, E. (advisory ed.) (1987) *The East German Economy*, London: Croom Helm.

Johnson, D. (1988a) 'Economic reforms in the People's Republic of China', *Economic Development and Cultural Change*, vol. 36, no. 3.

—— (1988b) 'Agriculture' in A. Cracraft (ed.) *The Soviet Union Today*, Chicago: University of Chicago Press.

Jones-Luong, P. and Weinthal, E. (2002) 'New friends, new fears in Central Asia', *Foreign Affairs*, vol. 81, no. 2.

Kamath, S. (1990) 'Foreign direct investment in a centrally planned developing economy: the Chinese case', *Economic Development and Cultural Change*, vol. 39, no. 1.

Kaminski, B., Wang, Z. and Winters, A. (1996) 'Export performance in transition economies', *Economic Policy*, no. 23.

Kane, P. (1988) *Famine in China (1958–1961): Demographic and Social Implications*, London: Macmillan.

Kojima, R. (1990) 'Achievements and contradictions in China's economic reform', *The Developing Economies*, vol. XXVIII, no. 4.

Koo, A. (1990) 'The contract responsibility system: transition from a planned to a market system', *Economic Development and Cultural Change*, vol. 35, no. 4.

Korzec, M. (1988) 'Contract labour, the right to work and new labour laws in the People's Republic of China', *Comparative Economic Studies*, vol. XXX, no. 2.

Kosta, J. (1987) 'The Chinese economic reform: approaches, results and prospects' in P. Gey, J. Kosta and W. Quaisser (eds) *Crisis and Reform in Socialist Economies*, London: Westview Press.

Kueh, Y. (1989) 'The Maoist legacy and China's new industrialization strategy', *China Quarterly*, no. 119.

—— (1992) 'Foreign investment and economic change', *China Quarterly*, no. 131.

Kung, J. (2000) 'Common property rights and land reallocations in rural China: evidence from a village survey', *World Development*, vol. 28, no. 4.

Lam, W. (2008) 'Hope for a better Tibet policy', *FEER*, April.

Lardy, N. (1998) 'China and the Asian contagion', *Foreign Affairs*, vol. 77, no. 4.

Lee, K. (1990) 'The Chinese model of the socialist enterprise: an assessment of its organization and performance', *Journal of Comparative Economics*, vol. 14, no. 3.

—— (1993) 'Property rights and the agency problem in China's enterprise reform', *Cambridge Journal of Economics*, vol. 17, no. 2.

Lee, P. (1986) 'Enterprise autonomy in post-Mao China: a case study of policy-making, 1978–83', *China Quarterly*, no. 105.

Li, D. (1998) 'Changing incentives for the Chinese bureaucracy', *American Economic Review*, Papers and Proceedings, May.

Li, W. (1997) 'The impact of economic reform on the performance of Chinese state enterprises, 1980–1989', *Journal of Political Economy*, vol. 105, no. 5.

Lin, C. (1995) 'The assessment: Chinese economic reform in retrospect and prospect', *Oxford Review of Economic Policy*, vol. 11, no. 4.

Lin, J. (1988) 'The household responsibility system in China's agricultural reform; a theoretical and empirical study', *Economic Development and Cultural Change*, vol. 36, no. 3 (Supplement).

—— (1990) 'Collectivization and China's agricultural crisis in 1959–61', *Journal of Political Economy*, vol. 98, no. 6.

—— (1992) 'Rural reforms and agricultural growth in China', *American Economic Review*, vol. 82, no. 1.

Lin, J., Cae, F. and Li, Z. (1998) 'Competition, policy burdens and state-owned enterprise reform', *American Economic Review*, Papers and Proceedings, May.

Ling, L. (1988) 'Intellectual responses to China's economic reforms', *Asian Survey*, vol. XXVIII, no. 5.

Ling, Z. and Zhongyi, J. (1993) 'From brigade to village community: the land tenure system and rural development in China', *Cambridge Journal of Economics*, vol. 17, no. 4.

Liu, Z. and Liu, G. (1996) 'The efficiency impact of the Chinese industrial reforms in the 1980s', *Journal of Comparative Economics*, vol. 23, no. 3.

Lockett, M. (1987) 'China's development strategy: the Seventh Five Year Plan and after', *Euro-Asia Business Review*, July.

Long, S. (1990) *China against the Tide*, London: EIU.

Lynch, D. (2008) 'Mr Ma's Taiwanese identity', *FEER*, March.

Ma, S. (1998) 'The Chinese route to privatization: the evolution of the shareholding system option', *Asian Survey*, vol. XXXVIII, no. 4.

McKinnon, R. (1992a) 'Taxation, money, and credit in a liberalizing socialist economy', *Economics of Planning*, vol. 25, no. 1.

—— (1992b) 'Taxation, money and credit in a liberalizing socialist economy' in C. Clague and G. Rausser (eds) *The Emergence of Market Economies in Eastern Europe*, Oxford: Basil Blackwell.

—— (1994) 'Financial growth and macroeconomic stability in China, 1978–92: implications for Russia and other transitional economies', *Journal of Comparative Economics*, vol. 18, no. 3.

McMillan, J. and Woodruff, C. (2002) 'The central role of entrepreneurs in transition economies', *Journal of Economic Perspectives*, vol. 16, no. 3.

McMillan, J., Whalley, J. and Lijing Zhu (1989) 'The impact of China's economic reforms on agricultural productivity growth', *Journal of Political Economy*, vol. 97, no. 4.

Mancours, K. and Swinnen, J. (2002) 'Patterns of agrarian transition', *Economic Development and Cultural Change*, vol. 50, no. 2.

Mao, Y. and Hare, P. (1989) 'Chinese experience in the introduction of a market mechanism into a planned economy: the role of pricing', *Journal of Economic Surveys*, vol. 3, no. 2.

Meng, X. and Zhang, J. (2001) 'The two-tier labour market in urban China. Occupational segregation and wage differentials between urban residents and rural migrants in Shanghai', *Journal of Comparative Economics*, vol. 29, no. 3.

Murrell, P. (1990) *The Nature of Socialist Economies: Lessons from Eastern European Foreign Trade*, Princeton, NJ: Princeton University Press.

—— (1992a) 'Evolutionary and radical approaches to economic reform', *Economics of Planning*, vol. 25, no. 1.

—— (1992b) 'Evolution in economics and in the economic reform of the centrally planned economies' in C. Clague and G. Rausser (eds) *The Emergence of Market Economies in Eastern Europe*, Oxford: Basil Blackwell.

—— (1993) 'What is shock therapy? What did it do in Poland and Russia?' *Post-Soviet Affairs*, vol. 9, no. 2.

Naughton, B. (1994) 'Chinese institutional innovation and privatization from below', *American Economic Review*, vol. 84, no. 2.

—— (1996) 'China's emergence and prospects as a trading nation', *Brookings Papers on Economic Activity*, no. 2.

Nellis, J. (1999) 'Time to rethink privatization in transition economies?', *Finance and Development*, vol. 36, no. 2.

Nolan, P. (1992) 'Transforming Stalinist systems: China's reforms in the light of Russian and East European experience', University of Cambridge, Discussion Paper on Economic Transition DPET 9203.

—— (1993) 'China's post-Mao political economy: a puzzle', *Contributions to Political Economy*, no. 12.

—— (1996a) 'Large firms and industrial reform in former planned economies: the case of China', *Cambridge Journal of Economics*, vol. 20, no. 1.

—— (1996b) 'China's rise, Russia's fall', *Journal of Peasant Studies*, vol. 24, nos 1 and 2.

Nolan, P. and Xiaoqiang, W. (1999) 'Beyond privatization: institutional innovation and growth in China's large state-owned enterprises', *World Development*, vol. 27, no. 1.

Nove, A. (1961) *The Soviet Economy*, London: Allen & Unwin.

OECD (2005) *Economic Survey of China 2005*, OECD, available www.oecd.org/documentprint/0,2744,en_2649

Pearson, M. (1991) 'The erosion of controls over foreign capital in China', *Modern China*, vol. 17, no. 1.

Perkins, D. (1988) 'Reforming China's economic system', *Journal of Economic Literature*, vol. XXVI, no. 2.

—— (1994) 'Completing China's move to the market', *Journal of Economic Perspectives*, vol. 8, no. 2.

Phillips, D. (1986) 'Special Economic Zones in China's modernisation: changing policies and changing fortunes', *National Westminster Review*, February.

Platte, E. (1994) 'China's foreign debt', *Pacific Affairs*, vol. 66, no. 4.

Pomfret, R. (1993) 'Mongolia's economic reforms: background, contents and prospects', *Economic Bulletin for Asia and the Pacific*, vol. XLIV, no. 1.

—— (2000a) 'Transition and democracy in Mongolia', *Europe–Asia Studies*, vol. 52, no. 1.

—— (2000b) 'Agrarian reform in Uzbekistan: why has the Chinese model failed to deliver?' *Economic Development and Cultural Change*, vol. 48, no. 2.

—— (2000c) 'The Uzbek model of economic development, 1991–99', *Economics of Transition*, vol. 8, no. 3.

Prasad, E. and Rumbaugh, T. (2003) 'Beyond the Great Wall', *Finance and Development*, vol. 40, no. 4.

Prybyla, J. (1985) 'The Chinese economy: adjustment of the system or systemic reform?' *Asian Survey*, vol. XXV, no. 5.

—— (1986) 'China's economic experiment: from Mao to market', *Problems of Communism*, vol. XXXV, no. 1.

—— (1987) 'On some questions concerning price reform in the People's Republic of China', University Park: Pennsylvania State University, Working Paper 9–87–16.

—— (1994) Review in *Economic Development and Cultural Change*, vol. 42, no. 3.

Pudney, S. and Wang, L. (1994) 'Housing and housing reform in urban China: efficiency, distribution and the implications for social security', LSE, EF no. 8.

Putterman, L. (1988) 'Group farming and work incentives in collective-era China', *Modern China*, vol. 14, no. 4.

Qian, Y. (1994) 'A theory of shortage in socialist economies based on the soft budget constraint', *American Economic Review*, vol. 84, no. 1.

Qian, Y. and Xu, C. (1993) 'Why China's economic reforms differ: the M-form hierarchy and entry/expansion of the non-state sector', *Economics of Transition*, vol. 1, no. 2.

Quaisser, W. (1987) 'The new agricultural reform in China: from the people's communes to peasant agriculture' in P. Gey, J. Kosta and W. Quaisser (eds) *Crisis and Reform in Socialist Economies*, London: Westview Press.

Rawski, T. (1994) 'Chinese industrial reform: accomplishments, prospects and implications', *American Economic Review*, vol. 84, no. 2.

Richman, B. (1969) *Industrial Society in Communist China*, New York: Random House.

Riskin, C. (1987) *The Political Economy of Chinese Development since 1949*, London: Oxford University Press.

Roy, D. (1990) 'Real product and income in China, Cuba, North Korea and Vietnam', *Development Policy Review*, vol. 8, no. 1.

Sachs, J. (1992) 'The economic transformation of Eastern Europe: the case of Poland', *Economics of Planning*, vol. 25, no. 1.

—— (1994) *Poland's Jump to the Market Economy*, Cambridge, MA: MIT Press.

—— (1995) 'Consolidating capitalism', *Foreign Policy*, no. 98.

—— (1996a) 'The transition at mid-decade', *American Economic Review*, Papers and Proceedings (May).

—— (1996b) 'Economic transition and the exchange rate regime', *American Economic Review*, Papers and Proceedings (May).

—— (1997) 'An overview of stabilization issues facing economies in transition' in W. Woo, S. Parker and J. Sachs (eds) (1997) *Economies in Transition: Comparing Asia and Eastern Europe*, London: MIT Press.

Sachs, J. and Woo, W. (1994) 'Structural factors in the economic reforms of China, Eastern Europe and the former Soviet Union', *Economic Policy*, no. 18.

—— (1996) 'China's transition experience reexamined', *Transition*, vol. 7, nos 3–4.

Schram, S. (1988) 'China after the 13th Congress', *China Quarterly*, no. 114.

Shakya, Tsering (2008) 'The gulf between Tibet and its exiles', *FEER*, May.

Shambaugh, D. (1989) 'The fourth and fifth plenary sessions of the 13th CCP Central Committee', *China Quarterly*, no. 120.

Shen Xiaofang (1990) 'A decade of direct foreign investment in China', *Problems of Communism*, March–April.

Sicular, T. (1988a) 'Plan and market in China's agricultural commerce', *Journal of Political Economy*, vol. 96, no. 2.

—— (1988b) 'Grain pricing: a key link in Chinese economic policy', *Modern China*, vol. 14, no. 4.

—— (1988c) 'Agricultural planning and pricing in the post-Mao period', *China Quarterly*, no. 116.

Skinner, G. (1985) 'Rural marketing in China: repression and revival', *China Quarterly*, no. 103.

Smyth, R. (1998) 'Recent developments in rural enterprise reform in China', *Asian Survey*, vol. XXXVIII, no. 8.

—— (2000) 'Should China be promoting large-scale enterprises and enterprise groups?' *World Development*, vol. 28, no. 4.

Solinger, D. (1989a) 'Urban reform and relational contracting in post-Mao China: an interpretation of the transition from plan to market', *Comparative Communism*, vol. XXII, nos 2 and 3.

—— (1989b) 'Capitalist measures with Chinese characteristics', *Problems of Communism*, vol. XXXVIII, January–February.

Stavis, B. (1989) 'The political economy of inflation in China', *Studies in Comparative Communism*, vol. XXII, nos 2 and 3.

Tam, On-Kit (1988) 'Rural finance in China', *China Quarterly*, no. 113.

Thurow, L. (1998) 'Asia: the collapse and the cure', *The New York Review of Books*, 5 February, vol. XLV, no. 2.

Tsai, K. (2008) 'China's complicit capitalists', *FEER*, January–February.

Tsang, S. (1996) 'Against "big bang" in economic transition: normative and positive arguments', *Cambridge Journal of Economics*, vol. 20, no. 2.

Ungar, E. (1987–8) 'The struggle over the Chinese community in Vietnam, 1946–86', *Pacific Affairs*, vol. 60, no. 4.

United Nations (1993) *World Economic Survey 1993*, New York: United Nations.

—— (2001) *World Economic and Social Survey 2001*, New York: United Nations.

—— (2006) *World Economic Situation and Prospects 2006*, New York: United Nations.

Wädekin, K.-E. (1982) *Agrarian Policies in Communist Europe*, Totowa, NJ: Rowman & Allanheld.

—— (1988) 'Soviet agriculture: a brighter prospect' in P. Wiles (ed.), *The Soviet Economy on the Brink of Reform*, London: Unwin Hyman.

—— (ed.) (1990a) *Communist Agriculture: Farming in the Far East and Cuba*, London: Routledge.

—— (1990b) *Communist Agriculture: Farming in the Soviet Union and Eastern Europe*, London: Routledge.

—— (1990c) 'Private agriculture in socialist countries: implications for the USSR' in E. Gray (ed.) *Soviet Agriculture: Comparative Perspectives*, Ames: University of Iowa Press.

Walder, A. (1989) 'Factory and manager in an era of reform', *China Quarterly*, no. 118.

Wall, D. (1991) 'Special economic zones and industrialisation in China', International Economics Research Centre at the University of Sussex, Discussion Paper no. 01/91.

—— (1993) 'China's economic reform and opening-up process: the Special Economic Zones', *Development Policy Review*, vol. 11, no. 3.

Wang, J. (1999) 'China's rural reform: the "rights" direction', *Transition*, vol. 10, no. 2.

Wang Jun (1989) 'The export-oriented strategy of China's coastal areas: evaluation and prospects', University of Leicester, Department of Economics, Discussion Paper no. 116 (September).

Wang, X. (1997) 'Rural empowerment of state and peasantry: grassroots democracy in rural China', *World Development*, vol. 25, no. 9.

Wang Xiao-qing (1993) '"Groping for stones to cross the river": Chinese price reform against the "big bang"', University of Cambridge, Discussion Paper DPET 9305.

Wang Zhonghui (1990) 'Private enterprise in China: an overview', *Journal of Communist Studies*, vol. 6, no. 3.

—— (1993) 'China's policies towards collective rural enterprises', *Small Enterprise Development*, vol. 4, no. 1.

Watson, A. (1988) 'The reform of agricultural marketing in China', *China Quarterly*, no. 113.

Weitzman, M. and Xu, C. (1993) 'Chinese township-village enterprises as vaguely defined co-operatives', LSE, CP no. 26.

—— (1994) 'Chinese township-village enterprises as vaguely defined co-operatives', *Journal of Comparative Economics*, vol. 18, no. 2.

Wen, G. (1993) 'Total factor productivity in China's farming sector, 1952–89', *Economic Development and Cultural Change*, vol. 42, no. 1.

White, G. (1987a) 'Cuban planning in the mid-1980s: centralisation, decentralisation and participation', *World Development*, vol. 15, no. 1.

—— (1987b) 'The politics of economic reform in Chinese industry: the introduction of the labour contract system', *China Quarterly*, no. 111.

—— (1988) 'State and market in China's labour reform', *Journal of Development Studies*, vol. 24, no. 4.

White, G. and Bowles, P. (1988) 'China's banking reforms: aims, methods and problems', *National Westminster Bank Quarterly Review*, November.

Wong, C. (1986) 'The economics of shortage and the problems of reform in Chinese industry', *Journal of Comparative Economics*, vol. 10, no. 4.

—— (1988) 'Interpreting rural industrial growth in post-Mao China', *Modern China*, vol. 14, no. 1.

—— (1989) 'Between plan and market: the role of the local sector in post-Mao reforms in China' in S. Gomulka, Ha Yong-Chool and Kim Cai-One (eds) *Economic Reforms in the Socialist World*, London: Macmillan.

—— (1991) 'Central–local relations in an era of fiscal decline', *China Quarterly*, no. 128 (December).

Wong, E. (1987) 'Recent developments in China's Special Economic Zones: problems and prognosis', *The Developing Economies*, vol. XXV, no. 1.

Woo, W. (1994) 'The art of reforming centrally planned economies: comparing China, Poland and Russia', *Journal of Comparative Economics*, vol. 18, no. 3.

—— (1997) 'Improving the performance of enterprises in transition' in W. Woo, S. Parker and J. Sachs (eds) *Economies in Transition: Comparing Asia and Eastern Europe*, London: MIT Press.

Woo, W., Hai, W., Jin, Y. and Fan, G. (1994) 'How successful has Chinese enterprise reform been? Pitfalls in opposite biases and focus', *Journal of Comparative Economics*, vol. 18, no. 3.

Woo, W., Parker, S. and Sachs, J. (eds) (1997) *Economies in Transition: Comparing Asia and Eastern Europe*, London: MIT Press.

World Bank (1996) *World Development Report: From Plan to Market*, New York: Oxford University Press.

—— (2002) 'The World Bank, privatization and enterprise reform in transition economies', *Transition*, vol. 13, no. 1.

Wu, H.-L. and Chen, C.-H. (2001) 'An assessment of outward foreign direct investment from China's transitional economy', *Europe-Asia Studies*, vol. 53, no. 8.

Wu, J. and Reynolds, B. (1988) 'Choosing a strategy for China's economic reform', *American Economic Review*, Papers and Proceedings, May.

Wu, Z. (1997) 'How successful has state-owned enterprise reform been in China?' *Europe–Asia Studies*, vol. 49, no. 7.

Yao, S. (2000) 'Economic development and poverty reduction in China over twenty years of reform', *Economic Development and Cultural Change*, vol. 48, no. 3.

Zhu Ling (1990) 'The transformation of the operating mechanism in Chinese agriculture', *Journal of Development Studies*, vol. 26, no. 2.

Zhu, Y. (1995) 'Major changes under way in China's industrial relations', *International Labour Review*, vol. 134, no. 1.

Zhuang, J. and Xu, C. (1996) 'Profit-sharing and financial performance in the Chinese state enterprises: evidence from panel data', *Economics of Planning*, vol. 29, no. 3.

Index

Abe, S. 650, 652–3, 685–6, 689, 691, 701, 703, 903
Ai Weiwei 458, 956–7, 815–19
Alibaba Group 457
Al Qaeda 357, 957
Amano, Y. 995, 1004
Apec (Asia-Pacific Economic Co-operation summit 882–3
Aso, T. 872–3
Auerswald, P. 5

Baidu 441, 443–7, 453–6, 968
Ban Ki-moon 1003–4
Bao Pu 1014
Bao Tong 1014–15
Barnett, R. 164
Basic Law (Hong Kong) 134, 138, 144–5, 148–9
Basic Law (Macao) 134
Bergersen 741–3, 828
Bernstein, R. 5
Black Hawk Safety Net 466
black jails (houses) 410, 866, 898, 929
Blix, H. 994
Bo Xilai 919, 950
Bo Yibo 666
Brown, G. 194–5, 224, 266, 285, 826
Bush, George W. 28, 172–3, 177–8, 205, 663, 709, 826, 840, 849, 853–4, 893, 990–3, 996

Cao Gangchuan 705
Cao Wenzhuang 549
Champa Phuntsok 190–1, 222
Chan, Anson 138–9, 141, 146, 148–9, 155, 959
Chan, Margaret 488, 531
Chang'e-2 932
Charter '08 404–9, 417
Chen Daojun 403
Chen Deming 989
Chen Guangcheng 388–9
Chen Liangyu 649–51, 655, 660, 671, 685, 699–700, 706, 753
Chen Shui-bian 11, 48–9, 52–8, 61, 67, 74–5, 78–9, 86, 107–8, 111–16, 127–30
Chen Shuqing 436
Chen Xitong 638, 649
Chen Zhu 585
Cheonan 1012
Chiang Kai-shek10–11, 47–8, 118
China-African Co-operation Summit 657
Ching Cheong 390, 399
Chongqing (corruption trials) 919–20, 932, 950, 998
Chui, Fernando 137
Clark, H. 583–4, 587
Clinton, B. 16, 171–2
Clinton, H. 460–2, 895–7, 906, 1011
Cohen, R. 5, 170
Comprehensive Test Ban Treaty 993
Cultural Revolution 164, 634, 652, 867, 1014
cyber-attacks (hacking) *see* Google
cyber-attacks (hacking) (Tibet) 305–8

Dalai Lama 13–14, 84, 123–6, 161 (*see* Chapter 4), 740, 757, 972, 981
Dalai (Dalai Lama) clique 192, 210, 217, 226, 230
Davidson, A. 969
death penalty statistics 382–8
Defence Policy Co-ordination Talks 897
Deng Xiaoping 17–20, 22, 25, 33, 470, 642, 664, 739, 866–7, 887, 798, 1014
DeWoskin, K. 560
Drummond, D. 967–8
Dui Qinglin 320

Dworkin, R. 13

earthquakes (starting with the one of 12 May 2008) 758–821, 979–85
East Turkestan 325–7, 855–8
East Turkestan Islamic Movement 333, 336, 338, 835–9, 847–50, 855
Edward Yu 459
Erlanger, S. 226
exchange rate policy 923, 953–4, 954–5, 987–9, 1010–11, 1015

Falun Gong 12, 16, 404, 413–14, 422–3, 964
Fang Lizhi 31
Fifty Cent Party 438
Firewall (Great) 446, 844, 926
Forney, M. 226
Frank Hsieh 55, 60–1, 67–8, 75, 78, 80
French, H. 161, 393, 552
Fu, Bob 840
Fu Xiancai 639
Fukuda, Y. 730–1, 757–8, 822, 826, 870–1, 872

G-2 902
G-20 987–8
Gang of Four 634–5, 867
Gao Zhisheng 389, 411, 418–19, 688, 878, 963–5
Gates, R. 147, 1015
Geithner, T. 987–9, 1011
Gen Huichang 707
Genghis Khan 8
Ghostnet 306
Gilley, B. 9
global financial crisis 887, 899, 952, 955
global warming (greenhouse gases) 675, 709, 914–15, 927–31; (Copenhagen climate change conference 934–40, 955–6)
Gong, Sasha 840
Gong Xiantian 677–8
Google 441, 443–7, 453–70, 966–76
Gore, A. 939
Great Western Development (Go West) policy 168
Green Dam [Green Dam-Youth Escort] 446–50
green GDP 23, 634
Guantanamo detainees 329–31, 337, 340–4, 380–1
Guo Quan 416–17
Gyalwang Karmapa (seveneeenth) Ogyen Trinley Dorje 267

hacking (Germany and the United States) 708, 728; *see also* cyber-attacks
Han dynasty 8
Hao Heping 549
harmonious society 22, 173, 415, 652, 654, 697, 1006
Harris, P. 166
Hatoyama, Y. 912
He Dongping 978
He Yafei 939
Hill, C. 667
Hillman, B. 169
Ho, Edmund 134–7
Hoogewerf, R. 918
Howard, J. 175
Hu Jia 389, 398, 400–2, 878, 964
Hu Jindou 393
Hu Jintao 14, 22–7, 68, 89,-90, 94, 118, 142–3, 168, 173, 205, 228–9, 264, 266, 269, 309, 350, 352–3, 365–6, 391, 431, 436, 470, 550, 589, 640 (*see* Chapter 8), 985–1011
Hu Shuli 921–3, 942
Hu Yaobang 664, 902, 998–9
Hua Guofeng 866–7
Huang Guangyu 944–5, 1008–9
Huang Ju 696
Huang Qi 417
Huangdi (Yellow Emperor) 9
hukou system 946–7, 956
Hurun list 918
hutongs 836

Ignatius, D. 21
Ilham Tohti 356, 364
Ip 154

Jeffries, I. 21, 30–1
Jenkins, S. 217
Ji, R. 971
Jia Qinglin 720
Jiang Qing 635, 867
Jiang Zemin 20–2, 24–5, 168, 172, 470, 637, 642, 649, 651–2, 655, 690, 710, 715–16, 720, 723, 756–7
Jin Renqing 682–3, 705–6
Jung Chang and Jon Halliday 634
Justin Lin 741

Kahn, J. 23
Kanxi Emperor 165
Karmapa Lama 164, 171, 192, 291
Kahn, J. 551
Kelsang Gyaltsen 262, 279, 287

Kissinger, H. 994
Koizumi, J. 642–4, 650–3
Kyoto Protocol 915, 936

Lam, W. 169, 470–1
Lan Chengzhang 664
Laogai (labour camp) 146
Lau, Emily 153
Lavrov, S. 743
Lee, J. 5
Lee, Martin 152, 155
Lee Myung Bak 1012–13
Li Changjiang 555, 562, 564, 585, 591–2
Li Daokui 988
Li Ka-shing 156
Li Keqiang 25, 715–17, 721–2-3
Li Peng 21, 1014
Li Xiannian 664
Li Yizhong 450
Li Zhaoxing 640, 657, 690
Li Zhi 351, 369
Liao Yiwu 419
Liu Xiaobo 405–7, 414, 417–18
Liu Yao 413
Liu Zhihua 638, 880–1
Locke, G. 989
Lodi (Gyaltsen) Gyari 247, 262, 265, 278–9, 286–7
Long March 10
Lu Gebgsong 400
Lunar probe 897–8
Lynch, D. 87

Ma Ying-jeou 11, 55, 57–8, 60, 64, 68–70, 75–82 (see throughout the rest of Chapter 2), 958–9
MacKinnon, R. 445
MacMahon line 170
McCain, J. 198
McDonald, S. 971
McLaughlin, K. 281
McNeil, D. 478
manipulation (currency) 986–7
Mao Tse-tung (Zedong) 10–11, 18, 164, 421, 634–5, 642, 652, 685–7
Medvedev, D. 868, 934, 936
Merkel, A 177, 207, 266, 708, 740
Microsoft 440, 970–2
Miliband, D. 285, 315
Miliband, E. 939
Ming dynasty 8, 10
Minxin Pei 24
Mokyr, J. 6
Mongol Yuan dynasty 8, 161, 163, 165

Nabarro, D. 477, 484
Nanjing massacre (Rape of Nanjing) 697, 699, 728–9
Needham, J. 6
Needham Question 6
Nuclear Non-proliferation Treaty 990–4, 1003, 1005
Nuclear Posture Review 990–2, 1005
Nuclear Threat Initiative 995
Nunn, S. 994

Obama, B. 28, 131, 313–14, 320, 322–3, 462, 892–3, 896, 902, 904, 916, 918, 923, 925–30, 934, 985–97, 1011, 1013
Ollman, G. 469
Olympic Games 26–7, 100, 180–3, 200–65, 269, 273–82, 321, 332, 336, 339, 397, 400, 403, 419, 441, 557, 601, 638, 688, 691, 701–3, 709, 731, 743–5, 746–50, 757, 821–66, 976, 985
Olympic medals won by China 863–6
one-child policy 32–46
One China policy 11, 63–4, 309
one country, two systems 13
Opium War 10, 137

Padma Choling 324
Panchen Lama (Gedhun Choekyi Nyima/ Gendun Choekyi Nyima; choice of the Dalai Lama) 173, 323–4
Panchen Lama (Gyaltsen Norben/ Gyaincain Norbu; choice of the Communist Party) 173, 323
Paulson, H. 648, 661
Pelosi, N. 198, 240, 314
Peng Gaofeng 412
People's Armed Police 911–12
Perry, B. 994
Pfaff, W. 12
pirate attacks 888–90
Pope Benedict XVI 420–1, 424–30
property law 651–2, 677–81
public ownership 719
Putin, V. 686, 833

Qian Xuesen 919
Qin dynasty 8
Qing (Manchu) dynasty 8, 113, 129, 161–3, 165, 171, 326
Qiu Xiaohua 670
Quan-Sheng Shu 883

Rebiya Kadeer 347, 354, 357, 359–60, 363–4, 373, 840

Recep Tayyip Erdogan 356
Rehnstrom, J. 517
Reporters Without Borders 202, 398
Rice, C. 69, 986
Rogge, J. 832, 845, 853
Rudd, K. 217, 224, 228

Samdhong Rinpoche 212
Sarkozy, N. 239, 244, 279–80, 292–3, 309, 312, 826, 854
Schultz, G. 994
scientific development 697, 717–18
Shadow (network) 972
Shakya, T. 166
Shang dynasty 8
Shanghai Co-operation Organization (SCO) 704, 868–9, 908
Shanghai World Expo (held in Shanghai from 1 May to 31 October 2010) 976, 1001–3
Shezhou 7 (capsule) 874–6
Shu Yulong 515
Singh, M. 737–8
Skype 439–40
snow storms (onset of severe storms in January 2008) 732
Song dynasty 8
Sperling, E.162
Spratlys 891
Start Treaty 991
Stewart, J. 459
Strategic and Economic Dialogue 902, 987, 1010
Sui dynasty 8
Sun Yat-sen 10, 635
super ministries 75–1

Tai Shen Kuo 741–2, 828
taikonauts 875
Taiwan Relations Act 131, 148
Tanag Jigme Zangpo 172
Tang dynasty 8
Teng Biao 399–400, 415
Three Gorges Dam 635, 639, 710–13
three represents 21, 723
Three-Self Patriotic Movement 431
Tian Chengping 673, 749
Tian Wenhua 621–2, 625
Tiananmen Square 12, 16–17, 19–20, 158, 201, 251, 44, 636, 648, 664, 739, 836, 849, 902, 905–7, 913, 1014
Tiangong-1 947–8
Tibet (start of violent protests on 14 March 2008) 184
Toyota 945–6
trains (high speed) 940–1
Troedsson, H. 474
Tsang, Donald 138 (*see* Chapter 3) 688, 960
Tung Chee-hwa 143

Uighurs (violent demonstations of July 2009) 344
unity and stability 12, 14

Wan Gang 690, 698
Wan Yanhai 977
Wang Hongju 932
Wang Keqin 977
Wang Lequan 328, 332, 369, 961–2
Wang Lixiong 16
Wang Rongqing 4093
Wei Jingsheng 840
Wei Xingzhu, Li Lu and Theresa Hesketh 4
Wen Jiabao 19, 22, 26, 168, 194, 294–6, 302, 590, 592, 610–11, 640 (*see* Chapter 8), 980–1013
Wen Qiang 950
Williams, Rowan (Archbishop of Canterbury) 422–3
Woeser 983–4
Wong, E. 170
World Uighur Congress 335, 339, 347, 375
Wu, Harry 16, 416
Wu Bangguo 22
Wu Gaoxing 906
Wu Heping 1007
Wu Shu-chen 126–7
Wu Yi 561, 717, 720

Xi Jinping 25, 685, 715–17, 721–3
Xia Changfa 416
Xia dynasty 8
Xiang Yuzhang 593
Xiao Yang 398
Xie Caiping 919–21, 950
Xie Xuren 705
Xie Zhenhua 940
Xinang Xiaoji 906
Xu Youyu 408
Xu Zhiyong 414–16
Xu Zongheng 908

Yahoo 434–5, 456, 968, 971–2
Yan Yiming 408
Yang Chunlin 399–400

Yang Jiechi 690, 840
Yang, Liwei 874
Yardley, J. 24, 164, 703
Yasukuni Shrine 638, 642–4, 664, 691, 703, 730, 903
Yin Tian 677
Yu (Emperor) 8
Yu Haufeng 399

Zen, Joseph (Cardinal Zen Ze-kiun) 142–3, 157, 423–4, 426, 636, 960–1
Zeng Qinghong 23, 651, 664, 716, 720
Zhai Zhigang 875–6
Zhang Chunxian 961
Zhang Hong 956
Zhang Maosheng 648
Zhang Qingli 192, 195, 217, 324
Zhang Weiqing 3, 37, 39–40
Zhang Zuhua 406, 408
Zhang Bing Zhi 965
Zhao Yan 388–90, 396–7
Zhao Ziyang 18–20, 398, 664, 739, 867, 1014
Zheng He 9–10, 890
Zheng Xiaoyu 541, 549–50, 552–3, 670–1
Zhou Dou 905
Zhou Xiaochuan 954–5
Zhou Yonglin 464
Zhou Zhengyi 726
Zhu Rongji 21–2
Zhu Weiqun 287–8, 320
Zizek, S. 166

For Product Safety Concerns and Information please contact our EU representative GPSR@taylorandfrancis.com
Taylor & Francis Verlag GmbH, Kaufingerstraße 24, 80331 München, Germany

www.ingramcontent.com/pod-product-compliance
Lightning Source LLC
Chambersburg PA
CBHW070611270326
41926CB00011B/1656

* 9 7 8 1 1 3 8 9 7 8 7 2 0 *